영어로 표현하기 힘든 각 분야별 문장과 회화의 해법

영어문장·회화 대사전

편저 : 대한영어교육연구원

TOEIC·TOEFL·TEPS·영문학도·대학원진학·대입
각종자격시험·국가고시·공무원시험 대비

 법문북스

머 리 말

우리나라의 모국어 뿐 아니라 어떤 언어든 학습해 나가는 과정은 '단어'에서 출발하여 그 합성체인 '문장'의 합성으로 이루어집니다. 인류의 역사와 더불어 발전해 온 개별 언어에는 저마다의 뿌리 깊은 특색을 지니고 있어서 단순한 암기방식에만 의존하다가는 학습의 한계에 부딪쳐 쉽게 그만두게 됩니다.

학습과정을 단계별로 나누고 그 첫 단계인 단어 학습에 도움을 주기 위하여 체계적으로 정리한 『Word Origins and Vocabulary 77,000』(법문출판사)와 『영어 어원 어휘 사전』(법문출판사)을 발간한 바 있으며, 이어서 영어 특유의 맛깔과 생동감을 느낄 수 있는 『영어 숙어란 무엇인가』(안산미디어)를 통하여 관용어가 생겨난 근원을 소개한 바 있습니다. 단순 논리대로라면 부분적 표현을 합성할 때 종합적인 의미가 될 것 같지만 그러한 원리가 전혀 통하지 않는 관용어에 대한 내용을 이 책에서 담고 있습니다.

언어의 학습은 논리나 이치보다는 사용에 있다는 점을 잊어서는 안 됩니다.

언어가 생활의 도구인 이상 문맥이나 상황을 통한 학습 보다 더 효율적 방법이 없다는 점에서 일상생활에서 자주 쓰이는 문장을 하나하나 확실히 익혀나갈 필요가 있다는 말이 됩니다. 다시 말해 영어다운 표현으로 된 쉽고도 유용한 영어다운 문장을 완전히 자신의 것으로 만드는 학습을 필요로 합니다.

외국어의 학습에는 어휘, 문법, 독해, 음성학, 회화 등 여러 부문으로 나눌 수 있겠지만, 이를 근원적인 관점에서 독해와 작문으로 대별해 볼 수 있을 것입니다. 외국어를 자국어로 변환시키는 독해와, 자국어를 외국어로 변환시키는 작문에 능숙해져야 하도록 노력해야 합니다.

여기에는 간단한 표현인데도 적재적소에 잘 떠오르지 않아 애먹을 때 쉽고도 유용하게 쓸 수 있는 문장들을 오랜 시간에 걸쳐 모아서 수록하였습니다.

너무나 간단하면서도 쉽게 잘 떠올리기 어려웠던 표현, 이런 유용한 표현들을 몰라 외국인을 접할 때 당황했던, 그리고 쉬운 시험문제에서도 자신 있게 정답을 고르지 못했던 어려움을 해소하는데 큰 도움을 드리고자 하는 충정이 담겨 있습니다. 다른 어떠한 교재에서도 찾기 어려운 알짜로 유용한 재미있는 표현들만을 풍부하게 모았다는 얘기이다. 내용별로 간단히 훑어보면 이디엄, 속담 및 명언, 교훈, 학술 지식, 시사, 정치, 경제, 사회, 어휘력 증진, 최근의 각종 시험문제의 예문 등을 어느 교재보다 풍부하게 실었습니다.

영어 공부가 좀 더 쉽고, 재미있고, 유용하게 느껴질 수 있도록 이 책을 통하여 독자의 영어실력 향상에 큰 도움이 되기를 바랍니다.

끝으로 이 책이 나오기까지 큰 도움을 주신 법문출판사 김현호 사장님, 편집부 직원들과 미주현지에서의 영어지식과 정보를 성심성의껏 협조해 준 이 책의 편찬자 정벨희(시카고에서 연수중)씨에게 진심으로 감사의 말씀을 드립니다.

2016년 04월 저자 올림

C·O·N·T·E·N·T·S

서 지난해 가장 큰 흥행을 기록한 영화의 하나다

외 **122**개

위대한 사람은 잊어버릴 줄 알거나 그보다 더 저쪽을 볼 수 있는 사람이다

---

41. | **WORDS**(말) 367

A different construction was put on the wording of your statement by each of them 외 **482**개

네가 한 말의 표현에 대하여 그들은 각기 다른 해석을 내렸어

---

42. | **REPUTATION**(명성) 413

A good name is sooner lost than won 외 **19**개

훌륭한 명성은 얻기보다 잃기가 쉽다

---

43. | **MEETING**(모임&만남) 415

A big crowd of people stuck around hoping to get a glimpse of him but he never showed up 외 **30**개

많은 사람들이 그를 보려고 떠나지 않고 있었으나 그는 나타나지 않았다

---

44. | **TROUBLES & PROBLEMS**(문제) 419

A new problem has popped up 외 **117**개

새로운 문제가 생겼어

---

45. | **PRODUCTS**(물건) 431

Almighty God, keep our wives from shopping sprees and protect

them from bargains they don't need or can't afford Almighty God, keep our wives from shopping sprees and protect them from bargains they don't need or can't afford 외 48개

전능하신 하나님 아버지, 우리의 아내들이 쇼핑에 미쳐 돌아가는 일이 없도록 역사 하여 주시고 세일이라 해서 필요하지도 않거나 분수에 넘치는 물건을 사는 일이 없도록 살펴 주시기를 기원합니다

A servant is known by his master's absence 외 28개

주인이 없을 때에 좋은 하인인지 알 수 있다

A couple of days in the cooler will straighten him up 외 77개

그를 며칠 간 교도소에 보내놓으면 정신 좀 차릴 거야

Anyone carrying matches, lighters, cooking equipment and(or) fuel in(into the) mountains and wooded ares would(will) be sternly punished 외 62개

누구든, 성냥, 라이터, 취사도구 및 연료를 산과 삼림이 우거진 곳으로 가지고 다니는 사람은 엄격히 처벌된다

A change is as good as a rest 외 58개

분위기 전환은 상큼한 기분을 주게 돼 있어

바쁘게 사는 것이 목표 있는 생활에 가장 근접하는 일이다

는 것이 목격됐다

100. **DRIVING**(운전) 1013

A little car can weave its way through other big cars and get to the front of a waiting line quickly 외 **85**개

소형차는 큰 차들의 틈바구니를 헤집고 나아가서 재빨리 신호대기중인 차량들의 선두로 나설 수 있다

101. **SALARY**(월급) 1023

After heated discussion they came down in favor of accepting the new pay offer 외 **24**개

그들은 열띤 논의 끝에 새로운 급여방식을 수용하는 쪽으로 결정했다

102. **CONSOLATIONS**(위로) 1027

After a month or two, it'll be plain sailing 외 **83**개

한 두 달만 지나면 순조롭게 진행 될 거야

103. **COMMITTEES**(위원회) 1037

An-do doesn't want to be a member just along for the ride 외 **29**개

안도는 재미로(명예뿐인) 회원이 되길 원치 않아

104. **BANK**(은행) 1041

A careful and impartial review of the bank reference and the two references you gave to us indicate that your company is experiencing considerable financial difficulties in

making prompt payments 외 **25**개

귀사가 거래하는 은행과 신용거래처 두 곳의 신중하고 공정한 의견은 귀사가 현재 대금 지급을 하기엔 심각한 자금 압박을 받고 있다고 말하고 있습니다

A man takes a drink, the drink takes another, and the drink takes the man 외 **158**개

사람이 술을 마시고, 술이 사람을 마시고, 술이 사람을 마신다

A bean sprout soup loaded with hot red pepper, is considered the best for recovering from a hangover 외 **214**개

매운 고추 가루를 탄 콩나물국을 숙취 회복에 최고로 친다

An-do just dug in his heels 외 **69**개

안도가 고집을 부렸어

A capital punishment is more reprehensible because it is officially sanctioned and done with great ceremony in the name of the society 외 **54**개

사형은 그것이 사회라는 이름으로 공식적으로 승인되어 커다란 의식 속에서 행해지므로 더욱 지탄을 받는다

약소하지만 선물로 드리지요

115. DAILY HABITS(일상 생활) 1249

**A hundred thousand won doesn't go very far these days,
with the prices rising all the time 외 468개**

물가가 오르기만 하니 십만원 이라야 얼마 못 가

116. SELF-ESTEEM(자신&자만) 1293

A man is valued as he makes himself valuable 외 33개

사람은 자신을 얼마나 가치 있는 사람으로 만드느냐에 따라 평가된다

117. FREEDOM(자유) 1297

**A hungry man is more interested in four sandwiches than
four freedoms 외 37개**

배고픈 사람에게는 네 가지 자유보다 네 개의 샌드위치가 낫다

118. TRIALS(재판) 1301

All the evidence makes in the same direction 외 36개

모든 증거가 같은 방향을 가리키고 있다

119. PROPOSAL(제안) 1305

All he has done is put a damper on every suggestion 외 67개

그가 한 일은 모든 제안에 대해 생트집 잡는 것이었어

의무감이 일에는 유용하나 대인관계에는 기분을 언짢게 하는 요인이 된다

the two references you gave to us indicate that your
company is experiencing considerable financial difficulties in
making prompt payments 외 87개

귀사가 거래하는 은행과 신용거래처 두 곳의 신중하고 공정한 의견은 귀
사가 현재 대금 지급을 하기엔 심각한 자금 압박을 받고 있다고 말하고
있습니다

A nice cool glass of beer(a paid vacation) is just what the
doctor ordered 외 35개

시원한 맥주 한 잔(유급휴가)이야 말로 내게 가장 필요한 것이다

Allowing unethical figures to appear on the TV programs
will only serve to numb the sense of viewers 외 29개

비도덕적인 인물들을 TV 프로그램에 출연시킨다는 것은 시청자들의 도
덕관념을 마비시킬 뿐이다

1. 가족   Family

A good father is a little bit of a mother
> ↳ 좋은 아버지는 약간의 엄마 역할도 한다

A happy family is but an earlier heaven
> ↳ 행복한 가정은 한 발 앞서 찾아 온 천국이다

A home without love is no more a home, than a body without a sound mind is a man
> ↳ 건전한 정신이 없는 육체가 인간이 아닌 것과 같이, 사랑이 없는 가정은 가정이 아니다

A lot of fortune came Doo-soo's way when his father retired
> ↳ 아버지가 은퇴하시자 두수에겐 거금이 생겼지

A man must cultivate himself and manage his family properly before he can govern the nation
> ↳ 수신제가 이후에 치국평천하

A man travels the world in search of what he needs and returns home to find it
> ↳ 사람은 자신이 필요로 하는 것을 찾아 세계로 돌아다니다가 집에 와서야 그것을 찾아내게 된다

A mother with a large brood never has a peaceful day
> ↳ 가지 많은 나무가 바람 잘 날 없다

A mother-in-law remembers not that she was once a daughter-in-law

---

▸ **cultivate**   prepare for crops, forster the growth of, refine   ▸ **brood**   family of young, sit on eggs to hatch

└ 시어머니는 며느리 적 생각 못한다

> (Set a beggar on horseback, and he'll ride to the devil 개구리가 올챙이 적 생각 못한다) 갑자기 부자가 되거나 높은 지위에 오른 사람은 올바로 판단하지 못한다.

A new mouth to feed. That's all they need
> └ 새 식구가 생기다니. 그들에겐 너무 힘든 일이지

A will gives detailed instructions to your family in case of your sudden death
> └ 유언장에는 사람이 갑자기 사망할 경우에 대비하여 가족들에게 상세히 전할 말을 명시해 두는 것이다

Accidents will happen in the best regulated families
> └ 불행한 일은 누구에게나 일어난다

> 사람의 지위 고하에 따라 불행한 일이 선별적으로 일어나는 것은 아니다. 불행이 언제 닥칠지 모르니까 항상 유비무환의 자세를 가져야 한다(=We must be ready, because accidents will come at an hour when we do not expect them).

After all this time, my parents are still romantic
> └ 많은 세월이 지났는데도 우리 부모님은 여전히 금실 좋아

All the boys in that school are trotting(running) after my daughter
> └ 저 학교에 다니는 모든 남학생들이 우리 딸을 졸졸 따라다니고 있다

All they need is another mouth to feed
> └ 그들에게 필요한 것은 아이를 하나(더) 가지는 것뿐이다

- **feed** give food to, eat, food for livestock
- **detail** small item or part, give details of
- **regulate** govern according to rule

Almighty God, keep our wives from shopping sprees and protect them from bargains they don't need or can't afford Almighty God, keep our wives from shopping sprees and protect them from bargains they don't need or can't afford
> ↳ 전능하신 하나님 아버지, 우리의 아내들이 쇼핑에 미쳐 돌아가는 일이 없도록 역사 하여 주시고 세일이라 해서 필요하지도 않거나 분수에 넘치는 물건을 사는 일이 없도록 살펴 주시기를 기원합니다

An apple doesn't fall far from the tree
> ↳ 핏줄은 못 속여

> 아들은 보통 당연히 아버지를 닮는다. 아들과 아버지가 아주 많이 닮아 있을 경우에는 '아들은 아버지의 분신(Chip off the old block)'이라고 한다. 여기서 'chip'은 'block'에서 떨어져 나온 조각이라는 뜻을 가지고 있다.
> (=Like father, like son)
> (=Blood will tell)

As a baseball player, he doesn't come up to his brother's shoulder
> ↳ 그가 야구선수로서는 형보다 못해

As you have been married for five years, it's time to start a family
> ↳ 이제 네가 결혼한 지 5년이나 됐으니 아이를 가져야 할 것 아니냐

Asking me to support my parents on my meager salary is too hard on me
> ↳ 변변찮은 월급으로 부모님을 공양하라는 것은 무리입니다

Boil not the pap before the child is born
> ↳ 아이도 낳기 전에 기저귀부터 장만하지(미리 설치지) 마라

> (=Cut no fish before you get them)
> (=Don't eat the calf in the cow's belly)

› **support** take sides with, provide with food clothing, and shelter, hold up or serve as a foundation for

› **meager** thin, scanty

Bong-soo has three mouths to feed
ㄴ 봉수는(부양할)가족이 셋이다

Bong-soo is always bragging(boasting) of his son, as if anybody cared
ㄴ 봉수는 남들이 들은 척도 안 하는 아들 얘기만 하고 있어

Bringing up children in the absence of an extended family is no easy task
ㄴ 가까운 친척들의 부재중에 이들의 아이들을 돌보는 것은 결코 쉬운 것이 아니다

Can she maintain the balancing act of pleasing her parents and her parent-in-law?
ㄴ 그녀가 친부모와 시부모 모두를 기쁘게 할 균형 있는 행동을 유지할 수 있을까?

Chan-soo can't sponge food from his relatives
ㄴ 찬수는 계속해서 친척에게 밥을 얻어먹고 지낼 순 없어

Confide in an aunt and the world will know
ㄴ 아주머니(숙모)한테 가만히 말해도 온 세상이 알게 돼있다

Dear(God) knows when I'll get home tonight so don't wait up for me
ㄴ 오늘밤 언제 집에 들어갈지 모르니 나 때문에 기다리지마

Do you keep the household accounts?
ㄴ 가계부를 적습니까?

Don't expect being a mother will be smooth sailing
ㄴ 엄마노릇이 누워 떡 먹기라고 생각지 말아라

Don't shoot the works on your daughter's wedding
ㄴ 딸 시집 보낼 때 무리하지 마세요

Even the porcupine thinks its young are soft and glossy
ㄴ 고슴도치도 제 새끼는 예쁘다고 한다

‣ **calf**   young cow or related mammal
‣ **brag**   to boast, to show off

‣ **maintain**   keep in an existing state(as of repair), sustain, declare

(=The beetle is a beauty in the eyes of its mother)
(=The crow thinks her own bird fairest)
(=The owl thinks its own young fairest)
(=No mother has a homely child)

Families prepare 'charye' for their deceased ancestors, serving rice, soup, side dishes, fruit, and rice cakes to spirits visiting their homes
　　↳ 가족들은 집으로 찾아오는 돌아가신 조상들의 귀신들에게 밥, 국, 찬, 떡 등을 올릴 차례를 준비한다

Families visit tombs to pay respects to their ancestors on the occasion of Chusok
　　↳ 가족들은 추석에 즈음하여 조상의 묘를 찾아 성묘를 한다

Family background and schooling are considered important in many arranged marriages
　　↳ 중매결혼에는 가문과 학력이 중시되는 때가 많다

Family ties are strong ties
　　↳ 피는 물보다 진해(팔은 안으로 굽어)

인간은 세상의 어떤 관계보다도 혈연관계를 중요시한다. 그러나 맹목적인 사랑이 아닌 능력에 맞게 대우하는 사랑을 말한다(A family connection will outweigh other relationships 혈연 관계가 다른 인간 관계보다 훨씬 앞선다).
(=Family sticks together)
(=Siblings are closer than friends)
(=Blood is thicker than water)

Gil-soo's parents always gives in too much
　　↳ 길수의 부모님은 너무 오냐오냐하고 애들을 길러

· **ancestor** one from whom an individual is descended　｜　· **occasion** favorable opportunity, cause, time of an event, special event

Han-soo took his responsibilities as a father seriously but in matters of discipline was rather too free with his hands
  ↳ 그는 진지하게 아버지로서의 책임을 떠맡았으나 훈육문제에 있어서는 툭하면 아이를 때렸다

He is a good boy to his parents
  ↳ 그는 그의 부모님에게는 좋은 아들이다

> (=He tries to make)

He is ready to make his parents happy
  ↳ 그는 효자다

He's on the outs with his father
  ↳ 그는 자기 아버지와 사이가 나빠

Her daughter's learning difficulties can be correctly diagnosed and treated
  ↳ 그 여자의 딸의 학습장애는 정확히 진단하여 교정할 수 있다

Her father's been in the pits ever since her mother passed away
  ↳ 그 여자의 어머니가 돌아가신 후 그 여자의 아버지는 생지옥이었지 뭐

His anguish at not being able to be at his father's deathbed preyed on his mind for a long time
  ↳ 그에게는 아버지의 임종을 못 본데 대한 고뇌가 오랫동안 마음을 괴롭혔다

His death will fall heavy on his family
  ↳ 그가 죽으면 가족들 살 길이 난감해

His family celebrates birthdays in a big way
  ↳ 그의 가족들은 생일을 성대하게 치른다

His mother got after him for tracking mud into the house

· **diagnose** identification of a disease from its symptoms

· **pass away** a formal term for 'die'

ㄴ 그의 어머니가 그에게 흙을 묻혀 집에 들어오지 말라고 야단치셨어

His parents will be riding on his coattails for the rest of their life
ㄴ 그 사람 능력 덕분에 그의 부모는 앞으로 호강하겠군

His son is breaking his neck to get into the university
ㄴ 그의 아들은 대학에 들어가려고 열심히 공부하고 있다

His strange personality runs in his family
ㄴ 그의 이상한 성격은 대물림이야

Home is where the heart is
ㄴ 네 마음이 있는 곳이 바로 집이다=가정은 마음의 지주다

How did you leave your parents?
ㄴ 떠날 때 양친은 어떠셨습니까?

I can't picture myself as a father yet
ㄴ 아직 아이의 아빠가 됐다는 실감이 안나

I did my daughter over for coming home late
ㄴ 딸아이가 늦게 집에 오기에 야단 쳐줬지

I wanted to buy it, but my mother bullied me out of it
ㄴ 사고싶었지만 어머니가 윽박질러 못 샀지

In Korea traditionally any mother-in-law provides her son-in-law with a feast fit for a king
ㄴ 한국에서는 전통적으로 장모가 사위에게 진수성찬으로 대접한다

In old times, property was usually handed down to the oldest son upon his father's death
ㄴ 옛날엔 보통 아버지의 사망 때 장남에게 재산을 대물림했다

Living on my uncle make me feel small
ㄴ 아저씨 댁에 기식하자니 눈치가 보여

› **coattail** rear flap of a man's coat
› **break one's neck** do one's best

› **picture** image or copy
› **bully** one who hurts or intimidates others

Lots of parents sweated bullets(blood) to put their children through colleges, but the children treat their parents like strangers
> ↳ 많은 부모들이 자녀들을 대학에 보내느라 뼈가 빠졌건만 그들은 그런 부모들을 언제 봤느냐는 듯이 대하기 일쑤다

Man-soo's father changed jobs several times a year, and the family was moved from pillar to post
> ↳ 만수의 아버지는 1년에 여러 번 직장을 옮겨서 가족들이 여기 저기 이사를 다녔어

Moon-soo's ship came in when he married into a wealthy family
> ↳ 문수는 부잣집에 장가들어 살판났어

Most of these migrant urban dwellers visit their home villages or towns, taking their families along
> ↳ 대부분의 이들 도시지역 이주자 주민들은 가족들을 데리고 고향 마을을 방문한다

Mother and child are both doing well
> ↳ 모자는 다 건강하다

Mother is always holding up my cousin to me
> ↳ 어머닌 늘 사촌형(동생)을 본받으라고 성화다

Mother wiped away our tears, helped us get over our grief and comforted us when life wasn't fair
> ↳ 어머니는 삶이 평탄하지 못할 때 우리의 눈물을 닦아주고 우리가 슬픔을 극복하도록 도와주고 위로해 주셨다

모성애를 나타내는 문장이다. 모성애는 모든 생명체가 가지고 있는 본능이다
(The mother's breath is always sweet = 어머니의 숨결은 언제나 달다).

- **urban** characteristic of a city
- **dweller** reside, keep the attention directed
- **grief** emotional suffering caused by or as if by bereavement, disaster

My brother is on his feet soon after the operation
┗ 형은 수술 후 곧 회복했어

My daughter has been under a cloud since her colleague's money disappeared
┗ 우리 딸은 동료의 돈이 없어진 후 의심을 사고 있어(**Under a cloud**에 **depress, scold**의 뜻도 있음)

My daughter has itchy feet
┗ 우리 딸은 역마살이 끼었어

My daughter thinks the world of me
┗ 우리 딸은 나를 가장 사랑하고 존경해요

My daughter ties up the bathroom every morning
┗ 우리 딸이 화장실을 오래 쓰는 통에 아무도 쓸 수 가 없어

My family comes first, my work next(second)
┗ 가족이 먼저고 일은 그 다음이야

My father feels much better now that he has gotten it out of his system
┗ 아버지는 겁내어 오던 일을 해치웠으니 훨씬 마음 편하게 되셨어

My father gave me a blank check to use his car for month
┗ 차를 맘대로 쓰라고 아버지가 허락하셨어

My father has a mind like a steel trap
┗ 아버지는 기억력이 매우 좋으셔

My father implanted good ideas that have stayed with me all my life
┗ 아버지는 내가 평생 가지고 있던 좋은 생각을 심어준 분이다

My father lay at death's door for a week, but he began to get better
┗ 아버지가 1주일 동안 사경을 헤매었으나 곧 나아지기 시작하셨어

My father remembered me on my birthday
┗ 아버지는 내 생일을 잊지 않고 선물을 주셨다

› **scold** criticize severely, person who scolds | › **implant** set firmly or deeply, fix in the mind or spirit

My father went through the roof when he saw what I did
　　↳ 내가 저지른 일을 보고 아버지가 노발대발 하셨어

My father won't hear of(to) it
　　↳ 아버지가 승낙을 안 하서

My friend cast out his daughter when she married against his wishes
　　↳ 우리 친구는 딸이 뜻을 거역해 결혼하자 다시는 안 본다며 의절을 선
　　언했어

My little nephew would always come trotting after me, annoying me a lot
　　↳ 내가 가는 곳마다 조카애가 성가시게 따라다녔다

My mother's mind is failing
　　↳ 어머닌 노망기가 있어

> (=My mother is getting senile)

My mother's teeth are all gone
　　↳ 어머니의 이(치아)가 전부 빠졌어

My parents wear their years well
　　↳ 우리 부모님은 연세가 많아도 정정하서

Nam-soo's parents gave him the third degree about the girl he meets
　　↳ 남수의 부모님은 그가 사귀는 아가씨에 대해서 자세히 물어보셨다

On my mother's grave
　　↳ 맹세할게

One father is more than a hundred schoolmasters
　　↳ 한 사람의 아버지는 백 명의 학교 선생님보다 낫다

Parents are answerable for the crimes of their children
　　↳ 부모들은 자녀들의 범죄에 대해 책임이 있다

· **go through the roof** is so angry that
one cannot bear the anger

· **annoy** disturb or irritate

Parents are much the same all the world over
ㄴ 부모님들은 어디로 가나 똑같아

Poor children wore chothes their brothers and sisters had grown out of
ㄴ 가난한 집 아이들은 형이나 누나가 몸이 커져서 더 이상 입지 못하게
된 옷을 물려받아 입었다

Pyung-soo put on a show of cheerfulness to set(put) his parents at ease
ㄴ 평수는 부모님을 안심시키려고 기분 좋은 척 했다

Sang-soo has a bad habit of spouting off about things that concerns only himself and his family
ㄴ 상수는 자신과 자기 가족 얘기만 잔뜩 늘어놓는 나쁜 버릇이 있다

Sang-soo's parents swelled with pride as they watched him receive the prize
ㄴ 상수의 부모님은 상수가 상을 받는 것을 보고 뿌듯해 했다

Send your beloved son on a journey
ㄴ 자식을 사랑하거든 여행을 보내어라

She could have averted a conflagration if any member of her family had reacted to the first flames
ㄴ 그녀의 가족 중 누구든 한 사람이라도 첫 번째 불길에 조치를 취했더라면 큰불은 피할 수 있었을 것이다

She couldn't bear to leave her parents and cried all the way to the station
ㄴ 그녀는 부모를 떠나는 발걸음이 떨어지지 않아 줄곧 눈물을 흘리면서 역까지 갔다

She decided to bow out gracefully and spend more time with her family
ㄴ 그녀는 깨끗이 물러나서 가족들과 더 많은 시간을 보내기로 결정했다

She is her mother all over even in personality
ㄴ 그 여자는 성격에서조차 자기 어머니를 꼭 닮았어

She looks more like her father than her mother

› **spout**   shoot forth in a stream, say pompously | › **swell**   enlarge, bulge, fill or be filled with emotion

↳ 그 여자는 엄마보다 아빠를 많이 닮았다

She resembles more her mother than her father

↳ 그녀는 자기 아버지 보다 어머니를 더 많이 닮았다

She tried to deflect the attention of the media by disowning her own son

↳ 그녀는 자신의 아들을 모르는 사람이라고 잡아뗌으로써 매스컴의 주목을 피하려 했다

She was badly(well) left

↳ 그 여자는 유족으로서의 생활이 어려웠다(넉넉했다)

She was intolerant of any member of the family to follow a different religion

↳ 그녀는 가족 중 누구든 다른 종교를 믿는 것을 허용하지 않았다

She was more wife than mother

↳ 그 여자는 아이들 보다 남편을 더 소중히 여기는 여자였다

She's been after her daughter all day to clean up her room

↳ 그 여자는 자기 딸에게 방 좀 치우라고 하루종일 성화다

She's his half-sister on his father's side

↳ 그 여자는 그의 이복누이이다

She's my soul sister

↳ 그 여자는 나하고 마음이 통해

She'll catch hell if her father gets hold of her

↳ 그 여자는 아버지에게 붙잡히기만 하면 혼이 날 것이다

Sook-hee nursed her father back to health

↳ 숙희는 아버지가 건강을 회복할 때까지 간호했다

Tai-ho knocks himself out everyday to support his family

↳ 태호는 가족을 위해 매일 열심히 일한다

Tai-jung is an heir to his mother's fine brain

› **deflect** turn aside

› **disown** repudiate

› **heir** one who inherits or is entitled to inherit property

ㄴ 태정인 어머니에게서 훌륭한 두뇌를 물려받았어

Tai-soo was heir to large estates
ㄴ 태수는 막대한 땅을 물려 받았어

Taking place for his sick father, he had to work for his brothers and sisters
ㄴ 앓고 계신 아버지를 대신해서 그는 동생들을 위해서 일했다

The average family is a great deal smaller than it used to be
ㄴ 평균 가족 수는 예전보다 매우 적다

The baby's talking was hardly intelligible except to its mother
ㄴ 아기가 하는 말은 아기엄마 외에는 알아듣지 못해

The biggest family problems are those caused by know-it-all kids and yes-it-all parents
ㄴ 가족의 가장 큰 문제는 모든 것을 아는 체하는 자녀와 그저 오냐오냐 하는 부모에 의해 발생한다

The exceptional zeal for education among Korean parents ensures that private tutoring will not disappear as long as the reality in the schools fails to meet their expectation
ㄴ 학교교육이 현실적으로 학부모들의 기대에 못 미치는 한 한국 학부모들의 유별난 교육열풍은 과외가 사라지지 않을 것임이 확실하다

The family experienced the whole gamut of suffering
ㄴ 가족은 온갖 고난을 겪었다

The four children are beginning to tax their parents' strength
ㄴ 그들 네 아이들은 부모들에게 정말 부담이 되고있어

The parents are the best judges of their children
ㄴ 부모만큼 자식을 아는 사람 없다

The project is intended to make it easier to make parents to keep in touch with their sons in the military

---

‣ **ensure** guarantee

‣ **gamut** entire range or series

‣ **judge** form an opinion, decide as a judge

↳ 이 안은 부모가 군에 있는 아들들에게 연락을 쉽게 취할 수 있도록 하는 의도에 있다

There is no way to be a perfect mother and million ways to be a good one
↳ 완벽한 어머니가 되는 길은 없지만 좋은 어머니가 되는 길은 많다

This is our family tradition to hand this ring down(on) from mother-in-law to daughter-in-law
↳ 시어머니가 며느리에게 이 반지를 물러주는 게 우리 집 전통이다

Virtues and happiness are mother and daughter
↳ 덕행과 행복은 어머니와 딸과의 관계다

Wan-soo is the black sheep of the family
↳ 완수는 집에서 내놓은 사람

We must learn to live together as brothers or perish together as fools
↳ 우리는 형제같이 같이 살지 않으면 바보같이 망하게 된다는 것을 깨달아야 한다

We never know the love of our parents for us until we have become parents
↳ 부모가 돼보지 않고서는 부모의 사랑을 모른다

When his father died of lung cancer, he saw the light and quit smoking
↳ 그의 아버지가 폐암으로 돌아가시자 깨달은바 있어 금연했다

Would you raise your hand against your own parents?
↳ 부모님에게 거역하고 나설 수 있겠나?

You seem to place honor above(before) your family
↳ 넌 가족보다 명예를 중히 여기는 것 같구나

You'll catch it from your father
↳ 너희 아버지한테 야단 맞을 거다

You'll understand your parents with age

› **perish** die or spoil
› **lung** breathing organ in the chest

› **virtue** moral excellence, effective or commendable quality, chastity

ㄴ 나이를 먹으면 부모님을 이해하게 될 거야

Your daughter is only in a phase

ㄴ 자네 딸은 잠시 그러는 것 뿐이야

Your daughter was burning up the(phone) line

ㄴ 너희 딸은 전화통에 불이 나더군

‣ **phase**   particular appearance or stage in
a recurring series of changes

2. 감정 & 기분   Emotion & Feeling

A change is as good as a rest
    ↳ 분위기 전환은 상큼한 기분을 주게 돼 있어

A good indignation brings out all one's power
    ↳ 훌륭한 분노는 온 힘을 발휘시킨다

A man is as old as he feels, and a woman as old as she looks
    ↳ 남자의 나이는 느끼기에 달렸고 여자의 나이는 얼굴에 나타난다

> 남자는 나이가 들어도 건강하기만 하고 젊다고 느끼기만 한다면 나이에 구애받지 않지만, 여자는 외모, 즉 겉으로 드러나는 나이에 많은 구애를 받는다. 아무리 화장을 해도 얼굴에 나타나는 나이는 속일 수 없기 때문이다.

A puzzled look(expression) crossed(passed) over his face
    ↳ 곤혹스러운 표정이 그의 얼굴을 스쳤다

A rude remark sprang to my lips, but I prevented myself from saying it just in time
    ↳ 쌍소리가 불쑥 튀어나오려 했지만 가까스로 때맞춰 참았다

A shiver went through me
    ↳ 전신이 오싹했어

> (=It chilled(scared) me to the bone)
> (=It freaked me out)

▸ **indignation** anger aroused by something unjust or unworthy
▸ **puzzle** confuse, attempt to solve
▸ **shiver** tremble

A sorrow is an itching place which is made worse by scratching
ㄴ 슬픔은 긁을수록 가려워지는 가려운 자리이다

All she wished was for the ground to open and swallow her
ㄴ 그 여자는 쥐구멍이라도 있으면 들어가 버리고 싶은 심정뿐이었어

All this attention is embarrassing
ㄴ 관심이 내게 쏠리니 쑥스럽네

All your insults are like water off a duck's back
ㄴ 아무리 욕해도 난 아무렇지 않아

Although old beyond her years, I felt she was emotionally immature and not ready for marriage
ㄴ 그 여자가 나이에 비해 어른스럽긴 해도 결혼까지는 아직 덜 성숙해 있었다

Anger make a rich man hated, and a poor man scorned
ㄴ 부자가 화를 내면 미움을 사게되고 가난한 사람이 화를 내면 멸시받게 된다

Anger restrained is wisdom gained
ㄴ 화를 참으면 지혜를 얻는다

Annoyed is no word for it
ㄴ 그냥 언짢은 정도가 아냐

(=I'm just about to up=blow up)

As he managed to sell his house for a tidy sum he was elated at the unexpected windfall
ㄴ 그가 상당히 좋은 값으로 집을 팔게되자 굴러 들어온 호박에 한껏 고무되었다

As soon as she made the remark, she could have bitten her tongue off
ㄴ 그 여자는 말을 꺼내자마자 자신이 내뱉은 말에 대해 후회했다

‣ **scorn**　emotion involving both anger and disgust　　‣ **windfall**　thing blown down by wind, unexpected benefit

Better by far you should forget and smile than you should remember and be sad
> ↳ 잊지 않고 슬퍼하는 것보다 잊어버리고 웃는 편이 훨씬 낫다

Bigotry may be roughly defined as the anger of men who have no opinions
> ↳ 편협은 대략 아무 의견이 없는 사람의 분노로 정의될 수 있다

Bong-soo told me where to get off
> ↳ 봉수가 내게 화를 내며 말했어

Chang-soo was cool, calm, and collected
> ↳ 창수는 당황하지도 않고, 놀라지도 않고, 침착했어

Chul-hee feels more himself
> ↳ 철희는 자신에 대한 긍지를 느끼고 있다

Couldn't be better
> ↳ 지금 기분 최고야

Delay is the antidote of anger
> ↳ 지체함은 노여움의 해독제이다

Did that piss you off?
> ↳ 그래서 열 받았나?

Divorce can provoke aberrant behavior on the part of both parents and children when emotional resources to deal with aberrant are completely drained
> ↳ 이혼은 이상행위를 다룰 정서수단이 완전히 없어지게 될 때 부모와 아이들 모두에게 일탈행위를 유발시킬 수 있다

Don't be ruled by your passions
> ↳ 감정에 치우쳐선 안 돼

Don't blow up over minor things
> ↳ 사소한 일로 화내지마

› **antidote** remedy for poison

› **piss off** annoyed or disturbed

› **provoke** incite to anger, stir up on purpose

Don't bottle up all your feelings
> ↳ 감정을 모두 억제하려고만 하지마

Don't get emotional on me
> ↳ 내게 감정으로 대하지마

Don't let anyone feel isolated
> ↳ 누구든 외톨이가 된(소외감이 드는) 기분으로 만들어선 안 돼

Don't steam
> ↳ 흥분하지마

> (=Calm down)
> (=Take it easy)

Don't work you bad temper off on me, I'm not to blame for the way you feel
> ↳ 너의 언짢은 감정을 나한테 화풀이하지 마라, 너의 그런 기분이 나 때문이 아니잖아

Don't you feel embarrassed?
> ↳ 부끄럽지 않니?

Dong-soo did a slow burn
> ↳ 동수는 점점 화가 났어

Dong-soo goes through a lot of emotional ups and downs
> ↳ 동수는 감정의 기복이 심해

Each and every one of us jumped for joy
> ↳ 우리는 너도나도 다 기뻐 날뛰었다

Ease(Relieve your strain)
> ↳ 긴장을 풀어

› **isolate** place or keep by itself   › **embarrass** cause distress and self-consciousness

> (=Take it easy)
> (=Take a deep breath)

Ed's going to explode when he sees this mess
↳ 에드가 이 엉망인 꼴을 보면 노발대발하겠다

Everyone feels this way
↳ 누구나 그런 기분일거다

Everything feels different somehow
↳ 감회가 새롭다

> (=It's like I'm seeing everything for the first time)
> (=Everything seems so strange)
> (=It doesn't feel the same as before)

Fear was gradually merged in curiosity
↳ 공포는 차츰 호기심으로 변해갔다

For better, for worse
↳ 어쩔 수 없지 뭐(기쁠 때나 슬플 때나)

Hate is a prolonged form of suicide
↳ 증오는 오랜 시간에 걸친 자살행위다

Hatred of dishonesty generally arises from fear of being deceived
↳ 증오는 대개 속임을 당할 우려에서 생겨난다

Hatred stirs up strife, but love covers all sins
↳ 미움은 다툼을 일으키지만 사랑은 모든 허물을 가리우느니라

He has it in for me
↳ 그 사람 내게 나쁜 감정을 가지고 있어

· **gradually** going by steps of degrees
· **merge** unite, blend

· **prolong** lengthen in time or extent
· **strife** conflict

He is all nerves
└ 신경이 날카로워져 있어

(=His nerves are on edge)

He made me feel second-best
└ 그가 와서 내가 뒷전에 밀려난 기분이야

He was much affronted at having his presence disregarded
└ 그는 자기의 존재를 무시당해 몹시 모욕을 느꼈다

He who is slow to anger keeps his anger longer
└ 성을 잘 내지 않는 사람이 성내면 오래 간다

He will have a fit
└ 그는 노발대발 할거다

He's just feeling his oats
└ 그는 의기양양해

Heaven's what I feel when I'm with you
└ 당신과 함께라면 천국에 있는 느낌

Her cruel remarks cut me to the quick
└ 그 여자 가시 돋친 한 마디에 기분 잡쳤어

Her heart was too full for words
└ 그녀는 감정이 북받쳐 말이 나오지 않았다

His words betrayed his anger
└ 말속에 가시

(=I could feel his anger in his words)

· **oat**   cereal grass or its edible seed
· **betray**   seduce, deliver to an enemy by

treachery, prove unfaithful to, reveal
unintentionally

How do you find yourself today?
> ↳ 오늘 기분이 어때?

> (=How goes it with you today?)

How does it feel being the top-dog in the Sales Department?
> ↳ 판매부의 부장된 기분이 어때?

Hyun-soo could have hurt you by telling what he knew, but he held fire
> ↳ 현수는 자기가 알고 있는 말을 내뱉어서 네 감정을 상하게 할 수 있었지만 참아준 거야

Hyun-soo is high but he is grounded
> ↳ 현수는 들떠있지만 절제하고 있어

Hyun-soo's been flying light since he got the word that he won the scholarship
> ↳ 현수는 장학금을 받게 됐다는 소식을 듣고 나서 붕 뜬 기분이야

I always have butterflies in my stomach
> ↳ 항상 가슴이 조마조마해

I am swamped with responsibilities
> ↳ 무거운 책임감을 느껴

I can't help myself
> ↳ 내 감정 억제 못해

I can't picture myself as a father yet
> ↳ 아직 아이의 아빠가 됐다는 실감이 안나

I can't tell you how pleased I am
> ↳ 말로 할 수 없을 만큼 기뻐

· **ground** force or bring down to the

· **swamp** deluge(as with water), wet spongy land

I did a slow burn
> ↳ 점점 화가 났다

I don't feel safe at all
> ↳ 전혀 맘이 안 놓여

> (=I feel so insecure)

I don't think I've ever felt like this
> ↳ 이런 기분 처음이야

I even love your faults
> ↳ 너의 단점까지 사랑해

I feel a bit lost
> ↳ 약간 멍한 기분

I feel like a fish out of water
> ↳ 어색해

> (=I feel so awkward)

I feel like I'm being forced to go
> ↳ 도살장에 끌려가는 기분이군

> (=I feel like I'm being dragged to the slaughterhouse)
> (=I feel like I'm going against my will)

I feel like my heart would break

▸ **drag** something dragged over a surface or through water, something that hinders | progress or is boring

ㄴ 하늘이 무너져 내리는 것만 같아

I feel out of it
ㄴ 난 소외감 느껴

I feel out of myself in this new line of business
ㄴ 새 일을 맡고 보니 어리벙벙해

I feel the empty place inside
ㄴ 마음속에 공허감 느껴

I felt a lump in my throat
ㄴ 감동했어

> (= I'm impressed)

I felt easier(relieved) after I said(had) my say
ㄴ 할 말을 다 하고 나니 개운해

I felt my ears burning yesterday
ㄴ 어제 내가 소문의 주인공이 되어 당혹스러웠어

I felt out of place(my element) there
ㄴ 거기선 어색한 기분이었어

I find that remark very offensive
ㄴ 지금 한 말 몹시 불쾌해

I hate myself
ㄴ 정말 미치겠다

I was all hot and bothered that things didn't turn out the way I wanted
ㄴ 일이 뜻대로 되질 않아서 애태웠지

I was so nervous I was left speechless(tongue-tied, the words stuck in

---

▸ **lump** mass of irregular shape, abnormal swelling, heap together

▸ **speechless** lose of power, act, or manner of speaking

my throat)
> ↳ 너무 떨려서 말이 안나왔어

I wish I could sink through the floor
> ↳ 쥐구멍에라도 들어가고 싶은 심정이야

> (=I wish the earth would swallow me up)

I'm agreeably disappointed
> ↳ 기우에 그쳐서 기쁘다

I'm dead serious
> ↳ 난 심각해

I'm feeling really overwhelmed stomach
> ↳ 한방 맞은 기분이야

> (=I feel like I've just been punched in the stomach)

I'm losing my patience
> ↳ 더 이상 참기 힘들어

I'm not even close to kidding
> ↳ 난 지금 장난할 기분 아냐

I'm not in the vein for work
> ↳ 일할 기분이 아냐

I'm not up to it
> ↳ 그럴 기분이 아냐

I'm really pissed off

· **overwhelm** overcome completely
· **vein** vessel that carries blood toward the

heart, distinctive nature or mode of expression

ㄴ 정말 열 받았어

I'm torn

ㄴ 내 마음은 찢어져

I've had enough of this

ㄴ 더 이상 못 참아

If you're patient in one moment of anger, you'll escape a hundred days of sorrow

ㄴ 한 순간의 화를 참으면 **100**일의 근심을 덜게된다

In a few minutes he had gone from violent anger to pathetic tears

ㄴ 잠시 후 그의 감정은 격렬한 분노에서 연민의 눈물로 바뀌었다

Is there any need to get steamed up about a trifle matter?

ㄴ 하찮은 일에 화를 내야만 하겠니?

It made my nose run(water)

ㄴ 코끝이 찡했어

(=It made my nose to twitch)
(=It made me sniffle)

It seemed very tongue in cheek

ㄴ 마치 놀림 당한 느낌이더군

It shows the way my mind was working then

ㄴ 그건 그 때 내 마음이 어디로 끌렸는지 보여주고 있어

It still bothers me

ㄴ 왠지 찝찝해

› **trifle** something of little value
› **twitch** move or pull with a sudden motion

› **sniffle** sniff repeatedly, speak with or as if with sniffling

> (=It still upsets me)
> (=It's still on my mind)

It's a bittersweet feeling
　　　ㄴ 시원섭섭해

It's just a groove in me
　　　ㄴ 그냥 행복한 느낌이 들어

It's when he's driving at high speeds that he feels truly alive
　　　ㄴ 그는 차를 쌩쌩 몰아야만 생기가 돈다

Jung-soo was nervous and couldn't speak at first; then he found his tongue
　　　ㄴ 정수가 처음에는 긴장해서 말이 안 나왔으나 이내 말문이 열렸어

Living on my uncle make me feel small
　　　ㄴ 아저씨 댁에 기식하자니 눈치가 보여

Let not the sun go down upon your wrath
　　　ㄴ 화가 나더라도 죄를 짓지 말고 해가 지기 전에 화를 풀어라

Lulu looked mad enough to eat nails
　　　ㄴ 루루가 엄청나게 화가 난 모양이야

Min-soo was boiling inside but he tried to cool it
　　　ㄴ 민수는 속으로 화가 났지만 참으려고 애썼어

Moon-hee is floating on air after her marriage
　　　ㄴ 문희는 결혼 후 붕 뜬 기분이야

Moon-ho doubled his fists in anger
　　　ㄴ 문호는 화가 나서 주먹을 불끈 쥐었다

Moon-soo was in a state
　　　ㄴ 문수는 초조해 하고 있었어

› **bittersweet** being at once both bitter and sweet, being both pleasant and sad

› **groove** long narrow channel, fixed routine

Mother wiped away our tears, helped us get over our grief and comforted us when life wasn't fair

    ㄴ 어머니는 삶이 평탄하지 못할 때 우리의 눈물을 닦아주고 우리가 슬픔을 극복하도록 도와주고 위로해 주셨다

> 모성애를 나타내는 문장이다. 모성애는 모든 생명체가 가지고 있는 본능이다
> (The mother's breath is always sweet = 어머니의 숨결은 언제나 달다).

My conscience pricks me

    ㄴ 양심에 찔려

My ears are smoking

    ㄴ 화가 나서 미치겠다

> (=I'm seeing red)

My emotions defy description

    ㄴ 감회를 말로 표현할 수 없군

My father feels much better now that he has gotten it out of his system

    ㄴ 아버지는 겁내어 오던 일을 해치웠으니 훨씬 마음 편하게 되셨어

My father went through the roof when he saw what I did

    ㄴ 내가 저지른 일을 보고 아버지가 노발대발 하셨어

My happiness is bitter-sweet

    ㄴ 시원섭섭한(착잡) 심정이야

> (=I have mixed feelings)

· **conscience** awareness of right and wrong   · **defy** challenge, boldly refuse to obey

· **prick** pierce slightly with a sharp point

My heart is in my mouth
      ㄴ 가슴이 조마조마하다

My heart was too full for words
      ㄴ 가슴이 벅차 말이 안나왔어

My legs got wobbly(unsteady)
      ㄴ 다리가 후들후들해

My voice was frozen with fear
      ㄴ 무서워서 목소리가 안나왔어

My wife gets sentimental in the spring
      ㄴ 집사람은 봄을 타

Neuron is a special cell in the body that is capable of sending along messages that represent feelings and commands to muscles
      ㄴ 뉴런은 체내의 특수세포로서 감정을 표현하거나 근육에게 명령하는 메시지를 전달하는 능력이 있다

Never let your personal emotions into your work
      ㄴ 개인감정을 업무에까지 개입시키지 마라

No need to get worked up
      ㄴ 흥분할 필요 없어

No one can make you feel inferior without your consent
      ㄴ 당신의 동의가 없다면 아무도 당신이 열등감을 느끼게 하지 못한다

Nothing sharpens sight like envy
      ㄴ 질투만큼 눈을 반짝반짝하게 해주는 것은 없다

Now she laughs, then she weeps
      ㄴ 그녀는 금세 웃다가 금세 운다

Of all the passions, fear weakens judgement
      ㄴ 모든 감정 중에서 두려움은 판단력을 약하게 한다

› **wobbly** trembling, move or cause to move with an irregular rocking motion

› **consent** give permission or approval

Once bitten, twice shy
> ↳ 자라보고 놀란 가슴 솥뚜껑보고 놀란다

One could tell his face was distorted by rage
> ↳ 그가 화가 나서 얼굴이 일그러졌다는 것은 누구나 알 수 있었다

Our joy knew no bounds
> ↳ 우린 한없이 기뻐했지

People began to feel a sneaking sympathy(sense) with him
> ↳ 사람들이 그에게 은근히 동정했다

Peter turned out to have a soft spot(center)
> ↳ 피터가 나중에는 안타까워했어

Politicians can do worse than display their emotions in public
> ↳ 정치인이 자기 감정을 대중 앞에 토로한다해서 뭐가 이상해

Pyung-soo put on a show of cheerfulness to set(put) his parents at ease
> ↳ 평수는 부모님을 안심시키려고 기분 좋은 척 했다

Sadness and gladness succeed each other
> ↳ 슬픔과 기쁨은 서로 교대한다

Sang-soo isn't angry yet, but he's doing a slow burn
> ↳ 상수가 지금 당장 화가 나 있는 건 아니지만 점점 울화통이 치밀 거야

Sang-soo's parents swelled with pride as they watched him receive the prize
> ↳ 상수의 부모님은 상수가 상을 받는 것을 보도 뿌듯해 했다

Serving one's passion is the greatest slavery
> ↳ 자신의 감정에 이끌리는 것이 가장 큰 굴종이다

She banged her hand on the table, fighting back tears of rage and frustration
> ↳ 그녀는 테이블을 쾅 치면서 분노와 좌절의 눈물을 삼켰다

| ‣**distort** twist out of shape, condition, or true meaning | ‣**rage** violent anger, vogue, be extremely angry or violent, be out of control |

She came unglued and cried her eyes out
↳ 그 여자는 제 정신을 잃고 펑펑 울었어

She couldn't keep the tears from her eyes
↳ 그녀는 흐르는 눈물을 억제할 수 없었다

She cried fit to break her heart
↳ 그 여자는 가슴이 터지게 울었다

She cut him to the quick when she called him a cheapskate
↳ 그녀가 그를 구두쇠라고 불러서 감정을 크게 상했다

She felt the mistress of the situation
↳ 그 여자는 무엇이든지 자기 뜻대로 안 되는 것이 없는 기분이었다

She rained on my parade
↳ 그 여자 때문에 기분 잡쳤어

She raises a red flag when she gets angry
↳ 그 여자가 화가 나면 경고 신호를 보내거든

She said that in the heat of the moment
↳ 그 여자는 그 때 격해져서 그렇게 말했다

She talks a mile a minute when mad
↳ 그 여자가 화나면 속사포같이 말을 쏟아놓지

She was a woman who gave free play to her emotions
↳ 그 여자는 자신의 감정대로 행동하는 사람이었어

She was trying to come on to me, but I found her unlucky
↳ 그 여자가 날 유혹하려 했지만 불쾌한 느낌이 들었어

She went ballistic when the dude called her a liar
↳ 그 기생오라비 녀석이 그 여자에게 거짓말쟁이라고 하자 그 여자가 발끈했어

She would give her world to lift you up
↳ 그녀는 네 기분을 돋우는 일이라면 어떠한 희생도 마다하지 않을 거야

▸ **mistress** woman in control, woman with whom a man lives unmarried

▸ **ballistic** science of projectile motion
▸ **dude** dangy

She's been trying to put it behind her, but she's still furious
> 그녀가 그 일을 덮어두려고 애써오고 있기는 하지만 아직도 화가 잔뜩 나 있다

She's laughing all over her face
> 그 여자는 희색이 만면해

She's now ten feet tall
> 그 여자는 지금 하늘을 날아오르는 기분이야

> (=She feels the top of the world)

Smiles gave way to deep sorrow
> 미소가 깊은 슬픔으로 바뀌었다

Sook-hee feels blue whenever summer comes(rolls around)
> 숙희는 여름을 잘 타

> (=Sook-hee gets down(depressed, sensitive) whenever summer comes)

Sook-hee is distracted between hope and fear
> 숙희는 희망과 불안으로 뒤숭숭해

Sung-soo is feeling like being slapped in the face
> 성수는 한 방 맞은 기분이야

> (=Sung-soo is feeling really overwhelmed)
> (=Sung-soo feels like he's been punched in the stomach)

> **furious** fierce or angry
> **blue** melancholy

> **distract** divert the mind or attention of

Surrendering herself to her feelings of shame, she killed herself
↳ 그 여자는 부끄러운 마음을 이기지 못하여 자살했다

Tai-ho stepped on someone's toes during the last campaign
↳ 태호는 지난 유세 중 누군가의 감정을 건드린 일이 있어

Tai-ho took on sadly when told the sad news
↳ 태호는 비보를 듣고 몹시 심란해 했다

Tai-ho was on edge(running in circles)
↳ 태호가 안절부절못하고 있었어

Tai-ho was sweating bullets, waiting for the results
↳ 태호는 결과를 기다리면서 초조했다

Tai-ho's temper is equal to any trial
↳ 태호는 어떤 일에도 화를 내지 않는다

Talking about freckles gets her going
↳ 그 여자에게 주근깨 얘기를 하면 열 받지

Tell me how you feel
↳ 네 감정을 얘기해봐

That man always looks over the top of his wire rim glasses when angry
↳ 저 사람이 화가 나면 언제나 철 테 안경너머로 쳐다본다

That really burns me up
↳ 열 받네

The abrupt shrill noise startled me and destroyed my concentration
↳ 갑자기 날카로운 소리가 나는 바람에 깜짝 놀라 집중력이 흩어졌다

The hatred between the two men never flickered out
↳ 두 사람 사이의 미운 감정은 사라지지 않았다

The idea that the gravitational pull of the moon affects human

---

› **trial** hearing and judgement of a matter in court

› **shrill** utter a piercing sound

› **flicker** waver, burn unsteadily

emotions is far from certain
> ↳ 달의 중력이 인간의 감정에 영향을 미친다는 생각은 결코 정확성이 있는 것이 아니다

The noises jarred on my ears(nerves)
> ↳ 그 소리가 나에게 거슬렸다

The sight of his homeland brought a lump to his throat
> ↳ 그는 고향 땅을 보게되자 감개가 무량했다

There's a feeling of conflict in the air
> ↳ 갈등의 기운이 감돌고 있다

There's no laugh in the air
> ↳ 세상에 웃음이 다 사라졌어

There's no need to fly off(at) the handle
> ↳ 흥분할 일이 아냐

> (=There's no need to get worked-up)

To treat an enemy with magnanimity is to blunt our hatred for him
> ↳ 적에게 관대함은 적에 대한 우리의 미운 감정을 누그러뜨린다

To wrong those we hate is to add fuel to our hatred
> ↳ 우리를 미워하는 사람을 학대함은 우리의 미운 감정에 기름 붓기이다

True compassion can only be felt in the hearts of those who have suffered the same situation
> ↳ 진정한 연민은 똑같은 상황을 겪어본 사람들의 마음속에서만 느껴질 수 있다

· **conflict** war, clash of ideas

· **magnanimity** noble or generous

· **blunt** not sharp, tactless, make dull

> '동병상련', '유유상종' 등의 사자성어와 같은 뜻이다. 같은 처지에 있거나 같은 공동체에 속해 있으면 서로의 마음을 잘 이해하고, 서로의 이익을 위해 행동한다(Likeness cause liking = Dog doesn't eat dog).

Try not to let your personal feelings enter into the decision
ㄴ 너의 개인 감정을 그 결정에 개입시키지 않도록 해라

Try not to make him feel put down
ㄴ 그가 이용당한 느낌이 들지 않게 해

Try not to wet your pants
ㄴ 너무 기뻐서 팬티에 오줌 싸지나마

We'd better give him lots of room today
ㄴ 오늘은 그 사람 기분 건드리지 말아야겠군

What is moral is what you feel good after and what is immoral is what you feel bad after
ㄴ 도덕적인 일은 사후에 기분이 좋은 일이고 비도덕적인 일은 사후에 기분이 안 좋은 일이다

When a man is angry, he cannot be in the right
ㄴ 성낸 사람은 올바를 수 없다

When a year comes to its end, we can't help feeling nostalgic
ㄴ 연말이 가까워지면 우리는 향수에 젖기 마련이다

When An-do won the lottery, he felt as though the world was his oyster
ㄴ 안도가 복권에 당첨되자 제 세상인 것 같은 기분이었지

When Sung-min was furious at Sung-soo, Sung-soo cracked a joke, and it cleared the air between them
ㄴ 성민이가 성수에게 몹시 화를 내자 성수가 농담을 꺼내어 분위기를 확 바꿔버렸어

· **moral** relating to principles of right and wrong

· **oyster** bivalve mollusk
· **furious** fierce or angry

When the nerd asked her age, she was angry and put him in his place
↳ 그 머저리가 그 여자의 나이를 묻자 화를 내면서 나무랐다

When wrath speaks, wisdom veils her face
↳ 분노가 말을 하면 지혜가 얼굴을 가린다(Anger begins with folly, and ends with repentance)

When you are feeling down, I'll pick you up
↳ 네가 실의에 빠지면 달래줄게

When you are upset, anything goes(nothing stands in your way)
↳ 넌 흥분하면 앞뒤를 못 가려

When you jump for joy, be aware that no one moves the ground from beneath your feet
↳ 기뻐서 펄쩍펄쩍 뛸 때에 뛰어내리는 발 밑에 누군가가 흙을 치워버리지나 않는지 주의하라

Why are you getting your jaws so tight?
↳ 왜 그리 화가 나 있나?(What made your jaw drop a mile? 넛 때문에 그리 놀란거냐?)

Why are you so keyed up about nothing?
↳ 아무 것도 아닌 일을 왜 흥분하고 야단이야

Why do you bend yourself out of shape?
↳ 왜 네가 화내는 거니?

Witnesses ought to stick to the facts and leave aside all emotion and sentiment
↳ 증인은 사실에 벗어나지 않게 증언해야 하며 감정과 정서는 배제해야 한다

Women are victims of green-eyed-monster
↳ 여성은 질투심에 사로잡히기 쉬워

Won-suck's heart was in his mouth
↳ 원석이가 마음이 조마조마했지

Wrath kills the foolish man

· **veil** sheer material to hide something or to cover the face and head, something that hides
· **folly** foolishness, something foolish

ㄴ 분노는 어리석은 사람을 죽인다

You are getting too emotional
ㄴ 넌 너무 감정적이야

You are making me uncomfortable(embarrassed)
ㄴ 몸둘 바를 모르겠습니다

> (=I feel uncomfortable)
> (=You are too much of it)

You need to have counseling to rid yourself of the anger that must have been stored up from those early years of abuse
ㄴ 넌 어린 시절에 받은 학대로 인하여 쌓인 노여움을 풀도록 전문가의 상담을 받을 필요가 있어

You seem to have a thing for her
ㄴ 그 여자에게 특별한 감정이 있는 것 같구나

You'll end up looking foolish
ㄴ 그러다 큰 코 다쳐

> (=You'll end up embarrassing yourself(making a fool of yourself))

You'll miss her more than you can say
ㄴ 넌 그 여자가 없어지면 몹시 서운하겠구나

Your complexion begins to gather color
ㄴ 너 혈색이 돌아오는구나

Your rudeness really burns me up
ㄴ 너의 무례한 짓은 정말 화가 난다

· **counsel**   advice, deliberation together
· **complexion**   hue or appearance of the skin

especially of the face
· **rudeness**   roughly made, impolite

3. 거래   Dealings

As he managed to sell his house for a tidy sum he was elated at the unexpected windfall
> 그가 상당히 좋은 값으로 집을 팔게되자 굴러 들어온 호박에 한껏 고무되었다

Beside yours, my share seems small
> 네 것에 비해 내 몫이 너무 적은 것 같다

Buy one, get one free
> 하나를 사면 하나를 서비스로 드립니다

Buying our house privately will cut out the middleman and save money on agent's fees
> 우리 집을 당사자 개인간에 사고 팔면 중개인 없는 거래여서 중개 수수료가 절약된다

Byung-soo made a bundle of money on this deal, but the downside is that it was real(very) risky
> 병수가 그 거래에서 거금을 벌었지만 뒤집어보면 정말 위험한 일이었어

Chan-soo earned(cleared) a cool five million dollars on that deal
> 찬수는 그 거래에서 5백만원씩이나 벌었다

Credit is a promise of a future payment in money or in kind given in exchange for present money, goods or services
> 신용거래는 현재의 거래에 대하여 사후에 현금, 상품, 또는 용역을

› **tidy** well ordered and cared for, large or substantial

› **middleman** dealer or agent
› **risk** exposure to loss or injury

제공하겠다는 약속이다

Creditors have better memories than debtors
> ↳ 채권자는 채무자 보다 기억력이 좋다

Don't push me into signing the contract
> ↳ 내게 계약을 강요하지 마시오

Even then losing that contract doesn't say much for(score up against) your skill in business
> ↳ 그렇더라도 그 계약을 놓치는 건 네 사업능력을 보여 준다는 면에서 나쁘게 작용할 것이다

Gil-soo bought the house for a song and sold it a few months later at a good price
> ↳ 길수는 집을 헐값에 사서 두 세 달 후 큰 이익보고 팔았어

Gil-soo sold Sung-min the car at a cheap price and included the tape recorder for good measure
> ↳ 길수는 성민이에게 차를 싸게 팔면서 녹음기를 덤으로 주었어

Half now, half upon completion
> ↳ 반은 지금 반은 끝내고 주시오

Have no dealings with him
> ↳ 그놈하고 거래(교제)하지마

He did a(some) horse trading and finally came away with a contract
> ↳ 그는 빈틈없는 협상으로 마침내 계약을 따냈어

He put on their honor to take no more than they paid for
> ↳ 그는 그들에게 돈 낸 것 이상은 가져가지 말라면서 양심에 맡겼다

He's been known to rip up any contract as soon as it is signed
> ↳ 그는 무슨 계약이고 체결하자마자 파기해버리는 사람으로 소문나 있어

Hyun-soo got a hole in one on that deal

▸ **measure** moderate amount, dimensions or amount, something to show

account

▸ **rip up** to tear up, to break

↳ 현수는 단 한 방에 그 거래를 성사시켰어

I am afraid we don't have any left
↳ 물건이 다 나갔습니다

I can't afford to let it go for any less
↳ 조금도 더 깎아 줄 수 없습니다

I hope we can find some common ground
↳ 타협점을 찾게되길 바란다

I thought we had a deal
↳ 얘기가 다 됐다고 생각했는데

I was ahead one million won in the deal
↳ 그 거래에서 백 만원 벌었지

If you back out of(from) your contract(promise), you'll have to pay the penalty to the firm
↳ 계약(약속)을 이행치 않으면 회사에 벌금을 물어야 해

If you buy the house, they will fling in a car
↳ 그 집을 사신다면 자동차를 얹어준답니다

If you pull off this deal, you'll be fixed for life
↳ 넌 이번 거래만 잘 해내면 팔자가 늘어질 거야

If you score big on that deal, you'll make a lot of dough
↳ 네가 이번에 크게 한 건 올리면 거금이 들어오는 거야

It's our final offer
↳ 이건 최종 가격(제안)입니다

It's quite good value if you look at all the extras
↳ 거기에 딸려오는 것을 고려하면 지불한 돈이 그만한 가치는 있어

It's time to close the books on this account
↳ 이제 이 건(거래처)에 대한 결산을 할 때다

› **firm**   securely fixed in place, strong or vigorous, not subject to change,   resolute

› **dough**   stiff mixture of flour and liquid

Let me make up to him for what he has suffered

    ↳ 그 분의 손해를 변상해 드리죠

Let the lion lie down with the lamb

    ↳ 상대에게 좀 양보해서 요구사항을 잠재워라

Let's make a deal by giving you a 5% discount

    ↳ 5% 할인해 드릴 테니 거래에 합의하십시다

Let's put it in writing

    ↳ 계약서를 쓰자(문서로 하자)

Let's recap the points on which we're in agreement

    ↳ 합의 사항을 재확인합시다

Let's split the difference

    ↳ 우리 타협하자(반으로 나누자)

Let's talk it out

    ↳ 말로 해결하자(협상하자)

> (=We can work this out)
> (=Let's discuss this like adults)
> (=Let's talk)
> (=Let's work this out)
> (=Let's make a deal)

Man-soo made out like a bandit on that deal

    ↳ 만수는 그 거래에서 거금을 벌었다

My assent to the proposal clinched the bargain

    ↳ 내가 그의 제안에 찬성하여 거래는 이루어졌다

Necessity never made a good bargain

‣ **clinch** fasten securely, settle, hold fast or firmly

‣ **necessity** very great need, something that is necessary, poverty

ㄴ 필요에 몰리면 유리한 거래가 되지 않는다

Nobody holds all the aces in this deal
ㄴ 이 거래에서 칼자루를 쥔 사람은 없어

Oh, I see. You have the upper hand
ㄴ 옳아, 배부른 흥정을 하자 이거로군

> 배부른 흥정이란 말은 유리한 입장에서 흥정을 한다는 뜻이다. Upper Hand는
> 팔씨름(Arm Wrestling)에서 위에 얹는 손이 유리하다는 것에서 나온 말이다.
> 거래를 성사시킬 때에 달변이나 처세술로 흥정을 할 때에 사용하는 속담이다.

Okay, let's shake(hands) on it
ㄴ 좋아, 그렇게 하기로 합의한 거야

On this deal, we can't afford to let anything slip(fall) through the cracks
ㄴ 이번 거래에서 무슨 일이나 경합대상에서 제외돼서는 안 돼

Once you've signed, you're bound to fulfill the terms of the deal
ㄴ 일단 서명하고 난 뒤에는 넌 모든 약정들을 법적으로 이행해야 돼

One should help bargaining and stop quarrels
ㄴ 흥정은 붙이고 싸움은 말려라

Please let us know your usual credit terms and what business information you require to open an account
ㄴ 우리는 귀사와의 외상계정을 개설하고자 하오니 이에 관련된 서류 또는 신용조건에 대해 알려 주십시오

Read the policy carefully, because the insurance agent may lead you on
ㄴ 보험대리인이 너를 속일지 모르니 증서를 잘 읽어봐

Sailing against the wind, he succeeded in winning the contract
ㄴ 그는 어려움을 이겨내고 계약을 따내었다

› **ace** one that excels, defeat or score well against(+out) | › **insure** guarantee against loss, make certain

Sang-soo may have to go through a hoop to get that contract
> ↳ 상수가 그 계약을 따려면 꽤 고생해야 할지 몰라

Somebody must have pulled the rug out(from under me) in my deal with Bong-soo
> ↳ 봉수와의 거래에 틀림없이 누군가가 훼방을 놓았어

Something's got to give
> ↳ 이 상태로 가서는 안 돼(양보 또는 타협안을 내놔야)

Take this as an earnest of the further payment
> ↳ 나중에 지불하겠다는 보증으로 이것을 받으시오

Thank you for your business
> ↳ 거래해 주셔서 감사합니다

That is the lowest price that I can let it go for
> ↳ 그것은 최하로 깎은 값입니다

That's my final offer
> ↳ 제가 해 드릴 수 있는 최저가격 입니다

The agreement is binding on all our parties
> ↳ 이 계약은 당사자 모두가 이행해야 한다

The new contract should keep our business on its feet for another year
> ↳ 이번 신규수주 덕분에 1년은 더 버틸 것 같다

The total number of transplants may decline due to the law banning organ-for-money dealings
> ↳ 총 장기이식 건수는 현금거래를 금하는 법으로 인하여 줄어들 수도 있다

The two parties couldn't hammer out a contract
> ↳ 쌍방이 계약에 대하여 논의했으나 합의에 이르지 못했어

Their company has pulled out all the stops because there is a lot of

---

› **hoop** circular strip, figure, or object
› **transplant** dig up and move to another

place, transfer from one body
part or person to another

competition for the contract
> ↳ 그 계약에 대한 경쟁이 치열하니 그 회사는 최선을 다해야해

Their policy requires that credit applicants complete the application before they can consider opening a line of commercial credit
> ↳ 그들의 방침은 신용거래를 원하는 사람들에게 신용거래 검토를 위해 신용거래 신청서를 작성토록 되어있다

Then you have to meet him halfway
> ↳ 그렇다면 그 사람하고 타협할 수밖에 없군

These rock-bottom prices won't last forever
> ↳ 이런 최저가는 날이면 날마다 오는 게 아닙니다

They are trying to iron out the difficulties connected to the new contract
> ↳ 그들은 신규 수주와 관련된 어려움을 타개해 나가려 하고 있다

They brought a laundry list of demands to the negotiation
> ↳ 그들은 협상에 내놓을 요구사항 세목들을 제시했다

They can't steal a march on and get the contract
> ↳ 그들이 우릴 앞질러 계약을 따내진 못해

They could hardly remain ahead of the orders coming in
> ↳ 그들은 수주를 감당하기에 힘들 지경이었어

They finally came together on the point at issue
> ↳ 그들은 쟁점 사항에 합의했다

They have to find some common ground upon which to build a solid arms agreement
> ↳ 그들은 무기협정을 체결하기 위한 서로간의 공통된 기반을 찾아내야 한다

They have to play along with his suggestion, although it's not exactly what they want
> ↳ 그의 제안이 꼭 그들의 원하는 바가 아니라 하더라도 동의하는 체 할

- **laundry** wash or iron fabrics
- **fluctuate** change rapidly especially up and down
- **currency** general use or acceptance, money

수밖에 없었다

They took advantage of wide fluctuations in currency rates to amass huge profits from monetary trading
> ↳ 그들은 큰 환율 폭을 이용하여 금융거래를 통한 막대한 이익을 챙겼다

They'll give you a good price
> ↳ 싸게 해 줄 거야

They(집, 물건) are going fast
> ↳ 살 사람(세입자)이 빨리 나서거든요

This contract will stand good for another year
> ↳ 이 계약은 아직도 1년은 더 갈 것이다

This is a one-shot deal
> ↳ 이런 장사는 두 번 다시없습니다(꼭 사십시오)

This man wants a line of credit
> ↳ 이 분이 외상거래를 원합니다

We are sold out at the moment
> ↳ 물건이 다 나갔습니다

We can be flexible=We can make some concessions
> ↳ 그 점은 양보의 여지가 있습니다

We can find a common ground
> ↳ 우린 타협점을 찾을 수 있을 거야

We don't need to settle for such best-of-the-worst compromises
> ↳ 우린 가장 나쁜 것 중에서 그나마 우수한 것을 골라야 한다는 식의 타협은 필요 없다

We must be careful about the small(fine) print
> ↳ 우린 부대(단서) 조항에 주의해야 한다

We must give credit where credit is due
> ↳ 우린 상벌이 공정해야 해

· **flexible** capable or being flexed, adaptable

· **concession** act of conceding, something

conceded, right to do business
on a property

We offer a late-night discount
    ↳ 심야에 할인해 드립니다

We only do business cash on the barrelhead
    ↳ 우린 현금거래만 해

What reduction do you make for a prolonged day?
    ↳ 호텔에 오래 머물면 할인해 줍니까?

What's your secret to get his account?
    ↳ 그와 거래선을 개척하게 된 비결이 뭐냐?

Wine and dine our potential customers before you enter negotiations
    ↳ 협상에 들어가기 전에 잠재 고객들에게 후하게 대접해라

Would you please inform us when we may expect the payment of this balance?
    ↳ 언제쯤 이 잔금을 지급해 주실 지 알려 주시겠습니까?

You are welcome to call us if you need additional names of credit references or require more information before granting credit
    ↳ 신용추천인이 추가로 필요하거나 신용증인을 위한 정보가 더 필요할 경우 전화를 주시면 감사하겠습니다

You can't bring him together on a price
    ↳ 가격문제에 그 사람 합의를 얻긴 글렀어

You have the upper hand
    ↳ 배부른 흥정이군

> 배부른 흥정이란 말은 유리한 입장에서 흥정을 한다는 뜻이다. Upper Hand는 팔씨름(Arm Wrestling)에서 위에 얹는 손이 유리하다는 것에서 나온 말이다. 거래를 성사시킬 때에 달변이나 처세술로 흥정을 할 때에 사용하는 속담이다.

You have to keep a poker face when haggling

· **potential** capable or becoming actual
· **grant** consent to, give, admit as true

· **haggle** argue in bargaining

↳ 흥정할 땐 표정관리를 잘 해야

You shouldn't lend yourself to such a transaction

↳ 그런 거래에 참여해선 안 돼

You'd better read the small(fine) print

↳ 단서조항(숨은 함정)을 잘 봐야해

You've got a deal

↳ 그렇게 합시다

Your subscription is due for renewal

↳ 귀하의 구독 기간이 만료되었으니 갱신하시기 바랍니다

Yung-soo received three new accounts

↳ 영수가 신규 거래처 세 군데를 받았어

Yung-soo stacked the cards against you with that client

↳ 영수가 그 고객을 상대로 네게 불리한 공작을 한 거야

▸ **transaction** business deal

▸ **renewal** make or become new, fresh, or

strong again, begin again, grant
or obtain an extension of

4. 거짓   Lies

Ask no questions and I'll tell you no lies
> ↳ 거짓말 하고싶지 않으니 묻지마

A lie has speed, but truth has endurance
> ↳ 거짓은 속도를 자랑하지만 진실은 인내력을 가지고 있다

Better a lie that heals than a truth that wounds
> ↳ 남에게 상처를 입히는 진실보다 상처를 낫게 해주는 거짓이 낫다

Byung-soo's innocent air is all put on
> ↳ 병수의 천진난만한 태도는 연기에 불과해

Chan-soo made up that story out of thin air
> ↳ 찬수가 터무니없는 거짓말을 만들어 낸 거야

Debtors are liars
> ↳ 돈이 거짓말한다

Do you have any proof that'll enable you to nail their lie to the counter?
> ↳ 그들의 말이 거짓임을 밝힐만한 증거라도 있니?

Don't crank it out of water
> ↳ 거짓말 만들어내지마

Every violation of truth is not only a sort of suicide in the liar, but is a stab at the health of human society
> ↳ 진실에 어긋나는 모든 일은 거짓말 한 사람의 자살일 뿐 아니라 인간 사회의 건전성에도 타격이 된다

False words are not only evil in themselves, but they infect the soul with it

---

▸ **crank** to turn a bent lever to operate a machine   ▸ **infect** contaminate with disease-producing matter

ㄴ 거짓말은 그 자체가 나쁠 뿐 아니라 그 거짓말은 정신까지 오염시킨다

Fancy Dong-soo's telling a lie!
　　ㄴ 동수가 거짓말을 하다니!

Hair perhaps divides the truthfulness and falsehood
　　ㄴ 머리카락 하나로 진실과 거짓을 가려낸다

He who serves two masters has to lie to one
　　ㄴ 두 주인을 섬기는 자는 한 주인에게는 거짓말을 할 수밖에 없다

How many voters drank in his lies?
　　ㄴ 얼마나 많은 유권자가 그 사람의 거짓말에 귀를 기울이겠니?

I can't tell a lie
　　ㄴ 거짓말 못하겠군

I'll have none of his lies and exaggerations
　　ㄴ 그 작자의 거짓말과 허풍이 내겐 안 통해

Lie if you must
　　ㄴ 변명할 생각마

Life is a system of half-truths and lies
　　ㄴ 인생은 반의 사실과 반의 거짓으로 된 체계이다

Never did I dream you had told a lie
　　ㄴ 네가 거짓말했으리라 곤 꿈에도 몰랐지

No one believes a liar when you tell the truth
　　ㄴ 콩으로 메주를 쓴대도 네 말은 못 믿겠구나(이솝이야기에서)

> 자주 쓰이는 영어 속담 중에 "You are crying wolf too often"이 있다. 이 것은 이솝이야기의 '양치기 소년'이라는 이야기에서 유래하였다. 양치기 소년 이 늑대가 나타났다고 거짓말을 여러 번 했기 때문에 진짜로 늑대가 나타났 을 때에는 아무도 믿지 않았다는 내용이다. 여기서 직역을 하면 "너는 늑대를 너무 여러 번 외쳤어"이고, 그렇기 때문에 믿을 수 없다는 뜻이다.

> **vote**　individual expression of preference in choosing or reaching a decision,　　right to indicate one's preference
>
> **exaggerate**　say more than is true

One falsehood spoils a thousand truths
ㄴ 한 가지의 거짓은 천 가지의 진실을 망친다

One lie makes many
ㄴ 거짓말은 거짓말을 낳아

Repetition doesn't transform a lie into a truth
ㄴ 거짓은 반복해서 말해도 거짓말이 참말로 바뀌지 않는다

Sang-soo didn't say in so many words
ㄴ 상수는 사실대로 말하지 않았어

She went ballistic when the dude called her a liar
ㄴ 그 기생오라비 녀석이 그 여자에게 거짓말쟁이라고 하자 그 여자가 발끈했어

She'll have none of your lies and exaggerations any more
ㄴ 그 여자는 더 이상 너의 거짓말과 허풍을 허용하지 않을 거야

Sin has many tools, but a lie is the handle which fits them all
ㄴ 죄를 저지르는데는 여러 가지 도구가 있으나 거짓말은 모든 죄에 다
들어맞는 손잡이이다

Take it from me, there's no falsehood whatever in my statement
ㄴ 제 진술에 조금도 거짓이 없음을 믿어주십시오

That's a groundless accusation
ㄴ 그건 사실무근이야

The best liar is who makes the smallest amount of lying to the longest way
ㄴ 가장 거짓말을 잘하는 사람은 거짓말을 가장 적게 하면서도 그것을
가장 길게 끌고 가는 사람이다

The truthful lip shall be established forever, but a lying tongue is but
for a moment
ㄴ 진실한 입술은 영원히 보존되거니와 거짓 혀는 눈깜짝일 동안 있을
뿐이니라

· **repetition** act or instance of repeating
· **ballistic** science of projectile motion
· **groundless** without a cause
· **accuse** charge with an offense

The whole affair was just a put-on
> ↳ 모든 게 거짓(공갈)이었어

There's no worse lie than a truth misunderstood who hear it
> ↳ 사실을 듣고서 그 사실을 오해하는 것 보다 더 나쁜 거짓말이 없다

There's nothing to what he said
> ↳ 그의 얘기는 알맹이가 없다(거짓말이다)

Time can shout the truth where words lie
> ↳ 말이 거짓을 지껄이고 있을 경우에도 시간은 진실을 외칠 수 있다

> 인간의 악행에 대한 처벌이나, 선행에 대한 보답은 즉시 일어나지 않을 수도 있지만 시간이 흐르면 틀림없이 일어난다. 하나님의 맷돌은 천천히 돌아가지만 아주 곱게 갈아진다는 뜻의 "The mills of God grind slowly, yet they grind exceeding small"과도 같은 뜻이다.

When we see a secret smile on his lips, he must be telling a lie
> ↳ 그가 입가에 살짝 미소를 지을 때는 거짓말을 하고 있는 게 틀림없어

Without lies humanity would perish of despair and boredom
> ↳ 거짓말이 없으면 인간은 절망과 권태감으로 죽게 될 것이다

You can't catch him out easily
> ↳ 그의 말이 거짓이라고 쉽게 밝혀내긴 어려울 거다

Your nose is growing
> ↳ 거짓말 마(거짓말할 때 피노키오의 코가 커짐)

▸ **grind** reduce to powder, wear down or sharpen by friction

▸ **exceed** go or be beyond the limit of, do better than

5. 건강   **Health**

Although we are excited about the prospect of living healthier and longer by virtue of the scientific feat, we must wait patiently for progress in the research

ㄴ 우리는 과학의 위업 덕분에 보다 건강하고 오래 살게 될 것이라는 전망에 흥분하고 있지만 연구의 진척을 차분히 기다려야 한다

An-do has it all together. Besides, he's got what it takes

ㄴ 안도는 건강하고 건전해요. 게다가 능(실, 재)력도 있고요

> 다재 다능한 사람을 가리켜 '팔방미인'이라고 한다. 이를 번역한다면 'man of many talents = 다재 다능한 사람'정도가 된다.

Apples are valued nowadays for their aid to digestion and their help in keeping teeth clean and healthy

ㄴ 사과는 소화를 돕고 이를 깨끗하게 하고 건강을 유지시켜줌으로써 오늘날 소중히 여겨진다

Chang-soo didn't take that crappy job for(due to) his health

ㄴ 창수가 좋아서 그 시시한 일을 하고 있는 게 아니다(목구멍이 포도청이라 하고 있는 거지)

Cigarette ads in magazines and newspapers carry a health warning because they are obliged to

---

· **prospect** extensive view, something awaited, potential buyer

· **crappy** unworthy, boring

· **oblige** compel, do a favor for

└ 잡지와 신문에 나오는 광고는 이들 회사의 의무 때문에 건강에 대한 광고를 싣는다

Danggwi not only helps stimulate circulation and manufacture blood, but it also purifies existing blood

└ 당귀는 혈액순환을 촉진하고 조혈작용을 도울 뿐만 아니라 몸에 있던 피를 정화하기도 한다

Drinking in moderation is good for heart and health

└ 적당한 음주는 심장과 건강에 좋다

> 술도 좋은 술을 적당히 마시면 건강에 이롭다. 우리의 선조들도 "적게 먹으면 약주요, 많이 먹으면 망주"라고 하였다. 서양에서는 좋은 포도주가 건강에 이롭다고 한다(Good wine makes good blood).

Every violation of truth is not only a sort of suicide in the liar, but is a stab at the health of human society

└ 진실에 어긋나는 모든 일은 거짓말 한 사람의 자살일 뿐 아니라 인간 사회의 건전성에도 타격이 된다

Everyone who is born, holds dual citizenship, in the kingdom of the well and in the kingdom of the sick

└ 사람은 누구에게나 두 가지 시민권이 있는데, 한 가지는 건강한 왕국의 시민권이고 다른 하나는 환자 왕국의 시민권이다

Feed by measure and defy the physician

└ 절제 있게 먹으면 의사가 필요 없다

Fewer than half of all adults fully understand kinds and amounts of exercise necessary for an effective physical fitness program

└ 모든 성인들 중에 반도 되지 않는 사람들이 효과적인 건강프로그램을 위해 필요한 운동의 종류와 양에 대해 완전히 이해하고 있지 못하고 있다

- **stimulate** make active
- **moderation** avoidance or extremes
- **dual** twofold
- **defy** challenge, boldly refuse to obey

Ginseng helps warm up the body, strengthen immunity and even fight cancer
> ↳ 인삼은 몸을 따뜻하게 하고 면역성을 강화시키며 암에 대한 저항력까지 강화해 준다

Good health is not the same as great physical strength
> ↳ 건강과 체력은 별개의 것이다

He is very well despite his age
> ↳ 나이에 불구하고 건강

He keeps fit by jogging four kilometers everyday and looks the picture of health to us
> ↳ 그는 매일 4킬로씩 조깅을 해서 건강의 표상처럼 보인다

Health authorities unveiled an array of measurements to protect people from various health risks
> ↳ 보건당국은 각종 질환의 위험으로부터 국민들을 보호하기 위한 일련의 조치들을 내 놓았다

Her health gave way completely
> ↳ 그 여자의 건강은 완전히 지탱할 수 없게 되었다

How did your physical go?
> ↳ 건강진단은 어떻게 됐어?

I got a second burst of wind then
> ↳ 그때 솟구치는 원기를 회복했지

I propose toast to the health of Mr. Oh
> ↳ 오 선생님의 건강을 위해 건배합시다

In course of time, his health began to fail
> ↳ 마침내 그의 건강이 나빠지기 시작했다

In the twenty first-century healthy people will live out their natural

---

› **despite** in spite of, contempt, malice, disadvantage

› **toast** drink in honor of someone or something

lifespan and die of old age
> 21세기를 맞아 건강한 사람들은 천수를 다하고 노환으로 죽게 될 것이다

It'll make you full of vim and vigor
> 그걸 먹으면 정력이 좋아진대

It's important to control weight through good diet and regular exercise so that unnecessary pressure does not weaken the joints
> 좋은 식단과 규칙적인 운동으로 체중을 조절하여 불필요한 압력이 관절을 약화시키지 않도록 하는 것이 중요하다

Jogging and push-ups will do you a world of good
> 조깅과 푸시업은 건강에 매우 좋다

Just as eating against one's will is injurious to health, so studying without a liking for it spoils the memory, and our brains retain nothing
> 싫은 것을 억지로 먹이는 것이 건강에 해롭듯이 싫은 것을 억지로 공부하는 것은 기억력을 망치게 되어 머리 속에 들어와도 남아있지 않게 된다

Lean-ness may serve as a health advantage in youth and middle age, but may reduce hardiness in old age
> 청년기와 중년일 때에 날씬한 것은 건강에 이점이 될 수 있지만 노년에는 저항력을 떨어뜨릴 수도 있다

Mother and child are both doing well
> 모자는 다 건강하다

My parents wear their years well
> 우리 부모님은 연세가 많아도 정정하셔

Natural herbs are considered not only medicinal drugs, but also health food
> 자연산 약용식물은 의약뿐만 아니라 건강식품으로도 여겨진다

Nobody is as hot to trot as he
> 저 사람은 정력이라면 끝내주는 사람이야

› **retain**   keep or hold onto, engage the service of

› **advantage**   superiority of position, benefit or gain

Our personal peace and good health are greater assets than any material wealth
> ↳ 우리 자신의 개인적인 평화와 건강은 어떤 물질적인 부보다도 큰 재산이다

> 건강에 대한 조언 중에 "궁핍은 건강의 어머니이다(Poverty is the mother of health)"와 "모든 무절제가 건강의 적이다(All immoderations are enemies to health)"가 있다. 건강을 위해서는 규칙적인 생활과 운동, 적당한 식사가 중요하다.

Peace in mind is no less necessary for our health than fresh air and sunlight
> ↳ 마음의 평화가 신선한 공기와 햇빛만큼이나 우리들 건강에 필요하다

Persuade him that you are not in business for your health
> ↳ 네가 재미로 회사를 다니는 게 아님을 그에게 인식시켜라

Preserving the health by too severe a rule is a wearisome malady
> ↳ 엄격한 규칙으로 건강을 유지하는 그 자체가 지루한 병이다

Rarely has a health campaign so quickly become a national obsession
> ↳ 건강 캠페인이 이토록 빠르게 전 국민을 사로잡게 된 적이 거의 없었다

Regular living will put him right
> ↳ 그가 규칙적인 생활을 하면 다시 건강을 회복할 것이다

She does calisthenics every morning to keep in condition(shape)
> ↳ 그 여자는 건강을 유지하기 위해 매일 아침 미용체조를 한다

She'll get a clean bill of health soon
> ↳ 그녀는 곧 아무 이상이 없다는 결과를 얻게 될 것이다

Sook-hee nursed her father back to health
> ↳ 숙희는 아버지가 건강을 회복할 때까지 간호했다

Success flows from health and intelligence
> ↳ 성공은 건강과 지혜로 이루어진다

› **wearisome** causing weariness
› **malady** disease or disorder

› **obsess** preoccupy intensely or abnormally

The benefits we'll get from a healthy diet will be well worth the sacrifice
> ㄴ 식이요법을 통해 받게될 이익은 그 희생에 대한 충분한 가치가 있다

> 잘 챙겨서 먹는 것이 건강에 좋다. 문명 국가일수록 기름진 음식을 많이 섭취하고 운동이 부족한 편안한 생활을 하기에 비만증에 걸리고 여러 가지 성인병에 걸린다. 요즘은 건강 때문만이 아니라 몸매 관리를 위해서 'Diet(식이요법)'을 한다.

The doctor gave me a clean bill of health
> ㄴ 의사는 내가 아주 건강하다고 했어

The first wealth is health
> ㄴ 건강은 최대의 재산이다

> 건강에 대한 조언 중에 "궁핍은 건강의 어머니이다(Poverty is the mother of health)"와 "모든 무절제가 건강의 적이다(All immoderations are enemies to health)"가 있다. 건강을 위해서는 규칙적인 생활과 운동, 적당한 식사가 중요하다.

The government will not stand idly by as they take public health hostage in the pursuit of financial gains
> ㄴ 정부는 그들이 경제적인 이익을 추구하여 국민의 건강을 볼모로 하는 그들을 좌시하지 않을 것이다

The healthy are happier than the wealthy
> ㄴ 건강한 사람은 부자보다 행복해

- **idly** worthlessly, inactive, lazily
- **hostage** person held to guarantee thats

promises be kept or demand met
- **pursuit** act or pursuing, occupation

The tongue of the wise promotes health
     ㄴ 지혜로운 자의 혀는 양약 같으니라

The trouble about always trying to preserve the health of the body is that it is so difficult to do without destroying the health of the mind
     ㄴ 신체의 건강을 항상 유지하려는데 따르는 문제점은 정신건강을 해치지 않고는 매우 어렵다는 점이다

The wish for healing has ever been the half of health
     ㄴ 병이 낫겠다는 소망만으로 반쯤 나은 것과 같다

These health warning posters show grieving relatives to drive home the point that drink-driving can kill
     ㄴ 이들 건강 주의 경고 포스터들은 음주운전이 살인을 부를 수도 있다는 심각한 연계성을 절실히 보여준다

They offer a salary and benefits package consistent with their leadership position in the field of nursing and health related facilities
     ㄴ 그들은 요양이나 시설관련 분야에서 근무하는 지휘자의 직위에 어울리는 봉급과 복리후생을 제공한다

They spend hours at the tennis court to keep themselves fit
     ㄴ 그들은 건강한 몸을 유지하려고 몇 시간씩 테니스를 친다

Three spoons a day supplies a generous portion of the building blocks needed for a healthy body
     ㄴ 하루에 세 티스푼씩을 먹으면 건강한 신체에 필요한 성분을 다량 공급해 준다

Vinegar helps fights germs, sooths stomach pains, heals cuts quicker and adds to our overall health
     ㄴ 식초는 멸균효과가 있고, 위통을 진정시키며, 상처를 빨리 낫게 하며, 건강을 전반적으로 좋게 해준다

- **grieve**   feel or cause to feel grief or sorrow
- **germ**   microorganism, source or rudiment
- **consistent**   being steady and regular
- **generous**   freely giving or sharing

We drink one another's health and spoil our own
> ↳ 우리는 서로의 건강을 위한답시고 술을 마시면서 우리 자신의 건강을 망친다

We should place health among the most valuable things
> ↳ 우리는 건강을 가장 중요한 것 중의 하나로 생각해야 한다

What some calls health, if purchased by perpetual anxiety about diet, is not much better than tedious disease
> ↳ 노심초사하면서 다이어트로 얻는 건강을 건강이라고 하는 사람도 있지만 지루한 병을 앓는 것보다 나을 것이 없다

When people make wise choices, the environment stays healthy
> ↳ 사람들이 현명한 선택을 할 때 환경은 건강하게 유지된다

Without a reliable source of reasonably priced electricity, it would be practically impossible to maintain a healthy economy
> ↳ 믿을만한 저렴한 가격의 전원이 없이는 건강한 경제를 유지하기가 사실상 불가능하다

Without health, we can't do anything worth doing
> ↳ 건강이 없이는 가치 있는 일을 할 수가 없어

You have to provide your employees with a healthy outlet for tension and stress
> ↳ 넌 종업원들의 긴장과 스트레스에 대한 건전한 해소대책을 마련해줘야 해

You seem to sharp as a tack
> ↳ 아직 정정하시군요

(=You seem to be fit as a fiddle)

> • **perpetual** continuing forever, occurring continually

> • **tension** tense condition, state of mental unrest or of potential hostility or opposition

6. 겉모습 　　　　　Appearances

A man is as old as he feels, and a woman as old as she looks
> ↳ 남자의 나이는 느끼기에 달렸고 여자의 나이는 얼굴에 나타난다

> 남자는 나이가 들어도 건강하기만 하고 젊다고 느끼기만 한다면 나이에 구애
> 받지 않지만, 여자는 외모, 즉 겉으로 드러나는 나이에 많은 구애를 받는다.
> 아무리 화장을 해도 얼굴에 나타나는 나이는 속일 수 없기 때문이다.

Are you going to let your hair grow long?
> ↳ 머리를 기를 생각이냐?

Be careful about your appearance
> ↳ 옷차림에 유의해야해

By dressing up as a man and wearing a wig she was able to give her pursuers the slip
> ↳ 그녀는 남장을 하고 가발을 써서 추적자들을 따돌릴 수 있었다

Byung-soon's got nice legs but she's flat as a board
> ↳ 병순이가 다리는 예쁘지만 유방은 없어

Do you think I'm getting a gut?
> ↳ 내가 점점 배가 나오는 것 같니?

Don't judge people by their appearances(looks)
> ↳ 외모로 판단하지 마라

> ・**pursue**　follow in order to overtake, seek to accomplish, engage in

> ・**gut**　intestine(pl), digestive canal, courage(pl)

> (=Don't judge a book by its cover)

Everybody wants to grow old gracefully
> ↳ 누구나 곱게 나이 먹기를(나이보다 젊어 보이기를) 원한다

Excuse my appearance
> ↳ 내 꼴이 말이 아니죠?(민망한 모습으로 손님을 맞을 때)

Exercise and a sensible diet will help you get your figure back
> ↳ 운동과 분별 있는 식사를 하면 너의 예전 몸매를 되찾게 될 것이다

Good looks run in their family
> ↳ 그 집안은 인물이 좋아

Good wine needs no bush
> ↳ 외모보다 마음씨

> (=Goodness often charms more than mere beauty)

He has a receding hairline
> ↳ 그는 머리가 조금 벗겨졌어

He has a sprinkling of gray hair(s)
> ↳ 그는 새치가 있어

He has a style all his own
> ↳ 그에겐 독특한 스타일이 있다

He has gray hair
> ↳ 그 사람은 백발(hairs가 아님)

Her hair hung in abundant masses over her shoulders
> ↳ 그녀의 머리털은 탐스럽게 어깨에 내려와 있었다

- **recede** move back or away, slant backward
- **sprinkle** scatter in small drops or particles

- **abundant** more than enough

Her long hair flowed down her shoulders
↳ 그녀의 긴 머리가 어깨에 늘어져 있었다

His appearance belies him
↳ 그 사람 겉보기와는 달라

His hair is already flecked with gray
↳ 그의 머리는 벌써 희끗희끗해

Hyun-soo never does the in thing
↳ 현수는 유행을 따르는 법이 없어

If you want to keep your figure, don't eat too much
↳ 몸매를 유지하려면 많이 먹지 마라

Ignorance, if recognized, is often more fruitful than the appearance of knowledge
↳ 무지를 깨닫기만 한다면 지식을 내보이는 것보다 값질 때가 많다

In-ho has clear-cut(well-defined, distinctive) features(attributes)
↳ 인호는 톡 튀는 외모를 가졌어

It just looks flashy
↳ 겉보기만 좋을 뿐이야

> (=It just appears glamorous)
> (=It's all flashy and no substance)

It often happens that reality proves different from appearance
↳ 세상에는 겉과 속이 다른 경우가 많아

It's a woman's duty to provide for the inner man, and a man's duty to provide for the outer woman
↳ 남자의 속을 깊게 하는 것은 여자의 할 일이고 여자의 겉모습을 꾸며

- **belie** misrepresent, prove false
- **fleck** streak or spot
- **flashy** showy
- **glamor** romantic or exciting attractiveness

주는 것은 남자의 할 일이다

Look at that man! All meat and no potatoes
  ↳ 저 남자 좀 봐. 엄청남 뚱뚱보야

Look at yourself in the mirror
  ↳ 거울을 한번 들여다 봐

Look what the cat(reindeer) dragged in
  ↳ 네 꼴이 그게 뭐니(얼굴에 멍이 들었거나 옷, 신발 등이 엉망일 때)

Lulu seemed to lost her looks
  ↳ 루루의 모습이 볼품없이 달라져 보이더군

Maintaining appearances is now out of the question
  ↳ 체면 따위를 생각 할 때가 아니다

My hair has gone out of curl
  ↳ 머리 컬이 풀렸어요

My hair has too many split ends
  ↳ 내 머리칼 끝이 너무 많이 갈라졌어

No matter how much he eats, he can't seem to fill out
  ↳ 그는 아무리 먹어도 살이 안 찌는 것 같아

People should be judged what's inside
  ↳ 사람을 외모로 판단해서는 안 된다

> 사람은 겉모습만 봐서 평가할 수 없고, 사귀어 봐야 안다. 열길 물 속은 알아도 한길 사람 속은 모르기 때문이다. 더 자주 쓰이는 표현으로 "Judge not a book by its cover = 그 표지로 서적을 판단하지 마라"가 있다.

She is a very nice shape
  ↳ 그 여자는 몸매가 근사해

• **substance**   essence or essential part, physical material, wealth
• **reindeer**   large deer of northern region
• **split**   devide lengthwise or along a grain

She likes to take care of her body
> ↳ 그 여자는 몸매에 신경을 써

She looks more like her father than her mother
> ↳ 그 여자는 엄마보다 아빠를 많이 닮았다

She may not be an oil-painting, but she's all right in her way
> ↳ 그 여자가 눈에 확 들어오는 건 아니지만 나름대로 괜찮아

She stood in the wind with her hair flying
> ↳ 그녀는 바람에 머리를 휘날리며 서 있었다

She wants to keep up appearances
> ↳ 그 여자는 체면을 살리기를 원하는 거야

She's trying to keep up appearances, but she lives off borrowed money
> ↳ 그녀는 체면치레를 위해 애쓰고 있지만 빚을 얻어서 산다

Somehow I'm losing the battle of the bulge
> ↳ 암만해도 난 배가 나오는가 봐

Sung-soo put in an appearance at work, but he goofed off all day
> ↳ 성수는 직장에 얼굴을 내밀었지만 하루종일 빈둥거리기만 했어

Tai-ho tips the scales at 73 kilograms
> ↳ 태호의 체중은 73킬로 나간다

That man looks much fatter in real life than he does on TV
> ↳ 저 사람은 TV에서 보다 실제로 더 뚱뚱해 보인다

That ugly girl is as dumb as she looks
> ↳ 저 못난 아가씨가 꼴값하고 있군

That's really tacky
> ↳ 정말 촌스러워

› **bulge** swelling projecting part, swell out
› **goof** blunder

› **tacky** cheap or gaudy, sticky to the touch

(=That's unfashionable)
(=He looks like a yokel)
(=He looks like a country bumpkin)
(=Looks so dumb)

The huge man seemed to dwarf the motorcycle he was riding
ㄴ 그 남자는 덩치가 커서 오토바이가 작아 보였다

Then you can just put in an appearance
ㄴ 그렇다면 그저 얼굴만 내밀어도 돼

There are no tall people who know how to behave
ㄴ 키 크고 싱겁지 않은 사람 없다

Things may be unpleasant, but I'll save(keep up) appearances
ㄴ 사정은 달갑지 않지만 체면치레는 해 드리겠습니다

Wan-soo has a natural wave in his hair
ㄴ 완수는 원래 곱슬머리야

What's a man without competency, what's a woman without looks
ㄴ 남자가 내세울 건 능력, 여자가 내세울 건 미모뿐이다

Where do you want your hair parted?
ㄴ 가르마는 어느 쪽으로 하십니까?

You are getting a gut
ㄴ 넌 배가 자꾸 나오는군

You can get into shape in no time
ㄴ 넌 곧 균형 있는 몸매가 될 거야

You have to burn off your fat
ㄴ 너 체중 좀 줄여야겠어

You look as if somebody's been dragging you backwards through hedges

---

▸ **dwarf** stunt, cause to seem smaller, one   ▸ **competency** capability
that is much below normal size

ㄴ 넌 누가 잡아 뜯어놓은 것 같이 몰골이 그 모양이냐

You look like a million dollars

ㄴ 너 신수가 훤해 보이는구나

You look something the cat dragged in

ㄴ 몰골이 그게 뭐니(트럭 운전사라도 널 병원에 데려가겠다)

(=You look green around the gills)
(=You could stop a truck)

Your appearance catches everyone's eyes

ㄴ 네 용모라면 모든 사람의 눈을 끌기에 충분해

› **gill**   organ of a fish for obtaining oxygen
from water

7. 격려   Encouragement

All things are easy, that are done willingly
    ㄴ 하겠다는 마음으로 하면 안 되는 일이 없다

> 속담 중에도 "뜻이 있는 곳에 길이 있다(Where there is a will, there is a way)"
> 라는 말이 있다. 아무리 힘들고 어려운 일이라도 목적을 가지고 끈기 있게 도전하면
> 안 되는 일이 없다는 뜻이다(=Nothing is impossible to a willing heart).

Hang in there
    ㄴ 포기하지마. 버티어봐

I am glad to hear it. I know you're relieved
    ㄴ 그것참 잘 됐구먼. 너도 안심이겠네

I sincerely wish your continued success
    ㄴ 건투를 빈다

If at first you don't succeed, try, try again
    ㄴ 칠전팔기하라

> "첫술에 배부르랴"라는 말이 있다. "시작이 반이다(Well begun, half done)"이런
> 속담도 있지만, 이는 시작하는 것이 어렵다는 것을 뜻하는 속담이고, 시작한 후에
> 노력을 하여 한 단계 한 단계 이루어 나가야 된다는 뜻을 가진 속담이 "첫술에 배부
> 르라(Rome was not built in a day)"이다(It takes three generations to
> make a gentleman = 훌륭한 사람은 하루아침에 만들어지지 않는다).

· **willing**   inclined or favorably disposed in mind, prompt to act, done, borne,   or accepted voluntarily or reluctance

It'll do you fine
    ↳ 그게 너한테 큰 도움이 될 거야

It'll go a long way
    ↳ 그건 두고두고 도움이 될 거야

It's a small price to pay
    ↳ 그 정도는 감수해야 해

It's all a mind game
    ↳ 그건 모두 마음먹기에 달렸어

It's worth a shot(try)
    ↳ 해볼만한 가치 있어(밑져야 본전)

Just do what you want
    ↳ 마음 내키는 대로 해

Just make the best of it
    ↳ 그 상황에서 최선을 다 하라

Keep up the good work
    ↳ 계속 수고해

Keep your feet on the ground and you'll do fine
    ↳ 넌 침착하게 해 나가면 잘 해낼 거야

Knock yourself out
    ↳ 되든 안되든 해봐라

Life lies before you
    ↳ 너의 인생은 지금부터다

Make it on your own
    ↳ 너의 길을 가도록 해

Make me proud of you
    ↳ 가서 잘해 봐

› **shot** act of shooting, attempt as at making
a goal, small pellets forming a charge

More power to you

      ↳ 건투를 빕니다. 잘 하셨군요

My all good wishes for your next step

      ↳ 너의 앞일이 잘 되기 바란다

No one is good from the beginning

      ↳ 처음부터 잘 하는 사람은 없어

> 실패하더라도 포기하지 말고 오뚝이처럼 일어나면 언젠가는 이룰 수 있다는 말이다.
> (=Every one starts off a beginner)
> (=No one starts off being good at something)

Now you are cooking. You've finished half already

      ↳ 잘해나가고 있군. 벌써 반이나 끝냈잖아

Once over this barrier, the rest will be plain sailing

      ↳ 이번 고비만 넘기면 나머지는 쉬워

Once you get the knack of it, you can do it

      ↳ 일단 요령만 터득하면 할 수 있어

Pull yourself together

      ↳ 힘내라

Push it right through the edge

      ↳ 끝까지 밀어 부쳐라

Put on an all-court pressing

      ↳ 전력투구해봐

Set your heart at ease about that

      ↳ 그 점에 대해서는 안심해

Should you climb up and up, you'll someday reach the top in the end

      ↳ 오르고 또 오르면 정상에 못 오를 것 없다

‣ **barrier** something that separates or obstruct

‣ **knack** clever way of doing something, natural aptitude

So let it out and let it in
> ↳ 이제 심호흡하고 마음을 가다듬어라

Stick with it, it'll pay off in the end
> ↳ 끈기 있게 한 우물을 파면 결국엔 보람이 있을 거다

Stop sticking your head in the sand and face reality
> ↳ 일을 피하지 말고 정면 돌파해라

Take in you losses in your stride and you'll be on your feet in no time
> ↳ 너의 손실에 의연하게 대처해 나가면 금방 자립해 나가게 될 것이다

Take it for a spin
> ↳ 한 번 해봐

> (=Give it a try)

That's the way to go
> ↳ 바로 그거야(잘 한다)

> (=You are doing the right way)
> (=There you go)

The darkest hour is that before the dawn
> ↳ 동트기 전이 가장 어두운 시간이다(절망하지 마라)

> 아무리 힘들고 어렵더라고 참고 견디면 좋은 일이 생긴다(An unfavourable situation will eventually change for the better = 계속되는 불행도 참 아내다 보면 기회가 온다).

› **stride** walk or run with long steps

› **dawn** grow light as the sun rises, begin to appear, develop, or be understood

The victory is not cheaply bought
↳ 승리란 쉽게 이루어지는 게 아니야

There's no more chances but this one
↳ 이런 기회는 두 번 다시 오지 않아

Things will balance out
↳ 공정한 결말이 될 거야

Things will come right
↳ 만사가 잘 될 거다

Things will turn around for you soon
↳ 너의 일은 잘 풀릴 거야

Things won't always go so bad
↳ 쥐구멍에도 볕 들 날 있다

Tomorrow is another day
↳ 내일 일은 내일 처리하라=내일이 있으니 용기를 잃지 마라

Try and do it in one way or another
↳ 어떻게 해서든 해봐

Try to hang in there another month
↳ 한달 만 더 버텨 봐

We must make the best of things
↳ 어렵더라도 참아야 해

We'll get there
↳ 그 일은 그 때 생각하자

When the going gets tough, the tough gets going
↳ 어려울 때일수록 힘을 내야 해

When you get the right procedures, you'll be more efficient
↳ 네가 일 머리를 터득하면 더욱 유능한 사람이 될 것이다

› **unfavorable** not approving, unkind
› **eventually** later on

› **procedure** way of doing something, series
of steps in regular order

Why don't you give it a shot?
　　↳ 한 번 해보지 그래

Wipe out all thought of it and have a another try
　　↳ 그 생각은 모두 잊어버리고 다시 한 번 노력해봐

You are bound to have your moments soon
　　↳ 머지않아 네게 때가 오게 돼있어

You can pull yourself through this time too
　　↳ 넌 이번에도 어려움을 잘 넘길 거야

You can take things as they come
　　↳ 넌 부딪쳐보고 대처해도 돼

┌─────────────────────────────┐
│ (=Just face it)   │
└─────────────────────────────┘

You must at least try
　　↳ 해 보기라도 해

You should go for it
　　↳ 꼭 한 번 해봐

You should hang in there and things will turn
　　↳ 굽히지 않고 버티면 문제는 해결될 것이다

┌───┐
│ (=There's a light at the end of the tunnel) │
└───┘

You will come into your own any day
　　↳ 넌 곧 인정받게 될 거야

You will come to no good

| ‣ **pull off** carry out despite difficulties | ‣ **hang in** refuse to become discouraged or intimidated |

　　　　↳ 네가 하는 일은 잘 안될 거다

You'll get it soon

　　　　↳ 넌 곧 잘 해내게 될 거야(**You almost got it** 조금만 잘하면 돼)

You'll get through it soon

　　　　↳ 넌 곧 그 일을 해낼 거야

You will come into your own any day

　　　　↳ 넌 곧 인정받게 될 거야

You're going to come into your own this year

　　　　↳ 올해 넌 인정받게 될 거야

You've been cooking with gas

　　　　↳ 넌 일을 잘 해내고 있구먼

Your day will come

　　　　↳ 네게도 좋은 날이 올 거다

Your encouragement will carry him through

　　　　↳ 한마디 격려라면 그가 어려움을 이겨낼 수 있을 거야

▸ **encourage**　inspire with courage and hope,
　　　　　　　foster

8. 겸손   **Modesty**

A little knowledge is dangerous
> ↳ 선무당 사람 잡아

A little wind kindles, much puts out the fire
> ↳ 약간의 바람은 불을 일으키지만 센바람은 불을 꺼버린다(중용 예찬)

> 중용이란 한쪽으로 치우침이 없고 항상 변함 없음을 말한다. 자신을 과소평
> 가나 과대평가 하지말고, 항상 겸손한 마음으로 중도를 걷는 것이 중요하다.
> 예부터 우리나라에서는 공자의 사상을 받들어 중용을 강조하였다.

A little wood will heat a little oven
> ↳ 송충이는 솔잎을 먹어야 한다

> 분수를 모르고 터무니없는 짓을 하거나 그런 짓을 하여 낭패를 보았을 때하는
> 말이다. 가장 자주 쓰이는 표현, "Don't try to bite off more than you can
> chew"는 직역을 하면 "자신이 씹을 수 있는 것보다 더 많은 음식을 한꺼번에 베
> 어 물지 마라"이며, 이는 자신의 능력껏 소신껏 일을 하라는 말이다.
> (=A little bird is content with a little nest)
> (=Let the cobbler stick to his last)

A poor man like you can't do what a rich man can do
> ↳ 너 같은 가난뱅이가 부자 흉내를 내서야 되겠나

· **kindle**   set on fire or start burning, stir up   · **cobbler**   shoemaker
· **content**   satisfied

Ambition knows no bound
     ㄴ 위를 쳐다보면 한이 없다

(=There's always something higher to aim for)

Any one can hold the helm when the sea is calm
     ㄴ 잔잔한 바다에서는 아무나 선장이 될 수 있다

(=In a calm sea, every man is a pilot)

Anybody can win unless there happens to be a second entry
     ㄴ 혼자 참가한다면 누구나 승자가 될 수 있다

Don't lose sight of your humble beginnings
     ㄴ 소박했던 옛일을 잊지 마라

Every oak has been an acorn
     ㄴ 모든 떡갈나무는 도토리이던 시절이 있다

He who speaks without modesty will find it difficult to make his words good
     ㄴ 겸손하지 않게 말하는 사람은 자신의 말을 귀담아 듣게 하기 어려울 것이다

Modesty is the only sure angle bait when you angle for praise
     ㄴ 칭찬을 받으려면 겸손함이 유일한 미끼가 된다

Seek that which may be found
     ㄴ 못 오를 나무는 쳐다 보지도 마라

Spare me your modesty
     ㄴ 겸손하시군요

The boughs that bear most hangs lowest

› **modesty**   having a moderate estimate of oneself, reserved or decent | thoughts or actions. li inmited in size, amount, or aim

ㄴ 벼는 익을수록 고개를 숙인다

The crow that mimics a cormorant gets drowned
ㄴ 까마귀가 가마우지 흉내를 냈다가는 물에 빠져 죽는다

The length of sky is just about the size of my ignorance
ㄴ 하늘의 길이는 바로 내가 얼마나 무지한가 하는 것과 비슷한 수준이다

The parish priest forgets that he has been a holy water clerk
ㄴ 개구리가 올챙이 적 생각 못한다

> (Set a beggar on horseback, and he'll ride to the devil 개구리가 올챙이 적 생각 못한다) 갑자기 부자가 되거나 높은 지위에 오른 사람은 올바로 판단하지 못한다.

When anyone is somebody, then no one is anybody
ㄴ 모두가 잘난 사람일 땐 아무도 잘난 사람이 아니다

You may ruin yourself by trying to ape your betters
ㄴ 잘난 사람 흉내내려다가 너 자신을 망칠 수가 있어

› **mimic** imitate closely, ridicule by imitation
› **parish** local church community
› **ape** imitate

9. 결과   Result

As some of the thinking now collapses with share prices, concrete consequences are beginning to emerge
    ㄴ 이 같은 생각이 주가폭락과 함께 붕괴되면서 구체적인 결과들이 나타나기 시작했다

Conversation is unlike a discussion, insofar as one is not trying to arrive at any definite conclusion
    ㄴ 대화란 어떤 명확한 결론에 도달하려고 하지 않는 점에 있어서 토론과 다르다

Ed took exception to a few of my conclusions
    ㄴ 에드는 나의 몇 가지 결론에 대하여 의의를 제기했다

If this remains untreated and accumulated for a long time, it can result in a stomach ulcer
    ㄴ 이 증세를 치료하지 않고 장기간 누적시켜 간다면 위궤양을 일으킬 수 있다

It was early days yet and I still had a few cards up my sleeve
    ㄴ 결론을 내리기에는 아직 이른 시기였지만 나는 몇 가지 비책을 준비해 두고 있었다

It's an open and shut case
    ㄴ 그건 결과가 빤한 사건

It's better to travel hopefully than to arrive
    ㄴ 결과보다 과정이 중요하다

› **collapse** fall in, break down physically or mentally, fold down

› **emerge** rise, come forth, or appear

› **insofar as** to the extent that

> 결과에 얽매이지 말고 전심전력을 하여 노력해야 한다. 진정한 성공이란 그
> 과정에 쏟아 넣는 노력이다(The true success is to labour).

It's the same result
> └ 엎어 치나 메어치나 지

> (=The results are the same)

Let's keep our opinions open until we have a chance to analyze the results
> └ 우리가 결과를 분석할 때까지 결정을 미루자

My heart(mind) misgives me about the result
> └ 결과가 걱정이다

Generally the planet is getting warmer as a result of the greenhouse effect
> └ 지구는 온실효과 때문에 점점 더워지고 있다

Give me a brief update on the meeting
> └ 회의 결과에 대해 간단한 상황만 알려 줘

Nations, like individuals, have to limit their objectives, or take the consequences
> └ 국민도 개인과 마찬가지로 그들의 목적을 제한해야하고 그렇지 않으
> 면 그 결과에 대해 책임을 져야한다

On May 2, a 3% price increase will become effective on all over vehicles as a result of increased production and labor costs
> └ 생산비 및 인건비 인상으로 자사의 전 차종에 대해 5월 2일자로 3%
> 의 가격인상이 있을 것입니다

Repeated attempts have been made without any noticeable result
> └ 여러 가지 해봤지만 별로 효과가 없었어

· **analyze** make an analysis of
· **misgive** doubt or concern

· **update** bring up to date
· **objective** aim or end of action

Speculation ran high as to the result
    ㄴ 결과에 대해 억측이 구구했지

The government always costs more and the results are worse than if we had handled ourselves
    ㄴ 정부가 하는 일은 항상 우리자신이 처리하는 것보다 비용이 많이 들고 그 결과도 더 나쁘다

The highest result of education is tolerance
    ㄴ 교육에서 얻는 최고의 결과는 너그러움이다

The insufferable pain of the impoverished masses outweighs any fear of the consequences of striking out against those in power
    ㄴ 피폐해진 대중들의 참을 수 없는 고통이 권력을 쥔 사람들에 대항해 일어남의 결과에 대한 두려움을 넘어설 정도였다

The outcome caught me off guard(was unexpected)
    ㄴ 예상 밖의 결과였어

The outcome is doubtful
    ㄴ 결과는 불투명해

The result tells its own tale
    ㄴ 결과를 보니 알만하군

The results exceed my hope
    ㄴ 기대이상이다

There's always the possibility that the poll results were manipulated by researchers to suit the purposes of those who commission them
    ㄴ 투표 여론조사의 결과는 조사자들이 자신들을 채용해준 사람들의 목적에 부합시키려고 조작될 가능성이 언제나 있다

We got nowhere
    ㄴ 결론을 얻지 못했어

› **speculate** think about things yet unknown, risk money in a business deal   in hope of high profit
› **impoverish** make poor

We shall see what we shall see
ㄴ 일의 결과는 아무도 몰라

What was the result of your blind date(marriage meeting)?
ㄴ 너 선본 결과가 어떻게 되었니?

You'll hear from us, one way or the other
ㄴ 결과가 어떻든 알려드리겠습니다

You'll take what's coming to you, whatever you do
ㄴ 무슨 일을 하던지 그 결과는 네게 돌아오게 돼있어

10. 결심 & 결정   **Decision**

A shootout decided the game after it was tied to 2 all
ㄴ 경기가 2대 2로 동점이 된 후 승부차기로 승부가 결정되었다

A strong man does not swerve from the right decisions
ㄴ 강한 사람은 올바른 결정에서 벗어난 일은 안 한다

After four years in prison, he decided to go(run) straight
ㄴ 그는 4년간 복역한 뒤에 바르게 살기로 결심했다(바르게 살았다)

An-do chickened out on us at the last minute
ㄴ 안도는 최종 순간에 우리와 동행(협조)하지 않기로 했어

**As she knows she's only been a let-down and this time she's resolved
to show a thing or two**
ㄴ 그녀는 자신이 시시한 존재였음을 알기 때문에 이번에는 뭔가를 보여
주려고 하고 있다

As the old bus route has become unpopular, they decided to discontinue it
ㄴ 종전의 버스노선에 이용자가 적어지자 그들은 버스운행을 중단시키기로 했다

Be your own judge
ㄴ 스스로 판단해

(=You're on your own)
(=Decide it by yourself)

› **route**   line of travel, send by a selected route   › **steel**   make able to resist

Bong-soo resigned himself to life in the army
  ↳ 봉수는 할 수 없이 군대생활을 하기로 했다

Byung-soo steeled his heart(himself) against his sufferings
  ↳ 병수는 모질게 마음먹고 고통에 아랑곳하지 않았다

Chang-ho reconciled himself to what was going to have to happen
  ↳ 창호는 어차피 닥칠 일에 대하여는 감수하기로 했어

Damn me but I'll do it
  ↳ 기어이 하고야 말겠다

Decision by the(a) majority is one of the most important principles of democracy
  ↳ 다수결은 민주주의의 가장 중요한 원리이다

Duck-soo intended to retire from active life, but fate decided otherwise
  ↳ 덕수는 사회활동에서 은퇴할 예정이었으나 운명이 이를 허락지 않았다

Every obstacle yields to stern resolve
  ↳ 단호한 결의 앞에 모든 장애는 굴복한다

Gil-soo relies on his guts for his decisions
  ↳ 길수는 모든 결정을 직감에 의한다

He made vain resolutions never to repeat the act
  ↳ 그가 다시는 그 행동을 되풀이하지 않겠다고 결심했으나 허사였다

Her assurance made me decide to venture it whatever the outcome
  ↳ 틀림없다는 그녀의 말에 죽이 되든 밥이 되든 결단을 내렸다

I don't take it lying down
  ↳ 그대로 용납지 않을 거다

I have been trying hard determined to do whatever it takes
  ↳ 이를 갈고 열심히 하고있어

› **majority** age of full civil rights, quantity more than half

› **obstacle** something that stands in the way or opposes

(=I've been gritting my teeth and trying hard)
(=I've been trying hard bent on success(determined to do better))

I'll get there someday
ㄴ 언젠가 해낼 거야

I'll see what I can do
ㄴ 될지 모르지만 해볼게

I'll try to make amends
ㄴ 만회하려고 노력할 꺼야

I'm going for good
ㄴ 다신 돌아오지 않을 거다

I'm going to do it even if it kills me
ㄴ 죽어도 이건 할거야

I'm going to stand pat
ㄴ 내 생각은 변함이 없어

I'm ready for whatever comes
ㄴ 무슨 일이 일어나든 준비돼있어

In for a penny, in for a pound. Let's go through with it
ㄴ 이미 내친걸음이다 끝까지 해보자

In-soo decides things for mere gain
ㄴ 인수는 무엇이나 손익을 따져 결정하는 사람

It boils down to a go-no-go decision
ㄴ 계속할거냐 중지할거냐의 문제야

It shall go hard but I'll do it
ㄴ 어떤 일이 있어도 하겠다

› **grit** hard sharp granule, material composed of granules, unyielding courage

› **pat** light tap, small mass, tap gently

It's better to die on your feet than live on your knees
> ↳ 굴욕을 당하느니 명예로운 죽음을 택하겠다

It's now or never
> ↳ 지금이 아니면 안 돼

It's your call
> ↳ 결정은 네 몫

Just make a call and stick with it
> ↳ 그냥 결정하고 그대로 따라

Let us see how things turn out before we decide
> ↳ 사태가 어찌 돌아가는지 보고 결정하자

Let's decide it by a show of hands
> ↳ 거수표결로 결정합시다

Let's have a go at it
> ↳ 한 번 해보자

Let's kick around some of the details and decide what projects to take
> ↳ 세부사항을 논의해서 어떤 사업을 해야할지 결정합시다

Let's show them(fools) what we can do
> ↳ 우리 실력을 한 번 보여주자

Let's take our chances
> ↳ 일단 해보자

Let's turn over a new leaf
> ↳ 새로운 마음으로 시작하자

Make your resolution stick
> ↳ 네 결심이 흔들려서는 안 돼

No time like the present
> ↳ 지금이야말로 기회다

· **resolution** process of resolving, firmness of purpose, statement of the opinion, will, or intent of a body

Not till the next time
↳ 이 다음엔 끊지(금주, 금연의 농담조 맹세)

Nothing is impossible to a determined mind
↳ 마음을 굳게 먹으면 안 되는 일이 없다

Now is the time to dive in
↳ 지금이야말로 과감하게 뛰어들 때야

Now is the time to make your move
↳ 이제 용단을 내릴 때다

Now try to pull yourself together and get through this crisis
↳ 이제 정신 차려서 이 위기를 극복하자

Only when you reach the end of the road with your decision-making
↳ 네 결정이 끝나야만 되는 거야

Remember your constant nagging only makes me all the more determined not to change my mind
↳ 네가 쉴새없이 잔소리 해봤자 내 마음이 확고히 변하지 않게 굳혀줄 뿐임을 잊지 마라

Sang-soo made decisions by the seat of his pants
↳ 상수는 경험으로 결정했다

She decided not to become a doctor because medicine is not her bag
↳ 그 여자는 의학이 취향에 맞지 않아 의사가 되지 않기로 결정했다

She decided to bow out gracefully and spend more time with her family
↳ 그녀는 깨끗이 물러나서 가족들과 더 많은 시간을 보내기로 결정했다

She decided to go ahead with pregnancy, although she knew her child was likely to be physically deformed and mentally retarded
↳ 그녀는 아이가 기형과 지진아가 될 가능성이 있다는 것을 알면서도 임신을 강행키로 했다

· **crisis** decisive or critical moment
· **nag** scold or urge continually, be persistently annoying
· **retard** hold back

Show no partiality in your decisions
     ↳ 판정에 편파성이 있으면 안 돼

Something must be done
     ↳ 이대로 가만있을 순 없어

Stay out of it, you don't have any say-so in this matter
     ↳ 넌 이 일에 발언(결정)권이 없으니 빠져 줘

Sung-ho is of several minds on the issue
     ↳ 성호는 이 문제에 결정을 못 내렸어

Tai-gyung decided to go for broke in the biggest race in the year
     ↳ 태경이는 연중 최대의 경주에서 최선을 다하기로(이판사판식 작전으로) 작정했다

The buck stops here
     ↳ 결정은 내가 한다. 모든 책임은 내가 진다

The decision is in the hands of the power that be
     ↳ 그 결정은 당국의 손에 달려있다

The degree of government involvement in private affairs became an embarrassment to the nation when it was revealed that directors had been contacted regarding their decisions
     ↳ 중역들은 결정을 내리는 과정에서 정부로부터 접촉을 받았다는 사실이 드러남으로써 민간 업무에 관한 정부의 개입정도는 나라를 떠들썩하게 만들었다

The show must go on
     ↳ 시작을 했으니 그만둘 수 없잖아

The singer thought he had fully made a name for himself and decided to ride off into the sunset at the height of his career
     ↳ 그 가수는 충분히 출세했다는 생각에서 인기 절정에서 무대에서 은퇴

› **involve**   draw in as a participant, relate closely, require as a necessary

part, occupy fully

› **reveal** make known, show plainly

하기로 결심했다

Then he decided to take the plunge
> ↳ 그러자 그는 결단을 내리기로 했다

There ain't nothing(anything) that I wouldn't do
> ↳ 내가 못할 일이 뭐가 있겠어

They decided not pull the historic house down
> ↳ 그들인 역사적인 가옥을 헐지 않기로 결정했다

They hashed out the matter and decided to adopt it
> ↳ 그들은 문제를 충분히 논의하고 그것을 채택하기로 했다

They suspect the prosecution's decision to probe draft-dodging allegations as part of the ruling party's ploy to dig up dirt on some opposition members
> ↳ 그들은 검찰의 병역기피 주장에 대한 조사를 여당이 야당의원들에 대한 비리를 들춰내려는 속셈의 일환이라고 의심했다

This agreement is a step back rather than a step forward
> ↳ 이 협정은 일보 전진이 아니라 일보 후퇴로군

This is a decision you should make after consulting your doctor and weighing your options carefully
> ↳ 너의 이 결정은 의사와 상의하고 무엇을 선택할지 신중히 검토한 다음 이루어져야 한다

This may be my one and only chance
> ↳ 이게 처음이자 마지막 기회일지 몰라

This move decides the game
> ↳ 이 한 수로 승부가 난다

Try not to let your personal feelings enter into the decision
> ↳ 너의 개인 감정을 그 결정에 개입시키지 않도록 해라

Try to keep what the company has decided, even if it goes against

---

▸ **plunge** thrust or dive into something	▸ **prosecute** follow to the end, seek legal
▸ **hash** chop into small pieces	punishment of

your personal opinions

    ㄴ 회사가 결정한 일은 네 생각과 어긋나더라도 따르도록 해라

Turn it over in your mind before you decide it

    ㄴ 그 일을 결정하기 전에 신중히 고려해 봐

We'll get there eventually

    ㄴ 우린 결국 그 일을 해내고 말 거야

We'll stick to our roads

    ㄴ 우린 그대로 나아가는 거야

Whatever you decide I'm all the way with you

    ㄴ 네가 어떻게 결정하든 전적으로 찬성이야

You are the one who calls the shot

    ㄴ 네가 결정권을 가진 사람이잖아

You laughed me out of my resolution

    ㄴ 네 웃음 때문에 모처럼의 결심이 흔들렸어

› **opinion** belief, judgement, formal statement
by an expert

11. 결혼   Marriage

A good marriage should hold together without considering the children
> ↳ 훌륭한 결혼은 아이들과 상관없이 깨어지지 않아야 한다

A happy marriage is the world's best bargain
> ↳ 행복한 결혼생활은 이 세상 최고의 계약이다

A marriage without conflicts is almost inconceivable as a nation without crises
> ↳ 충돌 없는 결혼생활은 위기 없는 국가처럼 있을 수 없는 일이다

A wedding anniversary is the celebration of love, trust, partnership, tolerance and tenacity. The order varies for any given year
> ↳ 결혼 기념일은 사랑, 믿음, 협조, 관용, 인내에 대한 축하이다. 그 중 무엇이 중요한가의 순서는 해마다 다르다

A wedding is an event, but marriage is an achievement
> ↳ 결혼식은 하나의 행사지만 결혼생활은 성취이다

After five years of marriage, they grew apart
> ↳ 그들은 결혼생활 5년이 지나자 성격차이가 드러났다

Although old beyond her years, I felt she was emotionally immature and not ready for marriage
> ↳ 그 여자가 나이에 비해 어른스럽긴 해도 결혼까지는 아직 덜 성숙해 있었다

As you have been married for five years, it's time to start a family
> ↳ 이제 네가 결혼한 지 5년이나 됐으니 아이를 가져야 할 것 아니냐

› **inconceivable**   unable to think of
› **crises**   decisive or critical moment

› **achieve**   gain by work or effort

Before getting married, you have to set your house in order
  ↳ 결혼하기 전에 주변정리부터 해

Can she maintain the balancing act of pleasing her parents and her parent-in-law?
  ↳ 그녀가 친부모와 시부모 모두를 기쁘게 할 균형 있는 행동을 유지할 수 있을까?

Chan-soo had a bit of whiskey to get corkscrewed to pop the question
  ↳ 찬수는 술김에 결혼 얘기를 꺼내보려고 위스키를 약간 마셨다

Couples contemplating divorce usually have second thoughts when they realize how it'll affect their children
  ↳ 이혼을 생각해보고 있는 부부들은 보통 그 이혼이 자녀들에게 어떤 영향을 줄 것인지 생각할 때 마음이 흔들린다

Divorce can provoke aberrant behavior on the part of both parents and children when emotional resources to deal with aberrant are completely drained
  ↳ 이혼은 이상행위를 다룰 정서수단이 완전히 없어지게 될 때 부모와 아이들 모두에게 일탈행위를 유발시킬 수 있다

Don't shoot the works on your daughter's wedding
  ↳ 딸 시집 보낼 때 무리하지 마세요

Ed is married, but he also has a woman on the side
  ↳ 에드는 결혼을 했지만 따로 사귀는 여자가 있다

Even the woman with a roving eye gets short shrift if she goes in for marriage-breaking
  ↳ 바람기 있는 여자라도 파경에 이르면 잠깐의 참회는 있다

Family background and schooling are considered important in many arranged marriages

---

· **parent-in-law** parent of the spouse
· **contemplate** view or consider thoughtfully

· **drain** draw off or flow off gradually or completely(+away), exhaust

↳ 중매결혼에는 가문과 학력이 중시되는 때가 많다

Gab-dol was heartbroken when Gab-soon married another man
↳ 갑순이가 다른 남자와 결혼하자 갑돌이는 가슴이 찢어지는 듯 했다

Getting a girl in old age isn't worth the candle
↳ 노년에 젊은 색시를 얻어봤자 소용없어

Go down the ladder when you marry a wife
↳ 장가를 들려거든 눈 높이를 낮추어라

He had a one night stand only
↳ 그 사람은 잠시 바람을 피웠을 뿐이야

He has the seven-year itch
↳ 그는 권태기에 들었어(wear of one's marriage)

He's been dreaming of marrying a girl from the right side of the track
↳ 그는 잘 사는 아가씨와 결혼할 꿈을 꾸고 있다

I feel like more of a commitment
↳ 결혼신청 해줄 때도 된 것 아니어요?

I was a bundle of nerves on my wedding day
↳ 결혼식 날 신경이 예민했었지

If you get her child, then you must marry her
↳ 그 여자가 네 아이를 가지면 결혼해야 해

If you want to stretch out your golden years, getting hitched isn't a bad idea
↳ 노후에 오래 살기를 원한다면 결혼하는 것이 좋을 것이다

Instead of working to keep their marriages, more and more people are taking the soft option and getting divorced
↳ 결혼생활을 지속시키기 위해 애써 나가기보다는 쉬운 길을 택하여 이혼하는 사람들이 점점 늘어나고 있다

▸ **seven-your itch** gotten bored of marriage
▸ **commitment** pledge

▸ **hitch** move by jerks, catch by a hook, hitchhike

It's been one thing after another since she got married
> ↳ 그녀가 결혼한 후 사고 연발이다

Keeping busy was the only thing that kept him from going to pieces during the divorce
> ↳ 그가 이혼하고 있을 동안 자제력을 잃지 않게 해준 유일한 것은 계속 바쁘게 일하는 것이었다

Love makes passion; but money makes marriage
> ↳ 사랑은 열정을 낳지만 돈은 결혼을 만든다

Man-soon just married him as her meal ticket
> ↳ 만순이는 경제적인 이유 때문에 그와 결혼했을 뿐이야

Marriage has many pains, but celibacy has no pleasure
> ↳ 결혼은 많은 고통을 수반하지만 혼자 살면 아무런 즐거움도 없다

Marriage is a covered dish
> ↳ 결혼은 해봐야 알아

Marriage is compared to a cage: birds outside it despair to enter, and birds within, to escape
> ↳ 결혼은 새장과 같다. 새장밖에 있는 새는 못 들어가서 안달이고, 새장안에 있는 새는 못 나가서 안달이다

Marriage is three parts love and seven parts forgiveness of sins
> ↳ 결혼은 3할의 사랑과 7할의 용서로 이루어진다

Married life is said to be a matter of give and take
> ↳ 결혼생활은 서로 타협(양보)하는데 있다

Marry first and love will follow
> ↳ 결혼하고 나면 사랑이 싹트게 돼있어

› **celibacy** state of being unmarried, abstention from sexual inter course

› **despair** lose all hope, loss of hope

이 속담은 조금은 구시대적이다. 요즘은 중매 결혼보다 연애 결혼을 훨씬 선호한다. 그러나 옛날에는 서양에서나 동양에서나 결혼은 집안끼리 정략적으로 이루어진 경우가 많았다. 따라서 우선 서로를 잘 모르는 상태에서 결혼을 했다고 하더라도 결혼하여 살다보면 사랑이 싹튼다는 발상이 맞아 떨어졌을 것이다.

Marrying a man is like buying something you've been admiring for a long time in a shop window
  ↳ 여자의 결혼은 가게 진열장에 오래 전부터 사고싶어했던 것을 사는 것과 같다

Matrimony is a school in which one learns too late
  ↳ 결혼이란 학교는 너무 늦게 배우게되는 학교다

Moon-hee is floating on air after her marriage
  ↳ 문희는 결혼 후 붕 뜬 기분이야

Moon-soo's ship came in when he married into a wealthy family
  ↳ 문수는 부잣집에 장가들어 살 판 났어

More belongs to marriage than four legs in a bed
  ↳ 결혼이란 잠자리를 같이하는 것만이 전부가 아니다

Most married people never remember the sweet nothings they were once told
  ↳ 결혼한 사람들의 대부분은 한때 주고받았던 사랑의 속삭임을 거의 기억하지 못한다

My friend cast out his daughter when she married against his wishes
  ↳ 우리 친구는 딸이 뜻을 거역해 결혼하자 다시는 안 본다며 의절을 선언했어

Nam-soo and Bong-hee keep house these days
  ↳ 남수하고 봉희는 결혼 안하고 동거하고 있어(she keeps house 그 여자는 가사를 돌보고 있어)

· **admire** have high regard for
· **matrimony** marriage

· **belong** be suitable, be owned, be a part of

No good can come of your marrying above yourself(station)
ㄴ 과분한 결혼을 해서 이로울 게 없어

Quarrels are the dowry which married folks bring one another
ㄴ 부부싸움은 결혼한 사람들이 각자 가지고 오는 결혼지참금이다

Remember your boss treats you as if you are an airhead just filling time before you get married
ㄴ 너의 사장은 네가 결혼 전에 시간이나 때우고 있는 골이 빈 사람인 것으로 여기고 있다는 것을 잊지 마라

Rumor has it that Sang-soo and Hyang-soon are washed up, but I don't believe it
ㄴ 상수와 향순이 파경이라는 소문이지만 난 안 믿어

She didn't want to marry him, but it was the lesser of the two evils
ㄴ 그 여자는 그와의 결혼을 원치 않았지만 다른 사람을 택한 것보다는 나았어

She's married, but she still screws around
ㄴ 그 여자는 결혼은 했지만 아직도 바람기가 있다

Sook-hee came close for the kill and Jung-soo knew he was soon to be married
ㄴ 숙희에 대한 정수의 청혼은 막바지에 이르렀고 정수는 곧 결혼하게 될 줄 알았어

That girl's been giving all the married men the eye
ㄴ 저 아가씨는 모든 유부남에게 추파를 던지고 다녀

The chains of marriage are so heavy that it takes two to bear them
ㄴ 결혼의 족쇄는 너무 무거워서 둘이 있어야 감당할 수 있다

The double whammy for him was divorcing his wife and getting sued
ㄴ 그에게 엎친 데 덮친 일은 이혼을 한데다 제소까지 당한 거야

The great thing about marriage is that it enables us to be alone

---

▸ **dowry** property a woman gives her husband in marriage

▸ **airhead** bubblehead

▸ **screw around** act indiscreetly

without feeling loneliness
> ↳ 결혼이 좋은 점은 혼자 있어도 외로움을 느끼지 않게 해 준다는 것이다

The marriage is no bed of roses
> ↳ 결혼이 결코 편하고 좋은 것은 아니다

The one charm of marriage is that it makes a life of deception absolutely necessary for both parties
> ↳ 결혼에서의 한가지 매력은 살아가는 동안 양측모두 속이는 것이 절대 불가피하게 된다는 점이다

The quality of our wedding rings you made does not correspond with that of the sample submitted to us
> ↳ 당신이 보여주신 샘플과 우리의 결혼 반지는 일치하지 않습니다

The sum which two married people owe to one another defies calculation
> ↳ 결혼한 사람들이 상대방에게 빚진 것을 계산하면 한이 없다

Their love matured into a marriage
> ↳ 두 사람은 사랑으로 결혼하게 됐어

Their marriage went sour after she caught him with another girl
> ↳ 그가 딴 여자와 만나다가 처에게 들켜서 결혼생활에 파경이 왔다

There's no point in paying good money for a wedding dress when you are going to wear it once
> ↳ 넌 한 번 입고 말 결혼식 드레스에 거금을 쓸 필요가 없어

They appear to be a story book couple, but in fact, their marriage is on the rocks
> ↳ 그들이 겉보기에 잉꼬부부 같지만 실은 결혼생활이 파탄 지경이야

They can't stay married if they go round and round all the time
> ↳ 그들이 늘 아옹다옹 한다면 결혼생활을 유지하지 못할 것이다

They happily married

› **charm** something with magic power, appealing trait, small ornament
› **deception** act or fact of deceiving, fraud
› **submit** yield, give or offer

↳ 금실 좋은

> 한국에서는 "깨가 쏟아진다"라고 하지만, 영어로는 "Storybook couple"즉, '소설 속의 부부'라고 한다. '신데렐라', '백설공주' 같은 서양의 고전 동화를 보면 언제나 왕자와 공주가 결혼하며 행복한 결말을 맞는다. 이에서 유래한 속담이다.
> (=They have a happy married life)
> (=They are the perfect married couple)
> (=They are a storybook couple)

They jumped over the broom-stick
    ↳ 그들은 찬물 떠놓고 결혼했지

They lived together in happy union till parted by death
    ↳ 그들은 백년해로했다

They shot the works(wad) and had a real fancy wedding
    ↳ 그들은 기둥뿌리 빠지게 거금을 들여서 호화판 결혼식을 올렸다

Wedlock is a padlock
    ↳ 결혼은 자물쇠

When a marriage works, nothing on earth can take its place
    ↳ 결혼생활이 제대로 될 때 이 세상 어떤 것도 결혼을 대신할 수 없다

When are you going to tie(untie) the knot?
    ↳ 언제 결(이)혼 해요?

When is the big day?
    ↳ 혼사 날이 언제니?

When we are getting married, our education enters(comes) into the picture
    ↳ 결혼할 땐 학력을 말하게 되어있어(학력이 중요시 됨)

Why did she marry such a mouse?
    ↳ 그 여자가 어째서 그런 꽁생원과 결혼을 했지?

· **bloom-stick** stick made with flowers
· **padlock** lock with U-shaped catch

· **knot** interlacing that forms a lump, base of a woody branch in the stem

12. 경쟁　　　　　　　　**Competitions**

A bad workman quarrels with the man who calls him that.

　　　ㄴ 서툰 일꾼은 자기더러 서툰 일꾼이라고 부르는 사람과 다툰다

> 자신의 약점을 인정하지 못하고, 고치려고 하지 않는 발전이 없는 사람을 일컫는 말이다. 흔히 "똥 묻은 개가 겨 묻은 개 나무란다"라는 속담을 많이 쓰며 이는 영어에서는 "The pot calls the kettle black = 냄비가 주전자보고 검다고 한다"라고 한다.

A real test will prove who(which) is better(stranger)

　　　ㄴ 길고 짧은 것은 대봐야 안다

> 어떤 일이든지 할 수 있다는 자신감과 긍정적인 생각이 중요하다. 시도해 보지도 않고 포기한다거나 자만심을 갖는 것은 옳지 못하다(Don't be a faint-heart and say, 'I'll never manage to do it' = 약한 마음을 갖고 그것이 안 될 것이라는 생각을 갖지 마라).
> (=You never know what you can do till you try)

All right, I have them taped

　　　ㄴ 걱정 마, 그들을 장(파)악하고 있으니까

An enemy is an enemy is an enemy

　　　ㄴ 적은 적일 뿐이다

An enemy's gift is ruinous and no gift at all

- **pot**　rounded container
- **kettle**　vessel for boiling liquids
- **faint-heart**　coward

ㄴ 적의 선물은 나를 망치려는 것이지 결코 선물이 아니다

Anybody's guess is nobody's guess
ㄴ 사람마다 예상이 다를 경우 누구의 예상도 옳다고 할 수 없다

Are they on this side or the other side?
ㄴ 그 사람들이 우리편이냐 적이냐?

At the end of the game, I gave him the best
ㄴ 게임이 끝나자 그에게 졌다고 인정했다

Back at the ranch, I've succeeded in reading his thoughts
ㄴ 본론으로 말하면 난 그의 속셈을 알아내게 되었어

Being ahead of the game is important to your business
ㄴ 네 사업은 경쟁력에 앞서는 일이 중요하다

Believe or not, I place you well behind him
ㄴ 믿거나 말거나 넌 그 사람보다 훨씬 뒤졌다고 생각해

Better thousand enemies outside than one inside
ㄴ 문안에 있는 한 명의 적보다 문 밖의 적 **100**명이 낫다

Bong-soo is ahead now, but I'll cut him off at the pass
ㄴ 봉수가 한 발 앞서고 있지만 선두에서 밀어내고 말 거야

Bong-soo is not on our side(of our number)
ㄴ 봉수는 우리편이 아냐

Bong-soo is out of the league with me
ㄴ 봉수는 나한텐 상대가 안 돼

Bong-soo is straining at the leash
ㄴ 봉수는 남보다 앞서려고 안달이야

Bong-soo is trying to dig up some dirt on me
ㄴ 봉수가 내게 흠집 낼 게 없을까 하고 기웃거리고 있어

· **ranch** establishment for the raising of cattle, sheep, or hoses, specialized farm

· **leash** line to h old an animal

Bong-soon called his bluff and said "Let's see you do it"

↳ 봉순이가 그에게 말로만 하지말고 보여주라면서"얼마나 잘하는지 어디 보자"라고 했어

Byung-soo extended an olive branch of sorts to you

↳ 병수가 네게 모종의 평화안을 제시했어

Catch him napping right away

↳ 그가 방심하고 있는 지금 당장 허를 찔러라

Catch him off balance with a lot of unexpected questions

↳ 그에게 예상하지 못한 질문공세를 펴서 허를 찔러라

Chan-ho is riding high

↳ 찬호는 물이 올랐어

(=Chan-ho is number one these days)
(=Chan-ho is on top of the world)
(=Chan-ho is above the competition)

Chang-soo is nowhere near as good as you

↳ 창수는 너하곤 비교(상대)가 안 돼

Chul-soo is licking his chops because he beat me at a card game yesterday

↳ 철수는 어제 카드게임에서 나한테 이겨서 승리를 만끽하고 있어

Control of a whole industry by a single company tends to eliminate competition

↳ 한 회사가 전체 산업을 장악하면 경쟁력이 없어지기 쉽다

Don't forget they are playing chicken with you

↳ 그들이 네가 나가떨어질 때까지 버티고 있다는 걸 잊지마

Every time he comes around, it puts me on my guard

▸ **bluff** rising steeply with a broad flat front, frank, cliff

▸ **lick** draw the tongue over, beat, stroke of the tongue, small amount

ㄴ 그가 여기로 오기만 하면 경계심이 생겨

Gil-soo can have your number fast
ㄴ 길수는 네 속셈을 재빨리 간파할 수 있어

Have(keep) him covered while I try to fetch help
ㄴ 내가 도움을 청해 올 때까지 그를 사격할 수 있는 거리에서 놓치지 마라

He has got the goods on you
ㄴ 그가 네 약점(발모)을 쥐고 있단 말이야

He's my despair
ㄴ 난 그 사람 발 밑에도 못 가

Higher export prices will weaken our competitive position in world markets
ㄴ 수출가 상승은 세계시장에서 우리의 경쟁력을 약화시킬 것이다

I'm on your plot
ㄴ 네 흉계는 알고있어

It is a little unkind to gloat over our competitors failure
ㄴ 경쟁자의 실패에 고소해 하는 것은 약간 심한 짓이다

It's time we took(brought) him down a peg or two
ㄴ 이제 그 사람 코를 꺾어 놓아야 할 때다

It's too late to draw back
ㄴ 이제 와서 물러설 수 없잖아

Jong-soo is always getting the jump on others
ㄴ 종수는 언제나 남들보다 한 발 앞서고 있다

Jung-soo can steal a march on you any day
ㄴ 정수는 언제라도 너를 앞지를(따돌릴) 수 있어

Jung-soo is trying to run the show
ㄴ 정수가 주도권을 잡으려는 거야

› **fetch** go or come after and bring or take back, sell for

› **plot** main story development, ground plan, small area of ground

Let any man come, I am his man
  ↳ 누구든지 오너라, 내가 상대해 주마

Let's avoid dog-eat-dog competition
  ↳ 서로 잡아먹기 경쟁은 그만두자

Man has the perpetual contest for wealth which keeps world in tumult
  ↳ 인간은 세상을 계속 동요 속에 있게 하는 부를 얻기 위해 끊임없이
  경쟁해왔다

Many people today vie with each other for extravagance
  ↳ 요즘 많은 사람들이 사치와 낭비의 경쟁을 벌이고 있어

Moon-ho must have been laughing up his sleeve as Tai-ho got the ax
  ↳ 태호가 목이 잘렸으니 문호가 속으로 고소해 하겠지

Most firms slip into questionable business practices as a way to keep paces with competitors
  ↳ 대부분의 회사들은 다른 경쟁자들에게 뒤지지 않기 위한 방편으로 의
  심스러운 행위를 은밀히 할 수 있다

Myung-soo has the goods on me
  ↳ 명수는 나에 대해 시시콜콜 알고(약점 쥐고)있어

Myung-soo is not going to make it easy for you
  ↳ 명수가 그리 호락호락하지 않을 거야

Nam-soo has your number from the start
  ↳ 남수는 처음부터 네 속셈으로 알고있어

Nam-soo just doesn't measure up to me in intelligence
  ↳ 남수가 지식(능)면에서 나하고 맞먹을 수 없어

Nobody has a look-in with him
  ↳ 그를 이길만한 사람은 아무도 없어

Nobody thinks he's got the better of you

- **perpetual**   continuing forever, occurring continually

- **extravagance**   wildly excessive, lavish, or costly

↳ 아무도 그가 너한테 이겼다고(너보다 이익 봤다고) 생각지 않아

Nothing succeeds like the appearance of success

↳ 성공한 것으로 보이는 것이 경쟁에 낫다

Now there'll be the devil to pay

↳ 후환이 두렵다

Once he hesitates, you'll have him

↳ 그가 망설이기만 하면 네게 당하는 거야

Once you hesitate, he'll have you

↳ 네가 망설이기만 하면 그에게 당하는 거야

Only initiating can capture the world

↳ 앞서가는 것만이 세상을 사로잡는다

Only when one knows the enemy and oneself well, is one able to win all the battles

↳ 적을 알고 나를 알면 백전백승이다

Our enemies approach nearer to truth in their judgements of us than we do ourselves

↳ 적은 우리를 판단함에 있어서 우리자신보다 더 진실에 가까이 접근한다

Our scientists are trying to beat them to the punch

↳ 우리의 과학자들은 선수를 치려고 노력하고 있어

Our wage levels should be brought into line with those of our competitors

↳ 우리의 임금 수준은 경쟁사들과 맞먹을 정도로 해야 한다

Security is the greatest enemy

↳ 방심은 금물

She doesn't stack up very well with you

↳ 그 여자는 너한테 비교가 안 돼

› **devil**   personified supreme spirit of evil, demon, wicked person

› **hesitate**   hold back especially in doubt, pause

She had to live in the fast lane for a time then
> ㄴ 그 여자는 그 당시 한 동안 남들과 경쟁하며 살아야 했다

She has you on the string any way
> ㄴ 아무튼 그 여자는 너를 검토대상에 넣어놓고 있어

She's got a hole in her head if she thinks I was born yesterday
> ㄴ 그 여자가 나를 만만하게 본다면 어리석은 생각이다

She's pitted against you this time
> ㄴ 그 여자가 이번엔 너하고 맞붙게 됐구먼

Somebody is going to give a dose of his own medicine someday
> ㄴ 누군가 언젠가는 그에게 같은 수법으로 보복할 것이다

Someday the law of the averages will catch up with them and they'll start winning
> ㄴ 언젠가는 평균의 법칙이 작용해서 그들이 이기기 시작할 것이다

Sung-gil is up against a tough opponent
> ㄴ 성길인 강한 상대를 만났어

That computer is head and shoulder above the competition
> ㄴ 저 컴퓨터는 경쟁상대 보다 훨씬 우수하다

The best man wins
> ㄴ 실력 있는 사람이 이기게 돼 있어

The competition will beat you
> ㄴ 넌 경쟁에서 뒤지게 돼

The cutthroat nature of the competition between candidates has added to our concerns
> ㄴ 후보자들 간의 치열한 경쟁이 우리의 우려를 가중시켜주고 있다

The first blow is the half the battle
> ㄴ 선수를 써야 남을 제압 할 수 있어

· **pit** stony seed of some fruits, remove the pit from

· **candidate** one who seeks an office or membership

The industry can do better in its competition with other economic sections only when it is run with transparency and accountability
> ↳ 이들 산업이 투명하고 책임을 다해야만 타 부문과의 경쟁에서이길 수 있게 된다

The other team was beating us, but we wouldn't say uncle
> ↳ 상대팀이 우릴 앞서고 있었지만 우린 굴하지 않았어

The rat race is unrelenting
> ↳ 격심한 생존경쟁이 끊이질 않는다

Their company has pulled out all the stops because there is a lot of competition for the contract
> ↳ 그 계약에 대한 경쟁이 치열하니 그 회사는 최선을 다 해야 해

There's no choice between the two
> ↳ 양자간의 우열은 없어

There's no comparison between he and you
> ↳ 그와 넌 너무 차이가 커

They are going to blow you out of the water
> ↳ 그들은 너를 아주 망치려고 하고 있어(배를 물 밖으로 밀어내면 움직일 수 없으니까)

They are out of the league
> ↳ 상대가 안 돼(약한 상대)

They'll do anything in their power to prevent us from coming out on top
> ↳ 그들은 할 수 있는 수단을 다하여 우리가 저희들에게 이기지 못하도록 기를 쓰고 나설 것이다

This time I'll cut him down to size
> ↳ 그 녀석 코를 납작하게 해 줄 테다

This year somebody else got there first
> ↳ 올해는 다른 사람이 앞질러 버렸어

- **transparent** clear enough to see through, obvious
- **accountable** responsible
- **unrelenting** not yielding or easing

Those who drop(fall) by the wayside will find it hard to catch up
↳ 남들에게 뒤지면 따라잡기 어려워

To treat an enemy with magnanimity is to blunt our hatred for him
↳ 적에게 관대함은 적에 대한 우리의 미운 감정을 누그러뜨린다

Try to detect the crack(chink) in her armour
↳ 그의 약점을 찾아내도록 해

We know your little ways
↳ 그런 유치한 수법쯤은 알고 있어

We should further try to sharpen our competitive edge
↳ 우리는 경쟁력을 강화시키기 위해 더 한층 노력해야 한다

We'll lead them into competition
↳ 우린 경쟁에서 그들을 앞설 것이다

We'll see which of us is master
↳ 누가 이기나 해보자

When the idea of winning in sports carried too excess, honorable competition can turn into disorder and violence
↳ 경기에 이기겠다는 생각이 지나치면 명예로운 경쟁의 원칙이 무질서
와 폭력으로 변할 수 있다

Why do I feel small in front of him?
↳ 왜 그 사람 앞에서면 열등감이 생기는지 모르겠어

You can't always outdo others
↳ 기는 놈 위에 나는 놈 있다

(=Greatness is comparative)
(=Everyone has his master)
(=There's always someone who do it a little better)

› **wayside** side of the road

› **magnanimity** noble or generous

› **excess** amount left over, eliminate the position of

You can't let up on your efforts to compete with other firms
> ㄴ 다른 회사와의 경쟁을 위한 노력을 소홀히 해서는 안 돼

You have found a good match(rival, opponent) in the person of Pil-soo
> ㄴ 넌 필수라는 호적수를 만났군

You have got to beat them to the punch(draw)
> ㄴ 그들보다 한발 앞서야 해

You have me there
> ㄴ 그 점에선 내가졌다

You have won me
> ㄴ 이제 항복했다

You ought to break down the wall of inferiority complex
> ㄴ 넌 열등감의 장벽을 헐어버려야 해

You've got a hole in your head if you think I'm a dupe
> ㄴ 나를 어수룩하게 생각한다면 큰 오산이다

You've got me there
> ㄴ 넌 내 약점을 잘도 잡아내는군

Your wild insults will surely draw fire from your opponents
> ㄴ 네가 마구 욕했다가는 상대방에게 공격 빌미를 제공할게 틀림없어

- **inferior** being lower in position, degree, rank or merit
- **complex** psychological problem
- **dupe** one easily deceived or cheated

13. 경제   **Economy**

A sharp rise in imports of crude oil is responsible for the fall in the nation's current account surplus

         ↳ 원유 수입의 급작스러운 증가가 국가의 경상수지 잉여 하락의 원인이다

All these measures aimed at insuring the health of other animals and stabilizing the nation's economy

         ↳ 이 모든 조치는 다른 동물들의 건강을 확보하고 국가경제를 안정시키는데 목적을 둔다

Allowing the pricing of houses entirely to market forces will undoubtedly raise housing prices greatly

         ↳ 주택가격책정을 전적으로 시장 실정에 맡기는 어떠한 결정도 주택가격을 크게 올릴 것이 틀림없다

Complaints about the profiteering will be more vociferous, if food supplies dwindle

         ↳ 식량공급이 줄어지면 부당 이익에 대한 불평이 더욱 요란해질 것이다

Control of a whole industry by a single company tends to eliminate competition

         ↳ 한 회사가 전체 산업을 장악하면 경쟁력이 없어지기 쉽다

Economic growth benefits the poor because it allows prosperity to be widely shared

         ↳ 경제성장은 그로 인한 번영을 널리 공유하게 됨에 따라 빈곤층에 이

▸ **stabilize** firmly established, mentally wellbalanced, steady

▸ **profiteer** one who makes an reasonable profit

익이 된다

Everyone favors reduced taxes and deep cuts in the budget
└ 누구나 감세와 대폭적인 예산삭감을 찬성해

Excess tax revenues should be used to support low income earners who bore the brunt of the economic hardships
└ 여분의 조세수입은 경제적 어려움을 정면으로 겪었던 저소득 근로자 들을 지원하는데 사용되어야 한다

Fiscal policy has to be changed to a tight one, focusing on contracting the budget deficit
└ 재정정책은 긴축재정으로 변환하여 재정적자를 줄여나가야 할 것이다

If taxes are confiscatory, the destruction of work incentives makes the better-off members of the community less productive
└ 조세가 몰수적인 성격을 띤다면 일하고자하는 동기의 파괴가 가진 계 층의 생산성을 떨어뜨리게 될 것이다

In this disorderly social environment. no sustained economic progress can be expected
└ 이런 무질서한 환경 속에서는 지속적인 경제발전을 기대할 수 없다

It takes more brain and effort to make out the income-tax form than it does to make the income
└ 소득을 올리는 것 보다 소득세 신고용지를 작성하는데 더 머리와 노 력을 요한다

Keeping inflation at the lowest possible level is a way of preventing the value of the won from fluctuating wildly
└ 인플레이션을 가능한 한 억제하는 것은 원화 가치의 변동을 막는 방법이다

Korean manufacturers posted record net profits last year, due to a decrease in costly interest payments combined with a surging demand

---

› **incentive** inducement to do something

› **surge** rise and fall in or as if in waves

› **sustain** provide with nourishment, keep going, hold up, suffer, support or prove

from consumers
> ↳ 지난해 국내 제조업자들이 수요 급증과, 이자비용 감소 등으로 사상 최대 순익을 올렸다

No one is completely sure what causes booms and depressions in free economies
> ↳ 자유경제에서 무엇이 경기팽창과 침체를 불러일으키는지 아무도 확신할 수 없다

One difficulty in isolating the components of economic movements is that those components are not completely independent of one another
> ↳ 경제활동의 요소들을 분리하는데 한가지 어려움은 그 요소들이 완전히 독립되어있지 않다는 것이다

One role of public finance is to channel surplus revenue to the poor and low income earners
> ↳ 재정의 역할 중 하나는 여분의 세입을 가난한 사람과 저소득층에게 배분하는 일이다

Our big spending brought Korean economy to its knees
> ↳ 우리 국민의 과소비가 한국경제를 형편없이 약하게 만들었어

Political stability is a requirement for overcoming any difficulty that may crop up in the nation's economy
> ↳ 국가경제에 돌출할 수 있는 난관을 극복해 나가는 데는 정치적 안정을 요한다

Possibilities of another economic crisis are strong and growing due to their attempts to boost the economy only for votes
> ↳ 그들이 득표만을 위하여 경제를 부양시키려고 함에 따라 또 다른 경제위기의 가능성이 커져만 가고 있다

Production got into high gear after the recession

▸ **finance** money resources(pl), management of money affairs, raise funds for

▸ **recession** departing procession, period of reduced economic activity

↳ 불경기 이후 처음으로 생산이 활기를 띠었다

Production revved up after the strike

↳ 파업후 생산은 활기를 띠었다

Raising the ceiling on the national debt will not address the cause of unemployment

↳ 국채를 늘이는 것은 실업의 원인을 해결하는 것이 아니다

Rising prices press most heavily on the poor and on people with fixed income

↳ 물가 오름은 가난한 사람과 고정 수입자들에게 큰 부담이 된다

Subsidiary(Incidental) expenses surpass the original outlay

↳ 보조금이 예산보다 더 많다

That explains why there are considerable gaps between what price statistics say and what housewives perceive on shopping trips

↳ 그것이 통계상의 물가와 주부들이 시장에서 느끼는 물가 사이에 상당한 간격이 있는 이유를 설명해준다

The budget is staggering under the burden of having to care for many people

↳ 예산은 많은 사람을 위해서 써야하는 부담을 안고 있다

The current steep upturn of the domestic economy may exhibit a severe downturn

↳ 현재 국내경제의 가파른 상승이 심한 하강국면으로 반전될지 모른다

The determination of the income structure during the economic crisis must be corrected to sustain economic growth

↳ 경제위기중의 소득구조 악화는 경제성장의 지속을 위해 교정되어야 한다

The economy is going to hell in a basket

↳ 경제가 급속히 악화되고 있군

▸ **subsidiary** furnishing support
▸ **incidental** subordinate, nonessential

▸ **perceive** realize, become aware of
▸ **stagger** overlap or alternate

The economy seems to be turning the corner
    ㄴ 경제가 호전되어가고 있는 듯 하다

The feeling that there is one law for the workers and another for the gentry did much to undermine faith in the justice of the income policy
    ㄴ 근로자 계층을 생각하지 않고 상류계층 만을 위하는 법은 소득정책의 공정성에 대한 신뢰감을 크게 저해한다

The industry can do better in its competition with other economic sections only when it is run with transparency and accountability
    ㄴ 이들 산업이 투명하고 책임을 다해야만 타 부문과의 경쟁에서이길 수 있게 된다

The most rigid economy would not make both ends meet
    ㄴ 아무리 절약해도 도저히 살아 갈 수가 없다

The nation's five economic organizations have called on the government to come up with countermeasures to halt the won's climb
    ㄴ 국내의 경제 5 단체는 정부에게 원화가치 인상을 저지시킬 대책마련을 요구했다

The need for the Korean economy to gain ground on the market on a stable basis is being felt more acutely now than ever
    ㄴ 한국 경제가 건실한 바탕 위에 세계시장에서 기반을 확보해야 할 필요성이 과거 어느 때 보다도 절실히 느껴진다

The outlook for this year's economy is good at least on paper
    ㄴ 올해 경제가 이론(문서)상으로는 좋아 보인다

This inflation pales before(beside) the one we had five years ago
    ㄴ 이 정도 물가 오름은 5년 전의 그것에 비하면 아무 것도 아니다

This is the only way for them to revive the impoverished economy and to save innocent people from starvation

---

› **gentry** people of good birth or breeding

› **rigid** lacking flexibility

› **countermeasure** something intended to retard or offset

┗ 이것은 그들이 가난에 찌들려 있는 경제를 소생시키고 죄 없는 국민들을 가난에서 구제해 주는 유일한 방법이다

Their suggestion for improving the nation's exports were very well put(said)

┗ 국가의 수출을 늘이겠다는 그들의 제안은 옳은 말이었다

True individual freedom can't exist without economic security and independence

┗ 경제적 안정과 독립 없이는 진정한 개인적 자유가 보장될 수 없다

We learned the hard way during our economic crisis how individual greed can disrupt civil society

┗ 우리는 경제위기를 겪는 가운데 개인의 욕심이 시민사회에 어떤 혼란을 가져올 수 있는가를 쓰라린 체험으로 배웠다

We should be embracing economic independence wholeheartedly

┗ 우리는 경제적인 상호의존성을 기꺼이 받아들여야 한다

When the government didn't have transparency, the fundamental structure of the economy weakened and economic progress ground to a halt

┗ 정부가 투명성이 없을 때 경제의 기본구조가 약화되어 경제발전이 정지되었다

When the rising prices are combined with a lack of jobs, many people suffer and the nation becomes poorer

┗ 물가가 오르는데 취업마저 어려워지면 나라가 점점 가난해진다

Without a reliable source of reasonably priced electricity, it would be practically impossible to maintain a healthy economy

┗ 믿을만한 저렴한 가격의 전원이 없이는 건강한 경제를 유지하기가 사실상 불가능하다

· **disrupt** throw into disorder
· **embrace** clasp in the arms, welcome, include

· **wholehearted** sincere

14. 경찰   Police Officers

A police comedy action centered on a cop fooling around at headquarters, was one of the biggest box-office draw in Korea last year

      ↳ 경찰서에서 빈둥거리는 형사 이야기를 그린 경찰 코미디 영화가 국내에서 지난해 가장 큰 흥행을 기록한 영화의 하나다

All he could do was to play for time until the police arrived

      ↳ 그가 할 수 있는 일은 경찰이 도착할 대 가지 버티는 것뿐이었다

At last the criminal's guilty conscience forced him to spill his guts to the police

      ↳ 결국 그 죄인은 죄책감에 시달려 속에 있는 것을 경찰에게 털어놓았다

By the time the cops got there, the suspect had flown the coop

      ↳ 경찰이 거기로 출동했을 때 용의자는 벌써 도망가고 없었다

Chan-soo pushed himself by the policeman and almost got arrested for doing so

      ↳ 찬수는 경찰을 밀치고 지나가다가 하마터면 그 때문에 체포될 번했어

Duck-soo coughed up the whole story for the police

      ↳ 덕수가 경찰에게 다 불어버렸어

Get your story straight before the police get here

      ↳ 경찰이 오기 전에 내용을 얘기해 다오

He gave his friend away to the police, hoping to escape punishment

      ↳ 그는 처벌을 면할 생각에서 친구의 행적을 경찰에 불어버렸다

| ▸ **headquarter**   command or administrative center | ▸ **suspect**   regarded with suspicion, one who is suspected as of a crime |

He spilled his guts to the cops
ㄴ 그가 모든 걸 경찰에 불어버렸어

Her clever convolutions left officers thoroughly perplexed
ㄴ 그녀의 교묘한 둘러대기가 경찰들을 완전히 당황케 했다

She alerted the police after she noticed an over-powering smell of putrid flesh coming from the cellar
ㄴ 그녀는 지하실에서 나는 시체 썩는 강한 냄새가 코에 들어오자 경찰에 신고했다

Sometimes unscrupulous employers even call the police to have foreign workers deported to avoid paying the salary money they owe
ㄴ 때로는 사업주가 고용인들에게 대한 급료 지급을 회피하기 위하여 외국인 근로자들을 추방시키도록 경찰에 신고하기까지 한다

The best safety device in a car is a rear-view mirror with a policeman in it
ㄴ 차량의 최고 안전장치는 경찰의 얼굴이 보이는 백미러이다

The cop waved on all the pedestrians
ㄴ 경찰이 모든 보행자에게 길을 건너가라는 수신호를 보냈다

The cops pasted a robbery on him
ㄴ 경찰이 그에게 절도죄를 뒤집어 씌웠어

The insurance claim can't be paid over until the accident has been reported to the police
ㄴ 사건이 경찰에 신고되어야 보험금이 지급된다

The long arm of the law always tap these street vendors on the shoulder
ㄴ 경찰들은 늘 노점상들에게 뇌물(정보)을 얻으려고 찾아온다

The police appealed for information concerning the whereabouts of the stolen car used in the robbery
ㄴ 경찰은 강도행위에 사용되었던 차의 소재에 대한 제보를 호소했다

> **unscrupulous** being or acting in total disregard of conscience, ethical principles or rights of others

The police are on his track
　　ㄴ 경찰이 그를 쫓고있어

The police are putting the heat on the motorists who show any signs of driving while under the influence(of alcohol)
　　ㄴ 경찰이 조금이라도 기미가 있는 음주운전자에게는 단속을 강화하고 있다

The police are questioning many people to get behind the bank robbery
　　ㄴ 경찰은 은행 떨이의 단서를 잡으려고 많은 사람을 신문하고 있어

The police arrived on the scene of the crime
　　ㄴ 경찰이 범죄 현장에 왔다

The police choked the information out of him
　　ㄴ 경찰은 강제로 그에게서 정보를 얻으려고 했어

The police figured that it was an inside job
　　ㄴ 경찰은 그 사건을 내부소행으로 추정했다

The police flashed his badge at the suspect
　　ㄴ 경찰이 용의자에게 재빨리 경찰배지를 내보였다

The police have coerced the defendant into making a false confession to the crime
　　ㄴ 경찰은 피고인에게 그 범죄에 대한 자백을 강요했다

The police may be able to make him cough out his story
　　ㄴ 경찰은 그가 부지중에 입을 열 수밖에 없도록 만들 것 같다

The police moved in on the drug dealers
　　ㄴ 경찰이 마약상 들을 덮쳤어

The police nailed the spies who broke cover
　　ㄴ 경찰이 정체가 드러난 간첩을 잡았어

The police numbered him with the most likely of the suspects
　　ㄴ 경찰이 그를 가장 유력한 용의자의 한 사람으로 포함시켰어

· **choke** hinder breathing, clog or obstruct
· **influence** power or capacity of causing

an effect in indirect or intangible ways

The police put a tail on him , but he lost him
ㄴ 경찰이 그에게 미행자를 붙였으나 그는 그 미행을 벗어났다

The police vice squad have made efforts to arrest girls who walk the streets so that they may cut down on prostitution
ㄴ 경찰의 풍기사범 단속반은 매춘을 단속하기 위해 거리의 여자들을 잡아들이는데 노력을 기울여왔다

The police were on his tail until he gave them the slip
ㄴ 경찰이 그를 미행하다가 따돌림당했다

The policeman turned a blind eye to the illegal practice and didn't ask them to give him chapter and verse
ㄴ 그 경찰은 불법행위를 눈감아주고 꼬치꼬치 캐묻지 않았다

The suspect matches(measures) up to the description the police have of the wanted thief
ㄴ 피의자는 경찰이 수배중인 도둑의 인상착의와 부합한다

The thief flew the coop before the police arrived
ㄴ 경찰이 오기 전에 도둑이 도망쳤어

The thief ran across the street with the police dog hot pursuit
ㄴ 도둑은 경찰견에게 바싹 쫓겨서 도로를 뛰어 건너갔다

They gave the police the slip
ㄴ 그들은 경찰을 따돌리고 달아났다

They hauled us in and booked every one of us
ㄴ 그들이 우리를 연행하여 일일이 이름을 적었어

They holed up(lay low, lay up) there for a few months until the police stopped looking for them
ㄴ 그들은 경찰이 찾지 않을 때까지 거기서 숨어 지냈다

Will the cops drag it out of him?
ㄴ 경찰이 그에게서 정보를 끌어낼 수 있을까?

▸ **prostitute** one who engages in sexual intercourse for pay

▸ **coop** confine in or as if in a coop
▸ **haul** draw or pull, transport or carry

15. 경험   **Experiences**

A moment's sight is sometimes worth a life's experience
    ↳ 잠깐 보는 것이 때로는 평생의 경험과 맞먹는다

> 시청각 경험의 중요성을 말해주는 속담이다. 요즘은 Mass Media 의 대중화
> 에 힘입어 시청각 경험이 점차로 쉬워지고 있다(=Seeing is believing).
> (=The proof of the pudding is in the eating)
> (=One eyewitness is better than two hear-so)

A wise man profits by his mistakes
    ↳ 현명한 사람은 실수도 좋은 경험으로 삼는다

> 보통 사람들은 자신의 경험으로 지혜를 쌓아 나간다. 좋은 경험과 나쁜 경험
> 을 통해 참된 지혜를 얻는다. 그보다 더 앞선 사람은 자신의 경험이 아닌 남
> 의 경험을 통해서도 지혜를 얻는다(By other's faults wise men correct
> their own = 현인은 남의 허물을 보고 스스로의 허물을 시정한다).

A youth without fire is followed by an old age without experience
    ↳ 열정 없는 젊음은 경험 없는 노년이 된다

Adventure makes life more colorful
    ↳ 인생의 다채로움은 모험을 하는데 있다

All he has done is make a song and dance about his experience

---

• **eyewitness**   person who actually sees
something happen

↳ 그가 한 일이란 게 자신의 경험에 대하여 무슨 소리인지도 모를 소리
만 잔뜩 늘어놓은 것 뿐이야

Although he stayed out of the Korean War, he always spins us a yarn about his daring deeds in the war

↳ 그는 **6.25** 전쟁 때 참전하지도 않았으면서 늘 우리들에게 무용담을
늘어놓는다

An old eagle is better than a young crow

↳ 썩어도 준치이다

(=An old poacher makes the best gamekeeper)

An-do will find out where the shoe pinches when he tries it on

↳ 안도는 경험을 통해서 문제점을 찾아 낼 거야

Bo-sun has gone through a lot lately

↳ 보선이에게 많은 일이 있었다

Bong-soo tried one thing and another

↳ 봉수는 이것저것 해봤어

Bong-soo tried this once and got his fingers burned

↳ 봉수가 전에 이걸 시도한 적이 있는데 아주 나쁜 경험이었어(혼났어)

Bong-soo's seen many a man meet his maker in the electric chair

↳ 봉수는 많은 사람들이 전기의자로 처형되는 것을 보아왔다

Bosun's really been going through the changes lately

↳ 보선이는 요즘 사는 게 뭔지 몸소 체험하고 있어

Byung-soo learned it in the gall of bitterness

↳ 병수는 쓰라린 고통을 당하고서야 그것을 알았다(흔한 표현 아님)

Byung-soo tried it each and every way

› **deed** exploit

› **poach** hunt or fish illegally

› **gall** sore on the skin caused by chafing

ㄴ 병수는 여러모로 해보았다

Come back wiser for experience

ㄴ 경험 쌓아 지혜롭게 돌아 오라

Dong-soo has done(seen) it all

ㄴ 동수는 많은 일을 해 본 경험이 많아(견문이 넓어)

Everyone is a prisoner of his own experience

ㄴ 모든 사람은 자신의 경험에 대한 포로이다

Experience is a comb which nature give us when we are bald

ㄴ 경험은 우리가 대머리가 되었을 때 쓰라고 자연이 우리에게 주는 선물이다

Experience keeps a dear school, but fools learn in no other

ㄴ 경험의 학교는 비싸게 먹히지만 어리석은 사람은 경험 외에 배울 방법이 없다

Gil-soo came to griefs(unstuck) when he tried to challenge people with more experience than himself

ㄴ 길수는 자기보다 훨씬 경험 많은 사람들에게 도전하려 했다가 크게 망신당했다

Gil-soo is experienced enough to be able to deliver the goods

ㄴ 길수는 충분히 그 일을 해낼 만큼 노련해

He that shoots often will at last hit the mark

ㄴ 자주 쏘다보면 결국 정곡을 맞추게 된다

실패하더라도 포기하지 말고 오뚝이처럼 일어나면 언젠가는 이룰수 있다는 말이다.
(=Every one starts off a beginner)
(=No one starts off being good at something)

I appreciate your time in reviewing my enclosed resume and would

---

▸ **comb**	toothed instrument for arranging the hair	▸ **resume**	summary of one's career and qualification

welcome the opportunity to meet and discuss my qualifications and experience with you
> ↳ 제 이력서를 읽어주셔서 감사 드리며 귀하를 뵙고 저의 자격과 경력에 대해서 더 많은 말씀을 드리고 싶습니다

I believe that my background, qualifications and work experience are well-suited to your company's specific requirements
> ↳ 저의 학력, 자격, 경력이 귀사의 요구조건에 잘 맞는다고 생각합니다

If he wants to move ahead in his job, he should take advice from more experienced workers
> ↳ 그가 업무에 앞서 나가려면 경험 많은 동료들에게 조언을 받아야 한다

It's a great way to polish(fatten, broaden) your horizons
> ↳ 그건 네 시야를 넓혀주지

Nothing can top that experience
> ↳ 그보다 좋은 경험은 없어

One picture is worth a thousand words
> ↳ 사람은 겪어봐야 알고 말은 타봐야 안다(백문이 불여일견)

시청각 경험의 중요성을 말해주는 속담이다. 요즘은 Mass Media 의 대중화에 힘입어 시청각 경험이 점차로 쉬워지고 있다(=Seeing is believing).
(=The proof of the pudding is in the eating)
(=One eyewitness is better than two hear-so)

Personal characteristics are persistent and relatively little influenced by training and experience
> ↳ 개인의 성격은 지속적이며 상대적으로 훈련이나 경험에 의해 거의 영향을 받지 않는다

· qualification special skill or experience for a job	**· persistent** go on resolutely in spite of difficulties, continue to exist

Put a finishing touch to him
> ↳ 그에게 좋은 경험을 주어라

Quite a few women have relatively painless births, but most found it an extremely painful experience
> ↳ 많은 여성들이 상대적인 무통 분만을 하지만 그래도 매우 고통스러운 것으로 밝혀졌다

Sang-soo made decisions by the seat of his pants
> ↳ 상수는 경험으로 결정했다

She was full primed and said nothing about her past history of prostitution
> ↳ 그녀에게 충분히 필요한 일을 주입시켰기 때문에 자신의 매춘 경험에 대해서는 입도 벙긋하지 않았다

The experience obtained him the appointment
> ↳ 그 경험이 인정되어 그는 그 지위에 임명되었다

The family experienced the whole gamut of suffering
> ↳ 가족은 온갖 고난을 겪었다

The frog in the well doesn't know the ocean
> ↳ 우물 안 개구리가 큰 바다를 알랴

Today's experience will knock some sense into me
> ↳ 오늘의 경험으로 내가 정신 좀 차릴 것 같다

Trouble brings experience and experience brings wisdom
> ↳ 고통은 경험을 주고 경험은 지혜를 준다

직접 경험은 책이나 학교에서 배운 지혜나 간접 경험을 통해 얻은 지혜보다 값진 것이다. "Seeing is believing = 백 번 듣는 것보다 한번 보는 것이 낫다"라는 속담도 경험의 중요성을 말해준다.

› **prime** fill or load, lay a preparatory coatting on | › **obtain** gain by effort, be generally recognized

We are healed of a suffering only by experiencing it to the full
↳ 사람은 고통을 한껏 당해봄으로써만이 그 고통에서 치유된다

You never know until you try
↳ 직접 안 해보면 몰라

> (=Experience teaches)

You never know what it's like unless you go through it yourself
↳ 그건 당해본 사람이나 알아

> (=Don't say you understand the pain unless you experienced it
> yourself)

Your experience in dealing with your office work will stand you in good stead no matter what line of work you go into
↳ 네가 앞으로 무슨 일을 하든 사무실 일 처리의 경험이 크게 유익할 것이다

‣ **stead**   one's place, job, or function
‣ **in good stead**   to advantage

16. 계절   Season

After the long hot dry summer, the soil is cracking up
    ↳ 장기간 비가 안 오는 여름 날씨에 땅이 갈라지고 있다

**After three hours of snow and rain, the roads were so slushed up
that they could not travel**
    ↳ 눈비가 온 끝이라 도로가 엉망이 돼서 그들은 길을 갈 수가 없었다

Another storm will leave the wheat flat
    ↳ 폭풍우가 한 번 더 오면 밀이 쓰러질 것이다

**At this time everybody winds up their annual work and reflects on
what they have done this year**
    ↳ 이맘때면 모두가 1년 간의 일을 마무리하고 올해 한 일을 되돌아본다

**At this time of the year snowbound roads mean crawling traffic and
delays for commuters**
    ↳ 이맘때쯤 해서 눈 때문에 다니지 못하게 되면 차가 기어다니게 되고
      통근자들의 지각사태가 난다

Do we have enough heating oil to last out this winter?
    ↳ 이 겨울을 넘길만한 난방용 기름이 우리한테 있나?

Fears were entertained that the railroad would be blocked by snow
    ↳ 눈으로 인해 철도가 불통되지 않을까 하고 걱정되었다

I shall be away for the summer
    ↳ 피서 계획 중

▸ **slush** partly melted snow
▸ **snowbound** trapped in snow

▸ **crawl**   move slowly as by drawing the
              body along the ground

In the summer he often sleeps in his birthday suit(in the raw)
> ↳ 여름이면 그는 발가벗고 자는 때가 많아

It seems that the yellow dust in the sky has become as regular as birds showing up in spring
> ↳ 봄철에 누른 색 먼지는 철새처럼 정기적으로 공중에 떠오는 것 같다

It's suddenly starting to feel a lot like summer
> ↳ 갑자기 완연한 여름이 된 것 같다

Keep yourself warm by rolling yourself up in(all) clothes
> ↳ 있는 옷 다 껴입고 몸을 따뜻하게 감싸라

Men are constantly on the lookout for seasonal food shortages and gluts
> ↳ 인간은 끊임없이 계절적인 식량부족과 과인에 대해 경계해 왔다

My wife gets sentimental in the spring
> ↳ 집사람은 봄을 타

Prices are higher at certain seasons and holidays than at other times of the year
> ↳ 물가는 일년중 다른 때 보다 어떤 계절이나 휴가 때 더 높다

Some cities have severe winters and uncomfortably hot summers, so we get the worst of both worlds
> ↳ 어떤 도시들은 겨울의 심한 추위와 여름의 불편한 더위로 양쪽 모두
> 나쁜 조건만 가지고 있다

Sook-hee feels blue whenever summer comes(rolls around)
> ↳ 숙희는 여름을 잘 타

> (=Sook-hee gets down(depressed, sensitive) whenever summer comes)

Spring is early to come this year than last year

· **birthday** suit naked body
· **raw** not cooked, not processed, not trained,

having the skin rubbed off, cold and damp, vulgar

↳ 올 봄은 작년보다 일러

Summer and fall slowly wore away as she waited for his return
↳ 그녀가 그의 돌아오기를 기다리고 있을 동안 여름과 겨울이 슬며시 지나갔다

The bushes may die back(down) in this cold autumn but they will grow again next spring
↳ 이 관목들은 이 추운 겨울에 지상부분이 말라죽을 수 있지만 다음 봄엔 다시 싹이 난다

The picture takes me back to the time I spent the summer in Busan
↳ 이 사진을 보니 부산에서 여름을 보냈던 때가 생각나는군

The scent of spring is in the air
↳ 향기로운 봄 냄새가 풍기는군

The summer is lingering
↳ 올 여름은 길기도 하다

The warm season doesn't seem likely visit us so soon
↳ 따뜻한 봄날이 좀처럼 올 것 같지 않아

There are signs of spring everywhere
↳ 사방에서 봄기운이 물씬 풍긴다

There's a big difference in temperature between morning and night
↳ 일교차가 심하군

There's a lot more sun these days
↳ 요즈음 해가 길어졌어

> (=The sunlight lasts longer these days)
> (=The days are growing longer these days)

This cold I've got in summer shouldn't happen to a dog

· **glut** fill to excess

· **bush** shrub, rough uncleared country, thick

tuft or mat

· **scent** smell, fill with odor

ㄴ 난 여름에 개도 안 하는 감기를 하고 있어

This time of the year is always busy; it becomes quiet again after summer
ㄴ 이맘때면 늘 바빠지고 여름이 지나면 수월해진다

This winter belies its name
ㄴ 올 겨울은 겨울답지 않다

Trees start to change colors
ㄴ 나무들이 단풍이 들기 시작한다

Unlike most cone-bearing trees, the larch shed its leaves in fall
ㄴ 낙엽송은 대부분의 다른 구과 식물들과는 달리 가을에 낙엽이 진다

We have to chop plenty of logs and stack them in the shed for winter
ㄴ 우리는 겨울을 나기 위해 통나무를 많이 패어서 헛간에 쌓아 두어야 했다

We'll have to bear hot weather this summer
ㄴ 올 여름은 더위를 각오해야 해

When a year comes to its end, we can't help feeling nostalgic
ㄴ 연말이 가까워지면 우리는 향수에 젖기 마련이다

When did your dog come in season(heat)?
ㄴ 너희 개는 언제 발정했니?

With the hottest season in full swing, people began to show big interest in it
ㄴ 혹서의 계절이 임박하자 사람들은 그 일(상품)에 관심을 보이기 시작했다

· **cone-bearing** produces cone-type fruit   small storage building
· **shed** give off, cause to flow or diffuse,   · **larch** conical evergreen

17. 고통 & 걱정 Anxiety & Worries

A lot of jobless people don't know where their meals are coming from
ㄴ 많은 실직자들은 끼니 걱정을 해야 할 지경이야

A man who suffers before it is necessary, suffers more than necessary
ㄴ 고통받을 일이 있기 전에 미리 고통받는 것은 필요이상으로 고통받는 일이다

A mind quite vacant is a mind distressed
ㄴ 마음이 텅 비어 있다는 것은 그 마음이 고통을 당하고 있다는 말이다

A tear dries quickly, especially when it is shed for the troubles of others
ㄴ 눈물은 빨리 마른다, 특히 남들의 고통에 대한 눈물일 때

A willing burden is no burden
ㄴ 자진해서 지는 짐은 무겁지가 않아

Accidents will happen in the best regulated families
ㄴ 불행한 일은 누구에게나 일어난다

사람의 지위 고하에 따라 불행한 일이 선별적으로 일어나는 것은 아니다. 불행이 언제 닥칠지 모르니까 항상 유비무환의 자세를 가져야 한다(=We must be ready, because accidents will come at an hour when we do not expect them).

Adversity makes a man wise
ㄴ 역경은 사람을 현명하게 만든다

› **vacant** not occupied, filled or in use, foolish or without expression

› **burden** something carried, something oppressive, cargo

> 사람은 역경을 통하여 참된 지혜를 얻는다. 또한 사람은 역경을 통하여 진정한 친구를 가려낼 수도 있다(Adversity makes strange bedfellows).

All these worries have put years on me
　ㄴ 이 골치 아픈 일 들이 나를 겉늙게 만들었어

All this pressure is making a wreck out of me
　ㄴ 이 모든 스트레스가 나를 파멸시키고 있는 것 같다

Are things getting you down?
　ㄴ 걱정되는(신경 쓰이는) 일이라도 있나?

As the threat of nuclear war receded, other things began to worry us
　ㄴ 핵전쟁의 위협이 수그러들자 다른 걱정이 생겨나기 시작했다

At that time, quite a lot of firms suffered from a shrinkage of(in) the work force
　ㄴ 그 당시 많은 회사들이 인력난으로 고통을 겪었다

Better a little chiding than a great deal of heart-break
　ㄴ 크게 가슴 아플 일보다 작은 꾸지람이 낫다

Better to cut the shoe than pinch the foot
　ㄴ 발을 죄는 고통보다는 신발을 찢는 게 낫다

Better worry about need than live without heed
　ㄴ 태평하게 사는 것보다 필요한 일에 걱정하며 사는 게 낫다

Bong-soo acts as if he had the weight(cares) of the world on his shoulders
　ㄴ 봉수는 세상걱정 혼자 다 하는 것 같아

Byung-soo learned it in the gall of bitterness

· **bedfellow** close associate
· **wreck** ruin or damage by breaking up

· **threat** expression of intention to harm, thing that threatens

    ↳ 병수는 쓰라린 고통을 당하고서야 그것을 알았다(흔한 표현 아님)

Byung-soo steeled his heart(himself) against his sufferings
    ↳ 병수는 모질게 마음먹고 고통에 아랑곳하지 않았다

Caught up in circles
    ↳ 꼬리를 무는 고민에 빠져들곤 해

Chan-soo has something to get off his chest
    ↳ 찬수에게는 고민이 좀 있다

Cruelty is more cruel, if we defer the pain
    ↳ 아파야 할 일을 뒤로 미룬다면 그 가혹함이 더욱 가혹해진다

Don't associate drinking with worrying
    ↳ 걱정되는 일이 있다고 해서 술을 마셔서는 안 돼

Don't be such a worry wart
    ↳ 걱정도 팔자군

> 이 속담은 두 가지 경우에 쓰인다. 첫째, 늘 걱정하는 사람을 뜻할 때에는 "You are a worry wart"라고 하고, 둘째, 남의 일에 쓸데없이 하는 사람에게는 "mind your own business"라고 말한다.

Don't consider painful what's good for you
    ↳ 당신에게 좋은 일을 고통으로 여기지 마라

Don't run to meet trouble
    ↳ 걱정을 사서하지 마라

Every one can master a grief but he that has it
    ↳ 슬픔을 지닌 장본인 외에는 누구나 그 슬픔을 이겨낼 수 있다

Everyone has his own difficulties to tackle
    ↳ 누구에게나 스스로 해결해야 할 어려움이 있다

› **cruel** causing suffering to others
› **associate** join in companionship or partnership, connect in thought

› **defer** postpone

Everyone knows he would soon burn with a low blue flame
　　└ 그가 말은 안 하지만 속 끓이고 있다는 건 누구나 알아

Everyone suffers wrong for which there's no remedy
　　└ 모든 사람은 치유할 수 없는 학대로 고통받는다

Genius is an infinite capacity for taking pains
　　└ 천재는 무한히 노력할 수 있는 능력에서 온다

Give me grace to listen to others describe their aches and pains
　　　　└ 저에게 남들이 고통과 통증을 설명할 때 들어줄 아량을 갖게 해 주시옵소서

Ground packs after a rain
　　└ 비 온 뒤에 땅 굳는다

Half the agony of living is waiting
　　└ 삶의 고뇌 중 절반은 기다림이다

He that goes a borrowing goes a sorrowing
　　└ 빚은 고생의 장본

> "Borrowing is sorrowing"이라는 음율이 맞는 속담이 있다. 내용은 직역하여 "빚을 지면 슬픈 신세가 된다"는 말이다.

His anguish at not being able to be at his father's deathbed preyed
on his mind for a long time
　　└ 그에게는 아버지의 임종을 못 본데 대한 고뇌가 오랫동안 마음을 괴롭혔다

His fear of going bankrupt has stayed with him for a long time
　　└ 그는 파산하지 않을까 하는 걱정이 오랫동안 뇌리에서 떠나지 않았다

I don't care about the world
　　└ 난 아무 걱정 없어

I don't(couldn't) care less

› **infinite**　having no limit or extending indefinitely, vast

› **bankrupt**　one required by law to forfeit assets to pay off debts

↳ 조금도 걱정 없어

I'm devoured by anxiety

↳ 애태우고 있는 중이야

If you're patient in one moment of anger, you'll escape a hundred days of sorrow

↳ 한 순간의 화를 참으면 **100**일의 근심을 덜게된다

If your desire be endless, your cares and fears will be so too

↳ 욕심이 끝이 없으면 근심 걱정도 끝이 없을 것이다

In every kind of adversity, the bitterest part of a man's affliction is to remember that he once was happy

↳ 어떤 역경에서나 사람에게 가장 쓰라린 고통은 그가 과거에 행복했다는 것을 기억하고 있다는 일이다

It's more pain to do nothing than something

↳ 아무 것도 안 하는 것은 무언가를 하는 것 보다 더 괴롭다

It's not for nothing that she gave you such anxiety

↳ 그 여자가 네 속을 썩인 데는 그만한 이유기 있기 때문이다

Leave behind cares of the past and worries for the future

↳ 과거에 힘들었던 일, 내일의 걱정은 뒤로 제켜라

Long ailments wear out pain, long hopes, and joy

↳ 긴 고통은 아픔도, 오랜 희망도, 기쁨도 사라지게 한다

Marriage has many pains, but celibacy has no pleasure

↳ 결혼은 많은 고통을 수반하지만 혼자 살면 아무런 즐거움도 없다

My heart(mind) misgives me about the result

↳ 결과가 걱정이다

One less thing to worry about

↳ 한가지 걱정은 덜었군

▸ **devour** consume ravenously

▸ **affliction** causation of pain and distress

One pain is lessened by another's anguish
> ↳ 다른 사람의 고통은 자신의 고통 하나를 가볍게 해준다

Only riveting my attention on my work can I forget my sorrows and worries
> ↳ 일에 몰두하는 것만이 내 슬픔과 고통을 잊는 길이다

Pain is forgotten where gain follows
> ↳ 이익이 있으면 고통을 잊어버린다

Pain makes man think, thought makes man wise, wisdom makes life endurable
> ↳ 고통은 사람을 생각하게 하고, 사색은 현명하게 하며, 지혜는 삶의 인내심을 키워준다

Pain of love lasts a lifetime
> ↳ 사랑의 아픔은 평생 남는다

Pyung-soo loves to pile on the agony and have everyone feel sorry for him
> ↳ 평수는 고통을 과장해서 모든 사람에게 동정을 사기를 좋아해

Sang-soo is worried about saving his own neck
> ↳ 상수는 책임을 면할 걱정만 하고 있다

She was fearful that(lest) the prize should escape her at the last moment
> ↳ 그 여자는 그 상을 막판에 놓치지 않을까 하고 걱정했다

Suffering need not be embittering but be a source of knowledge
> ↳ 고난이 반드시 가혹할 필요는 없지만 지식의 원천이 될 수는 있다

That TV program about cruelty to women brought thousands of letters from worried viewers
> ↳ 여성에게 잔인했던 그 텔레비전 프로를 우려하는 수 천 통의 시청자 편지가 쇄도했다

The family experienced the whole gamut of suffering

- **rivet** fastening with a rivet, devoting
- **embitter** make bitter

ㄴ 가족은 온갖 고난을 겪었다

The fool knows after he's suffered
ㄴ 어리석은 자는 당해봐야 안다

Too much rest itself becomes a pain
ㄴ 너무 쉬는 것은 고통이다

Two in distress makes sorrow less
ㄴ 슬픔을 같이 나누면 가벼워진다

> "백지장도 맞들면 낫다"라는 한국 속담과 비슷한 뜻이다. 협력의 중요성과 친구의 고마움을 함께 나타낸 속담이다.
> (=Many hands make light work)
> (=Grief is lessened when imparted to others)

We are healed of a suffering only by experiencing it to the full
ㄴ 사람은 고통을 한껏 당해봄으로써만이 그 고통에서 치유된다

We'll cross the bridge when we come to it
ㄴ 내일 일은 내일 걱정해도 돼

When you worry you make it double
ㄴ 걱정은 할수록 커진다

You are free from bread and butter worries
ㄴ 생활 걱정은 없겠구나

You look as if you've gone through the mill
ㄴ 너 엄청 고생한 것 같구나

You may put your mind at rest on that point
ㄴ 그 점에 있어서는 염려 안 해도 돼

You might enjoy it if you can't avoid it

· **mill**   building in which grain is ground into flour, manufacturing plant

· **avoid**   keep away from, prevent the occurrence of, refrain from

ㄴ 피할 수 없는 고통은 즐겨라

> 어려운 환경에 처하더라도 불평만 할 것이 아니라 최선을 다하라는 말이다.
> 우리의 능력으로 바꿀 수 없는 일은 인정하여야 한다(What can't be
> cured must be endured = 주어진 환경에서 최선을 다하라).

> cure restore to health, remedy
> endure last, suffer patiently, tolerate

18. 공부 & 학교   Studies & Schools

A literal translation is not always the closest to the original meaning
> ↳ 직역이 언제나 원 의미에 가장 가까운 것은 아니다

A major application of the science of the logic is to help distinguish between correct and incorrect reasoning
> ↳ 논리학을 사용하는 주된 이유는 정확한 추론과 정확하지 못한 추론을 구별하기 위함이다

A number is an abstraction that has no physical existence
> ↳ 숫자는 물리적 형체가 없는 추상적 개념이다

After their business went down the drain, he started up his own vocational school
> ↳ 그들의 사업이 무너지자 그는 자신 소유의 직업학교를 시작했다

All talking is barred during a study period
> ↳ 공부 시간 중 잡담을 금한다

All the boys in that school are trotting(running) after my daughter
> ↳ 저 학교에 다니는 모든 남학생들이 우리 딸을 졸졸 따라다니고 있다

All the students fought against time to complete the test
> ↳ 모든 학생들은 기를 쓰고 시간 내에 시험 답안지를 작성해 나갔다

Art students who imitate the techniques of master artists too well may lose their own creative ability
> ↳ 예술을 공부하는 학생들이 스승이 되는 예술가의 기술을 너무 잘 모

- ▸ **literal** being exactly as started
- ▸ **logic** science of reasoning

- ▸ **distinguish** perceive as different, set apart, discern, make outstanding

방하면 자기들 자신의 창의력을 잃을 수 있다

Bong-soo doesn't like math, but he made the best of it
ㄴ 봉수는 수학을 좋아하지 않지만 불평 없이 해냈다

Corporal punishment has become a thing of the past in most schools
ㄴ 대부분의 학교에서 체벌은 옛날 얘기이다

Don't think the test will be a tea party
ㄴ 그 시험을 식은 죽 먹기로 여기지마

Examination papers are usually marked on the basis of 100
ㄴ 시험은 보통 **100**점 만점으로 채점해

Examinations help form the habit of thinking quickly
ㄴ 시험은 재빨리 생각하는데 도움을 준다

Experience keeps a dear school, but fools learn in no other
ㄴ 경험의 학교는 비싸게 먹히지만 어리석은 사람은 경험 외에 배울 방법이 없다

Family background and schooling are considered important in many arranged marriages
ㄴ 중매결혼에는 가문과 학력이 중시되는 때가 많다

Get it all together and go back to school
ㄴ 정신을 똑바로 차려서 학업을 계속해라

Gil-soo is just going through the motions
ㄴ 길수는 공부(일) 하는 척 할 뿐이야

Gil-soo'll go up to university next year
ㄴ 길수는 내년 대학에 진학할 거야

Go over it point by point
ㄴ 하나하나 차근하게 복습해 나가라

He didn't go to college for nothing

- **corporal** bodily, low-ranking non-commissioned officer in the army
- **examination** test by questioning

ㄴ 그가 대학에 헛 다닌 게 아냐

He made a feint of studying hard, though(while) actually listening to the radio

ㄴ 그가 실은 라디오를 듣고 있었는데 열심히 공부하는 것처럼 가장했다

He works days and goes to school nights

ㄴ 낮에 일하고 밤에 학교에 다녀

High school students and older must pay full fare

ㄴ 고교생 이상은 어른 요금입니다

His lecture was interesting and to the point

ㄴ 그의 강의는 재미있고 핵심을 짚었다

His son is breaking his neck to get into the university

ㄴ 그의 아들은 대학에 들어가려고 열심히 공부하고 있다

How do you stand in your class?

ㄴ 네 성적은 반에서 몇 등이냐?

Hyun-soo finally has a handle on his statistical theory

ㄴ 현수가 드디어 통계학 이론을 이해하는데 성공했어

Hyun-soo's been flying light since he got the word that he won the scholarship

ㄴ 현수는 장학금을 받게됐다는 소식을 듣고 나서 붕 뜬 기분이야

I can't make this equation come out

ㄴ 아무래도 이 방정식은 못 풀겠어

I have laid an egg on my test

ㄴ 시험은 아주 망쳤어

I'm a little behind

ㄴ 진도가 좀 늦은 편이야

· **feint** mock attack intended to distract attention

· **lecture** instructive talk

· **statistics** numerical facts collected for study

In old times, students worshiped the ground their teachers walked on
ㄴ 예전 학생들은 선생님들을 매우 존경했었다

It doesn't make no mind(matter) if we have college degrees or not
ㄴ 우리가 대학을 나왔거나 아니거나 상관없어

It ended up with a bad result after long and careful preparation
ㄴ 십년 공부 나무아미타불이다

It'll be of little avail to persue our studies without any goal in view
ㄴ 목표를 잡지 않고 공부만 하는 것은 거의 소용이 없다

Jung-soo got through school by the seat of his pants
ㄴ 정수는 운이 좋아 학교를 마쳤다(운이 나쁘거나 줄서기를 잘 못한 것 포함)

Jung-soo hit the jackpot with the exam
ㄴ 정수는 시험에서 크게 성공했어

Just as eating against one's will is injurious to health, so studying without a liking for it spoils the memory, and our brains retain nothing
ㄴ 싫은 것을 억지로 먹이는 것이 건강에 해롭듯이 싫은 것을 억지로 공부하는 것은 기억력을 망치게 되어 머리 속에 들어와도 남아있지 않게 된다

Keep motivation high to maximize learning
ㄴ 학습효과를 극대화하도록 학습동기를 높여라

Lots of parents sweated bullets(blood) to put their children through colleges, but the children treat their parents like strangers
ㄴ 많은 부모들이 자녀들을 대학에 보내느라 뼈가 빠졌건만 그들은 그런 부모들을 언제 봤느냐는 듯이 대하기 일쑤다

Man-soo has a natural bent for mathematics
ㄴ 만수가 수학에는 타고났어

Many children were running off and had to stay home from school
ㄴ 많은 아동들이 배탈이 나서 학교를 쉬게됐다

· **avail** be of use or make use, use
· **worship** reverence toward a divine being

or supernatural power, expression of reverence, extravagant respect or devotion

Matrimony is a school in which one learns too late
　　ㄴ 결혼이란 학교는 너무 늦게 배우게되는 학교다

Nobody in my division has got in the back door
　　ㄴ 우리 과에 뒷문으로 들어온 사람은 없어

Nobody's keyed up for the exam this time
　　ㄴ 아무도 이번 시험에 긴장하고 있는 사람은 없어

Nothing could be more detrimental to the good name of the school than
the imprisonment of the headmaster for immoral activities with students
　　　　ㄴ 학생들에게 부도덕한 행위를 했다는 이유로 교장선생님이 감옥에 가
　　　　는 것보다 더 명문학교의 이름을 손상시키는 일은 없을 것이다

Once I start the paper, the paper seems to write itself
　　ㄴ 일단 논문을 쓰기 시작하니까 저절로 술술 써지는 것 같다

Only with a practice can we master a foreign language
　　ㄴ 어학은 첫째도 연습, 둘째도 연습이다

Our teacher doesn't miss anything
　　ㄴ 우리 선생님은 그냥 넘기는 게 없어

Physical torture belonged to the dim and distant past
　　ㄴ 체벌이 있던 시절은 가물가물한 옛날 얘기다

Put all other things out of your mind and concentrate on your study
　　ㄴ 다른 생각은 다 떨쳐버리고 공부에 전념해라

Pyung-soo has learned English to good purpose
　　ㄴ 평수는 영어공부를 해서 상당한 성과가 있었다

Quite a few women have relatively painless births, but most found it
an extremely painful experience
　　　　ㄴ 많은 여성들이 상대적인 무통 분만을 하지만 그래도 매우 고통스러운
　　　　것으로 밝혀졌다

- **division** distribution, part of a whole
- **detrimental** damage

- **immoral** not moral

Rectify your old posture of learning by trying to persue truth on your own instead of relying on others
> ↳ 남들에게 의지하지 않고 자력으로 진실을 추구하여 공부하려던 예전 의 자세를 고쳐라

Rule out neatly any words which you do not wish the examiner to read
> ↳ 시험관이 읽지 않게 하고싶은 단어는 모두 깨끗이 선을 그어 지워라

Sang-soo has failed four classes in school. he'll drop the other shoe and quit altogether any day now
> ↳ 상수가 네 번씩이나 수업에 빠졌어. 차제에 학교를 아주 그만 둘 것 같아

School boys used to be less indulged than they are now
> ↳ 옛날 학생들은 지금 학생들보다 더 엄격하게 다루어졌다

Schools must be first and foremost in learning
> ↳ 학교는 배우는 일을 최우선으로 해야 한다

Set him straight about the importance of good grade in school
> ↳ 학교에서 좋은 점수를 따는 게 얼마나 중요한지 그에게 바르게 지도해 줘

She claims that, from a medical point of view, mixed-sex classes at school have a negative effect
> ↳ 교육적 관점에서 볼 때 남녀 공학은 부정적인 효과가 있다고 주장한다

She desperately scribbled down the answers, being aware of how the minutes were ticking away
> ↳ 그녀는 1분 1초 재깍재깍 시간의 흐름을 인식하면서 사력을 다해 답 안을 갈겨 써 내려갔다

She doesn't know math from a hole in the ground
> ↳ 그 여자는 수학 '수'자도 몰라

She scarcely made the grade in math
> ↳ 그녀는 수학과목에서 가까스로 통과했다

> ‣ **posture** bearing of the body
> ‣ **indulge** yield to the desire of or for

> ‣ **scribble** write hastily or carelessly
> ‣ **foremost** first in time, place, or order

She sweated blood to finish her composition on time
> ↳ 그녀는 시간 내에 작문을 끝내려고 기를 썼어(sweat blood=be worried or work hard)

She was bullied at school, but she refuses to talk about it whenever I try to broach the matter
> ↳ 그녀는 학교에서 행패를 당했지만 내가 그 얘길 꺼낼 때마다 말하기를 거부한다

She was scarcely able to make the grade in statistics
> ↳ 그 여자는 가까스로 통계학에서 낙제점을 면할 수 있었다

She's going to do an about face and concentrate on her study
> ↳ 그 여자는 생각을 완전히 바꾸어 공부에 전념하려고 한다

Some people start out to train career in medicine, but drop(fall) by the wayside
> ↳ 어떤 사람들은 직업의사가 되려고 공부하다가 도중에 팽개치곤 해

Students are trickling into the classroom
> ↳ 학생들이 삼삼오오 교실로 들어가고 있다

Suck-ho aced out the history
> ↳ 석호는 요행히 역사 시험에 합격했어

Sung-ho passed with flying colors(did well)
> ↳ 성호는 거뜬히 합격했어

Sung-min really knows a thing or two about statistics
> ↳ 성민이는 통계라면 도사

Sung-soo put me in the way of a lot of materials on the subject of my paper
> ↳ 성수는 내 논문 주제에 대한 많은 자료를 알려주었다

Tai-gyung just squeaked through the exam

> • **scarcely** barely, almost not

> • **compose** create or put together, calm, set type

ㄴ 태경인 턱걸이해서 시험에 합격했어

Tai-ho was afraid to talk to the teacher, so I piped up
ㄴ 태호가 겁이 나서 선생님에게 말을 못하기에 내가 큰 소리로 말했지

Tai-soo is going to take the rest of the day off
ㄴ 태수는 조퇴하려고 하고 있어

That student's grades are everywhere
ㄴ 저 학생의 성적은 오르락내리락 해

(=That student's grade vary a lot)

That's probably an apple for the teacher, and not to be accepted
ㄴ 그건 일종의 뇌물이니 안 받는 게 제일이야

The Constitutional Court ruled that a law banning out-of-school tutoring is unconstitutional and infringes the basic rights of the people more than is necessary
ㄴ 헌법재판소는 과외 금지가 헌법에 어긋나며 국민의 기본권을 필요 이상으로 침해하는 것이라고 판결했다

The course is very demanding that you can't afford to be slack about your assignments
ㄴ 그 과정은 매우 힘들어서 어영부영 학습할 여유가 없어

The exceptional zeal for education among Korean parents ensures that private tutoring will not disappear as long as the reality in the schools fails to meet their expectation
ㄴ 학교교육이 현실적으로 학부모들의 기대에 못 미치는 한 한국 학부모들의 유별난 교육열풍은 과외가 사라지지 않을 것임이 확실하다

The friends we rub up against in our early years in school make a

---

› **constitutional** the basic law of an organized body or the document containing it

› **vary** alter, make or be of different kind

great difference to our future
> ㄴ 초년 학생시절에 사귄 친구가 우리의 장래에 큰 영향을 미친다

The sparrow near a school sings a primer
> ㄴ 서당개 3년에 풍월 한다

> "서당개 삼 년에 풍월을 읊는다"는 속담은 아주 유용하게 많이 쓰인다. "The sparrow near a school sings a primer"는 "학교 주변의 참새는 1학년 교재를 따라한다"로 직역된다. 이는 어깨너머로 배운다는 말과도 뜻이 같다.

The students trooped into the school for roll call in the morning
> ㄴ 학생들은 아침 출석 부르기에 안 빠지려고 학교로 몰려갔다

The teacher had to urge the students along(forward, on) in the last few months before the exam
> ㄴ 그 교사는 학생들에게 시험 전 몇 달 동안 공부를 열심히 하라고 다그칠 수밖에 없었다

There's all the more reason for studying hard
> ㄴ 그러기에 더욱 더 열심히 공부해야 해

They are divided on the quality on the teaching in the university
> ㄴ 그들은 대학의 교수 자격에 대하여 의견이 엇갈리고 있다

They offer crash courses in accounting and word process
> ㄴ 그들은 회계와 워드프로세스의 속성과정을 개설해놓고 있어

This qualification exam will separate the men from the boys
> ㄴ 이 적성검사는 적성이 맞는 사람과 맞지 않는 사람을 구별해 줄 것이다

This seminar did me a world of good
> ㄴ 이 세미나는 내게 큰 도움이 됐어요

Try to be relax before exam, and you'll deal with(approach) it in a

---

› **urge** earnestly plead for or insist on, try to persuade, impel to a course of

activity

› **sparrow** small singing bird

better frame of mind
> ↳ 시험 전에 긴장을 풀도록 해라, 그러면 보다 나은 마음상태로 대처할 수 있을 것이다

Use the following words in a sentence
> ↳ 다음 단어로 문장을 만들어라

We can have that a wee try(performance test)
> ↳ 성능시험을 해야겠군

We must study hard to keep up with the times
> ↳ 우리는 시대에 뒤지지 않도록 열심히 공부해야 한다

What you learn in your school time should carry over into adult life
> ↳ 학교에서 배우는 건 어른이 되었을 때 필요한 것이다

When he suddenly dropped out of school, things came to a boil
> ↳ 그가 갑자기 학교를 그만두자 집안이 발칵 뒤집혔지

When we are getting married, our education enters(comes) into the picture
> ↳ 결혼할 땐 학력을 말하게 되어있어(학력이 중요시 됨)

Why don't you get your act together and go on to the university
> ↳ 정신 좀 차리고 대학에 진학해야지

Will school keep all day?
> ↳ 오늘 수업이 종일 있나?

With her life back on track, she studies hard
> ↳ 그 여자는 본래의 생활로 되돌아와서 열심히 공부하고 있다

With the examination at hand, everyone is nervous
> ↳ 시험이 다가오자 모두가 긴장해 있다

With two questions left in the exam, I drew a blank
> ↳ 시험문제 두 개를 남겼는데 도무지 생각이 안 나더라

With your degree the sky is the limit

· **wee** very small

· **performance** act or process of performing, public presentation

ㄴ 너의 이 학위만 있으면 너의 발전은 무한대야

You are playing at studying for my sake

ㄴ 나한테 잘 보이려고 건성으로 공부하고 있잖아(**Play at**=장난치다, 건성으로 하다)

You have nothing on them because they also have graduated from university

ㄴ 그들도 대학을 나왔으니 너라고 그들보다 나을 것도 없다

You must learn multiplication table by rote

ㄴ 넌 구구단을 외워야 해

You will get nowhere if you work by fits and starts

ㄴ 공부(일)를 하다 말다 해서는 아무 것도 안 돼

You'll be crippled in your future career unless you have a good command of English

ㄴ 영어를 잘 구사하지 못하면 너의 전도에 큰 장애가 될 것이다

You've got to learn what you need in the school of hard knocks to be successful

ㄴ 성공하려면 험한 세파를 이겨내는데 필요한 것을 배워야 한다

You've made a dog's dinner(breakfast) of your attendance register

ㄴ 넌 출석부를 개판으로 만들어놨군

› **sake**   purpose or reason, one's good or benefit

› **multiplication**   increase, short method of repeated addition

19. 공연 & 연설   Performances & Speeches

As he droned on, the listeners(audience) fell asleep one by one
> ↳ 그가 데데한 소리만 늘어놓자 청중들이 하나씩 잠이 들어버렸다

Be careful not to play(talk) down to your hearers, they are very sensitive about being treated as stupid
> ↳ 청중들이 바보취급 당하는 일에 매우 민감하니 수준을 낮추어 얘기하지 않도록 해라

Bong-soo is trying to hold the stage
> ↳ 봉수가 남들의 주목을 끌려고 하고 있어(hold the stage 는 "관중을 끌다"의 뜻도 됨)

Byung-soo stumbled through his speech and fled from the stage
> ↳ 병수는 더듬거리면서 연설을 마치고 도망치듯이 연단을 물러났다

Chang-soo carried his hearers along(away) with his speech
> ↳ 창수의 연설은 청중들을 매료시켰다

Did you enjoy your stay with us?
> ↳ 계속 즐겁게 시청 하셨습니까?

Edison played the recognizable production of his voice back to an astonished audience
> ↳ 에디슨은 두려움에 가득 찬 청중들에게 자신의 목소리인지를 식별할 만한 목소리를 들려주었다

Everything(The performance) went off well

- **drone** make a dull monotonous sound
- **stumble** speak or act clumsily
- **flee** run away
- **astonish** amaze

↳ 만사가(공연이) 잘 되었다(성공했다)

Gil-soo gave a good account of himself throughout the performance
↳ 길수는 공연 중 내내 잘 해냈다

He always colors up his adventures to please his listeners(audience)
↳ 그는 늘 듣는 사람들을 즐겁게 해 주려고 모험담에 그럴듯한 살을 붙인다

His agitation fell flat
↳ 그의 선동연설은 아무런 효과가 없었다

His acting carried the house
↳ 그의 연기가 만장의 박수를 받았어

His closing words brought the whole crowd to their feet, cheering wildly
↳ 그의 마지막 말에 사람들이 열광적으로 환호하며 기립박수를 보냈다

His latest play is a very different kettle of fish
↳ 그의 가장 최근 플레이는 전혀 평소의 그 답지 않았어

How can we ensure that our message reaches the maximum number of listeners
↳ 우리가 전할 말을 어떻게 하면 가장 많은 청취자에게 확실히 전달할 수 있을까?

In-ho's talk made a hit(points) with the audience
↳ 인호의 얘기는 청중들에게 감명을 주었어(점수를 땄어)

It won't be easy for me to hold the attention of the large audience over 50 minutes
↳ 50분이 넘도록 큰 군중이 흥미를 잃지 않도록 하기는 쉬운 일이 아니다

Keep your hearers interested, don't let them go off the boil
↳ 듣는 사람에게 흥미를 잃지 않게 하라, 시들하게 내버려두지 마라

Make sure you get someone who won't talk above the people's heads
↳ 사람들이 알아듣지도 못할 소리를 하는 연사를 모셔오지 않도록 해라

‣ **agitation**   try to arouse public feeling, excite or trouble the mind of

‣ **crowd**   large number or people, collect or cram together

Most of the audience tuned out during the last part of the lecture
ㄴ 대부분의 청중들은 강의의 후반부에 시들하게 듣는 둥 마는 둥 했다

Please fit your remarks to the audience
ㄴ 말씀을 청중의 수준에 맞춰 주십시오

Reverend King had the unique ability to exhilarate congregation with gentle but electrifying speeches
ㄴ 킹 목사는 부드럽지만 깜짝 놀라게 하는 연설로 군중들의 기분을 들 뜨게 하는 특별한 능력을 가지고 있었다

Sang-soo paid all that money to see the concert and slept through the whole thing
ㄴ 상수는 그 큰돈을 주고 음악회에 갔다가 내내 잠만 쿨쿨 자고 왔다

Sang-soo stole the show even though he was on stage for not more than five minutes
ㄴ 상수는 무대에 오른 지 5분을 넘기지 않았지만 인기를 독차지했다

Sitting in the hot seat is much more trying in the being in the audience
ㄴ 가시방석에 앉아 있는 것은 구경하는 것 보다 훨씬 힘들다

Somebody made the speaker lost his train of thought
ㄴ 누군가가 연사에게 방해를 해서 무엇을 말하려고 했던가를 잊어버렸다

The annual Miss Korea pageant features over 100 would-be beauty queens, each aspiring to be throned as the most beautiful woman in Korea
ㄴ 매년 열리는 미스코리아 대회에는 한국에서 가장 아름다운 여성으로서의 권좌에 오르길 열망하는 100명 이상의 지망생들이 참가한다

The audience seemed mesmerized by the sound of her voice
ㄴ 청중은 그녀의 목소리에 취한 듯 했다

The audience was spellbound by the fine performance
ㄴ 관객들은 그 묘(연)기에 취했다

› **remark** passing comment

› **reverend** clergyman

› **congregation** assembly of people at worship, religious group

The crowd drifted out after the performance
↳ 공연이 끝나지 군중들은 뿔뿔이 흩어져 갔다

The entire gathering was carried away by his speech
↳ 청중은 그의 열띤 연설에 감동되었어

The lecturer larded his long speech with some amusing stories
↳ 강사는 긴 강의에 재미있는 얘기를 곁들였다

The monkey ran away with the whole performance
↳ 공연에서 원숭이가 최고 인기였어

The more you make audience work, the more involved they become
↳ 네가 청중들을 점점 더 흥분시키면 그들은 점점 더 열중하게 될 것이다

The noise of the passing plane drowned out his lecture
↳ 비행기 소음으로 그의 강의를 못 들었어

The professor's lecture bored the pants off of us
↳ 그 교수의 강의는 정말 따분했어

The speaker radiated enthusiasm for the cause
↳ 연사는 자기주장을 위해서 열의를 쏟았다

There was a ripple of rather lukewarm applause
↳ 그저 미지근한 박수가 한 차례 있었을 뿐이다

There's no arranged seating
↳ 지정석은 없습니다

(=You can sit anywhere you like)
(=It doesn't matter where you sit)

They caught fire at my words and began to cheer
↳ 그들은 내 말에 흥분하더니 환호하기 시작했다

› **lard**　insert or cover with strips of fat for cooking

› **radiate**　issue rays or in rays, spread from a center

Wan-soo is good at whipping the crowd into a fever of excitement
ㄴ 완수는 군중들을 흥분의 도가니로 몰아넣는데 능숙해

We can't appreciate his performance very much
ㄴ 그 사람 연기는 별거 아니야

What'll follow is a presentation
ㄴ 이어서 발표가 있겠습니다

When he warmed up to his subject, his speech became very interesting
ㄴ 그의 주제가 열기를 띠자 연설이 매우 재미있게 진행되었다

Work in a few jokes when you are preparing your speech
ㄴ 연설을 준비할 때 농담 몇 마디를 넣어라

You don't review the performance; you just pick them apart(to pieces)
ㄴ 넌 연기를 비평하는 게 아니라 그저 혹평만 하고 있어

Your excellent presentation came across(over) well, so all the time they spent was worth it
ㄴ 당신의 훌륭한 발표는 성공적이었고 그들이 소비한 시간은 그만한 가치가 있었다

Your jokes would not go over with that type of audience
ㄴ 너의 농담이 그런 타입의 청중에게는 먹혀들지 않을 거야

› **appreciate** value justly, be grateful for, increase in value

› **presentation** showing or introducing before the public

20. 교육 & 배움   Education & Learning

A book is made better by good readers and clearer by good opponents
> ↳ 훌륭한 독자는 훌륭한 책을 만들고 저자의 훌륭한 적은 그 책의 내용
> 을 더욱 명료하게 해 준다

A good example is the best sermon
> ↳ 훌륭한 모범이 최고의 설교이다

A good father is a little bit of a mother
> ↳ 좋은 아버지는 약간의 엄마 역할도 한다

A good horse should be seldom spurred
> ↳ 준마에게 박차를 가해서는 안 된다

> (=Never spur a willing horse)

Acquiring education is the principal way of gaining status in culture that generally stresses achievement, skillfulness, and upward mobility
> ↳ 교육을 받는 것이 전반적으로 성취도와 기술, 상향적 사회이동을 강
> 조하는 문화에서 사회적 지위를 얻는 일차적 방법이다

An ounce of practice is worth a pound of precept
> ↳ 교훈보다 실행이 중요하다

- **opponent** one that opposes
- **sermon** lecture on religion or behavior

- **spur** pointed device used to urge on a horse, urge on

> 말하기는 쉬워도 행하기는 어렵다. 어른들도 아이들에게 부끄러운 모습을 보이는 일이 종종 있다. 아이들이 올바르게 자라기 위해서는 부모와 선생을 포함한 어른들의 모험이 중요하다(=Practice what you preach).

An-do has been taught to rise above his selfish considerations
  ↳ 안도는 이기적인 생각을 넘어설 수 있는 교육을 받았다

As the twig is bent, so grows the tree
  ↳ 될성부른 나무는 떡잎부터 알아본다

> 아이가 큰 인물이 될지 못될지는 어려서부터 알 수 있다는 말이다(=If something can go wrong, it will).
> (=A fine child becomes a fine gentleman)
> (=Sandalwood is fragrant even in seed-leaf)
> (=Genius displays even in childhood)

Better unborn than untaught
  ↳ 안 배울 바엔 태어나지 않는 게 낫다

Better untaught than ill taught
  ↳ 잘못 배우는 것보다는 안 배우는 게 낫다

Birchen twigs break no ribs
  ↳ 매 맞아 뼈 부러지지 않는다(엄한 훈육의 교훈)

> 대부분의 나라에서는 어렸을 때의 올바른 교육이 아이의 미래를 정한다고 생각한다. 심한 체벌은 문제이지만, 적당히 엄격한 교육은 필요하다.
> (=The rod breaks no bones)
> (=Spare the rod and spoil the child)

› **selfish**　taking care of oneself without regard for others

› **fragrant**　sweet-smelling
› **rib**　curved bone joined to the spine

Books and friends should be few and good
ㄴ 책과 친구의 수는 적어야 좋고 내용이 알차야 한다

Books operate powerfully on the soul both for good and evil
ㄴ 책은 좋건 나쁘건 간에 정신에 큰 영향을 미친다

Children are better at learning languages than adults
ㄴ 아이들은 어른들보다 언어학습에 뛰어나다

Children should learn from their mistakes
ㄴ 아이들은 실수해 가면서 배워야 한다

Confucius once taught us that males and females should not sit together after they have reached the age of seven
ㄴ 공자님은 남녀가 7세가 되면 같이 앉지 못 한다고 가르치셨다

Curiosity is the wick in the candle of hearing
ㄴ 호기심은 배움이라는 촛불의 심지이다

Don't spoil him
ㄴ 애를 오냐오냐하지 마라

(=He is growing up spoiled)
(=Don't let him have his way)

Early training means more than late learning
ㄴ 젊어서 고생은 사서한다

Education is a necessity because automation has replaced unskilled labor in many fields of work
ㄴ 많은 업무분야에서 자동화가 미숙련 노동자들을 대체함에 따라 교육은 필수적이다

Education is the ability to listen to almost anything without losing

---

› **Confucius** a Chinese philosopher
› **curious** eager to learn, strange

› **wick** cord that draws up oil, tallow, or wax to be burned

your temper or self-confidence
> ㄴ 교육이란 화내지 않고 자신감을 잃지 않으며 거의 모든 것을 경청하는 능력이다

Every real teacher is myself in disguise
> ㄴ 모든 참된 스승은 자신의 가장된 모습이다

Getting a good education boils down to hard work and dedication
> ㄴ 좋은 교육을 받는다는 것은 근면과 헌신으로 요약된다

Gil-soo's parents always gives in too much
> ㄴ 길수의 부모님은 너무 오냐오냐하고 애들을 길러

Give extra love to the lovely
> ㄴ 미운 자식 떡 하나 더 준다

Good books are for good readers
> ㄴ 좋은 책에는 좋은 독자가 있어야 한다

Good judgement is not necessarily proportional to education
> ㄴ 훌륭한 판단력은 반드시 교육과 비례하는 것은 아니다

Han-soo took his responsibilities as a father seriously but in matters of discipline was rather too free with his hands
> ㄴ 그는 진지하게 아버지로서의 책임을 떠맡았으나 훈육문제에 있어서는 툭하면 아이를 때렸다

He ploughed through the pile of books
> ㄴ 그는 산더미 같은 책을 힘들여 읽어갔다

He that nothing questions nothing learns(He that questions nothing learns nothing)
> ㄴ 아무 것도 묻지 않는 사람은 아무 것도 배우지 못해

Her daughter's learning difficulties can be correctly diagnosed and treated
> ㄴ 그 여자의 딸의 학습장애는 정확히 진단하여 교정할 수 있다

› **self-confidence** trusting oneself
› **dedicate** set apart for a purpose, address

to someone as a compliment

His theory has taken on among the younger scholars
> ㄴ 그의 학설은 소장파 학자들 사이에 인기가 있었다

I just watched and learned
> ㄴ 그냥 어깨너머로 배웠어

> "서당개 삼 년에 풍월을 읊는다"는 속담은 아주 유용하게 많이 쓰인다. "The sparrow near a school sings a primer"는 "학교 주변의 참새는 1학년 교재를 따라한다"로 직역된다. 이는 어깨너머로 배운다는 말과도 뜻이 같다.
> (=I just learned by watching(observing))
> (=I just caught on by observing)

I will teach you to ignore my words
> ㄴ 내 말 안 들으면 혼 낼 거다

If you want your children to improve, let them overhear the nice things you say about them to others
> ㄴ 당신의 자녀가 나아지기를 원한다면 다른 사람들에게 그들의 칭찬을 하면서 그들이 엿듣게 하라

If you want your children to keep their feet on the ground, put some responsibility on their shoulders
> ㄴ 자녀가 땅에 두 발을 굳게 디디기를 원한다면 그들의 어깨에 책임을 지워라

In the twenty-first century, the education and skills of the work force will end up being the dominant competitive weapon
> ㄴ 21세기는 노동력과 교육과 기술이 지배적인 경쟁무기가 될 것이다

It's her labor of love to teach us Japanese
> ㄴ 그 여자는 자신이 좋아서 우리에게 일본어를 가르치는 거야

It's through practice and mistakes that language improvement occurs

---

‣ **observe** conform to, celebrate, see, watch, or notice, remark

‣ **overhear** hear without the speaker's knowledge

ㄴ 어학 실력 향상은 훈련과 실수를 통하여 이루어진다

Learning in one's youth is engraved in stone

ㄴ 젊어서 배우는 것은 돌에 새겨진다

Most books now available simply enumerate words without identifying any proper etymological thread running through them

ㄴ 현재 시중에 나와있는 대부분의 책들은 책의 내용 속에 흐르고있는 어원적 실마리를 제대로 적시하지 못한 채 단지 단어들을 나열하고 있음에 불과하다

No man is born wise or learned

ㄴ 태어날 때부터 현명하거나 배우고 나온 사람은 없다

아무리 위대한 사람도 태어났을 때부터 위대하지는 않았다. "Alexander himself was once a crying babe 알렉산더 대왕도 한 때는 우는 아기였다"라는 말이 있다. 예전엔 왕족이 있어서 태어날 때부터 고귀한 사람이 있었기 때문에 "Not every man is born with a silver spoon in his mouth 모두 입에 은수저를 물고 태어난 것은 아니다"라는 말이 있었지만, 요즘은 모두 평등하기 때문에 태생으로 운명이 결정 나는 일은 드물다.

Now I've got it down pat

ㄴ 이제 완전히 배웠어

One is never too old to learn

ㄴ 배우는데 나이가 없다

사람은 평생을 배워도 모자라 다는 뜻이다. 요즘은 여러 문화 센터, 인터넷 강좌, 노인대학 등을 통하여 나이가 든 후에도 배움의 길을 가는 사람들이 늘어나고 있다.

Read these books at your leisure

ㄴ 틈 날 때 이 책들을 가만히 읽어봐(묵독)

▸ **enumerate** count, list	**etymologies**
▸ **etymology** history of a word, study of	▸ **leisure** free time, comfort, convenience

Reading is to the mind what exercise is to the body
> ↳ 독서가 정신에 필요한 것은 운동이 신체에 필요한 것과 같다

She was uneducated, but let that pass
> ↳ 그 여자가 교육은 못 받았지만 그건 그렇다고 치자

Some people never learn
> ↳ 끝까지 정신 못 차리는 사람이 있어

The aim of education is not of the facts but of the values
> ↳ 교육의 목적은 사실에 대한 지식이 아닌 기치에 대한 지식을 얻는데 있다

The art of teaching is the art of assisting discovery
> ↳ 가르치는 기술이란 발견하도록 도와주는 기술이다

The best way to learn a foreign language is to immerse oneself in it totally, speaking nothing else, for a period of a few years
> ↳ 외국어를 배우는 최상의 길은 다른 언어를 사용하지 말고 그 외국어 만을 몇 년간 말하면서 학습에 전념하는 일이다

The grammar is learned through language use, not through memorizing grammar rules, and it becomes internalized
> ↳ 문법은 문법 자체를 외우는 게 아닌 언어의 사용을 통하여 배워져서 자신의 것으로 된다

The highest result of education is tolerance
> ↳ 교육에서 얻는 최고의 결과는 너그러움이다

The information acquired should be used in a way that helps voters make good choices
> ↳ 조사를 통해 얻어지는 정보는 유권자들이 올바른 선택을 하도록 도와 주는 방향으로 이용되어야 한다

The lips of righteous feed many
> ↳ 의인의 입술은 여러 사람을 교육시킨다

The roots of education is bitter, but the fruit is sweet
> ↳ 교육의 뿌리는 쓰지만 그 열매는 달다

> • **aim** point or direct, direct one's efforts
> • **assist** help

> • **immerse** plunge or dip especially into liquid

The use of television in the auditorium is a departure from generally held views of education
> ↳ 강당에서 텔레비전을 사용하는 것은 평상시 생각하는 교육방식과는 상이한 것이다

These ridiculers are usually those who are not willing to put the necessary effort into learning English
> ↳ 이와 같이 비웃는 사람들은 대개 영어를 배우는데 필요한 노력을 기울이지 않는 사람들이다

Those who can, do; those who cannot, teach
> ↳ 제대로 할 줄 아는 사람은 직접 행하고, 제대로 못하는 사람은 남에게 가르친다

Those who wish to be learned to fools, seem fool to the learned
> ↳ 어리석은 자들에게 배운 사람으로 보이고 싶어하는 사람은 배운 사람에게 어리석은 사람으로 보여진다

To make your children capable of honesty is the beginning of education
> ↳ 자녀들을 정직하게 가르치는 것이 교육의 시작이다

To teach is to learn twice over
> ↳ 가르친다는 것은 반복해서 배우는 일이다

Use makes perfect
> ↳ 배우기보다 익히기

> '익히기', 즉 '반복하기'가 배움을 완전하게 한다. 특히 어학을 배움에 있어서는 반복 학습이 가장 중요하다. 더욱 자주 쓰는 표현으로는 'Practice makes perfect'가 있다.

We learn throughout our lives chiefly through our mistakes and pursuits of our fault assumption
> ↳ 사람은 일생동안 주로 실수와의 그릇된 가정을 통하여 배운다

> ‣ **auditorium**   room or building used for public gatherings

> ‣ **ridicule**   laugh at or make fun of
> ‣ **assumption**   something assumed

21. 과학　　　　　　　　　　Science

A body weighs less the farther it gets from the earth
> ↳ 물체가 지구에서 멀어질수록 무게는 가벼워진다

Although we are excited about the prospect of living healthier and longer by virtue of the scientific feat, we must wait patiently for progress in the research
> ↳ 우리는 과학의 위업 덕분에 보다 건강하고 오래 살게 될 것이라는 전망에 흥분하고 있지만 연구의 진척을 차분히 기다려야 한다

An accumulation of facts is no more a science than a heap of stones is a house
> ↳ 돌무더기를 쌓아올린 것이 집이 아니듯이 사실들을 쌓아 올린 것도 과학이 아니다

As gases are cooled, their molecules move more and more slowly
> ↳ 개스는 차가와 지면서 분자들의 운동이 점점 느려진다

Better solid-waste management in the future will require a combination of resource recovery and resource reduction
> ↳ 장래에 고체 폐기물을 잘 처리하는 것은 자원 재생과 자원 절약 모두를 위해 필요하다

Both lightening rods and lightening cables are constructed of materials that are good conductors electronically
> ↳ 피뢰침과 피뢰도선은 양호한 전도체로 만든다

· **heap**　pile, throw or lay in a heap
· **molecule**　small particle of matter

· **conductor**　thing that can be a channel for

By tracking the eye of a hurricane, forecasters can determine the speed at which a storm is moving

ㄴ 기상통보관들은 허리케인의 중심점을 추적하여 허리케인의 이동속도를 알 수 있다

Conversely, if we knew the luminosity of stars, we could calculate the distance from the Earth

ㄴ 반대로 우리가 별들의 광도를 안다면 지구와의 거리를 계산할 수 있을 것이다

Each time a species dies off, a complex series of genetic codes vanishes from the earth

ㄴ 생물의 한 종이 소멸할 때마다 복잡한 일련의 유전 정보도 지구상에서 사라지게 된다

Generally the planet is getting warmer as a result of the greenhouse effect

ㄴ 지구는 온실효과 때문에 점점 더워지고 있다

It's believed that the formation of the sun, the planets, and other stars began with the condensation of an interstellar gas cloud

ㄴ 태양, 행성들, 그리고 다른 별들의 형성은 별들간에 기운의 응축으로 형성되었다고 믿어지고 있다

Light is propagated through the air in a straight line

ㄴ 빛은 대기를 일직선으로 통과하여 전달된다

Most of the theories about its origins assume that the earth began in a gaseous state, moved through a liquid state, and finally became partly solid

ㄴ 지구의 기원에 관한 대부분의 이론은 지구가 가스상태로 시작하여 액체상태를 거쳐 부분적으로 고체가 되었다고 가정한다

Neuron is a special cell in the body that is capable of sending along messages that represent feelings and commands to muscles

---

› **species** biological grouping of closely related organisms

› **genetic** biology dealing with heredity or variation

ㄴ 뉴런은 체내의 특수세포로서 감정을 표현하거나 근육에게 명령하는 메시지를 전달하는 능력이 있다

Neutrals are neutral in the sense that they have neither a positive nor a negative charge

ㄴ 중성자는 양극도 음극도 아니라는 의미에서 중성적이다

Oil dispersed in water forms the most frequently occurring colloidal solutions

ㄴ 물에 퍼진 기름은 가장 빈번하게 발생하는 콜로이드 용액을 형성한다

On the hottest days, the heat transfer process works in reverse, so the environment actually heats up our body

ㄴ 가장 더운 날이면 열 전달 과정이 반대로 흐르게 되어서 사실상 주변에 있는 열이 우리의 몸을 뜨겁게 만든다

Once the safety of gene-engineered food is fully proven, a revolutionary chance can be expected in the global agricultural production

ㄴ 유전자 조작식품의 안전성이 증명되기만 하면 세계 농업생산의 혁명적 변동을 기대할 수 있게 된다

Particles with similar electric charges repel each other

ㄴ 전하량이 같은 분자는 서로 반발한다

Power derived from water creates no pollution and uses up no irreplaceable fuel resources

ㄴ 물에서 얻는 동력은 공해를 일으키지 않으며 대체 불가능 연료자원을 고갈시키지도 않는다

Science is different to the value of the ends for which the means are used

ㄴ 과학에 있어서는 사용할 수단의 목적에 대한 가치와는 무관하다

Science is pushing the limits

ㄴ 과학이 극단으로 치닫고있다

· **colloid** tiny particles in suspension with a fluid

· **particle** small bit

· **repel** drive away, disgust

Science may be learned by rote, but wisdom not
　　ㄴ 학문은 기계적으로 배울 수도 있지만 지혜는 그렇지 않다

Scientific achievements do more harm than good unless they are rightly used
　　ㄴ 과학이 이룬 업적은 바르게 쓰여지지 않는 한 이로움 보다 해로움이 더 많다

Scientists already learned to build and maintain artificial wombs to give premature infants a fighting chance
　　ㄴ 과학자들은 이미 인공자궁을 만들고 유지하여 조산아에게 살아날 수 있는 기회를 제공하는 법을 알게되었다

Scientists can't predict what'll happen to the earth's atmosphere if the ozone layer continues to be depleted
　　ㄴ 과학자들은 오존층이 파괴될 때 지구의 대기에 어떤 일이 일어날지 예측하지 못한다

Steam condenses to water when it comes into contact with a surface
　　ㄴ 증기가 물체의 표면에 닿으면 응축된다

Steaming the leaves, then baking them, prevents oxidation or fermentation of the leaves so that they remain green
　　ㄴ 이런 잎들을 쪄서 구우면 산화 또는 발효를 막게 되어 녹색을 유지하게 된다

The amounts of each in order of names are 50%, 30% and 20% respectively
　　ㄴ 그 성분은 앞서 밝힌 순서대로 **50%, 30%, 20%**씩 들어있다

The bacteria and molds that cause decay and fermentation in food can't thrive without moisture
　　ㄴ 부패와 발효를 일으키는 박테리아와 곰팡이는 습기가 없으면 번성할 수 없다

The bodies of living creatures are organized into many different systems, each of which has a certain function

---

↳ 생명체는 많은 다양한 기관으로 형성되며 각 기관은 나름대로의 기능이 있다

The data have confirmed that the damage to the ozone layer is not confined to the southern hemisphere

↳ 그 자료는 오존층의 파괴가 남반구에 한하지 않음을 확인해 주었다

The different attraction of the sun and the moon has a direct effect on the rising and falling of the tides

↳ 태양과 달의 인력 차가 조수의 높낮이에 직접 영향을 준다

The greater an object's mass, the harder it is to put it into motion

↳ 물체의 질량이 클수록 그 물체를 움직이게 하기 어렵다

The idea that the gravitational pull of the moon affects human emotions is far from certain

↳ 달의 중력이 인간의 감정에 영향을 미친다는 생각은 결코 정확성이 있는 것이 아니다

The jet stream is a narrow current of fast-flowing air

↳ 제트기류란 빠른 속도로 지나가는 공기의 좁은 흐름이다

The moon has no more light than a stone has

↳ 달이 발광체가 아닌 것은 돌이나 마찬가지다

The natural state of a body is a state of rest, and unless a force acted upon it to maintain motion, a moving body would come to rest

↳ 물체의 자연스러운 상태는 휴식의 상태이며 만약 동작을 계속 유지시키기 위해 어떤 힘을 가하지 않는다면 움직이는 물체는 정지하게 될 것이다

The objective of science is to discover uniformities in nature and to formulate these as laws on the basis of which predictions are made

↳ 과학의 목표는 자연 속에서 통일성을 찾아내어, 예측되는 법칙으로 이 통일성을 공식화하는 것이다

The quantum theory states that energy is given off and absorbed in

---

- **confirm** ratify, verify
- **tide** alternate rising and falling of the sea

- **mass** expanse or magnitude

tiny definite units called quanta or photons
ㄴ 양자이론에 의하면 에너지는 방출되어 양자 혹은 광자라고 부르는 작은 입자에 흡수된다

The scientists noted that opposition to genetically modified foods had come mostly from rich countries
ㄴ 과학자들은 유전자변형 식량에 대한 반대가 대부분 잘 사는 나라에서 제기되고 있다고 지적했다

The sun is a gaseous sphere, not a solid body like the earth
ㄴ 태양은 지구처럼 고체가 아니고 가스상태의 구이다

The sun's rays can penetrate to the sea to a depth of twenty meters
ㄴ 태양광선은 바다 밑 **20**미터까지 침투해 들어간다

The tide never goes out so far but it always comes in again
ㄴ 썰물이 아무리 멀리 빠져나가더라도 언제나 밀물이 되어 되돌아온다

The tides fluctuate with the phase of the moon
ㄴ 조수는 달의 상(像)에 따라 변한다

There's some attractive force operating between the bodies of the solar system
ㄴ 태양계에 있는 물체들 간에는 어떤 인력이 작용한다

Two suns can't shine in one sphere
ㄴ 하늘에 두 태양이 있을 수 없다

Under current conditions, water exists on Mars only in the form of water vapor in the atmosphere, and ice at its poles
ㄴ 현 상태에서 화성의 물은 단지 대기중 수증기나 극지방의 얼음 형태로 존재한다

Vacuum is a space that has no matter in it
ㄴ 진공은 그 안에 아무 물질도 없는 공간을 말한다

· **proton**   positively charged particle

· **penetrate**   enter into, permeate, see into

· **sphere**   round body, range of action or influence

Water can wear away rock after a long time
> ↳ 물은 오랜 세월을 지나면서 바위를 깎아 내린다

> 불가능한 일이라도 끊임없이 노력하면 이루어진다는 뜻이다. 물(Dripping)은 끊임없는 성실한 노력을 뜻한다(He that shoots often at last shall hit the mark = 여러 번 쏘는 자는 결국 표적을 맞춘다).

Water freezes in cracks of rocks, it expands and causes the rocks to split
> ↳ 물이 바위틈에서 얼면 부피가 불어나서 바위를 쪼개지게 한다

When a magnet is immersed in liquid oxygen, its pulling power in intensified
> ↳ 자석을 액체산소 속에 넣으면 자력이 강화된다

When battery acid gets on our clothe, it will eat away at the material and leave holes
> ↳ 건전지에 있는 산이 우리의 옷에 묻으면 물질을 부식시켜 구멍을 낸다

When heat travels by conduction, it moves through a material without carrying it
> ↳ 열이 전도작용을 통해 이동할 때 물질을 운반하지 않고 물질을 통해 이동한다

· **magnet** body that attracts iron
· **intense** extreme, deeply felt

· **eat away** consume or wear away gradually

22. 구매   **Purchase**

A big house like that is going to cost you a nice piece of change
      ㄴ 저런 큰집을 사려면 큰돈이 들어야 해

After he bought that house, the bottom dropped out of the market and he lost a lot of money
      ㄴ 그가 집을 사고 난 뒤 집 값이 바닥으로 떨어져 큰 손해를 보았다

Almighty God, keep our wives from shopping sprees and protect them from bargains they don't need or can't afford Almighty God, keep our wives from shopping sprees and protect them from bargains they don't need or can't afford
      ㄴ 전능하신 하나님 아버지, 우리의 아내들이 쇼핑에 미쳐 돌아가는 일이 없도록 역사 하여 주시고 세일이라 해서 필요하지도 않거나 분수에 넘치는 물건을 사는 일이 없도록 살펴 주시기를 기원합니다

As the item you purchased is covered by our unconditional refund and replacement policy, we can give you a full refund
      ㄴ 귀하가 구입하신 품목은 저희 회사의 환불 및 반품 대상품목에 들어 있으므로 전액 환불해 드리겠습니다

Before buying a new appliance, compare the characteristics of similar products and their warranties, which protect your purchase
      ㄴ 새로운 가전제품을 사기전에 유사상품들의 특징들과 보증서들을 비교 검토 하셔야 구매한 물건들에 대해 보호받으실 수 있습니다

› **spree**   burst of indulging in something
› **refund**   give or put back (money)

› **warranty**   guarantee of the integrity of a product

Bong-soo will buy it if the price is within reason
　　ㄴ 가격이 적당하면 봉수가 그걸 살 것이다

Bulk buying has enabled the company to cut costs
　　ㄴ 회사에서 대량으로 구입함에 따라 비용을 절감할 수 있게 되었다

Buying a good car won't come cheap, but it's worth it for you
　　ㄴ 좋은 차를 사는 건 비싸게 먹히지만 네게 그만한 가치는 있다

Buying our house privately will cut out the middleman and save money on agent's fees
　　ㄴ 우리 집을 당사자 개인간에 사고 팔면 중개인 없는 거래여서 중개 수
　　　료가 절약된다

Can I buy them singularly?
　　ㄴ 낱개로 살 수 있습니까?

(=Can you break up the set?)

Can you come down a little more?
　　ㄴ 조금 더 깎아줄 수 없겠습니까?

Could you put it on my credit card?
　　ㄴ 카드로 지급해도 되나요?

Do I get a discount if I buy in bulk?
　　ㄴ 대량으로 사면 할인해 줍니까?

(=Do you give discounts on volume purchases?)

Do you have that many on hand?

· **bulk** magnitude, indigestible fibrous food residues, large mass, major portion,　　have bulk

ㄴ 그만한 수량의 재고가 있습니까?

Do you make any discount for cash?

ㄴ 현금으로 사면 할인해 줍니까?

Double-check the bill carefully before paying to ensure there are no hidden additional costs

ㄴ 잘 안 보이게 비용을 덧붙인 것이 없는지 지불 전에 계산서를 재삼 잘 확인하여라

Enclosed is our bill; please remit

ㄴ 계산서를 동봉하였으니 송금해 주십시오

Everything is worth what its purchaser will pay for it

ㄴ 모든 물건은 구매자가 지불하려는 만큼의 가치가 있다

Getting out of debt must be placed before(above) buying anything new

ㄴ 빚을 갚는 것이 새로운 것을 사는 것 보다 우선돼야 한다

Give me something trendy

ㄴ 그냥 유행하는 것으로 주세요

How much do they come(amount) to altogether?

ㄴ 모두 합해서 얼마죠?

I bought it on impulse(impulsively, without thinking)

ㄴ 그건 충동구매로 샀지

I have a limited budget

ㄴ 가진 돈이 빠듯해요(물건 살 때)

I want to stay under 200,000 won

ㄴ 20만원 미만 자리를 원합니다

I wanted to buy it, but my mother bullied me out of it

ㄴ 사고싶었지만 어머니가 옥박질러 못 샀지

It would be greatly appreciated if you paid in cash

› **trendy** prevailing tendency, direction, or style
› **impulse** a moving force, sudden inclination

ㄴ 현금으로 지불해 주시면 매우 고맙겠습니다

It's not necessarily better to stagger the payments rather than pay so much all at once

ㄴ 큰돈을 일시불로 내는 것 보다 분할 식으로 하는 것이 반드시 나은 것은 아니다

It's sold in packs of ten

ㄴ 열 개 묶음으로 팝니다

Let's not hoard(hog)

ㄴ 사재기를 하지 맙시다

Marrying a man is like buying something you've been admiring for a long time in a shop window

ㄴ 여자의 결혼은 가게 진열장에 오래 전부터 사고싶어했던 것을 사는 것과 같다

Nothing is free in this world

ㄴ 세상에 공짜는 없어

(=Everything has a price in this world. Put it down((Charge the sum) to my credit(account)) 내 앞으로 달아주십시오

Put it on my tab

ㄴ 외상으로 해주세요

(=Could you give it to me on credit?)
(=I'll pay it later)

Put on any additional expenses in here

› **necessary** indispensable item, inevitable, compulsory, positively needed

› **hoard** hidden accumulation
› **expense** cost

ㄴ 추가요금이 있다면 여기다 적어 둬

Put the tab on my accounts
ㄴ 외상 좀 합시다

Run out the totals again
ㄴ 다시 합계를 내봐

She is a good(excellent) bargain hunter
ㄴ 그 여자는 싼 물건을 기막히게 잘 찾아다녀

Sometimes goods are sold at a loss
ㄴ 때로는 상품을 손해보고 팔 때도 있어

Sometimes I get carried away but I usually buy reasonably
ㄴ 때론 내가 정도에 지나치기도 하지만 대개는 분별 있게 구매한다

The buyers should look at the both(other) side of the coin
ㄴ 물건을 사는 사람은 눈에 안 보이는 부분까지 잘 살펴야 한다

The dearer it is the cheaper
ㄴ 싼 게 비지떡(지불한 정도의 값어치는 있어)

> (=You got what you paid for)
> (=You were penny-wise and pound foolish)

The price of this bicycle is ten thousand won, take it or leave it
ㄴ 이 자전거는 십만원 이하로는 안되니 사고 아니고는 맘대로 해

The quality of our wedding rings you made does not correspond with that of the sample submitted to us
ㄴ 당신이 보여주신 샘플과 우리의 결혼 반지는 일치하지 않습니다

They are available in sets of five
ㄴ 다섯 개 한 조로 살 수 있습니다

› **loss** something lost   › **dearer** a person or thing highly valued or loved, something expensive

They are compulsive bargain-hunters
> ㄴ 그 사람들은 바겐세일이라면 가만히 못 있어

They must have seen you coming
> ㄴ 바가지 썼군

They sell apples, 300 won each
> ㄴ 사과 한 개당 300원에 팔아

They sell it in units of a ten
> ㄴ 그들은 그걸 열 개 단위로 팔아

They tried to palm that painting as a real Kim-hong-do
> ㄴ 그들은 그 그림을 진짜 김홍도의 작품이라고 속여 팔려고 했다

They wouldn't sell for less than the stated price
> ㄴ 그들은 고시가격보다 싸게 팔지 않을 것이다

This is a one-shot deal
> ㄴ 이런 장사는 두 번 다시없습니다(꼭 사십시오)

This is better, and(but) again it costs much
> ㄴ 이건 좋긴 하지만 값이 비싸다

This is merely a case of distance lending enhancement to the view
> ㄴ 이건 멀리서 보았기 때문에 흠집이 눈에 안 들어왔을 뿐이야

This is much the better of the two
> ㄴ 이것이 이 둘 중 훨씬 좋다

This last thing will bring the bill to over ten thousand won
> ㄴ 이 마지막 물건까지 합해서 계산이 만원 넘는다

This man wants a line of credit
> ㄴ 이 분이 외상거래를 원합니다

This merchandise can go for nothing
> ㄴ 이 상품은 개 값이야

· compulsion coercion, irresistible impulse	**· merchandise** goods bought and sold, buy and sell
· enhancement improving in value	

We go by price tag
    ↳ 우린 정찰제로 팝니다

We have them on hand
    ↳ 재고준비 있습니다

> (=We have them in stock)

What is the lowest price you'll go down to?
    ↳ 최하로 싸게 해서 얼마입니까?

What price range do you have in mind?
    ↳ 생각하시는 가격수준은 얼마입니까?

Will you chalk(notch, log, clock, score) it up to me?
    ↳ 내 이름으로(외상으로) 달아주시오(**=charge it to, charge it against my account**)

You can argue the price down, but it does you no good
    ↳ 물건값을 우겨서 깎을 순 있어도 그게 너한테 이롭진 않아

You can either pay in one lump or in the installments
    ↳ 일시불이나 분할 납부할 수 있습니다

You can find that cheaper
    ↳ 더 싸게 살 수 있어

> (=You can find a better deal)

You can save on(up for) a new stereo set if you shop wisely
    ↳ 요령 있게 쇼핑을 하면 새 오디오를 살 돈은 저축될 거야

You may take your choice
    ↳ 좋은 것으로 골라잡아라

› **chalk**　mark with chalk

› **range**　variation within limits

› **notch**　v-shaped hollow

› **installment**　partial payment

23. 국가   **Nation**

A man must cultivate himself and manage his family properly before he can govern the nation
> ㄴ 수신제가 이후에 치국평천하

A man's wife has more power over him than the state has
> ㄴ 아내는 남편에게 국가보다 더 큰 힘을 가지고 있다

A marriage without conflicts is almost inconceivable as a nation without crises
> ㄴ 충돌 없는 결혼생활은 위기 없는 국가처럼 있을 수 없는 일이다

All port cities generally have lots of establishments catering to sailors on shore leave
> ㄴ 어느 항구도시나 일반적으로 선원들의 기항을 겨냥한 시설들이 많다

Barbed wire and concrete walls delineate the DMZ that physically separate the two Korea
> ㄴ 철조망과 콘크리트 벽이 두 개의 한국을 물리적으로 분리해 놓고있는 비무장지대를 표시하고 있다

During the Korean War, Korean soldiers disputed every inch of ground
> ㄴ 한국전쟁 때 한국군은 한 치의 땅이라도 양보하지 않으려고 항쟁했다

Every corner of the nation is within a day's reach of everybody
> ㄴ 전국이 일일 생활권에 있다

Every nation has its own peculiar character

- **shore** land along the edge of water
- **barb** sharp projection pointing backward
- **delineate** sketch or portray
- **DMZ** demilitarized zone

↳ 각 국민은 제각기 고유한 국민성을 갖고 있다

Facing a common enemy keeps the nation together

↳ 국가 공동의 적을 앞에 두면 국민이 단합하게 된다

For a state to survive more than a fleeting historical moment, it must have the loyalty of its residents

↳ 국가가 절박한 역사적인 순간에서 살아남기 위하여 국가는 주민의 충성심을 얻어내어야 한다

For the good of our country, we must be willing to go the extra mile, to work harder and demand less

↳ 우리나라의 이익을 위해서 우리는 최선을 다해서 봉사하고, 더 열심히 일하며, 더 적게 요구하여야 한다

History teaches us that men and nations behave wisely once they have exhausted all other alternatives

↳ 역사는 국민과 국가에게 모든 대안이 고갈됐을 때 현명하게 행동한다는 것을 가르쳐 준다

Korea is always the most volatile hot spot

↳ 한국은 늘 일촉즉발의 화약고다

Korea possesses the potential and wisdom to meet any challenge

↳ 한국은 어떠한 난관도 이겨낼 수 있는 저력과 지혜를 가지고 있다

Myung-dong is the cream of Seoul

↳ 명동은 서울의 노른자위

Nations, like individuals, have to limit their objectives, or take the consequences

↳ 국민도 개인과 마찬가지로 그들의 목적을 제한해야하고 그렇지 않으면 그 결과에 대해 책임을 져야한다

No race can prosper till it learns there is as much dignity in tilling a

---

› **fleet** pass rapidly
› **loyal** faithful to a country, cause or friend

› **resident** a person who lives in a certain place

field as in writing a poem
> ㄴ 땅을 가는 것이 시를 쓰는 만큼이나 품위 있는 일임을 알지 못하는 민족은 번영할 수 없다

Nobody wants to make a rod for himself to save their country
> ㄴ 그들의 나라를 구하기 위하여 서서 고생하려는 사람은 없다

One should love one's country
> ㄴ 사람은 누구나 자기 나라를 사랑할 줄 알아야

Patriotism cuts across all ages and sexes of Korean society
> ㄴ 애국심은 한국의 남녀노소를 초월한다

Patriotism sat loose on them
> ㄴ 그들에게 애국심 따위는 아무래도 좋았다

Quite a few people do not fly their national flags over their doors on national holidays
> ㄴ 국경일에 국기를 달지 않는 집이 많아

Rarely has a health campaign so quickly become a national obsession
> ㄴ 건강 캠페인이 이토록 빠르게 전 국민을 사로잡게 된 적이 거의 없었다

Seoul is bursting at the seams with people
> ㄴ 서울은 사람 때문에 미어져 터질 지경이야

Seoul is where it's at any time(where the action is)
> ㄴ 서울은 사람들이 모여드는 곳이지(돈벌이가 있는, 활동무대가 넓은, 재미있는)

Such radiant cultural heritage, timeless fragrance of tradition, and unique culture are the pride of every Korean
> ㄴ 찬란한 문화유산, 은은한 전통의 향기, 문화적 독창성은 한국인의 자부심이다

The battle for people's mind is more important than military struggle

---

› **loose** not restrained	› **seam** line of junction of 2 edges
› **obsess** preoccupy intensely or abnormally	› **radiant** glowing, beaming with happiness

ㄴ 민심을 얻기 위한 전쟁은 군대를 동원한 전투보다 중요하다

The degree of government involvement in private affairs became an embarrassment to the nation when it was revealed that directors had been contacted regarding their decisions

ㄴ 중역들은 결정을 내리는 과정에서 정부로부터 접촉을 받았다는 사실이 드러남으로써 민간 업무에 관한 정부의 개입정도는 나라를 떠들썩하게 만들었다

The dirty acquisition comes from an adulteration of our culture brought by money-hungry, greedy outsiders

ㄴ 그 더러운 이익추구는 돈에 굶주리고 탐욕스러운 외부인들이 들여온 우리 문화의 불순물이다

The driving force of a nation lies in its spiritual purpose, made effective by free, tolerant but unremitting national will

ㄴ 국가의 원동력은 자유롭고 인내하면서도 끈질긴 국가의 의지로 발효되는 목표에 있다

The language of a people often reflects its characteristics

ㄴ 한 민족의 언어는 흔히 그 민족의 특성을 반영한다

The scientists noted that opposition to genetically modified foods had come mostly from rich countries

ㄴ 과학자들은 유전자변형 식량에 대한 반대가 대부분 잘 사는 나라에서 제기되고 있다고 지적했다

The youth of a nation are the trustees of prosperity

ㄴ 나라의 젊은이들은 번영의 책임을 진다

Their fraudulent gambling made front pages across the country

ㄴ 그들의 사기도박이 온 나라의 관심사로 떠올랐다

Their outmoded attitudes are dragging the country back into the

---

- **acquisition** a gaining or something gained
- **adulterate** make impure by mixture
- **spiritual** relating to the spirit or sacred matters, deeply religious

twentieth century

    ㄴ 그들의 낡은 태도가 나라를 **20**세기로 퇴보시키고 있다

There are good curio shops in this city to set off the disadvantages of frequent traffic congestions

    ㄴ 이 도시에는 잦은 교통혼잡의 불편함을 보상해 줄만한 좋은 골동품상들이 있다

They gloried in giving their lives for their country

    ㄴ 그들은 나라를 위해 목숨을 바치는 것을 자랑으로 여겼어

This monument was built to perpetuate the memory of the national hero

    ㄴ 이 기념비는 국민적 영웅을 기념하기 위해 건립되었다

To the extent that we are a democracy we share a responsibility in what our country does

    ㄴ 민주국가인 이상 우리는 국가가 하는 일에 대하여 책임을 분담하고 있는 셈이다

We hoist our national flags at half mast on the Memorial Day

    ㄴ 우리는 현충일에 반기를 게양한다

We must change our way of thinking if we are to put the nation on its feet after all these struggles

    ㄴ 이 모든 어려움 끝에 나라가 바르게 돌아가자면 우리의 사고방식을 바꿔야 한다

You were wide of the mark when you said you knew who's who in Korea

    ㄴ 네가 한국에서 내노라하는 사람을 안다고 말하는 건 헛 다리 짚는 소리야

· **congest** overcrowd or overfill

· **monument** structure erected in remembrance

· **perpetuate** make perpetual

· **hoist** lift

24. 군대   Military

A civil defense drill is in progress(being conducted)
> ↳ 지금 민방위 훈련중이다

An army marches(travels) on its stomach
> ↳ 군대는 배가 불러야 싸울 수 있다

Basic military training is rigorous so that the trainees do not slack up
> ↳ 기초군사훈련은 훈련병들이 군기가 빠지지 않도록 엄격히 진행된다

Bong-soo mustered out of service well before his time was up
> ↳ 봉수는 만기가 되기 훨씬 전에 군에서 제대했어

Bong-soo resigned himself to life in the army
> ↳ 봉수는 할 수 없이 군대생활을 하기로 했다

By joining the army late, he was ranked below many men much younger than himself
> ↳ 그는 군에 늦게 가서 자기보다 훨씬 나이 적은 사람들의 졸병노릇을 했다

Countless allegations have been raised about the wrongdoing concerning the conscription
> ↳ 병역에 관해 수없이 많은 비리 주장이 제기되었다

Dong-soo is divided between joining the army and taking a job
> ↳ 동수는 군에 입대할지 취직을 할지 마음을 정하지 못하고 있다

Draft irregularities have long been a serious social issue symbolizing the conflict between the rich and the poor in this country

---

- **civil** relating to citizens, polite, relating to or being a law-suit
- **slack up** get loose
- **drill** strict training and instruction

ㄴ 병역비리는 이 나라의 가진 자 못 가진 자 사이의 갈등을 상징하는 심각한 사회문제가 되어왔다

Had it not been for the sacrifices of our armed forces, most of us would have starved to death or might be leading a miserable life

ㄴ 군인들의 희생이 없었다면 우리들은 굶어죽거나 비참한 생활을 하게 되었을 것이다

It's not proper to suppose that all of those who did not perform military service have violated the law

ㄴ 군 복무를 하지 않았다 해서 모두가 법을 어겼다고 여기는 것은 온당하지가 않다

Joining the army might improve your chances of getting out of that humdrum job

ㄴ 군에 입대하면 그 따분한 일에서 너를 벗어나게 해 줄지도 몰라

Jung-soo's joined the army and lived off post

ㄴ 정수는 군에 입대해서 영외에 거주했다

Jung-tai was my captain in the army, but now the shoe is on the other foot

ㄴ 군에서는 정태가 우리 중대장이었지만 지금은 나의 부서에서 일 하고 있어

Marksmen are trained to be accurate at long range

ㄴ 저격수는 먼 거리에서도 정확히 사격할 수 있도록 훈련받는다

Officers and men were just beginning to find their feet then

ㄴ 그러자 장교와 사병들은 경험과 지식을 쌓기 시작했다

Tai-ho gave her a snow job on his army career

ㄴ 태호는 그녀에게 자신의 군대경력을 그럴듯하게 얘기했어

The project is intended to make it easier to make parents to keep in touch with their sons in the military

ㄴ 이 안은 부모가 군에 있는 아들들에게 연락을 쉽게 취할 수 있도록

› **stave** narrow strip of wood, break a hole in, drive away

› **violate** act with disrespect or disregard of, rape, desecrate

하는 의도에 있다

There are too many chiefs and not enough Indians
> ↳ 대장만 많고 병사는 없군

Vivid in memory are the grim faces of those motionless young soldiers clad in uniform
> ↳ 군복차림으로 부동자세를 취하고 있는 젊은 군인들의 섬짓한 모습이 생생하다

While Gab-dol was in the army, Gab-soon kept the home fires burning
> ↳ 갑돌이가 군에 가 있을 동안 갑순이가 집 지키며 살림을 했다

You have grown slack
> ↳ 군기 빠졌군

(=You are not on your toes)

· **vivid**   lively, brilliant, intense or sharp
· **clad**   covered, proved with a covering

· **grim**   harsh and forbidding in appearance, relentless

25. 꿈 & 희망   Dreams & Wishes/Hopes

A stately mansion? You can't get there from here
> ↳ 근사한 저택이라? 꿈도 야무지군

All I want now is to do my own thing
> ↳ 지금 내가 하고싶은 일은 내가 원(좋아)하는 일이다

All she wished was for the ground to open and swallow her
> ↳ 그 여자는 쥐구멍이라도 있으면 들어가 버리고 싶은 심정뿐이었어

All we can hope is that our mistakes won't be expensive and we don't make them again
> ↳ 우리가 바랄 수 있는 것은 우리의 실수가 큰 부담이 되지 않고 같은 실수를 반복하지 않기를 바라는 것뿐이다

An-do is burning for only another look at Sook-hee
> ↳ 안도는 숙희를 한 번만이라도 더 보길 간절히 바랐어

As yet we have nothing in prospect(no prospects)
> ↳ 아직은 아무런 가망이 없다

At first, we hope too much, later on, not enough
> ↳ 사람은 처음엔 너무 많은 것을 바라다가 나중엔 그 희망이 너무 적어진다

Bong-soo puts himself ahead of his colleagues and expects special treatment
> ↳ 봉수는 자신을 동료들보다 중요한 사람으로 생각하고 특별 대우를 기대하고 있어

Bong-soo wants a clean break with the past

› **stately** having impressive dignity

ㄴ 봉수는 과거를 깨끗이 청산하기 바라고 있어

Byung-soo wanted a job where he would be calling the shots himself

ㄴ 병수는 자신이 책임지고 지휘할 수 있는 일을 원했다

Chan-soo had to write off the debt as hopeless

ㄴ 찬수는 빌려 준 돈이 회수 희망이 없다고 보고 결손처분 해야 했다

Cross my heart and hope to die

ㄴ 정말이지 믿어 줘

Don't ask for the moon

ㄴ 터무니없는걸 바라지마

Don't be a free swinger

ㄴ 허황한 욕심을 품지마

Don't expect that jack-off to get ahead in life

ㄴ 저 식충이 녀석에게 잘 되리라는 기대는 하지마

Don't hold your breath

ㄴ 기대 하지마

Don't lose your grip on your dreams

ㄴ 꿈을 포기하지 마라

Don't you wish!

ㄴ 아서라(터무니없는 기대), 그렇게 된다면 좋겠지

(=You wish!)

Dong-soo's dreams have fallen apart

ㄴ 동수의 꿈은 산산조각 났다

Doo-soo deceived(deluded) himself with dreams of success but they

---

- **grip** seize or hold firmly
- **jack-off** a person who does nothing

- **swinger** a person who moves rapidly in an arc

never came true
ㄴ 두수는 성공하리라는 헛된 꿈을 꾸어왔지만 그 꿈은 이루어지지 않았다

Dreams go by contraries
ㄴ 꿈은 현실과 반대

(=Dreams are lies)

Everybody wishes that loud mouth would put a cork in it
ㄴ 저 떠버리가 입 좀 다물어주길 모두가 바라고 있다

Feel it in your mind's eye
ㄴ 그 일을 마음속에 그려봐라

Few people expect to go over the top before the beginning of January
ㄴ 1월초가 되기 전에 목표를 달성하리라고 기대하는 사람은 거의 없어

Get real
ㄴ 꿈 깨라

Gil-soo hoped against hope, and everything worked out
ㄴ 길수는 가망 없는 일에 희망을 걸었는데 만사가 잘 풀렸어

Give up pining after what you can't get
ㄴ 얻을 수 없는 것을 탐내지 마라

He begins to die that quits his desire
ㄴ 소망을 포기하는 사람은 죽어가기 시작한 사람이다

인간은 살아가면서 여러 가지 절망에 부딪히는데, 이럴 때마다 희망을 버리면 실수가 없다. "하늘이 무너져도 솟아날 구멍이 있다(If the sky falls we shall catch larks)"고 하였다(Hope springs eternal = 희망의 샘은 영원히 샘솟는다).
(=He's perspective)

· **contrary** opposite in character, nature, or position, mutually opposed, un-　favorable, uncooperative or stubborn

He doesn't want anything like labor
> ㄴ 그는 힘든 일 따위는 바라지 않는다

He hopes that all your efforts don't go for naught(nothing)
> ㄴ 그는 너의 노력이 성공하기를 바라고 있어

He is(a) pie in the sky for you
> ㄴ 꿈 좀 깨라, 그는 네게 그림의 떡이야

He pinned his hopes on being rescued soon
> ㄴ 그는 곧 구조되리라는 희망을 걸었다

He wants to ride the gravy trains
> ㄴ 그는 금 방석을 원하는 거야

He who does something against his will is unhappy
> ㄴ 자신의 희망에 반하는 일을 하는 사람은 불행한 사람이다

He who doesn't hope to win has already lost
> ㄴ 승리를 바라지 않는 사람은 벌써 진 것이다

Her remarkable life and tragic death poignantly express the hopes and disappointments of a whole generation
> ㄴ 그녀의 눈부신 생애와 비극적인 죽음은 모든 세대들의 희망과 절망을 찡하게 표현해준다

He's been dreaming of marrying a girl from the right side of the track
> ㄴ 그는 잘 사는 아가씨와 결혼할 꿈을 꾸고 있다

Hope is a great falsifier of truth
> ㄴ 희망은 진실을 크게 왜곡시킨다

Hope is brightest when it dawns from fear
> ㄴ 두려움에서 싹트는 희망이 가장 밝은 희망이다

Hope springs eternal, that's what it is
> ㄴ 살아있는 한 희망은 있어

▸ **gravy** sauce made from thickened juices of cooked meat

▸ **poignant** emotionally painful, deeply moving
▸ **falsify** mislead

Hyun-soo's hope is in sight
> ↳ 현수에게 서광이 비쳐

I guess you have just made all my dreams come true
> ↳ 그대는 내가 꿈꾸어 오던 이상적인 여인(남자)

I had a crazy(wild or ridiculous) dream
> ↳ 개꿈 꾸었지 뭐

I have nothing left to wish for
> ↳ 그밖에는 아무 것도 바라는 게 없다

I hope to tell you she's a knockout
> ↳ 말이야 바로 말이지 그 여자 끝내주는 미인이야

I sincerely wish your continued success
> ↳ 건투를 빈다

I wish I could sink through the floor
> ↳ 쥐구멍에라도 들어가고 싶은 심정이야

> (=I wish the earth would swallow me up)

I wish you every success
> ↳ 하시는 일마다 성공하시기 바랍니다

If chance will have me king
> ↳ 만일 내가 왕이 된다면

If she thinks she can hit the jack-pot from buying lots of lottery tickets, she must be living in a fool's paradise
> ↳ 그 여자가 복권을 망상이 사서 한몫 보려고 한다면 헛된 꿈을 꾸고 있는 거야

- **knockout** something sensationally attractive
- **sincere** genuine or honest
- **sink** submerge or descent
- **paradise** place of bliss

In a few more years I'll be able to get ahead
> ↳ 몇 년 안 가서 흑자 낼 수 있을 거야

In dreams and in love nothing is impossible
> ↳ 꿈과 사랑에는 불가능이 없다

In many children's dreams they often relive their fears and they thought they were being attacked
> ↳ 어린이들은 꿈속에서 무서움과 공격당했던 기억을 회상하는 때가 많다

Keep your hopes within bounds
> ↳ 될성싶지도 않은 일은 바라지도 마라

Let's wish!
> ↳ 희망을 갖자

Life is but an empty dream
> ↳ 인생은 일장춘몽이다

Long ailments wear out pain, long hopes, and joy
> ↳ 긴 고통은 아픔도, 오랜 희망도, 기쁨도 사라지게 한다

My all good wishes for your next step
> ↳ 너의 앞일이 잘 되기 바란다

My friend cast out his daughter when she married against his wishes
> ↳ 우리 친구는 딸이 뜻을 거역해 결혼하자 다시는 안 본다며 의절을 선언했어

Never did I dream you had told a lie
> ↳ 네가 거짓말했으리라 곤 꿈에도 몰랐지

Never in his wildest dreams he imagined that he would get the gold medal
> ↳ 그는 금메달을 따리라고는 꿈에도 상상하지 못했다

People wish to be liked, not to be endured with patient resignation
> ↳ 사람들은 남들이 좋아해 주기를 원하지만 체념으로 참아주기를 바라
> 지는 않는다

› **relive** live over again(as in the imagination) | › **resign** give up deliberately, give over without resistance

Please circulate internally as you may wish
    ↳ 필요하다고 판단하시는 곳에 내부적으로 배포하여 주십시오

She wants to live in a lonely corner out of reach of the noisy world
    ↳ 그녀는 시끄러운 세상에서 떨어진 외딴 곳에 살고싶어 해

She wished to be all in all to him
    ↳ 그 여자는 그에게 가장 사랑하는 사람이 되고 싶었다

Snap out of your fantasy
    ↳ 꿈같은 생각은 집어치워

Some people expect the main computer to able to do all the donkey work
    ↳ 메인 컴퓨터가 따분한 일을 다 해 줄 것으로 기대하는 사람들도 있다

Sook-hee is distracted between hope and fear
    ↳ 숙희는 희망과 불안으로 뒤숭숭해

Tailor your desire to the measure of your abilities
    ↳ 능력에 맞게 소망을 가져라

Ten thousand men possess ten thousand hopes
    ↳ 십 만 명의 사람은 십 만 가지의 희망을 가지고 있다

That cut at all my hopes
    ↳ 이로서 희망은 사라졌어

The experiment didn't pan out well as we hoped
    ↳ 그 실험은 우리가 바랐던 만큼 잘 되지 않았어

The government is hoping to ease import restrictions soon
    ↳ 정부는 수입제한제도를 완화하기를 희망하고 있다

The results exceed my hope
    ↳ 기대이상이다

The wish for healing has ever been the half of health
    ↳ 병이 낫겠다는 소망만으로 반쯤 나은 것과 같다

›**snap** break suddenly with a sharp sound   ›**distract** divert the mind or attention of

›**fantasy** imagination

Their changes are beyond my wildest dreams(hopes)
> ↳ 그들은 꿈에도 생각 못했을 만큼 변했어

Their hope is to ride the boss's coattail
> ↳ 그들의 희망은 힘있는 상사의 덕을 보자는 것이다

There are situations in which hope and fear run together, in which they mutually destroy one another
> ↳ 희망과 두려움이 동행할 경우도 있으며 이 경우 이들은 서로를 파괴한다

They wish you wouldn't press more beer on them when they have already refused politely
> ↳ 그들이 정중히 사양하면 더 이상 맥주를 억지로 권하지 않길 바라고 있어

Those who wish to be learned to fools, seem fool to the learned
> ↳ 어리석은 자들에게 배운 사람으로 보이고 싶어하는 사람은 배운 사람에게 어리석은 사람으로 보여진다

To lose weight and to achieve their dream of a slimmer body, many people skip meals or go on fad diet
> ↳ 많은 사람들은 체중을 줄이고 보다 날씬한 몸매를 유지하겠다는 꿈을 실현시키기 위해 끼니를 거르거나 요즈음 유행식인 식단을 이용한다

We are still hoping
> ↳ 우린 희망을 버리지 않아

We do not wish people or things we find amusing to be other than they are
> ↳ 우린 재미있는 사람들이나 물건들이 있는 그대로이기를 바란다

We must live out our dreams to transform them into action
> ↳ 우리의 꿈을 실현하고 이를 행동으로 옮겨야 해

We wake from one dream into another dream
> ↳ 사람은 하나의 꿈을 깨고 나면 또 다른 꿈을 꾸게 된다

· **beyond** farther, besides, out of the reach of | · **mutually** given or felt by one another in equal amount, common

> 사람은 살아 있는 한, 꿈을 꾸며 희망을 가지게 마련이다. 희망이 없는 삶은
> 죽은 것과 마찬가지이기 때문이다(While there is life, there is hope 살
> 아 있는 한 희망은 있다).

What we fear comes to pass more speedily than what we hope
   ↳ 두려워하는 것은 희망하는 것 보다 빨리 지나간다

When the devil was ill, he wish to be a monk; when the devil was recovered, he was devil as before
   ↳ 화장실 갈 때 마음 다르고 올 때 마음 다르다

> 환경에 따라 태도와 입장이 바뀌어진다. 직역하면 "악마가 병에 걸리면 수도
> 승이 되길 원하지만, 병이 나으면 다시 악마가 된다"이다. 사람의 마음은 시
> 시각각 변한다는 것을 말한다.

Wishers were ever fools
   ↳ 어리석은 자는 헛된 희망에 의지한다

You are my dream come true
   ↳ 그대는 내가 꿈에 그리던 사람

You are our last hope(chance, bastion, line of defence)
   ↳ 넌 우리의 마지막 보루다

You are the only one I dream of
   ↳ 꿈속에도 그리는 단 한사람

You don't have to fluctuate between hopes and fears
   ↳ 일희일비해서는 안 돼

You must build your dreams on reality
   ↳ 꿈은 현실에 기반을 두고 세워야 해

· **monk** member of a religious order living in a monastery

· **fluctuate** change rapidly especially up and down

You'd better keep your hopes within bounds
　　↳ 가망 없는 일은 바라지 말아야 해

Your hopes were dashed
　　↳ 너의 희망은 사라졌어

Your hopes will crystalize into a fact
　　↳ 너의 희망은 현실로 구체화 될 것이다

Your wish is my command
　　↳ 분부만 하시죠

›dash　knock or hurl violently or impetuously,　　　　　　move quickly
　　　　smash, ruin, perform or finish hastily,

26. 기계　　　　　　　Machinery

A dynamiter is used to measure muscle power
　　ㄴ 근력계는 근력을 측정하는 데 쓰인다

A mis-stroke will jam the typewriter keys
　　ㄴ 타자를 잘못 치면 타자기 키가 움직이지 않아

A thinking robot? That's a new one to me
　　생각하는 로봇이라? 야, 그거 놀랠 노자네

Am I glad to see you! The computer's down and I can't figure out why
　　ㄴ 마침 잘 왔다. 컴퓨터가 고장났는데 어디가 잘못됐는지 모르겠다

> (=Just the person I wanted to see! The computer's down and I
> can't figure out why)

An-do can do 6,000 keystrokes an hour
　　ㄴ 안도는 시간당 **6,000**타를 쳐

An-do doesn't know a thing about computers
　　ㄴ 안도는 컴퓨터라곤 모르잖아

As far as computers are concerned, they've already cornered the market
　　ㄴ 컴퓨터라면 그들이 이미 시장을 다 휘어잡고 있다

Can you debug the program to make it run right?
　　ㄴ 이 컴퓨터 프로그램이 제대로 가동되도록 점검해 줄 수 있겠니?

‣ **dynamiter**　explosive made of nitroglycerin
‣ **jam**　press into a close or tight position, cause to become wedged so as to be unworkable

Chang-soo knows computers cold(inside out, backwards and forwards)
> ㄴ 창수가 컴퓨터라면 빠삭해

Computer skills are necessary in any profession, whereas some people refuse to learn these skills out of fear
> ㄴ 컴퓨터기술은 거의 모든 직업에 필요한데 반하여 어떤 사람들은 두려움 때문에 이 기술을 배우기를 거부한다

Computers'll be drug on the market any day
> ㄴ 머지 않아 컴퓨터가 많아 남아 돌 거야

Do you think the floor will bear up under the weight of the new machinery?
> ㄴ 마루바닥이 새로 구입한 기계무게를 감당할 것 같니?

Edison attached a telephone diaphragm to the needle in the telegraph repeater to produce a recording that could be played back
> ㄴ 에디슨은 재생 가능한 녹음기를 만들기 위하여 전신자동중계장치에 있는 바늘에 진동판을 붙였다

Have you fed the data into the computer?
> ㄴ 컴퓨터에 자료 입력했니?

He can put the elevator into use(service) as soon as he finishes the repairs
> ㄴ 그가 수리를 끝내는 대로 엘리베이터는 가동될 수 있을 것이다

He found a way to defeat your security system
> ㄴ 그가 보안 시스템에 허점을 발견했어(컴퓨터)

Her computer lost the file by a power failure
> ㄴ 그녀의 컴퓨터의 전원이 꺼져서 파일들을 잃었다

My computer is causing trouble again. Uh oh. Here we go again
> ㄴ 컴퓨터가 또 이상이야. 어이쿠. 또 시작이야

She can do 3,000 strokes an hour

› **telegraph** system for communication by electrical transmission of

coded signals
› **security** safety

　　　↳ 그 여자는 한 시간에 **3,000**타를 친다

Some people expect the main computer to able to do all the donkey work

　　　↳ 메인 컴퓨터가 따분한 일을 다 해 줄 것으로 기대하는 사람들도 있다

The washing machine was rattling away so we could hardly hear each other speak

　　　↳ 세탁기가 시끄럽게 움직이고 있어서 서로의 얘기가 들리지 않았다

▸ **rattle**　make a series of clattering sounds, say briskly, confuse or upset

27. 기억   **Memories**

A good memory is one trained to forget the trivial
> ↳ 우수한 기억력은 시시한 일을 잊어버리는데 단련되는 일이다

A strong memory is commonly coupled with infirm judgement
> ↳ 강한 기억력은 보통 허약한 판단력과의 결합으로 이루어진다

Age tells on one's memory
> ↳ 나이를 먹으면 기억력이 둔해져

(=Memory weakens with age)

Creditors have better memories than debtors
> ↳ 채권자는 채무자 보다 기억력이 좋다

Give me a moment and it'll come to me. I'm drawing a blank at the moment
> ↳ 시간을 좀 주면 기억이 날 것 같아. 지금은 기억이 잘 안나

He's dead from the memory of the world
> ↳ 그는 세상에서 버림받았어

He's got a memory like a sieve(sponge)
> ↳ 그는 건망증이 심해

His memory liveskka
> ↳ 그에 대한 추억은 아직도 생생해(그의 이름은 아직도 기억나)

> **trivial** of little importance
> **infirm** feeble from age

> **sieve** utensil with holes to separate particles

In every kind of adversity, the bitterest part of a man's affliction is to remember that he once was happy
> ↳ 어떤 역경에서나 사람에게 가장 쓰라린 고통은 그가 과거에 행복했다는 것을 기억하고 있다는 일이다

In many children's dreams they often relive their fears and they thought they were being attacked
> ↳ 어린이들은 꿈속에서 무서움과 공격당했던 기억을 회상하는 때가 많다

In plucking the fruit of the memory one runs the risk of spoiling its bloom
> ↳ 추억의 과실을 따는 사람은 그 열매가 될 꽃을 망가뜨리는 위험을 범하고 있는 것이다

Just as eating against one's will is injurious to health, so studying without a liking for it spoils the memory, and our brains retain nothing
> ↳ 싫은 것을 억지로 먹이는 것이 건강에 해롭듯이 싫은 것을 억지로 공부하는 것은 기억력을 망치게 되어 머리 속에 들어와도 남아있지 않게 된다

Moon-soo has an memory like an elephant
> ↳ 문수는 기억력이 굉장히 좋아

My memory doesn't go back so far
> ↳ 그렇게 옛날 일까진 생각이 안나

My memory of that is incomplete
> ↳ 기억이 잘 안 납니다

Our memories are independent of our wills
> ↳ 우리의 기억은 우리의 의지와는 별개이다

Please don't bring back those blotted-out memories
> ↳ 나의 지워(잊어)졌던 기억을 되살아나게 하지마

She has a brain like a sieve and always forget the secret number
> ↳ 그녀는 너무 기억력이 나빠서 늘 비밀번호를 잊어버린다

▸ **pluck** pull off or out, tug or twitch	▸ **independent** not relying for support
▸ **incomplete** not finished	▸ **blotted-out** forgotten, dried

The acts of good men live after them in our memories
> ↳ 훌륭한 사람들의 행동은 그들이 죽은 후에도 우리의 기억에 남는다

The incident stuck in my memory
> ↳ 그 사건은 내 기억에 뚜렷이 남아 있었어

The memory is still fresh(vivid) in my mind
> ↳ 아직도 그 기억이 생생해

> (=I remember it as if it were yesterday)

The memory of my late uncle revives unexpectedly from time to time
> ↳ 문득문득 돌아가신 아저씨 생각이 난다

The memory of those who died is very green
> ↳ 죽은 사람들에 대한 기억이 매우 생생하다

The memory remains with us
> ↳ 그 추억은 아직도 우리의 가슴에 남아있다

The memory represents to us not what we choose but what we please
> ↳ 추억은 우리가 선택한 바를 보여주는 것이 아니라 우리가 좋아하는 것을 보여준다

The sweetest memory is that which involves something one should have not done
> ↳ 가장 달콤한 추억은 그가 해서는 안 되는 일에 끼여들었던 추억이다

The picture takes me back to the time I spent the summer in Busan
> ↳ 이 사진을 보니 부산에서 여름을 보냈던 때가 생각나는군

This monument was built to perpetuate the memory of the national hero
> ↳ 이 기념비는 국민적 영웅을 기념하기 위해 건립되었다

› **late** recently deceased
› **green** vivid, fresh

› **represent** serve as a sign or symbol or

Vivid in memory are the grim faces of those motionless young soldiers clad in uniform

ㄴ 군복차림으로 부동자세를 취하고 있는 젊은 군인들의 섬짓한 모습이 생생하다

28. 나쁜 관계   Bad Relationships

After a few months of being ignored, Bong-soo withdrew into himself
ㄴ 봉수가 몇 달 동안 무시당하고 보니 남들과의 교제를 끊었어

An-do's been keeping(himself) to himself
ㄴ 안도는 줄곧 남과의 교제를 끊고 있어

As I treat, so will I treat you
ㄴ 당신이 대접한대로 당신을 대접하겠다

Bong-doo is all bad news to me
ㄴ 봉두는 정말 싫어

Bong-soo raised a few good points, but An-do shot him down immediately
ㄴ 봉수가 몇 가지 좋은 안을 제기했지만 안도가 즉각 묵살해버렸다

Chan-soo made(took) a quiet dig at me
ㄴ 찬수가 은근히 날 꼬아 주더군

Doo-chul let him slip through his fingers
ㄴ 두철이가 그를 놓쳐버렸어

Doo-man is ready to walk out on you if you tell him where to get off
ㄴ 네가 두만이에게 자꾸 싫은 소리하면 금방이라도 등을 돌릴 거야

Don't get emotional on me
ㄴ 내게 감정으로 대하지마

Don't work you bad temper off on me, I'm not to blame for the way you feel

---

› **withdraw** take back or away, call back
or retract, go away, terminate

one's participation in or use of

ㄴ 너의 언짢은 감정을 나한테 화풀이하지 마라, 너의 그런 기분이 나 때문이 아니잖아

Ed's ears must have been burning today

ㄴ 오늘 에드는 귀가 간질간질 할 거다

He dared not look me in the face

ㄴ 감히 내 얼굴을 바로 보지 못했어

He has it in for me

ㄴ 그 사람 내게 나쁜 감정을 가지고 있어

He parted company with me years ago

ㄴ 그는 몇 년 전부터 나하고 교제를 끊었어

He still remembers(holds) it against me

ㄴ 그는 아직도 내게 꽁하게 생각하고 있어

He's been back-talking me

ㄴ 그녀석이 내 험담하고 다닌다지

He's on the outs with his father

ㄴ 그는 자기 아버지와 사이가 나빠

He's taking it out on you

ㄴ 그가 네게 화풀이하고 있는 거야

He's the grossest

ㄴ 그 사람 밥맛 떨어져

His company is too warm for me

ㄴ 그와 같이 있는 건 너무 불편해

His view always jars with mine

ㄴ 그의 의견은 언제나 내 의견과 어긋나

How can you leave me on the mat?

ㄴ 날 문전박대 하다니

› **gross** glaringly noticeable, bulky, vulgar

› **jar** have a harsh or disagreeable effect, vibrate or shake

Hyun-soo has set you up
ㄴ 너 현수의 함정에 빠졌군

I can't stand the sight of him
ㄴ 그 녀석 꼴도 보기 싫어

I noticed you cut me dead whenever you see me
ㄴ 날 볼 때마다 모른 척 하더군

I really put him in his place
ㄴ 그 사람에게 건방지다고 야단을 쳐줬지

I refuse to deal with him
ㄴ 그 사람과 사귀는 건 질색

I shall see the back of you
ㄴ 네 꼴 좀 안 봤으면 좋겠다

I won't be lorded over
ㄴ 나한테 큰소리 못 치게 할거다

I won't look at him
ㄴ 그를 보지 않기로(상대하지 않기로) 했다(두 가지 뜻)

I won't see him in a hurry
ㄴ 그 사람은 두 번 다시 만나고 싶지 않아(in a hurry=쾌히)

I'll see you smart
ㄴ 혼내주고 말 테다(두고보자)

I'll settle your hash this time
ㄴ 이번엔 끽소리 못하게 해주지

I'll sin him alive
ㄴ 그 사람 혼내 줄 거야

I'll teach you a lesson
ㄴ 혼내주겠다

· **lord** rule over someone
· **hash** talk about(+over), chop into small pieces

· **sin** commit a sin

I'm only concerned to see the back of you
　　↳ 네가 가 주길 바랄 뿐이야

I've been thrown away like an old shoe
　　↳ 헌신짝 같이 버림받았어

> 오래 사귀던 사람을 버릴 때 쓰는 속담은 동·서양이 같다. 한국에서 헌신짝을 버린다고 하듯이, 영어에서는 "Throw away like an old shoe"라고 한다.

I've not been able to live up to(meet) your expectations
　　↳ 네 기대에 부응치 못했어

In-ho made out he hadn't seen me
　　↳ 인호는 나를 못 본체 했어

Is there any green in my eye?
　　↳ 내가 만만해 보이니?

It's ten to one he'll tan(dress) your hide
　　↳ 네가 그에게 혼날 건 뻔해

It's too late to make up(apologize) to me
　　↳ 사과하기엔 너무 늦었어

It's too much to ask of me
　　↳ 그것을 내게 바라는 것은 무리다

Jealousy is no more than feeling alone against smiling enemies
　　↳ 질투는 미소짓고 있는 적에 대해 혼자 가지고 있는 적대감에 불과하다

Jong-soo called me names in public
　　↳ 종수가 사람들 앞에서 날 욕했어

Make as if you don't see him
　　↳ 그를 못 본 척 해라

› **apologize**　make an apology, say sorry | › **jealousy**　suspicious of a rival or of one
　　　　　　　　　　　　　　　　　　　　　　　　　believed to enjoy an advantage

Man-soo doesn't even know I exist
> ↳ 만수는 나 따위엔 안중에도 없어

Nam-soo was as hard as nails
> ↳ 남수가 무척 차갑게 굴더군

Nobody crossed me up but he ratted on me
> ↳ 아무도 나를 배신하지 않았는데 그가 나를 밀고했어

Placed between them I find my position awkward
> ↳ 그들 사이에 끼어서 입장이 난처하다

Sang-soo will nail you to the wall if he finds out what you've done
> ↳ 네가 한 짓을 상수가 알기라도 한다면 혼 줄이 날거다

Send him to me whenever he gets out of line and I'll discipline him
> ↳ 언제든지 그가 말을 듣지 않을 때 나한테 보내면 내가 야단을 쳐 줄께

She is trying to get something on me so she can dress me down
> ↳ 그 여자는 내 꼬투리를 잡아서 야단 치려고 하고 있어

She's in my face too much
> ↳ 그 여자는 나를 너무 괴롭혀

She's so demanding she's beginning to drive us to drink
> ↳ 그 여자는 너무 자기위주라 우릴 달달 볶고있어

She's trying to push your buttons by making snide remarks to you
> ↳ 그 여자는 네게 헐뜯는 말을 해서 너를 조종하고 있는 거야

She's trying to turn them against you
> ↳ 그녀가 그들로 하여금 네게 등을 돌리게 만들고 있는 거야

Somebody needs to put him in his place
> ↳ 누군가가 그에게 싫은 소리 좀 해줘야겠다

Sung-hee is indifferent to you
> ↳ 성희가 너 따윌 안중에 두겠니('무관심'의 뜻도 됨)

▸ **cross up** betray	▸ **awkward** clumsy, embarrassing
▸ **rat on** betray one's associate	▸ **snide** subtly ridiculing

Sung-mo wants a dressing down
ㄴ 성모를 혼내줘야겠어

That fellow always talks about you behind your back and pretends to be nice to you when he meets you
ㄴ 저 녀석은 네가 없을 때 늘 험담하고 널 만날 때면 착한 척 해

That guy tried to bleed the villagers dry(white)
ㄴ 저 녀석이 마을 사람들을 알거지가 되게 알겨먹으러 했어

That man barged into me in the shop
ㄴ 저 사람이 가게에서 마구 부딪쳐 왔어

That poisoned his mind against me
ㄴ 그 일로 그가 내게 편견을 갖게 됐어

The chemistry with you is not right
ㄴ 너하고는 생리적으로 안 맞아

The hatred between the two men never flickered out
ㄴ 두 사람 사이의 미운 감정은 사라지지 않았다

The illicit practices of certain entertainers might have far-reaching consequences by sending the wrong message to young people
ㄴ 일부 연예인들의 불법행위는 젊은이들에게 나쁜 의미를 전달함으로써
큰 영향을 주는 결과가 될 수 있다

The relation between them began to sour
ㄴ 그 사람들 사이가 틀어지기 시작했어

There's a lot of bad blood between Moon-soo and Dong-soo
ㄴ 문수와 동수 사이에는 나쁜 감정이 깊어

There's still too much bad blood between us
ㄴ 우리 사이엔 아직도 악감이 많아

They are always at each other's throats

› **bleed** lose or shed blood, feel distress
› **barge** move rudely or clumsily

› **illicit** not lawful
› **sour** become disagreeable

ㄴ 그들은 늘 티격태격 이야

They bred bad blood
ㄴ 그들은 원수지간이 됐다

They hate each other like poison
ㄴ 그들은 서로 몹시 싫어해

They left him entirely out of their conversation
ㄴ 그들은 그를 완전히 따돌리고 말상대도 안 해줬다

They seem to keep their own company
ㄴ 그들은 남들과의 접촉을 꺼리는 눈치였어

They started to grow apart
ㄴ 그들의 사이는 점점 벌어지기 시작했다

They went away on their several ways
ㄴ 그들은 각기 다른 길로 사라져 갔다

They've long been at their loggerheads with her over a small plot of land
ㄴ 그들은 그 작은 땅 문제로 그녀와 오랫동안 사이가 좋지 않아

This is a deal-breaker
ㄴ 이러면 같이 일 못해

Those two do not mix well
ㄴ 그 두 사람은 사이가 안 좋아

Try to keep your nose out of the stuff that doesn't concern you
ㄴ 너하고 관계없는 일에 끼어 들지마

We are history
ㄴ 우리 사이는 끝났어

We are not effective in working together
ㄴ 우린 손발이 안 맞아

› **at loggerhead** in disagreement
› **compatible** harmonious

› **deal-breaker** a person who is hard to work with

> (=We are not compatible)
> (=Working with you is like pulling tooth)

We are not on the same wavelengths
　　ㄴ 우린 사고방식이 달라

We don't see eye to eye on anything
　　ㄴ 너랑 나랑은 전혀 맞지 않아

We grew apart from each other over the years
　　ㄴ 세월이 가면서 우리는 차츰 멀어지게 되었어

We see each other very little
　　ㄴ 우리는 서로 거의 안 만나

We should set him straight
　　ㄴ 그 사람 손 좀 봐줘야 할까봐

Why don't you too get together?
　　ㄴ 어째서 너희 둘은 마음이 안 맞니?

Woo-sung is difficult of access(approach)
　　ㄴ 우성인 가까이 하기 어려워

You are all wrong for me
　　ㄴ 너와 난 맞질 않아

You are nothing like me
　　ㄴ 넌 나하곤 딴판이군

> (=You are very different from me)

You are obsessed with(about) it

· **wavelength** distance from crest to crest in the line of advance of a wave
· **access** capability of way of approaching

ㄴ 넌 병적이야

(=It has taken you over)

You are really putting me through the mill
ㄴ 날 정말 못살게 구는군

You are the cause that I was abused
ㄴ 너 때문에 욕먹었잖아

You are the limit
ㄴ 너한테 더 이상은 못 참아

You can't order me around(about)
ㄴ 네가 뭔데 이래라 저래라 하는 거냐

You could have been anyone at all
ㄴ 많고 많은 사람 중에 하필 너냐

You got me up against a wall
ㄴ 날 궁지에 몰고 있군

You have failed me - What have you done to me?
ㄴ 내게 해준 게 뭐야 - 네가 나한테 그럴 수 있니?

You have to clear the air and stop using bad language about each other
ㄴ 넌 긴장상황을 진정시키고 나서 상대방과 서로 욕지거리를 하지 말아야 해

You presume to order me about
ㄴ 네가 뭔데 명령이야

You treat me like a slave
ㄴ 상전이 따로 없군

You're a real thorn in my(the) side(an eyesore)

· **presume**   assume authority without right to do so, take for granted

· **thorn**   sharp spike on a plant or a plant bearing these

ㄴ 넌 정말 눈에 가시로군

정말 싫고 보기 싫은 사람을 '눈에 가시'라고 칭한다. 영어에서는 'Thorn in my side(옆구리에 가시)'나 'Eyesore(눈을 아프게 하는 것)'이라고 한다.

You're better off without him
ㄴ 넌 그가 없는 게 훨씬 나아

You've got another think(thing) coming if you he'll be at your beck and call
ㄴ 그가 네 시키는 대로 할 줄 알았다간 큰 오산이다

Your very face puts me off
ㄴ 네 꼴만 봐도 밥맛 떨어져

Your vindictive, malignant and disgusting mudslinging aimed at defaming me has got to come to an end
ㄴ 나를 망신시키려는 의도에서 내게 대한 너의 그 앙심 깊고, 악의차고, 넌더리나는 중상모략은 끝내야 한다

› **beck** summons
› **vindictive** seeking or meant for revenge

› **mudslinging** using invective against a political opponent

29. 나이   Age

A man is as old as he feels, and a woman as old as she looks
> ↳ 남자의 나이는 느끼기에 달렸고 여자의 나이는 얼굴에 나타난다

> 남자는 나이가 들어도 건강하기만 하고 젊다고 느끼기만 한다면 나이에 구애받지 않지만, 여자는 외모, 즉 겉으로 드러나는 나이에 많은 구애를 받는다. 아무리 화장을 해도 얼굴에 나타나는 나이는 속일 수 없기 때문이다.

A youth without fire is followed by an old age without experience
> ↳ 열정 없는 젊음은 경험 없는 노년이 된다

Age creeps up on us
> ↳ 우린 모르는 사이에 나이를 먹어가고 있어

Age is a bad traveling companion
> ↳ 나이는 나쁜 길동무이다

Age stamped her with lines
> ↳ 그 여자는 나이를 먹어 얼굴에 주름이 잡혔다

Age tells on one's memory
> ↳ 나이를 먹으면 기억력이 둔해져

> =Memory weakens with age

‣ **creep**   crawl, grow over a surface like ivy   ‣ **stamp**   impress with a mark

‣ **companion**   close friend, one of a pair

Although old beyond her years, I felt she was emotionally immature and not ready for marriage

ㄴ 그 여자가 나이에 비해 어른스럽긴 해도 결혼까지는 아직 덜 성숙해 있었다

Although young, he has the makings of a first-class salesman

ㄴ 그는 젊지만 일류 판매원의 자질을 갖추고 있다

An old man is twice a boy

ㄴ 늙으면 아이가 된다더라

At about forty, he was finally evened out

ㄴ 그는 40줄에 들어서서야 제정신을 차렸다

Better children weep than old man

ㄴ 어릴 때의 눈물 난 훈육이 노년의 슬픔보다 낫다(흔한 표현은 아님)

By joining the army late, he was ranked below many men much younger than himself

ㄴ 그는 군에 늦게 가서 자기보다 훨씬 나이 적은 사람들의 졸병노릇을 했다

Chang-soo is now old enough to fend for himself

ㄴ 창수는 충분히 자활할만한 나이지

Chang-soo's father carries off his age well

ㄴ 창수 아버지는 나이가 들어도 정정하시다

Confucius once taught us that males and females should not sit together after they have reached the age of seven

ㄴ 공자님은 남녀가 7세가 되면 같이 앉지 못 한다고 가르치셨다

Don't pick up after children who are old enough to keep their own things in order

ㄴ 자기 물건을 정돈해 놓을만한 나이의 아이들을 위해 뒤치다꺼리 해 주지마

Everybody wants to grow old gracefully

ㄴ 누구나 곱게 나이 먹기를(나이보다 젊어 보이기를) 원한다

› **even out** make or become even

› **fend** ward off(+off)

Gather roses while you may
└ 젊어서 즐겨라

Getting a girl in old age isn't worth the candle
└ 노년에 젊은 색시를 얻어봤자 소용없어

Growing old is like being increasingly penalized for crime you haven't committed
└ 나이를 먹는다는 것은 저지르지도 않은 죄에 대해 점점 가혹한 벌을 받고 있는 것과 같다

Growth for the sake of growth is the ideology of the cancer cell
└ 성장을 위한 성장은 암세포의 논리이다

Growth itself contains the germ of happiness
└ 성장(숙) 그 자체에 행복의 씨앗이 들어있다

He is aging rapidly
└ 그 분 많이 늙으신 것 같아

He is very well despite his age
└ 나이에 불구하고 건강

He saw the elderly man across the street
└ 그는 나이든 남자를 길 건너로 모셔드렸다

(see across＝accompany someone across a dangerous area)

His face is lined with age(suffering)
└ 그의 얼굴은 나이(고생)로 인해 주름 투성이다

He's nearly 70, but he's still going strong
└ 그는 **70**에 가깝지만 아직도 원기 왕성하다

· **penalize** put a penalty on
· **ideology** body of beliefs
· **germ** microorganism, source of rudiment
· **elderly** past middle age

He's quite silly in his old age
> ↳ 그는 나이가 들어 망령이 났어

He's thirty-nine going on forty
> ↳ 그 사람은 서른 아홉 이지만 곧 마흔이 돼

Heavy work in youth is quiet resting in old age
> ↳ 젊어서 고생은 사서도 한다

High school students and older must pay full fare
> ↳ 고교생 이상은 어른 요금입니다

His face is lined with age(suffering)
> ↳ 그의 얼굴은 나이(고생)로 인해 주름 투성이다

His physical wreck at only 40 is a high price for his success in show business
> ↳ 나이가 겨우 40에 몸을 크게 망친 것은 연예계에서의 성공에 대한 값으로는 가혹하다

I am feeling my age - I don't feel my age
> ↳ 요즘 나이가 들어가는걸 느껴 - 요즘 나이를 잊고 살아요

I do want to turn(put) the clock back to my childhood days
> ↳ 정말이지 어린 시절로 되돌아 가고싶다

If we are not foolish young, we are foolish old
> ↳ 젊어서 어리석은 짓을 해보지 않으면 나이를 먹어서 어리석어진다

If you want to stretch out your golden years, getting hitched isn't a bad idea
> ↳ 노후에 오래 살기를 원한다면 결혼하는 것이 좋을 것이다

In his face wrinkles ploughed by time
> ↳ 그의 얼굴은 나이로 인해 주름살 투성이 이다

In the twenty first-century healthy people will live out their natural

---

› **stretch** spread or reach out, become extended without breaking

› **wrinkle** crease or small fold on a surface (as in the skin or in cloth)

lifespan and die of old age
> ↳ 21세기를 맞아 건강한 사람들은 천수를 다하고 노환으로 죽게 될 것이다

It's just a phase that youngsters go through
> ↳ 젊은이들이니까 한때 그러고 마는 거야

Jung-tai looks young, but in reality, he is past fifty
> ↳ 정태가 젊어 보이지만 실은 50을 넘었어

Lean-ness may serve as a health advantage in youth and middle age, but may reduce hardiness in old age
> ↳ 청년기와 중년일 때에 날씬한 것은 건강에 이점이 될 수 있지만 노년에는 저항력을 떨어뜨릴 수도 있다

Most hearing problems in later life are connected to prolonged exposure to loud noises during youth
> ↳ 노년에 생기는 대부분의 난청 문제는 젊었을 때 오랫동안 소음에 노출됨에 연관된다

My friend was getting old then long before his time
> ↳ 친구는 그 때 나이보다 훨씬 겉늙어 있었다

My parents wear their years well
> ↳ 우리 부모님은 연세가 많아도 정정하셔

Nobody can hold their drink as well as they could when they were young
> ↳ 젊었을 때만큼 술을 마시고 견디는 사람은 아무도 없다

Now, she's feeling her age
> ↳ 이제 그 여자는 나이가 들었다는 것을 실감하고 있어

Old age plowed furrows in her face
> ↳ 나이가 그녀의 얼굴에 깊은 주름을 잡아놓았다

Old people these days tend to keep to themselves
> ↳ 요즈음의 노인들은 고독하게 지내게 마련이다

› **hardiness**　ability to withstand adverse conditions

› **expose**　deprive of shelter or protection, subject to light, make known

One is never too old to learn
    ↳ 배우는데 나이가 없다

> 사람은 평생을 배워도 모자라 다는 뜻이다. 요즘은 여러 문화 센터, 인터넷 강좌, 노인대학 등을 통하여 나이가 든 후에도 배움의 길을 가는 사람들이 늘어나고 있다.

Our youth we can have but today
    ↳ 젊음은 쉬 늙는다

Patriotism cuts across all ages and sexes of Korean society
    ↳ 애국심은 한국의 남녀노소를 초월한다

People aged 60 and older who have a certain type of high blood pressure and who are particularly thin face have higher risks of stroke and death
    ↳ 60세 이상인 사람으로서 특정한 종류의 고혈압이 있고 특히 얼굴이 야윈 사람이 더 뇌졸중에 걸리거나 사망할 위험이 더 크다

Regrets are natural property of gray hairs
    ↳ 머리가 희끗희끗해지면 당연히 후회가 따른다

She was already well advanced in years when she began it
    ↳ 그 여자 분이 그 일을 시작했을 때에는 이미 상당히 나이가 들어있었다

She's already over the hill
    ↳ 그 여자는 벌써 나이가 들었어

She's getting a little long in tooth
    ↳ 그 여자가 나이를 먹었거든

She's not much below fifty
    ↳ 그 여자는 쉰 살 가까이 됐어

She's too young to end up in cement city

‣ **stroke**   sudden shock of heart or other organs, act of swinging or   striking, sudden action

↳ 그 여자가 죽기에는 너무 아까운 나이다

Spare when you are young, and spend when you are old
↳ 젊어서 벌고 노후에 써라

Superiors and adults must be honest and upright if subordinates and youth are to be
↳ 윗물이 맑아야 아랫물이 맑다

윗사람의 행동이 아랫사람의 행동을 결정한다. 아이들은 부모의 행동을 따라 하며, 평사원들은 부장급, 사장급 사람들을 본 받기 마련이다. 한국에서는 "윗물이 맑아야 아랫물이 맑다"라고 하며, 영어로는 "The fish always stinks from the head downward 생선은 머리부터 썩는다"라고 하는데, 이는 그리스의 격언에서 기원하였다.

The foolhardy youngster got to close to the edge of the cliff and had to be rescued
↳ 그 무모한 젊은이는 절벽 끝에 너무 가까이 다가갔다가 남들의 구조를 받아야 했다

The longer we live, the more we feel we are like other persons
↳ 나이를 먹을수록 더욱더 자신이 남과 같다는 것을 느끼게 된다

The older generation are respectful of tradition
↳ 나이든 사람들은 전통을 존중한다

The passion of the young are vice in the old
↳ 젊음의 정열이 노년에게는 해가 된다

The sagacity and serenity that comes with maturity are supposed to compensate for the degeneration of the corporeal self
↳ 나이가 들면서 찾아오는 지혜와 온화함은 신체상의 퇴화를 보상해 주게 되어있게 마련이다

▸ **passion** strong feeling especially of anger, love, or desire

▸ **compensate** offset or balance, repay
▸ **corporeal** physical or material

The unsettled and impatient youth was a rotten apple in the barrel
> ↳ 안정되지 못하고 잘 참지 못하는 젊은이는 사회에 악영향을 미쳤다

> 하나가 전체에게 나쁜 영향을 미친다는 말이다. 영어 속담에는 여러 가지가 있는데, 가장 자주 쓰이는 표현은 "One rotten apple spoils the barrel 썩은 사과 하나가 한 통을 썩게 한다"이다. 악한 한 사람이 한 가문, 한 나라를 욕되게 하는 것은 "It is an ill bird that fouls its own nest 자기의 둥지를 더럽히는 새는 나쁜 새이다"로 표현한다.
> (=One scabbed sheep will mar a whole flock)
> (=A hog that's bemired endeavors to bemire others)

The way it's done in Korea is for the younger people offer their seats to the older people
> ↳ 한국에서는 젊은 사람이 나이 든 사람들에게 자리를 양보하는 것이 통례이다

The young man knows the rules, but the old man knows the exceptions
> ↳ 젊은이는 규칙을 알지만 노인은 예외를 안다

The young man went to pieces when the judge said he would have to go to prison
> ↳ 판사가 젊은이를 징역형에 처한다고 하자 그는 정신(자제력)을 잃었다

The younger generation is better prepared
> ↳ 나중 난 뿔이 더 우뚝하다

The youngster has a lot to learn about this world
> ↳ 젊은이는 세상사를 잘 몰라

The youth of a nation are the trustees of prosperity
> ↳ 나라의 젊은이들은 번영의 책임을 진다

They vary in age from 10 to 15

› **scab** protective crust over a sore or wound, worker taking a striker's job

› **bemire** soil with mud or dirt, drag through or sing in mire

↳ 그들의 나이는 **10**살부터 **15**살까지로 다양해

Those who love the young best stay young longest
↳ 젊음을 사랑하는 사람이 가장 길게 젊음을 유지한다

Those youngsters have too much pocket money for their own good
↳ 그 젊은이들에게는 용돈이 너무 많아 탈이다

Though old, he has a spirit
↳ 그가 몸은 늙어도 마음은 젊다

Thousands upon thousands of youngsters set out to be film stars but only a handful make it
↳ 무수한 젊은이들이 일류배우를 지망하지만 성공하는 사람은 불과 소수이다

To be adult is to be alone
↳ 어른이 된다는 것은 고독해진다는 것이다

Understanding and love require a wisdom that comes only with age
↳ 이해와 사랑은 나이를 먹어야만 찾아온다

We are not getting younger
↳ 우린 항상 젊어 있는 게 아냐

We are too young to be scrimping everyday
↳ 젊은 우리가 뭐 그런 걸 쫀쫀하게 그런 걸 아까워할 게 있나

We are young only once
↳ 청춘은 한 번 뿐이다

Well, I mean, death's(ages) something that comes to us all
↳ 죽음(나이 먹음)은 누구에게나 오게 돼 있다 이 말이야

When the nerd asked her age, she was angry and put him in his place
↳ 그 머저리가 그 여자의 나이를 묻자 화를 내면서 나무랐다

With us, once a man over forty loses his own particular job, he's done for
↳ 우리들에게 있어서, 마흔 살이 넘어서 해오던 직업을 잃으면 모든 게 끝이다

› **spirit** life-giving force
› **handful** small amount, one grab of a hand

› **scrimp** economize greatly

Years know more than books
└ 노인의 지혜는 책보다 낫다

You are young man, act like one
└ 젊은이가 젊은이답게 행동해야지

You haven't aged(changed) a bit
└ 전혀 나이를 안 드셨네요(변하지 않으셨네요)

You'll understand your parents with age
└ 나이를 먹으면 부모님을 이해하게 될 거야

Your age is showing
└ 나이는 못 속여

Youth is a stuff will not endure
└ 청춘은 쉬 늙는다

Youth is half the battle
└ 젊음으로 반은 이긴 셈이다

Youth is the time to study wisdom; old is time to practice it
└ 젊어서는 지혜를 배우고 나이가 들어서는 실행할 때다

Youth is when you blame all your troubles on your parents; maturity is when you learn that everything is the fault of the younger generation
└ 젊어서는 모든 잘못을 부모 탓으로 돌리고 나이 들면 젊은이 탓임을 안다

‣ **youth** period between childhood and maturity, young man, youngperson

‣ **wisdom** accumulated learning, good sense

30. 날씨   **Weather**

A dam is a thick bank or wall built to control water and prevent flooding
> ↳ 댐은 수량을 통제하고 홍수를 예방하려는 목적으로 축조한 두터운 둑이나 제방이다

A flash flood watch is in effect
> ↳ 집중호우주의보가 발효중이다

After the storm, comes the calm
> ↳ 비 온 뒤에 땅 굳는다

> 아무리 힘들고 어렵더라고 참고 견디면 좋은 일이 생긴다(An unfavourable situation will eventually change for the better = 계속되는 불행도 참아내다 보면 기회가 온다).

After three hours of snow and rain, the roads were so slushed up that they could not travel
> ↳ 눈비가 온 끝이라 도로가 엉망이 돼서 그들은 길을 갈 수가 없었다

Another storm will leave the wheat flat
> ↳ 폭풍우가 한 번 더 오면 밀이 쓰러질 것이다

Blame this wind!
> ↳ 젠장, 바람이 불다니!

By tracking the eye of a hurricane, forecasters can determine the

---

- **flood**   great flow of water over the land, overwhelming volume
- **bank**   rising ground along a body of water
- **flash**   appear or pass suddenly, instant

speed at which a storm is moving
> ↳ 기상통보관들은 허리케인의 중심점을 추적하여 허리케인의 이동속도를 알 수 있다

Close the door after you, the rain is increasing in force
> ↳ 비가 세차게 내리고있으니 문을 닫고 들어와

Clouds appeared and rain ensued
> ↳ 구름이 끼더니 비가 왔다(ensue는 필연의 결과를 동반한다는 말)

Cloudy with occasional shower likely
> ↳ 구름 끼고 때에 따라 천둥과 구름 예상

Do you think your hat will stay on in this high wind?
> ↳ 이렇게 센바람에 모자가 안 날아갈 것 같으냐?

Do you want to share(use) this umbrella with me?
> ↳ 저와 우산을 같이 쓸까요?

Down came the rain in torrents
> ↳ 비가 억수같이 왔다

Frequent floodings eventually obliterated all traces of the community that used to live there
> ↳ 잦은 홍수 때문에 결국 거기 살던 마을 사람들이 살던 흔적마저 없어져버렸다

Generally the planet is getting warmer as a result of the greenhouse effect
> ↳ 지구는 온실효과 때문에 점점 더워지고 있다

Hot isn't the word. It's scorching
> ↳ 더운 정도가 아니라 지글지글 한다

How it snows(rains)!
> ↳ 눈이(비가) 많이도 오네!

It looks like raining on and off today

· **torrent** rushing stream, tumultuous outburst

· **trace** track, tiny amount or residue

· **scorch** burn the surface of

ㄴ 오늘은 비가 오다가 그치다가 할 것 같다

It might rain, and again it might not
ㄴ 비가 올 것도 같고 안 올 것도 같다

It sure is hot. Don't you know it!
ㄴ 정말 더워. 그래, 네 말대로야!

It's sheeting(pelting, pouring) down outside, hadn't you better wait a few minutes before going out?
ㄴ 밖에 비가 억수로 쏟아지고 있으니 몇 분 기다렸다가 가는 게 어때?

It's the piping hot coffee in cold weather
ㄴ 추운 날씨엔 따뜻한 커피가 최고야

Lots of big trees came crashing down in yesterday's storm
ㄴ 어제 비바람에 많은 큰 나무가 우지끈 쓰러졌다

Luckily all the rice was in before the rain began
ㄴ 다행히 비가 오기 전에 벼를 다 거두어 들였다

My car won't kick over because weather's too cold this morning
ㄴ 오늘아침 날씨가 너무 추워서 시동이 잘 안 걸려

On the hottest days, the heat transfer process works in reverse, so the environment actually heats up our body
ㄴ 가장 더운 날이면 열 전달 과정이 반대로 흐르게 되어서 사실상 주변에 있는 열이 우리의 몸을 뜨겁게 만든다

Rain or shine, he never un-bends
ㄴ 그는 비가 오나 눈이오나 하루도 편히 쉬는 날이 없다

Rains or none, it's nothing to us
ㄴ 비가 오든 안 오든 우리하곤 상관없어

She had just made it to the house when the heavens opened
ㄴ 그 여자는 막 비가 억수로 쏟아질 때 집에 돌아갔다

› **sheeting** material in the form of sheets or suitable for making sheets   › **pour** rain hard, flow or supply copiously

Sleet fell continuously and turned the winding dirt road into a river of slippery mud
> ↳ 진눈깨비가 계속 내려서 구불구불한 비포장도로가 진흙 진창으로 변해버렸다

Southern districts will become hotter the next few days with the higher temperature exaggerated by the heat wave
> ↳ 남부지역은 앞으로 며칠 간 열파로 인해 더욱 기승을 떨치는 고온으로 더 더운 날씨가 될 것이다

Such hot weather in-disposes anyone to work hard
> ↳ 이렇게 더워서는 누구나 일 할 마음이 없어진다

Temperatures range today from the low 1 to the high 15 degrees centigrade
> ↳ 오늘 기온은 최하 섭씨 1도에서 최고 15도까지이다

The coldest weather is yet to come
> ↳ 본격적인 추위는 지금부터 시작이야

The crops were beaten down by heavy rain
> ↳ 큰비가 와서 농작물이 쓰러졌다

The drought has taken its toll, and the population of the country is greatly reduced
> ↳ 가뭄은 아물기 어려운 큰 피해를 남겼고 전국의 인구는 크게 줄었다

The farmers are taking(bringing) the rice in early this year because of clear weather
> ↳ 금년에는 맑은 날씨 덕분에 농민들이 벼를 일찍 수확하고 있다

The fine day added to our pleasure
> ↳ 날씨가 좋아서 더 즐거웠다

The flood water from the storm backed up the pipes for the dirty water

---

‣ **centigrade** Celsius, metric unit used to measure temperature

‣ **population** people or number of people in a country or area

↳ 큰비로 불어난 물이 파이프에 꽉 차서 더러운 물이 안 빠져

The heat didn't decrease its tone in the least
↳ 더위가 조금도 누그러지지 않았어

The heavy overnight snow was attributed to clusters of clouds carrying snow being pushed over the Korean peninsula by a cold front
↳ 밤새 내린 폭설은 한반도에 들이닥친 한랭전선이 동반한 구름 대 때문인 것으로 보인다

The heavy rain spoiled the long-awaited holiday
↳ 비가 와서 모처럼의 휴일을 망쳤어

The heavy snow warning remains in effect for the southwestern regions
↳ 남서부지역에서는 대설주의보가 계속 발효중이다

The pier had been beaten by countless storms and was slowly starting to disintegrate
↳ 그 부두는 무수한 폭풍에 시달려 천천히 붕괴되어갔다

The rain wore away at the stone through time
↳ 세월이 흐르면서 빗물이 돌을 깎아 내렸다

불가능한 일이라도 끊임없이 노력하면 이루어진다는 뜻이다. 물(Dripping)은 끊임없는 성실한 노력을 뜻한다(He that shoots often at last shall hit the mark = 여러 번 쏘는 자는 결국 표적을 맞춘다).

The rainstorm was pelting against the window
↳ 폭풍우가 세차게 유리창을 때리고 있다

The rainstorms have laid all the crops low
↳ 폭풍우로 농작물이 모조리 쓰러졌다

The snow was not so deep and we pushed through
↳ 눈은 그리 깊지 않아서 우리는 헤치고 나아갔지

▸ **pier** support for a bridge span, deck or wharf built out over water, pillar ▸ **disintegrate** break into parts or small bits

The snowstorm was preceeded by a sharp drop in atmospheric pressure
> ↳ 기압이 갑자기 떨어지더니 폭설이 왔다

The storm rained out the game
> ↳ 폭풍우로 게임이 취소됐어

The sun beat down mercilessly on the dry earth
> ↳ 태양이 마른땅에 사정없이 내려 쬐고 있었다

The sun broke through after days of rain
> ↳ 며칠간 비가 오더니 해가 나왔다

The sunshine bodes well for our picnic today
> ↳ 화창한 날씨를 보니 오늘 야유회는 잘 될 것 같다

The temperature sank below the freezing mark today
> ↳ 오늘 기온이 영하로 떨어졌어

The thermometer gave(stood at) 30 degree
> ↳ 온도계가 30도를 가리켰어

The turbulent river, swollen by the heavy rain, rushed down to the sea
> ↳ 큰비로 물이 불어 강물이 요동치며 바다로 흘러 들어갔다

The weather forecast often turns out to be wrong
> ↳ 일기예보는 틀릴 때가 많아

The weather is all we could wish for
> ↳ 날씨가 바랄 나위 없이 좋다

The weather is fine for the time of the year
> ↳ 예년에 비해 날씨가 좋다

They'll offer prayers for rain if the rain keeps off until tomorrow
> ↳ 내일까지 비가 오지 않으면 그들은 기우제를 지낼 것이다

This month is scorching dry, and last month it rained almost everyday. Our weather is feast or famine
> ↳ 이번 달에는 찌는 듯한 가뭄이 계속되고 있고 지난달엔 거의 매일 비

› **thermometer** instrument for measuring temperature

› **turbulent** causing violence or disturbance, marked by agitation or tumult

가 왔다. 비(일광)가 너무 많거나 적어서 탈이다

This shelter is framed to resist any storm
> ↳ 이 피신처는 어떤 폭풍에도 견딜 수 있게 만들어졌다

This warm weather should bring the crops along
> ↳ 따뜻한 날씨 덕분에 농작물이 잘(빨리) 익을 것이다

We had a week of alternate rain and sunshine
> ↳ 일주일 동안 번갈아 비가 왔다 햇볕이 났다 했다

We have a stomachful with this heat
> ↳ 우리는 이 정도 더위는 참아낼 수 있어

We have a sudden frost
> ↳ 꽃샘추위

We have seven degrees of frost today
> ↳ 오늘은 영하 7도

We shall start if it's fine; if not, not
> ↳ 날씨가 좋으면 떠날 것이고 나쁘면 안 떠날 것이다

Weather permitting, we shall set off on our journey as originally planned
> ↳ 날씨만 좋으면 우린 당초 계획대로 여행을 떠날 것이다

We'll have to bear hot weather this summer
> ↳ 올 여름은 더위를 각오해야 해

When it rains, it pours
> ↳ 모든 일은 한꺼번에 닥쳐오게 돼 있어

> 나쁜 일은 한꺼번에 온다. 이럴 때에는 "Adding insult to injury 다친데에 모욕길
> 이 더한다"라고 하거나 "When it rains, it pours 비가 오면 쏟아진다"라고 한다.

Yesterday's storm brought lots of trees to the ground
> ↳ 어제 큰비로 많은 나무가 쓰러졌다

› **frost** freezing temperature, ice crystals on a surface

› **journey** a going from one place to another

31. 남자 & 여자   Male & Female

A guy feels his status is quite literally the true meaning of himself as a man
    ↳ 남자는 자신의 신분과 지위가 자신이 진정한 남자인가를 평가하는 척
      도라고 믿는다

A man is a man, you know
    ↳ 남자는 다 늑대다

A man is as old as he feels, and a woman as old as she looks
    ↳ 남자의 나이는 느끼기에 달렸고 여자의 나이는 얼굴에 나타난다

> 남자는 나이가 들어도 건강하기만 하고 젊다고 느끼기만 한다면 나이에 구애
> 받지 않지만, 여자는 외모, 즉 겉으로 드러나는 나이에 많은 구애를 받는다.
> 아무리 화장을 해도 얼굴에 나타나는 나이는 속일 수 없기 때문이다.

A man's meat is too often a woman's poison
    ↳ 남자에게 득이 되는 것이 흔히 여자에게는 독이 된다

A pessimistic woman can complement an optimistic man, and vise versa
    ↳ 비관적인 여자는 낙관적인 남자를 보충해 주고 그와 반대로 보충해
      줄 수도 있다

A woman only sees what we don't do
    ↳ 여자는 남자가 자기에게 해 주지 않는 것만 따진다

A woman prefers a man without money to money without a man

▸ **literally**   exactly as stated   ▸ **complement**   something that completes

▸ **pessimistic**   inclination to expect the worst   ▸ **vice versa**   with the order reversed

ㄴ 여자는 남자 없는 돈보다는 돈 없는 남자를 택한다

A woman will doubt everything you say except if it compliments herself
ㄴ 여자는 자신에 대한 찬사 외에는 무슨 말을 해도 의심한다

A woman's whole life is a history of the affections
ㄴ 여자의 전 생애는 애정의 역사이다

A woman's work is never done
ㄴ 여자의 일은 끝이 없어

After all he's just a man
ㄴ 뭐라 해도 그는 어엿한 남자다

All the boys in that school are trotting(running) after my daughter
ㄴ 저 학교에 다니는 모든 남학생들이 우리 딸을 졸졸 따라다니고 있다

Although he looks ugly, he is in good with a lot of girls
ㄴ 그의 외모는 볼품 없지만 여자들에게 인기 있어

An-do has been anguishing over his unreturned(unrequited) love for her
ㄴ 안도는 그 여자에 대한 짝사랑으로 번민하고 있다

Brigands demand your money or your life, whereas women require both
ㄴ 산적은 당신의 돈이나 생명을 요구하지만 여자는 그 둘 다를 요구한다

Byung-soo eats out of her palm
ㄴ 병수는 그 여자 시키는 대로 해

Chang-soo is too chicken-shit to go up and talk to her
ㄴ 창수는 너무 소심해서 그녀에게 말을 붙여보지 못하고 있어

Charming young ladies are right up my alley
ㄴ 젊은 여자들 비위 맞추는 게 내 주특기

Confucius once taught us that males and females should not sit together after they have reached the age of seven
ㄴ 공자님은 남녀가 7세가 되면 같이 앉지 못 한다고 가르치셨다

› **unrequited** not making return for or to
› **brigand** bandit

› **alley** narrow passage between buildings, place for bowling

Distant is the relationship between man and woman
> 멀고도 가까운 것이 남녀간의 관계이다

Don't be familiar with that girl
> 저 아가씨에게 치근대지마

Don't forget that old habits die hard and she likes to fool around
> 사람의 버릇은 고쳐지지 않는 법인데 그 여자는 바람기가 있다는 점을 잊지 마라

Don't go snitching to her
> 그 여자에게 고자질하지마

Don't push her to get it done
> 그 여자에게 그 일을 독촉하지 마라

Don't touch a sore point with her
> 그 여자 속 뒤집어놓을 소린 하지 마라

Don't try to reason him out of his obstinacy
> 그의 고집을 꺾으러 하지마

Don't you bigmouth this, but she's going to have a baby
> 소문내지마, 그 여자 아이 가졌어

Duck-soo was out sowing his wild oats last night
> 덕수는 어젯밤 나가서 바람을 피웠어

Each succeeding year stole away something from her beauty
> 연년이 쌓이는 세월 속에 그 여자는 아름다움을 잃어갔다

Ed made tremendous efforts to erase from his mind the fact that she had broken his mind
> 에드는 그녀에게서 입은 상처를 지우려고 무척 노력했다

Even the woman with a roving eye gets short shrift if she goes in for marriage-breaking

---

▸ **familiar** closely acquainted
▸ **habit** usual behavior

▸ **sore** causing pain or distress, severe or intense, angry

↳ 바람기 있는 여자라도 파경에 이르면 잠깐의 참회는 있다

For a man, what he does is what he is

↳ 남자에게는 그가 하는 일이 바로 그 사람이 누구인가를 말해준다

Flatter her a little, and she'll pull in her horns

↳ 그 여자는 조금 주어주면 누그러질 거야

He couldn't work late because his mind kept jumping the track to thinking about the new girl in the office

↳ 그는 사무실에 새로 온 여직원 생각으로 마음이 흔들려 늦게까지 일 할 수 없었다

He did want to get within the wind of her

↳ 그는 그녀의 체취라도 맡을 수 있는 거리에 다가가기를 절실히 원했다

He followed her for three blocks, and then got the slip

↳ 그가 그 여자를 세 구획까지 쫓아간 다음 놓쳐버렸다

He is just not performing but she's terrific at her job

↳ 그는 자기 일은 제대로 못해내고 있지만 그 여자는 자신의 일을 완벽 하게 해내고 있다

He keeps paying blackmail to a woman who has something on him

↳ 그는 자신의 약점을 쥐고 있는 여자에게 계속 돈을 갈취 당하고 있어

Hee-jung is one of the best girls going

↳ 희정인 요즘 보기 드문 아가씨

Her chastity remains in a question

↳ 그 여자가 정절을 지켰는지는 의문시된다

I don't feel drawn toward her

↳ 그 여자에게는 매력을 못 느끼겠어

I don't want to unload her

↳ 그녀를 떼어버리고 싶지 않아

› **chaste** abstaining from all or unlawful sexual relations, modest or decent, severely simple

I hope to tell you she's a knockout
↳ 말이야 바로 말이지 그 여자 끝내주는 미인이야

I know you put a bun in her oven
↳ 네가 그 여자에게 임신시킨걸 알고있어

I saw the man himself
↳ 바로 그 남자를 보았다니까

If she said something, he was sure to say another
↳ 그녀가 무슨 말만하면 그가 꼭 반대한다

In his youth, he excited some admiration among the girls
↳ 그도 젊었을 때 처녀들한테 인기가 있었다

It comes from a girl of twenty who's living in a fool's paradise
↳ 그건 20대 처녀의 헛된 기대에서 온다

It's a woman's duty to provide for the inner man, and a man's duty to provide for the outer woman
↳ 남자의 속을 깊게 하는 것은 여자의 할 일이고 여자의 겉모습을 꾸며주는 것은 남자의 할 일이다

It's a woman's privilege to change her mind
↳ 변하는 게 여자의 마음 아니겠어

우리나라 속담 중에 '여자의 마음은 갈대'라는 말이 있다. 여자가 변덕이 심하다는 뜻이다. 영어 속담 중에도 비슷한 'A woman is a weathercock'라는 표현이 있다. 'Weathercock'은 지붕 위에서 풍향에 따라 움직이는 닭 모양의 풍향계를 뜻한다. 풍향에 따라 시시각각 변하는 것을 비유한 표현이다.

Love is all in all to woman
↳ 여자에게는 사랑이 전부이다

› **bun** sweet biscuit or roll
› **admire** have high regard for

› **weathercock** weather vane shaped like a rooster

Man's hardheartedness is utterly disarmed by the tears of a woman
> ↳ 여자의 눈물에는 장부의 철석같은 간장도 녹는다

Many male superintendents consider that it is not acceptable for women to assume leadership roles
> ↳ 남자 관리자들은 여성이 관리자 역할을 맡는 것을 허용할 수 없다고 여긴다

Many women have home ties
> ↳ 많은 여자들은 가정에 묶여있다

Men are prone to treat women as inferiors
> ↳ 남자는 여자를 열등한 사람으로 다루기 일쑤다

Mi-gyung intoxicated him with her smiling eyes
> ↳ 미경인 눈웃음으로 그를 녹였어

Most likely, she's in her flowers(menses)=She seems to have a little visitor
> ↳ 그 여자는 아마 생리중인가 봐

Myung-soo had to mess her face up then
> ↳ 그때 명수는 그 여자를 한방 때려줄 수밖에 없었어

No is no negative in a woman's mouth
> ↳ 여자의 거절은 거절이 아니다

Not only does a guy live through his work, his work is who he is
> ↳ 남성은 그의 일로서 사는 것일 뿐 아니라 그의 일 자체가 그 사람이 어떤 사람인가를 말해준다

Put a private detective on her to see if she's meeting another man
> ↳ 그 여자가 다른 사람을 만나고 다니는지 탐정을 붙여봐라

Quite a few women have relatively painless births, but most found it an extremely painful experience
> ↳ 많은 여성들이 상대적인 무통 분만을 하지만 그래도 매우 고통스러운 것으로 밝혀졌다

- **role** part to play, function
- **intoxicate** make drunk

- **mense** monthly discharge of blood from the uterus(=menstruation)

She is known to as exercising female power over that matter
> ↳ 그 여자는 그 일에 대하여 치맛바람을 발휘하고 있는 것으로 알려져 있다

She keeps turning up like a bad penny
> ↳ 꼴도 보기 싫은 그 여자가 자꾸만 나타난단 말이야

She was trying to come on to me, but I found her unlucky
> ↳ 그 여자가 날 유혹하러 했지만 불쾌한 느낌이 들었어

She won't give you a tumble
> ↳ 그 여잔 널 거들떠보지도 않을 거야

She's gone six month
> ↳ 그 여잔 임신 6개월

She's got a bun in her oven
> ↳ 그 여자 아이 가졌어

Sook-hee doesn't give her heart to just anyone
> ↳ 숙희는 아무에게나 마음을 주는 여자가 아니다

Stop going after girls and get a proper job
> ↳ 여자들 꽁무니만 쫓아다니는 것 그만하고 제대로 된 직장을 찾아라

Summer and fall slowly wore away as she waited for his return
> ↳ 그녀가 그의 돌아오기를 기다리고 있을 동안 여름과 겨울이 슬며시 지나갔다

Temptations, unlike opportunities, will always give you second chances
> ↳ 기회와는 달리 유혹은 항상 두 번째 기회를 준다

That chick is putty in my hands
> ↳ 그 아가씨는 내가 시키는 대로 해

That ugly girl is as dumb as she looks
> ↳ 저 못난 아가씨가 꼴값하고 있군

That's a girl for you

› **temptation** act of tempting, something that tempts	› **chick** girl, young chicken or bird
	› **putty** doughlike cement

ㄴ 여자 애들은 다 그런 거야

That's he
ㄴ 바로 저 남자야

The beginning of understanding men is understanding how men act at work
ㄴ 남자를 이해하는 것은 남자가 직장에서 어떻게 행동하는가를 이해할 때 시작된다

The best partners are those who match your level
ㄴ 가장 좋은 짝은 자기수준에 맞는 사람이다

The scramble to win his heart stems from their judgement
ㄴ 그들이 앞다투어 그의 마음을 끌고싶어 하는 것은 그들의 판단에서 비롯된다

The way I see it, he's just playing hard
ㄴ 내가 보기에 그는 그냥 통겨 보는 거야

There are men and men
ㄴ 남자면 다 남자인줄 아나

There must be Mr. Right out there for you
ㄴ 네게 딱 맞는 남자가 어딘가에 있을 거야

There should be a law against girls going around half-naked
ㄴ 여자들이 반쯤 벗은 모양으로 돌아다녀서는 안 돼

Vanity is a common vice to woman
ㄴ 여자에게는 허영이 따르게 마련이다

Virtue is more important than anything else for a woman
ㄴ 도둑의 때는 벗어도 화냥질 때는 못 벗는다

We've been over this
ㄴ 우린 이젠 끝난 일

What was the result of your blind date(marriage meeting)?

› **scramble** clamber clumsily around, struggle for possession of something, mix together

› **stem** derive, make progress against

ㄴ 너 선 본 결과가 어떻게 되었니?

What's a man without competency, what's a woman without looks
ㄴ 남자가 내세울 건 능력, 여자가 내세울 건 미모뿐이다

When all is said and done, she is a woman
ㄴ 뭐니뭐니해도 그 여자는 여자다운 여자다

When I'm done with my crying, I'm done with you
ㄴ 실컷 울고 나서 너와 헤어질 거다

When it comes to acting as a go-between, he's up with professionals
ㄴ 중매서는 일이라면 그가 프로급이다

Who's the light bulb over there?
ㄴ 저기 있는 임신한 여자는 누구니?

Woman as she is, she is equal to a man
ㄴ 여자지만 남자에 못지 않아

Woman is woman
ㄴ 여자는 역시 여자일 뿐이야

Women are victims of green-eyed-monster
ㄴ 여성은 질투심에 사로잡히기 쉬워

Women have many faults, but the worst of them all is that they are too pleased with themselves and take too little pains to please the men
ㄴ 여자들에게는 많은 결함이 있는데 그 중에서도 가장 나쁜 것은 자신들에게 너무 만족해하고 남자들을 위해서 거의 아무 수고도 하지 않는다는 점이다

You are just like all the other men
ㄴ 당신도 다른 남자들과 똑 같군

You are the man(real man, man's man)
ㄴ 넌 정말 사내다운 사내구나

- **go-between** matchmaker
- **light bulb** rounded or pear-shaped object that lights up when connected to electricity

You are too much to take
> ㄴ 당신은 내게 너무 과분해

You can suit yourself about leaving or staying
> ㄴ 떠나든 말든 맘대로 해

You can't ride on his coattail all the time
> ㄴ 넌 늘 그의 옷자락만 잡고(그의 힘만 믿고) 있을 수는 없잖아

You can't run away from me
> ㄴ 날 버리고 떠나면 안돼요

You have a good taste in women
> ㄴ 넌 여자 보는 눈이 있구나

You'd better get out of her face
> ㄴ 그녀를 성가시게 하지마

You'll be history if you have a fling at other guys
> ㄴ 다른 남자들하고 바람을 피웠다간 끝장인줄 알아

You'll miss her more than you can say
> ㄴ 넌 그 여자가 없어지면 몹시 서운하겠구나

· **fling** move brusquely, throw, attempt, period
of self-indulgence

· **more than one can say** very much

32. 노력 Effort

All my efforts to help him went down the drain
ㄴ 그를 도우려던 나의 모든 노력은 허사가 됐다

All their efforts went for nothing
ㄴ 그 사람들의 노력은 수포로 돌아갔다

Bong-soo kept his nose to the grindstone, but all he got for his effort was a kick in the teeth(pants)
ㄴ 봉수는 뼈빠지게 일했지만 노력에 대한 칭찬은커녕 욕만 먹었다

Bong-doo pulled out all the stops
ㄴ 우린 전력을 다했다

Ed made tremendous efforts to erase from his mind the fact that she had broken his mind
ㄴ 에드는 그녀에게서 입은 상처를 지우려고 무척 노력했다

Genius is an infinite capacity for taking pains
ㄴ 천재는 무한히 노력할 수 있는 능력에서 온다

He hopes that all your efforts don't go for naught(nothing)
ㄴ 그는 너의 노력이 성공하기를 바라고 있어

He tried to lay his future course
ㄴ 그는 장래에 나아갈 길을 위해 노력했다

Hurling their arms and legs about wildly, they kept afloat but wasted much effort

---

· **grindstone** stone used in grinding
· **hurl** throw with violence

ㄴ 그들은 물 속에서 손발을 마구 허우적거리면서 가라앉지는 않았지만 힘이 많이 소진됐다

I'll try to make amends

ㄴ 만회하려고 노력할 꺼야

Instead of wasting energy in extended partisan confrontation, they should join in efforts to tackle the many crucial issues pending

ㄴ 그들은 더 이상 당파간 대결대신 많은 중요 현안들을 처리하는 데 합심해 노력해 나가야 한다

It takes more brain and effort to make out the income-tax form than it does to make the income

ㄴ 소득을 올리는 것 보다 소득세 신고용지를 작성하는데 더 머리와 노력을 요한다

Just try to buddy up to her and pretend you are interested in what she's doing

ㄴ 그저 그 여자와 친해지도록 노력하고 그 여자가 하는 일에 관심 있는 척 해

Many huge monuments built over some people's graves in an effort to achieve some degree of immortal presence long after their death are disgusting

ㄴ 죽은 지 오랜 후에도 상당한 정도로 불멸의 존재로 인식됨을 달성해 보려는 시도에서 무덤에 거대한 많은 비석들을 세우는 것은 역겹다

My efforts were rewarded with success

ㄴ 노력한 덕분에 성공했어

No sweet without sweat

ㄴ 땀 없이 단 맛을 볼 수 없다

(=You don't get something for nothing)

· **amend** improve, alter in writing

· **partisan** adherent, guerrilla

· **confront** oppose or face

· **pending** while awaiting, not yet decided

No work can be done without concentration and self-sacrifice and toil and doubt
ㄴ 집중, 자기희생, 수고, 의심이 없이는 아무 일도 되지 않는다

None of these unproductive debates between the ruling and opposition camps is helpful to their efforts to recover confidence of voters
ㄴ 여야간의 이러한 비생산적인 논쟁은 그들이 유권자들의 신뢰를 회복 하려고 기울이는 노력에 전혀 도움이 되지 않는다

Nothing great in the world has been accomplished without passion
ㄴ 위대한 일 치고 열정 없이 이루어진 일없다

(=Nothing great was ever achieved without enthusiasm)

Nothing great is easy
ㄴ 위대한 일 치고 쉬운 일이 없다

Nothing is worth having that can't be gained without labor
ㄴ 노력 없이 얻는 것 치고 값진 일없다

Nothing venture, nothing gain
ㄴ 호랑이 굴에 들어가야 호랑일 잡는다

노력의 중요성을 말해주는 속담이다. 무슨 일이든지 용기를 가지고 적극적으 로 부딪혀야 좋은 결과를 볼 수 있다.

Only after week's of vain efforts, did the right ideas occur to me
ㄴ 몇 주일동안 헛된 노력을 한 후에야 겨우 적절한 생각이 떠올랐다

Our scientists are trying to beat them to the punch

› **debate** discuss a question by argument | › **enthusiasm** strong excitement of feeling or its cause

↳ 우리의 과학자들은 선수를 치려고 노력하고 있어

People of average intelligence who persevere often carry the day over bright people who lack staying power

↳ 보통의 머리이면서도 끝까지 노력하는 사람이 머리만 좋고 지구력이 없는 사람을 제치고 승리하는 경우가 흔히 있다

Sang-soo strained every nerve to win the game

↳ 상수는 경기에 이기려고 온갖 노력을 다 했다

She has a field day trying to learn all the new programs

↳ 그 여자는 새 프로그램을 익히려는 노력이 대단하다

Success has crowned his efforts

↳ 그의 노력은 성과를 거두었어

Sung-ho did the little he could

↳ 성호는 미력하나마 최선을 다했다

Sung-soo can make the basketball team if he puts his back to it

↳ 성수는 노력만 하면 농구팀에 낄 수 있어

That only occurs when you put your heart into it

↳ 정성을 다할 때 얘기지

That's quite a good effort

↳ 잘된 일이군(노력한 보람이 있을 때)

The chairman made tremendous efforts to keep the issue from getting discursive, penetrating to the heart of the matter at hand

↳ 사회자는 논의가 옆으로 나가는 것을 막으면서 문제의 핵심을 뚫을 수 있도록 무한히 애를 썼다

The conglomerate pledged to speed up its downsizing efforts during recent financial jitters caused by the liquid problem of its financial arm

↳ 그 기업그룹은 금융계열사의 유동성 문제로 야기된 최근의 자금 불안감

> ▸ **conglomerate** made up of diverse parts, form into a mass
>
> ▸ **downsize** reduce in size
> ▸ **jitter** extreme nervousness

이 팽배해진 가운데 조직의 축소개편 노력을 가속시킬 것을 다짐했다

The government and the ruling party argue that the increasing debt has stemmed from their efforts to clean up the problems created under the rule of past administration
> ㄴ 정부와 여당은 늘어나는 빚을 전 정권이 저지른 문제점들을 정리해 나가는 노력에서 생겨난 것이라고 주장한다

The police vice squad have made efforts to arrest girls who walk the streets so that they may cut down on prostitution
> ㄴ 경찰의 풍기사범 단속반은 매춘을 단속하기 위해 거리의 여자들을 잡아들이는데 노력을 기울여왔다

The ruling and opposition parties are making all-out efforts to win a majority in the next general elections
> ㄴ 여야는 오는 총선에서 다수의석당의 위치를 확보하려고 전면적인 노력을 기울이고 있다

There are two ways of rising in the world, either by your own industry or by the folly of others
> ㄴ 출세에는 두 가지 방법이 있는데 하나는 자신의 노력이고 하나는 다른 사람의 바보짓이다

These ridiculers are usually those who are not willing to put the necessary effort into learning English
> ㄴ 이와 같이 비웃는 사람들은 대개 영어를 배우는데 필요한 노력을 기울이지 않는 사람들이다

This is worthy of your time and effort
> ㄴ 이건 승부를 걸어 볼만한 일이야

To see what is in front of one's nose requires a constant struggle
> ㄴ 당신의 코앞에 있는 것을 보는데도 끊임없는 노력이 필요하다

› **administration** process of managing, persons responsible for managing   › **folly** foolishness, something foolish

Toil conquers everything
↳ 노력으로 안 되는 일이 없다

We should further try to sharpen our competitive edge
↳ 우리는 경쟁력을 강화시키기 위해 더 한층 노력해야 한다

We should labor for better future
↳ 우린 보다 나은 미래를 위해 노력해야 해

We went all out but it was not appreciated
↳ 우린 전력을 다 했지만 알아주지 않더군

Wipe out all thought of it and have a another try
↳ 그 생각은 모두 잊어버리고 다시 한 번 노력해 봐

Without addressing these humanitarian issues, no genuine progress is expected in the effort for reconciliation
↳ 이들 인도적인 문제들을 외면하고서는 화해를 위한 노력에서 아무런 진전도 기대할 수 없다

Why are always putting his efforts down?
↳ 넌 어째서 그의 노력을 경시하니?

You can't let up on your efforts to compete with other firms
↳ 다른 회사와의 경쟁을 위한 노력을 소홀히 해서는 안 돼

You must sow before you can reap
↳ 노력 없이 성과 없어

> 직역하면 "뿌린 대로 거둔다"이다. 씨를 뿌리는 노력이 있어야 결과도 있다는 뜻이다. "Every herring must hang by its own gill＝콩 심은데 콩 나고, 팥 심은데 팥 난다"와도 일맥상통한다.

Your hard work will someday come to fruition

› **reap** cut or clear with a scythe or machine | › **gill** organ of a fish for obtaining oxygen from water

ㄴ 너의 노력 한 만큼의 결실은 언젠가 꼭 올 거야

Your sincere efforts made the recent fund-raising activity successful one

ㄴ 귀하의 진실한 노고로 최근의 모금운동은 성공적인 결과를 보게 되었습니다

› **fund-raising** ask for and collect fund

Your sincere efforts made the recent fund-raising activity successful one.

33. 농담   Jokes

A rich man's joke is always funny
ㄴ 부자의 농담은 언제나 재미있다(웃어주어야 하니까)

All hell broke loose All of a sudden, he cracked up everybody with a joke
ㄴ 그는 갑자기 농담 한 마디로 모든 사람을 웃겼다

Clumsy jesting is no joke
ㄴ 서툰 농담은 농담이 아니다

Did I miss a joke?
ㄴ 혹시 농담 아냐?

Don't turn it off with a joke
ㄴ 농담으로 얼버무리지마

Don't you take a joke?
ㄴ 농담도 못하나?

I don't mean what I say
ㄴ 농담이야

I know you have a stock of jokes
ㄴ 너 농담 잘 하는 거 알고있지

I took a joke
ㄴ 조롱 당하고도 참았지

I'm not even close to kidding
ㄴ 난 지금 장난할 기분 아냐

- **clumsy** lacking dexterity, nimbleness, or grace, tactless
- **jest** witty remark
- **kidding** deceive as a joke, tease

It's a big joke
  ㄴ 정말 웃기는 일이지

Many a true word is spoken in jest
    ㄴ 수많은 진담이 농담으로 말해진다

> 사자성어 중에 '언중유골'이라는 성어가 있다. 사람의 감정을 상하게 할 수도 있는 진실을 농담으로 말하는 것이 인간 관계를 유연하게 이끌어 나가는 지혜이다.

She made a joke and it cleared the air between them
    ㄴ 그 여자가 농담을 하자 그들 사이의 오해가 풀렸다

Smile when you say that
    ㄴ 농담이겠지

The joke was on you
    ㄴ 그 농담은 너를 두고 한 것이었어

The truest jests sound worst in guilty ears
    ㄴ 진실한 농담이 죄 있는 사람에게는 가장 귀에 거슬린다

There's many a true word said in jest
    ㄴ 농담 속이 진실 있다

> 사자성어 중에 '언중유골'이라는 성어가 있다. 사람의 감정을 상하게 할 수도 있는 진실을 농담으로 말하는 것이 인간 관계를 유연하게 이끌어 나가는 지혜이다.

When Sung-min was furious at Sung-soo, Sung-soo cracked a joke, and it cleared the air between them
    ㄴ 성민이가 성수에게 몹시 화를 내자 성수가 농담을 꺼내어 분위기를 확 바꿔버렸어

› **guilt** fact of having committed an offense, feeling of responsibility for offenses

Work in a few jokes when you are preparing your speech
↳ 연설을 준비할 때 농담 몇 마디를 넣어라

Your continual goofing off has got past a joke
↳ 너의 계속되는 농땡이는 그냥 넘어갈 일이 아냐

Your jokes would not go over with that type of audience
↳ 너의 농담이 그런 타입의 청중에게는 먹혀들지 않을 거야

You must not jest about serious problems
↳ 진지한 문제를 농으로 돌려선 안 돼

· **goof off**   waste time(+off or around),
blunder

34. 농업   Agriculture

A successful farm must produce food over and above what's necessary for basic requirements
> ↳ 성공적인 농가가 되려면 기본적인 필요량 이상의 식량을 생산해야 한다

After the long hot dry summer, the soil is cracking up
> ↳ 장기간 비가 안 오는 여름 날씨에 땅이 갈라지고 있다

Although Pyung-soo put much fertilizer on his field, his vegetable crop has failed
> ↳ 평수는 밭에 비료를 두 배 주었음에도 불구하고 채소 농사는 흉작이었다

An acre is the amount of land a yoke of oxen can plow in one day
> ↳ 에이커는 황소 두 필이 하루에 갈 수 있는 밭의 넓이이다

Another storm will leave the wheat flat
> ↳ 폭풍우가 한번 더 오면 밀이 쓰러질 것이다

Bananas that are to be shipped a long way are picked when they are green
> ↳ 멀리 보낼 바나나는 덜 익었을 때 수확한다

Barley does well after beans
> ↳ 콩을 심은 뒤에는 보리가 잘 돼

Drought and pestilence dogged the poor farmers' footsteps
> ↳ 가뭄과 역병이 불쌍한 농민들을 떠나지 않았다

Even after a bad harvest there must be sowing
> ↳ 수확이 흉작이었더라도 씨는 뿌려야한다

› **fertilizer** something added to fertilize the soil   › **oxen** bovine mammal and especially a castrated bull

Luckily all the rice was in before the rain began
ㄴ 다행히 비가 오기 전에 벼를 다 거두어 들였다

Many farmers are pouring away gallons of milk that has gone sour everyday
ㄴ 많은 농장에서 매일 다량의 쉬어진 우유를 쏟아버린다

Once the safety of gene-engineered food is fully proven, a revolutionary chance can be expected in the global agricultural production
ㄴ 유전자 조작식품의 안전성이 증명되기만 하면 세계 농업생산의 혁명적 변동을 기대할 수 있게 된다

Pears ripen signaling the advance of harvest season
ㄴ 배는 수확기가 왔음을 알리면서 익어간다

Rice has been turned golden yellow
ㄴ 벼가 황금빛으로 물들었다

Slash-and-burn farmers work one farm of land until it is exhausted, then move on to virgin soil and start again
ㄴ 화전민들은 땅의 힘이 고갈될 때까지 농사를 짓다가 또 새로운 땅으로 이동하여 다시 시작한다

The bad rice crop this year puts it at a premium
ㄴ 올해 벼 흉작으로 쌀값이 올랐어

The crops are coming on nicely
ㄴ 농사 작황은 좋아

The crops were beaten down by heavy rain
ㄴ 큰비가 와서 농작물이 쓰러졌다

The farmer has strived to slip bonds of earth in vain
ㄴ 그 농부는 땅의 속박에서 벗어나려고 몸부림 쳤으나 허사였다

The farmers are taking(bringing) the rice in early this year because of clear weather

---

› **virgin** natural and unspoiled

› **premium** bonus, sum over the stated value, sum paid for insurance, high value

ㄴ 금년에는 맑은 날씨 덕분에 농민들이 벼를 일찍 수확하고 있다

The farmers have a way of trapping locusts at night, using bright lights

ㄴ 농부들은 밝은 등불을 이용하여 밤에 메뚜기들을 잡는법을 잘 알고 있다

The rainstorms have laid all the crops low

ㄴ 폭풍우로 농작물이 모조리 쓰러졌다

The rice didn't crop well this year

ㄴ 금년 벼농사는 흉작이다

(=The rice crop has failed this year)

The rice is coming on this year

ㄴ 올해 벼 작황이 좋다(**His business came on splendidly** 그의 사업은 잘 됐어)

The woman was looking forlornly at her gutted roofless house and the farmer pointed at his seared seed potatoes

ㄴ 여인은 지붕이 다 타버린 집을 쓸쓸히 쳐다보고 있었고 농부는 그을린 씨감자를 가리켰다

They ploughed in(back) loose leaves of vegetable crop to enrich the soil

ㄴ 그들은 땅을 걸게 하려고 흩어진 채소 잎사귀들을 땅속으로 도로 들어가게 갈아엎었다

This warm weather should bring the crops along

ㄴ 따뜻한 날씨 덕분에 농작물이 잘(빨리) 익을 것이다

This year's rice crop is up on the last year's

ㄴ 금년 벼농사는 작년 수준을 웃돈다

We must enact necessary policies to aid poor farmers who barely eke out an existence farming

---

- **forlorn** deserted, wretched
- **sear** scorch

- **enact** make into law, act out
- **eke out** barely gain with effort

ㄴ 우리는 농사로 근근히 생계를 이어가는 농민들을 도우는 데에 필요한
정책을 수립해야 한다

**While the soil is nice and soft after the rain, let's prick out some
tomato plants that we have grown from seed**

ㄴ 비 온 뒤에 땅이 좋고 부드러울 때에 우리가 종자를 뿌려 기른 토마
토 모종을 옮겨 심자

You could do better with this chisel

ㄴ 이 끌을 쓰면 더 나을텐데

**You shouldn't burn out your field by planting the same crop every
year for many years**

ㄴ 매년 같은 작물을 반복 경작해서 지력을 고갈시켜서는 안 돼

› **prick**   tear or small wound made by a
point, something sharp or pointed

› **chisel**   sharp-edged metal tool

35. 능력   **Ability**

A bad workman always blames his tools
> ㄴ 선무당이 장고 나무란다

> 서투른 무당이 장구 탓만 하듯 기술이 부족한 자가 자기 기술의 미숙함을 반성하지 않고 도구만 나쁘다고 해봐야 아무런 진전이 없다. 훌륭한 기술자는 일이 잘못되면 그 책임을 자신에게 돌리는 사람이다.

A bad workman quarrels with the man who calls him that
> ㄴ 서툰 일꾼은 자기더러 서툰 일꾼이라고 부르는 사람과 다툰다

> 자신의 약점을 인정하지 못하고, 고치려고 하지 않는 발전이 없는 사람을 일컫는 말이다. 흔히 "똥 묻은 개가 겨 묻은 개 나무란다"라는 속담을 많이 쓰며 이는 영어에서는 "The pot calls the kettle black = 냄비가 주전자보고 검다고 한다"라고 한다.

A dog is not considered good because of his barking, but a man is because of his ability to talk
> ㄴ 잘 짖는다고 해서 훌륭한 개가 아니지만, 말 잘하는 사람은 훌륭한 사람으로 대우받는다

A good tongue is a good weapon
> ㄴ 말 잘 하는 것도 훌륭한 무기다

› **workman**   laboring man, employed man

Ability varies from person to person
> 사람에 따라 능력은 천차만별

Although young, he has the makings of a first-class salesman
> 그는 젊지만 일류 판매원의 자질을 갖추고 있다

An-do can do 6,000 keystrokes an hour
> 안도는 시간당 6,000타를 쳐

An-do has it all together. Besides, he's got what it takes
> 안도는 건강하고 건전해요. 게다가 능(실 · 재)력도 있고요

다재 다능한 사람을 가리켜 '팔방미인'이라고 한다. 이를 번역한다면 'man of many talents = 다재 다능한 사람'정도가 된다.

An-do has the Midas touch
> 안도의 손에만 가면 신품 같이 돼(안 되는 일이 없어)

Are you going to put him through the paces?
> 그의 능력을 시험해보려는 거냐?

Art students who imitate the techniques of master artists too well may lose their own creative ability
> 예술을 공부하는 학생들이 스승이 되는 예술가의 기술을 너무 잘 모방하면 자기들 자신의 창의력을 잃을 수 있다

Bong-soo has a number of irons in the fire, and manages to keep all of them hot
> 봉수는 여러 가지 일을 하고 있는데 다 잘 해나가고 있다

Calligraphy comes naturally to him
> 그의 글씨는 타고났어

Chan-ho is riding high
> 찬호는 물이 올랐어

› **talent** natural mental, creative, or artistic ability

› **calligraphy** beautiful penmanship

(=Chan-ho is number one these days)
(=Chan-ho is on top of the world)
(=Chan-ho is above the competition)

Chang-soo is a man of fair words
> ↳ 창수는 말주변이 좋아

Deny a strong man his due, and he'll take all he can get
> ↳ 실력자에게는 그의 몫을 주지 않더라도 그가 취할 수 있는 것은 모두 취한다

Education is the ability to listen to almost anything without losing your temper or self-confidence
> ↳ 교육이란 화내지 않고 자신감을 잃지 않으며 거의 모든 것을 경청하는 능력이다

Elephants have an ability to emit and hear sounds that are below the thresh-hold of human hearing
> ↳ 코끼리는 인간의 청각한계 아래에 있는 소리를 내고 듣는 능력을 가지고 있다

Even the expert can fall into the trap of ignoring evidence that contradicts his or her own intellectual performance
> ↳ 심지어 전문가조차도 자신의 지적인 수행능력에 배치되는 증거를 무시하는 함정에 빠질 수 있다

자신의 전문분야라고 해도 사람이면 실수도 할 수 있다는 말이다. 흔히 "원숭이도 나무에서 떨어진다"는 표현을 쓰고, 이는 영어 속담으로는 "Even Homer sometimes nods"라고 한다. 'Homer'는 기원전에 'Illiad'와 'Odyssey'를 쓴 유명한 그리스의 시인이다. 이런 사람도 가끔씩은 존다는 뜻이다.

Exposed topsoil can lose its ability to support plant growth and to hold moisture

---

· **deny**   declare untrue, disavow, refuse to grant

· **emit**   give off or out
· **threshold**   beginning stage

ㄴ 노출된 표토는 식물의 성장을 도와줄 능력과 습기를 머금는 능력을 잃게된다

Genius is an infinite capacity for taking pains
ㄴ 천재는 무한히 노력할 수 있는 능력에서 온다

Genius is the ability to put into effect what's in his(one's) mind
ㄴ 천재는 마음속에 있는 것을 실행하는 능력이다

He can barely read and write
ㄴ 그는 거의 읽고 쓸 줄 몰라

He has a long way to go
ㄴ 그의 실(능)력은 아직 멀었어

He is up with professionals
ㄴ 그는 프로급 솜씨야

He never lost the common touch
ㄴ 그는 일반대중들의 생각을 읽는 감각을 잃는 적이 없어

He now feels his legs
ㄴ 그는 이제 그의 능력을 가늠할 수 있게 됐어

He scarcely knows his letters
ㄴ 그는 낫 놓고 기역자도 몰라

His parents will be riding on his coattails for the rest of their life
ㄴ 그 사람 능력 덕분에 그의 부모는 앞으로 호강하겠군

His reputation bears no proportion to his ability
ㄴ 그의 평판이 그의 능력하고는 맞지 않아

Jin-ho is natural
ㄴ 진호는 타고났어

Luck always comes to those who believe their ability and cope with difficulties

---

· **reputation** one's character or public esteem
· **cope** deal with difficulties

ㄴ 행운은 항상 자신의 능력을 의심하지 않고 어려움에 맞서 가는 사람에게 찾아온다

Most human beings go through life only partially aware of the full range of their abilities

ㄴ 대부분의 사람들은 자신들이 가진 능력 전체범위의 일부분만 인식한 채 인생을 살아간다

Natural barriers to equality begin with the unequal distribution of natural abilities

ㄴ 평등에 장애가 되는 원초적인 장벽은 재능이 불균등하게 분배되는데서 시작된다

Neuron is a special cell in the body that is capable of sending along messages that represent feelings and commands to muscles

ㄴ 뉴런은 체내의 특수세포로서 감정을 표현하거나 근육에게 명령하는 메시지를 전달하는 능력이 있다

Our increased knowledge and skill may augment our capacity for evil if our purposes are unwise

ㄴ 우리의 목적이 어리석다면 우리에게 늘어난 지식과 기술이 나쁜 일에 대처할 능력을 증가시킬 수 있다

Reverend King had the unique ability to exhilarate congregation with gentle but electrifying speeches

ㄴ 킹 목사는 부드럽지만 깜짝 놀라게 하는 연설로 군중들의 기분을 들뜨게 하는 특별한 능력을 가지고 있었다

She can do 3,000 strokes an hour

ㄴ 그 여자는 한 시간에 **3,000**타를 친다

Sometimes a talent may lie inactive for years before it is awaken

ㄴ 어떤 재능은 가만히 있다가 깨어나는 경우가 흔히 있다

Strike a spark out of him

ㄴ 그 사람 재능을 발휘시켜 봐(중요한 일을 맡겨봐)

· **augment** enlarge or increase
· **spark** tiny hot and glowing particle, smallest beginning or germ, visible electrical discharge

Suck-ho is master of English
ㄴ 석호는 영어가 자유자재

Tailor your desire to the measure of your abilities
ㄴ 능력에 맞게 소망을 가져라

That incubus of debt will greatly hinder his ability to perform his duty
ㄴ 그 빚이라는 부담이 그의 직무수행에 큰 장애물이 되고 있다

The opportunity gave vent to her genius, which might have been consigned to oblivion
ㄴ 그 기회가 그녀의 천재성을 발휘시키게 해 주었고, 그렇지 않았으면 그 천재성이 망각되고 말았을 것이다

This work is far beyond your capacity
ㄴ 네 능력으로 이 일은 어림없어

Wan-soo thinks he is withering on the vine nobody has chosen him
ㄴ 완수는 아무도 그를 써(선택해)주지 않으니 능력을 썩히게 될 것이란 생각을 하고 있다

What's a man without competency, what's a woman without looks
ㄴ 남자가 내세울 건 능력, 여자가 내세울 건 미모뿐이다

When I read his editorial I realized he's a natural with writing
ㄴ 그가 쓴 사설을 읽어보았더니 그에게 타고난 글 솜씨가 있다고 느꼈어

You are letting your talents go to waste
ㄴ 재능을 썩히고 있군

You can't give full scope to your ability without training
ㄴ 재능을 닦지 않고는 네 능력을 충분히 발휘 할 수 없다(scope=opportunity)

You have it in you(what it takes)
ㄴ 네겐 남이 모르는 능력 있어

You have plenty of ability, but fail in patience
ㄴ 넌 능력은 있지만 인내심이 없어

- **plenty** more than adequate number or amount
- **scope** extent, room for development
- **patience** habit or fact of being patient

36. 데이트　　　　　　　　　　　**Dating**

All my roads lead to you
> ↳ 내 앞의 길은 모두 너를 향하고 있어

An-do is burning for only another look at Sook-hee
> ↳ 안도는 숙희를 한 번만이라도 더 보길 간절히 바랬어

Are you holding out on me?
> ↳ 내 발목을 잡겠다는 거니?

Are you seeing anyone?
> ↳ 너 사귀는 사람 있니?

Are you trying to move on his date?
> ↳ 넌 그의 애인을 꼬시겠다는 거니?

Being with you makes me happy
> ↳ 당신과 함께 있는 건 즐거워

Bong-soo(has) got his mind set on you
> ↳ 봉수의 맘은 네게 가 있어

Bong-soon is willing to kiss Dong-soo, but is not willing to go to all the way with him
> ↳ 봉순인 동수에게 키스까진 할 용의가 있지만 그가 요구하는 대로 다 하려고 하진 않는다

Byung-soo has got something going on with Sook-hee
> ↳ 병수가 숙희하고 연애하고 있어

▸ **burn for**　earnestly long for
▸ **advance**　bring or move forward, promote

Charming young ladies are right up my alley
ㄴ 젊은 여자들 비위 맞추는 게 내 주특기

Chan-soon made advances on(a pass at) every male she encountered
ㄴ 찬순이는 남자라는 남자는 모두 치근댔어

Chang-moon's has been chasing after girls for year, but he's already over the hill
ㄴ 창문이는 노상 아가씨들 꽁무니만 쫓아 다녔지만 이젠 한물 갔어

Crater face over there is trying to put the moves on you
ㄴ 저 쪽에 있는 여드름자국 투성이 녀석이 너를 꼬시려 한다 이 말이군

Did you see the shameless way she was chucking(hurling, throwing, flinging) herself at him?
ㄴ 그 여자가 창피한 줄도 모르고 그에게 매달리는 것 보았니?

Do you want a piece of that?
ㄴ 그 여자 어떻게 해보고싶어?

Don't come between Jung-soo and Mi-yun
ㄴ 정수와 미연이 사이에 끼어 들어 파경으로 이끌지마

Don't dare to touch me
ㄴ 내 몸에 손대기만 해봐라

Don't give her a glad eye
ㄴ 그 여자에게 추파 던지지마

(=Don't make googoo eyes to her)

Don't let her rest till she consents
ㄴ 그녀가 승낙할 때까지 떼를 써라

▸ **chase** follow trying to catch, drive away	▸ **chuck** give up
▸ **crater** volcanic depression	▸ **googoo eye** temptation

Don't let him kick you around
↳ 그 사람이 널 함부로 대하게 내버려둬선 안 돼

Don't let him pump you
↳ 그의 유도신문에 넘어가선 안 돼

Don't let him slip through your fingers this time
↳ 이번엔 그를 놓치지 마라

Don't play doctor with anybody any more
↳ 더 이상 남의 옷을 벗기고 만지는 짓은 하지마

Don't play games
↳ 튕기지마(**He likes the chase** 그는 튕기는 것 좋아해)

> (=Come on, I don't like a chasing game)

Don't play hard-to-get with me any more
↳ 더 이상 내게 내숭떨지마

Don't show him your hand too soon
↳ 그에게 너무 빨리 속마음을 보여주지 마라

Don't you think she's had a basinful(bellyfull) of your company this week?
↳ 그 여자가 이번 주 내내 지겹도록 너와 같이 있어주었다고 생각 안 해?

Dong-soo keeps strike out when it comes to the opposite sex
↳ 동수가 이성관계에서는 계속 실패야

Doo-soo and Yung-hee clicked with each other as soon as they met
↳ 두수와 영희는 만나자마자 서로 좋아했다

Duck-soo's been deceiving his girl friend with other girls
↳ 덕수는 여자친구를 배신한 채 다른 여자들을 사귀어 왔어

› **basin** large bowl or pan
› **bellyfull** full in stomach
› **click** make or cause to make a click

Ed is married, but he also has a woman on the side
 ↳ 에드는 결혼을 했지만 따로 사귀는 여자가 있다

Ever since they met, they've been a real item
 ↳ 그들이 만난 이래 줄곧 염문이 끊이질 않아

Every Jack has his Jill
 ↳ 짚신도 짝이 있다

> Jack 과 Jill은 아주 평범한 영어 이름으로 이 속담에서는 Jack은 남자, Jill
> 은 여자를 대표한다. 어떤 남자라도 그에게 맞는 여자가 있다는 얘기이다.

Gil-soo will grow on you after a while
 ↳ 곧 길수가 네 마음에 들게 될 것이다

Gil-soo oscillated between Sook-hee and Soon-mee
 ↳ 길수는 숙희를 택할지 순미를 택할지 망설였어

Girls that aren't coy are a turn off after a couple of dates
 ↳ 내숭이 없는 여자를 조금만 사귀어보면 매력이 없어진다

Guys need the patience to go after a girl until he wins her over
 ↳ 여자를 얻으려면 열 번을 찍는 인내력을 필요로 한다

Gyung-hee has had her eye on you for some time now
 ↳ 경희가 네게 마음을 두고 있어

Have no dealings with him
 ↳ 그놈하고 거래(교제)하지마

He has been having an affair
 ↳ 다른 여자와 깊이 사귀고 있어

He poisoned her mind against me
 ↳ 그 사람 때문에 그녀가 나를 싫어해

› **oscillate** swill back and forth | › **affair** something that related to or involves
› **coy** shy or pretending shyness | one

He wants to get to know her, but he always remains tongue-tied before her'
    ↳ 그는 그녀와 친해보고 싶어하지만 그녀 앞에 서면 늘 입이 안 떨어져

Heaven's what I feel when I'm with you
    ↳ 당신과 함께라면 천국에 있는 느낌

He'll have her in the palm of his hand shortly
    ↳ 그는 곧 그 여자를 장악하게 될 거야

He's a real operator when it comes to getting his way with women
    ↳ 그는 여자를 다루는데 진짜 이골난 수완 꾼 이다

He's been giving you the eye all day
    ↳ 그는 하루 종일 네게 눈길을 주었어

He's got four girls on the string
    ↳ 그에게는 맘대로 골라잡을 수 있는 아가씨가 네 명이나 있다

He's her be-all, and end-all
    ↳ 그는 그녀의 전부이다

He's trying to come on to me
    ↳ 그가 나한테 치근대고 있어

Her boyfriend has been stepping out on her
    ↳ 그녀의 남자친구가 바람을 피우고 있어

Her life is with you now
    ↳ 이제 그녀에게는 네가 더 중요해

Her quick-witted response hit him where it hurt
    ↳ 그녀의 재치 있는 응대가 그의 아픈 곳을 찔렀다

His heart started racing when she called his name
    ↳ 그 여자가 그의 이름을 부르자 심장이 마구 뛰기 시작했다

How often have I not watched him?
    ↳ 그를 눈 여겨 본 일이 몇 번인지 모른다

› **operator** person who performs work or an operation, person who manages | › **response** act of responding, answer

Hyun-soo might ask you out, but don't hold your breath
ㄴ 현수가 네게 데이트 신청할지 모르지만 김칫국은 마시지 마라

> "Don't count your chickens before they are hatched 떡 줄 사람은 생각도 안 하는데 김칫국부터 마시지 마라" 직역하면 "알이 부화하기도 전에 닭부터 세지 마라"이다(= It's ill waiting for dead men's shoes 신발을 갖기 위해 신발 주인이 죽기를 바라는 것은 헛된 일이다).

Hyun-soo's been going out with a hot number
ㄴ 현수는 잘 빠진 여자하고 데이트 중이야

I bet they'll never make it
ㄴ 그 짝은(couple) 절대 이뤄지지 않을 거야

I guess you have just made all my dreams come true
ㄴ 그대는 내가 꿈꾸어 오던 이상적인 여인(남자)

I have a boy(girl) friend
ㄴ 난 사귀는 사람이 있어요

> (=I'm not single
> (=I have a relationship)
> (=I'm with somebody)
> (=I'm not available)

I wouldn't two-time you
ㄴ 널 속이고 바람피지 않을게

I'm seeing someone else
ㄴ 만나는(데이트하는) 사람 있어요

› **hatch** emerge from an egg

› **wag** sway or swing from side to side or to and fro

If you go out with other girls, tongues will wag
↳ 네가 딴 여자들과 어울린다면 입들이 가만 안 있을 거다

In his youth, he excited some admiration among the girls
↳ 그도 젊었을 때 처녀들한테 인기가 있었다

It comes from a girl of twenty who's living in a fool's paradise
↳ 그건 **20**대 처녀의 헛된 기대에서 온다

It will take years for her to get you out of her system
↳ 그녀가 너를 잊어버리기까지는 몇 년이 걸릴 것이다

It won't take your cheating on me
↳ 몰래 다른 여자(남자)와 만나고 다니는 건 용서하지 않아

It's a match made in heaven
↳ 천생연분이야

> '하늘이 맺어준 인연'이라는 뜻이다. 'Match'는 '한 쌍'이라는 뜻이고,
> 'Heaven'은 천국, 즉 하늘이라는 뜻이다.

Jin-soo got(had) stars in his eyes when he met his blind date
↳ 진수는 낯선 데이트 상대와 만났을 때 들떠 있었어

Jung-ah flew to his arms as he got off the ship
↳ 그가 배에서 내리자 정아는 와락 그의 품에 안겼어

Just try to buddy up to her and pretend you are interested in what she's doing
↳ 그저 그 여자와 친해지도록 노력하고 그 여자가 하는 일에 관심 있는 척 해

Look how she's throwing herself at him
↳ 저 여자 그에게 달라붙는 것 좀 봐

· **cheat** on   deceive

Myung-hee is fluctuating between you and him
ㄴ 명희가 너냐 그 사람이냐 망설이고 있어

Nam-soo has been making time with Soon-hee
ㄴ 남수는 순희하고 연애중이야

Nam-soo was two-timing Song-hee with Myung-sook
ㄴ 종수는 송희를 속이고 명숙이와 어울렸어(송희가 배우자 또는 애인일 경우)

Nam-soo's parents gave him the third degree about the girl he meets
ㄴ 남수의 부모님은 그가 사귀는 아가씨에 대해서 자세히 물어보셨다

No use making a pass at her, she's already taken
ㄴ 그 여자는 임자 있는 몸이니 치근거려야 소용없어

Now that An-do and Nan-hee are through(broke up), Nan-hee is getting back to circulation
ㄴ 안도와 난희가 헤어졌으니 난희하고는 데이트할 수 있게되었어

Now there's a woman who likes her spaghetti
ㄴ 야, 너 국수 잘도 먹는구나(여자에게)

Oh, Sung-mee is my dreamboat
ㄴ 정말이지 성미는 나의 이상형이야

Once she is in love with him, it'll be difficult to tear her away
ㄴ 그녀가 그에게 일단 빠지게되면 떼어놓기는 어려워

Sang-soo and Hang-soon have had an on-again, off-again romance for years
ㄴ 상수와 행순이는 만났다 헤어지고 또 만났다 헤어지기를 오랫동안 해 오고 있어

Sang-soo has a crush on Myung-hee. I'll never know what he sees in him
ㄴ 상수가 명희에게 빠져있어. 상수의 어디가 좋은 건지 알 수가 없어

Sang-soo has a thing(something) going on with Hyang-soon
ㄴ 상수는 향순이와 연애하고 있다

› **give third degree** ask all about | › **dreamboat** ideal thing or person one dreamed of

Sang-soo warships the ground she walked on
  ↳ 상수는 그 여자에게 헌신적이야

Sang-soo's been playing fast and loose with Hang-soon's affections
  ↳ 상수는 행순이의 애정을 노리개쯤으로 여기고 있어

She boots me up=She turns me on
  ↳ 그 여자 싹 맘에 들어

She could have been anyone in the world
  ↳ 그 여자는 그냥 스쳐 가는 사람일 수도 있었어

She doesn't even know you're alive
  ↳ 창수가 너 따위를 거들떠보기나 하는 줄 아나

She dumped Duck-soo and attended a matchmaking meeting with another man
  ↳ 그녀는 덕수를 차버리고 다른 남자와 맞선을 보았다

She enjoys rubbing elbows with foreigners
  ↳ 그 여자는 외국인과 사귀기를 좋아한다

She flung herself at you
  ↳ 그 여자가 네게 매달렸단 말이군

She is hooking me up with Soo-sung
  ↳ 그 여자가 날 수성이하고 맺어주기로 주선 중이야

She is not right for me
  ↳ 그 여잔 내게 안 맞아(안 어울려)

She makes my heart skip a beat
  ↳ 그녀는 내 맘을 설레게 해

She walks all over him
  ↳ 그 여잔 그를 쥐고 흔들고 있어

› **boot up** satisfy

› **dump** unload or discard in a mass

› **rub** use pressure and friction on a body

She was on to him at first sight
> ↳ 그 여자는 첫 눈에 그를 꿰뚫어 보았다

She wished to be all in all to him
> ↳ 그 여자는 그에게 가장 사랑하는 사람이 되고싶었다

She'd eat someone as green as you for breakfast(dinner) alive
> ↳ 그 여자가 너 같은 영계는 철저히 이용하고 차버릴 거야

She's been playing musical beds for years
> ↳ 그 여자는 오랫동안 여러 남자하고 놀아났어

She's going to hit on you
> ↳ 그 여자가 널 꼬시려 해

She's got it very badly over you
> ↳ 그 여자가 네게 홀딱 빠져있단 말이야

Somebody will put the arm on you to get you out with him
> ↳ 누군가가 너에게 데이트하자고 대들 것이다

Soo-me comes on too strong
> ↳ 수미는 너무 적극적으로 나와

Sook-hee hinted to Moon-soo that she wanted to break up, but he didn't get the message(picture, word)
> ↳ 숙희가 문수에게 절교의 뜻을 비쳤으나 문수는 알아채지 못했어

Sook-hee hit Jong-soo between the eyes the moment he saw her
> ↳ 종수는 숙희를 보자마자 홀딱 빠져버렸어

Sook-hee moved in on Jung-hee's boy friend and now they are not talking to each other
> ↳ 숙희가 정희의 남자친구를 가로채는 바람에 이제 서로 말도 안하고 지내

Stay focused on me
> ↳ 나를 두고 한눈 팔지마

› **skip** move with leaps, read past or ignore   › **break up** end a relationship
› **hint** give a glue

(=Keep your attention on me)
(=Don't look away from me)
(=Don't even think about it)

Sung-mi is working him so hard
> ↳ 성미가 그에게 꼬리를 치고있어

(=Sung-mi is working him big time)
(=Sung-mi is flirting with him)

Sung-soo is so attached to me
> ↳ 성수는 내게 정이 듬뿍 들었어

(=Sung-soo already has my heart)
(=Sung-soo is already such a big part of me)

Sung-soo really turned me on at first sight
> ↳ 성수한테 첫눈에 빠졌어

Tai-gyung is going to put the hard word(moves, make) on Ji-yung
> ↳ 태경이가 지영일 꼬시려 한단 말이야

Tai-ho's had an eye on you
> ↳ 태호가 널 지켜봐 왔지

Tell me that we belong together
> ↳ 우린 인생을 함께 할거라고 말해 줘

That fish was a fox
> ↳ 그 여자는 매력적이었어

› **flirt** be playfully romantic, trifle

› **belong** be suitable, be owned, be a part of

That girl's been giving all the married men the eye
ㄴ 저 아가씨는 모든 유부남에게 추파를 던지고 다녀

That guy's dropped a bundle on Sung-mee lately
ㄴ 저 녀석이 요즘 성미에게 거금을 쓰고 다녀

That type of girl must be your cup of tea
ㄴ 넌 저런 타입의 여자를 좋아할 것 같아

The couple finally opened their hearts to each other
ㄴ 두 사람은 마침내 서로 정이 들게 되었다

The day will come when you'll get along with him
ㄴ 그 사람하고 잘돼갈 때가 올 거다

The flowers you gave her speak volumes
ㄴ 그 여자에게 꽃을 주다니 보통 사이가 아닌가봐(**speak volumes=be full of meaning**)

The gigolo began to show his true colors and wreck their relationship by seeing another woman
ㄴ 그 제비족은 본색을 드러내기 시작하더니 다른 여자를 만나면서 그들의 관계가 금이 가기 시작했다

There's a fire in my heart
ㄴ 내 가슴이 불타고 있어

There's something likable about her
ㄴ 그 여자에게는 어딘지 호감이 가

They are perfect for each other
ㄴ 그들은 궁합이 잘 맞아

(=They have good chemistry)
(=They were made for each other)

› **gigolo** man living on the earnings of a woman

› **asunder** into separate pieces, separated

They have gone together for two years
    ↳ 그들은 2년간 애인으로 사기고 있어

They two have seem to have got a thing going
    ↳ 그 두 사람은 서로 잘돼 가는 것 같다

Those two are meant to be
    ↳ 저 두 사람은 천생연분이야

'하늘이 맺어준 인연'이라는 뜻이다. 'Match'는 '한 쌍'이라는 뜻이고, 'Heaven'은 천국, 즉 하늘이라는 뜻이다.

We went all the way
    ↳ (데이트에서)우린 결혼단계까지 다 갔어

We'll always have Paris together
    ↳ 우린 헤어져도 영원히 잊지 못해

What was the result of your blind date(marriage meeting)?
    ↳ 너 선 본 결과가 어떻게 되었니?

Whenever I'm near him my heart misses(skips) a beat(stands still)
    ↳ 그 사람 옆에만 가면 가슴이 두근거려(심장이 멎는 느낌이야)

Why are you hanging around my boy?
    ↳ 왜 내 남자친구 주변에서 얼쩡거리니?

You are all I am thinking of
    ↳ 너만을 생각해

You are all that I know of
    ↳ 내겐 오직 그대 뿐

You are my dream come true
    ↳ 그대는 내가 꿈에 그리던 사람

‣ **groove** long narrow channel, fixed routine

You are my one and only
　　ㄴ 오직 당신뿐이에요

You are my reason for the step in my groove
　　ㄴ 당신이 있음으로써 난 매일 매일 삶을 한 걸음씩 살아가고 있어요

You are my survival, you are my living proof
　　ㄴ 그대는 내 삶의 이유이자 존재의 의미

You are still the one
　　ㄴ 당신은 변함없는 내 사랑

You are the one I belong to
　　ㄴ 당신은 내 마음을 가져간 사람

You are the one I want for life
　　ㄴ 당신은 내가 일생을 함께 하기 원하는 사람

You are the only one I dream of
　　ㄴ 꿈속에도 그리는 단 한사람

You just run to these arms
　　ㄴ 내 품으로 달려오기만 하면 돼

You make me feel like heaven
　　ㄴ 당신 덕분에 천국에 있는 느낌

You mean everything to me
　　ㄴ 너 없이는 못살아

> (=I can't live without you)
> (=You mean the world to me)

You seem to have a thing for her

‣ **survive**　remain alive or in existence, outlive
　　　　or outlast

ㄴ 그 여자에게 특별한 감정이 있는 것 같구나

You were made for me
ㄴ 그대는 나를 위해 태어난 사람

You'll never get to first base with a girl like Sook-hi
ㄴ 넌 숙희 같은 여자하고는 데이트 근처에도 못 가겠군

You've got your eyes glued to her
ㄴ 넌 그 여자에게서 눈을 못 떼는군

Your rudeness lost you her favor
ㄴ 너의 무례한 짓이 그 여자의 호의를 잃게 만든 거야

› **glue** substance used for sticking things togethe

› **rudeness** impoliteness

› **favor** approval, partiality, act of kindness

37. 도둑   Thieves

A bad padlock invites a pick-lock
> ↳ 시원찮은 자물쇠는 따고 들어올 도둑을 불러들인다

A few bank robbers acted out the bank robbery they committed last week
> ↳ 은행강도 몇 명이 지난주에 저질렀던 은행강도 행위를 재연했다

A few minutes after the thief left she got it all(pulled herself) together and called the police
> ↳ 도둑이 가버린 몇 분 후 그 여자는 정신을 차리고 경찰에 전화했어

A thief believes everybody steals
> ↳ 도둑은 모든 다른 사람들을 도둑으로 안다

A thief has a bad conscience and is apt to give himself away
> ↳ 도둑이 제발 저리다

Alone and unsupported, he'll be reduced to stealing
> ↳ 그가 혼자 남아 의지할 데 없게되면 도둑질을 하게 될 것이다

As no one was looking, they helped themselves to gems and other valuables
> ↳ 아무도 보는 사람이 없어지자 그들은 보석과 귀중품을 훔쳐갔다

Bolt you door fast against possible burglary
> ↳ 도둑이 들지 않도록 문단속을 잘 해라

Ed got this thing with his five-finger discount
> ↳ 에드는 이걸 슬쩍해서 손에 넣었다

Ed is a four-time loser, twice for burglary and twice for armed robbery

---

▸ **padlock**   lock with a U-shaped catch
▸ **apt**   suitable, likely, quick to learn

▸ **valuable**   worth a lot of money, being of great importance or use

ㄴ 에드는 절도 2범, 강도 2범인 전과 4범이다

He that steals a pin will steal an ox

ㄴ 바늘도둑이 소도둑 된다

이 속담은 마치 직역한 것 같이 영어와 우리나라 속담이 비슷하다. Pin 은 바늘과 같이 작은 것, ox 는 소와 같이 크고 값이 많이 나가는 것을 대표한다. 이는 동, 서양이 모두 농업 사회를 토대로 발전했다는 것을 나타낸다. (=He that thieves an egg will thieve an ox)

Her assailant knocked her to the ground and ran(made) off with her handbag

ㄴ 그녀를 공격한 사람은 그녀를 쓰러뜨리고 핸드백을 훔쳐서 달아났다

Her house was burgled(robbed) last night and she took a day off work today

ㄴ 그녀의 집이 어젯밤 도둑을 맞아서 오늘은 허락 받아 직장을 안 나왔다

He's a four-time loser

ㄴ 그는 전과 4범

Little thieves are hanged, but great ones escape

ㄴ 송사리 도둑은 벌을 받고 큰 도둑은 잡히지 않는다

Now you have been caught stealing the goods, you won't be able to bluff your way out of this one

ㄴ 물건을 훔치다 붙잡혔으니 이번엔 아니라고 빠져나갈 수 없겠지

Once a thief always a thief

ㄴ 몸에 밴 습성은 쉽게 버리지 못한다

▸ **assail**　attack violently

한 번 몸에 밴 습관이 얼마나 중요한 것인지를 알려주는 속담이다. 비슷한 뜻으로 쓰이는 "Once a beggar, always a beggar 한번 거지는 언제나 거지이다"와 "What's learned in the cradle is carried to the grave 요람에서 배운 것은 무덤까지 간다"도 있다.

One thief informed against others
↳ 도둑 한 사람이 패거리의 다른 사람을 밀고했다

Opportunity makes the thief
↳ 견물생심

좋은 물건을 보면 가지고 싶은 마음이 생기게 마련이다. 거기다 관리까지 허술하다면 다른 사람으로 하여금 도둑질을 하고 싶은 충동을 느끼게 한다. 비슷한 뜻으로 "A postern door makes a thief 뒷문이 도적을 만든다"도 쓰인다.

Pick-pockets always watch our every move closely, watching for the most adventitious moment to steal our money
↳ 소매치기들은 늘 우리의 모든 동작을 면밀히 지켜보면서 돈을 훔치기에 가장 우발적인 순간을 노린다

Procrastination is the thief of time
↳ 뒤로 미루는 것은 시간을 도둑맞는 일이다

Robbers broke into the gallery and made off with paintings to the value of 20 million won
↳ 도둑들이 화랑에 침입하여 **2**천만원 상당의 그림을 훔쳐갔다

Some sticky-fingered guy swiped my money yesterday
↳ 어떤 손버릇 나쁜 녀석이 내 돈을 어제 훔쳐갔다

Something tells me that he pulled a convenience store job and got

---

› **beggar** one that begs

› **cradle** baby's bed

› **pick-pocket** one who steals from pockets

› **adventitious** accidental

out of town
> ↳ 그가 편의점을 털어서 달아나 버렸다는 생각이 든다

The theft must have been an inside job considering only the staff knew the money was there
> ↳ 돈이 거기 있었다는 것을 직원들만이 알았던 점으로 보아 도난사건은 내부 소행이 틀림 없을 것이다

That crook tried to do me out of everything I have
> ↳ 그 사기꾼이 내가 가진 모든 걸 등쳐먹으러 했어

That sly con artist can take you to the cleaners any time
> ↳ 그 교활한 사기꾼은 언제라도 널 땡전 한푼 없이 알겨먹을 수 있어

That's an instance of evil-doer's audacity
> ↳ 도둑이 매를 든다더니 뻔뻔스럽기는

The burglar made off(away) with all the money in the safe
> ↳ 도둑은 금고 안에 있던 돈 전부를 훔쳐 가버렸다

The burglars sawed their way through the protective metal bars
> ↳ 도둑들은 방호철창을 톱으로 썰고 들어왔다

The pickpocket planted the wallet on a passerby
> ↳ 소매치기는 그 지갑을 지나가는 사람의 주머니에 슬쩍 넣었다

The postern door make thief and whore
> ↳ 나쁜 짓을 하고도 빠져나갈 수 있는 뒷문은 도둑과 창녀를 만든다

허술한 관리와 법의 불공평함이 범죄를 부추긴다는 뜻이다. 좋은 물건을 보면 가지고 싶은 마음이 생긴다는 뜻을 가진 '견물생심(見物生心) Opportunity makes the thief'와도 비슷한 뜻이다.

The robber came out of the jewelry shop and jumped into his car

---

- **sly**   given to or showing secrecy and deception
- **audacity**   boldness or insolence
- **passerby**   pedestrian

↳ 강도는 보석상에서 달려나와 자신의 차에 뛰어 올라탔다

The robber lit out on a stolen car which was waiting for him outside the shop

↳ 강도는 가게밖에 있던 차를 훔쳐 타고 급히 달아났다

The robbers lie low after holding up the bank

↳ 도둑들은 은행떨이 한 후 눈에 안 띄게 숨어 지냈어

The suspect matches(measures) up to the description the police have of the wanted thief

↳ 피의자는 경찰이 수배중인 도둑의 인상착의와 부합한다

The thief flew the coop before the police arrived

↳ 경찰이 오기 전에 도둑이 도망쳤어

The thief whipped away the purse

↳ 도둑이 지갑을 낚아채 갔어

The thieves got away as clean as a whistle, leaving nothing behind but an empty safe

↳ 도둑은 빈 금고만 남긴 채 흔적도 없이 사라졌다

The thieves got in through the window, but we found no sign of a break-in

↳ 도둑이 창문을 통해 들어왔지만 우리는 도둑이 든 것을 발견하지 못했다

The thieves sang from the same song sheet

↳ 도둑들은 미리 입을 맞춰 놓았다

The years, like a thief in the night, stole what I was

↳ 세월이 어느새 나의 모습을 앗아가 버렸다

They had broken into the house while we were away, and turned the place inside out looking for money

↳ 그들은 우리가 집을 비운 사이에 무단침입해서 돈이 있는지 샅샅이 뒤졌다

› **whistle** device by which a shrill sound is produced, shrill clear sound made by a whistle or through the lips

› **fraud** trickery

Thieves are made, not born
> ↳ 도둑의 씨가 있는 게 아니다

This fraud list will be circulated to all local police offices
> ↳ 이 사기꾼 명부는 전 지방 경찰서에 배포될 것이다

Two employees were killed in the line of duty when they tried to stop a robbery
> ↳ 종업원 두 명이 근무 중 강도를 잡으려다가 피살됐다

Who should come into my room at night but a thief?
> ↳ 도둑이 아닌 다음에야 밤중에 내 방에 누가 들어오겠나

▸ **thief** one that steals

38. 돈   **Money**

A friend in court is better than a penny in purse
 ↳ 높은 자리에 있는 친구는 지갑 속의 돈보다 낫다

A good doctor can net(clear) over 50 million won a year
 ↳ 괜찮은 의사라면 1년에 5천만원 이상의 순수익을 올린다

A hundred thousand won doesn't go very far these days, with the prices rising all the time
 ↳ 물가가 오르기만 하니 십만원이라야 얼마 못 가

A lot of fortune came Doo-soo's way when his father retired
 ↳ 아버지가 은퇴하시자 두수에겐 거금이 생겼지

A quarter of my income goes in(on) for housing
 ↳ 월급에서 평균 4분의 1은 주거비에 들어간다

A woman prefers a man without money to money without a man
 ↳ 여자는 남자 없는 돈보다는 돈 없는 남자를 택한다

After he sold his house, he was ten million won to the good(ahead of the game)
 ↳ 그는 집을 팔아 천만원 이익을 봤어

After only a few years, he's wallowing in money and property
 ↳ 그는 불과 몇 년 안 가서 돈이며 재산이 풍족해졌어

All is because of money
 ↳ 돈이 원수다

· **net** remaining after deductions, have as profit   · **income** money gained(as from work or investment)

An-do came by the money honestly
　　ㄴ 안도는 정직하게 돈을 벌었어

An-do has all kinds of money
　　　ㄴ 안도는 부자

> (=An-do has money to burn)
> (=An-do is made of money)

An-do is a little bit short lately
　　　ㄴ 안도가 요즘 돈이 좀 쪼들려

An-do is loaded(wasted, shit-faced)
　　　ㄴ 안도는 돈이 많아(꽤 취했어)

Anyone who(Whoever) pays the fiddler(piper) calls the shots
　　　ㄴ 누구든 비용을 부담하는 사람이 결정권을 가지다

As the safe was indestructible, the money and jewels were intact
　　　ㄴ 금고가 튼튼했기 때문에 돈과 귀금속은 무사했다

Better an empty purse than an empty head
　　　ㄴ 주머니가 빈 것은 머리가 빈 것보다 낫다

Blow the expense
　　　ㄴ 경비 따위는 생각지 마라

Bong-doo broke(emptied) his piggy bank
　　　ㄴ 봉두는 저금통을 탈탈 털었어

> (=Bong-doo took(pulled) out all his savings)

· **fiddler**　person who plays violin　　　· **expense**　cost
· **indestructible**　not able to destroy

Bong-doo pulled money out of thin air(a hat)
> ↳ 봉두는 어디서 돈을 잘도 만들어내는군

Bong-soo is really going to clean up
> ↳ 봉수는 떼돈 벌게 생겼어

Bong-soo was then down to his last ten thousand won
> ↳ 그때 봉수에게 가진 거라곤 만원밖에 없었어

Brigands demand your money or your life, whereas women require both
> ↳ 산적은 당신의 돈이나 생명을 요구하지만 여자는 그 둘 다를 요구한다

Buying our house privately will cut out the middleman and save money on agent's fees
> ↳ 우리 집을 당사자 개인간에 사고 팔면 중개인 없는 거래여서 중개 수수료가 절약된다

Byung-soo can't pin(fix) the bribery on me
> ↳ 병수는 내가 뇌물을 받았다고 뒤집어씌울 수 없어

Byung-soo is flatter than a pancake
> ↳ 병수는 땡전한푼 없어(흔한 표현 아님)

Byung-soo will stretch a dollar
> ↳ 병수는 돈 변통을 잘해

Byung-soo won't bankroll your spending spree any more
> ↳ 네가 돈을 물쓰듯하는 이상 병수가 네게 돈을 빌려주지 않을 것이다

Can this money carry you through this month?
> ↳ 이 돈이면 이 달을 넘길 수 있나?

Can you balance a coin on its edge?
> ↳ 이 동전을 가장자리로 세워놓을 수 있겠니?

Can you take my car in exchange(as a trade)?
> ↳ 받을 돈 대신 차를 가져가시면 안되겠습니까?

› **bribery** corrupt or influence by gifts, something offered or given in bribing

› **bankroll** supply of money

Cessation of work is not accompanied by cessation of expenses
> ↳ 일을 그만둔다해서 지출이 없어지는 것이 아니다

Chan-soo already earmarked some money for his own use
> ↳ 찬수는 자기가 쓸 돈을 얼마간 따로 꿍쳐 놨어

Chan-soo can't command the sum
> ↳ 찬수는 그렇게 큰돈을 마음대로 못해

Chan-soo earned(cleared) a cool five million dollars on that deal
> ↳ 찬수는 그 거래에서 5백만원씩이나 벌었다

Chang-soo is sitting on a gold mine
> ↳ 창수는 금 방석에 앉아있어

Credit is a promise of a future payment in money or in kind given in exchange for present money, goods or services
> ↳ 신용거래는 현재의 거래에 대하여 사후에 현금, 상품, 또는 용역을 제공하겠다는 약속이다

Dig down deep this time
> ↳ 이번엔 돈 좀 후하게 내봐

Do you think I have the golden goose that lays the golden eggs?
> ↳ 난 뭐 도깨비 방망이라도 가진 줄(돈이 무한정 있는줄) 아나?

Do you think I'm loaded or something?
> ↳ 내가 재력가라도 되는 줄 아는 모양이군

Dollars go everywhere
> ↳ 달러는 어디서나 쓰여

Don't drop the balls, or you'll lose big bucks
> ↳ 허투루 했다가는 거금을 놓친단 말이야

Don't flash a wad like that around here
> ↳ 여기서 돈 뭉치를 함부로 내보이지 마라(**Don't flash your money**

- ▸ **cessation**　a halting
- ▸ **earmark**　designate for a specific purpose
- ▸ **loaded**　full of burden or money
- ▸ **buck**　dollar

around 돈 자랑하며 돌아다니지마)

Don't forget you shouldn't be blinded by money
ㄴ 돈을 탐하면 안 된다는 것을 잊지 마라

Don't fritter away all your money and time
ㄴ 보람 없는 일에 돈과 시간을 허비해선 안 돼

Don't inflate your bill with extra costs
ㄴ 추가 비용을 덧붙여서 계산을 부풀리지 마

Don't max out all your credit cards
ㄴ 신용카드를 쓸 수 있는 한도까지 다 써서는 안 돼

Don't throw good money after bad
ㄴ 손해를 거듭 봐선 안 돼

Dong-soo scared(scraped) up the money for his speeding ticket
ㄴ 동수는 겨우 속도위반 벌금을 마련했어

Doo-chul grossed over two million won this month
ㄴ 두철인 이 달에 2백 만원 수익을 올렸어

Doo-soo is sixty thousand won in the hole this month
ㄴ 두수는 이 달 6십원 적자야

Duck-soo spends money like water
ㄴ 덕수는 돈을 물쓰듯해

Ed is rumored to have money coming out of his ears
ㄴ 에드는 엄청난 부자라고 소문이 나 있어

Ed's friend threw him a lifeline in the form of a million won loan when he was in a pinch
ㄴ 에드가 어려움을 당했을 때 그의 친구가 백만원을 빌려줘서 구원해 주었다

Enclosed please find a check for 5 million won
ㄴ 5백만원의 수표를 동봉하니 받아주시기 바랍니다

› **inflate** expand or increase abnormally
› **scrap** fight

› **loan** money borrowed at interest, something lent temporarily

Everybody thinks the accountant had his hand in the till
ㄴ 모두들 경리가 돈을 훔친 것으로 생각한다

Everything is sky high
ㄴ 모든 물가가 천정부지다

Financial success is not in the cards for me this month
ㄴ 이 달은 내가 경제적으로 잘 될 것 같지 않다

Frankly speaking, it makes me uncomfortable to see him splashing his money about(around)
ㄴ 솔직히 그가 돈을 마구 쓰는 건 내 마음이 편치 않아

Gil-soo doesn't make enough money to even get by
ㄴ 길수의 수입은 이럭저럭 살아가기에도 벅찰 정도야

Gil-soo has a golden thumb, and is very rich
ㄴ 길수는 돈을 잘 벌어서 큰 부자다

Gil-soo has not a penny to his name
ㄴ 길수에게는 땡전한푼 없어

Government departments have been urged to cut down on bureaucracy in order to save money
ㄴ 정부 부처들은 예산절감을 위해 관료적인 형식절차를 줄여나가야 했다

Gun-mo is obsessed with making money
ㄴ 건모는 돈 버는데 미친 사람

Has your ship come home?
ㄴ 큰돈이라도 들어왔나?

He accepted a lot of money under the table
ㄴ 그 사람은 뒷구멍으로 많은 돈을 받았어

He always counts the pennies and risks the pounds
ㄴ 그는 늘 푼돈을 시시콜콜 따지다가 큰돈을 놓칠 상황에 빠지곤 해

› **accountant** one skilled in accounting
› **splash** scatter

› **bureaucracy** body of government officials, unwieldy administrative system

Penny 와 Pound 는 영국의 화폐 단위로서, Penny는 작은 단위, Pound는 큰 단위이다. 여기서는 각각 푼돈과 큰돈을 대표한다. 작은 돈에 신중을 기하다가 큰 손해를 보는 경우에 쓰이는 속담이다(=Penny-wise and pound-foolish).

He arrived on the money(dot)
> ㄴ 그는 정확히 제 시간에 왔어

He doesn't miss a trick when it comes to making money
> ㄴ 돈 버는 일이라면 그 사람은 절대 기회를 안 놓쳐

He earns(makes) good money, but he is very extravagant so it doesn't last very long
> ㄴ 그가 돈은 잘 벌지만 워낙 잘 쓰기 때문에 별로 오래 가지 못해

어리석은 자는 큰돈을 쥐어줘도 금방 탕진하거나 사기를 당하지만, 지혜로운 자는 적은 돈이라도 잘 모으고 관리한다. 영리한 부자가 탄생하기 위해서는 바보들의 희생이 따른다는 뜻도 된다(= A fool and his money are soon parted).

He hardly makes a dent in his money all month
> ㄴ 그는 한 달 내내 돈을 써도 줄어든 표가 없을 만큼 부자다

He has no desire but to make a fortune
> ㄴ 그 사람은 재산 모으기에 여념이 없어

He has nothing to call his own
> ㄴ 그는 빈털터리야

He is a good provider(has a golden thumb)
> ㄴ 그는 돈을 잘 벌어다주어

He is a man of no resources

· **dent** small depression
· **desire** strong conscious impulse to have,

be, or do something, something desired

↳ 그는 심심해 하고 있어. 그에게는 재산이 없어(두 가지 뜻이 있음)

He is going to put the bite on you

↳ 그가 네게 돈을 갈취하(꾸)려고 하고 있어

He is low(deep) in his pocket

↳ 그 사람 돈 없(있)어

He is not fit for riches who is afraid to use them

↳ 쓰기를 꺼리는 사람에게 부는 어울리지 않는다

He is not so poor that he can't buy it

↳ 그가 그걸 못 살만큼 가난하지는 않아

He is paying something approaching half his income just to have a roof over his head

↳ 그는 소득에서 거의 절반을 집 장만에 다 쓴다

He is spending money like nobody's business

↳ 그는 돈을 물 쓰듯 해오고 있어

He is very upfront about wanting money

↳ 그 사람은 대놓고 돈을 요구해

He keeps paying blackmail to a woman who has something on him

↳ 그는 자신의 약점을 쥐고 있는 여자에게 계속 돈을 갈취 당하고 있어

He made a fortune at(in) a stroke

↳ 그는 일확천금을 벌었어(**There's no such thing as fast money** 일확천금이란 없어)

He makes a good living

↳ 그는 돈을 잘 번다

He must be rolling in dough

↳ 그 사람 돈방석에 앉았겠군

He once did me out of a large sum of money

‣ **upfront** easy-going
‣ **dough** stiff mixture of flour and liquid

↳ 그는 언젠가 내게 거액의 돈을 사기 쳤다

He that has no silver in his purse should have silver in his tongue
↳ 주머니가 빈 사람은 말주변이라도 있어야 한다

He wanted to get his money's worth
↳ 그는 본전을 뽑고 싶었던 거야

> (=He wanted to get a good run for his money)
> (=He wanted to make the best use of his money)

He was caught diverting the company's money into his own bank account
↳ 그는 회사 자금을 자신의 은행 계좌에 유용하다가 들통났어

He wouldn't miss a million won
↳ 그는 백만원쯤은 예사로 알 것이다

He's out to make a fast buck
↳ 그는 쉽게 큰돈을 벌려고 애쓰고 있어

He's trying to angle fame by money
↳ 그는 돈으로 명예를 낚으려 하고 있어

Her ascription of the failure to lack of money is not honest
↳ 그녀가 실패한 것을 돈 부족으로 돌리는 것은 정직하지 못한 것이다

Her money goes on clothes
↳ 그 여자의 돈은 옷 사는데 다 들어간다

High school students and older must pay full fare
↳ 고교생 이상은 어른 요금입니다

His law office turned out to be a money-spinner and was always full
↳ 그의 법률사무소는 돈방석이 되면서 늘 손님이 가득했다

› **divert** turn from a course or purpose,
distract, amuse

His mind is on fire to make money
└ 그는 돈 모으는데 혈안 돼 있어

His wife is always beefing about money
└ 그의 부인은 늘 돈 때문에 불평한다

How can you go through your allowance so fast?
└ 어쩜 용돈을 그리도 빨리 써버리니?

How is sugar(the dollar)?
└ 설탕(달러) 시세 어때?(이해하지 못할 수도 있음)

How much front money do we need?
└ 착수(선불)금은 얼마나 필요해?

How much money are we talking about?
└ 어느 정도 금액을 말씀하시는 겁니까?

Hyun-soo lost track of his expenditures, and some of his checks bounced
└ 찬수는 돈 지출을 소홀히 하여 수표에 부도가 좀 났어

I have a tight pocketbook
└ 주머니 사정이 좋지 않아

I have no one but you to turn to borrow money
└ 너 말고 내게 돈 꿔줄 사람이 어디 있겠니

I need money for this and that
└ 이런 저런 일로 돈이 많이 들어

(=There are many drains on my purse)

I want to see the color of your money
└ 주머니 사정을 알고 싶어

› **beef** complain	› **bounce** spring back, make bounce
› **expenditure** act of using or spending	› **pocketbook** purse, financial resource

I want to stay under 200,000 won
↳ **20만원 미만 자리를 원합니다**

I was ahead one million won in the deal
↳ 그 거래에서 백 만원 벌었지

I'll buy, you fly
↳ 내가 돈을 낼 테니 네가 사와

I'll pay the day after tomorrow, not before
↳ 모레 갚을게 그 이전엔 안 돼

I'll stand in with you in this expense
↳ 이 비용은 분담할게

I'm cleaned out
↳ 땡전한푼 없어

If interest rates do not shoot up, property should remain a good investment
↳ 금리가 치솟지 않는다면 부동산에 투자해 볼만하다

If you need any money, just say the word
↳ 돈이 필요하면 말만해

If you score big on that deal, you'll make a lot of dough
↳ 네가 이번에 크게 한 건 올리면 거금이 들어오는 거야

If you take away his money, he's nothing
↳ 그 사람은 돈 빼면 별 볼일 없어

If your business ever gets off the ground, you may make some bucks
↳ 네 사업이 시작만 좋으면 돈을 좀 벌게 될 것이다

In former times, there was a deal of spending in a thousand won
↳ 예전엔 천원이면 꽤 쓸게 있었지

In those days takings didn't cover expenses
↳ 그 당시에는 아무리 벌어도 적자였어

› **rate** quantity, amount, or degree measured
in relation to some other quantity

In-ho has yet to make two million won a month
> ↳ 인호는 월 이백만원은 벌어야 해

In-soo shelled out a lot of money for his new car
> ↳ 인수는 새 차 구입에 큰 돈 들었어

Intrinsic values can't be priced in dollars and cents
> ↳ 고유한 가치는 돈으로 가치를 매길 수 없다

Is a million won anything to sneeze at?
> ↳ 백만원이 누구 이름인줄 아나

Is the money good?
> ↳ 돈벌인 잘 되니?

It amounts to little short of three thousand won
> ↳ 총액은 거의 **30만원**에 달해

It can't be had for love or money
> ↳ 그건 절대로 손에 넣을 수 없어

It just goes to show you that the political world is moved by money
> ↳ 정치의 세계는 돈으로 움직인다는 게 명백해

It takes more brain and effort to make out the income-tax form than it does to make the income
> ↳ 소득을 올리는 것 보다 소득세 신고용지를 작성하는데 더 머리와 노력을 요한다

It turned up trumps after all, and the firm made a lot of money
> ↳ 그 일이 결국 예상외로 잘되어 그 회사는 큰돈을 벌었다

It was my little all
> ↳ 이것은 얼마 안 되는 나의 전 재산이다

It won't do any good to touch me for money
> ↳ 나한테 와서 돈을 청해봤자 소용없어

› **shell** hard or tough outer covering

› **intrinsic** essential, actual

› **sneeze** force the breath out with sudden and involuntary violence

It'll undoubtedly cut into our profits
    ㄴ 보나마나 우리 수익이 줄어들 것이다

It's a tiny percentage of the total income
    ㄴ 그건 총 수입에 비해 얼마 안 되는 몫의 비용이다

It's not enough to amount to buying a glass of beer
    ㄴ 맥주 한잔 살만한 돈도 못 돼

It's our custom to give money during holidays as a token of appreciation
    ㄴ 명절에 감사의 표시로 돈을 주는 것이 우리의 관습이다

It's our final offer
    ㄴ 이건 최종 가격(제안)입니다

It's quite good value if you look at all the extras
    ㄴ 거기에 딸려오는 것을 고려하면 지불한 돈이 그만한 가치는 있어

Korea saw its trade deficit swell to $12 billion so far this month
    ㄴ 한국은 이 달 들어 무역수지 적자가 **12**억불로 늘어났다

Let's cash up some money to have a party
    ㄴ 돈을 좀 추렴해서 회식하자

Let's chip in some money for his farewell gift
    ㄴ 그에게 줄 작별선물 사게 돈을 좀 추렴하자

Let's have separate checks(pay our own bills). I'm a little short
    ㄴ 각자 내기로 하자. 난 돈이 약간 모자라

Let's see if we can get them wholesale and save ourselves some money
    ㄴ 그 물건들을 도매로 사서 얼마간의 돈이라도 절약할 수 있을지 한 번 보자

Little good comes of gathering
    ㄴ 돈은 벌기만 할 게 아니라 쓸 줄도 알아야 한다

› **deficit** shortage especially in money   › **wholesale** sale of goods in quantity usually for resale by a retail merchant

> "돈이 돈을 낳는다 Money begets money"라는 말이 있다. 아무리 큰 재산이라도 쌓아두면 그 자리에 머물지만, 아무리 적은 재산이라도 적당한 곳에 투자하면 큰 이익을 볼 수도 있다. 지혜로운 자는 경기를 잘 파악하여 적절한 곳에 투자하여 돈을 늘리는 사람이다.

Lots of people keep their money loose in their pockets
ㄴ 돈을 주머니에 아무렇게나 넣어 다니는 사람이 많아

Love makes passion; but money makes marriage
ㄴ 사랑은 열정을 낳지만 돈은 결혼을 만든다

Love of money is common to all
ㄴ 돈보고 싫어하는 사람 없다

> 돈이 인생에 아주 중요한 가치를 가지게 되었다. 돈이 삶에 최고는 아니지만, 사람의 삶을 좌우하는 잣대중의 하나가 된 것은 사실이다(= No one spits on money).

Make money as much as possible and live a rich life
ㄴ 돈은 개 같이 벌어서 정승 같이 써라(쓴다)

> (=Miserly savings, and lavish spending)
> (=Narrow gathered, wisely spent)

Man-soo made out like a bandit on that deal
ㄴ 만수는 그 거래에서 거금을 벌었다

Many public servants have clean hands as regards money
ㄴ 많은 공무원들이 금전문제에 깨끗해

· **misery**   suffering and want caused by distress or poverty

· **regard**   consideration, feeling or approval or liking, friendly greeting(pl)

Million one is a good sum of money
> ↳ 백만원이면 상당한(큰) 돈이지

Money alone sets all the world in motion
> ↳ 돈만 있으면 세상은 돌아가게 되어있다

Money burns a hole in my pocket
> ↳ 주머니에 돈이 붙어있질 않아

Money can't buy love
> ↳ 돈으로 사랑을 살수는 없어

Money comes and goes
> ↳ 돈은 있다가도 없고 없다가도 있어

> (=Money goes(flies) in and out)
> (=It's easy to gain money and lose money)

Money doesn't always make sense
> ↳ 돈이 반드시 사람의 가치기준이 되는 것은 아니다

Money enables one to do a lot of things
> ↳ 돈이 있으면 여러 가지 일을 할 수 있다

Money gone, friends gone
> ↳ 돈 떨어지면 죽는 날이다

Money is bound to tell
> ↳ 돈은 효과가 나게 돼 있어

Money is like a sixth sense without which you can't make a complete use of the other five
> ↳ 돈은 육감과 같아서

돈이 없으면 다른 오감을 충분히 활용하지 못하게 된다

· **gain** profit, obtaining of profit or possessions, increase

Money is no consideration
ㄴ 돈은 문제가 아냐

Money is not everything
ㄴ 돈이 전부가 아니다(**Money's everything**의 반대)

Money is really tight for me
ㄴ 요즘 돈에 쪼들리고 있어

> (=I'm cash-strapped)

Money is useful only when you get rid of it
ㄴ 돈이 수중에 없을 때에만 필요한 일이 생긴다

Money kept in a savings account accrues to us with interest
ㄴ 은행에 예금을 하면 이자가 붙는다

Money may procure pleasure but not happiness
ㄴ 돈으로 향락은 살 수 있을지 몰라도 행복은 사지 못한다

Money takes to its wings
ㄴ 돈이란 날개가 달린 듯이 없어지는 법이다

Money talks loud
ㄴ 돈이면 안 되는 게 없어

> (=Money opens all doors)
> (=Money can buy anything)
> (=All things are obedient to money)

Money will come and go
ㄴ 돈은 돌고 도는 것

› **accrue** be added by periodic growth
› **procure** get possession of

› **wing** movable paired appendage for flying

Moon-soo has little more money than Moon-ho
>↳ 문호와 마찬가지로 문호에겐 돈이 없어

Much money and time are spent to prepare sacrificial food to offer the spirits of ancestors
>↳ 조상신들에게 드릴 제사음식을 준비하느라고 많은 돈과 시간이 소비된다

Much of his wealth remains on paper
>↳ 그의 재산의 대부분은 장부상의 계산에 불과하다

My daughter has been under a cloud since her colleague's money disappeared
>↳ 우리 딸은 동료의 돈이 없어진 후 의심을 사고 있어(**Under a cloud**에 **depress, scold**의 뜻도 있음)

My money can bulk up to a fortune if I save everything I can
>↳ 내가 가능한 모든 돈을 저축하면 목돈으로 불어날 수 있다

My money is on Jong-soo to win the race
>↳ 종수가 레이스에 이기는데 돈을 걸었다

My son gave me some song and dance about how he needed money
>↳ 우리아들은 무엇 때문에 돈이 필요하다고 자꾸 들볶았다

Nam-chul already profited to the tune of billion won
>↳ 남철인 벌써 **10억**이나 벌었어

No money, no honey
>↳ 돈 없으면 애인도 떨어져

No one spits on money
>↳ 돈에 침 뱉는 사람 없다

돈이 인생에 아주 중요한 가치를 가지게 되었다. 돈이 삶에 최고는 아니지만, 사람의 삶을 좌우하는 잣대 중의 하나가 된 것은 사실이다.

› **wealth** abundant possessions or resources, profusion

› **tune** melody, correct musical pitch, harmonious relationship

Not a day goes by without our children asking for the pocket money
> ↳ 아이들이 용돈을 달라고 졸라대지 않고 넘어가는 날이 하루도 없다

One would like to pull one's own
> ↳ 전 제 돈으로 사고싶어요

Our budget is stretched to the limit
> ↳ 예산이 없어

Pick-pockets always watch our every move closely, watching for the most adventitious moment to steal our money
> ↳ 소매치기들은 늘 우리의 모든 동작을 면밀히 지켜보면서 돈을 훔치기에 가장 우발적인 순간을 노린다

Please credit hundred thousand won against my account
> ↳ 내 통장에 십만원 입금해 줘(**I have debited ten thousand won against your account** 네 통장에서 십만원 뺐다)

Plenty of money often draws(brings) out the worst in some people
> ↳ 돈이 많다는 것이 어떤 사람들에게는 가장 추악한 면을 드러나게 해주는 일이 흔히 있다

Pyung-soo's got fish-hooks in his pocket
> ↳ 평수는 돈 내는데 인색해

Robbers broke into the gallery and made off with paintings to the value of 20 million won
> ↳ 도둑들이 화랑에 침입하여 2천만원 상당의 그림을 훔쳐갔다

Roping him into giving us control over his money is where I come in
> ↳ 그에게 가서 그의 돈 관리를 우리에게 넘겨주도록 틀어놓는 일은 내가 해야 할 일이다

Sang-soo paid all that money to see the concert and slept through the whole thing

---

- **debit** record as a debit
- **gallery** room or building for exhibiting art

└ 상수는 그 큰돈을 주고 음악회에 갔다가 내내 잠만 쿨쿨 자고 왔다

Sang-soo stormed off and came back with hat in hand when he ran out of money

└ 상수는 휑 하니 떠났다가 돈이 떨어지자 공손한 태도로 돌아왔다

She always keeps a decent amount of money for those emergencies

└ 그녀는 늘 그런 예상치 못했던 일에 대비해서 상당한 액수의 돈을 따로 비축해 두고 있다

She embezzled large amounts of money to finance her gambling and eventually was caught

└ 그녀는 노름 돈을 대느라고 큰 액수의 공금을 유용하다가 결국 잡혔다

She faced the music after her involvement in the money were brought to light

└ 그녀는 금전수수사건에 관련되어 있다는 소문이 밝혀진 후 자진해서 책임을 졌다

She had very little money and had a hard time, but she had weathered through

└ 그 여자에게는 돈이 거의 없어서 고생을 했지만 억척같이 살아나갔다

She has more money than sense when she bought that luxury car

└ 그 여자가 거금을 들여 고급 차를 산 것은 지각없는 짓이다

She lost the game, but she gave them a run for their money

└ 그 여자는 게임에 졌지만 잘 싸웠다

She need(ought)to have her head examined for loaning money to that dead beat

└ 남의 돈이라곤 갚을 줄을 모르는 그 사람에게 그 여자가 돈을 빌려주다니 뭔가에 홀렸군

She offered to pay for his meal when he made a big thing of having

---

‣ **emergency** condition requiring prompt action
‣ **embezzle** steal(money) by falsifying records

no money
> ↳ 그가 돈이 없다고 엄살을 떨자 그 여자가 식대를 내겠다고 나섰다

She was at a loss to explain the roller-coaster slides and surges on the money markets
> ↳ 그 여자는 통화시장의 급격한 등락현상을 설명하는데 당황했다

She's trying to keep up appearances, but she lives off borrowed money
> ↳ 그녀는 체면치레를 위해 애쓰고 있지만 빚을 얻어서 산다

Since when have you developed a taste for money?
> ↳ 너 언제부터 돈맛 들였니?

So soon as there is any talk of money, he cools down
> ↳ 그는 돈 얘기만 나오면 시들해져

Some foreign bank was laundering money for a fifteen percent cut
> ↳ 어떤 외국은행이 15%의 수수료를 받고 돈 세탁을 해 주었대

Some public servants feather their own nest by getting money from contractors
> ↳ 일부 공무원들은 건설업자들에게 뇌물을 받아 사복을 채운다

Some stick-fingered guy swiped my money yesterday
> ↳ 어떤 손버릇 나쁜 녀석이 내 돈을 어제 훔쳐갔다

Somebody like Jung-soo, who came up the hard way, understands reality better than a person who always had money
> ↳ 정수같이 가난(어려움)을 체험으로 배운 사람은 늘 돈이 아쉬운 줄 모르는 사람보다 현실을 잘 이해한다

Sometimes unscrupulous employers even call the police to have foreign workers deported to avoid paying the salary money they owe
> ↳ 때로는 사업주가 고용인들에게 대한 급료 지급을 회피하기 위하여 외국인 근로자들을 추방시키도록 경찰에 신고하기까지 한다

› **roller-coster slides** sudden increase or decrease

› **surge** rise and fall in or as if in waves

› **launder** wash or iron fabrics

Soo-man is making money hand over fist
↳ 수만이는 떼돈을 벌어

Stop sponging off money all the time
↳ 늘 돈만 뜯어내려고 하지마

Sung-ho's wife can stretch a dollar
↳ 성호의 부인은 돈을 잘 변통해 와

Sung-mo is in for two million won
↳ 성모는 이백만원 투자했어

Tai-gyung is rolling in the money because he won the lottery
↳ 태경이는 복권에 당첨되어 돈이 많아

Tai-ho made a clean sweep of the office to find the lost money
↳ 태호는 잃어버린 돈을 찾으려고 샅샅이 사무실을 뒤졌다

Ten thousand won doesn't go far these days
↳ 요즘 만원이래야 별로 쓸게 없어

That car cost the equivalent of my year's salary
↳ 저 차는 내 1년 월급에 맞먹는 비용이 들었어

That money-lender has been bleeding me white with his high rate of interest
↳ 저 고리업자가 고리를 붙여서 나를 망하게 하고 있어

That won't break the bank
↳ 그런다고 파산하지는 않아

That would be throwing good money after bad
↳ 본전 건지려다 더 망하는 꼴이지 뭐

That's my final offer
↳ 제가 해 드릴 수 있는 최저가격 입니다

That's where the money comes
↳ 그렇게 하면 돈이 생겨

› **sweep** move over with speed and force, move or extend in a wide

› **equivalent** equal

The bank has threatened to call in all money lent
↳ 은행은 모든 대출금을 회수하겠다고 으름장이다

The balance of account is against(for) me
↳ 차감 계정 결과 차입(대출)이 있다

The bill amounts(adds up, figures up) to twenty thousand won
↳ 계산이 이만원 나왔다

The burglar made off(away) with all the money in the safe
↳ 도둑은 금고 안에 있던 돈 전부를 훔쳐 가버렸다

The correct fare will be deducted from the amount recorded on the ticket
↳ 정확한 요금이 티켓에 표시된 금액에서 공제될 것이다

The cost of medical care is out of sight these days
↳ 요즘 의료비가 터무니없이 비싸다

The cost worked out at 7 pounds
↳ 비용은 7파운드로 산정 되었다

The credit card goes everywhere
↳ 그 신용카드는 어디서나 통한다

The crooked lawyer did them out of twenty million won
↳ 그 악덕변호사는 그들에게서 이천만원을 우려먹었다

The fare costs more after midnight
↳ 심야엔 할증료가 붙습니다

The fare is not on meter
↳ 차비를 미터기로 받지 않습니다

The government will soon move to halt the won's slide against the dollar
↳ 정부는 달러에 대한 원화 가치 하락에 조치를 취할 것이다

The learning of books that you do not make your own wisdom is

---

› **lent** give for temporary use, furnish
› **deduct** subtract

› **crook** bent or curved tool or part, thief
› **lawyer** legal practitioner

money in the hands of other in time of need
> 자신의 지혜로 만들 수 없는 책을 공부한다는 것은 돈이 필요할 때 남의 주머니에 있는 것과 같다

The love of money is the root of all evil
> 돈에 대한 사랑이 모든 악의 근원이다

신약성서 '디모데 전서'에서 유래한 속담이다. 이 세상의 모든 범죄는 금전, 즉 돈 때문에 일어난다고 해도 과언이 아니다.

The man was involved in green-washing some of the bribe money
> 그는 뇌물의 일부를 돈 세탁하는데 연루되었다

The money I had is gone
> 내가 가졌던 돈은 바닥났어

The money(time, effort, expense) is worth it
> 그만한 가치는 있어

The oiling companies are raking in lots of money selling all that heating oil
> 석유 회사들은 난방용 연료를 팔아 큰돈을 벌어들이고 있다

The price of this bicycle is ten thousand won, take it or leave it
> 이 자전거는 십만원 이하로는 안되니 사고 아니고는 맘대로 해

The real estate operator turned a pretty penny in selling that house
> 그 부동산 업자는 그 집을 팔아서 거금을 벌었다

The robbers lie low after holding up the bank
> 도둑들은 은행떨이 한 후 눈에 안 띄게 숨어 지냈어

The theft must have been an inside job considering only the staff knew the money was there
> 돈이 거기 있었다는 것을 직원들만이 알았던 점으로 보아 도난사건은

‣ **bribe** corrupt or influence by gifts, something offered or given in bribing

‣ **real estate** property in houses and land

내부 소행이 틀림없을 것이다

The total number of transplants may decline due to the law banning organ-for-money dealings

　　　ㄴ 총 장기이식 건수는 현금거래를 금하는 법으로 인하여 줄어들 수도 있다

The wining-and-dining revelations will unravel the plan to use taxpayer money

　　　ㄴ 뇌물성 접대 사실이 드러나면 국민의 세금을 사용하려던 계획이 밝혀
　　　질 것이다

Their plan fizzled out for lack of money

　　　ㄴ 그들의 계획은 돈이 없어서 흐지부지 끝났어

Then money will take care of itself

　　　ㄴ 그러면 돈은 저절로 벌리게 돼있어

There are still enough of these little leaks to drain off millions from the public treasury

　　　ㄴ 국가 재원으로부터 수십 억 달러의 돈을 들어먹을 이 작은 구멍들은
　　　아직도 있다

There's an off chance of getting the money back

　　　ㄴ 돈을 되돌려 받기란 쉽지 않다

There's money in it

　　　ㄴ 그거 돈 되겠는걸

There's more to life than money(success , this office)

　　　ㄴ 돈(성공)만이 인생의 전부가 아니다

There's no point in paying good money for a wedding dress when you are going to wear it once

　　　ㄴ 넌 한 번 입고 말 결혼식 드레스에 거금을 쓸 필요가 없어

These rock-bottom prices won't last forever

▸ **revelation** act of revealing, something enlightening of astonishing

▸ **leak** enter or escape through a leak, become or make known

↳ 이런 최저가는 날이면 날마다 오는 게 아닙니다

These things cost money, and I just haven't enough

↳ 그런 것들은 공짜가 아니고 내게 그만큼 충분한 돈은 없어

They are convinced the salesman did them out of lots of money

↳ 그들은 판매원이 큰돈을 떼어먹었다고 확신하고 있다

They can just scrape along(by) the little money she earns from her sewing

↳ 그들은 그 여자가 버는 작은 돈으로 연명이나 할 정도야

They had broken into the house while we were away, and turned the place inside out looking for money

↳ 그들은 우리가 집을 비운 사이에 무단침입해서 돈이 있는지 샅샅이 뒤져다

They hardly have enough money to keep body and soul together

↳ 그들은 겨우 밥이나 먹고살기에도 급급할 정도야

They joined hands(forces) to raise money when the church burned down

↳ 교회가 전소되자 그들은 모금에 협력했다

They made lots of money from cooking the books before the fraud investigators caught them

↳ 그들은 부정행위 조사단에게 적발되기 전 장부를 조작해서 거금을 벌었다

They sell apples, 300 won each

↳ 사과 한 개당 **300**원에 팔아

They'll chip in top dollar to buy him a neat present

↳ 그에게 근사한 선물을 하기 위한 일이라면 그들이 후하게 돈을 낼 것이다

They'll give you a good price

↳ 싸게 해 줄 거야

They've tried to keep a considerable amount of money tucked away for their retirement

↳ 그들은 퇴직에 대비해서 상당한 금액을 따로 저축해왔다

· **convince** cause to believe

· **scrape** remove by drawing a knife over,

clean or smooth by rubbing, get together

This high entrance fee will keep out the lower orders
↳ 이렇게 비싼 입장료라면 돈 없는 서민들이 들어가기 어려울 것이다

This last thing will bring the bill to over ten thousand won
↳ 이 마지막 물건까지 합해서 계산이 만원 넘는다

This money is safe in your hands
↳ 이 돈은 네게 맡기는 게 안심이군

This money should clear your debt
↳ 이 돈을 갚으면 너에 대한 빚은 없어지는 거야

This parcel contains a certificate check for that amount
↳ 이 소포에는 그 금액에 대한 지불보증수표가 들어있었다

Those with money never become guilty but those without money are always guilty
↳ 유전무죄 무전유죄로군

Those youngsters have too much pocket money for their own good
↳ 그 젊은이들에게는 용돈이 너무 많아 탈이다

Two million won for that job isn't hay
↳ 그 일에 이백만원이 뉘 집 아이 이름이 아냐

Vending machine eats my money
↳ 자판기가 돈을 다 먹어

Violating the traffic law cost me hundred thousand won
↳ 교통위반으로 십만원 물었다

Wan-soo did a sloppy job, so he may be whisle for his money
↳ 완수는 건성으로 일했기 때문에 돈을 받지 못할 것이다

We are cutting it fine
↳ 시간(돈)이 없어

› **parcel** lot, package, divide into portions

› **youngster** young person, child

› **vend** sell

› **sloppy** muddy, untidy

We are drowning in bills, not money to pay them with
    ↳ 돈은 없는데 고지서 투성이군

We can get some money back if we return the empties to the shop
    ↳ 우리는 빈 병 등을 가게에 가져가면 약간의 돈을 환불받는다

We gave them a run for their money
    ↳ 우린 선전(투)했어

We can get some money back if we return the empties to the shop
    ↳ 우리는 빈 병 등을 가게에 가져가면 약간의 돈을 환불받는다

We have to hold(draw) the line at this kind of expenditure
    ↳ 우린 이런 경비까지는 쓸 수 없어

We have to save money with an eye to the future
    ↳ 우린 장래를 위해 저축해야 해

We must pay the tax by the due date, or a penalty fee will be
    ↳ 세금을 납기 내에 내지 않으면 가산금이 붙어

We should get at least our money's worth
    ↳ 우린 최소한 본전치기는 해야 해

What kind of money can I make?
    ↳ 돈은 얼마나 벌 수 있을까?

What's $5 equivalent to Korean won?
    ↳ 5달러는 한국의 원으로 얼마냐?

Whatever turns a buck
    ↳ 돈만 된다면 야

When it comes to money-making, they play hard ball
    ↳ 그들은 돈벌이라면 수단방법을 가리지 않는다

When money speaks the world(truth) is in silence
    ↳ 돈이 말을 하면 세상(진실)이 침묵한다

▸ **penalty** punishment for crime, disadvantage, loss, or hardship due to an action

▸ **silence** state of being without sound

When people get together they bow to the pig and put money into the pig's mouth
> ㄴ 사람들이 모두 모일 때에 그 돼지 앞에서 절을 하고 돼지주둥이에 돈을 넣는다

Where there is muck there is money
> ㄴ 궂은 일 있는 곳에 돈 있다

While money isn't everything, it does keep you in touch with your children
> ㄴ 돈이 전부는 아니지만 돈은 당신과 아이들을 교류시키는 큰 힘이 된다

Whoever plays deep must necessarily lose his money or his character
> ㄴ 큰 도박을 하면 누구나 반드시 돈 아니면 품위를 잃게 된다

With a million won, I can manage
> ㄴ 백 만원만 있으면 어떻게 될 것 같다

With money in your pocket, you are wise and you are handsome and you sing well too
> ㄴ 돈이 있으면 현명한 사람도 되고, 멋쟁이도 되고, 노래까지 잘 하는 사람이 된다

Won-suck did me out of a large sum of money
> ㄴ 원석인 내게 거액 사기를 쳤어

Won-suck has a deep pocket
> ㄴ 원석인 돈이 많아

Won-suck is million won to the good
> ㄴ 원석인 백만원 벌었어

Would you chip in(with) some money on a gift for Sung-woo's housewarming?
> ㄴ 성우네 집들이 선물 사는데 추렴 좀 안 할래?

You can get an advance of one million won on your salary

· **bow** submit, bend the head or body

· **handsome** sizable, generous, nice-looking

· **housewarming** party to celebrate moving into a house

ㄴ 넌 월급에서 백만원 가불할 수 있어

(=You can draw one million won against your salary)

You can withdraw your money from the cash dispensers
ㄴ 현금인출기에서 현금을 인출할 수 있다

You can't bring him together on a price
ㄴ 가격문제에 그 사람 합의를 얻긴 글렀어

You can't exact a single cent from me
ㄴ 내게 한 푼도 강요해선 안 돼

You can't go wrong for 500 won
ㄴ 500원 정도라면 밑져야 본전이지

You pay your money and take your choice
ㄴ 돈 있는 곳에 명령 있어

돈의 위력을 나타낸 속담은 여러 가지가 있다. "Money makes the mare to go 돈은 당나귀도 가게 한다"와 "A golden key can open any door 돈이면 개도 명첨지다"가 그것이다. 두 가지다 돈만 가지면 세상만사 안되는 것이 없다는 것이다.
(=He who pays the piper calls the tune)
(=Money is power)

You shouldn't anticipate your income
ㄴ 수입을 예상하여 미리 돈을 써서는 안 돼

You were paid with some bad paper
ㄴ 네가 부도(위조)수표를 받았단 말이군

▸ **dispense** portion out, make up and give out(remedies)   ▸ **anticipate** be prepared for, look forward to

You won't buy me off, I'll see you in hell first
ㄴ 내게 돈으로 때우려 했다가는 큰 오산이다

You'll be fired if you have your hand in the till
ㄴ 넌 돈을 착복했다가는 해고야

Your credit card is maxed out
ㄴ 손님의 신용카드는 대출초과입니다

You look like a million dollars
ㄴ 너 신수가 훤해 보이는구나

Your money will be gone before you know it unless you are careful
ㄴ 주의하지 않으면 네 돈은 어느새 없어질 거야

· **unless** except on condition that

39. 동물   **Animal**

A cat ran into the road, causing the cyclist to swerve
> ↳ 고양이가 도로에 뛰어들어 자전거를 타고 가던 사람이 방향을 틀었다

A dragon's appearance has been regarded not only as an auspicious sign, but also as a mysterious object of folk worship in Korea
> ↳ 한국에서 용의 출현은 상서로운 조짐일 뿐 아니라 사람들이 숭배하는 신비의 대상으로 여겨왔다

A good horse should be seldom spurred
> ↳ 준마에게 박차를 가해서는 안 된다

(=Never spur a willing horse)

A little bird told me
> ↳ 소문으로 들었다

A little mouse popped out of the drawer
> ↳ 서랍에서 쥐가 한 마리 팔짝 뛰어나왔다

A little wood will heat a little oven
> ↳ 송충이는 솔잎을 먹어야 한다

· **auspicious** favorable

· **mystery** religious truth, something not   understood, puzzling or secret quality or state

분수를 모르고 터무니없는 짓을 하거나 그런 짓을 하여 낭패를 보았을 때하는 말이다. 가장 자주 쓰이는 표현, "Don't try to bite off more than you can chew"는 직역을 하면 "자신이 씹을 수 있는 것보다 더 많은 음식을 한꺼번에 베어 물지 마라"이며, 이는 자신의 능력껏 소신껏 일을 하라는 말이다.
(=A little bird is content a little nest)
(=Let the cobbler stick to his last)

A loaf of bread is better than the song of many birds
ㄴ 금강산도 식후경

인생의 즐거움도 배가 부른 연후에야 누릴 수 있다는 뜻이다. 사람이 살아가는데 있어서 의식주가 가장 중요하며, 이중에서도 가장 중요하고 인간의 목숨과도 연관이 있는 것이 바로 식(食)이다. 이 영어 속담을 직역하면 "한 덩이의 빵이 많은 새들의 노래 소리보다 낫다"이다.

A marsupial is an animal whose babies are raised in a pouch in the mother's body
ㄴ 유대류는 어미의 몸에 있는 주머니에서 새끼를 기르는 동물이다

A pig that has two owners is sure to die of hunger
ㄴ 주인이 둘인 돼지는 굶어죽게 마련이다

여러 사람이 같이 하는 일은 서로 책임을 미루게 되어 결국엔 망한다는 뜻이다. 아리스토텔레스는 정치론에서 "A matter common to most men receives least attention 많은 사람이 관심을 갖는 일은 항상 소홀히 취급된다"고 하였다.

A traveller without knowledge is a bird without wings
ㄴ 지식 없는 여행자는 날개 없는 새와 같다

· **marsupial** Australian mammal that nourishes young in an abdominal pouch

· **pouch** small bag, bodily sac

All these measures aimed at insuring the health of other animals and stabilizing the nation's economy
↳ 이 모든 조치는 다른 동물들의 건강을 확보하고 국가경제를 안정시키는데 목적을 둔다

All your insults are like water off a duck's back
↳ 아무리 욕해도 난 아무렇지 않아

Although it was a race against time, he walked like a duck in(on) its bottom
↳ 그는 시간을 다투는데도 어기적어기적 걸었다

An acre is the amount of land a yoke of oxen can plow in one day
↳ 에이커는 황소 두 필이 하루에 갈 수 있는 밭의 넓이이다

An old eagle is better than a young crow
↳ 썩어도 준치이다

(=An old poacher makes the best gamekeeper)

Animal rights groups are opposed to testing health products on animals
↳ 동물 애호가 협회는 동물을 대상으로 건강식품을 실험하는 것에 반대한다

Anyone who takes milk from an unhealthy cow will be contravening public health regulations
↳ 누구든 건강하지 않은 소에서 난 우유를 마시는 사람은 공중위생상의 규정을 어기는 것이 된다

Aristocracy in a republic is like a chicken whose head is cut off
↳ 공화국에서의 금권정치는 머리가 잘려 나간 닭과 같다

Bats flit about in the twilight
↳ 박쥐는 어두워지면 날아다닌다

· **aristocracy** upper class
· **flit** dart

· **twilight** light from the sky at dusk or dawn

Be careful not to come down on the wrong horse
> ↳ 줄을 잘못 서지 않도록 주의해라

Better a living dog than a dead lion
> ↳ 죽은 정승은 살아있는 개보다 못하다

Better be a free bird than a captive king
> ↳ 갇힌 왕보다 맘대로 날아다니는 새가 낫다

Birds of a feather flock together
> ↳ 가재는 게 편

> '동병상련', '유유상종' 등의 사자성어와 같은 뜻이다. 같은 처지에 있거나 같은 공동체에 속해 있으면 서로의 마음을 잘 이해하고, 서로의 이익을 위해 행동한다(Likeness cause liking = Dog doesn't eat dog).

Boil not the pap before the child is born
> ↳ 아이도 낳기 전에 기저귀부터 장만하지(미리 설치지) 마라

> (=Cut no fish before you get them)
> (=Don't eat the calf in the cow's belly)

Burn not your house to frighten the mouse away
> ↳ 쥐가 놀라 도망가게 하려고 집을 태우지 마라(빈대 한 마리 잡으려고 초가삼간 태우지 마라)

Call the bear 'uncle' till you are safe across the bridge
> ↳ 다리를 무사히 건널 때까지는 곰에게 잘못했다고 빌어라

› **frighten** suddenly fear

경솔하게 굴지말고 끝까지 신중을 기하라는 뜻이다. 비슷한 뜻으로 "Don't whistle until you are out of the wood 숲 속을 완전히 빠져나오기 전에는 휘파람을 불지 말라"가 있다. 숲 속을 거의 빠져나왔더라도 휘파람을 불면 맹수들을 유인할 수도 있기 때문에 끝까지 조심하라는 것을 말한다.

Chan-soo can't sit still for a moment, he is a can of worms
> ↳ 찬수는 한시도 가만히 있지 못하는 좀이 쑤시는 사람이야

Chang-soo is a lion at home and a mouse abroad
> ↳ 창수는 집안에서만 큰소리치고 밖에선 꼼짝도 못한다

(=Chang-soo is bully at home but a coward abroad)
(=Chang-soo is bossy at home but timid elsewhere)

Curiosity killed the cat
> ↳ 호기심도 정도가 있어야지

Cut that fish tale(story) out
> ↳ 그런 헛소리하지 마라

'Fish story'는 '과장된 이야기'라는 뜻이다.

Dead drunk, he looked as red as a lobster
> ↳ 고주망태가 된 그의 얼굴은 삶은 문어 같았다

Do nothing hastily but catching flies
> ↳ 파리 잡을 때 외에는 어떤 일도 서둘지 마라

- **worm** move or cause to move in a slow and indirect way
- **bossy** boss-like
- **timid** lacking in courage or self-confident

> "성급하면 손해본다(Haste makes waste)"라는 속담이 있다. 서둘다가 괜히 손해본다는 뜻이다. 비슷한 뜻을 가진 속담으로는 "Make haste, less speed (급할수록 천천히 가라)"와 "Make haste slowly(천천히 서둘러라)"가 있다.

Do you think I have the golden goose that lays the golden eggs?
  ↳ 난 뭐 도깨비 방망이라도 가진 줄(돈이 무한정 있는줄) 아나?

Do you think I'm a clay pigeon?
  ↳ 나를 동네북으로 아나?(clay pigeon 에는 '누워 떡 먹기'의 뜻이 있음)

Dogs bark but the caravan goes on
  ↳ 남이 무어라 하든 자기 할 일만 하면 된다

> 사람은 남의 의견을 수렴하지만 자신이 옳다고 생각하는 일은 추진할 수 있어야 한다. 로미오와 줄리엣에서는 "남의 말은 그리 중요한 것이 아니다. 장미꽃을 다른 이름으로 부르더라도 장미의 향기는 달라지지 않는다(What's in a name? That which we call a rose by any other name would smell as sweet)"라는 대사가 있다.

Dogs wag their tails not so much to(in love with) you as to(with) your bread
  ↳ 개가 꼬리를 흔드는 것은 당신 때문이 아니라 당신 빵 때문이다(아부에 대한 경계)

Don't be a camel sticking his nose under the tent
  ↳ 그렇게 참견하지마

Don't buy that fish, it's crawling with flies
  ↳ 그 생선은 파리가 득시글거리는데 사지마

Don't forget they are playing chicken with you

› **pigeon** stout-bodied short-legged bird

› **bark** make the sound of a dog

› **caravan** travelers journeying together

› **camel** large hoofed mammal of desert

↳ 그들이 네가 나가떨어질 때까지 버티고 있다는 걸 잊지마

Don't have a cow
↳ 징징거리지마

Don't have(hold) a big tiger by the tail. You've already bit off more than you can chew
↳ 큰 일을 벌려놓지 마라. 넌 벌써 과욕을 부리고 있어

Don't like being a small(little) fish in a big pond
↳ 시시한 사람으로 안주할 생각은 하지마

Don't make a pig of yourself
↳ 돼지같이 욕심부리지마

Don't make him feel like a fish out of water
↳ 그가 서먹서먹하지 않게 해줘

Don't put the cart before the horse
↳ 주객을 전도하지 마라

Don't sell the skin before you have killed the bear
↳ 너구리 굴 보고 빚돈 내 써서는 안 돼

Don't spur a willing horse
↳ 필요이상으로 재촉하지 마라

Don't wake a sleeping dog
↳ 일을 시끄럽게 만들지 마라

Doo-soo's accomplishment was for the birds
↳ 두수가 해낸 건 별거 아냐

Elephants have an ability to emit and hear sounds that are below the thresh-hold of human hearing
↳ 코끼리는 인간의 청각한계 아래에 있는 소리를 내고 듣는 능력을 가지고 있다

Even the porcupine thinks its young are soft and glossy

› **cart** wheeled vehicle
› **accomplish** do, fulfill, or bring about

ㄴ 고슴도치도 제 새끼는 예쁘다고 한다

> (=The beetle is a beauty in the eyes of its mother)
> (=The crow thinks her own bird fairest)
> (=The owl thinks its own young fairest)
> (=No mother has a homely child)

Every cloud has a silver lining
ㄴ 전화위복(쥐구멍에도 볕들 때 있다)

> 아무리 힘들고 어렵더라고 참고 견디면 좋은 일이 생긴다(An unfavourable situation will eventually change for the better = 계속되는 불행도 참아내다 보면 기회가 온다).
> (=Every dog has his day)

Every dog is valiant at his own door
ㄴ 자기집 문 앞에서는 모든 개가 용감하다

Fables are parables that assign human characteristics to animals to teach a lesson about human nature
ㄴ 우화란 인간의 본성에 관한 교훈을 가르치기 위해 인간의 특성을 동물들에게 부여한 비유담이다

Fish and guests stink after three days(old)
ㄴ 가는 손님은 뒤 꼭지도 예쁘다

> 직역하면 "생선과 손님은 사흘이 지나면 썩는 냄새가 난다"이다. 손님으로 가면 빠른 시일 내에 돌아오라는 얘기이다. 아무리 반가운 손님도 시간이 지남에 따라 부담스러워지기 때문이다(= A constant guest is never welcome).

› **fable** legendary story, story that teaches a lesson

› **parable** simple story illustrating a moral truth

Fish are not caught by a bird call
> ↳ 산에 가야 범을 잡고 물에 가야 고기를 잡는다

Fish or cut bait
> ↳ 하려면 똑똑히 하고 아니면 그만둬. 양단간에 결정해

Generally one animal only kills another for food, and rarely does an animal kill a member of its own species
> ↳ 일반적으로 짐승은 먹을 것을 구하기 위해서만 다른 짐승을 죽이며 자기 종족을 죽이는 경우는 극히 드물다

Get organized and stop running around like a hen with its head cut off(in circles)
> ↳ 정신 좀 차리고 호떡집에 불난 것처럼 허둥대지마

> "Running around like a hen with its head cut off"는 한국식으로 표현하면 "호떡집에 불났다"이다. 양계장에서 닭 잡는 날의 혼란스러움에 빗대어 만든 속담이다.

Grasshoppers thrive in May and June
> ↳ 메뚜기도 오뉴월이 한창이다

Hares may pull the dead lion by the beard
> ↳ 토끼도 죽은 사자는 깔본다

He did a(some) horse trading and finally came away with a contract
> ↳ 그는 빈틈없는 협상으로 마침내 계약을 따냈어

He has seen the elephant
> ↳ 그는 세상 물정을 아는 사람이다

He has so many pigs and chickens, he can hardly keep track of them
> ↳ 그는 돼지와 닭을 너무 많이 길러서 어느 우리(닭장)에 몇마리 있는지도 몰라

He is a white egg laid by a black hen

· **bait** lure especially for catching animals
· **hen** female domestic fowl
· **grasshopper** leaping plant-eating insect
· **thrive** grow vigorously, prosper

ㄴ 그는 개천에서 용 난 격이다

> 한국에서 용은 귀함을 대표하지만, 서양에서는 괴물, 악마를 뜻한다. 따라서 비슷한 뜻으로 'A white egg laid by a black hen(검은 닭이 난 하얀 알)' 이나, 'A rag to riches story(누더기에서 부자가 된 이야기)'가 쓰인다.

He keeps a dog and barks himself
ㄴ 그는 남들에게 일을 시켜놓고 스스로 해 버린다

He that steals a pin will steal an ox
ㄴ 바늘도둑이 소도둑 된다

> 이 속담은 마치 직역한 것 같이 영어와 우리나라 속담이 비슷하다. Pin 은 바늘과 같이 작은 것, ox 는 소와 같이 크고 값이 많이 나가는 것을 대표한다. 이는 동, 서양이 모두 농업 사회를 토대로 발전했다는 것을 나타낸다.
> (=He that thieves an egg will thieve an ox)

He used to be a habitual jailbird, but he'll go straight(straighten out, straighten up) this time
ㄴ 그가 왕년엔 큰집에 뻔질나게 드나들었지만 이번엔 맘 잡을 거야

He who has been bitten by a snake fears a piece of string
ㄴ 뱀에게 물려본 사람은 한 가닥 실만 보아도 무서워한다

> 가혹한 경험은 쉽게 머리에서 잊혀지지 않는다. Shy 는 '부끄러운'의 뜻이 아닌 '무서운'의 뜻이다(=A burnt child dreads the fire 불에 놀란 아이 부지깽이만 봐도 놀란다).

Heavy fines must be imposed on dog owners who are negligent about

---

· **jailbird** person confined in jail
· **impose** establish as compulsory, take

unwarranted advantage(+on or upon)

controlling their animals

↳ 개들을 잘못 관리하는 주인들에게는 과중한 벌금이 부과돼야 해

His latest play is a very different kettle of fish

↳ 그의 가장 최근 플레이는 전혀 평소의 그 답지 않았어

Honey catches more flies than vinegar

↳ 꿀은 식초보다 파리를 더 많이 잡는다(친절 권장)

친절하게 대하는 것은 말은 쉽지만 실천이 쉽지가 않다. 그러나 친절은 손해도 나지 않고, 자신에게 이로운 처세술이다.

How many pigs do we have at last count?

↳ 우리가 지난번에 세어봤을 때 돼지가 몇 마리였지?

I always have butterflies in my stomach

↳ 항상 가슴이 조마조마해

I am not going to be made a cat's paw of him

↳ 난 그 사람 앞잡이 노릇은 안 할거야

I feel like a fish out of water

↳ 어색해

(=I feel so awkward)

I have other fish to fry

↳ 다른 할 일이 있어

I think I've to just go home and kick the dog

↳ 종로에서 뺨맞고 한강에서 눈 흘길 수밖에 없게됐군

‣ **vinegar** acidic liquid obtained by fermentation

‣ **paw** foot of a 4-legged clawed animal

엉뚱한 상대에게 화풀이하는 상황을 말한다. 서양에서는 "집에 가서 애꿎은 개를 발로 찬다"는 표현을 쓴다.

I work for chicken feed(peanuts)
ㄴ 쥐꼬리 월급 받고있어

(=I'm making slave wages)

If it were a snake, it would bite you
ㄴ 업은 아이 3년 찾는다

바로 곁에 있는 것을 찾지 못할 때에 쓰이는 표현이다. 서양에서는 "그것이 뱀이라 면 당신을 물겠다"라고 하고, 이는 뱀이 물 정도로 가까이 있는 데도 알아채지 못한 다는 뜻이다(The husband is always the last to know 등잔 밑이 어둡다).

If you drink like a fish you should expect to feel sick the following day
ㄴ 술을 그렇게 마구 마셔대면 다음날 몸이 안 좋을 것은 각오해야 해

It seems that the yellow dust in the sky has become as regular as birds showing up in spring
ㄴ 봄철에 누른 색 먼지는 철새처럼 정기적으로 공중에 떠오르는 것 같다

It shouldn't happen to a dog
ㄴ 그 생각만 해도 지긋지긋해

It's as difficult as the argument over whether which come first chickens or the eggs
ㄴ 그건 닭이 먼저냐 달걀이 먼저냐 하는 논쟁만큼이나 어렵다

› **wage** engage in, payment for labor or services, compensation

› **forbid** prohibit, order not to do something

It's forbidden to import goods derived from animals on endangered species list
　　ㄴ 멸종위기 명단에 들어있는 동물로 만든 상품은 수입이 금지되어 있다

It's just a white elephant for me
　　ㄴ 빛 좋은 개살구다

It's like catching two pigeons with one bean
　　ㄴ 도랑 치고 가재잡고

It's like having the fox guard the hen-house
　　ㄴ 고양이한테 생선가게 맡긴 꼴이군

It's the last straw that breaks the camel's back
　　ㄴ 작은 일일지라도 한도를 넘으면 돌이킬 수 없게 된다

It's the power of speech which discriminates(differentiates) man from the animals
　　ㄴ 말을 할 수 있다는 점이 사람과 동물을 확실히 구별해준다

It's the tail wagging the dog
　　ㄴ 본말이 전도된 꼴이군. 하극상이로군

It's time to get on your horse
　　ㄴ 이제 떠날 준비해야지

It's unfair to ask a fish to pay for the bait he was caught with
　　ㄴ 잡힌 물고기에게 미끼 값을 내라는 건 좀 심하다

It's unlawful to try to duck out of paying taxes
　　ㄴ 납세를 피하려는 것은 불법이다

Laws catch flies, but let hornets go free
　　ㄴ 법은 큰 고기는 놓아주고 송사리만 잡는다

Let sleeping dogs lie
　　ㄴ 긁어 부스럼 만들지마

› **straw**　grass stems after grain is removed, tube for drinking

› **discriminate**　distinguish, show favor or disfavor unjustly

> 그냥 놔두면 될 것을 건드려서 화를 자초할 때 쓰이는 속담이다. 영어에서는
> "자는 개(호랑이)는 깨우지 마라", "구더기 깡통은 열지 마라" 등으로 쓴다.
> (=That would be opening a can of worms)
> (=Wake not sleeping lion)

Let the dog see the rabbit
  ↳ 도움이 안될 일에는 나서지 말고 구경이나 해

Let the lion lie down with the lamb
  ↳ 상대에게 좀 양보해서 요구사항을 잠재워라

Let's avoid dog-eat-dog competition
  ↳ 서로 잡아먹기 경쟁은 그만두자

Life is full of troubles(and trials)
  ↳ 인생은 고난과 시련에 가득 차 있다

> 인생을 고난으로 표현한 속담은 여러 가지가 있다. "Life is pilgrimage 인
> 생은 순례의 여행이다", "We must eat a peck of dirt before we die 살
> 다 보면 인생의 쓴맛을 보게 마련이다" 등이다.
> (=If wishes were horses, beggars would ride)

Little fishes slip through nets, but great fishes are taken
  ↳ 작은 물고기들은 그물은 빠져나가지만 큰 물고기들은 잡힌다

Lobsters can reproduce claws when these are torn off
  ↳ 바다가재는 집게발이 떨어져 나가도 재생할 수 있다

Lots of insects have met their death playing about a flame
  ↳ 많은 곤충들이 불꽃 주위에 접근하다가 죽었다

Love me, love my dog

› **peck** unit of dry measure equal to 9 quarts | › **reproduce** produce again or anew, bear offspring

↳ 처가 집 말뚝보고 절한다

> 진정으로 사랑을 한다면 그 사람의 단점은 물론, 주변의 모든 것이 이뻐 보이기 마련이다. 영국의 "Love me, love my dog"와 우리나라의 "처가집 말뚝보고 절한다"는 비슷한 뜻이지만, 영국의 속담은 의무, 즉 넉넉한 사랑을 요구하는 것이고, 우리나라의 속담은 당연히 그렇다는 것을 명기해 준 것이다.

Man differs from brutes in that he thinks
↳ 사람은 생각한다는 점에서 동물과 다르다

Man, when perfected, is the best animals, but, when separated from law and justice, he's the worst of all
↳ 사람이 완벽해 진다면 동물 중 가장 훌륭한 동물이지만, 법과 도리를 벗어나게 되면 가장 나쁜 동물이다

Marriage is compared to a cage: birds outside it despair to enter, and birds within, to escape
↳ 결혼은 새장과 같다. 새장밖에 있는 새는 못 들어가서 안달이고, 새장밖에 있는 새는 못 나가서 안달이다

Moles bore their way under our garden
↳ 두더지가 우리 집 정원 밑으로 구멍을 뚫고 다닌다

Monkey see, monkey do
↳ 남의 흉내를 내고있단 말이군

Moon-soo has a frog in the throat
↳ 문수는 목이 쉬어있어

> (=Moon-soo has lost his voice)

› **brute** beast, brutal person
› **mole** small burrowing mammal

› **bore** pierce, make by piercing, cylindrical hole or its diameter

Moon-soo has an memory like an elephant
> ↳ 문수는 기억력이 굉장히 좋아

Moon-soo put a flea in my ear
> ↳ 문수가 내게 듣기 싫은 소릴 했어(경고했어)

Most crocodiles will eat anything they capture and overpower
> ↳ 대부분의 악어들은 잡아서 제압할 수 있는 것이면 무엇이나 먹는다

Most tree frogs change their color to harmonize with their background
> ↳ 대부분의 나무에 사는 개구리들은 자신들의 주위환경과 맞게 색깔을 바꾼다

My dogs are killing me after walking around town all day
> ↳ 온 종일 시내를 돌아다녔더니 발이 아파

My handwriting is nothing but chicken scratches
> ↳ 내 필적은 괴발개발이야

Necessity turns lion into fox
> ↳ 필요는 사자를 여우로 만든다

Never try to teach a pig to sing, because it'll waste your time and annoy the pig
> ↳ 돼지에게 노래를 가르치려 하지 마라, 그런 일은 시간낭비인 데다가 돼지를 괴롭히는 일이기 때문이다

New born calves don't fear tigers
> ↳ 갓 태어난 송아지는 호랑이를 무서워하지 않는다(하룻강아지)

너무 어리석어서 겁이 없는 사람을 보고하는 속담이다. 비슷한 뜻으로는 "Fools rush in where angels fear to tread 바보들은 천사들이 두려워하는 곳으로 돌진한다"와 "Nothing so bold as a blind mare 눈 먼 당나귀는 무서운 것이 없다"가 자주 쓰인다.

› **handwriting** form of writing peculiar to a person
› **tread** step on or over, walk, press or crush with the feet

자신이 노력한 일의 대가를 남이 받을 때 쓰는 속담이다. 요즘 같이 노동에 대한 착취가 빈번한 사회에서 자주 쓰이는 말이다. 더 자주 쓰이는 표현으로는 "One man sows and another man reaps 파종하는 놈 따로, 거둬 가

No one believes a liar when you tell the truth
　　↳ 콩으로 메주를 쑨데도 네 말은 못 믿겠구나(이솝이야기에서)

자주 쓰이는 영어 속담 중에 "You are crying wolf too often"이 있다. 이것은 이솝이야기의 '양치기 소년'이라는 이야기에서 유래하였다. 양치기 소년이 늑대가 나타났다고 거짓말을 여러 번 했기 때문에 진짜로 늑대가 나타났을 때에는 아무도 믿지 않았다는 내용이다. 여기서 직역을 하면 "너는 늑대를 너무 여러 번 외쳤어"이고, 그렇기 때문에 믿을 수 없다는 뜻이다.

Nobody thinks their own dog is a nuisance to other people
　　↳ 자기가 기르는 개가 남에게 폐가 된다고 생각하는 사람이 없다

Nobody will open a can of worms
　　↳ 괜히 시끄러운 문제를 일으킬 사람은 없어

그냥 놔두면 될 것을 건드려서 화를 자초할 때 쓰이는 속담이다. 영어에서는 "자는 개(호랑이)는 깨우지 마라", "구더기 깡통은 열지 마라" 등으로 쓴다.

One arrow doesn't bring down two birds
　　↳ 화살 한 대로 두 마리의 새를 명중시킬 수 없다

· **nuisance**　something annoying
· **arrow**　slender missile shot from a bow

340

두 가지 일을 한꺼번에 할 수 없다는 것을 말해주는 속담이다. "You can not eat the cake and have it 케이크를 먹기도 하고 가지기도 할 수는 없다"와 "A door must either be shut or open 문은 닫히거나 열리거나 둘 중에 하나밖에 될 수 없다"도 자주 쓰이는 표현이다.

One beats the bush and another catches the birds
> ↳ 재주는 곰이, 돈은 되놈이

Only recently have the data on differences in life spans among animal species become adequate for statistical analysis
> ↳ 최근에 와서야 동물의 수명 차이에 관한 자료가 통계분석을 하기에 충분하기에 이르렀다

Pheasants have short stubby wings which enable them to fly very fast and low
> ↳ 꿩은 빨리 그리고 낮게 날 수 있는 짧고 짙은 날개를 가졌다

Prices are higher at certain seasons and holidays than at other times of the year
> ↳ 물가는 일년 중 다른 때 보다 특정 계절이나 휴가 때 더 높다

Pyung-soo wants to be a big fish in a small pond
> ↳ 평수는 용의 꼬리보다 뱀 머리가 되기를 원한다

Roasted sparrow and Soju go together best
> ↳ 참새구이와 소주는 최고로 잘 맞아

She finally got the monkey off her back
> ↳ 그 여자는 결국 골치 아픈 문제를 해결했어

She praised her dog and rewarded him a tidbit when her dog obeyed her instructions

---

› **analysis** examination of a thing to determine its parts, psychoanalysis

› **pheasant** long-tailed brilliantly colored game bird

↳ 그녀는 개가시키는 대로하자 칭찬을 하면서 먹을 것을 한 입 감 주었다

She stood glued to the spot, unable to take her eyes off the strange animal that was approaching
↳ 그녀는 이상한 동물에게서 눈을 떼지 못한 채 꼼짝 못하고 서 있었다

Some insects often escape observance because of protective coloring
↳ 곤충 가운데는 보호색 때문에 눈에 안 띄는 것이 있다

Some people expect the main computer to able to do all the donkey work
↳ 메인 컴퓨터가 따분한 일을 다 해 줄 것으로 기대하는 사람들도 있다

Stay clear of the insects which may be carrying dangerous diseases
↳ 위험한 질병을 지니고 있을지도 모르는 곤충들을 피하도록 해라

That fish was a fox
↳ 그 여자는 매력적이었어

That fish will soon be caught that nibbles at every bait
↳ 아무 미끼나 물어보는 물고기는 쉽게 잡힌다(호기심과 참견의 경계)

That safari gave us a chance to see wild animals in their natural habitat
↳ 그 탐험여행으로 야생동물들을 그들의 서식지에서 볼 기회를 얻었다

That's for the birds
↳ 그런 수에는 안 넘어가

The best fish smells when they are three days old
↳ 귀한 손님도 사흘만 넘기면 귀찮아진다

> 직역하면 "생선과 손님은 사흘이 지나면 썩는 냄새가 난다"이다. 손님으로 가면 빠른 시일 내에 돌아오라는 얘기이다. 아무리 반가운 손님도 시간이 지남에 따라 부담스러워 지기 때문이다(= A constant guest is never welcome).

The big bird swooped down on the mouse and carried it off for its meal

---

▸ **nibble** small bite, bite gently or bit by bit
▸ **safari** hunting expedition in Africa

▸ **habitat** place where a plant or animal naturally occurs

ㄴ 큰 새는 쥐를 덮쳐 물고는 먹으려고 물고 날아갔다

The bird is(has) flown

ㄴ 그는 날아가 버렸어(범인, 빚쟁이, 애인 등)

The birds numbered in the thousands

ㄴ 새떼가 수천 마리였다

The cat got his tongue

ㄴ 그 사람 부끄러워서 말못했지

The cat shot in the room with the dog after it

ㄴ 고양이는 개한테 쫓겨서 후닥닥 방으로 달려 들어왔다

The chickens that you have turned loose have got to come home to roost

ㄴ 넌 죄를 지었으니 벌을 받아 싸지 뭐

> "Curses, like chickens, come home to roost"라는 속담은 자신이 남에게 해를 끼치면 자신에게 그 해가 돌아온다는 뜻이다.

The crow that mimics a cormorant gets drowned

ㄴ 까마귀가 가마우지 흉내를 냈다가는 물에 빠져 죽는다

The dead pheasant spiraled down into the valley, where the hunting dog picked it up

ㄴ 죽은 꿩이 빙글빙글 돌면서 골짜기로 떨어지자 사냥개가 물어왔다

The deer pelted along, with the dog giving chase

ㄴ 사슴은 개에게 쫓겨서 죽어라하고 달렸다

The dog bites the stone, not him who throws it

ㄴ 개는 돌을 던진 사람을 놔두고 돌을 깨문다

The dog had an accident on the rug

ㄴ 개가 카펫에 똥을 쌌어

› **curse** call down injury upon, swear at, afflict

› **spiral** circling or winding around a single point or line

The dog minds well
> ↳ 그 개는 시키는 대로 잘 해

The farmers have a way of trapping locusts at night, using bright lights
> ↳ 농부들은 밝은 등불을 이용하여 밤에 메뚜기들을 잡는 법을 잘 알고 있다

The fish latched on to the bait
> ↳ 물고기가 미끼를 물었다

The frog in the well doesn't know the ocean
> ↳ 우물 안 개구리가 큰 바다를 알랴

The frog shot out its tongue and caught a fly
> ↳ 개구리가 재빨리 혀를 내밀어 파리를 잡아먹었다

The happiness and unhappiness of a rational, social animal depend on his or her deeds
> ↳ 이성적이고 사회적인 동물의 행복과 불행은 그들의 행위에 달렸다

The higher the animal in the evolutionary chain, the more it can learn and the less it depends on instinct
> ↳ 진화의 사슬에 있어서 고등동물일수록 더 잘 배우고 본능에 덜 의존한다

The kitten nestled up against its mother
> ↳ 새끼 고양이가 어미에게 바싹 붙어 앉았다

The little puppies squeezed themselves together to get a better chance at some food
> ↳ 작은 강아지들이 조금이라도 먹이를 잘 먹으려고 마구 같이 몰려들었다

The lobster poked its antennae out of the little cave
> ↳ 새우는 굴에서 더듬이를 밖으로 내밀었다

The miser and the pig are of no use until dead
> ↳ 구두쇠와 돼지는 죽기 전엔 쓸모가 없다

The monkey ran away with the whole performance
> ↳ 공연에서 원숭이가 최고 인기였어

› **evolution** process of change by degrees

› **instinct** natural talent, natural inherited or subconsciously motivated behavior

The mouse nibbled away at the huge cheese
ㄴ 쥐가 커다란 치즈를 갉아먹었다

The net of the sleeper catches fish
ㄴ 소발에 쥐잡기다

The pigeons will peck up all the grains that we throw on the ground for them
ㄴ 우리가 뿌리는 모이는 비둘기들이 다 쪼아먹을 것이다

The rabbit doubled back on me, and I lost its trail
ㄴ 토끼가 내가 있는 방향으로 되돌아 뛰어 오는 바람에 종적을 놓쳤어

The refugees on that asylum complained that the food served was not enough to feed a fly
ㄴ 수용소에 있던 난민들은 음식이 간에 기별도 안 간다고 불평이었다

The snake coiled itself around the branch of the tree
ㄴ 뱀은 나뭇가지를 잡아 또아리를 틀었다

The snake wound into a tight coil
ㄴ 뱀이 단단한 또아리를 틀었다

The sparrow is sorry for the peacock at the burden of its tail
ㄴ 참새는 공작의 거추장스러운 꼬리를 보고 안됐다고 생각한다

The sparrow near a school sings a prime
ㄴ 서당개 3년에 풍월 한다

"서당개 삼 년에 풍월을 읊는다"는 속담은 아주 유용하게 많이 쓰인다. "The sparrow near a school sings a primer"는 "학교 주변의 참새는 1학년 교재를 따라한다"로 직역된다. 이는 어깨너머로 배운다는 말과도 뜻이 같다.

▸ **trail** path or evidence left by something

▸ **asylum** refuge, institution for care especially of the insane

The stronger prey upon the weaker
> ↳ 약육강식

> (Big fish eat little fish) 약한 것은 결국 강한 것에게 먹히고 만다. 다윈
> 은 먹이사슬을 이론화 한 후 인간 사회에도 약육강식의 법칙을 적용시켰다.
> 강자 밑의 약자는 제대로 능력을 발휘하지 못한다.

The tiger leaped from his crouching position to bring down his quarry
> ↳ 호랑이는 사냥감을 낚아 채려고 웅크린 자세에서 펄쩍 뛰었다

The trouble is that he's a big frog in a small pond
> ↳ 문제는 그가 골목대장(우물 안 개구리)으로 끝나서는 안 된다는 점이다

The world is going to the dogs
> ↳ 세상은 말세다

The world is your oyster
> ↳ 세상은 넓고 할 일은 많다

The years, months, days, and hours have their corresponding 12 animal symbols
> ↳ 연, 월, 일, 시간에는 각각 해당되는 상징의 12 동물이 있다

The young bird found its wing
> ↳ 새 새끼는 자라서 날 수 있게 되었다

There are as good fish in the sea as ever came out of it
> ↳ 기회는 얼마든지 더 있다

There are no birds in last year's nest
> ↳ 산천은 의구한데 인걸은 간데 없네

> 인간의 흥망 성쇠는 참으로 무상하다. 모든 인간사는 환경에 따라 변하고 시
> 대가 바뀜에 따라 환경조차 변해 버렸다(Circumstances have altered).

· **crouch** stoop over

· **quarry** prey

· **oyster** bivalve mollusks

· **correspond** match(+to)

There's no need to throw him to the wolves yet
ㄴ 아직 그에게 힘든 일을 시킬 필요는 없어

They are trying to throw him to the wolves
ㄴ 그들은 그를 희생양으로 삼으려는 거야

They can hardly keep the wolf from the door
ㄴ 그 사람들 사업(살림)은 버티기 힘들 정도야

They dropped(died) like flies in that battle
ㄴ 그들은 그 전투에서 파리목숨처럼 죽어갔다

They had kittens when they found out what was going on
ㄴ 그들이 일의 진행을 보고는 당황해 했다

This animal reaches its maturity in about three years
ㄴ 이 동물은 약 3년이면 어른으로 성장하게 된다

This cold I've got in summer shouldn't happen to a dog
ㄴ 난 여름에 개도 안 하는 감기를 하고 있어

This dog minds well
ㄴ 이 개는 시키는 대로 잘 해

This fish will not keep good overnight
ㄴ 이 생선은 하룻밤 지나면 상할 것이다

This is the fish that got away
ㄴ 놓친 고기가 더 큰 법

> 놓쳐 버린 기회를 아쉬워 할 때 쓰는 표현이다. 낚시꾼들이 놓친 고기가 컸다고 과장을 하고 허풍을 자주 떨기 때문에, 'Fish story'라는 말을 '과장된 이야기'라는 표현으로 쓰기도 한다.

To mention the wolf's name is to see the same

· **alter** make different
· **get away** escape

↳ 호랑이가 제 말하면 온다

> 화제에 오르고 있는 사람이 마침 나타난다는 뜻으로 동,서양을 막론하고 자주 쓰이는 표현이다. 더 자주 쓰이는 표현으로 "Talk of the devil, and he is bound to appear 악마에 대해 말을 하면 그가 나타난다"가 있다.

Try not to back the wrong horse
> ↳ 승산 없는 사람을 지지(원) 하지마

Untrained fierce dogs ought to be destroyed before they attack people
> ↳ 훈련이 안 된 사나운 개는 사람을 물기 전에 없애버려야 한다

Villainous weeds grow in uncultivated minds and they are the haunt of toad
> ↳ 마음을 교화시키지 않으면 지독한 잡초가 자라고 그 잡초 속에 두꺼비가 우글거린다

Wan-soo is the black sheep of the family
> ↳ 완수는 집에서 내놓은 사람

Warm and fragrant breezes carry the warbles and chirps of birds rejoicing the blessings of sweet life
> ↳ 따사롭고 향기로운 미풍이 달콤한 삶의 축복을 받으면서 기뻐하는 새들의 지저귐과 짹짹거리는 소리를 싣고 온다

We are like ignorant shepherds living on a site where great civilization once flourished
> ↳ 우리는 위대한 문명이 번영했던 곳에 살고있는 셰퍼드 개만큼 역사에 대해 무식하다

We imagine ourselves more different from other animals than we are
> ↳ 우리는 실제보다 더 우리자신이 다른 동물들과 다르다고 생각한다

We'd better see which way the cat jumps

› **fierce** violently hostile or aggressive, intense, menacing looking

› **haunt** visit often, visit or inhabit as a ghost, place habitually frequented

ㄴ 상황을 보고 판단하자

When An-do won the lottery, he felt as though the world was his oyster
> 안도가 복권에 당첨되자 제 세상인 것 같은 기분이었지

When did your dog come in season(heat)?
> ㄴ 너희 개는 언제 발정했니?

When people get together they bow to the pig and put money into the pig's mouth
> ㄴ 사람들이 모두 모일 때에 그 돼지 앞에서 절을 하고 돼지주둥이에 돈을 넣는다

When pigs fly
> ㄴ 절대 안 돼(허용 불가)

When the cock is drunk, he forgets about the hawk
> ㄴ 수탉이 술에 취하면 매 따위는 안중에도 없다

When the fox preaches, beware your geese
> ㄴ 여우가 설교를 하거든 거위를 채어 가지 않을까 조심하라

When the mouse laughs at the cat, there's a hole nearby
> ㄴ 쥐가 고양이에게 웃을 때에는 바로 옆에 쥐구멍이 있기 때문이다(용기의 한계)

When we love animals and children too much, we love at the expense of them
> ㄴ 동물과 아이들을 너무 사랑한다면 그들을 망치면서 사랑하는 것이다

Who eats his cock alone must saddle his horse alone
> ㄴ 닭고기를 혼자 먹는 사람은 말 멍에도 혼자 채워야 한다

Who will not feed the cats, must feed the mice and rats
> ㄴ 고양이에게 밥을 안 주는 사람은 쥐에게 밥을 주어야 한다

Why are you running around like chickens with their heads cut off?
> ㄴ 호떡집에 불났나?

› **hawk** small or medium-sized day-flying bird of prey

› **beware** be cautious

› **nearby** near

"Running around like a hen with its head cut off"는 한국식으로 표현
하면 "호떡집에 불났다"이다. 양계장에서 닭 잡는 날의 혼란스러움에 빗대어
만든 속담이다.

Why did she marry such a mouse?
　　　↳ 그 여자가 어째서 그런 꽁생원과 결혼을 했지?

Wild horses can't draw any information out of him
　　　↳ 항우가 와도 저 사람에게서 정보는 캐내지 못해

**Worker bees labor for the good of the hive by collecting food,
caring for the young, and expanding the nest**
　　　↳ 일벌들은 식량을 수집해 오고, 새끼들을 양육하고, 집을 넓히면서 벌
　　　　집을 위해 일한다

Worms will do us for bait
　　　↳ 지렁이로 미끼를 하지

Would you teach a fish how to swim?
　　　↳ 공자 앞에 문자 쓰려고 그래?

박식한 사람 앞에서 아는 체 하는 사람을 비웃을 때 쓰는 말이다. 직역하면
"물고기에게 수영을 가르친다"이다.

You are giving me goose bumps
　　　↳ 닭살 돋게 하네

(=You make my flesh creep)

You brought you pigs to a fine(pretty) market
　　　↳ 넌 엉뚱한 짓을 한 거야

› **saddle** seat for riding on horseback
› **hive** colony of bees

› **goose bumps** cheesy feelings expressed
　　　　　　　　　as projecting of skin

You can catch more flies with honey than with vinegar
└ 식초보다 꿀이 더 많은 파리를 잡는다(부드러움은 강함을 이긴다)

You can't make them do a donkey work
└ 그 사람들에게 따분한 일을 시킬 수는 없어

You have to go to bed with chickens and get up early too
└ 넌 일찍 자고 일찍 일어나야 해

You look like the cat that ate canary
└ 눈감고 아웅 이군

"The cat that ate the canary 카나리아를 잡아먹은 고양이"란 한국 속담으로 표현하면 "눈감고 아웅한다"이다. 이는 자신이 잘못한 일을 다른 사람이 모를 것이라 생각하고 시치미 떼는 상황을 말한다. 영어 속담은 주인이 아끼는 카나리아를 잡아먹고 시치미 떼는 고양이에 비유하였다.

You look something the cat dragged in
└ 몰골이 그게 뭐니(트럭 운전사라도 널 병원에 데려가겠다)

(=You look green around the gills)
(=You could stop a truck)

You've made a dog's dinner(breakfast) of your attendance register
└ 넌 출석부를 개판으로 만들어놨군

Your goose will be cooked
└ 너한테 큰 일 나겠구나

Your thinking went out with the horse
└ 그런 낡아빠진 생각으로 뭘 할래

› **canary** yellow or greenish finch
› **attend** handle or provide for the care of something, accompany, be present at

40. 마음   **Mind & Heart**

A great mind is one that can forget or look beyond itself
    ↳ 위대한 사람은 잊어버릴 줄 알거나 그보다 더 저쪽을 볼 수 있는 사람이다

A home without love is no more a home, than a body without a sound mind is a man
    ↳ 건전한 정신이 없는 육체가 인간이 아닌 것과 같이, 사랑이 없는 가정은 가정이 아니다

A mind quite vacant is a mind distressed
    ↳ 마음이 텅 비어 있다는 것은 그 마음이 고통을 당하고 있다는 말이다

All things are easy, that are done willingly
    ↳ 하겠다는 마음으로 하면 안 되는 일이 없다

> 속담 중에도 "뜻이 있는 곳에 길이 있다(Where there is a will, there is a way)"라는 말이 있다. 아무리 힘들고 어려운 일이라도 목적을 가지고 끈기 있게 도전하면 안 되는 일이 없다는 뜻이다(=Nothing is impossible to a willing heart).

An interesting thought just past through my mind
    ↳ 재미있는 생각이 막 떠올랐어

Bong-soo(has) got his mind set on you
    ↳ 봉수의 맘은 네게 가 있어

> **distress** suffering, misfortune, state of danger or great need
> **willingly** favorably disposed in mind, promptly acting

Bong-soo has a Puritanical mind
ㄴ 봉수는 융통성 없는 사람이다

> (=Bong-soo is a straight arrow)

Bong-soo will come around(change his mind in a favorable way)
ㄴ 봉수는 우리편이 될 거야

Books operate powerfully on the soul both for good and evil
ㄴ 책은 좋건 나쁘건 간에 정신에 큰 영향을 미친다

Calamity is the touchstone of a brave mind
ㄴ 용기가 있는지는 위험에 부딪쳐봐야 안다

Chance favors a prepared mind
ㄴ 기회는 준비된 사람의 편이다

Chul-soo was so tied up with his work that it slipped his mind
ㄴ 철수가 일에 너무 몰두하다보니 그걸 깜박 잊어버린 거야

Concentrate(Focus) on what you are doing
ㄴ 한눈 팔지마

> (=Keep your mind on what you are doing)

Cross my heart and hope to die
ㄴ 정말이지 믿어 줘

Deceit is in the heart of those who devise evil, but counselors of peace have joy
ㄴ 일을 꾀하고자 하는 자의 마음에는 속임수가 있고 화평을 하는 자에

› **touchstone**   test or criterion of genuineness or quality

› **devise**   invent, plot, give by will
› **counselor**   a person who gives advises

게는 화락이 있다

Deep down in his heart he still loves her

    ↳ 그의 마음 한 구석엔 그녀를 사랑하는 마음이 남아있어

Don't get your hopes up

    ↳ 마음을 비워라

(=Don't expect to win)

Don't show him your hand too soon

    ↳ 그에게 너무 빨리 속마음을 보여주지 마라

Don't waffle about. Make up your mind

    ↳ 엉거주춤 하지 말고 마음을 정해라

Don't wear your heart on your sleeve

    ↳ 맘속에 있는 대로 표시(말) 해선 안 돼

Double-think means the power of holding two contradictory beliefs in one's mind simultaneously

    ↳ 이중사고란 두 가지의 모순된 신념을 동시에 가진다는 말이다

Ed made tremendous efforts to erase from his mind the fact that she had broken his mind

    ↳ 에드는 그녀에게서 입은 상처를 지우려고 무척 노력했다

False words are not only evil in themselves, but they infect the soul with it

    ↳ 거짓말은 그 자체가 나쁠 뿐 아니라 그 거짓말은 정신까지 오염시킨다

Feel it in your mind's eye

    ↳ 그 일을 마음속에 그려봐라

Fix it well in your mind

› **waffle** equivocate

› **contradictory** contrary

› **simultaneously** occurring or operating at the same time

ㄴ 머리 속에 잘 간직해 둬

Follow your heart
ㄴ 마음 내키는 대로(진정 원하는걸) 해

Genius is the ability to put into effect what's in his(one's) mind
ㄴ 천재는 마음속에 있는 것을 실행하는 능력이다

Gil-soo is here but really he's gone
ㄴ 길수가 몸은 여기 메여 있지만 마음은 어디론가 나가버렸어

Happiness is beneficial for the body, but it is grief that develops the powers of mind
ㄴ 행복은 신체에 이롭지만 슬픔은 마음에 힘을 길러준다

Have you ever had someone steal your heart away?
ㄴ 누군가에게 마음을 뺏겨 본 일이 있나?

He catches on quick
ㄴ 그 사람 눈치가 빨라

(=He's a good mind reader)

He couldn't work late because his mind kept jumping the track to thinking about the new girl in the office
ㄴ 그는 사무실에 새로 온 여직원 생각으로 마음이 흔들려 늦게까지 일 할 수 없었다

He doesn't know his own mind
ㄴ 그는 술에 술 타고 물에 물 탄 사람이야

He goes heart and soul into anything
ㄴ 그는 무슨 일이고 열심히 해

· **beneficial** being of benefit grief
· **develop** grow, increase, or evolve gradually;

cause to grow, increase, or reach full potential

He had enough presence of mind to rescue his friend from the wreckage
ㄴ 그는 매우 침착하게 잔해에서 친구를 구조했다

He has a black heart
ㄴ 뱃속 검은 놈

He is already such a big part of me
ㄴ 난 그에게 정이 많이 들었어

> (=He has my heart)
> (=I'm so attached to him)

He poisoned her mind against me
ㄴ 그 사람 때문에 그녀가 나를 싫어해

He that is of a merry heart has a continual feast
ㄴ 즐거운 마음을 가지는 것은 계속되는 잔치에 가는 것과 같다

He's not a bad man at heart
ㄴ 그는 본래 악인이 아냐

His anguish at not being able to be at his father's deathbed preyed on his mind for a long time
ㄴ 그에게는 아버지의 임종을 못 본데 대한 고뇌가 오랫동안 마음을 괴롭혔다

His ex-flame still holds a special place deep in her heart for him
ㄴ 그의 옛 애인은 아직도 마음 속 깊이 그를 사모하고 있다

His mind is on fire to make money
ㄴ 그는 돈 모으는데 혈안 돼 있어

Home is where the heart is
ㄴ 네 마음이 있는 곳이 바로 집이다=가정은 마음의 지주다

› **attach** seize legally, bind by personalities, join

› **feast** large or fancy meal, religious festival

I couldn't find it in my heart to do so
↳ 차마 그러지 못했지

I miss you with every beat of my heart
↳ 정말 당신을 보고싶어

In his mind's eye, he'll picture what's going to happen
↳ 그의 육감으로 무슨 일이 일어날지 예상할 것이다

In my state of mind, all cats are gray in the dark
↳ 지금 심정으로는 이런 것 저런 것을 구분할 상황이 아냐

It doesn't make no mind(matter) if we have college degrees or not
↳ 우리가 대학을 나왔거나 아니거나 상관없어

It shows the way my mind was working then
↳ 그건 그 때 내 마음이 어디로 끌렸는지 보여주고 있어

It weighs on my mind
↳ 그거 부담되네

It's a woman's privilege to change her mind
↳ 변하는 게 여자의 마음 아니겠어

우리나라 속담 중에 '여자의 마음은 갈대'라는 말이 있다. 여자가 변덕이 심하다는 뜻이다. 영어 속담 중에도 비슷한 'A woman is a weathercock'라는 표현이 있다. 'Weathercock'은 지붕 위에서 풍향에 따라 움직이는 닭 모양의 풍향계를 뜻한다. 풍향에 따라 시시각각 변하는 것을 비유한 표현이다.

It's all a mind game
↳ 그건 모두 마음먹기에 달렸어

It's all in your mind
↳ 그건 네 마음먹기에 달렸다

› **beat** single stroke or pulsation, rhythmic stress in poetry or music, strike   repeatedly, defeat(+down), act or arrive before, throb

It's difficult to plan anything with him because he doesn't know his own mind
> ↳ 그는 우유부단해서 같이 계획을 세우기가 어려워

It's indelibly impressed upon my mind
> ↳ 그 일은 내 머리에서 사라지지 않아

Just as our eyes need light in order to see, our minds need ideas in order to conceive
> ↳ 우리의 눈이 보는데는 빛이 필요하듯이 우리의 마음에 아이디어가 있어야 궁리를 하게 된다

Just do what you want
> ↳ 마음 내키는 대로 해

Keeping his heart on what he wanted and ignoring everything else, he made a success in life
> ↳ 그는 자신이 원하는 일에만 마음을 쏟고 다른 모든 것을 무시하면서 성공을 이루어내었다

Let him into your heart
> ↳ 마음으로 그를 받아들여라

Let's cast our minds back to the first meeting
> ↳ 우리가 처음 만났던 때의 기억을 되살려 보자

Let's turn over a new leaf
> ↳ 새로운 마음으로 시작하자

Little minds are attracted by little minds
> ↳ 소인은 하찮은 일에 흥미를 가져

Love looks not with the eyes, but with the mind
> ↳ 사랑은 눈으로 보는 것이 아니라 마음으로 본다

Men are not prisoners of fate, but only prisoners of their own minds

---

› **indelible**　not capable of being removed or erased

› **in order to**　to perform something

› **conceive**　think of, become pregnant

ㄴ 사람은 운명의 포로가 아니라 자기 마음의 포로이다

My father has a mind like a steel trap
　　　　ㄴ 아버지는 기억력이 매우 좋으셔

My heart bleeds for you in your sorrow
　　　　ㄴ 네가 슬퍼하니 내 마음이 아파

My heart(mind) misgives me about the result
　　　　ㄴ 결과가 걱정이다

My mind is torn between the two choices
　　　　ㄴ 이럴까 저럴까 망설이는 중이야

My mind keeps ringing on the problem
　　　　ㄴ 내 마음은 줄곧 그 문제에만 가 있다

My mind keeps wandering from my work
　　　　ㄴ 일이 손에 안 잡혀

```
(=I can't concentrate(focus) on my work)
(=I can't pay my attention to my work)
```

My mind was on other things
　　　　ㄴ 깜박했어

```
(=I was preoccupied)
```

My mother's mind is failing
　　　　ㄴ 어머닌 노망기가 있어

```
(=My mother is getting senile)
```

> **fate**　cause beyond human control held to determine events, end or outcome

> **tear**　separate or pull apart by force, move or act with violence or haste

Myung-soo is a man with a mind of his own
ㄴ 명수는 줏대가 있는 사람이다

Myong-soo marks the time and pays no mind to the job
ㄴ 명수는 시간만 죽이면서 일에는 마음을 쓰지 않아

Nothing is impossible to a determined mind
ㄴ 마음을 굳게 먹으면 안 되는 일이 없다

Peace in mind is no less necessary for our health than fresh air and sunlight
ㄴ 마음의 평화가 신선한 공기와 햇빛만큼이나 우리들 건강에 필요하다

Politeness is the art of selecting among one's real thoughts
ㄴ 예의바름이란 진짜 속마음 중에서 어떤 것을 드러낼지의 선택이다

Put all other things out of your mind and concentrate on your study
ㄴ 다른 생각은 다 떨쳐버리고 공부에 전념해라

Reading is to the mind what exercise is to the body
ㄴ 독서가 정신에 필요한 것은 운동이 신체에 필요한 것과 같다

Regrets and recriminations only hurt your soul
ㄴ 후회와 남의 탓 하기는 자신의 마음만 상하게 할 뿐이다

Remember your constant nagging only makes me all the more determined not to change my mind
ㄴ 네가 쉴새없이 잔소리 해봤자 내 마음이 확고히 변하지 않게 굳혀줄 뿐임을 잊지 마라

She makes my heart skip a beat
ㄴ 그녀는 내 맘을 설레게 해

She understood me heart to heart
ㄴ 그 여자는 진심으로 나를 이해했어

So let it out and let it in

▸ **determine** decide on, establish, or settle, find out, be the cause of

▸ **politeness** mark of correct social conduct

▸ **select** take by preference

↳ 이제 심호흡하고 마음을 가다듬어라

Sook-hee doesn't give her heart to just anyone

↳ 숙희는 아무에게나 마음을 주는 여자가 아니다

Stop chopping around(about) and make up your mind

↳ 이랬다저랬다 하지말고 마음을 정해라

Such hot weather in-disposes anyone to work hard

↳ 이렇게 더워서는 누구나 일할 마음이 없어진다

Sung-soo is so attached to me

↳ 성수는 내게 정이 듬뿍 들었어

(=Sung-soo already has my heart)
(=Sung-soo is already such a big part of me)

Suspicion always haunts the guilty mind

↳ 죄 있는 사람에게는 항상 의심이 따라다닌다

Tell me any idea that may occur(flash) your mind

↳ 느낀 점이 있으면 무엇이든지 말씀해 주세요

That poisoned his mind against me

↳ 그 일로 그가 내게 편견을 갖게 됐어

The battle for people's mind is more important than military struggle

↳ 민심을 얻기 위한 전쟁은 군대를 동원한 전투보다 중요하다

The direction of the mind is more important than its progress

↳ 마음의 방향은 마음의 진행보다 중요하다

The face is no index to the heart

↳ 얼굴이 곱다고 마음씨가 고운 건 아니다

› **suspicion** act of suspecting something, trace

› **occur** be found or met with, take place, come to mind

The idea flash through my mind
↳ 그 생각이 번개같이 머리를 스쳤다

The loneliness after his wife's death made my heart bleed
↳ 부인을 잃은 그의 외로움에 내 가슴이 아팠어

The problem sat heavy on my mind
↳ 그 문제가 내 마음을 무겁게 눌렀다

The scramble to win his heart stems from their judgement
↳ 그들이 앞다투어 그의 마음을 끌고싶어 하는 것은 그들의 판단에서 비롯된다

The soul which is not at peace with itself can't be at peace with the world
↳ 마음이 평화롭지 못한 사람은 세상을 편안히 살아갈 수 없다

The thought flashed through my mind
↳ 그 생각이 마음에 언 듯 떠올랐다

The trouble about always trying to preserve the health of the body is that it is so difficult to do without destroying the health of the mind
↳ 신체의 건강을 항상 유지하려는데 따르는 문제점은 정신건강을 해치지 않고는 매우 어렵다는 점이다

The unrequited love festered in her mind
↳ 짝사랑 때문에 그녀의 마음은 괴로웠다

The way to a man's heart is through his stomach
↳ 남자의 사랑을 얻으려면 그가 좋아하는 음식을 만들어 줘라

The writer's life seethes within but not without
↳ 글 쓰는 사람의 삶은 마음속에서 끓고 밖으로는 끓지 않는다

There's a fire in my heart
↳ 내 가슴이 불타고 있어

They are all of a mind(size)

‣ **scramble** struggle for possession of something

‣ **soul** person

‣ **destroy** kill or put an end to

↳ 전부 같은 마음(크기)이다

They mark their time and pay no mind to the job
↳ 그들은 퇴근시간만 기다리고 일에는 관심 없어

Though old, he has a spirit
↳ 그가 몸은 늙어도 마음은 젊다

To love is to admire with the heart; to admire is to love with the mind
↳ 사랑이란 진심으로 존경하는 것이며 존경이란 마음을 다해 사랑하는 것이다

Try to be relax before exam, and you'll deal with(approach) it in a better frame of mind
↳ 시험 전에 긴장을 풀도록 해라, 그러면 보다 나은 마음상태로 대처할 수 있을 것이다

Try to rid your mind of such obsolete ideas
↳ 그런 시대에 뒤진 생각들을 마음속에서 내버리도록 해

True compassion can only be felt in the hearts of those who have suffered the same situation
↳ 진정한 연민은 똑 같은 상황을 겪어본 사람들의 마음속에서만 느껴질 수 있다

> '동병상련', '유유상종' 등의 사자성어와 같은 뜻이다. 같은 처지에 있거나 같은 공동체에 속해 있으면 서로의 마음을 잘 이해하고, 서로의 이익을 위해

Turn it over in your mind before you decide it
↳ 그 일을 결정하기 전에 신중히 고려해 봐

Vast chasms can be filled, but the heart of man never
↳ 매우 큰 틈새들은 메울 수 있지만 사람의 마음은 메울 수 없다(만족을 모른다)

Villainous weeds grow in uncultivated minds and they are the haunt of toad
↳ 마음을 교화시키지 않으면 지독한 잡초가 자라고 그 잡초 속에 두꺼

· **frame** plan, formulate, construct or arrange, enclose in a frame
· **obsolete** no longer in use
· **compassion** pity

비가 우글거린다

What the eye doesn't see, the heart won't grieve over(crave for)
 ↳ 차라리 보지 않으면 슬퍼할(가지고싶은) 일도 없으련만

> 좋은 물건을 보면 가지고 싶은 마음이 생기게 마련이다. 거기다 관리까지 허술
> 하다면 다른 사람으로 하여금 도둑질을 하고 싶은 충동을 느끼게 한다. 비슷한
> 뜻으로 "A postern door makes a thief 뒷문이 도적을 만든다"도 쓰인다.

What the heart thinks, the mouth speaks
 ↳ 마음에 품은 것은 입 밖으로 나오게 돼있어

What price range do you have in mind?
 ↳ 생각하시는 가격수준은 얼마입니까?

We must harden our hearts and ignore them
 ↳ 우린 마음을 단단히 먹고 그런 일을 무시해야 해

We should obey the spirit, not the letter, of the law
 ↳ 법률의 조문이 아니라 정신을 따라야 한다

When by force subdue men, they do not submit to him in heart
 ↳ 힘으로 사람을 굴복시킨다면 마음속으로 굴복하지 않을 것이다

When the devil was ill, he wish to be a monk; when the devil was recovered, he was devil as before
 ↳ 화장실 갈 때 마음 다르고 올 때 마음 다르다

> 환경에 따라 태도와 입장이 바뀌어진다. 직역하면 "악마가 병에 걸리면 수도
> 승이 되길 원하지만, 병이 나으면 다시 악마가 된다"이다. 사람의 마음은 시
> 시각각 변한다는 것을 말한다.

When the idea of winning in sports carried too excess, honorable

---

› **obey** follow the commands or guidance of, behave in accordance with

› **subdue** bring under control, reduce the intensity of

competition can turn into disorder and violence
> ↳ 경기에 이기겠다는 생각이 지나치면 명예로운 경쟁의 원칙이 무질서
> 와 폭력으로 변할 수 있다

Whenever I'm near him my heart misses(skips) a beat(stands still)
> ↳ 그 사람 옆에만 가면 가슴이 두근거려(심장이 멎는 느낌이야)

Whether she carries on or not is all in the mind
> ↳ 그 여자가 해낼 수 있을지는 그 여자의 마음(의지)에 달렸다

Why the change of heart?
> ↳ 어째서 심경의 변화를 일으켰지?

(=what made your change of heart?)

Without the rich heart, wealth is an ugly beggar
> ↳ 마음이 풍족하지 않은 부자는 몰골 사나운 거지이다

You can follow your heart in this matter
> ↳ 이 일에는 마음 내키는 대로 해

You have a heart of gold
> ↳ 넌 맘씨가 곱구나

You may put your mind at rest on that point
> ↳ 그 점에 있어서는 염려 안 해도 돼

You must make up your mind to that
> ↳ 넌 체념하고 받아들여(각오해)야 해

You need someone to whom you can pour your heart out
> ↳ 네게는 마음을 털어놓을 만한 사람이 있어야 해

You'll succeed if you put your mind to it
> ↳ 넌 맘만 먹으면 그 일을 해낼 수 있어

› **wealth** abundant possessions or resources, profusion

› **beggar** one that begs
› **make up one's mind** decide

You're out of your mind
> ㄴ 네가 제정신이냐? 돌았군 돌았어

> (＝You've got to be out of your mind)

Your friend's name flitted through my mind, only to be forgotten again
> ㄴ 네 친구 이름은 언 듯 생각이 났다가도 그저 잊어버려져

▸ **flit**　dart

41. 말   Words

A different construction was put on the wording of your statement by each of them
> ↳ 네가 한 말의 표현에 대하여 그들은 각기 다른 해석을 내렸어

A dog is not considered good because of his barking, but a man is because of his ability to talk
> ↳ 잘 짖는다고 해서 훌륭한 개가 아니지만, 말 잘 하는 사람은 훌륭한 사람으로 대우받는다

A good tongue is a good weapon
> ↳ 말 잘 하는 것도 훌륭한 무기다

A man is hid under his tongue
> ↳ 혀의 아래에는 사람의 모습이 가려져 있다

A man of his words, and not of his deed, is like a garden of weed
> ↳ 말만 많고 실천이 없는 사람은 잡초만 우거진 정원과 같다

A person is a bore who talks when you wish him to listen
> ↳ 당신의 말을 들어주기를 원하는 사람이 안 듣고 말을 할 때 그가 바로 따분한 사람이다

A story doesn't lose in the telling
> ↳ 말이란 흔히 과장되는 법(말에는 꼬리가 붙게 마련)

A tale is never lost in the telling
> ↳ 말은 되풀이하면 커지게 마련이다

› **statement**   something stated, financial summary

› **deed**   exploit, document showing ownership

› **weed**   unwanted plant

A word before is worth two behind
  ↳ 사전의 한 마디는 사후의 두 마디와 맞먹는다

A word here may be in order
  ↳ 이쯤에서 한 마디 해도 좋을 것 같다

A word in your ear
  ↳ 귀 좀 빌리자(한 마디 할게 있어)

Abstract words are beyond the ken of children
  ↳ 추상적인 말은 아이들에게 이해하기 어렵다

Against his will he was swept along by my cogent words
  ↳ 그는 본의 아니게 나의 힘있는 말에 설득 당했다

All talking is barred during a study period
  ↳ 공부 시간 중 잡담을 금한다

All you have done so far is talk in circles
  ↳ 지금까지 네가 한 것이라곤 했던 말을 또 하고 또 한 것 뿐이야

An-do's insult left me speechless
  ↳ 안도의 모욕을 당하고 나니 말도 안 나왔어

Annoyed is no word for it
  ↳ 그냥 언짢은 정도가 아냐

Anything you say can be used against you
  ↳ 네가 한 말은 네게 불리하게 작용할 수 있다

Anything you say
  ↳ 뭐든 말만 해

Are you directing your remark at(to) me?
  ↳ 내게 한 말이냐?

Are you getting somewhere with Moon-Soo?
  ↳ 문수하고는 얘기가 잘 돼가니?

› **sweep** move over with speed and force
› **abstract** not representing something specific

› **cogent** compelling or convincing

Are you in a position to say that?
> ↳ 그렇게 말할 자격 있니?

> (=Are you entitled to say that?)

As poetry is the harmony of words, so music is that of notes
> ↳ 시가 말의 조화이듯이 음악은 선율의 조화이다

As soon as she made the remark, she could have bitten her tongue off
> ↳ 그 여자는 말을 꺼내자마자 자신이 내뱉은 말에 대해 후회했다

Be careful not to let your tongue run away with you again
> ↳ 또다시 말을 못 참는 일이 없도록 조심해

Be careful not to shoot from the hip
> ↳ 준비 없이 행동(말) 하지 않도록 주의해

Be careful what you say
> ↳ 함부로 말하지마

> (=Watch what you say)
> (=Watch your mouth)
> (=Don't say things you'll regret).

Be sure to your own word
> ↳ 말한 건 지켜야 해

> (=Be true to your own word)
> (=Do what you promised you would do)

· **entitle** name, give a right to

· **harmony** musical combination of sounds, pleasing arrangement of parts, lack of conflict, internal calm

Better say nothing than nothing to the purpose
↳ 아무 요령 없는 말을 하느니보다 가만히 있는 것이 낫다

Better the foot slip than the tongue
↳ 실언보다는 실족이 낫다

Big mouth
↳ 잔소리 되게 하네(**motor mouth, magpie, windbag, talking machine**)

Bong-soo is always bragging(boasting) of his son, as if anybody cared
↳ 봉수는 남들이 들은 척도 안 하는 아들 얘기만 하고 있어

Bong-soo told me where to get off
↳ 봉수가 내게 화를 내며 말했어

Bong-soon called his bluff and said "Let's see you do it"
↳ 봉순이가 그에게 말로만 하지말고 보여주라면서 "얼마나 잘하는지 어디 보자"라고 했어

Brevity is the soul of wit
↳ 말은 짧을수록 좋아

> 말이란 뜻을 전달하기 위한 수단이다. 거창하고 긴 말은 말의 초점을 흐릴 뿐만 아니라, 진실성이 없어진다. 비슷한 뜻으로 "Short answer is often the most eloquent 간단한 말은 웅변과 같다"도 쓰인다.

Byung-soo's remarks put the matter wrong
↳ 찬수의 말이 사태를 악화시켰다

Can I digress for a moment?
↳ 잠시 본론에서 벗어나도 되겠습니까?

Can you get it through your head?
↳ 그게 무슨 말인지 납득이 가니?

› **bluff** deceive by pretense
› **brevity** shortness or conciseness

› **eloquent** forceful and persuasive in speech

Can you run that by me again?
    ↳ 다시 한번 말해 줄 수 있겠니?

Chang-soo always talks in circles
    ↳ 창수는 늘 겉도는 소리만 하고 있어

Chang-soo is a man of fair words
    ↳ 창수는 말주변이 좋아

Chang-soo is too chicken-shit to go up and talk to her
    ↳ 창수는 너무 소심해서 그녀에게 말을 붙여보지 못하고 있어

Chang-soo was tongue-tied on what to say
    ↳ 창수는 무슨 말을 해야할지 몰랐다

> (=Chang-soo didn't know just what to say)
> (=Chang-soo was fumbling for words)

Come and get an eyeful(earful) of this
    ↳ 와서 이걸 좀 봐(내 말 좀 들어봐)

Come off it
    ↳ 객쩍은 소리 마

> (=Stop that nonsense)

Conversation is unlike a discussion, insofar as one is not trying to arrive at any definite conclusion
    ↳ 대화란 어떤 명확한 결론에 도달하려고 하지 않는 점에 있어서 토론과 다르다

‣ **chicken-shit** small-minded, petty

‣ **tongue-tied** speechless

‣ **fumble** fail to hold something properly

Conversation teaches more than meditation
 ↳ 대화는 명상보다 더 많은 것을 가르쳐 준다

Could you be more specific?
 ↳ 좀더 구체적으로 말씀해 주시겠습니까?

Cut that fish tale(story) out
 ↳ 그런 헛소리하지 마라

> Fish Tale(Story) 는 과장된 이야기를 말한다.

Cut to the chase
 ↳ 단도직입(본론만)으로 말해

> (=Just get to the point)

Deeds are better than words
 ↳ 말보다 실천

Different people say different things all the time
 ↳ 사람마다 하는 말이 달라

Do not be afraid to speak because you are afraid of what others may think of you
 ↳ 다른 사람들이 당신을 어떻게 생각할까 두려워서 말하기를 두려워 말라

Do those chatterboxes ever stop talking big?
 ↳ 저 수다쟁이들의 허풍은 못 말린다니까

Do you have to bark your orders out at everyone?
 ↳ 아무한테나 이래라 저래라 명령조로 말해야 하니?

· **meditation** contemplation
· **specific** definite or exact

· **chase** follow trying to catch, drive away

Do you want me to give you a rundown?
↳ 개요를 말해줄까?

Do you want me to simplify it more
↳ 말귀를 못 알아들어

Don't ask me. I take the fifth
↳ 내게 묻지마. 난 말 안 하기로 했으니까

Don't beat around the bush, come straight to the point
↳ 변죽만 울리지 말고 요점을 말해

Don't believe a person on his bare word
↳ 남의 말만 듣고 믿어선 안 돼

Don't breathe a word of this
↳ 입도 벙끗 말아라

Don't change the subject
↳ 말 돌리지마

Don't chop(cut) me off
↳ 내 말 막지마(안 끝났어)

Don't cut the grass from under my feet(pick at my words or find fault with my remark)
↳ 말꼬리 물고늘어지지지마(방해하지마)

(=Don't pick at(nitpick, criticize) everything I say)
(=Don't pick at my every word)

Don't get me started on the food
↳ 음식얘기는 꺼내지도 마라

› **chatterbox** incessant talker
› **bare** naked, not concealed, empty, leaving

nothing to spare, plain, make or lay bare

Don't give me a line
> ↳ 마음에도 없는 소리하지마

Don't give me any of that nonsense
> ↳ 그 따위 소리 마

Don't give me none of your noise
> ↳ 그런 헛소리하지마

Don't give me that cock-and-bull story
> ↳ 말도 안 되는 소리하지마

Don't give me that line about how hard things are for you
> ↳ 네가 얼마나 어려운 처지에 있는지 장황하게 늘어놓지마

Don't give me that
> ↳ 그런 소리 마

(=Don't talk like that)

Don't let anyone say you're talking to hear your own voice
> ↳ 남들에게서 네가 말이 많다는 소릴 듣게 해선 안 돼

Don't let yourself loose
> ↳ 함부로 지껄이지마

Don't say anything you don't mean
> ↳ 마음에 없는 말하지마

Don't shoot yourself in the foot
> ↳ 경솔하게 말하지마

(=Don't put your foot into your mouth)
(=Don't say the wrong thing)

› **cock-and-bull story** an absurd story, sheer nonsense, a lie, a   hoax, a fabrication

Don't shuffle; give a clear answer
↳ 얼렁뚱땅 하지 말고 똑똑히 말해

Don't speak out of order
↳ 차례가 아닐 때 말하지 마라

Don't speak out of place
↳ 자다가 봉창 두드리지마

Don't speak too soon
↳ 그렇게 말하기는 아직 일러

Don't speak with a forked tongue
↳ 일구이언하지마

Don't speak with your mouth full
↳ 입에 음식을 넣은 채 말하지마

Don't split hairs about who's to blame for such trifles
↳ 그런 하찮은 일에 누구 잘못인지 따위의 시시콜콜한 얘기는 집어 치워

Don't tell me that. What I don't know won't(can't) hurt me
↳ 그런 건 내게 말하지마. 모르면 기분 상할 일도 없으니까

Don't tell the whole world
↳ 사사로운 일을 남들에게 얘기하지마

Don't try to have the last word
↳ 억지쓰지마

Don't turn it off with a joke
↳ 농담으로 얼버무리지마

Don't use bad language
↳ 상소리 하지마

Don't want to communicate
↳ 아무 말도 하고싶지 않아(**I**가 생략되어 있음)

‣ **shuffle** mix together, walk with a sliding movement

‣ **fork** divided into branches, move with a fork

Don't wear your heart on your sleeve
    ↳ 맘속에 있는 대로 표시(말) 해선 안 돼

Dong-soo let that idea slip out before he thought
    ↳ 동수는 무심코 그 생각을 입 밖에 내고 말았다

Doo-chul gave me a long song and dance about his new car
    ↳ 두철인 새 차를 샀다고 한참 얘길 늘어놓았어

Doo-soo can't have the last word
    ↳ 두수에겐 결정권이 없어

Duck-soon is getting diarrhea of the mouth(jawbone)
    ↳ 덕순이가 또 끝없는 얘길 늘어놓는군

Each has his own claims
    ↳ 누구에게나 할 말은 있다

Ed is a charitable person? Tell me another one
    ↳ 에드가 자선가라고? 소가 웃겠군

Ed's foul language in the office caused our eyebrows to rise
    ↳ 에드가 사무실에서 상스러운 말을 하는 바람에 우리가 놀랐어

End of the story
    ↳ 그게 전부(다)야

> (=Period)
> (=That's all she wrote)

Enough with your sarcasm
    ↳ 비꼬지마

> (=Stop making sarcastic remarks)

› **jawbone** use public persuasion to influence behavior

› **claim** demand of right or ownership, declaration, something claimed

Everybody wishes that loud mouth would put a cork in it
ㄴ 저 떠버리가 입 좀 다물어주길 모두가 바라고 있다

Everyone wants to have(get) his say in this matter
ㄴ 이 일에는 누구나 한 마디씩 하고싶어해

Excuse my slip of the tongue
ㄴ 실언을 용서해 주세요

False words are not only evil in themselves, but they infect the soul with it
ㄴ 거짓말은 그 자체가 나쁠 뿐 아니라 그 거짓말은 정신까지 오염시킨다

First learn the meaning of what you say, and then speak
ㄴ 자신이 하는 말의 뜻을 파악한 다음 말하라

Flattery will get you everywhere
ㄴ 말 한마디에 천 량 빚 갚는다

> (=Good words are worth much and cost little)

Flexing vocabulary runs right through me
ㄴ 하지 못한 말들이 입에서 맴돌고 있어

Gil-soo's rude remark got to me for a while
ㄴ 길수의 험한 말에 한동안 속상했다(get to 에는Please 또는 Entice라
는 반대의 뜻도 있음)

Give me a blow by blow account
ㄴ 아주 좀 자세히 얘기 해

Good words without deeds are rushes and reeds
ㄴ 행동이 따르지 않는 말은 골풀과 갈대와 같다

Great talkers are not great doers
ㄴ 말 잘하는 사람 치고 실행이 따르는 사람 없다

› **excuse** pardon, release from an obligation, justify

› **flattery** praising insincerely
› **flex** bend

"빈 수레가 요란하다 Empty vessels make the greatest noise"와도 뜻이 통한다. 말이 많고 허풍이 많은 사람일수록 실천이 뒤따르는 사람은 드물다.

He concocted the whole story from dribs and drabs of gossip
　↳ 그는 토막 얘기들을 묶어서 얘기를 만들어 내었다

He didn't say so in so many words
　↳ 그는 사실대로 말하지 않았다

He goes off on tangents to no end
　↳ 그는 두서(목적)없는 말을 해 옆으로 새버려

He had his word stack in his throat
　↳ 그는 목이 메어 말을 잇지 못했다

He is all mouth and no chops
　↳ 그 사람은 입만 살고 행동이 없어

He is closed about his own affairs
　↳ 자기 일을 좀처럼 말하지 않아

He is not good himself who speaks well of everybody alike
　↳ 누구에게나 똑같이 좋게 말하는 사람은 그 사람 자신이 좋은 사람이 아니다

He is talking in circles again
　↳ 그 사람 또 횡설수설이군

He is the last word in architecture
　↳ 그는 건축의 최고 권위자이다

He left the remark unnoticed
　↳ 그는 그 말을 대수롭지 않게 여겼다

He must have dropped his buckets when he said that
　↳ 그가 그 말을 했을 땐 실언이 틀림없어

› **architecture**　building design, style of building

› **bucket**　pail, hustle, move about hurriedly or jerkily

He put his foot in his mouth
> 그 사람 무례한 말을 마구 했어

He rambled on for almost two hours without really saying anything
> 그는 실제 알맹이도 없이 거의 두 시간이나 얘기했다

He rambles on and on, so I try to avoid getting into conversations with him
> 그는 같은 말을 또 하고 또 해서 그와의 대화를 피하려고 해

He runs off at the mouth all the time(has diarrhea of mouth)
> 그는 항상 말이 너무 많아

He that has no silver in his purse should have silver in his tongue
> 주머니가 빈 사람은 말주변이라도 있어야 한다

He that speaks lavishly shall hear as knavishly
> 말을 마구 하는 사람은 그만큼 험한 말을 듣게 되어있다

He was muddling on(along), and nobody could follow what he was trying to say
> 그가 어물어물 넘어가는 바람에 아무도 무슨 말을 하려는지 이해할 수 없었다

He was through talking to you
> 그는 기분 나빠 네게 말을 안 한 거야

He weighs his words carefully
> 말을 허투루 하는 사람이 아니다

He who guards his mouth preserves his life, but he who opens wide his lips shall have destruction
> 입을 지키는 자는 그 생명을 보전하나 입술을 크게 벌리는 자에게는 멸망이 오느니라

He who restrains his lips is wise

› **lavish** expending or expended profusely

› **muddle** make, be, or act confused, make a mess of, waste(+away)

ㄴ 입술을 제어하는 자는 지혜가 있느니라

He who speaks without modesty will find it difficult to make his words good
　　ㄴ 겸손하지 않게 말하는 사람은 자신의 말을 귀담아 듣게 하기 어려울 것이다

He who talks more is sooner exhausted
　　ㄴ 말은 많이 할수록 빨리 지친다(할 말이 없어진다)

He's always telling, never doing
　　ㄴ 그는 언제나 말만하고 실행은 하지 않는다

He's off the track(on the wrong track)
　　ㄴ 잘 나가다가 삼천포로

Her cruel remarks cut me to the quick
　　ㄴ 그 여자 가시 돋친 한 마디에 기분 잡쳤어

Her speech was full of contradictory statements
　　ㄴ 그녀의 말에는 모순된 발언 투성이였다

His closing words brought the whole crowd to their feet, cheering wildly
　　ㄴ 그의 마지막 말에 사람들이 열광적으로 환호하며 기립박수를 보냈다

His last novel had all the marks of having been written in haste
　　ㄴ 그의 지난번 소설은 허겁지겁 쓴 게 틀림없어

His rambling way of talking is getting us nowhere
　　ㄴ 그의 얘기는 이랬다저랬다 해서 종잡을 수 없었다

His speech was all form and no content
　　ㄴ 그의 연설은 말이 연설이었지 알맹이가 없었다

His speech was stumbling and disjointed
　　ㄴ 그의 말은 더듬거리며 횡설수설 종잡을 수 없었다

His word is law
　　ㄴ 그의 말은 들어야 해

· **novel** long invented prose story
· **stumble** speak or act clumsily

· **disjoint** separate the parts of, separate at the joints

His words and actions do not correspond
ↄ 그는 언행이 일치하지 않아

His words betrayed his anger
ↄ 말속에 가시

(=I could feel his anger in his words)

His words have a ring of truth
ↄ 그의 말에는 진실이 담겨있다

How could you have the gut to say so?
ↄ 어디서 감히 그런 말이 나와?

How dare you say such a thing?
ↄ 감히 네가 어찌 그런 말을

How else can I say it?
ↄ 그렇게 밖에 말할 수 없잖아

Hyun-soo could have hurt you by telling what he knew, but he held fire
ↄ 현수는 자기가 알고 있는 말을 내 뱉어서 네 감정을 상하게 할 수 있
었지만 참아준 거야

I can't find the right word
ↄ 적당한 말이 생각나지 않는군

I can't find the word to describe it
ↄ 말로 표현 할 수 없을 정도야

I can't put my finger(a label) on it
ↄ 꼬집어 말할 순 없어

(=It escapes me)

› **betray**   seduce, deliver to an enemy by treachery, prove unfaithful to

› **dare**   have sufficient courage, urge or provoke to contend

I can't tell you how pleased I am
ㄴ 말로 할 수 없을 만큼 기뻐

I couldn't get a word in edge-ways(edgewise)
ㄴ 내가 한마디 끼어 들 틈이 없었어

I don't want to hear that kind of talk
ㄴ 그런 소린 듣고싶지 않아

I felt easier(relieved) after I said(had) my say
ㄴ 할 말을 다 하고 나니 개운해

I find that remark very offensive
ㄴ 지금 한 말 몹시 불쾌해

I gave you all I had
ㄴ 있는 그대로 말했어

I give my word for that
ㄴ 그 사실은 내가 보증하지

(=I'd give my word for that)

I have to tell you something
ㄴ 분명히 말해 주지

I have words with you
ㄴ 따질게 좀 있어

I heard their conversation but didn't listen to what they said
ㄴ 그들이 말하는 소린 들었지만 무슨 말을 하는지는 못 들었어

I hope to tell you she's a knockout
ㄴ 말이야 바로 말이지 그 여자 끝내주는 미인이야

▸ **relieve** free from a burden or distress, release from a post or duty, | break the monotony of ▸ **offensive** causing offense

I speak under correction
↳ 내 말이 틀릴지 모르지만 말할게

I spoke too soon
↳ 내가 잘 모르면서 함부로 말한 것 같군

I told you time and time again
↳ 몇 번이나 얘기했잖아

I want straight talk
↳ 똑바로 말해

I was coming to that
↳ 내 말이 그 말이야

I was so nervous I was left speechless(tongue-tied, the words stuck in my throat)
↳ 너무 떨려서 말이 안나왔어

I will teach you to ignore my words
↳ 내 말 안 들으면 혼 낼 거다

I won't have you say such things
↳ 너한테 그런 말 듣고싶지 않아

I would die before I told you about it
↳ 죽어도 너한테 얘기 안해

I wouldn't go so far as to say that
↳ 그렇게까지 말하진 않겠어

I wouldn't tell a piss-ant like you
↳ 내가 알더라도 너 같은 어린애 같은 사람에겐 말 안 해(piss-ant=어리석고 무가치한 사람)

I'll confine myself to making a few remarks
↳ 몇 마디하고서 그치렵니다

- **confine** restrain or restrict to a limited area, put in prison
- **afraid** filled with fear
- **escape** get away or get away from

I'll just come to the point
> ↳ 요점만 말할게

I'll let myself loose
> ↳ 기탄 없이 말하지

I'm afraid your point escapes me
> ↳ 이야기의 요점을 잘 모르겠습니다

I'm inclined to disbelieve his words
> ↳ 난 그의 말이 도저히 믿기지 않아

I'm sorry for my own words
> ↳ 내가 한 말을 후회하고 있어

I'm sorry you asked
> ↳ 말하기 싫은데

I'm speaking English
> ↳ 내 말 잘 들어

If I have told you once, I've told you a thousand times
> ↳ 몇 번 얘기해야 알겠나

If there isn't anything to it, don't spread it
> ↳ 확실한 근거가 없으면 그런 말을 퍼뜨리지 마라

If you need any money, just say the word
> ↳ 돈이 필요하면 말만 해

If you value your life, never say a word
> ↳ 입도 벙긋 안 하는 게 신상에 이로워

Ill words are bellow to a slackening fire
> ↳ 잘못된 말은 꺼져 가는 불길을 살려 일으키는 풀무이다

In the multitudes of words sin is not lacking
> ↳ 말이 많으면 허물을 면하기 어렵다

- **incline** tend toward an opinion
- **disbelieve** hold not to be true or real

- **slacken** make or become slack or less active

In-ho came back when I told him the whole story
> ↳ 인호에게 모든 얘길 해 줬더니 마음이 돌아서더군

In-ho is just a smooth talker
> ↳ 인호는 말재간이 뛰어나

(=He's so charming with words)

In-ho knows what he is talking about
> ↳ 인호의 말은 진짜(전문가)

It bears on this conversation
> ↳ 말이 나왔으니 말인데

It is clear what you are driving at
> ↳ 네가 무슨 말을 하는지 알겠어

It slipped out(of my mouth)
> ↳ 얼떨결에 말이 나왔어(실언)

(=It was a slip of the tongue)
(=I wasn't thinking)
(=It was out before I knew it)
(=I said the wrong thing)
(=I didn't mean what I said)

It's a slim excuse
> ↳ 그건 속보이는 소리야

It's better to use simple words
> ↳ 말은 간단할수록 좋다

‣ **multitude** great number
‣ **sin** offense against God

‣ **slim** slender, scanty
‣ **excuse** justification, apology

말이란 뜻을 전달하기 위한 수단이다. 거창하고 긴 말은 말의 초점을 흐릴 뿐만 아니라, 진실성이 없어진다. 비슷한 뜻으로 "Short answer is often the most eloquent 간단한 말은 웅변과 같다"도 쓰인다.

It's hard to say what it is
> ㄴ 뭔지 말로써 설명하기 어려운(=**Words can't say it**)

It's in vain to speak reason where it'll not be heard
> ㄴ 들어주지 않으면 이치에 맞는 말도 쓸모가 없다

It's just a figure of speech
> ㄴ 말이 그렇다는 거지

It's just talk
> ㄴ 그건 말 뿐이야(행동이 안 따르는, 또는 괜한 엄살뿐인)

It's no use paying me a blackmail
> ㄴ 입막음 돈 줘도 소용없어(다 불어버릴 테니까. **blackmail**을 "공갈치다"로 받아들일 수도 있음)

It's not easy to bring her out of her shell
> ㄴ 그 여자를 터놓고 얘기하게 만드는 건 쉽지 않아

It's not the words that matter so much as the way we say them
> ㄴ 문제가 되는 것은 말 자체가 아니고 말하는 방법이다

It's not what you say to people, but it's the way you say it
> ㄴ 말이란 '아'다르고 '어'달라

It's only words
> ㄴ 그건 말 뿐이야

It's the power of speech which discriminates(differentiates) man from the animals
> ㄴ 말을 할 수 있다는 점이 사람과 동물을 확실히 구별해준다

› **vain** of no value, unsuccessful, conceited
› **figure** illustration, patter or design

› **shell** hard or tough outer covering

It's the same old story every time
> ↳ 매번 똑같은 소리야

Jung-ah had her mouth full and couldn't get the words out
> ↳ 정아는 입에 밥이 들어있어서 말하기 힘들었어(get something out 은 "입이 안 떨어지다"의 듯도 있음)

Jung-soo was nervous and couldn't speak at first; then he found his tongue
> ↳ 정수가 처음에는 긴장해서 말이 안 나왔으나 이내 말문이 열렸어

Jung-soo's last few words were lost in the strange sounds
> ↳ 정수의 마지막 몇 마디는 이상한 소리 때문에 못 들었어

Just because he asked you not to talk so loud, there's no need to go to the other extreme and remain completely silent
> ↳ 그가 네게 큰 소리로 얘기하지 말라고 했다해서 아주 입을 다물고 있을 필요는 없어

Keep a still tongue in your head
> ↳ 말을 삼가서 해

Keep it close to your chest
> ↳ 아무에게도 말하지 말고 혼자만 알고 있어라

(=Don't show your hand)

Less of your nonsense
> ↳ 허튼 소리 작작 해

Let me have a word with you
> ↳ 잠깐 한마디할게 있다

Let your hair down and tell me what you really think
> ↳ 속마음을 열고 정말 무슨 생각을 하고 있는지 말해봐

Let your speech be better than silence, or be silent

› **nervous** relating to or made up of nerves, easily excited, fearful

› **complete** having no part lacking, finished

› **silent** having or producing no sound

ㄴ 말을 하려면 침묵보다 나은 말을 하고 그렇지 않으면 침묵하라

Let's cut the chitchat

ㄴ 잡담은 그만 합시다

Let's keep to the subject; we are trying to reach an agreement, not have a conversation

ㄴ 우리는 잡담을 하려는 게 아니라 합의를 끌어내려는 것인 만큼 주제만 얘기하기로 합시다

Let's pad out this paragraph a little

ㄴ 이(구)절에 말을 덧붙여 말을 좀 늘이자

Let's pass the time of day here

ㄴ 여기서 이런 저런 얘기나 좀 나누자

Let's put a lid on the vulgar language

ㄴ 상스런 말은 삼가 합시다

Let's shoot(bat, fan) the breeze over a cup of coffee

ㄴ 커피 한잔하면서 얘기(잡담)나 좀 하자

Let's talk about it face to face

ㄴ 만나서 얘기하자

Let's talk it out

ㄴ 말로 해결하자(협상하자)

(=We can work this out)
(=Let's discuss this like adults)
(=Let's talk)
(=Let's work this out)
(=Let's make a deal Little remains to be said)

Live my words everyday

ㄴ 매일매일 내 말을 실천하며 살아라

- **lid** movable cover
- **vulgar** offensive in manner or language
- **bat** wink or blink
- **fan** stir to activity

Look at all this rubbish and broken glass everywhere. Words fail me
ㄴ 사방에 널려있는 이 쓰레기며 유리조각 좀 봐. 말이 안 나오네

Look who's talking
ㄴ 남 말하고 있네

Many a true word is spoken in jest
ㄴ 수많은 진담이 농담으로 말해진다

> 사자성어 중에 '언중유골'이라는 성어가 있다. 사람의 감정을 상하게 할 수도 있는 진실을 농담으로 말하는 것이 인간 관계를 유연하게 이끌어 나가는 지혜이다.

Mark my words
ㄴ 내 말 잘 들어

Mention was made of you
ㄴ 네 말이 나왔지

Mere words are not enough
ㄴ 말로 때우는 건 안 돼

Min-ho's acts belies his words
ㄴ 민호는 언행이 다른 사람이야

Modulating the sound of the words we say adds feeling, intentions or emphasis to them
ㄴ 말하는 단어들의 소리를 조절함으로써 그 말에 감정이나 의도, 혹은 강조의 의미를 덧붙이게 된다

Moon-hee has a liberal tongue
ㄴ 문희는 때와 장소를 가리지 않고 지껄여

Moon-joo's speech was stumbling and disjointed
ㄴ 문주의 말은 더듬거리고 횡설수설 종잡을 수 없었어

▸ **intention** purpose
▸ **emphasis** stress

▸ **liberal** not stingy, narrow, or conservative

Moon-soo put a flea in my ear
ㄴ 문수가 내게 듣기 싫은 소릴 했어(경고했어)

Moon-soo told me a story that wouldn't hold water
ㄴ 문수는 내게 사실이 아닌 얘길 했던 거야

Moon-soo's words are mouth-made
ㄴ 문수의 말은 입 발린 소리야

More have repented speech than silence
ㄴ 침묵의 후회보다 말을 했던 후회가 더 많다

> (=Speak fitly or be silent wisely)

My gorge rose at his words
ㄴ 그의 말을 듣고있자니 욕지기났어

My heart can talk to you
ㄴ 일일이 말 안 해도 알잖아

My heart was too full for words
ㄴ 가슴이 벅차 말이 안 나왔어

My lips are sealed
ㄴ 절대 말 안 할게

My voice was frozen with fear
ㄴ 무서워서 목소리가 안나왔어

Nice words for nice words
ㄴ 가는 말이 고와야 오는 말이 곱다

No amount of words can make up for something
ㄴ 입이 열 개라도 할 말이 없다

- **repent** turn from sin, regret
- **fit** suitable, qualified, sound in body
- **gorge** narrow ravine
- **seal** affix a seal to, close up securely

Not in so many words
> ↳ 꼭 그렇게 말했다는 건 아니야

Not on your life, I didn't say that
> ↳ 난 결코 그런 말은 하지 않았어

Not what goes into the mouth defiles a man; but what comes out of the mouth, this defiles a man
> ↳ 입에 들어가는 것이 사람을 더럽게 하는 것이 아니라 입에서 나오는 그것이 사람을 더럽게 하느니라

Nothing will come out of all this talk
> ↳ 이렇게 이야기만 해봤자 소용없어

Now you speak my language
> ↳ 이제야 말(마음)이 통하는군

Now, you are catching on
> ↳ 이제 말귀가 통하는군

Once she starts chatting, it's impossible to switch her off
> ↳ 그 여자가 한번 입을 열기만 하면 그칠 줄 몰라

One never repents of having spoken too little
> ↳ 할 말을 적게 한 일을 후회하는 일은 없다

> 말이란 뜻을 전달하기 위한 수단이다. 거창하고 긴 말은 말의 초점을 흐릴 뿐만 아니라, 진실성이 없어진다. 비슷한 뜻으로 "Short answer is often the most eloquent 간단한 말은 웅변과 같다"도 쓰인다.

One picture is worth a thousand words
> ↳ 사람은 겪어봐야 알고 말은 타봐야 안다(백문이 불여일견)

› **make up** invent, become reconciled, compensate for, try to win

one's favor(+to)
› **catch on** understand, become popular

> 시청각 경험의 중요성을 말해주는 속담이다. 요즘은 Mass Media 의 대중화
> 에 힘입어 시청각 경험이 점차로 쉬워지고 있다(＝Seeing is believing).
> (＝The proof of the pudding is in the eating)
> (＝One eyewitness is better than two hear-so)

Only one understands a word should one try to use it
  ↳ 말은 그 뜻을 이해한 뒤 써야

Our conversation was delightfully informal
  ↳ 우리의 대화는 스스럼없어서 기분이 좋았다

Our new plan came apart at the seams when his tongue slipped
  ↳ 그가 실언을 하는 바람에 우리 계획은 망가졌다

Out of the mouth comes the evil
  ↳ 입이 화근

Outspoken advice is(sounds) harsh to the ear
  ↳ 바른 말은 귀에 거슬린다

> 자신의 결점을 꼬집어서 말하는 충고를 들을 때에는 기분이 좋을 수가 없다.
> 그렇기 때문에 함부로 남에게 충고를 해서는 안되고, 충고를 들어서 기분이
> 나쁘더라도 받아들일 수 있는 아량이 있어야 한다.
> (＝Unpleasant advice is a good medicine)
> (＝A good medicine taste bitter)

Pay no attention. He's just a hip-shooter
  ↳ 신경 쓰지마. 그 사람은 조심 없이 말하는 사람이니까

People will talk
  ↳ 세상은 말이 많아

› **informal** without formality or ceremony, for ordinary or familiar

› **seam** line of junction of 2 edges, layer of a mineral

Please be more specific
> ↳ 좀더 구체적으로 말해봐

> (=Please explain it in more detail)
> (=Can you give me more details about it?)

Please correct me if I'm wrong
> ↳ 얘기 중 틀린 것 고쳐줘라

Please don't break in on us just now
> ↳ 지금은 우리들의 얘기에 끼어 들지 마십시오

Please fill me in on what happened in my absence
> ↳ 내가 없을 때 무슨 일이 있었는지 말해 줘

Please forgive the interruption
> ↳ 말씀 중에 죄송합니다(**Don't interrupt so** 말을 끝까지 들어봐)

Please pass the word around
> ↳ 말 좀 전해 줘

> (=Let everyone know)
> (=Get the word out)

Please tell me the end of the story, put me out of my misery
> ↳ 얘기의 결말을 말해주고 맘 조리게 하지 말아 줘

Politicians say anything to get votes, but once the elections are over, they don't act on their words
> ↳ 정치인들은 득표를 위해 온갖 말을 늘어놓지만 선거가 끝나고 나면 그들이 한 말을 이행치 않는다

· **interrupt**　intrude so as to hinder or end continuity

· **politic**　practice of government and managing of public affairs

Put a lid in it
> ↳ 그만 떠들어

Put in a good word for me with the higher-ups
> ↳ 위 분들에게 말 좀 잘 해줘

Read my lips
> ↳ 내 말을 믿어

Remember your constant nagging only makes me all the more determined not to change my mind
> ↳ 네가 쉴새없이 잔소리 해봤자 내 마음이 확고히 변하지 않게 굳혀줄 뿐임을 잊지 마라

Repeat the message often enough, and it'll be firmly fixed in the subconscious
> ↳ 전하고싶은 말을 자주 몇 번이고 반복 말하면 사람들의 잠재의식 속에 확고히 자리잡게 될 것이다

Rule out neatly any words which you do not wish the examiner to read
> ↳ 시험관이 읽지 않게 하고싶은 단어는 모두 깨끗이 선을 그어 지워라

Sang-soo didn't say in so many words
> ↳ 상수는 사실대로 말하지 않았어

Sang-soo slapped Min-soo for speaking out of turn
> ↳ 민수가 나설 데가 아닌데 입을 열자 상수가 따귀를 때려줬다

Sang-soo spilled his guts to me
> ↳ 상수는 속에 있는 말을 다 털어놨어

Sang-soo's slurring his words. He's had one too many
> ↳ 상수는 혀가 잘 안 돌아. 벌써 취했어

Sang-soo's story just doesn't add up
> ↳ 상수의 말은 앞뒤가 맞지 않아

‣ **subconscious** existing without conscious awareness   ‣ **neat** not diluted, tastefully simple, orderly and clean

Saying and doing are two thing
     ↳ 말로는 쉬워도 실천은 어렵다

> "To say is one thing; to practice is another"와 같은 뜻이다. 직역하면
> "말하는 것은 한가지이고, 실천하는 것은 다른 것이다"이다. "말로 만리장성
> 쌓는다"는 말이 있듯이, 말은 쉬워도 실천은 몇 배로 어렵다.
> (=From word to deed is a great space)

Set the action to the word
     ↳ 말한 대로 행하라

Sharp's the word
     ↳ 서둘러라(**Mum's the word** 입 다물어)

She always babbles like a brook whenever she finds anyone to talk to
     ↳ 그녀는 누구든 얘기할 상대만 있으면 늘 수다를 떤다

She always chips(breaks) into other people's conversation, irrespective of time or place
     ↳ 그녀는 시도 때도 없이 남의 이야기에 끼여든다

She always shoots straight from the shoulder
     ↳ 그녀는 늘 솔직히 말한다

She always talks her way out of her duty
     ↳ 그녀는 늘 자기 책임을 말로 얼버무리고 빠져나간다

She always uses flowery speeches
     ↳ 그 여자는 늘 미사여구를 늘어놓는다

She ever talks a mile a minute
     ↳ 그 여자는 쉴새없이 지껄여

She is all talk and no action

▸ **babble** utter meaningless sounds, talk foolishly or too much	▸ **brook** tolerate, small stream
	▸ **irrespective of** without regard to

ㄴ 그 여잔 입만 살았어

> (=She never does what she says)
> (=She has no follow-through)
> (=She's full of empty promises)

She likes the sound of her own voice
　　　ㄴ 그 여자는 한 번 말을 꺼내면 그칠 줄을 몰라

She made the statement in a news conference
　　　ㄴ 그 여자는 기자회견에서 그와 같이 말했다

She said almost nothing worth listening to
　　　ㄴ 그 여자는 거의 들을 가치가 없는 말만 늘어놓았다

She said that in the heat of the moment
　　　ㄴ 그 여자는 그 때 격해져서 그렇게 말했다

She seemed to have lost thread of her remarks
　　　ㄴ 그 여자는 자기가 무슨 말을 하다가 잊어버린 것 같았다

She shoots off her mouth every time we meet her
　　　ㄴ 그 여자는 우릴 만날 때마다 쉴새없이 지껄여

She talks a mile a minute when mad
　　　ㄴ 그 여자가 화나면 속사포같이 말을 쏟아놓지

She was bullied at school, but she refuses to talk about it whenever I try to broach the matter
　　　ㄴ 그녀는 학교에서 행패를 당했지만 내가 그 얘길 꺼낼 때마다 말하기를 거부한다

She whispered it to me as soon as she was out of earshot
　　　ㄴ 그녀는 그들이 들을 수 있는 거리를 벗어나자 그 사실을 내게 가만히 말했다

‣ **conference** meeting to exchange views	‣ **broach** introduce for discussion
‣ **thread** train of thought	‣ **whisper** speak softly

She zipped through her speech
> ↳ 그 여자는 잽싸게 지껄여댔다

She's tongue-tied
> ↳ 그녀는 할 말을 잃었어

Simple believes every word, but the prudent man considers well his steps
> ↳ 어리석은 자는 온갖 말을 믿으나 슬기로운 자는 행동을 삼가느니라

Since it bears on this conversation
> ↳ 말이 나왔으니 말인데

Since power with words is a mark of successful people, provision is made for increasing their vocabulary on a systematic basis
> ↳ 말의 힘이 성공한 사람들의 특징이기 때문에 너의 어휘를 체계적으로 늘리기 위한 준비가 되어있다

Some man or other spoke to me on the street
> ↳ 누군가가 거리에서 내게 말을 걸었어

Some people often use foreign words in preference to perfectly acceptable Korean language
> ↳ 완벽하게 알아들을 수 있는 우리말을 젖혀놓고 외래어를 즐겨 쓰는 사람들이 있다

Some say one thing, some another
> ↳ 이렇게 말하는 사람도 있고 저렇게 말하는 사람도 있다

Somebody told me so, I forgot who
> ↳ 누군가 그렇게 말했는데 누군지 모르겠어

Sometimes your own remarks argue against you
> ↳ 자신이 뱉은 말이 네게 불리하게 작용할 수도 있어

Sook-hee moved in on Jung-hee's boy friend and now they are not talking to each other
> ↳ 숙희가 정희의 남자친구를 가로채는 바람에 이제 서로 말도 안하고 지내

Speech is the mirror of the action

‣ **system** arrangement of units that function together, regular order	‣ **foreign** situated outside a place or country and especially one's

ㄴ 말은 행동의 거울이다

Stick to the point
ㄴ 말 돌리지마

Stop jerking(jacking) me around and give me the information I need
ㄴ 헛소리 집어치우고 내게 필요한 정보나 좀 줘

Stop putting your words into my mouth
ㄴ 내가 하지도 않은 말을 했다고 하지마

Such a word is known to the man in the street
ㄴ 그런 말은 누구나 다 안다

Tai-gyung is going to put the hard word(moves, make) on Ji-yung
ㄴ 태경이가 지영일 꼬시려 한단 말이야

Tai-ho was afraid to talk to the teacher, so I piped up
ㄴ 태호가 겁이 나서 선생님에게 말을 못하기에 내가 큰 소리로 말했지

Tai-ho's remarks were strikingly different in substance and in tone from previous ones
ㄴ 태호의 말은 이전에 했던 말과는 내용과 어조에서 사뭇 달랐다

Tai-soo was about to tell the secret but he bit his words back
ㄴ 태호는 비밀을 말하려 하였으나 말을 참았다

Take back what you just said to me
ㄴ 지금 내게 한 말 취소해

Talk is cheap
ㄴ 말이야 쉽지

(=That's not as easy as it sounds)
(=Talking about it is easy)
(=That's easier said than done)

· **substance** essence or essential part, physical material, wealth

· **previous** having hone, happened, or existed before

Talk sense to a fool and he calls you foolish
↳ 어리석은 사람에게 사리에 맞는 말을 하면 당신더러 바보라고 할 것이다

Talk will not avail without work
↳ 실행 없이 말만 앞세우는 건 소용없어

Talkers are no great doers
↳ 말이 능숙한 사람은 실천이 없어

(=The greatest talkers are the least doers)
(=He who gives a fair words feeds you with an empty spoon)

Talking about it is one thing, doing it is another
↳ 말로 하는 것과 실제로 그 일을 하는 것과는 달라

Talking to him is like talking to a brick wall
↳ 그에게 잔소리 해봤자 쇠귀에 경 읽기다

마음에 있지 않으면 들어도 들리지 않고 보아도 보이지 않는다(There's none so blind as those who will not see = There's none so deaf as those who will not hear).

Tell him exactly what you are getting at
↳ 무슨 말을 하려는 건지 그에게 정확히 말해줘라

Tell it like it is
↳ 이실직고해

(=Tell your story without diverging from the truth)

> ‣ **avail** be of use or make use
> ‣ **blind** lacking or quite deficient in ability to

see, not intelligently controlled, having no way out

Tell me any idea that may occur(flash) your mind
> ↳ 느낀 점이 있으면 무엇이든지 말씀해 주세요

Tell me the flip side of this matter before I make a judgement
> ↳ 내가 판단을 내리기 전에 이 일의 이면에 있는 내용을 얘기해 다오

Tell not all you know, believe not all you hear, do not all you able
> ↳ 안다고 다 말하지 말며, 듣는다고 다 믿지 말며, 할 수 있다고 다 하지 마라

That boring woman was going to keep talking till kingdom come
> ↳ 그 지겨운 여자의 얘기는 끝없이 이어질 태세였어

That fellow always talks about you behind your back and pretends to be nice to you when he meets you
> ↳ 저 녀석은 네가 없을 때 늘 험담하고 널 만날 때면 착한 척 해

That goes without saying
> ↳ 말할 필요 없이 그렇지 뭐

That is a clincher
> ↳ 더 이상 할 말 없어

That is not good language which all understand not
> ↳ 아무도 이해하지 못하는 말은 좋은 말이 아니다

That man would chew the fat(rag) for hours with anyone who would join him
> ↳ 그 사람은 상대해 주는 사람이 있으면 몇 시간이고 얘기를 하곤 했어

That story simply doesn't hang together
> ↳ 그 얘기는 도무지 조리(앞뒤)가 안 맞아

That tells a tale
> ↳ 거기에는 사정이 있다

That toilet(potty) mouth is offending us again
> ↳ 저 쌍소리 잘하는 녀석이 또 우리에게 듣기 거북한 소릴 하고 있어

› **diverge** move in different directions, differ
› **fellow** companion or associate, man or boy

That'll bear out what I said in even more detail
↳ 그건 내가 한 말을 더 상세히 증명해 줄 거야

That'll teach you not to talk to me like that
↳ 이제 다시는 내게 그런 식으로 못되게 말하진 않겠지

That's easy for you to say!
↳ 당신에겐 별거 아니겠죠(쉬운 일이겠죠)＝말은 쉽지(내심으로)

That's enough back talk from you
↳ 건방진 소리 그만 해

That's not the end of the story
↳ 그게 전부가 아냐

That's what I say
↳ 내 말이 그 말

The baby's talking was hardly intelligible except to its mother
↳ 아기가 하는 말은 아기엄마 외에는 알아듣지 못해

The best way to keep one's word is not to give it
↳ 약속을 지키는 최선의 방법은 약속을 하지 않는 것이다

**The best way to learn a foreign language is to immerse oneself in it
totally, speaking nothing else, for a period of a few years**
↳ 외국어를 배우는 최상의 길은 다른 언어를 사용하지 말고 그 외국어
　　만을 몇 년간 말하면서 학습에 전념하는 일이다

The cat got his tongue
↳ 그 사람 부끄러워서 말못했지

The eternal talker neither hears nor learns
↳ 끝없이 얘기하는 사람은 남의 말을 듣지도 않고 배우지도 않는다

The fact lends probability to story
↳ 이 사실로 보면 그 얘긴 그럴듯해

· **intelligible** understandable
· **except** omit, excluding, but

· **immerse** plunge or dip especially into
liquid, engross

The language will not bear repeating
　　ㄴ 그 말은 입에 담기도 싫어

The most deadly of wild beasts is a backbiter
　　ㄴ 가장 지독한 짐승은 남이 없을 때 험담하는 사람이다

The noise was so loud that it drowned out our talk
　　ㄴ 소음이 너무 커서 우리들의 얘기가 들리지 않았다

The right to be heard doesn't automatically include the right to be taken seriously
　　　　ㄴ 남에게 얘기할 수 있는 권리는 자동적으로 경청 받을 권리까지 포함
　　　　하는 것은 아니다

The suppressed words gushed(poured) from her lips
　　　　ㄴ 참았던 말이 한꺼번에 그녀의 입에서 나왔다

The words 'give up' are not in my vocabulary
　　　　ㄴ 내 사전에 포기라는 단어는 없어

> (=Failure is not a word in my vocabulary)
> (=I don't know the meaning of the 'give up')

The words don't come out right
　　　　ㄴ 딱 맞는 말이 잘 안 떠올라

Their accounts tally with each other
　　　　ㄴ 그들의 얘기는 일치해

Their face to face talks squared the matter
　　　　ㄴ 그들은 얼굴을 맞대고 얘기해서 문제를 풀었다

There are talkers and there are doers
　　　　ㄴ 허풍떨고있네

‣ **suppress**　keep from being known, put an end to by authority　　‣ **gush**　pour forth violently or enthusiastically

(=You are all blow and no go)

There is no logic in your remark
> ↳ 앞뒤가 안 맞는 소리를 하는군

There's many a true word said in jest
> ↳ 농담 속에 진실 있다

사자성어 중에 '언중유골'이라는 성어가 있다. 사람의 감정을 상하게 할 수도 있는 진실을 농담으로 말하는 것이 인간 관계를 유연하게 이끌어 나가는 지혜이다.

There's no talking to you
> ↳ 너하곤 얘기가 안 되는군

There's nothing busier than an idle rumor
> ↳ 할 일없는 소문보다 나쁜 것은 없다

There's nothing to what he said
> ↳ 그의 얘기는 알맹이가 없다(거짓말이다)

These are words to that song
> ↳ 이게 그 노래의 가사야

These words from your mouth sound queer
> ↳ 네가 이런 소리를 하니 이상해

They caught fire at my words and began to cheer
> ↳ 그들은 내 말에 흥분하더니 환호하기 시작했다

They do least who talk most
> ↳ 다변가일수록 실천이 적다

They hung on my every word

· **logic** science of reasoning, sound reasoning
· **idle** worthless, inactive, lazy

· **queer** differing from the usual or normal

ㄴ 그들은 내가 하는 말을 한 마디도 안 놓치고 들었어

Thinking back to what I said in front of her really makes me want to squirm

ㄴ 그녀 앞에서 했던 말을 생각하면 정말 몸둘 바를 모르게 된다

This avowal is strong enough to kill any speculation about a rift between you and me

ㄴ 이 공언은 너와 나 사이의 불화에 대한 억측을 잠재우기에 충분해

This is just a digression, but I'd like to share this with you

ㄴ 이 얘기하곤 상관없는 얘기지만 너와 함께 나누고 싶어

This is way out of line

ㄴ 초점에서 한참 벗어난 얘기

This word takes an accent on the second syllable

ㄴ 이 단어에는 두 번째 음절에 강세가 있다

Those things which proceed out of the mouth come from the heart, and defile a man

ㄴ 입에서 나오는 것들은 마음에서 나오나니 이것이야말로 사람을 더럽게 하느니라

Those were his exact words

ㄴ 그 사람이 말한 그대로야

Though he says so, he doesn't mean so much

ㄴ 입으론 그렇지만 속으론 그렇지도 않아

Though I'm ashamed to say, it means(brings) no money

ㄴ 치사한 소리 같지만 그건 돈벌이가 안 돼

Time can shout the truth where words lie

ㄴ 말이 거짓을 지껄이고있을 경우에도 시간은 진실을 외칠 수 있다

Time is subject to less distortion than the spoken language

· **squirm** wriggle
· **avowal** declare openly

· **speculation** thinking about things yet unknown

↳ 시간은 입으로 하는 말보다 덜 왜곡된다

To bandy words with a foolish person is a waste of time
↳ 어리석은 자와 말을 주고받는 건 시간낭비다

Tongues are wagging
↳ 입방아들이 가만히 있질 않고 있어

Try a little arm-twisting if nice talk won't work
↳ 좋은 말로 안되거든 약간 을러봐

Try and draw So-hi out
↳ 소희를 구슬려 말 좀 하게 해봐

Try to go behind his words
↳ 말뜻의 이면을 캐봐라

Try to put(lay) some sweet lines on him
↳ 그에게 부드럽게 잘 말해 봐

Try what kind words will do
↳ 친절히 말을 걸어봐(그러면 될 테니까)

Use the following words in a sentence
↳ 다음 단어로 문장을 만들어라

Wan-soo is just warming over ideas he's heard from other people
↳ 완수는 남들에게 주워들은 얘기를 그대로 말하고 있을 뿐이야

Wan-soo is not good for words
↳ 완수는 말주변이 없어

Wan-soo said something nice to me for the first time in a long while
↳ 완수가 오랜만에 내게 듣기 좋은 소릴 하더군

Wan-soo said their proposal was incredible, or words to that effect
↳ 완수는 그 사람들의 제안이 믿을 수 없다던가

‣ **band** unite for a common end, enclose with a band

‣ **arm-twist** force, compel, coerce
‣ **incredible** too extraordinary to be believed

We are out of synch with each other
ㄴ 우린 말이 안 통해

We couldn't hear him over the static
ㄴ 잡음 때문에 그의 말이 안 들렸어

We have no word on it yet
ㄴ 그 일에 대해 아직 아무 연락을 못 받았다

We heard them talking, but didn't listen to what they said
ㄴ 우리가 그들이 얘기하는 소리는 들었지만 무엇을 말했는지 귀를 기울여 듣진 않았다

We shouldn't talk about that here
ㄴ 그런 얘기는 하기 곤란해

We tried to draw Chang-ho out of his shell, but without success
ㄴ 우린 창호에게 입을 열도록 해보았으나 잘 되지 않았어

We tried to get her to talk to Bong-soo, but she stayed in her shell
ㄴ 우린 그 여자로 하여금 봉수에게 말을 붙여보도록 해 봤으나 계속 입을 다물고 있었어

Well, that's a nice thing to say!
ㄴ 정말 터무니없는 말을 해버렸군

What goes around comes around
ㄴ 가는 말이 고와야(자업자득)

What he does is out of keeping with his words
ㄴ 그의 행동은 말과 일치하지 않아

What I'm going to say is off the record
ㄴ 내가 말하는 건 여기서 그치기로 하자

What possessed you to say such a thing?
ㄴ 도대체 무슨 생각으로 그런 말을 하는 거냐?

- **synch** = synchronize
- **synchronize** cause to agree in time

- **static** noise on radio or television from electrical disturbances

What raises that commonplace above banality is the obvious sincerity behind it
> ↳ 그 흔한 말을 진부한 표현 이상으로 높여주는 것은 그 말 뒤에 있는 성실성이다

What she said missed the point
> ↳ 그녀의 말은 핵심을 벗어났다

What the heart thinks, the mouth speaks
> ↳ 마음에 품은 것은 입 밖으로 나오게 돼있어

What you do is out of keeping with your words
> ↳ 넌 언행이 일치하지 않아

What you said is a force to be reckoned with
> ↳ 네가 한 말은 무시 못할 영향력이 있어

What you said is neither here no there
> ↳ 네가 한 말은 전혀 별개의 문제야

What you say doesn't click with me at all
> ↳ 네가 하는 말은 전혀 와 닿지 않아

What you say passes the bounds of common sense
> ↳ 네 말은 상식을 벗어나

What's the good word?
> ↳ 재미가 어때?

When the word is out it belongs to another
> ↳ 한번 내뱉은 말은 되돌릴 수 없다

Whispered words are heard afar
> ↳ 가만히 속삭이는 소리는 멀리 들린다

Who knows but that he may be right
> ↳ 혹시 그의 말이 맞을지도 몰라

- **commonplace** cliché, ordinary
- **banal** ordinary and uninteresting
- **obvious** plain or unmistakable
- **sincerity** genuine or honesty

Whoever gossips to you will gossip about you
> 당신에게 남의 얘기를 하는 사람은 당신의 얘기를 남에게도 할 것이다

Why are you putting word in my mouth?
> 왜 하지도 않은 말을 했다고 그래

> (=Why are you lying about what I said?)
> (=Why are you twisting around my words?)

Will you permit me a few words?
> 몇 마디 말씀드려도 되겠습니까?

Words are but wind, but blows unkind
> 말은 바람에 불과하지만 그것도 매정한 바람이다

Words calculated to catch everyone may catch no one
> 모든 사람의 귀를 의도적으로 솔깃하게 하려 했다가는 아무에게도 관심을 끌지 못할 수 있다

Words cut more than swords
> 말은 검보다 더 깊이 벤다

Words failed me
> 기가 막혀 말이 안 나왔어. 입이 안 떨어졌어

Words have a way of coming true
> 말이 씨 된다

> (=Words sometimes do come true)
> (=Don't estimate the power of words)
> (=What you say surprisingly come true)

· **permit** give approval for, make possible   processes, judge, rely(+on, +upon)
· **calculate** determine by mathematical

Words have wings, and can't be recalled
> ↳ 말에는 날개가 있어서 주워 담을 수가 없다

Words of praise seldom fall from his lips
> ↳ 좀처럼 그에게 칭찬 받기 힘들어

Words stuck in my throat
> ↳ 말이 잘 안나왔다

Words without actions are of little use
> ↳ 실천이 안 따르는 말은 소용없어

You are digressing(losing focus, getting side-tracked) again
> ↳ 또 얘기가 옆길로 새는군

You are driving it to the ground again
> ↳ 또 그 소릴 장황하게 늘어놓고 있는 거잖아

You are going a bit too far
> ↳ 그런 말은 너무 심해

You are missing the point
> ↳ 말뜻을 이해 못하는군

You are supposed to use careful language
> ↳ 말씨를 조심해야해

You are talking like a saint
> ↳ 공자님 같은 소리만 하는군

You attach a strange meaning to what I say
> ↳ 내 말을 이상하게 생각하는구나

You can accept me at my own currency
> ↳ 내가 말하는 그대로 믿어도 돼

You can never tell
> ↳ 단정할 수 없지

› **recall** call back, remember, revoke

› **seldom** not often

› **suppose** assume to be true, expect, think probable

You can't go by(on) what he says
ㄴ 그 사람 얘긴 믿을게 못돼

You don't have a leg to stand on
ㄴ 넌 입이 열 개라도 할 말이 없어

You don't have to rub my nose in it
ㄴ 창피한 얘기 좀 그만 해라

You give a false color to your statement(conduct)
ㄴ 정말인 것 같이 말(행동)하고 있군

You go behind my words
ㄴ 내 말의 진위를 의심하고 있군

You have my word
ㄴ 약속하지

You have said your(little) piece, so go on home
ㄴ 네 할말은 다 들었으니 날 좀 내버려둬

You may well say so
ㄴ 지당한 말씀

You mustn't breathe a word of it
ㄴ 한마디도 해선 안 돼

You need not take his stories at face value
ㄴ 그의 말을 액면대로 받아들일 필요 없어

You only waste your words
ㄴ 넌 입만 아플 분이야

You say just everyone to hear
ㄴ 듣기 좋은 말만 해

(=You really kiss up to me)

› **conduct** management, behavior

You should take a good line(game)
  ↳ 자신 있게 말해야 해

You shouldn't say that
  ↳ 그런 말씀 마세요

You shouldn't take her word for it
  ↳ 그 여자의 말대로 믿어선 안 돼

You're better than your word
  ↳ 넌 약속 이상으로 해냈구나

You're not talking, you're just making a noise
  ↳ 그게 말이라고 하니, 넌 꼭 쓸데없는 말만하고 있어

You're talking to the wall
  ↳ 쇠귀에 경 읽기야

> 마음에 있지 않으면 들어도 들리지 않고 보아도 보이지 않는다(There's
> none so blind as those who will not see = There's none so deaf
> as those who will not hear).
> (=He always turns deaf ear)

You've said it all
  ↳ 네가 말한 그대로가 전부야

Your bare word isn't enough
  ↳ 그런 말만으로는 믿을 수 없어

Your last few words were lost in the strange sounds
  ↳ 너의 마지막 몇 마디는 이상한 소리 때문에 못 들었다

Your remark cut me to quick(heart)
  ↳ 말씀이 가슴에 사무칩니다

› **kiss up** flatter, praise
› **wall** structure for defense or for enclosing

something, upright enclosing part of a
building or room

Your remarks deviate from the truth
　ㄴ 네 말은 사실과 동떨어져

Your story doesn't add up
　ㄴ 네 말은 앞뒤가 맞질 않아

Your tongue can make or break you
　ㄴ 말 한마디로 천냥 빚 갚는다

Your words are more than I deserve
　ㄴ 분에 넘치는 말씀입니다

Your words ring(sound) true
　ㄴ 정말같이 들리네

▸ **deviate** change especially from a course or standard

▸ **deserve** be worthy of

42. 명성   **Reputation**

A good name is sooner lost than won
ㄴ 훌륭한 명성은 얻기보다 잃기가 쉽다

A good name keeps its luster in the dark
ㄴ 훌륭한 명성은 어둠 속에서 그 광택이 있다

A great man will be remembered for his achievements
ㄴ 호랑이는 죽어서 가죽을 남기고 사람은 죽어서 이름을 남긴다

> (=A man dies; his name remains)

Any firm can be tainted to a great extent by dishonesty and sharp practice
ㄴ 어느 회사나 부 정직과 교활한 행위로 명성을 크게 손상할 수 있다

Because of his fame(renown), there's always a line of visitors before his door
ㄴ 그의 명성이 널리 알려져 그의 집은 문전성시다

Brave men's deeds live after them
ㄴ 용기 있는 사람의 위업은 사후에도 남는다

Chang-soo carved out a name for himself in business
ㄴ 창수는 자력으로 사업가로서의 명성을 얻었다

Despite his reputation as a trouble-maker, he's a good listener
ㄴ 그가 사고뭉치라고 소문이 나 있지만 남의 말은 잘 들어준다

· **achievement** things gained by work or effort   · **taint** affect or become affected with something bad and decay

Don't tarnish my reputation
↳ 내 얼굴에 먹칠하지마

> (=Don't embarrass me)
> (=Don't make me look bad)

Fame is narrowest at its source and broadest afar off
↳ 명성은 가까이에서 보면 작지만 멀리 떨어질수록 커진다

Fame usually comes to those who are thinking about something else
↳ 명예는 대개 다른 생각을 하고 있는 사람에게 찾아온다

He is the last word in architecture
↳ 그는 건축의 최고 권위자이다

He was in the job for ten years and certainly left his mark
↳ 그는 10년 동안 재직하면서 큰 업적을 남겼다

He's doing his best to save face
↳ 그는 명성을 얻으려고 최선을 다하고 있다

His reputation bears no proportion to his ability
↳ 그의 평판이 그의 능력하고는 맞지 않아

One who has the reputation of an early riser may safely lie abed till noon
↳ 일찍 일어나는 것으로 알려진 사람이 정오까지 일어나지 않을 수도 있다

Our reputation will be reestablished if their complaints peter out
↳ 그들의 불평이 사그라지면 우리의 명성은 재확립 될 것이다

She left a great name behind her
↳ 그 여자는 위대한 이름을 남기고 세상을 떠났다

Stack your reputation on the success of this invention
↳ 이번 발명의 성공에 네 명예를 걸어라

· **proportion** relation of one part to another or to the whole with respect to magnitude, quantity, or degree

· **peter out** diminish gradually

43. 모임 & 만남   Meeting

A big crowd of people stuck around hoping to get a glimpse of him but he never showed up
> ↳ 많은 사람들이 그를 보려고 떠나지 않고 있었으나 그는 나타나지 않았다

Are you going to blow off the meeting?
> ↳ 회의를 빼 먹으(망치)려는 거냐?

Byung-soo drove home the point at the meeting
> ↳ 병수는 모임에서 핵심을 찔렀다

Chan-soo fell to pieces and didn't attend the meeting
> ↳ 찬수는 속이 뒤틀려서 모임에도 안 나왔어

Give me a brief update on the meeting
> ↳ 회의 결과에 대해 간단한 상황만 알려 줘

I'd like to get things under way
> ↳ (회의를)시작할까요?

It was a chance meeting
> ↳ 우연히 만났을 뿐이야

It was a thousand chances to one that I shall see him
> ↳ 내가 그를 만나게 될 일은 확실했지

I've already set about contacting every surviving member of our class to arrange a reunion
> ↳ 난 이미 반창회를 준비하려고 우리 반의 모든 생존 동창들에게 연락

▸ **attend**   handle or provide for the care of something, accompany, be present

▸ **brief**   short of concise

▸ **update**   bring up to date

을 착수했어

Let's cast our minds back to the first meeting
↳ 우리가 처음 만났던 때의 기억을 되살려 보자

Make sure that your picnic doesn't clash with the alumni meeting
↳ 너의 야유회 날자가 동창회와 중복이 안되도록 해

No concrete agreement came out of the meeting
↳ 그 모임에서 아무런 구체적 합의가 없었어

Now, let's move on to a new question
↳ 이제 새로운 문제를 논의해 보기로 하자

Often time is wasted in staff meetings because participants have not studied the issues prior to the meeting
↳ 참가자들이 회의 전에 토의 주제에 대하여 연구하지 않았기 때문에 직원회의는 시간이 낭비되는 일이 많다

Our meeting broke up without reaching any agreement
↳ 우리의 모임은 아무런 합의 없이 끝났어

Our seminar is rolling along nicely
↳ 우리의 세미나는 원만하게 진행되고 있어

See that no one is left out at the conference
↳ 회의에 빠지는 사람이 없도록 해야 해

She came away from the meeting with a heightened awareness of environmental problems
↳ 그녀가 회의에서 돌아올 때에는 환경문제에 대해 더욱 인식이 강화되어 있었다

She went to the business meeting in her shirt-sleeves
↳ 그 여자는 허술한 차림으로 사업상의 모임에 참석했다

That impulsive man yelled at them and stormed out of meetings on

---

› **seminar** conference or conferencelike study
› **heighten** increase in amount or degree

› **awareness** realization or consciousness

several occasions
> ↳ 다혈질인 그 사람은 여러 번 째 그들에게 소리를 치면서 회의장에서 불쑥 나가버렸다

The chairman called to order and the meeting began
> ↳ 의장이 개회를 선언하자 회의가 시작되었다

The chairman made tremendous efforts to keep the issue from getting discursive, penetrating to the heart of the matter at hand
> ↳ 사회자는 논의가 옆으로 나가는 것을 막으면서 문제의 핵심을 뚫을 수 있도록 무한히 애를 썼다

The meeting was like a three-ring circus
> ↳ 그 회의는 온통 뒤죽박죽이었어(**like a three-ring circus**에는 **very busy**의 뜻도 있음)

The meeting's been bumped(moved) up to this afternoon
> ↳ 회의시간이 오늘 오후로 앞당겨졌어

They have regular meetings where workers are given an opportunity to air their grievances
> ↳ 그들은 정기적으로 고충을 토로할 모임을 갖는다

Today three meetings clash
> ↳ 오늘은 세 건의 모임이 중복된다

Understanding human need is half the job of meeting them
> ↳ 사람들에게 필요한 것이 무엇인지를 아는 것은 그 필요에 응하는 일의 절반이다

Will you favor me with your company at our meeting?
> ↳ 모임에 참석해 주시겠습니까?

You are not supposed to shoot your wad at the meeting
> ↳ 회의에서 할 말을 다 해선 안 돼

· **bump up** advance a date

· **wad** little mass, soft mass of fibrous material, pliable plug to retain a power charge

44. 문제　Troubles & Problems

A new problem has popped up

ㄴ 새로운 문제가 생겼어

A problem arose from left field

ㄴ 엉뚱한 곳에서 문제가 생겼어

A tear dries quickly, especially when it is shed for the troubles of others

ㄴ 눈물은 빨리 마른다, 특히 남들의 고통에 대한 눈물일 때

A trouble shared is a trouble halved

ㄴ 슬픔을 같이 나누면 낫다

> "백지장도 맞들면 낫다"라는 한국 속담과 비슷한 뜻이다. 협력의 중요성과 친구의 고마움을 함께 나타낸 속담이다.
> (=Many hands make light work)
> (=It's good to have company in trouble)

All he does is crank out troubles

ㄴ 그가 하는 일이라곤 사고만 저지르는 것뿐이다

All is a riddle, and the key to a riddle is another riddle

ㄴ 모든 것이 수수께끼이고 그 수수께끼를 푸는 단서는 또 다른 수수께끼이다

All I got from my trouble was a kick in the pants(teeth), and that's that

ㄴ 애써 도와줬더니 욕이나 실컷 얻어먹은 게 전부야

· **tear** drop of salty liquid that moistens the eye
· **arise** get up, originate

· **halve** divide into halves, reduce to half

Although I had some trouble with my car, I kept my chin up(kept a stiff upper lip
↳ 차에 약간의 문제가 생겼지만 침착하게 대처했어

An-do will find out where the shoe pinches when he tries it on
↳ 안도는 경험을 통해서 문제점을 찾아낼 거야

And there's(that's) the end of the matter
↳ 그것으로 끝이다

Can you get them round the table to agree on this point?
↳ 그들이 이 문제에 합의할 수 있도록 협상 테이블로 끌어 올 수 있겠나?

Chan-ho held himself together through all his troubles
↳ 찬호는 모든 어려움 가운데도 정신을 가다듬고 버티었어

Chang-soo is at his wit's end with this problem
↳ 창수는 이 문제 처리를 난감해 하고 있어

Don't consider this problem from your own angle
↳ 그 문제를 너의 독자적인 각도에서 고찰해선 안 돼

Don't make a(federal) case out of nothing
↳ 아무 것도 아닌 걸 가지고 큰 문제를 만들지마

Don't run to meet trouble
↳ 걱정을 사서하지 마라

Don't trouble trouble till trouble troubles you
↳ 고통이 당신을 괴롭히기 전에는 고통에 손대지 마라

Emergency services are on hand in case there is any trouble
↳ 유사시에 대비하여 응급서비스가 준비되어 있습니다

Everybody gave me advice about what to do with my problem but kept his own counsel
↳ 모두가 내 문제에 대해 한 마디씩 했는데도 그는 자신의 생각을 말하

· **pinch** compress painfully
· **federal** of or constituting a government with | power distributed between a central authority and constituent units

지 않았어

Everybody knows where he stands on the issue
> ↳ 그가 이 문제에 대해 어떤 입장인지 누구나 알고 있다

Friends show their love in time of trouble, not in happiness
> ↳ 친구는 행복할 때가 아닌 어려울 때 애정을 나타낸다

> 어려움에 부딪혀 봐야 진정으로 친구를 알아 볼 수 있다는 말이다. 더 자주 쓰이는 표현으로 "A friend in need is the friend indeed 필요할 때 옆에 있어주는 친구가 진정한 친구이다"가 있다.

Give me some places to call in case of trouble
> ↳ 사고 날 경우 연락처를 좀 가르쳐 주시오

Hardly had he escaped before the unexpected problem came up
> ↳ 그가 도망치기 무섭게 예상 밖의 문제가 발생했다

Have you been keeping out of trouble?
> ↳ 요즘 별일 없나?

He is fully justified in leaving the matter untouched
> ↳ 그가 그 문제를 손대지 않고 있는 데에는 충분한 이유가 있어서였다

Hyun-soo kept out of trouble by keeping to himself
> ↳ 현수는 남들과 접촉을 끊음으로써 말썽이 안 생기게 했어

I take leave to consider the matter settled
> ↳ 본 건은 낙착된 것으로 간주합니다

If a new car is having teething troubles, nine times out of ten free servicing is available
> ↳ 새 차의 길들이기(초창기 어려움)에 문제가 있으면 대개의 경우 해당 지역에서 서비스를 제공받는다

It can save you a lot of trouble if you'll listen to reason

· **counsel** advice, deliberation together
· **indeed** without question

· **justify** prove to be just, right, or reasonable

┗ 남의 충고를 따르면 많은 어려움을 피할 수 있어

It requires the understanding and cooperation of everyone in the country to resolve the problems created by this outbreak

┗ 이번 발생한 문제점들을 해결하기 위해 전 국민적 이해와 협조가 요망된다

It's tempting to criticize others and turn a blind eye to all the problems of your own

┗ 남들을 마구 헐뜯고 자신의 문제점을 덮어두고자 하는 유혹에 끌려들기 쉽다

Just clear the decks and concentrate only on the important problems first

┗ 불필요한 요소를 없애고 중요한 문제에만 주의를 기울여라

Let's address ourselves to the matters at hand

┗ 현안 문제부터 해결하자

Let's concentrate on one problem at a time

┗ 문제를 하나 하나 생각해 보자

Life is full of troubles(and trials)

┗ 인생은 고난과 시련에 가득 차 있다

> 인생을 고난으로 표현한 속담은 여러 가지가 있다. "Life is pilgrimage 인생은 순례의 여행이다", "We must eat a peck of dirt before we die 살다 보면 인생의 쓴맛을 보게 마련이다" 등이다.
> (=If wishes were horses, beggars would ride)

Look before you leap and you won't get into trouble

┗ 사전에 주의하면 어려운 일은 없을 것이다

> 무엇이든 실행하기 전에 심사숙고하라는 뜻이다. 직역하면 "뛰기 전에 잘 살펴라"이다. 한국 속담으로 "돌다리도 두드려 보고 건너라"와 비슷하다.

› **cooperate** act jointly
› **resolve** find an answer to, make a formal

resolution
› **outbreak** sudden occurrence

Maintain your car regularly, or you're just inviting trouble
↳ 차를 정기적으로 정비해 두지 않으면 화를 자초하게 돼

Many troubles of life can be spared when you learn to say "No"
↳ "아니오"라고 말하기를 제대로 배울 때 많은 문제들이 지나쳐 갈 수 있다

Minority problems lack the immediacy in a homogeneous culture
↳ 동질문화 속에서는 소수민족 문제가 급박하지 않다

Most hearing problems in later life are connected to prolonged exposure to loud noises during youth
↳ 노년에 생기는 대부분의 난청 문제는 젊었을 때 오랫동안 소음에 노출됨에 연관된다

My computer is causing trouble again. Uh oh. Here we go again
↳ 컴퓨터가 또 이상이야. 어이쿠. 또 시작이야

My mind keeps ringing on the problem
↳ 내 마음은 줄곧 그 문제에만 가있다

Nobody has any trouble making a go of it
↳ 그 일을 원만하게 추진하는데 애먹는 사람은 아무도 없어

Nothing between your ears, that's your trouble
↳ 넌 머리가 텅 비었다는 게 문제야

Pack up your troubles in your old kid-bag
↳ 걱정 꺼리는 가방 속에 다 넣어두어라

Please give me some places to call in case of trouble
↳ 사고가 날 경우의 연락처를 가르쳐 주세요

Please render this problem down to the considerations that are important to us
↳ 이 문제를 우리가 중요시할 사항으로 좀 요약해 줘

Please straighten up and fly right before you get into trouble

---

› **maintain** keep in an existing state, sustain, declare

› **homogeneous** of the same or a similar kind

› **prolong** lengthen in time or extent

ㄴ 어려운 일 당하기 전에 자세를 고쳐서 바르게 행동해라

Problems are only opportunities in work clothes
ㄴ 문제점은 단지 작업복 차림의 기회일 뿐이다

Put two and two together and come up with a solution to the problem
ㄴ 이것저것 종합추리해서 문제의 해결책을 찾아라

Sang-soo's trouble is that he tends to spread himself too thin so that nothing gets done properly
ㄴ 상수의 문제점은 이것저것 마구 해서 아무것도 제대로 되는 게 없다는 점이다

She finally got the monkey off her back
ㄴ 그 여자는 결국 골치 아픈 문제를 해결했어

She immersed herself in work so as to stop thinking about the problem
ㄴ 그녀는 그 문제를 더 이상 생각하지 않기 위해 일에 몰두했다

She just stumbled on the answer to the problem purely by chance
ㄴ 그녀는 순전히 요행으로 문제의 답을 알아냈다

She's a very fastidious woman but her exhaustive reporting is well worth the trouble
ㄴ 그녀는 몹시 까다로운 여자지만 그녀의 철저한 보도는 충분히 그 수고의 가치가 있다

She's vicious to find a way out of trouble
ㄴ 그녀는 곤경을 벗어나려고 물불을 가리지 않아

Some people say they could do without the children causing trouble
ㄴ 말썽이나 일으키는 자식들은 없는 게 좋겠다고 푸념하는 사람들이 있다

Stay on this medicine for another day to see if your stomach trouble improves
ㄴ 너의 배탈이 나아질지 이 약을 하루만 더 먹어봐라

› **vicious** wicked, savage, malicious
› **medicine** preparation used to treat disease, science dealing with the cure of disease

Thank you for going the trouble
> ↳ 수고해줘서 고마워

That is a real chicken-and-egg problem
> ↳ 인과관계를 알 수 없는 일

That issue seems to have slipped between the cracks and become forgotten
> ↳ 그 문제는 흐지부지해져서 잊혀져버린 것 같다

The biggest family problems are those caused by know-it-all kids and yes-it-all parents
> ↳ 가족의 가장 큰 문제는 모든 것을 아는 체하는 자녀와 그저 오냐오냐 하는 부모에 의해 발생한다

The central bank sees lower interest rates as a sure-fire solution to the banks' bad debt problems
> ↳ 중앙은행은 일반은행들의 악성 채권문제 해결법으로 이자율을 낮추는 것을 확실한 방법으로 보고 있다

The conglomerate pledged to speed up its downsizing efforts during recent financial jitters caused by the liquid problem of its financial arm
> ↳ 그 기업그룹은 금융계열사의 유동성 문제로 야기된 최근의 자금 불안감 이 팽배해진 가운데 조직의 축소개편 노력을 가속시킬 것을 다짐했다

The continuous problems turned us out in a few weeks
> ↳ 계속되는 문제점들이 우리를 몇 주 동안 맥빠지게 만들었어

The government and the ruling party argue that the increasing debt has stemmed from their efforts to clean up the problems created under the rule of past administration
> ↳ 정부와 여당은 늘어나는 빚을 전 정권이 저지른 문제점들을 정리해 나가는 노력에서 생겨난 것이라고 주장한다

The problem is now to keep the oil consumption down without

> • **central** constituting or being near a center, essential or principal
> • **debt** sin, something owed
> • **jitter** extreme nervousness

affecting the nation's industry

    ㄴ 문제는 국가의 산업에 영향을 미치지 않고 기름 소비를 어떻게 낮추느냐 하는 것이다

The problem sat heavy on my mind

    ㄴ 그 문제가 내 마음을 무겁게 눌렀다

The question of pay mushroomed into a major problem

    ㄴ 급여문제가 갑자기 주요 문제로 대두되었어

The rub(thing) is that I'm in an impossible position

    ㄴ 문제는 내가 어려운 상황에 빠져있다는 것이다

The small matter ripened into a large problem in a short time

    ㄴ 얼마 안 가서 작은 일이 큰 문제로 커졌어

The trouble about always trying to preserve the health of the body is that it is so difficult to do without destroying the health of the mind

    ㄴ 신체의 건강을 항상 유지하려는데 따르는 문제점은 정신건강을 해치지 않고는 매우 어렵다는 점이다

The trouble is that he's a big frog in a small pond

    ㄴ 문제는 그가 골목대장(우물 안 개구리)으로 끝나서는 안 된다는 점이다

The troubles in that refugee camp are overcrowding and a lack of basic amenities

    ㄴ 난민수용소의 문제점은 수용인원의 과밀과 편의시설의 부족이다

The weekly makes a feature of economic problems

    ㄴ 그 주간지는 경제기사를 특종으로 다루고 있다

There's more to be the problem than meets the eye

    ㄴ 그 문제는 겉보기와는 달라

There's trouble brewing

    ㄴ 말썽이 생기고 있어

▸ **mushroom** grow rapidly	▸ **overcrowd** excessively crowd
▸ **rub** difficulty	▸ **brew** make by fermenting or infusing

These troubles are all of your own making
    ↳ 이런 말썽은 다 네가 자초한 거야

They had only thirty minutes to discuss the problem and Jong-soo held the stage for most of it
    ↳ 그들은 그 일을 겨우 **30분** 정도 논의했을 뿐 나머지는 거의 다 종수가 주도적으로 말을 다 해버렸어

They keep mute and silent about it
    ↳ 그들은 그 문제에 침묵으로 일관하고 있어

They've been having trouble keeping pace with their colleagues
    ↳ 그들은 동료들에게 뒤지지 않으려고 애를 먹고 있어

This is at the bottom of the trouble
    ↳ 이게 그 사건의 원인

This issue must be resolved(clarified)
    ↳ 이 문제는 짚고 넘어가야 해

(=We must resolve this problem)

This medicine works wonders on woman's problems, such as the dizziness and pain frequently associated with menstruation
    ↳ 이 약은 현기증 및 생리불순으로 인한 통증과 같은 여성 병에 특효가 있다

This question involves embarrassing explanation
    ↳ 이 문제에는 구차한 설명이 필요하다

Tomorrow will worry its own trouble
    ↳ 내일 일은 내일 염려해도 된다

Trouble brings experience and experience brings wisdom
    ↳ 고통은 경험을 주고 경험은 지혜를 준다

› **mute** unable to speak, silent
› **clarify** make or become clear

› **menstruation** monthly discharge of blood from the uterus

> 직접 경험은 책이나 학교에서 배운 지혜나 간접 경험을 통해 얻은 지혜보다 값진 것이다. "Seeing is believing = 백 번 듣는 것보다 한번 보는 것이 낫다"라는 속담도 경험의 중요성을 말해준다.

Trouble can call out(forth) a person's best qualities
    ↳ 고통은 사람의 가장 훌륭한 면을 발휘시킬 수 있다

Trouble comes along when we least expect it
    ↳ 사고란 우리가 가장 안 일어날것으로 생각할 때 닥쳐온다

Trouble is shadow to life
    ↳ 인생은 괴로움이 따르게 마련

> 인생을 고난으로 표현한 속담은 여러 가지가 있다. "Life is pilgrimage 인생은 순례의 여행이다", "We must eat a peck of dirt before we die 살다 보면 인생의 쓴맛을 보게 마련이다" 등이다.

Try not to cover up your troubles while things worsen
    ↳ 문제가 악화되고 있는데 고민거리를 덮어버리려고 하지 마라

Unable to solve its financial problems, the club disbanded
    ↳ 그 클럽은 재정문제를 해결하지 못해서 해산했다

We can't let the matter rest at that(there)
    ↳ 문제를 그대로 방치해 둘 수 없다

We have no room for accommodation on this controversial issue
    ↳ 우리는 논쟁의 핵이 되고 있는 이 문제에 대하여 융통의 여지가 없다

We must consider this and that aspect of the matter
    ↳ 문제의 여러 가지 면을 고려해야 한다

We must get to the bottom of the problem

› **disband** break up the organization of
› **accommodation** providing things needed

› **controversy** clash of opposing views

ㄴ 우린 문제의 진상을 규명해야해

We must hang together when one of us in trouble
ㄴ 우리들 중 한 사람이 어려움에 처할 때 우린 단합해야 해

We'll go through the problem carefully
ㄴ 문제를 신중히 검토해 보자

We'll iron out all these little matters first
ㄴ 우리는 이런 작은 일들을 먼저 해소(처리) 해 나가겠습니다

What I think doesn't carry any weight in this matter
ㄴ 이 일에 내가 어떻게 생각하느냐 하는 것은 크게 중요하지 않아

Wine is the best broom for troubles
ㄴ 고통을 잊게 해 주는데는 술이 최고다

Wrinkling our brows won't solve a single one of our personal problems
ㄴ 얼굴은 찌푸린다고 우리들의 개인적인 문제점이 하나라도 해결되지는
않을 것이다

You have made even more bigger problems(things whose)
ㄴ 혹 떼려다가 혹 붙였군

> (=You have created more problems)
> (=You've ended up making things worse)

You have to attack the problem at the grass roots
ㄴ 문제의 핵심을 찔러야

You have to face the problem face to face
ㄴ 문제를 정면돌파 해야해

You must not jest about serious problems
ㄴ 진지한 문제를 농으로 돌려선 안 돼

▸ **broom** implement for sweeping
▸ **brow** forehead
▸ **root** source, essential core

You must not leave any seed of future trouble
↳ 뒤 탈없게 해

You should hang in there and things will turn
↳ 굽히지 않고 버티면 문제는 해결될 것이다

(=There's a light at the end of the tunnel)

You'd better study the problem before you shoot off your face(mouth)
↳ 무책임하게 주절대기 전에 문제를 파악해야해

You'll be in trouble if you don't go by the numbers
↳ 규정(절차)대로 하지 않으면 곤란해

Youth is when you blame all your troubles on your parents; maturity is when you learn that everything is the fault of the younger generation
↳ 젊어서는 모든 잘못을 부모 탓으로 돌리고 나이 들면 젊은이 탓임을 안다

- **tunnel** underground passageway
- **maturity** fully grown or developed

- **generation** living beings constituting a single step in a line of descent

45. 물건   **Products**

Almighty God, keep our wives from shopping sprees and protect them from bargains they don't need or can't afford Almighty God, keep our wives from shopping sprees and protect them from bargains they don't need or can't afford

     ↳ 전능하신 하나님 아버지, 우리의 아내들이 쇼핑에 미쳐 돌아가는 일이 없도록 역사 하여 주시고 세일이라 해서 필요하지도 않거나 분수에 넘치는 물건을 사는 일이 없도록 살펴 주시기를 기원합니다

As the item you purchased is covered by our unconditional refund and replacement policy, we can give you a full refund

     ↳ 귀하가 구입하신 품목은 저희 회사의 환불 및 반품 대상품목에 들어 있으므로 전액 환불해 드리겠습니다

Before buying a new appliance, compare the characteristics of similar products and their warranties, which protect your purchase

     ↳ 새로운 가전제품을 사기전에 유사상품들의 특징들과 보증서들을 비교 검토 하셔야 구매한 물건들에 대해 보호받으실 수 있습니다

Business in Seoul fell(went into a decline), as not many people could afford to purchase goods

     ↳ 사람들이 물건을 살 형편이 안 되고 보니 서울의 사업경기가 약해졌다

Contrary to the description on the instruction manual, the speed of sending documents is so slow and oftentimes the papers don't go in properly

     ↳ 안내설명서에 나와 있는 것과는 달리(팩스의) 전송속도가 너무 느리

• **policy**   course of action selected to guide decisions | • **warranty**   guarantee of the integrity of a product

고 자주 종이가 들어가지 않습니다

Credit is a promise of a future payment in money or in kind given in exchange for present money, goods or services
> ↳ 신용거래는 현재의 거래에 대하여 사후에 현금, 상품, 또는 용역을 제공하겠다는 약속이다

Everything is worth what its purchaser will pay for it
> ↳ 모든 물건은 구매자가 지불하려는 만큼의 가치가 있다

He used the opportunity of appearing on TV to give his product a plug
> ↳ 그는 TV에 출연해서 자기회사 제품을 선전할 기회로 활용했다

I am afraid we don't have any left
> ↳ 물건이 다 나갔습니다

In-ho's insight for products is getting better
> ↳ 인호가 제품을 보는 눈이 점점 나아지고 있군

It's a product that is marketable these days
> ↳ 이게 요즘 잘 나가는 제품이다

It's forbidden to import goods derived from animals on endangered species list
> ↳ 멸종위기 명단에 들어있는 동물로 만든 상품은 수입이 금지되어 있다

It's quite marketable
> ↳ 그건 꽤 시장성이 있어

It's what the market is crying for
> ↳ 이건 시장에서 원하던 제품

Lots of customers are really sold on the quality of their products
> ↳ 많은 고객들은 그들 제품의 질을 신뢰한다

Our products have more advantages over similar goods in the market
> ↳ 우리 제품들이 시장에서 타사 제품보다 더 많은 장점을 가지고 있다

▸ **insight** understanding
▸ **marketable** productive

▸ **advantage** superiority of position, benefit or gain

Please pick up your circular for items on sale
> ↳ 저희들의 세일 상품에 대한 광고지를 가져가시기 바랍니다

Really? You could have fooled me. I thought they were top quality
> ↳ 정말이냐? 난 그게 아니라고 생각했어. 최고품이라고 생각했단 말이야

Quite a lot of factories grind out their products
> ↳ 적지 않은 공장에서 제품을 날림으로 마구 만들어 내고 있어

Please let me explain excellent features of this newly developed product
> ↳ 이번에 새로 개발된 이 제품의 탁월한 성능에 대해 말씀드리겠습니다

She is clever enough to know that if she offers one product at a low price, customers will rise to the bait, come into her shop, and then buy other goods
> ↳ 그 여자는 한 가지 물건을 싼값에 팔 때 손님들이 달려들게 되어 가게로 몰려오고 덩달아 다른 상품도 잘 팔리게 된다는 것쯤은 충분히 알만큼 영리해

She's been hawking any bargain articles
> ↳ 그 여자는 난장에서 아무거나 싸구려 물건들을 소리치며 팔고 있다

State-of-the-art optical technology is incorporated in this product
> ↳ 이 제품을 만드는데 첨단 과학기술을 이용했다

The goods lie wasting in the warehouse
> ↳ 상품들은 창고에 방치되어 있다

The new product clicked with customers
> ↳ 신상품은 인기가 있었어

The other shoppers had already snapped up all that product
> ↳ 다른 손님들이 그 상품을 재빨리 다 사 가버렸어

The quality of finished product depends on the raw materials from which it is made

---

- **hawk** offer for sale by calling out in the street
- **nay** negative vote
- **article** item or piece

ㄴ 완제품의 질은 그것을 만드는 원료에 달려있다

There's a good market for consumer goods

ㄴ 소비재 수요가 많아

These items are going very fast(selling like hot cakes)

ㄴ 이들 물건은 불티나게 팔리고 있어

These knapsacks are made with specially padded straps so that they do not rub against the shoulders

ㄴ 이 배낭들은 어깨에 시달리지 않도록 특수하게 가죽끈을 덧붙여 만들었다

They are busy tieing up the loose ends in the new design

ㄴ 그들의 새 디자인은 마무리가 한창이다

They(집, 물건) are going fast

ㄴ 살 사람(세입자)이 빨리 나서거든요

This article is above changes in the fashion

ㄴ 이 물건은 유행을 타지 않습니다

This article is moving well(slow to move)

ㄴ 이 상품은 잘(안) 나가

This desk accommodates its shape and size to person's position

ㄴ 이 책상은 사람의 지위에 따라 모양과 규격이 조절된다

This is a hot item everyone is looking for

ㄴ 이게 누구나 찾는 잘 나가는 물건입니다

This is a red-hot item

ㄴ 이게 요즘 잘 나갑니다

This is well-known(noted) product of this region

ㄴ 이건 이 지방 명물이다

This product numbered among the most popular developed during the

---

- **knapsack** case for carrying supplies
- **strap** narrow strip of flexible material used

for fastening

- **fashion** prevailing custom or style

last month
> ↳ 이 제품은 지난달에 개발한 최고 인기 상품의 하나다

We are sold out at the moment
> ↳ 물건이 다 나갔습니다

What you see is what you get
> ↳ 상품은 전시되어 있는바와 같습니다

When business is good, people are buying up even the cats and dogs
> ↳ 경기가 좋아지면 평소에 안 나가던 상품도 잘 나가

Will you be getting more in?
> ↳ 물건이 더 들어옵니까?

With the hottest season in full swing, people began to show big interest in it
> ↳ 혹서의 계절이 임박하자 사람들은 그 일(상품)에 관심을 보이기 시작했다

You can argue the price down, but it does you no good
> ↳ 물건값을 우겨서 깎을 순 있어도 그게 너한테 이롭진 않아

You can only estimate what a thing is worth to you
> ↳ 물건의 가치는 사람에게 얼마나 가치 있는가에 따라 평가된다

You can save on(up for) a new stereo set if you shop wisely
> ↳ 요령 있게 쇼핑을 하면 새 오디오를 살 돈은 저축될 거야

You have known to have butterfingers
> ↳ 넌 물건 잘 떨어뜨리기로 유명하잖아

› **estimate** judge the approximate value, size, or cost

› **butterfinger** incautious person, a person who drops things too often

46. 믿음   Trust

A servant is known by his master's absence
> ↳ 주인이 없을 때에 좋은 하인인지 알 수 있다

After that incident lots of people pulled the rug from under him
> ↳ 그 사건 이후 그는 많은 사람들의 지지를 잃었다

Any attempts to revive the outdated campaign tactics of using regional rivalries to drum up support will further exacerbate the loss of public confidence in politicians
> ↳ 표를 모으기 위해 지역감정을 부추기는 낡은 전략을 부활시키려는 어떠한 시도도 정치인에 대한 신뢰상실을 악화시킬 것이다

Because of his double-dealing, he lost our trust
> ↳ 그는 표리부동해서 우리의 신뢰를 잃었다

Belief in the worth of individual is the key to a democratic society
> ↳ 개인의 가치에 대한 신뢰는 민주주의사회의 핵심이다

Believe nothing of what you hear, and only half of what you see
> ↳ 귀로들은 것은 아무 것도 믿지 말고 눈으로 본 것은 반만 믿어라

Better one safe way than a hundred on which you can't reckon
> ↳ 믿을 수 없는 백 가지 방법보다 한 가지의 안전한 방법이 낫다

Credit is everything for a merchant
> ↳ 장사꾼에게는 신용이 무엇보다 중요해

Cross my heart and hope to die

- **tactic**   action as part of a plan
- **rival**   competitor, peer

- **exacerbate**   make more violent, bitter, or severe

ㄴ 정말이지 믿어 줘

Don't believe a person on his bare word

ㄴ 남의 말만 듣고 믿어선 안 돼

Don't con me into believing what you said

ㄴ 네 말을 믿어달라고 우기지마

Don't go by what he says, he's very untrustworthy

ㄴ 그 사람 믿지 못할 사람이니 그 사람 말만 믿고 판단해선 안 돼

Evidence of trust begets trust

ㄴ 신뢰한다는 증거가 신뢰를 낳는다

Friendship, stability, and trust are frequently mentioned as criteria for a worthwhile relationship between two people

ㄴ 우정, 안정성, 신뢰가 두 사람간의 가치 있는 관계의 기준으로 종종 언급된다

Give(Allow) me the benefit of the doubt

ㄴ 속는 셈치고 믿어 줘

Have faith and stay the course

ㄴ 믿음을 가지고 초지일관하자(계속 나아가자)

He can be trusted to give a good account of himself

ㄴ 그가 훌륭하게 해낼 것으로 믿어도 돼

He has gained(lost) currency with the world

ㄴ 그는 사회의 신용을 얻어(잃어)

He that does not speak truth to me does not believe me when I speak truth

ㄴ 진실을 말하지 않는 사람은 남이 진실을 말할 때 믿지 않는다

I'll try to be worthy of your trust

ㄴ 신임에 부응토록 하겠습니다

› **worthwhile** being worth the time or effort spent | › **doubt** be uncertain about, mistrust, consider unlikely

I'm inclined to disbelieve his words
> ↳ 난 그의 말이 도저히 믿기지 않아

If you believe that, you'll believe anything
> ↳ 그런 걸 믿는다면 못 믿을 일이 어디 있어(분별력 없고 줏대 없는 사
> 람에게)

Our democracies must build a culture of mutual trust and respect and re-learn the value of strategic thinking
> ↳ 우리의 민주주의는 상호신뢰와 존중의 문화를 증진시키고 전략적 사
> 고의 가치를 다시 배워나가야 한다

There are numbers who believe it
> ↳ 그걸 믿는 사람들이 꽤 많아

There can be no progress if people have no faith in tomorrow
> ↳ 내일에 대한 신뢰가 없으면 진보가 없다

They trust him as far as they can throw him
> ↳ 그들은 그를 전혀 신뢰하지 않아

They'll believe it until we get proof to the contrary
> ↳ 우리가 그렇지 않다는 증거를 얻을 때까지 그들은 그렇게 믿을 것이다

To believe with certainty, we must begin with doubting
> ↳ 확실히 믿기 위해 우리는 의심하며 시작해야 한다

▸ **proof** evidence of a truth or fact | ▸ **faith** allegiance, belief and trust in God, confidence, system of religious beliefs

47. 범죄   Crime

A couple of days in the cooler will straighten him up
      ㄴ 그를 며칠 간 교도소에 보내놓으면 정신 좀 차릴 거야

A man fitting that description was seen leaving the house shortly after the crime was committed
      ㄴ 범죄가 자행된 지 잠시 후 공시한 인상착의가 같은 한 남자가 집을 떠나는 것이 목격됐다

A reckless driver who crashes into another car may be guilty of a crime in endangering public safety
      ㄴ 무모하게 다른 차와 충돌하는 운전자는 공동의 안전을 위협하는 죄를 짓는 짓이다

All sin tends to be addictive, and the terminal point of addiction is what's call damnation
      ㄴ 모든 죄악은 중독성이 있고 이 중독이 중증이 되면 이른바 파멸이 된다

Chan-soo was framed(up)
      ㄴ 찬수는 죄를 뒤집어썼어

Chang-ho mouthed(snitched, ratted) on Bong-soo and got him arrested
      ㄴ 창호가 봉수를 밀고해서 봉수가 체포됐어

Confusion betrayed his guilt
      ㄴ 허둥대다가 그의 죄가 탄로 났어

Crime and punishment grow on one stem

› **cooler** cool time or place, composure   › **additive** substance added to another
› **reckless** lacking caution   › **damnation** curse, insulting languages

ㄴ 범죄와 처벌은 같은 줄기에서 자란다

Crimes and poverty often go together

ㄴ 범죄와 가난은 종종 함께 한다

Did the punishment really fit the crime?

ㄴ 그 처벌이 정말 그 죄과에 합당했을까?

Ed got arrested flying kites

ㄴ 에드는 부도수표를 사용하다가 붙잡혔다(이해하지 못하는 경우도 있음)

Ed got off easy with a fine only

ㄴ 에드는 벌금만으로 가볍게 풀려났어

Evidence put him in the clear

ㄴ 그는 증거에 의해 혐의가 풀렸다

For their money, you'd be better off forgetting about the lawsuit

ㄴ 그들의 의견으로는 너의 소송 따위는 그만두는 게 좋겠다는 거야

Gil-soo has enough goods on you

ㄴ 길수는 네 발목(네게 불리한 증거)을 쥐고 있어

Growing old is like being increasingly penalized for crime you haven't committed

ㄴ 나이를 먹는다는 것은 저지르지도 않은 죄에 대해 점점 가혹한 벌을 받고 있는 것과 같다

Half the sins of mankind are caused by the fear of boredom

ㄴ 인간 범죄의 절반은 권태에 대한 두려움에서 생겨난다

He paraded the suspects in front of the victim

ㄴ 그는 용의자들을 피해자 앞에 도열시켰어

Her sins are all blotted out

ㄴ 그녀의 전과는 모두 말소됐다

Her testimony was inconsistent with their observations at the time of

---

▸ **parade** pompous display, ceremonial formation and march

▸ **blot out** make obscure or insignificant, destroy

the robbery
> ↳ 그녀의 증언은 강도사건 당시 그들이 본 것과는 맞지 않았다

If they can't prove he pulled the robbery, he'll walk
> ↳ 그들이 그의 강도행위에 증거를 대지 못하면 무죄로 풀려날 거야

It's time we stamped out all the street crime in our town
> ↳ 지금 바로 우리가 나서서 노상범죄를 뿌리뽑아야 한다

Lack of love in early children can induce criminal behavior in the young
> ↳ 어릴 적 사랑의 결핍은 청년기에 범죄행위로 빠지게 할 수 있다

Let's not beg the question and call them criminals
> ↳ 확정된 것도 아니니 아직 죄인이라고 부르지 말기로 하자

Lulu's attempt to frame Jim for crime back-fired
> ↳ 룰루가 짐에게 죄를 뒤집어씌우려던 일은 역효과가 났다

Moon-soo had better mend his way or he's going to end up in prison
> ↳ 문수가 행동을 고치지 않으면 교도소 가게 되어있어

Most of them have prices on their heads
> ↳ 그들의 대부분은 상금이 걸려있어

Nobody has a more sacred obligation to obey the law than those who make the law
> ↳ 법을 만드는 사람만큼 그 법을 더 잘 지켜야할 사람은 없다

One good bang in the arm leads to another
> ↳ 마약주사는 결국 중독되고 만다

Parents are answerable for the crimes of their children
> ↳ 부모들은 자녀들의 범죄에 대해 책임이 있다

Plead not guilty to the charge of kidnapping, but guilty to the lesser charge of robbery
> ↳ 유괴혐의를 불지 말고 형량이 좀 작은 강도행위를 자백해라

› **sacred** set apart for or worthy of worship
› **plead** argue for or against in court, answer to a charge or indictment, appeal earnestly

Poverty and ignorance combined to lead him into such a crime
ㄴ 그는 가난과 무지가 겹쳐 그런 범죄를 저지르게 되었다

Sang-soo sputtered(spluttered) out his story of the crime that he witnessed
ㄴ 상수는 범죄를 목격한 내용을 잽싸게 말했다

Several escaped prisoners are on the loose in this area
ㄴ 탈옥수 몇 명이 이 지역에서 도주 중에 있어

Spot checks by customs officers led to the arrest of several jewelry smugglers
ㄴ 세관원의 통관점검으로 몇 건의 보석 밀수를 검거하게 되었다

Suspicion always haunts the guilty mind
ㄴ 죄 있는 사람에게는 항상 의심이 따라다닌다

The movement to crack down on gangsters is getting up steam
ㄴ 깡패들을 소탕하려는 움직임은 더욱 거세어지고 있어

The wounds on his face lend(give) color to his story that he was beaten by his fellow criminals
ㄴ 그의 얼굴에 있는 상처로 인해 동료 재소자들에게 얻어맞았다는 얘기가 그럴듯해 보인다

That alone covers a multitude of sins
ㄴ 그것만으로도 다른 모든 결함을 보상하고도 남는다

That fellow got thrown into the cooler last night for creating a disturbance
ㄴ 그 녀석은 어젯밤 소란을 피워서 수감되었다

That guy always gets away with murder
ㄴ 저 사람은 늘 못된 짓하고도 걸려들지는 않아

That man will get sent up for a long time now
ㄴ 저 사람은 이제 오랫동안 콩밥 먹어야 할거야

The act is forbidden under penalty of death

· **smuggle** import or export secretly or illegally
· **wound** injury in which the skin is broken

↳ 그 행위는 이를 범하면 사형에 처한다는 규정 하에 금지되고 있다

The atrocious murderer felt no compunction at having taken a human life
↳ 흉악한 살인자는 사람을 살해할 때 양심의 가책이 없었다

The chickens that you have turned loose have got to come home to roost
↳ 넌 죄를 지었으니 벌을 받아 싸지 뭐

"Curses, like chickens, come home to roost"라는 속담은 자신이 남에게 해를 끼치면 자신에게 그 해가 돌아온다는 뜻이다.

The cockpit crew plotted course to the nearest airport to oust the culprit from the plane
↳ 승무원들은 범인을 항공기에서 내보내기 위해 가장 가까운 공항 쪽으로 항로를 잡았다

The conviction for bribery will jeopardize the future of him
↳ 그는 뇌물수수에 대한 유죄판결로 앞날이 위태롭게 될 것이다

The criminal was able to screw every penny out of that helpless man by threatening to give the photograph to his wife
↳ 범인은 속수무책이 된 그에게 그 사진을 부인에게 보내겠다고 을러서 알거지가 되도록 알겨먹었다

The emphasis on the unpleasantness of the human trade misses an important underlying point
↳ 인신매매의 불쾌한 면에 대해서만 강조하는 것은 그 이면의 중요성을 간과하는 것이다

The ex-convict's anecdote ranged from his days as a shoplifter to his life as a fortuneteller
↳ 그 출소자의 일화는 가게 들치기에서 점쟁이로 살아가기까지에 걸쳐있었다

› **atrocious** appalling or abominable
› **compunction** remorse

› **cockpit** place for a pilot, driver, or helmsman

The gangsters put the squeeze on all the merchants
> ↳ 깡패들이 모든 상인들에게서 돈을 뜯어갔어

The gangsters shake the shop owners down every month
> ↳ 깡패들이 매월 상점 주인들을 등쳐먹고 있어

The grapevine wasn't right. He's innocent
> ↳ 남들에게서 들은 얘기는 사실과 달랐다. 그에게는 죄가 없어

The hit-man already gunned down the key-witness
> ↳ 살인청부업자는 벌써 중요 목격자를 사살했다

The hooligan edged closer, gripping the ax tightly in his hand
> ↳ 그 불한당은 도끼를 손에 꼭 쥐고 천천히 다가갔다

The horrible scene sent shivers down his spines
> ↳ 그는 끔찍한 광경에 간담이 서늘해졌다

The illicit practices of certain entertainers might have far-reaching consequences by sending the wrong message to young people
> ↳ 일부 연예인들의 불법행위는 젊은이들에게 나쁜 의미를 전달함으로써 큰 영향을 주는 결과가 될 수 있다

The judge threw the book at him for a gamut of felony charges running from the armed robbery to trickery
> ↳ 판사는 그가 무장강도에서 사기범에 이르기까지 모든 범죄를 종횡무진 하게 저질러왔기 때문에 그를 엄벌에 처했다

The police arrived on the scene of the crime
> ↳ 경찰이 범죄 현장에 왔다

The punishment was only a slap on the wrist
> ↳ 그 처벌은 솜방망이에 불과해

The statement is exactly what it says
> ↳ 그 진술은 말한 그대로다

- **grapevine** secret information, rumor
- **hooligan** thug

- **illicit** not lawful
- **felony** serious crime

The suspect was kept in custody
> ↳ 용의자는 구류 중이었다

The terrorist threatened to release a lethal biochemical agent into the water reservoirs
> ↳ 테러리스트는 급수 저수지에 치명적인 생물학적 약제를 살포하겠다고 위협했다

The whistle blower put Mr. Big behind bars for five years
> ↳ 밀고자의 밀고로 인해 두목이 5년간 교도소에 들어가 있었다

They are trying to nip the crime in the bud before it gets serious
> ↳ 그들은 범죄가 심각해지기 전에 미연에 방지하려고 하고 있다

They are trying to reconstruct the crime from all the separate pieces of information
> ↳ 그들은 모든 흩어진 정보를 종합해서 범죄를 재구성(연)해 보려고 하고 있다

They made lots of money from cooking the books before the fraud investigators caught them
> ↳ 그들은 부정행위 조사단에게 적발되기 전 장부를 조작해서 거금을 벌었다

They tried to worm the story out of her in vain
> ↳ 그들은 그녀에게서 내막을 슬며시 알아내려 했으나 허사였다

They went over the scene of the crime with a fine-tooth comb for clues
> ↳ 그들은 단서를 찾기 위해 현장을 샅샅이 조사했다

They'll believe it until we get proof to the contrary
> ↳ 우리가 그렇지 않다는 증거를 얻을 때까지 그들은 그렇게 믿을 것이다

They've got him dead to rights on that charge
> ↳ 그들은 그 건에 대해서 옴짝달싹 못하게 만들어놨어(현장증거 등)

Try to catch him padding his expense accounts
> ↳ 그가 자신의 지출계정을 날조해 불린 것을 잡아내도록 해

- **biochemical** chemistry dealing with organisms
- **reservoir** place where something is kept

in store
- **bud** undeveloped plant shoot

Two blacks(wrongs) do not make a white(right)

ㄴ 다른 사람이 다 그런다고 해서 죄과가 정당화되진 않는다

We must fit the punishment to the crime

ㄴ 처벌은 범죄의 수준에 맞추어야 한다

Who is in fault suspects everyone

ㄴ 죄를 지은 사람은 모두를 의심한다

(=He that commits a fault, thinks everyone speaks of it)

You can't get away from murder, as they'll remain focussed

ㄴ 그들이 계속 주시할 터이니 넌 그 일에 무사히 넘어갈 수는 없을 것이다

· **expense** cost

· **commit** turn over to someone for safekeeping

in store

or confinement, perform or do, pledge

48. 법   Law

Anyone carrying matches, lighters, cooking equipment and(or) fuel in(into the) mountains and wooded ares would(will) be sternly punished

↳ 누구든, 성냥, 라이터, 취사도구 및 연료를 산과 삼림이 우거진 곳으로 가지고 다니는 사람은 엄격히 처벌된다

Anyone who takes milk from an unhealthy cow will be contravening public health regulations

↳ 누구든 건강하지 않은 소에서 난 우유를 마시는 사람은 공중위생상의 규정을 어기는 것이 된다

Contracts inconsistent with the law are not binding

↳ 불법계약서는 구속력을 갖지 못한다

Countless sewage treatment plants break the law by dumping highly toxic substances into rivers

↳ 무수한 하수처리장에서 맹독성 물질을 강물에 버리는 범법행위를 하고 있다

Don't lay down the law to me

↳ 내게 이래라 저래라 하지(야단치지) 마

Even then your action didn't constitute lawful behavior

↳ 그렇더라도 네 행동은 합법적인 것이 아니었어

Few former prisoners remain on the right side of the law for very long after they have been freed

↳ 전과자들이 풀려난 후 상당한 기간동안 법을 잘 지키는 사람은 별로 없다

› **match** piece of wood or paper material with a combustible tip

› **contravene** go or act contrary to

› **sewage** liquid household waste

Having seized the power, he arrogated himself the right to change the law
> ㄴ 그가 권력을 잡더니 권력을 남용하여 법을 고쳤다

His law office turned out to be a money-spinner and was always full
> ㄴ 그의 법률사무소는 돈방석이 되면서 늘 손님이 가득했다

His word is law
> ㄴ 그의 말은 들어야 해

In line with the historic implementation of a law acknowledging brain death, the government launched a state-run agency to manage all matters related to organ transplants
> ㄴ 정부는 뇌사를 인정하는 장기이식에 관한 법률 시행과 연계해 장기이식을 총괄하기 위한 공공기구를 발족시켰다

Interest groups taking illegal job actions to capitalize on the general election will be punished in accordance with the law
> ㄴ 총선 분위기에 편승하여 불법행위를 하는 이익집단들은 법에 따라 처벌될 것이다

Is there any law against double-dippers?
> ㄴ 월급을 두 군데서 받으면 안 되는 일이라도 있나?

Is there any law against my eating out?
> ㄴ 나라고 외식 못 하라는 법 있나?

It won't take a long time before the newly implemented law gets on the right track
> ㄴ 새로 실시되는 법이 본 궤도에 오른 이상 그리 긴 시간이 필요치 않을 것이다

It'll make us think the law is an ass
> ㄴ 그래봤자 그 일에 법을 적용하는 게 얼마나 멍청한 짓인가 하는 생각이 들게 할 뿐이다

› **acknowledge** admit as true, admit the authority of, express thanks for

› **capitalize** turn something to advantage

It's no use raging at(against)the unjust laws; there's nothing we can do to change them
  ㄴ 불공정한 법에 대해서 분통해 해도 소용없어; 그런 법을 우리가 나서서 고쳐놓을 수 없잖아

It's not proper to suppose that all of those who did not perform military service have violated the law
  ㄴ 군 복무를 하지 않았다 해서 모두가 법을 어겼다고 여기는 것은 온당하지가 않다

It's unlawful to try to duck out of paying taxes
  ㄴ 납세를 피하려는 것은 불법이다

Laws are silent in time of war
  ㄴ 전시에는 법이 침묵한다

Laws catch flies, but let hornets go free
  ㄴ 법은 큰 고기는 놓아주고 송사리만 잡는다

Laws too gentle are seldom obeyed; too severe, seldom executed
  ㄴ 법이 너무 무르면 지켜지기가 어렵고 너무 엄하면 시행이 어렵다

Let's go by the book
  ㄴ 법대로 하자

Liberty is the right to do what the laws permit
  ㄴ 자유는 법률이 허용한 권리이다

Man, when perfected, is the best animals, but, when separated from law and justice, he's the worst of all
  ㄴ 사람이 완벽해 진다면 동물 중 가장 훌륭한 동물이지만, 법과 도리를 벗어나게 되면 가장 나쁜 동물이다

Might makes right
  ㄴ 법은 멀고 주먹은 가깝다

· **unjust** not reasonable, incorrect or improper, immoral or illegal

· **tax** charge by authority for public purposes

'Might' 에는 '힘'과 '권력' 이라는 뜻이 있고, 'Right' 에는 '정의', '권력' 이라는 뜻이 있다. 여기서 'Might' 는 '힘', 'Right' 는 '정의'라는 뜻을 가지고 있다. 따라서 직역하면 "힘이 정의를 만든다'가 된다.

Negotiable instruments such as personal checks may ordinarily be transferred to another person by endorsement
> ↳ 개인수표와 같은 양도가능 약속어음은 보통 배서를 통해 남에게 양도
> 될 수 있다

New lord, new laws
> ↳ 주인이 바뀌면 법도 바뀐다

Nobody ever got arrested for bending the law
> ↳ 합법적으로 남을 속인 죄로 잡혀 간 사람은 없어

Nobody has a more sacred obligation to obey the law than those who make the law
> ↳ 법을 만드는 사람만큼 그 법을 더 잘 지켜야할 사람은 없다

Rich or poor, we are all subject to the law of this country
> ↳ 부자든 가난한 사람이든 우리는 모두 나라법의 영향을 받는다

She was flabbergasted to learn that she didn't legally own the house she bought
> ↳ 그녀는 자기가 산 집이 법적으로 자기 소유가 아니라는 것을 알고 어
> 이가 없었다

She's a law unto herself
> ↳ 그 여자는 제 맘대로야

Survival is part of the law of the jungle
> ↳ 생존은 약육강식의 일부이다

› **endorse** sign one's name to

› **sacred** set apart for or worthy of worship,

› worthy or reverence

› **flabbergast** astound

(Big fish eat little fish) 약한 것은 결국 강한 것에게 먹히고 만다. 다윈은 먹이사슬을 이론화 한 후 인간 사회에도 약육강식의 법칙을 적용시켰다. 강자 밑의 약자는 제대로 능력을 발휘하지 못한다.

The constitution stipulates the separation of the state and religion to prevent the interference in one by the other
ㄴ 헌법은 서로간의 간섭을 방지하기 위해 정·교의 분리를 규정하고 있다

The Constitutional Court ruled that a law banning out-of-school tutoring is unconstitutional and infringes the basic rights of the people more than is necessary
ㄴ 헌법재판소는 과외 금지가 헌법에 어긋나며 국민의 기본권을 필요 이상으로 침해하는 것이라고 판결했다

The court's function is to protect us from these murderers and maniacs
ㄴ 법원의 기능은 이들 살인자들과 미친 사람들로부터 우리를 보호해 주는데 있다

The crooked lawyer did them out of twenty million won
ㄴ 그 악덕변호사는 그들에게서 이천만원을 우려먹었다

The law can't be enforced against the man who is the law's master
ㄴ 법을 주무르는 사람의 뜻을 거슬러서 그에게 법을 적용할 수는 없다

The law must take its course
ㄴ 법이 왜곡돼서는 안 돼

The law would do more for part-time workers if the union wasn't so blinkered
ㄴ 노조가 옹졸하게 나오지만 않았더라면 그 법은 파트타임 근로자들에게 도움이 되었을 것이다

The legislature should revise the election law in order to make up

---

· **enforce** compel, carry out
· **blinker** a blinking light

· **legislature** organization with authority to make laws

for this problem and other shortcomings
> ↳ 입법부는 이 문제와 다른 결함들을 보완하기 위해 선거법을 개정해야 한다

The long arm of the law always tap these street vendors on the shoulder
> ↳ 경찰들은 늘 노점상들에게 뇌물(정보)을 얻으려고 찾아온다

The more laws, the more offenders
> ↳ 법이 많으면 범법자가 많다

The new law on organ donation would sharply increase the number of transplants using organs of the brain-dead
> ↳ 장기 기증에 대한 새로운 법은 뇌사자의 장기를 이용한 장기이식 건수를 급격히 늘일 것이다

The potential for misusing or abusing the human genes for commercial and other unethical purposes would make it necessary to enact special laws
> ↳ 상업적 및 다른 목적으로 인간의 유전자를 오용 또는 남용할 가능성으로 인해 특별법을 시행할 필요성이 생겼다

The present law shall take effect on after Jan. 1
> ↳ 이 법은 1월 1일 이후 발효

The shallow consider liberty a release from all law, from every constraint
> ↳ 생각이 얕은 사람들은 자유를 모든 법률과 모든 구속으로부터의 해방으로 여긴다

The total number of transplants may decline due to the law banning organ-for-money dealings
> ↳ 총 장기이식 건수는 현금거래를 금하는 법으로 인하여 줄어들 수도 있다

There should be a law against girls going around half-naked
> ↳ 여자들이 반쯤 벗은 모양으로 돌아다녀서는 안 돼

These notorious laws reflect the past dark days when our political system remained highly authoritarian

---

› **gene** complex chemical unit of a chromosome that carries heredity

› **shallow** not deep, not intellectually profound

↳ 이들 악명 높은 법률은 우리의 정치제도가 대단히 독재주의였던 지난
날의 암흑시대를 반영해 준다

They must operate within the law by ensuring that an acceptable standard of work is carried out
↳ 그들은 받아들일 수 있는 수준의 사업실적을 보증함으로써 기준의 범위 내에서 일해야 한다

This law carries a 30day mandatory jail sentence for anyone who deliberately neglect the safety for elderly people leaving them unattended for long periods of time
↳ 이 법은 오랫동안 고의로 노인을 돌보지 않고 내버려 둔 사람에게 누구나 **30**일간 강제 교도형을 부과토록 돼있다

This rule will go into abeyance until it has received president's approval
↳ 이 법은 대통령 재가를 얻을 때까지 실행이 중단된다

To explain any aspect of society the sociologist must determine the law influencing human behavior
↳ 사회의 어떤 양상을 설명하기 위해서 사회학자는 사회적인 맥락에서 인간 행동에 영향을 주는 법칙을 알아내야 한다

Under the new law physicians will be limited to diagnosing patients and writing prescriptions
↳ 새로운 법에 따라 의사들은 환자들은 진료하고 처방전을 써주는 것으로 제한 받게된다

We must obey the law, not excepting the king
↳ 우린 모두 법을 지켜야하고 임금님도 예외일 수는 없다

We should obey the spirit, not the letter, of the law
↳ 법률의 조문이 아니라 정신을 따라야 한다

Where drums beat, laws are silent

‣ **prescription** written direction for the preparation and use of a medicine　　　or the medicine prescribed

ㄴ 북소리 나는 곳에 법은 침묵한다(전쟁 때는 법이 소용없다)

Who would give a law to lovers?

　　ㄴ 사랑엔 법이 없다

49. 변화   Change

A change is as good as a rest
↳ 분위기 전환은 상큼한 기분을 주게 돼 있어

A change would do this place a world of good
↳ 변화를 주면 이 곳이 훨씬 좋아질 거야

A new era is dawning now
↳ 이제 새 시대가 열리고 있어

A new pragmatism is replacing the old emphasis on the size, prestige and face
↳ 크기, 명성, 체면을 생각했던 옛 생각은 새로운 실용주의로 바뀌고 있다

After that things changed
↳ 그 후 사정이 달라졌다

All things have changed from what they were 5years ago
↳ 모든 것이 5년 전에 비해 변모했다

Bong-soo will come around(change his mind in a favorable way)
↳ 봉수는 우리편이 될 거야

Bong-soo will soon get into the swing of things
↳ 봉수는 곧 새로운 환경에 적응하게 될 거야

Bosun's really been going through the changes lately
↳ 보선이는 요즘 사는 게 뭔지 몸소 체험하고 있어

Can the leopard change his spots?

· **era**   period of time associated with something

· **pragmatism**   practical approach to problems

· **prestige**   estimation in the eyes of people

ㄴ 제 버릇 개 주랴

Change your act
ㄴ 레퍼터리 바꿔 주시오

(=We need a new act)

Companies that are slow to respond to customers' ever-changing needs will find themselves squeezed out by those possessing the necessary celerity
ㄴ 끊임없이 변하는 고객의 요구에 응하는 속도가 느린 회사들은 필요한 민첩성을 갖춘 회사들에게 밀려나게됨을 알게 될 것이다

Do not hesitate to make any necessary changes as you think(see) fit
ㄴ 적절하다고 생각되면 주저하지 말고 필요에 맞게 변경시켜라

Don't change the subject
ㄴ 말 돌리지마

Gil-soo hasn't been the same since that time
ㄴ 길수는 그 이후 달라졌어

Having seized the power, he arrogated himself the right to change the law
ㄴ 그가 권력을 잡더니 권력을 남용하여 법을 고쳤다

He began to sing a different tune
ㄴ 그의 태도가 달라지기 시작했어

It's a new ball game
ㄴ 상황이 달라졌어

It's a woman's privilege to change her mind
ㄴ 변하는게 여자의 마음 아니겠어

› **celerity** speed
› **hesitate** hold back especially in doubt, pause

> 우리나라 속담 중에 '여자의 마음은 갈대'라는 말이 있다. 여자가 변덕이 심하다는 뜻이다. 영어 속담 중에도 비슷한 'A woman is a weathercock'라는 표현이 있다. 'Weathercock'은 지붕 위에서 풍향에 따라 움직이는 닭 모양의 풍향계를 뜻한다. 풍향에 따라 시시각각 변하는 것을 비유한 표현이다.

It's no use raging at(against)the unjust laws; there's nothing we can do to change them

      ↳ 불공정한 법에 대해서 분통해 해도 소용없어; 그런 법을 우리가 나서서 고쳐놓을 수 없잖아

Lawyers and painters can soon change white to black

      ↳ 변호사와 화가는 흰 것을 금방 검게 만들 수 있다

Liberals tend to favor more immediate social change than do conservatives

      ↳ 진보주의자들은 보수주의자들 보다 더 신속한 사회변화를 선호하는 경향이 있다

Love is more afraid of change than destruction

      ↳ 사랑은 깨지는 것보다 바뀌는 것을 더 두려워한다

Man-soo's father changed jobs several times a year, and the family was moved from pillar to post

      ↳ 만수의 아버지는 1년에 여러 번 직장을 옮겨서 가족들이 여기 저기 이사를 다녔어

Most tree frogs change their color to harmonize with their background

      ↳ 대부분의 나무에 사는 개구리들은 자신들의 주위환경과 맞게 색깔을 바꾼다

Not to change the subject…

      ↳ 좀 다른 얘기지만…

Now I could never change you

      ↳ 이제 와서 당신 마음을 돌릴 수 없겠군요

· **liberal**   party of government backing not stingy, narrow, or conservative view

· **conservative**   political party acting cautiously, and historically

Remember your constant nagging only makes me all the more determined not to change my mind

ㄴ 네가 쉴새없이 잔소리 해봤자 내 마음이 확고히 변하지 않게 굳혀줄 뿐임을 잊지 마라

Please change the record

ㄴ 제발 또 그 소리 좀 작작 해

She finally turned the tables in the last round

ㄴ 그녀는 드디어 막판에 대세를 바꿔 놓았다

Since I got a job, a lot of water passed under the bridge

ㄴ 내가 취직하고 난 후에 많은 것이 변했다

That idea changed the current of history

ㄴ 그 사상이 역사의 흐름을 바꾸어 놓았다

That's the rub of the green

ㄴ 그건 갑작스런 계획 변경이군

The growing clamor for political reform has brought about change among lawmakers

ㄴ 커져 가는 정치개혁의 요구는 국회의원들에게 변화를 가져다주었다

The only way for them to prove changes is to conduct the upcoming elections in a fair and transparent manner

ㄴ 그들이 변했다는 것을 보여주는 유일한 길은 오는 선거를 공정하고 투명하게 치르는 일이다

The rapid changes in the market placed the bank stocks at a premium

ㄴ 주식시장의 변동으로 은행주 값이 확 올랐어

The word 'variable' is a nice way of putting "watchout"

ㄴ '변화'라는 말은 "조심하라"는 말을 듣기 좋게 표현한 것이다

The world is always changing

▸ **current** occurring in or belonging to the present

▸ **reform** make or become better especially by correcting bad habits

↳ 세상은 늘 변해

Their behavior should suffice to illustrate how social attitudes are changing
↳ 그들의 행동은 사회풍조가 어떻게 변하고 있는가를 잘 보여주기에 충분할 것이다

Their changes are beyond my wildest dreams(hopes)
↳ 그들은 꿈에도 생각 못했을 만큼 변했어

Things have changed greatly
↳ 형편이 많이 달라졌어

This article is above changes in the fashion
↳ 이 물건은 유행을 타지 않습니다

Time changes and we with time
↳ 10년이면 강산도 변한다

Time changes everything
↳ 세월이 지나면 모든 게 변해

Time changes
↳ 지금이 어느 때니? 시대가 변했어

Time change, people change
↳ 시대가 변하니 사람도 변하는구나

Time won't change anything
↳ 시간이 간다고 달라질건 아무 것도 없어

Times are changing
↳ 요즘 세상이 그래(**Times have changed** 세상이 많이 변했어)

(=You can't expect the world stand still)

Trees start to change colors
↳ 나무들이 단풍이 들기 시작한다

› **suffice** be sufficient
› **illustrate** explain by example, provide with   pictures or figures
› **stand still** stay without moving

We must change our way of thinking if we are to put the nation on its feet after all these struggles
> ↳ 이 모든 어려움 끝에 나라가 바르게 돌아가자면 우리의 사고방식을 바꿔야 한다

Wan-soo is more changeable than a weathercock
> ↳ 완수는 변덕이 죽 끓듯 해

> 변덕이 심한 사람들을 보고 'Weathercock'이라고 한다. 이는 지붕 위에 있는 닭 모양의 풍향계이다. 바람의 방향에 따라 시시각각 변하는 모양을 빗댄 말이다.

When the vocal codes vibrate it changes sound that the mouth produce
> ↳ 성대를 진동시키면 입에서 나는 목소리가 달라진다

Why the change of heart?
> ↳ 어째서 심경의 변화를 일으켰지?

> (=what made your change of heart?)

You can't change(mend) your ways
> ↳ 제 버릇 개 못 주는군

> (=You can't change who you are)
> (=You can't change your spots)

You have changed a lot
> ↳ 너 몰라보게 변했구나

You shouldn't change your lane too often or all of a sudden
> ↳ 차선을 자주 바꾸거나 갑자기 차선을 바꿔서는 안 돼

▸ **vibrate** move or cause to move quickly back and forth or side to side, respond sympathetically

▸ **spot** blemish, distinctive small part, location

50. 부 & 빈곤　　Wealth & Poverty

A gift in season is a double favor to the needy
　　　ㄴ 가난한 사람에게 때맞게 주는 선물은 갑절의 은혜가 된다

A poor man like you can't do what a rich man can do
　　　ㄴ 너 같은 가난뱅이가 부자 흉내를 내서야 되겠나

> 분수를 모르고 터무니없는 짓을 하거나 그런 짓을 하여 낭패를 보았을 때하는
> 말이다. 가장 자주 쓰이는 표현, "Don't try to bite off more than you can
> chew"는 직역을 하면 "자신이 씹을 수 있는 것보다 더 많은 음식을 한꺼번에 베
> 어 물지 마라"이며, 이는 자신의 능력껏 소신껏 일을 하라는 말이다.
> (=A little bird is content with a little nest)
> (=Let the cobbler stick to his last)

A rich man's joke is always funny
　　　ㄴ 부자의 농담은 언제나 재미있다(웃어주어야 하니까)

All wealth is relative; so is its absence
　　　ㄴ 모든 부는 상대적이고 모든 빈곤도 상대적이다

An-do has all kinds of money
　　　ㄴ 안도는 부자

> (=An-do has money to burn)
> (=An-do is made of money)

> **season**　division of the year, customary time for something

> **relative**　person connected with another by blood or marriage

Anger make a rich man hated, and a poor man scorned
> ㄴ 부자가 화를 내면 미움을 사게되고 가난한 사람이 화를 내면 멸시받게 된다

Bank loans are often refused to poorer borrowers because the risk of default is greater
> ㄴ 가난한 사람들은 채무를 이행치 못할 위험성이 큼에 따라 은행대출이 거부되는 일이 흔히 있다

Crimes and poverty often go together
> ㄴ 범죄와 가난은 종종 함께 한다

Discussions about poverty are laden with value judgments and are often motivated by political rather than humanitarian concerns
> ㄴ 빈곤에 대한 논의는 가치판단이 개입되며 인도적인 관심보다는 정치적인 동기에서 이루어지는 일이 더 흔하다

Draft irregularities have long been a serious social issue symbolizing the conflict between the rich and the poor in this country
> ㄴ 병역비리는 이 나라의 가진 자 못 가진 자 사이의 갈등을 상징하는 심각한 사회문제가 되어왔다

Economic growth benefits the poor because it allows prosperity to be widely shared
> ㄴ 경제성장은 그로 인한 번영을 널리 공유하게 됨에 따라 빈곤층에 이익이 된다

He is not fit for riches who is afraid to use them
> ㄴ 쓰기를 꺼리는 사람에게 부는 어울리지 않는다

He is not poor that has not much, but he that craves much
> ㄴ 가진 것이 적다고 가난한 것이 아니라 욕심이 많은 사람이 가난한 사람이다

› **motivate** provide with a motive

› **draft** select usually on a compulsory basis

› **crave** long for

> "돈이 돈을 낳는다 Money begets money"라는 말이 있다. 아무리 큰 재산이라도 쌓아두면 그 자리에 머물지만, 아무리 적은 재산이라도 적당한 곳에 투자하면 큰 이익을 볼 수도 있다. 지혜로운 자는 경기를 잘 파악하여 적절한 곳에 투자하여 돈을 늘리는 사람이다.

He prefers honest poverty to dishonest richness
　　 ↳ 그는 청빈한 가난뱅이가 될지언정 부정한 부자가 되기를 원치 않는다

He's rich enough that he wants for nothing
　　 ↳ 그는 부자여서 부족한 게 없다

In a fight the rich man tries to save his face, the poor man his coat
　　 ↳ 싸움에서 부자는 체면을 생각하고 가난한 사람은 옷을 생각한다

In all labor there's profit, but chatter leads only to poverty
　　 ↳ 모든 수고에는 이익이 있어도 입술의 말은 궁핍을 이룰 뿐이다

In many parts of the world the poor are going without food so that the rich can live in luxury
　　 ↳ 세계의 많은 지역에서 가난한 사람들이 끼니를 거르고있기 때문에 부자인 사람들이 호화롭게 산다

It is better to be rich than die rich
　　 ↳ 부자로 죽는 것보다 부자로 사는 것이 낫다

It isn't as if I were poor
　　 ↳ 나를 가난하다고 하는 말은 아닐 테지

It's easier to commend poverty than to endure it
　　 ↳ 가난을 찬양하기는 쉬워도 참아내기는 어렵다

Laziness travels so slowly that poverty soon overtakes
　　 ↳ 게으름은 걸음이 너무 느려서 가난이 곧 따라잡는다

Lean liberty is better than fat slavery

· **comment**　statement of opinion or remark
· **overtake**　catch up with

· **consecrate**　declare sacred, devote to a solemn purpose

ㄴ 예속된 풍족함 보다 가난한 자유가 낫다

Man has the perpetual contest for wealth which keeps world in tumult
ㄴ 인간은 세상을 계속 동요 속에 있게 하는 부를 얻기 위해 끊임없이 경쟁해왔다

Many people paled at the notion that they would always be poor
ㄴ 많은 사람들은 언제나 가난에 찌들려야 할 생각을 하니 맥이 빠졌어

Moon-soo's ship came in when he married into a wealthy family
ㄴ 문수는 부잣집에 장가들어 살 판 났어

Mother Teresa's consecration to the task of helping the poor has accentuated the affliction of the poverty
ㄴ 가난한 사람들을 돕는 테레사 수녀의 헌신은 세계에서 수백만이 고통받는 가난의 고통을 부각시켜 주었다

Much of his wealth remains on paper
ㄴ 그의 재산의 대부분은 장부상의 계산에 불과하다

Myself poor, I understand the situation
ㄴ 나 자신도 가난하기에 그 사정이야 알지

Nam-soo too wanted to live in wealth and honor, but he couldn't quite turn the trick
ㄴ 남수도 부귀영화를 원했지만 소원대로 되진 않았어

Narrowing the gap between the rich and poor should receive the government's highest priority
ㄴ 정부는 빈부격차를 줄이는 것을 최고의 우선 과제로 해야한다

No man has tasted full flavor of life until he has known poverty, love, and war
ㄴ 가난, 사랑, 전쟁을 알기 전에는 아무도 인생을 안다고 할 수 없다

One role of public finance is to channel surplus revenue to the poor

---

› **accentuate** stress or show off by a contrast | › **finance** money resources(pl), management of money affairs

and low income earners
> ↳ 재정의 역할 중 하나는 여분의 세입을 가난한 사람과 저소득층에게 배분하는 일이다

Our personal peace and good health are greater assets than any material wealth
> ↳ 우리 자신의 개인적인 평화와 건강은 어떤 물질적인 부보다도 큰 재산이다

Plain living is nothing but voluntary poverty
> ↳ 검소한 삶은 자청한 가난일 뿐이다

Policies that are intended to redistribute income or wealth from the haves to the have-nots can be counter-productive
> ↳ 소득과 부를 가진 자에게서 못 가진 자에게 재분배토록 하는 의도의 정책은 생산성 향상에 역행한다

Poor and liberal, rich and covetous
> ↳ 빈곤한 사람은 인색하지 않고 부자인 사람은 욕심이 많아

Poor children wore clothes their brothers and sisters had grown out of
> ↳ 가난한 집 아이들은 형이나 누나가 몸이 커져서 더 이상 입지 못하게 된 옷을 물려받아 입었다

Poverty and ignorance combined to lead him into such a crime
> ↳ 그는 가난과 무지가 겹쳐 그런 범죄를 저지르게 되었다

Poverty is no disgrace, but it's a great inconvenience
> ↳ 가난이 수치는 아니지만 크게 불편하다

가난하면 사람이 비굴해지고 비참한 일도 자주 생긴다. 그래서 가난하면 두 배의 노력과 인내가 필요하다. 그래서 부지런하고 자신의 신념을 따르는 삶을 살더라도 부가 따르지 않는 것은 치욕은 아니지만, 불편하다는 것이다.

▸ **voluntary** done, made, or given freely and without expecting compensation, relating to or controlled by the will

Poverty is the worst guard of chastity
> ↳ 가난은 정절은 지키는데 가장 나쁜 파수꾼이다

Poverty obstructs the road to virtue
> ↳ 가난은 선으로 가는 길을 방해한다

Pyung-ho is not poor, only he seems such
> ↳ 평호가 가난한 게 아니라 단지 가난하게 보일 뿐이다

Rich or poor, we are all subject to the law of this country
> ↳ 부자든 가난한 사람이든 우리는 모두 나라법의 영향을 받는다

Riches alone make no man happy
> ↳ 돈만 있다고 행복해 지는 건 아니다

Riches have wings
> ↳ 부자는 망하기 쉽다(요즘 부자는 망하지도 않지만)

Riches rather enlarge than satisfy appetites
> ↳ 부는 많을수록 욕심을 채워주는 것이 아니라 욕심을 더 키워준다

Riches serve a wise man and command a fool
> ↳ 부자는 현명한 사람에게 봉사하고 바보를 부려먹는다

Riches stink in a heap, but spread abroad make the earth fruitful
> ↳ 부를 쌓아 두면 냄새가 나지만 널리 퍼지면 열매를 맺게 한다

Sang-soo rubs shoulders with rich people only
> ↳ 상수는 돈 많은 사람들하고만 사귄다

Somebody like Jung-soo, who came up the hard way, understands reality better than a person who always had money
> ↳ 정수같이 가난(어려움)을 체험으로 배운 사람은 늘 돈이 아쉬운 줄 모르는 사람보다 현실을 잘 이해한다

Superfluous wealth can buy superfluities only
> ↳ 넘치는 부는 필요 이상의 것을 사게 만들뿐이다

▸ **appetite** natural desire especially for food, preference

▸ **abroad** over a wide area, outside one's country

The age of miracle is not past
> ↳ 벼락부자라도 될지 누가 아나(벼락감투라도 쓸지 누가 아나)

The battle is not always to the rich
> ↳ 부자가 언제나 이기는 것은 아니다

The disparity between the slum quarters and the homes of the wealthy is no aberration
> ↳ 빈민촌과 부자들의 집이 차이가 난다는 것은 전혀 이상할 일이 아니다

The equitable distribution of resources and wealth should be a priority of the government
> ↳ 자원과 부의 공정한 배분이 정부의 우선 과제여야 한다

The government must try to distribute the country's wealth, so that they help those who need it most
> ↳ 정부는 국가의 부를 가장 필요로 하는 사람들을 도울 수 있도록 국가
> 의 부를 분배해야 한다

The first wealth is health
> ↳ 건강은 최대의 재산이다

The healthy are happier than the wealthy
> ↳ 건강한 사람은 부자보다 행복해

The higher the hills, the lower the grass
> ↳ 부자일수록 더 째째하다

The rich become richer, while the poor sank into the deeper poverty
> ↳ 빈익빈 부익부가 더욱 심화되어갔다

The rich knows not who is his friend
> ↳ 부자는 누가 자신의 친구인지 모른다

The rich man has lived well and not done a stroke of work all his life
> ↳ 그 부자는 유복하게 살면서 평생 일이라고는 하나도 안 했다

› **miracle** event that cannot be explained by known laws of nature

› **disparate** different in quality or character

› **aberration** deviation or distortion

The rich man is wise in his own eyes, but the poor who has understanding searches him out
> 부자는 자기를 지혜롭게 여겨도 명철한 가난한 자는 자신을 살펴 아느니라

The poor men in the street don't know any better
> 가난한 일반 서민들은 어찌해야할지 모르고 있어

The surest way to remain poor is to be an honest man
> 가난을 면할 수 없는 가장 확실한 길은 정직한 사람이 되는 것이다

There are countries in which unnecessary poverty prevails because the people as a whole are unaware of methods whereby it can be relieved
> 국민전체가 가난에서 벗어날 수 있는 방법을 모르기 때문에 피할 수 도 있는 가난을 겪고있는 나라들이 있다

There is considerable evidence that poverty is the outcome of inappropriate policies and poorly-designed legal institutions
> 빈곤이 부적절한 정책과 부실하게 설계된 법적인 제도로 인한다는 상 당한 증거가 있다

There's no virtue that poverty destroys not
> 가난은 모든 덕행을 파괴한다

These days the richer become richer, while the poorer sink into deeper poverty
> 요즈음 가난한 사람들은 더욱 궁핍 속으로 빠져드는 반면, 부자들은 더욱 부자가 되어가고 있다

They are little better than beggars
> 그들은 거지나 다름없었어

They are upstarts who live off the tit
> 그들은 별로 하는 일없이 잘 사는 졸부들이다

This is the only way for them to revive the impoverished economy and to save innocent people from starvation
> 이것은 그들이 가난에 찌들려 있는 경제를 소생시키고 죄 없는 국민

▸ **prevail** triumph, urge successfully (+on or upon), be frequent, widespread, or dominant

▸ **unaware** not aware

들을 가난에서 구제해 주는 유일한 방법이다

We have no more right to consume happiness without producing it than to consume wealth without producing it
> ↳ 우리는 부를 만들어내지 않고 그 부를 소비할 권리가 없듯이 행복도 만들지 않고 소비할 권리가 없다

Wealth is not his who has it, but he who enjoys it
> ↳ 돈은 가진 사람의 것이 아니라 쓰는 사람의 것이다

"돈이 돈을 낳는다 Money begets money"라는 말이 있다. 아무리 큰 재산이라도 쌓아두면 그 자리에 머물지만, 아무리 적은 재산이라도 적당한 곳에 투자하면 큰 이익을 볼 수도 있다. 지혜로운 자는 경기를 잘 파악하여 적절한 곳에 투자하여 돈을 늘리는 사람이다.

Wealth stays with us a little moment if at all
> ↳ 부는 우리에게 머무르더라도 잠깐 뿐이다

When a man is reduced to want, the beggars in him crops out
> ↳ 사람이 가난해지면 거지근성이 나온다

When poverty comes in at the door, love flies out of the window
> ↳ 가난이 현관문으로 들어서면 사랑이 창문 밖으로 달아난다

가난해지면 의식주 해결이 힘들어 지기 때문에 인정이 사라지고 갈등이 늘어나는 것이 사실이다. 금실이 좋던 부부도 가난이 오면 싸움이 잦아진다.

Without the rich heart, wealth is an ugly beggar
> ↳ 마음이 풍족하지 않은 부자는 몰골 사나운 거지이다

You are poor now, but you'll see better days
> ↳ 넌 지금은 가난하지만 앞으로 잘살게 될 거다

51. 부부   **Couple**

A man's best possession is a sympathetic wife
> ↳ 남자에게 최고의 소유는 마음 맞는 아내이다

A man's wife has more power over him than the state has
> ↳ 아내는 남편에게 국가보다 더 큰 힘을 가지고 있다

A wife loves out of duty, and duty leads to constraint, and constraint kills desire
> ↳ 아내는 의무감에서 사랑하게 되고, 그 의무감은 구속이 되고, 그 구속은 욕망을 말살시킨다

As(Because) my wife was away last night, I had to fend for myself for dinner
> ↳ 어제 밤에 집사람이 없어서 내가 손수 저녁을 마련해야 했다

Behind every successful man there stands a woman
> ↳ 성공한 사람의 뒤에는 부인의 내조가 있게 마련

Choose a wife rather by your ear than eye
> ↳ 아내를 고를 때 눈으로 고르지 말고 귀로 골라라

Couples contemplating divorce usually have second thoughts when they realize how it'll affect their children
> ↳ 이혼을 생각해보고 있는 부부들은 보통 그 이혼이 자녀들에게 어떤 영향을 줄 것인지 생각할 때 마음이 흔들린다

Discreet wives sometimes have no ears or eyes

· **sympathy** ability to understand or share the feelings or interest or another

· **fend** ward off(+off)

ㄴ 소에게 한 말은 탈이 없어도 아내에게 한 말은 퍼져나간다

Don't be such a wuss with your wife

ㄴ 아내한테 그렇게 쥐어 살지마

Don't step out on your wife

ㄴ 집사람 놔두고 바람피우지마

Dong-soo's wife is expecting

ㄴ 동수의 처가 곧 출산한대

Doo-man's wife always takes him to task for his drinking

ㄴ 두만의 아내는 그가 술 마실 때마다 꾸중을 해

For every quarrel a man and a wife have before others, they have a hundred when alone

ㄴ 부부가 남들 앞에서 한번 싸운다면 그들만 있을 때에 백번을 싸운다

He has been carrying on with his wife's best friend

ㄴ 아내의 가장 친한 친구와 바람을 피워

He is very selfish, but his wife goes to the other extreme of being too anxious to curry favor with me

ㄴ 그가 너무 이기적인데 반면 그의 처는 너무 내 비위를 맞추려고 안달이다

He's a perfect husband=He's everything a husband should be

ㄴ 그는 남편으로선 더할 나위 없다

He's got a thing about his wife's incessant nagging

ㄴ 그는 부인의 끝없는 잔소리를 듣기 싫어하고 있어

His wife is always beefing about money

ㄴ 그의 부인은 늘 돈 때문에 불평한다

His wife is giving him the third degree

ㄴ 그의 부인이 그에게 꼬치 꼬치 캐어묻고 있어

› **discreet** capable of keeping a secret

› **anxious** uneasy, earnestly wishing

› **curry favor** seek favor by flattery

His wife's been on his back for months to fix the big leak there
ㄴ 그의 부인이 그에게 몇 달 동안 졸라서 거기 크게 새는 곳을 고치고있어

His wife, consumed with jealousy, shadowed him hoping to catch him with his lover
ㄴ 그의 처는 질투심에 불타 그가 정부와 함께 있는 것을 덮치려고 미행했다

How can you do(live) without your wife?
ㄴ 부인 없이 어떻게 지내려고 그러세요?

Hyuyn-soo will hear from his wife when she comes home
ㄴ 현수는 집사람이 집에 돌아올 때면 한마디(싫은 소리) 듣게 돼 있어

Jin-soo kicked his wife aside and took up with a young chick(younger woman)
ㄴ 진수는 부인을 내쫓고 새파란 아가씨와 사귀었어

Let me introduce my intended to you
ㄴ 장래 아내 될 사람을 소개 드립니다

Love me, love my dog
ㄴ 처가 집 말뚝보고 절한다

> 진정으로 사랑을 한다면 그 사람의 단점은 물론, 주변의 모든 것이 이뻐 보이기 마련이다. 영국의 "Love me, love my dog"와 우리나라의 "처가집 말뚝보고 절한다"는 비슷한 뜻이지만, 영국의 속담은 의무, 즉 넉넉한 사랑을 요구하는 것이고, 우리나라의 속담은 당연히 그렇다는 것을 명기해 준 것이다.

Man and wife must help each other, for better or for worse
ㄴ 부부는 장래에 잘 살건 못살건 서로 협조해 나가야 한다

Marital disputes are a waste of time and energy
ㄴ 부부싸움은 칼로 물 베기다

- **leak** enter or escape through a leak, become or make known
- **jealously** suspicious of a rival or of one believed to enjoy an advantage

> (=Marital disputes never last long)
> (=Marital disputes are soon patched up)
> (=There's no point in having marital disputes)
> (=The couple are inseparably bound up by love)

My husband is a good provider
ㄴ 내 남편은 돈을 잘 벌어다 줘

My wife gets sentimental in the spring
ㄴ 집사람은 봄을 타

My wife got after me to hang up the clothes
ㄴ 집사람이 내게 옷을 걸어놓으라고 성화였어

My wife's been hounding me to see a doctor
ㄴ 집사람이 병원에 가 보라고 성화야

My wife's cleanness is bred in the bone
ㄴ 우리 집사람의 청결성은 타고났어

My wife's getting gray her hair because of our three children
ㄴ 집사람은 세 아이 치다꺼리로 머리가 세고 있다

Nam-soo must be laughing up his sleeve as his nagging wife is dead
ㄴ 바가지 긁는 부인이 죽었으니 남수가 화장실에서 웃고 있겠지

Nam-soo's wife's constant nagging puts a tax on his patience
ㄴ 남수의 처가 끝없이 잔소리를 해서 그를 참을 수 없게 하고 있다

Sang-soo's wife's got another one in the oven
ㄴ 상수의 처는 또 아이를 가졌어

She got sidetracked in her talk about her husband
ㄴ 그 여자는 남편 얘기가 나오자 슬쩍 화제를 돌렸다

She is everything a wife should be

› **marital** relating to marriage

› **dispute** argue, deny the truth or rightness of, struggle against or over

↳ 그 여자는 아내로서는 최고다

> (=She's a perfect wife)

She just basks in the glory of a successful husband although she's never achieved much herself
>↳ 그 여자는 이렇다하게 해 놓은 것 없이 성공한 남편의 영광을 한껏 누리고 있을 뿐이다

She was more wife than mother
>↳ 그 여자는 아이들 보다 남편을 더 소중히 여기는 여자였다

She'd jump through the hoop for her husband
>↳ 그녀는 남편을 위해서라면 물불을 안 가려

She's no oil painting, but she'll make a excellent wife for you
>↳ 그녀가 외모는 볼품 없지만 네겐 훌륭한 색시가 될 것이다

Sung-ho's wife can stretch a dollar
>↳ 성호의 부인은 돈을 잘 변통해 와

Sung-soo sound his wife's praises far and wide
>↳ 성수는 어디를 가나 부인 칭찬만 해

The calmest husbands make the stormiest wives
>↳ 고요한 남편은 폭풍 같은 아내를 만든다

The couple are inseparably bound up by love
>↳ 부부싸움은 칼로 물 베기다

The criminal was able to screw every penny out of that helpless man by threatening to give the photograph to his wife
>↳ 범인은 속수무책이 된 그에게 그 사진을 부인에게 보내겠다고 을러서 알거지가 되도록 알겨먹었다

> ‣ **bask** enjoy pleasant warmth
> ‣ **hoop** circular strip, figure, or object

> ‣ **calm** period or condition of peacefulness or stillness

The husband is always the last to know
 ↳ 아내에 관한 일은 남편이 제일 몰라

The loneliness after his wife's death made my heart bleed
 ↳ 부인을 잃은 그의 외로움에 내 가슴이 아팠어

The man who is always the life of the party will be the death of his wife
 ↳ 항상 파티에서 잘 나가는 남자를 둔 부인은 죽을 맛이다

Their domestic battle is nothing new in this neighborhood
 ↳ 그들의 부부싸움은 이 동네에서 잘 알려져 있다

They appear to be a story book couple, but in fact, their marriage is on the rocks
 ↳ 그들이 겉보기에 잉꼬부부 같지만 실은 결혼생활이 파탄 지경이야

They are a double paycheck couple
 ↳ 맞벌이 부부

They are a story book couple
 ↳ 그들은 깨가 쏟아지고 있어

> 한국에서는 "깨가 쏟아진다"라고 하지만, 영어로는 "Storybook couple" 즉, "소설 속의 부부"라고 한다. '신데렐라', '백설공주', '인어공주' 같은 서양의 고전 동화를 보면 언제나 왕자와 공주가 결혼하며 행복한 결말을 맞는다. 이에서 유래한 속담이다.

They are man and wife in everything but name
 ↳ 그들은 사실상의 부부이다

They have cleaved only to each other for their entire lives
 ↳ 그들은 평생 서로를 위해 정조를 지켰어

They made a scene last evening
 ↳ 그들은 어젯밤 부부싸움을 했어

▸ **paycheck** check showing the salary

We have a weekend marriage
> ↳ 우린 주말부부

While Gab-dol was in the army, Gab-soon kept the home fires burning
> ↳ 갑돌이가 군에 가 있을 동안 갑순이가 집 지키며 살림을 했다

Who has a fair wife needs more than two eyes
> ↳ 예쁜 처를 둔 사람이 마음 편할 날 없다

> (=Please your eye and plague your heart)

Working women need helping husbands
> ↳ 직장 여성에겐 외조 잘하는 남편이 최고

You can bear your own faults, and why not a fault in your wife?
> ↳ 당신은 자신의 허물에 그리도 관대하면서 아내의 허물을 참지 못하는가?

You really caught him on the raw when you mentioned his wife
> ↳ 네가 그의 아내 얘기를 꺼낸 것은 정말 그의 아픈데를 건드렸을 거야

You'll make an ideal couple
> ↳ 너희들은 천생연분이 될 거야

Your wife would kill you if she got wind of this
> ↳ 자네 부인이 이것을 알아챘다면 자넨 끝장이야

› **plague** disastrous evil, destructive contagious bacterial disease   › **ideal** imaginary, perfect

52. 부탁   **Requests**

Asking Bong-soo is wasting your breath
> ↳ 봉수에게 부탁해봐야 소용없어

Can I bum a cigarette off you?
> ↳ 담배 한 대 있어?

Can I check my valuables with you?
> ↳ 귀중품을 맡아 주시겠습니까?(**I'd like my valuables back** 맡긴 귀중품을 돌려주십시오)

Can I put in my two cents?
> ↳ 제 의견을 덧붙여도 될까요?

Can I share your umbrella?
> ↳ 우산 좀 같이 쓰십시다

> (=Can I walk under your umbrella?)

Can we make it off the record?
> ↳ 비밀로 하기로 합시다

Can you get everything on him?
> ↳ 그 사람에 대한 모든 걸 알아줄 수 있나?

Can you make just one exception?
> ↳ 한 번만 봐 주십시오

› **valuable**   worth a lot of money, being of great importance or use

Can you oblige(us) with a song?
　　　ㄴ 노래 한 곡 해 주시겠습니까?

Can you run that by me again?
　　　ㄴ 다시 한번 말해 줄 수 있겠니?

Can you smooth over this matter?
　　　ㄴ 네가 이 일을 수습할 수 있겠니?

Can you sweat any information out of him?
　　　ㄴ 그에게서 정보 좀 얻어낼 수 있겠나?

Can you take(let) these pants in(out)?
　　　ㄴ 이 바지 좀 넓혀(줄여) 주시겠어요?

Change your act
　　　ㄴ 레퍼터리 바꿔 주시오

> (=We need a new act)

Clear the way(decks)
　　　ㄴ 길 좀 비켜주세요

Coming through, please
　　　ㄴ 좀 지나가겠습니다

> (=Could I get by, please)

Could everyone come up front?
　　　ㄴ 앞쪽으로 와 주시겠습니까?(회의장에서)

Could I be excused?

- **oblige**　comper, do a favor for
- **act**　thing done, law, main division of a play

ㄴ 일어나도 되겠습니까?(먼저 자리 뜰 때)

Could I get by?

ㄴ 앞을 좀 지나가도 되겠습니까?

Could you be more specific?

ㄴ 좀더 구체적으로 말씀해 주시겠습니까?

Could you clean the fish?

ㄴ 비늘과 내장을 제거해 주시겠어요?

Could you fix another one?

ㄴ 한 잔 더 주시겠어요?

Could you go for a cup of tea?

ㄴ 차 한 잔 드릴까요?

Could you have a person paged for me?

ㄴ 사람 좀 찾아주세요(사람 찾는 방송 부탁합니다)

Could you let me go with a warning?

ㄴ 경고정도로 처리해 줄 수 없겠습니까?

Could you let us know when the shipment comes in?

ㄴ 언제 선적물이 들어오는지 알려주시겠어요?

Could you move over(down) a little so we can have some room

ㄴ 자리가 생기게 좀 죄어 앉아(서) 주시겠습니까?

Could you please put your car at my disposal today?

ㄴ 오늘 네 차를 좀 사용할 수 있겠나?

Could you put it on my credit card?

ㄴ 카드로 지급해도 되나요?

Could you put that more simply?

ㄴ 조금 설명을 해 주시겠어요?

· **page**   summon by repeated calls
· **disposal**   give a tendency to, settle

Could you save my seat for me?
 ↳ 제 자리 좀 봐 주시겠습니까?(잠시 자리 뜰 때)

Could you squeeze a little?
 ↳ 좀 지나가겠습니다

Could you start the ball rolling?
 ↳ 먼저 발언해 주시겠습니까?

Could you take it full-length
 ↳ 전신 사진으로 찍어 줘

Cut me some slack, will you
 ↳ 좀 봐 줘

Direct this letter to my business(home) address
 ↳ 이 편지를 직장(집) 주소로 해주세요

Do what you can to keep construction dust to a minimum
 ↳ 가능한 한 건설 공사장 먼지를 최소화하도록 해 주시오

Don't fail to let me know
 ↳ 꼭 알려 주시오

Easy does it with these articles
 ↳ 이 물건들을 조심해서 다뤄 주세요

Excuse me, I need to get through(by)
 ↳ 실례지만 지나가겠습니다

Excuse my slip of the tongue
 ↳ 실언을 용서해 주세요

Gangway!
 ↳ 짐이요 짐!(길 좀 비켜 주세요!)

Gil-soo's gone above(over) and beyond the call of duty
 ↳ 길수는 부탁한 것 이상으로 해 놓았다

· **slack** careless, not taut, not busy
· **gangway** passage in or out

Give him hell if he interrupts you in the middle of making a recording
↳ 네가 녹음할 때 방해하거든 혼을 좀 내 줘라

Give it a few more days
↳ 며칠만 더 기다려 줘

Give me a candid hearing
↳ 편견 없이 들어다오

Give me grace to listen to others describe their aches and pains
↳ 저에게 남들이 고통과 통증을 설명할 때 들어줄 아량을 갖게 해 주시옵소서

Grab one while you are at it
↳ 네 것 가져오면서 내 것도 하나 갖다 줘

I beg a favor of you
↳ 청이 하나 있어

I beseech your favor
↳ 간절히 부탁합니다

I need it yesterday
↳ 아주 급히 필요해

I need it right away
↳ 지금 당장 필요해

I would like to have your favor
↳ 선처해 주시기 바랍니다

Is it too much for you to handle(manage)?
↳ 무리한 부탁(주문)인가?

(=Am I asking too much?)

› **interrupt** intrude so as to hinder or end
  continuity

› **candid** frank, unposed
› **beseech** entreat

Just shoot(take) it from the waist up
↳ 사진을 상반신만 찍어주세요

Keep me company
↳ 내 옆에 있어 줘

Keep me posted on the developments in our plans while I'm away
↳ 내가 없을 동안 우리 계획의 진행을 쭉 알려줘

Keep some coffee around in case anyone wants it
↳ 누가 커피를 찾을지 모르니 준비해 놓으세요

Keep your hand on that to steady it
↳ 움직이지 않게 손으로 꾹 눌러 잡아 줘

Let it slide this time
↳ 한번만 봐줘

Let me know before we can go public with this
↳ 이것을 일반에 공개하기 전에 내게 알려줘

Let me know soon whether it is yes or no
↳ 가부간 곧 알려줘

Let's have a game and see how skillful you are
↳ 한 수 가르쳐 주십시오

Make like a janitor and open the door for us
↳ 수위인체 하고 우리에게 문을 열어 줘

Make your account illustrative rather than descriptive
↳ 이 내용을 서술하기보다 예를 들어 설명해 다오

Never ask of who has, but of him who wishes you well
↳ 가진 사람에게 부탁하지 말고 당신이 잘되기를 바라는 사람에게 부탁하라

Not to ask is not to be denied
↳ 부탁하지 않으면 거절당할 일이 없다

› **waist** narrowed part of the body between chest and hips

› **janitor** person who has the care of a building

Oh, Sung-mee, I couldn't ask you to do that
　　ㄴ 아이, 성미야, 그것까지 너한테 부탁할 수 있나

One trespass more I must make on your patience
　　ㄴ 한번 더 신세 지겠습니다

Please bear with me another day
　　ㄴ 하루만 더 참아주시오

Please circulate internally as you may wish
　　ㄴ 필요하다고 판단하시는 곳에 내부적으로 배포하여 주십시오

Please collate all these documents and scrutinize each one to assess whether it's valuable or garbage
　　ㄴ 이 서류들을 대조해서 각각의 서류가 가치있는 것인지 쓰레기인지 자
　　　세히 검토해 주시오

Please come and give life to the event
　　ㄴ 꼭 참석하여 자리를 빛내 주시기 바랍니다

> (=Please honor us with your presence)
> (=Your presence will be greatly appreciated)

Please compress his speech into something brief without losing the main ideas
　　ㄴ 그의 연설문 주제를 손상없이 간략하게 요약해 주시오

Please cover for me
　　ㄴ 나 대신 좀 해줘

Please credit hundred thousand won against my account
　　ㄴ 내 통장에 십만원 입금해줘(**I have debited ten thousand won against
　　　your account** 네 통장에서 십만원 **뺐다**)

· **trespass**　sin, unauthorized entry onto some-　　·　**collate**　compare carefully, assemble in order
　　one's property

Please crush up a little
ㄴ 자리를 좀 죄어 주십시오

Please direct all the mail to Mr. Gim when it is delivered
ㄴ 우편물이 배달될 때 김 선생님에게 보내 주시기 바랍니다

Please draw me a rough map
ㄴ 약도를 그려 주실 수 있겠습니까

Please drop these books at the library
ㄴ 이 책들을 도서관에 좀 반납해 줘

Please fit your remarks to the audience
ㄴ 말씀을 청중의 수준에 맞춰 주십시오

Please get back to me about that
ㄴ 그 일은 나중에 알려줘

Please give me some places to call in case of trouble
ㄴ 사고가 날 경우의 연락처를 가르쳐 주세요

Please have an eye out for the bus
ㄴ 버스가 오는지 잘 지켜봐 줘

Please have more consideration for him who has grown gray in his service
ㄴ 오랫동안 성실히 봉사해준 그를 좀 생각해 주십시오

Please hold down the fort till I get back
ㄴ 돌아올 때까지 잠시 내가 하던 일 좀 봐줘

Please inform me of the course of the affair(business)
ㄴ 일의 진행을 알려 주시오

Please keep my place in this queue a moment
ㄴ 잠시 자리 좀 봐 줄래?(기다리는 열에서 잠시 이탈할 때)

Please keep out from under my feet
ㄴ 방해 좀 하지마

· **library** place where books are kept for use, collection of books   · **queue** search, braid of hair

Please keep the discussion on track
↳ 이 논의를 예정대로 진행시켜 주시오

Please let me get by
↳ 좀 지나가겠습니다

Please let me hear you play a piece
↳ 한 곡 들려(연주해) 주십시오

Please pane the bumps off(away) so that the board is perfectly smooth
↳ 판자가 완전히 반들반들하게 울퉁불퉁한걸 좀 깎아주세요

Please pick up your circular for items on sale
↳ 저희들의 세일 상품에 대한 광고지를 가져가시기 바랍니다

Please point out where I am on this map
↳ 이 지도에 현재 위치를 가리켜 주세요

Please remind me if there is anything amiss on my part
↳ 부족한 점이 있으면 일깨워 주십시오

Please render this problem down to the considerations that are important to us
↳ 이 문제를 우리가 중요시 할 사항으로 좀 요약해 줘

Please run this ad in your paper for three days
↳ 이 광고를 3일간 귀지에 실어 주십시오

Please send this as unaccompanied baggage
↳ 별송 화물로 해 주십시오

Please shoot the package(over) to me immediately
↳ 소포를 내게 급히 좀 보내 줘

Please sign the duplicate of the enclosed order form and return it to us as your acknowledgement
↳ 주문서의 사본에 수취확인 서명 후 저희에게 반송해 주십시오

‣ **amiss** in the wrong way, wrong

‣ **ad** advertisement

‣ **duplicate** consisting of 2 identical items, being just like another

Please slide your hand over that wall to see if you can feel any crack
    ㄴ 벽에 균열이 있는지 살며시 쓰다듬어봐 줘

Please stay a little longer in your debt
    ㄴ 빚 상환을 조금만 늦춰주세요

Please stop distracting conversations
    ㄴ 사담을 중단해 주십시오

Please strike a pose for the camera
    ㄴ 사진 찍게 포즈 취해주세요

> (＝Please pose for the camera)

Please untie(undo, untangle, loosen) this thread
    ㄴ 이 꼬인 실을 좀 풀어 줘

She did it as a favor for me
    ㄴ 그 여자는 내 부탁으로 그 일을 한 거야

Stop standing there like a couple of stiffs and give me some help
    ㄴ 장승(죽은 사람)처럼 서있지 말고 날 좀 도와줘

Tai-ho began with soft entreaties and ended with threats
    ㄴ 태호는 부탁 조로 나오더니 막판에는 협박 조로 나왔다

Teach me the trick
    ㄴ 비법을 좀 알려 주세요

> (＝Let me in on the secret)
> (＝Show me the inside trick)

› **pose** assume a posture or attitude, propose, pretend to be what one is not

› **entreat** ask earnestly

We need your help every step of the way
> ↳ 우린 처음부터 끝까지 네 도움이 필요해

When you come up for air, I have a favor to ask of you
> ↳ 잠깐 숨 돌릴 때 부탁이 하나 있어

Why don't you pop over for a moment?
> ↳ 잠시 나한테 와 줄 수 있겠나?

Would you please inform us when we may expect the payment of this balance?
> ↳ 언제쯤 이 잔금을 지급해 주실 지 알려 주시겠습니까?

Would you put a plug in for me?
> ↳ 나를 위해 남들에게 얘기 좀 해줘

You're talking to the wrong man
> ↳ 번지수가 틀려(엉뚱한 사람에게 부탁할 때)

53. 분위기   **Atmosphere**

A change is as good as a rest
> ↳ 분위기 전환은 상큼한 기분을 주게 돼 있어

All is silent
> ↳ 만물이 고요하다(**All were silent** 모두가 침묵했다)

An uncomfortable silence fell on the room
> ↳ 방안에 어색한 침묵이 흘렀어

An-do keyed his speech to the occasion
> ↳ 안도는 그 자리의 분위기에 맞춰 얘기했어

Chang-soo is having a hard time(job) getting Sunday laziness out of his blood
> ↳ 창수는 태평한 일요일 분위기를 벗어나는데 애를 먹고있어

Clear the air in this stuffy room
> ↳ 이 방의 탁한 공기를 환기 시켜라

For one awkward moment he saw the funny side of the situation
> ↳ 어색해진 순간 그는 나쁜 쪽을 안 보고 재미있는 쪽으로 받아들였다

It was like being a stranger in a strange land
> ↳ 그건 촌닭 장에 갖다놓은 꼴이었지(어색하고 낯선 상황)

It's embarrassing to watch
> ↳ 눈꼴사나워(민망한 상황)

> (=It's an embarrassing sight)
> (=I feel embarrassed(uncomfortable) watching it)

› **occasion** favorable opportunity, cause, time   › **stuffy** lacking fresh air, unimaginative or
         of an event, special event   pompous

Let's liven things up
↳ 분위기 좀 띄워볼까(바람 좀 잡아볼까)

> (=Let's liven up the place)

Making quick profits seems to be the order of the day
↳ 투기 분위기가 지배하고 있는 것 같다

Not a lot of action here
↳ 여긴 조용하군

Our boss is disinclined to attenuate our high spirits by marring the atmosphere
↳ 우리 사장은 분위기를 망쳐가며 우리들의 좋은 기분을 망가뜨릴 사람이 아니다

Our boss will take a drastic measure and won't let the contumacious, discordant behavior of any employees ruin the harmonious atmosphere
↳ 사장은 단호한 태도로 직장의 조화로운 분위기를 깨는 어떤 직원의 불손하고 거슬리는 행동도 가만두지 않을 것이다

Recreation facilities need atmosphere
↳ 휴양지는 분위기가 있어야 해

She really knows what buttons to push
↳ 그 여자는 분위기 파악에 능해(성질 건드리는 것, 기분 좋게 하는 것)

That's lame(uncool)
↳ 썰렁해(분위기 죽었어)

> (=It's so dead in here)
> (=Who died?)

- **profit** valuable return, excess of the selling price of goods over cost
- **attenuate** make or become thin, weaken
- **drastic** extreme or harsh

The air is charged with tension
> ↳ 긴장감이 넘치고 있다

The bachelor didn't know where to look
> ↳ 그 총각은 매우 어색해 했다

The party was turning into a shouting match between the host and guests
> ↳ 파티장은 주인과 손님간에 고성이 오가는 소란한 분위기로 변했다

When Sung-min was furious at Sung-soo, Sung-soo cracked a joke, and it cleared the air between them
> ↳ 성민이가 성수에게 몹시 화를 내자 성수가 농담을 꺼내어 분위기를
> 확 바꿔버렸어

Who's going to break the ice?
> ↳ 어색한 분위기를 누가 깨지?(처음 시작할 때의 서먹서먹한 분위기)

Why all this ceremony today?
> ↳ 오늘은 왜 이리 서먹서먹해?

You ruined the mood
> ↳ 분위기 잡쳤잖아

▸ **tension**   tense condition, state of mental unrest or of potential hostility or opposition   ▸ **bachelor**   holder of lowest 4-year college degree, unmarried man

54. 비밀   **Secret**

Bong-soo dropped a bombshell when he revealed the secret
↳ 봉수가 비밀을 털어놓자 대단한 충격이 일어났어

Can we make it off the record?
↳ 비밀로 하기로 합시다

Don't blunder(blurt) out your company secrets again
↳ 또 회사 비밀을 불쑥 말하지마

Don't tell a soul
↳ 아무에게도 말하지마

He is trying to pump you for your company secrets
↳ 그는 네게서 회사 기밀을 얻어내려는 거야

He must have kept something back from me
↳ 그가 내게 뭔가 숨기고 있음이 틀림없어

He's getting much too personal
↳ 그는 시시콜콜한 개인 비밀을 너무 건드려

I have something for your private ear
↳ 비밀히 말할게 있어

Secret fire is discerned by its smoke
↳ 세상에 비밀은 없어

She found she couldn't keep her secret from becoming public knowledge
↳ 그녀는 자신의 비밀이 새는 것을 어찌할 수 없었다

· **bombshell** bomb, great surprise
· **blunder** move clumsily, make a stupid   mistake, lose through carelessness(+away)

She has a brain like a sieve and always forget the secret number
↳ 그녀는 너무 기억력이 나빠서 늘 비밀번호를 잊어버린다

She promised never to reveal her secrets on pain of death
↳ 그 여자는 목숨을 걸고라도 그 비밀을 지키겠다고 약속했다

She's privy to some of their most secret documents
↳ 그들은 몇몇 가장 중요한 기밀문서들에 은밀히 간여하고 있다

Sung-man dropped a bombshell when he revealed the secret
↳ 성만이가 비밀을 터뜨려 큰 소동이 일어났어

Tai-soo was about to tell the secret but he bit his words back
↳ 태호는 비밀을 말하러 하였으나 말을 참았다

Teach me the trick
↳ 비법을 좀 알려 주세요

> (=Let me in on the secret)
> (=Show me the inside trick)

The secret is common property
↳ 그 비밀은 누구나 알아

The secret is only now beginning to rise to the surface; he kept it successfully for many years
↳ 그 비밀은 이제야 드러나게 되었고, 그는 몇 년씩이나 이 비밀을 잘 도 숨겨왔다

The secret let(filtered) out before it was officially reported
↳ 그 비밀은 공식 보도 이전에 새어나갔다

The secret of happiness is to fill one's life with activity
↳ 행복의 비결은 인생을 활동적으로 사는 일이다

· **privy** private or secret

· **filter** pass through a filter, remove by means of a filter

The secret percolated through the office until everyone knew
↳ 그 비밀은 차츰 사무실에 새어나오더니 모두가 알게 됐다

There's nothing so secret but it comes to light
↳ 탄로되지 않는 비밀은 없다

When the time is right, I'll tell you
↳ 때가되면 다 말해주지

When we see a secret smile on his lips, he must be telling a lie
↳ 그가 입가에 살짝 미소를 지을 때는 거짓말을 하고 있는 게 틀림없어

Your secret plans must not go down on papers
↳ 너의 비밀 계획이 기록으로 남아선 안 돼

Your secret's safe with me
↳ 비밀은 보장하지

‣ **percolate** trickle or cause to trickle down
through a substance

55. 비즈니스   **Business**

A guest sees more in an hour than the host in a year
> ↳ 주인이 1년간 보고 아는 것 이상을 손님은 한 시간에 보고 안다

Accounting figures must be consistent with the information given in the annual report
> ↳ 회계상의 수치는 연차보고서의 것과 일치해야 한다

Accounts are coming in very slowly
> ↳ 지금은 장사가 잘 안 돼

Advertisers always play up the good qualities of the house for sale and fail to mention its disadvantage
> ↳ 광고주들은 팔려는 집의 장점만 내세우고 불리한 점은 어물쩍 넘어간다

After their business went down the drain, he started up his own vocational school
> ↳ 그들의 사업이 무너지자 그는 자신 소유의 직업학교를 시작했다

All sales of the drug were suspended after it was properly tested
> ↳ 그 약은 정식 검사를 거친 뒤 모드 판매가 중단되었다

All supermarkets are full of people stocking up for the long holidays
> ↳ 모든 슈퍼마켓은 연휴에 대비해 물건을 사 두려는 사람들로 가득하다

All's fair in love and business
> ↳ 사랑과 사업에는 수단을 가리지 않는다

▸ **figure**   be important, calculate   ▸ **advertise**   call public attention to

▸ **annual**   occurring once a year

사랑과 성공은 쟁취라는 말이 있다. 용기를 내서 부딪혀야 하는 것이 사랑과 비즈니스이기 때문이다. 비슷한 어구 중에는 "All is fair in love and war 사랑과 전쟁에는 수단을 가리지 않는다"도 있다. 또한 사랑의 용기를 말한 속담 중에는 "None but the brave deserve the fair 용감한 자만이 미인을 차지한다"도 있다.

As expected it was gravy all the way
　　ㄴ 그건 예상대로 거저먹기였어

As far as computers are concerned, they've already cornered the market
　　ㄴ 컴퓨터라면 그들이 이미 시장을 다 휘어잡고 있다

As the prospects of bankruptcy loom large, life is getting tough for small businesses
　　ㄴ 부도가 날 전망이 무겁게 다가오자 영세사업체들의 생존이 어려워지고 있다

Base gains are the same as losses
　　ㄴ 비열한 이익은 손실이다

Be careful not to blow a deal
　　ㄴ 고객 놓치지 않게 주의해야해

Be careful not to flog it to death, or your customers will lose interest
　　ㄴ 같은 소리를 또 하고 또 해서 손님들의 흥미가 덜어지지 않도록 해

Be careful not to price yourself out of business(market)
　　ㄴ 너무 비싼 값을 매겨서 물건이 안 팔려 사업이 망하지 않도록 주의해

Be your own boss
　　ㄴ 자기 사업을 해라

(=Start your own business)

· **corner** give into a corner, get a corner on, turn a corner

· **loom** appear large and indistinct or impressive

Being ahead of the game is important to your business
┗ 네 사업은 경쟁력에 앞서는 일이 중요하다

Better modify your investment plans according to new circumstances
┗ 투자계획을 새로운 상황에 맞추어 수정하지 그래

Big-time spenders come out of the closet
┗ 큰손들이 움직이기 시작하는군

Bong-soo's business fattened up on low interest rates and light taxes
┗ 봉수의 사업은 낮은 이자율과 낮은 세금 덕분에 잘 되었지

Bong-soo's business fell apart like a house of cards
┗ 봉수의 사업은 사상누각처럼 망했어

'사상누각', 즉 '모래 위의 집' 이다. 비슷한 뜻으로 '공중누각'이라는 표현도 있고, 이는 영어에는 'Castle in the air'라는 비슷한 표현이 있다. 또한 'House of cards' '카드로 지은 집'라는 표현도 쓰인다.

Business dropped off drastically in the retail stores
┗ 소매점의 고객이 뚝 떨어졌다

Business in Seoul fell(went into a decline), as not many people could afford to purchase goods
┗ 사람들이 물건을 살 형편이 안 되고 보니 서울의 사업경기가 약해졌다

Business turns around all the time
┗ 사업은 잘 되다가도 잘 안되고 잘 안되다가도 잘 된다

Byung-soo's business was wisely managed, and it kept out of the hole
┗ 창수의 사업은 잘 운영되었기 때문에 빚은 지지 않았다

Can you keep this business on its feet for another year?
┗ 이 사업을 1년 더 버티어 낼 수 있겠나?

· **modify** limit the meaning of, change
· **castle** fortified building

· **retail** sell in small quantities directly to the consumer

Chan-soo's business was done(doomed) after the fire that burned down his office
> ㄴ 찬수의 사무실이 전소되는 바람에 사업이 망했어

Consumer sales are so slack that many smaller manufacturers are(have gone) out of business
> ㄴ 판매가 부진하여 소규모 제조업체들이 도산하고 있다

Customers are always right
> ㄴ 손님은 왕

Dealing with awkward customers is my strong suit
> ㄴ 다루기 힘든 사람을 잘 다루는 게 내 특기잖니

Does the advertising bring in any business?
> ㄴ 광고를 하면 일거리가 들어오나?

Don't forget that your customers are worth their weight in gold
> ㄴ 너의 고객이야말로 매우 소중하다는 것을 잊지 마라

Don't give your customers a runaround any more
> ㄴ 더 이상 네 고객들에게 이리 가라 저리 가라 하지 마라

Don't mix business with pleasure
> ㄴ 공과 사를 구분하라

Don't price yourself out of the market
> ㄴ 터무니없이 비싼 값을 불러서 물건이 팔리지 않게 하지마

Don't saddle yourself with such a big debt before you are sure of your professional success
> ㄴ 사업상 성공이 보장되기 전에는 그 큰 빚을 떠맡지 마라

Duck-soo's business may go any day
> ㄴ 덕수의 사업은 언제 망할지 몰라

· **doom** judgment, fate, ruin, condemn, fix the fate of(+to)

· **runaround** evasive or delaying action
· **saddle** put a saddle on

Even then losing that contract doesn't say much for(score up against) your skill in business

↳ 그렇더라도 그 계약을 놓치는 건 네 사업능력을 보여 준다는 면에서 나쁘게 작용할 것이다

Futurists envision the disappearance of advertising as consumers flock to services providing unbiased information

↳ 미래학자들은 소비자들이 편견 없는 정보를 제공하는 서비스로 몰리면서 광고가 사라질 것이라고 전망한다

Gil-soo followed in my footsteps and went into real estate

↳ 길수는 나를 따라 부동산업에 뛰어들었다

He can't wait to get his hooks into their business

↳ 그는 그들의 사업을 손에 넣으려고 부심하고 있어

He gathered his courage to take the plunge, resign from his job and start his own business

↳ 그는 용단을 내어서 모험을 걸어 직장을 그만 두고 자신의 사업을 시작했다

He has a constant stream of visitors(customers)

↳ 문전성시

He is spending money like nobody's business

↳ 그는 돈을 물 쓰듯 해오고 있어

He makes a great business of it

↳ 그는 힘겨워하고 있어(감당을 못하고 있어)

He's got both feet on the ground with his business

↳ 그는 자신의 사업에 관하여는 현실적인 사람이다

High interest rates will force many small businesses to go bust(fold)

↳ 높은 이자율은 영세 기업들을 파산시킬 것이다

His 'quality first' policy brought him success in business

‣ **envision**   picture to oneself

‣ **footstep**   step, distance covered by a step,

footprint

‣ **unbiased**   not influenced by prejudice

ㄴ 그는 품질위주의 영업방침으로 성공했다

His law office turned out to be a money-spinner and was always full
ㄴ 그의 법률사무소는 돈방석이 되면서 늘 손님이 가득했다

Hyun-soo couldn't build up his business, but he held his own
ㄴ 현수가 사업 확장은 못했지만 사업기반은 유지하고 있었다

I'll be doing this for a long time
ㄴ 하루 이틀 할 장사가 아니잖아

(=This is a long-term thing)

If he plays his cards right, he'll go places in this business
ㄴ 그가 잘만 한다면 이 사업에서 성공할 것이다

If you can't attract more customers, you'll wither on the vine
ㄴ 네가 고객을 더 끌지 못하면 실패하고 말 것이다

If your business ever gets off the ground, you may make some bucks
ㄴ 네 사업이 시작만 좋으면 돈을 좀 벌게 될 것이다

In this business, it's either a feast or a famine
ㄴ 이 사업은 도 아니면 모다

In-ho kept off(out of) dirty business
ㄴ 인호는 더러운 장사에 손대지 않았어

It's either looks or bust in her business
ㄴ 그 여자가 하는 일에는 미모가 뛰어나지 않으면 끝장이다

It's our policy to hold down our profit margin and sell as much as possible
ㄴ 우리는 박리다매의 방침을 취하고 있다

Jin-ro builds better mouse-traps

‣ **stream** flow in a stream, pour out streams   ‣ **wither** shrivel, lose or cause to lose energy, force, or freshness

ㄴ 진로가(손님 끌게) 물건은 잘 만들어

Joo-yung plowed all the profits back into the expansion of the business
ㄴ 주영이는 모든 이익을 사업확장에 재투자했다

Let's kick around some of the details and decide what projects to take
ㄴ 세부사항을 논의해서 어떤 사업을 해야할지 결정합시다

Let's try to crown our project with perfection
ㄴ 우리의 사업에 유종의 미를 거두도록 합시다

Lulu will surely make a go of her business she enters
ㄴ 루루는 시작한 사업에서 확실히 성공 할거야

Mr. Gim is out of the picture and Mr. Nam runs the store
ㄴ 김씨는 일을 그만두고 남씨가 가게를 보고 있어

Mr. Sohn has something going for himself with his business
ㄴ 손씨는 그의 사업에 성공했어

My business just managed to break even this month
ㄴ 이 달엔 겨우 적자나 면할 정도야

My cut is ten percent if I make the sale
ㄴ 내가 판매한 금액의 10%가 내 몫이다

My sales figures dropped behind what they should have been
ㄴ 나의 판매 실적은 기준치에 못 미쳤어

Nobody knew he was the fast-talker in the insurance business
ㄴ 그 작자가 보험업계에서 대단한 사기꾼인줄을 아무도 몰랐다

Nobody wants to shackle himself to troublesome visitors
ㄴ 귀찮은 손님에게 매달리길 좋아하는 사람이 어디 있니

Now that all our difficulties lie behind us, we can get on with our business
ㄴ 이제 어려움은 지나갔으니 사업을 추진할 수 있게 되었다

· **project** planned undertaking, design or plan, protrude, throw forward
· **shackle** metal device to bind legs or arms, fasten with shackles

One way that works every time is to convince the buyer that lots of other people want to buy that
> ↳ 확실히 효과 있는 방법으로는 구매자에게 다른 사람들이 그걸 사겠다고 줄을 서 있다는 것을 인식시키는 것이다

Our business must stay in the black to keep on
> ↳ 회사가 살아남으려면 흑자를 유지해야해

Our business showings last month went through the roof
> ↳ 지난 달 영업 실적은 왕창 올랐어

Punctuality is the soul of business
> ↳ 약속을 잘 지킴은 사업에 있어서 핵심이 된다

> 약속을 잘 지키는 사람은 신용을 얻게 된다. 사회 생활에서 신용만큼 중요한 것이 없다(Punctuality is the duty of politeness of kings 약속을 잘 지키는 것은 신사의 의무이다).

Riding on a growing demand, his business enjoyed a big profit last month
> ↳ 그의 사업은 수요증가에 힘입어 지난 달 큰 수익을 올렸다

Roadside produce stands usually offer lower price fruits and vegetables than supermarkets
> ↳ 도로변 농산물 판매소는 대개 슈퍼마켓보다 값이 싸다

Sang-soo has to sell himself to the customers if he wants to advance in business
> ↳ 상수가 사업에 성공하려면 손님들에게 자기선전을 잘 해야 해

Sang-soo's store is being liquidated
> ↳ 상수는 점포정리 중이야

› **punctual** prompt
› **roadside** strip of land along a road

› **liquidate** pay off, dispose of

(=Sang-soo is closing his door)
(=Sang-soo is shutting down)

Send up a trial balloon before you start the project
   ↳ 사업을 시작하기 전에 성공여부를 타진해 보아라

She gobbled her lunch down then dashed off to her next client
   ↳ 그녀는 점심을 후닥닥 해 치우고 다음 고객을 만나려고 달려나갔다

She has to shoot straight in business or her company will fail
   ↳ 그 여자가 정직하게 사업을 하지 않으면 회사가 실패하고 말 것이다

She is clever enough to know that if she offers one product at a low price, customers will rise to the bait, come into her shop, and then buy other goods
   ↳ 그 여자는 한 가지 물건을 싼값에 팔 때 손님들이 달려들게 되어 가게로 몰려와 덩달아 다른 상품도 잘 팔리게 된다는 것쯤은 충분히 알만큼 영리해

She is in charge and has a free hand with this project
   ↳ 그녀는 책임을 지고 이 사업에 재량권을 가지고 있다

She left a document alleging that he had fraudulently misappropriated client's funds
   ↳ 그녀는 그가 고객자금의 착복했다고 주장하는 서류를 남겼다

She made a go of his computer business and made a fortune
   ↳ 그녀는 컴퓨터 사업에 성공해서 큰돈을 벌었다

She's been hawking any bargain articles
   ↳ 그 여자는 난장에서 아무거나 싸구려 물건들을 소리치며 팔고 있다

She's running a works(work이 아님)
   ↳ 그 여자는 공장을 운영하고 있어

› **gobble** eat greedily
› **fraud** trickery

Sound business allows us only a narrow margin of profit
ㄴ 건전한 장사는 이익이 적어

That ex-army-officer runs his business with a rod of iron
ㄴ 그 육군장교출신의 관리자는 사업을 군대식으로 운영한다

That man's typical sales tactic is to play on people's greed in order to make them buy more than they need
ㄴ 저 사람의 전형적인 판매전략은 사람들의 욕심을 이용하여 필요이상의 물건을 사게 하는 것이다

That store is fresh out of bananas
ㄴ 저 가게는 바나나를 막 다 팔아버렸어

That'll blow a hole in our projects for this month
ㄴ 그렇게되면 이 달 장사는 망치는 거야

The best fish smells when they are three days old
ㄴ 귀한 손님도 사흘만 넘기면 귀찮아진다

The bullish market will boost our sales volume by 6%
ㄴ 시황이 강 추세인 만큼 매상고는 6%나 증가할 것이다

The business is on its last legs
ㄴ 그 사업체는 파산직전에 와있어

The business showings didn't come up to my standards
ㄴ 영업 실적이 맘에 차지 않았어

The customers reactions are positive
ㄴ 소비자들의 반응은 좋아

The locality brings a great deal of business
ㄴ 장소(목)가 좋아야 장사가 잘 된다

The market for their products is going down
ㄴ 그들의 상품 구매력이 약화되고 있다

· **typical** having the essential characteristics of a group ｜ · **boost** raise, promote

The new contract should keep our business on its feet for another year
　ㄴ 이번 신규수주 덕분에 1년은 더 버틸 것 같다

The other shoppers had already snapped up all that product
　ㄴ 다른 손님들이 그 상품을 재빨리 다 사 가버렸어

The quality should stay up without increasing the price
　ㄴ 높은 품질은 가격인상 없이 유지되어야 한다

The sale will pull a lot of customers in
　ㄴ 세일을 하면 많은 손님을 끌어올 것이다

The store hasn't any; you'll have to do without
　ㄴ 가게에는 팔지 않으니 그냥 지낼 수밖에

The store rolled all its prices back for the sale
　ㄴ 그 점포에서는 세일을 하려고 모든 가격을 다 내렸어

The time will soon come for me to bow out and let a younger person to take my place
　ㄴ 자리를 물려주고 젊은 사람이 나를 대신할 때가 멀지 않았다

The worth of a thing is best known by the want of it
　ㄴ 물건의 가치는 그것이 없어졌을 때 가장 잘 알 수 있다

Their bottom-line output target is to produce three motors a week
　ㄴ 그들의 최소한 목표는 주당 3대의 모터를 생산하는 것이다

Then people will beat a path to your door
　ㄴ 그땐 너의 고객이 문전성시를 이루겠지

There's a good market for consumer goods
　ㄴ 소비재 수요가 많아

There's always a line of visitors before his door
　ㄴ 그의 집은 문전성시다

› **snap** bite at something, utter angry words, break suddenly with a sharp sound

› **output** amount produced

These items are going very fast(selling like hot cakes)
ㄴ 이들 물건은 불티나게 팔리고 있어

They are going the distance on this project
ㄴ 그들은 이 사업을 끝까지 해내고 있어

They are half on business and half on pleasure
ㄴ 그들은 업무 겸 관광차 온 거야

They can hardly keep the wolf from the door
ㄴ 그 사람들 사업(살림)은 버티기 힘들 정도야

They do very well at this hotel
ㄴ 이 여관은 서비스가 좋아

They have already conducted the test market to get reliable data
ㄴ 그들은 믿을 수 있는 자료를 얻으려고 이미 시험판매를 해 보았다

They increased the efficiency by 20% by streamlining the production line
ㄴ 그들은 생산과정을 재정비해서 능률을 20% 올렸다

They swing into high gear around nine o'clock in preparation for their customers
ㄴ 그들은 아홉 시가 되면 손님맞이 준비로 일손이 바빠진다

They've been getting nowhere fast in that project
ㄴ 그들은 그 사업에 전혀 진척이 없어

They've got a new model in the pipeline
ㄴ 그들은 새 모델제품을 개발중이다

This project is going in the right direction
ㄴ 이 사업은 제대로 되고 있어

This trade is above business fluctuation
ㄴ 이 장사는 경기를 잘 안 탄다

› **efficient** working well with little waste
› **streamline** made with contours to reduce ┆ air or water resistance, simplified, modernized

Try to charge it off as a business expenses
ㄴ 그건 사업 경비로 처리하자

Uncompetitive small businesses must eventually belly up
ㄴ 경쟁력이 약한 작은 업체는 결국 모두 도산할 수밖에 없어

We can get some money back if we return the empties to the shop
ㄴ 우리는 빈 병 등을 가게에 가져가면 약간의 돈을 환불받는다

We got the official go-ahead yesterday
ㄴ 어제 공식 허가가 났지

We must gear production to the new demand
ㄴ 새로운 수요에 맞게 생산을 조정해야해

We should like to have your custom
ㄴ 많이 애호(용)해 주시기 바랍니다

We've already gone over the top
ㄴ 우린 이미 초과달성

What line(of business) are you in?
ㄴ 무슨 사업하십니까?

When business is good, people are buying up even the cats and dogs
ㄴ 경기가 좋아지면 평소에 안 나가던 상품도 잘 나가

When Koreans start a business, they have a unique ceremony for good luck on the first day of the business
ㄴ 한국인들은 사업을 시작할 때 행운이 따르기를 기원하면서 사업 첫날 독특한 의식을 치른다

When the business lets up, we'll be able to see the light of day
ㄴ 사업이 좀 수그러들면 한가해질 수 있을 것이다

Wine and dine our potential customers before you enter negotiations
ㄴ 협상에 들어가기 전에 잠재 고객들에게 후하게 대접해라

› **belly up** bankrupt, go out of business | › **unique** being the only one of its kind, very unusual

Within the warranty periods, all repairs are free
ㄴ 보증기간 내의 수리는 무료

Without some dissimulation, no business can be carried on at all
ㄴ 약간의 가면 없이는 장사 자체가 전혀 이루어지지 않는다

You can make a go of your business
ㄴ 넌 사업에 성공할 것이다

You can't succeed in business without taking certain risks
ㄴ 사업에서 어느 정도 위험을 감수하지 않고서는 성공할 수 없다

You have to break the bottleneck of the project
ㄴ 사업의 애로를 타개해 나가야 해

You have to learn how to dress windows when you work there
ㄴ 넌 거기서 일할 때 상품 진열 법을 배워야 해

You wrote(rubber) a bad check
ㄴ 지난번 어음이 부도났습니다

(＝You bounced your last check)

Your business has a long connection
ㄴ 단골이 많군요

Your business licence comes up for renewal every three years
ㄴ 너의 사업 허가증은 매 3년마다 갱신해야 해

Your business will get off the ground soon
ㄴ 네 사업은 곧 잘 풀려 갈 것이다

· **dissimulate** hide under a false appearance · **bottleneck** place or cause of congestion
· **risk** exposure to loss or injury

56. 빛   Debt

A promise made is a debt unpaid
> ↳ 약속을 하는 일은 갚지 않은 빛을 짊어지는 일이다

A small loan makes a debtor, a great one, an enemy
> ↳ 작은 빛은 빛쟁이를 만들고 큰 빛은 원수를 만든다

At the end of the last year he was in the clear(hole)
> ↳ 작년 말 그는 탈 빛 했어(빛을 지고 있었어)

Can I see a statement showing all accrued interest?
> ↳ 전체 발생한 이자에 대해서 알려 주시겠습니까?

Chan-soo had to write off the debt as hopeless
> ↳ 찬수는 빌려 준 돈이 회수 희망이 없다고 보고 결손처분 해야 했다

Cut me some slack, I can't pay it all right back
> ↳ 웬만큼 독촉 해줘, 전액을 곧바로 갚을 수는 없어

Debtors are liars
> ↳ 돈이 거짓말한다

Don't saddle yourself with such a big debt before you are sure of your professional success
> ↳ 사업상 성공이 보장되기 전에는 그 큰 빛을 떠맡지 마라

Ever rising interest rates are nibbling away at our profits
> ↳ 오르기만 하는 이자율이 우리의 이익금을 잠식해 들어가고 있다

Four more paychecks and I'll be out of the hole

› **loan**   money borrowed at interest, something lent temporarily, permission to use

› **accrue**   be added by periodic growth
› **nibble**   bite gently or bit by bit

↳ 네 달치 월급만 받으면 빚은 면하게 될 거야

Getting deeply in debt to a loan-shark finally led him to his suicide
↳ 그의 고리대금업자에게 지게된 큰 빚이 자살을 불러왔다

Getting out of debt must be placed before(above) buying anything new
↳ 빚을 갚는 것이 새로운 것을 사는 것 보다 우선돼야 한다

He that goes a borrowing goes a sorrowing
↳ 빚은 고생의 장본

"Borrowing is sorrowing"이라는 음율이 맞는 속담이 있다. 내용은 직역하여 빚을 지면 슬픈 신세가 된다는 말이다.

He was very easy with me on the debt
↳ 그는 내게 빚 독촉을 안 했어

How can you be out from under that loan?
↳ 넌 어떻게 그 빚을 갚아 낼 거냐?

How much interest will your loan bear?
↳ 당신 돈의 이자는 얼마입니까?

Hyun-soo's got in hock by overusing his credit card
↳ 현수는 신용카드를 많이 써서 빚더미에 올라 있어

I'll pay the day after tomorrow, not before
↳ 모레 갚을게 그 이전엔 안 돼

In-ho promised to make good on his debts
↳ 인호는 빚을 갚겠다고 약속했어

Interest gnaws at a man's substance with invisible teeth
↳ 이자는 빚진 사람의 재산을 보이지 않는 이빨로 갉아먹는다

Pay me a fraction of the usual monthly payment so that I don't have to worry about your defaulting on the loan

---

› **suicide** act of killing oneself purposely, one who commits suicide

› **hock** pawn
› **overuse** excessively use

↳ 내가 너의 채무 불이행에 대해 걱정할 필요가 없도록 평소 월 불입금
의 일부라도 상환해 줘

Please stay a little longer in your debt
↳ 빚 상환을 조금만 늦춰주세요

Raising the ceiling on the national debt will not address the cause of unemployment
↳ 국채를 늘이는 것은 실업의 원인을 해결하는 것이 아니다

Rising prices press most heavily on the poor and on people with fixed income
↳ 물가 오름은 가난한 사람과 고정 수입자들에게 큰 부담이 된다

She was unusually easy with me on that debt
↳ 그녀는 보통 때와 달리 그 빚을 전혀 독촉하지 않았다

She's almost out of the red
↳ 그녀는 빚을 거의 다 갚아가고 있다

> (=She's nearly in the red)
> (=She's almost on easy street)

She's trying to keep up appearances, but she lives off borrowed money
↳ 그녀는 체면치레를 위해 애쓰고 있지만 빚을 얻어서 산다

Short debts make long friends
↳ 빚을 빨리 갚아야 우정이 길어져

> 가까운 사이일수록 금전 관계를 조심해야 한다는 뜻이다. 친구끼리의 빚 독촉도
> 곤란하고, 돈을 갚지 못하는 입장도 곤란하다. 비슷한 뜻으로 "Lend your
> money and lose your friend" "돈을 빌려주면 친구를 잃는다"도 쓰인다.

› **ceiling** overhead surface of a room, upper
　　　　　limit

Stop spending so fast or you'll land yourself in debt
ㄴ 그렇게 마구 돈을 써 대다가는 빚쟁이가 되고 말겠군

That incubus of debt will greatly hinder his ability to perform his duty
ㄴ 그 빚이라는 부담이 그의 직무수행에 큰 장애물이 되고 있다

That loan-shark has lived off the blood of others by charging usurious interest
ㄴ 고리대금업자는 높은 이자를 받아서 남의 피를 빨아먹고 살아왔다

That money-lender has been bleeding me white with his high rate of interest
ㄴ 저 고리업자가 고리를 붙여서 나를 망하게 하고 있어

The central bank sees lower interest rates as a sure-fire solution to the banks' bad debt problems
ㄴ 중앙은행은 일반은행들의 악성 채권문제 해결법으로 이자율을 낮추는 것을 확실한 방법으로 보고 있다

The government and the ruling party argue that the increasing debt has stemmed from their efforts to clean up the problems created under the rule of past administration
ㄴ 정부와 여당은 늘어나는 빚을 전 정권이 저지른 문제점들을 정리해 나가는 노력에서 생겨난 것이라고 주장한다

The interest rate is going out of sight(skyrocketing)these days
ㄴ 요즘 이자율이 천정부지로 오르고 있어

The ruling and opposition camps are urged to cooperate in seeking effective ways to reduce the state debt
ㄴ 여·야는 나라의 빚을 줄이기 위한 효과적인 방법을 찾는데 협조해야 한다

Their plan to pay off their debts by borrowing more would be a non-starter
ㄴ 돈을 더 빌려서 있는 빚을 갚겠다는 그들의 계획은 보나마나 실패다

There'll be a long struggle for us to pay off all our debts, but we'll

---

· **incubi** evil spirit, nightmare, one that oppresses like a nightmare

· **hinder** obstruct or hold back

· **skyrocket** shooting firework, rise suddenly

soon get there
>↳ 우리의 빚을 다 갚자면 오랫동안 힘들겠지만 머지 않아 이루어질 것이다

They will dun you for your debt day and night
>↳ 빚쟁이들이 널 가만 두지 않을 거다

This money should clear your debt
>↳ 이 돈을 갚으면 너에 대한 빚은 없어지는 거야

With government debts rising so fast, it's preposterous to use the excess taxes for purposes other than reducing it
>↳ 정부의 부채가 이토록 빨리 늘어나고 있는데 여분의 조세로 이를 줄이는데 쓰지 않고 다른 목적으로 쓰는 것은 모순이다

You'd better cough up what you owe me
>↳ 나한테 꿔간 돈 갚아야 할걸

▸ **pay off** pay in full, bribe, inflict retribution on, yield returns

▸ **dun** hound for payment of a debt

▸ **preposterous** absurd

57. 사건   Incidents

A bullet flew past his head and shattered the vase on the mantlepiece
    ↳ 실탄은 그의 머리위로 날아와서 벽난로 장식 위의 꽃병을 박살냈다

A mixture of paint and gasoline oozed out of the bottom of the tub
    ↳ 휘발유를 섞은 페인트가 큰 통의 밑바닥에서 흘러나왔다

A number of mobs forced their way in, pushing security guards aside
    ↳ 다수의 폭도들이 경비원들을 밀어젖히고 힘으로 밀고 들어왔다

A settlement was reached at the eleventh hour
    ↳ 사태는 마지막 순간에 타결됐어

A tire rolled across the road and went crashing into the pilothouse
    ↳ 타이어 하나가 도로를 굴러 넘어와서 조타실에 쾅 하고 부딪쳐왔다

Affairs are smoothing down
    ↳ 사태는 수습돼가고 있다

After that incident lots of people pulled the rug from under him
    ↳ 그 사건 이후 그는 많은 사람들의 지지를 잃었다

All hell broke loose
    ↳ 온통 뒤죽박죽 이었어

All I can do is(to) pick up the pieces
    ↳ 이젠 사태를 수습하는 수밖에 없어

And I just have got to let it go
    ↳ 그냥 되는 대로 내버려 놔둘 수밖에 없어

› **shatter** smash or burst into fragments   › **mob** large disorderly crowd, criminal gang
› **mantelpiece** shelf above a fireplace

All of us joined in to swell the chorus of admiration
↳ 우리들 모두가 소리 높여 찬양하였다

As the safe was indestructible, the money and jewels were intact
↳ 금고가 튼튼했기 때문에 돈과 귀금속은 무사했다

Blinded by soap, I had to fumble about for the door
↳ 나는 얼굴에 비누칠을 해서 앞이 안 보이는 가운데 출입문을 더듬어 찾았다

Boards and bricks scattered in every(any) which way
↳ 판자며 벽돌이 사방으로 흩어졌어

Bong-soo carried on for an hour after he fell from his desk
↳ 봉수는 책상에서 떨어진지 한 시간이나 아프다고 엄살(호들갑)을 떨었어

Bong-soo dealt a(the) door a tremendous blow but it remained intact
↳ 봉수는 대문을 크게 쳤지만 문은 그대로였다

Bong-soo stopped dead in his tracks when he heard the scream
↳ 봉수는 비명소리에 놀라 딱 멈춰 섰다

Bringing this chaos under control is at the top of the agenda
↳ 이 혼란을 진정시키는 것이 급선무다

By a stroke of the devil's own luck, the bullet sped straight to its mark
↳ 요행히도 실탄이 휙 날아가 목표물을 정통으로 맞혔다

By Friday, poor Sung-mee didn't know if(whether) she was coming or going
↳ 금요일이 되자 딱하게 된 성미는 어쩔 줄 몰랐다

Byung-soo bobbed up just when they were sure that he had left
↳ 병수가 틀림없이 가버렸다고 생각할 때 느닷없이 나타난 거야

Chang-soo has been carrying on all morning
↳ 창수는 아침나절 내내 울고불고 야단이다

Do we not all spend the greater part of our lives under the shadow

---

› **chorus** group of singers or dancers, part of a song repeated at intervals, | composition for a chorus

› **intact** undamaged

of an event that has not yet come to pass?
> ↳ 우리 모두는 아직 다가오지 않은 사건의 그늘 아래서 인생의 태반 이상을 소비하고 있지 않을까?

Do you have any theory about the case?
> ↳ 그 일에 뭐 집히는 일이라도 있나?

Doctors took to the streets yesterday demanding a redress of the nation's medical system
> ↳ 의사들은 어제 의료서비스제도의 개정을 요구하면서 거리로 뛰쳐나갔다

Donations began to nose-dive after several allegations of fraud were made against the charity accountant
> ↳ 자선단체의 회계 담당자에 대한 몇 건의 배임행위 주장이 제기된 후 기부 실적이 뚝 떨어지기 시작했다

Dong-soo dashed back to the burning house without a second thought
> ↳ 동수는 즉각 불타고있는 집으로 다시 뛰어들었다

Doo-chul couldn't rest under such an accusation
> ↳ 두철인 그런 비난을 받고 가만히 있을 수 없었다

Doo-chul was under house arrest
> ↳ 두철인 가택연금을 당했었다

Forgetfulness transforms every occurrence into a non-occurrence
> ↳ 망각은 일어났던 모든 사건들을 없었던 일로 변형시켜준다

Get down and stay down until I tell you the danger is over
> ↳ 위험상황이 끝났다고 내가 말 할 때까지 몸을 굽히고 일어나지 말고 있어라

He beat about in the water, trying not to drown
> ↳ 그는 물에 빠지지 않으려고 물 속에서 허우적거렸다

He has gone to a wake
> ↳ 그는 초상집에 갔다

› **nose-dive** decrease sharply

› **allege** state as a fact without proof

› **sorely** causing pain or distress, severe or intense, angry

(=He has gone to pay his respects)

He is sorely perplexed to account for the situation
　　ㄴ 그는 사태를 설명하는데 몹시 쩔쩔매고 있었다

He lost himself in the crowd and escaped me
　　ㄴ 그는 군중 속에 가리워져 보이지 않았다

He passed out(fainted) but he rolled(came)(a)round when we threw drops of water on his face
　　ㄴ 그는 정신을 잃었지만 우리가 그의 얼굴에 물을 뿌리자 정신을 차렸다

He was involved in the private tutoring scandal engulfing the country
　　ㄴ 그는 온 나라를 떠들썩하게 한 과외 사건에 연루되었어

His accounts of what happened approached the truth, but there were a few errors
　　ㄴ 발생한 사건에 대한 그의 설명은 사실에 가까웠으나 다소 잘못이 있었다

Hurling their arms and legs about wildly, they kept afloat but wasted much effort
　　ㄴ 그들은 물 속에서 손발을 마구 허우적거리면서 가라앉지는 않았지만 힘이 많이 소진됐다

Hyun-soo's in the hot seat on this matter
　　ㄴ 현수는 이 일로 좌불안석이다

I am glad to be well out of this matter
　　ㄴ 이번 일에서 빠진 건 다행이지 뭐

I couldn't find it in my heart to do so
　　ㄴ 차마 그러지 못했지

I couldn't have acted otherwise

・**faint** cowardly or spiritless, weak and dizzy, lacking vigor, indistinct

・**engulf** swallow up

ㄴ 그럴 수밖에 없었어

I lost you in a crowd
ㄴ 난 군중 속에서 널 잃어버린 거야

I missed the train before I knew where I was
ㄴ 아차 하는 순간에 기차를 놓쳤어

I missed the train by the second
ㄴ 간발의 차이로 열차를 놓쳤어

If he remains for more than a minute, pull him out, he may be drowning
ㄴ 그가 1분 이상 물위로 올라오지 않으면 익사할 수도 있으니까 끌어 내어라(**How long can you remain under water?** 물 속에서 숨을 멈추고 얼마나 있겠니?)

If the flames reach the gas tank the whole place will go up
ㄴ 불길이 개스 탱크에 미치면 그 곳 전체가 폭발 할 것이다

In a last-minute about-face, a leading doctor's group canceled plans to protest the medical reform program
ㄴ 의료계 주요그룹이 의료법 개정안에 항의하여 전국적인 무기한 휴진에 들어가기로 한 방침을 막판 태도변화로 철회했다

In-ho needs some time to pick up the pieces of his life after the accident
ㄴ 인호는 사고 후 뒷수습을 하는데 얼마간의 시간이 필요해

In-ho was lost in the crowd
ㄴ 인호는 군중 속에서 안보였어

It benefited more than double the number of people than it would have in the past
ㄴ 그것은 과거에 입을 수 있었던 수혜자에 비해 곱절 이상의 혜택을 주었다

It was done accidently-on-purpose
ㄴ 그건 우연을 가장한 고의성에서 일어난 일이다

· **glad** experiencing or causing pleasure, joy, or delight, very willing

· **otherwise** in a different way, in different circumstances, in other respects

It was early days yet and I still had a few cards up my sleeve
> 결론을 내리기에는 아직 이른 시기였지만 나는 몇 가지 비책을 준비해 두고 있었다

It was great to beat all the odds
> 예상을 뒤엎고 이겨내어 굉장했어

It was nothing short of fantastic
> 그건 완전히 환상적이었어

It will stand them on their heads
> 그 일은 그들을 혼란에 빠뜨릴 것이다

It's an open and shut case
> 그건 결과가 뻔한 사건

It's not long before he lost himself in the crowd
> 이윽고 그는 군중 속으로 사라졌다

Jin-soo squeaked by me in the hall way only to find himself blocked by another
> 진수는 복도에서 겨우 나를 비켜 나아갔지만 또 다른 사람에게 길을 막혔다

Keep on his tail and don't let him out of your sight
> 그를 계속 미행하고 시야에서 놓치지 마라

Keep on your toes and report anything that you see
> 경계를 늦추지 말고 이상한 것을 보면 연락해 줘

Let us offer for a moment silent prayer for the victims
> 희생자들에게 잠시 묵도를 올립시다

Let's let it ride for now
> 일단 사태를 관망해 보자

Let's reconstruct a full picture of what happened, based on the evidence before us

---

> **odd** being only one of a pair or set, not divisible by 2 without a remainder, queer

> **squeak** make a thing high-pitched sound

ㄴ 이러한 상황에서 사건의 전모를 추리해 보자

Let's send up a trial balloon and see what we'll find out
ㄴ 어떻게 될지 알아보게 여론을 한번 떠보자

Let's wait until things cool off
ㄴ 사태가 가라앉을 때까지 기다려보자

Many new discoveries have been brought to light
ㄴ 많은 새 사실이 밝혀졌어

Moon-ho's prestige and honor are on the line
ㄴ 문수의 위신과 명예가 위기에 놓여있다

Moon-soo missed his footing as spread-eagled in the mud
ㄴ 문수가 발이 삐끗 하더니 진흙바닥에 큰 대자로 쓰러졌다

My sixth sense told me that he went to hospital incognito, where she confidentially underwent the plastic surgery
ㄴ 내 육감으로 그 여자는 신분을 숨긴 채 병원으로 가서 성형수술을 받았다는 걸 알았다

Nam-soo was numbered with the transgressors
ㄴ 남수가 위반자 속에 들어 있었어

No less serious is the damage caused by mountain fires on the east coast
ㄴ 동해안 산불로 인한 피해가 이에 못지 않게 심각한 문제이다

Nobody came and laid any claim to the watch I found
ㄴ 아무도 내게 와서 주운 시계의 임자라고 나서지 않았어

Nothing short of a miracle could have saved him
ㄴ 기적이 아니고서는 살아날 수 없었을 것이다

Nothing, unless a miracle, could save him
ㄴ 기적이 아니고서는 그를 구할 수 없을 거다

Now they are in the clear

- **balloon** swell out
- **spread-eagle** lie flat
- **incognito** with one's identity concealed
- **transgressor** sinner

ㄴ 이제 그들은 위험을 벗어났다

Now we should do something about it
ㄴ 정말 뭔가 조치를 취해야 할 때다

People came from far and wide
ㄴ 여기 저기서 사람들이 모였지

Popular feelings run high
ㄴ 여론이 들끓고 있어

Quite a little crowd collected
ㄴ 상당히 많은 사람들이 모여 있었다

Sang-soo looked suspicious at first, but something about the whole case didn't ring true
ㄴ 처음에는 상수가 의심스러워 보였으나 그 일의 전말은 정말 같이 들리지 않았다

Sang-soo made(cut) a big splash
ㄴ 상수는 세상의 이목을 한 몸에 받았다

Sang-soo snatched his hand away from the hot pan with a cry of pain
ㄴ 상수는 뜨거움에 비명을 지르면서 냄비에서 손을 확 뗴었다

Several miners hung by a thread while the rescuers worked toward them
ㄴ 몇 명의 광원들은 구조대가 굴진 해 들어갈 동안 생명이 경각에 달려 있었다

She stepped on the floorboards that had rotted away and her foot went right through the floor
ㄴ 그녀가 썩어 문드러진 마루청을 밟자 발이 곧바로 마루바닥까지 빠져 들어갔다

Somebody keeps in the back ground
ㄴ 흑막 인물이 있어

Someone must be at the bottom of this affair

› **a little** many

› **splash** scatter a liquid on

› **snatch** try to grab something suddenly, seize or take away suddenly

↳ 누군가 이 사건 뒤에서 충동질하고 있음이 틀림없어

Sometimes circumstances alter cases
↳ 때로는 상황논리가 적용돼

Sure enough it did happen
↳ 아니나 다를까, 그 일이 터지고 말았다

Take care of the matter before it attracts public attention
↳ 일이 표면화되기 전에 처리해라

That event has really put a lot of years on me
↳ 그 사건 때문에 정말 십 년은 감수했어

That was my darkest hour, but the rescuers turned up and everything was suddenly brighter
↳ 그 때가 내겐 가장 절망적인 순간이었지만 구조대가 나타났고 급속히 모든 일이 풀려갔다

The crowd surged forward and the fence gave way under the strain
↳ 군중이 앞쪽으로 쏠리자 울타리가 누르는 힘에 못 이겨 무너졌다

The crowd trickled away(out) until only a few were left
↳ 군중들이 점점 줄어 겨우 몇 명밖에 안 남게 되었다

The demonstrators flew on by
↳ 시위대들은 계속 쏜살같이 지나갔다

The explosion sent them scattering, screaming hysterically
↳ 폭발이 일어나자 그들은 사방으로 흩어지면서 발작하듯 비명을 질렀다

The foolhardy youngster got to close to the edge of the cliff and had to be rescued
↳ 그 무모한 젊은이는 절벽 끝에 너무 가까이 다가갔다가 남들의 구조를 받아야 했다

The gold bullion has traveled from hand to hand until it got back to

---

› **rot** undergo decomposition

› **surge** rise and fall in or as if in waves

› **strain** excessive tension or exertion

› **trickle** run in drops or a thin stream

its owner
> ↳ 그 금괴는 여러 사람들의 손을 거치다가 주인의 손에 들어갔다

The ground is contaminated by chemicals which have leaked from the storage tank over the last 30 years
> ↳ 지난 30년에 걸쳐 저장탱크에서 새어나온 화학물질로 토양이 오염되었다

The incessant unpleasant incidents began to tarnish his respectable image
> ↳ 그에게 끊이지 않는 불유쾌한 사건들이 그의 훌륭한 인상을 더럽혀오기 시작했다

The incident stuck in my memory
> ↳ 그 사건은 내 기억에 뚜렷이 남아 있었어

The interests of anti-abortionists and pro-choicers are in a collision course
> ↳ 낙태 반대론자와 낙태 지지론자들의 관심은 서로 충돌하고 있다

The juice(electricity) made it's way into our village at that time
> ↳ 그 때 우리 마을에 전기가 들어왔어

The level of human indifference reached by the urban dwellers has become frightening
> ↳ 도시주민들이 보여주는 무관심은 놀라울 정도에 이르렀다

The measure will be now put into effect at the earliest possible
> ↳ 그 대책은 조속한 시일 내에 시행될 것이다

The minority is sometimes right; the majority always wrong
> ↳ 소수가 때로는 옳지만 다수는 항상 잘못이다

The more fit individuals in every generation will leave a few more offspring than the unfit so
> ↳ 세대에 있어서 적응자는 부적응자 보다 몇 명의 자손을 더 남긴다

The terrain of the burning areas provided no access for the fire engines and their crew

---

· **tarnish** make or become dull or discolored

· **abortion** removal or induced expulsion of **a fetus**

↳ 화재가 난 지역은 소방차와 소방대원들의 진입이 쉽지 않았다

The whole village was laid flat by the earthquake

↳ 마을은 지진으로 전체가 붕괴됐다

Then the fur began to fly

↳ 그러자 소동이 일어나기 시작했어

There were a big scuffle and vandalism but nobody saw them coming

↳ 큰 난투극이 일어나고 난장판이 일어났지만 아무도 이를 미리 감지하지 못했다

They are going to have a devil of a time cleaning up this mess

↳ 그들이 이 난장판을 정리하자면 죽을 맛일 것이다

They are trying to smooth things over

↳ 그들은 사태를 원만히 수습하려고 하고 있어

They brought the sunken ship to the surface

↳ 그들은 침몰한 배를 인양했다

They crossed the border minutes after the explosion and made a clean getaway

↳ 그들은 폭발 직후 국경을 넘어서 용케 도망쳤다

They folded their arms and waited for hell to break loose

↳ 그들은 팔짱만 끼고 난장판이 되기를 기다리고 있었다

They played the water along the left side of the burning office building

↳ 그들은 불타고 있는 사무실 건물의 왼쪽 편에 물을 뿌렸다

They rampaged through the streets, hell-bent on destruction

↳ 그들은 마구 때려부수는데 혈안 되어 거리를 누비고 다녔다

They've been accused of whipping crowds up into frenzies of violent hatred

↳ 그들은 군중들을 격렬한 증오의 광란으로 몰아넣었다는 비난을 받고 있다

Things have come out against us

> ‣ **scuffle** struggle at close quarters, shuffle one's feet | ‣ **vandal** one who willfully defaces or destroys property

ㄴ 사태가 불리하게 됐어

Things have gotten out of hand(control)=Things have gone too far(to extremes)

ㄴ 사태가 걷잡을 수 없게 됐어

Things haven't got going yet

ㄴ 사태가 아직 진전되진 않았어(본 궤도에 오르지 않아)

This puts another complexion on the accident

ㄴ 이로서 사건의 양상은 또 바뀐다

58. 사고   Accidents

A cat ran into the road, causing the cyclist to swerve
> ↳ 고양이가 도로에 뛰어들어 자전거를 타고 가던 사람이 방향을 틀었다

A white cab came out of nowhere and rolled over him
> ↳ 별안간 하얀 택시가 나타나서 그를 치었어

Accidents will happen in the best regulated families
> ↳ 불행한 일은 누구에게나 일어난다

> 사람의 지위 고하에 따라 불행한 일이 선별적으로 일어나는 것은 아니다. 불행이 언제 닥칠지 모르니까 항상 유비무환의 자세를 가져야 한다(=We must be ready, because accidents will come at an hour when we do not expect them).

After a long investigation into the accident, faulty warning lights were found to be the cause
> ↳ 사고에 대해 장기간 조사한 끝에 잘못된 경고신호등이 사고 원인인 것으로 밝혀졌다

An oil tanker came careering along the road, banging into all other vehicles in its path
> ↳ 유조차가 거리를 질주해 오면서 마주치는 모든 차량을 마구 부딪쳤다

Go to the bath-room before we leave so that you won't have an accident in the car

---

· **swerve**   move abruptly aside from a course   · **career**   vocation, go at top speed
· **investigate**   study closely and systematically

ㄴ 차 타고 가다가 화장실 갈 일 없도록 출발 전에 화장실 다녀오너라

He barely missed being knocked down by the car
ㄴ 그는 하마터면 차에 치일 번했다

In-ho needs some time to pick up the pieces of his life after the accident
ㄴ 인호는 사고 후 뒷수습을 하는데 얼마간의 시간이 필요해

It was done accidently-on-purpose
ㄴ 그건 우연을 가장한 고의성에서 일어난 일이다

It's been one thing after another since she got married
ㄴ 그녀가 결혼한 후 사고 연발이다

It's found that most drivers are over the limit in a large proportion of the accidents
ㄴ 사고 중 많은 비율은 대부분의 운전자들이 허용 음주량을 초과해서 일어나는 것으로 밝혀졌다

Jung-soo narrowly escaped being killed in the accident
ㄴ 정수는 하마터면 사고로 죽을 번했어

Lines of vehicles backed up for several kilometers because of the accident
ㄴ 사고 때문에 차량 행렬이 몇 킬로미터씩 늘어섰다

Make it clear to them that the accident wasn't only your fault
ㄴ 그 사고가 네 잘못이 아니라는 것을 그들에게 밝혀라

Speed demons burning up the road often cause accidents
ㄴ 자동차 속도광은 사고 내는 일이 많아

Sung-ho could only give a disconnected account of the accident
ㄴ 성호는 사고에 대하여 단편적인 얘기밖에 할 수밖에 없었어

The accident brought home to him the evil of drinking while driving
ㄴ 그는 사고를 보고 음주 운전이 얼마나 나쁜가를 절감하게 되었어

The accident left him with several broken ribs and dislocated right arm

› **demon** evil spirit

        ↳ 그 사고로 그는 갈비뼈가 몇 개 부러지고 오른팔이 탈구됐다

The committee was called into being to discover the causes of accident
        ↳ 사고원인 규명을 위한 위원회가 생겨났다

The dog had an accident on the rug
        ↳ 개가 카펫에 똥을 쌌어

The insurance claim can't be paid over until the accident has been reported to the police
        ↳ 사건이 경찰에 신고되어야 보험금이 지급된다

The news of the accident really tore me up
        ↳ 사고 소식에 정말 상심했다

The wound will scar over, but his leg will never be the same as it was before the accident
        ↳ 그의 상처는 흉터를 남긴 채 아물겠지만 다리는 이전의 상태로는 회복될 수 없을 겁니다

They denied their liability in the accidents, but that was only the standard insurance company response
        ↳ 그들은 그 사고에 대한 책임을 부인했지만 그것은 단지 배상청구에 대하여 표준적으로 취하는 보험회사의 반응일 뿐이다

This puts another complexion on the accident
        ↳ 이로서 사건의 양상은 또 바뀐다

Thoughts about the accident, little by little, passed into oblivion
        ↳ 사고에 대한 생각이 차츰 잊혀져갔어

Traffic tailed back for ten kilometers when the highway was blocked by the accident
        ↳ 고속도로가 사고로 막혔을 때 차량이 10킬로도 넘게 늘어섰다

We are living on borrowed time in that accident

› **dislocate** move out of the usual or proper place

› **committee** panel that examined or acts on something

ㄴ 우리가 그 사고에서 살아남은 건 정말 다행이다

We do more to decimate our population in automobile accidents than we do in war

ㄴ 전쟁에서보다 자동차 사고에서 더 많은 사람들이 죽는다

‣ **decimate** destroy a large part of
something

59. 사람   **People**

A good man is hard to find
      ↳ 세상에 착한 사람이 그리 흔한 게 아니다

A person's attention is attracted not so much by the intensity of different signals as by their context, significance, and information contents
      ↳ 사람의 주의력은 서로 다른 신호들의 강도보다는 신호들의 상황, 중요성, 그리고, 정보의 내용에 보다 더 끌린다

An ideal is a standard by which people judge real phenomena
      ↳ 이상이란 사람들이 그것에 의해서 판단하는 표준이다

An-do has a big house, but I wouldn't change places
      ↳ 안도가 큰집을 가졌다해서 그 사람 처지가 되고싶진 않아

An-do is accident-prone
      ↳ 안도는 사고뭉치다

> (=Disasters follow An-do everywhere)

All great discoveries are made by men whose feelings run ahead of their thinking
      ↳ 모든 위대한 발명은 느낌이 생각보다 앞서가는 사람들에 의해 이루어진다

Dong-soo goes through a lot of emotional ups and downs
      ↳ 동수는 감정의 기복이 심해

▸ **context**   words surrounding a word or phrase

▸ **phenomena**   observable fact or event, prodigy

Each human being is unique, unprecedented, and un-repeatable
> ㄴ 사람은 제각기 별나고, 그 사람과 같은 사람은 이전에도 없었고 이후
> 에도 없을 것이다

Every human being must be valued as such irrespective of his social positions
> ㄴ 모든 인간은 그의 사회적인 지위에 상관없이 인간 그 자체로 평가받
> 아야 한다

Every other man is a piece of myself, for I am a part and a member of mankind
> ㄴ 모든 다른 사람들은 나 자신의 한 조각이다, 왜냐하면 나는 전 인류
> 의 일원이기 때문이다

Every virtue(quality) has its attendant vice(defect)
> ㄴ 사람은 누구에게나 장점에 따르는 결점이 있게 마련

> (=Everyone has the defects of his own qualities(virtues))

Everyone has a skeleton in his closet
> ㄴ 털어 먼지 안 나는 사람 없다

> 누구에게나 한두 가지 결점은 있다는 뜻이다. "Everyone has a skeleton
> in his closet 모든 사람은 창고에 해골을 가지고 있다"는 것은 공포 영화에
> 서 가장 선해 보이는 사람이 결국에는 범인임이 드러나는 것을 빗댄 표현이다.
> (=Everyone has his faults(short comings))
> (=No one is without their faults)
> (=Everyone makes mistakes)

Gil-soo is a man with a lot to be grateful(thankful) for

- **unprecedented** unlike or superior to anything known before
- **mankind** human race
- **skeleton** bony framework

↳ 길수는 복이 많은 사람이다

Gil-soo is here but really he's gone
↳ 길수가 몸은 여기 메여 있지만 마음은 어디론가 나가버렸어

Gil-soo now only has the guts and bluffs
↳ 이제 길수는 배짱과 허풍 뿐이야

Great and good are seldom the same man
↳ 한 사람이 위대함과 착함을 동시에 갖추기는 어렵다

Has the world another man to show like him?
↳ 세상에 그런 사람 또 있을까?

He can be a little slow
↳ 그는 둔한 면이 있어

He can't see wood(the woods) for the trees
↳ 그는 작은 것만 보고 큰 것(숨은 것, 장래성)을 못 봐

He catches on quick
↳ 그 사람 눈치가 빨라

(=He's a good mind reader)

He consults his own convenience only
↳ 자기 형편 좋을 대로만 해

He doesn't care about keeping up with the times
↳ 그는 시속 따위에 얽매이는 사람이 아냐

He doesn't know beans about statistics
↳ 통계라곤 쥐뿔도 모르는 사람

He doesn't know his own mind

· **bluff** deceive by pretense
· **statistics** numerical facts collected for study

· **conscience** awareness of right and wrong

ㄴ그는 술에 술 타고 물에 물 탄 사람이야

He doesn't want to miss a thing
ㄴ그는 하나(한 순간)도 놓치기 싫어해

He has a black heart
ㄴ뱃속 검은 놈

He has no conscience
ㄴ어떤 나쁜 일이라도 하는 사람

He is a bit too slow
ㄴ그는 눈치가 없어

(=He is slow at taking hints)
(=He is blind(tactless, insensitive))

He is a handful
ㄴ그 사람 말썽꾼이야(**It's a handful** 그건 골치 아픈 일이야)

He is a nose of wax with other people
ㄴ남이 하자는 대로하는 사람

He is always on the take
ㄴ그는 뇌물을 밝히는 사람

He is always setting people to rights
ㄴ그는 늘 남들에게 타박을 준다

He is always the one who has the brain-waves
ㄴ그는 늘 묘안이 준비되어있는 사람이다

He is blind to all arguments
ㄴ고집불통

· **tactless** lacking sense of proper thing to
say or do

자신의 생각만을 옳다고 고집하는 독불장군형의 인간이 얼마나 상대하기 힘든 사람인가를 말해주는 속담이다. 듣는 것(hear) 대신에 보는 것(see)으로 대치하기도 한다(None are so blind as those who will not see).

He is himself again
> 그 사람 제정신 차렸어(정상으로 돌아왔어)

He is in a world of his own(by himself)
> 그는 자기 일 밖에 몰라

He is master of the situation
> 그는 형세에 능숙하게 대처(임기응변)하는 사람이다

He is not catching on
> 대책 없는 애

(=He hasn't a clue)
(=His light isn't turning on)

He is nothing but a big bag of wind
> 진짜 대단한 허풍쟁이

He is pig-headed
> 그는 벽창호야

He is quite a character
> 괴짜

He is the kind of person who means what he means
> 그는 한다면 한다는 사람이야

He looks possessed
> 신들린 사람 같아

> **clue**   piece of evidence that helps solve a problem

> **pig-headed**   stubborn

He is blind to all arguments
      ↳ 고집불통

> 자신의 생각만을 옳다고 고집하는 독불장군형의 인간이 얼마나 상대하기 힘든 사람인가를 말해주는 속담이다. 듣는 것(hear) 대신에 보는 것(see)으로 대치하기도 한다(None are so blind as those who will not see).

He is going to please himself and let the world go hang
      ↳ 그는 즐기기만 하고 무슨 일이 어떻게 돌아가든 개의치 않을 심산이야

He is quite content to take the cash and let the credit go
      ↳ 그는 나중 일을 생각지 않고 눈앞의 이익에만 만족하고 있어

He likes to dish it out, but he doesn't(can't) take it
      ↳ 그는 남을 꾸짖는 것만 좋아하지 남의 꾸짖음을 들어주지는 못해

He loves to be admired
      ↳ 그는 추어주기만 하면 좋아해

He put up a brave face(front)
      ↳ 그 사람 낯두껍더라

> 'Thick-skinned'는 '두꺼운 얼굴'을 나타내고, 'Brazen-faced' 는 '철판을 깐 얼굴'을 나타낸다.

He says one thing and, means another
      ↳ 그는 말과 뱃속이 달라

He seems to be a man with his feet planted firmly on the ground
      ↳ 그는 아주 분별력 있는 사람 같아

He sounded very sorry for himself

› **dish out** give freely

› **brazen** made of brass, bold

ㄴ 그 사람 참 처량한 것 같더군

He that fears you present will hate you absent
ㄴ 사람을 면전에서 두려워하는 사람은 그 사람이 없을 때 욕하는 사람이다

He that shows his purse, longs to be rid of it
ㄴ 지갑을 내다보이는 사람은 그 지갑을 털리고싶어하는 사람이다

He that thinks himself wisest, is generally the greatest fool
ㄴ 자신이 가장 슬기롭다고 생각하는 사람은 대개 가장 어리석은 사람이다

He uses his learning to the best advantage
ㄴ 되 글을 말글로 써먹는 사람

He who keeps instruction is in the way of life, but he who refuses reproof goes astray
ㄴ 훈계를 지키는 자는 생명 길로 행하지만 징계를 버리는 자는 그릇되게 가느니라

He who never says "no" is no true man
ㄴ 거절을 못하는 사람은 제대로 된 사람이 아니다

He who would be cured of his ignorance must confess it
ㄴ 무지에서 벗어나고 싶은 사람은 자신의 무지를 고백해야 한다

He who's being carried doesn't realize how far the town is
ㄴ 실려 가는 사람은 가는 곳이 얼마나 먼지 알지 못한다

He'll get you out of doing all that grunt work
ㄴ 그 사람이라면 그런 따분한 일에서 널 구해 줄 거야

He'll go the whole nine yards for me
ㄴ 그는 나를 위해서 무엇이든지 할 사람이다

He returned to what was his real existence
ㄴ 그는 본래의 모습으로 되돌아갔다

He's a man capable of doing anything

▸**confess** acknowledge or disclose one's misdeed, fault, or sin; declare

faith in
▸**grunt** deep guttural sound

↳ 그는 무슨 일이고 서슴지 않을 사람이다

He's a nice guy, but there's nobody home
↳ 그가 사람은 좋지만 머리 텅 비었어

He's boring with a capital 'B'
↳ 참 따분한 사람이지

He's got a memory like a sieve(sponge)
↳ 그는 건망증이 심해

He's just feeling his oats
↳ 그는 의기양양해

He's like the rest of us
↳ 그 사람도 사람이다

He's no worse than the others
↳ 그도 다른 사람과 다를 바 없어

He's not a bad man at heart
↳ 그는 본래 악인이 아냐

He's not a fool but he can tell that
↳ 그가 그 정도 모를 바보는 아니다

He's not above cheating
↳ 그는 속이고도 남을 사람이다

He's not exactly an excellent worker, but he would pass in a crowd
↳ 그가 반드시 크게 뛰어난 사람은 아니지만 보통정도는 될 거야

He's quick of eye(sight)
↳ 그는 눈치가 빨라

(=He has quick(sharp) eyes)

› **cheat** deprive through fraud or deceit, violate
rules dishonestly

He's quick to get angry and quick to get over it
↳ 성질은 급해도 뒤가 없는 사람이다

He's slow in speaking
↳ 그는 입이 무거워

(=He's slow of tongue(speech))

Hee-jung knows where to draw the line
↳ 희정인 자기 분수를 알아

Her integrity is beyond dispute
↳ 그녀가 청렴하다는 것은 의심의 여지가 없어

His good qualities overbalance his shortcomings
↳ 그의 장점은 단점을 보완하고도 남는다

I have nothing to call my own
↳ 난 빈털터리야

I just came into my own
↳ 당연한 권리를 받았을 뿐이야

I won't bite you
↳ 난 무서운(나쁜) 사람이 아냐

I wouldn't put it past him
↳ 그 사람이라면 그러고도 남을 사람이지

I'm afraid you're in the "I'm-OK-you-are-not syndrome"
↳ 넌 남 탓만 하는 사람 같군

I'm not given that way
↳ 난 그런 짓 할 사람이 아니야

· **overbalance**   exceed in weight, value, or importance; cause to lose balance

· **syndrome**   particular group of symptoms

I'm nothing, if not critical
　　↳ 입바른 것만이 나의 장점(입바른 것 빼면 시체)

I'm sure you more than deserve the recognition
　　↳ 넌 인정을 받고도 남을 사람

I'm wondering I'm blind
　　↳ 내가 왜이리 어리석은지 몰라(이해 못할 수도 있음)

If anyone keeps bugging Jim any longer, he may cancel their Christmas
　　↳ 이제 더 이상 짐을 괴롭히는 사람이 있다면 그런 사람을 죽일지도 몰라

If you give him an inch, he'll take a mile
　　↳ 사람을 건져놓으면 보따리 내놔라 한다

> 좋은 일을 해주고 고마움은 커녕 원망을 들을 때 쓰는 말이다. 직역하면 "1 인치만큼을 주면 1마일만큼을 달라고 한다"이고 더 자주 쓰는 표현으로 "To get more kicks than half pence 반 펜스(적은 돈의 단위)를 받고 그만큼보다 더 차인다"가 있다.

In nine cases out of ten nature pulls one way and human nature the other
　　↳ 본능과 인간성은 서로 반대로 작용하는 수가 많다

In-ho is a regular fellow
　　↳ 인호는 기분 좋은 사람(호남아)

In-soo decides things for mere gain
　　↳ 인수는 무엇이나 손익을 따져 결정하는 사람

In-soo learns things so fast(easily, instantly)
　　↳ 인수는 눈썰미가 있다

> (=In-soo can mimic things easily)

· **recognition**　act of recognizing or state of being recognized

· **instantly**　in a moment

It is comparison that makes men happy or miserable
ㄴ 사람은 남들과의 비교를 통해서 행복해지거나 비참해진다

It takes all her time to look after herself
ㄴ 그 여자는 자기 자신을 추스려 나가기에도 급급해

It takes three generations to make a gentleman
ㄴ 훌륭한 사람은 하루아침에 만들어지지 않는다

> 훌륭한 사람이 되려면 본인의 노력도 필요하지만, 주위의 보살핌과 격려도 못지않게 중요하다. 비슷한 말로 "Rome was not built in a day 로마는 하루아침에 만들어 진 것이 아니다"와 "Success doesn't come overnight 성공은 하룻밤 사이에 이루어지지 않는다"가 있다.

It's par for the course for her
ㄴ 그 여자가 그러는 건 흔히 있는 일이야

It's ploughers of lonely furrows who get there
ㄴ 그걸 해내는 사람은 혼자서 묵묵히 일하는 사람이다

It's tempting to criticize others and turn a blind eye to all the problems of your own
ㄴ 남들을 마구 헐뜯고 자신의 문제점을 덮어두고자 하는 유혹에 끌려들기 쉽다

It's the one who talks big who is really the coward
ㄴ 큰소리 치는 녀석 치고 겁쟁이 아닌 녀석이 없다

It's the power of speech which discriminates(differentiates) man from the animals
ㄴ 말을 할 수 있다는 점이 사람과 동물을 확실히 구별해준다

Jung-tae is a rotten apple to spoil it for the rest of us
ㄴ 정태는 미꾸라지 한 마리가 웅덩이 전체를 흐려놓을 사람이다

› **par** stated value, common level, accepted standard or normal condition   ┊   › **furrow** trench made by a plow, wrinkle or groove

하나가 전체에게 나쁜 영향을 미친다는 말이다. 영어 속담에는 여러 가지가 있는데, 가장 자주 쓰이는 표현은 "One rotten apple spoils the barrel 썩은 사과 하나가 한 통을 썩게 한다"이다. 악한 한 사람이 한 가문, 한 나라를 욕되게 하는 것은 "It is an ill bird that fouls its own nest 자기의 둥지를 더럽히는 새는 나쁜 새이다"로 표현한다.
(＝One scabbed sheep will mar a whole flock)
(＝A hog that's bemired endeavors to bemire others)

King Se-jong is as great a man as ever lived
ㄴ 세종대왕은 다시없는 위대한 인물이다

Luck is not something you can mention in the presence of self-made man
ㄴ 자력으로 일어난 사람 앞에서 행운을 들먹거릴 일이 아니다

Luckiest in gambling is who he knows just when to rise and go home
ㄴ 도박에서는 언제 자리를 떠서 집으로 가는 것이 좋은지를 아는 사람이 가장 운 좋은 사람이다

Lulu is not up-to-date on literary trends
ㄴ 루루가 문학에는 문외한이다

(＝Lulu doesn't follow the literary scene)

Man differs from brutes in that he thinks
ㄴ 사람은 생각한다는 점에서 동물과 다르다

Man has always preferred egocentric fantasy to reality
ㄴ 인간은 늘 현실보다 자기중심적 환상을 더 좋아해 왔다

Man has the perpetual contest for wealth which keeps world in tumult
ㄴ 인간은 세상을 계속 동요 속에 있게 하는 부를 얻기 위해 끊임없이 경쟁해왔다

· **literate** able to read and write

· **trend** prevailing tendency, direction, or style

· **egocentric** self-centered

Man is apt to overlook his own fault
  ↳ 사람은 자기 잘못을 못보고 넘기기 쉬워

Man is the only creature that consumes without production
  ↳ 사람은 생산하지 않으면서 소비하는 유일한 동물이다

Man masters nature not by force but by understanding
  ↳ 사람은 자연을 힘으로 정복하는 것이 아니라 이해함으로써 정복해야한다

Man pines to live but can't endure the days of his life
  ↳ 사람은 애타게 살고싶어 하면서도 나날의 삶을 견뎌내지 못한다

Man's real life is happy, chiefly because he's ever expecting that it soon will be so
  ↳ 인간의 실제 생활은 행복하다, 주된 원인은 그가 행복해 지리라고 기대하기 때문이다

Man, when perfected, is the best animals, but, when separated from law and justice, he's the worst of all
  ↳ 사람이 완벽해 진다면 동물 중 가장 훌륭한 동물이지만, 법과 도리를 벗어나게 되면 가장 나쁜 동물이다

Mankind apparently finds it easier to drive away adversity than to retain prosperity
  ↳ 인간은 분명히 번영을 유지하기보다 역경을 물리치기가 쉽다

Many a man's vices have at first been nothing worse than good qualities run wild
  ↳ 인간의 많은 악이 처음에는 좋은 점들이 난폭해졌다는 사실에 불과하다

Many people are lost without their personal computers
  ↳ 많은 사람들이 개인용 컴퓨터가 없어지면 어쩔 줄 몰라한다

Many people are turned off by the abundant attention being paid to it
  ↳ 많은 사람들은 너도나도 그 일에 관심을 갖는데 대해 식상해 하고 있다

› **pine** lose health through distress, yearn for intensely

› **apparent** visible, obvious, seeming

Many people consider body odor unpleasant and antisocial
↳ 많은 사람들은 체취를 불쾌하고 반사회적인 것으로 여긴다

Many people paled at the notion that they would always be poor
↳ 많은 사람들은 언제나 가난에 찌들려야 할 생각을 하니 맥이 빠졌어

Many people today vie with each other for extravagance
↳ 요즘 많은 사람들이 사치와 낭비의 경쟁을 벌이고 있어

Mean fellows will advertise themselves at the expenses of others
↳ 소인은 자기를 내세우고 남을 헐뜯는다

Mediocre minds generally condemn everything that passes their understanding
↳ 평범한 사람들은 일반적으로 자기가 이해하지 못하는 모든 것을 비난한다

Men are constantly on the lookout for seasonal food shortages and gluts
↳ 인간은 끊임없이 계절적인 식량부족과 과인에 대해 경계해 왔다

Men are more prone to revenge injuries than to requite kindness
↳ 사람은 친절에 대한 보답보다는 해를 입은 데 대한 앙갚음을 하기 쉽다

Men are not prisoners of fate, but only prisoners of their own minds
↳ 사람은 운명의 포로가 아니라 자기 마음의 포로이다

Men are not what they are born, but what they become
↳ 사람은 어떤 환경에서 태어났는가가 아니라 어떻게 되느냐가 중요하다

Men are often reached by flattery
↳ 사람은 흔히 아첨에 흔들리기 쉽다

Men cling to life even at the cost of enduring great misfortune
↳ 사람은 큰 고생을 참아가면서 삶에 애착한다

Men seldom give pleasure when they are not pleased themselves
↳ 사람은 자신이 기쁘지 않으면서 남에게 기쁨을 주지는 않는다

▸ **mediocre** not very good | ▸ **revenge** inflict harm or injury in return for a wrong, desire to return evil

Men understand the worth of blessings only when they have lost them
ↄ 사람은 가지고 있던 복을 잃어봐야 그 복의 가치를 안다

Most human beings have almost an infinite capacity for taking things for granted
ↄ 대부분의 인간은 만사를 당연시하는 거의 무한한 능력을 가지고 있다

Most people are voting with their feet
ↄ 대부분의 사람들이 싫은 곳에는 잘 안 간다

Mountains of gold wouldn't seduce some men, yet flattery would break them down
ↄ 산더미 같은 금으로도 유혹할 수 없지만 아첨에는 무너지는 사람들도 있다

Myung-soo is a man with a mind of his own
ↄ 명수는 줏대가 있는 사람이다

Nam-chul can read the signs of the times
ↄ 남철인 시류를 아는 사람이다

Nam-chul is naturally funny
ↄ 남철인 원래 재미있는 사람이다

Nam-soo's face maligns him
ↄ 남수는 얼굴과 딴판으로 착한 사람이다

No man is a dead-end kid from the day he was born
ↄ 처음부터 싹수가 틀린 사람은 아무도 없다

No man is an island, nor are a man and a woman
ↄ 인간은 아무도 고립해서 살 수 없고, 남자든 여자든 예외는 없다

No man is born wise or learned
ↄ 태어날 때부터 현명하거나 배우고 나온 사람은 없다

› **bless**   consecrate by religious rite, invoke divine care for, make happy

› **malign**   wicked, malignant, speak evil of

아무리 위대한 사람도 태어났을 때부터 위대하지는 않았다. "Alexander himself was once a crying babe 알렉산더 대왕도 한 때는 우는 아기였다"라는 말이 있다. 예전엔 왕족이 있어서 태어날 때부터 고귀한 사람이 있었기 때문에 "Not every man is born with a silver spoon in his mouth 모두 입에 은수저를 물고 태어난 것은 아니다"라는 말이 있었지만, 요즘은 모두 평등하기 때문에 태생으로 운명이 결정 나는 일은 드물다.

No man is good enough to govern other man without that others' consent
ㄴ 상대방의 동의 없이 그 사람을 지배할 만큼 훌륭한 사람은 없다

No man is good for anything who has not some particle of obstinacy to use upon occasion
ㄴ 가끔씩 약간의 고집도 없는 사람은 쓸모가 없다

No man is justified in doing evil on the ground of expediency
ㄴ 편의를 이유로 나쁜 짓을 하는 사람은 아무도 정당화되지 못한다

No man is so bad but he may have some redeeming points
ㄴ 아무리 나쁜 사람도 장점은 있다

아무리 악한 사람에게도 한두 가지 좋은 점이 있기 마련이다. 따라서 자신과 마음이 안 맞는 사람이거나 사회에서 평판이 안 좋은 사람이라도 좋은 점은 인정해 주어야 한다. "Give the devil his due 싫은 사람도 좋은 점은 인정해라"

No man is wise enough or good enough to be trusted with unlimited power
ㄴ 무제한의 권리를 부여받고도 현명하거나 훌륭할 수 있는 사람은 없다

No man was ever great by imitation
ㄴ 남의 흉내를 내서 위대해진 사람은 없다

Nobody will open a can of worms
ㄴ 괜히 시끄러운 문제를 일으킬 사람은 없어

‣ **particle** small bit
‣ **redeem** regain, free, or rescue by paying a price, atone for, free from sin, convert into something of value

그냥 놔두면 될 것을 건드려서 화를 자초할 때 쓰이는 속담이다. 영어에서는 "자는 개(호랑이)는 깨우지 마라", "구더기 깡통은 열지 마라" 등으로 쓴다.

None can hold fortune still and make it last
↳ 행운을 진득이 오래 붙들고 있을 수 있는 사람은 없다

Nothing is good for whom nothing is bad
↳ 아무 거나 있어도 나쁘지 않는 사람에게는 아무 것도 좋은 것이 없다

Nothing we do could ever stop this born malcontent's grumbling
↳ 이 불평분자에게는 어떻게 해 주더라도 그의 투덜거림을 막을 수 없을 것이다

One essence of being human is that one does not seek perfection
↳ 인간이기 위한 요소의 하나는 그가 완벽을 추구하는 것이 아니라는 점이다

One nice thing about the egoist: they don't talk about other people
↳ 이기주의자들에게 한가지 좋은 점: 그들은 남에 대한 이야기를 전혀 하지 않는다

Only one who has learned much can fully appreciate his ignorance
↳ 충분히 배운 사람만이 자신의 무지를 충분히 깨달을 수 있다

Our task now is to create a man within our self
↳ 우리의 당면 과제는 우리의 자아 내에서 새로운 인간을 창조하는 일

People wish to be liked, not to be endured with patient resignation
↳ 사람들은 남들이 좋아해 주기를 원하지만 체념으로 참아주기를 바라지는 않는다

Pyung-soo prefers honest poverty to dishonest richness
↳ 평수는 불의를 하여 부자가 되는 것보다 오히려 청빈을 택하는 사람이다

Pyung-soo wants to be a big fish in a small pond
↳ 평수는 용의 꼬리보다 뱀 머리가 되기를 원한다

· **grumble** mutter in discontent

· **egoist** someone who believes that self-interest is the motive for action

Sang-ho isn't given that way
↳ 상호는 그런 사람이 아냐

Sang-soo is a master at shooting himself in the foot
↳ 상수는 자기 발등 찍는데는 선수야

Sang-soo is smart enough to quit while he's ahead
↳ 상수는 잘 나갈 때 충분히 그만둘 줄 알만큼 현명한 사람이다

Sara is as nutty as a fruitcake
↳ 사라는 덜 떨어진 사람

Se-hyung blows hot and cold
↳ 세형인 편의주의자(변덕쟁이)

Se-ri is stuck-up because of that
↳ 그 때문에 세리는 콧대가 높아

Selfishness inheres in human nature
↳ 이기심은 인간성에 내재한다

She doesn't like having her name bandied about
↳ 그 여자는 여기저기 이름 퍼뜨리는걸 싫어해

She has a quick eye=She catches on quickly=She is very perceptive
↳ 그 여자는 눈치가 빨라

She is a wet blanket and puts a damp on everything
↳ 그 여자는 흥을 깨는 사람이라서 모든 일에 찬물을 끼얹는다

She is chastity personified
↳ 그녀는 정절의 귀감이다

She knows how to doctor the figures
↳ 그 여자가 숫자를 조작하는데는 선수다

She seems to have known it all along
↳ 그 여자는 그 일을 진작부터 알고 있었던 것 같다

· **inhere** be inherent

· **bandy** exchange in rapid succession

· **perceptive** showing perception

· **personify** represent as a human being

She seems to relish the limelight(spotlight)
> ㄴ 그 여자는 세인의 주목받기를 좋아하는 것 같다

She should see how the other half lives
> ㄴ 그 여자는 자신과 다른 처지에 있는 사람들이 있다는 걸 이해해야 해

She was a woman living in a nondescript brick-house in the boonies
> ㄴ 그녀는 오지에서 평범한 벽돌집에서 살던 여자였다

She'll take a flyer(hike, walk) if things get a little tough=She's the first rat to leave the ship
> ㄴ 그 여자는 별 볼일 없을(위험할) 때 맨 먼저 떠날 사람이다

She's a as good a girl as ever was
> ㄴ 그녀는 참으로 착한 소녀

She's a great woman, if ever there was one
> ㄴ 그 여자처럼 훌륭한 여자는 없어

She's a law unto herself
> ㄴ 그 여자는 제 맘대로야

She's a miser with a capital M
> ㄴ 그 여자는 수전노 중의 수전노다

She's a real National Statistical Office woman
> ㄴ 그 여자는 정말 통계청에 충실한 사람이다

Small minds are much distressed by little things
> ㄴ 마음이 좁은 사람은 작은 일에 매우 고통받는다

Some are born great; some achieve greatness; and some have greatness thrust upon him
> ㄴ 태어날 때 위대한 사람도 있고, 자신의 힘으로 위대해 지는 사람도
> 있으며, 타인의 힘으로 위대해 지는 사람도 있다

Some of the people who used to come to our church have fallen by

---

› **relish** keen enjoyment, highly seasoned sauce, enjoy	› **miser** person who hoards money
	› **thrust** shove forward, stab or pierce

the wayside(from grace)
↳ 종전에 우리 교회에 나오던 몇 사람이 타락해 버렸어

Some people are glued to their tubes
↳ 텔레비전 앞에서 떠나지 못하는 사람들도 있다

Some people are so fond of ill-luck that they run half-way to meet it
↳ 어떤 사람들은 너무 불운을 즐겨서 그 불운이 다가오는 도중에 맞이한다

Some people have all the luck
↳ 어떤 사람들은 이래도 잘 되고 저래도 잘 돼

Some people just don't know when to quit
↳ 적당한 때(정도)를 모르는 사람도 있어

Some people often use foreign words in preference to perfectly acceptable Korean language
↳ 완벽하게 알아들을 수 있는 우리말을 젖혀놓고 외래어를 즐겨 쓰는 사람들이 있다

Some people start out to train career in medicine, but drop(fall) by the wayside
↳ 어떤 사람들은 직업의사가 되려고 공부하다가 도중에 팽개치곤 해

Some talented people burn themselves out
↳ 너무 과한 활동을 해서 수명을 다하지 못하는 재능 있는 사람들도 있다

Such a remark will not take the starch out of him at all
↳ 그에게 그런 소리 했다해서 전혀 수그러들 사람이 아냐

Such people are history
↳ 요즘 그런 사람이 어디 있나

Tae-ho is a little(slightly) wanting
↳ 태호는 약간 모자란(둔한) 사람

Tai-ho is still as sharp as a tack

› **starch** nourishing carbohydrate from plants also used in adhesives and laundering

    ↳ 태호가 아직은 머리가 잘 돌아

Tai-ho wouldn't be going on this wild-goose chase
    ↳ 태호는 이런 뜬구름 잡는 일을 할 사람이 아니야

That lazybones hardly earns his keep around here
    ↳ 저 게으름뱅이는 여기서 거의 밥값도 못 하고 있어

That man is a name to conjecture with in many communities
    ↳ 저 사람은 여러 곳에서 내노라 하는 사람이다

That man is the one of the heavies around here
    ↳ 저 사람이 여기서는 힘깨나 쓰는 사람이야

That man lined his pocket(purse) by permitting contractors to use poor building materials
    ↳ 저 사람이 건설업자들에게 부실건축자재 사용을 허용해 준 사람이다

That snobbish always gets sententious about living a righteous life and then goes about his own sinful life when no one is watching
    ↳ 그 속물근성의 위선자는 늘 올바르게 사는 현명한 사람인체 하다가 아무도 보는 사람이 없으면 죄로 가득 찬 삶을 살고있다

That swindler is clever enough to twist the truth until it fits his needs
    ↳ 그 사기꾼이라면 능히 자신의 필요에 맞아 들어갈 때까지 사실을 왜곡할 수 있어

That toilet(potty) mouth is offending us again
    ↳ 저 쌍소리 잘하는 녀석이 또 우리에게 듣기 거북한 소릴 하고 있어

That wheeler-dealer is in with most of the judges in town
    ↳ 그 수단꾼은 시내에 있는 거의 모든 판사들과 친해

That's just the way he is
    ↳ 그는 못 말리는 사람이다

› **snobbish** acting superior to others
› **sententious** using pompous language

› **swindler** person who cheats of money or property

(=He's clueless(hopeless))
(=He can't be helped)

The better gamester, the worse man
ㄴ 놀음은 더 잘하는 사람일수록 더 나쁜 사람이다

The man has gone God knows where
ㄴ 그 사람은 인기척도 없이 사라졌어

The man is resting on a cane
ㄴ 남자가 지팡이를 짚고 서 있다

The man who can own up his error is greater than who merely knows how to avoid making it
ㄴ 자신의 실수를 털어놓을 수 있는 사람은 단지 실수를 피할 줄 아는 사람보다 훌륭하다

죄를 짓느냐 짓지 않느냐가 문제가 아니라 죄를 고백하고 반성하고 고치려고 노력을 하는 것이 중요한 것이다. 죄를 짓지 않는 인간은 없기 때문이다 (Confession can be described as a medicine that heals the mind = 고백은 마음의 상처를 치료하는 치료제와 같다).

The man who does evil to another does evil to himself
ㄴ 남에게 못된 짓을 하는 사람은 자기 자신에게 못된 짓을 하는 것이다

남을 욕하거나 저주하면 결국에는 자신에게 다시 돌아온다는 말이다. 남에게 상처를 주는 말은 하지 말아야 한다는 뜻과 일맥상통한다(Reckless words pierce like a sword = 무분별한 말은 칼과 같이 사람을 찌른다).

· **gamester** gambler

· **cane** slender plant stem, a tall woody grass or reed, stick for walking or beating

The more the merrier(better)
　　ㄴ 사람이 많을수록 좋지

(=Everyone is invited to come)
(=You're more than welcome to come)

The most fortunate people in the world may be those who are conscious of what they are doing
　　ㄴ 가장 운이 좋은 사람들은 아마 자신들이 무엇을 하고 있는지 의식하고 있는 사람들일 것이다

The most important evils that mankind have to consider are those which they inflict upon each other through stupidity or malevolence
　　ㄴ 인간이 고려해야 할 중요한 해악들은 인간의 어리석음이나 적의를 통해서 서로에게 가하는 해악이라고 생각할 수 있다

The profound thinker always suspects that he is superficial
　　ㄴ 심오한 사상가는 늘 자신이 수박 겉 핥기를 하고 있는 것 아닌가 하고 생각한다

The progress of rivers to the ocean is not so rapid as that of man to error
　　ㄴ 바다로 흘러가는 강물의 진행은 사람이 실수 쪽으로 나아가는 것만큼은 빠르지 않다

There are a quite a few that fit that description
　　ㄴ 그 설명과 일치하는 사람(것)들이 상당히 많다

There are numbers who believe it
　　ㄴ 그걸 믿는 사람들이 꽤 많아

There was nobody present who didn't know it
　　ㄴ 거기 있었던 사람들 중 그걸 모르는 사람은 없었어

There's a devil inside everyone
　　ㄴ 인간에게는 누구나 악마적 본성이

· **inflict** give by or as if by hitting
· **malevolent** malicious or spiteful
· **profound** marked by intellectual depth or insight, deeply felt

There's a sucker born every minute
> ↳ 어수룩한 사람이 하나 둘 인줄 아나

There's no such thing as the perfect man
> ↳ 완벽한 사람이란 존재하지 않는다

There's nothing to choose between bad tongues and wicked ears
> ↳ 남의 험담을 들어주는 사람은 그 험담을 하는 사람과 다를 바 없다

They just don't want to seem like grave-dancers
> ↳ 그들은 남들의 불행에 편승해서 잘 되보려고 하는 사람으로 비쳐지지
> 않길 바랄 뿐이다

They know enough who know how to learn
> ↳ 어떻게 배워야 할지 아는 사람은 충분한 학식이 있는 사람이다

They know me and my kind
> ↳ 그들은 내가 어떤 사람인지 잘 알아

Those who apply themselves too much to little things become incapable of great ones
> ↳ 작은 일에 전념하는 사람은 큰 일을 해 내기가 어렵다

Those who give consent are accomplices in whatever follows
> ↳ 동의하는 사람은 그 후에 일어난 어떤 문제에 대하여도 공범자이다

Those who live by bread alone will submit, for the sake of it, to the vilest abuse
> ↳ 빵만으로 사는 사람은 그 빵 때문에 가장 창피한 모욕에 굴복해야 한다

To do him justice, we must say he is a cheap skate
> ↳ 공정히 말해서 그는 구두쇠다

To know the great man dead is compensation for having to live with the mediocre
> ↳ 이미 죽은 사람의 위대함을 인정해 주는 것은 그가 평범한 사람들과
> 같이 살았던데 대한 보상이다

To look at him, you'd never think he's such a snob

› **sucker** easily deceived person

› **sake** purpose or reason, one's good or

benefit

› **vile** thoroughly bad or contemptible

↳ 그의 모습으로만 본다면 그런 속물로 생각되지 않을 것이다

To put it in an extreme way, he's the scum of mankind
↳ 극단적으로 말하면 그는 인간쓰레기다

To the mean all becomes mean
↳ 천박한 사람에게는 모든 것이 천박해 진다

Tyson can beat the other guy with one hand tied behind his back
↳ 타이슨은 상대방을 손쉽게 이길 수 있다

Understanding human need is half the job of meeting them
↳ 사람들에게 필요한 것이 무엇인지를 아는 것은 그 필요에 응하는 일의 절반이다

Unto the pure all things are pure
↳ 마음이 순수한 사람에게는 모든 것이 순수하게 보인다

> 순수한 사람은 남도 자신과 같이 순수하다고 믿고 사람을 대한다. 마음이 깨끗한 사람은 어떠한 유혹도 뿌리 칠 수 있다. 그러나 악한 사람들도 또한 다른 사람들도 자신과 같다고 생각하기 때문에 자신의 입장을 주장한다.

Vast chasms can be filled, but the heart of man never
↳ 매우 큰 틈새들은 메울 수 있지만 사람의 마음은 메울 수 없다(만족을 모른다)

Wan-soo doesn't know how the wind blows
↳ 완수는 눈치코치가 없어

Wan-soo is more changeable than a weathercock
↳ 완수는 변덕이 죽 끓듯 해

> 변덕이 심한 사람들을 보고 'Weathercock'이라고 한다. 이는 지붕 위에 있는 닭 모양의 풍향계이다. 바람의 방향에 따라 시시각각 변하는 모양을 빗댄 말이다.

› **scum**   filthy film on a liquid

› **chasm**   gorge

Wang-soo knows his way around
ㄴ 왕수는 자신이 할 일을 잘 알아

We find good(bad) in everybody
ㄴ 누구에게나 좋은(나쁜)점은 있게 마련이다

> 누구에게나 한두 가지 결점은 있다는 뜻이다. "Everyone has a skeleton in his closet 모든 사람은 창고에 해골을 가지고 있다"는 것은 공포 영화에서 가장 선해 보이는 사람이 결국에는 범인임이 드러나는 것을 빗댄 표현이다.
> (=Everyone has his faults(short comings))
> (=No one is without their faults)
> (=Everyone makes mistakes)

We like to read others but we do not like to be read
ㄴ 사람은 남을 이해하고 싶어 하지만 남이 자기를 이해하는 것은 좋아하지 않는다

What destroys one man preserves another
ㄴ 어떤 사람을 망치는 일은 다른 사람을 살려준다

When by force subdue men, they do not submit to him in heart
ㄴ 힘으로 사람을 굴복시킨다면 마음속으로 굴복하지 않을 것이다

When you interrupt somebody, you do so because you are a bad listener
ㄴ 당신이 남의 말을 가로막는다면 당신이 잘 들어주지 못하는 사람이기 때문이다

Who chatters to you will chatters of you
ㄴ 당신에게 수다떠는 사람은 다른 사람에게 당신에 대한 수다를 떨 것이다

Who comes uncalled, sits unserved
ㄴ 초대받지 않고 간 사람은 앉을 자리를 얻지 못한다

Who escapes a duty, avoids a gain
ㄴ 의무를 피하는 자는 이익도 얻지 못한다

‣ **subdue** bring under control, reduce the intensity of

Who will not feed the cats, must feed the mice and rats
  ↳ 고양이에게 밥을 안 주는 사람은 쥐에게 밥을 주어야 한다

Whoever let it pass(let him get away with it) is to blame, too
  ↳ 그것을 묵인하는 사람에게도 책임이 있다

Whoever wants to leave, go ahead. Otherwise, we are staying
  ↳ 갈 사람은 가고 있을 사람만 있기로 하자

Without heroes we are all plain and don't know how far we can go
  ↳ 영웅이 없으면 우리가 어디까지 갈 수 있는지 알지 못한다

Women molesters are becoming more and more active on jam-packed subways, harassing thinly dressed women passengers
  ↳ 빽빽한 지하철에서 치한들이 날뛰면서, 노출이 심한 여성들을 괴롭히고 있다

Won-suck does himself fairly well
  ↳ 원석인 호화판이야

(=Won-suck lives like a prince)

Woo-sung has to do everything his way
  ↳ 우성인 독불장군

자신의 생각만을 옳다고 고집하는 독불장군형의 인간이 얼마나 상대하기 힘든 사람인가를 말해주는 속담이다. 듣는 것(hear) 대신에 보는 것(see) 으로 대치하기도 한다(None are so blind as those who will not see).
(=Woo-sung doesn't listen to anyone but himself)
(=Woo-sung wants to be in charge of everything)
(=Everyone has to do everything he wants)

You are a diamond in the rough

› **molest** annoy especially by improper or rough handling

› **harass** worry and impede by repeated raids, annoy continually

ㄴ 넌 장래성이 있는 사람

You are a fat lot of use
ㄴ 넌 전혀 도움이 안 돼

You are a lock
ㄴ 넌 보장된 사람이잖아(따 놓은 당상이다)

You are a major pain in the ass
ㄴ 넌 참 피곤한 존재군

(=You get on my nerves)

You are all mouth and no chops
ㄴ 넌 입만 살고 실천이 없어

You are along for the ride
ㄴ 넌 곁다리야

You are always on my case
ㄴ 툭 하면 트집이로군

(=You are too ready to find fault with me)

You are always there to answer the bell
ㄴ 넌 항상 성실히 책임을 다 하거든

You are asking me to put up with a lot
ㄴ 넌 내게 대단한 인내를 요구하는군

You are so naive
ㄴ 순진하긴

You are so transparent
ㄴ 속보인다 속보여

› **lock** fastener using a bolt, enclosure in a canal to raise or lower boats

› **naive** innocent and unsophisticated, easily deceived

(=I can read you like a book)

You can't get blood from a stone
↳ 무정한 사람한테 동정을 구할 수 없어

> Blood 는 인간의 감정을 뜻하고 Stone 은 지독한 사람, 무정한 사람을 뜻한다(잔인하고 무정한 사람에게는 동정이나 자비를 기대하지 말라 You won't get pity or sympathy from someone who is completely unfeeling).

You can't lump Byung-soo and Chan-soo together
↳ 병수와 찬수를 똑 같은 사람으로 봐서는 안 돼

You don't have a leg up on anyone
↳ 넌 남들보다 잘난 구석이 하나도 없어

You have a heart of gold
↳ 넌 맘씨가 곱구나

You have a lot going for you
↳ 너 복이 터졌구나

You have a lot of expectations
↳ 넌 눈이 높구나

(=That's a tall order)

You have known to have butterfingers
↳ 넌 물건 잘 떨어뜨리기로 유명하잖아

You look big
↳ 잘난 체 하는군

· **lump**   mass of irregular shape, abnormal swelling

You must not follow your bent
ㄴ 맘 내키는 대로해서는 안 돼

You ought to know him better
ㄴ 넌 그 사람을 잘못 봤어

You started off with a bang and ends with a whimper
ㄴ 넌 용두사미로구나

> '용두사미(龍頭蛇尾)'란 '작심삼일'과 비슷한 말이다. 거창하게 시작해 놓고 흐지부지 끝나는 것을 설명한 말이다. 영어로는 "Starts off with a bang and ends with a whimper 큰소리로 시작해서 낑낑대며 끝난다"이다.

You're really thick-skinned(brazen-faced)
ㄴ 넌 정말 낯두껍구나

> 'Thick-skinned'는 '두꺼운 얼굴'을 나타내고, 'Brazen-faced'는 '철판을 깐 얼굴'을 나타낸다.

Your nose is turned up
ㄴ 너 콧대가 높군

> (=You have your nose in the air)

· **whimper** cry softly

· **turn up** discover or appear, happen unexpectedly

60. 사랑   Love

A god could hardly love and be wise
>↳ 신이라 하더라도 사랑에 빠지면 현명할 수 없다

> "Love is blind 사랑에 빠지면 눈이 먼다"라는 얘기가 있다. 사랑과 이성은 공존할 수 없다는 뜻이다(Love and reason do not go togther).

A home without love is no more a home, than a body without a sound mind is a man
>↳ 건전한 정신이 없는 육체가 인간이 아닌 것과 같이, 사랑이 없는 가정은 가정이 아니다

A wife loves out of duty, and duty leads to constraint, and constraint kills desire
>↳ 아내는 의무감에서 사랑하게 되고, 그 의무감은 구속이 되고, 그 구속은 욕망을 말살시킨다

A woman's whole life is a history of the affections
>↳ 여자의 전 생애는 애정의 역사이다

Adultery is the application of democracy to love
>↳ 간음은 민주주의를 사랑에 적용하는 것이다

All my roads lead to you
>↳ 내 앞의 길은 모두 너를 향하고 있어

› **desire** feel desire for, request   › **adultery** sexual unfaithfulness of a married person

All's fair in love and business
↳ 사랑과 사업에는 수단을 가리지 않는다

> 사랑과 성공은 쟁취라는 말이 있다. 용기를 내서 부딪혀야 하는 것이 사랑과 비즈니스이기 때문이다. 비슷한 어구 중에는 "All is fair in love and war 사랑과 전쟁에는 수단을 가리지 않는다"도 있다. 또한 사랑의 용기를 말한 속담 중에는 "None but the brave deserve the fair 용감한 자만이 미인을 차지한다"도 있다.

An-do has been anguishing over his unreturned(unrequited) love for her
↳ 안도는 그 여자에 대한 짝사랑으로 번민하고 있다

An-do is carrying a torch for Yun-hee, even though she's in love with you
↳ 연희가 널 사랑하고 있는데도 안도는 연희를 짝사랑하고 있어

Are you seeing anyone?
↳ 너 사귀는 사람 있니?

Be off with the old love before you are on with the new
↳ 새롭게 사랑을 하기 전에 옛 사랑을 정리해라(끝내라)

Being with you makes me happy
↳ 당신과 함께 있는 건 즐거워

Bong-soo(has) got his mind set on you
↳ 봉수의 맘은 네게 가 있어

Byung-soo has got something going on with Sook-hee
↳ 병수가 숙희하고 연애하고 있어

Caution in love is the most fatal to true happiness
↳ 사랑의 신중함은 진정한 행복에 치명적 장애이다

Chan-soo slipped his arm round Sook-hee's waist
↳ 찬수는 숙희의 허리를 껴안았다

› **anguish** suffer distress or sorrow | › **fatal** causing death or ruin
› **torch** flaming light

Concentrate(Focus) on what you are doing
↳ 한눈 팔지마

(=Keep your mind on what you are doing)

Craft must have clothes, but truth loves to go naked
↳ 책략에는 옷을 입혀야 하지만 진실은 옷을 벗고있기를 좋아한다

Deep down in his heart he still loves her
↳ 그의 마음 한 구석엔 그녀를 사랑하는 마음이 남아있어

Don't get physical with anyone
↳ 남들에게 완력으로 대해선 안 돼(**get physical** 에는 **touch someone in love-making**)이란 뜻도 있음

Don't you know how much you mean to me?
↳ 네가 내게 얼마나 소중한지 알잖아

Every one loves justice in the affairs of others
↳ 남의 일에는 누구나 정의를 중히 여긴다

First love dies hard
↳ 첫사랑은 잊을 수 없는 것

Friends show their love in time of trouble, not in happiness
↳ 친구는 행복할 때가 아닌 어려울때 애정을 나타낸다

어려움에 부딪혀 봐야 진정을 친구를 알아 볼 수 있다는 말이다. 더 자주 쓰이는 표현으로 "A friend in need is the friend indeed 필요할 때 옆에 있어주는 친구가 진정한 친구이다"가 있다.

Friendship admits the difference of character, as love does that of sex

---

· **craft** occupation requiring special skill(pl), craftiness, structure designed to   provide transportation

ↄ 우정은 성격 차를 용납한다, 사랑에서 이성을 허용하듯이

Give extra love to the lovely
ↄ 미운 자식 떡 하나 더 준다

Hang-soon thinks he loves her, but he's just stringing her along
ↄ 행순이는 그가 자신을 사랑하는 줄 알고 있지만 그는 그저 사랑하는 척 하면서 다른 남자에게 못 가게 붙들고만 있는 거야

Hatred stirs up strife, but love covers all sins
ↄ 미움은 다툼을 일으키지만 사랑은 모든 허물을 가리우느니라

Have you ever had someone steal your heart away?
ↄ 누군가에게 마음을 뺏겨 본 일이 있나?

Have you got your eyes then?
ↄ 그러면 봐둔 사람이 있다는 거니?

He flung his arms around my neck
ↄ 그는 급히 내 목을 끌어안았다

He is already such a big part of me
ↄ 난 그에게 정이 많이 들었어

> (=He has my heart)
> (=I'm so attached to him)

He put his arms around her neck and planted a kiss on her face
ↄ 그는 그녀의 목을 끌어안고 얼굴에 키스 세례를 퍼부었다

He used to be a habitual jailbird, but he'll go straight(straighten out, straighten up) this time
ↄ 그가 왕년엔 큰집에 뻔질나게 드나들었지만 이번엔 맘 잡을 거야

He who loves others is constantly loved by them

· **stir** move slightly, prod or push into activity(+up), mix by continued circular movement
· **strife** conflict

    ㄴ 남을 사랑하는 사람은 끊임없이 사랑을 받는다

Heaven's what I feel when I'm with you
    ㄴ 당신과 함께라면 천국에 있는 느낌

Her love boat has hit an iceberg, and it's in danger of sinking
    ㄴ 그녀가 탄 사랑의 배는 빙산에 부딪쳐 가라앉을 위기에 빠져있다

Her swashbuckling life of romance is now but a farce
    ㄴ 그녀의 사랑에 대한 허황한 삶은 이제 단지 하나의 익살극 일 뿐이다

His ex-flame still holds a special place deep in her heart for him
    ㄴ 그의 옛 애인은 아직도 마음 속 깊이 그를 사모하고 있다

His wife, consumed with jealousy, shadowed him hoping to catch him with his lover
    ㄴ 그의 처는 질투심에 불타 그가 정부와 함께 있는 것을 덮치려고 미행했다

However rare true love may be, it is less so than true friendship
    ㄴ 진정한 사랑을 아무리 찾기 어렵다해도 진정한 우정만큼 찾기 어렵지는 않다

Human's love is often but the encounter of two weaknesses
    ㄴ 인간의 사랑은 양쪽의 약점이 서로 만나는데 불과한 경우가 많다

I even love your faults
    ㄴ 너의 단점까지 사랑해

I love you in your very own way
    ㄴ 있는 그대로의 당신을 사랑해

I miss you with every beat of my heart
    ㄴ 정말 당신을 보고싶어

If you judge people, you have no time to love them
    ㄴ 남을 비판하면 그들을 사랑할 틈이 없다

In dreams and in love nothing is impossible
    ㄴ 꿈과 사랑에는 불가능이 없다

› **swashbuckler** boasting blustering soldier or daredevil

› **farce** satirical comedy with an improbable plot, ridiculous action

It can't be had for love or money
> ↳ 그건 절대로 손에 넣을 수 없어

It was just a one night stand long time ago
> ↳ 그건 오래된 하룻밤 풋사랑이야

It was love at first sight(=fall in love with a person at first sight)
> ↳ 첫눈에 반했지

It's her labor of love to teach us Japanese
> ↳ 그 여자는 자신이 좋아서 우리에게 일본어를 가르치는 거야

It's not the perfect but the imperfect that's in need of our love
> ↳ 사랑에는 완전한 것이 아닌 불완전한 것을 필요로 한다

Lack of love in early children can induce criminal behavior in the young
> ↳ 어릴 적 사랑의 결핍은 청년기에 범죄행위로 빠지게 할 수 있다

Let him into your heart
> ↳ 마음으로 그를 받아들여라

Love arrives on tiptoe and bangs the door when it leaves
> ↳ 사랑은 발끝으로 다가오며 떠날 때는 문을 꽝 닫고 간다

Love conquers all, hate heals nothing
> ↳ 사랑은 모든 걸 이겨내지만 증오는 아무 것도 치유 못해

Love dies only when growth stops
> ↳ 사랑이 성장을 멈추면 식고 만다

Love doesn't just sit there, like a stone: it has to be made, like bread, re-made all the time, made new
> ↳ 사랑은 돌처럼 항상 제자리에 있지 않다. 그것은 빵이 만들어지듯 만들어져야 하며 항상 다시 만들어지며 새롭게 거듭나야 하는 것이다

Love doesn't make the world go around. Love is what makes the ride worthwhile

---

› **induce** persuade, bring about

› **tiptoe** the toes of the feet, supported on tiptoe, walk quietly or on tiptoe

↳ 사랑이 세상을 돌아가게 하지는 않지만 세상살이를 살만한 것으로 만들어준다

Love endures only when the lovers love many things and not merely each other

↳ 사랑이 지속되려면 연인들이 상대방만이 아닌 세상의 많은 것들을 함께 사랑하는 마음이 있어야 한다

Love is a game that two can play and both win

↳ 사랑이란 둘이 출전해서 둘 다 이길 수 있는 경기이다

Love is a two-way street

↳ 사랑은 상호적인 것

Love is all in all to woman

↳ 여자에게는 사랑이 전부이다

Love is more afraid of change than destruction

↳ 사랑은 깨지는 것보다 바뀌는 것을 더 두려워한다

Love laughs at distance

↳ 사랑엔 국경이 없어

(=Love will find a way)

Love looks forward, hate looks back, anxiety has eyes all over its head

↳ 사랑은 앞을 내다보고, 증오는 과거를 돌아보고, 근심은 사면팔방을 돌아본다

Love looks not with the eyes, but with the mind

↳ 사랑은 눈으로 보는 것이 아니라 마음으로 본다

Love makes passion; but money makes marriage

↳ 사랑은 열정을 낳지만 돈은 결혼을 만든다

‣ **passion** strong feeling especially of anger, love, or desire; object of affection

Love me as(like) I am, warts and all

ㄴ 내 모습 그대로 사랑해다오

Love me, love my dog

ㄴ 처가 집 말뚝보고 절한다

> 진정으로 사랑을 한다면 그 사람의 단점은 물론, 주변의 모든 것이 이뻐 보이기 마련이다. 영국의 "Love me, love my dog"와 우리나라의 "처가집 말뚝보고 절한다"는 비슷한 뜻이지만, 영국의 속담은 의무, 즉 넉넉한 사랑을 요구하는 것이고, 우리나라의 속담은 당연히 그렇다는 것을 명기해 준 것이다.

Love of fame is common to all

ㄴ 누구에게나 명예욕은 있다

Love of money is common to all

ㄴ 돈보고 싫어하는 사람 없다

> 돈이 인생에 아주 중요한 가치를 가지게 되었다. 돈이 삶에 최고는 아니지만, 사람의 삶을 좌우하는 잣대중의 하나가 된 것은 사실이다.
> (=No one spits on money)

Love of nature is a common language that can transcend political and social boundaries

ㄴ 자연에 대한 사랑은 정치적 사회적 경계선을 초월할 수 있는 공통의 언어이다

Love truth, but pardon error

ㄴ 진실을 사랑하되 실수를 용서하라

Love understands love

› **wart** small projection on the skin caused by a virus, wart-like protuberance

› **boundary** line marking extent or separation

↳ 사랑은 해 본 사람이 안다

Love won't pay the bills

↳ 사랑이 밥 먹여 주나

Lovers' quarrels are soon mended

↳ 부부싸움은 칼로 물 베기

> (=Lover's anger is short-lived)

Marry first and love will follow

↳ 결혼하고 나면 사랑이 싹트게 돼있어

> 이 속담은 조금은 구시대적이다. 요즘은 중매 결혼보다 연애 결혼을 훨씬 선호
> 한다. 그러나 옛날에는 서양에서나 동양에서나 결혼은 집안끼리 정략적으로 이
> 루어진 경우가 많았다. 따라서 우선 서로를 잘 모르는 상태에서 결혼을 했다고
> 하더라도 결혼하여 살다보면 사랑이 싹튼다는 발상이 맞아 떨어졌을 것이다.

Misery loves company

↳ 동병상련이다

> '동병상련', '유유상종' 등의 사자성어와 같은 뜻이다. 같은 처지에 있거나 같
> 은 공동체에 속해 있으면 서로의 마음을 잘 이해하고, 서로의 이익을 위해
> 행동한다(Likeness cause liking = Dog doesn't eat dog).

Money can't buy love

↳ 돈으로 사랑을 살 수는 없어

My love for you will never die

› **pardon** excuse of an offense, free from penalty

› **misery** suffering and want caused by distress or poverty

ㄴ 당신에 대한 나의 사랑은 결코 식지 않을 것이다

> (=Now I belong to you from this day until forever)
> (=Time will never change the way I feel about you)
> (=My life is all yours)

Nam-soo has been making time with Soon-hee
　　　ㄴ 남수는 순희하고 연애중이야

Never love unless you can bear with all the faults of him
　　　ㄴ 남의 단점을 참아낼 수 없다면 사랑을 하지 마라

No man has tasted full flavor of life until he has known poverty, love, and war
　　　ㄴ 가난, 사랑, 전쟁을 알기 전에는 아무도 인생을 안다고 할 수 없다

Once she is in love with him, it'll be difficult to tear her away
　　　ㄴ 그녀가 그에게 일단 빠지게되면 떼어놓기는 어려워

Once you get the load of it, you'll love it
　　　ㄴ 일단 네가 그걸 자세히 보고 나면 좋아하게 될 것이다

One can't love and be wise
　　　ㄴ 사랑에 빠지고도 현명할 수는 없다

> "Love is blind 사랑에 빠지면 눈이 먼다"라는 얘기가 있다. 사랑과 이성은 공존할 수 없다는 뜻이다(Love and reason do not go togther).

One should love one's country
　　　ㄴ 사람은 누구나 자기 나라를 사랑할 줄 알아야

Pain of love lasts a lifetime

› **taste**　try or determine the flavor of, eat or drink in small quantity

› **flavor**　quality that effects the sense of taste, something that adds flavor

↳ 사랑의 아픔은 평생 남는다

Pleasures of love lasts but a moment
↳ 사랑의 즐거움은 잠깐 뿐이다

Politicians love to create grassroots movements
↳ 정치인들은 민중운동을 일으키기를 좋아한다

Sang-mi fell in love with Woo-sung at first sight
↳ 상미는 우성이에게 첫눈에 반해 =**It was love at first sight**

She wished to be all in all to him
↳ 그 여자는 그에게 가장 사랑하는 사람이 되고 싶었다

She'll love you and leave
↳ 그 여자의 네게 대한 사랑은 잠깐의 불장난일 거야

Tell me that we belong together
↳ 우린 인생을 함께 할거라고 말해 줘

That you still love me is neither here no there
↳ 네가 아직도 나를 사랑하든 안 하는 나한테는 상관없어

The couple are inseparably bound up by love
↳ 부부싸움은 칼로 물베기다

The course of true love never did run smooth
↳ 사랑에는 장애가 따르게 마련이다

The love inside, you take it with you
↳ 마음속 사랑은 영원히 간직할 수 있어

The love of money is the root of all evil
↳ 돈에 대한 사랑이 모든 악의 근원이다

신약성서 '디모데 전서'에서 유래한 속담이다. 이 세상의 모든 범죄는 금전, 즉 돈 때문에 일어난다고 해도 과언이 아니다.

▸ **grassroots**　begin from the bottom

The supreme happiness of life is the conviction that we are loved
ㄴ 인생 최고의 행복은 자신이 사랑을 받고 있다는 확신이다

The true course of love never did run smooth
ㄴ 진정한 사랑에 장애가 없을 수 없다

The unrequited love festered in her mind
ㄴ 짝사랑 때문에 그녀의 마음은 괴로웠다

The way to a man's heart is through his stomach
ㄴ 남자의 사랑을 얻으려면 그가 좋아하는 음식을 만들어 줘라

Their love matured into a marriage
ㄴ 두 사람은 사랑으로 결혼하게 됐어

They are trying to reduce their difficult relationship to a simple form of shared love and common interests
ㄴ 그들은 어려워진 관계를 서로간의 사랑과 상호이익이라는 단순한 형태로 이끌어 가려고 애쓰고 있다

Those who love the young best stay young longest
ㄴ 젊음을 사랑하는 사람이 가장 길게 젊음을 유지한다

Those whom we love we can hate
ㄴ 사랑할 수 있는 사람은 미워할 수도 있다

Thousands are hated, but none is ever loved without a real cause
ㄴ 증오를 받는 사람은 수없이 많지만 진정한 이유 없이 사랑을 받는 사람은 아무도 없다

Time, which strengthens friendship, weakens love
ㄴ 시간은 우정을 두텁게 하지만 사랑은 약하게 한다

사랑은 시간이 지나면 퇴색한다는 뜻이다. 비슷한 뜻으로 'Love me little, love me long 사랑은 가늘고 길게도 많이 쓰인다. 직역하면 '나는 조금씩 오래 사랑하라'이다. '백년해로'란 말을 결혼하는 커플들에게 많이 얘기하지만 말처럼 쉽지만은 않다.

› **supreme** highest in rank or authority, greatest possible

› **fester** pus-filled sore, form pus, become more bitter or malignant

To love and be loved is to feel the sun from both sides
↳ 사랑하고 사랑 받는 것은 앞뒤로 햇빛을 느끼는 것이다

To love is to admire with the heart; to admire is to love with the mind
↳ 사랑이란 진심으로 존경하는 것이며 존경이란 마음을 다해 사랑하는 것이다

To really know someone is to have loved and hated him in turn
↳ 사람을 제대로 알려면 그를 사랑도 해보고 미워도 해봐야 한다

Two things only a man cannot hide: that he drunk and that he is in love
↳ 인간이 숨길 수 없는 두 가지가 있는데 하나는 술 취한 것이고 하나는 사랑에 빠진 것이다

Understanding and love require a wisdom that comes only with age
↳ 이해와 사랑은 나이를 먹어야만 찾아온다

We are never hesitating to become the fated ones
↳ 운명적 사랑을 이루는데 주저하지 않는다

We are still going strong
↳ 우리의 사랑은 변함 없이 확고해

We love without reason, and without reason we hate
↳ 사람은 이유 없이 사랑하고 이유 없이 미워한다

We never know the love of our parents for us until we have become parents
↳ 부모가 되보지 않고서는 부모의 사랑을 모른다

When a man is in love he endures more than at other times
↳ 사람이 사랑에 빠지면 다른 때보다 참을성이 많아진다

When poverty comes in at the door, love flies out of the window
↳ 가난이 현관문으로 들어서면 사랑이 창문 밖으로 달아난다

> 가난해지면 의식주 해결이 힘들어 지기 때문에 인정이 사라지고 갈등이 늘어나는 것이 사실이다. 금실이 좋던 부부도 가난이 오면 싸움이 잦아진다.

› **wisdom** accumulated learning, good sense | › **fate** cause beyond human control held to determine events, end or outcome

When we love animals and children too much, we love at the expense of them
> ↳ 동물과 아이들을 너무 사랑한다면 그들을 망치면서 사랑하는 것이다

Where love fails we espy all faults
> ↳ 사랑이 식으면 온갖 허물을 들춰낸다

Where there is love, there's pain
> ↳ 사랑이 있는 곳에 아픔이 있다

Where there is no jealousy there's no love
> ↳ 질투가 없으면 사랑도 없다

Who does not sufficiently hate vice, does not sufficiently love virtue
> ↳ 악을 철저히 미워하지 않는 사람은 선을 깊이 사랑하지 않는다

Who would give a law to lovers?
> ↳ 사랑엔 법이 없다

You must be crossed in love
> ↳ 너 누굴 짝사랑하고 있군

› **espy** catch sight of
› **sufficient** adequate

› **cross in** trapped in

61. 사회   Society

A capital punishment is more reprehensible because it is officially sanctioned and done with great ceremony in the name of the society

    ㄴ 사형은 그것이 사회라는 이름으로 공식적으로 승인되어 커다란 의식 속에서 행해지므로 더욱 지탄을 받는다

A new pragmatism is replacing the old emphasis on the size, prestige and face

    ㄴ 크기, 명성, 체면을 생각했던 옛 생각은 새로운 실용주의로 바뀌고 있다

Addicts may be viewed as losers on society's margins

    ㄴ 마약 중독자는 소외계층의 패배자로 비쳐질 수 있다

All progress means war with society

    ㄴ 모든 진보는 사회와의 싸움이다

Allowing unethical figures to appear on the TV programs will only serve to numb the sense of viewers

    ㄴ 비도덕적인 인물들을 **TV** 프로그램에 출연시킨다는 것은 시청자들의 도덕관념을 마비시킬 뿐이다

Any mistake or wrongdoing concerning the use of public funds should be tracked down so that appropriate measures can be taken to prevent a repetition

    ㄴ 공공기금의 사용에 관한 어떠한 착오나 비행도 단속하여 재발을 방지할 수 있는 적절한 조치를 취해야 한다

· **sanction** approve
· **numb** lacking feeling

Anyone who is eccentric and lacks social skills usually becomes the fifth wheel in social functions

ㄴ 성격이 괴팍하고 사교술이 능하지 못한 사람은 사교모임에서 외톨이 가 된다

Belief in the worth of individual is the key to a democratic society

ㄴ 개인의 가치에 대한 신뢰는 민주주의사회의 핵심이다

Censorship reflects a society's lack of confidence in itself

ㄴ 검열은 한 사회가 스스로에 대해 자신이 없다는 증거이다

Cultural exchange should go both ways

ㄴ 문화는 쌍방이 교류해야 한다

Culture takes a back-seat again to modernization

ㄴ 문화가 현대화 때문에 또 뒷전으로 밀려난다는 애기로군

Doctors took to the streets yesterday demanding a redress of the nation's medical system

ㄴ 의사들은 어제 의료서비스제도의 개정을 요구하면서 거리로 뛰쳐나갔다

Doctors won't be able to avoid public condemnation if they continue to push their plans to boycott services for patients

ㄴ 의사들이 환자들의 진료를 거부하겠다는 계획을 강행한다면 국민들의 비난을 면치 못할 것이다

Draft irregularities have long been a serious social issue symbolizing the conflict between the rich and the poor in this country

ㄴ 병역비리는 이 나라의 가진자 못가진자 사이의 갈등을 상징하는 심각 한 사회문제가 되어왔다

During war we imprison the rights of man

ㄴ 전시에는 인권을 감옥에 가둬 둔다

Every human being must be valued as such irrespective of his social

---

· **eccentric** odd in behavior, being off center   · **censor** one with power to suppress anything objectionable

positions
> ↳ 모든 인간은 그의 사회적인 지위에 상관없이 인간 그 자체로 평가받아야 한다

Every violation of truth is not only a sort of suicide in the liar, but is a stab at the health of human society
> ↳ 진실에 어긋나는 모든 일은 거짓말 한 사람의 자살일 뿐 아니라 인간 사회의 건전성에도 타격이 된다

Giving self-starters autonomy can be a powerful reward
> ↳ 솔선해서 일하는 사람들에게 보다 많은 자율권을 주는 것은 큰 보상일 수 있다

Heavy fines must be imposed on dog owners who are negligent about controlling their animals
> ↳ 개들을 잘못 관리하는 주인들에게는 과중한 벌금이 부과돼야 해

In line with the historic implementation of a law acknowledging brain death, the government launched a state-run agency to manage all matters related to organ transplants
> ↳ 정부는 뇌사를 인정하는 장기이식에 관한 법률 시행과 연계해 장기이식을 총괄하기 위한 공공기구를 발족시켰다

In many countries introduction of free contraceptives led to an increase in promiscuity
> ↳ 어떤 나라에서나 피임약(기구)를 마구 도입함으로써 성생활 문란을 가져왔다

It manifested what citizens can obtain in the face of various obstacles when they are determined to realize their goals
> ↳ 시민들이 목적달성을 위해 결의할 때 갖가지 장애들에 부딪치더라도 얻어낼 수 있는 것이 뭔가를 보여주었다

· **autonomy**   self-governing
· **negligent**   marked by neglect

It requires the understanding and cooperation of everyone in the country to resolve the problems created by this outbreak
　　　　ㄴ 이번 발생한 문제점들을 해결하기 위해 전 국민적 이해와 협조가 요망된다

It's time to get rid of the decadence that has crept into every aspect of our society
　　　　ㄴ 사회의 모든 측면에 배어든 퇴폐를 추방해야 할 때다

It's to the common advantage that street traffic should be well controlled
　　　　ㄴ 거리 교통이 잘 통제돼야 한다는 것은 공동의 이익이 된다

Jobs are one of the evaluations of the success on any society
　　　　ㄴ 직업은 어느 사회에서나 성공 여부를 평가하는 기준이 될 수 있다

Justice must not only be done, it must be seen to be done
　　　　ㄴ 정의가 이루어져야 한다는 것만으로는 부족하고 누구나 볼 수 있게 실현되어야 한다

Liberals tend to favor more immediate social change than do conservatives
　　　　ㄴ 진보주의자들은 보수주의자들 보다 더 신속한 사회변화를 선호하는 경향이 있다

Love of nature is a common language that can transcend political and social boundaries
　　　　ㄴ 자연에 대한 사랑은 정치적 사회적 경계선을 초월할 수 있는 공통의 언어이다

Patriotism cuts across all ages and sexes of Korean society
　　　　ㄴ 애국심은 한국의 남녀노소를 초월한다

People must free themselves from society's prejudices and

· **decadent** deterioration
· **creep** crawl, grow over a surface like ivy

stereo-types
> 사람들은 사회의 편견과 고정관념에서 벗어나야 한다

Planned mergers of agricultural and livestock federation are grid-locked in factional disputes
> 예정되었던 농·축협의 통합은 파벌싸움으로 교착상태에 빠져있다

Public morals are very lax(sadly decayed) these days
> 요즘 풍기가 너무 문란해

Public opinion is a force to be reckoned with
> 여론의 힘은 무시할 수 없어

Society is not so naive
> 세상살이가 그리 만만한 게 아냐

(=Everything has a price)

Society now is connected through a huge web of networks and well on its way to becoming integrated into a borderless society
> 사회는 이제 거대한 정보망으로 연결되어 국경 없는 사회로 통합되어 나가고 있다

Tax thresh-holds should be raised drastically to protect those on lower wages
> 면세점은 저소득층 보호를 위해 크게 높여야 한다

That project involves an unacceptable risk to public safety
> 그 사업은 일반 국민들의 안전에 허용할 수 없는 위험을 내포하고 있다

The burgeoning public cries public cries for transparent politics have been expressed through the civil society movement to expedite

---

· **stereo-type** something conforming to a general pattern

· **burgeon** grow
· **expedite** carry out or handle promptly

political reform with the power of the people

  ↳ 투명한 정치를 부르짖으면서 생겨난 시민들의 소리는 국민의 힘으로
  개혁을 앞당기겠다는 시민단체운동으로 표현되고 있다

The call for a better society must be reconciled with the demands of ordinary people

  ↳ 보다 나은 사회에 대한 욕구는 보통 사람들의 요망과 조화를 이루어
  야 한다

The civic movement appeared too naive and idealistic against the backdrop of such a muddy political culture

  ↳ 시민단체운동은 이런 혼탁한 정치문화의 배경에 대항하기에 너무 순
  수하고 이상적인 것으로 보인다

The civil society's movement reminded politicians of the sobering fact that they can no longer carry on with their shameful traditions and undemocratic practices

  ↳ 시민단체운동은 부끄러운 전통과 비민주적 관행을 더 이상 계속 이어
  갈 수 없다는 엄연한 사실을 정치인들에게 상기시켜 주었다

The enormous en-equality is the real cause of speculative investment in property, which remains a leading social issue in Korea

  ↳ 그 막심한 불평등이 한국의 주요 사회문제로 되어 온 부동산 투기의
  진정한 원인이다

The fit must not leave the weak marginalized and the weak must empower themselves to cope with the challenges

  ↳ 우위에 있는 계층은 어려운 사람들을 사회적으로 소외시켜서는 안되
  며 어려운 사람들은 힘을 내어서 어려움에 대처해 나가야한다

The media likes public figures that project a distinctly good or bad image because either extreme makes the news more interesting

  ↳ 언론은 어느 쪽이든지 뉴스를 흥미 있게 만들기 때문에 두드러지게

› **sober** not drunk, serious or solemn
› **cope** deal with difficulties

좋거나 아니면 나쁜 이미지를 드러내는 공인을 선호한다

The media turned him into an idol
↳ 언론이 그를 우상으로 만들었어

The more individuals there are following their own bent, the healthier we are as a society
↳ 개인별 취향을 추구하는 사람이 많아질수록 더 건전한 사회가 된다

The nation is stunned by a series of revelation exposing the moral laxity rampant in our society
↳ 우리 사회에 팽배한 도덕적 해이를 드러내는 일련의 폭로로 나라 전체가 놀라고 있다

The ongoing campaign by civic groups to boycott corrupt and dishonest politicians has already gained public support
↳ 현재 진행중인 부패하고 부정직한 정치인에 대한 시민단체의 낙선 (천)운동은 벌써 일반대중의 지지를 얻고 있다

The only way to achieve true success is to express yourself completely in service to society
↳ 진정한 성공을 이룰 수 있는 유일한 방법은 사회를 위하여 최선을 다하는 것이다

The press should be the good mirror of society
↳ 신문은 사회를 제대로 반영해 주어야 한다

The proportion of urban dwellers who are originally migrants from rural areas is astonishing
↳ 이전에 농촌지역에서 살다가 이주해 온 도시지역 주민 수의 비율이 엄청나다

The refugees on that asylum complained that the food served was not enough to feed a fly

---

› **laxity** not strict or tense
› **rampant** widespread

› **boycott** refrain from dealing with

↳ 수용소에 있던 난민들은 음식이 간에 기별도 안 간다고 불평이었다

The rejection campaign was an ultimatum of a sort from the people to the politicians to wake up from their chronic malaise and backwardness

↳ 이 거부운동은 정치인들의 고질적인 병폐와 구태를 벗어나 각성을 요구하는 국민의 최후통첩이다

The troubles in that refugee camp are overcrowding and a lack of basic amenities

↳ 난민수용소의 문제점은 수용인원의 과밀과 편의시설의 부족이다

The unsettled and impatient youth was a rotten apple in the barrel

↳ 안정되지 못하고 잘 참지 못하는 젊은이는 사회에 악영향을 미쳤다

하나가 전체에게 나쁜 영향을 미친다는 말이다. 영어 속담에는 여러 가지가 있는데, 가장 자주 쓰이는 표현은 "One rotten apple spoils the barrel 썩은 사과 하나가 한 통을 썩게 한다"이다. 악한 한 사람이 한 가문, 한 나라를 욕되게 하는 것은 "It is an ill bird that fouls its own nest 자기의 둥지를 더럽히는 새는 나쁜 새이다"로 표현한다.

Their behavior should suffice to illustrate how social attitudes are changing

↳ 그들의 행동은 사회풍조가 어떻게 변하고 있는가를 잘 보여주기에 충분할 것이다

There is tremendous pressure to keep up face in our society

↳ 우리사회는 체면치레라는 보이지 않는 압력이 있다

There must be a shift in political emphasis from individual profit to social equality

↳ 정치적으로 강조돼야 할 것은 개인의 이익에서 사회적 평등으로의 전

· **malaise** sense of being unwell
· **suffice** be sufficient

환이다

They are trying to work out measures to spend surplus tax revenue for the less privileged in society
> ㄴ 그들은 소외계층을 위해 잉여세입을 사용할 계획을 마련하고 있다

This is the only way for them to revive the impoverished economy and to save innocent people from starvation
> ㄴ 이것은 그들이 가난에 찌들려 있는 경제를 소생시키고 죄 없는 국민들을 가난에서 구제해 주는 유일한 방법이다

This world is a weak-to-the-wall society
> ㄴ 세상은 약육강식이다

> (Big fish eat little fish) 약한 것은 결국 강한 것에게 먹히고 만다. 다윈은 먹이사슬을 이론화 한 후 인간 사회에도 약육강식의 법칙을 적용시켰다. 강자 밑의 약자는 제대로 능력을 발휘하지 못한다.

To explain any aspect of society the sociologist must determine the law influencing human behavior
> ㄴ 사회의 어떤 양상을 설명하기 위해서 사회학자는 사회적인 맥락에서 인간 행동에 영향을 주는 법칙을 알아내야 한다

We learned the hard way during our economic crisis how individual greed can disrupt civil society
> ㄴ 우리는 경제위기를 겪는 가운데 개인의 욕심이 시민사회에 어떤 혼란을 가져올 수 있는가를 쓰라린 체험으로 배웠다

We should meet our responsibility to the next generation by maintaining our fiscal discipline
> ㄴ 우리는 재정 원칙을 준수함으로써 다음 세대를 위한 책임을 다 해야

· **disrupt** throw into disorder
· **fiscal** relating to money

한다

You are not a man of the society(world)
ㄴ 넌 세상 물정을 잘 몰라

(=You're out of touch with the world)

Your conduct in society was impeccable
ㄴ 사람들 앞에서 너의 행동은 나무랄 데 없었다

· **impeccable** faultless

62. 사회 생활   Social Life

A good man is hard to find
> ↳ 세상에 착한 사람이 그리 흔한 게 아니다

All he needs is a ball park figure
> ↳ 그는 어림치만 알면 돼

All the usual people were there
> ↳ 늘 오는 사람들이 거기 다 모여있었어

Be just before you are generous
> ↳ 관대하기에 앞서 공정히 하라

Be on sure ground before you suspect anyone
> ↳ 공연히 남을 의심해선 안 돼(자주 쓰이지는 않음)

Better mad with the rest of the world than wise alone
> ↳ 혼자 현명하기보다는 세상의 다른 사람들과 더불어 함께 미치는 게 낫다

Beware of the man who does not return your blow
> ↳ 매 맞고도 가만히 있는 사람을 주의하라

Beware the people weeping when they bare the iron and
> ↳ 압제에서 벗어나면서 우는 사람들을 주의하라

Bong-soo is more than a little cracked
> ↳ 봉수는 머리가 돌아도 보통 돈 게 아냐

Bong-soo just snapped

· **generous** freely giving or sharing

ㄴ 봉수는 잠시 머리가 돌았던 거야

Bong-soo was very careful not to blow his cover
ㄴ 봉수는 정체(의중)를 드러내지 않으려고 신중을 기했다

Bong-soo won't notice anything but what relates to himself
ㄴ 봉수는 자기와 관련 없는 일에는 어떤 일에도 주의를 기울이지 않아

By and large the more question you ask in a survey, the less polite people tend to be
ㄴ 대체로 사람들은 조사시 질문을 많이 할수록 불친절해지기 쉽다

Byung-soo has my measure to an inch
ㄴ 병수는 나에 대하여 속속들이 알고 있어(흔한 표현 아님)

Byung-soo never learned to subordinate his needs to anyone else's
ㄴ 병수는 다른 사람의 일을 자신의 일보다 중시할 줄 몰랐다

Byung-soo will get his feet off the ground
ㄴ 병수는 곧 자리를 확고히 잡게 될 것이다

Campus life can be beautiful and rewarding in spite of the unfavorable factors that can frustrate your ambitious goals
ㄴ 대학생활은 비록 불리한 요인들이 야심에 찬 목표를 좌절시킬지라도 아름답고 값진 일일 수 있다

Chan-ho's complaint is nothing new
ㄴ 찬호의 불평은 늘 하던 거잖아

Chang-soo is going to have a go at a comeback
ㄴ 창수는 재기를 시도할 거야

Chang-soo is a lion at home and a mouse abroad
ㄴ 창수는 집안에서만 큰소리치고 밖에선 꼼짝도 못한다

› **survey** look over and examine closely, make a survey of

› **frustrate** block, cause to fail

(=Chang-soo is bully at home but a coward abroad)
(=Chang-soo is bossy at home but timid elsewhere)

Come on, get into the swing of things
       ㄴ 자 이제 남들과 어울려서 살아(해) 나가자

Dealing with awkward customers is my strong suit
       ㄴ 다루기 힘든 사람을 잘 다루는 게 내 특기잖니

Don't be so conscious about others
       ㄴ 남의 눈치 볼 거 없어

(=Don't worry about what others may think)

Don't burn your bridge behind you
       ㄴ 배수진을 치지 마라

'배수지진(背水之陣)'이란 "강을 등지고 진을 친다"라는 뜻으로 사마천의 사기에 나오는 내용이다. 도망갈 곳이 없으면 죽기 살기로 싸우기 때문에 오히려 더 어려운 곳에다 진을 치라는 내용이다. 그러나 잘못하면 자신을 궁지에 몰아넣는 수가 있다. 때에 따라서 위기 상황에는 배수진이 필요하기도 하다 (Desperate diseases must have desperate remedies 중병에는 극약 처방이 필요하다). 이는 암 치료를 위한 항암치료를 빗댄 말이다. 항암치료는 암세포뿐만 아니라 정상적인 세포까지도 파괴하는 부작용이 있기 때문이다.

Don't burn your bridges, you might need their help someday
       ㄴ 돌이킬 수 없는 사이를 만들지 마라. 언젠가 그들의 도움을 필요로 할지 모르니까

› **desperate** hopeless, rash, extremely intense
› **remedy** medicine that cures, something   that corrects an evil or compensates for a loss

Don't call me Mr. it's very distant
      ↳ 우리 서먹서먹하게 **Mr.**라 부르지 말자

Don't forget people who made you what you are today
      ↳ 오늘의 네가 있기까지 도와준 사람들을 잊지 마라

Don't forget to return the favor
      ↳ 신세 진 일은 잊지 말고 갚아라

Don't get me set up as an outsider
      ↳ 날 이방인 취급 마

Don't get physical with anyone
      ↳ 남들에게 완력으로 대해선 안 돼(**get physical** 에는 **touch someone in love-making**)이란 뜻도 있음)

Don't give them the back of your hand
      ↳ 그들을 함부로 대하지마

Don't hang(ride) on to somebody else's coattails
      ↳ 남에게 신세를 지지 마라

Don't have a double standard
      ↳ 사람차별 하지마

Don't interfere with other people's comfort
      ↳ 다른 사람을 불편하게 하지마

Don't jostle everyone around
      ↳ 아무에게나 함부로 대하지마

Don't let anyone feel isolated
      ↳ 누구든 외톨이가 된(소외감이 드는) 기분으로 만들어선 안 돼

Don't let anyone say you have a long bottom
      ↳ 아무에게도 엉덩이가 무겁다는 말을 듣지 않도록 해

Don't let anyone say you're talking to hear your own voice

· **interfere** collide or be in opposition, try to run the affairs of others   · **jostle** push or shove

↳ 남들에게서 네가 말이 많다는 소릴 듣게 해선 안 돼

Don't let anyone think you're a loose cannon
↳ 남들에게서 못 말리는 위험인물(떠버리)이란 소릴 들어선 안 돼

Don't make him feel like a fish out of water
↳ 그가 서먹서먹하지 않게 해줘

Don't mix business with pleasure
↳ 공과 사를 구분하라

Don't nose into another's affairs
↳ 남의 일에 끼어 들지마

Don't step into something that doesn't concern you
↳ 무관한 일에 끼어 들지 마라

Don't stick your nose into other people's private affairs
↳ 남의 사생활에 간섭하지마

Don't try to be all think to all men
↳ 모든 사람의 마음에 들려고 하지 마라

Don't try to make him the heavy because he's watching out for his own interests
↳ 그가 자신의 이익만 챙긴다고 매도하지마

Don't try to weasel out of your responsibility
↳ 책임을 벗어나려고 하지마

Doo-soo can't have the last word
↳ 두수에겐 결정권이 없어

Doo-soo knows his part inside out(through and through)
↳ 두수는 자기 역(할)을 속속들이 알고 있어

Doo-soo is getting the silent treatment
↳ 두수는 점점 찬밥 신세가 되어가고 있어

- **cannon**   artillery piece
- **weasel**   small slender flesh-eating mammals

Doo-soo put himself out on a limb
> ↳ 두수는 자신을 불리한 입장으로 밀어 넣고 말았어

Doo-soo's accomplishment was for the birds
> ↳ 두수가 해낸 건 별거 아냐

Draw a sharp line between public and private affairs
> ↳ 공과 사를 엄격히 구분하라

Duck-soo intended to retire from active life, but fate decided otherwise
> ↳ 덕수는 사회활동에서 은퇴할 예정이었으나 운명이 이를 허락지 않았다

Eat to please yourself, but dress to please others
> ↳ 자신을 위해서 먹고 남을 위해서 옷을 입어라

Ed is eager to get in on the act
> ↳ 에드가 한몫 끼고싶어 안달이야

Envy shoots at others, and wounds herself
> ↳ 질투는 남을 향해 쏘지만 자신이 다친다

Everything depends on him
> ↳ 그 사람이 하기 나름이다

> (=He is the one in charge)
> (=He makes the choices)
> (=It's up to him)

Every human being must be valued as such irrespective of his social positions
> ↳ 모든 인간은 그의 사회적인 지위에 상관없이 인간 그 자체로 평가받아야 한다

› **limb**   projecting appendage used in moving
            or grasping, tree branch

Every one loves justice in the affairs of others
 ↳ 남의 일에는 누구나 정의를 중히 여긴다

Every other man is a piece of myself, for I am a part and a member of mankind
 ↳ 모든 다른 사람들은 나 자신의 한 조각이다, 왜냐하면 나는 전 인류의 일원이기 때문이다

Everything I've done is on the up and up
 ↳ 내가 한 일은 모두 정당하다

Everything is funny as long as it is happening to others
 ↳ 남들에게 닥치는 일은 무슨 일이나 재미있다

Everything told against me
 ↳ 모든 건이 내게 불리했다

Everywhere we go, people are much the same
 ↳ 어디를 가나 사람은 대개 같다

Few people today are reduced to tears by the sight of the disabled people begging
 ↳ 요즈음 지체불구자들이 구걸하는 것을 보고 눈물을 흘리는 사람은 거의 없다

For a while I was lost to the world
 ↳ 한동안 난 세상에서 외톨이가 되었지

Get Dong-soo to help you
 ↳ 동수한테 도움을 받아라

Get him off my back
 ↳ 그 사람을 나한테서 좀 떼 내 줘

Gil-soo has exceeded his authority
 ↳ 길수가 월권을 한 거지

▸ **disabled** handicapped

Gil-soo is a man with a finger in every pie in our office
↳ 우리 사무실에서 길수는 약방에 감초지

Had I known you then, I would have given you what help I could
↳ 그 당시 널 알았다면 모든 도움을 줬을 텐데

He already filled the bill
↳ 그는 이미 기대에 부응했어

He finally gave me the slip
↳ 그는 끝내 나를 따돌리고 말았어

He had his back to us
↳ 우리에게 등 돌렸어

He has been keeping a high(low) profile
↳ 그는 남의 눈에 띠(안 띠)려고 노력하고 있어

He has taken me in more than once
↳ 그 사람한테 속은 게 한 두 번이 아냐

He heaped coals of fire on your head
↳ 그가 네게 악을 선으로 갚았군

He intoned that the enemy had been the within the gate
↳ 그는 믿는 도끼에 발등 찍혔다고 탄식했다

> "믿는 도끼에 발등 찍혔다"에 해당하는 영어 표현은 "Stabbed in the back 등을 찔렸다"이다. 또한 강아지가 주인의 손을 무는 상황에 비유하여 "Bite the hand that feeds you 먹이를 주는 손을 문다"라고도 한다.

He is always name-dropping
↳ 그는 늘 누구누구를 잘 안다고 들먹거려

He is always trying to get in(good) with the people in charge

---

‣ **profile** picture in outline
‣ **intone** chant

ㄴ 그는 늘 관계(책임)자들에게 환심을 사려고 해

He is very selfish, but his wife goes to the other extreme of being too anxious to curry favor with me

ㄴ 그가 너무 이기적인데 반면 그의 처는 너무 내 비위를 맞추려고 안달이다

He kept making mistakes and became red in the face

ㄴ 그는 계속 실수를 해서 곤혹스럽게 됐다

He of all men should set an example

ㄴ 누구보다 먼저 그가 모범을 보여야 한다

He set a good example to them

ㄴ 그는 그들에게 좋은 본보기를 남겼어

> (His work serves as an example to the others 그가 하는 일은 타의 모범이 된다)

He that can't obey, can't command

ㄴ 남에게 복종하지 않는 자는 남에게 명령할 수 없다

He that respects not is not respected

ㄴ 남을 존경해야 남에게 존경받는다

> "가는 말이 고와야 오는 말도 곱다"라는 속담이 있듯이, 사회 생활을 하면서 누구나 자신이 대접받고 싶은 데로 남을 대접하면 싸우는 일은 전혀 없을 것이다. 이에 해당하는 영어 속담은 "Do as you would be done by 대접받고 싶은 데로 대접하라"이다(＝Respect a man, he'll do the more).

He that would govern others, first should be master of himself

---

- **respect** consider deserving of high regard
- **master** subdue, become proficient in

ㄴ 남을 지배하려는 자는 자신부터 먼저 지배해야 한다

He turned even his errors to good account(good use)

ㄴ 그가 실수는 했을망정 교훈은 얻었다

> 성공을 하기 위해서는 도전을 해야 하고, 여러 시행착오를 겪은 후에야 비로
> 소 참된 성공을 맛볼 수 있다. 신이 아닌 인간이기 때문에 완벽하지 못하기
> 때문이다(He who makes no mistakes makes nothing 실수를 하지 않는
> 사람은 아무것도 만들지 못한다).

He was buried alive

ㄴ 그는 세상에서 매장되었다

He went to the funeral just for the ride

ㄴ 그는 내키지 않지만 다른 속셈이 있어서 참여하는 거야

He who rebukes a man will find more favor afterward

ㄴ 남에게 싫은 소리를 하는 자는 나중에 더욱 사랑 받느니라

Hospitality consists in a little fire, a little food and an immense quiet

ㄴ 환대란 불을 좀 지펴주고, 음식을 좀 내주며 조용히 해주는 것이다

How could you behave so shamefully in public?

ㄴ 여러 사람 앞에서 그런 추태를 보이다니

How have you put up with him treating you like dirt for all the years?

ㄴ 그가 그토록 긴 세월에 걸쳐 너를 개떡같이 취급해 오는 것을 어떻게 참아왔나?

Hyun-soo hedged his bet to reduce a possible loss

ㄴ 현수는 생길지도 모르는 손실을 줄이기 위해 양쪽에 걸었다

Hyun-soo's been a real hot property here

› **rebuke** reprimand sharply

› **immense** vast

› **hedge** protect oneself against loss, evade the risk of commitment

↳ 현수가 여기선 없어선 안 되는(인기 있는) 사람이다

I am not going to be made a cat's paw of him
↳ 난 그 사람 앞잡이 노릇은 안 할거야

I am not good at personal relationships
↳ 난 사람들과 잘 친하지 못해

I can't fill your shoes
↳ 네가 하던 일을 감당하기엔 역부족이야

I carved out a career for myself
↳ 난 자력으로 사회에 진출한 사람

I don't want this conversation to become public
↳ 이 이야기는 남에게 알리고 싶지 않아

I don't like to be classed with such fellows
↳ 나를 저런 사람들하고 같이 취급하면 곤란해

I refer myself to your generosity
↳ 당신의 관대한 처분을 바랄 뿐입니다

I took a joke
↳ 조롱당하고도 참았지

I will do whatever you want me to do
↳ 시키는 대로 다 할게

I won't be dictated to
↳ 남의 지시는 안 받기로 했어

(=No one shall dictate me)

I won't sit back and watch it

› **dictate** speak for a person or a machine to record, command

ㄴ 가만히 보고 있을 순 없어

I'll support you fully

ㄴ 발벗고 나서주지

(=I'll give you my full support)
(=You may have my full support)

I'll teach you the do's and dont's

ㄴ 너에게 규칙(할 일과 안 할 일)을 알려주지

I'm not fit to be seen

ㄴ 이대로 남의 앞에 나설 순 없어

I've been done

ㄴ 감쪽같이 속았어

I've tried to make myself generally useful

ㄴ 여러모로 도움이 되려고 애썼습니다

If anything goes wrong, she'll take the heat

ㄴ 무슨 일이고 잘못 되기라도 하면 그녀가 뒤집어쓰게 돼 있어

If he catches them taking bribes, He'll string(hang) them out to dry

ㄴ 그들이 뇌물을 받다가 그에게 걸리면 뜨거운 맛을 보게 될 것이다

If you can't beat them, join them

ㄴ 꺾을 수 없는 상대라면 싸우지 말고 그들을 내편으로 만들어라=힘
(실력) 앞에는 못 당해

If you do happen to bump into one of them, he stares at you as if you had no right to walk on the street where he walks

ㄴ 혹시 네가 그들을 만난다면, 그들은 네가 길을 걸어갈 권리도 없는
사람으로 취급할 것이다

› **bribe** corrupt ot influence by gifts

In the country of the blind, the one-eyed is the king
> 호랑이 없는 골에 토끼가 왕이다

> 잘난 사람이 없는 사회에서 못난 사람이 잘난 체 하는 것을 빗댄 말이다. 한
> 국 속담 "호랑이 없는 끝에 토끼가 왕이다"와 비슷한 "When the cat's
> away, the mice will play 고양이가 없으면 쥐가 판친다"도 쓰인다.

Injuries may be forgiven, but not forgotten
> 남을 해치고 용서받을 수 있을지 모르지만 잊혀지게 하지는 못할 것
> 이다

It all depends on what you mean by "help"
> "돕는다"는 말이 어느 정도의 도움인지에 따라 다르지

It takes all sorts to make a world
> 세상엔 온갖 사람들이 어울려 살아가게 마련이야

It was hard for him to reconcile himself to the disagreeable state
> 그가 비위에 거슬리는 일을 감수하기는 어려웠다

It's awful to be at somebody's beck and call
> 남이 시키는 대로 한다는 건 견디기 어려운 일이다

It's more than his job's worth to take a bribe
> 그가 뇌물을 받는다면 모가지 내놓고 받아야 해

Jack is as good as his master
> 지위가 낮다고 해서 상관보다 못한 것이 아니다

Jin-soo can play second fiddle to no one
> 진수는 독불장군(남의 밑에 일 못해)

Joo-yung is a first-rate leader who knows how to call the tune(shots)
> 주영이는 사람을 어떻게 다뤄야 하는지 잘 아는 일류 관리자이다

· **injury** hurt, damage, or loss sustained
· **fiddle** move the hands restlessly

Let him get his feet wet first
> ↳ 우선 그에게 적응훈련부터 시키자

Life is a process where people mix and match, fall apart and come back together
> ↳ 인생은 섞여서 어울리고, 헤어졌다가 다시 함께 되돌아가는 과정이다

Losers are always in the wrong
> ↳ 이기면 충신, 지면 역적

Many ex-convicts complain they are kept at an arm's length when people find out(discover) their criminal past
> ↳ 어느 출소자나 사람들이 자신들의 전과에 대해 알게되면 거리를 두려 한다고 불평한다

Mi-gyung rates with all the colleagues
> ↳ 미경인 전 동료들간에 인기 있어

Moon-ho has a really good bedside manner
> ↳ 문호는 사람(환자)을 무척 능숙하게 다룰 줄 알아

My poor academic background is keeping me down(back) in life
> ↳ 나는 낮은 학력 때문에 사회생활에 불리해(keep back에는 "유급 또는 낙제시키다"의 뜻이 있음)

Nam-soo has quickly entrenched himself in the new office, and is liked by everyone
> ↳ 남수는 새로운 사무실에서 재빨리 자리잡았고 모두가 그를 좋아한다

None is as deaf as those who won't hear
> ↳ 남의 말을 안 듣는 사람보다 더 귀먹은 사람은 없어

> 자신의 생각만을 옳다고 고집하는 독불장군형의 인간이 얼마나 상대하기 힘든 사람인가를 말해주는 속담이다. 듣는 것(hear) 대신에 보는 것(see)으로 대치하기도 한다(None are so blind as those who will not see).

· **entrench** establish in a strong position

Nothing marred the unanimity of the proceedings
> ↳ 만장일치로 처리하는데 지장이 되는 것은 없었다

One drop of poison infects the whole ton of wine
> ↳ 미꾸라지 한 마리가 온 웅덩이를 흐린다

하나가 전체에게 나쁜 영향을 미친다는 말이다. 영어 속담에는 여러 가지가 있는데, 가장 자주 쓰이는 표현은 "One rotten apple spoils the barrel 썩은 사과 하나가 한 통을 썩게 한다"이다. 악한 한 사람이 한 가문, 한 나라를 욕되게 하는 것은 "It is an ill bird that fouls its own nest 자기의 둥지를 더럽히는 새는 나쁜 새이다"로 표현한다.
(=One scabbed sheep will mar a whole flock)
(=A hog that's bemired endeavors to bemire others)

Our control over is getting out of range
> ↳ 그들에 대한 저지력이 능력을 벗어나고 있어

People of every walk of life are gathered
> ↳ 각계각층 사람들이 모여있어

Pyung-soo will soon get with the program
> ↳ 평수는 곧 본격적으로 참여 할거야

Sang-soo is just stringing along
> ↳ 상수는 득이라도 볼까해서 편드는 척 할 뿐이야

She couldn't bear to be made a fool of herself
> ↳ 그 여자는 바보취급 당하는 게 견딜 수 없었어

She has already broken the rules; I can't let it pass this time
> ↳ 그녀가 이미 규정을 어겼으니 이번엔 그냥 넘어갈 수 없어

She has been able to carve out an enviable position in the broadcast journalism industry

---

› **unanimity** showing no disagreement, formed with the agreement of all

› **envy** resentful awareness of another's advantage, object of envy

↳ 그녀는 방송산업에서 부러워할 만한 지위를 개척해 나가고 있다

She's got strings attached
↳ 그 여자는 백이 있어

Spread the table, and contentions will cease
↳ 식탁을 차리고 나면 말다툼이 사라진다

Take him under your wing until he gets adjusted
↳ 그가 자리잡을 때까지 보살펴줘라

That guy table-hopped all night and talked to almost everyone in the bar
↳ 저 녀석은 교제를 넓히려고 술집 안에 있는 거의 모든 좌석마다 돌아다니면서 모든 손님들과 밤새워 얘기를 걸었다

That man is going hat in hand to him to get a grant
↳ 저 사람은 보조금을 받기 위해 그에게 굽실거리고 있는 거야

The enemy agents try to sow discontent among the people
↳ 적의 첩자들은 사람들 사이에 불만을 부추기고 있다

The first thing to learn in intercourse with others is non-interference with their own ways of being happy
↳ 남들과의 교제에서 먼저 알아야 할 것은 그들 고유의 특수한 방식으로 행복해지는데 대한 불간섭이다

The general feeling is against you
↳ 넌 일반의 호감을 못 사고 있어

The grassroots isn't organized on most issues
↳ 일반대중은 대부분의 문제에 있어서 조직화 되어있지 않다

The IMF crisis pulled him under
↳ 그는 아이엠에프 때문에 망했어

The IMF times drove us back on our life savings

· **contention** state of contending
· **cease** stop

↳ 아이엠에프가 닥치고 보니 평생 저축한 돈을 쓸 수밖에 없게 되었어

The rule covers all cases

↳ 이 규칙은 모든 경우에 적용돼

The rule stands

↳ 그 규칙은 아직도 유효하다(**Let that word stand** 그 단어는 그대로 두어라)

The unsettled and impatient youth was a rotten apple in the barrel

↳ 안정되지 못하고 잘 참지 못하는 젊은이는 사회에 악영향을 미쳤다

> 하나가 전체에게 나쁜 영향을 미친다는 말이다. 영어 속담에는 여러 가지가 있는데, 가장 자주 쓰이는 표현은 "One rotten apple spoils the barrel 썩은 사과 하나가 한 통을 썩게 한다"이다. 악한 한 사람이 한 가문, 한 나라를 욕되게 하는 것은 "It is an ill bird that fouls its own nest 자기의 둥지를 더럽히는 새는 나쁜 새이다"로 표현한다.
> (=One scabbed sheep will mar a whole flock)
> (=A hog that's bemired endeavors to bemire others)

There is strength in numbers

↳ 수가 많은 것이 강점이다

There's no rules

↳ 특별한 원칙은 없어

There's sucker born every minute

↳ 어디로 가나 봉은 있게 마련이다

These rules not made to be flung aside lightly

↳ 이 규칙은 가볍게 무시할만한 게 아니다

They are encouraged to make a voluntary contribution

↳ 그들은 자진해서 기부하도록 권유받는다

› **voluntary** done, made, or given freely and without expecting compensation

They are not content with the crumbs from the table
↳ 그들은 떡고물 정도로는 양이 차지 않아

They are trying to throw him to the wolves
↳ 그들은 그를 희생양으로 삼으려는 거야

They don't do it for nothing
↳ 그 사람들이 할 일 없어 그런 줄 아나?

They have got him on a pedestal
↳ 그들은 그를 우상화해 오고있다

This rule reads several ways
↳ 이 규칙은 귀에 걸면 귀고리, 코에 걸면 코 고리다

(=This rule admits of several interpretations)

Uniforms symbolize the oneness of the spirit and coordination essential to the winning
↳ 유니폼은 승리하는데 필수적인 단일정신과 일치를 상징한다

We are tied down by the rules
↳ 우리는 규칙에 묶여있다

We are under the gun right now
↳ 우린 압력(부담, 스트레스)을 받고 있어

We beat the odds together
↳ 우린 함께 난국을 헤쳐 나왔어

We figure on not more than 100
↳ 백 명을 넘지 않을 거야

We use confidential access numbers(security numbers)

▸ **crumb** small fragment
▸ **pedestal** support or foot of something upright

ㄴ 우린 여기서 비밀번호를 사용하지

Welcome to the club!
　　ㄴ 너만 당하는 게 아니라 나도 당했어

When the fox preaches, beware your geese
　　ㄴ 여우가 설교를 하거든 거위를 채어 가지 않을까 조심하라

Where might is master, justice is servant
　　ㄴ 불의가 통하면 도리가 안 통해

'Might'에는 '힘' 과 '권력'이라는 뜻이 있고, 'Right'에는 '정의', '권력'이라는
뜻이 있다. 여기서 'Might'는 '힘', 'Right'는 '정의'라는 뜻을 가지고 있다. 따
라서 직역하면 "힘이 정의를 만든다"가 된다.

Where there is no might right loses itself
　　ㄴ 힘이 없는 곳에서는 정의가 힘을 잃게 된다

Who eats his cock alone must saddle his horse alone
　　ㄴ 닭고기를 혼자 먹는 사람은 말 멍에도 혼자 채워야 한다

Why are you always furtive(in your manner)?
　　ㄴ 어째서 넌 늘 남의 눈치를 살피니?

Why are you always selling yourself short?
　　ㄴ 넌 왜 항상 낮춰 말하니?

You are not fit to be seen
　　ㄴ 이대로 남 앞에 나서면 안 돼

You are out of order
　　ㄴ 그건 규칙(법)에 어긋나

You have to put out some feelers to find out what's going on here
　　ㄴ 여기서 무슨 일이 일어나고 있는지 알려면 안테나를 좀 세워야 해

· **furtive**　slyly or secretly done

You need to reach out and meet people
ㄴ 넌 교제를 넓혀 사람들을 좀 만나야 해

You see in others who you are
ㄴ 다른 사람들을 통해서 자신을 알게된다

You‘ve been making your presence felt there already
ㄴ 넌 거기서 이미 없으면 표가 나는 존재가 돼버렸어

Your rudeness will come home to roost
ㄴ 남한테 무례하게 굴다간 남에게 무례한 대접을 받게될 것이다

> 남을 욕하거나 저주하면 결국에는 자신에게 다시 돌아온다는 말이다. 남에게
> 상처를 주는 말은 하지 말아야 한다는 뜻과 일맥상통한다(Reckless words
> pierce like a sword = 무분별한 말은 칼과 같이 사람을 찌른다).

‣ **pierce** enter or thrust into or through,
penetrate, see through

63. 산업   Industry

Better solid-waste management in the future will require a combination of resource recovery and resource reduction

    ↳ 장래에 고체 폐기물을 잘 처리하는 것은 자원 재생과 자원 절약 모두를 위해 필요하다

Control of a whole industry by a single company tends to eliminate competition

    ↳ 한 회사가 전체 산업을 장악하면 경쟁력이 없어지기 쉽다

Our many forest experts and scientific silvi-cultural practices are powerful resources we can be proud of

    ↳ 우리에게 많은 산림 전문가들이 있다는 것과 우리의 과학적인 조림활동은 자랑할만한 큰 자원이다

The electronic industry will bounce back to what it was in the good old days

    ↳ 전자산업이 왕년의 호황을 회복할 것이다

The embryonic wind industry is anxious to persuade people to use this new form of energy

    ↳ 이제 막 태동기에 있는 풍력에너지 산업부문에서는 사람들에게 이 신형 에너지의 사용을 설득하는데 노심초사하고 있다

The full effects of power shortage will make themselves felt soon

    ↳ 사람들은 곧 확연한 전력부족을 실감케 될 것이다

▸ **eliminate**   get rid of

▸ **embryo**   living being of its earliest stages of development

64. 삶 & 인생   Life

A busy life is the nearest thing to a purposeful life
> ↳ 바쁘게 사는 것이 목표 있는 생활에 가장 근접하는 일이다

A busy man has many calls on time
> ↳ 바쁜 사람은 뭔가에 시간을 많이 빼앗긴다

A full belly counsels well
> ↳ 목구멍이 포도청

> (=The hungry belly has no ears)
> (=It beats living on welfare)
> (=It's a living)
> (=It's a way to make a buck)
> (=It's one way to make a living)

A lot of jobless people don't know where their meals are coming from
> ↳ 많은 실직자들은 끼니 걱정을 해야 할 지경이야

A lot of youngsters these days live in sin
> ↳ 요즘 많은 젊은이들은 죄를 지으며 살고 있다

A recumbent lifestyle accelerates your decline
> ↳ 태만한 생활방식은 노화를 촉진시킨다

> **welfare**   prosperity relief
> **recumbent**   lying down

A successful man can't realize how hard an unsuccessful man finds life
> ↳ 성공한 사람은 실패한 사람의 어려운 삶을 알지 못한다

A useless life is early death
> ↳ 쓸데없는 인생은 일찍 죽는 것과 같다

A woman's whole life is a history of the affections
> ↳ 여자의 전 생애는 애정의 역사이다

After all, here today and gone tomorrow
> ↳ 그 일(인생)이 언제까지고 그대로 있을 줄 아나

All our yesterdays are summarized in our now, and all the tomorrows are ours to shape
> ↳ 모든 과거는 오늘 우리의 모습으로 요약되어있고 모든 미래는 우리가 만들어 가야할 일이다

All this talk of the happiest days of our life is only bunkum to us
> ↳ 동심에 돌아간 시절의 얘기를 해 봤자 우리에겐 부질없을 뿐이다

As he grew up in the boonies(boondocks), he doesn't know much about city life
> ↳ 그는 오지에서 자라나서 도시생활에 대해서는 별로 몰라

As one door closes, another one opens
> ↳ 사람이 죽으라는 법은 없다

> 아무리 큰 어려움이 있어도 헤쳐나갈 방도가 있다는 뜻이다. 자주 쓰는 속담으로 "If the sky falls we shall catch larks 하늘이 무너져도 솟아날 구멍이 있다"가 있다. 직역하면 "하늘이 무너지면 종달새를 잡을 수 있다"이며, 이는 하늘이 무너질까봐 노심초사하는 사람을 위로하는 뜻이다.

› **bunkum** nonsense
› **boondocks** rural area

Be street-smart(wise)
> ↳ 세상물정을 익혀라(**He has street-smarts** 그는 그 곳 사정에 밝아)

Better worry about need than live without heed
> ↳ 태평하게 사는 것보다 필요한 일에 걱정하며 사는 게 낫다

Bong-soo has a new lease on life
> ↳ 봉수가 완쾌 됐으니 명은 길겠군

Bosun's really been going through the changes lately
> ↳ 보선이는 요즘 사는 게 뭔지 몸소 체험하고 있어

Brigands demand your money or your life, whereas women require both
> ↳ 산적은 당신의 돈이나 생명을 요구하지만 여자는 그 둘 다를 요구한다

Busiest time finds the most leisure time
> ↳ 가장 바쁜 사람에게 가장 여가가 많다

Byung-soo tried to start over(off) with a clean slate
> ↳ 병수는 새 출발하려고 했다

Campus life can be beautiful and rewarding in spite of the unfavorable factors that can frustrate your ambitious goals
> ↳ 대학생활은 비록 불리한 요인들이 야심에 찬 목표를 좌절시킬지라도 아름답고 값진 일일 수 있다

Certain defects are necessary for the existence of individuality
> ↳ 개인이 생존하는데 있어서 일정한 허물은 부득이하다

Chang-ho's whole life is before him
> ↳ 창호의 인생은 지금부터다

Chang-soo didn't take that crappy job for(due to) his health
> ↳ 창수가 좋아서 그 시시한 일을 하고 있는 게 아니다(목구멍이 포도청이라 하고 있는 거지)

› **heed** pay attention, attention

Choon-ho has run up a lot of bills
ㄴ 춘호는 셈할게 많아

Choon-ho lives without life
ㄴ 춘호는 인생의 맛을 모르고 사는 거야

City dwellers are in a rush
ㄴ 도시 사람들은 시간에 쫓겨

Come in out of the rain(come down to earth)and learn to live within your means
ㄴ 현실로 돌아와서 수입 한도 내에서 살아야 해

Come out from under quickly and start a new life
ㄴ 빨리 궁지에서 벗어나 새 삶을 시작해라

Cut your coat according to your cloth
ㄴ 분수에 맞게 살아라

"분수에 맞게 살아라"는 교훈이 있다. 이는 영어로 "Cut your coat according to your cloth 몸에 맞게 옷을 맞춰 입어라"라고 표현한다.

Day alternates with night
ㄴ 낮과 밤은 번갈아 온다

Death is but an instant, life a long torment
ㄴ 죽음은 순간이지만 삶은 고문이다

Do something with your life
ㄴ 살아있는 동안 무엇인가를 해라

Do we not all spend the greater part of our lives under the shadow of an event that has not yet come to pass?
ㄴ 우리 모두는 아직 다가오지 않은 사건의 그늘 아래서 인생의 태반 이

· **torment**　extreme pain or anguish or a source of this

상을 소비하고 있지 않을까?

Do you keep the household accounts?
　　　↳ 가계부를 적습니까?

Doing nothing is doing ill
　　　↳ 아무 일도 안 하는 것은 나쁜 일을 하는 것이다

Don't expect that jack-off to get ahead in life
　　　↳ 저 식충이 녀석에게 잘 되리라는 기대는 하지마

Don't forget to keep a tally of everything that you spend
　　　　↳ 네가 지출하는 모든 계산을 잊지 말고 적어둬라

Don't just breeze along through life
　　　　↳ 인생을 얼렁뚱땅 살아선 안 돼

Don't live in a happy-go-lucky way
　　　　↳ 되는대로 살아선 안 돼

Don't miss out on life
　　　　↳ 인생을 즐기며 살아라

Don't try and run my life
　　　　↳ 나에게 이런 저런 간섭하지마

Doo-chul lives for it
　　　　↳ 두철인 그걸 낙으로 살아

Doo-soo's early life is a closed book
　　　　↳ 두수가 전에 무얼 했는지는 아무도 몰라

Easy street is what I really want now
　　　　↳ 이제 정말 편하게 살고싶어

Duck-soo intended to retire from active life, but fate decided otherwise
　　　　↳ 덕수는 사회활동에서 은퇴할 예정이었으나 운명이 이를 허락지 않

> ‣ **tally**　recorded amount, add or count up,
> 　　　match

았다

Even though prices have risen drastically, the government is not entirely to blame

↳ 물가가 엄청나게 올랐지만 정부만의 탓은 아니다

Every three years or so he pulls up his roots(stakes), moves to another city and starts again

↳ 그는 매번 3년 남짓 어느 곳이든 살다가 다른 도시로 옮겨 거기서 다시 시작해

Everyday brings its bread with it

↳ 산 입에 거미줄 치랴

Everyone has a right to enjoy his liberty, and much more his life

↳ 모든 사람이 자신의 권리를 누릴 권리가 있는데 하물며 자신의 삶을 누리는 것은 당연하다

Everyone has his own life

↳ 누구에게나 나름대로의 삶이 있어

Everyone's destiny is in his hands

↳ 사람의 운명은 자기 손에 달렸다

Everything eventually comes back to number one

↳ 모든 일이 결국은 본인에게 돌아오게 돼 있어

Everything goes by turns

↳ 세상은 돌고 도는 것

Everything happens to everybody sooner or later if there's time enough

↳ 시간이 충분하다면 언젠가는 모든 일은 모든 사람에게 닥쳐온다

Everything in nature has its own course and different degree of growth

---

› **stake** small post driven into the ground, bet, prize in a contest

↳ 모든 것이 자연에서 각기 제 갈길이 있고 각기 다르게 성장한다

Everything is not what you see

↳ 세상 모든 일이 보이는 그대로인 것은 아니다

Everything is sky high

↳ 모든 물가가 천정부지다

Fate finds for every man

↳ 모든 사람에게 운명이 있다

Few people are cheerful when they haven't even got roofs over their heads

↳ 살아갈 집마저 없는데도 쾌활해지는 사람은 거의 없다

Few things go right in life. Just learn to take the rough with the smooth

↳ 인생살이에 늘 제대로 돌아가기란 거의 없는 법이다. 신산 고초를 겪어나가는 방법을 배워 나가도록 해라

Financial success is not in the cards for me this month

↳ 이 달은 내가 경제적으로 잘 될 것 같지 않다

Folly is perennial and yet the human race has survived

↳ 인간의 바보짓은 영원하지만 그래도 인간은 생존해 왔다

For six years everything in his life seemed to be coming up roses

↳ 6년 동안 그의 일은 최고로 잘 되어 나가는 것 같았다

Four more paychecks and I'll be out of the hole

↳ 네 달치 월급만 받으면 빚은 면하게 될 거야

Games and recreation provide a release from tension and make people both more willing and fitting to resume their daily routines

↳ 게임과 레크레이션은 긴장이완을 제공하고 사람들의 일상생활을 기꺼이 다시 시작하고 잘 적응하게 한다

▸ **perennial**   present at all seasons of the year, continuing of live from   year to year

Get a life
ㄴ 그렇게 할 일이 없나

Gil-soo got away with his skin intact
ㄴ 길수는 구사일생으로 살아났다

Gil-soo has been keeping a low profile
ㄴ 길수는 조용히 살고 있어

Gil-soo let himself go yesterday and was the life of the party
ㄴ 어제 길수가 분위기잡고 나서서 파티를 확 살렸지

Had it not been for the sacrifices of our armed forces, most of us would have starved to death or might be leading a miserable life
ㄴ 군인들의 희생이 없었다면 우리들은 굶어죽거나 비참한 생활을 하게 되었을 것이다

He does himself fairly well
ㄴ 그는 꽤 호화롭게 산다

He enjoys living out of a suitcase
ㄴ 그는 떠돌이생활을 즐겨한다

He has already had long enough innings
ㄴ 그는 충분히 장수했어(수명, 활동, 전성기 등)

He has everything going for him
ㄴ 그에게는 아쉬운 것이 없다

He has it made
ㄴ 그는 없는 게 없어

He has seen much of life
ㄴ 그는 세상의 쓴맛 단맛을 다 본 사람이다

He has seen nothing of life
ㄴ 그는 세상 물정을 몰라

· **sacrifice** the offering of something precious
to s deity or the thing offered

He has seen the elephant
↳ 그는 세상 물정을 아는 사람이다

He hit it big
↳ 그 사람 땡 잡았어

> (=He hit the jackpot)

He is lifeless who is faultless
↳ 허물이 없다는 것은 생명이 없다는 것이다

He knows where his interests lie
↳ 이해득실에 밝은 사람

He knows which side his bread is buttered on
↳ 자기 이익을 챙길 줄 아는 사람

He lived in a lonely corner of reach out of the noisy world
↳ 그는 시끄러운 세상에서 떨어진 외딴곳에 살고있었다

He lives next door to us(two doors away from)
↳ 옆집에 살아

He musn't let himself get into a rut
↳ 그는 판에 박힌 생활을 해서는 안 된다

He noses a job in everything
↳ 그는 무슨 일이나 자기 이익 되는 일을 찾아낸다(사전에 흔히 수록된 표현이나 이해하지 못할 수도 있음)

He tried to lay his future course
↳ 그는 장래에 나아갈 길을 위해 노력했다

He was advised to go slow for a time, to give his heart a rest
↳ 그는 심장에 휴식을 줄 수 있도록 당분간 한적한 생활을 하도록 권유

· **jackpot** sum of money won
· **nose** defeat narrowly, pry, inch ahead

받았다

He was cut off in the prime of manhood
> ↳ 한창때 요절

He was destined to plod the path of toil
> ↳ 그는 고생길로 가야할 운명이었다

He was greatly admired until he began tripping up on his own standards
> ↳ 그는 자신이 세운 기준에 스스로 걸려들 때까지만 해도 매우 존경받았다

He who guards his mouth preserves his life, but he who opens wide his lips shall have destruction
> ↳ 입을 지키는 자는 그 생명을 보전하나 입술을 크게 벌리는 자에게는 멸망이 오느니라

He who keeps instruction is in the way of life, but he who refuses reproof goes astray
> ↳ 훈계를 지키는 자는 생명 길로 행하지만 징계를 버리는 자는 그릇 가느니라

He's a bird in a gilded cage
> ↳ 그가 겉으로는 화려해 보여도 구속된 생활을 하고 있는 거야

He's hanging on to life by a single hair
> ↳ 그는 절대절명의 궁지에 몰려있어

He's having one of his bad days
> ↳ 지금 그는 한참 어려운 때를 당하고 있는 중이다

He's in bad shape
> ↳ 그는 곤경에 처했어

· **plod** walk heavily or slowly, work laboriously and monotonously

· **toil** work hard and long

· **gild** cover with or as if with gold

(=He's in hot water)

Heavy work in youth is quiet resting in old age
> ↳ 젊어서 고생은 사서도 한다

Her life is with you now
> ↳ 이제 그녀에게는 네가 더 중요해

Her remarkable life and tragic death poignantly express the hopes and disappointments of a whole generation
> ↳ 그녀의 눈부신 생애와 비극적인 죽음은 모든 세대들의 희망과 절망을 찡하게 표현해준다

Her swashbuckling life of romance is now but a farce
> ↳ 그녀의 사랑에 대한 허황한 삶은 이제 단지 하나의 익살극 일 뿐이다

Hilly districts in the suburbs of the cities where people live from hand to mouth are called Daldongnae
> ↳ 하루 벌어 하루 먹는 사람들이 사는 도시근교의 고지대를 '달동네'라 한다

His career was paved with good intentions
> ↳ 그의 생애는 선의로 일관되어있었다

His life has only a few years to run(go)
> ↳ 그의 수명은 몇 년밖에 안 남았어

His life is a total disaster
> ↳ 그의 생활은 개판이야

His parents will be riding on his coattails for the rest of their life
> ↳ 그 사람 능력 덕분에 그의 부모는 앞으로 호강하겠군

Honesty is for the most part less profitable than dishonesty
> ↳ 대부분의 경우 정직한 것은 부정직한 것에 비해 손해를 본다

· **poignant** emotionally painful, deeply moving
· **suburb** residential area adjacent to a city

Honesty is the guiding principle of my life
ㄴ 정직은 나의 처세술이다

> 정직하면 대대손손 그 복을 받게 된다는 얘기가 있다(It pays to be honest) 정직함이 사람의 됨됨이를 말해주는 척도가 될 수 있다.(Honesty is the best policy 정직은 최상의 정책이다).

Hyun-soo is used to living out of a suitcase
ㄴ 현수는 여행자 같은 간소한 생활에 익숙해 있어

I had my glory days(=good old days)
ㄴ 한때 나도 잘 나갔는데

I have been lucky, knock on wood
ㄴ 내겐 행운이 따랐어, 앞으로도 그래야 하는데

I just filled the suitcase full of regrets
ㄴ 후회만 가득할 뿐이야

I merely opened my eyes to what I knew
ㄴ 이제야 눈이 뜨인 거야

I never knew a better time
ㄴ 그처럼 신났던 적이 없어

I shall be grateful to you all my life
ㄴ 이 은혜는 평생 잊지 않겠습니다

I try to push myself
ㄴ 난 스스로를 채찍질 하고있어

› **grateful** thankful or appreciative

(=I try to go the extra mile)
(=I try to excel in what I do)
(=I try to really apply myself)

I would do this, that, and the other
└ 여러 가지 손을 대봤지

I would rather stay than otherwise
└ 난 차라리 머물고 싶다

I'd give 100%
└ 전력을 다할게

I'm a man of the world, though I say it myself
└ 내가 말하긴 뭣하지만 난 세상물정을 좀 알아

I'm not the man that I once was
└ 예전의 내가 아냐

I'm quite well where I am
└ 현 상태에 만족

I'm very well where I am
└ 난 현재의 위치에 만족한다

If I'm lucky at first, I don't press my work
└ 처음에 잘 됐다해서 계속 요행을 바라진 않아

If life were eternal all interest and anticipation would vanish
└ 인생이 영원하다면 모든 관심과 기대가 사라질 것이다

If one is to lead one's life efficiently, one must separate what's essential from what's not
└ 능률적인 생활을 영위하려면 필요한 일과 그렇지 않은 일을 구별해야 한다

› **excel** do extremely well or far better than

If you pull off this deal, you'll be fixed for life
↳ 넌 이번 거래만 잘 해내면 팔자가 늘어질 거야

If you value your life, never say a word
↳ 입도 벙긋 안 하는 게 신상에 이로워

If you win the lottery, you'll be set up
↳ 네가 복권만 당첨되면 팔자가 늘어지는 거야

Ignorance is not innocence but sin
↳ 무지는 순진함이 아니라 죄이다

In all labor there's profit, but chatter leads only to poverty
↳ 모든 수고에는 이익이 있어도 입술의 말은 궁핍을 이룰 뿐이다

In life, there are ups and downs
↳ 인생에는 좋을 때도 있고 나쁠 때도 있어

> 살다 보면 모든 일이 잘 될 때도 있고, 잘 안 될 때도 있는 법이다. 한국 속
> 담에는 "양지가 음지 되고, 음지가 양지된다"라는 표현이 있고, 영어 속담에
> 는 "Life is full of ups and downs"가 있다.

In our life there is a single color; as on an artist's palette, which provides the meaning of life and art
↳ 우리의 삶에는 화가의 팔레트처럼 삶과 예술의 의미를 주는 한가지 색깔이 있다

In the way of righteous is life, and in its pathway there's no death
↳ 의로운 길에 생명이 있나니 그 길에는 사망이 없느니라

In with the luck, out with the devil
↳ 복은 들어오고 화는 물러가라

In-ho needs some time to pick up the pieces of his life after the

---

› **chatter** utter rapidly succeeding sounds, talk fast or too much

› **righteous** acting or being in accordance with what is just or moral

accident
　　　↳ 인호는 사고 후 뒷수습을 하는데 얼마간의 시간이 필요해

In-soo is still green to the ways of the world
　　　↳ 인수는 아직 세상 물정에 어두워

Instead of extricating yourself from situations in which you feel uncomfortable, try to face them and overcome them
　　　↳ 불편한 상황을 피해가기 보다 정면으로 맞서서 극복하도록 해라

Is this what life is at(after) all?
　　　↳ 이렇게 라도 살아야 하나?

> (=Is this how I'm to live my life?)

It doesn't make no mind(matter) if we have college degrees or not
　　　↳ 우리가 대학을 나왔거나 아니거니 상관없어

It has been up quick and down quick with me
　　　↳ 내 인생은 부침이 심했어

> 살다 보면 모든 일이 잘 될 때도 있고, 잘 안 될 때도 있는 법이다. 한국 속담에는 "양지가 음지 되고, 음지가 양지된다"라는 표현이 있고, 영어 속담에는 "Life is full of ups and downs"가 있다.

It is every man for himself and the devil takes the hindmost
　　　↳ 자신의 일을 자기가 돌보지 않으면 버림받고 말게 돼

It matters not how long the man lives, but how he lives=It's not how long, but how well we live
　　　↳ 얼마나 오래 사느냐가 아니라 얼마나 사람답게 사느냐가 중요하다

‣ **extricate** set or get free from an entanglement or difficulty

‣ **hindmost** fathest to the rear

It was fun while it lasted
> ↳ 그 때가 좋았지

It won't be over till the fat lady sings
> ↳ 사람팔자 알 수 없다

It's a bad plan that admits of no modification
> ↳ 수정의 여지가 없는 계획은 나쁜 계획이다

It's a sign of the times
> ↳ 세상이 그렇게 되어가고 있어

It's a twist of fate
> ↳ 기구한 운명이군

> (=It was meant to happen this way)
> (=It's pure destiny)

It's all due to the stars you were born under
> ↳ 그건 다 네 팔자소관

It's all I can do to keep my head above water with the work I have
> ↳ 주어진 일에 급급할 정도로 어렵게 지내고 있어

It's all in your(a) life time
> ↳ 모두 네 운명이다

It's all or nothing with me
> ↳ 그 일에 내 사활이 걸렸어

It's all part of the battle of life
> ↳ 세상사가 원래 그래

It's an enemy who keeps you straight
> ↳ 적이 있음으로써 바르게 살아가게 된다

· **modify** limit the meaning of, change

It's difficult always to live by our principles
> ↳ 언제나 원칙대로만 살기는 어렵다

It's my life
> ↳ 내 인생은 내가 알아서 해

> (=Don't meddle in my affairs)
> (=Don't tell me how to live my life)

It's neck or nothing
> ↳ 죽느냐 사느냐 하는 일이다

It's not easy to do well in life
> ↳ 이 세상을 잘 헤쳐나가기가 그리 쉬운 일은 아니다

> (=It's not easy to be successful in life)
> (=It's not easy to get on well in society)

It's not the mountain we conquer but ourselves
> ↳ 우리가 정복하는 것은 산이 아니라 우리 자신이다

It's only in adventure that some people succeed in knowing themselves
> ↳ 모험을 통해서만이 자기 자신을 알게되는 사람들도 있다

It's sad to see him mooning(moping) about the house like this
> ↳ 그가 집안에서 울적한 세월을 보내고 있는 게 안 됐어

It's such a fight for me to survive from payday to payday
> ↳ 이 달 월급을 타면 저 달 월급을 탈 때까지 빠듯하게 살고 있어

It's too late to spare when the bottom is bare

‣ **meddle** interfere

ㄴ 바닥이 드러난 다음 절약해봤자 때는 늦다

It's vanity to desire a long life and to take no heed of a good life
ㄴ 장수를 소망하면서 훌륭한 삶을 소홀히 함은 허영이다

It's very difficult to get ahead of the game
ㄴ 어려움을 이기고 일을 이뤄(출세해) 나간다는 건 매우 힘든 일이야

Jealousy becomes subordinate to the need to survive in times of exigency
ㄴ 위기상황에서는 질투심이 살아남는다는 필요에 종속된다

Jin-soo lives well
ㄴ 진수는 잘 살아('풍족하게' 및 '깨끗하게'의 두 가지 뜻)

Jong-soo takes life easy
ㄴ 종수는 태평하게 살아

Jung-tae retired last year, and is going stir crazy now
ㄴ 정태는 작년에 퇴직했는데 지금은 좀이 쑤셔서 못 견딘다

Just as fear encourages life, fear protects it
ㄴ 두려움은 인생을 위태롭게 하는 만큼 그것을 막아준다

Lady luck is smiling on me
ㄴ 내게 행운이 따르고 있어

Learn to concentrate as early in life as possible
ㄴ 될 수 있는 한 젊을 때부터 주의를 집중하는 법을 배워라

Learn to obey before you command
ㄴ 남에게 명령하기 전에 남의 명령을 듣는 것을 배워라

Let's live it up while we can
ㄴ 할 수 있을 때 즐기며 살자

Life gives me a high
ㄴ 난 내 생활을 즐기고 있어

› **vanity**　futility or something that is futile, undue pride in oneself, makeup table

› **exigency**　urgent need, requirements of the situation(pl)

Life has a value only when it has something valuable as its object
　ㄴ 인생은 그 목적으로 가치 있는 것을 지녀야만 가치가 있다

Life is a continued struggle to be what we are not, and to do what we can't
　ㄴ 인생은 현재의 자신이 아닌 자신이 되어보려는 것과 할 수 없는 일을 해 보려는 계속된 몸부림이다

Life is a maze in which we take the wrong turning before we have learned to walk
　ㄴ 인생은 우리가 걸어가기를 배우기도 전에 방향을 잘못 잡아 나아가는 미로이다

Life is a process where people mix and match, fall apart and come back together
　ㄴ 인생은 섞여서 어울리고, 헤어졌다가 다시 함께 되돌아가는 과정이다

Life is a system of half-truths and lies
　ㄴ 인생은 반의 사실과 반의 거짓으로 된 체계이다

Life is a tragedy wherein we sit as spectators for a while and then act our part in it
　ㄴ 인생은 한 동안 구경꾼으로 앉아 있다가 그 다음은 무대에 올라가게 되는 비극의 하나이다

Life is all like that
　ㄴ 산다는 게 다 그런 거지 뭐

> (=It's about the same with everybody)
> (=It can happen to any one)
> (=That's how people get along with their life)

‣ **maze**　confusing network of passages, bewilder

‣ **spectator**　one who looks on

Life is an irreversible process and for that reason its future can never be a repetition of the past
> ↳ 인생은 되돌릴 수 없는 과정이기에 인생의 장래는 결코 과거의 반복이 될 수 없다

Life is but an empty dream
> ↳ 인생은 일장춘몽이다

Life is earnest and real
> ↳ 삶은 진지하고 엄숙한 것이다

Life is ephemeral and it's what happens after death that's important
> ↳ 인생은 덧없는 것이고 중요한 것은 사후에 어떻게 될 것이냐 이다

Life is for each man a solitary cell whose walls are mirrors
> ↳ 각 개인에게 인생은 거울 붙인 벽으로 된 독방에 갇힌 것이다

Life is for the living
> ↳ 인생은 살아있는 사람을 위한 것이다

Life is full of surprises
> ↳ 오래 살고 볼일이야(희한한 일을 다 보는군)

Life is full of troubles(and trials)
> ↳ 인생은 고난과 시련에 가득 차 있다

인생을 고난으로 표현한 속담은 여러 가지가 있다. "Life is pilgrimage 인생은 순례의 여행이다", "We must eat a peck of dirt before we die 살다 보면 인생의 쓴맛을 보게 마련이다" 등이다.
(=If wishes were horses, beggars would ride)

› **ephemeral** short-lived
› **solitary** alone, secluded, single

Life is full of ups and downs
> ↳ 양지가 음지 된다. 살다보면 좋을 때도 있고 나쁠 때도 있다

> 살다 보면 모든 일이 잘 될 때도 있고, 잘 안 될 때도 있는 법이다. 한국 속 담에는 "양지가 음지 되고, 음지가 양지된다"라는 표현이 있고, 영어 속담에 는 "Life is full of ups and downs"가 있다.

Life is half spent before one knows what life is
> ↳ 인생이 무엇인지 알기도 전에 반은 지나가 버린다

Life is just one damned thing after another
> ↳ 인생살이는 시름의 연속이다

> 인생을 고난으로 표현한 속담은 여러 가지가 있다. "Life is pilgrimage 인 생은 순례의 여행이다", "We must eat a peck of dirt before we die 살 다 보면 인생의 쓴맛을 보게 마련이다" 등이다.

Life is life, whether spent in tears or laughter
> ↳ 울어도 한평생, 웃어도 한평생

Life is like playing a violin solo in public and learning the instrument as one goes on
> ↳ 인생은 대중 앞에서 바이올린을 연주하는 것과 같고 연주해 가면서 배우게 된다

Life is like riding a bicycle. You don't fall off unless you stop pedaling
> ↳ 삶은 자전거 타기와 같다. 페달을 밟는 한 떨어지지 않는다

· **solo** performance by only one person

Life is no picnic

↳ 산다는 것이 쉬운 것이 아니다

Life is the art of drawing sufficient conclusions from insufficient premises

↳ 인생은 불충분한 전제에서 충분한 결론을 끌어내는 기술이다

Life is to be enjoyed; not simply endured

↳ 인생은 즐기기 위한 것이지 참아내기만 하려는 것이 아니다

Life isn't always what you like

↳ 세상사 생각대론 안 돼

Life lies before you

↳ 너의 인생은 지금부터다

Life must be first consideration

↳ 우선 살고 봐야 할 일이다

Life protracted is woe

↳ 질질 끌며 사는 것은 고통이다

Life takes the long way round to circumvent barrenness

↳ 인생은 무미건조함을 피해 나아가는 긴 우회로이다

Like it or not, that's life

↳ 세상살이를 운명으로 받아들일 수밖에 없다

사람에게는 모두다 타고난 운명이 있다. 자신이 자신의 삶을 위해서 열심히 노력할 수는 있지만, 결국에는 모두 운명에 맡기는 것이다. 그래서 어떠한 절망이 있더라도 운명에 순종하라고 하였다(What must be, must be 피할 수 없는 운명에는 순종하여라).

· **protract** prolong

· **woe** deep suffering, misfortune

· **barrenness** unproductiveness of life, uninteresting

Live life by the minute

         ↳ 인생을 최대한 즐겨라

> (=Enjoy every moment)
> (=Make the most of your life)
> (=Live life to the fullest)

Lives come and go

         ↳ 인생은 한 번 왔다 가는 것

Make money as much as possible and live a rich life

         ↳ 돈은 개 같이 벌어서 정승같이 써라(쓴다)

> (=Miserly savings, and lavish spending)
> (=Narrow gathered, wisely spent)

Make the most of your life

         ↳ 인생을 후회 없이 살아라

Man pines to live but can't endure the days of his life

         ↳ 사람은 애타게 살고싶어 하면서도 나날의 삶을 견뎌내지 못한다

Man's real life is happy, chiefly because he's ever expecting that it soon will be so

         ↳ 인간의 실제 생활은 행복하다, 주된 원인은 그가 행복해 지리라고 기
           대하기 때문이다

Many city dwellers yearn for the idyllic life of the country

         ↳ 많은 도시 거주자들은 시골의 목가적인 생활을 동경한다

› **lavish** expending or expended profusely | › **idyllic** poem describing peaceful country life, fit subject for an idyll

Many new discoveries have been brought to light
ㄴ 많은 새 사실이 밝혀졌어

Many troubles of life can be spared when you learn to say "No"
ㄴ "아니오" 라고 말하기를 제대로 배울 때 많은 문제들이 지나쳐 갈 수 있다

Men cling to life even at the cost of enduring great misfortune
ㄴ 사람은 큰 고생을 참아가면서 삶에 애착한다

Min-gyoo lives by his wits
ㄴ 민규는 남들에게 사기 치면서 살고있지

Min-ho lives very near
ㄴ 민호는 이웃에(검소하게) 산다(두 가지 뜻)

Most human beings go through life only partially aware of the full range of their abilities
ㄴ 대부분의 사람들은 자신들이 가진 능력 전체범위의 일부분만 인식한 채 인생을 살아간다

Mother wiped away our tears, helped us get over our grief and comforted us when life wasn't fair
ㄴ 어머니는 삶이 평탄하지 못할 때 우리의 눈물을 닦아주고 우리가 슬픔을 극복하도록 도와주고 위로해 주셨다

> 모성애를 나타내는 문장이다. 모성애는 모든 생명체가 가지고 있는 본능이다(The mother's breath is always sweet = 어머니의 숨결은 언제나 달다).

› **cling** adhere firmly, hold on tightly

My best days are behind me
↳ 좋은 시절 다 갔어

> (=I lost my get-up and go)

My father implanted good ideas that have stayed with me all my life
↳ 아버지는 내가 평생 가지고있던 좋은 생각을 심어준 분이다

My whole life just fell into place
↳ 인생의 모든 일이 잘 풀리기 시작했어

Naked come we into the world and naked shall we depart
↳ 맨손으로 왔다가 맨손으로 가는 게 인생이다(공수래 공수거)

> "인생은 빈손으로 와서 빈손으로 간다"라는 말을 흔히 쓴다. 한국에서는 한문 성어를 이용하여 '공수래 공수거'라는 말을 많이 하지만, 영어에서는 'Naked body 빈 몸'이라는 표현을 쓴다.
> (=Naked I came into the world, and naked I shall go out of it)

Nam-soo too wanted to live in wealth and honor, but he couldn't quite turn the trick
↳ 남수도 부귀영화를 원했지만 소원대로 되진 않았어

Necessity is the mother of invention
↳ 궁하면 통한다

› **depart** go away or away from, die

절실히 필요할 때에는 보통 때에 생각지도 못했던 해결책이 나오게 마련이다. 보통 "Necessity is the mother of invention"을 직역하여 "필요는 발명의 어머니다"를 쓴다. 인간의 모든 발명은 인간의 삶을 더 윤택하고 편리하게 만들기 위한 필요에서 비롯되었다.

No life is without its regrets
↳ 후회 없는 삶이란 없다

No man has tasted full flavor of life until he has known poverty, love, and war
↳ 가난, 사랑, 전쟁을 알기 전에는 아무도 인생을 안다고 할 수 없다

No matter how famous he became, he never lost sight of the fact that he had born in slums
↳ 그는 아무리 유명해져도 자신이 빈민가 출신이라는 사실을 잊지 않았다

Nobody in all the world is safe from unhappiness
↳ 불행을 피할 수 있는 사람은 아무도 없다

사람의 지위 고하에 따라 불행한 일이 선별적으로 일어나는 것은 아니다. 불행이 언제 닥칠지 모르니까 항상 유비무환의 자세를 가져야 한다(=We must be ready, because accidents will come at an hour when we do not expect them).

Nobody is so unhappy as he supposes
↳ 자신이 생각하는 것만큼 불행한 사람은 아무도 없어

Nothing is beneath you if it is in the direction of your life
↳ 살기 위한 일이라면 아무 것도 창피할 일이 없다

Nothing is certain but death and taxes

‣ **suppose** assume to be true, expect, think probable ┊ ‣ **beneath** below

↳ 인생에 있어서 확실한 건 죽음과 세금이다

Nothing is miserable unless you think it is

↳ 비참하다고 생각하지 않는 한 비참한 일은 없다

Nothing is more unbearable than the sheer drudgery of that job

↳ 순전히 그 따분한 일만 하는 것 보다 더 견딜 수 없는 일이 없다

Nothing is obnoxious as other people's luck

↳ 다른 사람의 행운보다 불쾌한 것이 없다(놀부)

남이 잘 되면 질투가 난다는 뜻이다. 질투를 표현할 때 "To turn green with envy 질투로 얼굴이 녹색이 된다"라고 한다. Green face 는 한국말로 창백함을 나타내는 표현이고, 이는 공포(fear), 질투심(jealousy), 아픔(sickness)을 나타낼 때 쓰인다.

Nothing is so good for an ignorant man as silence

↳ 잘 모르는 사람에게는 가만히 있는 것보다 상책이 없다

Nothing is troublesome that we do willingly

↳ 자진해서 하는 일은 성가시지 않다

Now he's living on borrowed time

↳ 그는 이제 새 생명을 얻어서 살고있어(기적같이 살아서)

Now she's had it never so good

↳ 이제 그 여자는 형편이 풀렸어(지금까지 형편이 풀리지 않았어)

Now this is the life

↳ 이제야 살맛이 나는군

Old sins cast long shadows

↳ 죄짓고는 못살아

One must have lived long to see how short life is

· **drudge** do hard or boring work
· **obnoxious** repugnant

ㄴ 오래 살아보지 않고서는 인생이 얼마나 짧은지를 알 수 없어

Our goal must be set at the highest possible horizon so we can work toward that goal step by step
ㄴ 우리의 목표를 가능한 한 최고 수준으로 세워야 그 목표를 향해 한 걸음씩 나아갈 수 있게 된다

Our life is but a span
ㄴ 사람의 일생은 짧아

Our life is what our thoughts make it
ㄴ 인생은 생각하기 나름이다

Our standard of living not only depends on our income, but also on the amount of leisure we enjoy
ㄴ 우리의 생활수준은 소득수준만이 아니라 즐길 수 있는 여가시간의 많음에 달려있다

Pain of love lasts a lifetime
ㄴ 사랑의 아픔은 평생 남는다

Please don't bring back those blotted-out memories
ㄴ 나의 지워(잊어)졌던 기억을 되살아나게 하지마

Put some life into your work
ㄴ 일에 좀 더 정력을 쏟아라

Put that heartbreak behind you and get on with your normal life again
ㄴ 그 비통함을 다 잊어버리고 정상적인 생활로 되돌아가라

Roll with the punches
ㄴ 세상이 더러워도 형편대로 살아

· **income** money gained as from work or investment

"분수에 맞게 살아라"는 교훈이 있다. 이는 영어로 "Cut your coat according to your cloth 몸에 맞게 옷을 맞춰 입어라"라고 표현한다.

Sang-soo doesn't have a pot to piss in
> ㄴ 상수는 알거지야

Sang-soo is a tumbleweed
> ㄴ 상수는 역마살이 끼었어

(=Sang-soo is always floating(drifting) from place to place)
(=Sang-soo's shoes are made of running leather)

Scatter with one hand, gather with two
> ㄴ 한 손으로 뿌리고(돈을 쓰고) 두 손으로 거두어라(벌어라)=분수 맞게 살아라

"분수에 맞게 살아라"는 교훈이 있다. 이는 영어로 "Cut your coat according to your cloth 몸에 맞게 옷을 맞춰 입어라"라고 표현한다.

She had her moments too
> ㄴ 그 여자도 잘 나가던 때가 있었어

She's just keeping the wolf from the door
> ㄴ 그녀는 겨우 입에 풀칠이나 하는 정도야

She's long sung the praise of country life and finally moved to Yong-in
> ㄴ 그녀는 오랫동안 전원생활에 찬사를 보내더니 끝내 용인으로 이사를 갔다

› **drift**   float or be driven along (as by a current), wander without purpose

Shrouds have no pockets
> ↳ 빈손으로 왔다가 빈손으로 간다

> "인생은 빈손으로 와서 빈손으로 간다"라는 말을 흔히 쓴다. 한국에서는 한문
> 성어를 이용하여 '공수래 공수거'라는 말을 많이 하지만, 영어에서는 'Naked
> body 빈 몸'이라는 표현을 쓴다.
> (=Naked I came into the world, and naked I shall go out of it)

Since the IMF times, most people have fallen on hard times
> ↳ 아이엠에프 이후 대부분의 사람들이 어려움을 겪게 됐어

So, your whole life seems to be going to pot? That makes two of us
> ↳ 그래서 네 인생이 망가진 것 같다고? 너만 그런 게 아니라 나도 그래

Society is not so naive
> ↳ 세상살이가 그리 만만한 게 아냐

> (=Everything has a price)

Socrates maintained that an unexamined life is not worth living
> ↳ 소크라테스는 시련 없는 삶은 살 가치가 없다고 말했다

Some people just drift through life
> ↳ 어떤 사람들은 인생을 보람 없이 빈둥거리며 살지

Somebody like Jung-soo, who came up the hard way, understands reality better than a person who always had money
> ↳ 정수같이 가난(어려움)을 체험으로 배운 사람은 늘 돈이 아쉬운 줄 모르는 사람보다 현실을 잘 이해한다

Someday your whole life will fall into place

· **shroud** cloth put over a corpse, cover or screen

┗ 언젠가 네 인생의 모든 일이 잘 풀릴 거다

Somehow life doesn't always pay off to those who are most insistent
┗ 왠지 모르지만 인생살이는 반드시 고집스러운 사람에게 보상이 돌아오는 건 아니다

Sometimes accidents happen in life from which we have need of a madness to excite ourselves successfully
┗ 우리의 삶에는 때로 우리 자신을 자극하여 성공할 수 있게 하는 미친 짓을 필요로 하는 사건이 생기기도 한다

Sometimes we may be buffeted by waves of adversity as we reach our goal
┗ 때로는 우리가 목표를 달성하기 위해 역경의 파도와 싸워나가야 할 때도 있다

Start planning on your second career while you are on your first one
┗ 현직에 있을 때 제 2의 인생을 설계하라

Such is life
┗ 그런 것이 인생이다

Sung-hi is her usual self again
┗ 성희는 본래의 모습으로 되돌아갔어

Sung-min lives on his own fancy
┗ 성민인 제멋에 살아

> (=Everyone got their own thing)

Sung-moon is a man of the world
┗ 성문이는 인생의 쓴맛 단맛을 다 봤어

Survival is part of the law of the jungle

· **buffet** hit especially repeatedly
· **fancy** liking, whim, imagination

ㄴ 생존은 약육강식의 일부이다

> (Big fish eat little fish) 약한 것은 결국 강한 것에게 먹히고 만다. 다윈은 먹이사슬을 이론화 한 후 인간 사회에도 약육강식의 법칙을 적용시켰다. 강자 밑의 약자는 제대로 능력을 발휘하지 못한다.

Tai-jung has to cut his own grass
> ㄴ 태정인 혼자 힘으로 살아가야 해

That is then, this is now
> ㄴ 그때는 그때고 지금은 지금이야

> (=Times have changed)
> (=That's all in the past)
> (=You are talking about the past)

That snobbish always gets sententious about living a righteous life and then goes about his own sinful life when no one is watching
> ㄴ 그 속물근성의 위선자는 늘 올바르게 사는 현명한 사람인체 하다가 아무도 보는 사람이 없으면 죄로 가득 찬 삶을 살고있다

That's life these days
> ㄴ 요즘은 다 그렇게 사는걸

That's the story of my life
> ㄴ 그건 내가 평생 해 왔던 일이야

That's what I've got to face
> ㄴ 그게 내가 받아들일 현실

The absent are always wrong(The absent party is always to blame)

› **sententious** using pompous language
› **absent** not present, keep oneself away

ↆ 잘못된 일은 모두 없는 사람의 몫으로 돌아간다

The art of life is to know how to enjoy a little and to endure much

ↆ 삶의 지혜는 적게 즐기고 많이 참는데 있다

The atrocious murderer felt no compunction at having taken a human life

ↆ 흉악한 살인자는 사람을 살해할 때 양심의 가책이 없었다

The banished dictator was relegated to a life of shame and isolation

ↆ 추방된 그 독재자의 생활은 치욕적이고 고립된 삶으로 전락했다

The best things in life are free

ↆ 인생에서 최고로 좋은 일은 돈이 들지 않고도 얻을 수 있는 것이다
(맑은 공기, 행복감, 아름다운 경관 등)

The devil looks after his own

ↆ 행운은 엉뚱한 사람에게 굴러가게 돼 있어

The devil tempts all idle men, but idle men tempt the devil

ↆ 악마는 모든 게으른 사람을 유혹하고 게으른 사람은 악마를 유혹한다

The drowning man is not troubled by rain

ↆ 큰 역경에 처한 사람에게는 작은 불편이 문제되지 않는다

The evil that men do lives after them

ↆ 생전에 지은 죄는 죽어서도 살아남는다

The ex-convict's anecdote ranged from his days as a shoplifter to his life as a fortuneteller

ↆ 그 출소자의 일화는 가게 들치기에서 점쟁이로 살아가기까지에 걸쳐 있었다

The fish market springs to life at dawn

ↆ 새벽이 되면 어시장이 활기를 띠지

The follies a man regrets are those he didn't commit when he had

---

· **banish** force by authority to leave a country, expel

· **relegate** govern according to rule, adjust to a standard

the opportunity
　　　↳ 사람은 기회가 주어졌을 때 바보짓을 해 보지 않은 것을 후회한다

The follies of one man is the fortune of another
　　　↳ 한 사람의 어리석은 짓은 다른 사람에게 행운이 된다

The future has a way of arriving unannounced
　　　↳ 미래는 미리 알리지 않고 다가온다

The future is the past again, entered through another gate
　　　↳ 미래는 또 다른 문으로 들어간 과거이다

The game of life is a game of boomerangs
　　　↳ 삶의 게임은 부메랑 게임이다

> 남을 욕하거나 저주하면 결국에는 자신에게 다시 돌아온다는 말이다. 남에게 상처를 주는 말은 하지 말아야 한다는 뜻과 일맥상통한다(Reckless words pierce like a sword = 무분별한 말은 칼과 같이 사람을 찌른다).

The gods give to mortals not everything at the same time
　　　↳ 신은 인간에게 모든 것을 동시에 주지는 않는다

The good die young
　　　↳ 곧은 나무가 먼저 찍힌다

> '미인박명(美人薄命)', "곧은 나무가 먼저 찍힌다"라는 말이 한국에선 자주 쓰인다. 세상에 이로운 사람이 요절할 때 아쉬움을 표현하는 말이다. 영어에서는 말 그래도 "The good die young 좋은 사람은 어려서 죽는다"라고 한다. (=The best go first)

The great and glorious masterpiece of man is to know how to live to

---

· **folly**　foolishness, something foolish
· **masterpiece**　great piece of work

purpose
> ↳ 사람에게 위대하고 영광스러운 걸작은 어떻게 목적을 위해 사는가 이다

The great end of life is not knowledge but action
> ↳ 인생의 큰 목표는 지식이 아닌 행동에 있다

The greatest mistake in life is to be continually fearing you'll make one
> ↳ 인생 최대의 잘못은 실수를 하지 않을까 하는 끝없는 우려이다

The lines in his face reflect a hard life
> ↳ 그의 얼굴에 새겨진 주름들은 그가 많은 고생을 했음을 보여준다

The man barely started his life before he lost it
> ↳ 그 사람은 인생을 채 시작하기도 전에 목숨을 잃었다

The man who has lived the longest is not he who has spent the greatest sensibility of life
> ↳ 인생을 가장 길게 산 사람은 가장 나이를 많이 먹은 사람이 아니라 인생을 가장 잘 맛보며 살아온 사람이다

The man who is lazy to work for his living is the most ready to beg or to steal
> ↳ 게을러서 생계를 위해 일하는 것조차 싫어하는 사람은 거지 노릇이나 절도 짓을 가장 하기 쉬운 사람이다

The mouth of righteous is a well of life, but the violence covers mouth of the wicked
> ↳ 의인의 입은 생명의 입이지만 악인의 입은 악을 머금었느니라

The paths of glory lead but to the grave
> ↳ 영광을 찾아가는 길은 죽음으로 끌려가는 길이다

The reckoning spoils the relish
> ↳ 즐거운 기분은 계산 때에 잡친다

> **reckon**　count or calculate, consider, rely (+on)
>
> **relish**　keen enjoyment, highly seasoned sauce (as of pickles)

The recompence of a man's hand will be rendered to him
　ㄴ 사람은 손으로 행한 대로 보상받으리라

The rich man has lived well and not done a stroke of work all his life
　ㄴ 그 부자는 유복하게 살면서 평생 일이라고는 하나도 안 했다

The secret of happiness is to fill one's life with activity
　ㄴ 행복의 비결은 인생을 활동적으로 사는 일이다

The soul which is not at peace with itself can't be at peace with the world
　ㄴ 마음이 평화롭지 못한 사람은 세상을 편안히 살아갈 수 없다

The strong must be just and the weak secure
　ㄴ 강자는 정의롭고 약자는 보호받아야 한다

The supreme happiness of life is the conviction that we are loved
　ㄴ 인생 최고의 행복은 자신이 사랑을 받고 있다는 확신이다

The third time is the charm
　ㄴ 세 번째는 행운이 따르는 법이다

The virtues of the past seem greater and its faults are reduced
　ㄴ 과거의 장점은 더욱 큰 것처럼 보이고 결점은 줄어든다

The wicked covets the catch of evil man, but the root of the righteous yields fruit
　ㄴ 악인은 불의의 이를 탐하나 의인은 그 뿌리로 인하여 결실 하느니라

The wicked flee when no man pursue
　ㄴ 악인은 아무도 쫓지 않는데도 도망치기 바쁘다

The wicked is ensnared by the transgression of his lips, but the righteous will come through trouble
　ㄴ 악인은 입술의 허물로 인하여 그물에 걸려도 의인은 환난에서 벗어나

‣ **recompense** give compensation to　　　‣ **transgression** sin
‣ **ensnare** snare

느니라

The writer's life seethes within but not without
    ㄴ 글 쓰는 사람의 삶은 마음속에서 끓고 밖으로는 끓지 않는다

There comes a time in every man's life when he has to think
    ㄴ 모든 사람의 삶에는 생각해야 할 때가 찾아온다

There is no fence against ill fortune'
    ㄴ 불운을 막을 울타리는 없다

There is the greatest practical benefit in making a few failures early in life
    ㄴ 초년에 몇 번 실패해보는 것은 실제로 큰 이익이 된다

There isn't enough hours in a day
    ㄴ 눈코 뜰 새 없이 바쁘다

There's more to life than money(success , this office)
    ㄴ 돈(성공)만이 인생의 전부가 아니다

There's those hold life cheap, but they are not our kind
    ㄴ 목숨을 늘 초개같이 여기는 사람도 있지만 우린 그렇지 않아

They have cleaved only to each other for their entire lives
    ㄴ 그들은 평생 서로를 위해 정조를 지켰어

They have gone through many twists and turns together during their lifetime
    ㄴ 그들은 평생 많은 우여곡절을 같이 겪어가며 살고있어

Things are escaped that promise us a smile
    ㄴ 행운이 한 번 이상 되풀이해서 찾아오기는 어려워

Things were better in old days
    ㄴ 옛날이 좋았지

· **seethe** become violently agitated
· **cleave** adhere

This is painted to the life
　　　↳ 이 그림은 실물대로 그렸어

Those days can't be brought back
　　　↳ 옛날로 되돌아 갈 순 없어

Those days have passed(gone) by the board
　　　↳ 그 시절은 아주 지나갔다

Those were times
　　　↳ 생각하면 신나는 세월이었지. 그 때가 정말 좋았어

Those who have never been ill are incapable of real sympathy for great many misfortunes
　　　↳ 앓아보지 않은 사람은 많은 불행에 참된 동정을 가질 수 없다

Time tames the strongest grief
　　　↳ 아무리 아픈 슬픔도 세월이 가면 누그러진다

To achieve great things we must live as though we were never going to die
　　　↳ 큰 일을 이루기 위해서는 영원히 죽지 않을 것처럼 살아야 한다

To be alive at all involves some risk
　　　↳ 살아 있다는 그 자체만으로도 어느 정도의 위험을 안고 있다는 말이다

To excel the past we must not allow ourselves to lose contact with it
　　　↳ 과거보다 나아지기 위해서는 과거와의 접속을 끊지 말아야 한다

To have a grievance is to a have purpose in life
　　　↳ 불만이 있다는 것은 삶의 목표가 있다는 것과 같다

To live with fear and not be afraid is the final test of maturity
　　　↳ 두려움을 안고 살면서도 그 두려움을 겁내지 않고 살수 있다는 것이 마지막 시험이다

To make a vow for life is to make oneself a slave

· tame changed from being wild to being controllable by man, docile, dull	**· vow** solemn promise to do something or to live or act a certain way

ㄴ 평생을 맹세한다는 것은 평생 종으로 살겠다는 것이다

To regret deeply is to live afresh
ㄴ 깊이 후회하는 것은 새 삶을 사는 것이다

To some life means pleasure, to others suffering
ㄴ 인생이란 어떤 사람에겐 기쁨을 뜻하고 어떤 사람에겐 괴로움을 뜻한다

Today increasing people are leading a catch-as-catch-can life
ㄴ 실지하루 벌어 하루 먹는 사람들이 늘어나고 있어

Trouble is shadow to life
ㄴ 인생은 괴로움이 따르게 마련

> 인생을 고난으로 표현한 속담은 여러 가지가 있다. "Life is pilgrimage 인생은 순례의 여행이다", "We must eat a peck of dirt before we die 살다 보면 인생의 쓴맛을 보게 마련이다" 등이다.

Two in distress makes sorrow less
ㄴ 슬픔을 같이 나누면 가벼워진다

> "백지장도 맞들면 낫다"라는 한국 속담과 비슷한 뜻이다. 협력의 중요성과 친구의 고마움을 함께 나타낸 속담이다.
> (=Many hands make light work)
> (=Grief is lessened when imparted to others)

Warm and fragrant breezes carry the warbles and chirps of birds rejoicing the blessings of sweet life
ㄴ 따사롭고 향기로운 미풍이 달콤한 삶의 축복을 받으면서 기뻐하는 새들의 지저귐과 쩍쩍거리는 소리를 싣고 온다

› **warble** melodious succession of low pleasing sounds, musical trill

› **chirp** short sharp sound like that of a bird or cricket

Was it not for public acceptance of a single yardstick of time, life would be unbearably chaotic

> ↳ 일반대중들이 시간에 대한 단순한 척도를 받아들이지 않는다면 인생은 참을 수 없을 정도로 혼란스러울 것이다

Waste not fresh tears over old griefs

> ↳ 묵은 슬픔 때문에 새로운 눈물을 허비하지 마라

We all have enough strength to bear the misfortunes of others

> ↳ 우리는 남들의 불행은 충분히 참아낼 만한 힘이 있다

We are all in a rut

> ↳ 우린 모두 다람쥐 쳇바퀴 돌기지

We are born crying, live complaining, and die disappointed

> ↳ 사람은 태어나면서 울고, 살면서 불평하고, 죽을 땐 불평한다

We can chart our future clearly and wisely only when we know the path which has led to the present

> ↳ 우리는 현재까지 이르렀던 경로를 알아야만 장래의 계획을 명료하고 슬기롭게 세울 수 있다

We don't see any reason why the devil should have all the good for tunes

> ↳ 어째서 악한 사람이 잘 되고 착한 사람이 안 되는지 알 수 없군

We don't see nature with our eyes, but with our understanding and hearts

> ↳ 우리는 자연을 눈으로 보는 것이 아니라 이해와 마음으로 본다

We feel hopeful about the future

> ↳ 우린 장래를 낙관해

We felt all the more keenly that life is all in vain

> ↳ 우린 인생의 무상함을 새삼 느꼈어

› **yardstick** measuring stick 3 feet long, standard for judging

› **keen** sharp, severe, enthusiastic, mentally alert

We had a mingled feeling of joy and sorrow
> ↳ 우린 희비가 엇갈렸어

We have no more right to consume happiness without producing it than to consume wealth without producing it
> ↳ 우리는 부를 만들어내지 않고 그 부를 소비할 권리가 없듯이 행복도 만들지 않고 소비할 권리가 없다

We have to find something to live for
> ↳ 우린 삶의 목표를 찾아야 한다

We have to save money with an eye to the future
> ↳ 우린 장래를 위해 저축해야 해

We learn throughout our lives chiefly through our mistakes and pursuits of our fault assumption
> ↳ 사람은 일생동안 주로 실수와의 그릇된 가정을 통하여 배운다

We may become the makers of our fate when we have ceased to pose as its prophets
> ↳ 우리가 운명의 예언자인 것처럼 하는 태도를 그만둘 때 운명의 창조자가 될 수 있다

We should help who are down and out
> ↳ 우린 곤궁한 사람들을 도와줘야 해

We wish we could be with you in your sorrow
> ↳ 당신의 슬픔을 같이 나누고 싶습니다

We'll bury the past and make a fresh start
> ↳ 우린 과거를 잊어버리고 새 출발 할거야

What can't be altered must be borne, not blamed
> ↳ 변경할 수 없는 일은 탓하지 말고 참아야 한다

What can't be cured must be endured

· **mingle** bring together or mix   · **prophet** one who utters revelations or predicts events

ㄴ 주어진 환경에서 최선을 다 하라

What goes up must come down
ㄴ 올라갈 때가 있으면 내려갈 때가 있어

What is necessary is never a risk
ㄴ 꼭 필요한 것은 모험이 아니다

What most counts is not to live, but to live aright
ㄴ 가장 중요한 것은 그냥 산다는 것이 아니라 바르게 사는데 있다

What the eye doesn't see, the heart won't grieve over(crave for)
ㄴ 차라리 보지 않으면 슬퍼할(가지고싶은) 일도 없으련만

What would life be if we had no courage to attempt anything?
ㄴ 무언가를 시도할만한 용기가 없다면 삶이 무슨 의미가 있겠는가

What you learn in your school time should carry over into adult life
ㄴ 학교에서 배우는 건 어른이 되었을 때 필요한 것이다

What's the use of saving life?
ㄴ 살아남은들 무슨 의미가 있겠나?

Whatever formed for long duration arrives slowly to its maturity
ㄴ 장시간에 걸쳐 형성된 것은 천천히 성숙해 나간다

Whatever is produced hastily goes hastily to waste
ㄴ 급히 만든 것은 급히 쓰레기장으로 간다

Whatever there be of progress in life comes not through adaption but through daring, through obeying the blind urge
ㄴ 인생의 진보가 있다면 적응에서가 아니라 대담하고 저돌적인 충동을 따르는데서 온다

When An-do won the lottery, he felt as though the world was his oyster
ㄴ 안도가 복권에 당첨되자 제 세상인 것 같은 기분이었지

· **urge** earnestly plead for or insist on, try to persuade, impel to a course of activity

· **oyster** bivalve mollusk

When are you going to take me out of this black hole?
　　↳ 언제쯤 날 이 슬픔에서 구해줄 건가요?

When money speaks the world(truth) is in silence
　　↳ 돈이 말을 하면 세상(진실)이 침묵한다

When the first fine rapture had worn off, he seemed none too pleased
　　↳ 그는 처음의 열광이 지나가자 그다지 즐거워하는 기색이 아니었다

When work is a duty, life is slavery
　　↳ 일이 의무일 때 삶은 노역이다

Where do you get off telling me how to run my life?
　　↳ 네가 뭔데 내 인생을 이래라 저래라 하는 거니?

Where do you plan to live out your days(life)?
　　↳ 여생을 어디서 보내실 계획입니까?

While we teach our children all about life, our children teach us what life is all about
　　↳ 우리가 아이들에게 삶에 대해 많은 것을 가르치는 반면, 아이들은 결국 우리들에게 산다는 것이 뭔지를 가르쳐 준다

Willing mind makes a light foot
　　↳ 의지가 있으면 발걸음이 가벼워진다

Wise living consists less in acquiring good habits than acquiring as few habits as possible
　　↳ 현명한 삶은 좋은 습관을 붙이는 것보다 오히려 가능한 한 나쁜 습관을 줄여나가는 데 있다

With her life back on track, she studies hard
　　↳ 그 여자는 본래의 생활로 되돌아와서 열심히 공부하고 있다

With the continued loss of blood, her life was steadily leaking away

---

· **rapture** spiritual or emotional ecstasy

↳ 그 여자는 계속되는 출혈로 생명을 잃어가고 있었다

With the progress of medicine, it'll become more and more common people to live until they have had their fill of life
↳ 의학의 발달로 사람들이 자신에게 주어진 천수를 다할 때까지 사는 것이 점점 흔하게 될 것이다

Yesterday is not ours to be recovered, but tomorrow is ours to win or lose
↳ 어제는 우리의 것으로 회복시킬 수 없는 날이지만, 내일은 우리가 얻을 수도 잃을 수도 있는 날이다

You are a long time dead
↳ 언제 죽을지 모르는 몸, 살았을 때 즐겨라(활동적으로 살아라)

You are not a man of the society(world)
↳ 넌 세상 물정을 잘 몰라

> (=You're out of touch with the world)

You are the one I want for life
↳ 당신은 내가 일생을 함께 하기 원하는 사람

You have a long future before you
↳ 넌 장래가 창창해

You have no idea how the world works
↳ 넌 세상 물정을 몰라

> (=You are still wet behind the ears)
> (=You don't know how things work in life)

› **society** companionship, community life, rich or fashionable class, voluntary group

You have the best life
     네 팔자가 상팔자다

> (=You have it easiest)
> (=You've got it made)
> (=You don't have a worry in the world)

You live in a make-believe world of your own
     ㄴ 넌 너 혼자만의 공상세계에 살고있어

You need a lot more information before making the right choice about which course to follow
     ㄴ 넌 어떤 길로 가야할지 바른 선택을 하기 위해 많은 정보가 필요하다

You never know what tomorrow might bring
     ㄴ 내일 어찌될지 아무도 몰라

You never know your luck
     ㄴ 사람팔자 알 수 없다

You should economize
     ㄴ 절약하며 살아야 해

You should take the world as you find it
     ㄴ 넌 세상 따라 살아야 해

You shouldn't lose touch with the world
     ㄴ 시대발전에 뒤지면 안 돼

You turned my life around
     ㄴ 당신이 내 일생을 바꿔 놓았어

You'd better get a life
     ㄴ 그런 식으로 살아서는 안 돼

‣ **economize** be thrifty

You'd better take long views
  ↳ 먼 장래를 생각해야 해

You're in a fool's paradise
  ↳ 넌 세상물정 모르고 잘난 척 하고 있는 거야

You've been over with this
  ↳ 이젠 끝난 일

You've had a stroke of luck
  ↳ 복 터졌구나

> (＝This is your lucky day)
> (＝The gods are on your side)

Your life and my life are two very different things
  ↳ 우린 전혀 다른 세상에 살고있어

· **paradise**　place of bliss
· **stroke**　rub gently

65. 상사   **Bosses**

A good public servant is not necessarily always at the boss's beck and call

    ↳ 상사가 하라는 대로하는 사람이 반드시 좋은 공무원이 아니다

An-do didn't cut much ice with his boss

    ↳ 안도의 말은 사장에게 잘 안 먹혀들었어

Are your talks with your boss getting anywhere?

    ↳ 사장과의 얘긴 잘 돼가니?

As our boss's on vacation, I've got the run of the place now

    ↳ 사장님이 휴가중이니 이제 여긴 내 맘대로야

Be your own boss

    ↳ 자기 사업을 해라

> (=Start your own business)

Bong-soo is trying to kiss(shine) up to our boss

    ↳ 봉수가 사장에게 아부하고 있는 거야

Boss or no, he shall regret it

    ↳ 사장이고 뭐고 그냥 안 두겠어

Can he measure up to the new boss's expectations?

    ↳ 그가 사장의 기대에 부응할 수 있을까?

› **beck** summons

Chan-soo has already fallen from grace with the boss
> ↳ 찬수는 이미 사장님한테 찍혔어

Chang-soo's got an in with the boss
> ↳ 창수는 사장에게 백 줄이 있어

Did the boss ream you out?
> ↳ 윗분이 야단 치셨어요?

Dong-soo wanted to bask in his boss's approval
> ↳ 동수는 사장의 승인을 받으려 했다

Doo-soo fell(lapsed) from his boss's grace when he left the office door unlocked the other day
> ↳ 두수는 일전에 사무실 문을 안 잠그고 나가서 사장님 눈밖에 났어

Doo-soo's got(needs) to get the boss's say-so before he goes ahead
> ↳ 그가 일을 추진하자면 사장의 결재가 있어야 한다

Ed used to be the boss's fair-haired boy, but now he's just like the rest of us
> ↳ 에드가 왕년엔 사장의 총애를 받았지만 지금은 우리들이나 똑같다

Ed's poor explanation of his being late didn't fly with the boss
> ↳ 늦게 출근한 에드의 구차한 변명이 사장에게 먹히지 않았다

From where I stand(my point of view, my perspective), our new boss has a lot of work to do
> ↳ 내가 보는 바로는 사장에게 일거리가 산더미 같이 있어

He came out smelling like a rose after his boss was indicted
> ↳ 그의 사장이 제소 당하자 그의 형편이 풀렸다

He has a good thing going, working at home without his boss
> ↳ 그는 감독하는 상사 없이 집에서 일하게 됐으니 잘된 일이지

› **ream** quantity of paper that is 480, 500, or 516 sheets

› **bask** enjoy pleasant warmth

› **indict** charge with a crime

He is a boss by name(in name only)
> ↳ 그는 명색만 사장일 뿐이야

He is in bad with the boss for his goofing off
> ↳ 그는 농땡이를 쳐서 사장한테 미운 털이 박혔어

He made a face at me when I was talking to the boss
> ↳ 사장에게 얘기를 막 하려는데 그가 내게 얼굴(표정)로 신호를 보
> 냈다

He's been playing up to the boss as usual
> ↳ 그는 늘 하던 대로 사장에게 알랑거리기나 하고 있지

He's just another boss
> ↳ 그도 그저(전임자와) 똑같은 윗사람일 뿐이야

His boss gives(puts) teeth to him
> ↳ 그의 상사가 그에게 힘을 실어주고 있어

How did your new idea rate with your boss?
> ↳ 너의 새 아이디어가 사장에게 어느 정도 호평을 얻었니?

Hyang-soon can't get anything across to the boss, because he just tunes her out
> ↳ 사장이 향순이의 말이라면 들은 척도 안 하니 무슨 일이나 사장을 설
> 득하기는 글렀어

I have a situation with the boss
> ↳ 난 사장에게 풀어야 할 문제가 있어

I was not conscious of my boss's presence in the room
> ↳ 윗분이 방에 계신걸 몰랐지

If you'll believe it, the man was our boss
> ↳ 놀래지마, 그 사람은 바로 우리 상사였어

In-ho has a lot of balls to say(speak) against his boss

› **ball** large formal dance

ㄴ 인호는 사장에게 거역할만한 용기가 있다

It's a point of honor with our boss

ㄴ 윗 분 체면에 관한 문제야

It's also good to keep in good with the boss

ㄴ 사장님 눈에 드니 역시 좋군

My boss told me to hold the port in the office in his absence

ㄴ 사장은 부재중에 내게 뒷일을 맡겼다

No boss, no work

ㄴ 왕초가 없으니 농땡이나 칠 수밖에

Not only does sucking up help your relationship with peers, it does wonders for the boss

ㄴ 칭찬(아부)은 동료들과의 관계개선에 도움을 줄 뿐 아니라 상사에게
신통한 효과가 있다

Now I'm my own boss(master)

ㄴ 이젠 내 세상이다

Our boss comes on as a philanthropist, but we all know him better

ㄴ 우리 사장님은 박애주의자로 자처하지만 우린 모두 그렇지 않다는 걸
잘 알지

Our boss is disinclined to attenuate our high spirits by marring the atmosphere

ㄴ 우리 사장은 분위기를 망쳐가며 우리들의 좋은 기분을 망가뜨릴 사람
이 아니다

Our boss is going to lower the boom

ㄴ 사장이 무섭게 나오려나봐

Our boss is not free and easy with us

ㄴ 우리 윗분은 우리에게 느슨하게 놔두질 않아

› **philanthropy** charitable act or gift or an
organization that distribute
such gifts

› **attenuate** make or become thin, weaken

Our boss keeps tabs on all the staff
ㄴ 윗분이 전 직원을 감시해

Our boss plans on putting tens of office staff out to pasture
ㄴ 사장이 우리 직원 수십 명을 해고시킬 계획을 하고 있다

Our boss runs a tight ship here
ㄴ 우리 윗분은 기강을 중시해

Our boss tries to get the best out of his staff members
ㄴ 우리 상사는 직원들을 통하여 최대의 성과를 올리려 하고 있어

Our boss wants to twist us around her little finger
ㄴ 우리 사장님은 우릴 완전히 주무르고 싶어해

Our boss warned him not to hang around the office
ㄴ 사장이 그에게 사무실에서 어영부영하지 말라고 경고했다

Our boss will give you the works if you're loafing off again
ㄴ 또 농땡이 쳤다간 사장님한테 혼날 거야

Our boss will take a drastic measure and won't let the contumacious, discordant behavior of any employees ruin the harmonious atmosphere
ㄴ 사장은 단호한 태도로 직장의 조화로운 분위기를 깨는 어떤 직원의
불손하고 거슬리는 행동도 가만두지 않을 것이다

Our boss won't sit still for his coming to work late
ㄴ 그가 늦게 출근하면 사장이 가만 안 둘걸

Our director didn't listen to our proposal, so we went over(above) him
ㄴ 우리 과장이 우리의 안을 들어주지 않아서 과장 위의 상사에게 가져
갔지

Our former boss, once the idol of our company, now lives in the total obscurity

---

▸ **pasture** graze, land used for grazing

▸ **loaf** waste time

▸ **obscure** dim or hazy, not well known, vague, make indistinct or unclear

↳ 한때 우리 회사의 우상이었던 사장이 지금은 세인들에게서 잊혀진 채 살고 있다

Our hard-ass boss work our tails off
↳ 인정사정 없는 우리 사장은 우리를 꽁지 빠지게 부려먹는다

Remember your boss treats you as if you are an airhead just filling time before you get married
↳ 너의 사장은 네가 결혼 전에 시간이나 때우고 있는 골이 빈 사람인 것으로 여기고 있다는 것을 잊지 마라

Sang-soo's making points with the boss by agreeing with everything he says
↳ 상수는 사장의 말이라면 무조건 예스 예스해서 점수를 따고있어

Seeing that she was in the presence of her superior, she whipped off her hat
↳ 그녀는 자신이 상사 앞에 서 있다는 것을 알고는 재빨리 모자를 벗었다

She always seems to have the boss's ear
↳ 그 여자는 늘 사장의 총애를 받는 것 같아

She has to show us who's the boss
↳ 그 여자는 윗사람다운 모습을 보여줘야 해

She'll have the boss convinced as she's a smooth operator(smoothie)
↳ 그녀는 설득을 잘하니까 사장도 꼭 설득할 꺼야

Some higher-ups in our office are making free with their secretaries
↳ 우리 사무실의 일부 상사들은 비서들에게 아무 일이나 시켜

Some muck-a-mucks from headquarters are coming down today
↳ 본사에서 거물급 인사들이 내려온다

Some of the office workers do sloppy work until the boss keeps after them

---

· **whip off**   take off very quickly

ㄴ 어떤 직원들은 사장이 자꾸 잔소리 안 하면 일을 성의 없이 해

Somehow he must have won(had) the boss's ear
ㄴ 어쨌든 그가 사장에게 무슨 조치를 취했음이 틀림없어

Soon he wormed his way into the boss's favor
ㄴ 얼마 안돼서 그는 차차 사장의 환심을 사게 됐다

Sucking up to the boss won't get you anywhere
ㄴ 사장에게 잘 보이려 해봤자 소용없어

The boss fired Sang-soo to make an example of him
ㄴ 본때를 보이기 위해 사장이 상수를 해고시켰어

The boss gave me a good salting down(talking to, dressing down) for no other reason than that
ㄴ 사장은 단지 그 이유만으로 나를 호되게 야단쳤다

The boss is all out to break the workers' balls to see if he can get them to quit
ㄴ 사장은 종업원들을 내쫓기 위해 그들의 기를 꺾어놓으려고 혈안이다

The boss really nailed Sung-soo to the wall(a cross)
ㄴ 사장님은 성수를 정말 호되게 호통쳤어(징계했어)

The boss seems to be down this morning
ㄴ 사장이 오늘 아침 저기압인 것 같아

The employer had to come up against the prejudices of many staff whenever he tried to introduce new working practices
ㄴ 사장은 새로운 작업방식을 도입하려고 할 때마다 많은 직원들이 가진 편견에 부딪쳐 어려움을 겪었다

The employer has sown the seeds of future conflict by sacking him
ㄴ 사장이 그를 해고함으로써 앞으로 갈등의 빌미를 만들게 되었다

The higher-ups began to tighten their screws

- **worm** move or cause to move in a slow and indirect way, to free from worms
- **salt down** to scold
- **sack** dismiss

ㄴ 윗분들이 우리 들에 대한 압력을 강화하기 시작했어

The higher-ups in some offices are all-out to clip their staff's wings
ㄴ 우리 사무실의 높은 분들은 직원들이 튈까봐 꺾어놓으려고 혈안이야

The talks with the boss bogged down on the question of working hours
ㄴ 사장과의 근로시간에 관한 얘기는 어려움에 봉착했다

Their hope is to ride the boss's coattail
ㄴ 그들의 희망은 힘있는 상사의 덕을 보자는 것이다

They accord varying degrees of affection and respect to their boss
ㄴ 그들은 정도의 차이는 있지만 사장에게 애정과 존경을 가지고 있다

They can't touch him when it comes to convincing the boss
ㄴ 사장을 설득하는 일에는 그들이 그 사람에게 상대가 안 돼

This maxim indicates everybody to be the boss of something small, rather than a follower of something big
ㄴ 이 속담은 누구나 큰 회사 같은 곳의 말단이 되기보다 하찮은 곳이라도 우두머리가 되라는 것을 말해준다

What you say is shot through with the praise for the boss
ㄴ 네 말은 상사에 대한 칭찬 일색이군

Working freelance means that you are your own boss and can work at your own pace
ㄴ 프리랜서로 일한다는 것은 자신이 경영자가 되어 자기 페이스대로 일한다는 것을 말한다

You have to put this document back to the boss's desk, with nobody the wiser
ㄴ 이 서류를 아무도 모르게 사장님 책상 위에 도로 갖다 놔야 해

You seem to have our boss's ear

> **bog** swamp, sink in or as if in a bog
> **accord** grant, agree, agreement

> **maxim** proverb

ㄴ 넌 윗분의 신임을 받고 있는 것 같구나

You shouldn't be more boss than the boss

ㄴ 넌 윗사람도 아닌 주제에 윗사람 이상으로 행동해선 안 돼

You will soon have(get) the new boss's number

ㄴ 너는 곧 신임 사장의 신임을 받게 될 거다

You'd better not fly in the face(teeth) of your boss

ㄴ 상사에게 대들어서는 안 돼

› **fly in**   stand against

66. 싸움   **Quarrels**

A bad workman quarrels with the man who calls him that
         ↳ 서툰 일꾼은 자기더러 서툰 일꾼이라고 부르는 사람과 다툰다

> 자신의 약점을 인정하지 못하고, 고치려고 하지 않는 발전이 없는 사람을 일
> 컫는 말이다. 흔히 "똥 묻은 개가 겨 묻은 개 나무란다"라는 속담을 많이 쓰
> 며 이는 영어에서는 "The pot calls the kettle black = 냄비가 주전자보
> 고 검다고 한다"라고 한다.

A full belly neither fights nor flies well
         ↳ 배가 부르면 잘 싸울 수도 잘 도망할 수도 없다

All progress means war with society
         ↳ 모든 진보는 사회와의 싸움이다

Another crack like this and I'll leave
         ↳ 한 번만 더 이런 쌍소릴 하면 난 갈 거야

Any misunderstanding can resolve itself into a quarrel
         ↳ 조금만 오해가 있어도 다툼이 될 수 있어

Are you giving me ultimatums?
         ↳ 한 번 해 보자는 거냐?

Are you going to make him pay?
         ↳ 그에게 앙갚음하겠다는 거니?

›**ultimatum**   final proposition or demand
                 carrying or implying a threat

Are you going to put the chill(freeze) on me?
↳ 나를 상대하지 않겠다(무시하겠다)는 거니?

As soon as microbes enter the body they would kill all living matter, if it were not for the tiny defenders that rush immediately to fight them
↳ 만일 침입자들과 싸우기 위해 즉시 달려가는 작은 방어 균이 없다면 세균이 몸 속에 들어가자마자 살아있는 모든 것을 죽일 것이다

At this rate, the next time you need my help you can whistle for it
↳ 이렇게 나간다면 다음에 내게 도움을 청해봤자 어림 반 푼 어치 없어

Better to flatter the devil than fight him
↳ 악마와 싸우기보다는 그를 추켜 주어라

Bong-soo and An-do patched their quarrel up
↳ 봉수와 안도는 싸움 끝에 화해했어

Bong-soo clawed his way up to the top, fighting at every step
↳ 봉수는 한 단계 한 단계 분투하여 영예의 자리에 오른 사람

Bong-soo gets quarrelsome in his cups
↳ 병수는 술만 먹으면 시비조로 나와

Bong-soo knocked Sang-do for a loop
↳ 봉수가 상도를 늘씬하게 패 주었어

Bong-soo stopped short of striking me
↳ 봉수는 나를 때릴 번 하다가 말았다

Do you have something against me?
↳ 내게 유감 있니?

Do you want to go one on one with me?
↳ 나하고 맞붙어 보겠다는 거냐?

Don't argue with that bruiser, or he'll punch your lights off(out)

‣ **put the chill on** ignore

‣ **bruiser** big husky man

‣ **microbe** disease-causing microorganism

‣ **loop** doubling of a line that leaves an opening

└ 그런 불한당하고 시비했다가는 뼈도 못 추려

Don't call me names if you like the way your teeth are arranged
└ 이빨이 성하고싶거든 날 욕하지마

Don't dare to touch me
└ 내 몸에 손대기만 해봐라

Don't fight a losing battle
└ 승산 없는 싸움(일, 게임) 하지마

(=Don't play losing games)

Don't get(become) personal with him any more
└ 그에게 더 이상 인신공격 하지마

Don't start with me
└ 내 성질 건드리지마

Don't you take the cake!
└ 너 참 뻔뻔하기도 하구나

Even fish-fights can be brutal
└ 여자들 싸움도 사나워질 수 있다

Evidence suggests that patients who show a fighting spirit exhibit stronger immune defenses against the spread of diseases than those who suffer stoically
└ 병과 싸울 의지가 있는 환자가 금욕적으로 견디는 환자들보다 병의 확산에 대한 강한 면역성을 보여준다

Flight was his only resource
└ 그는 도망칠 밖에 별 도리가 없었다

› **brutal** like a brute and especially cruel
› **stoical** showing indifference to pain

For every quarrel a man and a wife have before others, they have a hundred when alone
> ↳ 부부가 남들 앞에서 한 번 싸운다면 그들만 있을 때에 백 번을 싸운다

Give him a taste of his own medicine
> ↳ 그가 한 것만큼 당하게 해줘라

Go ahead and make my day
> ↳ 뼉다귀가 성하고 싶거든 네 맘대로 해봐=네 맘대로 해봐, 난 각오하고 있어

Hatred stirs up strife, but love covers all sins
> ↳ 미움은 다툼을 일으키지만 사랑은 모든 허물을 가리우느니라

He dared me to fight
> ↳ 덤빌 테면 덤비라고 그가 내게 대들었어

He flung me a stream of abuse
> ↳ 그는 내게 마구 욕지거리를 퍼부었다

He has a score to settle with you
> ↳ 그가 네게 따질 일이 있어

He is going to fight his way back
> ↳ 그는 싸워 이겨 낼 거야

He pulled the fighting boys apart and sent them home
> ↳ 그는 싸우는 소년들을 뜯어말려 집으로 돌려보냈다

He ran between the people all day, trying to settle the argument
> ↳ 그는 다투고 있는 두 사람 사이를 왔다 갔다 하면서 문제를 해결하려고 했다

He reeled back when the heavy blow landed on his chin
> ↳ 그는 강한 펀치가 턱에 작렬하자 비틀거리며 물러났다

He turns(puts) us off with his scowling

› **reel** wind on a reel, pull in by reeling

› **scowl** make a face in expression of displeasure

↳ 그가 우릴 노려보는 통에 정나미가 뚝 떨어져

He waded through slaughter to the throne

↳ 그는 피비린내 나는 싸움을 치르고 왕위를 차지하였다

Hightail it out of here if any fight breaks out

↳ 싸움이라도 일어나거든 여기서 피해버려라

His eyes flashed back defiance

↳ 그도 똑같이 노려보며 반항의 빛을 보였다

I can fight with him with one arm tied behind my back

↳ 그 사람이라면 쉽게 맞서 싸울 수 있어

I don't know what you have against me

↳ 무슨 원한이 있는 거냐?

I have to fight the clock

↳ 시간을 다투고있어

If they do me any harm I'll return tit for tat

↳ 그들이 내게 해코지하면 나도 가만 안 있어

If you shoot your bolt now, your defeat will be just a matter of time

↳ 지금 최후수단을 다 써버린다면 너의 패배는 시간문제다

In a fight the rich man tries to save his face, the poor man his coat

↳ 싸움에서 부자는 체면을 생각하고 가난한 사람은 옷을 생각한다

In-soo gave him a sound thrashing within an inch of his life

↳ 인수가 그 사람을 초죽음이 되게 패 주었어

It takes two to make a quarrel

↳ 상대가 없으면 싸움이 안 돼

› **wade** move with difficulty

› **hightail** leave the place

› **defiance** act or state of defying

› **thrash** thresh, beat, move about violently

> "손바닥도 마주쳐야 소리가 난다"라는 한국 속담이 있다. 영어에서는 "It takes two to tango 탱고를 추기 위해서는 두 명이 필요하다"라고 한다. 이는 싸움뿐만 아니라 협력을 필요로 할 때에도 쓰인다.

It's such a fight for me to survive from payday to payday
　　　　ㄴ 이 달 월급을 타면 저 달 월급을 탈 때까지 빠듯하게 살고있어

Jung-soo and Sang-man were having an argument, and I got caught in the middle(cross-fired)
　　　　ㄴ 정수와 상만이가 다투고 있어 내 입장이 난처하게 됐어

Let'em all come
　　　　ㄴ 얼마든지 오라고(덤비라고) 해

Lovers' quarrels are soon mended
　　　　ㄴ 부부싸움은 칼로 물 베기

(=Lover's anger is short-lived)

Most quarrels amplify a misunderstanding
　　　　ㄴ 대부분의 싸움은 오해를 더 크게 만든다

My fingers itch for quarrel
　　　　ㄴ 싸우고 싶어 손이 근질거린다

Never contend with a man who has nothing to lose
　　　　ㄴ 아무 것도 잃을 게 없는 사람과 다투지 마라

One should help bargaining and stop quarrels
　　　　ㄴ 흥정은 붙이고 싸움은 말려라

Quarrels are the dowry which married folks bring one another

| ‣ **amplify**　make louder, stronger, or more thorough | ‣ **dowry**　property a woman gives her husband in marriage |

ㄴ 부부싸움은 결혼한 사람들이 각자 가지고 오는 결혼지참금이다

Quarrels wouldn't last long if the fault was only on one side

ㄴ 한 쪽만 잘못이 있는 싸움은 오래가지 않는다

Sung-gyoo's sent you after me

ㄴ 성규가 날 노리고(해치려고) 널 보냈군

The art of self-defense is not a combative art, but an art of discipline and defense

ㄴ 호신술은 싸움을 하기 위한 기술이 아니라 수양과 자기방어를 위한 기술이다

The best defence is a good offence

ㄴ 공격이 최선의 방어다

The innocent bystander often gets beaten up

ㄴ 고래싸움에 새우등 터진다

The quarrels of friends are the opportunities of foes

ㄴ 친구의 싸움이 적에게는 기회가 된다

The small argument boiled over into a serious quarrel

ㄴ 사소한 논쟁이 심각한 말다툼으로 커졌다

They always fight and make up on a regular basis

ㄴ 그들은 늘 금방 싸우다가 화해하다 하고 있어

They fought hand to hand

ㄴ 주먹다짐이 벌어졌어

They parted company with each other over a financial quarrel

ㄴ 그들은 대수롭지 않은 금전 문제로 서로 싸우더니 갈라섰어

They traded blows and wrestled for several minutes, each of them refusing to give way

ㄴ 그들은 물러나지 않고 몇 분 동안 주먹다짐을 하면서 맞붙어 싸웠다

▸ **combat** fight
▸ **bystander** spectator

They've been quarreling, each accusing the other of being responsible for the error
> ↳ 그들은 제각기 서로 상대방에게 잘못의 책임이 있다고 비난하면서 싸워오고 있다

Thoughts about the accident, little by little, passed into oblivion
> ↳ 사고에 대한 생각이 차츰 잊혀져 갔어

To dispute a drunkard is to debate with an empty house
> ↳ 술주정뱅이와 논쟁하는 것은 빈집과 말씨름하는 것과 같다

Victory is to him who fights the longest
> ↳ 승리는 끝까지 싸우는 사람의 것이다

Vinegar helps fights germs, sooths stomach pains, heals cuts quicker and adds to our overall health
> ↳ 식초는 멸균효과가 있고, 위통을 진정시키며, 상처를 빨리 낫게 하며, 건강을 전반적으로 좋게 해준다

Violence broke loose in Seoul last night
> ↳ 어제 밤 서울에 폭력이 난무했다

What matters is that you put up a good fight
> ↳ 중요한 건 네가 최선을 다 하는 것이다

When it comes to dividing an estate, the politest men quarrel
> ↳ 재산분배 문제에 있어서는 아무리 점잖은 사람이라도 싸운다

You are lowing yourself by picking a quarrel over such a trifling matter
> ↳ 그런 사소한 일로 싸운다는 것은 네 위신에 관한 문제다

You can make up a quarrel, but it will always show where it was patched
> ↳ 싸움을 화해할 수는 있으나 그 싸움이 봉합된 자리는 결코 지워지지

› **soothe** calm or comfort
› **trifle** something of little value or importance

않는다

You have to fight fire with fire
　ㄴ 이열치열이야

> 한국의 속담 '이열치열(以熱治熱)'과 비슷하게 영어에는 "Fight fire with fire 불은 불로 다스려라"라는 말이 있다. 이 말은 적을 물리치려면 적의 전술로 대응해야 한다는 뜻이다. 비슷한 말로 "Like cures like"도 있다.

> **fire** light or heat and especially the flame of something burning, destructive · burning of somethin(as a house), enthusiasm, discharge or firearms

67. 선&악   Virtue & Vice

Don't paint people with their warts
↳ 선악을 있는 그대로 표시해서는 안 돼

Every vice has its excuse ready
↳ 모든 악은 변명을 준비해 두고 있다

Every vice is only an exaggeration of a necessary and virtuous function
↳ 모든 악은 필요하고도 이로운 역할은 가장하는데 불과하다

Evil enters like a needle and spreads like an oak tree
↳ 악이 들어오면 새끼를 쳐서 나간다

Extremes in wickedness make for extremes in goodness
↳ 악에 강한 자는 선에도 강하다

Hypocrisy is the homage which vice pays to virtue
↳ 위선은 악덕이 미덕에게 보내는 존경의 표시이다

It's the function of vice to keep virtue within reasonable bounds
↳ 악은 덕으로 하여금 적절한 한계를 지키게 해준다

Many a man's vices have at first been nothing worse than good qualities run wild
↳ 인간의 많은 악이 처음에는 좋은 점들이 난폭해졌다는 사실에 불과하다

Miseries are attendant upon vice
↳ 죄악에는 불행이 따른다

· **hypocrisy** a feigning to be what one is not   · **homage** reverent regard

More people are flattered into virtue than bullied out of vice
   ↳ 을러서 악행을 안 하게 된 사람보다 칭찬으로 덕을 행하게 된 사람이 많다

Poverty obstructs the road to virtue
   ↳ 가난은 선으로 가는 길을 방해한다

The absence of vices adds so little to the sum of one's virtues
   ↳ 악이 없다는 것은 쌓아둔 덕에 거의 보탬이 되지 않는다

The existence of virtue depends entirely upon its use
   ↳ 덕성의 존재는 그 덕성의 필요성에 달려있다

The function of wisdom is to discriminate between good and evil
   ↳ 지혜의 기능은 선악을 구분하는 것이다

The good or evil of man lies within his own will
   ↳ 선이나 악은 그 사람의 의지에 있다

The greatest pleasure is to do a good action by stealth, and to have it found out by chance
   ↳ 몰래 선행을 한 다음 그것이 우연히 말해지게 되는 것이 가장 큰 기쁨이다

The love of money is the root of all evil
   ↳ 돈에 대한 사랑이 모든 악의 근원이다

> 신약성서 '디모데 전서'에서 유래한 속담이다. 이 세상의 모든 범죄는 금전, 즉 돈 때문에 일어난다고 해도 과언이 아니다.

The most important evils that mankind have to consider are those which they inflict upon each other through stupidity or malevolence
   ↳ 인간이 고려해야 할 중요한 해악들은 인간의 어리석음이나 적의를 통

› **stealth** secret or underhand procedure
› **inflict** give by or as if by hitting

해서 서로에게 가하는 해악이라고 생각할 수 있다

The object of reporting is to find good or evil in a story by ironing out the distracting wrinkles of complexity
> ㄴ 보도의 목적은 초점을 흐리는 복잡성을 다 제거함으로써 선하거나 악한 무엇인가를 찾아내는데 있다

The virtues of the past seem greater and its faults are reduced
> ㄴ 과거의 장점은 더욱 큰 것처럼 보이고 결점은 줄어든다

There's no virtue that poverty destroys not
> ㄴ 가난은 모든 덕행을 파괴한다

Vanity is a common vice to woman
> ㄴ 여자에게는 허영이 따르게 마련이다

Vice grows in small steps
> ㄴ 악은 작은 걸음으로 자라난다

Vice makes virtue shine
> ㄴ 악이 있기에 선이 빛난다

Vices are ingredients of virtues just as poisons are ingredients of remedies
> ㄴ 독약이 치료약의 재료이듯이 악은 덕의 재료이다

Virtue and vice, evil and good, are siblings
> ㄴ 덕과 악, 좋은 것과 나쁜 것은 형제자매이다

Virtue is more important than anything else for a woman
> ㄴ 도둑의 때는 벗어도 화냥질 때는 못 벗는다

Virtue is praised by all, but practised by few
> ㄴ 덕은 모든 사람이 칭송하지만 행하는 사람은 거의 없다

Virtue itself turns vice, being misapplied
> ㄴ 선이 잘못 사용되면 그 자체가 악이 된다

- **object** purpose
- **misapply** apply wrongly

Virtue must shape itself in deed
　　└ 덕은 행동함으로써 생겨나야 한다

Virtue triumphs over vice
　　└ 선인은 흥하고 악인은 망해

Virtue wouldn't go to such lengths if vanity did not keep her company
　　└ 허영심을 동반하지 않은 덕행은 그리 멀리 가지 않을 것이다

Virtues and happiness are mother and daughter
　　└ 덕행과 행복은 어머니와 딸과의 관계다

Virtues are virtues only to those who can appreciate them
　　└ 덕은 그 덕을 제대로 이해하는 사람에게만 덕이다

We are more apt to catch the more vices of others than their virtues
　　└ 사람은 덕행보다 악행을 더 잘 지적하기 쉽다

We look for good on earth and can't recognize it
　　└ 우리는 세상의 선을 구하지만 그것을 알아보지 못한다

We make a ladder of our vices, if we trample those same vices underfoot
　　└ 악을 짓밟는 것은 그 악이 기어오르는 사다리를 만드는 것이다

We tolerate without rebuke the vice with which we have grown familiar
　　└ 친숙해진 악에 대해서는 말없이 참는다

When the bad imitates the good, there's no knowing what mischief is intended
　　└ 악이 선의 흉내를 낼 때에는 어떤 못된 짓이 숨이 있는지 모른다

Where there is music, there can be no evil
　　└ 음악이 있는 곳에 악이 있을 수 없다

› **triumph**　victory of great success

› **underfoot**　under the feet, in the way of another

Who does not sufficiently hate vice, does not sufficiently love virtue

ㄴ 악을 철저히 미워하지 않는 사람은 선을 깊이 사랑하지 않는다

'

‣ **sufficient**　adequate

68. 설득   **Persuasion**

Against his will he was swept along by my cogent words
    ↳ 그는 본의 아니게 나의 힘있는 말에 설득 당했다

Asking him to turn over a new leaf was just like talking to a brick wall
    ↳ 그에게 새 사람이 되라고 해봤자 소용이 없었어

Bong-soo will come around(change his mind in a favorable way)
    ↳ 봉수는 우리편이 될 거야

Can you bring him around to your way of thinking?
    ↳ 그를 설득해서 동의를 얻어낼 수 있겠나?

Can you find a way to persuade the fence-hangers to come over to our side?
    ↳ 마음을 정하지 못한 사람들을 우리편으로 설득해 올 방법이 없을까?

Can you get them round the table to agree on this point?
    ↳ 그들이 이 문제에 합의할 수 있도록 협상 테이블로 끌어 올 수 있겠나?

Can't you get something in balance? You go from one extreme to another
    ↳ 중간을 택하면 안되겠니? 넌 도 아니면 모잖아(죽기 아니면 까무러치기야)

How can I persuade you of my plight?
    ↳ 어떻게 하면 나의 곤란한 입장을 이해할 수 있겠니?

Hyang-soon can't get anything across to the boss, because he just

---

› **cogent**   compelling or convincing
› **plight**   bad state

tunes her out
　　↳ 사장이 향순이의 말이라면 들은 척도 안 하니 무슨 일이나 사장을 설득하기는 글렀어

It would be regrettable if any violence were to succeed as a result of the failure in gentle persuasion
　　↳ 조용히 설득하지 못해서 폭력이라도 일어난다면 유감스러운 일이다

Now I could never change you
　　↳ 이제 와서 당신 마음을 돌릴 수 없겠군요

Once you get the load of it, you'll love it
　　↳ 일단 네가 그걸 자세히 보고 나면 좋아하게 될 것이다

Persuade him that you are not in business for your health
　　↳ 네가 재미로 회사를 다니는 게 아님을 그에게 인식시켜라

See it from other person's point of view(perspective)
　　↳ 다른 사람의 입장에서 생각을 좀 해 봐

She'll get it through your head if it takes all day
　　↳ 그 여자는 하루종일 걸려서라도 너를 설득하려 들것이다

She'll have the boss convinced as she's a smooth operator(smoothie)
　　↳ 그녀는 설득을 잘하니까 사장도 꼭 설득할 꺼야

She's been trying to have her perverted views colored by them, taking advantage of their weakness
　　↳ 그녀는 그들의 약점을 이용해서 자신의 비뚤어진 생각을 그들에게 물들이려 해 오고 있다

That man can sell ice to an Eskimo
　　↳ 저 사람이라면 누구라도 설득할 수 있어(발가벗겨 놔도 살 사람)

That nice-looking girl thinks she can bring her charm into play when she's trying to persuade you to what she want

---

· **pervert** corrupt or distort

└ 그 예쁘게 생긴 아가씨가 자기가 원하는 것을 이루어 내기 위해 너를 설득하려고 할 때 자신의 매력을 활용할 수 있다고 생각하고 있어

That salesman caught them off guard with his sales pitch

└ 저 판매원은 그들의 허술한 틈을 이용하여 그럴듯한 입담으로 설득했다

The landlord was persuaded to hold(stay) his hand till other accommodation was found for the occupying tenants

└ 세입자들이 이사할 곳은 마련할 때까지 참아달라고 집주인을 설득했다

They can't touch him when it comes to convincing the boss

└ 사장을 설득하는 일에는 그들이 그 사람에게 상대가 안 돼

They must bring the rest of the committee around to their point of view

└ 그들은 여타 위원들을 자신들의 견해에 동의하도록 설득해야 한다

To please people is a great step towards persuading them

└ 사람들을 기쁘게 하는 것이 그들을 설득하는 큰 발걸음이다

We only admit to minor faults to persuade ourselves that we have no major ones

└ 우리에게 중대한 허물이 없다는 것을 우리 자신에게 설득하려고 단지 작은 허물만을 자백한다

We should try to feed them some carrots

└ 그들을 설득해 우리편으로 만들어야 해

Would you persuade, speak of interest, not of reason

└ 남을 설득하려거든 이치로 설득하지 말고 흥미 있는 말로 설득하라

You got somewhere with him

└ 너 그를 설득했군 그래

- **landlord** owner of property
- **tenant** one who occupies a rented dwelling

69. 설명   Descriptions & Instructions

A man fitting that description was seen leaving the house shortly after the crime was committed

         ㄴ 범죄가 자행된 지 잠시 후 공시한 인상착의가 같은 한 남자가 집을 떠나는 것이 목격됐다

A will gives detailed instructions to your family in case of your sudden death

         ㄴ 유언장에는 사람이 갑자기 사망할 경우에 대비하여 가족들에게 상세히 전할 말을 명시해 두는 것이다

Make your account illustrative rather than descriptive

         ㄴ 이 내용을 서술하기보다 예를 들어 설명해 다오

My emotions defy description

         ㄴ 감회를 말로 표현할 수 없군

Myung-soo's explanation may be read in several ways

         ㄴ 그의 설명은 여러 가지로 해석할 수 있다

She praised her dog and rewarded him a tidbit when her dog obeyed her instructions

         ㄴ 그녀는 개가시키는 대로하자 칭찬을 하면서 먹을 것을 한 입 감 주었다

That explanation satisfied me

         ㄴ 이제야 이해가 가는군

› **defy**   challenge, boldly refuse to obey
› **tidbit**   choice morsel

(=That explains everything)

The suspect matches(measures) up to the description the police have of the wanted thief
> ↳ 피의자는 경찰이 수배중인 도둑의 인상착의와 부합한다

There are a quite a few that fit that description
> ↳ 그 설명과 일치하는 사람(것)들이 상당히 많다

This question involves embarrassing explanation
> ↳ 이 문제에는 구차한 설명이 필요하다

· **match up** be or provide the equal of, fit or go together

70. 성격   **Personality**

A cynic is a man who knows the price of everything and the value of nothing
> ↳ 냉소주의자는 모든 것의 가격은 알지만 가치는 모르는 사람이다

A man of too much integrity is politely shunned by others
> ↳ 맑은 물에는 물고기가 모이지 않는다

A pessimistic woman can complement an optimistic man, and vise versa
> ↳ 비관적인 여자는 낙관적인 남자를 보충해 주고 그와 반대로 보충해 줄 수도 있다

An-do draws the line at using violence
> ↳ 안도는 폭력 쓰는 걸 용서하지 않아

An-do has his nose up in the air
> ↳ 안도는 거만해

An-do has it all together. Besides, he's got what it takes
> ↳ 안도는 건강하고 건전해요. 게다가 능(실, 재)력도 있고요

> 다재 다능한 사람을 가리켜 '팔망미인'이라고 한다. 이를 번역한다면 'man of many talents = 다재 다능한 사람' 정도가 된다.

An-do's abrasive personality will offend even the most patient of them

---

› **shun** keep away from

› **vice versa** with the order reversed

› **abrasive** tending to abrade, causing irritation

    ㄴ 안도의 거친 성격에는 아무리 참을성 있는 사람일지라도 참아내지 못
    할 거야

Anyone who is eccentric and lacks social skills usually becomes the fifth wheel in social functions
    ㄴ 성격이 괴팍하고 사교술이 능하지 못한 사람은 사교모임에서 외톨이
    가 된다

Anyone who is out of step or tries to be individualistic will be ignored or ridiculed
    ㄴ 누구든 남들과 어울리지 않거나 개인주의로 나가는 사람은 무시되거
    나 놀림을 받게 될 것이다

Are you always this lukewarm about everything?
    ㄴ 넌 언제나 모든 일에 이렇게 뜨뜻미지근하냐?

Bigotry may be roughly defined as the anger of men who have no opinions
    ㄴ 편협은 대략 아무 의견이 없는 사람의 분노로 정의될 수 있다

Bong-soo has a Puritanical mind
    ㄴ 봉수는 융통성 없는 사람이다

(=Bong-soo is a straight arrow)

Bong-soo has broad shoulders
    ㄴ 봉수는 포용력이 있어

Bong-soo is down-to-earth and the sort of man with no pretensions
    ㄴ 봉수는 순수하고 견실한 사람이다

Bong-soo is more stingy than frugal
    ㄴ 봉수는 검약하다기 보다는 인색해

‣ **pretension** insincere effort, deception
‣ **frugal** thrifty

Bong-soo won't notice anything but what relates to himself
> ↳ 봉수는 자기와 관련 없는 일에는 어떤 일에도 주의를 기울이지 않아

Bong-soon has big ears
> ↳ 봉순이는 꼬치꼬치 캐묻기를 좋아해

Byung-ho is as innocent as a new-born baby
> ↳ 병호는 정말 깨끗해

Caprice runs in his blood
> ↳ 변덕이 죽 끓는 게 그 사람 내력

Chan-soo can't sit still for a moment, he is a can of worms
> ↳ 찬수는 한시도 가만히 있지 못하는 좀이 쑤시는 사람이야

Chang-ho has the patience of a saint(Job)
> ↳ 창호는 돌부처 같은 인내심을 가졌어

Chang-ho likes to dish it out, but he hates to take it in
> ↳ 창호는 남에게 욕(꾸짖기)은 잘 하지만 남에게 욕먹는 건 싫어해

Chang-ho really plays it safe(enough)
> ↳ 창호는 정말 신중해

Chang-soo has a forbidding countenance but he wouldn't hurt a fly
> ↳ 창수가 얼굴은 험상궂지만 그렇게 순할 수 없어

Chang-soo has well-rounded corners
> ↳ 창수는 모가 나지 않는 사람이다

Chang-soo is too chicken-shit to go up and talk to her
> ↳ 창수는 너무 소심해서 그녀에게 말을 붙여보지 못하고 있어

Chang-soo is very good(much) in command of himself
> ↳ 창수는 자제력이 대단해

Chang-soo never fails to please
> ↳ 창수는 절대 남의 비위를 건드리지 않아

▸ **countenance** face or facial expression

Chul-soo is not hard to please
　　ㄴ 철수는 까다로운 사람이 아냐

Circuitous and ambiguous prevaricating comes naturally to her
　　ㄴ 그녀에게는 우회적이고 애매 모호한 얼버무림이 쉬운 일이다

Doesn't he take the cake!
　　ㄴ 그 사람 뻔뻔스럽기 짝이 없어

Doo-chul really knows how to hit below the belt
　　ㄴ 병수는 참으로 치사한 사람이다

Doo-soo does not like to be fussed over
　　ㄴ 두수는 남들이 치켜세우는 걸 좋아하지 않아

Doo-soo is a man of strong individuality
　　ㄴ 두수는 개성이 강해

Duck-soo appears dismissive in public but he's in fact a caring person
　　ㄴ 덕수가 남들 앞에서는 무정해 보이지만 실은 인정 있는 사람이다

Every nation has its own peculiar character
　　ㄴ 각 국민은 제각기 고유한 국민성을 갖고 있다

Friendship admits the difference of character, as love does that of sex
　　ㄴ 우정은 성격 차를 용납한다, 사랑에서 이성을 허용하듯이

Gi-jae always gives of himself when he is needed
　　ㄴ 기재는 언제고 그를 필요로 할 때면 시간과 노력을 아끼지 않고 도와 준다

Gil-soo can't live giving in to others
　　ㄴ 길수는 지고는 못살아

Have a straight forward personality(=no-nonsense)

› **prevaricate**　deviate from the truth
› **peculiar**　characteristic of only one, strange

↳ 성격이 시원 시원

He always plans ahead
  ↳ 그는 계획성 있는 사람이다

He is rather retiring in disposition
  ↳ 그는 상당히 내성적이야

He rose above petty jealousies then
  ↳ 그는 그때 시시한 질투심 따위는 초월하고 있었다

He turns green with envy
  ↳ 그는 사촌이 논 사면 배아픈 사람이다

남이 잘 되면 질투가 난다는 뜻이다. 질투를 표현할 때 "To turn green with envy 질투로 얼굴이 녹색이 된다"라고 한다. Green face 는 한국말로 창백함을 나타내는 표현이고, 이는 공포(fear), 질투심(jealousy), 아픔(sickness)을 나타낼 때 쓰인다.

He's a poor(sore) loser
  ↳ 지고는 못살아

(=He cries sour grapes)

He's been a little edgy
  ↳ 그는 신경이 좀 날카로워

(=He's been a bit high-strung(on edge))

He's his own man

‣ **disposition** act or power of disposing of,
          arrangement, natural attitude

ㄴ 그 사람은 주관이 뚜렷해

His character comes out in what he has said
ㄴ 그가 한 말에 그의 성격이 나타난다

His strange personality runs in his family
ㄴ 그의 이상한 성격은 대물림이야

I've eased up
ㄴ 내 성질 많이 죽었다

It goes against the grain with me
ㄴ 그건 내 성미에 안 맞아

It's difficult to plan anything with him because he doesn't know his own mind
ㄴ 그는 우유부단해서 같이 계획을 세우기가 어려워

It's my nature
ㄴ 그건 내 천성인가 봐

It's not my cup of tea
ㄴ 그건 내 스타일이 아냐

> (=It's not my thing(style))
> (=It isn't for me)

It's not my line to interfere
ㄴ 남의 일에 간섭하는 건 내 성미에 맞지 않아

Jealousy is deeply ingrained in human nature
ㄴ 질투는 인간본성에 깊이 배어 있다

Lulu loves to be in the limelight(likes to keep in the background)
ㄴ 루루는 남의 앞에 나서길 좋아해(싫어해)

› **ease up** relieve from distress, lessen the tension of, make easier

› **ingrain** work into the texture or moral or mental makeup

Min-ho looks mild-mannered, but actually he has a passionate temperament
> ↳ 민호가 보기에는 온순하나 실제로는 성깔이 있다

My wife's cleanness is bred in the bone
> ↳ 우리 집사람의 청결성은 타고났어

Nam-soo has nerve
> ↳ 남수는 뻔뻔스러워

> (=Nam-soo is really cheeky(brash))
> (=Nam-soo does just whatever he pleases)

Nam-soo's true nature was eventually revealed
> ↳ 시간이 지나면서 남수의 본성이 드러났다

Now you are showing your true colors
> ↳ 이제야 본색이 드러나는군

People say he's tough but the opposite is true
> ↳ 사람들은 그를 거칠다고 하지만 알고 보면 부드러운 남자야

People's character comes out in what they have said
> ↳ 사람들이 말하는데서 그들의 인격이 나온다

Personal characteristics are persistent and relatively little influenced by training and experience
> ↳ 개인의 성격은 지속적이며 상대적으로 훈련이나 경험에 의해 거의 영향을 받지 않는다

She is her mother all over even in personality
> ↳ 그 여자는 성격에서조차 자기 어머니를 꼭 닮았어

Soft and fair goes far

· **temperament** characteristic frame of mind

↳ 부드럽고 순하면 이겨

Some people are molded by their admirations, others by their hostilities
↳ 어떤 사람들의 성격은 남들에 대한 경탄에서 이루어지고 어떤 사람들은 남들에 대한 적대감에서 이루어진다

The thing that counts is character
↳ 중요한 건 인격

We are not naturally bad
↳ 타고날 때 나쁜 사람은 없어

We are opposites
↳ 우리는 성질이 극과 극이다

> (=We are totally different)

Whoever plays deep must necessarily lose his money or his character
↳ 큰 도박을 하면 누구나 반드시 돈 아니면 품위를 잃게 된다

You have a quite a personality
↳ 넌 매우 개성적이야

> (=You have a lot of character)

You've got a short fuse
↳ 성미 급하시구먼

You've got the common touch
↳ 넌 붙임성이 있군

› **mold** shape in or as if in a mold

› **fuse** tube lighted to transmit fire to an explosive

71. 성공　　　　　　　　　　　　　Success

A minute's success pays for the failure of years
　　　↳ 한 순간의 성공은 1년간의 실패를 보상한다

A prosperous fool is a grievous burden
　　　↳ 성공한 어리석은 자는 사회악이다

A successful man can't realize how hard an unsuccessful man finds life
　　　↳ 성공한 사람은 실패한 사람의 어려운 삶을 알지 못한다

After he sold his house, he was ten million won to the good(ahead of the game)
　　　↳ 그는 집을 팔아 천만원 이익을 봤어

After only a few years, he's wallowing in money and property
　　　↳ 그는 불과 몇 년 안 가서 돈이며 재산이 풍족해졌어

All my work is falling into place
　　　↳ 모든 일이 잘 풀리고 있어

(=Everything is going like clockwork(working out perfectly))

All of us come out ahead in the end
　　　↳ 결국 우리 모두 이익을 볼 거다

All these things cooperated to make this work a success

▸ **wallow**　roll about in deep mud, live with excessive pleasure

▸ **clockwork**　machinery containing small gears

ㄴ 모든 상황이 겹쳐서 이 일이 성공했다

An-do began from the bottom of the ladder
ㄴ 안도는 미천한 출신에서 입신한 사람

As your company rewards enterprising employees with accelerated promotions and responsibilities, you'll go far into the job
ㄴ 너희 회사가 진취적인 사원에게 빠른 승진과 책임 있는 일의 보임을 보장하고 있으니 넌 그 직무에서 성공할 것이다

Back at the ranch, I've succeeded in reading his thoughts
ㄴ 본론으로 말하면 난 그의 속셈을 알아내게 되었어

Behind every successful man there stands a woman
ㄴ 성공한 사람의 뒤에는 부인의 내조가 있게 마련

Bong-soo clawed his way up to the top, fighting at every step
ㄴ 봉수는 한 단계 한 단계 분투하여 영예의 자리에 오른 사람

By the look of your huge house and new car, you are getting up in the world
ㄴ 너의 큰집이며 새 차를 보니 출세했구나

Chance has nothing to do with his present success
ㄴ 그의 성공은 우연한 일이 아니다

Chang-soo will carry everything before him
ㄴ 창수는 크게 성공할 것이다

Don't saddle yourself with such a big debt before you are sure of your professional success
ㄴ 사업상 성공이 보장되기 전에는 그 큰 빚을 떠맡지 마라

Every failure is a stepping stone to success
ㄴ 실패는 성공의 디딤돌이다

Everything fell into his lap

‣ **enterprise** an undertaking, business organization, initiative

‣ **ranch** establishment for the raising of cattle, sheep, or horses; specialized farm

ㄴ 모든 일이 그의 뜻대로 되었다

Everything is coming up roses
  ㄴ 만사가 잘 되고있어

Everything is falling into place(going like clockwork, working perfectly)
  ㄴ 매사가 척척 맞아 들어가는군

> (=All my work is falling into(a) place)

Everything is in working order
  ㄴ 매사 순조롭게 되어가다

Everything went like clockwork
  ㄴ 모든 일이 차질 없이 진행 됐어

Everything went off without a hitch
  ㄴ 모든 일이 순조롭게 진행되었다

Everything went smoothly on the line today
  ㄴ 오늘은 모든 작업이 순조로웠다

Everything(The performance) went off well
  ㄴ 만사가(공연이) 잘 되었다(성공했다)

Failure is the condiment that gives success its flavor
  ㄴ 실패는 성공의 묘미를 더해주는 조미료

Failure may be an orphan, but success always has many parents
  ㄴ 실패하면 혼자 책임져야 하지만 성공하면 너도나도 공로자라고 나선다

Failures are rehearsals for success
  ㄴ 실패는 성공의 예행연습이다

› **hitch** jerk, sudden halt
› **orphan** child whose parents are dead

Gil-soo hoped against hope, and everything worked out
　　　ㄴ 길수는 가망 없는 일에 희망을 걸었는데 만사가 잘 풀렸어

Gil-soo pulled in(a notch) and smiled at his success at losing weight
　　　ㄴ 길수는 혁대를 한 매듭 줄이고서 체중 감량 성공에 흡족해 했다

Hard work is a sure avenue to success
　　　ㄴ 근면은 성공에 이르는 확실한 길

He finally got(had) his way, as he does in such matters
　　　ㄴ 그는 평소 그런 일에 대처하듯이 결국 그 일을 해냈어

He fought his way to success
　　　ㄴ 그는 고군분투해서 이겨냈다

He hopes that all your efforts don't go for naught(nothing)
　　　ㄴ 그는 너의 노력이 성공하기를 바라고 있어

He is a white egg laid by a black hen
　　　ㄴ 그는 개천에서 용 난 격이다

> 한국에서 용은 귀함을 대표하지만, 서양에서는 괴물, 악마를 뜻한다. 따라서
> 비슷한 뜻으로 'A white egg laid by a black hen(검은 닭이 난 하얀 알'
> 이나, 'A rag to riches story(누더기에서 부자가 된 이야기)'가 쓰인다).

He rose from the ranks to become a foremost industrialist
　　　ㄴ 그는 밑바닥에서 입신하여 일류 실업자가 되었다

He rose through the ranks due to his hard work
　　　ㄴ 그는 열심히 일해서 평사원으로부터 빨리 출세했다

He set up the fortune of today out of nothing
　　　ㄴ 그는 맨주먹으로 지금의 부를 이뤘다

He won with everything against him

> · **avenue**　way of approach, broad street
> · **foremost**　first in time, place, or order

↳ 그는 인간승리를 이루어 내었다

> (=He beat all the odds)
> (=He succeeded with no hope of success)

He'll do something with his life
↳ 그는 크게 성공할 것이다

Her tenacity was what finally carried the day
↳ 그녀의 집념이 결국 성공으로 이끌었다

His 'quality first' policy brought him success in business
↳ 그는 품질위주의 영업방침으로 성공했다

His physical wreck at only 40 is a high price for his success in show business
↳ 나이가 겨우 **40**에 몸을 크게 망친 것은 연예계에서의 성공에 대한 값으로는 가혹하다

His triumph has a sting in its tail
↳ 그의 승리는 개운치 않은 뒷맛을 남기고 있다

I have been trying hard determined to do whatever it takes
↳ 이를 갈고 열심히 하고 있어

> (=I've been gritting my teeth and trying hard)
> (=I've been trying hard bent on success(determined to do better))

I must succeed this time or never
↳ 이번이야말로 성공해야해

› **tenacity** holding fast, retentive
› **grit** press with a grating noise

I sincerely wish your continued success
　　ㄴ 건투를 빈다

I tried with varying success
　　ㄴ 해서 성공 할 때도 있었고 못할 때도 있었어

I wish you every success
　　ㄴ 하시는 일마다 성공하시기 바랍니다

If at first you don't succeed, try, try again
　　ㄴ 칠전팔기하라

"첫술에 배부르랴"라는 말이 있다. "시작이 반이다(Well begun, half done)"
이란 속담도 있지만, 이는 시작하는 것이 어렵다는 것을 뜻하는 속담이고, 시
작한 후에 노력을 하여 한 단계 한 단계 이루어 나가야 된다는 뜻을 가진 속
담이 "첫술에 배부르랴(Rome was not built in a day)"이다(It takes
three generations to make a gentleman = 훌륭한 사람은 하루아침에
만들어지지 않는다).

If he plays his cards right, he'll go places in this business
　　ㄴ 그가 잘만 한다면 이 사업에서 성공할 것이다

In the end I'll come through with flying colors
　　ㄴ 결국 난 성공할 것이다

In the end, the odds are in your favor
　　ㄴ 결국엔 네게 승산이 있어

It looks like we made it
　　ㄴ 우리가 해낸 것 같아

It's still the end of the rainbow
　　ㄴ 그러면 더욱더 만사형통이지

・**vary**　alter, make or be of different kinds

Jin-shil really made a name for herself in show business

  ↳ 진실인 연예계에서 출세(성공)했어

Jobs are one of the evaluations of the success on any society

  ↳ 직업은 어느 사회에서나 성공 여부를 평가하는 기준이 될 수 있다

Just play it cool and he'll probably appoint you because of your past success

  ↳ 그저 차분하게 해나가면 아마 전에 네가 거둔 성과 덕분에 네가 임명될 것이다

Keeping his heart on what he wanted and ignoring everything else, he made a success in life

  ↳ 그는 자신이 원하는 일에만 마음을 쏟고 다른 모든 것을 무시하면서 성공을 이루어내었다

Let success or failure be on my head

  ↳ 성패는 내 책임이다

Lulu will surely make a go of her business she enters

  ↳ 루루는 시작한 사업에서 확실히 성공 할거야

Mr. Sohn has something going for himself with his business

  ↳ 손씨는 그의 사업에 성공했어

My efforts were rewarded with success

  ↳ 노력한 덕분에 성공했어

Nobody will go for broke when the odds are stacked against him

  ↳ 성공할 확률이 적은데 무모하게 대들 사람은 없어

Nothing succeeds like the appearance of success

  ↳ 성공한 것으로 보이는 것이 경쟁에 낫다

One can't grudge success to such a worthy man

  ↳ 그런 훌륭한 사람이 성공한 것을 시기할 사람은 없어

· **evaluate** appraise
· **grudge** be reluctant to give

One should be careful of small things if one is aiming to achieve great successes
ㄴ 큰 일을 이루기 위해서는 작은 일도 소홀히 해서는 안 돼

Only some people have it to make it in the show business
ㄴ 연예계에서 성공할 수 있는 사람은 그리 많지 않아

Pil-soo succeeded even though he had two strikes against him
ㄴ 필수는 매우 불리한 입장에도 불구하고 성공했다

Sailing against the wind, he succeeded in winning the contract
ㄴ 그는 어려움을 이겨내고 계약을 따내었다

Send up a trial balloon before you start the project
ㄴ 사업을 시작하기 전에 성공여부를 타진해 보아라

She just basks in the glory of a successful husband although she's never achieved much herself
ㄴ 그 여자는 이렇다하게 해 놓은 것 없이 성공한 남편의 영광을 한껏 누리고 있을 뿐이다

She made a go of his computer business and made a fortune
ㄴ 그녀는 컴퓨터 사업에 성공해서 큰돈을 벌었다

She'll be prosperous yet
ㄴ 그 여자가 언젠가는 성공할 것이다

She'll never succeed in ingratiating herself into my good graces
ㄴ 그 여자가 아무리 애교를 떨어도 내 마음에 들 수는 없어

She's really made something of herself
ㄴ 야, 그 여자 성공했네

She's running a one-man show in which they have overcome the hurdle in order to attain success
ㄴ 그들이 장애물을 극복하고 성공해 온 데는 그녀가 북 치고 장구 치고

› **bask** enjoy pleasant warmth
› **ingratiate** gain favor for (oneself)

다 해 오고 있기 때문이다

Since power with words is a mark of successful people, provision is made for increasing their vocabulary on a systematic basis
> ↳ 말의 힘이 성공한 사람들의 특징이기 때문에 너의 어휘를 체계적으로 늘리기 위한 준비가 되어있다

Sometimes accidents happen in life' from which we have need of a madness to excite ourselves successfully
> ↳ 우리의 삶에는 때로 우리 자신을 자극하여 성공할 수 있게 하는 미친 짓을 필요로 하는 사건이 생기기도 한다

Stack your reputation on the success of this invention
> ↳ 이번 발명의 성공에 네 명예를 걸어라

Success doesn't come overnight
> ↳ 천리 길도 한 걸음부터

> '천릿길도 한 걸음부터'는 작은 일부터 차근차근하여 큰 일을 이뤄야 한다는 뜻이다. 자주 쓰는 영어 속담은 'A journey of a thousand miles begins with a single step'이며 이는 '리'를 'mile'로만 썼을 뿐, 한국 속담과 뜻이 같다. (=Little by little and bit by bit)

Success flows from health and intelligence
> ↳ 성공은 건강과 지혜로 이루어진다

Success has crowned his efforts
> ↳ 그의 노력은 성과를 거두었어

Success is not permanent. The same is also true of failure
> ↳ 성공은 영원하지 않다. 실패도 마찬가지다

Successful people need more challenge and stimulation than others

---

- **permanent** lasting
- **stimulate** make active

↳ 성공할 사람에게는 보다 더 많은 도전과 자극이 필요하다

The last thing you should do is to rest on your laurels
↳ 성공에 도취해서 방심해선 안 돼

The only way to achieve true success is to express yourself completely in service to society
↳ 진정한 성공을 이룰 수 있는 유일한 방법은 사회를 위하여 최선을 다 하는 것이다

The pursuit of success is a religion to him
↳ 그는 입신출세에 전념하고 있어

The secret of success is constancy to success
↳ 성공의 비결은 목적에 대한 일관성이다

The subtlety was successful that he was able to throw them off the trail
↳ 그 속임수가 성공을 거두어서 그는 그들을 따돌릴 수 있었다

The success of most things depends on knowing how it will take to succeed
↳ 대부분의 성공은 성공하는데 무엇이 필요한가를 아는데 달려있다

The toughest thing about success is that you've got to keep being a success
↳ 성공에서 가장 어려운 점은 계속 성공하는 일이다

The true road to preeminent success in any line is to make yourself master of that line
↳ 어떤 분야에서 눈에 띄게 성공하기 위해서는 그 분야의 전문가가 되 어야 한다

The way to rise is to obey and please
↳ 성공의 방법은 남의 말을 따르고 남을 기쁘게 하는 일이다

‣ **subtle** hardly noticeable, clever
‣ **preeminent** having highest rank

There are two ways of rising in the world, either by your own industry or by the folly of others
> ↳ 출세에는 두 가지 방법이 있는데 하나는 자신의 노력이고 하나는 다른 사람의 바보짓이다

There's more to life than money(success , this office)
> ↳ 돈(성공)만이 인생의 전부가 '아니다

There's much more to his success than luck
> ↳ 그의 성공이 운이 따랐기 때문만은 아니다

They succeeded in isolating extreme left by winning massive popular support
> ↳ 그들은 대중의 큰 지지에 힘입어 극좌분자를 색출하는데 성공했다

They succeeded in their cost-cutting program by getting rid of a fourth of their manpower
> ↳ 그들은 인력의 1/4을 감원시킴으로써 비용절감에 성공했다

They will come through with flying colors in the end
> ↳ 그들은 결국 고생 끝에 성공을 거둘 것이다

This is your lifetime chance to give your all to succeed in the male-dominated world of finance
> ↳ 이번엔 네가 남자 위주의 금융계에서 성공하기 위해 전력을 다해야 할 일생에 한 번 있을만한 절호의 기회다

Too much success can ruin you as surely as too much failure
> ↳ 지나친 실패가 사람을 확실히 망치듯 지나친 성공도 사람을 망칠 수 있다

We have to make this job successful whatever the cost
> ↳ 어떤 대가를 치러도 이 일은 성공시켜야 해

We tried to draw Chang-ho out of his shell, but without success

---

› **massive** being a large mass, large in scope

ㄴ우린 창호에게 입을 열도록 해보았으나 잘 되지 않았어

You can make a go of your business
ㄴ넌 사업에 성공할 것이다

You can't succeed in business without taking certain risks
ㄴ사업에서 어느 정도 위험을 감수하지 않고서는 성공할 수 없다

You have rested on your laurels too long
ㄴ넌 지난번 성공에 너무 오래 안주하고 있어

You made your way through difficulties
ㄴ너 출세했구나

You should never allow their unwillingness to become successful to prevent you from becoming successful
ㄴ그들의 내키지 않는 마음이 당신의 성공을 저해하는데 성공할 정도로 허용해서는 안 된다

You'll succeed if you put your mind to it
ㄴ넌 맘만 먹으면 그 일을 해낼 수 있어

You'll surely get promoted; you have everything going for you
ㄴ모든 일이 네게 유리하게 돌아가고 있으니 틀림없이 성공할거야

You've got to learn what you need in the school of hard knocks to be successful
ㄴ성공하려면 험한 세파를 이겨내는데 필요한 것을 배워야 한다

Your sincere efforts made the recent fund-raising activity successful one
ㄴ귀하의 진실한 노고로 최근의 모금운동은 성공적인 결과를 보게 되었습니다

Your success is on the horizon. You know what you're doing
ㄴ너의 성공이 눈앞에 다가왔어. 넌 정말 훌륭하게 해내고 있어

› **laurel** small evergreen tree, honor

72. 생각 ─────────── **Thoughts**

A man can never be hindered from thinking whatever he chooses
　　↳ 사람이 맘대로 생각하는걸 누가 막으랴

A penny for your thoughts
　　↳ 뭘 그리 멍하니 생각해?

A thinking robot? That's a new one to me
　　↳ 생각하는 로봇이라? 야, 그거 놀랠 노자네

Act quickly, think slowly
　　　　↳ 행동(실천)은 빨리, 생각은 천천히

All great discoveries are made by men whose feelings run ahead of their thinking
　　　　↳ 모든 위대한 발명은 느낌이 생각보다 앞서가는 사람들에 의해 이루어
　　　　　진다

All you have to do is to do as you think right
　　　　↳ 네가 할 일은 네가 옳다고 생각하는 대로하기만 하면 돼

An interesting thought just past through my mind
　　　　↳ 재미있는 생각이 막 떠올랐어

An-do has been taught to rise above his selfish considerations
　　　　↳ 안도는 이기적인 생각을 넘어설 수 있는 교육을 받았다

An-do thought I was not all there
　　　　↳ 안도는 내가 돌았다고 생각했나봐

› **hinder**　obstruct or hold back

As some of the thinking now collapses with share prices, concrete consequences are beginning to emerge
> ↳ 이 같은 생각이 주가폭락과 함께 붕괴되면서 구체적인 결과들이 나타나기 시작했다

Back at the ranch, I've succeeded in reading his thoughts
> ↳ 본론으로 말하면 난 그의 속셈을 알아내게 되었어

Better bad now than worse later
> ↳ 지금은 나쁘더라도 나중 일을 생각해야 해

Bong-soo thought that he was the star of the team until he got the business from his coach
> ↳ 봉수는 코치한테 혼나기 전까지는 자기가 팀에서 스타라고 생각했어

Bong-soo went out of there feeling sorry for himself
> ↳ 봉수는 자신이 한심하다는 생각이 들어 거기서 나왔어

By no stretch of the imagination
> ↳ 아무리 생각해 보아도 힘들 거야

Byung-soo has his head in the clouds
> ↳ 병수는 비현실적인 생각을 하고 있어(**Your plan is a house of cards** 네 계획은 비현실적이야)

Can you bring him around to your way of thinking?
> ↳ 그를 설득해서 동의를 얻어낼 수 있겠나?

Couples contemplating divorce usually have second thoughts when they realize how it'll affect their children
> ↳ 이혼을 생각해보고 있는 부부들은 보통 그 이혼이 자녀들에게 어떤 영향을 줄 것인지 생각할 때 마음이 흔들린다

Cut out that knee-jerk reaction and think them through
> ↳ 덮어놓고 대답하지 말고 잘 생각해서 대답해

› **emerge** rise, come forth, or appear
› **contemplate** view or consider thoughtfully

Deep-six the trash
ㄴ 쓸데없는 생각 버려

Do not be afraid to speak because you are afraid of what others may think of you
ㄴ 다른 사람들이 당신을 어떻게 생각할까 두려워서 말하기를 두려워 말라

Do not hesitate to make any necessary changes as you think(see) fit
ㄴ 적절하다고 생각되면 주저하지 말고 필요에 맞게 변경시켜라

Do you think he doesn't know his way around?
ㄴ 그를 아무 것도 모르는 사람으로 아나?

Do you think I have the golden goose that lays the golden eggs?
ㄴ 난 뭐 도깨비 방망이라도 가진 줄(돈이 무한정 있는줄) 아나?

Do you think I'm loaded or something?
ㄴ 내가 재력가라도 되는 줄 아는 모양이군

Do you think your hat will stay on in this high wind?
ㄴ 이렇게 센바람에 모자가 안 날아갈 것 같으냐?

Does that ring a bell?
ㄴ 이제 생각나나?

Don't give it another thought(a second thought)
ㄴ 그 일은 이제 잊어버려

> (=Don't sweat it)

Don't think the test will be a tea party
ㄴ 그 시험을 식은 죽 먹기로 여기지마

Don't you think she's had a basinful(bellyfull) of your company this

---

› **sweat** work or cause to work hard
› **basinful** amount that fills the basin

week?
> ↳ 그 여자가 이번 주 내내 지겹도록 너와 같이 있어주었다고 생각 안 해?

Dong-soo dashed back to the burning house without a second thought
> ↳ 동수는 즉각 불타고있는 집으로 다시 뛰어들었다

Dong-soo let that idea slip out before he thought
> ↳ 동수는 무심코 그 생각을 입 밖에 내고 말았다

Double-think means the power of holding two contradictory beliefs in one's mind simultaneously
> ↳ 이중사고란 두 가지의 모순된 신념을 동시에 가진다는 말이다

Even the porcupine thinks its young are soft and glossy
> ↳ 고슴도치도 제 새끼는 예쁘다고 한다

> (=The beetle is a beauty in the eyes of its mother)
> (=The crow thinks her own bird fairest)
> (=The owl thinks its own young fairest)
> (=No mother has a homely child)

Everybody thinks the accountant had his hand in the till
> ↳ 모두들 경리가 돈을 훔친 것으로 생각한다

Examinations help form the habit of thinking quickly
> ↳ 시험은 재빨리 생각하는데 도움을 준다

Fame usually comes to those who are thinking about something else
> ↳ 명예는 대개 다른 생각을 하고 있는 사람에게 찾아온다

Hang-soon thinks he loves her, but he's just stringing her along
> ↳ 행순이는 그가 자신을 사랑하는 줄 알고 있지만 그는 그저 사랑하는 척 하면서 다른 남자에게 못 가게 붙들고만 있는 거야

· **contradict** state the contrary of
· **fame** public reputation

He couldn't work late because his mind kept jumping the track to thinking about the new girl in the office
> ↳ 그는 사무실에 새로 온 여직원 생각으로 마음이 흔들려 늦게까지 일할 수 없었다

He is a fool that thinks not that another thinks
> ↳ 남도 생각이 있다는 것을 생각지 못하는 사람은 바보다

He that thinks himself wisest, is generally the greatest fool
> ↳ 자신이 가장 슬기롭다고 생각하는 사람은 대개 가장 어리석은 사람이다

His thoughts have been nothing but you for years
> ↳ 몇 년 동안 그의 생각은 너한테만 가 있었다

How can you think other than logically?
> ↳ 어찌 논리적이 아닌 방식으로 생각할 수 있겠는가?

Hyun-soo screwed up my train of thought
> ↳ 현수가 나의 정리되고 있는 생각을 흩으러 놨어

I lost my train of thought
> ↳ 내가 무슨 말을 했더라

I think I have claim on your compassion
> ↳ 조금은 내 맘을 알아줘야지

I think I'll pass
> ↳ 싫어(사양하겠어)

I think it's quite the opposite
> ↳ 그 반대라고 생각해

I thought I'd seen everything
> ↳ 난 내가 다 아는 일이라고 생각했지

I thought my number was up yesterday
> ↳ 어제는 죽는 줄만 알았다

› **screw up** bungle, disturb

› **compassion** pity

I'm going to stand pat
  ↳ 내 생각은 변함이 없어

If a man takes no thought about what is distant, he'll find sorrow near at hand
  ↳ 사람이 먼 일을 생각지 않으면 눈앞에 슬픔이 닥쳐온다(공자)

If she thinks she can win the game, she's riding for a fall
  ↳ 그 여자가 게임에 이길 수 있다고 생각한다면 무모한(가망 없는) 짓이다

If you know what's good for you, don't let him know what you really think
  ↳ 네가 그렇게 생각하는 것을 드러내지 않는 것이 너 자신을 위하는 일이야

In many children's dreams they often relive their fears and they thought they were being attacked
  ↳ 어린이들은 꿈속에서 무서움과 공격당했던 기억을 회상하는 때가 많다

It is the thought that counts
  ↳ 중요한 건 마음 쏨쏨이야

(=The thought is what matters)

It is thinking that makes what we read ours
  ↳ 읽은 것을 우리 것으로 만들어 주는 것은 사고이다

It isn't worth a thought
  ↳ 생각할 가치도 없어

It shouldn't happen to a dog
  ↳ 그 생각만 해도 지긋지긋해

· **pat** tap gently

It'll make us think the law is an ass

    ↳ 그래봤자 그 일에 법을 적용하는 게 얼마나 멍청한 짓인가 하는 생각이 들게 할 뿐이다

It's later than you think

    ↳ 네 생각처럼 어물어물 할 틈이 없어

It's the thought that counts

    ↳ 무슨 일이나 정성이 중요=먹(받)은 걸로 칠게

Let your hair down and tell me what you really think

    ↳ 속마음을 열고 정말 무슨 생각을 하고 있는지 말해봐

Let's give a(some) thought to that matter

    ↳ 그 일을 한 번 생각해 보자

Look at the big picture

    ↳ 넓게(잘) 생각해 봐

Man differs from brutes in that he thinks

    ↳ 사람은 생각한다는 점에서 동물과 다르다

My daughter thinks the world of me

    ↳ 우리 딸은 나를 가장 사랑하고 존경해요

My father implanted good ideas that have stayed with me all my life

    ↳ 아버지는 내가 평생 가지고 있던 좋은 생각을 심어준 분이다

Nobody can follow your thinking if you talk a blue streak

    ↳ 그처럼 청산유수 같이 주워섬기면 아무도 네 생각을 이해하지 못해

Nobody thought he was destined for greatness

    ↳ 그가 큰 인물이 되리라는 것을 아무도 생각지 못했다

Nobody thought it would come to this

    ↳ 일이 이 지경이 될 줄 아무도 생각 못했지

Nothing is miserable unless you think it is

› **streak**　move fast

› **destine**　designate, assign, or determine in advance; direct

ㄴ 비참하다고 생각하지 않는 한 비참한 일은 없다

Oh, I lost my train of thought

ㄴ 아, 뭘 얘기하려고 했는지 잊어버렸어

Only after week's of vain efforts, did the right ideas occur to me

ㄴ 몇 주일동안 헛된 노력을 한 후에야 겨우 적절한 생각이 떠올랐다

Our democracies must build a culture of mutual trust and respect and re-learn the value of strategic thinking

ㄴ 우리의 민주주의는 상호신뢰와 존중의 문화를 증진시키고 전략적 사고의 가치를 다시 배워나가야 한다

Our life is what our thoughts make it

ㄴ 인생은 생각하기 나름이다

Pain is forgotten where gain follows

ㄴ 이익이 있으면 고통을 잊어버린다

Pain makes man think, thought makes man wise, wisdom makes life endurable

ㄴ 고통은 사람을 생각하게 하고, 사색은 현명하게 하며, 지혜는 삶의 인내심을 키워준다

Petty officials are given no scope for original thought

ㄴ 말단공무원에게는 창의적인 생각을 할 여지가 없다

Politeness is the art of selecting among one's real thoughts

ㄴ 예의바름이란 진짜 속마음 중에서 어떤 것을 드러낼지의 선택이다

Put that in your pipe and smoke it

ㄴ 곰곰이 생각을 좀 해봐라

Rational thought is interpretation according to a scheme which we can't escape

ㄴ 이치에 맞는 생각이란 피할 수 없는 계획에 의한 해석이다

› **mutual** given or felt by one another in equal amount, common

› **scheme** crafty plot, systematic design

Sang-soo's bright idea will give them a needed shot in the arm
　　ㄴ 상수의 기발한 생각이 그들에게 필요한 활력소가 될 것이다

See it from other person's point of view(perspective)
　　ㄴ 다른 사람의 입장에서 생각을 좀 해봐

She immersed herself in work so as to stop thinking about the problem
　　ㄴ 그녀는 그 문제를 더 이상 생각하지 않기 위해 일에 몰두했다

She's got a hole in her head if she thinks I was born yesterday
　　ㄴ 그 여자가 나를 만만하게 본다면 어리석은 생각이다

Some people still cling to the fallacy that she is in the wrong
　　ㄴ 어떤 사람들은 아직도 그녀가 잘못한 것이라는 잘못된 생각을 고수하고 있다

Somebody made the speaker lost his train of thought
　　ㄴ 누군가가 연사에게 방해를 해서 무엇을 말하려고 했던가를 잊어버렸다

Take a day or two to think about it
　　ㄴ 잘 생각해봐

> (=Think it over)

Take whatever measure you think the best
　　ㄴ 무엇이든지 적절하다고 생각되는 조치를 취하라

That's a consideration
　　ㄴ 그건 좀 생각해 볼 문제로군

The idea didn't work in practice
　　ㄴ 생각은 그럴듯했지만 실용성은 없었다

‣ fallacy false idea, false reasoning

The idea flash through my mind
↳ 그 생각이 번개같이 머리를 스쳤다

The idea kept running through my head
↳ 그 생각이 끊임없이 머리에 떠올랐어

The only sure way against bad ideas is better ideas
↳ 나쁜 생각을 반대하고 나설 수 있는 확실하고도 유일한 수단은 그보다 나은 생각이 있을 때이다

The profound thinker always suspects that he is superficial
↳ 심오한 사상가는 늘 자신이 수박 겉 핥기를 하고 있는 것 아닌가 하고 생각한다

The singer thought he had fully made a name for himself and decided to ride off into the sunset at the height of his career
↳ 그 가수는 충분히 출세했다는 생각에서 인기 절정에서 무대에서 은퇴하기로 결심했다

The thought flashed through my mind
↳ 그 생각이 마음에 언 듯 떠올랐다

There comes a time in every man's life when he has to think
↳ 모든 사람의 삶에는 생각해야 할 때가 찾아온다

There is a difference between not thinking of someone and forgetting him
↳ 누군가를 생각하지 않는 것과 잊는 것에는 차이가 있다

There is nothing either good or bad but thinking makes it so
↳ 좋고 나쁨이 따로 있는 것이 아니라 사람의 생각 속에 있다

They found out that no idea would come; their brains seemed to be lying fallow
↳ 그들은 묘안이 떠오르지 않고 머리도 잘 돌아가지 않고 있는 것만 같

› **profound** marked by intellectual depth or insight, deeply felt

› **fallow** land plowed but not planted

왔다

They thought the bank robbery was an inside job
ㄴ 그들은 그 은행강도를 내부 자에 의한 소행으로 생각했다

Think nothing of it
ㄴ 신경 쓰지마

This feverish cold often kicks back when we think we are better
ㄴ 이 열 감기는 낫는다고 생각할 때 도지는 수가 많다

Thoughts about the accident, little by little, passed into oblivion
ㄴ 사고에 대한 생각이 차츰 잊혀져갔어

To look at him, you'd never think he's such a snob
ㄴ 그의 모습으로만 본다면 그런 속물로 생각되지 않을 것이다

Try to rid your mind of such obsolete ideas
ㄴ 그런 시대에 뒤진 생각들을 마음속에서 내버리도록 해

Use your brain
ㄴ 생각을 좀 해봐라

Wan-soo thinks he is withering on the vine nobody has chosen him
ㄴ 완수는 아무도 그를 써(선택해)주지 않으니 능력을 썩히게 될 것이란 생각을 하고 있다

We must change our way of thinking if we are to put the nation on its feet after all these struggles
ㄴ 이 모든 어려움 끝에 나라가 바르게 돌아가자면 우리의 사고방식을 바꿔야 한다

What I think doesn't carry any weight in this matter
ㄴ 이 일에 내가 어떻게 생각하느냐 하는 것은 크게 중요하지 않아

What the heart thinks, the mouth speaks
ㄴ 마음에 품은 것은 입 밖으로 나오게 돼있어

› **fever** abnormal rise in body temperature, state of heightened emotion

› **obsolete** no longer in use

What you think doesn't go with my view
ㄴ 네 생각은 내 생각과 어긋나

Who planted that silly idea in your head?
ㄴ 누가 네게 그런 바보 같은 생각을 하게 만들었지?

Who would(could) have thought?
ㄴ 전혀 믿을 수 없어

Wipe out all thought of it and have a another try
ㄴ 그 생각은 모두 잊어버리고 다시 한 번 노력해 봐

Would you share your thoughts with the others?
ㄴ 네 생각을 다른 사람에게 얘기해 보지 그래

You are all I am thinking of
ㄴ 너만을 생각해

You are always in my thoughts
ㄴ 항상 당신의 행복을 빕니다

You are long way out if you think that
ㄴ 그리 생각한다면 한참 오산하고 있는 거야

You attach a strange meaning to what I say
ㄴ 내 말을 이상하게 생각하는구나

You can(are free to) think what you want
ㄴ 착각은 자유다

(=You can believe whatever you want)
(=You are entitled to think what you want)

You must think I'm something

› **silly** foolish or stupid
› **entitle** name, give a right to

↳ 제가 특별하다고 생각하나보죠

You think they are on my tails

↳ 내가 그들과 놀아난다고 생각하는 모양이지

You think too much

↳ 과민반응이야

You'd better read between the lines'

↳ 깊이 생각하는 게 좋아

You've got a hole in your head if you think I'm a dupe

↳ 나를 어수룩하게 생각한다면 큰 오산이다

Your bright idea does you credit

↳ 그 기발한 생각은 훌륭해

Your thinking went out with the horse

↳ 그런 낡아빠진 생각으로 뭘 할래

› **dupe** one easily deceived or cheated

73. 세상   World

A change would do this place a world of good
> ↳ 변화를 주면 이 곳이 훨씬 좋아질 거야

A happy marriage is the world's best bargain
> ↳ 행복한 결혼생활은 이 세상 최고의 계약이다

A man travels the world in search of what he needs and returns home to find it
> ↳ 사람은 자신이 필요로 하는 것을 찾아 세계로 돌아다니다가 집에 와서야 그것을 찾아내게 된다

A wonder lasts but nine days
> ↳ 세상을 떠들썩하게 하는 일도 곧 잊혀지게 된다

All the world knows it
> ↳ 그건 세상이 다 아는 일

An ever increasing number of people throughout the world are exposing themselves to foods containing high level of artificial ingredients
> ↳ 전 세계적으로 점점 많은 사람들이 인공성분이 많이 함유된 식품에 노출되고 있다

An-do is not long for this world
> ↳ 안도는 오래 살지 못할 것이다

Anything goes these days

▸ **ingredient** one of the substances that make up a mixture

ㄴ 요즘 세상엔 별 일이 다 있어

Are there enough oil supplies to see the world to(through to) the end of the century?

ㄴ 세기말까지 기름 공급이 유지될 수 있을까?

Better be out of the world than out of the fashion

ㄴ 유행에 뒤지느니 지구를 떠나겠단 말이군

Better mad with the rest of the world than wise alone

ㄴ 혼자 현명하기보다는 세상의 다른 사람들과 더불어 함께 미치는 게 낫다

Bong-soo acts as if he had the weight(cares) of the world on his shoulders

ㄴ 봉수는 세상걱정 혼자 다 하는 것 같아

By the look of your huge house and new car, you are getting up in the world

ㄴ 너의 큰집이며 새 차를 보니 출세했구나

Chan-ho is riding high

ㄴ 찬호는 물이 올랐어

(=Chan-ho is number one these days)
(=Chan-ho is on top of the world)
(=Chan-ho is above the competition)

Common sense suits itself to the ways of the world

ㄴ 상식은 세상의 이치에 따르는 것이다

Confide in an aunt and the world will know

· **confide** share private thoughts, reveal in confidence

· **aunt** sister of one's father or mother, wife of one's uncle

└ 아주머니(숙모)한테 가만히 말해도 온 세상이 알게 돼있다

Count not him among your friends who'll retail your privacies to the world

└ 당신의 개인적인 일을 여기 저기 떠들고 다니는 사람을 친구로 삼지 말라

Don't tell the whole world

└ 사사로운 일을 남들에게 얘기하지마

For a while I was lost to the world

└ 한동안 난 세상에서 외톨이가 되었지

Has the world another man to show like him?

└ 세상에 그런 사람 또 있을까?

Having all the time in the world is hard for an office worker

└ 사무원에게 시간이 남아돈다는 것은 흔한 일이 아니다

He has been to the four corners of the world(country)

└ 그는 전 세계(국)에 안 가본 곳이 없어

He has gained(lost) currency with the world

└ 그는 사회의 신용을 얻어(잃어)

He is in a world of his own(by himself)

└ 그는 자기 일 밖에 몰라

He lived in a lonely corner of reach out of the noisy world

└ 그는 시끄러운 세상에서 떨어진 외딴곳에 살고 있었다

He wanted to swim a good time, but that it was a world record surprised him

└ 그는 수영에서 좋은 기록을 내고싶었을 뿐이지만 막상 세계기록을 내고 보니 놀랐다

He's dead from the memory of the world

› **retail**   sell in small quantities directly to the consumer

      └ 그는 세상에서 버림받았어

Higher export prices will weaken our competitive position in world markets

      └ 수출가 상승은 세계시장에서 우리의 경쟁력을 약화시킬 것이다

His idea is out of this world

      └ 그의 생각은 훌륭해

How's the world treating(using) you?

      └ 어떻게 지내니?

I can't bring myself to conform to the ways of the world

      └ 아무래도 시류에 따를 마음이 내키지 않아

I don't care about the world

      └ 난 아무 걱정 없어

I wouldn't have missed it for the world

      └ 절대 놓칠 수 없었지

In many parts of the world the poor are going without food so that the rich can live in luxury

      └ 세계의 많은 지역에서 가난한 사람들이 끼니를 거르고 있기 때문에 부자인 사람들이 호화롭게 산다

In-soo is still green to the ways of the world

      └ 인수는 아직 세상 물정에 어두워

In the new world of e-commerce, there's concern that information is being exchanged more easily, resulting in unwelcome intrusions into consumers' personal lives

      └ 새로운 전자 상거래 세계에서는 정보가 한층 용이하게 교환되며 결과적으로 소비자들의 사생활을 침범하는 결과를 낳게 된다는 문제가 있다

I'm a man of the world, though I say it myself

› **commerce** business

› **intrude** thrust in, encroach

↳ 내가 말하긴 뭣하지만 난 세상물정을 좀 알아

It is the end of the world
↳ 세상 말세로군

It just goes to show you that the political world is moved by money
↳ 정치의 세계는 돈으로 움직인다는 게 명백해

It just happens
↳ 세상사가 다 그런 거란다

It often happens that reality proves different from appearance
↳ 세상에는 겉과 속이 다른 경우가 많아

It takes all sorts to make a world
↳ 세상엔 온갖 사람들이 어울려 살아가게 마련이야

It's not the end of the world
↳ 세상이 끝난 건 아니잖아

It's nothing unusual in the world
↳ 세상엔 그런 일도 더러 있어

Jogging and push-ups will do you a world of good
↳ 조깅과 푸시업은 건강에 매우 좋다

Just sit back and watch the world go by
↳ 가만히 앉아서 세상 돌아가는 일이나 구경해(자중해라)

Keep up on what's going on in this world
↳ 세계 각국에서 일어나는 일에 귀를 기울여라

Korea ranked 11th among the trading nations in the world
↳ 한국은 세계의 무역국들 중 11위였다

Korea topped the world list in per capita consumption of liquor
↳ 한국은 1인당 음주 소비에서 세계 제1위였다

› **per capita** by or for each person | › **liquor** liquid substance and especially a distilled alcoholic beverage

Laugh, and the world will laugh with you; weep, and you weep alone

ㄴ 웃으면 만인이 따라 웃어줄 것이고, 울면 혼자 울게 될 것이다

> 늘 웃는 사람은 인복이 있지만, 찡그린 사람에게는 아무도 따르지 않는다
> 는 뜻이다. 사회 생활을 위해서는 웃는 낯, 즉 표정 관리가 중요하다. "웃
> 는 낯에 침 못 뱉는다 A soft answer turneth away wrath"와도 뜻이
> 통한다.

Lots of workers just don't move up in the world

ㄴ 많은 근로자들은 입신이라곤 못해(이름이라곤 못내)보고 살아

Love doesn't make the world go around. Love is what makes the ride worthwhile

ㄴ 사랑이 세상을 돌아가게 하지는 않지만 세상살이를 살만한 것으로 만
들어준다

Man has the perpetual contest for wealth which keeps world in tumult

ㄴ 인간은 세상을 계속 동요 속에 있게 하는 부를 얻기 위해 끊임없이
경쟁해왔다

Money alone sets all the world in motion

ㄴ 돈만 있으면 세상은 돌아가게 되어있다

My daughter thinks the world of me

ㄴ 우리 딸은 나를 가장 사랑하고 존경해요

Naked come we into the world and naked shall we depart

ㄴ 맨손으로 왔다가 맨손으로 가는 게 인생이다(공수래 공수거)

› **turneth** old form of 'turns'
› **weep** shed tears

"인생은 빈손으로 와서 빈손으로 간다"라는 말을 흔히 쓴다. 한국에서는 한문 성어를 이용하여 '공수래 공수거'라는 말을 많이 하지만, 영어에서는 'Naked body 빈 몸'이라는 표현을 쓴다.
(=Naked I came into the world, and naked I shall go out of it)

Newspapers keep us in contact with the events of the world
> ↳ 신문 덕분에 세계에서 일어나는 일을 접할 수 있다

Nobody in all the world is safe from unhappiness
> ↳ 불행을 피할 수 있는 사람은 아무도 없다

사람의 지위 고하에 따라 불행한 일이 선별적으로 일어나는 것은 아니다. 불행이 언제 닥칠지 모르니까 항상 유비무환의 자세를 가져야 한다(=We must be ready, because accidents will come at an hour when we do not expect them).

Nothing great in the world has been accomplished without passion
> ↳ 위대한 일 치고 열정 없이 이루어진 일없다

(=Nothing great was ever achieved without enthusiasm)

Nothing in the world I could keep from you
> ↳ 네게는 아무 것도 숨길 게 없어

Nothing in the world I would keep from you
> ↳ 네게 뭐가 아까울 게 있겠니

Nothing is free in this world
> ↳ 세상에 공짜는 없어

› **keep from** protect, guard

(=Everything has a price in this world)

Once he falls asleep, he's dead to the world
↳ 그가 일단 잠들고 나면 세상 모르고 잔다

One can't weep for the entire world
↳ 세상의 모든 슬픈 일에 대하여 울어줄 수는 없다

Only initiating can capture the world
↳ 앞서가는 것만이 세상을 사로잡는다

Parents are much the same all the world over
↳ 부모님들은 어디로 가나 똑같아

Reading these papers will keep you posted on the latest happenings in the world
↳ 이 신문들을 읽으면 최근의 세계정세에 밝게 된다

Sam-shik has been all over the world
↳ 삼식인 세계 도처에 안 가본 데가 없어

She could have been anyone in the world
↳ 그 여자는 그냥 스쳐 가는 사람일 수도 있었어

She wants to live in a lonely corner out of reach of the noisy world
↳ 그녀는 시끄러운 세상에서 떨어진 외딴 곳에 살고싶어해

She's in the blissful ignorance of the world
↳ 그 여자는 세상 물정을 모르고 잘난 척 한다

She's not having you wandering down the street drunk for all the world to see
↳ 네가 많은 사람 보는 앞에서 술에 취해 거리를 싸돌아다니는 꼴을 그 여자가 가만히 두지 않을 거야

› **initiate** start, induct into membership
› **blissful** completely happy, heavenly

Some cities have severe winters and uncomfortably hot summers, so we get the worst of both worlds
> ㄴ 어떤 도시들은 겨울의 심한 추위와 여름의 불편한 더위로 양쪽 모두 나쁜 조건만 가지고 있다

Small world
> ㄴ 세상 참 좁구먼

Sung-hi is dead to the world
> ㄴ 성희는 세상 모르게 자고있어

Sung-moon is a man of the world
> ㄴ 성문이는 인생의 쓴맛 단맛을 다 봤어

The history of the world is none other than the progress of the conscience of the freedom
> ㄴ 세계역사는 바로 양심의 자유의 진로이다

The most fortunate people in the world may be those who are conscious of what they are doing
> ㄴ 가장 운이 좋은 사람들은 아마 자신들이 무엇을 하고 있는지 의식하고 있는 사람들일 것이다

The practice of forgiveness is our most important contribution to the healing of the world
> ㄴ 용서는 세상의 상처를 치유하는데 가장 큰 몫을 한다

The soul which is not at peace with itself can't be at peace with the world
> ㄴ 마음이 평화롭지 못한 사람은 세상을 편안히 살아갈 수 없다

The times are out of joint
> ㄴ 어지러운 세상이야

The trend toward computerization of an ever-increasing number of

---

· **computerization** using electronic data processing machine called

computrer

airline function is accelerating rapidly and is beginning to embrace even the world's smallest carriers
> ↳ 항공사들은 점점 증가하고 있는 기능을 전산화하는 경향이 가속화되고 있으며 이러한 추세가 소규모 항공사에까지 미치기 시작했다

The whole world is on your case
> ↳ 온 세상이 네게 손가락질하고 있어

The whole world is upside down
> ↳ 세상은 뒤죽박죽이군

The world is a ladder for some to go up and some down
> ↳ 세상이라는 사다리에는 어떤 사람은 올라가고 어떤 사람은 내려간다

The world is always changing
> ↳ 세상은 늘 변해

The world is coming to an end
> ↳ 말세다 말세(=What is this world coming to?)

The world is going to the dogs
> ↳ 세상은 말세다

The world is his that enjoys it
> ↳ 세상은 그 세상을 즐길 줄 아는 사람의 것이다

The world is just the way it is
> ↳ 세상이란 그런 거야

The world is your oyster
> ↳ 세상은 넓고 할 일은 많다

The youngster has a lot to learn about this world
> ↳ 젊은이는 세상사를 잘 몰라

There are more things in heaven and earth than are dreamed of in your philosophy

---

› **embrace**　clasp in the arms, welcome, include

↳ 세상에는 상상도 못할 일이 얼마든지 있다

There are some things we don't know

↳ 세상엔 우리가 알지 못 하는 게 있어

There are two ways of rising in the world, either by your own industry or by the folly of others

↳ 출세에는 두 가지 방법이 있는데 하나는 자신의 노력이고 하나는 다른 사람의 바보짓이다

There is a sign of unrest in the world

↳ 요즘 세상이 어수선해

They've been keeping themselves unspotted from the world

↳ 그들은 세속에 물들지 않고 살아오고 있어

This failure won't be the end of the world

↳ 이번 실패로 끝장나는 건 아냐

This is your lifetime chance to give your all to succeed in the male-dominated world of finance

↳ 이번엔 네가 남자 위주의 금융계에서 성공하기 위해 전력을 다해야 할 일생에 한 번 있을만한 절호의 기회다

This means the world to me

↳ 이건 내게 중요해(의미가 있어)

This seminar did me a world of good

↳ 이 세미나는 내게 큰 도움이 됐어요

This world is a weak-to-the-wall society

↳ 세상은 약육강식이다

› **dominate** have control over, rise high above

> (Big fish eat little fish) 약한 것은 결국 강한 것에게 먹히고 만다. 다윈은 먹이사슬을 이론화 한 후 인간 사회에도 약육강식의 법칙을 적용시켰다. 강자 밑의 약자는 제대로 능력을 발휘하지 못한다.

Times are changing= You can't expect the world stand still
　　　↳ 요즘 세상이 그래(**Times have changed** 세상이 많이 변했어)

We have to keep more in touch with the world development
　　　↳ 우리는 좀 더 세계정세를 잘 알아야 한다

What an age we are living in
　　　↳ 더러운 세상이로군

What the people will say I'm quite ignorant of
　　　↳ 세상이 뭐라 할지 난 전혀 몰라

What's the world coming to?
　　　↳ 세상이 어떻게 돌아가는 거냐?

When An-do won the lottery, he felt as though the world was his oyster
　　　↳ 안도가 복권에 당첨되자 제 세상인 것 같은 기분이었지

When money speaks the world(truth) is in silence
　　　↳ 돈이 말을 하면 세상(진실)이 침묵한다

When the war ended, Korea was carved up by the powers of the world
　　　↳ 전쟁이 끝나자 한국은 강대국들에 의해 분단되었다

With things going like this, the world has fallen on evil days
　　　↳ 이쯤 되면 세상은 말세다

You are not a man of the society(world)
　　　↳ 넌 세상 물정을 잘 몰라

· **keep in touch with**　be aware of, be acquaint of

(=You're out of touch with the world)

You don't need to carry the weight of the world on your shoulders
　　ㄴ 너무 걱정하지 마라

You have all the time in the world
　　ㄴ 시간은 얼마든지 있어

You have no idea how the world works
　　ㄴ 넌 세상 물정을 몰라

(=You are still wet behind the ears)
(=You don't know how things work in life)

You live in a make-believe world of your own
　　ㄴ 넌 너 혼자만의 공상세계에 살고있어

You mean everything to me
　　ㄴ 너 없이는 못살아

(=I can't live without you)
(=You mean the world to me)

You ought to see something of the world
　　ㄴ 세상을 볼 줄 알아야지

You should take the world as you find it
　　ㄴ 넌 세상 따라 살아야 해

You shouldn't lose touch with the world
　　ㄴ 시대발전에 뒤지면 안 돼

› **make-believe** a pretending to believe

74. 소문   **Rumor**

A little bird told me
> ↳ 소문으로 들었다

Confide in an aunt and the world will know
> ↳ 아주머니(숙모)한테 가만히 말해도 온 세상이 알게 돼있다

Don't you bigmouth this, but she's going to have a baby
> ↳ 소문내지마, 그 여자 아이 가졌어

Ed is rumored to have money coming out of his ears
> ↳ 에드는 엄청난 부자라고 소문이 나 있어

Every detail of the scandal came to a head
> ↳ 스캔들의 전모가 드러났어

He's been known to rip up any contract as soon as it is signed
> ↳ 그는 무슨 계약이고 체결하자마자 파기해 버리는 사람으로 소문나 있어

I felt my ears burning yesterday
> ↳ 어제 내가 소문의 주인공이 되어 당혹스러웠어

If you go on behaving like that, you'll get yourself talked about in the office
> ↳ 네가 계속 이렇게 행동하면 사무실에서 소문나겠다

In-soo is in on most of the gossip that's usually floating around there
> ↳ 인수는 주변에서 떠도는 대부분의 얘기 거리에 대해 훤해

It's rumored that he has been up against it for some time

‣ **scandal** disgraceful situation, malicious gossip
‣ **gossip** rumor or report of an intimate nature

ㄴ그는 한 동안 형편이 궁하게 되었다는 소문이다

Mandela let his worst-kept secret out of the bag
　　　ㄴ 만델라는 무성했던 소문을 사실로 밝혔다

Moon-ho's relationship with the scandal came under scrutiny
　　　ㄴ 문호의 스캔들 관계는 철저히 조사를 받았어

Not everyone repeats gossip. Some improve it
　　　ㄴ 모든 사람들이 뜬소문을 반복하는 것은 아니다. 어떤 이들은 그것에
　　　살을 붙인다

Rumor has it that Sang-soo and Hyang-soon are washed up, but I don't believe it
　　　ㄴ 상수와 향순이 파경이라는 소문이지만 난 안 믿어

Rumors circulate rapidly
　　　ㄴ 소문은 금방 퍼져

Rumors have been getting round(going about) the government's big deal
　　　ㄴ 정부의 빅딜에 대한 소문이 퍼지고 있다

Run that report back to its source
　　　ㄴ 소문의 출처를 밝혀라

Seems there's a new scandal in this city every time we turn around
　　　ㄴ 이 도시에는 날이면 날마다 새로운 스캔들이 터져 나오는 것 같아

Spread the rumor around, and we'll cut them off at the knees
　　　ㄴ 소문을 널리 퍼뜨리면 그들은 얼굴을 들고 다닐 수 없게 될 거야

Stop noising that rumor around
　　　ㄴ 그 소문을 여기저기 퍼뜨리고 다니지마

Ten good turns lie dead and one ill deed report abroad does spread
　　　ㄴ 열 번 잘한 일은 다 사라져도 한 번 잘못했다는 소문은 잘도 퍼진다

› **scrutiny** careful inspection

The rumor is spreading(getting abroad), the rest is history
    ↳ 그 소문은 퍼져 나가고, 더 이상 얘기 안 해도 아는 일이잖아

The rumor quickly passed round the village
    ↳ 그 소문은 금방 마을에 퍼졌다

The scandal has done for our party
    ↳ 그 추문으로 우리 당은 완전히 매장되었다

There is an off-color rumor about him
    ↳ 그에 관한 추잡한 소문이 나돌고 있다

There's a nasty rumor about Jung-soo going around
    ↳ 정수에 대한 고약한 소문이 나돌고 있어

There's a rumor going the rounds that Sang-ho will get promoted
    ↳ 상호가 승진할 것이라는 소문이 파다해

There's not an atom of truth in the rumor
    ↳ 그 소문은 전혀 사실무근이었다

There's nothing busier than an idle rumor
    ↳ 할 일 없는 소문보다 나쁜 것은 없다

They are nosing around trying to find more information about the scandal
    ↳ 그들은 그 추문에 대한 정보를 더 알아내려고 탐색하고 있다

What's the buzz?
    ↳ 무슨 소문이니?

What's told in the ear of a man is often heard a hundred miles away
    ↳ 발 없는 말이 천리 간다

Wild rumors are in the air
    ↳ 터무니없는 소문이 퍼져 있다

› **nasty** filthy, indecent, malicious or spiteful   › **buzz** make a low humming sound
› **idle** worthless, inactive, lazy

You always beat me to the draw(punch) when it comes to getting new stories

ㄴ 소식통으로는 네가 늘 한발 앞서는군

You should run the report back to its source

ㄴ 넌 소문의 출처를 밝혀야 해

› **punch**　strike with the fist, perforate with
a punch

75. 소식   **News**

After a few years we lost track of each other
↳ 몇 년 지난 후 우리는 소식이 끊겼어

After a year or two we lost track of each other
↳ 2~3년 후 우리는 서로 소식이 끊어지고 말았다

Bong-doo is all bad news to me
↳ 봉두는 정말 싫어

Don't you bigmouth this, but she's going to have a baby
↳ 소문내지마, 그 여자 아이 가졌어

Each reporter is trying to get the jump on the others with the story of the scandal
↳ 신문기자들은 저마다 그 스캔들의 기사를 다른 기자들 보다 앞질러 보도하려고 기를 쓰고 있어

He has never been heard of since
↳ 그 후 전혀 그의 소식은 못 들었어

> (=Nothing has been heard of him since)

He just dropped out of sight after that
↳ 그는 그 후 소식이 끊겼어

He's good news in many ways

› **track** awareness of a progression

ㄴ 그는 여러 가지 면에서 나무랄 데 없는 사람이다

Hyun-soo's been flying light since he got the word that he won the scholarship

ㄴ 현수는 장학금을 받게됐다는 소식을 듣고 나서 붕 뜬 기분이야

I have some late-breaking news

ㄴ 바로 전에 들어온 새로운 뉴스가 있다

It's no news to you(us)

ㄴ 뻔할 뻔 자야

Let me apologize for my silence

ㄴ 오랫동안 소식 전하지 못해 죄송합니다

Let's see what the bad news is

ㄴ 계산(청구서, 고지서)이 얼마나 나왔는지 어디 보자

Maintaining objectivity and a sense of balance are cardinal rules for all self-respecting members the media news

ㄴ 객관성과 균형감각의 유지는 새로운 대중매체의 모든 자존심 있는 종사자들에게 핵심적인 규칙이다

My ears itch for information

ㄴ 소식을 알고 싶어

Newspapers should not give currency to frightening news without making sure of their facts

ㄴ 신문이 사실 확인도 안하고 겁주는 뉴스를 보도해서는 안 된다

No news is good news

ㄴ 무소식이 희소식이다

> **cardinal** of basic importance

'무소식이 희소식'이란 말은 영어 속담이나 한국 속담이나 같이 쓰인다. 영어로는 'No news is good news'이다. 소식에 대한 속담 중에 "Bad news travels quickly 나쁜 소문은 빨리 퍼진다"도 있다.

Once he hears the news, he'll be laughing out of the wrong side of his mouth
> 그가 이 소식을 듣고 보면 들떴던 마음이 싹 가시겠군

She faced the music after her involvement in the money were brought to light
> 그녀는 금전수수사건에 관련되어 있다는 소문이 밝혀진 후 자진해서 책임을 졌다

Tai-ho took on sadly when told the sad news
> 태호는 비보를 듣고 몹시 심란해 했다

The news knocked me off my feet(socks off, me out)
> 그 소식에 나는 깜짝 놀랐어

That's news from nowhere
> 그건 뻔할 뻔 자야(누구나 다 알아)

That's quite news to me
> 금시초문인데

The good news followed on the neck of the letter
> 그 편지에 이어 좋은 소식이 전해졌어

The news of the accident really tore me up
> 사고 소식에 정말 상심했다

The news scared me out of ten years' of life
> 그 소식을 듣고 10년 감수하게 놀랐다

The news was expected momentarily

· momentarily for a moment, at any moment

ↆ 사람들이 이제나저제나 하고 뉴스를 기다렸어

The news was flashed over Korea

ↆ 그 뉴스는 삽시간에 한국에 퍼져 나갔다

The reporters fired away at the news conference

ↆ 기자들이 기자회견에서 질문공세를 펴왔다

You may spring news on her now that the prize will be awarded to her

ↆ 넌 지금 그 여자에게 입상하게 될 것이라는 놀라운 소식을 얘기해도 돼

› **flash**　appear or pass suddenly

› **award**　give(something won or deserved)

76. 속담   Proverb

A bad workman always blames his tools
      ㄴ 선무당이 장고 나무란다

> 서투른 무당이 장구 탓만 하듯 기술이 부족한 자가 자기 기술의 미숙함을 반성하지 않고 도구만 나쁘다고 해봐야 아무런 진전이 없다. 훌륭한 기술자는 일이 잘못되면 그 책임을 자신에게 돌리는 사람이다.

A broken egg can never be mended
      ㄴ 엎질러진 물이다

> 이미 저질러져서 돌이킬 수 없는 일을 두고 '엎질러진 물'이라고 한다. 이 표현에 해당하는 영어 속담은 "A broken egg can never be mended 깨진 계란은 다시 고칠 수 없다"와 "It is no use crying over spilt milk 이미 쏟아진 우유를 보고 울어봐야 소용없다"이다.

A closed mouth catches no flies
      ㄴ 가만히 있으면 중간은 간다

A full gut is better than moral precepts
      ㄴ 배부름은 도덕적 교훈보다 낫다

A great cry and little wool. The mountains have brought forth a mouse

---

‣ **precept** rule of action or conduct

ㄴ 태산명동에서 한 필

A journey of a thousand miles is a single step
　　　ㄴ 천리 길도 한 걸음부터

> '천릿길도 한 걸음부터'는 작은 일부터 차근차근하여 큰 일을 이뤄야 한다
> 는 뜻이다. 자주 쓰는 영어 속담은 'A journey of a thousand miles
> begins with a single step'이며 이는 '리'를 'mile'로만 썼을 뿐, 한국
> 속담과 뜻이 같다.
> (=High buildings have deep foundations)
> (=Big things have small beginnings)
> (=Little by little goes a long way)
> (=Success doesn't come overnight)
> (=Little by little and bit by bit)
> (=To reach the top you may ascend step by step)

A little wind kindles, much puts out the fire
　　　ㄴ 약간의 바람은 불을 일으키지만 센바람은 불을 꺼버린다(중용 예찬)

> 중용이란 한쪽으로 치우침이 없고 항상 변함 없음을 말한다. 자신을 과
> 소평가나 과대평가 하지말고, 항상 겸손한 마음으로 중도를 걷는 것이
> 중요하다. 예부터 우리나라에서는 공자의 사상을 받들어 중용을 강조하
> 였다.

A little wood will heat a little oven
　　　ㄴ 송충이는 솔잎을 먹어야 한다

› **ascend**　move upward
› **kindle**　set on fire or start burning, stir up

분수를 모르고 터무니없는 짓을 하거나 그런 짓을 하여 낭패를 보았을 때하는 말이다. 가장 자주 쓰는 표현에는 "Don't try to bite off more than you can chew"이 있는데, 직역을 하면 "자신이 씹을 수 있는 것보다 더 많은 음식을 한꺼번에 배어 물지 마라"이며, 이는 자신의 능력껏 소신껏 일을 하라는 말이다.
(=A little bird is content with a little nest)
(=Let the cobbler stick to his last)

A loaf of bread is better than the song of many birds
└ 금강산도 식후경

인생의 즐거움도 배가 부른 연후에야 누릴 수 있다는 뜻이다. 사람이 살아가는데 있어서 의식주가 가장 중요하며, 이중에서도 가장 중요하고 인간의 목숨과도 연관이 있는 것이 바로 식(食)이다. 이 영어 속담을 직역하면 "한 덩이의 빵이 많은 새들의 노래 소리보다 낫다"이다.

A pig that has two owners is sure to die of hunger
└ 주인이 둘인 돼지는 굶어죽게 마련이다

여러 사람이 같이 하는 일은 서로 책임을 미루게 되어 결국엔 망한다는 뜻이다. 아리스토텔레스는 정치론에서 "A matter common to most men receives least attention 많은 사람이 관심을 갖는 일은 항상 소홀히 취급된다"고 하였다.

› **hunger** craving or urgent need for food, strong desire

› **attention** concentration of the mind on something, notice or awareness

A pretext is never wanting
> ↳ 핑계 없는 무덤 없다

A servant is known by his master's absence
> ↳ 주인이 없을 때에 좋은 하인인지 알 수 있다

A small leak will sink a ship
> ↳ 가랑비에 옷 젖는다

A soft answer turned away wrath
> ↳ 웃는 낯에 침 뱉으랴

> 웃음으로 어떠한 나쁜 상황도 대처할 수 있다는 얘기이다. "A soft answer turneth away wrath 부드러운 대답은 화를 없앤다"는 성서에서 유래한 말로서 구어를 사용한 것이 특징이다.

A stitch in time saves nine
> ↳ 호미로 막을 일을 가래로 막는다

> 모든 일은 때가 있다는 얘기이다. 호미, 즉 작은 노력으로 막을 수 있는 일을 때를 놓쳐 가래, 즉 큰 노력으로 막게 됐을 때 하는 말이다. 영어로는 "A stitch in time saves nine 때에 맞는 한 땀이 아홉 땀을 절약한다"이다.
> (=An ounce of prevention is worth a pound of cure)

A thief has a bad conscience and is apt to give himself away
> ↳ 도둑이 제발 저리다

A tree often transplanted, bears not much fruit
> ↳ 우물을 파도 한 우물을 파라

› **pretext** falsely stated purpose
› **transplant** dig up and move to another place, transfer from one body part or person to another

(=Three removals are as bad as a fire)

After the feast comes the reckoning
↳ 잔치 뒤에 허리가 휜다

After the meeting,(the) wishing is in vain
↳ 닭 쫓던 개 지붕 쳐다보는 격이군

After the storm, comes the calm
↳ 비 온 뒤에 땅 굳는다

아무리 힘들고 어렵더라고 참고 견디면 좋은 일이 생긴다(An unfavourable situation will eventually change for the better = 계속되는 불행도 참아내다 보면 기회가 온다).

All clouds not bring rain
↳ 겉만 보고 속단하지 마라

(=All are not thieves that dogs bark at)
(=Not all clouds bring rain)

All covet all lose
↳ 멧돼지 잡으려다 집돼지 잃어

All that's fair must fade
↳ 화무십일홍(권불십년)

Although it rains, cast not away the watering pot
↳ 비가 오더라도 물뿌리개를 내버리지 마라

‣ **fade** wither, lose or cause to lose freshness
or brilliance, grow dim

‣ **cast** throw

An empty sack can't stand upright
> ↳ 빈 자루는 바로 서지 못한다(가난한 자의 허약성)

An oak is not felled in one stroke
> ↳ 참나무는 한 번 찍어 넘어지지 않는다

An old eagle is better than a young crow
> ↳ 썩어도 준치이다

> (=An old poacher makes the best gamekeeper)

An-do only added fuel to the fire
> ↳ 안도는 불난 집에 부채질만 했지 뭐

> (=An-do only rubbed salt into the an open wound)

As the saying goes, nobody is without his faults
> ↳ 속담에 있듯이 털어 먼지 안 나는 사람 없지

> 누구에게나 한두 가지 결점은 있다는 뜻이다. "Everyone has a skeleton in his closet 모든 사람은 창고에 해골을 가지고 있다"는 것은 공포 영화에서 가장 선해 보이는 사람이 결국에는 범인임이 드러나는 것을 빗댄 표현이다.
> (=Everyone has his faults(short comings))
> (=No one is without their faults)
> (=Everyone makes mistakes)

› **sack** bag

› **poacher** a person who hunts or fishes illegally

As the twig is bent, so grows the tree

ㄴ 될성부른 나무는 떡잎부터 알아본다

> 아이가 큰 인물이 될지 못될지는 어려서부터 알 수 있다는 말이다(=If something can go wrong, it will)
> (=A fine child becomes a fine gentleman)
> (=Sandalwood is fragrant even in seed-leaf)
> (=Genius displays even in childhood)

As we sow, so shall we reap

ㄴ 콩 심은 데 콩 나고 팥 심은 데 팥 난다

Ask a stupid(silly) question and you'll get a stupid(silly) answer

ㄴ 현문현답, 우문우답

> (=Like question, like answer)

Better a living dog than a dead lion

ㄴ 죽은 정승은 살아있는 개보다 못하다

Better authentic mammon than bogus god

ㄴ 엉터리 신보다는 진짜 부자가 낫다

Better be a free bird than a captive king

ㄴ 갇힌 왕보다 맘대로 날아다니는 새가 낫다

Better late than never

ㄴ 매도 먼저. 늦어도 안 하는 것보다 나아

Better not a hero than work oneself up into heroism by shouting

ㄴ 거짓말로 떠들어서 영웅이 되느니 보다 안되는 게 낫다

· **twig** small branch
· **mammon** material wealth especially when seen as having a debasing influence

Better starve free than be a fat slave
ㄴ 살찐 종이 되기보다는 편히 굶는 것이 낫다

Better to go about than fall into the ditch
ㄴ 도랑에 빠지는 것보다는 피해 가는 것이 낫다

Beware lest you lose the substance by grasping at the shadow
ㄴ 그림자를 잡으려다 실체를 놓치지 않는지 주의하라

Birds of a feather flock together
ㄴ 가재는 게 편

> '동병상련', '유유상종' 등의 사자성어와 같은 뜻이다. 같은 처지에 있거나 같은 공동체에 속해 있으면 서로의 마음을 잘 이해하고, 서로의 이익을 위해 행동한다(Likeness cause liking = Dog doesn't eat dog).

Blue are the hills that are far away
ㄴ 동네 무당 보다 건너 마을 무당이 용하다

> "남의 떡이 커 보인다"라는 말이 있다. 영어로는 "The grass is greener on the other side of the fence 남의 집 정원에 잔디가 더 파래 보인다"가 자주 쓰인다. 또한 "Blue are the hills that are far away 멀리 있는 언덕이 푸르러 보인다"도 많이 쓰인다.

Burn not your house to frighten the mouse away
ㄴ 쥐가 놀라 도망가게 하려고 집을 태우지 마라(빈대 한 마리 잡으려고 초가삼간 태우지 마라)

By a small sample we may judge the whole piece
ㄴ 한 가지를 보면 열 가지를 안다

› **lest** for fear that

› **grasp** take the seize firmly, understand

Call the bear 'uncle' till you are safe across the bridge
↳ 다리를 무사히 건널 때까지는 곰에게 잘못했다고 빌어라

> 경솔하게 굴지말고 끝까지 신중을 기하라는 뜻이다. 비슷한 뜻으로 "Don't whistle until you are out of the wood 숲 속을 완전히 빠져나오기 전에는 휘파람을 불지 말라"가 있다. 숲 속을 거의 빠져나왔더라도 휘파람을 불면 맹수들을 유인할 수도 있기 때문에 끝까지 조심하라는 것을 말한다.

Chang-soo is like a kid in a candy store
↳ 참새(창수)가 방앗간을 그냥 지나가겠나

> (=That's something like a home away from home to me)

Civility costs nothing
↳ 예의 발라 손해날 것 없다

> 솔로몬은 '사람이 예의 바르면 자기 자신에게 유익하고 사람이 잔인하면 자기 자신에게 해를 끼친다(A kind man benefits himself, but a cruel man brings trouble on himself)'고 하였다. 예의는 어디에서나 지켜야 할 사회 생활의 필수 덕목이다. 'Civility'는 'Politeness'로 대체 할 수 있다.

Common proverb seldom lies
↳ 흔히 쓰는 속담에 틀린 말없다

Constant dripping wears away the stone
↳ 끊임없이 떨어지는 물방울이 바위를 깎아 내린다

▸ **proverb** short meaningful popular saying
▸ **wear** decay by use or by scraping

불가능한 일이라도 끊임없이 노력하면 이루어진다는 뜻이다. 물(Dripping)은 끊임없는 성실한 노력을 뜻한다(He that shoots often at last shall hit the mark = 여러 번 쏘는 자는 결국 표적을 맞춘다).

Covetousness breaks the sack
↳ 욕심이 지나치면 자루가 찢어진다(바다는 메워도 사람의 욕심은 못 메워)

(=Covetousness is always filling a bottomless vessel)
(=Greedy people have long arms)

Creaking doors hang the longest
↳ 삐걱거리는 문이 오래간다(쭉정이 밥 3년)

Curiosity killed the cat
↳ 호기심도 정도가 있어야지

Distance lends enhancement to the view
↳ 사돈과 뒷간은 멀어야 한다

Do as I say, not as I do
↳ 난 바담 '풍' 해도 넌 바람 '풍' 해라

"진리를 전하는 사람을 보고 판단하지 말고 진리 자체를 보라"라는 뜻이다. 인간은 말로는 모든 진리를 보여줄 수 있어도 행동으로는 그럴 수가 없다. 따라서 이 속담과 같이 쓰이는 명언 중에는 실천을 강조하는 명언이 많다.
(=Practice what you preach 말한 대로 행하라)
(=Carry out in action 행동으로 실행하라)

› **vessel** container for a liquid
› **enhancement** improve in value

Do nothing hastily but catching flies
↳ 파리 잡을 때 외에는 어떤 일도 서둘지 마라

Do your best, and God will do the rest
↳ 진인사대천명

(＝Do your duty and leave the rest to the gods)

Dogs bark but the caravan goes on
↳ 남이 무어라 하든 자기 할 일만 하면 된다

Don't back him into a corner
↳ 개도 도망갈 구멍을 만들어놓고 쫓아라(이해하지 못할 경우도 있음)

적을 궁지로 몰아가면 궁지에 몰린 사람은 사생결단을 하기 때문에 온 힘을 다해 달려들기 마련이다. 때문에 "개도 도망갈 구멍을 만들어놓고 쫓아라"라는 말이 생겼다. 영어로는 "It is good to make a bridge of gold to a flying enemy"라고 한다.

Don't cut off your nose to spite your face
↳ 누워 침 뱉기야

다른 사람을 해치려다가 결국은 자신에게 해가 돌아간다는 뜻이다. 한국에서는 '누워서 침 뱉기'가 있고, 영어로는 비슷한 'Spit in the wind 바람에 침 뱉기'와 "Piss in the wind 바람에 오줌누기'가 있다. 바람을 마주보고 침을 뱉거나 오줌을 누면 결국 자신한테도 돌아오는 법이다. 조금 더 점잖은 표현으로는 "Cut off your nose to spite your face 코를 깎아서 얼굴을 망친다'가 있다.

› **spite** treat insultingly

Don't look up the tree you can't climb
ㄴ 못 오를 나무는 쳐다보지도 마라

Don't put the cart before the horse
ㄴ 주객을 전도하지 마라

Don't rock the boat
ㄴ 긁어 부스럼 만들지 말라

그냥 놔두면 될 것을 건드려서 화를 자초할 때 쓰이는 속담이다. 영어에서는 "자는 개(호랑이)는 깨우지 마라", "구더기 깡통은 열지 마라" 등으로 쓴다.

Don't sell the skin before you have killed the bear
ㄴ 너구리 굴 보고 빚돈 내 써서는 안 돼

Drawn wells are seldom dry
ㄴ 물을 길어내는 샘은 여간해서 마르지 않는다

Empty vessels make the greatest sound
ㄴ 빈 수레가 요란하다

Even Homer sometimes nods
ㄴ 원숭이도 나무에서 떨어진다

Even the porcupine thinks its young are soft and glossy
ㄴ 고슴도치도 제 새끼는 예쁘다고 한다

(=The beetle is a beauty in the eyes of its mother)
(=The crow thinks her own bird fairest)
(=The owl thinks its own young fairest)
(=No mother has a homely child)

› **draw** extract
› **cart** wheeled vehicle

Every cloud has a silver lining

↳ 전화위복(쥐구멍에도 볕 들 때 있다)

> 아무리 힘들고 어렵더라고 참고 견디면 좋은 일이 생긴다.
> (An unfavourable situation will eventually change for the better
> = 계속되는 불행도 참아내다 보면 기회가 온다)
> (=Every dog has his day)

Every dog is valiant at his own door

↳ 자기집 문 앞에서는 모든 개가 용감하다

Every flow has its ebb

↳ 권불십년이다

Every path has a puddle

↳ 어느 길에나 패인 곳이 있다(결함 없는 것이 없다)

Every school boy knows it

↳ 그건 삼척동자도 알아

> (=It's a household name(word))

Extremes meet

↳ 천재와 광인은 종이 한 장 차이다

> 이 세상에는 좋은 것과 나쁜 것이 따로 있는 것이 아니고 사람의 생각에 의
> 해서 결정된다. 좋은 것이 상황에 따라서는 나쁜 것이 될 수도 있고, 그 반대
> 가 될 수도 있다. 선(善) 의 반대는 악(惡) 이지만 악(惡)이 없이는 선(善)
> 도 아무런 의미가 없다.
> (=Genius is but one remove from insanity)

▸ **valiant** brave or heroic
▸ **ebb** outward flow of the tide, decline

Fields have eyes and woods have ears
　　ㄴ 낮말은 새가 듣고 밤 말은 쥐가 듣는다

> 말조심의 중요성을 말해주는 속담이다. 한국에서는 동물을 이용하여 뜻을 전
> 달하였지만, 영어 속담에서는 자연 그대로를 이용한다. "Fields have eyes,
> and woods have ears 들에 눈이 있고 나무에 귀가 있다"

Fish and guests stink after three days(old)
　　ㄴ 가는 손님은 뒤 꼭지도 예쁘다

> 직역하면 "생선과 손님은 사흘이 지나면 썩는 냄새가 난다"이다. 손님으로 가면
> 빠른 시일 내에 돌아오라는 얘기이다. 아무리 반가운 손님도 시간이 지남에 따
> 라 부담스러워 지기 때문이다(= A constant guest is never welcome).

Fish are not caught by a bird call
　　ㄴ 산에 가야 범을 잡고 물에 가야 고기를 잡는다

For want of a nail(horse), the sho(=rider) is lost
　　ㄴ 새 잡아 잔치 할 일 소 잡아 잔치한다(호미로 막을 일 가래로 막는다)

> 모든 일은 때가 있다는 얘기이다. 호미, 즉 작은 노력으로 막을 수 있는 일을
> 때를 놓쳐 가래, 즉 큰 노력으로 막게 됐을 때 하는 말이다. 영어로는 "A
> stitch in time saves nine 때에 맞는 한 땀이 아홉 땀을 절약한다"이다.
> (=Spare at the spigot and let it out at the bunghole)

Good for the liver may be bad for the spleen
　　ㄴ 간에 좋은 것은 지라에 나쁠 수도 있다(모두에게 좋을 수는 없다)

· **spleen** organ for maintenance of the blood

Great boast and small roast
ㄴ 소문난 잔치에 먹을 것 없어

> (=Much noise and no substance)

Hares may pull the dead lion by the beard
ㄴ 토끼도 죽은 사자는 깔본다

He that steals a pin will steal an ox
ㄴ 바늘도둑이 소도둑 된다

> 이 속담은 마치 직역한 것 같이 영어와 우리나라 속담이 비슷하다. Pin 은 바늘과 같이 작은 것, ox 는 소와 같이 크고 값이 많이 나가는 것을 대표한다. 이는 동, 서양이 모두 농업 사회를 토대로 발전했다는 것을 나타낸다.
> (=He that thieves an egg will thieve an ox)

He that would eat the fruit(nut) must climb(crack) the tree(shell)
ㄴ 부뚜막의 소금도 집어넣어야 짜다

> 무슨 일이든 노력이 있어야 가능하고 노력하여 성취한 일은 보다 값지다. 과일이 달려 있어도 올라가서 따와야 먹을 수 있다는 뜻이다. 게으른 사람은 먹지도 말라는 말과도 같은 뜻이다.

He is a white egg laid by a black hen
ㄴ 그는 개천에서 용 난 격이다

· **hare**   long-eared mammal related to the rabbit

한국에서 용은 귀함을 대표하지만, 서양에서는 괴물, 악마를 뜻한다. 따라서 비슷한 뜻으로 "A white egg laid by a black hen(검은 닭이 난 하얀 알 이나), A rag to riches story(누더기에서 부자가 된 이야기)"가 쓰인다.

Honey catches more flies than vinegar
ㄴ 꿀은 식초보다 파리를 더 많이 잡는다(친절 권장)

친절하게 대하는 것은 말은 쉽지만 실천이 쉽지가 않다. 그러나 친절은 손해 도 나지 않고, 자신에게 이로운 처세술이다.

I think I've to just go home and kick the dog
ㄴ 종로에서 뺨맞고 한강에서 눈 흘길 수밖에 없게됐군

엉뚱한 상대에게 화풀이하는 상황을 말한다. 서양에서는 "집에 가서 애꿎은 개를 발로 찬다"는 표현을 쓴다.

If it were a snake, it would bite you
ㄴ 업은 아이 3년 찾는다

바로 곁에 있는 것을 찾지 못할 때에 쓰이는 표현이다. 서양에서는 "그것이 뱀이라면 당신을 물겠다"라고 하고, 이는 뱀이 물 정도로 가까이 있는 데도 알아채지 못한다는 뜻이다(The husband is always the last to know 등 잔 밑이 어둡다).

If it's all the same, take whatever you like
ㄴ 이왕이면 다홍치마

› **vinegar** acidic liquid obtained by fermentation

(=If you have to choose, choose the best)
(=Other things being equal, choose the better one)

If you don't like the heat, get out of the kitchen
> ↳ 절이 싫으면 중이 떠나라

꼭 필요한 불편에 대해 불평을 해서는 안 된다는 뜻이다. 맘에 안 맞는 직장이나 희망도 없는 사업에 매달려 불평만 하고 있을 것이 아니라 빨리 다른 일을 찾아보라는 충고이다. 그래서 영어로 "If you don't like the heat, get out of the kitchen 열이 싫으면 부엌에서 나가라"라고 한다.

Ignorance is bliss
> ↳ 모르는 게 약이다

알아서 좋은 일이 있지만, 몰라야 될 일도 있는 법이다. 언제나 좋은 일만 생길 수는 없기 때문이다. 한국에서는 "모르는 게 약이다"라고 하지만, 영어로는 "Ignorance is bliss 무지는 곧 안심이다"라고 한다. 무엇인지 알기 전에는 걱정을 할 필요는 없기 때문이다.

It proves the truth of the proverb
> ↳ 그 속담이 맞다는 걸 알 수 있어

It takes more than pearls to make a necklace
> ↳ 구슬이 세 말이라도 꿰어야 보배다

It's done a disappearing act
> ↳ 개똥도 약에 쓰려니까 없군

It's easy to miss what's in front of you(under your nose=staring in

---

› **bliss**   complete happiness, heaven or paradise

your face)

↳ 등잔 밑이 어두워

It's just a white elephant for me

↳ 빛 좋은 개살구다

(=That's only fool's gold)

It's like a smokestack in here

↳ 너구리 잡는구나(=smokers den)

It's like catching two pigeons with one bean

↳ 도랑 치고 가재잡고

It's like having the fox guard the hen-house

↳ 고양이한테 생선가게 맡긴 꼴이군

It's mere child's play

↳ 식은 죽 먹기야

아주 쉬운 일을 '누워서 떡 먹기'나 '식은 죽 먹기'라고 한다. 영어로는 "It's mere child's play 어린 아이 놀음이다", 혹은 "It's a piece of cake 케일 한 조각이다"라고 한다.

It's unfair to ask a fish to pay for the bait he was caught with

↳ 잡힌 물고기에게 미끼 값을 내라는 건 좀 심하다

Laugh, and the world will laugh with you; weep, and you weep alone

↳ 웃으면 만인이 따라 웃어줄 것이고, 울면 혼자 울게 될 것이다

› **smokestack** chimney through which smoke is discharged

늘 웃는 사람은 인복이 있지만, 찡그린 사람에게는 아무도 따르지 않는다는 뜻이다. 사회 생활을 위해서는 웃는 낯, 즉 표정 관리가 중요하다. "웃는 낯에 침 못 뱉는다 A soft answer turneth away wrath"와도 뜻이 통한다.

Leave a sinking ship rather than stay around
ㄴ 무거운 절보다는 가벼운 중이 떠나라

Let sleeping dogs lie
ㄴ 긁어 부스럼 만들지마

그냥 놔두면 될 것을 건드러서 화를 자초할 때 쓰이는 속담이다. 영어에서는 "자는 개(호랑이)는 깨우지 마라", "구더기 깡통은 열지 마라"등으로 쓴다.
(=That would be opening a can of worms)
(=Wake not sleeping lion)

Light gains make a heavy purse(purses)
ㄴ 티끌 모아 태산

작은 노력들이 큰 성공을 가져다 준다는 뜻이다. 작은 돈이 모여서 큰돈이 되는 것이고, 밑바닥부터 시작하여 높은 자리까지 올라가는 것이다. 영어로는 "Little drops of water makes the mighty ocean 물방울들이 모여서 대양이 된다" 또는 "Many a little makes a mickle 적음이 모여서 많음이 된다"라고 한다. 또한 돈을 얘기할 때에는 "Take care of the pence, and the pounds will take care of themselves 펜스(작은 돈의 단위)를 돌보면 파운드(큰돈의 단위)는 저절로 따라 올 것이다"

Listeners hear no good of themselves=Ignorance is bliss
ㄴ 들으면 병이요, 안 들으면 약이다

› **purse**　bag or pouch for money and small objects, financial resource, prize money

› **mickle**　quiet a much

알아서 좋은 일이 있지만, 몰라야 될 일도 있는 법이다. 언제나 좋은 일만 생길 수는 없기 때문이다. 한국에서는 "모르는 게 약이다"라고 하지만, 영어로는 "Ignorance is bliss 무지는 곧 안심이다"라고 한다. 무엇인지 알기 전에는 걱정을 할 필요는 없기 때문이다.

Man proposes, God disposes
ㄴ 세상일은 인력으로 되지 않는다

Many hands make light work
ㄴ 백짓장도 맞들면 낫다

Many strokes can overthrow the oaks
ㄴ 여러 번 찍으면 참나무도 넘어간다

Men trip not on mountains, they stumble on stones
ㄴ 사람은 산에 걸려 넘어지는 게 아니라 돌부리에 걸려 넘어진다(사소한 일에 주의 촉구)

Misery loves company
ㄴ 동병상련이다

'동병상련', '유유상종' 등의 사자성어와 같은 뜻이다. 같은 처지에 있거나 같은 공동체에 속해 있으면 서로의 마음을 잘 이해하고, 서로의 이익을 위해 행동한다(Likeness cause liking = Dog doesn't eat dog).

Names and natures do often agree
ㄴ 보기 좋은 떡이 먹기도 좋다

Never shoot, never hit
ㄴ 쏘지 않으면 맞지도 않는다

› **overthrow** upset, bring to defeat
› **stumble** lose one's balance or fall in

walking or running, speak or act clumsily

> 직역하면 "뿌린 대로 거둔다"이다. 씨를 뿌리는 노력이 있어야 결과도 있다는 뜻이다. "Every herring must hang by its own gill=콩 심은 데 콩 나고, 팥 심은 데 팥 난다"와도 일맥상통한다.

New born calves don't fear tigers
ㄴ 갓 태어난 송아지는 호랑이를 무서워하지 않는다(하룻강아지)

> 너무 어리석어서 겁이 없는 사람을 보고하는 속담이다. 비슷한 뜻으로는 "Fools rush in where angels fear to tread 바보들은 천사들이 두려워하는 곳으로 돌진한다"와 "Nothing so bold as a blind mare 눈 먼 당나귀는 무서운 것이 없다"가 자주 쓰인다.

No one believes a liar when you tell the truth
ㄴ 콩으로 메주를 쑨데도 네 말은 못 믿겠구나(이솝이야기에서)

> 자주 쓰이는 영어 속담 중에 "You are crying wolf too often"이 있다. 이것은 이솝이야기의 '양치기 소년'이라는 이야기에서 유래하였다. 양치기 소년이 늑대가 나타났다고 거짓말을 여러 번 했기 때문에 진짜로 늑대가 나타났을 때에는 아무도 믿지 않았다는 내용이다. 여기서 직역을 하면 "너는 늑대를 너무 여러 번 외쳤어"이고, 그렇기 때문에 믿을 수 없다는 뜻이다.

Oaks may fall when reeds stand the storm
ㄴ 갈대가 폭풍에 버틸 때 참나무는 쓰러질 수도 있다

Old chains gall less than new
ㄴ 구관이 명관이다

· **herring** narrow-bodied Atlantic food fish
· **gall** chafe, irritate or vex

곁에 있을 때에는 느끼지 못해도 없어지고 나면 그 빈자리가 느껴지게 마련이다. 한국에서는 "구관이 명관이다"라고 하지만, 영어로는 글자 그대로 "You don't know what you've got until you've lost it 자신이 가지고 있는 것을 잃어보지 않고서야 무엇을 가지고 있는지 모른다"라고 한다.
(=Old shoes are easiest)
(=You don't know what you have got until you have lost it)
(=Old is good)

Once bitten, twice shy
ㄴ 자라보고 놀란 가슴 솥뚜껑보고 놀란다

가혹한 경험은 쉽게 머리에서 잊혀지지 않는다. Shy 는 '부끄러운'의 뜻이 아닌 '무서운'의 뜻이다(=A burnt child dreads the fire 불에 놀란 아이 부지깽이만 봐도 놀란다).

Once on shore, we pray no more
ㄴ 뒷간에 갈 적 다르고 뒷간에서 올 적 다르다

One arrow doesn't bring down two birds
ㄴ 화살 한 대로 두 마리의 새를 명중시킬 수 없다

두 가지 일을 한꺼번에 할 수 없다는 것을 말해주는 속담이다. "You can not eat the cake and have it 케이크를 먹기도 하고 가지기도 할 수는 없다"와 "A door must either be shut or open 문은 닫히거나 열리거나 둘 중에 하나밖에 될 수 없다"도 자주 쓰이는 표현이다.

One bad general is better than two good ones
ㄴ 한 사람의 시원찮은 장군은 똑똑한 장군 둘이 있는 것보다 낫다(불화

› **dread** feel extreme fear or reluctance
› **general** senior commissioned officer

에 대한 경고)

One beats the bush and another catches the birds

ㄴ 재주는 곰이, 돈은 되놈이

> 자신이 노력한 일의 대가를 남이 받을 때 쓰는 속담이다. 요즘 같이 노동에 대한 착취가 빈번한 사회에서 자주 쓰이는 말이다. 더 자주 쓰이는 표현으로 는 "One man sows and another man reaps 파종하는 놈 따로, 거둬 가 는 놈 따로 있다"라 있다.

One can't behave rudely to a flattering person

ㄴ 웃는 낯에 침 뱉으랴

> 웃음으로 어떠한 나쁜 상황도 대처할 수 있다는 얘기이다. "A soft answer turneth away wrath 부드러운 대답은 화를 없앤다"는 성서에서 유래한 말 로서 구어를 사용한 것이 특징이다.

One puts merit(credit) upon oneself when things go well, and blame one's ancestor when not

ㄴ 잘되면 제 탓, 못되면 조상 탓

One rotten apple spoils the barrel

ㄴ 미꾸라지 한 마리가 웅덩이 물 다 흐려

> merit   praiseworthy quality, rights and wrongs of a legal case(pl), deserve

> 하나가 전체에게 나쁜 영향을 미친다는 말이다. 영어 속담에는 여러 가지가
> 있는데, 가장 자주 쓰이는 표현은 "One rotten apple spoils the barrel
> 썩은 사과 하나가 한 통을 썩게 한다"이다. 악한 한 사람이 한 가문, 한 나라
> 를 욕되게 하는 것은 "It is an ill bird that fouls its own nest 자기의
> 둥지를 더럽히는 새는 나쁜 새이다"로 표현한다.
> (=One scabbed sheep will mar a whole flock)
> (=A hog that's bemired endeavors to bemire others)

People only fear its heights, standing at the foot of the mountain
　　　ㄴ 사람이 제 아니 오르고 뫼만 높다 하더라

Respect is greater at a distance
　　　ㄴ 동네 무당보다 건너 마을 무당이 더 용하다

> "남의 떡이 커 보인다"라는 말이 있다. 영어로는 "The grass is greener on
> the other side of the fence 남의 집 정원에 잔디가 더 파래 보인다"가
> 자주 쓰인다. 또한 "Blue are the hills that are far away 멀리 있는 언
> 덕이 푸르러 보인다"도 많이 쓰인다(=Intimacy lessens fame).
> (=far fowls have fair feathers)

Right will prevail in the end
　　　ㄴ 사필귀정이다

> (=Nothing goes uncorrected for long)
> (=Justice has long arms)

Rome was not built in a day
　　　ㄴ 첫술에 배부르랴

· **scab** protective crust over a sore or wound,　　· **mar** damage
worker taking a striker's job

> "첫술에 배부르랴"라는 말이 있다. "시작이 반이다(Well begun, half done)"
> 이란 속담도 있지만, 이는 시작하는 것이 어렵다는 것을 뜻하는 속담이고, 시
> 작한 후에 노력을 하여 한 단계 한 단계 이루어 나가야 된다는 뜻을 가진 속
> 담이 "첫술에 배부르랴(Rome was not built in a day)"이다(It takes
> three generations to make a gentleman = 훌륭한 사람은 하루아침에
> 만들어지지 않는다).

Superiors and adults must be honest and upright if subordinates and youth are to be
> ㄴ 윗물이 맑아야 아랫물이 맑다

> 윗사람의 행동이 아랫사람의 행동을 결정한다. 아이들은 부모의 행동을 따라
> 하며, 평사원들은 부장급, 사장급 사람들을 본 받기 마련이다. 한국에서는
> "윗물이 맑아야 아랫물이 맑다"라고 하며, 영어로는 "The fish always
> stinks from the head downward 생선은 머리부터 썩는다"라고 하는데,
> 이는 그리스의 격언에서 기원하였다.

Talk of the devil and you'll hear the flutter of their wings
> ㄴ 호랑이도 제 말하면 온다

> 화제에 오르고 있는 사람이 마침 나타난다는 뜻으로 동,서양을 막론하고 자
> 주 쓰이는 표현이다. 더 자주 쓰이는 표현으로 "Talk of the devil, and he
> is bound to appear 악마에 대해 말을 하면 그가 나타난다"가 있다.

That fish will soon be caught that nibbles at every bait
> ㄴ 아무 미끼나 물어보는 물고기는 쉽게 잡힌다(호기심과 참견의 경계)

That is the case of "sowing the wind and reaping the whirlwind"

› **flutter** flap the wings rapidly, move with quick wavering or flapping motions, behave in an agitated manner

› **whirlwind** whirling wind storm

└ 되로 주고 말로 받는 꼴이군

That's sour grapes

    └ 못 먹는 감 찔러나 보자는 말이군

> 자신이 갖지 못할 바에 다른 사람도 가지지 못했으면 하는 것이 사람의 심리
> 이다. 한국에서는 "못 먹는 감 찔러나 본다"나 "못 먹는 밥에 재 뿌린다"라고
> 하며, 이에 가장 가까운 영어 표현은 "Sour grapes 신 포도"이다. 유명한
> 이솝우화 중에서 포도를 따지 못한 여우가 "저것은 신 포도일 것이다"라고 자
> 신을 위로하는 데서 비롯된 것이다.

That's the case of "the blind leading the blind"

    └ 선무당이 생사람 잡는군

> "A little knowledge is dangerous 얕은 지식은 위험하다"라는 말이 있다.
> 한국에서는 "선무당이 생사람 잡는다"라고 한다.

Thatch your roof before the rain

    └ 비가 오기 전에 지붕을 이어라(유비무환)

The bait hides the hook

    └ 미끼에는 후크가 숨겨져 있다

The cobbler's children go bare foot

    └ 대장간에 식칼 없다

> 마땅히 있어야 할 곳에 없는 상황을 "대장간에 식칼 없다"라고 표현한다. 영
> 어로는 "The cobbler's children go bare foot 구두장이의 아이들이 맨발
> 로 다닌다"라고 한다.

› **thatch**   cover with thatch, covering with
matted straw

The darkest hour is that before the dawn

ㄴ 동트기 전이 가장 어두운 시간이다(절망하지 마라)

> 아무리 힘들고 어렵더라고 참고 견디면 좋은 일이 생긴다(An unfavourable situation will eventually change for the better = 계속되는 불행도 참아내다 보면 기회가 온다).

The devil takes the hindmost

ㄴ 매도 먼저 맞는 게 낫다

The end justifies the means

ㄴ 모로 가도 서울만 가면 된다

> 과정이야 어떻든 목적지에 닿기만 하면 된다는 뜻을 가진 속담은 "모로 가도 서울만 가면 된다"이고 영어로는 "The end justifies the means 목적은 수단을 정당화한다"이다.

The grass is greener on the other side of the fence

ㄴ 남의 떡이 커 보여

> "남의 떡이 커 보인다"라는 말이 있다. 영어로는 "The grass is greener on the other side of the fence 남의 집 정원에 잔디가 더 파래 보인다"가 자주 쓰인다. 또한 "Blue are the hills that are far away 멀리 있는 언덕이 푸르러 보인다"도 많이 쓰인다.

The net of the sleeper catches fish

ㄴ 소발에 쥐잡기다

The peerless peak of Taesan is still under the sky

› **peerless** having no equal

ㄴ 태산이 높다하되 하늘 아래 뫼이로다

The plot thickens

ㄴ 점입가경이군

The postage costs more than the goods

ㄴ 배보다 배꼽이군

The snipe need not to criticize the woodcock

ㄴ 사돈이 남 말하고 있군

(=The eyes that see all things else see not itself)

The sparrow is sorry for the peacock at the burden of its tail

ㄴ 참새는 공작의 거추장스러운 꼬리를 보고 안됐다고 생각한다

The sparrow near a school sings a prime

ㄴ 서당개 3년에 풍월 한다

"서당개 삼년에 풍월을 읊는다"는 속담은 아주 유용하게 많이 쓰인다. "The sparrow near a school sings a primer"는 "학교 주변의 참새는 1학년 교재를 따라한다"로 직역된다. 이는 어깨너머로 배운다는 말과도 뜻이 같다.

The squeaky(speaking) wheel gets the grease

ㄴ 우는 아이에게 젖 준다

› **snipe** bird of marshy areas

› **woodcock** common shore-bird or Europe and Africa

맘에 들지 않는 일을 참기보다는 상황에 맞는 불평도 필요하다는 뜻이다. 물에 물 탄 듯 술에 술 탄 듯 한 사람은 결국에는 무시를 당하기 마련이다. 이에 해당하는 표현은 "The squeaky wheel gets the grease 삐걱거리는 바퀴에 기름을 친다"이다.
(=You'll get nothing without asking)

The worst wheel of the cart always creaks most
ㄴ 빈 수레가 요란하다

There are no birds in last year's nest
ㄴ 산천은 의구한데 인걸은 간데 없네

인간의 흥망 성쇠는 참으로 무상하다. 모든 인간사는 환경에 따라 변하고 시대가 바뀜에 따라 환경조차 변해 버렸다(Circumstances have altered).

They stumble that runs fast
ㄴ 빨리 달리는 사람은 넘어지기 쉽다

This is the fish that got away
ㄴ 놓친 고기가 더 큰 법

놓쳐 버린 기회를 아쉬워 할 때 쓰는 표현이다. 낚시꾼들이 놓친 고기가 컸다고 과장을 하고 허풍을 자주 떨기 때문에, 'Fish story'라는 말을 '과장된 이야기'라는 표현으로 쓰기도 한다.

This maxim indicates everybody to be the boss of something small, rather than a follower of something big
ㄴ 이 속담은 누구나 큰 회사 같은 곳의 말단이 되기보다 하찮은 곳이라도 우두머리가 되라는 것을 말해준다

› **creak** squeak

Those who live in glass-houses should not throw stones
> ↳ 자식 있는 사람은 남의 자식 욕 못해

Those who push themselves forward can expect to take a beating
> ↳ 모난 돌이 정 맞는다

> (=A tall tree catches much wind)

To mention the wolf's name is to see the same
> ↳ 호랑이가 제 말하면 온다

> 화제에 오르고 있는 사람이 마침 나타난다는 뜻으로 동·서양을 막론하고 자주 쓰이는 표현이다. 더 자주 쓰이는 표현으로 "Talk of the devil, and he is bound to appear 악마에 대해 말을 하면 그가 나타난다"가 있다.

What goes around comes around
> ↳ 가는 말이 고와야(자업자득)

> 자기가 한 일이나 말에 대해 책임을 져야 한다는 말이다. '자업자득 As you make your bed, so you must lie upon it'이나 "뿌린 데로 거둔다 You must sow, before you reap"과도 뜻이 통한다. 일상 대화에서는 "He got what he bargained(asked) for"이라고도 한다.

When it rains, it pours
> ↳ 모든 일은 한꺼번에 닥쳐오게 돼있어

· **bound** intending to go, be a boundary of

> 나쁜 일은 한꺼번에 온다. 이럴 때에는 "Adding insult to injury 다친데에 모욕같이 더한다"라고 하거나 "When it rains, it pours 비가 오면 쏟아진 다"라고 한다.

When the blind leads the blind, both shall fall into the ditch
　　ㄴ 장님이 장님을 인도하면 둘 다 구덩이에 빠진다

> 어리석은 자가 어리석은 자를 인도하면 결국에는 둘 다 화를 면하지 못한다 는 뜻이다. 공자는 "아는 것을 안다고 하고 모르는 것을 모른다고 하는 것이 참으로 아는 것이다"라고 하였다. 자신이 모르는 것은 인정할 수 있는 겸손함 도 겸비한 사람이 진정한 현인이다.

Would you teach a fish how to swim?
　　ㄴ 공자 앞에 문자 쓰려고 그래?

> 박식한 사람 앞에서 아는 체 하는 사람을 비웃을 때 쓰는 말이다. 직역하면 "물고기에게 수영을 가르친다"이다.

You can't scratch your own back
　　ㄴ 중이 제 머리 못 깎는다

You can't see beyond the end of your nose
　　ㄴ 등잔 밑이 어두워

> 바로 곁에 있는 것을 찾지 못할 때에 쓰이는 표현이다. 서양에서는 "그것이 뱀이라 면 당신을 물겠다"라고 하고, 이는 뱀이 물 정도로 가까이 있는 데도 알아채지 못한 다는 뜻이다(The husband is always the last to know 등잔 밑이 어둡다).

▸ **scratch** scrape or dig with or as if with claws or nails, cause to move　|　gratingly

You have to fight fire with fire
└ 이열치열

> 한국의 속담 '이열치열(以熱治熱)'과 비슷하게 영어에는 "Fight fire with fire 불은 불로 다스려라"라는 말이 있다. 이 말은 적을 물리치려면 적의 전술로 대응해야 한다는 뜻이다. 비슷한 말로 "Like cures like"도 있다.

You're talking to the wall
└ 쇠귀에 경 읽기야

> 마음에 있지 않으면 들어도 들리지 않고 보아도 보이지 않는다(There's none so blind as those who will not see = There's none so deaf as those who will not hear).
> (=He always turns deaf ear)

You're trying to get blood from a turnip
└ 벼룩의 간을 빼먹고 있군

› **turnip** edible root of an herb

77. 속음   **Deceit**

Deceit is in the heart of those who devise evil, but counselors of peace have joy
> ↳ 일을 꾀하고자 하는 자의 마음에는 속임수가 있고 화평을 하는 자에게는 화락이 있다

Doo-chul cheated me under the name of friendship
> ↳ 두철이는 우정이란 이름으로 나를 속였어

Doo-chul is just leading you down the garden path
> ↳ 두철인 널 속이고 있을 뿐이다

Duck-soo's been deceiving his girl friend with other girls
> ↳ 덕수는 여자친구를 배신한 채 다른 여자들을 사귀어 왔어

Fool me once, shame on you; fool me twice, shame on me
> ↳ 네가 나를 한 번 속이는 것은 너의 수치요, 두 번 속이는 것은 나의 수치다

Hatred of dishonesty generally arises from fear of being deceived
> ↳ 증오는 대개 속임을 당할 우려에서 생겨난다

He has taken me in more than once
> ↳ 그 사람한테 속은 게 한 두 번이 아냐

He was deceived by his own trick
> ↳ 제 꾀에 제가 넘었어

He's not above cheating

▸ **devise** invent, plot, give by will

ㄴ 그는 속이고도 남을 사람이다

I fell for it

ㄴ 감쪽같이 속았어

It's more tolerable to be refused than deceived

ㄴ 거절은 참을 수 있어도 속는 건 참지 못한다

No man so wise but he may be deceived

ㄴ 아무리 현명한 사람도 속을 때가 있다

Nobody can put anything over on me

ㄴ 어느 누구도 나를 속일 수는 없다

Pyung-soo pulled a fast one on me

ㄴ 평수가 나를 감쪽같이 속였어

She had a fast one pulled over her

ㄴ 그녀는 감쪽같이 속았어

She's trying to put something over on you

ㄴ 그 여자가 뭔가 너를 속이려하고 있어

Tai-ho played anyone false who trusted him

ㄴ 태호는 그를 믿는 모든 사람들을 속였어

The one charm of marriage is that it makes a life of deception absolutely necessary for both parties

ㄴ 결혼에서의 한가지 매력은 살아가는 동안 양측 모두 속이는 것이 절대 불가피하게 된다는 점이다

They must have been done in by that foxy salesman

ㄴ 그들은 그 교활한 외판원에게 속아넘어간 게 틀림없어

They must have put something over on us to share the expenses of disposing trash

ㄴ 그들이 우리에게 쓰레기 처리비용을 분담시키는데는 뭔가 속임수가

‣ **tolerable** capable of being endured, moderately good

‣ **deception** act or fact of deceiving, fraud

있음이 틀림없어

They tried to palm that painting as a real Kim-hong-do
> 그들은 그 그림을 진짜 김홍도의 작품이라고 속여 팔려고 했다

We are never so easily deceived as when we imagine we are deceiving others
> 남을 속이고 있다고 생각하고 생각할 때만큼 쉽게 우리자신이 속아넘어갈 때가 없다

Who will not be deceived must have as many eyes as hairs on his head
> 속지 않으려면 머리카락 수만큼의 눈이 있어야 한다

You are nicely left again
> 너 또 속은 게로군

You can't fool(please) the people all the time
> 모든 사람을 언제나 속일(즐겁게 할) 수는 없다

You caught a weasel asleep
> 넌 생사람 눈 빼 먹었군(약은 사람을 속였군)

You have been had
> 너 당했구나

> (=You have been taken for a ride)

> **weasel** small slender flesh-eating mammals

78. 스포츠 & 운동　Sports & Exercises

A shutout decided the game after it was tied to 2 all
ㄴ 경기가 **2**대 **2**로 동점이 된 후 승부차기로 승부가 결정되었다

A team which is full of enthusiasm is more likely to win
ㄴ 열의가 많은 팀이 이기기 쉽다

After Jong-soo had been on for several minute, the other team's defeat became certain
ㄴ 종수가 게임에 출장한지 몇 분이 안되어서 상대팀이 질 수밖에 없게 되었다

After staying behind the leading runner for most of the race, Yung-joh suddenly passed him and won
ㄴ 영조는 경기 중 거의 내내 선두주자의 뒤를 따라가다가 갑자기 추월 해서 우승했다

After the game the stadium poured the crowds into the streets
ㄴ 시합이 끝나자 군중들이 거리로 쏟아져 나왔다

After the game, the winning team could be heard crowing their heads off in the locker room
ㄴ 게임이 끝나자 라커룸에서 이긴 팀의 환호하는 소리를 들을 수 있었다

As a baseball player, he doesn't come up to his brother's shoulder
ㄴ 그가 야구선수로서는 형보다 못해

As a lame duck, there's not much he can do and he's run out of gas

---

> **shutout**　game or contest in which one side fails to score

> **lame**　having a limb disabled, weak

↳ 그는 레임덕 상태에 들어가서 할 수 있는 일도 별로 없고 의욕도 잃어버렸다

At the end of the game, I gave him the best

↳ 게임이 끝나자 그에게 졌다고 인정했다

Being a star soccer player goes to Jong-soo's head

↳ 종수가 이름 있는 축구선수가 되더니 교만해졌어

Bong-soo thought that he was the star of the team until he got the business from his coach

↳ 봉수는 코치한테 혼나기 전까지는 자기가 팀에서 스타라고 생각했어

Byung-soo can't do anything as long as the ball is in your court

↳ 이제 공이 네게 와 있는 이상 병수로서는 어떻게 해 볼 수 없게 되어 있어

Can you whip the players into shape before the game?

↳ 게임 전에 선수들의 몸 만들기를 해낼 수 있겠습니까?

Chang-soo can't do a single chin-up

↳ 창수는 턱걸이라고는 한 개도 못 한다

Crowds flocked after him when he left the ball-park

↳ 그가 야구장을 떠날 때 군중들이 몰려들었다

Don't fling your arms and legs like that, make the proper swimming strokes

↳ 아무렇게나 손발을 허우적거리지 말고 제대로 수영동작을 취해라

Don't forget your legs can go to sleep if you swim a long distance

↳ 장거리 수영을 하면 다리에 쥐가 날 수 있다는 걸 잊지 마라

Don't let the other fellows get(have) the(a) jump on you at the beginning of the race

↳ 경기를 시작할 때 다른 사람들에게 뒤지지 않도록 해

› **flock** group of animals or people

Exercise and a sensible diet will help you get your figure back
> ↳ 운동과 분별 있는 식사를 하면 너의 예전 몸매를 되찾게 될 것이다

Exercise is as good a way as any to lose unwanted weight
> ↳ 운동은 불필요한 체중을 줄이는데 매우 좋은 방법이다

Fewer than half of all adults fully understand kinds and amounts of exercise necessary for an effective physical fitness program
> ↳ 모든 성인들 중에 반도 되지 않는 사람들이 효과적인 건강프로그램을 위해 필요한 운동의 종류와 양에 대해 완전히 이해하고 있지 못하고 있다

Four straight losses got the team down
> ↳ 팀이 4연패하자 맥이 빠졌다

Frankly our team enjoyed the home-court(field) advantage
> ↳ 솔직히 우리 팀은 홈그라운드의 이점을 톡톡히 봤다

Get the kinks out of your body gradually before taking exercise in earnest
> ↳ 본격적인 운동을 하기 전에 조금씩 몸을 풀어라

Gil-soo was a good boxer until he became rich and went to seed
> ↳ 기수는 돈이 붙고 한물 가기 전까지는 훌륭한 권투선수였어

He keeps fit by jogging four kilometers everyday and looks the picture of health to us
> ↳ 그는 매일 4킬로씩 조깅을 해서 건강의 표상처럼 보인다

He let out a yell of triumph as he tumbled into the water
> ↳ 그는 물 속으로 뛰어들면서 승리의 환호를 올렸다

He scored the game-winning goal and was named the most valuable player of the match
> ↳ 그가 결승골을 넣음으로써 최우수 선수가 됐다

› **sensible** intelligent, aware or conscious
› **kink** short tight twist or curl, cramp

He wanted to swim a good time, but that it was a world record surprised him
> ↳ 그는 수영에서 좋은 기록을 내고싶었을 뿐이지만 막상 세계기록을 내고 보니 놀랐다

How do you stand among the runners in your class?
> ↳ 넌 달리기 할 때 반에서 몇 번째 가니?

How I want them to win the game!
> ↳ 그들이 시합에서 제발 이겨주었으면!

Hyun-soo made three hits in five at bat
> ↳ 현수는 야구에서 5타수 3안타를 쳤다

In the shallow end of the pool the water comes up to my waist
> ↳ 풀의 얕은 끝 부분은 허리까지 물이 온다

It was nip and tuck until the final 20 seconds
> ↳ 그 경기는 마지막 20초까지 막상막하하였어

It's a game-ending homer
> ↳ 끝내기 홈런이군

It's advisable to run a fast race after limbering ourselves up first
> ↳ 빠른 달리기를 하기 전에 몸을 푸는 것이 바람직하다

It's important to control weight through good diet and regular exercise so that unnecessary pressure does not weaken the joints
> ↳ 좋은 식단과 규칙적인 운동으로 체중을 조절하여 불필요한 압력이 관절을 약화시키지 않도록 하는 것이 중요하다

Jogging and push-ups will do you a world of good
> ↳ 조깅과 푸시업은 건강에 매우 좋다

Jong-bum surely can play baseball
> ↳ 종범인 야구 하나는 끝내주는 선수

› **limber** supple or agile

Let's set our sights on the championship this time
↳ 이번엔 우승을 한 번 노려보자

Lewis was so fast that everyone else was left standing
↳ 루이스는 너무 빨라서 모든 사람들을 훨씬 앞질렀다

Life is like riding a bicycle. You don't fall off unless you stop pedaling
↳ 삶은 자전거 타기와 같다. 페달을 밟는 한 떨어지지 않는다

Losing the game was a slap in the face for him
↳ 게임에 진다는 게 그에게는 모욕적인 일이었다

Lots of scalpers are all out to cash in on the popularity of baseball
↳ 많은 암표 상들이 야구의 인기에 편승해서 야구팬들의 주머니를 긁어 내는데 혈안 되어 있다

Lulu leads her opponent by a two-to-one margin
↳ 루루는 상대방을 2대 1로 앞서 있다

Maybe I'm going out on a limb by saying this, but I expect her to lose the game
↳ 이렇게 말하면 틀릴지 모르지만 그 여자는 게임에서 질 것 같아

Moon-soo got a second wind and won the game
↳ 문수가 갑자기 힘을 내어 그 게임을 이겼어

Moon-soo is a strong player but his opponent has youth on his side
↳ 문수는 강한 선수지만 그의 상대선수는 젊음이라는 이점을 가지고 있다

Moon-soo is on the ball in tennis
↳ 문수는 테니스를 잘 해

My money is on Jong-soo to win the race
↳ 종수가 레이스에 이기는데 돈을 걸었다

Never in his wildest dreams he imagined that he would get the gold

---

› **scalp** skin and flesh of the head

› **limb** projecting appendage used in moving or grasping

medal
> ↳ 그는 금메달을 따리라고는 꿈에도 상상하지 못했다

No offence, but I hate tennis
> ↳ 듣기 거북할지 모르지만 테니스는 싫어

Only two games separated them from total victory
> ↳ 그들은 단 두 게임이 부족해서 완전한 승리를 얻지 못했다

Our team was behind but the pitcher on the other team blew up and we got the winning runs
> ↳ 우리 팀이 뒤졌지만 상대팀 투수가 난조에 빠져 우리가 결승점을 올렸지

Our team won in a shoot-out
> ↳ 우리 팀이 승부차기로 이겼어

> (=We won the shoot-out to win the game)

Reading is to the mind what exercise is to the body
> ↳ 독서가 정신에 필요한 것은 운동이 신체에 필요한 것과 같다

Sang-soo can run fast for a short distance, but he has no staying power
> ↳ 상수가 단거리 달리기에는 빠르지만 뒷심이 없어

Sang-soo pulled a muscle and scratched the game
> ↳ 상수는 근육을 삐어서 경기를 포기했다

Sang-soo strained every nerve to win the game
> ↳ 상수는 경기에 이기려고 온갖 노력을 다 했다

Se-ri completed a wire-to-wire victory
> ↳ 세리는 시종일관 선두를 지켰어

› **pitch** throw

Seok-joo fired just from the outside of the penalty box, hitting the left goalpost and landing inside the net
> ↳ 석주가 페널티박스 바로 외곽에서 슛을 터뜨리자 공은 골포스트를 맞고 그물 안으로 빨려 들어갔다

Shall I dust him off?
> ↳ 경고를 한 번 줄까?(투수가 위협구를 던지면 타자가 쓰러졌다 일어나 먼지를 터는데서)

She does calisthenics every morning to keep in condition(shape)
> ↳ 그 여자는 건강을 유지하기 위해 매일 아침 미용체조를 한다

She lost the game, but she gave them a run for their money
> ↳ 그 여자는 게임에 졌지만 잘 싸웠다

She put on a quite a show
> ↳ 그녀는 멋진 경기를 보여줬다

She won the match by default this time
> ↳ 그녀는 이번에 부전승을 거두었다

She's a tennis player of sorts only
> ↳ 그 여자는 그저 테니스를 조금 치는 정도야

Sook-hee was always cow's tail for running
> ↳ 달리기에서 숙희는 늘 꼴찌를 맡아했어

Stand on your tiptoe and stretch as high as you can, then relax slowly
> ↳ 발끝으로 서서 최대한 높이 기지개를 켜고 천천히 긴장을 풀어라

Stand with your feet shoulder-width apart and swing your golf club back, keeping eye on the ball
> ↳ 양발을 어깨 넓이로 벌리고 서서 공을 쳐다보면서 골프채를 뒤로 휘둘러라

› **dust off** warn

Sung-ho is one of these(those) players
> ㄴ 성호는 시시한 선수야

Sung-soo can make the basketball team if he puts his back to it
> ㄴ 성수는 노력만 하면 농구팀에 낄 수 있어

Swimming right after drinking and eating is a no-no
> ㄴ 음주와 식사직후 수영은 금물이야

Tai-gyung decided to go for broke in the biggest race in the year
> ㄴ 태경이는 연중 최대의 경주에서 최선을 다하기로(이판사판식 작전으로) 작정했다

Take your game to the next level
> ㄴ 작전(게임)의 수준을 한 단계 높여라

Tennis is right down my alley
> ㄴ 테니스 하면 나잖아

That shattered the teen sensation's own record of 1:42 flat set in New York Jan. 20
> ㄴ 이는 10대 돌풍인 그가 지난 1월 20일 뉴욕에서 자신이 수록한 1분 42초 플랫을 깬 것이다

The ball went out of play and the whistle was blown
> ㄴ 공이 경기장 밖으로 나가자 심판이 호각을 불었어

The best way to beat obesity is to stick to a good diet and exercise plan
> ㄴ 비만을 극복하는 최선의 길은 좋은 식단과 운동이다

The chances are two to one against us
> ㄴ 형세는 2대 1로 우리에게 불리해

The chances stand even
> ㄴ 승산은 반반이다

› **shatter** smash or burst into fragments
› **obese** extremely fat

The coach is bound to get it in the neck
ㄴ 감독이 호되게 당하겠군

The coach pitted his best players against the other team
ㄴ 코치는 그의 가장 나은 선수들을 뽑아 다른 팀과 시합을 붙였어

The coach will send you to the showers if you play badly
ㄴ 네가 게임에 시원찮으면 감독이 교체시킬 거야

The crowds outside the ball park began to thin out
ㄴ 야구장 밖의 군중들이 흩어지기 시작했다

The game comes naturally to them
ㄴ 그 게임이 그들에겐 쉬워

The game could go either way
ㄴ 어떤 결과가 나올지 장담 못해

The game kept us on the edge of our seats from the very beginning
ㄴ 게임은 처음부터 손에 땀을 쥐게 했다

The ground played well(badly)
ㄴ 운동장은 상태가 좋았다(나빴다)

The ground rang with the cheers of the crowd
ㄴ 운동장에는 관중들의 환호가 울려 퍼졌다

The horses ran the race neck and neck
ㄴ 경마에서 말들이 막상막하로 달렸어

The number of people suffering from obesity due to poor diet and lack of exercise has grown sharply
ㄴ 잘못된 식단과 운동부족에서 오는 비만으로 고통받는 사람들의 수가 급격히 늘어났다

The race is not to the swift, nor the battle to the strong
ㄴ 경주에서 빠른 자가 반드시 이기는 것도 아니고 전투에서 강한 자가

› **pit** form pits in
› **swift** moving with great speed

반드시 이기는 것도 아니다

The race was nosed out just a few meters before the finish line
> ↳ 그 경주는 결승선 몇 미터 앞두고 간신히 이겼어

The referee ordered him off the field
> ↳ 심판이 그에게 퇴장명령을 내렸어

The right fielder made a shoestring catch to end the inning
> ↳ 우익수가 가까스로 공을 잡아 공수 교대가 됐지

The score's been knotted for the last twenty minutes
> ↳ 지난 20분 동안 득점 변동이 없었다

The soccer game was a cliff-hanger
> ↳ 축구경기가 아슬아슬했다

The storm rained out the game
> ↳ 폭풍우로 게임이 취소됐어

The team is making a lead, so they are trying to run the clock
> ↳ 그 팀은 이기고 있어서 시간을 끌려고 해

The team played right up to the last minute, and then they lost
> ↳ 그 팀이 마지막 순간까지 앞서 갔으나 결국은 지고 말았다

The umpire in the game must be above suspicion of supporting one side over the other
> ↳ 게임의 심판이 한 쪽에 편들고 있음이 틀림없어

They are two points down with three minutes to play
> ↳ 그들은 경기시간 3분을 남기고 2점을 뒤지고 있다

They came from behind to win
> ↳ 그들은 역전승 했다

They edged out the Giants and are now in first place
> ↳ 그들은 자이언스 팀을 겨우 이겨 1위가 됐다

› **knot** interlacing that forms a lump
› **umpire** arbitrator, sport official

They give losers a second chance(the benefit of the doubt)
> ↳ 시합은 패자 부활전이 있어

They remained together for most of the race, until a leader at last came to the front
> ↳ 그들은 코스의 대부분을 거의 같이 달리다가 결국 한 사람이 선두로 나섰다

They spend ours at the tennis court to keep themselves fit
> ↳ 그들은 건강한 몸을 유지하려고 몇 시간씩 테니스를 친다

They turned a five-point deficit with only two minutes left into a three point victory in overtime
> ↳ 그들은 게임종료 2분을 남기고 5점차로 뒤졌다가 연장전에서 3점 차의 승리로 이끌었다

They won(lost) by a close call
> ↳ 가까스로(애석하게) 이겼지(졌지)

This is a breath-taking game=The game is neck-and-neck
> ↳ 손에 땀을 쥐는 경기

This move decides the game
> ↳ 이 한 수로 승부가 난다

To which team will fortune smile in neck and neck game?
> ↳ 팽팽한 전력의 양 팀 중 승리의 여신은 누구를 택할까?

Two teams played to a scoreless tie
> ↳ 두 팀은 0대 0으로 비겼다(**It was one to one draw** 1대 1로 비겼다)

Uniforms symbolize the oneness of the spirit and coordination essential to the winning
> ↳ 유니폼은 승리하는데 필수적인 단일정신과 일치를 상징한다

Wan-soo's tennis went daily from bad to worse

› **deficit** shortage especially in money
› **symbolize** serve as a symbol of

ㄴ 완수의 테니스 실력은 나날이 나빠졌다

We live to have another game

ㄴ 게임 하는 게 오늘만 날이냐

We were patting ourselves for winning when the final whistle blew

ㄴ 마지막 호각이 불어 우리가 이기자 기뻐했지

We won a victory over them that really pinned their ears back

ㄴ 우리는 그들에게 참패를 안기는 승리를 얻었다

We'd better resign ourselves to the fact that they are much better players than we

ㄴ 그들이 우리보다 경기 실력이 훨씬 낫다는 것을 받아들이는 게 좋을 것 같다

What an amazing comeback!

ㄴ 대단한 역전승이군

What's the lie of the land?

ㄴ 상황이 어때?(lie＝형세, 방향 *골프코스의 지형에서)

When the idea of winning in sports carried too excess, honorable competition can turn into disorder and violence

ㄴ 경기에 이기겠다는 생각이 지나치면 명예로운 경쟁의 원칙이 무질서와 폭력으로 변할 수 있다

Whenever he received each blow from his opponent, he writhed on the floor

ㄴ 그는 상대방에게서 펀치를 얻어맞을 때마다 바닥에 쓰러져 몸부림쳤다

Where did you come in? I came in second in the running race

ㄴ 너 몇 등 했니? 달리기에서 2등 했다

Whether Jung-ho or Sang-ho is a better player is an unknown quantity

---

› **writhed**　move or proceed with twists and turns

↳ 정호가 나은 선수인지 상호가 나은지는 미지수야

Who are you playing against?
↳ 상대팀이 누구니?

Who came first in the race?
↳ 경주에서 누가 우승했지?

With his team losing(trailing) 75:77 the head coach was compelled to bring his star back on
↳ 팀이 75대 77로 근소하게 뒤지자 감독은 스타선수를 다시 출장시켰다

With some more practice, we might be able to whip(lick) the team into shape for this month's game
↳ 조금만 더 연습하면 이번 달 시합에 나가 볼만하게 만들 수도 있을 거야

You can't go swimming without getting wet
↳ 호랑이 굴에 들어가야 호랑이를 잡는다

You were so near to winning the game
↳ 넌 그 게임을 이길 뻔했지

You won the six games in a row but the law of average will catch up with them in no time
↳ 넌 여섯 게임을 연승했지만 곧 몇 번 져서 평균치 정도 될 것이다

You'd better wear conspicuous fluorescent clothing for safety when riding your bicycle
↳ 자전거를 탈 때에는 안전을 위해 눈에 띄는 형광복을 입는 게 좋겠다

Your balls have no legs today
↳ 오늘 너의 공은 속도가 없어

Yung-joh can swim with the best of his colleagues
↳ 영조는 그의 동료 누구에게 못지 않게 헤엄을 잘 쳐

▸ **compel** cause through necessity

▸ **fluorescent** emission of light after initial absorption

Yung-joh finished the race with flying colors
ㄴ 영조는 의기양양하게 달리기 경기를 끝냈어

Yung-joh is an excellent runner. It's in his blood
ㄴ 영조는 달리기에 매우 뛰어나. 타고났어

Yung-joh made many points and saved the day
ㄴ 영조가 여러 점을 득점해서 불리한 상황을 유리한 상황으로 돌려놓았어

› **save the day** become a champion or a
hero

79. 습관 & 버릇   Habits

A bad habit is easy to get into and hard to get rid(out) of
> ↳ 나쁜 버릇이 붙기는 쉬워도 버리긴 어려워

Be careful not to glide into bad habits
> ↳ 나쁜 버릇 붙이지 않도록 주의해야 해

Bong-soo gets quarrelsome in his cups
> ↳ 병수는 술만 먹으면 시비조로 나와

Can the leopard change his spots?
> ↳ 제 버릇 개 주랴

Chul-hee will grow out of his bed-wetting
> ↳ 철희는 자라서 자다가 오줌 싸는 버릇은 없어질 것이다

Don't forget that old habits die hard and she likes to fool around
> ↳ 사람의 버릇은 고쳐지지 않는 법인데 그 여자는 바람기가 있다는 점을 잊지 마라

Dong-soo has a habit of going off the deep end about anything
> ↳ 동수는 무슨 일에 나 깊이 빠져드는 버릇이 있어

Everybody has a way of his(her) own
> ↳ 누구에게나 독특한 버릇이 있다

Examinations help form the habit of thinking quickly
> ↳ 시험은 재빨리 생각하는데 도움을 준다

His rule is to take a rubdown with a wet towel every morning

▸ **glide**   move or descend smoothly and effortlessly   ▸ **rubdown**   brisk rubbing of the body

ㄴ 매일 아침 냉수마찰을 하는 것이 그의 습관이다

It's easy to relapse into lazy habits when we have been away from work for a while

ㄴ 한동안 일손을 놓고 지내면 도로 게으른 버릇에 빠져들기 쉽다

My baby's got the habit of kicking his covers off himself in his sleep

ㄴ 우리 아이는 자면서 이불을 걷어차는 버릇이 생겼어

Once a thief always a thief

ㄴ 몸에 밴 습성은 쉽게 버리지 못한다

> 한 번 몸에 밴 습관이 얼마나 중요한 것인지를 알려주는 속담이다. 비슷한 뜻으로 쓰이는 "Once a beggar, always a beggar 한번 거지는 언제나 거지이다"와 "What's learned in the cradle is carried to the grave 요 람에서 배운 것은 무덤까지 간다"도 있다.

Once a use forever a custom

ㄴ 제 버릇 개 못 줘(Custom is a second nature)

Once you get a habit, it'll stay with you

ㄴ 일단 버릇이 되면 고쳐지지 않아

Please make a practice of being on time for work

ㄴ 출근시간에 늦지 않는 습관을 기르도록 해

Sang-soo has a bad habit of spouting off about things that concerns only himself and his family

ㄴ 상수는 자신과 자기 가족 얘기만 잔뜩 늘어놓는 나쁜 버릇이 있다

The habit of smoking while drinking grew upon Jin-soo

ㄴ 진수에게는 술을 마시면서 담배를 피우는 습관이 생겼어

There's no more miserable human being than one in whom nothing is

---

› **relapse** recurrence of illness after a period of improvement

› **spout off** say pompously

habitual but indecision

    ↳ 우유부단 외에 아무 습관적인 것을 가지지 못한 사람만큼 비참한 사람은 없다

What's bred in the bone will not go out of the flesh

    ↳ 세 살 버릇 여든까지

Wise living consists less in acquiring good habits than acquiring as few habits as possible

    ↳ 현명한 삶은 좋은 습관을 붙이는 것보다 오히려 가능한 한 나쁜 습관을 줄여나가는 데 있다

You can't change(mend) your ways

    ↳ 제 버릇 개 못 주는군

> (=You can't change who you are)
> (=You can't change your spots)

▸ **acquire**   gain

80. 승진   **Promotion**

All the employees are in their glory whenever they get promoted
> ↳ 모든 종업원들은 승진 때 가장 기뻐한다

An-do has been promoted, and it's about time considering all the hard work he has put in
> ↳ 안도가 승진을 하였는데, 지금까지 열심히 일해 온 것으로 보아 승진할 때가 온 것이다

As your company rewards enterprising employees with accelerated promotions and responsibilities, you'll go far into the job
> ↳ 너희 회사가 진취적인 사원에게 빠른 승진과 책임 있는 일의 보임을 보장하고 있으니 넌 그 직무에서 성공할 것이다

Believe it or not, I got promoted yesterday
> ↳ 놀라지마, 어제 날짜로 승진했어

Doo-chul persevered at his job and got promoted in no time
> ↳ 두철인 업무에 열중하여 빠른 기간에 승진했어

He rose through the ranks due to his hard work
> ↳ 그는 열심히 일해서 평사원으로부터 빨리 출세했다

His promotion caused a lot of static
> ↳ 그의 승진에는 말이 많아

How long will it be before you can move me up?
> ↳ 나를 승진시키는데 얼마나 걸리겠습니까?

· **persevere** persist
· **static** relating to bodies or forces at rest, ot moving, relating to stationary charges of electricity

I know you are in line for the promotion
ㄴ 당신이 승진 대상이라며

Jin-hee has the inside track for the promotion because she had the best marks
ㄴ 진희가 최고 점수를 얻었으니 승진에 유리해

Nobody will steer you toward the right choices or show you how to climb the corporate ladder
ㄴ 너에게 바른 진로의 선택이나 회사에서 어떻게 승진해 올라가야 할지 가르쳐 줄 사람은 아무도 없다

Promotion goes by merit
ㄴ 승진은 공로 여하에 달렸다

Recently female workers have no difficulties in climbing up the management ladder
ㄴ 요즈음 여성 근로자들은 중역진으로 승진하는데 어려움이 없다

Responsibility goes with promotion
ㄴ 승진이 되면 책임이 따른다

Sang-hee is next in line for promotion
ㄴ 다음 승진은 상희 차례

She had her head in the clouds until her friend was promoted
ㄴ 그 여자는 자기 친구가 승진할 때까지 건성으로 일하고 있었다

She's been moving up quickly
ㄴ 그녀는 빨리 승진을 해 오고 있다

She's sore over the fact that she wasn't promoted
ㄴ 그 여자는 승진을 못해 속상해 하고 있다

There's a rumor going the rounds that Sang-ho will get promoted
ㄴ 상호가 승진할 것이라는 소문이 파다해

‣ **steer** direct the course of, guide

Trying to get a promotion here is like knocking your head against a brick wall
> ↳ 여기서 승진을 바라보다가는 철저한 좌절감만 맛볼 뿐이다

When he failed to get promotion it came as a body blow to him
> ↳ 그가 승진을 못하게 되자 크게 실망하게 되었다

Where do I stand in regards to the promotion?
> ↳ 나의 승진 가능성은 어떻습니까?

You got your promotion clinched
> ↳ 너의 승진은 따 놓은 당상이야

You'll surely get promoted; you have everything going for you
> ↳ 모든 일이 네게 유리하게 돌아가고 있으니 틀림없이 성공할거야

▸ **clinch** fasten securely, settle, hold fast or firmly

81. 시간   **Time**

A 10 minute walk will get you there
       ↳ 10분 정도 걸으면 도착할거야

A ball game(It) is not over until it's over
       ↳ 사람팔자 시간문제다

> (=No one can foretell his destiny)

A busy man has many calls on time
       ↳ 바쁜 사람은 뭔가에 시간을 많이 빼앗긴다

A couple of days in the cooler will straighten him up
       ↳ 그를 며칠 간 교도소에 보내놓으면 정신 좀 차릴 거야

A few minutes after the thief left she got it all(pulled herself) together and called the police
       ↳ 도둑이 가버린 몇 분 후 그 여자는 정신을 차리고 경찰에 전화했어

A good doctor can net(clear) over 50 million won a year
       ↳ 괜찮은 의사라면 1년에 5천만원 이상의 순수익을 올린다

A good salesman will not encroach on his customer's time
       ↳ 훌륭한 판매원은 고객에게 시간을 낭비시키지 않는다

A guest sees more in an hour than the host in a year
       ↳ 주인이 1년간 보고 아는 것 이상을 손님은 한 시간에 보고 안다

› **encroach**   to enter gradually or stealthily upon another's property or rights

› **host**   one who receives or entertains guests

A minute's success pays for the failure of years
　　ㄴ 한 순간의 성공은 1년간의 실패를 보상한다

A protracted illness wears out filial devotions
　　　　ㄴ 긴 병에 효자 없다

> (=A long visit(stay) wears out welcome)
> (=Enthusiasm is short-lived)

A settlement was reached at the eleventh hour
　　　　ㄴ 사태는 마지막 순간에 타결됐어

A whole lot of precious time
　　　　ㄴ 귀중한 시간이 엄청나게 필요해

A wonder lasts but nine days
　　　　ㄴ 세상을 떠들썩하게 하는 일도 곧 잊혀지게 된다

After a few months of being ignored, Bong-soo withdrew into himself
　　　　ㄴ 봉수가 몇 달 동안 무시당하고 보니 남들과의 교제를 끊었어

After a few years we lost track of each other
　　　　ㄴ 몇 년 지난 후 우리는 소식이 끊겼어

After a month or two, it'll be plain sailing
　　　　ㄴ 한 두 달만 지나면 순조롭게 진행될 거야

After a year or two we lost track of each other
　　　　ㄴ 2~3년 후 우리는 서로 소식이 끊어지고 말았다

After all this time, my parents are still romantic
　　　　ㄴ 많은 세월이 지났는데도 우리 부모님은 여전히 금실 좋아

After five years of marriage, they grew apart
　　　　ㄴ 그들은 결혼생활 5년이 지나자 성격차이가 드러났다

‣ **filial** relating to, or befitting a son or daughter

‣ **devotion** religious fervor, the fact or state of being dedicated and loyal

After four years in prison, he decided to go(run) straight
> 그는 4년간 복역한 뒤에 바르게 살기로 결심했다(바르게 살았다)

After Jong-soo had been on for several minute, the other team's defeat became certain
> 종수가 게임에 출장한지 몇 분이 안되어서 상대팀이 질 수밖에 없게 되었다

After only a few years, he's wallowing in money and property
> 그는 불과 몇 년 안 가서 돈이며 재산이 풍족해졌어

After three hours of snow and rain, the roads were so slushed up that they could not travel
> 눈비가 온 끝이라 도로가 엉망이 돼서 그들은 길을 갈 수가 없었다

All government workers have had their salaries frozen for three years
> 모든 공무원들의 봉급이 3년간 동결되었다

All he could do was to play for time until the police arrived
> 그가 할 수 있는 일은 경찰이 도착할 때 까지 버티는 것뿐이었다

All passengers should pass through the security area one hour before scheduled flight
> 모든 승객께서는 비행기 출발 한 시간 전에 보안 검색 열을 통과해야 합니다

All that was before your time
> 그건 다 네가 태어나기 전의 일

All that's fair must fade
> 화무십일홍(권불십년)

All these worries have put years on me
> 이 골치 아픈 일 들이 나를 겉늙게 만들었어

All things have changed from what they were 5 years ago

▸ **wallow** to roll oneself about sluggishly in or if in deep mud

▸ **fade** wither, to lose or cause to lose freshness

ㄴ 모든 것이 5년 전에 비해 변모했다

Although it was a race against time, he walked like a duck in(on) its bottom

ㄴ 그는 시간을 다투는데도 어기적어기적 걸었다

An-do can do 6,000 keystrokes an hour

ㄴ 안도는 시간당 **6,000**타를 쳐

An-do chickened out on us at the last minute

ㄴ 안도는 최종 순간에 우리와 동행(협조)하지 않기로 했어

An-do never seemed to be in the same job for more than three months at a time

ㄴ 안도는 한 직장에서 세 달 이상 눌러앉아 있질 못하는 것 같았어

An-do rushed the special medicine to the pharmacy in a race against the clock

ㄴ 안도는 시각을 다투어 그 특수 약을 구하려고 약방으로 달려갔다

Are you available today?

ㄴ 오늘 시간 좀 있어?

As she knows she's only been a let-down and this time she's resolved to show a thing or two

ㄴ 그녀는 자신이 시시한 존재였음을 알기 때문에 이번에는 뭔가를 보여 주려고 하고 있다

As there was such a crowd in the street, I kept running around in circles trying to find you

ㄴ 길거리에 인파가 너무 많아서 너를 찾느라고 시간만 잔뜩 허비했다

As time goes by, more and more people come forward to donate organs

ㄴ 세월이 흐름에 따라 장기를 기증하겠다고 나서는 사람들이 점점 늘어

› **donate** make a gift of

› **organ** periodical, animal or plant structure with special function

나고 있다

As you have been married for five years, it's time to start a family
↳ 이제 네가 결혼한 지 5년이나 됐으니 아이를 가져야 할 것 아니냐

At the end of the last year he was in the clear(hole)
↳ 작년 말 그는 탈 빚 했어(빚을 지고 있었어)

At this rate I'm going, I doubt I'll be home tonight before twelve
↳ 이렇게 가다간 밤 열두 시전에 집에 가게 될지 의문이다

At this time everybody winds up their annual work and reflects on what they have done this year
↳ 이맘때면 모두가 1년간의 일을 마무리하고 올해 한 일을 되돌아본다

At this time of the year snowbound roads mean crawling traffic and delays for commuters
↳ 이맘때쯤 해서 눈 때문에 다니지 못하게 되면 차가 기어다니게 되고 통근자들의 지각사태가 난다

Back in the old days, I used to drink
↳ 왕년엔 술 좀 마셨지

Because we refuse to astray from the path, we are doing something that would have seemed unimaginable seven years ago
↳ 우리는 이러한 원칙을 고수했기 때문에 7년 전에는 할 수 없었던 일들을 현재 추진하고 있다

Bong-soo carried on for an hour after he fell from his desk
↳ 봉수는 책상에서 떨어진지 한 시간이나 아프다고 엄살(호들갑)을 떨었어

Bong-soo mustered out of service well before his time was up
↳ 봉수는 만기가 되기 훨씬 전에 군에서 제대했어

Busiest time finds the most leisure time

› **snowbound** slippery with snow
› **crawl** move slowly

› **commute** travel back and forth regularly
› **astray** off the right way

↳ 가장 바쁜 사람에게 가장 여가가 많다

By joining the army late, he was ranked below many men much younger than himself

    ↳ 그는 군에 늦게 가서 자기보다 훨씬 나이 적은 사람들의 졸병노릇을 했다

By the end of the two-week tour, they were dragging their asses(butts, feet)

    ↳ 그들은 2주에 걸친 여행 끝에 몹시 지쳐있었다

Byung-soo busted a gut to get there on time

    ↳ 병수는 시간 안에 거기에 도착하려고 꼬리가 빠지게 달려갔다

Can this money carry you through this month?

    ↳ 이 돈이면 이 달을 넘길 수 있나?

Can you keep this business on its feet for another year?

    ↳ 이 사업을 1년 더 버티어 낼 수 있겠나?

Can you move(push) the date back a little?

    ↳ 날짜를 조금 늦출 수 있겠나?

Can you stall(play) for time till the end of the year?

    ↳ 연말까지 시간을 늦춰줄 수 있겠니?

Chan-soo bowed out as a train engineer after ten years of railroading

    ↳ 찬수는 철도 사업에 10년 근무한 후 기관사 직을 그만 두었어

Chang-moon's has been chasing after girls for year, but he's already over the hill

    ↳ 창문이는 노상 아가씨들 꽁무니만 쫓아 다녔지만 이젠 한물 갔어

Chang-soo is having a hard time(job) getting Sunday laziness out of his blood

    ↳ 창수는 태평한 일요일 분위기를 벗어나는데 애를 먹고있어

› **bust** burst or break, tame

› **stall** delay, evade, or keep a situation going to gain advantage of time

Chang-soo's been cooking the books for years, but the auditors have never caught it
> ↳ 창수가 회계장부를 몇 년씩이나 조작해 왔지만 감사원이 적발하지 못했어

Do you have a time for a quick one?
> ↳ 한잔 할 시간 있니?

Don't dawdle over your meal, we don't want to be late for the train
> ↳ 기차시간 늦으면 안되니까 밥 먹는데 꾸물대지마

Don't fritter away all your money and time
> ↳ 보람없는 일에 돈과 시간을 허비해선 안 돼

Don't get after me all the time
> ↳ 나를 노상 들볶(괴롭히)지마(get after 에는 "추격하다"의 뜻도 있음)

Don't kill yourself to get here in time
> ↳ 무리하게 시간 내에 여기 오려고 하지마

Don't let the grass grow under your feet
> ↳ 시간낭비 하지 마라

Don't linger over your meal, we don't have all day
> ↳ 우린 급하니까 밥 먹는데 시간 끌지 말자

Don't try to earn time
> ↳ 시간만 벌려고 하지마

Don't you think it's time we sent in the second string?
> ↳ 이제 제2진을 내보내는 게 어때?

Doo-chul grossed over two million won this month
> ↳ 두철인 이 달에 2백만원 수익을 올렸어

Doo-soo began to saw wood(logs) twenty seconds after his head hit the pillow

---

› **auditor** person who examines financial accounts

› **dawdle** waste time, loiter
› **linger** be slow to leave or act

ㄴ 두수는 드러누워 **20**초가 되자마자 코를 골기 시작했다

Doo-soo is sixty thousand won in the hole this month
ㄴ 두수는 이 달 **6**만원 적자야

During(the) rush hours, there's always a lot of pushing and shoving to get on trains
ㄴ 러시아워 시간에는 열차를 타기 위해 항상 밀고 비집고 들어가야 한다

Each succeeding year stole away something from her beauty
ㄴ 연년이 쌓이는 세월 속에 그 여자는 아름다움을 잃어갔다

Ed has done time on a number of occasions
ㄴ 에드는 여러 차례 복역한 일이 있다

Even a beauty can get wearing after a while
ㄴ 미인이라도 시간이 가면 실증날 수 있어

Even if there's no time for breakfast, you must not go without
ㄴ 아침 먹을 시간이 없다고 해도 아침을 걸러선 안 돼

Every minute seems like a thousand
ㄴ 일각이 여삼추다

힘든 일을 하거나 무엇을 기다릴 때에는 시간이 늦게 가는 것처럼 느껴진다. 이럴 때에는 "일각이 여삼추다"라는 말을 쓴다. 한 순간이 삼년 같다는 말이다. 영어로는 "Every minute seems like a thousand 일분이 천 분 같다"라는 표현을 쓴다. 아주 지루할 때에는 "Time drags 시간이 질질 끈다"라는 표현을 쓰기도 하는데, 이는 "Time flies 시간이 날아간다"와 반대되는 표현이다.

Every three years or so he pulls up his roots(stakes), moves to another city and starts again
ㄴ 그는 매번 **3**년 남짓 어느 곳이든 살다가 다른 도시로 옮겨 거기서

› **shove** push, along, aside, or away

다시 시작해

Everyone really cut loose and had a very good time
↳ 우리들은 진짜 흥청거리면서 아주 재미있게 보냈다

Everything happens to everybody sooner or later if there's time enough
↳ 시간이 충분하다면 언젠가는 모든 일은 모든 사람에게 닥쳐온다

Few people expect to go over the top before the beginning of January
↳ 1월초가 되기 전에 목표를 달성하리라고 기대하는 사람은 거의 없어

Financial success is not in the cards for me this month
↳ 이 달은 내가 경제적으로 잘될 것 같지 않다

Fish and guests stink after three days(old)
↳ 가는 손님은 뒤 꼭지도 예쁘다

직역하면 "생선과 손님은 사흘이 지나면 썩는 냄새가 난다"이다. 손님으로 가면 빠른 시일 내에 돌아오라는 얘기이다. 아무리 반가운 손님도 시간이 지남에 따라 부담스러워지기 때문이다(=A constant guest is never welcome).

For some years he's held the fields
↳ 그는 몇 년 동안 버티어 왔다

Gil-soo hasn't been the same since that time
↳ 길수는 그 이후 달라졌어

Gil-soo'll go up to university next year
↳ 길수는 내년 대학에 진학할 거야

Gil-soo's time schedule conflicts with the concert

▸ **conflict** war, clash of ideas, clash

↳ 길수의 스케줄은 음악회하고 어긋나

Give it a few more days
↳ 며칠만 더 기다려 줘

Guilt doesn't pass with time
↳ 시간이 간다고 죄가 없어지는 게 아냐

Having all the time in the world is hard for an office worker
↳ 사무원에게 시간이 남아돈다는 것은 흔한 일이 아니다

He doesn't care about keeping up with the times
↳ 그는 시속 따위에 얽매이는 사람이 아냐

He hardly makes a dent in his money all month
↳ 그는 한 달 내내 돈을 써도 줄어든 표가 없을 만큼 부자다

He has drifted about like a rudderless ship for three years
↳ 그는 3년간 정처 없이 떠돌아 다녔다

He left the company after 30 years' service without a single black mark against him
↳ 그는 30년간 단 하나의 과오도 없이 회사를 물러났다

He rambled on for almost two hours without really saying anything
↳ 그는 실제 알맹이도 없이 거의 두 시간이나 얘기했다

He was in the job for ten years and certainly left his mark
↳ 그는 10년 동안 재직하면서 큰 업적을 남겼다

He's on for six o'clock tomorrow morning
↳ 그는 내일 아침 여섯 시에 약속이 있어

His first trip abroad wound him up and he talked almost three hours
↳ 그의 첫 해외여행으로 얘기가 쌓여서 세 시간씩이나 얘기했다

His life has only a few years to run(go)
↳ 그의 수명은 몇 년밖에 안 남았어

▸ **dent** small depression

▸ **rudderless** a boat or aircraft without steering device in rear

His proposal is dead in the water this year
↳ 그의 제안이 금년 중에는 거론도 안 돼

His thoughts have been nothing but you for years
↳ 몇 년 동안 그의 생각은 너한테만 가 있었다

His wife's been on his back for months to fix the big leak there
↳ 그의 부인이 그에게 몇 달 동안 졸라서 거기 크게 새는 곳을 고치고 있어

Hit the ground running or you'll never make it in time
↳ 최고 속력으로 가지 않으면 시간 안에 못 가

How have you put up with him treating you like dirt for all the years
↳ 그가 그토록 긴 세월에 걸쳐 너를 개떡같이 취급해 오는 것을 어떻게 참아왔나?

I am against the clock
↳ 시간이 촉박해

I count the hours until that day
↳ 그날이 오기를 손꼽아 기다리고 있어

I have been averaging 20 minutes to get a taxi
↳ 택시 잡는데 20분이나 걸렸어

I have many demands(claims) on my time
↳ 여러 가지로 시간을 뺏기는 일이 많아

I have to fight the clock
↳ 시간을 다투고 있어

I kept(remained) standing for an hour
↳ 한시간이나 계속 서 있었어(**keep on standing**은 "몇 번이고 일어서다"임)

› **average** be usually, fine the mean of
› **demand** ask for with authority, require

I know your three minutes
> ↳ 네가 말하는 **3**분이란 믿을 수가 없어(이해 못할 수도 있음)

I lost count(track) of time
> ↳ 시간 가는 줄 몰랐지

> (=I don't know how I lost track of time)

I'll be doing this for a long time
> ↳ 하루 이틀 할 장사가 아니잖아

> (=This is a long-term thing)

If he remains for more than a minute, pull him out, he may be drowning
> ↳ 그가 **1**분 이상 물위로 올라오지 않으면 익사할 수도 있으니까 끌어 내어라

> (How long can you remain under water? 물 속에서 숨을 멈추고 얼마나 있겠니?)

If this remains untreated and accumulated for a long time, it can result in a stomach ulcer
> ↳ 이 증세를 치료하지 않고 장기간 누적시켜간다면 위궤양을 일으킬 수 있다

If you judge people, you have no time to love them
> ↳ 남을 비판하면 그들을 사랑할 틈이 없다

› **drown** suffocate in water, overpower or become overpowered

› **accumulate** collect or pile up

If you make the 9:00 a.m flight, you'll be able to make the connecting flight to Seoul
> ↳ 오전 아홉 시 비행기를 놓치지 않으면 서울로 가는 연결 비행기를 탈 수 있을 것입니다

If you shoot your bolt now, your defeat will be just a matter of time
> ↳ 지금 최후수단을 다 써버린다면 너의 패배는 시간문제다

If you're patient in one moment of anger, you'll escape a hundred days of sorrow
> ↳ 한 순간의 화를 참으면 100일의 근심을 덜게된다

In a few more years I'll be able to get ahead
> ↳ 몇 년 안 가서 흑자 낼 수 있을 거야

In old times, property was usually handed down to the oldest son upon his father's death
> ↳ 옛날엔 보통 아버지의 사망 때 장남에게 재산을 대물림했다

In old times, students worshiped the ground their teachers walked on
> ↳ 예전 학생들은 선생님들을 매우 존경했었다

In-ho has yet to make two million won a month
> ↳ 인호는 월 이백만원은 벌어야 해

In-ho needs some time to pick up the pieces of his life after the accident
> ↳ 인호는 사고 후 뒷수습을 하는데 얼마간의 시간이 필요해

It might be done on time, but I wouldn't make book(bank) on it
> ↳ 제 시간에 될 수도 있겠지만 내기를 걸고 싶을 정도는 아냐

It takes some time to dry him out
> ↳ 그가 술을 깨자면 시간이 좀 걸릴 것이다

It takes time to do it right

› **pick up** improve, put in order, take hold of and lift, collect, tidy, take | into a vehicle, acquire by chance, learn, increase or improve

ㄴ 제대로 하려면 시간이

It took an hour for me to come to
ㄴ 내가 정신을 차리는데 한 시간 걸렸어

It was nip and tuck until the final 20 seconds
ㄴ 그 경기는 마지막 20초까지 막상막하였어

It won't be easy for me to hold the attention of the large audience over 50 minutes
ㄴ 50분이 넘도록 큰 군중이 흥미를 잃지 않도록 하기는 쉬운 일이 아니다

It won't take a long time before the newly implemented law gets on the right track
ㄴ 새로 실시되는 법이 본 궤도에 오른 이상 그리 긴 시간이 필요치 않을 것이다

It'll take a few months for them to get into the swing of things
ㄴ 그들이 익숙해지기까지는 두 세 달 걸릴 것이다

It'll take some time for that fact to sink in
ㄴ 그게 완전히 이해되려면 시간이 좀 걸리겠지

It's about one hour one way
ㄴ 거기 까진 편도로 약 한시간 걸려

It's already well on in the night
ㄴ 벌써 밤이 깊었군

It's been around for some time now
ㄴ 그게 생긴지 꽤 오래 됐어

It's going(getting) on for a lunch time
ㄴ 그럭저럭 점심시간이 되어가는군

It's still long before the day draws in

› **nip**   biting cold, tang, pinch or bite
› **tuck**   fold in a cloth

ㄴ 해가 저물려면 아직 멀었다

It's time for a timeout
ㄴ 이제 그만 놀 시간이다

It's time to put our hand to the plow
ㄴ 자, 일 할 시간이다

Jin-hee knocked herself out to get there on time
ㄴ 진희는 기를 쓰고 시간 안에 거기에 도착하려고 애를 썼어

Jung-tae retired last year, and is going stir crazy now
ㄴ 정태는 작년에 퇴직했는데 지금은 좀이 쑤셔서 못 견딘다

Keep a good cut of beef for me every week
ㄴ 매주 상등 쇠고기 한 덩이를 내 몫으로 떼어놓아 주어라

Korea saw its trade deficit swell to $1.2 billion so far this month
ㄴ 한국은 이 달 들어 무역수지 적자가 12억불로 늘어났다

Korean manufacturers posted record net profits last year, due to a decrease in costly interest payments combined with a surging demand from consumers
ㄴ 지난해 국내 제조업자들이 수요 급증과, 이자비용 감소 등으로 사상 최대 순익을 올렸다

Let's make every minute count
ㄴ 시간을 유용하게 쓰자

Man-soo's father changed jobs several times a year, and the family was moved from pillar to post
ㄴ 만수의 아버지는 1년에 여러 번 직장을 옮겨서 가족들이 여기 저기 이사를 다녔어

Most banks allow us to space out our payments over several years
ㄴ 대부분 은행은 대출자에게 몇 년에 걸쳐 상환하게 해준다

› **timeout** suspension of play in an athletic game

› **deficit** shortage especially in money

Much money and time are spent to prepare sacrificial food to offer the spirits of ancestors
> ↳ 조상신들에게 드릴 제사음식을 준비하느라고 많은 돈과 시간이 소비된다

My business just managed to break even this month
> ↳ 이 달엔 겨우 적자나 면할 정도야

My father gave me a blank check to use his car for month
> ↳ 차를 맘대로 쓰라고 아버지가 허락하셨어

My father lay at death's door for a week, but he began to get better
> ↳ 아버지가 1주일 동안 사경을 헤매었으나 곧 나아지기 시작하셨어

My parents wear their years well
> ↳ 우리 부모님은 연세가 많아도 정정하셔

My time is my own
> ↳ 내 시간은 내 맘대로야

Myong-soo marks the time and pays no mind to the job
> ↳ 명수는 시간만 죽이면서 일에는 마음을 쓰지 않아

Nam-chul can read the signs of the times
> ↳ 남철인 시류를 아는 사람이다

Nam-soo has been making time with Soon-hee
> ↳ 남수는 순희하고 연애중이야

Nine-tenths of wisdom is being wise in time
> ↳ 대부분의 지혜는 시간이 가면서 생겨난다

No person will have occasion to complain of the want of time who never loses any
> ↳ 시간을 허비하지 않는 사람은 시간이 없다고 푸념할 겨를이 없다

Now is the time to dive in

› **sacrificial** precious things offered to a deity

› **dive in** get started in certain field

ↄ 지금이야말로 과감하게 뛰어들 때야

Now is the time to make your move

ↄ 이제 용단을 내릴 때다

Often time is wasted in staff meetings because participants have not studied the issues prior to the meeting

ↄ 참가자들이 회의 전에 토의 주제에 대하여 연구하지 않았기 때문에 직원회의는 시간이 낭비되는 일이 많다

One hour's cold will spoil seven year's warming

ↄ 일순간의 잘못으로 공든 탑도 무너진다

> (=One slip of the knife will spoil the work of months)

One of the greatest disadvantages of hurry is that it takes such a long time

ↄ 서두름에서 오는 가장 큰 손해는 그 서두름으로 인하여 오히려 매우 오랜 시간이 걸린다는 점이다

Only after week's of vain efforts, did the right ideas occur to me

ↄ 몇 주일동안 헛된 노력을 한 후에야 겨우 적절한 생각이 떠올랐다

Our business showings last month went through the roof

ↄ 지난 달 영업 실적은 왕창 올랐어

Our costliest expenditure is time

ↄ 사람에게 가장 큰비용은 시간이다

Our membership has been rolling up for the past few years

ↄ 우리의 회원 수가 지난 몇 년 동안 점점 늘어나고 있다

Please run this ad in your paper for three days

ↄ 이 광고를 3일간 귀지에 실어 주십시오

▸ **prior to** coming before in time, order, or importance

▸ **expenditure** act of using or spending

Prices are higher at certain seasons and holidays than at other times of the year

ㄴ 물가는 일년 중 다른 때 보다 특정 계절이나 휴가 때 더 높다

Procrastination is the thief of time

ㄴ 뒤로 미루는 것은 시간을 도둑맞는 일이다

Quit wasting time. Fish or cut bait

ㄴ 헛 시간 보내지마. 똑똑히 하던지 아니면 그만 둬

Remember your boss treats you as if you are an airhead just filling time before you get married

ㄴ 너의 사장은 네가 결혼 전에 시간이나 때우고 있는 골이 빈 사람인 것으로 여기고 있다는 것을 잊지 마라

Riding on a growing demand, his business enjoyed a big profit last month

ㄴ 그의 사업은 수요증가에 힘입어 지난 달 큰 수익을 올렸다

Sang-soo and Hang-soon have had an on-again, off-again romance for years

ㄴ 상수와 행순이는 만났다 헤어지고 또 만났다 헤어지기를 오랫동안 해 오고 있어

Sang-soo stole the show even though he was on stage for not more than five minutes

ㄴ 상수는 무대에 오른 지 5분을 넘기지 않았지만 인기를 독차지했다

See you at five if I don't hear otherwise

ㄴ 나한테 별다른 얘기가 없으면 다섯 시에 올게

She can do 3,000 strokes an hour

ㄴ 그 여자는 한 시간에 3,000타를 친다

She decided to bow out gracefully and spend more time with her

---

· **procrastinate** put something off until later
· **airhead** bonehead, stupid

family
> ㄴ 그녀는 깨끗이 물러나서 가족들과 더 많은 시간을 보내기로 결정했다

She desperately scribbled down the answers, being aware of how the minutes were ticking away
> ㄴ 그녀는 1분 1초 재깍재깍 시간의 흐름을 인식하면서 사력을 다해 답안을 갈겨 써 내려갔다

She ever talks a mile a minute
> ㄴ 그 여자는 쉴새없이 지껄여

She sweated blood to finish her composition on time
> ㄴ 그녀는 시간 내에 작문을 끝내려고 기를 썼어(sweat blood=be worried or work hard)

She's been counting the hours(days) since that day
> ㄴ 그 여자는 그 날 이후 일각이 여삼추로(하루가 멀다하고) 기다리고 있다

힘든 일을 하거나 무엇을 기다릴 때에는 시간이 늦게 가는 것처럼 느껴진다. 이럴 때에는 "일각이 여삼추다"라는 말을 쓴다. 한 순간이 삼년 같다는 말이다. 영어로는 "Every minute seems like a thousand 일분이 천 분 같다"라는 표현을 쓴다. 아주 지루할 때에는 "Time drags 시간이 질질 끈다"라는 표현을 쓰기도 하는 데, 이는 "Time flies 시간이 날아간다"와 반대되는 표현이다.

She's been laboring under that mistaken idea for years now
> ㄴ 그 여자는 수년동안 그런 착각 속에 빠져 있는 거야

She's been playing musical beds for years
> ㄴ 그 여자는 오랫동안 여러 남자하고 놀아났어

She's been working against the clock, trying to meet deadlines
> ㄴ 그녀는 마감시간에 맞추려고 시간과의 싸움을 해 오고 있다

· **scribble** write hastily or carelessly | · **deadline** time by which something must be finished

Shin-jah looks like a fashion page from the 60s
ㄴ 신자는 60년대의 케케묵은 스타일 같아

Short skirts will be back next year
ㄴ 내년에는 짧은치마가 다시 유행 할 것이다

Sometimes a talent may lie inactive for years before it is awaken
ㄴ 어떤 재능은 가만히 있다가 깨어나는 경우가 흔히 있다

Spring is early to come this year than last year
ㄴ 올 봄은 작년보다 일러

Sung-soo puts in five hours a day reading
ㄴ 성수는 독서하는데 하루 다섯 시간 사용한다

Tai-gyung decided to go for broke in the biggest race in the year
ㄴ 태경이는 연중 최대의 경주에서 최선을 다하기로(이판사판식 작전으로) 작정했다

That event has really put a lot of years on me
ㄴ 그 사건 때문에 정말 십 년은 감수했어

That kind of hat went out years ago
ㄴ 그런 모자는 몇 년 전부터 사람들이 안 쓰더라

That man will get sent up for a long time now
ㄴ 저 사람은 이제 오랫동안 콩밥 먹어야 할거야

That shattered the teen sensation's own record of 1:42 flat set in New York Jan. 20
ㄴ 이는 10대 돌풍인 그가 지난 1월 20일 뉴욕에서 자신이 수록한 1분 42초 플랫을 깬 것이다

That'll blow a hole in our projects for this month
ㄴ 그렇게되면 이 달 장사는 망치는 거야

The best fish smells when they are three days old

› **talent** natural mental, creative, or artistic ability

› **shatter** smash or burst into fragments

↳ 귀한 손님도 사흘만 넘기면 귀찮아진다

> 직역하면 "생선과 손님은 사흘이 지나면 썩는 냄새가 난다"이다. 손님으로 가면 빠른 시일 내에 돌아오라는 얘기이다. 아무리 반가운 손님도 시간이 지남에 따라 부담스러워지기 때문이다(= A constant guest is never welcome).

The best way to learn a foreign language is to immerse oneself in it totally, speaking nothing else, for a period of a few years
> ↳ 외국어를 배우는 최상의 길은 다른 언어를 사용하지 말고 그 외국어 만을 몇 년간 말하면서 학습에 전념하는 일이다

The bus line launched with a lot of fanfare and fizzled out just in one month
> ↳ 요란하게 떠들어대며 착수한 버스노선이 한 달만에 흐지부지 끝나버 렸다

The continuous problems turned us out in a few weeks
> ↳ 계속되는 문제점들이 우리를 몇 주 동안 맥빠지게 만들었어

The darkest hour is that before the dawn
> ↳ 동트기 전이 가장 어두운 시간이다(절망하지 마라)

> 아무리 힘들고 어렵더라고 참고 견디면 좋은 일이 생긴다(An unfavourable situation will eventually change for the better = 계속되는 불행도 참 아내다 보면 기회가 온다).

The effect of the medicine will go off(wear off, pass off, pass away) after five hours or so
> ↳ 다섯 시간 정도 지나면 약 기운이 없어질 것이다

› **fanfare** a sounding of trumpets, showy display | › **fizzle** fizz, fail, failure

The farmers are taking(bringing) the rice in early this year because of clear weather
> ㄴ 금년에는 맑은 날씨 덕분에 농민들이 벼를 일찍 수확하고 있다

The gangsters shake the shop owners down every month
> ㄴ 깡패들이 매월 상점 주인들을 등쳐먹고 있어

The ground is contaminated by chemicals which have leaked from the storage tank over the last 30 years
> ㄴ 지난 30년에 걸쳐 저장탱크에서 새어나온 화학물질로 토양이 오염되었다

The impossible takes a longer time
> ㄴ 불가능한 일은 좀 더 시간을 요할 뿐 결국은 할 수 있다

The last 5 minutes determine the issue
> ㄴ 최후의 5분이 중요해

The longer you vacillate, the less time you'll have to do anything worthwhile
> ㄴ 오래 망설일수록 가치 있는 일을 할 수 있는 시간이 더 짧아진다

The memory of my late uncle revives unexpectedly from time to time
> ㄴ 문득문득 돌아가신 아저씨 생각이 난다

The new contract should keep our business on its feet for another year
> ㄴ 이번 신규수주 덕분에 1년은 더 버틸 것 같다

The picture takes me back to the time I spent the summer in Busan
> ㄴ 이 사진을 보니 부산에서 여름을 보냈던 때가 생각나는군

The rain wore away at the stone through time
> ㄴ 세월이 흐르면서 빗물이 돌을 깎아 내렸다

› **vacillate** waver between courses or opinions

불가능한 일이라도 끊임없이 노력하면 이루어진다는 뜻이다. 물(Dripping)은 끊임없는 성실한 노력을 뜻한다(He that shoots often at last shall hit the mark = 여러 번 쏘는 자는 결국 표적을 맞춘다).

The ride to the village seemed to take only half the time
> 차를 타고 그 마을까지 가는데는 생각보다 훨씬 짧은 시간밖에 안 걸렸다

The score's been knotted for the last twenty minutes
> 지난 **20**분 동안 득점 변동이 없었다

The secret is only now beginning to rise to the surface; he kept it successfully for many years
> 그 비밀은 이제야 드러나게 되었고, 그는 몇 년씩이나 이 비밀을 잘도 숨겨왔다

The small matter ripened into a large problem in a short time
> 얼마 안 가서 작은 일이 큰 문제로 커졌어

The talks with the boss bogged down on the question of working hours
> 사장과의 근로시간에 관한 얘기는 어려움에 봉착했다

The teacher had to urge the students along(forward, on) in the last few months before the exam
> 그 교사는 학생들에게 시험 전 몇 달 동안 공부를 열심히 하라고 다그칠 수밖에 없었다

The team is making a lead, so they are trying to run the clock
> 그 팀은 이기고 있어서 시간을 끌려고 해

The team played right up to the last minute, and then they lost
> 그 팀이 마지막 순간까지 앞서 갔으나 결국은 지고 말았다

- **ripe** fully grown, developed, or prepared
- **bog** swamp, sink in or as if in a bog

The weather is fine for the time of the year
> 예년에 비해 날씨가 좋다

The whistle blower put Mr. Big behind bars for five years
> 밀고자의 밀고로 인해 두목이 5년간 교도소에 들어가 있었다

The years are rolling by(gliding by, going by)
> 세월은 빨라

(=Time flies)

The years rolled on(by), and soon they were old and gray
> 세월이 흘러 어느새 그들은 나이가 들고 반백이 되었다

The years, like a thief in the night, stole what I was
> 세월이 어느새 나의 모습을 앗아가 버렸다

The years, months, days, and hours have their corresponding 12 animal symbols
> 연, 월, 일, 시간에는 각각 해당되는 상징의 12 동물이 있다

Their bottom-line output target is to produce three motors a week
> 그들의 최소한 목표는 주당 3대의 모터를 생산하는 것이다

There are few things of which we are apt to be so wasteful as time
> 시간만큼 허비하기 쉬운 것도 별로 없다

There is a good time coming
> 곧 좋은 시절이 올 거다

There's a sucker born every minute
> 어수룩한 사람이 하나 둘 인줄 아나

There's a time for everything

▸ **correspond** match(+to), communicate by letter

▸ **symbol** something that represents or suggests another thing

↳ 모든 일에는 때가 있어

There's a time and place for everything

↳ 매사가 때와 장소에 따라 다르다

There's not a moment to lose

↳ 한 시도 지체할 수 없어

They are two points down with three minutes to play

↳ 그들은 경기시간 **3**분을 남기고 **2**점을 뒤지고 있다

They debated for three hours, just talking in a circle(circles)

↳ 그들은 세 시간씩이나 토론을 벌였지만 아무런 진척이 없었어

They had only thirty minutes to discuss the problem and Jong-soo held the stage for most of it

↳ 그들은 그 일을 겨우 **30**분 정도 논의했을 뿐 나머지는 거의 다 종수가 주도적으로 말을 다 해버렸어

They have gone together for two years

↳ 그들은 **2**년간 애인으로 사귀고 있어

They held out for several years against the policy of the company

↳ 그들은 회사의 방침에 맞서서 몇 년씩이나 싸웠다

They holed up(lay low, lay up) there for a few months until the police stopped looking for them

↳ 그들은 경찰이 찾지 않을 때까지 거기서 숨어 지냈다

They made it under the wire

↳ 그들은 겨우 제 시간에 되었어

They may find time for a quick one

↳ 그 사람들이 한잔 할 정도의 시간은 있을 거야

They really missed out on wonderful time

↳ 그들은 정말 멋진 시간을 놓친 거야

› **debate** discuss a question by argument

They swing into high gear around nine o'clock in preparation for their customers
> ↳ 그들은 아홉 시가 되면 손님맞이 준비로 일손이 바빠진다

They turned a five-point deficit with only two minutes left into a three point victory in overtime
> ↳ 그들은 게임종료 **2**분을 남기고 **5**점차로 뒤졌다가 연장전에서 **3**점 차의 승리로 이끌었다

They were exhausted as they had been working for three hours at a stretch to finish it
> ↳ 그들은 일을 끝내려고 세 시간씩이나 단숨에 쉬지 않고 일해서 녹초가 되었다

They were saved by the bell
> ↳ 시간이 그들을 살렸어

They will get the feel of the job after they've been there a few months
> ↳ 그들이 두 세 달 지나면 업무에 대한 감을 잡게 될 것이다

They'll arrive here in plenty of time
> ↳ 그들은 시간 안에 넉넉히 여기 도착할 것이다

They'll understand you with time
> ↳ 그들은 시간이 지나면 널 이해할 것이다

They've lived in Seoul 50 years upwards
> ↳ 그들은 **50**년 이상 서울에 살고 있다

Things are running behind, and you'll not finish on time
> ↳ 넌 일이 늦어지고 있어서 시간 내에 끝내지 못하겠군

Thirty years ago there might not have been a dry eye in the house
> ↳ **30**년 전이었다면(여기 모인)모든 사람이 눈물을 흘렸을 것이다

› **overtime** extra working time

› **plenty** more than adequate number or amount

This contract will stand good for another year
    ㄴ 이 계약은 아직도 1년은 더 갈 것이다

This is a fine time of night to come back home
    ㄴ 이렇게 밤늦게 집에 돌아오는 녀석이 어디 있어

This law carries a 30 day mandatory jail sentence for anyone who deliberately neglect the safety for elderly people leaving them unattended for long periods of time
    ㄴ 이 법은 오랫동안 고의로 노인을 돌보지 않고 내버려 둔 사람에게 누구나 30일간 강제 교도형을 부과토록 돼있다

This record has been gathering dust on my shelves for the past twenty years
    ㄴ 이 레코드는 지난 20년간 선반에 얹힌 채 한번도 쓰인 일이 없어

This style is quite the thing this year
    ㄴ 이 스타일은 올해 큰 유행이다

This time of the year is always busy; it becomes quiet again after summer
    ㄴ 이맘때면 늘 바빠지고 여름이 지나면 수월해진다

This trip will keep me away from home for two weeks
    ㄴ 이번 여행으로 2주동안 집에 있지 않게 될 거야

This work has taken all my time
    ㄴ 이 일을 하는데 애 먹었다

(=I've had a time doing this work)

This year somebody else got there first
    ㄴ 올해는 다른 사람이 앞질러 버렸어

‣ **mandatory**   obligatory, person given a mandate

This year's rice crop is up on the last year's
ㄴ 금년 벼농사는 작년 수준을 웃돈다

To bandy words with a foolish person is a waste of time
ㄴ 어리석은 자와 말을 주고받는 건 시간낭비다

Those who make the worst of time are the first to complain of its brevity
ㄴ 시간을 가장 나쁘게 쓰는 사람이 시간이 짧다고 제일먼저 불평하는 사람이다

Thousands of people poured along the street during the rush hour
ㄴ 출퇴근 시간에 수 천명의 인파가 길거리를 따라 쏟아져 나왔다

Time brings all things to pass
ㄴ 시간이 가면 모든 일이 지나간다

Time can shout the truth where words lie
ㄴ 말이 거짓을 지껄이고 있을 경우에도 시간은 진실을 외칠 수 있다

> 인간의 악행에 대한 처벌이나, 선행에 대한 보답은 즉시 일어나지 않을 수도 있지만 시간이 흐르면 틀림없이 일어난다. 하나님의 맷돌은 천천히 돌아가지만 아주 곱게 갈아진다는 뜻의 "The mills of God grind slowly, yet they grind exceeding small"도 같은 뜻이다.

Time can turn days and nights into nothing
ㄴ 시간은 밤과 낮을 무로 만들어줄 것이다

Time changes and we with time
ㄴ 10년이면 강산도 변한다

Time changes everything
ㄴ 세월이 지나면 모든 게 변해

› **brevity**   shortness or conciseness

Time changes
> ↳ 지금이 어느 때니? 시대가 변했어

Time change, people change
> ↳ 시대가 변하니 사람도 변하는구나

Time deals gently only with those who take it gently
> ↳ 시간은 자기를 부드럽게 대하는 사람만을 부드럽게 대해준다

Time does not seem to pass at a constant rate to all men
> ↳ 시간의 흐름이 모든 사람에게 일정하지는 않은 것 같다

Time dragged toward my vacation
> ↳ 그럭저럭 휴가 때가 다가왔군

Time flew by so fast that it was so dark before we knew it
> ↳ 시간이 너무 빨리 지나가서 어느새 밤이 되었어

Time flies deep into the night
> ↳ 밤은 점점 깊어간다

Time goes by
> ↳ 시간(세월)은 간다

Time got you
> ↳ 시간 다 됐습니다

(=Time put you out)

Time has jammed the pipe up with dust
> ↳ 오랜 시간에 먼지가 끼어서 파이프가 막혔어

Time heals what reason can't
> ↳ 이치로 안 되는 일은 시간이 해결한다

› **jam** press into a close or tight position, cause to become wedged so as to be unworkable

› **heal** make or bocome sound or whole

시간이 가면 잊혀진다, 즉 "세월이 약이다"라는 속담에 해당하는 영어 속담은
여러 가지가 있다.
(= Time heals all wounds)
(= Time is a great healer)
(= Time works wonders)
(= Time cures all things)

Time in its aging course teaches all things
        ↳ 시간은 지나는 길에 모든 것을 가르쳐준다

Time is a file that wears and makes no noise
        ↳ 시간은 슬면서도 아무 소리를 내지 않는 줄이다

Time is on the side of the oppressed
        ↳ 시간은 피압박자들의 편이다

Time is on your side
        ↳ 네 문제는 시간이 해결해 줄 것이다

Time is subject to less distortion than the spoken language
        ↳ 시간은 입으로 하는 말보다 덜 왜곡된다

Time is the only purgatory
        ↳ 시간만이 참된 속죄를 준다

Time is working against us
        ↳ 시간을 끌수록 불리해

Time once lost never returns
        ↳ 잃어버린 시간은 돌아오지 않아

Time passes quickly when I'm absorbed in reading an interesting book
        ↳ 재미있는 책읽기에 빠지면 시간 가는 줄 몰라

▸ **oppress** persecute, weigh down   ▸ **purgatory** intermediate state after death for purification by expiating sins

Time presses

       ↳ 일각의 여유도 없다

Time spent in vice or folly is doubly lost

       ↳ 해악과 어리석은 일에 소비된 시간은 곱절의 손실이다

Time tames the strongest grief

       ↳ 아무리 아픈 슬픔도 세월이 가면 누그러진다

Time was when we ate from hand to mouth

       ↳ 우리가 호구지책으로 살아가던 때가 있다

Time was when we had no child then

       ↳ 그 땐 아이가 없던 때였거든

Time will ease your pain

       ↳ 시간이 지나면 잊혀질 것(You will get over it = Time will heal your pains = You will forget in due time)

Time will heal your wound

       ↳ 시간이 약

시간이 가면 잊혀진다, 즉 "세월이 약이다"라는 속담에 해당하는 영어 속담은 여러 가지가 있다.
(= Time heals all wounds)
(= Time is a great healer)
(= Time works wonders)
(= Time cures all things)

Time will tell

       ↳ 시간이 지나봐야 알아

Time won't change anything

       ↳ 시간이 간다고 달라질건 아무 것도 없어

› **vice** immoral habit, depravity

Time, which strengthens friendship, weakens love
> ↳ 시간은 우정을 두텁게 하지만 사랑은 약하게 한다

> 사랑은 시간이 지나면 퇴색한다는 뜻이다. 비슷한 뜻으로 'Love me little, love me long 사랑은 가늘고 길게'도 많이 쓰인다. 직역하면 "나는 조금씩 오래 사랑하라"이다. '백년해로'란 말을 결혼하는 커플들에게 많이 얘기하지만 말처럼 쉽지만은 않다.

Times are changing
> ↳ 요즘 세상이 그래(**Times have changed** 세상이 많이 변했어)

> (=You can't expect the world stand still)

Timing is everything
> ↳ 시간을 지키는 일이 무엇보다 중요해

To bandy words with a foolish person is a waste of time
> ↳ 어리석은 자와 말을 주고받는 건 시간낭비다

To begin another investigation with the general elections two months away is enough to raise suspicions about their motivations
> ↳ 총선을 2개월 앞두고 또다시 조사를 하겠다는 것은 그들의 동기에 대해 충분히 의문을 제기할 만한 일이다

Try to hang in there another month
> ↳ 한달 만 더 버텨 봐

Was it not for public acceptance of a single yardstick of time, life would be unbearably chaotic
> ↳ 일반대중들이 시간에 대한 단순한 척도를 받아들이지 않는다면 인생

› **suspicion** act of suspecting something
› **chaotic** complete disorder

은 참을 수 없을 정도로 혼란스러울 것이다

Water can wear away rock after a long time
　　ↄ 물은 오랜 세월을 지나면서 바위를 깎아 내린다

> 불가능한 일이라도 끊임없이 노력하면 이루어진다는 뜻이다. 물(Dripping)은 끊임없는 성실한 노력을 뜻한다(He that shoots often at last shall hit the mark = 여러 번 쏘는 자는 결국 표적을 맞춘다).

We are cutting it fine
　　ↄ 시간(돈)이 없어

We are supposed to improve each hour
　　ↄ 우린 시간을 활용할 줄 알아야

We checked her into the hospital for two days
　　ↄ 우린 그 여자를 이틀간 입원 시켰다

We had a big time
　　ↄ 신나는 시간이었어

We had a good long talk about olden times
　　ↄ 우린 옛이야기로 꽃을 피웠어

We grew apart from each other over the years
　　ↄ 세월이 가면서 우리는 차츰 멀어지게 되었어

We must study hard to keep up with the times
　　ↄ 우리는 시대에 뒤지지 않도록 열심히 공부해야 한다

We should have enough time to establish a statistical base
　　ↄ 우리에게는 통계의 근거로 삼을 자료를 얻으려면 충분한 시간이 필요하다

We should proportion our time out more evenly among our different

---

› **statistical**　numerical facts collected for study
› **base**　fundamental part, beginning point

activities
> ↳ 우리는 시간을 여러 활동에 보다 고르게 배분해야 한다

What time shall we make it?
> ↳ 몇 시에 만날까요?

> (=When is the best time for you?)
> (=When do you have time?)
> (=What time is good for you?)

When a year comes to its end, we can't help feeling nostalgic
> ↳ 연말이 가까워지면 우리는 향수에 젖기 마련이다

When the time is right, I'll tell you
> ↳ 때가되면 다 말해주지

Where did the time go?
> ↳ 벌써 시간이 그렇게 됐나?

Working twenty hours a day completely burned him out
> ↳ 그는 하루 20시간을 일하자 완전히 녹초가 되었다

You can get into shape in no time
> ↳ 넌 곧 균형 있는 몸매가 될 거야

You have all the time in the world
> ↳ 시간은 얼마든지 있어

You have been disappointed to have passed over the last month
> ↳ 너 지난번 승진에 누락되어 실망했었어

You haven't been out later than ten o'clock
> ↳ 넌 열시 넘게 밖에 있어본 적이 없잖아

You look like the way you did ten years ago

› **nostalgic** wistful yearning for something past

ㄴ 너 **10**년 전 모습이 변하지 않았군

You may catch him in(out) 10 o'clock
ㄴ 열 시에는 그가 집(사무실)에 있(없)을 지 몰라

You will come into your own any day
ㄴ 넌 곧 인정받게 될 거야

You're going to come into your own this year
ㄴ 올해 넌 인정받게 될 거야

Your business licence comes up for renewal every three years
ㄴ 너의 사업 허가증은 매 **3**년마다 갱신해야 해

Your day will come
ㄴ 네게도 좋은 날이 올 거다

Your excellent presentation came across(over) well, so all the time they spent was worth it
ㄴ 당신의 훌륭한 발표는 성공적이었고 그들이 소비한 시간은 그만한 가치가 있었다

Your old slippers have been kicking around here for months
ㄴ 너의 헌 슬리퍼는 몇 달씩이나 여기 팽개쳐져 있어

Youth is the time to study wisdom; old is time to practice it
ㄴ 젊어서는 지혜를 배우고 나이가 들어서는 실행할 때다

‣ **presentation** introducing, bring before the public

‣ **kick around** strike out or hit with the foot for long period of time

You may catch him (when) 10 o'clock

You will come into your own any day

You're going to come into your own this year

Your business comes up for renewal every three years

Your day will come

Your excellent presentation came across(over) well, so all the time they spent was worth it

Your old slippers have been kicking around in... for months

...when the time to study (taken), old is time to imagine it

82. 시작   **Beginning**

A beard well lathered is half shaved
> ↳ 시작이 반이다

> 계획은 거창해도 막상 시작하기가 힘든다는 말이다. 우리나라의 "시작이 반이다"
> 를 직역해 놓은 것 같이 영어로는 "Well begun is half done"이라고 한다.
> (=Once start(begin), you're halfway there)
> (=The beginning is the half part, the rest is easy)

Byung-soo tried to start over(off) with a clean slate
> ↳ 병수는 새 출발하려고 했다

Come out from under quickly and start a new life
> ↳ 빨리 궁지에서 벗어나 새 삶을 시작해라

Don't let the other fellows get(have) the(a) jump on you at the beginning of the race
> ↳ 경기를 시작할 때 다른 사람들에게 뒤지지 않도록 해

Don't lose sight of your humble beginnings
> ↳ 소박했던 옛일을 잊지 마라

Every three years or so he pulls up his roots(stakes), moves to another city and starts again
> ↳ 그는 매번 3년 남짓 어느 곳이든 살다가 다른 도시로 옮겨 거기서
> 다시 시작해

· **lather**   foam, form or spread lather
· **humble**   not proud or haughty, not pretentious

Everything has a beginning
> ↳ 모든 일에 시작이 있는 법이다

> 계획만으로 끝나면 안되고 시작을 해야 한다는 뜻이다. 속담이라기보다는 충고, 명언에 가깝다. "It is the first step that is troublesome 모든 일은 그 시작이 가장 어렵다"라는 말도 자주 쓴다.

Few people expect to go over the top before the beginning of January
> ↳ 1월초가 되기 전에 목표를 달성하리라고 기대하는 사람은 거의 없어

For six years everything in his life seemed to be coming up roses
> ↳ 6년 동안 그의 일은 최고로 잘 되어나가는 것 같았다

Gil-soo always starts out like a gang-buster but fades in the stretch
> ↳ 길수는 항상 시작은 요란해도 마무리가 시들해

> '용두사미(龍頭蛇尾)'란 '작심삼일'과 비슷한 말이다. 거창하게 시작해 놓고 흐지부지 끝나는 것을 설명한 말이다. 영어로는 "Starts off with a bang and ends with a whimper 큰소리로 시작해서 낑낑대며 끝난다"이다.

He who would climb the ladder must begin at the bottom
> ↳ 사다리를 오르려는 사람은 바닥에서 시작해야 한다

I'm beginning to feel very sick
> ↳ 속이 울렁거리네

I'm beginning to get the picture
> ↳ 이제 무슨 뜻인지 알 것 같아

I'm just beginning

› **whimper** cry softly

↳ 지금까지는 맛 배기

> (=I'm just getting started)
> (=I'm just warming up)
> (=I'm just getting warmed up)

Jung-ah's baby was just beginning to find his feet
↳ 정아의 아이는 이제 막 걸음마를 시작했어

Knowledge of what's possible is the beginning of happiness
↳ 가능한 일이 무엇인지 아는 것이 행복의 시작이다

Let's beat(get) the show on the road
↳ 본격적으로 시작해볼까

Let's get going(rolling)
↳ 슬슬 시작할까

> (=Let's get the show on the road)

No one is good from the beginning
↳ 처음부터 잘하는 사람은 없어

> 실패하더라도 포기하지 말고 오뚝이처럼 일어나면 언젠가는 이룰 수 있다는 말이다.
> (=Every one starts off a beginner)
> (=No one starts off being good at something)

Officers and men were just beginning to find their feet then
↳ 그러자 장교와 사병들은 경험과 지식을 쌓기 시작했다

› **officer** one charged with law enforcement, one who holds an office of trust or authority, one who holds a commission in the armed forces

She's so demanding she's beginning to drive us to drink

↳ 그 여자는 너무 자기위주라 우릴 달달 볶고있어

The beginning of understanding men is understanding how men act at work

↳ 남자를 이해하는 것은 남자가 직장에서 어떻게 행동하는가를 이해할 때 시작된다

The four children are beginning to tax their parents' strength

↳ 그들 네 아이들은 부모들에게 정말 부담이 되고있어

The game kept us on the edge of our seats from the very beginning

↳ 게임은 처음부터 손에 땀을 쥐게 했다

The show must go on

↳ 시작을 했으니 그만 둘 수 없잖아

The trend toward computerization of an ever-increasing number of airline function is accelerating rapidly and is beginning to embrace even the world's smallest carriers

↳ 항공사들은 점점 증가하고 있는 기능을 전산화하는 경향이 가속화되고 있으며 이러한 추세가 소규모 항공사에까지 미치기 시작했다

They were not on the right track from the beginning

↳ 그들은 첫 단추부터 잘못 끼웠다

To believe with certainty, we must begin with doubting

↳ 확실히 믿기 위해 우리는 의심하며 시작해야 한다

To make your children capable of honesty is the beginning of education

↳ 자녀들을 정직하게 가르치는 것이 교육의 시작이다

Wan-soo is beginning to throw his weight around

↳ 완수가 폼을 잡기 시작하는군

› **certainty** settlement, truth

83. 식당 & 주문   Restaurants & Ordering

Allow me to replenish your glass with some more beer
> ↳ 맥주를 좀더 따라 드릴까요?

Are you adding it to your order?
> ↳ 별도(추가)로 주문하는 겁니까?

(=Is that a separate order?)
(=Do you want that as well?)

Are you being attended to?
> ↳ (손님에게)주문 하셨습니까?

Are you being helped(served)?
> ↳ 주문하셨어요?

Can I entice you with a piece of cake?
> ↳ 과자 하나 먹어볼래?

(=Can I oblige you with a piece of cake?)

Can I help you to some more soup?
> ↳ 수프를 좀 더 드시겠습니까?

Can I tempt you with another glass of beer?

‣ **replenish** stock or supply anew   ‣ **tempt** coax or persuade to do wrong, attract or provoke

ㄴ 맥주 한 잔 더 하시겠습니까?

Can I top off your glass?

ㄴ 술을 더(첨가해서) 따를까요?

Could you fix another one?

ㄴ 한 잔 더 주시겠어요?

Could you go for a cup of tea?

ㄴ 차 한 잔 드릴까요?

Covers are laid for five

ㄴ 5인분의 식사가 나왔군

Did you remember to take care of the waiter?

ㄴ 웨이터에게 팁 주는 것 잊지 않았겠지?

Do you want to order dinner in?

ㄴ 저녁을 배달시켜 먹을 거냐?

Gratuities are included in the bill

ㄴ 팁은 계산서에 포함되어 있습니다

It's on the house

ㄴ 이건 서비스입니다(접객업소 등)

It's really deplorable to see so much food left over in restaurants

ㄴ 식당에서 많은 음식을 남긴다는 것은 참으로 한심한 일이다

Leave the car behind

ㄴ 차는 두고 가세요(음주 손님에게)

Make another one for the gentleman

ㄴ 남자 분에게 한 잔 더 따라 드리세요

Make mine double

ㄴ 곱빼기로 주세요(자장면 따위)

· **gratuity** tip

· **deplore** regret strongly

Make out separate checks, please
> ↳ 따로 따로 계산해 주세요

May I take your order?
> ↳ 주문하시겠어요?

Please hold the mustard
> ↳ 겨자는 넣지 말아 주십시오(음식 조리)

Please hold the onions and red pepper
> ↳ 양파와 고추는 넣지 말아주세요

She ordered three lunch boxes to go
> ↳ 그 여자가 도시락 세 개를 싸달라고 주문했어

That restaurant padded the bill for our dinner
> ↳ 저 식당은 우리에게 저녁 식대 바가지를 씌웠어

That restaurant was one of my ports of call in Seoul
> ↳ 서울에서는 저 식당에 자주 갔었지

That tavern can rob you blind if you don't watch out
> ↳ 저 술집에서 주의하지 않으면 호되게 바가지 쓰는 수가 있어

That tavern is a good place to get gypped(diddled)
> ↳ 저 술집에 가면 바가지 쓰기 십상이다

The bill amounts(adds up, figures up) to twenty thousand won
> ↳ 계산이 이만원 나왔다

The bill came out at(to) far more than I expected
> ↳ 계산서가 예상보다 너무 많이 나왔어

The bill didn't come to much
> ↳ 계산서(요금)가 별로 안나왔어

The mixture of fish, rice and eggs goes by the name of kedgeree in

---

‣**tavern** establishment where liquors aresold to be drunk on the premises

‣**gyp** cheat, trickery

most restaurants
> ↳ 생선, 쌀, 계란을 섞어서 만든 것을 대부분의 식당에서는 케저리라고 부른다

There was a discrepancy between what we ordered and what's on the bill
> ↳ 우리와 주문한 것과 계산서 내용과는 틀린 것이 있었다

This can serve five persons
> ↳ 이건 5인분입니다

(=This is for five servings)
(=This contains five servings)

Two hamburgers to stay(go)
> ↳ 여기서 먹고(싸 가지고) 갈 햄버거 두 개 주세요

We are still waiting for the lunch
> ↳ 주문한 점심식사가 아직 안 나왔습니다

We'd better go earlier to beat the crowd in the restaurant
> ↳ 사람들이 붐비기 전에 식당에 빨리 가자

Were you out hunting for the meat?
> ↳ 돼지를 사냥해서 잡아오는 겁니까?(주문한 돼지고기가 오래 걸릴때)

What it'll be?
> ↳ 뭘 드시겠어요?

What name should I make the reservation under?
> ↳ 누구 이름으로 예약할까요?

What's taking our order so long?
> ↳ 주문한 게 왜 이리 늦어

› **discrepancy** difference or disagreement

› **reservation** act of reserving or something reserved, limiting condition

What's your normal turnaround?
> ↳ 주문(신청)하면 얼마나 걸립니까?

Where's your service?
> ↳ 서비스가 이게 뭡니까?

"Can I fill a glass again?" "Can a duck swim?"
> ↳ "한 잔 더 따라 드릴까요?" "물어보면 잔소리지"

› **turnaround**   reversal in thinking or acting, time required for a round trip

84. 신문   **Newspapers**

All successful newspapers are ceaselessly querulous and bellicose
> 모든 성공한 신문들은 끊임없이 시끄럽고 호전적이다

Cigarette ads in magazines and newspapers carry a health warning because they are obliged to
> 잡지와 신문에 나오는 광고는 이들 회사의 의무 때문에 건강에 대한 광고를 싣는다

Each reporter is trying to get the jump on the others with the story of the scandal
> 신문기자들은 저마다 그 스캔들의 기사를 다른 기자들보다 앞질러 보도하려고 기를 쓰고 있어

Four hostile newspapers are more to be feared than a thousand bayonets
> 네 개의 악의 찬 신문은 천 개의 총검보다 무섭다

He couldn't keep the lid on this any longer. The press has already got wind of it
> 그는 이 일을 쉬쉬할 수 없게 됐어. 기자들이 벌써 냄새를 맡았거든

It featured all the newspapers
> 그건 전 신문에 대서특필 됐어

It was a small thing but the newspapers had blown it up until it seemed important

---

- **querulous** fretful or whining
- **bellicose** pugnacious

- **bayonet** dagger that fits on the end of a rifle

↳ 사소한 일인데도 무슨 대단한 일이나 되는 것처럼 신문에 과장 보도 했지 뭐

Many of our newspapers and television networks still tend to be subservient to the authorities

↳ 많은 우리의 신문과 텔레비전 방송은 아직도 정부당국의 시녀노릇을 하는 경향이 있다

Newspaper reporters must be primed with facts before they start to write their article

↳ 신문기자들은 기사를 쓰기 전에 사실을 파악해야 한다

Newspapers acclaimed Whang Young-Jo an exemplary national hero, extolled the virtues of his diligent, assiduous training

↳ 신문에서는 황영조 선수를 크게 칭찬하고, 그의 근면함, 정성을 다하 는 미덕을 높이 칭찬했다

Newspapers keep us in contact with the events of the world

↳ 신문 덕분에 세계에서 일어나는 일을 접할 수 있다

Newspapers should not give currency to frightening news without making sure of their facts

↳ 신문이 사실 확인도 안하고 겁주는 뉴스를 보도해서는 안 된다

Please double-check all the facts before you run this story

↳ 이 기사를 게재하기 전에 재차 확인하여라

Please run this ad in your paper for three days

↳ 이 광고를 3일간 귀지에 실어 주십시오

Plug it in your next newspaper column

↳ 요 다음 신문 칼럼에 그걸 계속 광고해

Reading these papers will keep you posted on the latest happenings in the world

---

› **subservient** obsequious submission   › **assiduous** diligent
› **extolled** praise highly

↳ 이 신문들을 읽으면 최근의 세계정세에 밝게 된다

Reporters shouldn't slant their stories against one political party

↳ 신문기자는 어느 한 정당에 불리하게 편향된 기사를 써서는 안 된다

She made the statement in a news conference

↳ 그 여자는 기자회견에서 그와 같이 말했다

She provides an endless supply of newsworthy stories which can hit the headlines

↳ 그녀는 대서특필 감 보도가치가 있는 뉴스 감을 끊임없이 제공해 준다

She, who is a reporter, pounded out the story, racing to meet the deadline

↳ 그 여기자는 마감시간에 대려고 서둘러 기사를 입력했다

That news will surely get his motor running

↳ 이만한 뉴스면 틀림없이 그가 후끈할 거야

The newspaper boy makes his rounds every morning

↳ 신문배달 소년은 매일아침 이 집 저 집 신문을 배달한다

The newspaper reported that radioactive waste had escaped from a damaged pipe, and polluted a large area of coast

↳ 방사선 폐기물이 파손된 파이프에서 새어나와 넓은 해안지역을 오염 시켰다고 신문이 보도했다

The object of reporting is to find good or evil in a story by ironing out the distracting wrinkles of complexity

↳ 보도의 목적은 초점을 흐리는 복잡성을 다 제거함으로써 선하거나 악 한 무엇인가를 찾아내는데 있다

The press reports blew the story out of all proportion(blew the story up)

↳ 신문이 그 건을 과장보도 했어

› **slant** present with a special viewpoint
› **radioactive** property of an element that

emits energy through nuclear disintegration

The press should be the good mirror of society
> ㄴ 신문은 사회를 제대로 반영해 주어야 한다

The public will not read articles unless they are seasoned(salted) with sex and violence
> ㄴ 사람들은 기사를 섹스와 폭력으로 짭짤하게 소금을 쳐야 읽어본다

The situation remains ominous although they are making reassuring statements to the press
> ㄴ 그들이 신문에 안심시키는 성명을 내고있지만 상황은 불길하다

The story of the bribery case was splashed all over the front page
> ㄴ 뇌물기사는 머리기사로 대서특필되었다

The weekly makes a feature of economic problems
> ㄴ 그 주간지는 경제기사를 특종으로 다루고 있다

These newspapers are full of partially dressed women in provocative poses
> ㄴ 이들 신문에는 거의 알몸을 드러낸 요염한 여성들이 잔뜩 실려있다

Your contribution to the bulletin had to be crowded out
> ㄴ 회보에는 지면관계상 귀하의 기고를 실리지 못했습니다

› **ominous** threatening
› **provoke** incite to anger, stir up on purpose

85. 실패   Failure

A minute's success pays for the failure of years
     ↳ 한 순간의 성공은 1년간의 실패를 보상한다

A number of factors militated against my success
     ↳ 난 여러 가지 원인으로 성공하지 못했어

Addicts may be viewed as losers on society's margins
     ↳ 마약 중독자는 소외계층의 패배자로 비쳐질 수 있다

After all I was no better than before
     ↳ 난 결국 도로아미타불이었어

After he bought that house, the bottom dropped out of the market and he lost a lot of money
     ↳ 그가 집을 사고 난 뒤 집 값이 바닥으로 떨어져 큰 손해를 보았다

All he does is crank out troubles
     ↳ 그가 하는 일이라곤 사고만 저지르는 것뿐이다

All he has done is gone((to go) on a wild goose chase
     ↳ 그 사람 하는 일은 허탕만 쳐왔어

All his honors and disgraces were swept under the rug
     ↳ 그의 모든 영욕은 묻혀버렸다

All his plans fell through
     ↳ 그의 모든 계획은 무산되었다

All I hope for is damage control

▸ **addict**   one who is psychologically or physiologically dependent (as on   a drug)

↳ 이제 피해가 최소화이기를 바랄 뿐이야

All my plans blew up in my face
↳ 진행 중이던 모든 계획을 망쳤어

All of his plans simply fell out(apart) at the seams
↳ 그의 모든 계획은 산산이 무너졌어

All these pains were for nothing
↳ 이 모든 노고도 다 허사였다

All these things have come full circle
↳ 모든 일이 빙 돌아서 원점으로 왔군

All they have been doing is going on a wild goose chase
↳ 그들은 여태껏 허탕만 쳐오고 있어

An inability to identify potential high-volume customers are a major failing of the marketing department, but the lack of credit in general has contributed to the company's poor performance
↳ 잠재적인 많은 고객을 찾아내지 못하는 것이 마케팅부의 중요 실패이
지만 전반적인 신용결여가 이 회사의 나쁜 실적의 원인이 되고 있다

An-do himself made this mess and he can't make his way out
↳ 안도 자신이 일을 엉망으로 만들었으니 돈주고 빠져 나오긴 틀렸어

At last Sung-ho got it through his head that he had failed the TOEIC test
↳ 성호는 마침내 토익 시험에 실패했다는 게 실감났다

Being young and resilient, he got over his failure quickly
↳ 그는 젊고 회복력이 빨라서 실패에서 상당히 빨리 벗어났다

Bong-soo's business fell apart like a house of cards
↳ 봉수의 사업은 사상누각처럼 망했어

› **seam** line of junction of 2 edges, layer   › **resilient** elastic
of a mineral

'사상누각', 즉 '모래 위의 집'이다. 비슷한 뜻으로 '공중누각'이라는 표현도 있고, 이는 영어에는 'Castle in the air'라는 비슷한 표현이 있다. 또한 'House of cards 카드로 지은 집'라는 표현도 쓰인다.

Byung-soo took a bath on any investment he made
> ↳ 병수는 무슨 투자에서나 왕창 손해만 봤어

Don't gloss over your role in this failure
> ↳ 이 실패에 대한 너의 역할에 대해 둘러치기 할 생각은 하지마

Doo-soo deceived(deluded) himself with dreams of success but they never came true
> ↳ 두수는 성공하리라는 헛된 꿈을 꾸어왔지만 그 꿈은 이루어지지 않았다

Duck-soo already cut a loss
> ↳ 덕수는 벌써 그 일(투기)에 손떼고 더 이상의 손실은 면했어

Events seemed to be conspiring to bring about this ruin
> ↳ 여러 가지 사정이 겹쳐서 그의 파멸을 가져온 것 같아

Every failure is a stepping stone to success
> ↳ 실패는 성공의 디딤돌이다

Everything he has done screwed up
> ↳ 그는 하는 일마다 실패했다

Everything we have done has gone down the chute(drain, tubes)
> ↳ 지금까지 한 일은 모두 허사로 돌아갔어

Everything went against me
> ↳ 만사가 꼬였어

Failure is the condiment that gives success its flavor
> ↳ 실패는 성공의 묘미를 더해주는 조미료

› **delude** mislead or deceive	› **chute** trough or passage
› **conspire** secretly plan an unlawful act	› **condiment** pungent seasoning

Failure may be an orphan, but success always has many parents
ㄴ 실패하면 혼자 책임져야 하지만 성공하면 너도나도 공로자라고 나선다

Failures are rehearsals for success
ㄴ 실패는 성공의 예행연습이다

He is cornered
ㄴ 이젠 끝장

> (=He's got his back to the wall)
> (=This is the end)
> (=All is over with him)

He's going to get it
ㄴ 그는 끝장이야

> (=He's history)

Her ascription of the failure to lack of money is not honest
ㄴ 그녀가 실패한 것을 돈 부족으로 돌리는 것은 정직하지 못한 것이다

His death followed close on his failure
ㄴ 그는 실패한지 얼마 후 결국 죽었다

His plan dropped((fell) through when it proved too costly
ㄴ 그의 계획은 비용이 너무 먹히게 되자 수포로 돌아갔다

I screwed up
ㄴ 다 틀렸어

I started out wrong
ㄴ 첫단추가 잘못되었군

› **rehearsal** practice session or performance
› **ascribe** attribute

> (=I got off on the wrong foot)
> (=I made a mistake from the very beginning(with him))

I'm on the confines of bankruptcy
     ㄴ 파산 직전이야

If at first you don't succeed, you are 99.9 percent of the population
     ㄴ 첫 번째 실패는 대부분의 사람들이 누구나 겪는다

It is a little unkind to gloat over our competitors failure
     ㄴ 경쟁자의 실패에 고소해 하는 것은 약간 심한 짓이다

It looks like it's a long shot
     ㄴ 가망이 희박해 보여

It never would have worked out
     ㄴ 애초에 가망 없었어

It was just like chasing my own tail
     ㄴ 애써온 성과가 거의 없었어

It's no go
     ㄴ 글렀어

Let success or failure be on my head
     ㄴ 성패는 내 책임이다

Once is enough for such a bitter trial and error
     ㄴ 이처럼 쓰라린 시행착오가 두 번 다시 있어서는 안 된다

Oh-yung overreached himself this time, aiming for the contract with the government
     ㄴ 오영이는 정부의 계약을 따려는 과도한 의욕 때문에 실패했다

Remember to keep off the delicate subject of his failure

› **gloat** think of something with pride or self-satisfaction | › **overreach** try or seek too much

ㄴ 그의 실패와 같은 민감한 화제를 피해라

She has to shoot straight in business or her company will fail
ㄴ 그 여자가 정직하게 사업을 하지 않으면 회사가 실패하고 말 것이다

Success is not permanent. The same is also true of failure
ㄴ 성공은 영원하지 않다. 실패도 마찬가지다

Tai-ho's obstinate refusal to tell you about his bankruptcy is typical of him
ㄴ 태호가 파산에 대해서 네게 말하기를 완강히 거부하는 것은 태호다운 모습이다

Taking all things into consideration, his attempt is not likely to turn out to be a success
ㄴ 모든 일을 종합할 때 그의 의도는 잘될 것 같지 않다

That unexpected flop is really starting to get me down
ㄴ 그 예상 밖의 실패가 정말 나를 맥빠지게 하고 있어

The new beauty shop folded up in less than a year
ㄴ 그 미장원은 1년도 안돼서 문 닫았어

The two companies preyed on each other to their mutual destruction
ㄴ 두 회사는 서로 잡아먹기를 하다가 같이 망했어

The whole project went down in flames
ㄴ 그 사업은 깡그리 실패했어

There can be no real freedom without the freedom to fail
ㄴ 실패할 자유 없이는 참된 자유가 없다

There is no failure except in no longer trying
ㄴ 더 이상 해보지 않을 때를 제외하고는 실패란 없다

There is the greatest practical benefit in making a few failures early in life

---

› **obstinate** stubborn

› **mutual** given or felt by one another in equal amount, common

↳ 초년에 몇 번 실패해보는 것은 실제로 큰 이익이 된다

They chalked up their defeat to his rashness
ㄴ 그들은 자신들의 패배를 그의 경솔함에 돌렸다

This failure could be a wake-up call for him
ㄴ 이번 실패가 그에게는 약이 될 수도 있다

This failure won't be the end of the world
ㄴ 이번 실패로 끝장나는 건 아냐

Too much success can ruin you as surely as too much failure
ㄴ 지나친 실패가 사람을 확실히 망치듯 지나친 성공도 사람을 망칠 수 있다

You may be disappointed if you fail, but you are doomed if you don't try
ㄴ 실패에는 실망이 따르지만 시도조차 안 하는 사람에게는 절망이 따른다

You may go to ruin(go bankrupt)for all I care
ㄴ 네가 망하든 말든 내 알 바 아니다

You want to see me fall flat on my face
ㄴ 내가 실패하는 꼴을 보고싶다 이 말이군

› **rashness**   hastiness in deciding or acting
› **doom**   judgment, fate, ruin, condomn

86. 아이들   **Children**

A baby sees things but does not conceive them as definite objects
> ↳ 갓난애는 물건이 보여도 그것을 뚜렷한 대상으로 지각하지 못한다

A good marriage should hold together without considering the children
> ↳ 훌륭한 결혼은 아이들과 상관없이 깨어지지 않아야 한다

Abstract words are beyond the ken of children
> ↳ 추상적인 말은 아이들에게 이해하기 어렵다

Adults can be so childish
> ↳ 어른이나 애나 똑같아!=어른들도 유치하긴!

> (=Sometimes adults are so childish)
> (=Sometimes adults act so childishly)

All their kindness will rub off on their children
> ↳ 그들의 친절성은 자녀들에게 이어져 내려갈 것이다

An old man is twice a boy
> ↳ 늙으면 아이가 된다더라

As the twig is bent, so grows the tree
> ↳ 될성부른 나무는 떡잎부터 알아본다

· **conceive** become pregnant, think of
· **ken** range of sight or understanding

> 아이가 큰 인물이 될지 못될지는 어려서부터 알 수 있다는 말이다(=If something can go wrong, it will).
> (=A fine child becomes a fine gentleman)
> (=Sandalwood is fragrant even in seed-leaf)
> (=Genius displays even in childhood)

Babies sleeping face down are at greater risk than those sleeping on their backs

ㄴ 엎드려 자는 아이들은 바로 누워 자는 아이들보다 더 위험하다

Boil not the pap before the child is born

ㄴ 아이도 낳기 전에 기저귀부터 장만하지(미리 설치지) 마라

> "Don't count your chickens before they are hatched 떡 줄 사람은 생각도 안 하는데 김칫국부터 마시지 마라" 직역하면 "알이 부화하기도 전에 닭부터 세지 마라"이다(= It's ill waiting for dead men's shoes 신발을 갖기 위해 신발 주인이 죽기를 바라는 것은 헛된 일이다).
> (=Cut no fish before you get them)
> (=Don't eat the calf in the cow's belly)

Boys will be boys

ㄴ 아이들은 아이들이야

Bringing up children in the absence of an extended family is no easy task

ㄴ 가까운 친척들의 부재중에 이들의 아이들을 돌보는 것은 결코 쉬운 것이 아니다

Childhood diseases such as measles and chicken-pox are highly epidemic(contagious)

> **measles** disease that is marked by red spots on the skin

> **epidemic** affecting many persons at one time
> **contagion** spread of disease by contact

↳ 홍역과 수두와 같은 소아병은 매우 전염성이 높다

Children are better at learning languages than adults
↳ 아이들은 어른들보다 언어학습에 뛰어나다

Children are the most expensive entertainment
↳ 아이들은 비용이 가장 비싸게 먹히는 오락이다

Children should learn from their mistakes
↳ 아이들은 실수해 가면서 배워야 한다

Couples contemplating divorce usually have second thoughts when they realize how it'll affect their children
↳ 이혼을 생각해보고 있는 부부들은 보통 그 이혼이 자녀들에게 어떤 영향을 줄 것인지 생각할 때 마음이 흔들린다

Divorce can provoke aberrant behavior on the part of both parents and children when emotional resources to deal with aberrant are completely drained
↳ 이혼은 이상행위를 다룰 정서수단이 완전히 없어지게 될 때 부모와 아이들 모두에게 일탈행위를 유발시킬 수 있다

Don't crash about the living room while I have visitors
↳ 손님들이 와 계실 동안 거실에서 쿵쿵거리면서 시끄럽게 굴지마

Don't pick up after children who are old enough to keep their own things in order
↳ 자기 물건을 정돈해 놓을만한 나이의 아이들을 위해 뒤치다꺼리 해주지마

Don't spoil him
↳ 애를 오냐오냐하지 마라

› **entertainment** amusement
› **aberrant** deviation or distortion

(=He is growing up spoiled)
(=Don't let him have his way)

Encourage your children to listen to(hear) good music, and its calming power will rub off on them
> 아이들에게 좋은 음악을 듣게 해주면 마음을 가라앉히는 힘이 그들에게 감화를 줄 것이다

Every child is dear to his parents
> 열 손가락 깨물어 안 아픈 손가락 없어

Every school boy knows it
> 그건 삼척동자도 알아

Even the porcupine thinks its young are soft and glossy
> 고슴도치도 제 새끼는 예쁘다고 한다

(=The beetle is a beauty in the eyes of its mother)
(=The crow thinks her own bird fairest)
(=The owl thinks its own young fairest)
(=No mother has a homely child)

Getting hurt like that is part and parcel of growing up
> 저렇게 다쳐가며 크는 것 아니겠니

Gil-soo's parents always gives in too much
> 길수의 부모님은 너무 오냐오냐하고 애들을 길러

Han-soo took his responsibilities as a father seriously but in matters of discipline was rather too free with his hand
> 그는 진지하게 아버지로서의 책임을 떠맡았으나 훈육문제에 있어서는

› **parcel** lot, package

› **discipline** field of study, training that corrects, molds, or perfects

톡하면 아이를 때렸다

He is blessed with good children

↳ 자식 복 있는 사람

He lowers the boom on his children staying out after midnight

↳ 그는 자정이 넘어서 들어오는 아이들에게 무섭게 나무란다

He takes his children in tow and shows them wherever he goes

↳ 그는 자기 아이들을 데리고 다니면서 어디로 가나 여봐란 듯이 자랑하고 다녀

He's a quick child

↳ 그는 머리회전이 빨라

Her baby isn't afraid of strangers

↳ 그 여자의 아이는 낯을 가리지 않아

If something can go wrong, it will

↳ 될성부른 나무는 떡잎부터 알아본다

아이가 큰 인물이 될지 못될지는 어려서부터 알 수 있다는 말이다(=If
something can go wrong, it will).
(=A fine child becomes a fine gentleman)
(=Sandalwood is fragrant even in seed-leaf)
(=Genius displays even in childhood)

If you get her child, then you must marry her

↳ 그 여자가 네 아이를 가지면 결혼해야해

If you want your children to improve, let them overhear the nice things you say about them to others

↳ 당신의 자녀가 나아지기를 원한다면 다른 사람들에게 그들의 칭찬을 하면서 그들이 엿듣게 하라

・tow　pull along behind

・**overhear**　hear without the speaker's knowledge

If you want your children to keep their feet on the ground, put some responsibility on their shoulders
> ↳ 자녀가 땅에 두 발을 굳게 디디기를 원한다면 그들의 어깨에 책임을 지워라

In many children's dreams they often relive their fears and they thought they were being attacked
> ↳ 어린이들은 꿈속에서 무서움과 공격당했던 기억을 회상하는 때가 많다

In some countries children and women are regarded as a source of cheap labor
> ↳ 어떤 나라에서는 어린이와 여성을 값 싼 노동력으로 여긴다

Is your baby potty-trained?
> ↳ 너희 아이는 대소변 가리니?

It'll take another month for the baby to feed itself
> ↳ 갓난애가 혼자서 먹기까지는 한 달은 더 걸릴 것이다

It's mere child's play
> ↳ 식은 죽 먹기야

> 아주 쉬운 일을 '누워서 떡 먹기'나 '식은 죽 먹기'라고 한다. 영어로는 "It's mere child's play 어린 아이 놀음이다", 혹은 "It's a piece of cake 케잌 한 조각이다"라고 한다.

It's usual for babies to do that
> ↳ 애들이 그렇게 하는 건 정상

Jung-ah's baby was just beginning to find his feet
> ↳ 정아의 아이는 이제 막 걸음마를 시작했어

Keep the children in line during the service

› **potty-train** teaching child to use small pot for urination or defecation

› **service** meeting for worship

↳ 예배시간 중 아이들이 얌전하게 있게 해야해

Lack of love in early children can induce criminal behavior in the young

↳ 어릴 적 사랑의 결핍은 청년기에 범죄행위로 빠지게 할 수 있다

Lots of parents sweated bullets(blood) to put their children through colleges, but the children treat their parents like strangers

↳ 많은 부모들이 자녀들을 대학에 보내느라 뼈가 빠졌건만 그들은 그런 부모들을 언제 봤느냐는 듯이 대하기 일쑤다

Many children were running off and had to stay home from school

↳ 많은 아동들이 배탈이 나서 학교를 쉬게됐다

Men are children of a larger growth

↳ 어른은 보다 크게 자라난 어린이일 뿐이다

Most of the fun seems to gone out of life since the children left home

↳ 아이들이 집을 떠난 후 즐거움이 사라진 것 같다

Mother and child are both doing well

↳ 모자는 다 건강하다

My baby doesn't nurse very well

↳ 아이가 젖을 잘 안 먹어

My baby's got the habit of kicking his covers off himself in his sleep

↳ 우리 아이는 자면서 이불을 걷어차는 버릇이 생겼어

My children eat me out of house and home

↳ 애들이 기둥뿌리 뽑아먹고 있다네

My children had to pig together with us in one small room then

↳ 그때 우리 아이들은 우리와 함께 단칸 방에서 우글우글 살았었다

My rule is that children should be seen and not heard

‣ **nurse** suckle, care for
‣ **pig** live crowdedly in a small house

↳ 아이들이 예절 있게 행동하게 하는 것이 나의 수칙이다

My wife's getting gray her hair because of our three children
↳ 집사람은 세 아이 치닥꺼리로 머리가 세고 있다

Never let your children ride on your coat-tail any longer
↳ 더 이상 당신 덕분에 아이들이 호사하는 일이 없도록 하시오

Not a day goes by without our children asking for the pocket money
↳ 아이들이 용돈을 달라고 졸라대지 않고 넘어가는 날이 하루도 없다

Our child doesn't take to strangers
↳ 우리 아이는 낯을 좀 가려

(=Our child is shy(bashful) in front of strangers)
(=Our child doesn't talk in front of strangers)

Parents are answerable for the crimes of their children
↳ 부모들은 자녀들의 범죄에 대해 책임이 있다

People drew aside so the children could pass
↳ 사람들은 어린이들이 지나갈 수 있도록 비켜주었어

Poor children wore clothes their brothers and sisters had grown out of
↳ 가난한 집 아이들은 형이나 누나가 몸이 커져서 더 이상 입지 못하게
된 옷을 물려받아 입었다

Pyung-soo pulled himself together to ensure that his children would survive the handicap of a broken home
↳ 평수는 아이들이 결손가정의 어려움에서 확고히 이겨낼 수 있도록 정
돈해 나갔다

Round the edge of this block so that your baby won't hurt himself in his mouth when eating

---

· **bashful** self-conscious
· **ensure** guarantee

ꀁ 이 덩어리를 너의 아기가 먹을 때 입이 다치지 않도록 가장자리에 모나지 않게 잘라라

She always blows a lot about her children

ꀁ 그 여자는 아이들 자랑이 끊이질 않아

She decided to go ahead with pregnancy, although she knew her child was likely to be physically deformed and mentally retarded

ꀁ 그녀는 아이가 기형과 지진아가 될 가능성이 있다는 것을 알면서도 임신을 강행키로 했다

She had to resign herself to bring up her baby alone

ꀁ 그녀는 체념하고 혼자 힘으로 아기를 양육해야 했다

Some people say they could do without the children causing trouble

ꀁ 말썽이나 일으키는 자식들은 없는 게 좋겠다고 푸념하는 사람들이 있다

Some people seem as if they can never have been children

ꀁ 어떤 사람들은 자신들이 어린 아이인 적이 없었던 것처럼 행동한다

Sometimes we like going back to our second childhood

ꀁ 우린 가끔씩 동심으로 돌아가고 싶어해

Tell your children they can't hang around while we are working

ꀁ 우리가 일하고 있을 때 여기에 얼씬거리지 말라고 아이들에게 말해 주십시오

That child is still bashful in front of strangers

ꀁ 저 아이는 아직도 낯을 가려

The baby's talking was hardly intelligible except to its mother

ꀁ 아기가 하는 말은 아기엄마 외에는 알아듣지 못해

The biggest family problems are those caused by know-it-all kids and yes-it-all parents

ꀁ 가족의 가장 큰 문제는 모든 것을 아는 체하는 자녀와 그저 오냐오냐

› **deform** distort, disfigure
› **retard** hold back

하는 부모에 의해 발생한다

The cobbler's children go bare foot
　 ↳ 대장간에 식칼 없다

> 마땅히 있어야 할 곳에 없는 상황을 "대장간에 식칼 없다"라고 표현한다. 영
> 어로는 "The cobbler's children go bare foot 구두장이의 아이들이 맨발
> 로 다닌다"라고 한다.

The fields where we played as children have been built up(over)
　 ↳ 우리가 뛰놀던 들이 건물로 꽉 찼다

The four children are beginning to tax their parents' strength
　 ↳ 그들 네 아이들은 부모들에게 정말 부담이 되고 있어

The kid is going through a phase where he wants his own way
　 ↳ 저맘때 아이는 뭐든지 제 맘대로 하려고 해

The kid wants for nothing
　 ↳ 그 애는 부족한 게 없어

The parents are the best judges of their children
　 ↳ 부모만큼 자식을 아는 사람 없다

There you are. That kid always gets his own way
　 ↳ 그거 봐(내 말 대로군). 그 애는 언제나 자기 생각대로 해

They came apart at the seams when their children got hurt
　 ↳ 그들은 아이들이 다치자 자제력을 잃었다

Time was when we had no child then
　 ↳ 그 땐 아이가 없던 때였거든

To make your children capable of honesty is the beginning of education

---

· **cobbler** shoemaker

↳ 자녀들을 정직하게 가르치는 것이 교육의 시작이다

Today we should educe and cultivate what is best in children

↳ 현대의 우리는 어린이의 소질을 찾아내어 키워야 한다

We expect our children grow away from us

↳ 우린 아이들이 자라서 독립할 것을 기대한다

We have to pen in the kids to keep them away from the traffic

↳ 아이들이 차 다니는 길에 나가지 않도록 못나가게 해야해

What's the use of children?

↳ 무자식 상팔자지

When is she due? She's due next month

↳ 그 여자 출산 일이 언제지? 내 달이야

When is your baby due?

↳ 출산 일이 언제입니까?

When we love animals and children too much, we love at the expense of them

↳ 동물과 아이들을 너무 사랑한다면 그들을 망치면서 사랑하는 것이다

While money isn't everything, it does keep you in touch with your children

↳ 돈이 전부는 아니지만 돈은 당신과 아이들을 교류시키는 큰 힘이 된다

While we teach our children all about life, our children teach us what life is all about

↳ 우리가 아이들에게 삶에 대해 많은 것을 가르치는 반면, 아이들은 결국 우리들에게 산다는 것이 뭔지를 가르쳐 준다

Whooping cough is a condition which occurs mainly in young children

↳ 백일해는 주로 어린아이에게 잘 일어나는 증세이다

▸ **educe** elicit, deduce
▸ **whoop** shout loudly

You have brought up(educated, raised) your children well
　ㄴ 자식농사 잘 지으셨군요

> (=You did a good job of raising your children)

You have got to show your children where you stand
　ㄴ 아이들에게는 행동으로 보여줘야 해

You need to have counseling to rid yourself of the anger that must have been stored up from those early years of abuse
　　ㄴ 넌 어린 시절에 받은 학대로 인하여 쌓인 노여움을 풀도록 전문가의 상담을 받을 필요가 있어

You put your children through the wringer
　ㄴ 넌 아이들을 심하게 다루는군

‣ **wring**　get by or as if by forcible exertion, pain

87. 아첨   Flattering

A flatterer's throat is an open sepulcher
> ↳ 아첨자의 목구멍은 입벌린 무덤이다

A wise king wouldn't want his friends and officials to lick his boots
> ↳ 현명한 왕이라면 그의 친구와 신하들에게 아부하기를 원치 않을 것이다

All your writing seems to pander to your higher-ups
> ↳ 네가 쓴 글은 모두 윗사람들 취향에 맞춰 쓴 것 같구나

Better to flatter the devil than fight him
> ↳ 악마와 싸우기보다는 그를 추켜 주어라

Beware of one who flatters unduly
> ↳ 당치도 않게 아첨하는 사람을 경계하라

Bong-soo is trying to kiss(shine) up to our boss
> ↳ 봉수가 사장에게 아부하고 있는 거야

Dogs wag their tails not so much to(in love with) you as to(with) your bread
> ↳ 개가 꼬리를 흔드는 것은 당신 때문이 아니라 당신 빵 때문이다(아부에 대한 경계)

Don't bother buttering him up
> ↳ 그에게 알랑거리려 애쓰지마

Flatter her a little, and she'll pull in her horns
> ↳ 그 여자는 조금 주어주면 누그러질 거야

▸ **sepulcher** burial vault
▸ **undue** excessive

▸ **pander** pimp, one who caters to others' desires or weaknesses

Flattery is a juggler, no kin unto sincerity
> ㄴ 아첨은 요술쟁이니 성실과는 전혀 친척이 되지 않는다

Flattery is all right if you don't inhale
> ㄴ 아첨은 거기에 빠지지만 않는다면 나쁘지 않다

Flattery will get you nowhere
> ㄴ 추켜세워 봤자 소용없어

He's been playing up to the boss as usual
> ㄴ 그는 늘 하던 대로 사장에게 알랑거리기나 하고 있지

If a man is vain, flatter, if timid, flatter, if boastful, flatter
> ㄴ 허영이 많은 사람, 소심한 사람, 허세가 심한 사람에게는 아첨하라

Imitation is the sincerest form of flattery
> ㄴ 모방은 가장 성실한 아부다

Men are often reached by flattery
> ㄴ 사람은 흔히 아첨에 흔들리기 쉽다

Mountains of gold wouldn't seduce some men, yet flattery would break them down
> ㄴ 산더미 같은 금으로도 유혹할 수 없지만 아첨에는 무너지는 사람들도 있다

Not only does sucking up help your relationship with peers, it does wonders for the boss
> ㄴ 칭찬(아부)은 동료들과의 관계개선에 도움을 줄 뿐 아니라 상사에게 신통한 효과가 있다

One can't behave rudely to a flattering person
> ㄴ 웃는 낯에 침 뱉으랴

› **juggle** manipulate for an often tricky purpose
› **inhale** breathe in

웃음으로 어떠한 나쁜 상황도 대처할 수 있다는 얘기이다. "A soft answer turneth away wrath 부드러운 대답은 화를 없앤다"는 성서에서 유래한 말로서 구어를 사용한 것이 특징이다.

Sometimes our judgment is overcome by sweet talk
ㄴ 때론 아첨으로 우리의 판단이 흐려져

There is no such flatterer than a man's self
ㄴ 자기 자신보다 자신에게 더 아부하는 사람은 없다

There must be absolutely no favoritism
ㄴ 절대 사바사바가 있어서는 안 돼

They flatter him all the time and he just laps it up
ㄴ 그들은 늘 그에게 아첨하고 그는 그걸 받아들이고 있어

› **favoritism** favoring particular person or thing

88. 아픔 & 약   Illness & Treatment

A bean sprout soup loaded with hot red pepper, is considered the best for recovering from a hangover
> ↳ 매운 고추 가루를 탄 콩나물국을 숙취 회복에 최고로 친다

A cold may develop into all kinds of illnesses
> ↳ 감기는 만 병의 근원이다

> (=A cold predisposes us to other diseases)

A good medicine tastes bitter
> ↳ 좋은 약은 입에 쓰다

> 자신의 결점을 꼬집어서 말하는 충고를 들을 때에는 기분이 좋을 수가 없다.
> 그렇기 때문에 함부로 남에게 충고를 해서는 안되고, 충고를 들어서 기분이
> 나쁘더라도 받아들일 수 있는 아량이 있어야 한다.
> (=Unpleasant advice is a good medicine)

A protracted illness wears out filial devotions
> ↳ 긴 병에 효자 없다

› **sprout** send out new growth
› **hangover** sick feeling following heavy drinking

› **predispose** cause to be favorable to something beforehand

> (=A long visit(stay) wears out welcome)
> (=Enthusiasm is short-lived)

A stroll in the fresh air took(conjured) his hangover away
> ↳ 맑은 공기를 마시면서 잠시 산책을 하고 나자 그의 숙취가 씻은 듯이 사라졌다

After his long illness, Sang-hee looked forward to getting back into circulation
> ↳ 상희는 병상에서 일어나서 평상시 생활로 되돌아가기를 고대했어

All interest in disease and death is only another expression of interest in life
> ↳ 질병과 죽음에 대한 모든 관심은 삶에 대한 관심의 또 다른 표현이다

All my strength is gone
> ↳ 힘이 완전히 빠졌어

All sales of the drug were suspended after it was properly tested
> ↳ 그 약은 정식 검사를 거친 뒤 모든 판매가 중단되었다

An-do rushed the special medicine to the pharmacy in a race against the clock
> ↳ 안도는 시각을 다투어 그 특수 약을 구하려고 약방으로 달려갔다

Antibiotics can be conveniently grouped according to species of microorganisms they inhibit
> ↳ 항생물질은 편의상 이들이 억제하는 미생물의 종류에 따라 분류될 수 있다

Apricot pits are especially good for those who have a dry, itchy throat
> ↳ 목이 마르고 가려운 사람에게 살구 씨가 특히 좋다

- **stroll** walk leisurely
- **conjure** summon by sorcery, entreat

- **antibiotic** substance that inhibits harmful microorganisms

Are you muffled up against the cold?
> ↳ 감기 안 들게 옷을 두껍게 입었니?

Are you short of breath at all?
> ↳ 조금이라도 숨이 차는 일이 있습니까?

Are you up or down today?
> ↳ 오늘 기분(몸 상태)이 좋으냐 나쁘냐?

As soon as microbes enter the body they would kill all living matter, if it were not for the tiny defenders that rush immediately to fight them
> ↳ 만일 침입자들과 싸우기 위해 즉시 달려가는 작은 방어 균이 없다면 세균이 몸 속에 들어가자마자 살아있는 모든 것을 죽일 것이다

As you broke the window, you have to take your medicine
> ↳ 네가 유리창을 깼으니 뒷일은 감수해야지

Backchul greatly activates and revitalizes the stomach as well as removes toxic waste trapped inside the stomach
> ↳ 백출은 위장에 남아있는 독성을 제거할 뿐 아니라 위를 활성화하고 새로운 활력을 준다

Better a tooth out than always aching
> ↳ 아프기만 하는 이빨은 뽑아버리는 게 낫다

Bong-soo came around almost immediately after he had passed out(fainted)
> ↳ 봉수는 기절하자마자 곧 정신을 차렸어

Bong-soo carried on for an hour after he fell from his desk
> ↳ 봉수는 책상에서 떨어진지 한 시간이나 아프다고 엄살(호들갑)을 떨었어

Bong-soo ended up painting the wall

› **revitalize**   give new life or vigor to

ㄴ 병수는 결국 토하고 말았어

> (=Byung-soo ended up puking his lunches)
> (=Byung-soo ended up losing his lunches)
> (=Byung-soo ended up tossing up his cookies)
> (=Byung-soo ended up talking to Ralph on the big white phone)
> (=Byung-soo ended up praying to the porcelain god)

Bong-soo had a big head and can't go to work this morning

ㄴ 오늘 아침 봉수는 숙취가 심해서 출근을 못 한다(**have a big head** 에
는 "자만하다"의 뜻도 있으며 잘 이해하지 못하는 경우도 있음)

Bong-soo has a new lease on life

ㄴ 봉수가 완쾌 됐으니 명은 길겠군

Bong-soo spent the whole night bowing to the porcelain altar

ㄴ 봉수는 밤새도록 토했다

Bruised or scalded skin can be more painful than broken bones

ㄴ 피부에 멍이 들거나 뜨거운 물에 데는 것은 뼈가 부러지는 것 보다
더 아플 수 있다

Byung-soo had to step into the breach when I got sick

ㄴ 내가 아플 때 병수가 내 일을 해줘야 했어

Chan-soo fell to pieces and didn't attend the meeting

ㄴ 찬수는 속이 뒤틀려서 모임에도 안 나왔어

Chang-doo is almost coming apart at the seams now

ㄴ 창두는 지금 거의 제정신을 못 차리고 있어

Childhood diseases such as measles and chicken-pox are highly epidemic(contagious)

ㄴ 홍역과 수두와 같은 소아병은 매우 전염성이 높다

· **puke** vomit

· **porcelain** fine-grained ceramic ware

· **scald** burn with hot liquid or steam, heat
to the boiling point

Constipation is mainly caused by toxic wastes trapped inside the intestines
> ↳ 변비는 주로 장의 내부에 배출되지 않고 있는 유독한 노폐물로 인해 발생한다

Danggwi not only helps stimulate circulation and manufacture blood, but it also purifies existing blood
> ↳ 당귀는 혈액순환을 촉진하고 조혈작용을 도울 뿐만 아니라 몸에 있던 피를 정화하기도 한다

Diseases are the interests of pleasure
> ↳ 질병은 쾌락의 이자이다

Doo-soo is still on the rebound
> ↳ 두수는 아직 회복중이야

Duck-soo is doing this on doctor's orders only, but he doesn't like it
> ↳ 덕수는 이 일을 어쩔 수 없어서 하는 것이지 좋아서 하는 게 아니다

Duck-soon is getting diarrhea of the mouth(jawbone)
> ↳ 덕순이가 또 끝없는 얘길 늘어놓는군

Everyone who is born, holds dual citizenship, in the kingdom of the well and in the kingdom of the sick
> ↳ 사람은 누구에게나 두 가지 시민권이 있는데, 한 가지는 건강한 왕국의 시민권이고 다른 하나는 환자 왕국의 시민권이다

Evidence suggests that patients who show a fighting spirit exhibit stronger immune defenses against the spread of diseases than those who suffer stoically
> ↳ 병과 싸울 의지가 있는 환자가 금욕적으로 견디는 환자들보다 병의 확산에 대한 강한 면역성을 보여준다

Extreme remedies are very appropriate for extreme diseases

› **constipation** difficulty of defecation

› **intestine** tubular part of the digestive system

› **diarrhea** abnormal discharge of loose matter from the bowels

┗ 극단적인 병에는 극단적인 처방이 가장 적절하다

Food doesn't taste good to us when we have a cold
　　┗ 감기가 들면 밥맛이 떨어진다

Ginseng is particularly effective for those who suffer from chronically cold hands and feet, bodily aches and pains
　　┗ 인삼은 특히 만성적으로 손발이 차며, 몸이 아프고 쑤시는 사람에게 효과가 크다

Give him a taste of his own medicine
　　┗ 그가 한 것만큼 당하게 해 줘라

Have you been on any medication for this pain?
　　┗ 이 통증 때문에 약을 드신 적이 있습니까?

He runs off at the mouth all the time(has diarrhea of mouth)
　　┗ 그는 항상 말이 너무 많아

He's already too far gone for any more operations to do much good
　　┗ 그는 이미 너무 병세가 악화돼서 더 이상 수술을 해 봤자 별로 좋아질 수 없어

He's on the danger list
　　┗ 중태

Her daughter's learning difficulties can be correctly diagnosed and treated
　　┗ 그 여자의 딸의 학습장애는 정확히 진단하여 교정할 수 있다

His sore arm is starting to act up again
　　┗ 그의 아픈 팔이 다시 도지기 시작했어

How long should I stay(remain) on these pills?
　　┗ 이 알약을 얼마동안 복용해야 합니까?

How soon can I be off this medicine? - I've been on this medicine

---

› **chronically** frequent or persistent

› **sore** causing pain or distress, severe or intense

for some weeks
> ㄴ 언제쯤 이 약을 안 먹어도 됩니까? - 이 약을 몇 주 째 먹고 있다

I feel a pain in the pit of my stomach
> ㄴ 명치가 아파

I feel like a ton of bricks fell on me
> ㄴ 몸이 천근 만근

> (=I feel like a hundred pounds)
> (=My muscles are screaming)

I have a knot in my leg
> ㄴ 다리에 알배다(근육통)

> (=have a sore calf)
> (=have a muscle-ache)

I have a pounding(splitting) headache
> ㄴ 머리가 지끈지끈 아파

I have canker sores in my mouth
> ㄴ 입안이 헐어서 쓰립니다

I itch all over
> ㄴ 온 몸이 가려워

I'm beginning to feel very sick
> ㄴ 속이 울렁거리네

I've got the sniffles
> ㄴ 코감기 걸렸어

- **calf** back part of the leg below the knee
- **pound** strike heavily, crush by beating
- **canker** mouth ulcer
- **sniffle** sniff repeatedly

If this remains untreated and accumulated for a long time, it can result in a stomach ulcer
> ↳ 이 증세를 치료하지 않고 장기간 누적시켜간다면 위궤양을 일으킬 수 있다

If you do not properly treat a cold, you may also develop arthritis or neuralgia
> ↳ 감기를 제대로 치료하지 않으면 관절염이나 신경통으로 발전할 수 있다

It's medicine, not scenery, for which a sick man must go searching
> ↳ 병든 사람은 경치 좋은 곳이 아닌 약을 찾아 헤매게 된다

Just stay at home and rest and let the illness run its course
> ↳ 집에서 쉬면서 병이 저절로 낫도록 기다려 봐

Laughter is the best medicine
> ↳ 웃으면 젊어지고 성내면 늙는다

Many children were running off and had to stay home from school
> ↳ 많은 아동들이 배탈이 나서 학교를 쉬게됐다

Many diseases are carried by bacteria that live in stagnant or slow-moving water
> ↳ 많은 질병은 고인 물이나 느리게 흐르는 물에 사는 박테리아에서 전파된다

Measles, colds, whooping coughs and typhoid fever are catching
> ↳ 홍역, 감기, 백일해, 장티부스는 전염된다

Measure is treasure medicine
> ↳ 절제(중용)가 보배다

› **ulcer** eroded sore
› **arthritis** inflammation of the joints

› **typhoid** relating to or being a communicable bacterial disease

> 중용이란 한쪽으로 치우침이 없고 항상 변함 없음을 말한다. 자신을 과소평가나 과대평가 하지말고, 항상 겸손한 마음으로 중도를 걷는 것이 중요하다. 예부터 우리나라에서는 공자의 사상을 받들어 중용을 강조하였다.
> (=Virtue is found in the middle)
> (=Safety lies in the middle course)

Moon-soo took his medicine like a man
> ↳ 문수는 남자답게 처벌을 감수했다

Most eye infections are contagious so it is advisable to avoid touching the eyes at all
> ↳ 대부분의 눈병은 전염성이 있으니 아예 눈을 만지지 않는 것이 바람직하다

Most stroke victims there have seriously impaired or slurred speech
> ↳ 거기 있는 대부분의 뇌졸중 환자들은 크게 손상을 입었거나 말을 똑똑히 하지 못하고 있다

My brother is on his feet soon after the operation
> ↳ 형은 수술 후 곧 회복했어

My fears, however, were not confirmed and he made an excellent recovery
> ↳ 하지만 내 염려는 기우였고 그는 훌륭하게 회복했어

My head is aching from it=It's making my head pound
> ↳ 골치 아프게 하는군

My leg's been acting up again
> ↳ 또 다리가 아프기 시작하는군

My muscles ache
> ↳ 몸이 뻐근해

› **contagious** spread of disease by contact
› **slur** malicious or insulting remark

(=I'm rather stiff)

Natural herbs are considered not only medicinal drugs, but also health food
↳ 자연산 약용식물은 의약뿐만 아니라 건강식품으로도 여겨진다

No herb(medicine) worked at all
↳ 백 약이 무효로군

Nothing he eats stay(keep, hold, stop) down today
↳ 오늘은 그가 먹는 것마다 토한다

Orange peel tea mixed with ginger is considered powerful remedy for people who suffer from first-stage cold
↳ 초기 감기로 고생하는 사람에게는 생강을 섞은 오렌지 껍질 차가 효험 있는 약으로 알려져 있다

Oriental herbal medicine plays an important role in providing the whole body with the nutritive substances it lacks
↳ 한약은 인체에서 부족한 성분을 제공해주는 중요한 역할을 한다

Outspoken advice is(sounds) harsh to the ear
↳ 바른 말은 귀에 거슬린다

자신의 결점을 꼬집어서 말하는 충고를 들을 때에는 기분이 좋을 수가 없다.
그렇기 때문에 함부로 남에게 충고를 해서는 안되고, 충고를 들어서 기분이
나빠더라도 받아들일 수 있는 아량이 있어야 한다.
(=Unpleasant advice is a good medicine)
(=A good medicine taste bitter)

People aged 60 and older who have a certain type of high blood

---

▸ **ginger** pungent aromatic spice from a tropical plant

▸ **oriental** culture derived from the eastern part of Asia

pressure and who are particularly thin face have higher risks of stroke and death

    ↳ 60세 이상인 사람으로서 특정한 종류의 고혈압이 있고 특히 얼굴이 야윈 사람이 더 뇌졸중에 걸리거나 사망할 위험이 더 크다

People with arthritis are burdened with sharp pain in almost every joint in their bodies

    ↳ 관절염이 있는 사람은 전신에 있는 거의 모든 관절에서 심한 통증으로 고생하게 된다

Perhaps that's what you've got to thank for the rheumatism that's crippling you today

    ↳ 아마 그게 너가 절뚝거리며 걷게한 류마티즘에게 감사해야 하는 이유일 것이다

Please make up this prescription

    ↳ 이 처방전대로 조제해 주세요

Recurring illness forced her to retire from work prematurely

    ↳ 그녀는 병이 재발해서 부득이 조기 퇴직했다

Sang-mi gained ground after being near death

    ↳ 상미는 죽도록 아프다가(망했다가) 많이 회복했어

She drinks some special potion made of a combination of steamed red ginseng, crushed young deer antler powder, and jujubes

    ↳ 그녀는 홍삼과 녹용가루, 대추를 넣어서 만든 보약을 먹고있어

She fought hard in vain against the affliction, refusing to let it rob her of her vigor

    ↳ 그녀는 그 병이 자신의 원기를 빼앗아 가기를 내버려두지를 않으면서 격렬히 투병했으나 허사였다

She suddenly toppled over and went into a convulsion

› **premature**   coming before the usual or proper time

› **convulsion**   violent involuntary muscle contraction

↳ 그녀는 갑자기 쓰러지더니 발작을 일으켰다

She was energetic woman who cut off her prime by scarlet fever

↳ 그녀는 정력적인 여성이었으나 한창때 성홍열로 요절했다

She's out sick

↳ 병가 중

Some people always keep a variety pills and medicines in their home

↳ 어떤 사람들은 늘 여러 가지 환약과 그 밖의 의약품을 가정에 비치해 둔다

Some plants produce irritating poisons that can affect a person even if he or she merely brush against them

↳ 일부 식물들은 그저 스치고만 지나가도 사람에게 영향을 줄 수 있는 염증을 일으키는 독소를 가지고 있다

Somebody is going to give a dose of his own medicine someday

↳ 누군가 언젠가는 그에게 같은 수법으로 보복할 것이다

Someone who regularly feels coldness in his/her hands is likely to have less resistance to catching a cold

↳ 손에서 규칙적으로 한기를 느끼는 사람은 감기에 대한 저항력이 약할 가능성이 있다

Something he ate this morning gave him the runs

↳ 그는 아침에 뭔가 잘못 먹어서 배탈이 났다

Stay clear of the insects which may be carrying dangerous diseases

↳ 위험한 질병을 지니고 있을지도 모르는 곤충들을 피하도록 해라

Stay on this medicine for another day to see if your stomach trouble improves

↳ 너의 배탈이 나아질지 이 약을 하루만 더 먹어봐라

Stop chain-smoking, or else you'll wind up a basket case

‣ **scarlet** bright red

ㄴ 담배 피우지마, 담배를 안 끊고선 네 병을 못 고쳐

Stop feeding the cancer genes

ㄴ 담배 좀 끊어

Such a hardy strain of the virus can make people ill for over a month

ㄴ 그런 끈질긴 종류의 바이러스는 사람들을 한 달 이상 씩 앓게 할 수 있다

Taken in moderation, wine is the best of all medicines

ㄴ 알맞게 마시면 술이 최고의 영약이다

> 술도 좋은 술을 적당히 마시면 건강에 이롭다. 우리의 선조들도 "적게 먹으면 약주요, 많이 먹으면 망주"라고 하였다. 서양에서는 좋은 포도주가 건강에 이롭다고 한다(Good wine makes good blood).

That medicine worked miracles

ㄴ 그 약은 신통하게 잘 들었다

That quack charged the earth for useless treatment

ㄴ 그 돌팔이 의사는 효과도 없는 온갖 치료를 해놓고 터무니없이 치료비를 청구했다

That's a cure which has long been handed down among the common people

ㄴ 그것은 오랫동안 민간에 전해 내려오는 치료법이다

The accident left him with several broken ribs and dislocated right arm

ㄴ 그 사고로 그는 갈비뼈가 몇 개 부러지고 오른팔이 탈구됐다

The anesthesiologist has to administer small doses of drugs to sedate

---

› **quack** one who pretends to have medical or healing skill

› **anesthesiology** branch of medicine dealing with anesthesia

the patient throughout the operation
> ㄴ 마취의사는 수술 중 내내 환자를 진정시키기 위해 소량의 약을 투여 해야 한다

The boy walked along as if favoring his sore foot
> ㄴ 소년은 아픈 다리를 다칠세라 가만가만 걸어갔다

The cold has been giving him a devil of a time
> ㄴ 그는 감기 때문에 매우 고생하고 있다

The direction and end are fixed and the patient never works backward
> ㄴ 환자의 가는 방향과 가는 곳은 정해져 있고 그 길을 역행해서 되돌아 오지는 않는다(의학의 한계)

The effect of the medicine will go off(wear off, pass off, pass away) after five hours or so
> ㄴ 다섯 시간 정도 지나면 약 기운이 없어질 것이다

The epidemic was nipped in the bud by a big flue shot campaign
> ㄴ 대대적인 독감 예방주사 운동으로 그 유행병을 초기에 없애버렸다

The herb should be taken in the form of a tea and imbibed as often as possible
> ㄴ 그 약초는 차로 만들어서 가능한 자주 복용해야 한다

The medicine starts to kick in
> ㄴ 약 기운이 막 오르는군

The nagging inflammation of the joints is generally caused by deposits of inorganic calcium in the cartilage of joints
> ㄴ 이 성가신 관절의 염증은 일반적으로 관절 연골 내에 무기 칼슘이 쌓 여서 일어난다

The number of people suffering from obesity due to poor diet and

---

› **flue** smoke duct

› **imbibe** drink

› **cartilage** elastic skeletal tissue

lack of exercise has grown sharply

↳ 잘못된 식단과 운동부족에서 오는 비만으로 고통받는 사람들의 수가 급격히 늘어났다

The officials assume that patients contracted the epidemic from contaminated underground water at the prayer house

↳ 관계 공무원들은 전염병에 걸린 환자들이 기도원의 오염된 지하수를 마신 데서 일어난 것으로 추정한다

The pain from his scalded ankles prevents mobility, thus allowing inflamed tissues to heal

↳ 그는 물에 덴 발목 때문에 곪아있는 조직이 낫도록 움직이지 못하게 되어있다

The plan prohibits physicians from selling medicines and does not allow pharmacists to prescribe without the doctor's prescription

↳ 이 지침에는 의사들의 매약을 금하고 약사들은 의사의 처방 없이 약을 조제하지 못하도록 되어있다

The process requires that this fresh herb be dipped in alcohol steamed and dried some nine times

↳ 이 생약초는 아홉 번 정도 알콜에 담그고, 찌고, 말리는 과정을 요한다

The quality of a medical care is much of a muchness

↳ 의료 서비스의 질은 그게 그거야

The recent rapid progress in medical science promises well for the future

↳ 최근 의학의 급속한 진보는 미래에 커다란 희망을 갖게 한다

The slaughtering of the livestock in the affected farms is unavoidable if the spread of the epidemic to the other area is to be curbed

↳ 전염병이 타 지역으로 퍼짐을 막으려면 전염됐던 사육농가의 가축도

› **tissue**   layer of cells forming a basic structural element of an animal   or plant body

› **slaughter**   butchering of livestock for market

살은 불가피하다

The sooner they get him to the hospital, the more chance he has of survival
└ 그들이 그를 병원에 빨리 데려 갈수록 살아날 가망성이 더 크다

The wish for healing has ever been the half of health
└ 병이 낫겠다는 소망만으로 반쯤 나은 것과 같다

The wound soon scabbed over and the was well on its way to healing
└ 상처에는 딱지가 앉고 상당히 나아져 가고 있었다

The wound will scar over, but his leg will never be the same as it was before the accident
└ 그의 상처는 흉터를 남긴 채 아물겠지만 다리는 이전의 상태로는 회복될 수 없을 겁니다

The wounded man levered himself up(out) on his elbow and shouted for help
└ 상처를 입은 사람은 힘들게 팔꿈치로 몸을 일으켜 도와달라고 소리쳤다

The wounds on his face lend(give) colors to his story that he was beaten by his fellow criminals
└ 그의 얼굴에 있는 상처로 인해 동료 재소자들에게 얻어 맞았다는 얘기가 그럴듯해 보인다

Then the remedy(cure) would be worse than the disease
└ 그랬다가는 병보다 처방이 더 나쁜 꼴이지

There could be mark left behind
└ 흉터가 남겠군요

(=There could be some scarring)

› scab   protective crust over a sore or wound

There exists a great reluctance to accept viruses as being importance in human cancer
> ↳ 바이러스가 인간의 암을 일으키는 중요한 인자라고 인정하기에는 아직 시기상조다

There is a salve for every sore
> ↳ 만가지 병에는 만가지 약이 있다

This cold I've got in summer shouldn't happen to a dog
> ↳ 난 여름에 개도 안 하는 감기를 하고 있어

This cold of mine just keeps lingering on
> ↳ 이번 감기는 떨어지지가 않네

This feverish cold often kicks back when we think we are better
> ↳ 이 열 감기는 낫는다고 생각할 때 도지는 수가 많다

This medicine is obtainable only on a physician's prescription
> ↳ 이 약은 의사의 처방 없이는 조제하지 않습니다

This medicine is used to arrest the development of the disease
> ↳ 이 약은 병이 더 이상 커지지 않도록 저지하는 데 쓰인다

This medicine lessens pain by blocking the signals from the affected area's nerves to the brain
> ↳ 이 약은 병에 걸린 부분의 신경에서 뇌로 신호를 보내는 것을 차단함으로써 통증을 덜어준다

This medicine should call your strength back
> ↳ 이 약은 원기를 회복시켜 드릴 겁니다

This medicine should work well on(work wonders with) your cold
> ↳ 이 약은 감기에 잘(신통하게) 들을 겁니다

This medicine will protect(safeguard) you against a return of the disease

---

› **reluctance**　state of being reluctant
› **salve**　medicinal oinment

ㄴ 이 약을 먹으면 병의 재발을 막아 줄 것이다

This medicine works wonders on woman's problems, such as the dizziness and pain frequently associated with menstruation

ㄴ 이 약은 현기증 및 생리불순으로 인한 통증과 같은 여성 병에 특효가 있다

Those who have never been ill are incapable of real sympathy for great many misfortunes

ㄴ 앓아보지 않은 사람은 많은 불행에 참된 동정을 가질 수 없다

'동병상련', '유유상종' 등의 사자성어와 같은 뜻이다. 같은 처지에 있거나 같은 공동체에 속해 있으면 서로의 마음을 잘 이해하고, 서로의 이익을 위해 행동한다(Likeness cause liking = Dog doesn't eat dog).

Those with this chronic condition are more likely swell up or grow fat if he consumes even a small amount of food

ㄴ 이 같은 만성적 증세가 있는 사람은 음식을 조금만 섭취해도 몸이 나거나 살이 찔 가능성이 커진다

Though the sore be healed, yet a scar may remain

ㄴ 상처는 나아도 흉터는 남는다

Thousand ills require a thousand cures

ㄴ 천 가지 병에는 천 가지 치료법이 있다

To be unable to bear an ill is itself a great ill

ㄴ 병에 이겨낼 수 없다는 그 자체가 병이다

Unless you are ready to walk around the city at noon wearing a gas mask, its almost tantamount to asking for horrible respiratory diseases

ㄴ 정오에 방독면을 쓰고 도시지역을 돌아다닐 준비가 되어있지 않다면

› **consume** eat or use up

› **tantamount** equivalent in value or meaning

› **respiration** act or process of breathing, energy-yielding oxidation in living matter

호흡기 질환을 자초하는 것이나 다름없다

Vinegar helps fights germs, sooths stomach pains, heals cuts quicker and adds to our overall health
> ↳ 식초는 멸균효과가 있고, 위통을 진정시키며, 상처를 빨리 낫게 하며, 건강을 전반적으로 좋게 해준다

Vitamin plays an important part in the function of the body
> ↳ 비타민은 신진대사에 중요한 역할을 한다

What some calls health, if purchased by perpetual anxiety about diet, is not much better than tedious disease
> ↳ 노심초사하면서 다이어트로 얻는 건강을 건강이라고 하는 사람도 있지만 지루한 병을 앓는 것보다 나을 것이 없다

When his father died of lung cancer, he saw the light and quit smoking
> ↳ 그의 아버지가 폐암으로 돌아가시자 깨달은바 있어 금연했다

When it heels over(up), there won't be any mark to show where it was
> ↳ 상처가 아물고 나면 어디가 다쳤던 자리인지 흉터가 남지 않을 거야

When the devil was ill, he wish to be a monk; when the devil was recovered, he was devil as before
> ↳ 화장실 갈 때 마음 다르고 올 때 마음 다르다

> 환경에 따라 태도와 입장이 바뀌어진다. 직역하면 "악마가 병에 걸리면 수도승이 되길 원하지만, 병이 나으면 다시 악마가 된다"이다. 사람의 마음은 시시각각 변한다는 것을 말한다.

Whooping cough is a condition which occurs mainly in young

› **tedious** wearisome from length or dullness
› **lung** breathing organ in the chest

children

↳ 백일해는 주로 어린아이에게 잘 일어나는 증세이다

Wine is best of all medicine

↳ 술은 백 약의 장이다

> 술도 좋은 술을 적당히 마시면 건강에 이롭다. 우리의 선조들도 '적게 먹으면 약주요, 많이 먹으면 망주'라고 하였다. 서양에서는 좋은 포도주가 건강에 이롭다고 한다(Good wine makes good blood).
> (＝Good wine engenders good blood)

With the continued loss of blood, her life was steadily leaking away

↳ 그 여자는 계속되는 출혈로 생명을 잃어가고 있었다

With the progress of medicine, it'll become more and more common people to live until they have had their fill of life

↳ 의학의 발달로 사람들이 자신에게 주어진 천수를 다할 때까지 사는 것이 점점 흔하게 될 것이다

Working too hard, coupled with not getting enough sleep, will make you ill

↳ 일을 너무 열심히 하면서 잠을 충분히 안자면 병나게 돼

Wounds can't be cured without searching

↳ 아픈 곳을 찾아내지 않고는 고칠 수 없다

You need some sort of medicine to clean you out

↳ 넌 설사약을 먹어야겠군

You'd better let your disease run its course

↳ 병이 저절로 나을 때까지 내버려두어라

Your illness threw my plans for the weekend out of gear

› **engender**   create

ㄴ 네가 아파서 주말 계획은 차질이 생겼어

You'd better let your disease run its course

ㄴ 병이 저절로 나을 때까지 내버려두어라

· **course** progress, ground over which something moves, part of a meal served at one   time, method of procedure, subject taught in a series of classes

89. 야단　　　　　　　　　　　　**Scolding**

Better a little chiding than a great deal of heart-break
↳ 크게 가슴 아플 일보다 작은 꾸지람이 낫다

Bong-soo thought that he was the star of the team until he got the business from his coach
↳ 봉수는 코치한테 혼나기 전까지는 자기가 팀에서 스타라고 생각했어

Byung-soo stepped out of line once too often and got bawled at
↳ 병수는 못된 짓을 너무 자주 해서 호되게 야단 맞았어

Castigating and punishing her would only exacerbate the shame she's suffering
↳ 그녀를 나무라고 벌주는 것은 수치심을 더 악화시킬 뿐이다

Chang-ho likes to dish it out, but he hates to take it in
↳ 창호는 남에게 욕(꾸짖기)은 잘 하지만 남에게 욕먹는 건 싫어해

Did the boss ream you out?
↳ 윗분이 야단 치셨어요?

Don't let yourself get cowed down by his heavy scolding
↳ 그에게 큰 꾸지람 받았다고 의기소침하지마

Doo-man's wife always takes him to task for his drinking
↳ 두만의 아내는 그가 술 마실 때마다 꾸중을 해

Ed's going to explode when he sees this mess
↳ 에드가 이 엉망인 꼴을 보면 노발대발하겠다

‣ **chid** scold
‣ **bawl** cry loudly

‣ **exacerbate** make more violent, bitter, or severe

Give him hell if he interrupts you in the middle of making a recording
↳ 네가 녹음할 때 방해하거든 혼을 좀 내줘라

He will haul us over the coals for not finishing on time
↳ 우린 제때 일을 못 끝냈다고 호되게 야단 맞을 것이다

He will have a fit
↳ 그는 노발대발 할거다

His mother got after him for tracking mud into the house
↳ 그의 어머니가 그에게 흙을 묻혀 집에 들어오지 말라고 야단치셨어

I did my daughter over for coming home late
↳ 딸아이가 늦게 집에 오기에 야단쳐줬지

I really put him in his place
↳ 그 사람에게 건방지다고 야단을 쳐줬지

I wanted to buy it, but my mother bullied me out of it
↳ 사고싶었지만 어머니가 윽박질러 못 샀지

I will teach you to ignore my words
↳ 내 말 안 들으면 혼낼 거다

I'll see you smart
↳ 혼내주고 말 테다(두고보자)

I'll sin him alive
↳ 그 사람 혼내 줄 거야

I'll teach you a lesson
↳ 혼내주겠다

It would have gone ill with me
↳ 혼날 뻔했어

‣ **haul** draw or pull, transport or carry

It'll cost you dear
> ㄴ 그 일 때문에 혼날 거다

It's ten to one he'll tan(dress) your hide
> ㄴ 네가 그에게 혼날 건 뻔해

Mother is always holding up my cousin to me
> ㄴ 어머닌 늘 사촌형(동생)을 본받으라고 성화다

My father went through the roof when he saw what I did
> ㄴ 내가 저지른 일을 보고 아버지가 노발대발 하셨어

Nobody is going to nail your ears back
> ㄴ 아무도 널 호되게 나무랄 사람은 없어

Sang-soo will nail you to the wall if he finds out what you've done
> ㄴ 네가 한 짓을 상수가 알기라도 한다면 혼 줄이 날거다

Send him to me whenever he gets out of line and I'll discipline him
> ㄴ 언제든지 그가 말을 듣지 않을 때 나한테 보내면 내가 야단을 쳐 줄게

She is trying to get something on me so she can dress me down
> ㄴ 그 여자는 내 꼬투리를 잡아서 야단치려고 하고 있어

She must be talked to
> ㄴ 그 여자는 혼내줘야 해

She's been after her daughter all day to clean up her room
> ㄴ 그 여자는 자기 딸에게 방 좀 치우라고 하루종일 성화다

She'll catch hell if her father gets hold of her
> ㄴ 그 여자는 아버지에게 붙잡히기만 하면 혼이 날 것이다

Sung-mo wants a dressing down
> ㄴ 성모를 혼내줘야겠어

That will fix his wagon
> ㄴ 그걸로 그 사람은 혼날 거다

· **tan** make or become brown (as by exposure to the sun)

The boss gave me a good salting down(talking to, dressing down) for no other reason than that

ㄴ 사장은 단지 그 이유만으로 나를 (호되게) 야단쳤다

The sting of a reproach is in the truth of it

ㄴ 꾸지람의 통렬함은 꾸짖는 내용의 진실성에 달려있다

They'll really give it to you if you don't keep straight

ㄴ 제대로 행동하지 않으면 그들에게 혼날 것이다

You shall smart for this

ㄴ 나중에 혼날 줄 알아라

You'll catch it from your father

ㄴ 너희 아버지한테 야단 맞을 거다

› **reproach**   disgrace, rebuke

90. 약속   Promises

A bargain's a bargain
> 약속은 약속

A promise is a promise after all
> 어쨌든 약속은 약속이다

A promise made is a debt unpaid
> 약속을 하는 일은 갚지 않은 빚을 짊어지는 일이다

All they have done is only a lick and a promise
> 그 사람들 해 놓은 일이란 날림(하는 둥 마는 둥)이야

Anytime you are ready
> 난 언제라도 좋아

Are you available today?
> 오늘 시간 좀 있어?

Be slow to promise, quick to perform
> 약속은 천천히, 실천은 빨리

Be sure to your own word
> 말한 건 지켜야 해

(=Be true to your own word)
(=Do what you promised you would do)

› **lick**   draw the tongue over, beat

Be that as it may, we'll have to make another appointment tomorrow
　　↳ 어차피 우리는 내일 다시 만날 약속을 해야해

Better break your word than do worse in keeping it
　　↳ 지켜서 해로울 약속은 깨는 것이 낫다

Can I move it up a day?
　　↳ 하루 앞당길 수 있을까요?

Can you fit(squeeze, crowd) in a game of bowling with me on the weekend?
　　↳ 주말에 보울링 한판 칠래?(crowd in 스케쥴에 넣어주다)

Can you move(push) the date back a little?
　　↳ 날짜를 조금 늦출 수 있겠나?

Can you stall(play) for time till the end of the year?
　　↳ 연말까지 시간을 늦춰줄 수 있겠니?

Credit is a promise of a future payment in money or in kind given in exchange for present money, goods or services
　　↳ 신용거래는 현재의 거래에 대하여 사후에 현금, 상품, 또는 용역을
　　　제공하겠다는 약속이다

Do you have a time for a quick one?
　　↳ 한잔 할 시간 있니?

Do you have anything on this evening?
　　↳ 오늘 저녁 무슨 계획(약속)이라도 있니?

Do you want to get out of a promise(back out of from a promise)?
　　↳ 약속을 취소하고 싶어?

Enemies' promises were made to be broken
　　↳ 적의 약속은 깨지기 위한 약속이다

Give it a few more days

› **bowling**　game in which balls are rolled
　　　　　to knock down pins

┗ 며칠만 더 기다려 줘

He is trying to sweep his failure to keep his election promise under the mat(carpet)
┗ 그는 선거공약을 지키지 못한 것을 슬며시 덮어두려고 하고 있다

He that promises too much means nothing
┗ 너무 많은 약속을 하는 사람은 그 약속의 의미가 없다

He'll hold you to it
┗ 넌 그에게 약속(계약)을 안 지킬 수 없어

He's on for six o'clock tomorrow morning
┗ 그는 내일 아침 여섯 시에 약속이 있어

His promises are merely wind
┗ 그의 약속은 빈말에 불과

How are you going to fill in this afternoon?
┗ 오늘 오후에 뭐하면서 시간 보낼 거니?

I am flexible
┗ 아무 때나 좋아

I haven't seen you alone
┗ 단둘이 한 번 만나자

I keep my end of the bargain
┗ 내가 한 약속은 지켜

I'll come through for you
┗ 약속은 지킬게

I'll take this to the grave
┗ 죽을 때까지 비밀을 지킬게

If you back out of(from) your contract(promise), you'll have to pay

---

‣ **sweep** remove or clean by a brush or a single forceful wipe

‣ **contract** binding agreement, establish or undertake by contract

the penalty to the firm
　　　↳ 계약(약속)을 이행치 않으면 회사에 벌금을 물어야해

In-ho promised to make good on his debts
　　　↳ 인호는 빚을 갚겠다고 약속했어

Is the Saturday still on you?
　　　↳ 토요일 약속 아직 변동 없는 거지?(약속 확인. 그러나 이해 못할 수 있음)

Keep this Saturday open
　　　↳ 이번 토요일 약속은 비워둬

Keep up your end of the bargain
　　　↳ 약속한 일은 지켜라

Let's beat(shoot, fan) the breeze over a cup of coffee
　　　↳ 커피 한잔하면서 이런 저런 얘기나 좀 하자

Let's bottom-line this project and break for coffee
　　　↳ 이 일은 마무리하고 커피 한잔하자

Let's get down to the tavern to dish some dirt
　　　↳ 술집에 가서 이런 저런 얘기나 좀 하자

Let's get together and compare notes
　　　↳ 언제 다시 만나 의견을 나눠봅시다

Let's go out and get juiced
　　　↳ 어디 나가서 한 잔 하지 그래

Let's have one for the road
　　　↳ 길 떠나기 전에 딱 한잔하자

Let's splurge on a lavish lunch today
　　　↳ 오늘 비싼데 가서 화끈하게 점심한번 먹자

Let's talk about it face to face

▸ **penalty**　punishment for crime, disadvantage, loss, or hardship due to an action

▸ **splurge**　indulge oneself

ㄴ 만나서 얘기하자

My calendar is full

ㄴ 벌써 계획(면회, 데이트 등)이 다 잡혀있어요

On Monday two meetings clash

ㄴ 월요일에는 약속이 두 개나 있다

Once we promise, we can't back out

ㄴ 일단 약속을 하면 거역하지 못해

Politicians often try to sway undecided voters by promising lower taxes

ㄴ 정치인들은 부동 투표자들에게 세금을 낮추어 준다고 약속함으로써 마음을 사로잡으려 한다

Promises and pie-crust are made to be broken

ㄴ 약속과 파이껍질은 깨지기 위해 만들어진다

Punctuality is the politeness of princes

ㄴ 약속을 잘 지키는 것이 예의의 근본이다

> 약속을 잘 지키는 사람은 신용을 얻게 된다. 사회 생활에서 신용만큼 중요한 것이 없다(Punctuality is the duty of politeness of kings 약속을 잘 지키는 것은 신사의 의무이다).

Punctuality is the soul of business

ㄴ 약속을 잘 지킴은 사업에 있어서 핵심이 된다

> 약속을 잘 지키는 사람은 신용을 얻게 된다. 사회 생활에서 신용만큼 중요한 것이 없다(Punctuality is the duty of politeness of kings 약속을 잘 지키는 것은 신사의 의무이다).

› **crust** hard surface layer

Reserve that day for me
　　↳ 스케줄 비워두세요

> (=Keep that day open for me)
> (=Don't make plans that day)
> (=Leave your schedule that day)

See you at five if I don't hear otherwise
　　↳ 나한테 별다른 얘기가 없으면 다섯시에 올게

She promised never to reveal her secrets on pain of death
　　↳ 그 여자는 목숨을 걸고라도 그 비밀을 지키겠다고 약속했다

The best way to keep one's word is not to give it
　　↳ 약속을 지키는 최선의 방법은 약속을 하지 않는 것이다

The recent rapid progress in medical science promises well for the future
　　↳ 최근 의학의 급속한 진보는 미래에 커다란 희망을 갖게 한다

The vow that binds too strictly snaps itself
　　↳ 너무 엄격히 구속하는 약속은 저절로 깨어진다

Their promises were full of hot air
　　↳ 그들의 약속은 알맹이 없는 말로 가득했다

They failed to deliver on their promise to provide fringe benefits
　　↳ 그들은 약속을 어기고 추가급여를 주지 않았다

They have already reneged on their commitment to full employment
　　↳ 그들은 이미 완전고용에 대한 공약을 어겼어

They tried to beg it off by claiming a previous engagement
　　↳ 그들은 선약이 있다고 그걸 거절하려 했다

› **fringe**　ornamental border of short hanging　　│　› **renege**　go back on a promise
　　　　threads or strips

Things are escaped that promise us a smile
> ↳ 행운이 한 번 이상 되풀이해서 찾아오기는 어려워

Treaties are like roses and girls. They last while they last
> ↳ 조약은 장미나 소녀와 같다. 그들은 지속되는 기간만큼만 지속된다

Vote for the man who promises least
> ↳ 공약이 제일 적은 사람에게 표를 찍어라

Vows made in storm are forgotten in calms
> ↳ 급할 때의 맹세는 편안할 때 다 잊어버린다

We are waiting anxiously to see if the group will remain faithful to its promise of reform
> ↳ 우리는 그 기업그룹이 구조조정 약속을 충실히 지킬지 눈 여겨 지켜보고 있다

We can't pin(nail) down the date just now
> ↳ 현재로서는 날짜를 확정 지울 수 없어

We promise according to our promise, and perform according to our fears
> ↳ 우리는 희망에 따라 약속하고 두려움에 따라 이행한다

We'd like to pay you a lightening(flying) visit
> ↳ 우린 너를 잠깐만 방문하고 싶어

What time shall we make it?
> ↳ 몇 시에 만날까요?

(=When is the best time for you?)
(=When do you have time?)
(=What time is good for you?)

› **treaty**   agreement between governments

Would this date suit you?
ㄴ 이 날이면 되겠어?

You always promise me the moon
ㄴ 넌 내게 터무니없는 약속만 하는군

You are far from promising
ㄴ 넌 사람되긴 틀렸어(싹수가 노래)

You have my word
ㄴ 약속하지

You have to meet him by appointment
ㄴ 그를 만나려면 약속을 해야해

You know I'm good for it
ㄴ 나 약속 잘 지키는 것 알잖아

You're better than your word
ㄴ 넌 약속 이상으로 해냈구나

▸ **appointment**   act of appointing, nonelective   a meeting
                    political job, arrangement for

91. 얼굴 & 화장   Faces & Makeups

A man is as old as he feels, and a woman as old as she looks
> ↳ 남자의 나이는 느끼기에 달렸고 여자의 나이는 얼굴에 나타난다

남자는 나이가 들어도 건강하기만 하고 젊다고 느끼기만 한다면 나이에 구애받지 않지만, 여자는 외모, 즉 겉으로 드러나는 나이에 많은 구애를 받는다. 아무리 화장을 해도 얼굴에 나타나는 나이는 속일 수 없기 때문이다.

Age stamped her with lines
> ↳ 그 여자는 나이를 먹어 얼굴에 주름이 잡혔다

All these worries have put years on me
> ↳ 이 골치 아픈 일들이 나를 겉늙게 만들었어

Although he looks ugly, he is in good with a lot of girls
> ↳ 그의 외모는 볼품 없지만 여자들에게 인기 있어

Be careful about which make-up you wear under these strong lights
> ↳ 이 강렬한 조명아래 무슨 화장을 해야할지 주의해라

Beautiful is my middle name
> ↳ '미인'하면 나잖아

Beauty won't make the pot boil
> ↳ 얼굴이 밥 먹여주나

› **stamp** pound with the sole of the foot or a heavy implement, impress with | with a mark, cut out with a die, attach a postage stamp to

아름다움이 좋은 것이지만, 시간이 지나면 퇴색하기 마련이다. "Beauty is but skin-deep 아름다움은 그저 살갗 한 겹 차이이다"라는 속담이 있다.

Chang-soo has a forbidding countenance but he wouldn't hurt a fly
ㄴ 창수가 얼굴은 험상궂지만 그렇게 순할 수 없어

Crater face over there is trying to put the moves on you
ㄴ 저 쪽에 있는 여드름자국 투성이 녀석이 너를 꼬시려 한다 이 말이군

Dead drunk, he looked as red as a lobster
ㄴ 고주망태가 된 그의 얼굴은 삶은 문어 같았다

Each succeeding year stole away something from her beauty
ㄴ 연년이 쌓이는 세월 속에 그 여자는 아름다움을 잃어갔다

Even a beauty can get wearing after a while
ㄴ 미인이라도 시간이 가면 싫증날 수 있어

Every time we frown, we are letting lines creep up on us like unwanted guests
ㄴ 우리가 얼굴을 찌푸릴 때마다 원치 않는 손님과 같은 주름살이 우리에게 다가오고 있다

Freckles, moles and warts on our face can sometimes be considered fashionable rather than distracting from our appearance
ㄴ 우리의 얼굴에 나는 주근깨, 점, 사마귀가 때론 외모를 손상시키기보다 멋지다고 여겨지는 때도 있다

Giving your face a good massage two or three times a week will help make your skin firm
ㄴ 일주일에 두 세 번 정도 잘 마사지하면 피부가 팽팽해져

Handsome is as handsome does
ㄴ 잘 생긴 사람은 얼굴값을 하게 돼있어

· **crater** volcanic depression
· **frown** scowl

· **freckle** brown spot on the skin

Her face is her fortune

↳ 그 여자 얼굴 빼고 나면 아무 것도 아니다

> 여성의 아름다움은 그 사람의 인생을 바꿀 수도 있다. 세계적인 미인인 클레오파트라와 양귀비 등은 그 아름다움으로 세기를 평정했었다. 그래서 "A fair face is half a fortune 아름다운 용모는 재산의 절반이다"라는 속담이 있다. 요즘은 취업에도 외모가 많이 관여되기 때문에 외모에 더욱 많은 비중을 둔다.

His face is lined with age(suffering)

↳ 그의 얼굴은 나이(고생)로 인해 주름 투성이다

His face is peppered with freckles

↳ 그의 얼굴은 주근깨 투성이다

If you don't prepare your skin properly, your makeup will be poorly done

↳ 피부상태가 안 좋으면 화장이 잘 될 리 없어

In his face wrinkles ploughed by time

↳ 그의 얼굴은 나이로 인해 주름살 투성이 이다

Looks can go only so far

↳ 예쁘게 보이는 것도 한 때일 뿐이다

Mi-gyung uses too much make-up

↳ 미경인 화장을 너무 짙게 해

My friend was getting old then long before his time

↳ 친구는 그 때 나이보다 훨씬 겉늙어 있었다

Nam-soo's face maligns him

↳ 남수는 얼굴과 딴판으로 착한 사람이다

› **makeup** cosmetics
› **malign** wicked, malignant, speak evil of

Old age plowed furrows in her face
> ↳ 나이가 그녀의 얼굴에 깊은 주름을 잡아놓았다

Pretty face, poor fate
> ↳ 미인박명

Put a good amount of cosmetic on your face
> ↳ 얼굴에 충분한 양의 화장품을 발라라

Pyung-soon is all lipstick and powder
> ↳ 평순이의 외모는 다 화장 발이야

She broke out in hives that didn't go away soon
> ↳ 그녀는 잘 낫지 않는 두드러기가 났었다

She is beautiful in her own conceit
> ↳ 제 딴에 미인인줄 아나봐

She was a beauty in her day
> ↳ 한창때 미인이었던 사람

She'll show us how to powder your face and remove the makeup
> ↳ 그녀는 화장법과 화장을 지우는 법을 가르쳐 줄 것이다

Squeeze a little amount onto the palm of your hand and spread the gel evenly through face
> ↳ 손바닥에 겔을 조금 짜내어서 얼굴에 고루 바르십시오

Sung-hee has a personal advantage
> ↳ 성희는 미인

Talking about freckles gets her going
> ↳ 그 여자에게 주근깨 얘기를 하면 열 받지

That ugly guy latched on to me at the party and I couldn't get rid of him
> ↳ 저 못생긴 녀석이 파티에서 달라붙어서 안 떨어져

▸ **furrow** trench made by a plow, wrinkle orgroove

▸ **latch** catch or get hold, catch that hold a door closed

That's just makeup
    ↳ 그건 다 화장 발 때문이야

(=You should see her without makeup)

The face is no index to the heart
    ↳ 얼굴이 곱다고 마음씨가 고운 건 아니다

The face of the tyranny is always mild at first
    ↳ 독재자들의 첫 인상은 늘 온화하다

The first thing you need is a good foundation
    ↳ 우선 기초화장을 잘 해야해

The lines in his face reflect a hard life
    ↳ 그의 얼굴에 새겨진 주름들은 그가 많은 고생을 했음을 보여준다

The woods are full of nice-looking girls up for grabs
    ↳ 나서기만 하면 많고 많은 게 잘 생긴 여자들이다

Ultra violet rays are what induce sunburn and tanning of the skin
    ↳ 자외선은 피부를 그을리고 태운다

When we keep our expression frown-free, the wrinkling know that they are not welcome
    ↳ 우리가 찡그리지 않는 표정을 유지해 나갈 때 주름살들은 멀어지게 될 것이다

You are much so prettier from close-up
    ↳ 너를 가까이서 뜯어보니 훨씬 더 예쁘다

You look like the way you did ten years ago
    ↳ 너 10년 전 모습이 변하지 않았군

› **tyranny** unjust use of absolute governmental power | › **induce** persuade, bring about

You look white as a ghost
ㄴ 너 얼굴이 백짓장 같이 희구나
Your complexion begins to gather color
ㄴ 너 혈색이 돌아오는구나

‣ **complexion**   hue or appearance of the
skin especially of the face

92. 여러 가지 상황들　Different Situations

At that time I didn't know where to turn(which way to turn)(whether I was coming or going)
> ↳ 그땐 뭐가 뭔지 몰랐어

Bellyaching will get you nowhere
> ↳ 투덜거려봤자 소용없어

Bong-soo can't squirm out of it
> ↳ 봉수는 발뺌할 수 없어

Circumstances alter cases
> ↳ 사정에 따라 이야기가 달라진다

Don't forget to earth up the roots firmly when you plant the tree
> ↳ 나무를 심을 때 뿌리에 흙을 단단히 덮어야 한다

Finders keepers, losers weepers
> ↳ 줍는 사람이 임자지(**Finding is keeping**)

'줍는 사람이 임자'라는 한국 속담을 영어로는 "Finders keepers, losers weepers 찾은 사람은 갖는 사람이고, 잃은 사람은 우는 사람이다"라고 한다.

Giving me the silent treatment will get you nowhere
> ↳ 나한테 입 닫고 있어봐야 별 수 없어

He is equal to the occasion

· **bellyache**　pain in the abdomen
· **squirm**　wriggle

ㄴ 그 사람은 어떤 경우에도 잘 대처해 나가고 있어

He made himself scarce

ㄴ 그는 슬그머니 가버렸다. 그는 틀어박혀서 좀처럼 나오지 않았다

He screwed Bong-soo out of what was due(to) Bong-soo

ㄴ 그는 봉수에게 돌아갈 것을 갈취해 갔어

He's got a bullet with their names on it

ㄴ 그는 그들을 쏘아 죽이려 하고 있어

He's just flying by the seat of his pants

ㄴ 그는 그저 감으로 때려잡아 해나가고 있는 거야

Her voice failed to carry across the noisy street

ㄴ 그녀의 목소리는 시끄러운 길 건너 편 까지 들려오지 않았다

Hindsight is always twenty-twenty(My eyesight is fifteen-fifteen 내시력은 1.5, 1.5이다)

ㄴ 늘 일이 터지고 나면 뭐가 옳은지 알게 돼 있어

How long do I have to keep this act up?

ㄴ 언제까지 이런 연극을 해야해?

Hyun-soo held his peace(tongue)

ㄴ 그는 침묵을 지켰어

I can't do enough to prove

ㄴ 증명할 만큼 행동할 수 없는 형편(이해 못할 수도 있음)

I can't get back to my old way(what I used to be)

ㄴ 옛날 방식으로 돌아갈 순 없어

I can't get over how everyone liked it

ㄴ 이렇게 마음에 들어 하시다니 놀랐습니다

I can't give you the exact number offhand

ㄴ 지금 당장 정확한 개수는 몰라

› **scarce** not plentiful, rare | › **offhand** without previous thought or preparation

I can't really say right now
> ↳ 지금은 뭐라 할 수 없어

I count the hours until that day
> ↳ 그날이 오기를 손꼽아 기다리고 있어

I cried myself blind
> ↳ 눈물이 앞을 가렸어

I did it for the best
> ↳ 그게 제일 좋겠다는 생각으로 한 일이다

I did so with good reason
> ↳ 그만한 이유가 있어서 그런 거야

I did the best I could
> ↳ 난 할 만큼 했어

> (=I did everything I could)
> (=I did all I could do)

I didn't use to do that
> ↳ 예전엔 나도 그런 거 안 했어

I don't know what is in store for me
> ↳ 앞일은 몰라

I don't know whether I'm coming or going
> ↳ 어찌해야 할지 모르겠다

I don't like to have somebody else tell me I ought to do this and that
> ↳ 남이 이래라 저래라 하는 잔소린 듣고 싶지 않아

▸ **cry oneself blind** burst into tears

I don't like to leave loose ends
ㄴ 확실히 해 두고 싶어(미결로 남기고 싶지 않아)

I don't mean roughing it for a bit
ㄴ 다소 불편한 건 개의치 않아

I happened to be by
ㄴ 때마침 내가 옆에 있었지

I have an idea, such as it is
ㄴ 별건 아니지만 내게도 생각은 있어

I have hurried into error
ㄴ 재촉을 받아 틀리게 됐어

I haven't one clue how to do it
ㄴ 도무지 방법이 안 떠오르네

I know better
ㄴ 그 정도엔 넘어갈 내가 아냐

I know it to my cost
ㄴ 그 일을 알기까진 큰 희생을 치렀어(그 일은 진저리 나)

I know nothing beyond this
ㄴ 이것 외는 아무 것도 몰라

I shall cut out unimportant details
ㄴ 중요하지 않은 사소한 건 생략할게

I shall use my discretion
ㄴ 내가 알아서 할게

I thought I'd seen everything
ㄴ 난 내가 다 아는 일이라고 생각했지

I understand your reservations
ㄴ 미심쩍어 하는 점은 이해해(**I have some reservations** 의문스러운 점

› **discretion** discreet quality, power of decision
          or choice

이 좀 있긴 해)

I'll handle the rest(matter)
> ↳ 뒷일은 내가 맡지(총대 멜게)

> (=I'll take the bullet(responsibility))

I'm beginning to get the picture
> ↳ 이제 무슨 뜻인지 알 것 같아

I'm just beginning
> ↳ 지금까지는 맛 배기

> (=I'm just getting started)
> (=I'm just warming up)
> (I'm just getting warmed up)

I'm open to conviction
> ↳ 도리에 따르겠습니다

I'm ready to come apart at the seams
> ↳ 미칠 지경이야

I've heard it the other way around
> ↳ 나는 다르게 들었어

If anything can go wrong, it will
> ↳ 조금이라도 잘못될 가능성이 있으면 잘못되고 말아

If anything is missing you'll have to answer to me
> ↳ 한 가지라도 없어지면 나한테 책임져야 해

If he knew, he wouldn't remain calm

› **conviction** act of convicting, strong belief

↳ 그가 안다면 가만있을 리 없지

If it sounds too good to be true, it probably is

↳ 얘기가 너무 잘 나간다 싶으면 그럴 리 없다는 생각이 들어

If they are shown once, they are shown a dozen(hundred) times

↳ 그건 백 번도 더 봤어

If you add it up

↳ 그 상황을 종합하면

If you are discovered, you're done for

↳ 넌 들키면 큰일이다

In an ordinary way, I should refuse

↳ 보통 때 같으면 거절할거다

In my state of mind, all cats are gray in the dark

↳ 지금 심정으로는 이런 것 저런 것을 구분할 상황이 아냐

In the middle of the sermon, the baby started crying. "Another country coming from" Jang-soo said

↳ 설교도중 아이가 울음을 터뜨리자, 장수 왈 "하필 이런 때에"(another country coming from은 엉뚱(뚱딴지)한 일이 돌발했을 때 하는 말임. 그러나 이해하지 못할 경우도 있음))

It boils down to this

↳ 요약하면 다음과 같아

It can go both ways

↳ 그건 양쪽 모두에게 해당될 수 있다

It comes and goes

↳ 좋아졌다 나빠졌다 해

It fell far short of the avowed level of the so-called renewal of blood

↳ 그것은 소위 새로운 피로 바꾼다는 언약과는 너무나 거리가 먼 것이다

▸ **sermon** lecture on religion or behavior

▸ **avow** declare openly

It is not altogether without reason
> ↳ 전혀 이유 없이 그런 건 아냐

It is reduced to conjecture
> ↳ 추측해 보는 수밖에 없어

It isn't as if I were poor
> ↳ 나를 가난하다고 하는 말은 아닐 테지

It lacked real punch
> ↳ 뭔가 딱 와 닿는 게 없었어

It makes a difference
> ↳ 그렇다면 차이가 나는걸

It might be done on time, but I wouldn't make book(bank) on it
> ↳ 제 시간에 될 수도 있겠지만 내기를 걸고 싶을 정도는 아냐

It seemed that he was still riding the wave then
> ↳ 그는 그때까지만 해도 잘 나가는 것 같았어

It was a near miss(narrow escape, close call)
> ↳ 하마터면 놓칠 번했다

It's a pretty sticky(complicated, tricky) situation
> ↳ 이거 곤란하게 됐군

It's a whole new ball game
> ↳ 전부 처음부터 다시 해야해

It's as good as new
> ↳ 감쪽같아(새것 같아)

› **complicate**   make complex or hard to
            understand

> (=It looks brand-new)
> (=It's all better)
> (=It's never been better)

It's been around for some time now
> ↳ 그게 생긴지 꽤 오래 됐어

It's been one disaster after another
> ↳ 산 너머 산이로군

It's going to be do or die
> ↳ 죽기 아니면 살기 식이야(이판사판)

> (=It's make or die)
> (=It's throwing caution or discretion to the wind)

It's got to be done without going back to square one
> ↳ 이 일은 도로아미타불 되는 일없도록 마무리지어야 한다

It's hard to understand the issues with all the hoopla surrounding him
> ↳ 그에게 온갖 유언비어가 난무하고 있어서 상황파악이 어려워

It's in a million pieces
> ↳ 산산조각이 났어

> (=It's smashed into smithereens)
> (=It's broken into bits)

It's in the pipeline

· **disaster** sudden great misfortune
· **smithereens** very small parts

↳ 진행 중

It's later than you think
↳ 네 생각처럼 어물어물 할 틈이 없어

It's like comparing apples and oranges
↳ 그건 비교를 못 하겠어

It's like pulling teeth
↳ 장난이 아니네. 정말 어려운 일이네

It's no use making a mystery(of it)
↳ 숨겨(시치미 떼)도 소용없어

It's no use trying to force it, it just won't go(in)
↳ 맞지 않으니 무리하게 밀어 넣어 봐야 소용없어

It's not over until the fat lady sings
↳ 결과는 두고봐야 알아

It's not the way I planned
↳ 그럴 생각이 아니었어

It's on its last leg
↳ 그건 간신히 지탱하고 있어

It's on-again, off-again
↳ 이렇게 될지 저렇게 될지 불확실해

It's only poetic justice
↳ 그건 인과응보일 뿐이야

It's the exception rather than the rule
↳ 다 그렇지는 않지만 예외적으로 그럴 수도 있다

It's the same result
↳ 엎어 치나 메어치나 지

(=The results are the same)

It's your call
> ↳ 결정은 네 몫

It's your funeral
> ↳ 그건 네가 알아서 할 일이다

It's your go
> ↳ 이제 네 차례(네가 둘 차례)

It(He) is something like a rose
> ↳ 그 일(그 사람)에 불만은 없어

Its future course is still uncertain
> ↳ 앞으로 어찌될지 몰라

Jung-soo has to clear(tie) up(the) loose ends
> ↳ 정수가 마무리해야해

Just follow the directions and you can't go wrong
> ↳ 지시(설명서)대로만 하면 잘못될 일은 없어

Just go and I'll take care of the rest(things over from here)
> ↳ 뒷일은 내게 맡기고 가봐

(=Just go and leave the rest up to me)

Just highlight all the positives and downplay the negatives
> ↳ 긍정적인 면을 부각시키고 부정적인 면을 슬쩍 넘겨라

Just make a call and stick with it
> ↳ 그냥 결정하고 그대로 따라

· **highlight** emphasize, be a highlight of
· **downplay** neglect, ignore

Just put him on ice until you have enough facts to go on
> ↳ 충분히 근거할 사실이 확보될 때까지 그의 처리는 보류하자

Just rough in to give an idea of the general look of the place
> ↳ 그 곳 전체 모양이라도 알 수 있게 대강만 그려 봐

Just sit back and let things happen(take care of themselves)
> ↳ 그저 굿만 보고 떡만 먹어

Just stick in a knife and see if it comes out clean
> ↳ 칼을 찔렀다가 빼어서 칼이 깨끗한지 보면 돼

Keep after him until he does
> ↳ 그가 할 때까지 계속 다그쳐라

Keep it that way
> ↳ 그렇게(하기로) 하자

Keep things within bounds
> ↳ 일의 한계(범위)를 벗어나지마

Keep your finger on the pulse of Seoul
> ↳ 서울에서 무슨 일이 일어나고 있는지 주시해

Keep your nose out of it
> ↳ 그 문제엔 좀 빠져 줘

Keep yourself on the right track
> ↳ 똑바로 해나가란 말이야

Leaf through this and see if there's anything wrong
> ↳ 이걸 쭉 훑어보고 틀린 데가 있는지 봐

Leave a two and half centimeter margin on the right hand side
> ↳ 용지의 왼쪽에 2.5센티의 여백을 남겨라

Leave him to his own devices
> ↳ 멋대로 하게 내버려둬

› **rough** not smooth, not calm, harsh, violent,
   or rugged, crudely or hastily done

Leave things as they are
ㄴ 현재 그대로 놔둬

Light(Build) a fire under him to get this taken care of immediately
ㄴ 당장 이 일을 처리하려면 그를 정신이 번쩍 나게 해줘야 해

Lots of innocent people on his sucker list
ㄴ 많은 죄 없는 사람들이 그의 희생양 명부에 올라있다

Many difficulties lie behind us, but greater ones lie ahead
ㄴ 많은 어려움이 지나갔지만 이보다 더한 어려움이 다가오고 있다

Many is the time that we haven't had enough to eat
ㄴ 우리가 충분히 먹을 게 없던 때가 많이 있었다

Marshall is well versed in things Korean, chapter and verse
ㄴ 마셜은 한국에 대해서 속속들이 잘 알고 있어

Maybe some other time
ㄴ 그러면 다음 기회에 하지 뭐

Min-ho was caught napping
ㄴ 민호가 방심하다 당했지

**Min-soo must have got my wires crossed, because that's not the way
I understood it**
ㄴ 내가 알고 있는 것과 다른 것을 보니 민수가 잘못 알고 있음이 틀림
없어

Monkey see, monkey do
ㄴ 남의 흉내를 내고있단 말이군

Moon-ho knows no better
ㄴ 문호가 아는 건 그 정도야

Moon-soo is expected to turn up at any moment
ㄴ 문수는 금방이라도 나타날 거야

› **verse**　line or stanza of poetry, poetry, short
division of a chapter in the Bible

More is meant than meets the ear
    ↳ 언외의 뜻이 있다

Much right you have to interfere with me!
    ↳ 내게 간섭할 권리가 많기도 하겠다(네가 뭔데…)

My butt is on fire
    ↳ 발등에 불이 떨어졌어

My fingers have been burned
    ↳ 내가 혼 줄이 났지

My gut tells me the same
    ↳ 나도 같은 예감이야

My hunch was right on the nose
    ↳ 내 예감이 적중했다

My mind is torn between the two choices
    ↳ 이럴까 저럴까 망설이는 중이야

Myself poor, I understand the situation
    ↳ 나 자신도 가난하기에 그 사정이야 알지

Myung-soo made a mess when trying to make a wooden box as he was not a carpenter
    ↳ 명수는 목수가 아니었기에 나무상자를 만들 때 엉망이 되었다

No matter how dry a desert may be, it's not necessarily worthless
    ↳ 사막이 아무리 메마르더라도 반드시 가치 없는 것은 아니다

No matter what happens, he always has an out
    ↳ 무슨 일이 일어나도 그는 늘 빠질 구멍을 준비해 놓고 있어

No resource was left for us
    ↳ 속수무책이었지

› **hunch**   assume or cause to assume a bent or crooked posture

› **carpenter**   one who builds with wood

Nobody but I know it
> ↳ 나 빼곤 아무도 몰랐어

Nobody but you know of it
> ↳ 너 외에는 아는 사람이 없어

Nobody can predict what course he'll follow at any moment
> ↳ 그가 어떤 순간에 어떤 노선을 따를지 아무도 예측할 수 없다

Nobody has time(use) for such old-fashioned methods
> ↳ 요즘 그런 낡은 방식을 좋아하는 사람은 아무도 없다

Nobody make an objection to the new incinerator so long as it isn't in their own backyard
> ↳ 자기가 사는 인근이 아니라면 소각(화장)로 설치에 반대하는 사람은 없다

None of us know what lies in store for us
> ↳ 앞일이 어찌될지 몰라

Not a complain escaped his lips
> ↳ 불평 한마디 없었어

Not much further
> ↳ 이제 얼마 안 남았어

Not only did he hear it but he saw it as well
> ↳ 그는 그 말을 들었을 뿐만 아니라 보기도 했다

Nothing is easy to the unwilling
> ↳ 하기 싫은 일 치고 쉬운 일없다

Nothing is good for everyone, but only relatively to some people
> ↳ 모든 사람에게 좋은 일은 없으나 상대적으로 좋을 수는 있다

Now I'm back on my feet
> ↳ 이제 경제적으로 혼자 설 수 있어

› **incinerate** burn to ashes

Now I've seen everything
  ↳ 별 걸 다 보는군

Now it's kind of petering out
  ↳ 그게 지금은 용두사미가 되고있어

> '용두사미(龍頭蛇尾)'란 '작심삼일'과 비슷한 말이다. 거창하게 시작해 놓고 흐지부지 끝나는 것을 설명한 말이다. 영어로는 "Starts off with a bang and ends with a whimper 큰소리로 시작해서 낑낑대며 끝난다"이다.

Of course it's no such thing
  ↳ 물론 그건 앞에 말한 그런 건은 아니다

Once this tree has rooted in this soil, it should grow well
  ↳ 이 나무가 일단 뿌리를 내렸으니 잘 자랄 거야

Put a tail on him and don't let him get away
  ↳ 그를 미행시켜서 놓치지 마라

Put everything else in one side, and how hell, was I to know the gun was loaded
  ↳ 세상에 총에 실탄이 들어있는 줄을 어떻게 알았겠나

Put up or shut up
  ↳ 내기를 하던지(증거를 보이던지) 입을 다물던지 해

Remember, this room is out of bounds
  ↳ 이 방이 출입금지구역이란 걸 몰라?

Repeated attempts have been made without any noticeable result
  ↳ 여러 가지 해 봤지만 별로 효과가 없었어

Right now, the details are better unsaid
  ↳ 지금 당장은 상세한 것을 말하지 않고 놔두는 게 낫겠다

› **attempt** make an effort toward

Rock hounding is a closed book to me
└ 난 수석이라면 '수'자도 몰라

Run your fingers over that paper to see if it's been embossed
└ 그 종이가 돋을 새김이 되어있는지 더듬어 보아라

Running my eye down the page, I caught sight of several mistakes
└ 페이지를 쭉 훑어 내려가다가 잘못된 곳을 여러 개 찾아냈다

Safety comes first when it comes to construction
└ 건설공사에는 안전이 제일

Sales of that book was taken off the market within a few years
└ 그 책은 출간한지 얼마 안 가서 끊어졌다

Sang-soo knows the score
└ 상수는 빠삭하게 잘 안다

Sang-soo still has several shots in his locker
└ 상수는 아직도 몇 가지 비책(잔여 분, 여력)을 남겨두고 있다

She applied on the off chance
└ 그녀는 요행을 바라고 응모했다

She doesn't have a prayer
└ 그 여자는 가망이 없어

She doesn't know which end(way) is up
└ 그 여자는 뭐가 뭔지 몰라

She has another enemy at the gate
└ 그 여자에게는 또 다른 일이 발등에 떨어졌다

She has cheated and swindled to get what she wanted, tempting fate
└ 그 여자는 모험을 무릅쓰고 원하는 것을 얻기 위해 남들을 속이고 사기를 쳤다

She has her own reasons for complaining

· **emboss** ornament with raised work
· **swindle** cheat of money or property

↳ 그 여자가 불평을 하는데는 나름대로의 이유가 있다

She has stirred the pot

↳ 그 여자는 상황을 더욱 복잡하게 만들었다

She is here understood

↳ 여기에 '그 여자'는 생략돼 있어

She is not what she seems

↳ 그 여자는 속에 뭔가 감추고 있어

She'll find some way to beat the rap

↳ 그 여자는 빠져나갈 구멍을 찾아낼 거야

She'll give you as good as she gets

↳ 그 여자는 네게 당하고 가만있지 않을 것이다

She'll go the distance

↳ 그 여자는 끝까지 해낼 거야

She'll go to any length(go all length)

↳ 그 여자는 무슨 일이고(철저히) 할거야

She'll make it up to you

↳ 그 여자는 네가 하자는 대로 할 거야

She'll put the bite on you

↳ 그 여자가 네게 졸라 댈 거다

She'll stay with it until it is

↳ 그 여자는 그 일을 끝낼 때까지 계속할 것이다

She's always imagining things

↳ 그 여자는 늘 있지도 않은 일을 멋대로 상상해

She's always ranting and raving about trifles

↳ 그 여자는 늘 시시콜콜한 일로 야단법석이야

› **rave** talk wildly in or as if in delirium
› **trifle** something of little value or importance

She's at zero hour right now
> ↳ 그 여자는 지금 결정적 순간에 와 있다

She's been counting the hours(days) since that day
> ↳ 그 여자는 그 날 이후 일각이 여삼추로(하루가 멀다하고) 기다리고 있다

She's been laboring under that mistaken idea for years now
> ↳ 그 여자는 수년동안 그런 착각 속에 빠져 있는 거야

She's getting tired of going on in the same grooves
> ↳ 그녀는 구습대로 고수해 나가는 데 지쳐있어

She's going to see the way winds are blowing
> ↳ 그 여자는 돌아가는 낌새를 살피려고 할거야

She's gone off to find herself a better hole
> ↳ 그 여자는 더 나은 곳을 찾아 떠났어

She's on top of current affairs
> ↳ 그 여자는 시사문제에 훤해

She's seeing straws in the wind
> ↳ 그 여자는 시대의 흐름을 보고 있는 거야

She's the big one that got away
> ↳ 그 여자는 잡았다 놓친 대어란 말이야

Since that day he has never looked back
> ↳ 그 날 이후 그는 결코 주저하지 않았다

So much for the easy part
> ↳ 쉬운 일은 간단히 해치웠어

Some folks must have been burning their ears tonight
> ↳ 오늘밤 누구누구는 남들의 입방아에 오른줄 알고 몹시 궁금해하겠군

Someday I'll manage to get it(all) together

› **groove** fixed routine

› **straw** grass stems after grain is removed, tube for drinking

↳ 머지 않아 나도 주변정리하고 정상으로 되돌아 갈 거야

Sometimes I can be careless and blind

↳ 가끔은 내가 덤벙거리고 멍청할 때가 있어

Soon-ho is up to here with it

↳ 순호는 그 일에 질려버렸어

Speculation ran high as to the result

↳ 결과에 대해 억측이 구구했지

Stay out of it, you don't have any say-so in this matter

↳ 넌 이 일에 발언(결정)권이 없으니 빠져 줘

Such is the case with me

↳ 나의 사정은 이렇다

Sung-gyoo doesn't know he's coming or going

↳ 성규는 할까 말까 하고 망설이고 있어

Sung-ho never ceased boasting of his skill

↳ 성호는 자기 솜씨를 두고두고 자랑했어

Sung-ho tried all manners of ways

↳ 성호는 모든 방법을 동원했어

Sung-mi got it for a song

↳ 성미는 그걸 거저 줍다시피 했어

Tai-ho just came in cold

↳ 태호는 준비 없이 왔어(**It's difficult to wing it** 즉흥적으로 해내긴 어려워)

Tai-ho tore down(along) the street

↳ 태호는 거리를 달려왔다

That complicates the matter

↳ 그 때문에 일이 복잡해지고 있어

› **speculate**   think about things yet unknown, risk money in a business deal   in hope of high profit

That doesn't excuse any of it
ㄴ 그걸로 모든 것이 용서될 수 없겠지

That guy is still a unknown quantity
ㄴ 저 사람에 대해선 아직 아는 바 없어

That guy must have put up a smoke screen to hide something
ㄴ 저 녀석이 뭔가를 숨기려고 연막을 친 게 틀림없어

That information has not yet passed his lips
ㄴ 아직 그에게서 그런 정보가 나온 일은 없어

That is a real chicken-and-egg problem
ㄴ 인과관계를 알 수 없는 일

That jumps with the spirit of the age
ㄴ 그건 시대정신과 일치해

That proves she's equal to the occasion
ㄴ 그게 바로 그 여자가 어떤 상황에도 잘 대처한다는 걸 보여주고 있어

That saves me a trip
ㄴ 내가 안가도 되겠군

That shall be my care
ㄴ 그건 내가 맡지

That takes the cake
ㄴ 그런 것은 들은 일이 없어

That was before your time
ㄴ 그건 네가 태어나기 전의 일이야

That was the(one) thing of all others he wanted to see(have)
ㄴ 그것은 다른 무엇보다도 그가 보고(갖고) 싶어했던 바로 그것이었다

That which needs to be proved can't be worth much
ㄴ 증명을 필요로 하는 일은 그다지 가치 있는 일이 아니다

› **quantity** something that can be measured
or numbered, considerable amount

That will fix his wagon
↳ 그걸로 그 사람은 혼 날거다

That'll take the wind out of her sails
↳ 그건 그를 쩔쩔매게 할거야

That's enough. Hold back. Save some for the others
↳ 이거면 됐어. 그만해. 다른 사람 몫도 남겨놔야지

That's just a shot in the dark
↳ 그건 억측에 불과해

That's more than can be said of me
↳ 그건 내겐 해당되지 않아

That's nothing to rave about
↳ 그까짓 것 가지고 뭘 큰소리냐

That's our case
↳ 그게 우리의 입장이야

That's the umpteenth time that I have told you to do that
↳ 그걸 해 놓으라고 몇 번씩이나 말해야 알겠니

That's to be expected
↳ 그건 있을 수 있는 일이다

That's what it says right there
↳ 바로 거기 적힌 그대로야

That's where it is at
↳ 상황이 그래

(=That's the way the situation is)

· **umpteenth** very numerous

That'll be the day
　　└ 그런 일은 절대 없을 거야

That's a clincher
　　└ 할 말은 더 이상 없다

The amount is so small that it hardly counts
　　└ 양이 너무 적어서 문제가 안 돼

The ball is in your court now
　　└ 이제 칼자루는 네게 있다

The benefits are denied me
　　└ 내겐 그런 혜택이 주어지지 않아

The bird is(has) flown
　　└ 그는 날아가 버렸어(범인, 빚쟁이, 애인 등)

The biter is bit(bitten)
　　└ 혹 떼려다가 혹 붙여

The buck stops here
　　└ 결정은 내가 한다. 모든 책임은 내가 진다

The cards are stacked against(in favor of) me
　　└ 난 불리(유리)한 입장

The criticism should be accompanied by suggestions of alternative solutions
　　└ 비판에는 대안이 될 해법이 제시되어야 한다

The detail needs to be ironed out
　　└ 세부사항은 조정돼야해

The difference between this and that is one of degree, not kind
　　└ 이것과 저것은 정도의 차이지 종류의 차이가 아니다

› **alternative** offering a choice

The entrance is marked with an arrow
> ↳ 입구 표지는 화살표로 되어있다

The experiment didn't pan out well as we hoped
> ↳ 그 실험은 우리가 바랐던 만큼 잘되지 않았어

The final test of a leader is that he leaves behind him in other men the conviction and the will to carry on
> ↳ 지도자에 대한 최종 평가는 그가 다른 사람들에게 남겨놓은 확신과 그 확신을 실행하려고 했던 의지이다

The first step is always the hardest
> ↳ 뭐든지 처음이 어렵다

The most useful thing about a principle is that it can always be sacrificed to expediency
> ↳ 원칙을 지키는데 가장 유용함은 언제나 편의의 희생물이 될 수 있다

The most vulnerable and yet most unconquerable of things is human vanity
> ↳ 가장 취약하면서도 가장 제어하기 어려운 것이 인간의 허영심이다

The new building has been changed from the ground up
> ↳ 새 건물은 근본부터(철저히) 고쳐졌어

The new road will pass over the dangerous railroad crossing
> ↳ 위험한 철도 건널목 위로 도로가 지나가게 될 것이다

The only shame is to have none
> ↳ 유일한 수치는 한 번도 부끄러운 일을 해 본적이 없다는 것이다

The plane made a smooth landing
> ↳ 비행기는 사뿐히 착륙했다

The reason is not far to seek
> ↳ 그 이유는 간단해

› **vulnerable** susceptible to attack or damage | › **vanity** futility or something that is futile, undue pride in oneself

The rest can be pictured to yourself
　　ㄴ 나머지는 네 상상에 맡기지

The reward of one duty done is the power to fulfill another
　　ㄴ 의무를 이행함에 따른 보상은 다른 의무를 하나 더 수행할 수 있게되는 힘이다

The same is true of everything
　　ㄴ 다른 모든 경우에도 마찬가지

The shoe is on the other foot
　　ㄴ 상황은 역전되었어

The situation is capable of improvement
　　ㄴ 사태는 개선의 여지가 있다

The situation is much the same with us
　　ㄴ 우리도 사정은 매 한가지야

The situation was embarrassing enough without having you rub it in
　　ㄴ 네가 몇 번이고 되풀이 말하지 않았더라도 사태가 난처하다는 것은 충분히 알고 있어

The solution is not far to seek
　　ㄴ 해답은 가까이 있어

The tide will turn to(against) you soon
　　ㄴ 형세는 곧 네게 유(불)리하게 될 것이다

The two sides are not even
　　ㄴ 양쪽이 똑같지 않아

The unknown always passes for the marvellous
　　ㄴ 알지 못하는 것은 늘 신기한 것으로 통한다

The urgent business forced him to deny himself to all callers
　　ㄴ 그는 급한 용무로 모든 방문객의 면회를 사절할 수밖에 없었다

› **marvellous**　surprising or amazing
› **urgent**　calling for immediate attention

The whole plan blew up
↳ 그 계획 모두가 무산되었다

The will is as good as the deed
↳ 무슨 일이나 의지가 중요

The worst is behind me now
↳ 이제 고비는 넘겼다

The worst of it is behind you and you can look forward to the future
↳ 그 일에서 최악의 상황은 끝났으니 이제 앞만 쳐다봐도 돼

Their aspersions, mud-sling and blackmail will be sure to backfire
↳ 그들의 비난, 중상모략, 공갈은 틀림없이 역효과가 날 것이다

Their hospitality was such as rarely experienced elsewhere
↳ 그들의 환대는 다른 곳에서는 좀처럼 볼 수 없는 것이었다

Their number amounts to eight hundred(hundreds가 아님)
↳ 그 수는 800가량 돼

Their plans haven't crystallized yet
↳ 그들의 계획은 아직 구체화되지 않았다

Theory and practice do not always go hand in hand
↳ 이론과 실제가 반드시 동행하지는 않아

There are always blind spots
↳ 언제나 맹점은 있게 마련이다

There are always wheels within wheels
↳ 옥상 옥(따로 승낙 받아야 할 일)은 늘 있는 법이거든

There are extenuating circumstances
↳ 거기엔 사정이 좀 있어

› **aspersion** remark that hurts someone's reputation

› **mud-sling** using invective against a political opponent

There are things you can't do for yourself
  ↳ 중이 제 머리 못 깎는다

There are two sides of every coin
  ↳ 모든 일에 양면성이 있다

There can be no progress if people have no faith in tomorrow
  ↳ 내일에 대한 신뢰가 없으면 진보가 없다

There is an edge to his voice this time
  ↳ 이번엔 그의 목소리에 심각함이 담겨있어

There is but one way open to us
  ↳ 우리의 나아갈 길은 하나 뿐이다

There is measure in all things
  ↳ 모든 일에 한계가 있다

(=There's a limit to everything)

There is no need to make a meal of it
  ↳ 그 정도 일로 힘들다고 엄살해야 소용없어

There isn't the least danger
  ↳ 위험은 전혀 없어(**There's not the least danger** : 적지 않은 위험이 있다. 발음시 **not**에 강세)

There lies difficulty
  ↳ 거기가 어려운 대목이다

There may be a remote possibility
  ↳ 만에 하나 있을까 말까한 일이다

There must be some gimmick
  ↳ 난 그게 사실이라고 생각지 않아

▸ **remote** far off in place or time, hard to reach or find, slight, distant in manner

▸ **gimmick** new and ingenious scheme, feature, or device

There you are
ㄴ 일의 결말이 이럴 수밖에 더 있겠니

There's a first time for everything
ㄴ 누구나 언젠가는 해보게(겪게) 될 것이다

There's a possibility of examples existing
ㄴ 선례가 있을 가능성도 있다

There's a way out of every situation, however bad
ㄴ 하늘이 무너져도 솟아날 구멍은 있다

There's been a big complication
ㄴ 일이 굉장히 꼬였어

There's been a lot of water under the bridge
ㄴ 이런 저런 일들이 많이 있었지

There's been times I'm confused
ㄴ 마음을 정하지 못한 때도 있었어

There's got to be a way
ㄴ 뭔가 방법이 있을 거야

There's movement all around
ㄴ 여기저기 사람들이 북적거려

There's never a dull moment
ㄴ 숨 쉴 틈도 없어

There's no blinking the fact that it would only aggravate the situation
ㄴ 그렇게 했다가는 사태를 악화시킬 뿐이라는 사실을 무시해서는 안 된다

There's no good in arguing with the inevitable
ㄴ 어쩔 수 없는 일을 가지고 왈가왈부해봤자 소용없다

There's no knowing how it'll come out
ㄴ 어떻게 될지 몰라

› **blink** wink, shine intermittently
› **aggravate** make more severe, irritate

There's no knowing what the future may bring forth
> ㄴ 다가올 일은 몰라

There's no need to kill yourself
> ㄴ 너무 무리할 필요 없어

There's no point in digging further for more information
> ㄴ 애써 더 이상 정보를 얻으려는 건 무의미해

There's no point in running our head against a brick wall
> ㄴ 우린 오르지도 못할 나무는 쳐다볼 필요도 없잖아

There's no precedent for it and the rest is history
> ㄴ 그 일은 선례가 없던 일이고 그 후의 일은 아시는 바와 같습니다

There's no real force without justice
> ㄴ 도리가 없이는 참된 힘을 발휘할 수 없다

There's no turning back
> ㄴ 이제 와서 돌이킬 수 없어

There's not much chance of that happening
> ㄴ 그건 하늘의 별 따기지

(=It's like asking for the moon)
(=The chances of that happening are one in a million(slim))

There's only just enough room to brush past in the crowd
> ㄴ 사람들 때문에 겨우 부딪치며 지나갈 틈밖에 없었다

These seeds germinated and sprouts shot up rapidly
> ㄴ 이들 종자는 발아해서 싹이 빨리 자랐다

These two things can't be mentioned in the same breath
> ㄴ 이 두 가지는 내용이 다른 얘기

› **precedent** something said or done earlier that serves as an example   › **germinate** begin to develop

They can rub along(through) somehow, although there's difficult time ahead
> ↳ 앞으로 그들에게 어려움이 있겠지만 그럭저럭 헤쳐나갈 수 있을 거야

They cut down trees and hollowed them out to make canoes
> ↳ 그들은 나무를 베어 넘기고 속을 파내어 커누를 만들었다

They don't want to jump on the bandwagon to be with it
> ↳ 그들은 단지 유행을 따르기 위해 시류에 편승하기를 원하지는 않아

They exhausted every possibility(possible means)
> ↳ 그들은 가능한 일은 다 해봤어

They have only kept it warm for you
> ↳ 그들은 그걸 네게 넘겨주려고 임시 대역을 하고 있었던 것 뿐이야

They jump on the bandwagon no matter what the cause is
> ↳ 그들은 대의(주의) 따위엔 상관없이 시류에 편승한다

They prefer the devil they know to the devil they don't
> ↳ 그들은 매를 맞아도 알고 맞는 것이 모르고 맞는 것 보다 좋다고 여긴다

They seem to be holding their fire
> ↳ 그들은 적절한 때를 기다리고 있는 것 같다

They should see the matter against the background of what has happened before
> ↳ 그들은 이전에 일어난 일에 비추어 생각해야해

They showed a distinct lack of enthusiasm when he told them his plan
> ↳ 그가 그들에게 그의 계획을 말하자 열의가 없음을 분명히 보여줬다

They want to walk before they run
> ↳ 그들은 단계별로 나아가길 원한다(기지도 못하면서 날려고 하지 않아)

› **hollow** having a cavity within

› **bandwagon** candidate, side, or movement gaining support

They were not themselves for some time
> ↳ 그들은 잠시 멍하니 있었어

They'd like to get this plan going
> ↳ 그들은 이 일이 추진되기를 바란다

Things are gliding back into bad ways
> ↳ 사태가 또 다시 나쁜 길로 가고 있어

Things are not what they used to be
> ↳ 만사가 예전 같지 않다

Things don't swing into high gear before noon
> ↳ 정오가 돼야 본격적으로 시작돼

Things past can't be recalled
> ↳ 지나간 일은 되돌릴 수 없다

Thirty years ago there might not have been a dry eye in the house
> ↳ **30**년 전이었다면(여기 모인)모든 사람이 눈물을 흘렸을 것이다

This can't be happening
> ↳ 귀신이 곡할 노릇이군

> (=I can't believe what's going on)
> (=This is unbelievable)

This couldn't have happened at a worse time
> ↳ 이렇게 안 좋을 때 이런 일이 일어나다니

This is not a thing to be passed over in silence
> ↳ 침묵하고 묵과할 일이 아니다

This kind of grass dies back every year
> ↳ 이런 풀은 매년 땅 위 부분이 말라죽고 뿌리에서 새싹이 나

›**gear** clothing, equipment, toothed wheel
that interlocks with another for
transmitting motion

This kind of thing bring out the best(worst) in me
> ↳ 이런 일은 나의 최선(악)을 발휘시키는(드러내게 하는) 일이다

This ticket is invalid if marked, rubbed, torn or otherwise defaced
> ↳ 이 표는 표시가 되어있거나 아니면 다르게 외관이 손상되어 있으면 무효가 된다

This time I'll not let you go
> ↳ 이번엔 사정 안 봐줄 거야

To become a popular religion, it's only necessary for a superstition to enslave a philosophy
> ↳ 인기 있는 종교가 되기 위해서는 반드시 미신이 철학을 노예로 삼아 야만 된다

Trim your plants regularly and don't let them grow too large and unwieldy
> ↳ 나무들을 정기적으로 다듬고 너무 자라서 다루기 어렵게 놔두지 마라

Tropical orchids are found in all shapes and sizes, and have a wide color range
> ↳ 열대성 난은 여러 가지 형태가 있고 색상도 다양하다

Try to find out what's the history on it
> ↳ 그 일의 연유를 알아봐

Try to find some place off the beaten track
> ↳ 사람들이 잘 안 다니는 곳을 찾아봐라

Try to get a grip on all the facts first
> ↳ 사실을 먼저 파악해야해

Try to look at things from where you are standing and be more tolerant
> ↳ 모든 일을 네가 처한 상황에서 생각하고 너그럽게 대하라

› **unwieldy** too big or awkward to manage easily

› **orchid** plant with showy 3-petal flowers or its flower

Under the circumstances, I can't do anything about it
   ↳ 사정이 사정이니 어쩔 수 없어

> (=I don't have any choice)
> (=There's nothing I can do)

Variety takes away satiety
   ↳ 다양성은 싫증을 물리친다
View the matter in the right light
   ↳ 사태를 바르게 보라

> (=Watch the development of affairs)

Wake up and smell the coffee
   ↳ 뒷다리 긁지마(상황판단을 제대로 하라)(**=keep up with the program**)

We all know better
   ↳ 우리가 그걸 모를 바보는 아니지

We are apt to overlook something worthwhile close at hand
   ↳ 우린 흔히 등잔 밑이 어두운 격이 되기 쉬워

> 바로 곁에 있는 것을 찾지 못할 때에 쓰이는 표현이다. 서양에서는 "그것이
> 뱀이라면 당신을 물겠다"라고 하고, 이는 뱀이 물 정도로 가까이 있는데도 알
> 아채지 못한다는 뜻이다(The husband is always the last to know 등잔
> 밑이 어둡다).

We are never so easily deceived as when we imagine we are deceiving

---

· **satiate** satisfy fully, surfeit

· **overlook** look down on, fail to see, ignore

others
> ↳ 남을 속이고 있다고 생각하고 생각할 때만큼 쉽게 우리자신이 속아넘어갈 때가 없다

We are playing for keeps, be careful of what you do
> ↳ 따먹은 건 돌려주지 않기로 하는 거니까 잘 알아서 해

We built(made) a fire under his feet, but it did no good
> ↳ 우린 그에게 자극을 줘봤지만 소용이 없었어

We can row a lot faster if we synchronize our strokes
> ↳ 우리가 팔의 움직임을 일치시키면 더 빨리 노를 저어갈 수 있을 것이다

We can't rest on our laurels
> ↳ 여기서 만족할 수는 없어

We carefully planned for almost every possibility
> ↳ 우린 거의 모든 가능성에 대비하여 만전을 기했다

We checked her into the hospital for two days
> ↳ 우린 그 여자를 이틀 간 입원 시켰다

We do not wish people or things we find amusing to be other than they are
> ↳ 우린 재미있는 사람들이나 물건들이 있는 그대로이기를 바란다

We don't all get our deserts
> ↳ 우린 당연한 보상을 얻지 못하는 경우도 있어

We got a classified situation
> ↳ 이건 극비상황이야

We got nowhere
> ↳ 결론을 얻지 못했어

We have come too far to turn back now
> ↳ 그만 두기엔 너무 늦었어

› **synchronize** occur or cause to occur at the same instant, cause to agree in time

We have some weakness in our program, but if we act too hastily we may cause the baby thrown out with the bath
> ↳ 우리 계획에 약간의 약점은 있지만 너무 조급히 굴다간 빈대 한 마리 잡다가 초가삼간 태우는 꼴이 돼

We have to shop around for an alternative
> ↳ 우린 대안을 찾아야해

We live in an age when birth and extraction are of no(little) account
> ↳ 지금은 가문을 따지는 시대가 아니다

We managed to break even
> ↳ 우린 겨우 본전 챙겼어

We may with advantage at times forget what we know
> ↳ 알고 있는 것을 잊어버리는 것이 유리할 때가 있다

We might have to call it quits
> ↳ 없었던 일로 해야할지 모르겠어

We must discriminate between the two cases
> ↳ 그것과 이것은 경우가 달라

We must harden our hearts and ignore them
> ↳ 우린 마음을 단단히 먹고 그런 일을 무시해야해

We need to remember that it can happen here
> ↳ 우린 그런 일을 남의 일이 아님을 잊지 말아야해

We need to talk to someone who has inside information
> ↳ 내부사정을 잘 아는 사람에게 알아봐야해

We often get in quicker by the back door than by the front
> ↳ 우리는 뒷문으로 들어가는 것이 앞문으로 들어가는 것보다 빠를 때가 흔히 있다

We shall never hear the last of it

› **discriminate** distinguish, show favor or disfavor unjustly

↳ 그건 언제까지나 사람들의 얘기 거리로 남을 것이다

We shall never see his like again
↳ 그와 같은 사람을 다시는 볼 수 없을 것이다

We shall see how things turn out
↳ 사태가 어찌 될지 곧 알게 될 것이다

We shall see what we shall see
↳ 일의 결과는 아무도 몰라

We should follow the instructions to the letter
↳ 우린 지시를 정확히 따라야 해

We should give him some head
↳ 그가 스스로 결정하게 해야 한다

We should have a fair crack of the whip
↳ 우리에게 공정한 기회가 주어져야 한다

We shouldn't get a swelled head about it
↳ 우리가 그 일로 우쭐해선 안 돼

We took care to preserve the trees where their presence was necessary
↳ 우리는 꼭 필요한 곳에 있는 나무를 보호하도록 주의했다

We'd better see which way the cat jumps
↳ 상황을 보고 판단하자

We've got a long way to go yet
↳ 지금부터가 큰 일이다

Well, he had done it this time
↳ 음, 이번엔 그가 일을 저질렀군

Well, the fat is in the fire now
↳ 그렇다면 큰일이 생겼군 그래

‣ **whip** move quickly, strike with something
slender and flexible, defeat

What followed is doubtful
> ↳ 그 뒤에 어떻게 되었는지 몰라

What has he got that I haven't got
> ↳ 그는 잘 되는데 나만 왜 안 되는 거지

What the eye sees not, the ear craves not
> ↳ 견물생심

좋은 물건을 보면 가지고 싶은 마음이 생기게 마련이다. 거기다 관리까지 허술하다면 다른 사람으로 하여금 도둑질을 하고 싶은 충동을 느끼게 한다. 비슷한 뜻으로 "A postern door makes a thief 뒷문이 도적을 만든다"도 쓰인다.

When did the old tree blow down?
> ↳ 저 큰 나무가 언제 바람에 쓰러졌지?

When going is tough, Dong-soo can always be depended on to carry the ball
> ↳ 일이 어렵게 되면 언제나 동수가 총대를 메게 된다

When I get all that out of my system, I'll feel much better
> ↳ 그걸 전부 배설하고 나면 훨씬 좋아질 것 같아

When she cries she gives it all she's got
> ↳ 그 여자가 울음을 터뜨리면 실컷 울어버린다

Wherever anyone is against his will, that's to him a prison
> ↳ 어디서나 본인의 뜻에 어긋나는 곳이면 거기가 그의 감옥이다

Whether she carries on or not is all in the mind
> ↳ 그 여자가 해낼 수 있을지는 그 여자의 마음(의지)에 달렸다

Who would expect things to come to this(such a pass)
> ↳ 일이 이렇게 될 줄 누가 알았으랴

› **expect** look forward to, consider probable
or one's due

Why don't you take a page from Chang-soo and do what he does
└ 창수 하는 걸 본 받아 그가 하는 대로 해 보렴

Wild horses can't draw any information out of him
└ 항우가 와도 저 사람에게서 정보는 캐내지 못해

You are led to reflect on what you have done
└ 네가 한 일을 반성하게 되었단 말이군

You are long way out if you think that
└ 그리 생각한다면 한참 오산하고 있는 거야

You are really missing out
└ 넌 좋은 기회를 놓치는 거야

You are running the chance
└ 한번 해보겠다 이말 이군

You are the one who calls the shot
└ 네가 결정권을 가진 사람이잖아

You can hardly generalize from only a few instances
└ 한 두 번 있었던 일에 비추어 일반적으로 그럴 것이라고 추단 하기는 어려워

You can't depend on your judgement when your imagination is out of focus
└ 상상이 초점을 벗어날 때는 자신의 판단을 믿을 수 없다

You can't go swimming without getting wet
└ 호랑이 굴에 들어가야 호랑이를 잡는다

You can't have such a windfall every day
└ 그런 횡재가 흔해빠진 줄 아니?

You can't make me stay
└ 날 붙들어 둘 순 없어

› **generalize**   reach a general conclusion especially on the basis of | particular instances

You caught me unprepared

    ㄴ 네게 허를 찔렸네

You don't have to spoon-feed me

    ㄴ 나를 한두 살 먹은 어린애로 아나. 일일이 내게 일러주지 않아도 돼

You don't know the half of it

    ㄴ 넌 상황을 잘 몰라서 그러는군. 그게 전부가 아냐

Were born with a silver spoon in your mouth

    ㄴ 넌 복에 겨워서 무엇이 불행인지 모르고 있는 거야

You don't know you are sitting on a volcano

    ㄴ 넌 위태로운 상황에 처한걸 모르는군

You don't know your ass from your elbow=You don't know your left hand from your right hand

    ㄴ 일의 진행을 파악하지 못하고 있군

You finally got even with him

    ㄴ 너 드디어 그에게 복수했구나

You fob off everything on to others

    ㄴ 넌 무슨 일이나 남에게 뒤집어씌우기만 하는군

You forget your privilege carries great responsibilities with it

    ㄴ 특권에 책임이 따른다는 것을 잊고 있군

You have come none too soon

    ㄴ 넌 정말 때 맞춰 왔구나

You have come to the parting of the ways

    ㄴ 넌 기로에 선거야

You have excessive concern for your face

    ㄴ 넌 체면을 너무 차리는구나

· **spoon-feed** present information to completely as to preclude in-   independent thought

You have hold on to yourself not to scream
↳ 소리를 지르지 않도록 자제해야 해

You have no idea what it is like for me
↳ 그게 어떤 건지 넌 몰라(입장이 다르니까)

You have only yourself to thank for it
↳ 그건 다 네 탓이야

You have to be on the ball
↳ 빠릿빠릿해야 해

You have to bluff yourself out of this mess
↳ 넌 요령 있게(속임수로라도) 이 난장판에서 빠져나가야 해

You have to even off(out) this surface
↳ 이 표면을 반반하게 해야 해

You have to go while the going is good
↳ 형편이 좋을 때 떠나야 해

You have to hold your end up
↳ 네 몫은 해야 해

You have to like it or lump it
↳ 싫어도 할 수 없어

You have to prove to everyone you weren't born yesterday
↳ 넌 모든 사람에게 바보가 아님을 보여줘야 해

You have to put up with it
↳ 그런 건 감수해야 해

> (=You just have to endure(overlook) it)

› **scream** cry out loudly and shrilly

You have to roll with the punches
↳ 유연하게 대처해야 해

You have to sink or swim
↳ 넌 성패간에 자력으로 헤쳐나가야 해

You have to take the fall for him if he pays you enough
↳ 그가 네게 충분히 보상해 준다면 그의 일에 책임을 져야 해

You have to take(answer for) the consequences
↳ 결과에 책임져야 해

You have to work through channels
↳ 넌 절차를 밟아야 해

You haven't seen anything yet
↳ 이제부터가 시작이야

You hit the nail right on the head
↳ 넌 정곡을 찔렀어

You learn something new everyday
↳ 그건(내가) 몰랐던 일이야

You look like the cat that ate canary
↳ 눈감고 아웅이군

> 'The cat that ate the canary 카나리아를 잡아먹은 고양이'란 한국 속담
> 으로 표현하면 "눈감고 아웅한다"이다. 이는 자신이 잘못한 일을 다른 사람이
> 모를 것이라 생각하고 시치미 떼는 상황을 말한다. 영어 속담은 주인이 아끼
> 는 카나리아를 잡아먹고 시치미 떼는 고양이에 비유하였다.

You may have this for keeps
↳ 네게 주마(가져도 좋아)

› **canary** yellow or greenish finch

You may spring news on her now that the prize will be awarded to her
> ↳ 넌 지금 그 여자에게 입상하게 될 것이라는 놀라운 소식을 얘기해도 돼

You missed the bus(point)
> ↳ 기회(요점)를 놓쳤군

You mix things up
> ↳ 넌 일을 뒤죽박죽으로 하는구나

You must have got your signals crossed
> ↳ 네가 틀림없이 잘못 알렸구나

You must think I'm something
> ↳ 제가 특별하다고 생각하나보죠

You need a strong stomach to overcome your weakness
> ↳ 너의 약점을 극복하려면 다부진 마음이 필요해

You never know what is enough unless you know what is more than enough
> ↳ 얼마나 많아야 필요이상으로 많은 것인지 알지 못하면 얼마나 있어야 충분한 것인지 모른다

You screwed up
> ↳ 네가 다 망쳤잖아

You see things in perspective
> ↳ 넌 사물을 보는 눈이 바르구나

You seem to be getting off the point
> ↳ 아무래도 주제를 벗어난 것 같습니다

You shall not serve me that trick twice
> ↳ 두 번 다시 그런 수에 안 넘어간다

You shall smart for this

· **perspective** apparent depth and distance in painting, view of things in their true relationship or importance

↳ 나중에 혼날 줄 알아라

You shall want for nothing

↳ 아쉬운 것 없이 해 주지

You should be prepared to follow it through

↳ 끝까지 해낼 태세가 되어 있어야 해

You should carry yourself well

↳ 훌륭하게 행동해야 해

You should keep to the straight and narrow

↳ 넌 근신하며 지내야 해

You should take things as they are

↳ 넌 현 상태에 만족해야 해

You sniffed around in the wrong area

↳ 넌 헛다리 짚었어

> (=You headed in the wrong direction)
> (=You didn't look in the right area)

You will be grounded

↳ 금족령이야

You will have to go through the proper channels

↳ 올바른 절차를 밟으셔야지요

You won't know until the results come out

↳ 뚜껑을 열어봐야 알아

> (=Nothing is definite until the results come out)

› **sniff** draw air audibly up the nose, detect
by smelling

You would see things differently if you put yourself in my place
> ↳ 네가 내 입장이라면 시각이 달라질 거다

You'd better cut your losses
> ↳ 손해가 적은 때에 손떼는 게 나아

You'd better keep your ears to the ground
> ↳ 상황 판단을 잘 해야 해

You'd better not show your face around here
> ↳ 넌 이제 이 근처에 얼씬도 안 하는 게 좋아

You'd better sit this one out
> ↳ 이번엔 좀 빠져 줘

You'd better start afresh with a clean slate
> ↳ 백지로 돌아가 새 출발하는 게 나아

You'd get out while the getting is good
> ↳ 빠져나갈 수 있을 때 빠져나가야 해

You'd light(let) up on him
> ↳ 그 사람에게 웬만큼 해 둬(부담을 줄여 줘)

You'll have to gild(sugar) the pill by telling him that he's doing such valuable work here that he can't be spared
> ↳ 그가 없으면 안 되는 값진 일을 하게 되는 것이라고 그를 잘 구슬려 둬야 할 것이다

You'll have to keep on(at) Bong-soo if you get anything done
> ↳ 무슨 일이고 하려면 봉수에게 자꾸 다그쳐야 해

You'll hear about this
> ↳ 넌 나중에 이 일로 꾸지람들을 거야

You'll hear from us, one way or the other
> ↳ 결과가 어떻든 알려 드리겠습니다

‣ **slate** dense fine-grained layered rock, roofing tile or writing tablet of slate

‣ **gild** cover with or as if with gold

You'll hear of this

↳ 추후에 알려 줄게

You'll take what's coming to you, whatever you do

↳ 무슨 일을 하던지 그 결과는 네게 돌아오게 돼 있어

You're always busy in other people's affairs

↳ 넌 늘 남의 일에 끼어 들고 있어

You're always playing me for a fool. I know better

↳ 날 항상 바보취급하고 있군. 그 정도는 나도 알아

You're asking for a good hiding(trouncing)

↳ 넌 호된 변을 자초하고 있어

You're now caught in a trap

↳ 넌 독 안에 든 쥐다

> 사방으로 막혀서 도망 갈 곳이 없는 사람을 보고 "독 안에 든 쥐다"라고 한다. 영어로는 'A rat in a trap 덫에 걸린 쥐'라고 한다. 쥐에 관한 속담은 영어와 한국 속담이 비슷하다. "쥐 죽은 듯하다"도 "as still as a mouse"라고 한다.

You're rather beforehand in your suspicions

↳ 의심하기엔 아직 일러

You've always been that way

↳ 넌 항상 그런 식이었어

You've got another thing(think) coming

↳ 그건 큰 착각이야

Your constant complaining cheapens you

↳ 늘 불평만 하고 있으니 사람 가치 떨어져

‣ **trounce** thrash, punish, or defeat severely

‣ **cheapen** discounted in price

Your fax didn't come through clearly
> ㄴ 네 팩스가 선명하지 않아

Your good nature can be presumed upon once too often
> ㄴ 넌 사람이 좋아서 남에게 이용당할 일이 너무 잦게 돼 있어

Your goose will be cooked
> ㄴ 너한테 큰일 나겠구나

› **presume**   assume authority without right
to do so, take for granted

93. 여행　　　　　　　　　　Traveling

A 10 minute walk will get you there
　　　↳ 10분 정도 걸으면 도착 할거야

A journey of a thousand miles is a single step
　　　↳ 천리 길도 한 걸음부터

'천릿길도 한 걸음부터'는 작은 일부터 차근차근하여 큰 일을 이뤄야 한다는 뜻이다. 자주 쓰는 영어 속담은 'A journey of a thousand miles begins with a single step'이며 이는 '리'를 'mile'로만 썼을 뿐, 한국 속담과 뜻이 같다.
(=High buildings have deep foundations)
(=Big things have small beginnings)
(=Little by little goes a long way)
(=Success doesn't come overnight)
(=Little by little and bit by bit)
(=To reach the top you may ascend step by step)

A man travels the world in search of what he needs and returns home to find it
　　　↳ 사람은 자신이 필요로 하는 것을 찾아 세계로 돌아다니다가 집에 와서야 그것을 찾아내게 된다

A path wound through the woods, leading us to the main road
　　　↳ 숲 속에는 구불구불한 오솔길이 있어서 우리는 큰 도로로 나가게 되었다

› **ascend** move upward

A road had been cut up the hillside
> ↳ 산허리에 길이 나 있었지

A road that doesn't lead to other roads always has to be retraced
> ↳ 다른 길로 연결이 안 되는 길로 갔다면 언제나 그 길로 되돌아 갈 수 밖에 없다

A sea voyage is full of subjects for meditation
> ↳ 바다명상은 충분한 명상의 소재를 제공한다

All passengers should pass through the security area one hour before scheduled flight
> ↳ 모든 승객께서는 비행기 출발 한 시간 전에 보안 검색 열을 통과해야 합니다

Are there any landmarks along the way?
> ↳ 길을 가면 길 찾는 표적이 될만한 게 있습니까?

Are we there?
> ↳ (목적지에) 다 왔어?

As I shall be quite happy just to share your ordinary family life, there's no need to take me round(around) showing me the sights
> ↳ 당신의 평소시 가족 생활처럼 같이 지내기만 해도 만족스러우니, 나를 데리고 여기저기 다니면서 구경시켜 줄 필요는 없습니다

Better ask twice than lose your way once
> ↳ 길을 한 번 잃는 것 보다 두 번씩이라도 물어보는 것이 낫다

Better to ask the way than go astray
> ↳ 길을 잃는 것 보다 길을 물어보는 게 낫다

By the end of the two-week tour, they were dragging their asses(butts, feet)
> ↳ 그들은 2주에 걸친 여행 끝에 몹시 지쳐 있었다

› **retrace**　trace again, go over again in reverse

› **landmark**　object that marks a boundary or serves as a guide, event that marks a turning point

Can I get some directions?

> ↳ 길 좀 물어보겠습니다

Can I make good connections for Seoul?

> ↳ 서울로 가는 연결 교통편이 있습니까?

Can I stop over on route?

> ↳ 도중에 내릴 수 있습니까?

Can you fit them all in your trunk?

> ↳ 그것들을 전부 네 트렁크에 넣을 수 있겠나?

Chang-soo cut short his tour to fly back

> ↳ 창수는 여행을 중단하여 귀국했다

Conference carried him to Tokyo

> ↳ 회의 차 도쿄에 갔다

Do I turn right here or at the next corner?

> ↳ 여기서 좌회전해야 합니까 아니면 다음 모퉁이에서 해야 합니까?

Do you have any preference about which airline you fly?

> ↳ 특별히 선호하는 항공사가 있습니까?

Don't dawdle over your meal, we don't want to be late for the train

> ↳ 기차시간 늦으면 안되니까 밥 먹는데 꾸물대지마

Don't draw apart from the group

> ↳ 일행에게서 따로 떨어지지마

Doo-man went to flag down a taxi

> ↳ 두만이는 택시 잡으러 갔어

Duck-soo's already left us high and dry

> ↳ 덕수는 우리를 고립무원에 빠뜨린 채 벌써 가버렸어

Follow this street to the first corner

> ↳ 모퉁이가 나올 때까지 이 거리를 쭉 가십시오

› **route** line of travel

› **flag** signal with a flag

Get out while the going(getting) is good
  ↳ 떠날 수 있을 때 떠나라

Get to the airport in good time, in case the airplane arrives early
  ↳ 비행기가 일찍 도착하는 일에 대비해서 여유있게 공항으로 가거라

Gil-soo does cover a lot of ground
  ↳ 길수는 여기저기 많이 돌아다녀

Gil-soo's going on a long trip to get(have) his head together
  ↳ 길수는 머리 좀 식히려고 긴 여행을 떠나려는 거야

Give me a brief tour of the city
  ↳ 시내를 한 바퀴 돌아주세요

Give me the numbers for traveling expenses
  ↳ 여행경비가 얼마냐?

Go to the bath-room before we leave so that you won't have an accident in the car
  ↳ 차 타고 가다가 화장실 갈 일 없도록 출발 전에 화장실 다녀오너라

Have you gotten over your jet lag?
  ↳ 시차병은 나았나요?

He has been to the four corners of the world(country)
  ↳ 그는 전 세계(국)에 안 가본 곳이 없어

He has drifted about like a rudderless ship for three years
  ↳ 그는 3년간 정처 없이 떠돌아 다녔다

He has traveled far and wide as he has itchy feet
  ↳ 그는 역마살이 끼여서 여기저기 많이 돌아다녔다

He is all hopped up about going over the ocean
  ↳ 그는 배를 타고 여행한다는데 신이 나 있어

· **lag**　fail to keep up, a falling behind

· **itch**　uneasy irritating skin sensation, skin disorder, persistent desire

He travels fastest who travels alone

↳ 여행은 혼자 하는 것이 가장 빨리 다닐 수 있다

He went on a trip to recharge his batteries

↳ 그는 재충전하러 여행 갔어

(=He went on a little getaway)

He who would travel happily must travel light

↳ 즐거운 여행을 하려면 가벼운 차림으로 하라

His first trip abroad wound him up and he talked almost three hours

↳ 그의 첫 해외여행으로 얘기가 쌓여서 세 시간씩이나 얘기했다

How about doing another round of window-shopping

↳ 아이쇼핑 한번 더하자

How long will the next train be?

↳ 다음 열차는 얼마나 기다려야 오죠?

If you make the 9:00 a.m flight, you'll be able to make the connecting flight to Seoul

↳ 오전 아홉 시 비행기를 놓치지 않으면 서울로 가는 연결 비행기를 탈 수 있을 것입니다

Is Samchunpo on the map?

↳ 삼천포가 널리 알려진(찾기 쉬운) 곳이냐?

Is this the road leading me to the seashore?

↳ 이 길로 가면 해변이 나옵니까?

Is your journey necessary?

↳ 꼭 그래야만 하는 거니?

· **getaway**　escape, a starting or getting under way

It always takes forever and a day at this airport
↳ 이 공항에는 그것 때문에 시간이 너무 걸려

It seems only the other day we went down to the airport to meet you
↳ 공항에 너를 맞으러 갔던 때가 엊그제만 같다

It would be just another block ahead
↳ 한 블록만 더 가면 있을 것입니다

It's about one hour one way
↳ 거기 까진 편도로 약 한시간 걸려

It's better to travel hopefully than to arrive
↳ 결과보다 과정이 중요하다

> 결과에 얽매이지 말고 전심전력을 하여 노력해야 한다. 진정한 성공이란 그 과정에 쏟아 붓는 노력이다(The true success is to labour).

It's time to get on your horse
↳ 이제 떠날 준비해야지

Just call us and we'll make Mt. Sorak come alive for you
↳ 전화만 해 주시면 설악산이 생생하게 눈앞에 다가올 여행 프로그램을 제공하겠습니다

Let's check out(visit) the plumbing before we go
↳ 떠나기 전에 화장실에 들러서 가자

Let's get our stuff together and get going
↳ 소지품을 챙겨서 떠나자

Let's go play in the fall leaves
↳ 우리 단풍놀이 가자(=Let's go see the fall foliage)

‣ **plumb** weight on the end of a line to show vertical direction

‣ **foliage** plant leaves

Let's hurry up to get(catch) up to our party
↳ 일행에 따라붙게 빨리 가자

Let's take advantage of the off-peak reduction for package holidays
↳ 휴일 여행 때 비수기 할인 기회를 활용하자

Let's try to find out if there are any flights to Seoul going cheap(any cheap flight going to Seoul)
↳ 싸게 먹히는 서울행 비행기편을 찾아보자

Look sharp, or you'll miss the train
↳ 우물쭈물 하다가는 기차 놓친다

My calling requires a good deal of traveling
↳ 난 직업상 출장이 많아

My sense of direction is terrible
↳ 난 길눈이 어두워

(=I get lost easily)

Nice to have you with us aboard
↳ 탑승하신 것을 환영합니다

(=Welcome aboard)

No rest room in the bus
↳ 버스 타기 전에 용변을 미리 보십시오

Not only do I like flying, but also like traveling by train
↳ 난 비행기여행 뿐만 아니라 기차여행도 좋아해

· **peak**   highest level
· **reduction**   amount lost in reducing

Our plan for the expedition was going fine till one of our members pulled the plug on it
> ↳ 우리의 탐사여행계획은 잘돼가다가 팀원 중 한 사람이 도중에 무산시켜 버렸다

Our train flashed through the station
> ↳ 기차는 역을 획 지나갔다

Our trip is a no-go because the airport is fogged in
> ↳ 공항에 안개가 끼었으니 우리의 여행계획은 취소다

Passengers near the door of the jam-packed bus risked being thrown out when it jolted out of the bus terminal
> ↳ 버스 터미널에서 만원버스가 덜컥거리며 떠나자 출입문 옆에 있던 승객들은 밖으로 떨어질 뻔했다

Passing inspection should be a priority
> ↳ 먼저 검사부터 통과해야 해

Please hold on a little longer. We'll be at a rest area soon
> ↳ 화장실 갈 일은 조금만 참아주세요. 휴게소에 곧 도착합니다

Sam-shik has been all over the world
> ↳ 삼식인 세계 도처에 안 가본 데가 없어

Send your beloved son on a journey
> ↳ 자식을 사랑하거든 여행을 보내어라

Stay on this street you are going, and you'll come to the post office
> ↳ 이 길로 곧장 가면 우체국이 있습니다

Store all food in plastic away from camp at night and when camp is unattended
> ↳ 밤에 혹은 텐트를 비워놓을 때에는 반드시 음식을 비닐봉지로 꼭 싸매어 둬라

▸ **jolt** move with a sudden jerky motion, give a jolt to

▸ **plastic** material that can be formed into rigid objects, films, or filaments

Take all your possessions with you and leave nothing on the ship
　　↳ 모든 소지품을 내리고 배 안에 아무 것도 남기지 마라

Taking a day-trip to the Mt. Halla and back was hard on my feet
　　↳ 한라산까지 당일치기로 갔다왔더니 다리에 무리가 갔다

That safari gave us a chance to see wild animals in their natural habitat
　　↳ 그 탐험여행으로 야생동물들을 그들의 서식지에서 볼 기회를 얻었다

The heaviest baggage for a traveller is an empty purse
　　↳ 여행자에게 가장 무거운 짐은 텅 빈 지갑이다

The long journey has done me in
　　↳ 긴 여행에 녹초 됐어

The ride to the village seemed to take only half the time
　　↳ 차를 타고 그 마을까지 가는데는 생각보다 훨씬 짧은 시간밖에 안 걸렸다

The road curves round the monument
　　↳ 도로가 그 기념탑 근처를 지나간다

The train just missed being destroyed(in the accident)
　　↳ 열차는 간신히 파손(사고)을 면했다

The train stopped short of the end of the track
　　↳ 열차는 선로의 끝에 약간 못 미치는 곳에 섰다

There are a number of passenger(ferry) boats plying between Inchon and Mokpo
　　↳ 인천과 목포를 오가는 여객선이 많이 있다

There's a big bookstore off the main street
　　↳ 길에서 몇 걸음 들어간 곳에 큰 서점이 있다

There's nothing like travel by air

‣ **safari** hunting expedition in Africa
‣ **monument** structure erected in remembrance

↳ 비행기 여행만큼 좋은 건 없다

They are half on business and half on pleasure
↳ 그들은 업무 겸 관광차 온 거야

They routed us around the congestion of the big city
↳ 그들은 우리를 대 도시의 혼잡을 피해서 가게 해(보내) 주었다

They went on a spending spree on a trip to Hawaii
↳ 그들은 하와이 여행에서 돈을 물 쓰듯 했다

This road leads to Seoul
↳ 이 길로 가면 서울로 가

This road will lead you to the station
↳ 이 길로 가면 역으로 갑니다

This trip will keep me away from home for two weeks
↳ 이번 여행으로 2주 동안 집에 있지 않게 될 거야

Tourists must get a glimpse of the abominable, dreadful conditions the native people actually endure
↳ 여행자들은 그 곳 사람들이 실제 참고 살아가는 구역질나는 지독한 상황을 보어야 한다

We'll be ready to move as soon as we pull ourselves together
↳ 우리는 소지(휴대)품을 챙기는 대로 떠날 것이다

Weather permitting, we shall set off on our journey as originally planned
↳ 날씨만 좋으면 우린 당초 계획대로 여행을 떠날 것이다

What landmarks are on the way?
↳ 도중의 경계표시(뚜렷한 표지물 또는 지형지물)를 알려주십시오

What time does the last train go?
↳ 막차가 몇 시에 떠납니까?

› **glimpse** take a brief look at

› **abominable** thoroughly unpleasant or revolting

What track does the next train leave from?
> ㄴ 다음 열차는 몇 번 선에서 떠납니까?

What's the airline distance between Seoul and Daejun?
> ㄴ 서울과 대전간 직선거리가 얼마냐?

When my ship comes in, I'll take a trip to Jeju-do
> ㄴ 목돈이 들어오면 제주 여행 갈 거야

Where does this street go?
> ㄴ 이 길로 가면 어디로 가지?

> (=Where this road lead to?)

Whom did you fly with?
> ㄴ 어느 항공사 비행기로 왔니?

You have to remain together while you are on this tour
> ㄴ 너희들은 여행 중 같이 다녀야 해

You'd better send ahead for room reservations at the hotel
> ㄴ 사전에 연락해서 호텔 예약을 해 두지 그래

You've done yourself well, haven't you, staying in the best hotel
> ㄴ 너 최고급 호텔에서 잠을 다 자고, 호강했군 그래

You've got a way to go yet till you reach Moon-san
> ㄴ 문산까지 가시려면 아직 멀어요

· **distance**　mearue of separation in space
or time, reserve

94. 예술   Art

A police comedy action centered on a cop fooling around at headquarters, was one of the biggest box-office draw in Korea last year

     ㄴ 경찰서에서 빈둥거리는 형사 이야기를 그린 경찰 코미디 영화가 국내에서 지난해 가장 큰 흥행을 기록한 영화의 하나다

A red-blooded scoundrel sometimes writes pretty verses which are entirely harmless in character

     ㄴ 불한당 같은 작가도 전적으로 순진한 성격묘사를 하고 있는 아름다운 시들을 써내는 때도 있다

Art students who imitate the techniques of master artists too well may lose their own creative ability

     ㄴ 예술을 공부하는 학생들이 스승이 되는 예술가의 기술을 너무 잘 모방하면 자기들 자신의 창의력을 잃을 수 있다

As poetry is the harmony of words, so music is that of notes

     ㄴ 시가 말의 조화이듯이 음악은 선율의 조화이다

At best, the movie was okay

     ㄴ 기껏해야 그저 그런 영화였어

Chul-hee's work will come into its own soon

     ㄴ 철희의 작품은 곧 각광을 받게 될 것이다

Doo-man is a big name on the rock music scene

› **scoundrel** mean worthless person

ㄴ 두만이가 록음악계에선 내노라 하는 사람이다

Encourage your children to listen to(hear) good music, and its calming power will rub off on them

ㄴ 아이들에게 좋은 음악을 듣게 해주면 마음을 가라앉히는 힘이 그들에게 감화를 줄 것이다

His book was favorably noticed in literary magazines

ㄴ 그의 책은 문예잡지에서 호평을 받았다

His pictures are much sought after

ㄴ 그의 그림은 인기가 대단해

I remember when trot was young

ㄴ 트로트가 한창때이던 때가 생각나

It tells you little

ㄴ 얻는 게 없어(소설, 영화, **TV** 등)

Life is like playing a violin solo in public and learning the instrument as one goes on

ㄴ 인생은 대중 앞에서 바이올린을 연주하는 것과 같고 연주해 가면서 배우게 된다

Literature flourishes best when it is a half a trade and half an art

ㄴ 문학은 반쯤 상업적이고 반쯤 예술적일 때 가장 번창한다

Making himself out to be some kind of expert in modern art is all he did

ㄴ 그가 한 일이라고는 자기가 제법 현대예술에 대한 전문가인체 한 것뿐이다

Many dances come and go

ㄴ 많은 춤들이 인기를 끌다가 시들해졌지

Music is not in my way

‣ **literary** relating to literature
‣ **flourish** thrive, wave threateningly

ㄴ 음악은 내게 취미에 맞지 않아

Music is nothing else but wild sounds civilized into time and tune
ㄴ 음악은 단지 박자와 선율에 맞추어 조화시킨 거친 소리일 뿐이다

Oil paintings look to advantage at a distance
ㄴ 유화는 거리를 두고 보아야 좋게 보인다

Poetry can never be adequately rendered in another language
ㄴ 시는 결코 다른 언어로 완전하게 번역될 수 없다

Rock concerts are big with the youngsters
ㄴ 록 음악회가 젊은이들에게 인기 있어

Sang-soo was on a winning streak then, but his next movie bombed at the box office
ㄴ 그는 그 때 한창 끝 발을 날렸지만 그의 그 다음 영화에서는 죽을 쑤었다

Shakespeare has given us human nature marvelously well
ㄴ 셰익스피어는 인간성을 놀라우리만큼 잘 묘사하고 있다

She got an unexpected chance to play the lead after the film's original star fell ill
ㄴ 당초에 주연키로 했던 인기배우가 몸이 아프게 되자 그녀가 예상 밖의 주연을 맡게 되었다

Some parts are rather slow=The film drags in some spots
ㄴ 영화가 지루하게 끄는 부분이 있어

Styles and fads in music may come and go, but the blues always seem to endure
ㄴ 음악의 양식과 일시적인 유행이 왔다가 사라지지만 블루스의 인기는 여전한 것 같다

Television has robbed the cinema of its former popularity

› **fad** briefly popular practice or interest

ㄴ 텔레비전이 영화의 옛 인기를 빼앗아 갔다

The art of self-defense is not a combative art, but an art of discipline and defense

ㄴ 호신술은 싸움을 하기 위한 기술이 아니라 수양과 자기방어를 위한 기술이다

The art of teaching is the art of assisting discovery

ㄴ 가르치는 기술이란 발견하도록 도와주는 기술이다

The difficulty of literature is not to write, but to write what you mean

ㄴ 문학의 어려움은 글을 쓰는 자체에 있는 것이 아니라 의도한 대로 쓰는데 있다

The most beautiful things are those that madness prompts and reason writes

ㄴ 가장 아름다운 글은 미친 듯한 열정의 충동과 이성으로 쓴 글이다

The movie has been playing to sold-out crowds since opening recently in many theaters

ㄴ 최근 많은 극장가에서는 그 영화가 연일 매진을 기록하며 상영되고 있다

The movie has gotten rave reviews for its fast-paced action scenes as well as the main story of a man and woman torn apart by ideological differences

ㄴ 그 영화는 빠르게 전개되는 액션장면과 서로 다른 이념 때문에 헤어진 남녀에 대한 얘기 구성으로 호평을 받고 있다

The painting has every indication of being genuine

ㄴ 그 그림은 아무리 보아도 진짜 같다

The tune goes like this

› **ideological** body of beliefs

› **genuine** being the same in fact as in appearance

ↄ 그 곡은 이렇게 되어있어

There are a lot of thrilling scenes in this film
ↄ 이 영화에는 아슬아슬한 장면이 많다

There are several scenes that are a bit corny=It has a bit corniness=Some parts are a bit corny
ↄ 진부한 대목이 여러 곳 있어

There's a double feature playing at the Cinema Hall
ↄ 시네마 홀에서 두 영화가 동시상영 되고있다

These are words to that song
ↄ 이게 그 노래의 가사야

They juiced up the movie with a little sex and violence
ↄ 그들은 영화에 약간의 섹스와 폭력을 가미해서 재미있게 만들었다

They sang to the accompaniment of a piano played by him
ↄ 그들은 그가 연주하는 피아노에 맞추어 노래했다

They tried to palm that painting as a real Kim-hong-do
ↄ 그들은 그 그림을 진짜 김홍도의 작품이라고 속여 팔려고 했다

This drama doesn't live up to the original(novel)
ↄ 이 드라마는 원작(소설)보다 못해

This film will soon flash back to earlier scene
ↄ 이 영화는 곧 회상(이전)장면으로 되돌아 갈 것이다

This is painted to the life
ↄ 이 그림은 실물대로 그렸어

This novel isn't half bad, though the plot doesn't really hang together
ↄ 이 소설은 구성에 조리가 안 맞는 면도 있으나 그런 대로 괜찮다

This song has the greatest hook
ↄ 이 노래가 제일 맘에 들어

› **corny** trite or tiresomely sentimental

This song makes my heart swell up(touches me)
ㄴ 이 노래를 들으면 가슴이 벅차

We are going to take a brief break to let you hear from our
sponsors before I continue to blast you with smashes from the past
ㄴ 잠시 협찬회사들의 광고를 들으면서 휴식시간을 가진 다음 불멸의 히
트곡을 들려 드리겠습니다

Where there is music, there can be no evil
ㄴ 음악이 있는 곳에 악이 있을 수 없다

Writing comes easily if you have something to say
ㄴ 뭔가 할 말이 있어야 글이 잘 써진다

You can keep yourself amused on the bus by listening to this music
ㄴ 버스를 탈 때 이 음악을 들으면 심심하지 않게 갈 수 있어

› **sponsor** one who assumes responsibility for another or who provides financial support

› **blast** violent gust of wind, explosion

95. 예절 & 친절   Politeness

A civil denial is better than a rude grant
> ↳ 정중한 거절은 퉁명스럽게 들어주는 것보다 낫다

A forced kindness deserves no thanks
> ↳ 억지 친절은 감사할 가치 없다

A gentleman should do the polite
> ↳ 신사는 예의바르게 행동해야 한다

About the only thing lost by politeness is a seat on a crowded bus
> ↳ 친절해서 손해본다 해봤자 만원버스에서 좌석 하나 잃는 정도뿐이다

All their kindness will rub off on their children
> ↳ 그들의 친절성은 자녀들에게 이어져 내려갈 것이다

An-do came by his kindness honestly
> ↳ 안도의 친절함은 집안 내력

Be gentle and don't break anybody
> ↳ 남에게 부드럽게 대하고 폐를 끼치지 마라

Be my guest. I'm in no rush
> ↳ 먼저 하십시오. 전 바쁘지 않으니까요

By and large the more question you ask in a survey, the less polite people tend to be
> ↳ 대체로 사람들은 조사시 질문을 많이 할수록 불친절해지기 쉽다

Men are more prone to revenge injuries than to requite kindness

---

› **grant**   consent to, give, admit as true | › **revenge**   inflict harm or injury in return for a wrong

ㄴ 사람은 친절에 대한 보답보다는 해를 입은 데 대한 앙갚음을 하기 쉽다

Better friendlier denial than unwilling compliance

ㄴ 마지못해서 하는 승낙보다 친절한 거절이 낫다

Byung-soo's work isn't the best but it'll fill the bill

ㄴ 병수의 작품이 최고는 아니지만 기준은 통과할 것이다

Chang-soo never fails to please

ㄴ 창수는 절대 남의 비위를 건드리지 않아

Civility costs nothing

ㄴ 예의 발라 손해날 것 없다

> 솔로몬은 '사람이 예의 바르면 자기 자신에게 유익하고 사람이 잔인하면 자기 자신에게 해를 끼친다(A kind man benefits himself, but a cruel man brings trouble on himself)'고 하였다. 예의는 어디에서나 지켜야 할 사회 생활의 필수 덕목이다. 'Civility'는 'politeness'로 대체 할 수 있다.

Didn't you have sense enough to offer your seat to the old lady?

ㄴ 그 노부인에게 자리를 양보할 생각 없습니까?

Do not forget little kindnesses and do not remember little faults

ㄴ 작은 친절을 잊지 말고 작은 허물을 탓하지 마라

Familiarity breeds contempt

ㄴ 친할수록 예의를 지켜야

> 처음 만나는 사람에게는 모두가 예의를 갖추지만, 친해지면 상대를 함부로 대하기 쉽다. 그렇지만 친한 사이일수록 거래도 조심해야 하며 예의도 지켜야 한다. 너무 친하면 공경하는 태도가 없어지지만, 거리를 두고 지내면 존경심을 갖게 된다(Familiarity breeds contempt, while rarity wins admiration).

- **compliance** obeyance
- **contempt** feeling of scorn, state of being

despised, disobedience to a court or legislature

He saw the elderly man across the street
> 그는 나이든 남자를 길 건너로 모셔드렸다

(see across＝accompany someone across a dangerous area)

He that respects not is not respected
> 남을 존경해야 남에게 존경받는다

(＝Respect a man, he'll do the more)

He was unnecessarily rude but he had the decency(grace) to apologize afterwards
> 그는 필요 이상으로 무례하였지만 그 후에 예의를 차려서 사과했다

Honey catches more flies than vinegar
> 꿀은 식초보다 파리를 더 많이 잡는다(친절 권장)

친절하게 대하는 것은 말은 쉽지만 실천이 쉽지가 않다. 그러나 친절은 손해도 나지 않고, 자신에게 이로운 처세술이다.

I was civil then
> 그땐 내가 예의를 갖췄거든

In-ho has shown me many kindnesses
> 인호가 내게 여러 가지 친절히 해주었어

It boils down to common courtesy
> 그건 결국 평범한 예절 문제야

› **decency**   good, right, or just, fairly good
› **courtesy**   courteous behavior

By and large the more question you ask in a survey, the less polite people tend to be

↳ 대체로 사람들은 조사시 질문을 많이 할수록 불친절해지기 쉽다

No respect

↳ 사람을 존경할 줄 모르는군

One can always be kind to people without whom one care nothing

↳ 아무런 상관없는 사람에게는 항상 친절할 수가 있다

Politeness is the art of selecting among one's real thoughts

↳ 예의바름이란 진짜 속마음 중에서 어떤 것을 드러낼지의 선택이다

Punctuality is the politeness of princes

↳ 약속을 잘 지키는 것이 예의의 근본이다

> 약속을 잘 지키는 사람은 신용을 얻게 된다. 사회 생활에서 신용만큼 중요한 것이 없다(Punctuality is the duty of politeness of kings 약속을 잘 지키는 것은 신사의 의무이다).

Sang-hi knows her manners

↳ 상희는 예의가 발라

See no evil, hear no evil, speak no evil

↳ 예가 아니면 보지도 말고 예가 아니면 듣지도 말고 예가 아니면 말하지 말라

> 이 격언은 세 마리의 원숭이가 각각 손으로 눈을 가리고, 귀를 가리고, 입을 막고 있는 모습에서 이 격언이 기원하였다. 성경에는 죄를 보고 듣는 것만으로도 죄를 범하는 것이라고 말하고 있다.

› **tend** show a tendency

› **punctual** prompt

Straightforwardness without the rules of propriety becomes rudeness
　　↳ 예의에 구속받지 않는 솔직함은 무례가 된다

Such was his kindness that we'll never forget him
　　↳ 그는 너무나 친절했기 때문에 우리는 그를 잊을 수 없다

The way it's done in Korea is for the younger people offer their seats to the older people
　　↳ 한국에서는 젊은 사람이 나이 든 사람들에게 자리를 양보하는 것이 통례이다

The wise forget insults, as the ungrateful a kindness
　　↳ 배은망덕한 사람이 남의 친절을 잊어버리듯이 현인은 모욕을 잊어버린다

There should be courtesy even between close friends
　　↳ 친한 사이에도 예절은 지켜야해

True power and true politeness are above vanity
　　↳ 진정한 권력과 진정한 예절은 허영심을 초월한다

Violence is just where kindness is vain
　　↳ 친절이 안 통하면 폭력이 정당화된다

Yielding a seat to an elderly has gone out of the window in these days
　　↳ 요즘 연장자에게 자리를 양보하는 일은 이미 사라져 버렸다

You have done me a various acts of kindnesses
　　↳ 신세 많이 졌습니다

You need not lavish kindness on those ungrateful people
　　↳ 그렇게 배은망덕한 사람들에게 친절히 대할 필요가 없다

You never lose by doing others a good turn
　　↳ 남에게 친절해서 손해 날 일없어

› **straightforward** frank or honest
› **yield** surrender, grant

› **propriety** standard of acceptability in social conduct

> 솔로몬은 '사람이 예의 바르면 자기 자신에게 유익하고 사람이 잔인하면 자기 자신에게 해를 끼친다(A kind man benefits himself, but a cruel man brings trouble on himself)'고 하였다. 예의는 어디에서나 지켜야 할 사회생활의 필수 덕목이다. 'Civility'는 'Politeness'로 대체 할 수 있다.

You should repay the favor(his kindness)=You should make it up to him=You should show your gratitude

ㄴ 그의 은혜는 갚아야 해

> **gratitude** state of being grateful

96. 오염   **Pollutions**

Although the emission volumes remain high, natural winds usually blow the pollutants away, keeping the dense of pollution in check
> ↳ 배출량은 높은 수치를 유지하고있으나 자연에서 오는 바람이 공해물질을 불어 없애 줌으로써 그 밀도를 억제해 준다

Exhaust gas has been incriminated in the city air pollution
> ↳ 도시의 배기 오염은 배기가스가 주범으로 지목되어 왔다

Factories are no longer allowed to spew out black smoke from their chimneys
> ↳ 공장들이 굴뚝에서 검은 연기를 내뿜는 것은 더 이상 허용되지 않는다

False words are not only evil in themselves, but they infect the soul with it
> ↳ 거짓말은 그 자체가 나쁠 뿐 아니라 그 거짓말은 정신까지 오염시킨다

Power derived from water creates no pollution and uses up no irreplaceable fuel resources
> ↳ 물에서 얻는 동력은 공해를 일으키지 않으며 대체 불가능 연료자원을 고갈시키지도 않는다

The government's action only increases suspicions that the public is not being warned about the dangers of rising pollution levels
> ↳ 정부의 그런 행동은 증가하고있는 대기오염의 위험수위에 대해 경고하지 않았다는 의심을 증폭시킬 뿐이다

▸ **emission** giving off or out

The ground is contaminated by chemicals which have leaked from the storage tank over the last 30 years

ㄴ 지난 30년에 걸쳐 저장탱크에서 새어나온 화학물질로 토양이 오염되었다

The newspaper reported that radioactive waste had escaped from a damaged pipe, and polluted a large area of coast

ㄴ 방사선 폐기물이 파손된 파이프에서 새어나와 넓은 해안지역을 오염시켰다고 신문이 보도했다

The officials assume that patients contracted the epidemic from contaminated underground water at the prayer house

ㄴ 관계 공무원들은 전염병에 걸린 환자들이 기도원의 오염된 지하수를 마신 데서 일어난 것으로 추정한다

The river was slowly turning brown and smelly from the dye-house waste

ㄴ 강물은 염색공장에서 나온 폐기물로 갈색을 띠고 냄새가 났다

The sewage spill was cause by a power failure at a treatment plant

ㄴ 그 하수의 오물유출은 하수처리 공장의 정전으로 일어났다

They have already made pioneering strides to curb the spread of water and air pollution

ㄴ 그들은 이미 수질 및 대기오염 확산을 저지할 선도적인 일을 추진해 오고 있다

They've been trying to soft-pedal the fact that their cars are polluting the air seriously

ㄴ 그들의 차가 아직도 대기를 심각하게 오염시키고 있다는 사실을 그들은 은폐시키려 기를 써 오고 있다

Toxic chemicals may permeate the soil, threatening the environment

ㄴ 유독성 화학물질은 토양에 스며들어서 환경에 위협이 될 수 있다

· **permeate** seep through, pervade

97. 옷   **Clothing**

Are you muffled up against the cold?
> ↳ 감기 안 들게 옷을 두껍게 입었니?

Better to cut the shoe than pinch the foot
> ↳ 발을 죄는 고통보다는 신발을 찢는 게 낫다

Bong-soo kept his nose to the grindstone, but all he got for his effort was a kick in the teeth(pants)
> ↳ 봉수는 뼈빠지게 일했지만 노력에 대한 칭찬은 커녕 욕만 먹었다

By dressing up as a man and wearing a wig she was able to give her pursuers the slip
> ↳ 그녀는 남장을 하고 가발을 써서 추적자들을 따돌릴 수 있었다

Byung-soo brushed up against the door, and some of the paint came off onto his coat
> ↳ 병수가 출입문에 약간 스쳐(부딪쳐)서 윗도리에 페인트가 묻었다

Chul-hee has grown out of all his clothes
> ↳ 철희가 몸이 자라서 입던 옷을 하나도 못 입게 되었어

Craft must have clothes, but truth loves to go naked
> ↳ 책략에는 옷을 입혀야 하지만 진실은 옷을 벗고있기를 좋아한다

Cut your coat according to your cloth
> ↳ 분수에 맞게 살아라

› **muffle** wrap up, dull the sound of

"분수에 맞게 살아라"는 교훈이 있다. 이는 영어로 "Cut your coat according to your cloth 몸에 맞게 옷을 맞춰 입어라"라고 표현한다.

Do you think your hat will stay on in this high wind?
    └ 이렇게 센바람에 모자가 안 날아갈 것 같으냐?

Don't leave your clothes(lying) around
    └ 옷을 아무렇게나 널어놓지마

Everything suits you well
    └ 넌 무얼 입어도 예뻐

(=You look beautiful in anything)

Half shirts are sexy
    └ 배꼽티는 야해(crop tops =half tops)

He wears many hats
    └ 그에게는 모자(감투, 역할)가 많아

He would give you the shirt off his back if you curry favor with him
    └ 네가 그의 비위만 잘 맞추면 있는 것 없는 것 다 줄 것이다

He'll sue your pants off if you are not obedient
    └ 네가 고분고분하게 나오지 않으면 그가 고소를 해서 큰돈이 들것이다

He's just flying by the seat of his pants
    └ 그는 그저 감으로 때려잡아 해나가고 있는 거야

Her ample figure was scarcely concealed by her scanty bathing suit
    └ 그녀의 꼭 끼는 수영복으로는 커다란 몸집을 거의 가리지 못했다

Her money goes on clothes

› **sue** bring legal action against
                                                        › **scanty** barely sufficient
› **conceal** hide

↳ 그 여자의 돈은 옷 사는데 다 들어간다

Her skirt fastens along one side
↳ 그녀의 스커트는 옆으로 채우게 되어있다

His shirt-sleeves were smeared with jam, berry-juice and butter
↳ 그의 셔츠 소매는 잼, 딸기주스, 버터가 묻어있었다

His shoes were caked with mud
↳ 그의 신발에는 진흙이 굳게 달라붙어 있었다

Hold(hang) on to your hat
↳ 놀라지 말아

I can't fill your shoes
↳ 네가 하던 일을 감당하기엔 역부족이야

I've been thrown away like an old shoe
↳ 헌신짝 같이 버림받았어

> 오래 사귀던 사람을 버릴 때 쓰는 속담은 동·서양이 같다. 한국에서 헌신짝을
> 버린다고 하듯이, 영어에서는 "Throw away like an old shoe"라고 한다.

If the shoe fits, wear it
↳ 마음에 찔린다면 네게 맞는 말이기 때문

In a fight the rich man tries to save his face, the poor man his coat
↳ 싸움에서 부자는 체면을 생각하고 가난한 사람은 옷을 생각한다

It doesn't matter what your clothes look like
↳ 옷이야 아무려면 어때

It looks as though you've been sleeping in it for a week
↳ 꾀죄죄한 네 옷 그 꼴이 뭐니

› **smear**   greasy stain

It's all the thing(the in thing) for youngsters today to wear Japanese blue jeans and demonstrate against Japan
> ↳ 요즘 젊은이들은 일본제 청바지를 입고 항일데모를 하는 게 유행병인 가 봐

It's you
> ↳ 너에게 정말 잘 어울린다(맞는다)

Jung-soo got through school by the seat of his pants
> ↳ 정수는 운이 좋아 학교를 마쳤다(운이 나쁘거나 줄서기를 잘못한 것 포함)

Jung-tai was my captain in the army, but now the shoe is on the other foot
> ↳ 군에서는 정태가 우리 중대장이었지만 지금은 나의 부서에서 일하고 있어

Keep your pants on
> ↳ 진정해

Keep yourself warm by rolling yourself up in(all) clothes
> ↳ 있는 옷 다 껴입고 몸을 따뜻하게 감싸라

Korean dress sets you off to advantage
> ↳ 넌 한복을 입으니 아주 돋보이네

Let me slip this coat on and see if it fits
> ↳ 이 코트를 입어서 맞는지 보자

Let me take it in just a little at the waist
> ↳ 이 옷의 허리를 조금 줄여 드리지요

Lots of people have been driven back on cheaper clothes by the rises in prices
> ↳ 물가가 오르자 많은 사람들이 싼 옷을 다시 입게 됐다

· **demonstrate**   show clearly or publicly, prove, explain

Make sure you do your coat up before going out
> ↳ 외출 전에 코트의 단추가 잘 채워졌는지 챙겨봐

Man-soon was quite a sight in that dress
> ↳ 만순이가 그 옷을 입으니 가관이더군

Mini-skirts are still going strong
> ↳ 미니스커트는 여전히 인기가 있다

Mini-skirts were a must for any women who wanted to keep up with the latest fashions then
> ↳ 그 당시 유행을 따라가려면 어느 여성에게나 미니스커트를 입는 게 필수였다

My dress does up at the back
> ↳ 내 옷은 뒤에서 단추를 채우도록 되어 있다

My elbow has worked through the sleeve
> ↳ 옷 팔꿈치가 차츰 닳아 떨어졌다

My new suit was a good fit and didn't need any alteration
> ↳ 새 양복은 잘 맞아서 고칠 데가 없었다

My shoes have worn down since I started walking so much
> ↳ 내가 이 신을 신고 많이 돌아다녔더니 해져버렸다

My shoes take a high polish
> ↳ 내 구두는 광이 잘 나

My shoes were caked with mud
> ↳ 내 신발에는 진흙이 달라붙었다

My socks keep slipping down
> ↳ 양말이 자꾸 미끄러져 내려오네

My wife got after me to hang up the clothes
> ↳ 집사람이 내게 옷을 걸어놓으라고 성화였어

› **alter** make different

› **polish** make smooth and glossy, develop or refine

Only the wearer knows where the shoe pinches
ㄴ 신발을 신어봐야 어디가 끼는지 안다

Please take it in just a little at the waist
ㄴ 옷의 허리부분을 조금 줄여주세요

Poor children wore clothes their brothers and sisters had grown out of
ㄴ 가난한 집 아이들은 형이나 누나가 몸이 커져서 더 이상 입지 못하게 된 옷을 물려받아 입었다

Problems are only opportunities in work clothes
ㄴ 문제점은 단지 작업복 차림의 기회일 뿐이다

Sang-soo has failed four classes in school. he'll drop the other shoe and quit altogether any day now
ㄴ 상수가 네 번씩이나 수업에 빠졌어. 차제에 학교를 아주 그만 둘 것 같아

Sang-soo made decisions by the seat of his pants
ㄴ 상수는 경험으로 결정했다

Sang-soo stormed off and came back with hat in hand when he ran out of money
ㄴ 상수는 휑 하니 떠났다가 돈이 떨어지자 공손한 태도로 돌아왔다

Sung-soo wears two hats
ㄴ 성수는 두 직업(부업)을 가졌어

She always looks as though(if) she's stepped out of a bandbox
ㄴ 그 여자는 늘 쏙 빼어 입고 다녀

She went to the business meeting in her shirt-sleeves
ㄴ 그 여자는 허술한 차림으로 사업상의 모임에 참석했다

She's done up in fine costume
ㄴ 그녀는 화려한 복장을 하고 있다

▸ **pinch** compress painfully

Shin-jah looks like a fashion page from the 60s
ㄴ 신자는 **60**년대의 케케묵은 스타일 같아

Short skirts will be back next year
ㄴ 내년에는 짧은치마가 다시 유행 할 것이다

Tai-hee's dressed in the height of the fashion
ㄴ 태희는 최신 유행복을 입고 있어

Tai-ho tore his new trousers on something sharp on the side of the car
ㄴ 태호는 차 옆의 뾰족한 무엇에 걸려서 새 바지를 찢었다

That kind of hat went out years ago
ㄴ 그런 모자는 몇 년 전부터 사람들이 안 쓰더라

The clothes at this department rank with those of the best places in Seoul
ㄴ 이 백화점에 있는 의류는 서울에 있는 어느 백화점의 옷에 못지 않다

The clothes that are out of fashion today will be back in tomorrow
ㄴ 오늘 유행이 지난 옷들은 내일이면 다시 유행하게 될 것이다

The dirt clinging to the collar can't be washed out
ㄴ 옷깃에 묻은 때가 지워지지 않는다

The fashion for half-shirts has gone
ㄴ 배꼽티의 유행은 지나갔어

The fashion has already taken the country by storm
ㄴ 그 유행은 벌써 전국을 휩쓸고 있어

The flattering shape of the blouse is much emphasized by this lace
ㄴ 그 블라우스가 잘 어울리는 모양은 이 레이스 때문에 더욱 돋보인다

The knees of these trousers have completely worn through
ㄴ 이 바지의 무릎이 완전히 해져서 구멍이 났다

· **wash out**　cause to fade by laundering, exhaust the strength or energy | of, fail to measure up, destroy by the force of water

The miniskirt rapidly made it's way into universal favor
ㄴ 미니스커트가 급속히 유행되었지

The shoe is on the other foot
ㄴ 상황은 역전되었어

The slit in the back of a man's coat is said to hark back to the days of horse-back riding
ㄴ 남자코트 뒷부분에 길게 트여진 것의 유래는 말을 타고 다니던 시절로 거슬러 올라간다

The smell still lingers in my clothes
ㄴ 옷에 아직도 냄새가 배어 있어

(=The smell still didn't come out of my clothes)
(=Smell is still in my clothes)

The tips of Jung-soo's toes poked through his socks
ㄴ 정수의 발가락이 양말을 뚫고 나왔더군

The trousers don't crease easily
ㄴ 이 바지는 주름이 잘 안 잡혀

There's no one size fits all
ㄴ 모든 경우에 다 들어맞는 치수란 없다

These clothes have a lot of static(too much static cling)
ㄴ 이 옷은 정전기가 잘 올라

These cloths hold colors better than others
ㄴ 이들 천은 다른 천 보다 색채유지가 잘 된다

These shoes don't even begin to fit me
ㄴ 이 신발은 도무지 맞지가 않아

· **linger** be slow to leave or act
· **poke** prod, dawdle

· **crease** line made by folding

These skirts are in
> ↳ 이 치마가 유행

This cloth will bear washing
> ↳ 이 천은 손빨래 할 수 있어

This dress is hooked at the back
> ↳ 이 옷은 뒤에서 잠근다

This is a flattering outfit
> ↳ 이 옷은 신체 결함(뚱뚱보, 홀쭉이, 임산부)을 잘 감춰주는군

This jacket won't go round me
> ↳ 이 웃옷은 작아서 못 입겠어

This one could serve in many capacities
> ↳ 이 옷은 여러 경우에 입을 수 있겠다

This scarf and your dress go well together
> ↳ 이 스카프하고 네 양복은 잘 어울려

This style is quite the thing this year
> ↳ 이 스타일은 올해 큰 유행이다

This sweater comes down to my knees
> ↳ 이 스웨터는 무릎까지 온다

Wait, I'm not decent yet
> ↳ 난 아직 옷을 안 입었어(목욕, 알몸상태)

Wan-soo is wearing a very different hat this time
> ↳ 완수가 이번엔 전혀 다른 역할을 하고 있어

We can whisk away(off) these little pieces of dirt that have go on your trousers
> ↳ 네 바지에 묻은 때는 간단히 털어 낼 수 있을 거야

| · **outfit** equipment for a special purpose | · **whisk** quick light sweeping or brushing motion |

We'd better bundle up
ㄴ 옷을 껴입어야겠어

When battery acid gets on our clothe, it will eat away at the material and leave holes
ㄴ 건전지에 있는 산이 우리의 옷에 묻으면 물질을 부식시켜 구멍을 낸다

When she's wearing a bathing suit, we can really see her spare tire
ㄴ 그 여자가 수영복을 입을 때 디룩디룩 허리 살이 보여

Where is the pair to this sock?
ㄴ 이 양말의 짝은 어디 있니?

Who are you putting on the dog(ritz) for?
ㄴ 누굴 위해 쏙 빼 입은 거지?

Why are all these clothes lying about?
ㄴ 이 옷들이 왜 마구 널려있어?

Will you check if my suit is ready to go
ㄴ 제 양복 맞춤(세탁)이 다 됐는지 확인해 주세요

You can leave your coat on
ㄴ 코트를 그냥 입고 있어도 돼

You don't know how to get a lot of milage out of a pair of shoes
ㄴ 넌 신발 한 켤레로 오래 신는 방법을 모르는군(**get a lot of milage** 는 "오래 쓰다"의 뜻)

You have ants in your pants
ㄴ 안절부절 못하는구나

You're wearing odd pair of shoes
ㄴ 신발을 짝짝이로 신었구나

Your dress is dragging on the ground
ㄴ 치마가 끌려요(=**skimming(touching) the floor**)

‣ **skim** read or move over swiftly

Your homely figures arose my sympathy and respect
ㄴ 너의 검소한 차림을 보니 동정과 존경심이 이는구나

Your old slippers have been kicking around here for months
ㄴ 너의 헌 슬리퍼는 몇 달씩이나 여기 팽개쳐져 있어

Your red tie really caught my eye(is really eye-catching)
ㄴ 빨간 타이가 눈에 확 띄네

Your shoelace is undone(=loose)
ㄴ 구두끈 풀렸어

(=Your shoes are untied)

Your skirt keeps riding up
ㄴ 네 치마가 자꾸 올라가는구나

Your socks don't match
ㄴ 양말이 짝짝(**=pair up =mismatching socks**)

Your zipper is open(down)
ㄴ 남대문 열렸어

(=Your garage is open)

› **homely** plain or unattractive

98. 용기   Courage

A great part of courage is the courage of having done things before
     ↳ 용기란 대부분이 그 일을 먼저 해놓는 용기를 말한다

A search behind enemy lines requires a tremendous test of our endurance and nerves
     ↳ 적진의 후방을 탐색하는 데는 대단한 참을성과 담력을 요한다

At that time, I couldn't dare to tell you the truth
     ↳ 그때 진실을 얘기할 용기가 없었죠

Brave men's deeds live after them
     ↳ 용기 있는 사람의 위업은 사후에도 남는다

Calamity is the touchstone of a brave mind
     ↳ 용기가 있는지는 위험에 부딪쳐봐야 안다

Courage is redefined by each generation
     ↳ 용기는 각 세대에 따라 다르게 정의된다

Fear can keep a man out of danger, but courage can support him in it
     ↳ 두려움은 사람을 위험에서 구하지만 용기가 이를 뒷받침한다

Fortune favors the brave(bold)
     ↳ 운명은 용기 있는 사람의 편이다

Gil-soo's guts were turned to water
     ↳ 길수의 용기가 꺾였어

Great things are done more through courage than wisdom

› **calamity** disaster | › **touchstone** test or criterion of genuineness or quality

ㄴ 큰 일은 지혜보다 용기를 통하여 이루어지는 일이 많다

He can be brave enough to do it

ㄴ 그는 용감한 사람이니 능히 해낼 거야

He gathered his courage to take the plunge, resign from his job and start his own business

ㄴ 그는 용단을 내어서 모험을 걸어 직장을 그만 두고 자신의 사업을 시작했다

He that forecasts all perils, will never sail the sea

ㄴ 모든 위험을 예고(측)하는 사람은 바다를 건너지 못한다

His courage brought the people through the war

ㄴ 그의 용기에 사람들이 전쟁에서 버티어 낼 수 있었다

His is a nature in which courage and caution meet

ㄴ 그는 용기와 신중함을 겸비한 사람이다

If he had a little encouragement, he could pull himself up by his own bootstraps

ㄴ 그에게 조금만 용기를 주었으면 자력으로 해낼 수 있었을 것이다

In-ho has a lot of balls to say(speak) against his boss

ㄴ 인호는 사장에게 거역할만한 용기가 있다

Necessity and opportunity make a coward valiant

ㄴ 필요와 계기는 겁쟁이를 용감하게 만들 수도 있다

Sang-ho's courage shone out in the middle of his misfortunes

ㄴ 상호의 용기는 역경을 겪는 가운데 발휘되었다

The weak in courage are strong in cunning

ㄴ 용기가 없는 자는 간계가 많아

What would life be if we had no courage to attempt anything?

ㄴ 무언가를 시도할만한 용기가 없다면 삶이 무슨 의미가 있겠는가?

› **plunge**	thrust or dive into something, begin an action suddenly	› **peril**	danger
		› **bootstraps**	unaided efforts

When the mouse laughs at the cat, there's a hole nearby
   └ 쥐가 고양이에게 웃을 때에는 바로 옆에 쥐구멍이 있기 때문이다(용기의 한계)

▷ **nearby** near

99. 외교   Foreign Affairs

An enormous number of foreigners were deported and imprisoned in an atmosphere of growing xenophobia
> 외국인 혐오증의 분위기 속에 엄청나게 많은 외국인들이 추방되고 투옥되었다

Cultural exchange should go both ways
> 문화는 쌍방이 교류해야 한다

Differences of language and customs are a barrier to understanding
> 언어 및 관습의 차이는 상호 이해에 대한 장벽이다

Don't telegraph your punches in any negotiations
> 어떤 협상에서나 부지중에 속을 드러내 보여선 안 돼

Enemy soldiers poured over the walls and conquered the country
> 적이 성벽을 넘어 몰려 들어와서 나라를 정복해버렸다

Facing a common enemy keeps the nation together
> 국가 공동의 적을 앞에 두면 국민이 단합하게 된다

Few people have ever managed to penetrate the insularity and stubbornness of the aborigines
> 원주민들의 편협성과 고집을 파악할 수 있었던 사람들은 거의 없었다

Heavily outnumbered, the invaders had no choice but to surrender
> 침략군은 중과부적으로 항복할 수밖에 없었다

Higher export prices will weaken our competitive position in world

---

› **xenophobia**   fear and hatred of foreign people and things

› **aborigine**   original inhabitant

markets
> ↳ 수출가 상승은 세계시장에서 우리의 경쟁력을 약화시킬 것이다

In many parts of the world the poor are going without food so that the rich can live in luxury
> ↳ 세계의 많은 지역에서 가난한 사람들이 끼니를 거르고있기 때문에 부자인 사람들이 호화롭게 산다

In some countries children and women are regarded as a source of cheap labor
> ↳ 어떤 나라에서는 어린이와 여성을 값 싼 노동력으로 여긴다

Keep up on what's going on in this world
> ↳ 세계 각 국에서 일어나는 일에 귀를 기울여라

Korea must find some new attractions to keep the foreigners rolling in
> ↳ 한국이 외국인을 계속해서 대거 유치하려면 매력 있는 방문지를 발굴해야 한다

Korea ranked 11th among the trading nations in the world
> ↳ 한국은 세계의 무역국들 중 11위였다

Korea topped the world list in per capita consumption of liquor
> ↳ 한국은 1인당 음주 소비에서 세계 제1위였다

Man-soo has put Korea on the map this time
> ↳ 이번엔 만수가 한국의 국위를 떨쳤다

Many employers in Korea are turning to South-East Asia for workers who are still not unwilling to sweat for their pay
> ↳ 한국의 많은 고용주들은 보수를 받기 위해 땀흘리며 일하기를 마다하지 않는 노동자들을 찾기 위해 동남아시아에 의존하고 있다

Many foreign workers are relegated to illegal alien status where low

---

· **rank**   vigorous in growth, unpleasantly strong-smelling

· **relegate**   remove to some less prominent position, assign to a particular class or sphere

pay and bad working conditions force them to flee their work-places
> ↳ 많은 외국인들은 낮은 급료와 열악한 근무조건으로 인해 직장을 이탈
> 하게되는 외국인의 신분으로 떨어지고 있다

Millions Japanese listened spellbound as they heard the Emperor speak in public for the first time
> ↳ 천황이 처음으로 국민들 앞에서 연설을 하자 수많은 일본 사람들은
> 홀린 듯이 경청했다

Minority problems lack the immediacy in a homogeneous culture
> ↳ 동질문화 속에서는 소수민족 문제가 급박하지 않다

Mother Teresa's consecration to the task of helping the poor has accentuated the affliction of the poverty
> ↳ 가난한 사람들을 돕는 테레사 수녀의 헌신은 세계에서 수백만이 고통
> 받는 가난의 고통을 부각시켜 주었다

Newspapers keep us in contact with the events of the world
> ↳ 신문 덕분에 세계에서 일어나는 일을 접할 수 있다

No country without an atom bomb could properly consider itself independent
> ↳ 핵무기 없는 나라는 제대로 독립성을 유지하고 있다고 볼 수 없다

One sword keeps another in the sheath
> ↳ 칼을 한 자루 빼어들고 있어야 칼집에 든 다른 칼을 빼어드는 것을
> 막을 수 있다(평화의 속성)

Our allies stood by us when war broke out
> ↳ 전쟁이 났을 때 우방 국가들이 도와주었다

Peace talks were held and both sides began to feel their way towards a truce
> ↳ 평화회의가 열리자 양측은 휴전협정을 향해 조심스럽게 나아갔다

› **consecrate** declare sacred, devote to a solemn purpose

› **accentuate** stress of show off by a contrast

Reading these papers will keep you posted on the latest happenings in the world

    ↳ 이 신문들을 읽으면 최근의 세계정세에 밝게 된다

Small and weak countries were necessarily compliant to the superpowers' every request even when their demands ran against small countries' national grain

    ↳ 약소국들은 강대국들의 요구가 약소국들의 기질에 어긋나더라도 고분고분 따라야 했다

Society now is connected through a huge web of networks and well on its way to becoming integrated into a borderless society

    ↳ 사회는 이제 거대한 정보망으로 연결되어 국경 없는 사회로 통합되어 나가고 있다

Some foreign bank was laundering money for a fifteen percent cut

    ↳ 어떤 외국은행이 15%의 수수료를 받고 돈 세탁을 해 주었대

The author sees the international in perspective

    ↳ 저자는 국제정세를 정확히 내다보고 있다

The biggest slice of the cake goes to the multinational oil companies

    ↳ 제일 큰 알짜는 다국적 석유회사들이 다 쓸어간다

The maxim of the British people is business as usual

    ↳ 영국인의 모토는 위기에 임해서도 태연자약 한다는 것이다

The settlers have usually divided up according to language and culture

    ↳ 이주민들은 보통 언어와 문화에 의해서 각각의 집단으로 나눠진다

The settlers soon merged with other peoples

    ↳ 이주민들은 곧 다른 민족과 융합되었다

There are countries in which unnecessary poverty prevails because

---

· **grain** seeds or fruits of cereal grasses

· **merge** unite, blend

the people as a whole are unaware of methods whereby it can be relieved

> ㄴ 국민전체가 가난에서 벗어날 수 있는 방법을 모르기 때문에 피할 수 도 있는 가난을 겪고있는 나라들이 있다

There's increased awareness of the global cooperation in the rehabilitation of degrades land

> ㄴ 퇴화된 토지를 회복시키기 위한 전 세계적인 협조의 중요성에 대한 인식이 커져가고 있다

Unless the nation's trade sees a turnaround, its targeted international balance of payments for this year might need to be adjusted

> ㄴ 대외무역수지가 반전되지 않는다면 올해 목표로 했던 국제수지 실적 을 조정해야할지도 모른다

We have to keep more in touch with the world development

> ㄴ 우리는 좀 더 세계정세를 잘 알아야 한다

When the war ended, Korea was carved up by the powers of the world

> ㄴ 전쟁이 끝나자 한국은 강대국들에 의해 분단되었다

Without addressing these humanitarian issues, no genuine progress is expected in the effort for reconciliation

> ㄴ 이들 인도적인 문제들을 외면하고서는 화해를 위한 노력에서 아무런 진정한 진전도 기대할 수 없다

› **degrade** reduce from a higher to a lower rank or degree, debase

› **adjust** fix, adapt, or set right

the people as a whole are unaware of methods whereby it can be relieved

There's increased awareness of the global cooperation in the rehabilitation of degraded land

Unless the nation's trade sees a turnaround, its targeted international balance of payments for this year might need to be adjusted

We have to keep pace in touch with the world development

When the war ahead, Karzacans carried on by the people of the world

Without analyzing these fundamental issues, no genuine progress is expected in the effort for remediation

100. 운전   Driving

A little car can weave its way through other big cars and get to the front of a waiting line quickly
> ↳ 소형차는 큰 차들의 틈바구니를 헤집고 나아가서 재빨리 신호대기중
> 인 차량들의 선두로 나설 수 있다

After twisting for a few kilometers the road straightens out here and driving is easier
> ↳ 이 도로는 몇 킬로만 구불구불하다가 여기부터 바른 길이 나오기 때
> 문에 운전하기가 쉬워져

Although I had some trouble with my car, I kept my chin up(kept a stiff upper lip
> ↳ 차에 약간의 문제가 생겼지만 침착하게 대처했어

Always yield to cars the right of way
> ↳ 직진하는 차에게 길을 항상 양보해야 해

At this time of the year snowbound roads mean crawling traffic and delays for commuters
> ↳ 이맘때쯤 해서 눈 때문에 다니지 못하게 되면 차가 기어다니게 되고
> 통근자들의 지각사태가 난다

Bong-soo saw the other car in the nick of time
> ↳ 봉수는 아슬아슬하게 다른 차를 보고 사고를 면했다

Can you drive a car with a manual transmission?

· **weave** form by interlacing strands or material, contrive, make a coherent whole

· **transmission** system of gears between a car engine and drive wheels

ㄴ 수동 변속 차를 운전할 수 있니?

Can you gain on(get ahead of) the car in front?

ㄴ 앞차를 추월할 수 있겠니?

Can you open up the engine a little?

ㄴ 차를 좀 빨리 몰 수 없겠니?

Can you squeeze a few kilometers out of this tank of gas before you fill up again?

ㄴ 주유소에 닿기 전에 차에 있는 기름으로 몇킬로 더 갈 수 있겠니?

Car after car goes by

ㄴ 자동차가 잇따라 지나가고 있다

Chan-ho nosed his car into the parking space and turned off the engine

ㄴ 찬호는 차를 주차장으로 몰고 들어가서 시동을 껐어

Chan-soo managed to ease(on) out of the parking space

ㄴ 찬수는 주차 공간에서 힘들여 조심스럽게 빠져 나왔어

Check to make sure your security belt is firmly fastened

ㄴ 안전벨트가 단단히 매어졌는지 확인해 봐라

Do I turn right here or at the next corner?

ㄴ 여기서 좌회전해야 합니까 아니면 다음 모퉁이에서 해야 합니까?

Don't drive drunk(under the influence)

ㄴ 음주 운전은 안 돼

(=Drinking and driving do not mix)
(=Don't drive under the influence)

> **gain** profit, obtaining of profit or possessions, increase

Don't let your eyes wander when you are driving
↳ 운전시 항상 도로를 주의해야 해

Don't tailgate that car, he must be drunk
↳ 저 차 운전자가 술 취한 게 틀림없으니 너무 바싹 따라가지마

Draw up alongside (of) that car
↳ 저 차 옆까지 따라붙어

Driving an automatic is easier than a stick shift
↳ 오토매틱 차 운전이 쉬워

Drop me off at the next corner
↳ 다음 모퉁이에서 내려 줘

Drunk driving kills and maims thousands of people on our roads every year
↳ 음주운전으로 노상에서 매년 수 천명의 사상자가 생긴다

Duck-soo dodged through heavy traffic to the front
↳ 덕수는 교통혼잡 속을 피해가며 선두로 나아갔다

Ed was too eliminated(elevated, embalmed) to drive home last night
↳ 에드는 어젯밤 너무 취해서 차를 몰고 집에 올 수 없었다(이해하지
못할 수도 있음)

Ed's too far-gone to drive
↳ 에드는 너무 취해서 운전을 못해

Full steam(speed) ahead
↳ 전 속력으로 가자

(=At full blast(tilt))

› **tailgate** drive dangerously close behind

› **alongside** along or by the side

› **embalm** preserve (a corpse)

Gil-soo jammed up the traffic when his car stalled
ㄴ 길수는 차가 멈칫거려(시동이 꺼져) 남들에게 교통 피해를 주었어

Give way to traffic coming in from the left
ㄴ 좌측에서 진입하는 차에게 길을 양보하시오

Half way up the hill, the engine gave out and they had to push the car the rest of the way
ㄴ 그들의 차가 언덕을 반쯤 올라가다가 엔진이 꺼져서 나머지 언덕길은 밀고 올라가야 했다

He scraped by the car that was blocking the way
ㄴ 그는 길을 막고 있는 차를 겨우 비켜 빠져나갔다

He was caught driving under the influence
ㄴ 그는 음주운전을 하다가 붙잡혔다

Here's your claim check
ㄴ 주차증 받아 가십시오

Hit the ground running or you'll never make it in time
ㄴ 최고 속력으로 가지 않으면 시간 안에 못 가

How did you take the wrong exit off the freeway?
ㄴ 어쩌다가 고속도로에서 엉뚱한 출구로 빠져 나오게 되었나?

I believe we are in the right direction
ㄴ 제대로(바른 방향으로) 가고있는 것 같아

If you'll get tanked up, who'll drive me home?
ㄴ 네가 술에 취하면 누가 나를 집까지 태워주나

In a panic he inadvertently pushed the accelerator instead of the brake
ㄴ 그는 엉겁결에 브레이크를 밟는다는 것이 가속기를 밟고 말았다

In driving, carefulness is the name of the game

· **inadvertent** unintentional

↳ 운전에는 안전운행이 관건이다

It's found that most drivers are over the limit in a large proportion of the accidents

↳ 사고 중 많은 비율은 대부분의 운전자들이 허용 음주량을 초과해서 일어나는 것으로 밝혀졌다

It's not unusual for me to be followed close behind by a car on a sidewalk

↳ 인도에서 자동차가 바싹 뒤에 다가와 있는 것이 드문 일이 아니다

It's open season on drunk drivers

↳ 지금 음주운전 일제단속기간이야

It's six kilometers there and back

↳ 거기까지는 왕복 6킬로다

It's to the common advantage that street traffic should be well controlled

↳ 거리 교통이 잘 통제돼야 한다는 것은 공동의 이익이 된다

It's when he's driving at high speeds that he feels truly alive

↳ 그는 차를 쌩쌩 몰아야만 생기가 돈다

Leave the car behind

↳ 차는 두고 가세요(음주 손님에게)

Let's do away with useless car trips

↳ 불필요한 자동차 운행을 줄입시다

Lines of vehicles backed up for several kilometers because of the accident

↳ 사고 때문에 차량 행렬이 몇 킬로미터씩 늘어섰다

Maintain your car regularly, or you're just inviting trouble

↳ 차를 정기적으로 정비해 두지 않으면 화를 자초하게 돼

‣ **proportion**　relation to one part to another or to the whole with respect 　to magnitude, quantity, or degree

‣ **sidewalk**　paved walk at the side of a road

Many cars cutting in cause heavy traffic

↳ 끼여드는 차들이 많아서 교통체증을 야기한다

Many cowboys in trucks cut in front of me

↳ 고속도로상에서 많은 난폭한 트럭 운전자들이 내 차를 앞질러 나아갔다

Mind backing up a little?

↳ 차(car) 좀 빼 주시겠어요?

Moon-soo's car must have been really moving when it hit the other car

↳ 문수가 다른 차를 들이받을 때 굉장히 과속이었음이 틀림없어

Move over into the bullet(passing) lane, this heavy truck is moving too slow

↳ 저 대형 트럭이 느림보이니 추월선으로 차선을 바꾸자

My car has clocked(logged) up 45,000 kilometers so

↳ 차의 주행기록은 45,000킬로이다

My car keeps acting up

↳ 내 차는 자꾸 말썽이야

My car won't kick over because weather's too cold this morning

↳ 오늘아침 날씨가 너무 추워서 시동이 잘 안 걸려

Nam-soo really had a time with that lousy jalopy he bought

↳ 남수는 그 형편없는 고물 차 때문에 애 먹었어

Nam-soo wants to borrow my car and try his wings

↳ 남수는 내 차를 빌려서 배운 운전솜씨를 실제 시험해 보고싶어해

No sooner had I stepped at the stop light than the car behind me crashed into me

↳ 정지신호에 서자마자 뒤에 있던 차가 들이받았어

· **jalopy** dilapidated automobile

Now that the private cars are banned in the bus-only lanes, it takes forever to drive across town
> ↳ 버스전용차선에 개인 승용차가 들어갈 수 없기 때문에 시내를 한 번 빠져 나오려면 시간이 많이 걸려

Please move your car or we'll have to have it towed
> ↳ 차량의 주인께서 차를 빼어주지 않으신다면 견인조치를 취하겠습니다

Pull over to the side of the road to let that big truck pass
> ↳ 저 큰 화물차가 지나가게 차를 한 쪽 길로 붙여라

Several cars went zooming past us
> ↳ 차가 몇 대 씽 하고 우리 옆을 지나갔다

She was on the wrong side of the road, swerving to miss another car
> ↳ 그녀는 다른 차를 피하려고 방향을 틀다가 잘못된 방향으로 들어갔다

Speed demons burning up the road often cause accidents
> ↳ 자동차 속도광은 사고 내는 일이 많아

That car is pulling out(leaving), so pull in to his space
> ↳ 저 차가 막 나가려고 하니 저기다 주차하자

That car is tailgating us
> ↳ 저 차가 우리를 바싹 쫓아오고 있어(**Get off my tail** 너무 바싹 따라 오지 마시오)

The 10 day rotation system is being implemented
> ↳ 10부제가 실시되고 있다

The accident brought home to him the evil of drinking while driving
> ↳ 그는 사고를 보고 음주 운전이 얼마나 나쁜가를 절감하게 되었어

The noise of the traffic became fainter and fainter until it had tapered off altogether
> ↳ 교통으로 인한 소음이 차차 약해지더니 아주 사라졌다

› **tow** pull along behind

› **taper** slender wax candle, gradual lessening of width in a long object

The speeding bus cut around the light pole and almost hit it
> ↳ 속력을 내어 달리던 버스가 전주 있는데서 홱 돌아서더니 하마터면 전주에 부딪칠 뻔했어

The taxi hurried along, gobbling up 4 kilometers
> ↳ 택시는 4킬로미터를 순식간에 지나서 서둘러 달렸다

The traffic jam is breaking up, so we can drive up
> ↳ 이제 길이 막히지 않으니까 차를 몰고 나아갈 수 있어

Then you won't mind taking a breath test
> ↳ 그럼 음주운전 측정을 해도 되겠군요

There are good curio shops in this city to set off the disadvantages of frequent traffic congestions
> ↳ 이 도시에는 잦은 교통혼잡의 불편함을 보상해 줄만한 좋은 골동품상들이 있다

There is a bunch-up ahead
> ↳ 길이 꽉 막혔어

There was a fender-bender and traffic slowed to a halt
> ↳ 접촉사고가 생겨서 차들이 길에 늘어서 버렸다

There's a lot of slow-and-go on the road right now due to rush hour
> ↳ 현재 러시아워로 인해 차가 가다가 서다가 하는 상태가 반복되고 있다

There's always a bottleneck on this part of the highway because it decreases from four lanes to two lanes
> ↳ 고속도로의 이 구간은 4차선에서 2차선으로 좁아지기 때문에 항상 병목현상이 생겨

These health warning posters show grieving relatives to drive home the point that drink-driving can kill
> ↳ 이들 건강 주의 경고 포스터들은 음주운전이 살인을 부를 수도 있다

› **gobble** make the noise of a turkey
› **curio** rare or unusual article

는 심각한 연계성을 절실히 보여준다

They took turns at the wheel for every hundred kilometers
　　　↳ 그들은 100킬로마다 바꿔가면서 운전했다

This car does 40 kilometers to the gallon
　　　↳ 이 차는 1 갤런으로 40킬로 달린다

This car will get you the best milage
　　　↳ 이 차는 연료 효율이 가장 좋아요

This is the place where we are supposed to cut off
　　　↳ 이쯤(큰 도로)에서 옆길로 빠져나가야 해

This morning I had a near missing driving over here
　　　↳ 오늘아침 여기로 운전해 오다가 부딪칠 뻔했다

Traffic is stalled because of all the drivers who are rubber-necking
　　　↳ 구경하는 운전자들 때문에 교통이 많이 막히고 있다

Turn right at the next fork
　　　↳ 삼거리에서 우회전 해 주세요

Use your turn signal
　　　↳ 깜박이 켜

Violating the traffic law cost me hundred thousand won
　　　↳ 교통위반으로 십만원 물었다

Watch out for the car in your blind-spot
　　　↳ 사각지대에 있는 차를 주의해야해

We pitched forward inside the car as we went over the bumpy road
　　　↳ 우리는 울퉁불퉁한 길을 달릴 때 차안에서 앞으로 확 쏠렸어

We went beyond the turnoff
　　　↳ 우린 빠지는 길을 지나쳐 버렸어

· **pitch**　fall headlong
· **turnoff**　place for turning off

When you try to cut in, drivers in the other lane behind you speed up instead of slowing down
> ㄴ 끼어 들기를 할 때면 뒤에 있던 차량들 대부분이 속력을 늦추는 게 아니라 오히려 가속을 한다

You should match the flow of traffic
> ㄴ 교통의 흐름에 따라 운전해야 해

You shouldn't change your lane too often or all of a sudden
> ㄴ 차선을 자주 바꾸거나 갑자기 차선을 바꿔서는 안 돼

› **lane** narrow way

101. 월급   Salary

After heated discussion they came down in favor of accepting the new pay offer
>ㄴ 그들은 열띤 논의 끝에 새로운 급여방식을 수용하는 쪽으로 결정했다

All government workers have had their salaries frozen for three years
>ㄴ 모든 공무원들의 봉급이 3년간 동결되었다

Asking me to support my parents on my meager salary is too hard on me
>ㄴ 변변찮은 월급으로 부모님을 공양하라는 것은 무리입니다

Chan-soo worked at two jobs in order to eke out a salary
>ㄴ 찬수는 봉급액수를 늘리려고 두 직장을 다녔어

Hard enough to call it a raise
>ㄴ 그 정도 가지고 월급 인상이라 할 수 있나

How much are you in your job?
>ㄴ 직장에서 얼마 받니?

I work for chicken feed(peanuts)
>ㄴ 쥐꼬리 월급 받고있어

> (=I'm making slave wages)

Our wage levels should be brought into line with those of our

---

› **meager**   thin, scanty
› **eke out**   barely gain with effort

competitors
> ㄴ 우리의 임금 수준은 경쟁사들과 맞먹을 정도로 해야 한다

Let him have it by reducing his pay by 10%
> ㄴ 그의 봉급을 10% 깎아서 본때를 보여줘라

Many employers in Korea are turning to South-East Asia for workers who are still not unwilling to sweat for their pay
> ㄴ 한국의 많은 고용주들은 보수를 받기 위해 땀흘리며 일하기를 마다하지 않는 노동자들을 찾기 위해 동남아시아에 의존하고 있다

Many foreign workers are relegated to illegal alien status where low pay and bad working conditions force them to flee their work-places
> ㄴ 많은 외국인들은 낮은 급료와 열악한 근무조건으로 인해 직장을 이탈하게되는 외국인의 신분으로 떨어지고 있다

Public servants(Government employees) must eat their honest bread
> ㄴ 공무원은 정직한 월급으로 살아야 한다

Pyung-soo puts a portion of his salary in the savings account each month
> ㄴ 평수는 월급의 일부를 매달 보통예금 계좌에 넣는다

Sometimes unscrupulous employers even call the police to have foreign workers deported to avoid paying the salary money they owe
> ㄴ 때로는 사업주가 고용인들에게 대한 급료 지급을 회피하기 위하여 외국인 근로자들을 추방시키도록 경찰에 신고하기까지 한다

That car cost the equivalent of my year's salary
> ㄴ 저 차는 내 1년 월급에 맞먹는 비용이 들었어

The question of pay mushroomed into a major problem
> ㄴ 급여문제가 갑자기 주요 문제로 대두되었어

They are going to hang tough on the salary raise

› **relegate** remove to some less prominent position, assign to a particular · class or sphere

› **alien** foreign

ㄴ 그들은 봉급인상을 강경하게 주장 할 태세다

They failed to deliver on their promise to provide fringe benefits

ㄴ 그들은 약속을 어기고 추가급여를 주지 않았다

They offer a salary and benefits package consistent with their leadership position in the field of nursing and health related facilities

ㄴ 그들은 요양이나 시설관련 분야에서 근무하는 지휘자의 직위에 어울리는 봉급과 복리후생을 제공한다

They'll get a big raise when the economy turns around

ㄴ 경기가 좋아지면 그들은 월급을 크게 올려 받을 것이다

Thousands of demonstrators demanded a bigger slice of cake

ㄴ 수천 명의 근로자들은 보다 나은 급료(배당)을 요구했다

What's the average starting wage in your line of work?

ㄴ 당신 직종의 평균 초임은 얼마입니까?

Will you advance me a month's salary?

ㄴ 한 달치 월급을 가불해 주시겠습니까?

You can get an advance of one million won on your salary

ㄴ 넌 월급에서 백만원 가불 할 수 있어

(=You can draw one million won against your salary)

· **fringe**   ornamental border of short hanging threads or strips

· **consistent**   being steady and regular

102. 위로   **Consolations**

After a month or two, it'll be plain sailing
> ↳ 한 두 달만 지나면 순조롭게 진행 될 거야

All is well
> ↳ 만사가 잘 될 거야(**All are well** 이 아님)

All my sympathy went out to her. I know how she felt
> ↳ 그 여자 정말 불쌍하더라. 얼마나 상심이 컸을지 알겠더라

All things are difficult before they are easy
> ↳ 처음부터 잘 할 수 있는 일은 아무 것도 없다

Better luck next time
> ↳ 다음에 잘 하자. 안됐군

Carry(Keep) on smiling
> ↳ 미소를 잃지마

Cheer up, the end is not yet
> ↳ 기운을 내, 아직 일이 끝난 것은 아냐

Deploring will not mend matters
> ↳ 한탄한다고 될 일이 아니잖아

Don't be cut up about the defeat
> ↳ 패배를 애석해 하지마

Don't dwell on the past
> ↳ 과거에 연연하지 마라

· **sympathy** expression of sorrow for another's misfortune
· **deplore** regret strongly
· **dwell** reside, keep the attention directed

> (=Don't think too much of what's already happened)

Don't eat your heart out
> ↳ 너무 슬퍼하지마

Don't fuss about so much. Things will take care of themselves
> ↳ 너무 수선 피우지마. 일은 저절로 잘 풀릴 테니까

Don't get your bowels in an uproar
> ↳ 너무 속상해 하지마

Don't get your nose out of joint
> ↳ 속상해(부러워) 하지마

Don't give it another thought(a second thought)
> ↳ 그 일은 이제 잊어버려

> (=Don't sweat it)

Don't let it bother you
> ↳ 신경 쓰지마

Don't let it get you down
> ↳ 그 일로 기죽지마

Don't let this matter pull you apart
> ↳ 이 일로 상심하지마

Don't let yourself get cowed down by his heavy scolding
> ↳ 그에게 큰 꾸지람 받았다고 의기소침하지마

Don't lose any sleep over the matter
> ↳ 그 일에 마음 쓰지마

· **fuss** pay undue attention or details

· **bowel** intestine(pl), inmost part(pl)

· **uproar** state of commotion or violent disturbance

Don't make it bad
└ 나쁘게 생각지마(비관하지마)

Don't put your nose out of joint
└ 언짢아하지마

Don't take it hard
└ 심각하게 받아들이지마

Don't tear yourself down(apart) for making a small error
└ 조그만 잘못에 자책하지마

Don't try to keep(hold) it in
└ 그걸 마음속으로만 삭이려 하지마

Don't turn on waterworks. Cheer up
└ 울지만 말고 용기를 내어라

Everything will be all right
└ 별일 없을 거다

> (=All will be fine)

Everything will come out all right
└ 만사가 잘 될 거야

Everything will come out in the wash
└ 다 잘 될 거다

Everything will come up roses
└ 만사가 잘 될 것이다

Go with the flow
└ 내버려둬. 마음 편하게 먹어라

‣ **waterworks**   system by which water is supplied(as to a city)   ‣ **bereaved**   suffering the death of a loved one

Hope for the best
> ↳ 좋은 일이 있을 거야(비관하지마)

I feel sympathetic to your situation
> ↳ 나라도 기분 나쁠 것이다

I sympathize with you in your bereavement
> ↳ 불행한 일에(사별, 사망 등) 대하여 애석히 생각합니다

I'm sorry I had to drop it on you
> ↳ 안 좋은 소식을 알려드려서 죄송합니다

I've been there
> ↳ 내가 겪어봐서 알지. 무슨 얘긴지 알아

It won't be a comfort to me
> ↳ 그 정도로는 위로가 안 돼

It's a massive weight around your neck
> ↳ 그건 큰 부담이겠군

It's not the end of the world
> ↳ 세상이 끝난 건 아니잖아

It's perfectly natural for you to feel that way
> ↳ 그렇게 생각하는 건 당연해

Join the club. Most of us did
> ↳ 너만 그런 줄(고통 당하는 줄) 아나? 우리 모두 그랬어

Join the club=Been there
> ↳ 너만 그런(고통스러운)게 아냐

Just let it go
> ↳ 이제 그만 잊어

Just let it in one ear and out the other
> ↳ 한쪽 귀로 듣고 한쪽 귀로 흘려라

• **massive** being a large mass, large in scope

(=Just let it pass without much thought)
(=Just ignore what he says)

Just sit tight
↳ 그냥 참을성 있게 기다려라

Keep a grip on you(yourself)
↳ 진정해

(=Calm down)

Keep your chin up. You must stop being blue
↳ 기운을 내. 우울한 얼굴은 그만 거둬

Keep your pants on
↳ 진정해

Let matters run(take) their course
↳ 일은 순리에 맡겨라

Let's put this matter behind us
↳ 이제 이 일은 과거로 돌리자

(=Let bygones be bygones)

Life goes on
↳ 다 그런 거야(감수해야해)

· **bygone** past

> (=That's the way it goes)

Life is all like that
> ↳ 산다는 게 다 그런 거지 뭐

> (=It's about the same with everybody)
> (=It can happen to any one)
> (=That's how people get along with their life)

Lift your cloudy look off and buck up
> ↳ 침통한 얼굴을 떨쳐 버리고 기운을 내

Most people offer condolence to those who have suffered pain, grief or misfortune just because it is expected of themselves
> ↳ 대부분의 사람들은 마땅히 그래야 한다고 생각하기 때문에 고통이나 슬픔 또는 불행을 겪는 사람들에게 조위를 표한다

Mother wiped away our tears, helped us get over our grief and comforted us when life wasn't fair
> ↳ 어머니는 삶이 평탄하지 못할 때 우리의 눈물을 닦아주고 우리가 슬픔을 극복하도록 도와주고 위로해 주셨다

> 모성애를 나타내는 문장이다. 모성애는 모든 생명체가 가지고 있는 본능이다
> (The mother's breath is always sweet = 어머니의 숨결은 언제나 달다).

My heart bleeds for you in your sorrow
> ↳ 네가 슬퍼하니 내 마음이 아파

(No), not by a long shot

· **buck** jerk forward, oppose, dislodge from a seat(+off)

· **condole** express sympathy

      ↳ 절대 그런 일은 없을 거야

Nobody would have done otherwise than you did

      ↳ 누구나 네가 한 것처럼 그렇게 할 수밖에 없었을 것이다

Perhaps it's all for the best

      ↳ 그래도 생각(보기)보다 낫다(그만하기 다행이다)

Please believe me that you have all my sympathy

      ↳ 충심으로 위로의 말씀을 드립니다

Please don't go out of your way to do it

      ↳ 그렇다고 너무 마음 쓰지 마세요

Put it out of your head

      ↳ 그 일은 더 생각하지 말아라

Put that behind you and make a fresh start

      ↳ 그 일은 잊어버리고 새로 시작해라

Put that heartbreak behind you and get on with your normal life again

      ↳ 그 비통함을 다 잊어버리고 정상적인 생활로 되돌아가라

Regrets will not(No repentance will) mend matters

      ↳ 후회해봤자 소용없어

She's not the only pebble on the beach

      ↳ 그 여자만 여자냐

Shouting doesn't solve anything

      ↳ 소리친다고 될 일이냐

Shun bad people as you would filth

      ↳ 더러운걸(똥을) 무서워서 피하나

Slow down and start smelling the roses now

      ↳ 이제 안정을 취하고 여유를 가져라

· **heartbreak** crushing grief

· **pebble** small stone

That's the way it goes=That's the way it plays(the mop flops, the cookie crumbles, the ball bounces)
    ↳ 어쩔 수가 없다(세상사가 다 그래)

The mill can't grind with the water that is past
    ↳ 흘러간 물로 물레방아를 돌릴 수 없다

> 알맞은 때를 놓치고 후회해 봐야 소용이 없다는 뜻이다. "엎질러진 물은 다시 담을 수 없다 It's no use crying over spilt milk"와도 비슷한 뜻이다. "It is no use sighing for the past 지난 일 때문에 한숨지어봐야 소용없다"

There are as good fish in the sea as ever came out of it
    ↳ 기회는 얼마든지 더 있다

Think nothing of it
    ↳ 신경 쓰지마

This too shall pass
    ↳ 이번 일도 지나갈 거야(세월이 약이다)

> (=Time can heal everything)

Time brings all things to pass
    ↳ 시간이 가면 모든 일이 지나간다

We'll cross the bridge when we come to it
    ↳ 내일 일은 내일 걱정해도 돼

Worse things happen at sea
    ↳ 그만하기 다행이다

You can't have everything

› **flop** flap, slump heavily, fail

› **sigh** audible release of the breath (as to express weariness)

      ㄴ 원하는 걸 다 가질 순 없어

(=You can't have it all)

You don't need to carry the weight of the world on your shoulders
      ㄴ 너무 걱정하지 마라

You look small
      ㄴ 넌 풀이 죽어 있구나

You were lucky not to have been hurt seriously
      ㄴ 그만하기 다행이다

(=It could have been worse)
(=You've got off chiefly)

› **chief** highest in rank, most important

103. 위원회   **Committees**

An-do doesn't want to be a member just along for the ride
> ↳ 안도는 재미로(명예뿐인) 회원이 되길 원치 않아

Don't fade from the scene(picture) because you are no longer a member of the club committee
> ↳ 이제 클럽위원이 아니라고 해서 뒷전에 앉아있지마

Don't try to weasel out of serving on the committee
> ↳ 위원회에서 할 일에서 빠져나가려고 하지 마라

Doo-chul is the leader of the movement in fact(reality) and in name
> ↳ 두철이는 명실공히 이 운동의 지도자다

Everything works that way here
> ↳ 여기선 그게 순리다

If you do that, I'm going to opt out of the club
> ↳ 네가 그렇게 하면 클럽에서 탈퇴하겠어

If you want to be one of us, you have to toe the line
> ↳ 네가 우리와 함께 일하고싶다면 명령에 따라야 해

If you work for us, you have nothing to lose
> ↳ 우리와 함께 일 해서 손해날거 없어

It's hoped that the members will pay their dues promptly
> ↳ 회원은 회비를 조속히 납입해 주십시오

It's just the way things work

· **opt** choose(+for)

· **prompt** ready and quick

↳ 그게 이곳의 법칙이야

It's only with the consent of the committee that the plan will go forward

↳ 그 계획이 추진되려면 위원회의 동의가 있어야 된다

New members must fit in with rest of the committee

↳ 신규 회원은 여타 위원들과 잘 어울려 나가야 해

Nobody will pull out of our club

↳ 우리 클럽에서 탈퇴할 사람은 아무도 없어

Our membership has been rolling up for the past few years

↳ 우리의 회원 수가 지난 몇 년 동안 점점 늘어나고 있다

Sung-soo's suggestion will be brought(put) forward to committee at a suitable date

↳ 성수의 제안은 적절한 날짜에 위원회에 회부될 것이다

The club is fronted by Mr. Joo who's been affiliated(associated) with other organizations in the past

↳ 그 클럽은 과거에 다른 단체에 가입했던 적이 있는 주씨를 대표로 내세우고 있다

The committee accepted the resignation of the members who benefited from the good-will gift giving

↳ 위원회는 떡값을 챙긴 위원들의 사표를 수리했다

The committee was called into being to discover the causes of accident

↳ 사고원인 규명을 위한 위원회가 생겨났다

There were a not enough people present for a quorum

↳ 참석자는 정족수 미달이었다

They are only 18 strong

▸ **consent** give permission or approval

▸ **affiliate** become a member or branch

▸ **quorum** required number of members present

ㄴ 그들의 인원은 **18**명 뿐이야

They must bring the rest of the committee around to their point of view
ㄴ 그들은 여타 위원들을 자신들의 견해에 동의하도록 설득해야 한다

They railroaded the motion through the committee
ㄴ 그들은 그 동의를 위원회에 회부하여 일사천리로 통과시켰다

They were much smaller in number than we
ㄴ 그들이 인원수로는 우리보다 훨씬 적었다

This meeting will draw us together better
ㄴ 이 모임으로 우리는 더욱 단합할 것이다

This practice should be done away with
ㄴ 이 관행은 폐지되야 해

This regulation is binding on everyone
ㄴ 누구든지 규칙은 지켜야 해

This room lends itself to small, intimate gatherings
ㄴ 이 방은 소규모의 친밀한 모임에 유용하게 사용된다

Those who have any legitimate grievance against the company can take it to the arbitration committee
ㄴ 회사에 정당한 불평이 있는 사람은 이를 조정위원회에 제기할 수 있다

Unable to solve its financial problems, the club disbanded
ㄴ 그 클럽은 재정문제를 해결하지 못해서 해산했다

› **railroad** force something hastily
› **arbitrate** settle a dispute as arbitrator

› **legitimate** lawfully begotton, genuine, conforming with law or accepted standards

104. 은행   **Bank**

A careful and impartial review of the bank reference and the two references you gave to us indicate that your company is experiencing considerable financial difficulties in making prompt payments

       ↳ 귀사가 거래하는 은행과 신용거래처 두 곳의 신중하고 공정한 의견은 귀사가 현재 대금 지급을 하기엔 심각한 자금 압박을 받고 있다고 말하고 있습니다

A few bank robbers acted out the bank robbery they committed last week

       ↳ 은행강도 몇 명이 지난주에 저질렀던 은행강도 행위를 재연했다

A large amount of money goes through banker's hands, but none of it is his

       ↳ 은행원은 하루에도 거금을 만지지만 자기 돈은 하나도 없다

Bank loans are often refused to poorer borrowers because the risk of default is greater

       ↳ 가난한 사람들은 채무를 이행치 못할 위험성이 커짐에 따라 은행대출이 거부되는 일이 흔히 있다

Bong-soo paid(put) a lot into his savings account this month

       ↳ 봉수는 이 달 많은 돈을 자신의 계좌에 입금했다

He was caught diverting the company's money into his own bank account

---

▸ **divert**   turn from a course or purpose, distract, amuse   ▸ **accrue**   be added by periodic growth

ㄴ 그는 회사 자금을 자신의 은행 계좌에 유용하다가 들통났어

Money kept in a savings account accrues to us with interest
ㄴ 은행에 예금을 하면 이자가 붙는다

Most banks allow us to space out our payments over several years
ㄴ 대부분 은행은 대출자에게 몇 년에 걸쳐 상환하게 해 준다

Now he is laughing(crying) all the way to the bank
ㄴ 이제 그는 은행가는 길 내내 웃으며(울며) 가게 된 거야(큰 돈을 벌었거나 망했을 때)

Our bank accounts must always stay in credit
ㄴ 우리의 은행 계좌에는 늘 잔고가 있어야 한다

Please credit hundred thousand won against my account
ㄴ 내 통장에 십만원 입금해 줘(I have debited ten thousand won against your account 네 통장에서 십만원 뺐다)

Some foreign bank was laundering money for a fifteen percent cut
ㄴ 어떤 외국은행이 **15%**의 수수료를 받고 돈 세탁을 해 주었대

Sook-hee's account balance remains classified
ㄴ 숙희의 은행구좌 잔고는 비밀에 부친다

That won't break the bank
ㄴ 그런다고 파산하지는 않아

The balance of account is against(for) me
ㄴ 차감 계정 결과 차입(대출)이 있다

The bank has threatened to call in all money lent
ㄴ 은행은 모든 대출금을 회수하겠다고 으름장이다

The central bank sees lower interest rates as a sure-fire solution to the banks' bad debt problems
ㄴ 중앙은행은 일반은행들의 악성 채권문제 해결법으로 이자율을 낮추는

· **classify** arrange in or assign to classes | · **capital**   wealth, total face value of a company's stock

것을 확실한 방법으로 보고 있다

The main function of a bank is to distribute capital efficiently by lending it to borrowers who'll be able to employ the money usefully and repay it
> ↳ 은행의 주된 기능은 돈을 유용하게 사용하고 갚을 능력이 있는 차용자들에게 빌려줌으로써 자본을 효율적으로 배분하는 일이다

The onus is on the banks to smooth fluctuations out in the exchange rate
> ↳ 환율이 크게 변동하지 않게 하는 것이 은행의 임무이다

The police are questioning many people to get behind the bank robbery
> ↳ 경찰은 은행털이의 단서를 잡으려고 많은 사람을 신문하고 있어

The rapid changes in the market placed the bank stocks at a premium
> ↳ 주식시장의 변동으로 은행주 값이 확 올랐어

The robbers lie low after holding up the bank
> ↳ 도둑들은 은행털이 한 후 눈에 안 띄게 숨어 지냈어

They thought the bank robbery was an inside job
> ↳ 그들은 그 은행강도를 내부 자에 의한 소행으로 생각했다

Time deposits accumulate higher interest than ordinary savings account
> ↳ 정기적금은 보통예금보다 이자율이 높다

Who are you banking with?
> ↳ 어느 은행에 거래하니?

› **onus** burden (as of obligation or blame)

105. 음료&술   Drinks & Liquor

A man takes a drink, the drink takes another, and the drink takes the man
> ↳ 사람이 술을 마시고, 술이 사람을 마시고, 술이 사람을 마신다

A nice cool glass of beer(a paid vacation) is just what the doctor ordered
> ↳ 시원한 맥주 한 잔(유급휴가)이야 말로 내게 가장 필요한 것이다

After six beers I was feeling no pain
> ↳ 맥주 여섯 잔에 취해버렸어

Alcohol doesn't like me, but I like it
> ↳ 술은 몸에 해롭지만 난 술을 좋아해

Allow me to replenish your glass with some more beer
> ↳ 맥주를 좀더 따라 드릴까요?

An-do had a glass too much
> ↳ 안도는 만취했어

> (=An-do is blind(dead) drunk)

Any liquor goes to my head
> ↳ 아무 술이나 마시기만 하면 취해

Back in the old days, I used to drink

· **vacation**　extended period of rest from routine

└ 왕년엔 술 좀 마셨지

Beer and Sojoo went to my head

└ 맥주하고 소주를 마셨더니 취하더군

Beer goes through very fast

└ 맥주를 마시면 화장실에 자주 가게 돼

Bong-soo gets quarrelsome in his cups

└ 병수는 술만 먹으면 시비조로 나와

Byung-soo drank me under the table

└ 병수가 나를 술에 골아 떨어지게 했어

Can I tempt you with another glass of beer?

└ 맥주 한 잔 더 하시겠습니까?

Can I top off your glass?

└ 술을 더(첨가해서) 따를까요?

Chan-soo dried out in two days

└ 찬수는 술 깨는데 이틀 걸렸어

Chan-soo had a bit of whiskey to get corkscrewed to pop the question

└ 찬수는 술김에 결혼 얘기를 꺼내보려고 위스키를 약간 마셨다

Chang-soo began to hit the bottle(booze, sauce)

└ 창수가 과음하기 시작했어

Cola always goes to my head

└ 콜라만 마셔도 취해요(**Don't let it go to your head** 는 "그만한 일로 우쭐해 하지마")

Could you fix another one?

└ 한 잔 더 주시겠어요?

Could you go for a cup of tea?

› **quarrelsome** cause conflict

› **booze** drink liquor to excess

› **corkscrew** device for drawing corks from bottles

┗ 차 한 잔 드릴까요?

Did you tie one on again?
┗ 또 술을 진탕 마셨나?

Do you take cream and sugar in your coffee?
┗ 커피에 크림이나 설탕 넣습니까?

Don't associate drinking with worrying
┗ 걱정되는 일이 있다고 해서 술을 마셔서는 안 돼

Don't drive drunk(under the influence)
┗ 음주 운전은 안 돼

(=Drinking and driving do not mix)
(=Don't drive under the influence)

Don't tailgate that car, he must be drunk
┗ 저 차 운전자가 술 취한 게 틀림없으니 너무 바싹 따라가지마

Doo-chul can drink any man under the table
┗ 술로 두철이를 당할 사람 없어

Doo-man's wife always takes him to task for his drinking
┗ 두만의 아내는 그가 술 마실 때마다 꾸중을 해

Doo-soo called for glasses all over
┗ 두수가 모두에게 잔을 돌리게 했지

Drinking in moderation is good for heart and health
┗ 적당한 음주는 심장과 건강에 좋다

› **moderate** avoiding extremes

> 술도 좋은 술을 적당히 마시면 건강에 이롭다. 우리의 선조들도 '적게 먹으면 약주요, 많이 먹으면 망주라고 하였다. 서양에서는 좋은 포도주가 건강에 이롭다고 한다(Good wine makes good blood).

Drunk driving kills and maims thousands of people on our roads every year
    ㄴ 음주운전으로 노상에서 매년 수 천명의 사상자가 생긴다

Eat at pleasure, drink by measure
    ㄴ 즐겁게 먹고 적당히 마셔라

Ed was too eliminated(elevated, embalmed) to drive home last night
    ㄴ 에드는 어젯밤 너무 취해서 차를 몰고 집에 올 수 없었다(이해하지 못할 수도 있음)

Ed's too far-gone to drive
    ㄴ 에드는 너무 취해서 운전을 못해

Four beers and he's already down
    ㄴ 저 사람 맥주 네 잔에 벌써 갔군

Give up drinking cold turkey(all at once) rather than taper off
    ㄴ 술을 차차 끊을게 아니라 딱 끊어

Go and get drunk
    ㄴ 실컷 취해봐!

Go easy on the So-ju
    ㄴ 소주 좀 작작 해라

He becomes quite another man(a troublesome drinker) when he drinks
    ㄴ 그는 술이 들어가면 딴 사람이 된다

He couldn't hold his liquor and got heeled on only two beers

· **maim** seriously wound or disfigure
· **embalm** preserve (a corpse)

· **taper** make or become smaller toward one end, diminish gradually

└ 그는 술이 약해서 겨우 맥주 두 잔에 취해버렸다

He is already half seas but does not wish to be thought so

└ 그는 벌써 취했지만 남들이 자기를 취했다고 생각하지 않길 바라(이해하지 못할 경우도 있음)

He lets himself go when he drinks

└ 그는 술만 마시면 자제력을 잃는다

He was caught driving under the influence

└ 그는 음주운전을 하다가 붙잡혔다

He's down at the beer hall soaking his face

└ 그는 술이 너무 취해서 맥주홀에서 뻗어있어

He's merry in his cups

└ 그는 술을 곱게 마셔

He's quite another man when the wine is in

└ 술이 취하면 딴 사람 같아

His true self is revealed when he drinks

└ 술 마시면 본성이 나와

How many shots did you have?

└ 몇 잔 마셨어?

Hyun-soo is not much of a drinker

└ 현수는 술을 별로 못해

Hyun-soo never touches the stuff

└ 현수는 술에 손도 못 대

I am getting tipsy

└ 술기운 돈다

› **soak** lie in a liquid, absorb

› **tipsy** unsteady or foolish from alcohol

> (=I am a little buzzed)

I drink straight out of(=from) the bottle
└ 병째 마셔

I said that under the influence of alcohol
└ 술김에 한 소리(be drunk when a person say that)

I'm fired up
└ 술이 막 오르는군

I'm sober as a judge
└ 난 말짱해(안 취했어)

If you drink like a fish you should expect to feel sick the following day
└ 술을 그렇게 마구 마셔대면 다음날 몸이 안 좋을 것은 각오해야 해

If you'll get tanked up, who'll drive me home?
└ 네가 술에 취하면 누가 나를 집까지 태워주나

In wine there's truth
└ 취중진담

It takes some time to dry him out
└ 그가 술을 깨자면 시간이 좀 걸릴 것이다

It won't go to my head
└ 그 정도로는 안 취해

It's not enough to amount to buying a glass of beer
└ 맥주 한잔 살만한 돈도 못 돼

It's only the first bottle that is expensive
└ 첫 번째 술병만이 비싼 술이다

› **buzz** make a low humming sound
› **sober** not drunk, serious or solemn

It's open season on drunk drivers
> ↳ 지금 음주운전 일제단속기간이야

It's the piping hot coffee in cold weather
> ↳ 추운 날씨엔 따뜻한 커피가 최고야

I'm not much of a drinker
> ↳ 난 술을 별로 못해

Jin-soo should stay at arm's length from any liquor(such a friend)
> ↳ 진수는 술이란 술(그런 친구)을 멀리 해야 해

Keep some coffee around in case anyone wants it
> ↳ 누가 커피를 찾을지 모르니 준비해 놓으세요

Korea topped the world list in per capita consumption of liquor
> ↳ 한국은 1인당 음주 소비에서 세계 제1위였다

Let him sleep off his drinking
> ↳ 그가 술이 깨게 잠을 재워라

Let him stew in his own juice
> ↳ 그가 자승자박하게 내버려 둬

Let me buy you a draft
> ↳ 맥주 한잔 살께

Let me take you to one more place for another drink(Let's go for another round somewhere)
> ↳ 2차로 딱 한잔만 더 하자

Let's beat(shoot, fan) the breeze over a cup of coffee
> ↳ 커피 한잔하면서 이런 저런 얘기나 좀 하자

Let's bottom-line this project and break for coffee
> ↳ 이 일은 마무리하고 커피 한잔하자

› **stew**   make a dish of boiled meat and vegetables

Let's drink till we drop
> ㄴ 취하도록 마셔보자

Let's go out and get juiced
> ㄴ 어디 나가서 한 잔 하지 그래

Let's knock off work today early and go have a few beers
> ㄴ 오늘은 일찍 퇴근해서 맥주나 한 잔 하러 가자

Let's shoot(bat, fan) the breeze over a cup of coffee
> ㄴ 커피 한잔하면서 얘기(잡담)나 좀 하자

Lewis raised(lifted) his glass of beer, Ed followed suit and we clinked glasses
> ㄴ 루이스가 맥주 잔을 들자 에드가 따라서 잔을 들었고 우리도 술잔을 부딪쳤다

Looks like he's had all he can take
> ㄴ 그가 너무 취한 것 같다

Many is the time I had beer at that beer hall
> ㄴ 저 맥주 집에서 맥주 마신 적이 많아

Milk is a suspension of nourishing materials in water
> ㄴ 우유는 물 속에 녹아있는 영양성분 물질의 현탁액이다

Never again did I sample alcohol in any shape or form
> ㄴ 술이라고는 입에도 안 댔어

No daylight!
> ㄴ 잔을 가득 채웁시다!

› **clink** make a slight metallic sound
› **nourish** promote the growth of

(=Fill it up)
(잔을 바다에 비유한다면 깊은 바다 속에 햇빛이 없기 때문이며, 젊은 세대
는 잘 안 쓰는 경향이 있음. 따라서 Fill it up 이 무난)

No thanks, I've sworn off drinking
    ㄴ 술을 끈기로 맹세했으니 고맙지만 사양이야

Nobody can hold their drink as well as they could when they were young
    ㄴ 젊었을 때만큼 술을 마시고 견디는 사람은 아무도 없다

One drop of poison infects the whole ton of wine
    ㄴ 미꾸라지 한 마리가 온 웅덩이를 흐린다

하나가 전체에게 나쁜 영향을 미친다는 말이다. 영어 속담에는 여러 가지가
있는데, 가장 자주 쓰이는 표현은 "One rotten apple spoils the barrel
썩은 사과 하나가 한 통을 썩게 한다"이다. 악한 한 사람이 한 가문, 한 나라
를 욕되게 하는 것은 "It is an ill bird that fouls its own nest 자기의
둥지를 더럽히는 새는 나쁜 새이다"로 표현한다.
(=One scabbed sheep will mar a whole flock)
(=A hog that's bemired endeavors to bemire others)

One heaping spoonful of coffee struck a happy medium
    ㄴ 커피를 한 스푼 고봉으로 해서 적당한 양으로 조절했다(한 스푼은 너
      무 많고 두 스푼은 너무 많을 때)

One of my friends rolled around(round) when I was getting coffee ready this morning
    ㄴ 오늘 오전 커피를 마시려 할 때 친구 하나가 불쑥 찾아왔다

Only four beers and he's out

> **swear** make or cause to make a solemn statement or promise under oath

> **medium** middle position or degree

ㄴ 그는 겨우 맥주 네 잔에 벌써 취해버렸어

Orange peel tea mixed with ginger is considered powerful remedy for people who suffer from first-stage cold

ㄴ 초기 감기로 고생하는 사람에게는 생강을 섞은 오렌지 껍질 차가 효
험 있는 약으로 알려져 있다

People who drink only to satisfy their thirst will consume about two-thirds of the water their body actually need

ㄴ 단지 갈증을 면하기 위해 물을 마시는 사람은 실제 그들의 몸이 요구
하는 물의 2/3정도 밖에 취하지 못하는 셈이다

Please freshen my drink

ㄴ 제 잔에 술을 더 부어 주세요

Please, hand round the tea

ㄴ 차(tea) 좀 내 오십시오

Quitting drinking should be your first order of business

ㄴ 넌 우선 술 끊는 것부터 실천해야 해

Roasted sparrow and Soju go together best

ㄴ 참새구이와 소주는 최고로 잘 맞아

Sang-hee poured the beer and the glass ran over

ㄴ 상희가 맥주를 따르자 맥주 잔이 넘쳤다

Sang-soo has been in a state of suspended animation

ㄴ 상수는 인사불성인 상태야

Sang-soo's slurring his words. He's had one too many

ㄴ 상수는 혀가 잘 안 돌아. 벌써 취했어

She drank so much before we got there that she fell asleep and missed all the fun of the fair

ㄴ 그 여자는 우리가 거기 가기 전에 너무 취한 채 잠이 들어 즐거운 행

‣ **quit** stop, leave
‣ **animation** liveliness, animated cartoon

사를 다 놓쳐버렸어

She'd sour the drink
> ↳ 저 여자 보면 술맛 떨어져

She's not having you wandering down the street drunk for all the world to see
> ↳ 네가 많은 사람 보는 앞에서 술에 취해 거리를 싸돌아다니는 꼴을 그 여자가 가만히 두지 않을 거야

She's through with alcohol
> ↳ 그 여자는 술 끊었어

Since then he hasn't touched a drop
> ↳ 그 이후 그는 술이라고는 한 방울도 안 마셨다

Soju is filling me up
> ↳ 이제 소주(술)를 더는 못 마시겠어

Step up to the tavern and name your poison
> ↳ 우선 술집으로 가서 무슨 술이 좋은지 말만 해

Sung-moon kept his head in his cups
> ↳ 성문이는 술에 취했어도 정신은 말짱했어

Taken in moderation, wine is the best of all medicines
> ↳ 알맞게 마시면 술이 최고의 영약이다

> 술도 좋은 술을 적당히 마시면 건강에 이롭다. 우리의 선조들도 '적게 먹으면 약주요, 많이 먹으면 망주'라고 하였다. 서양에서는 좋은 포도주가 건강에 이롭다고 한다(Good wine makes good blood).

That brought a chill to the merry-making
> ↳ 그 바람에 모처럼 올랐던 취흥이 깨졌다

› **wander** move about aimlessly
› **chill** make or become cold or chilly

That guy is carrying a load again
ㄴ 저 친구가 또 취했군

That guy is falling-down drunk
ㄴ 저 친구는 취해서 몸도 못 가누는군

That you were drunk doesn't justify your violating the rule
ㄴ 술이 취했다해서 규칙을 위반해도 좋다는 이유는 될 수 없어

That's enough to drive me to drink
ㄴ 거 참 짜증나는군

That's my limit
ㄴ 술은 더 이상 못합니다(술, 음식을 사양할 때)

The accident brought home to him the evil of drinking while driving
ㄴ 그는 사고를 보고 음주 운전이 얼마나 나쁜가를 절감하게 되었어

The herb should be taken in the form of a tea and imbibed as often as possible
ㄴ 그 약초는 차로 만들어서 가능한 한 자주 복용해야 한다

The Soju has begun to its work
ㄴ 소주가 막 오르는군

The tantalizing aroma of coffee made him stop before the cafe
ㄴ 그는 감질나게 하는 커피 향에 끌려서 커피점으로 들어섰다

The wine has weakened you
ㄴ 술 취했군

There was plenty of food and booze, and a good time was had by all
ㄴ 음식도 술도 풍성했고 모두가 즐거웠어

They are being quite cynical that the reason why we have such a large turnout is that we are serving refreshments
ㄴ 그들은 우리가 음료수를 제공하기 때문에 참석자들이 그렇게 많은 것

› **justify** prove to be just, right, or reasonable
› **imbibe** drink

› **tantalize** tease or torment by keeping something desirable just out of each

이라는 냉소적인 태도이다

They are only here for the beer
　　↳ 그들에겐 염불보다 잿밥이지

They began to let their hair down and chat over tea and cookies
　　↳ 그들은 긴장을 풀고 차와 커피를 들면서 얘기를 나누었다

They may find time for a quick one
　　↳ 그 사람들이 한잔 할 정도의 시간은 있을 거야

They wish you wouldn't press more beer on them when they have already refused politely
　　↳ 그들이 정중히 사양하면 더 이상 맥주를 억지로 권하지 않길 바라고 있어

This is my favorite watering hole
　　↳ 여기가 내 단골 술집이야

This Soju really packs a wallop(is really strong)
　　↳ 이 소주는 정말 독해

Those guys spend a lot of time at the fill-mill(tavern)
　　↳ 저 친구들은 술집에서 노닥거리는 때가 많다

To dispute a drunkard is to debate with an empty house
　　↳ 술주정뱅이와 논쟁하는 것은 빈집과 말씨름하는 것과 같다

Too much of drinking is bad for you
　　↳ 과음은 좋지 않아

Two things only a man cannot hide: that he drunk and that he is in love
　　↳ 인간이 숨길 수 없는 두 가지가 있는데 하나는 술 취한 것이고 하나는 사랑에 빠진 것이다

Wake up and smell the coffee

· **wallop**　powerful blow, ability to hit hard, defeat soundly, hit hard

ㄴ 뒷다리 긁지마(상황판단을 제대로 하라)(=keep up with the program)

We are going to make the bars all night
ㄴ 우린 오늘 밤새워 술집 순례에 나서기로 했어

We can't get through the day without at least one cup of coffee
ㄴ 우리는 최소한 한 잔의 커피를 마시지 않고는 하루도 보낼 수 없다

We drank till our tongues tripped
ㄴ 우린 혀가 꼬부라지게 술을 마셔댔어

We drink one another's health and spoil our own
ㄴ 우리는 서로의 건강을 위한답시고 술을 마시면서 우리 자신의 건강을 망친다

We enjoy our glass now and then
ㄴ 우린 가끔 술 한잔씩 해

When the cock is drunk, he forgets about the hawk
ㄴ 수탉이 술에 취하면 매 따위는 안중에도 없다

When the wine is in, wit(truth) is out
ㄴ 술먹은 개

Whenever he drinks he almost goes out of his head
ㄴ 그 사람 술만 마시면 제정신이 아냐

While he was talking to us he polished off a whole bottle of beer
ㄴ 그는 우리들에게 이야기하면서 맥주 한 병을 쭉 마셨다

Why are you driving me to drink?
ㄴ 왜 날 달달 볶고있지?

Wine is a turncoat
ㄴ 술은 마실 때 좋지만 뒤끝이 안 좋다

Wine is best of all medicine
ㄴ 술은 백 약의 장이다

· **trip** step lightly, stumble or cause to stumble
· **turncoat** traitor

> 술도 좋은 술을 적당히 마시면 건강에 이롭다. 우리의 선조들도 '적게 먹으면 약주요, 많이 먹으면 망주'라고 하였다. 서양에서는 좋은 포도주가 건강에 이롭다고 한다(Good wine makes good blood).
> (=Good wine engenders good blood)

Wine is the best broom for troubles
　　　↳ 고통을 잊게 해 주는데는 술이 최고다

You drank too much to carry
　　　↳ 술에 취해 비틀거리더군

You fell off the wagon again
　　　↳ 또 술잔을 입에 댔단 말이군

You had one too many
　　　↳ 취하셨군요(You are drunk보다 훨씬 정중한 말)

You like coffee, but it doesn't like you
　　　↳ 너는 커피를 좋아하지만 몸에 안 좋아

You may drink if you want, but you must not be drowned in your liquor
　　　↳ 술을 마시는 건, 좋지만 술이 사람을 마셔선 안 돼

You may get the back-door trot if you drink cold beer
　　　↳ 찬 맥주를 마시면 설사가 날지도 몰라

You seemed to be more than a little(bit) tipsy
　　　↳ 너 상당히 취한 것 같더라

You'll drink yourself out of your job
　　　↳ 그러다간 술로 직장을 잃게 돼

▸ **broom**　flowering shrub, implement for sweeping

▸ **trot**　moderately fast gait of a horse with diagonally paired legs moving together

106. 음식&맛   Foods & Tastes

A bean sprout soup loaded with hot red pepper, is considered the best for recovering from a hangover
> ↳ 매운 고추 가루를 탄 콩나물국을 숙취 회복에 최고로 친다

A broken egg can never be mended
> ↳ 엎질러진 물이다

> 이미 저질러져서 돌이킬 수 없는 일을 두고 '엎질러진 물'이라고 한다. 이 표현에 해당하는 영어 속담은 "A broken egg can never be mended 깨진 계란은 다시 고칠 수 없다"와 "It is no use crying over spilt milk 이미 쏟아진 우유를 보고 울어봐야 소용없다"이다.

A diet is what helps a person gain weight more slowly
> ↳ 식이요법이란 살이 천천히 붙도록 도와주는 것이다

A good medicine tastes bitter
> ↳ 좋은 약은 입에 쓰다

> 자신의 결점을 꼬집어서 말하는 충고를 들을 때에는 기분이 좋을 수가 없다. 그렇기 때문에 함부로 남에게 충고를 해서는 안되고, 충고를 들어서 기분이 나쁘더라도 받아들일 수 있는 아량이 있어야 한다.
> (=Unpleasant advice is a good medicine)

› **spill**   cause or allow unintentionally to fall, flow, or run out

A fish bone was stuck in my throat for a while

ㄴ 생선뼈가 목에 걸려 얼마동안 넘어가지 않았어

A full gut is better than moral precepts

ㄴ 배부름은 도덕적 교훈보다 낫다

A hungry man is more interested in four sandwiches than four freedoms

ㄴ 배고픈 사람에게는 네 가지 자유보다 네 개의 샌드위치가 낫다

A hungry stomach has no ears

ㄴ 배가 고프면 아무 소리도 귀에 안 들어온다

A loaf of bread is better than the song of many birds

ㄴ 금강산도 식후경

> "Running around like a hen with its head cut off"는 한국식으로 표현
> 하면 "호떡집에 불났다"이다. 양계장에서 닭 잡는 날의 혼란스러움에 빗대어
> 만든 속담이다.
> (=The belly has no ears)

A lot of jobless people don't know where their meals are coming from

ㄴ 많은 실직자들은 끼니 걱정을 해야 할 지경이야

Acorns were good till bread was found

ㄴ 빵이 생기기 전에는 도토리가 훌륭한 양식이었다

Add some garlic to season it

ㄴ 마늘로 양념하면 돼

After the spirits of ancestors taste the food on New Year's day, it'll be served as the first meal of the year to the family

---

· **precept** rule of action or conduct
· **acorn** nut of the oak

↳ 설날 아침 조상들이 음식을 맛본 후 그 음식은 가족들에게 주어지는 새해 첫 음식이 된다

All this running worked up quite an appetite today

↳ 이렇게 한참 달리기를 했더니 오늘은 밥맛이 돌아왔다

All's good in famine

↳ 배고프면 무엇이나 맛있다

An ever increasing number of people throughout the world are exposing themselves to foods containing high level of artificial ingredients

↳ 전 세계적으로 점점 많은 사람들이 인공성분이 많이 함유된 식품에 노출되고 있다

An-do force himself to eat(take, have a few mouthfuls)

↳ 안도는 식사를 하는 둥 마는 둥 했어

Apples are valued nowadays for their aid to digestion and their help in keeping teeth clean and healthy

↳ 사과는 소화를 돕고 이를 깨끗하게 하고 건강을 유지시켜줌으로써 오늘날 소중히 여겨진다

Apricot pits are especially good for those who have a dry, itchy throat

↳ 목이 마르고 가려운 사람에게 살구 씨가 특히 좋다

Bananas that are to be shipped a long way are picked when they are green

↳ 멀리 보낼 바나나는 덜 익었을 때 수확한다

Better beans and bacons in piece than cakes and ale in fear

↳ 두려움 속의 케이크와 에일맥주 보다는 평화 속의 콩과 베이컨이 낫다

Better starve free than be a fat slave

▸ **appetite** natural desire especially for food, preference

▸ **apricot** peachlike fruit

ㄴ 살찐 종이 되기보다는 편히 굶는 것이 낫다

Bong-soo portioned out the cake carefully, making sure everyone got an equal share

ㄴ 봉수는 모든 사람에게 같은 양이 돌아가도록 조심스레 케익을 나누었다

Burn off the calories before you eat the food

ㄴ 음식을 먹기 전에 칼로리부터 먼저 연소시켜라

Byung-soo is flatter than a pancake

ㄴ 병수는 땡전한푼 없어(흔한 표현 아님)

Can I entice you with a piece of cake?

ㄴ 과자 하나 먹어볼래?

(=Can I oblige you with a piece of cake?)

Can I help you to some more soup?

ㄴ 수프를 좀 더 드시겠습니까?

Chang-soo's cake came out right this time

ㄴ 창수의 케익이 이번엔 잘 나왔어

Chobap is rice-balls topped with slices of raw fish

ㄴ 초밥은 주먹밥에 생선회를 얹은 것이다

Come and get some hamburgers before Dong-soo polish them all off

ㄴ 동수가 햄버거를 다 먹어치우기 전에 얼른 가서 좀 먹어라

Complaints about the profiteering will be more vociferous, if food supplies dwindle

ㄴ 식량공급이 줄어지면 부당 이익에 대한 불평이 더욱 요란해질 것이다

Could you clean the fish?

· **oblige** compel, to a favor for
· **vociferous** noisy and insistent

· **profiteer** one who makes an unreasonable profit

↳ 비늘과 내장을 제거해 주시겠어요?

"Did you bake the cakes yourself?" - "Yes, with my own fair hands"

↳ "그 케익을 네가 구웠니?" - "그럼요. 제가 직접 구웠죠"

Doesn't he take the cake!

↳ 그 사람 뻔뻔스럽기 짝이 없어

Don't buy that fish, it's crawling with flies

↳ 그 생선은 파리가 득시글거리는데 사지마

Don't get me started on the food

↳ 음식얘기는 꺼내지도 마라

Don't just gobble your food down

↳ 음식을 게걸스레 먹기만 해서는 안 돼

Don't play(toy) with your food

↳ 음식을 먹지는 않고 건드리기만 해선 안 돼

Don't skip(miss) meals

↳ 끼니를 거르지 마라

(=Eat at every mealtime)

Don't speak with your mouth full

↳ 입에 음식을 넣은 채 말하지마

Don't trifle with your meal

↳ 음식을 깨지락거리지마

Doo-chul ate three helpings of beef

↳ 두철인 쇠고기 3인분을 먹었어

During the ceremony, the host sets the table with food, rice cakes,

---

· **gobble** eat greedily

· **trifle** eat greedily

and the head of a pig
↳ 사업주는 음식과 떡을 차려놓은 상위에 돼지머리를 올려놓는다

Eat at pleasure, drink by measure
↳ 즐겁게 먹고 적당히 마셔라

Eat to please yourself, but dress to please others
↳ 자신을 위해서 먹고 남을 위해서 옷을 입어라

Even a few pieces of cake will take the edge off your hunger
↳ 케이크 몇 조각이지만 너의 허기를 조금은 면하게 해 줄 것이다

Even if there's no time for breakfast, you must not go without
↳ 아침 먹을 시간이 없다고 해도 아침을 걸러선 안 돼

Every oak has been an acorn
↳ 모든 떡갈나무는 도토리이던 시절이 있다

Everyday brings its bread with it
↳ 산 입에 거미줄 치랴

Families prepare 'charye' for their deceased ancestors, serving rice, soup, side dishes, fruit, and rice cakes to spirits visiting their homes
↳ 가족들은 집으로 찾아오는 돌아가신 조상들의 귀신들에게 밥, 국, 찬, 떡 등을 차례 올릴 차례를 준비한다

Fat paunches have lean pates(heads)
↳ 배가 부르면 머리가 텅비게 된다

Food comes first, then morals
↳ 배가 불러야 도덕이 있다

Food doesn't taste good to us when we have a cold
↳ 감기가 들면 밥맛이 떨어진다

Get on with your food before it gets cold
↳ 식기 전에 드세요

› **decease** death
› **paunch** large belly

Gil-soo ate so much that he was bursting at the seams
ㄴ 봉수는 배가 터지게 먹어댔어

Gil-soo is a man with a finger in every pie in our office
ㄴ 우리 사무실에서 길수는 약방에 감초지

Ginseng helps warm up the body, strengthen immunity and even fight cancer
ㄴ 인삼은 몸을 따뜻하게 하고 면역성을 강화시키며 암에 대한 저항력까지 강화해 준다

Ginseng is particularly effective for those who suffer from chronically cold hands and feet, bodily aches and pains
ㄴ 인삼은 특히 만성적으로 손발이 차며, 몸이 아프고 쑤시는 사람에게 효과가 크다

Good wine needs no bush
ㄴ 외모보다 마음씨

Grapes are in now
ㄴ 포도가 제철

Half a loaf is better than no bread(none)
ㄴ 소량이라도 없는 것 보다 낫지

He ate a little more than he should have
ㄴ 그는 과식했어

He has a finger in every pie
ㄴ 그는 약방의 감초다

He is(a) pie in the sky for you
ㄴ 꿈 좀 깨라, 그는 네게 그림의 떡이야

· **immune**   not liable especially to disease

> 한국과 영어 속담 중에 뜻이 일치하는 것이 여러 가지 있다. "Pie in the sky 그림의 떡"도 음식을 사용하여 표현했다는 점에서 비슷하다. 이 말은 선거철에 후보들이 이루지 못할 공약을 제시할 때에 많이 쓰인다.

He that would eat the fruit must climb the tree
ㄴ 부뚜막의 소금도 집어넣어야 짜다

> 무슨 일이든 노력이 있어야 가능하고 노력하여 성취한 일은 보다 값지다. 과일이 달려 있어도 올라가서 따와야 먹을 수 있다는 뜻이다. 게으른 사람은 먹지도 말라는 말과도 같은 뜻이다.

He whose belly is full believes not him who is fasting
ㄴ 자기 배가 부르면 남의 배고픈 줄 모른다

His car has many nice options which are sort of the icing(frosting) on the cake
ㄴ 그의 차에는 덤(금상첨화)이라 할 수 있는 멋진 옵션이 많이 붙어있어

> "좋은 데 더 좋은 것을 더한다"는 뜻이다. 영어로는 'Icing on the cake 케익위의 크림'이라고 한다. 케익만으로도 맛있는데, 거기에 크림을 더해 더욱 맛있어 졌다는 얘기이다. Icing 대신에 Frosting 으로 대체 할 수도 있다.

His shirt-sleeves were smeared with jam, berry-juice and butter
ㄴ 그의 셔츠 소매는 잼, 딸기주스, 버터가 묻어있었다

Honey catches more flies than vinegar
ㄴ 꿀은 식초보다 파리를 더 많이 잡는다(친절 권장)

› **smear** greasy stain, spread, smudge, slander

친절하게 대하는 것은 말은 쉽지만 실천이 쉽지가 않다. 그러나 친절은 손해
도 나지 않고, 자신에게 이로운 처세술이다.

Hospitality consists in a little fire, a little food and an immense quiet
> ↳ 환대란 불을 좀 지펴주고, 음식을 좀 내주며 조용히 해주는 것이다

How is sugar(the dollar)?
> ↳ 설탕(달러) 시세 어때?(이해하지 못할 수도 있음)

How long will it keep(last)?
> ↳ 얼마동안 먹어도 됩니까?(식품)

Hunger finds no fault with the cookery
> ↳ 시장이 반찬이다

배가 고프면 무슨 음식이던지 달게 느껴지게 마련이다. "시장이 좋은 반찬이
다"는 영어로 "Hunger is the spice of food"나 "Hunger is the best
sauce"라고도 한다.
(=All's good in a famine)

Hyun-soo needs extra calories like a hole in the head
> · ↳ 현수에게 여분의 칼로리는 전혀 필요 없어

I ate with a capital 'E'
> ↳ 실컷 먹었지

I feel like some munchies
> ↳ 군것질이 생각나네

I must cut out starchy foods
> ↳ 난 전분 식품을 피해야 해

I work for chicken feed(peanuts)

· **immense** vast

· **munch** chew

· **starchy** nourishing carbohydrate from plants
also used in adhesives and
laundering

ㄴ 쥐꼬리 월급 받고있어

(=I'm making slave wages)

I would rather starve than eat this
ㄴ 이걸 먹느니 차라리 굶고 말지

If I could stop blimping out(overeating), I could lose some weight
ㄴ 과식(비만)을 피할 수만 있다면 체중을 좀 줄일 수 있으런만

In many parts of the world the poor are going without food so that the rich can live in luxury
ㄴ 세계의 많은 지역에서 가난한 사람들이 끼니를 거르고 있기 때문에 부자인 사람들이 호화롭게 산다

Is there any law against my eating out?
ㄴ 나라고 외식 못 하라는 법 있나?

Is there anything to eat?
ㄴ 안주 있습니까?

It comes in bite-size pieces
ㄴ 한입 크기로 나옵니다(식료상품 출하)

It looks very appetizing
ㄴ 구미가 당기는군

(=It makes me feel hungry)
(=It is wetting my appetite)

It turns me off
ㄴ 입맛 떨어지네

› **blimp** small airship holding form by pressure of contained gas

› **appetizing** tempting to the appetite

It's like catching two pigeons with one bean
> ↳ 도랑 치고 가재잡고

It's like comparing apples and oranges
> ↳ 그건 비교를 못 하겠어

Jiwhang can be a great help for people who get easily stressed and fatigued working long hours
> ↳ 지황은 장시간 일을 해서 쉽게 스트레스가 쌓이고 쉽게 피곤해지는 사람에게 큰 도움이 된다

Jiwhang helps prevent the symptoms of senility and supplements the substances essential for marrow production
> ↳ 지황은 노화현상을 막아주고 골수형성에 꼭 필요한 성분을 보충해준다

Jung-tae is a rotten apple to spoil it for the rest of us
> ↳ 정태는 미꾸라지 한 마리가 웅덩이 전체를 흐려놓을 사람이다

하나가 전체에게 나쁜 영향을 미친다는 말이다. 영어 속담에는 여러 가지가 있는데, 가장 자주 쓰이는 표현은 "One rotten apple spoils the barrel 썩은 사과 하나가 한 통을 썩게 한다"이다. 악한 한 사람이 한 가문, 한 나라를 욕되게 하는 것은 "It is an ill bird that fouls its own nest 자기의 둥지를 더럽히는 새는 나쁜 새이다"로 표현한다.
(=One scabbed sheep will mar a whole flock)
(=A hog that's bemired endeavors to bemire others)

Just tell him there'll be lots of delicious food and he'll rise to the bait
> ↳ 그에게 맛있는 음식이 많이 있다고만 하면 올 거야

Keep a good cut of beef for me every week
> ↳ 매주 상등의 쇠고기 한 덩이를 내 몫으로 떼어놓아 주어라

› **fatigue** weariness from labor or use
› **senile** mentally deficient through old age

› **marrow** soft tissue in the cavity of bone

Kimchi is prepared with Chinese cabbage and many other natural ingredients, then stored underground in clay containers to ferment for at least three weeks
ㄴ 김치는 배추와 여러 가지 자연산 재료들을 섞어 질그릇에 넣어 땅 속에서 최소한 **3**주 이상 발효시켜 만든다

Let's divide the watermelon among us three
ㄴ 이 수박을 쪼개서 우리 셋이 나눠먹자

Let's eat, drink, and be merry, for tomorrow is another day
ㄴ 내일은 내일이니 오늘을 즐기자

Let's fair out this pizza
ㄴ 이 피자를 고루 나누어주자

Let's flock(get, gather) around the birthday cake
ㄴ 생일 케익 옆에 둥그렇게 모이자

Let's splurge on a lavish lunch today
ㄴ 오늘 비싼데 가서 화끈하게 점심한번 먹자

Licorice root counteracts the effects of poisons and helps to increase and harmonize effects of other herbs
ㄴ 감초는 독성을 중화시키고 다른 한약재들의 효능을 강화시키고 조화시켜 준다

Look at this nice spread
ㄴ 야, 진수성찬이군

Love doesn't just sit there, like a stone: it has to be made, like bread, re-made all the time, made new
ㄴ 사랑은 돌처럼 항상 제자리에 있지 않다. 그것은 빵이 만들어지듯 만들어져야 하며 항상 다시 만들어지며 새롭게 거듭나야 하는 것이다

Men are constantly on the lookout for seasonal food shortages and

---

· **ferment** cause or undergo fermentation
· **splurge** indulge oneself

· **counteract** lessen the force of

gluts

  ↳ 인간은 끊임없이 계절적인 식량부족과 과잉에 대해 경계해 왔다

Mustard is a good sauce, but mirth is better

  ↳ 겨자가 좋은 소스지만 즐거움은 더 좋은 소스이다

My stomach is already growling

  ↳ 벌써부터 배에서 꼬르륵 소리가 난다

Natural herbs are considered not only medicinal drugs, but also health food

  ↳ 자연산 약용식물은 의약뿐만 아니라 건강식품으로도 여겨진다

No dish pleases all palates alike

  ↳ 모든 입맛에 다 맞는 음식은 없다

Nothing comes amiss to a hungry man

  ↳ 시장이 반찬

배가 고프면 무슨 음식이던지 달게 느껴지게 마련이다. "시장이 좋은 반찬이다"는 영어로 "Hunger is the spice of food"나 "Hunger is the best sauce"라고도 한다.

Now there's a woman who likes her spaghetti

  ↳ 야, 너 국수 잘도 먹는구나(여자에게)

Nowadays more and more people prefer natural flavoring ingredients to artificial ones

  ↳ 요즈음에는 인공 조미료 보다 천연 조미료를 더 좋아한다

Once the safety of gene-engineered food is fully proven, a revolutionary chance can be expected in the global agricultural production

---

- **glut** fill to excess
- **mirth** gladness and laughter
- **palate** roof of the mouth, taste

↳ 유전자 조작식품의 안전성이 증명되기만 하면 세계 농업생산의 혁명
적 변동을 기대할 수 있게 된다

One rotten apple spoils the barrel
  ↳ 미꾸라지 한 마리가 웅덩이 물 다 흐려

> 하나가 전체에게 나쁜 영향을 미친다는 말이다. 영어 속담에는 여러 가지가
> 있는데, 가장 자주 쓰이는 표현은 "One rotten apple spoils the barrel
> 썩은 사과 하나가 한 통을 썩게 한다"이다. 악한 한 사람이 한 가문, 한 나라
> 를 욕되게 하는 것은 "It is an ill bird that fouls its own nest 자기의
> 둥지를 더럽히는 새는 나쁜 새이다"로 표현한다.
> (=One scabbed sheep will mar a whole flock)
> (=A hog that's bemired endeavors to bemire others)

**Orange peel tea mixed with ginger is considered powerful remedy for
people who suffer from first-stage cold**
  ↳ 초기 감기로 고생하는 사람에게는 생강을 섞은 오렌지 껍질 차가 효
  험 있는 약으로 알려져 있다

Our apples run large(small) this year
  ↳ 금년에는 사과가 크(작)다

Pears ripen signaling the advance of harvest season
  ↳ 배는 수확기가 왔음을 알리면서 익어간다

Please don't pick(peck) at your food
  ↳ 음식을 깨죽거리고 먹지마

Please hold the mustard
  ↳ 겨자는 넣지 말아 주십시오(음식 조리)

Please hold the onions and red pepper
  ↳ 양파와 고추는 넣지 말아주세요

· **signal** communicate or notify by signals
· **peck** at nag(+at)

Please pass the snacks around to everyone
ㄴ 모든 사람에게 간식을 좀 나눠주어라

Pop this chicken in the microwave and it'll be ready in no time
ㄴ 이 닭고기를 전자레인지에 넣으면 금방 먹을 수 있게 될 거야

Promises and pie-crust are made to be broken
ㄴ 약속과 파이껍질은 깨지기 위해 만들어진다

Public servants(Government employees) must eat their honest bread
ㄴ 공무원은 정직한 월급으로 살아야 한다

Ripe bananas peels easily
ㄴ 익은 바나나는 껍질이 잘 벗겨져

Roadside produce stands usually offer lower price fruits and vegetables than supermarkets
ㄴ 도로변 농산물 판매소는 대개 슈퍼마켓보다 값이 싸다

Roasted sparrow and Soju go together best
ㄴ 참새구이와 소주는 최고로 잘 맞아

Salt has good side and bad side and it's best when taken in moderation
ㄴ 소금은 좋은 면과 나쁜 면을 모두 가지고 있으므로 적당히 섭취하는 것이 제일 좋다

Salt plays an important part in the function of the body
ㄴ 소금은 신진대사에 중요한 역할을 한다

Sara is as nutty as a fruitcake
ㄴ 사라는 덜 떨어진 사람

Save some bread for me
ㄴ 빵은 내 몫을 남겨야 해

She drinks some special potion made of a combination of steamed

---

‣ **ripe** fully grown, developed, or prepared

red ginseng, crushed young deer antler powder, and jujubes
> ㄴ 그녀는 홍삼과 녹용가루, 대추를 넣어서 만든 보약을 먹고 있어

She was occupied sorting out the best fruits
> ㄴ 그녀는 가장 좋은 과일을 고르고 있었다

Stockpiling food is a selfish thing to do
> ㄴ 식료품 사재기는 이기심이다

Tai-soo ate dry bread
> ㄴ 태수는 빵에 아무 것도 안 바르고 먹었다(마른 빵이 아님)

Take a step close to a healthier body by adding a spoonful of vinegar to your diet today
> ㄴ 오늘 식사에 한 티스푼의 식초를 첨가해서 더욱 건강한 신체로 가꾸어 나가라

Take those persimmons which they seems are bit green
> ㄴ 좀 푸릇푸릇한 감을 골라라

Temperature is of vital importance when storing fresh food such as vegetables, meat, and fish
> ㄴ 채소류, 육류, 어류 같은 신선식품을 저장하는데는 온도가 중요하다

That dish is hard to make
> ㄴ 그건 손이 많이 가는 음식이다

> (=That dish takes a lot of work to do(time to make))
> (=Cooking that dish is not easy)

That hungry guy garbaged down(bolted down, gobbled up) almost everything
> ㄴ 저 배고픈 녀석이 거의 닥치는 대로 먹어치웠다

▸ **sort** classify
▸ **stockpile** reserve supply

▸ **persimmon** tree with orange-colored edible fruit

That store is fresh out of bananas
> ↳ 저 가게는 바나나를 막 다 팔아버렸어

That type of girl must be your cup of tea
> ↳ 넌 저런 타입의 여자를 좋아할 것 같아

That's icing on the cake
> ↳ 그건 금상첨화야

> "좋은 데 더 좋은 것을 더한다"는 뜻이다. 영어로는 "Icing on the cake 케익위의 크림"이라고 한다. 케익만으로도 맛있는데, 거기에 크림을 더해 더욱 맛있어 졌다는 얘기이다. Icing 대신에 Frosting 으로 대체 할 수도 있다.

That's probably an apple for the teacher, and best not to be accepted
> ↳ 그건 일종의 뇌물이니 안 받는 게 제일이야

That's sour grapes
> ↳ 못 먹는 감 찔러나 보자는 말이군

> 자신이 갖지 못할 바에 다른 사람도 가지지 못했으면 하는 것이 사람의 심리이다. 한국에서는 "못 먹는 감 찔러나 본다"나 "못 먹는 밥에 재 뿌린다"라고 하며, 이에 가장 가까운 영어 표현은 'Sour grapes 신 포도'이다. 유명한 이솝우화 중에서 포도를 따지 못한 여우가 "저것은 신 포도일 것이다"라고 자신을 위로하는 데서 비롯된 것이다.

The bacteria and molds that cause decay and fermentation in food can't thrive without moisture
> ↳ 부패와 발효를 일으키는 박테리아와 곰팡이는 습기가 없으면 번성할 수 없다

The dinner is being delivered as we speak

· **decay** decline in condition, break down chemically or fall into a state of ruin

· **thrive** grow vigorously, prosper

ㄴ 저녁식사가 지금 막 배달됐다

The flavor of field mushrooms leaves the cultivated commercial product standing

ㄴ 자연산 버섯의 향은 영업적으로 양식한 버섯에 비해 뛰어나다

The frosting(icing) on the cake is that I can earn more overtime

ㄴ 게다가 시간외 근무수당도 더 벌 수 있게 됐으니 금상첨화지 뭐

> "좋은 데 더 좋은 것을 더한다"는 뜻이다. 영어로는 'Icing on the cake 케익위의 크림'이라고 한다. 케익만으로도 맛있는데, 거기에 크림을 더해 더욱 맛있어 졌다는 얘기이다. Icing 대신에 Frosting 으로 대체 할 수도 있다.

The mere smell put him off the food

ㄴ 그는 냄새만 맡고도 식욕이 없어졌다

The mixture of fish, rice and eggs goes by the name of kedgeree in most restaurants

ㄴ 생선, 쌀, 계란을 섞어서 만든 것을 대부분의 식당에서는 케저리라고 부른다

The molds that cause decay and fermentation in food can't thrive without moisture

ㄴ 음식의 부패와 발효를 일으키는 곰팡이는 습기 없이 번성할 수 없다

The mouse nibbled away at the huge cheese

ㄴ 쥐가 커다란 치즈를 갉아먹었다

The process requires that this fresh herb be dipped in alcohol steamed and dried some nine times

ㄴ 이 생약초는 아홉 번 정도 알콜에 담그고, 찌고, 말리는 과정을 요한다

The roots of education is bitter, but the fruit is sweet

· **nibble**   bite gently or bit by bit

↳ 교육의 뿌리는 쓰지만 그 열매는 달다

The scientists noted that opposition to genetically modified foods had come mostly from rich countries
↳ 과학자들은 유전자변형 식량에 대한 반대가 대부분 잘 사는 나라에서 제기되고 있다고 지적했다

The smell of garlic and ginger lingered on in the kitchen
↳ 주방에는 마늘과 생강 냄새가 가시지 않았다

The table was groaning with good things for the many guests to eat
↳ 많은 손님들이 먹을 음식으로 식탁은 상다리가 휘게 차려져 있었다

The tasty food they served here put this place on the map
↳ 그 사람들이 내놓는 맛있는 음식 때문에 여기가 유명해졌어

The unsettled and impatient youth was a rotten apple in the barrel
↳ 안정되지 못하고 잘 참지 못하는 젊은이는 사회에 악영향을 미쳤다

> 하나가 전체에게 나쁜 영향을 미친다는 말이다. 영어 속담에는 여러 가지가 있는데, 가장 자주 쓰이는 표현은 "One rotten apple spoils the barrel 썩은 사과 하나가 한 통을 썩게 한다"이다. 악한 한 사람이 한 가문, 한 나라를 욕되게 하는 것은 "It is an ill bird that fouls its own nest 자기의 둥지를 더럽히는 새는 나쁜 새이다"로 표현한다.
> (=One scabbed sheep will mar a whole flock)
> (=A hog that's bemired endeavors to bemire others)

There was plenty of food and booze, and a good time was had by all
↳ 음식도 술도 풍성했고 모두가 즐거웠어

There're not apples enough to go around
↳ 모두에게 돌아갈 만큼의 사과는 없어

There's little difference between a feast and belly-full

▸ **groan** moan, creak under a strain
▸ **booze** drink liquor to excess

ㄴ 배를 채우는데는 잘 먹고 못 먹고 가 상관없다

There's no fruit which is not bitter before it is ripe
ㄴ 익기 전에 쓰(떫)지 않은 과일 없다

There's nothing in the jam to preserve it against spoilage
ㄴ 잼에 방부제 같은 건 넣지 않았다

These watermelons will not keep good overnight
ㄴ 이 수박들은 하룻밤 지나면 상할 거다

They are like peas and carrots
ㄴ 그들은 붙어 다니는 짝꿍이야

They are practically giving away vegetables
ㄴ 그들은 채소를 정말 싸게 팔고 있어

They ate so much they almost burst at their seams
ㄴ 그들은 배가 터지게 먹었다

They have any kind of food you want on tap
ㄴ 그들은 당신이 원하는 어떤 음식이든 준비해 놓고 있다

They sell apples, 300 won each
ㄴ 사과 한 개당 **300**원에 팔아

They were late with lunch
ㄴ 그들은 늦게 점심을 먹었어

They've had enough with fried potatoes
ㄴ 그들은 이제 튀긴 감자라면 지긋지긋해

This agar goes right through me
ㄴ 이 우무는 몸에 들어가면 바로 나간다

This is a meal fit for a king
ㄴ 진수성찬이로군

· **spoil** plunder, pillage, ruin, rot

· **agar** substance from seaweed used in laboratory cultures

This piece of meat has your name on it
ㄴ 이 마지막 고기 한 점은 네 거야

This soup has lasting taste
ㄴ 이 국물 시원하다

This soup needs something to pick it up
ㄴ 이 수프에 뭔가 빠진 것 같아

This soup wants a touch of salt
ㄴ 이 국은 싱거워

This table is groaning with food
ㄴ 상다리가 휘어지는군

Those who live by bread alone will submit, for the sake of it, to the vilest abuse
ㄴ 빵만으로 사는 사람은 그 빵 때문에 가장 창피한 모욕에 굴복해야 한다

Those with this chronic condition are more likely swell up or grow fat if he consumes even a small amount of food
ㄴ 이 같은 만성적 증세가 있는 사람은 음식을 조금만 섭취해도 몸이 나거나 살이 찔 가능성이 커진다

Thousands of demonstrators demanded a bigger slice of cake
ㄴ 수천 명의 근로자들은 보다 나은 급료(배당)을 요구했다

To lose weight and to achieve their dream of a slimmer body, many people skip meals or go on fad diet
ㄴ 많은 사람들은 체중을 줄이고 보다 날씬한 몸매를 유지하겠다는 꿈을 실현시키기 위해 끼니를 거르거나 요즈음 유행식인 식단을 이용한다

Try to eat your meal, You've nibbled(picked, pecked) at it
ㄴ 밥을 제대로 좀 먹어라, 먹는 둥 마는 둥 하지 말고

Try and see

‣ **submit**　yield, give or offer
‣ **abuse**　attack with words, misuse, mistreat

ㄴ 먹어봐야 맛을 알지

Try not to slurp in your soup

ㄴ 국을 홀쩍홀쩍 소리내며 먹지 않도록 해

Upon the clearing of the sacrificial table, the attendants are given a treat of food and drink

ㄴ 제사상을 물리자마자 제관들은 음복음식을 먹고 마시게 된다

Vinegar helps fights germs, sooths stomach pains, heals cuts quicker and adds to our overall health

ㄴ 식초는 멸균효과가 있고, 위통을 진정시키며, 상처를 빨리 낫게 하며, 건강을 전반적으로 좋게 해준다

We ate rice rolled in seaweed

ㄴ 우린 김밥을 먹었지

We have gone through all the pizza

ㄴ 피자 다 먹어버렸네

We played a good knife and fork

ㄴ 우린 배불리 먹었어

We should try to feed them some carrots

ㄴ 그들을 설득해 우리편으로 만들어야 해

We've got hamburgers coming out of our ears in the canteen at work

ㄴ 우린 직장 구내 매점에서 햄버거를 배가 터지게 먹었다

We've got to go halves on the rest of the apples

ㄴ 남은 사과는 우리 모두가 고루 나눠가져야 해

What a spread(feast)

ㄴ 진수성찬이군

› **slurp** eat or drink noisily

› **canteen** place of recreation for servicemen, water container

> (=We'll eat in style today)

Who eats his cock alone must saddle his horse alone
　　　　ㄴ 닭고기를 혼자 먹는 사람은 말 멍에도 혼자 채워야 한다

Who made the hamburger(mincemeat)out of my paper?
　　　　ㄴ 누가 내 서류를 엉망으로 만들어놨어?

You can catch more flies with honey than with vinegar
　　　　ㄴ 식초보다 꿀이 더 많은 파리를 잡는다(부드러움은 강함을 이긴다)

You can eat with a capital 'E' there
　　　　ㄴ 거기 가면 실컷 먹을 수 있어

You won't be long(in) starving
　　　　ㄴ 넌 얼마 안 있어 배고파 올 것이다

‣ **mincemeat**　finely chopped mixture especially
　　　　　　　　of raisins, apples, and spices

(=We'll eat in style today)

Who eats his cock alone must saddle his horse alone
　　ㄴ 닭고기를 혼자 먹는 사람은 말 멍에도 혼자 채워야 한다

Who made the hamburger(mincemeat)out of my paper?
　　ㄴ 누가 내 서류를 엉망으로 만들어놨어?

You can catch more flies with honey than with vinegar
　　ㄴ 식초보다 꿀이 더 많은 파리를 잡는다(부드러움은 강함을 이긴다)

You can eat with a capital 'E' there
　　ㄴ 거기 가면 실컷 먹을 수 있어

You won't be long(in) starving
　　ㄴ 넌 얼마 안 있어 배고파 올 것이다

▸ **mincemeat** finely chopped mixture especially
　　　　　of raisins, apples, and spices

107. 의견 & 토론   Opinions & Arguments

An-do just dug in his heels
     ↳ 안도가 고집을 부렸어

Bigotry may be roughly defined as the anger of men who have no opinions
     ↳ 편협은 대략 아무 의견이 없는 사람의 분노로 정의될 수 있다

Bong-soo is backward in giving people his views
     ↳ 봉수는 남에게 자기 의견을 말하기를 싫어한다

Byung-soo rested his argument on trivialities
     ↳ 병수는 하찮은 것을 논거로 자기 주장을 내세웠다

Can I put in my two cents?
     ↳ 제 의견을 덧붙여도 될까요?

Can we patch up our differences?
     ↳ 우리가 견해차를 조정(수습할 수 있을까?)

Chan-ho called for a show of hands and I took the count
     ↳ 찬호가 거수로 결정하자고 해서 내가 수를 세었지

Chan-soo chimed in with his opinion
     ↳ 찬수는 그의 의견에 동의했다(맞장구 쳤다)

Conversation is unlike a discussion, insofar as one is not trying to arrive at any definite conclusion
     ↳ 대화란 어떤 명확한 결론에 도달하려고 하지 않는 점에 있어서 토론

▸ **trivial** of little importance

과 다르다

Discussions among ourselves led us nowhere

ㄴ 우리끼리 의논해봤자 소용이 없었어

Dong-soo's comments struck home with me

ㄴ 동수의 의견은 깨달음을 주었어

Each has his own claims

ㄴ 누구에게나 할 말은 있다

Ed took exception to a few of my conclusions

ㄴ 에드는 나의 몇 가지 결론에 대하여 의의를 제기했다

For their money, you'd be better off forgetting about the lawsuit

ㄴ 그들의 의견으로는 너의 소송 따위는 그만두는 게 좋겠다는 거야

Hash it over again to reach an agreement

ㄴ 충분히 토의해서 합의를 끌어내어라

He disavowed any share in the plot

ㄴ 그는 음모에 관계없다고 부인했다

He has said his piece(has given his opinion)

ㄴ 그가 소신을 밝혔어

He held his course through good and evil report

ㄴ 그는 남이 뭐라든 개의치 않고 자신의 방침대로 관철시켰다

He slurred over the details to carry over his point

ㄴ 그는 주장을 관철하기 위해 세부 사항을 얼버무렸다

His view always jars with mine

ㄴ 그의 의견은 언제나 내 의견과 어긋나

I'll get a second opinion

ㄴ 남들에게 물어봐야겠어(확인 등)(다른데 가서도 또 물어보지 그래)

› **disavow** deny responsibility for

› **jar** have a harsh or disagreeable effect, vibrate or shake

> (=Let me get a second opinion)
> (=Maybe you need a second opinion)

In his book, anyone who disagrees with him is an enemy
ㄴ 그의 말에 의하면 그와 의견이 맞지 않는 사람은 모두 적이라는군

Let's get together and compare notes
ㄴ 언제 다시 만나 의견을 나눠봅시다

Let's keep our opinions open until we have a chance to analyze the results
ㄴ 우리가 결과를 분석할 때까지 결정을 미루자

Let's push our demand to the last
ㄴ 우리의 주장을 끝까지 관철하자

Let's settle our differences over the matter
ㄴ 그 문제의 의견차이를 조정하자

Most people kept(themselves) to themselves most of the time, and rarely expressed any opinion
ㄴ 대부분의 사람들이 대부분의 시간에 가만히 있기만 하고 의견이라곤 거의 제시하지 않았다

Much has been said for and against it
ㄴ 찬반이 많았지

My opinion carries little weight around here
ㄴ 여기선 내 의견이 별로 반영되지 않아

Myung-soo is already one opinion on this
ㄴ 명수는 요지부동이야

› **analyze** make an analysis of

> (=Myung-soo's mind is set(made up))

Nobody supported his supposition that the earnings should be pooled
> ↳ 수입의 일부를 공동자금으로 하자는 그의 제안을 아무도 지지하지 않았다

Nobody will know where your head is at(where you are coming from)
> ↳ 너의 의중이 무엇인지 누가 알겠나

Not in my book
> ↳ 내 생각은 달라

Oh-jin ventured his opinion studying my face
> ↳ 오진이는 내 눈치를 봐 가면서 의견을 제시했어

One way and another, there were a lot of talks
> ↳ 여러 가지 얘기가 나왔지

Public opinion became vocal about the new financial policy
> ↳ 새로운 정책에 대한 여론이 분분해졌다

Pyung-soo never fails to rip into his opponents, showing the weakness of their arguments
> ↳ 평수는 상대방의 논거에 약점을 들추면서 놓치지 않고 공격한다

Sang-ho sat tight until the members accepted the plan
> ↳ 상호는 그 안이 받아들여질 때까지 입장을 바꾸지 않았다

Such a proposal may be received with rather ill grace
> ↳ 그런 제의는 불쾌하게 받아들여질 수 있어

Suck-ho's argument carries little conviction
> ↳ 석호의 주장은 별로 설득력이 없어

› **pool** contribute to a common fund

› **venture** risk or take a chance on, put forward

That argument doesn't pass the idiot test
> ㄴ 그러한 주장은 어리석기 짝이 없다

That disposes of your point
> ㄴ 그걸로 네 주장은 해결된다

That view gained ground among them
> ㄴ 그 견해는 그들 사이에 지지를 얻었다

That's pretty weak
> ㄴ 그건 순 억지

(=That's a weak argument)
(=That's not a very strong argument)
(=you have no basis for your position)

The argument led nowhere
> ㄴ 그 논쟁은 결론 없이 끝났다

The domestic political scene is rife with all kinds of allegations of all political conspiration
> ㄴ 국내 정치권에서는 온갖 음모 주장이 난무하고 있다

The government and the ruling party argue that the increasing debt has stemmed from their efforts to clean up the problems created under the rule of past administration
> ㄴ 정부와 여당은 늘어나는 빚을 전 정권이 저지른 문제점들을 정리해
> 나가는 노력에서 생겨난 것이라고 주장한다

The speaker radiated enthusiasm for the cause
> ㄴ 연사는 자기주장을 위해서 열의를 쏟았다

There's something to both arguments

> • **allege**   state as a fact without proof
> • **conspiration**   an act of conspiracy

┗ 양 쪽 다 일리 있어

There's the rub, for it is a claim that can be neither wholly admitted nor wholly dismissed

┗ 그 요구를 모두 수용할 수도 모두 거절할 수도 없다는 게 문제다

They are divided in opinion

┗ 중구난방(**They are divided on this matter**그들은 이 문제에 대해 의견이 엇갈려 있어)

(=You can't shut the doors of other peoples' mouths)

They are too set in their ways

┗ 그들은 너무 생각이 굳어 있어

They debated for three hours, just talking in a circle(circles)

┗ 그들은 세 시간씩이나 토론을 벌였지만 아무런 진척이 없었어

They had only thirty minutes to discuss the problem and Jong-soo held the stage for most of it

┗ 그들은 그 일을 겨우 **30**분 정도 논의했을 뿐 나머지는 거의 다 종수가 주도적으로 말을 다 해버렸어

They hashed out the matter and decided to adopt it

┗ 그들은 문제를 충분히 논의하고 그것을 채택하기로 했다

They have covered a lot of ground

┗ 그들은 여러 가지를 논의했다

They see eye to eye on many things, but this is not one of them

┗ 그들은 많은 문제에 의견이 일치하지만 이번 일은 그렇지 않아

They still have a few details to hash out

┗ 그들에게는 아직도 결말이 나도록 상의해야 할 세부사항이 남아있어

› **hash** talk about, chop into small pieces

Try to keep what the company has decided, even if it goes against your personal opinions
>↳ 회사가 결정한 일은 네 생각과 어긋나더라도 따르도록 해라

We have to debate pros and cons of this matter
>↳ 우린 이 일에 찬반토론을 해야해

We see eye to eye on many things
>↳ 우린 많은 문제에서 의견이 일치해

We were divided in our opinions
>↳ 의견이 분분했지

We would like to invite your opinions
>↳ 여러분의 고견을 듣고 싶습니다

Whatever you decide I'm all the way with you
>↳ 네가 어떻게 결정하든 전적으로 찬성이야

Winning him in an argument is as easy as cutting butter(margarine) with a knife
>↳ 토론에서 그를 이기는 것쯤이야 식은 죽 먹기지

You are out in the left field
>↳ 네 말은 아주 틀린 거야

You can't argue your way out of this
>↳ 이 문제에서 변설로 빠져나갈 생각 마

You should speak up for yourself
>↳ 네 의견을 당당히 말 해

Yung-soo will have it so
>↳ 영수는 그렇게 주장할거야

› **pro** favorable argument or person, in favor
› **con** against, opposing side or person

108. 이름   **Names**

A capital punishment is more reprehensible because it is officially sanctioned and done with great ceremony in the name of the society
> ↳ 사형은 그것이 사회라는 이름으로 공식적으로 승인되어 커다란 의식 속에서 행해지므로 더욱 지탄을 받는다

A good name is sooner lost than won
> ↳ 훌륭한 명성은 얻기보다 잃기가 쉽다

A good name keeps its luster in the dark
> ↳ 훌륭한 명성은 어둠 속에서 그 광택이 있다

A great man will be remembered for his achievements
> ↳ 호랑이는 죽어서 가죽을 남기고 사람은 죽어서 이름을 남긴다

> (=A man dies; his name remains)

Are they going to name names?
> ↳ 그들이 대상(비행 등)자들을 거명 하겠다는 거니?

Beautiful is my middle name
> ↳ '미인'하면 나잖아

Chang-soo began to call off the names on the list
> ↳ 창수가 명단을 보고 호명했다

Chang-soo carved out a name for himself in business

- **reprehend**   express disapproval of
- **luster**   brightness from reflected light

ㄴ 창수는 자력으로 사업가로서의 명성을 얻었다

Don't call me names if you like the way your teeth are arranged
ㄴ 이빨이 성하고 싶거든 날 욕하지마

Doo-chul cheated me under the name of friendship
ㄴ 두철이는 우정이란 이름으로 나를 속였어

Doo-chul is the leader of the movement in fact(reality) and in name
ㄴ 두철이는 명실공히 이 운동의 지도자다

Doo-man is a big name on the rock music scene
ㄴ 두만이가 록음악계에선 내노라 하는 사람이다

Gil-soo has not a penny to his name
ㄴ 길수에게는 땡전한푼 없어

He's got a bullet with their names on it
ㄴ 그는 그들을 쏘아 죽이려 하고 있어

He's starting to name names
ㄴ 그가 관련자 이름을 대기 시작했어

His heart started racing when she called his name
ㄴ 그 여자가 그의 이름을 부르자 심장이 마구 뛰기 시작했다

His house stands in his name
ㄴ 그의 이름은 그의 명의로 되어있어

I am trying to think of his name but I keep drawing a blank
ㄴ 그 사람 이름을 생각해 내려고 애쓰지만 자꾸 까먹어

I didn't catch your name
ㄴ 성함을 잊어버렸습니다

In driving, carefulness is the name of the game
ㄴ 운전에는 안전운행이 관건이다

· **blank**   empty, free from writing, lacking
expression

It stands in my name
ㄴ 그건 내 명의로 돼 있어

Jong-soo called me names in public
ㄴ 종수가 사람들 앞에서 날 욕했어

Moon-ho's name stands at the bottom of the list
ㄴ 문호의 이름이 명단 끝에 있어

My name in Korean alphabet goes like this
ㄴ 홍길동. 내 이름은 한글로 '홍 길동'이라고 써

My name leads the list
ㄴ 내 이름이 맨 앞에 나와 있어

My mind seemed to go blank for a few minutes, but I soon remembered his name
ㄴ 난 몇 분 동안 생각이 멍해졌지만 곧 그의 이름이 생각났다

Names and natures do often agree
ㄴ 보기 좋은 떡이 먹기도 좋다

Nothing could be more detrimental to the good name of the school than the imprisonment of the headmaster for immoral activities with students
ㄴ 학생들에게 부도덕한 행위를 했다는 이유로 교장선생님이 감옥에 가는 것보다 더 명문학교의 이름을 손상시키는 일은 없을 것이다

Our fingers had gone dead and we couldn't write our names
ㄴ 우리는 손가락이 곱아서 이름을 쓸 수가 없었다

Patience is the name of the game in fishing
ㄴ 낚시에서 가장 중요한 것은 인내심이다

People will pay attention to you if you throw his name around a bit
ㄴ 그의 이름을 조금만 팔아도 사람들이 네게 관심을 보일 거야

> **detriment** damage
> **headmaster** male head of a private school

Sang-soo spun out at the sound of his name, ready to defend himself
> ↳ 상수는 자신의 이름을 부르는 소리에 방어자세를 취하면서 홱 돌아섰다

She doesn't like having her name bandied about
> ↳ 그 여자는 여기저기 이름 퍼뜨리는걸 싫어해

She left a great name behind her
> ↳ 그 여자는 위대한 이름을 남기고 세상을 떠났다

Step up to the tavern and name your poison
> ↳ 우선 술집으로 가서 무슨 술이 좋은지 말만 해

The amounts of each in order of names are 50 %, 30% and 20 % respectively
> ↳ 그 성분은 앞서 밝힌 순서대로 **50%, 30%, 20%**씩 들어있다

The mixture of fish, rice and eggs goes by the name of kedgeree in most restaurants
> ↳ 생선, 쌀, 계란을 섞어서 만든 것을 대부분의 식당에서는 케저리라고 부른다

The singer thought he had fully made a name for himself and decided to ride off into the sunset at the height of his career
> ↳ 인기절정인 그 가수는 충분히 출세했다는 생각에 무대에서 은퇴하기로 결심했다

There'll be no name-calling in this house
> ↳ 집안에서 욕을 해선 안 돼

They are man and wife in everything but name
> ↳ 그들은 사실상의 부부이다

They hauled us in and booked every one of us
> ↳ 그들이 우리를 연행하여 일일이 이름을 적었어

They mentioned no man by name

> • **spin** revolve or cause to revolve extremely fast
>
> • **haul** draw or pull, transport or carry

↳ 그들은 아무도 거명 하지 않았다

This car has my name on it
　　　↳ 이 차 맘에 쏙 든다

This piece of meat has your name on it
　　　↳ 이 마지막 고기 한 점은 네 거야

Though he never uses your name, the allusion to you is obvious
　　　↳ 그가 너를 직접 거명 하진 않았지만 은근히 너를 가리키는 건 분명해

To mention the wolf's name is to see the same
　　　↳ 호랑이가 제 말하면 온다

Wan-soo whipped round(whirl about, whirl round) to the mention of his name
　　　↳ 완수는 자신의 이름을 부르는 소리를 듣고 휙 돌아보았다

What name shall I give?
　　　↳ 누구시라 할까요?

```
(=Who's calling?)
(=May I have your name?)
```

What name shall I say?
　　　↳ 누구시라고 여쭐까요?

What name should I make the reservation under?
　　　↳ 누구 이름으로 예약할까요?

When he heard his name called, he pricked up his ears
　　　↳ 그의 이름이 호명되자 신경을 곤두세우고 들었어

You are welcome to call us if you need additional names of credit

---

‣ **allude**　refer indirectly
‣ **prick**　pierce slightly with a sharp point

references or require more information before granting credit
> ↳ 신용추천인이 추가로 필요하거나 신용증인을 위한 정보가 더 필요할
> 경우 전화를 주시면 감사하겠습니다

Your friend's name flitted through my mind, only to be forgotten again
> ↳ 네 친구 이름은 언 듯 생각이 났다가도 그저 잊어버려져

Your name flashed across the television screen
> ↳ 네 이름이 텔레비전 화면에 확 지나가더구나

› **grant** consent to, give, admit as true

109. 이야기　　　　　　　　　　　　**Stories**

A dull subject like this is enough to switch me off
　　↳ 이런 시시한 얘기는 나한테는 너무나 흥미가 떨어져

A fable is a story intended to teach a moral truth
　　↳ 우화는 도덕적 진실을 가르치려는 의도가 담긴 이야기다

A sentence that isn't coherent is hard to understand
　　↳ 조리 없는 문장은 이해하기 힘들어

All this talk of the happiest days of our life is only bunkum to us
　　↳ 동심에 돌아간 시절의 얘기를 해 봤자 우리에겐 부질없을 뿐이다

Allegories are still written today although modern authors generally prefer less abstract, more personal symbolism
　　　　↳ 현대의 작가들이 덜 추상적이고 더 개인적인 상징을 선호하지만 우화는 오늘날에도 여전히 사용되고 있다

As the topic is too broad, you can branch out
　　↳ 주제가 광범위하니 일부(지엽)만 다뤄도 돼

Bong-soo is always bragging(boasting) of his son, as if anybody cared
　　↳ 봉수는 남들이 들은 척도 안 하는 아들 얘기만 하고 있어

Duck-soo coughed up the whole story for the police
　　↳ 덕수가 경찰에게 다 불어버렸어

Each reporter is trying to get the jump on the others with the story of the scandal

---

› **coherent**　able to stick together, logically consistent

› **allegory**　story in which figures and actions are symbols of general truths

↳ 신문기자들은 저마다 그 스캔들의 기사를 다른 기자들 보다 앞질러
보도하려고 기를 쓰고 있어

**Fables are parables that assign human characteristics to animals to
teach a lesson about human nature**

↳ 우화란 인간의 본성에 관한 교훈을 가르치기 위해 인간의 특성을 동
물들에게 부여한 비유담이다

Fact(Truth) is stranger than fiction

↳ 사실이 소설보다 더 기이하다

**For this part of the story I can't do better than read from my notes
of the case**

↳ 이 부분에 관한 얘기로는 내가 이 사건을 메모해 둔 것을 읽어보는
게 나아

Get your story straight before the police get here

↳ 경찰이 오기 전에 내용을 얘기해 다오

He gave his friend away to the police, hoping to escape punishment

↳ 그는 처벌을 면할 생각에서 친구의 행적을 경찰에 불어버렸다

He spilled his guts to the cops

↳ 그가 모든 걸 경찰에 불어 버렸어

Her writing style is often convoluted and full of extraneous language

↳ 그녀의 문체는 복잡하고 쓸데없는 말들이 들어있는 경우가 종종 있다

I can read the whole story in your face

↳ 얼굴에 다 씌었군

In-ho's talk made a hit(points) with the audience

↳ 인호의 얘기는 청중들에게 감명을 주었어(점수를 땄어)

It's an old story

↳ 뻔할 뻔 자지

› **parable** simple story illustrating a moral
truth   › **convolute** twist

Make sure you get someone who won't talk above the people's heads
└ 사람들이 알아듣지도 못할 소리를 하는 연사를 모셔오지 않도록 해라

Modern fairy stories have their roots in ancient myths and folklore
└ 현대의 동화는 옛 신화와 설화에 뿌리를 둔다

Please double-check all the facts before you run this story
└ 이 기사를 게재하기 전에 재차 확인하여라

Pyung-soo's earlier books were very popular, but have been put in the shade by his latest story
└ 평수가 이전에 썼던 책들이 매우 인기가 있었지만 최근에 쓴 소설에 비하면 아무 것도 아니다

Reading such silly stories, you'll pervert your taste for good books
└ 그런 저속한 얘기를 읽는다면 양서에 대한 취미를 상실하게 될 것이다

Reporters shouldn't slant their stories against one political party
└ 신문기자는 어느 한 정당에 불리하게 편향된 기사를 써서는 안 된다

Sang-soo sputtered(spluttered) out his story of the crime that he witnessed
└ 상수는 범죄를 목격한 내용을 잽싸게 말했다

She provides an endless supply of newsworthy stories which can hit the headlines
└ 그녀는 대서특필 감 보도가치가 있는 뉴스 감을 끊임없이 제공해 준다

She, who is a reporter, pounded out the story, racing to meet the deadline
└ 그 여기자는 마감시간에 대려고 서둘러 기사를 입력했다

So soon as there is any talk of money, he cools down
└ 그는 돈 얘기만 나오면 시들해져

Stories must be allowed to mature in the cask

▸ **folklore** customs and traditions of a people | ▸ **sputter** talk hastily and indistinctly in excitement, make popping sounds

ㄴ 이야기는 숙성할 때까지 통에 담아두어야 한다

Talking about freckles gets her going

ㄴ 그 여자에게 주근깨 얘기를 하면 열받지

Tell me how you feel

ㄴ 네 감정을 얘기해 봐

That's an old story

ㄴ 흔한 일이지

That's the story

ㄴ 일이 그렇게 된 거야

That's the story of my life

ㄴ 그건 내가 평생 해 왔던 일이야

The lecturer larded his long speech with some amusing stories

ㄴ 강사는 긴 강의에 재미있는 얘기를 곁들였다

The movie has gotten rave reviews for its fast-paced action scenes as well as the main story of a man and woman torn apart by idealogical differences

ㄴ 그 영화는 빠르게 전개되는 액션장면과 서로 다른 이념 때문에 헤어진 남녀에 대한 얘기 구성으로 호평을 받고 있다

The noises jarred on my ears(nerves)

ㄴ 그 소리가 나에게 거슬렸다

The police may be able to make him cough out his story

ㄴ 경찰은 그가 부지중에 입을 열 수밖에 없도록 만들 것 같다

The press reports blew the story out of all proportion(blew the story up)

ㄴ 신문이 그 건을 과장보도 했어

The sight of his homeland brought a lump to his throat

› **freckle** brown spot on the skin | › **lard** insert or cover with strips of fat for cooking

↳ 그는 고향 땅을 보게되자 감개가 무량했다

The stories were neither of them true

↳ 어느 쪽의 이야기도 진실이 아니었다

The story comes pat to the occasion

↳ 얘기가 그 경우에 딱 들어맞는군

The story of the bribery case was splashed all over the front page

↳ 뇌물기사는 머리기사로 대서특필되었다

The story you use has been worked to death many time and is no longer interesting

↳ 너의 그 얘긴 지겹게 써먹었던 터라 더 이상 흥미가 없어

The tale is so long, nor have I heard it out

↳ 그 얘기는 너무 길어서 끝까지 들어본 적이 없다

The wounds on his face lend(give) color to his story that he was beaten by his fellow criminals

↳ 그의 얼굴에 있는 상처로 인해 동료 재소자들에게 얻어맞았다는 얘기가 그럴듯해 보인다

They are a story book couple

↳ 그들은 깨가 쏟아지고 있어

> 한국에서는 '깨가 쏟아진다'라고 하지만, 영어로는 'Storybook couple' 즉, '소설 속의 부부'라고 한다. '신데렐라', '백설공주' 같은 서양의 고전 동화를 보면 언제나 왕자와 공주가 결혼하며 행복한 결말을 맞는다. 이에서 유래한 속담이다.

They tried to worm the story out of her in vain

↳ 그들은 그녀에게서 내막을 슬며시 알아내려 했으나 허사였다

They'll be clear if they all stick to the same story

‣ **tale** story of anecdote, falsehood

ㄴ 그들이 모두 입을 맞춘다면 무죄로 판정될 것이다

This fact lends probability to the story
> ㄴ 이 사실로 보면 그 얘기가 그럴듯하다

This is a jumble of words
> ㄴ 이 글은 두서가 없어

> (=This writing is poorly constructed)
> (=This is difficult to read and understand)

To resume our story, your behavior isn't in keeping
> ㄴ 각설하고 너의 행동은 상식 선을 벗어나고 있어

What's the story on it?
> ㄴ 그게 어떻게 된 일이냐?

You can boil the long story down to a long sentence
> ㄴ 그 긴 얘기는 긴 문장 하나로 줄일 수 있어

You have to keep your preamble succinct and to the point
> ㄴ 넌 서문을 간결하고 요령 있게 써야 해

You need not take his stories at face value
> ㄴ 그의 말을 액면대로 받아들일 필요 없어

Yours is a real rags to riches story
> ㄴ 너 정말 개천에서 용 났구나

> 한국에서 용은 귀함을 대표하지만, 서양에서는 괴물, 악마를 뜻한다. 따라서 비슷한 뜻으로 'A white egg laid by a black hen(검은 닭이 난 하얀 알)' 이나, 'A rag to riches story(누더기에서 부자가 된 이야기)'가 쓰인다.

› **jumble** mix in a disorderly mass

› **preamble** introduction

› **succinct** brief

110. 인내   **Patience**

A lie has speed, but truth has endurance
> ↳ 거짓은 속도를 자랑하지만 진실은 인내력을 가지고 있다

A little impatience spoils great plans
> ↳ 작은 일을 참지 못하면 큰 일을 못한다

A search behind enemy lines requires a tremendous test of our endurance and nerves
> ↳ 적진의 후방을 탐색하는 데는 대단한 참을성과 담력을 요한다

An-do's abrasive personality will offend even the most patient of them
> ↳ 안도의 거친 성격에는 아무리 참을성 있는 사람일지라도 참아내지 못
> 할 거야

Chang-ho has the patience of a saint(Job)
> ↳ 창호는 돌부처 같은 인내심을 가졌어

Forbearance consists in bearing what is unbearable
> ↳ 자제심이란 참을 수 없는 것을 참는 데 있다

Genius is but a greater aptitude for patience
> ↳ 천재는 참을성을 조금 더 가진 사람 일 뿐이다

Guys need the patience to go after a girl until he wins her over
> ↳ 여자를 얻으려면 열 번을 찍는 인내력을 필요로 한다

He who is impatient waits twice
> ↳ 조급해 하면 두 번을 기다리게 된다

▸ **abrasive**   tending to abrade, causing irritation
▸ **aptitude**   capacity for learning, natural ability

If you're patient in one moment of anger, you'll escape a hundred days of sorrow
> ↳ 한 순간의 화를 참으면 100일의 근심을 덜게 된다

I'm losing my patience
> ↳ 더 이상 참기 힘들어

It's easier to commend poverty than to endure it
> ↳ 가난을 찬양하기는 쉬워도 참아내기는 어렵다

It's in the garden of patience that strength grow best
> ↳ 인내의 정원에서 강인한 힘이 가장 잘 자란다

Life is to be enjoyed; not simply endured
> ↳ 인생은 즐기기 위한 것이지 참아내기만 하려는 것이 아니다

Man pines to live but can't endure the days of his life
> ↳ 사람은 애타게 살고 싶어 하면서도 나날의 삶을 견뎌내지 못한다

Men cling to life even at the cost of enduring great misfortune
> ↳ 사람은 큰 고생을 참아가면서 삶에 애착한다

Nam-soo's wife's constant nagging puts a tax on his patience
> ↳ 남수의 처가 끝없이 잔소리를 해서 그를 참을 수 없게 하고 있다

Nothing important can be achieved without perseverance
> ↳ 인내 없이는 아무런 중요한 일도 이루어질 수 없다

One must draw the line somewhere
> ↳ 참는데도 한계가 있어

One trespass more I must make on your patience
> ↳ 한번 더 신세 지겠습니다

Pain makes man think, thought makes man wise, wisdom makes life endurable
> ↳ 고통은 사람을 생각하게 하고, 사색은 현명하게 하며, 지혜는 삶의

› **pine** lose health through distress, yearn for intensely

› **trespass** sin, unauthorized entry onto someone's property

인내심을 키워준다

Patience in the old injuries invites new ones
> ↳ 피해를 입고도 참아주기만 하면 또 다른 해를 입게 된다

Patience is the best medicine
> ↳ 인내는 최고의 약이다

Patience is the name of the game in fishing
> ↳ 낚시에서 가장 중요한 것은 인내심이다

People wish to be liked, not to be endured with patient resignation
> ↳ 사람들은 남들이 좋아해 주기를 원하지만 체념으로 참아주기를 바라지는 않는다

Possess yourself in patience
> ↳ 꾹 눌러 참아라

Pyung-soo adopted a posture of patience and compromise toward the protestors
> ↳ 그는 시위자들에게 인내와 협상의 자세를 보여주었다

She has had all she can take
> ↳ 그 여자는 참고 또 참았다

Styles and fads in music may come and go, but the blues always seem to endure
> ↳ 음악의 양식과 일시적인 유행이 왔다가 사라지지만 블루스의 인기는 여전한 것 같다

That guy tries my patience
> ↳ 저 친구 참 성가셔

The art of life is to know how to enjoy a little and to endure much
> ↳ 삶의 지혜는 적게 즐기고 많이 참는데 있다

The driving force of a nation lies in its spiritual purpose, made

---

· **posture** bearing of the body, strike a pose   · **compromise** settle differences by mutual concessions

effective by free, tolerant but unremitting national will

       ㄴ 국가의 원동력은 자유롭고 인내하면서도 끈질긴 국가의 의지로 발효되는 목표에 있다

The real test of endurance(patience) lies in bearing the unbearable=To endure what's unendurable is true endurance

       ㄴ 참을 수 없는 것을 참는 것이 정말 참는 것이다

The unsettled and impatient youth was a rotten apple in the barrel

       ㄴ 안정되지 못하고 잘 참지 못하는 젊은이는 사회에 악영향을 미쳤다

> 하나가 전체에게 나쁜 영향을 미친다는 말이다. 영어 속담에는 여러 가지가 있는데, 가장 자주 쓰이는 표현은 "One rotten apple spoils the barrel 썩은 사과 하나가 한 통을 썩게 한다"이다. 악한 한 사람이 한 가문, 한 나라를 욕되게 하는 것은 "It is an ill bird that fouls its own nest 자기의 둥지를 더럽히는 새는 나쁜 새이다"로 표현한다.
> (=One scabbed sheep will mar a whole flock)
> (=A hog that's bemired endeavors to bemire others)

Tourists must get a glimpse of the abominable, dreadful conditions the native people actually endure

       ㄴ 여행자들은 그 곳 사람들이 실제 참고 살아가는 구역질나는 지독한 상황을 보어야 한다

When a man is in love he endures more than at other times

       ㄴ 사람이 사랑에 빠지면 다른 때보다 참을성이 많아진다

With the trowel of patience we dig out roots of truth

       ㄴ 인내의 삽으로 진실을 캐낸다

You are asking me to put up with a lot

       ㄴ 넌 내게 대단한 인내를 요구하는군

› **abominable**   thoroughly unpleasant or revolting

› **trowel**   tools for spreading or smoothing, garden scoop

You had better school yourself in some patience
ㄴ 넌 참을성을 좀 길러야 해

You have plenty of ability, but fail in patience
ㄴ 넌 능력은 있지만 인내심이 없어

You may have much to lose by precipitate action and much to gain from patience
ㄴ 넌 경솔한 짓을 했다가는 손해보기 십상이고 참아서 이익 볼일이 많아

Youth is a stuff will not endure
ㄴ 청춘은 쉬 늙는다

› **precipitate** cause to happen quickly or   out of a liquid
abruptly, cause to separate

111. 인사 & 감사   Salutations & Thanks

A forced kindness deserves no thanks
    ㄴ 억지 친절은 감사할 가치 없다

All my best wishes for your(the) future
    ㄴ 앞날에 축복을 보낸다

Am I glad to see you! The computer's down and I can't figure out why
    ㄴ 마침 잘 왔다. 컴퓨터가 고장났는데 어디가 잘못됐는지 모르겠다

> (=Just the person I wanted to see! The computer's down and I can't figure out why)

Been keeping cool
    ㄴ 잘 지내고 있어(**I've**가 생략되어 있슴)

Come back when you can stay longer
    ㄴ 시간 날 때 또 오너라

Don't I know you from somewhere?
    ㄴ 어디선가 만난 적이 있던가요?

Don't stay away so long
    ㄴ 조만(금명)간 또 오세요

Excuse me, but don't I know you from somewhere?

▸ **deserve**   be worthy of

↳ 실례합니다만, 어디서 만난 적이 있던가요?

Excuse my appearance
↳ 내 꼴이 말이 아니죠?(민망한 모습으로 손님을 맞을 때)

Fancy meeting you here
↳ 너를 여기서 만나다니

Give thanks in all circumstances
↳ 범사에 감사하라

Have I the pleasure of addressing Mr. Bahk?
↳ 박 선생님이십니까?

Have you been keeping out of trouble?
↳ 요즘 별일 없나?

He has made me what I am
↳ 내가 이만큼이라도 된 건 그분 덕분이지

How are you keeping?
↳ 넌 어떻게 지내니?

How are you making out in your job?
↳ 하는 일은 잘돼가니?

How have I been? Don't ask
↳ 어떻게 지냈느냐고? 말도 마

How's the world treating(using) you?
↳ 어떻게 지내니?

I appreciate your coming here on such a short notice
↳ 급히 연락했는데도 와줘서 고마워

I don't believe I've had the pleasure
↳ 초면인 것 같습니다

· **address** direct one's remarks to, mark an
address on

I don't want to wear out my welcome
> ↳ 너무 자주 와서 죄송합니다

I don't want to be rude, but I have to leave early
> ↳ 실례지만 좀 일찍 가봐야겠습니다

I hope you are all keeping well
> ↳ 모두 안녕하시길 빕니다

I only have myself to thank
> ↳ 스스로를 탓할 수밖에

I shall be grateful to you all my life
> ↳ 이 은혜는 평생 잊지 않겠습니다

I shall come if nothing interferes
> ↳ 사정이 허락하면 올께

I shall not expect you till I see you
> ↳ 오고싶을 때 오십시오

I want you to be my eyes and ears
> ↳ 내 몫까지 즐기고 와

I wish you all the best
> ↳ 잘 되기 바란다(헤어질 때)

I won't be a moment
> ↳ 잠깐 실례하겠습니다

(=I won't be long)

I'll keep you in touch
> ↳ 연락줄께

› **interfere**   collide or be in opposition, try
   to run the affairs of others

I've been expecting you
> ↳ 오시길 기다리고 있었습니다

It takes so little to make him thankful
> ↳ 그는 조그만 일에도 고마워한다

It's been a while
> ↳ 오랜만이군

It's our custom to give money during holidays as a token of appreciation
> ↳ 명절에 감사의 표시로 돈을 주는 것이 우리의 관습이다

I'll do my poor best
> ↳ 미력하나마 최선을 다하겠습니다

Let me apologize for my silence
> ↳ 오랫동안 소식 전하지 못해 죄송합니다

Let me introduce my intended to you
> ↳ 장래 아내 될 사람을 소개 드립니다

Look, who's there
> ↳ 어이구 이게 누구야

(=Look, who I've got here)

Long tarrying takes all the thanks away
> ↳ 오래 꾸물대면 모든 감사한 마음이 없어진다

My ears itch for information
> ↳ 소식을 알고싶어

My thanks go out to you all

› **tarry**   be slow in leaving

    ↳ 모든 분들에게 사의를 표합니다

Now I must cut
    ↳ 이제 실례합니다(자리 뜰 때)

Please accept a slight token of my gratitude
    ↳ 변변찮으나 감사의 뜻으로 드립니다

Please call on me whenever it suits you
    ↳ 언제라도 형편 닿을 때 와 주십시오

Send my best wishes to everyone
    ↳ 모두에게 안부 전해 줘

Thank you for a job well done
    ↳ 재임 중의 업적에 사의를 표합니다

Thank you for going the trouble
    ↳ 수고해줘서 고마워

Thank you for nothing
    ↳ 내 걱정 마(**Thank you anyway** 라고 응답 할 때와는 달리 도와준답시고 오히려 일을 그르칠 때 내뱉는 말)

Thank you for your business
    ↳ 거래해 주셔서 감사합니다

Thank you for your time and attention(cooperation and contribution)
    ↳ 바쁘신 중에 참석해 주셔서 감사합니다

Thank you very much for your taking time out of your schedule
    ↳ 바쁘신 중에 시간을 내 주셔서 감사합니다

Thanks for getting back to me so quickly
    ↳ 빨리 응답해 주셔서 감사합니다

Thanks for the offer
    ↳ 말만 들어도 고마워

› **cooperate**   act jointly
› **contribute**   give or help along with others

That's not a happy hi
> ↳ 어째 인사말이 시원찮군

This is to request the honor of your presence at a brief ribbon cutting ceremony at Jejoo Airport on July 17, 1999.
> ↳ 1999년 7월 17일 제주공항에서 거행될 개통식에 귀하께서 참석해 주시기 바랍니다

We don't see you much around here
> ↳ 오랜만입니다

Well, well, if it isn't Mr. Joo
> ↳ 아니, 주 선생님 아니십니까

What's cooking?
> ↳ 어떻게 지내?

You have done lots of good turns for me
> ↳ 여러 가지 나를 위해 애를 많이 써주셨군요

You have done me a various acts of kindnesses
> ↳ 신세 많이 졌습니다

You'll be glad someday
> ↳ 언젠가 고마워 할거다

> (=You'll appreciate it someday)
> (=Someday you'll look back in appreciation)

Your timing is perfect
> ↳ 마침 잘 왔다

> (=You couldn't come at a better time)

› **various** being many and unlike

112. 인체   **Human Body**

A bit of white skin peeked out
      └ 하얀 살결이 약간 드러나 보였다

A body weighs less the farther it gets from the earth
      └ 물체가 지구에서 멀어질수록 무게는 가벼워진다

A bullet flew past his head and shattered the vase on the mantlepiece
      └ 실탄은 그의 머리위로 날아와서 벽난로 장식 위의 꽃병을 박살냈다

A faint smile played on his lips
      └ 엷은 미소가 그의 입가를 스쳤다

A fish bone was stuck in my throat for a while
      └ 생선뼈가 목에 걸려 얼마동안 넘어가지 않았어

A full belly counsels well
      └ 목구멍이 포도청이다

> (=The hungry belly has no ears)

A full belly neither fights nor flies well
      └ 배가 부르면 잘 싸울 수도 잘 도망할 수도 없다

A good tongue is a good weapon
      └ 말 잘 하는 것도 훌륭한 무기다

A hungry stomach has no ears

‣ **peek out**   look furtively
‣ **counsel**   advice, deliberation together

╚ 배가 고프면 아무 소리도 귀에 안 들어온다

A large amount of money goes through banker's hands, but none of it is his

╚ 은행원은 하루에도 거금을 만지지만 자기 돈은 하나도 없다

A man is hid under his tongue

╚ 혀의 아래에는 사람의 모습이 가려져 있다

A man who works with his hand and his brain, and his heart is an artist

╚ 손과 머리와 가슴으로 일하는 사람은 예술가이다

A puzzled look(expression) crossed(passed) over his face

╚ 곤혹스러운 표정이 그의 얼굴을 스쳤다

A rude remark sprang to my lips, but I prevented myself from saying it just in time

╚ 쌍소리가 불쑥 튀어나오려 했지만 가까스로 때맞춰 참았다

After the game, the winning team could be heard crowing their heads off in the locker room

╚ 게임이 끝나자 라커룸에서 이긴 팀의 환호하는 소리를 들을 수 있었다

All my plans blew up in my face

╚ 진행 중이던 모든 계획을 망쳤어

All night you ground your teeth, keeping me awake

╚ 네가 밤새도록 이를 가는 바람에 잠을 못 잤다

An army marches(travels) on its stomach

╚ 군대는 배가 불러야 싸울 수 있다

An organ is a group of tissues capable of performing some special function

╚ 신체기관이란 어떤 특수한 기능을 이행할 수 있는 일단의 조직들이다

▸ **prevent** keep from happening or acting

▸ **crow** make the loud sound of the cock, gloat

Anyone with his head screwed on straight wouldn't have done something so dumb
> ↳ 제정신이 있는 사람이라면 그런 멍청한 짓을 하려고 안 했을 것이다

Apples are valued nowadays for their aid to digestion and their help in keeping teeth clean and healthy
> ↳ 사과는 소화를 돕고 이를 깨끗하게 하고 건강을 유지시켜줌으로써 오늘날 소중히 여겨진다

Apricot pits are especially good for those who have a dry, itchy throat
> ↳ 목이 마르고 가려운 사람에게 살구 씨가 특히 좋다

As a baseball player, he doesn't come up to his brother's shoulder
> ↳ 그가 야구선수로서는 형보다 못해

As an independent organization we have enough elbow room to try out new methods
> ↳ 이제 독립된 기관으로서 새로운 방법을 시험해 볼 여지가 생겼다

As soon as microbes enter the body they would kill all living matter, if it were not for the tiny defenders that rush immediately to fight them
> ↳ 만일 침입자들과 싸우기 위해 즉시 달려가는 작은 방어 균이 없다면 세균이 몸 속에 들어가자마자 살아있는 모든 것을 죽일 것이다

As soon as she made the remark, she could have bitten her tongue off
> ↳ 그 여자는 말을 꺼내자마자 자신이 내뱉은 말에 대해 후회했다

As time goes by, more and more people come forward to donate organs
> ↳ 세월이 흐름에 따라 장기를 기증하겠다고 나서는 사람들이 점점 늘어

› **independent** not governed by another, not requiring or relying on some-   thing or somebody else, not easily influenced

ㄴ 나고 있다

At last Sung-ho got it through his head that he had failed the TOEIC test
　　ㄴ 성호는 마침내 토익 시험에 실패했다는 게 실감났다

At least I landed on both feet when it was all over
　　ㄴ 그 일이 끝났을 때 난 무사히 버텨냈어

Babies sleeping face down are at greater risk than those sleeping on their backs
　　ㄴ 엎드려 자는 아이들은 바로 누워 자는 아이들보다 더 위험하다

Backchul greatly activates and revitalizes the stomach as well as removes toxic waste trapped inside the stomach
　　ㄴ 백출은 위장에 남아있는 독성을 제거할 뿐 아니라 위를 활성화하고 새로운 활력을 준다

Be careful not to get any on your fingers when you are putting on the glue
　　ㄴ 아교를 바를 때 손가락에 묻지 않도록 해

Be careful not to get off on the wrong foot
　　ㄴ 처음부터 잘 되게 주의해

Be careful not to let your tongue run away with you again
　　ㄴ 또다시 말을 못 참는 일이 없도록 조심해

Be careful not to run the needle into your finger by mistake
　　ㄴ 잘못해서 바늘에 손가락이 찔리지 않도록 주의해

Being a star soccer player goes to Jong-soo's head
　　ㄴ 종수가 이름 있는 축구선수가 되더니 교만해졌어

Better a tooth out than always aching
　　ㄴ 아프기만 하는 이빨은 뽑아버리는 게 낫다

› **risk**　exposure to loss or injury
› **toxic**　poisonous

Better the foot slip than the tongue
　　↳ 실언보다는 실족이 낫다

Better to cut the shoe than pinch the foot
　　↳ 발을 죄는 고통보다는 신발을 찢는 게 낫다

Beware of bedroom eyes
　　↳ 유혹의 눈길에 주의하라

Birchen twigs break no ribs
　　↳ 매 맞아 뼈 부러지지 않는다(엄한 훈육의 교훈)

> 대부분의 나라에서는 어렸을 때의 올바른 교육이 아이의 미래를 정한다고 생
> 각한다. 심한 체벌은 문제이지만, 적당히 엄격한 교육은 필요하다.
> (=The rod breaks no bones)
> (=Spare the rod and spoil the child)

Bong-soo acts as if he had the weight(cares) of the world on his shoulders
　　↳ 봉수는 세상걱정 혼자 다 하는 것 같아

Bong-soo has broad shoulders
　　↳ 봉수는 포용력이 있어

Bong-soo kept his nose to the grindstone, but all he got for his effort was a kick in the teeth(pants)
　　↳ 봉수는 뼈빠지게 일했지만 노력에 대한 칭찬은 커녕 욕만 먹었다

Bong-soon has big ears
　　↳ 봉순이는 꼬치꼬치 캐묻기를 좋아해

Break a leg
　　↳ 잘해봐

› **birch**　deciduous tree with close-grained wood

Bruised or scalded skin can be more painful than broken bones
> ↳ 피부에 멍이 들거나 뜨거운 물에 데는 것은 뼈가 부러지는 것 보다
> 더 아플 수 있다

Byung-soo eats out of her palm
> ↳ 병수는 그 여자 시키는 대로 해

Byung-soo will get his feet off the ground
> ↳ 병수는 곧 자리를 확고히 잡게 될 것이다

Byung-soo will land on his feet
> ↳ 병수는 어려운 상황에서 잘 벗어날 것이다

Byung-soon's got nice legs but she's flat as a board
> ↳ 병순이가 다리는 예쁘지만 유방은 없어

Can you keep this business on its feet for another year?
> ↳ 이 사업을 1년 더 버티어 낼 수 있겠나?

Can you get it through your head?
> ↳ 그게 무슨 말인지 납득이 가니?

Chan-soo put a bug in my ear
> ↳ 찬수가 내게 귀띔(경고, 부추김) 하더군

Chan-soo slipped his arm round Sook-hee's waist
> ↳ 찬수는 숙희의 허리를 껴안았다

Constipation is mainly caused by toxic wastes trapped inside the intestines
> ↳ 변비는 주로 장의 내부에 배출되지 않고 있는 유독한 노폐물로 인해
> 발생한다

Critics say that the government is turning a blind eye to signs of overheating to press ahead with expansionary policy in an attempt to gain votes

---

> ▸ **constipation** difficulty of defecation
> ▸ **expansionary** act or process of expansion

ㄴ 비평가들은 정부가 투표의 지지율을 높이려고 확장정책을 밀고 나가
기 위해 과열증세를 무시하고 있다고 비난하고 있다

Discreet wives sometimes have no ears or eyes
ㄴ 소에게 한 말은 탈이 없어도 아내에게 한 말은 퍼져나간다

Don't beat(bang) your head against a brick wall
ㄴ 바보짓 그만둬

Don't bite the hand that feeds you
ㄴ 배은망덕한 짓은 하지 마라

Don't burn your fingers on the stock market
ㄴ 주식에 손대었다가 큰코 다치지 않도록 해

Don't call me names if you like the way your teeth are arranged
ㄴ 이빨이 성하고 싶거든 날 욕하지마

Don't clutter your head up with unimportant details
ㄴ 하찮은 일로 머리 속을 어지럽게 하지마

Don't cut off your nose to spite your face
ㄴ 누워 침 뱉기야

다른 사람을 해치려다가 결국은 자신에게 해가 돌아간다는 뜻이다. 한국에서
는 '누워서 침 뱉기'가 있고, 영어로는 비슷한 'Spit in the wind 바람에 침
뱉기'와 'Piss in the wind 바람에 오줌누기'가 있다. 바람을 마주보고 침을
뱉거나 오줌을 누면 결국 자신한테도 돌아오는 법이다. 조금 더 점잖은 표현
으로는 "Cut off your nose to spite your face 코를 깎아서 얼굴을 망친
다"가 있다.

Don't dive in head first
ㄴ 무모한 짓 하지마

› **discreet** capable of keeping a secret
› **clutter** fill with things that get in the way

(=Don't make a leap in the dark)

Don't eat your heart out
> ㄴ 너무 슬퍼하지마

Don't fling your arms and legs like that, make the proper swimming strokes
> ㄴ 아무렇게나 손발을 허우적거리지 말고 제대로 수영동작을 취해라

Don't forget your legs can go to sleep if you swim a long distance
> ㄴ 장거리 수영을 하면 다리에 쥐가 날 수 있다는 걸 잊지 마라

Don't give her a glad eye
> ㄴ 그 여자에게 추파 던지지마

(=Don't make googoo eyes to her)

Don't give them the back of your hand
> ㄴ 그들을 함부로 대하지마

Don't hide(bury) your head in the sand
> ㄴ 현실도피(눈감고 아옹) 식으로 나와선 안 돼

'The cat that ate the canary 카나리아를 잡아먹은 고양이'란 한국 속담으로 표현하면 "눈감고 아웅한다"이다. 이는 자신이 잘못한 일을 다른 사람이 모를 것이라 생각하고 시치미 떼는 상황을 말한다. 영어 속담은 주인이 아끼는 카나리아를 잡아먹고 시치미 떼는 고양이에 비유하였다.

Don't just mouth off

> **bury** deposit in the earth, hide

↳ 나설 차례가 아닐 때 나서지 마라

Don't just stand there with your bare face hanging out
↳ 그냥 그렇게 바보 같은 얼굴로 서 있지마

Don't let all this praise go to your head
↳ 칭찬 좀 들었다고 우쭐해 하지마

Don't let him slip through your fingers this time
↳ 이번엔 그를 놓치지 마라

Don't let the grass grow under your feet
↳ 시간낭비 하지 마라

Don't let this opportunity slip though your fingers
↳ 이번 기회를 놓치지 마라

Don't let your eyes wander when you are driving
↳ 운전 시 항상 도로를 주의해야 해

Don't shake your leg, it's bad luck
↳ 다리 떨지마, 복 나간다

(=It causes(or brings) bad luck)
(=It's unlucky)

Don't shoot yourself in the foot
↳ 경솔하게 말하지마

(=Don't put your foot into your mouth)
(=Don't say the wrong thing)

Don't shove your idea down my throat

· **shove** push along, aside, or away

↳ 네 생각을 내게 강요하지마

Don't show him your hand too soon

↳ 그에게 너무 빨리 속마음을 보여주지 마라

Don't speak with a forked tongue

↳ 일구이언하지마

Don't speak with your mouth full

↳ 입에 음식을 넣은 채 말하지마

Don't stick your neck out

↳ 위험을 자초하지마

Don't stick your nose into other people's private affairs

↳ 남의 사생활에 간섭하지마

Don't try to palm(pass) that idea off as your own

↳ 그 안을 네가 내놓은 것처럼 하지 마라

Don't wear your heart on your sleeve

↳ 맘속에 있는 대로 표시(말) 해선 안 돼

Doo-chul let him slip through his fingers

↳ 두철이가 그를 놓쳐버렸어

Drinking in moderation is good for heart and health

↳ 적당한 음주는 심장과 건강에 좋다

술도 좋은 술을 적당히 마시면 건강에 이롭다. 우리의 선조들도 '적게 먹으면 약주요, 많이 먹으면 망주'라고 하였다. 서양에서는 좋은 포도주가 건강에 이롭다고 한다(Good wine makes good blood).

Duck-soon is getting diarrhea of the mouth(jawbone)

↳ 덕순이가 또 끝없는 얘길 늘어놓는군

▶ **private** belonging to a particular individual or group

▶ **diarrhea** abnormal discharge of loose matter from the bowels

Ed is rumored to have money coming out of his ears
> ↳ 에드는 엄청난 부자라고 소문이 나 있어

Ed's ears must have been burning today
> ↳ 오늘 에드는 귀가 간질간질 할 거다

Ed's foul language in the office caused our eyebrows to rise
> ↳ 에드가 사무실에서 상스러운 말을 하는 바람에 우리가 놀랐어

Emergency services are on hand in case there is any trouble
> ↳ 유사시에 대비하여 응급서비스가 준비되어 있습니다

Even the woman with a roving eye gets short shrift if she goes in for marriage-breaking
> ↳ 바람기 있는 여자라도 파경에 이르면 잠깐의 참회는 있다

Every detail of the scandal came to a head
> ↳ 스캔들의 전모가 드러났어

Everybody thinks the accountant had his hand in the till
> ↳ 모두들 경리가 돈을 훔친 것으로 생각한다

Everybody wishes that loud mouth would put a cork in it
> ↳ 저 떠버리가 입 좀 다물어주길 모두가 바라고 있다

Everyone has a skeleton in his closet
> ↳ 털어 먼지 안나는 사람 없다

누구에게나 한두 가지 결점은 있다는 뜻이다. "Everyone has a skeleton in his closet 모든 사람은 창고에 해골을 가지고 있다"는 것은 공포 영화에서 가장 선해 보이는 사람이 결국에는 범인임이 드러나는 것을 빗댄 표현이다.
(=Everyone has his faults(short comings))
(=No one is without their faults=Everyone makes mistakes)

› **rove** wander without definite direction

Everyone's destiny is in his hands
> ↳ 사람의 운명은 자기 손에 달렸다

Excuse my slip of the tongue
> ↳ 실언을 용서해 주세요

Fields have eyes and woods have ears
> ↳ 낮말은 새가 듣고 밤 말은 쥐가 듣는다

> 말조심의 중요성을 말해주는 속담이다. 한국에서는 동물을 이용하여 뜻을 전달하였지만, 영어 속담에서는 자연 그대로를 이용한다. "Fields have eyes, and woods have ears 들에 눈이 있고 나무에 귀가 있다"

Get the kinks out of your body gradually before taking exercise in earnest
> ↳ 본격적인 운동을 하기 전에 조금씩 몸을 풀어라

Gil-soo got his feet on the ground and is hard at work
> ↳ 길수는 땅에 발을 딱 붙이고 열심히 일하고 있다

Gil-soo has a golden thumb, and is very rich
> ↳ 길수는 돈을 잘 벌어서 큰 부자다

Gil-soo is a man with a finger in every pie in our office
> ↳ 우리 사무실에서 길수는 약방에 감초지

Gil-soo's going on a long trip to get(have) his head together
> ↳ 길수는 머리 좀 식히려고 긴 여행을 떠나려는 거야

Ginseng is particularly effective for those who suffer from chronically cold hands and feet, bodily aches and pains
> ↳ 인삼은 특히 만성적으로 손발이 차며, 몸이 아프고 쑤시는 사람에게 효과가 크다

› **earnest** serious state of mind

› **suffer** experience pain, loss, or hardship; permit

Good for the liver may be bad for the spleen
> ↳ 간에 좋은 것은 지라에 나쁠 수도 있다(모두에게 좋을 수는 없다)

Gyung-hee has had her eye on you for some time now
> ↳ 경희가 네게 마음을 두고 있어

Han-soo took his responsibilities as a father seriously but in matters of discipline was rather too free with his hands
> ↳ 그는 진지하게 아버지로서의 책임을 떠맡았으나 훈육문제에 있어서는 툭하면 아이를 때렸다

Happiness always looks small while you hold it in your hand
> ↳ 손에 들어온 행복은 늘 작아 보인다

Have you got your eyes then?
> ↳ 그러면 봐둔 사람이 있다는 거니?

He doesn't know whether(if) he's on his head or heels
> ↳ 그는 정신없이 바빠(그의 일은 두서가 없어)

He flung his arms around my neck
> ↳ 그는 급히 내 목을 끌어안았다

He gave ear to my advice
> ↳ 그는 내 충고를 들어줬어

He is all mouth and no chops
> ↳ 그 사람은 입만 살고 행동이 없어

He had a very worried look on his face
> ↳ 그는 몹시 근심스러운 표정이었어

He had his back to us
> ↳ 우리에게 등 돌렸어

He had his word stack in his throat
> ↳ 그는 목이 메어 말을 잇지 못했다

› **fling** move brusquely, throw

He has a black heart
    ↳ 뱃속 검은 놈

He has a finger in every pie
    ↳ 그는 약방의 감초다

He has more goodness in his little finger than you have altogether
    ↳ 그는 너보다 훨씬 훌륭한 사람이야

He has traveled far and wide as he has itchy feet
    ↳ 그는 역마살이 끼여서 여기저기 많이 돌아다녔다

He heaped coals of fire on your head
    ↳ 그가 네게 악을 선으로 갚았군

He is a good provider(has a golden thumb)
    ↳ 그는 돈을 잘 벌어다 주어

He is a nose of wax with other people
    ↳ 남이 하자는 대로 하는 사람

He is all mouth and no chops
    ↳ 그 사람은 입만 살고 행동이 없어

He is dragging his feet on this project
    ↳ 그는 이 계획을 일부러 질질 끌고 있어

He is just putting on a brave face
    ↳ 그는 그저 태연한 체 할 뿐이야

He is paying something approaching half his income just to have a roof over his head
    ↳ 그는 소득에서 거의 절반을 집 장만에 다 쓴다

He kept making mistakes and became red in the face
    ↳ 그는 계속 실수를 해서 곤혹스럽게 됐다

› **heap** pile, throw or lay in a heap | › **approach** move nearer or be close to, make initial advances or efforts toward

He made a face at me when I was talking to the boss
> ↳ 사장에게 얘기를 막 하려는데 그가 내게 얼굴(표정)로 내게 신호를 보냈다

He never lets the grass grow from under his feet
> ↳ 그는 행동이 민첩해(기회를 안 놓쳐)

He now feels his legs
> ↳ 그는 이제 그의 능력을 가늠할 수 있게 됐어

He passed out(fainted) but he rolled(came)(a)round when we threw drops of water on his face
> ↳ 그는 정신을 잃었지만 우리가 그의 얼굴에 물을 뿌리자 정신을 차렸다

He put his arms around her neck and planted a kiss on her face
> ↳ 그는 그녀의 목을 끌어안고 얼굴에 키스 세례를 퍼부었다

He put his finger and thumb in his mouth and gave a piercing whistle
> ↳ 그는 손가락을 입에 넣고 귀청이 떨어지게 휘파람을 불었다

He put his foot in his mouth
> ↳ 그 사람 무례한 말을 마구 했어

He put up a brave face(front)
> ↳ 그 사람 낯두껍더라

'Thick-skinned' 는 '두꺼운 얼굴'을 나타내고, 'Brazen-faced'는 '철판을 깐 얼굴' 을 나타낸다.

He reeled back when the heavy blow landed on his chin
> ↳ 그는 강한 펀치가 턱에 작렬하자 비틀거리며 물러났다

He runs off at the mouth all the time(has diarrhea of mouth)

› **pierce** enter or thrust into or through
› **reel** wind on a reel, pull in by reeling

ㄴ 그는 항상 말이 너무 많아

He seems to be a man with his feet planted firmly on the ground

ㄴ 그는 아주 분별력 있는 사람 같아

He that has no silver in his purse should have silver in his tongue

ㄴ 주머니가 빈 사람은 말주변이라도 있어야 한다

He was advised to go slow for a time, to give his heart a rest

ㄴ 그는 심장에 휴식을 줄 수 있도록 당분간 한적한 생활을 하도록 권유
받았다

**He who guards his mouth preserves his life, but he who opens wide
his lips shall have destruction**

ㄴ 입을 지키는 자는 그 생명을 보전하나 입술을 크게 벌리는 자에게는
멸망이 오느니라

He who restrains his lips is wise

ㄴ 입술을 제어하는 자는 지혜가 있느니라

He whose belly is full believes not him who is fasting

ㄴ 자기 배가 부르면 남의 배고픈 줄 모른다

He would have my head

ㄴ 난 모가지야

(=My head's gonna roll)

He'll have her in the palm of his hand shortly

ㄴ 그는 곧 그 여자를 장악하게 될 거야

He's been giving you the eye all day

ㄴ 그는 하루 종일 네게 눈길을 주었어

He's doing his best to save face

· **restrain** limit or keep under control
· **palm** conceal in the hand

ㄴ 그는 명성을 얻으려고 최선을 다하고 있다

He's down at the beer hall soaking his face

ㄴ 그는 술이 너무 취해서 맥주홀에서 뻗어 있어

He's got both feet on the ground with his business

ㄴ 그는 자신의 사업에 관하여는 현실적인 사람이다

He's retired as a player, but he keeps his hand in by giving us tennis lessons

ㄴ 그가 테니스 선수로서는 은퇴했지만 우리들에게 레슨을 해주면서 손을 놓지는 않고 있다

Hee-jung is eating out of your hand

ㄴ 희정인 네가 죽으라면 죽는시늉이라도 하는 사람이잖아

Her hair hung in abundant masses over her shoulders

ㄴ 그녀의 머리털은 탐스럽게 어깨에 내려와 있었다

Her heart was too full for words

ㄴ 그녀는 감정이 북받쳐 말이 나오지 않았다

Her long hair flowed down her shoulders

ㄴ 그녀의 긴 머리가 어깨에 늘어져 있었다

His boss gives(puts) teeth to him

ㄴ 그의 상사가 그에게 힘을 실어주고 있어

His closing words brought the whole crowd to their feet, cheering wildly

ㄴ 그의 마지막 말에 사람들이 열광적으로 환호하며 기립박수를 보냈다

His eyes flashed back defiance

ㄴ 그도 똑같이 노려보며 반항의 빛을 보였다

His eyes made the round of the room

ㄴ 그는 방을 휘 둘러보았다

› **abundant** more than enough
› **defiance** act or state of defying

His face fell
> ㄴ 그 사람 실망의 빛이 보였어

His face is lined with age(suffering)
> ㄴ 그의 얼굴은 나이(고생)로 인해 주름 투성이다

His face is peppered with freckles
> ㄴ 그의 얼굴은 주근깨 투성이다

His heart started racing when she called his name
> ㄴ 그 여자가 그의 이름을 부르자 심장이 마구 뛰기 시작했다

His sore arm is starting to act up again
> ㄴ 그의 아픈 팔이 다시 도지기 시작했어

How are you with your hands?
> ㄴ 네 솜씨 좀 보고싶은데

Hurling their arms and legs about wildly, they kept afloat but wasted much effort
> ㄴ 그들은 물 속에서 손발을 마구 허우적거리면서 가라앉지는 않았지만 힘이 많이 소진됐다

Hyun-soo held his peace(tongue)
> ㄴ 그는 침묵을 지켰어

Hyun-soo needs extra calories like a hole in the head
> ㄴ 현수에게 여분의 칼로리는 전혀 필요 없어

Hyun-soo needs your stupid advice like a hole in the head
> ㄴ 현수가 뭐가 아쉬워서 너의 서푼어치 조언이 필요하겠니

Hyun-soo threw up his hands in disgust and quit his job
> ㄴ 현수는 속이 뒤틀려서 손을 털어 버리고 직장을 그만 두었어

I always have butterflies in my stomach
> ㄴ 항상 가슴이 조마조마해

› **pepper** season with pepper
› **disgust** strong aversion

I can fight with him with one arm tied behind my back
> ↳ 그 사람이라면 쉽게 맞서 싸울 수 있어

I can hardly believe my ears
> ↳ 그 말은 정말 놀라운 일이네

I can read the whole story in your face
> ↳ 얼굴에 다 씌었군

I can't put my finger(a label) on it
> ↳ 꼬집어 말할 순 없어

> (=It escapes me)

I can't put my hands on anything
> ↳ 일이 손에 안 잡혀

I don't want to go over your head, but I will if necessary
> ↳ 당신을 무시하고 당신 상사에게 따지고 싶지 않지만 계속 이러시면 어쩔 수 없어요

I feel a pain in the pit of my stomach
> ↳ 명치가 아파

I feel it in my bones
> ↳ 내 짐작이 틀림없어

I feel like my heart would break
> ↳ 하늘이 무너져 내리는 것만 같아

I felt a lump in my throat
> ↳ 감동했어

› **label** identification slip, identifying word or phrase

(=I'm impressed)

I felt my ears burning yesterday
> ㄴ 어제 내가 소문의 주인공이 되어 당혹스러웠어

I have a frog in my throat
> ㄴ 목이 쉬었어

(=I have lost my voice)

I have a knot in my leg
> ㄴ 다리에 알배다(근육통)

(=have a sore calf)
(=have a muscle-ache)

I have a weak stomach
> ㄴ 난 비위가 약해

(=I lose my appetite easily)
(=I can't take it)

I have been trying hard determined to do whatever it takes
> ㄴ 이를 갈고 열심히 하고 있어

› **determine**   decide on, establish, or settle;
           find cut; be the cause of

> (=I've been gritting my teeth and trying hard)
> (=I've been trying hard bent on success(determined to do better))

I have canker sores in my mouth
　　↳ 입안이 헐어서 쓰립니다

I have something for your private ear
　　↳ 비밀히 말할게 있어

I know them like the back of my hand
　　↳ 그 사람들이야 손바닥 들여다보듯 알지

I know you have your feet on the ground
　　↳ 넌 사려분별이 있는 사람이잖아

I merely opened my eyes to what I knew
　　↳ 이제야 눈이 뜨인 거야

I miss you with every beat of my heart
　　↳ 정말 당신을 보고 싶어

I threw some water on my face
　　↳ 고양이 세수했어(후닥닥 세수를 하는 둥 마는 둥 했을 때)

> (=I couldn't wash my face properly)
> (=I quickly washed my face)

I want you to be my eyes and ears
　　↳ 내 몫까지 즐기고 와

I was so nervous I was left speechless(tongue-tied, the words stuck in my throat)

▸ **canker** mouth ulcer

└ 너무 떨려서 말이 안나왔어

I'm feeling really overwhelmed stomach
└ 한방 맞은 기분이야

(=I feel like I've just been punched in the stomach)

I'm not in the vein for work
└ 일 할 기분이 아냐

I've got two left feet
└ 저는 춤을 잘 못춰요

If he makes(offers) new proposals, we should seize them with both hands
└ 그가 새로운 제안들은 내 놓는다면 감지덕지 할 일이지

If you go out with other girls, tongues will wag
└ 네가 딴 여자들과 어울린다면 입들이 가만 안 있을 거다

If you hold your tongue, no one will be any wiser
└ 네가 잠자코 있으면 누가 알겠나

If you twist my arm
└ 꼭 해야한다면

(=If you insist)

If you want your children to keep their feet on the ground, put some responsibility on their shoulders
└ 자녀가 땅에 두 발을 굳게 디디기를 원한다면 그들의 어깨에 책임을 지워라

▸ **overwhelm** overcome completely

Ignorance is the womb of monsters
> ㄴ 무지는 괴물들이 생겨나는 자궁이다

Imagine how big my eyes got!
> ㄴ 내가 얼마나 놀랐겠는가 상상을 해봐

In a fight the rich man tries to save his face, the poor man his coat
> ㄴ 싸움에서 부자는 체면을 생각하고 가난한 사람은 옷을 생각한다

In an instant I was again on my feet
> ㄴ 난 곧 일어났어

In his face wrinkles ploughed by time
> ㄴ 그의 얼굴은 나이로 인해 주름살 투성이다

In his mind's eye, he'll picture what's going to happen
> ㄴ 그의 육감으로 무슨 일이 일어날지 예상할 것이다

In line with the historic implementation of a law acknowledging brain death, the government launched a state-run agency to manage all matters related to organ transplants
> ㄴ 정부는 뇌사를 인정하는 장기이식에 관한 법률 시행과 연계해 장기이식을 총괄하기 위한 공공기구를 발족시켰다

In man an increase in body heat results in dilation of the peripheral blood vessels, which cause blushing and facilitates cooling
> ㄴ 인체 내에서 체온이 상승하면 말초혈관이 팽창하고 이로 인해 얼굴이 붉어지고 기관이 냉각한다

In the shallow end of the pool the water comes up to my waist
> ㄴ 풀의 얕은 끝 부분은 허리까지 물이 온다

Industry is fortune's right hand, and frugality her left
> ㄴ 근면은 행운의 오른손이고 검소함은 왼손이다

Interest gnaws at a man's substance with invisible teeth

▸ **womb** uterus	▸ **peripheral** outer boundary
▸ **dilate** swell or expand	▸ **frugality** thrifty

ㄴ 이자는 빚진 사람의 재산을 보이지 않는 이빨로 갉아먹는다

Is there any green in my eye?

ㄴ 내가 만만해 보이니?

Is there any need to rub my nose in it(rub it in)?

ㄴ 그 일을 두고두고 들먹거려야 하겠니?

It chilled(scared) me to the bone

ㄴ 등골이 오싹했다

(=It freaked me out)

It made my nose run(water)

ㄴ 코끝이 찡했어

(=It made my nose to twitch)
(=It made me sniffle)

It seemed very tongue in cheek

ㄴ 마치 놀림 당한 느낌이더군

It slipped out(of my mouth)

ㄴ 얼떨결에 말이 나왔어(실언)

(=It was a slip of the tongue)
(=I wasn't thinking)
(=It was out before I knew it)
(=I said the wrong thing)
(=I didn't mean what I said)

· **freak**   something abnormal or unusual,
enthusiast

It sounds strange in your mouth
> ↳ 네가 그럴 말을 하니 이상하게 들린다

It sticks out like a sore thumb
> ↳ 그건 너무 튀어

It takes more brain and effort to make out the income-tax form than it does to make the income
> ↳ 소득을 올리는 것보다 소득세 신고용지를 작성하는데 더 머리와 노력을 요한다

It will stand them on their heads
> ↳ 그 일은 그들을 혼란에 빠뜨릴 것이다

It won't go to my head
> ↳ 그 정도로는 안 취해

It'd be better all around if you'd take that thing off your eyes
> ↳ 그 일을 관심 밖으로 내보내는 것이 어느 모로 보나 훨씬 낫다

It'll be hard for you to quit gambling once you get your feet wet
> ↳ 노름에 한번 손대면 끊기 힘든다

It'll take a lot of elbow grease
> ↳ 그걸 해내자면 꽤 힘들 거야

It's a massive weight around your neck
> ↳ 그건 큰 부담이겠군

It's a must that we brush our teeth after every meal
> ↳ 우린 매 식사 후 반드시 양치질을 해야 한다

It's all I can do to keep my head above water with the work I have
> ↳ 주어진 일에 급급할 정도로 어렵게 지내고 있어

It's as plain as the nose on your face
> ↳ 그건 뻔한 거잖아

› **grease** thick oily material or fat, smear or lubricate with grease

It's better to die on your feet than live on your knees
 ↳ 굴욕을 당하느니 명예로운 죽음을 택하겠다

It's coming out(written on) of your face
 ↳ 네 얼굴에 씌었어

It's easy to miss what's in front of you(under your nose=staring in your face)
 ↳ 등잔 밑이 어두워

> 바로 곁에 있는 것을 찾지 못할 때에 쓰이는 표현이다. 서양에서는 "그것이 뱀이라면 당신을 물겠다"라고 하고, 이는 뱀이 물 정도로 가까이 있는 데도 알아채지 못한다는 뜻이다(The husband is always the last to know 등잔 밑이 어둡다).

It's like pulling teeth
 ↳ 장난이 아니네. 정말 어려운 일이네

It's not that easy. It'll cost him his neck this time
 ↳ 그렇게 쉽게 끝날 일이 아냐. 이번엔 그의 목이 걸려 있어

It's on its last leg
 ↳ 그건 간신히 지탱하고 있어

It's out of my hands
 ↳ 이젠 네 손을 떠났어

It's stamped on your forehead
 ↳ 네 얼굴에 다 씌었어

It's staring you in the face
 ↳ 네 눈(코) 앞에 있잖아

It's tempting to criticize others and turn a blind eye to all the

---

› **stare** look intently with wide-open eyes

problems of your own
> ↳ 남들을 마구 헐뜯고 자신의 문제점을 덮어두고자 하는 유혹에 끌려들기 쉽다

It's time to put our hand to the plow
> ↳ 자, 일할 시간이다

Jin-soo got(had) stars in his eyes when he met his blind date
> ↳ 진수는 낯선 데이트 상대와 만났을 때 들떠 있었어

Jung-ah flew to his arms as he got off the ship
> ↳ 그가 배에서 내리자 정아는 와락 그의 품에 안겼어

Jung-ah had her mouth full and couldn't get the words out
> ↳ 정아는 입에 밥이 들어있어서 말하기 힘들었어(get something out은 "입이 안 떨어지다"의 뜻도 있음)

Jung-ah's baby was just beginning to find his feet
> ↳ 정아의 아이는 이제 막 걸음마를 시작했어

Jung-soo was nervous and couldn't speak at first; then he found his tongue
> ↳ 정수가 처음에는 긴장해서 말이 안 나왔으나 이내 말문이 열렸어

Jung-tai was my captain in the army, but now the shoe is on the other foot
> ↳ 군에서는 정태가 우리 중대장이었지만 지금은 나의 부서에서 일하고 있어

Just as eating against one's will is injurious to health, so studying without a liking for it spoils the memory, and our brains retain nothing
> ↳ 싫은 것을 억지로 먹이는 것이 건강에 해롭듯이 싫은 것을 억지로 공부하는 것은 기억력을 망치게 되어 머리 속에 들어와도 남아있지 않

▸ **injury** hurt, damage, or loss sustained

▸ **retain** keep or hold onto, engage the services of

게 된다

Just as our eyes need light in order to see, our minds need ideas in order to conceive
  ↳ 우리의 눈이 보는데는 빛이 필요하듯이 우리의 마음에 아이디어가 있어야 궁리를 하게 된다

Just let it in one ear and out the other
  ↳ 한쪽 귀로 듣고 한쪽 귀로 흘려라

> 남의 말에 주의를 기울이지 않는 사람을 두고 쓰거나, 잔소리에 시달리는 사람을 위로할 때 쓰이는 말이다. 영어에는 "In one ear and out the other 한 귀로 들어오고 다른 귀로 나간다"라는 한국 속담과 비슷한 속담이 있다.
> (=Just let it pass without much thought)
> (=Just ignore what he says)

Keep a still tongue in your head
  ↳ 말을 삼가서 해

Keep on your toes and report anything that you see
  ↳ 경계를 늦추지 말고 이상한 것을 보면 연락해 줘

Keep your chin up. You must stop being blue
  ↳ 기운을 내. 우울한 얼굴은 그만 거둬

Keep your finger on the pulse of Seoul
  ↳ 서울에서 무슨 일이 일어나고 있는지 주시해

Keep your hand on that to steady it
  ↳ 움직이지 않게 손으로 꾹 눌러 잡아 줘

Keep your hands to yourself
  ↳ 남의 것(깨지는 것) 손대지마(아이들에게는 "남을 때리지마"이고, 어른들에게는 "내 몸에 손대지마"가 될 수 있음)

▸ **pulse** arterial throbbing caused by heart contractions

▸ **steady** firm in position or sure in movement, calm or reliable

Keep your nose out of it
> ↳ 그 문제엔 좀 빠져 줘

Let him get his feet wet first
> ↳ 우선 그에게 적응훈련부터 시키자

Let success or failure be on my head
> ↳ 성패는 내 책임이다

Let your fingers do the walking
> ↳ 손가락으로 짚어가며 찾아봐라

Let's address ourselves to the matters at hand
> ↳ 현안 문제부터 해결하자

Let's decide it by a show of hands
> ↳ 거수표결로 결정합시다

Let's get on with the job at hand first
> ↳ 우선 현안문제부터 처리하자

Let's not overplay our hand
> ↳ 무리한 짓은 말자

Let's put our heads together
> ↳ 중지를 모읍시다

Let's talk about it face to face
> ↳ 만나서 얘기하자

Look me in the face eyeball to eyeball(face to face)
> ↳ 내 얼굴을 똑바로 쳐다봐

Loose lips sink ships
> ↳ 느슨한 입은 전함을 함몰시킨다

Losing the game was a slap in the face for him
> ↳ 게임에 진다는 게 그에게는 모욕적인 일이었다

▸ **overplay** act excessively

▸ **eyeball** organ of sight consisting of a globular structure

Love looks forward, hate looks back, anxiety has eyes all over its head

ㄴ 사랑은 앞을 내다보고, 증오는 과거를 돌아보고, 근심은 사면팔방을 돌아본다

Love looks not with the eyes, but with the mind

ㄴ 사랑은 눈으로 보는 것이 아니라 마음으로 본다

Make sure you get someone who won't talk above the people's heads

ㄴ 사람들이 알아듣지도 못할 소리를 하는 연사를 모셔오지 않도록 해라

Man-soo shot himself in the foot

ㄴ 만수는 화를 자초했어

Many hands make light work

ㄴ 백짓장도 맞들면 낫다

Many public servants have clean hands as regards money

ㄴ 많은 공무원들이 금전문제에 깨끗해

Many taxpayers are up in arms when they got their tax bills

ㄴ 많은 납세자가 고지서를 받아보고는 화를 내었다

Mi-gyung intoxicated him with her smiling eyes

ㄴ 미경인 눈웃음으로 그를 녹였어

Moon-hee has a liberal tongue

ㄴ 문희는 때와 장소를 가리지 않고 지껄여

Moon-ho doubled his fists in anger

ㄴ 문호는 화가 나서 주먹을 불끈 쥐었다

Moon-soo has a frog in the throat=Moon-soo has lost his voice

ㄴ 문수는 목이 쉬어있어

Moon-soo put a flea in my ear

ㄴ 문수가 내게 듣기 싫은 소릴 했어(경고했어)

› **intoxicated** make drunk
› **flea** leaping bloodsucking insect

More is meant than meets the ear
> ↳ 언외의 뜻이 있다

Most eye infections are contagious so it is advisable to avoid touching the eyes at all
> ↳ 대부분의 눈병은 전염성이 있으니 아예 눈을 만지지 않는 것이 바람직하다

Most of them have prices on their heads
> ↳ 그들의 대부분은 상금이 걸려있어

Most people are voting with their feet
> ↳ 대부분의 사람들이 싫은 곳에는 잘 안간다

My fingers itch for quarrel
> ↳ 싸우고 싶어 손이 근질거린다

My body won't listen to me=My energy level has dropped=I'm not feeling well=My body is feeling week
> ↳ 몸이 전혀 말을 안들어

My brain isn't working today
> ↳ 오늘은 머리가 잘 안돌아

My brother is on his feet soon after the operation
> ↳ 형은 수술 후 곧 회복했어

My butt is on fire
> ↳ 발등에 불이 떨어졌어

My daughter has itchy feet
> ↳ 우리 딸은 역마살이 끼었어

My ears are ringing=I have a ringing noise in my ear
> ↳ 귀가 멍멍해

My ears are smoking=I'm seeing red

› **contagious** spread of disease by contact, disease spread by contact

ᄂ 화가 나서 미치겠다

My ears itch for information
ᄂ 소식을 알고싶어

My elbow has worked through the sleeve
ᄂ 옷 팔꿈치가 차츰 닳아 떨어졌다

My fingers have been burned
ᄂ 내가 혼줄이 났지

My fingers have gone stiff from lack of practice
ᄂ 연습을 안 했더니 손가락이 굳었어

My fingers itch for quarrel
ᄂ 싸우고 싶어 손이 근질거린다

My friend stabbed me in the back
ᄂ 믿는 도끼에 발등 찍혔어

> "믿는 도끼에 발등 찍혔다"에 해당하는 영어 표현은 "Stabbed in the back 등을 찔렸다"이다. 또한 강아지가 주인의 손을 무는 상황에 비유하여 "Bite the hand that feeds you 먹이를 주는 손을 문다"라고도 한다.

My head is aching from it=It's making my head pound
ᄂ 골치 아프게 하는군

My head is spinning
ᄂ 머리가 핑핑 돈다

My heart is in my mouth
ᄂ 가슴이 조마조마하다

My hunch was right on the nose
ᄂ 내 예감이 적중했다

› **stiff** not bending easily, tense, formal   › **hunch** assume or cause to assume a bent or crooked posture

My leg's been acting up again
↳ 또 다리가 아프기 시작하는군

My legs got wobbly(unsteady)
↳ 다리가 후들후들해

My lips are sealed
↳ 절대 말 안할게

My mother's mind is failing=My mother is getting senile
↳ 어머닌 노망기가 있어

My mother's teeth are all gone
↳ 어머니의 이(치아)가 전부 빠졌어

My muscles ache=I'm rather stiff
↳ 몸이 뻐근해

My stomach is already growling
↳ 벌써부터 배에서 꼬르륵 소리가 난다

My wife's cleanness is bred in the bone
↳ 우리 집사람의 청결성은 타고났어

Myung-soo had to mess her face up then
↳ 그때 명수는 그 여자를 한방 때려줄 수밖에 없었어

Nam-soo's face maligns him
↳ 남수는 얼굴과 딴판으로 착한 사람이다

Nature and books belong to the eyes that see them
↳ 자연과 책은 알아보는 눈을 가진 사람의 것이다

Neuron is a special cell in the body that is capable of sending along messages that represent feelings and commands to muscles
↳ 뉴런은 체내의 특수세포로서 감정을 표현하거나 근육에게 명령하는 메시지를 전달하는 능력이 있다

· **wobble** move or cause to move with an irregular rocking motion

· **neuron** nerve cell

No is no negative in a woman's mouth
　　ㄴ 여자의 거절은 거절이 아니다

Nobody is going to nail your ears back
　　ㄴ 아무도 널 호되게 나무랄 사람은 없어

Nobody will know where your head is at(where you are coming from)
　　ㄴ 너의 의중이 무엇인지 누가 알겠나

Not a complain escaped his lips
　　ㄴ 불평 한마디 없었어

Not what goes into the mouth defiles a man; but what comes out of the mouth, this defiles a man
　　ㄴ 입에 들어가는 것이 사람을 더럽게 하는 것이 아니라 입에서 나오는 그것이 사람을 더럽게 하느니라

Nothing between your ears, that's your trouble
　　ㄴ 넌 머리가 텅 비었다는 게 문제야

Now I can hold my head up again
　　ㄴ 이제 다시 당당하게 나가도 되겠군

Now I'm back on my feet
　　ㄴ 이제 경제적으로 혼자 설 수 있어

Officers and men were just beginning to find their feet then
　　ㄴ 그러자 장교와 사병들은 경험과 지식을 쌓기 시작했다

Often a noble face hides filthy ways
　　ㄴ 고상한 얼굴로 더러운 수단을 덮어 가리는 일은 흔히 있다

Oh, I see. You have the upper hand
　　ㄴ 옳아. 배부른 흥정을 하자 이거로군

▸ **defile**　make filthy or corrupt, profane or dishonor

▸ **filthy**　repulsive dirt or refuse

배부른 흥정이란 말은 유리한 입장에서 흥정을 한다는 뜻이다. Upper Hand는
팔씨름(Arm Wrestling)에서 위에 얹는 손이 유리하다는 것에서 나온 말이다.
거래를 성사시킬 때에 달변이나 처세술로 흥정을 할 때에 사용하는 속담이다.

Oh-jin ventured his opinion studying my face
> ↳ 오진이는 내 눈치를 봐 가면서 의견을 제시했어

Old age plowed furrows in her face
> ↳ 나이가 그녀의 얼굴에 깊은 주름을 잡아놓았다

On our office picnic, we count our noses(heads)
> ↳ 사무실 야유회 때 우린 인원 점검을 해

On the hottest days, the heat transfer process works in reverse, so the environment actually heats up our body
> ↳ 가장 더운 날이면 열 전달 과정이 반대로 흐르게 되어서 사실상 주변
> 에 있는 열이 우리의 몸을 뜨겁게 만든다

Once he hears the news, he'll be laughing out of the wrong side of his mouth
> ↳ 그가 이 소식을 듣고 보면 들떴던 마음이 싹 가시겠군

One could tell his face was distorted by rage
> ↳ 그가 화가 나서 얼굴이 일그러졌다는 것은 누구나 알 수 있었다

One feature of the brain in all primates is its division into hemispheres
> ↳ 모든 영장류가 가지고 있는 뇌의 한가지 특징은 반구체로 나누어져
> 있다는 점이다

One good bang in the arm leads to another
> ↳ 마약주사는 결국 중독되고 만다

One good head is better than a hundred strong arms

› **distort** twist out of shape, condition, or true meaning

› **primate** highest-ranking bishop, mammal of the group that includes man and monkeys

↳ 훌륭한 두뇌 하나는 힘센 손 백개 보다 낫다

One learns to know oneself best behind one's back

↳ 자기가 없을 때 남들이 하는 말을 들어봐야 자기를 가장 잘 알 수 있다

Oriental herbal medicine plays an important role in providing the whole body with the nutritive substances it lacks

↳ 한약은 인체에서 부족한 성분을 제공해주는 중요한 역할을 한다

Our body gets rid of the extra heat from muscular activity by dissipating it into the cooler surrounding air

↳ 우리의 몸은 근육활동으로 생겨나는 열을 주변의 보다 서늘한 공기 중으로 발산함으로써 제거한다

Our boss wants to twist us around her little finger

↳ 우리 사장님은 우릴 완전히 주무르고 싶어해

Our fingers had gone dead and we couldn't write our names

↳ 우리는 손가락이 곱아서 이름을 쓸 수가 없었다

Our new plan came apart at the seams when his tongue slipped

↳ 그가 실언을 하는 바람에 우리 계획은 망가졌다

Out of the mouth comes the evil

↳ 입이 화근

Outspoken advice is(sounds) harsh to the ear

↳ 바른 말은 귀에 거슬린다

자신의 결점을 꼬집어서 말하는 충고를 들을 때에는 기분이 좋을 수가 없다. 그렇기 때문에 함부로 남에게 충고를 해서는 안되고, 충고를 들어서 기분이 나쁘더라도 받아들일 수 있는 아량이 있어야 한다.
(=Unpleasant advice is a good medicine)
(=A good medicine taste bitter)

› **dissipate** break up and drive off, squander, drink to excess

People aged 60 and older who have a certain type of high blood pressure and who are particularly thin face have higher risks of stroke and death
> ↳ 60세 이상인 사람으로서 특정한 종류의 고혈압이 있고 특히 얼굴이 야윈 사람이 더 뇌졸중에 걸리거나 사망할 위험이 더 크다

People with arthritis are burdened with sharp pain in almost every joint in their bodies
> ↳ 관절염이 있는 사람은 전신에 있는 거의 모든 관절에서 심한 통증으로 고생하게 된다

Perspiration eliminates about one fourth of the total amount of heat that the body generates
> ↳ 땀은 몸이 발산하는 전체 열의 1/4을 제거한다

Please don't jump down on his throat(all over him)
> ↳ 그 사람 호되게 나무라지 마

Please have an eye out for the bus
> ↳ 버스가 오는지 잘 지켜봐 줘

Please keep out from under my feet
> ↳ 방해 좀 하지마

Poke your hand through this crack and see if you can reach any coins there
> ↳ 이 벌어진 틈 사이로 손을 푹 집어넣어 거기 동전이 있는지 찾아봐

Politicians who are in the public eye have a responsibility to behave in a sensible way
> ↳ 세인의 주목을 받는 정치인은 지각 있는 행동을 할 책임이 있다

Pull in your ears and mind your own business
> ↳ 못들은 일로 하고 네 일이나 해

▸ **perspire** sweat
▸ **poke** prod, dawdle

Put a good amount of cosmetic on your face
ㄴ 얼굴에 충분한 양의 화장품을 발라라

Put it out of your head
ㄴ 그 일은 더 생각하지 말아라

Read my lips
ㄴ 내 말을 믿어

Reading is to the mind what exercise is to the body
ㄴ 독서가 정신에 필요한 것은 운동이 신체에 필요한 것과 같다

Remembering faces is a process that take place in the central cortex, the most highly evolved area of the brain
ㄴ 얼굴을 기억하는 것은 뇌에서 가장 많이 진화된 부분인 대뇌피질에서 발생하는 과정이다

Round the edge of this block so that your baby won't hurt himself in his mouth when eating
ㄴ 이 덩어리를 너의 아기가 먹을 때 입이 다치지 않도록 가장자리에 모나지 않게 잘라라

Run your fingers over that paper to see if it's been embossed
ㄴ 그 종이가 돋을 새김이 되어있는지 더듬어 보아라

Running my eye down the page, I caught sight of several mistakes
ㄴ 페이지를 쭉 훑어 내려가다가 잘못된 곳을 여러개 찾아냈다

Salt plays an important part in the function of the body
ㄴ 소금은 신진대사에 중요한 역할을 한다

Sang-soo is a master at shooting himself in the foot
ㄴ 상수는 자기 발등 찍는데는 선수야

Sang-soo has the world on his shoulders
ㄴ 상수에게는 책임이 많아

› **cortex** outer or covering layer of an organism or part

› **evolve** develop or change by degrees

Sang-soo is worried about saving his own neck
  ↳ 상수는 책임을 면할 걱정만 하고 있다

Sang-soo pulled a muscle and scratched the game
  ↳ 상수는 근육을 삐어서 경기를 포기했다

Sang-soo rubs shoulders with rich people only
  ↳ 상수는 돈 많은 사람들하고만 사귄다

Sang-soo snatched his hand away from the hot pan with a cry of pain
  ↳ 상수는 뜨거워 비명을 지르면서 뜨거운 냄비에서 손을 확 뗴었다

Sang-soo stormed off and came back with hat in hand when he ran out of money
  ↳ 상수는 횡 하니 떠났다가 돈이 떨어지자 공손한 태도로 돌아왔다

Sang-soo's bright idea will give them a needed shot in the arm
  ↳ 상수의 기발한 생각이 그들에게 필요한 활력소가 될 것이다

Sang-soo's eyes are in his stomach
  ↳ 상수의 머리 속에는 먹는 것밖에 없어

Scientists already learned to build and maintain artificial wombs to give premature infants a fighting chance
  ↳ 과학자들은 이미 인공자궁을 만들고 유지하여 조산아에게 살아날 수 있는 기회를 제공하는 법을 알게 되었다

She always shoots straight from the shoulder
  ↳ 그녀는 늘 솔직히 말한다

She banged her hand on the table, fighting back tears of rage and frustration
  ↳ 그녀는 테이블을 쾅 치면서 분노와 좌절의 눈물을 삼켰다

She came unglued and cried her eyes out

› **snatch** try to grab something suddenly, seize or take away suddenly

› **frustrate** block, cause to fail

ㄴ그 여자는 제 정신을 잃고 평평 울었어

She couldn't keep the tears from her eyes
ㄴ그녀는 흐르는 눈물을 억제할 수 없었다

She enjoys rubbing elbows with foreigners
ㄴ그 여자는 외국인과 사귀기를 좋아한다

She got one of her fingers trapped in the door
ㄴ그녀는 손가락이 문에 끼었다

She had her head in the clouds until her friend was promoted
ㄴ그 여자는 자기 친구가 승진할 때까지 건성으로 일하고 있었다

She has a brain like a sieve and always forget the secret number
ㄴ그녀는 너무 기억력이 나빠서 늘 비밀번호를 잊어버린다

She has something for your private ear
ㄴ그 여자가 네게 은밀히 할 얘기가 있데

She passed her hands over her face
ㄴ그녀는 손으로 얼굴을 매만졌다

She rubbed suntan lotion onto her arms and legs
ㄴ그 여자는 팔과 다리에 선탠 로션을 묻혔다(일부러 바른 게 아님)

She shoots off her mouth every time we meet her
ㄴ그 여자는 우릴 만날 때마다 쉴새없이 지껄여

She stepped on the floorboards that had rotted away and her foot went right through the floor
ㄴ그녀가 썩어 문드러진 마루청을 밟자 발이 곧바로 마루바닥까지 빠져 들어갔다

She stood glued to the spot, unable to take her eyes off the strange animal that was approaching
ㄴ그녀는 이상한 동물에게서 눈을 떼지 못한 채 꼼짝 못하고 서 있었다

‣promote advance in rank, contribute to the growth, development, or prosperity of

‣**floorboards** boards used to cover flooring

She wears her feet(is on the go) for us
> 그 여자는 우리를 위해 동분서주 하고 있어

She went down on her knees and began to pray
> 그 여자는 무릎을 꿇고 기도하기 시작했다

She'll get it through your head if it takes all day
> 그 여자는 하루종일 걸려서라도 너를 설득하려 들것이다

She's getting a little long in tooth
> 그 여자가 나이를 먹었거든

She's going to do an about face and concentrate on her study
> 그 여자는 생각을 완전히 바꾸어 공부에 전념하려고 한다

She's got a hole in her head if she thinks I was born yesterday
> 그 여자가 나를 만만하게 본다면 어리석은 생각이다

She's got two left feet
> 그 여자는 도무지 춤 솜씨가 늘지 않아

She's in my face too much
> 그 여자는 나를 너무 괴롭혀

She's laughing all over her face
> 그 여자는 희색이 만면해

Shut up before I mace your face up
> 박살내기 전에 입 닥쳐

Some folks must have been burning their ears tonight
> 오늘밤 누구누구는 남들의 입방아에 오른줄 알고 몹시 궁금해 하겠군

Somehow he managed to slip through their fingers
> 어쨌든 그는 그들에게서 빠져나갔어

Someone who regularly feels coldness in his/her hands is likely to

---

› **concentrate** gather together, make stronger, fix
one's attention on one thing

have less resistance to catching a cold
> ↳ 손에서 규칙적으로 한기를 느끼는 사람은 감기에 대한 저항력이 약할 가능성이 있다

Sometimes he has his fingers in the till
> ↳ 그는 가끔씩 회사(가게)에서 돈을 슬쩍 훔쳐

Sook-hee hit Jong-soo between the eyes the moment he saw her
> ↳ 종수는 숙회를 보자마자 홀딱 빠져버렸어

Spread the rumor around, and we'll cut them off at the knees
> ↳ 소문을 널리 퍼뜨리면 그들은 얼굴을 들고 다닐 수 없게 될 거야

Spread the umbrella over your head
> ↳ 머리에 우산을 받쳐라

Stand with your feet shoulder-width apart and swing your golf club back, keeping eye on the ball
> ↳ 양발을 어깨 넓이로 벌리고 서서 공을 쳐다보면서 골프채를 뒤로 휘둘러라

Stay on this medicine for another day to see if your stomach trouble improves
> ↳ 너의 배탈이 나아질지 이 약을 하루만 더 먹어봐라

Stop breathing down my neck, I make mistakes when I'm being watched
> ↳ 옆에서 지켜보지마, 누가 지켜보면 실수한단 말이야

Stop putting your words into my mouth
> ↳ 내가 하지도 않은 말을 했다고 하지마

Stop sticking your head in the sand and face reality
> ↳ 일을 피하지 말고 정면 돌파해라

Stretch your foot to the length of your blanket

▸ **resistance** act of resisting, opposition to electric current

▸ **blanket** heavy covering for bed

↳ 당신의 발을 담요의 길이까지만 뻗어라

Sung-gyoo has a very good hand

↳ 성규는 매우 글씨를 잘 써

(=Sung-gyoo's handwriting is very good)

Sung-soo is feeling like being slapped in the face

↳ 성수는 한 방 맞은 기분이야

(=Sung-soo is feeling really overwhelmed)
(=Sung-soo feels like he's been punched in the stomach)

Sung-moon kept his head in his cups

↳ 성문이는 술에 취했어도 정신은 말짱했어

Sung-soo set(put) his hand to the plow

↳ 성수는 큰 일에 착수했다

Sweating a lot while taking a bath or sauna for an extended period of time can cause extreme fatigue and greatly harm to the body

↳ 긴 시간 목욕이나 사우나를 하면서 땀을 많이 흘리는 것은 극도의 피로를 가져오고 몸에 크게 해로울 수 있다

Tai-ho always sets tongues wagging by his actions

↳ 태호는 늘 자기 행동으로 입방아에 오르고 있어

Tai-ho stepped on someone's toes during the last campaign

↳ 태호는 지난 유세 중 누군가의 감정을 건드린 일이 있어

Tai-ho's had an eye on you

↳ 태호가 널 지켜봐 왔지

▸ **wag** sway or swing from side to side or to and fro

▸ **campaign** series of military operations or of activities meant to gain a result

Tai-jung is an heir to his mother's fine brain
  ↳ 태정인 어머니에게서 훌륭한 두뇌를 물려받았어

Tai-jung just sat on his hands
  ↳ 태정인 전혀 도와주려고 하지 않더군

Take a step close to a healthier body by adding a spoonful of vinegar to your diet today
  ↳ 오늘 식사에 한 티스푼의 식초를 첨가해서 더욱 건강한 신체로 가꾸어 나가라

Take his praise as a kind of lip service
  ↳ 그의 칭찬을 입 발린 소리쯤으로 알아라

Take in you losses in your stride and you'll be on your feet in no time
  ↳ 너의 손실에 의연하게 대처해 나가면 금방 자립해 나가게 될 것이다

Taking a day-trip to the Mt. Halla and back was hard on my feet
  ↳ 한라산까지 당일치기로 갔다왔더니 다리에 무리가 갔다

That chick is putty in my hands
  ↳ 그 아가씨는 내가 시키는 대로 해

That computer is head and shoulder above the competition
  ↳ 저 컴퓨터는 경쟁상대보다 훨씬 우수하다

That girl's been giving all the married men the eye
  ↳ 저 아가씨는 모든 유부남에게 추파를 던지고 다녀

That guy has sticky fingers
  ↳ 저 친구 손버릇이 나빠

That toilet(potty) mouth is offending us again
  ↳ 저 쌍소리 잘하는 녀석이 또 유리에게 듣기 거북한 소릴 하고 있어

The accident left him with several broken ribs and dislocated right arm

---

· **compete** strive to win

· **offend** sin or act in violation; hurt, annoy, or insult

↳ 그 사고로 그는 갈비뼈가 몇 개 부러지고 오른팔이 탈구됐다

The agency is already facing a serious challenge from a private organization that promotes organ transplants between people with no blood relation

↳ 이 기구는 혈연관계가 없는 기증자와 이식 대상자 사이의 장기이식운 동을 펴고있는 민간기구로부터 벌써 거센 반발에 직면하고 있다

The answer's staring you in the face

↳ 네 얼굴에 답이 쓰였어

The battle was won by brain rather than brawn

↳ 전투는 완력이 아닌 두뇌로 승부가 났다

The boy walked along as if favoring his sore foot

↳ 소년은 아픈 다리를 다칠세라 가만가만 걸어갔다

The business is on its last legs

↳ 그 사업체는 파산직전에 와있어

The cat got his tongue

↳ 그 사람 부끄러워서 말못했지

The coach is bound to get it in the neck

↳ 감독이 호되게 당하겠군

The cobbler's children go bare foot

↳ 대장간에 식칼 없다

> 마땅히 있어야 할 곳에 없는 상황을 "대장간에 식칼 없다"라고 표현한다. 영 어로는 "The cobbler's children go bare foot 구두장이의 아이들이 맨발 로 다닌다"라고 한다.

The color mounted to her face as she saw him staring at her

‣ **brawn** muscular strength ‣ **mount** increase in amount, get up on, put in position

ㄴ 그 여자는 그가 자신을 뚫어지게 쳐다보고 있는 걸 보고 얼굴을 확 붉혔다

The decision is in the hands of the power that be
ㄴ 그 결정은 당국의 손에 달려있다

The eyes are not responsible when the mind does the seeing
ㄴ 마음을 통해 볼 때엔 눈에게 책임이 없다

The face is no index to the heart
ㄴ 얼굴이 곱다고 마음씨가 고운 건 아니다

The face of the tyranny is always mild at first
ㄴ 독재자들의 첫 인상은 늘 온화하다

The gold bullion has traveled from hand to hand until it got back to its owner
ㄴ 그 금괴는 여러 사람들의 손을 거치다가 주인의 손에 들어갔다

The hooligan edged closer, gripping the ax tightly in his hand
ㄴ 그 불한당은 도끼를 손에 꼭 쥐고 천천히 다가갔다

The idea kept running through my head
ㄴ 그 생각이 끊임없이 머리에 떠올랐어

The kidneys control overall balance of vital fluids in the body, which in turn directly influence the energy level and equilibrium of the body
ㄴ 신장은 체내의 체액을 전체적으로 조절하고 나아가서 이것이 체내의 활력과 균형수준에 직접 영향을 준다

The learning of books that you do not make your own wisdom is money in the hands of other in time of need
ㄴ 자신의 지혜로 만들 수 없는 책을 공부한다는 것은 돈이 필요할 때 남의 주머니에 있는 것과 같다

▸ **bullion** gold or silver especially in bars

The left hand doesn't know what the right hand is doing
↳ 하고 있는 일이 제 각각이구먼

The lines in his face reflect a hard life
↳ 그의 얼굴에 새겨진 주름들은 그가 많은 고생을 했음을 보여준다

The lips of righteous feed many
↳ 의인의 입술은 여러 사람을 교육시킨다

The long arm of the law always tap these street vendors on the shoulder
↳ 경찰들은 늘 노점상들에게 뇌물(정보)을 얻으려고 찾아온다

The mouth is the gate of misfortune
↳ 입이 화근이다

The mouth of righteous is a well of life, but the violence covers mouth of the wicked
↳ 의인의 입은 생명의 입이지만 악인의 입은 악을 머금었느니라

The nagging inflammation of the joints is generally caused by deposits of inorganic calcium in the cartilage of joints
↳ 이 성가신 관절의 염증은 일반적으로 관절 연골 내에 무기 칼슘이 쌓여서 일어난다

The new law on organ donation would sharply increase the number of transplants using organs of the brain-dead
↳ 장기 기증에 대한 새로운 법은 뇌사자의 장기를 이용한 장기이식 건수를 급격히 늘일 것이다

The noises jarred on my ears(nerves)
↳ 그 소리가 나에게 거슬렸다

The pain from his scalded ankles prevents mobility, thus allowing inflamed tissues to heal

---

▸ **vendor** seller

▸ **deposit** put away for safekeeping, give as a pledge, lay or put down

ㄴ 그는 물에 덴 발목 때문에 곪아있는 조직이 낫도록 움직이지 못하게
되어있다

**The policeman turned a blind eye to the illegal practice and didn't
ask them to give him chapter and verse**
ㄴ 그 경찰은 불법행위를 눈감아주고 꼬치꼬치 캐묻지 않았다

The punishment was only a slap on the wrist
ㄴ 그 처벌은 솜방망이에 불과해

The recompence of a man's hand will be rendered to him
ㄴ 사람은 손으로 행한 대로 보상받으리라

**The rich man is wise in his own eyes, but the poor who has
understanding searches him out**
ㄴ 부자는 자기를 지혜롭게 여겨도 명철한 가난한 자는 자신을 살펴 아
느니라

The shoe is on the other foot
ㄴ 상황은 역전되었어

The sight of his homeland brought a lump to his throat
ㄴ 그는 고향 땅을 보게되자 감개가 무량했다

The size of the pupil is affected by mental activity
ㄴ 눈동자의 크기는 정신활동에 영향을 받는다

The stillest tongue can be the truest friend
ㄴ 가만히 있는 혀가 참된 친구가 될 수 있다

The suppressed words gushed(poured) from her lips
ㄴ 참았던 말이 한꺼번에 그녀의 입에서 나왔다

The tips of Jung-soo's toes poked through his socks
ㄴ 정수의 발가락이 양말을 뚫고 나왔더군

The tongue is sharper than the sword=The tongue stings

· **recompense** give compensation to

· **pupil** dark central opening of the iris of
the eye

ㄴ 혀는 칼보다 예리하다

The tongue is the rudder of the ship

ㄴ 혀는 배의 키이다

The tongue of idle persons is never still

ㄴ 할 일 없는 사람의 혀는 가만히 있지를 못한다

The tongue of the wise promotes health

ㄴ 지혜로운 자의 혀는 양약 같으니라

The total number of transplants may decline due to the law banning organ-for-money dealings

ㄴ 총 장기이식 건수는 현금거래를 금하는 법으로 인하여 줄어들 수도 있다

The toxins in alcohol become trapped inside your body and wreak havoc on it

ㄴ 알콜 속에 있는 독소가 체내에 남아 해악을 끼치게 된다

The truthful lip shall be established forever, but a lying tongue is but for a moment

ㄴ 진실한 입술은 영원히 보존되거니와 거짓 혀는 눈깜짝일 동안 있을 뿐이니라

The violent fall occasioned him to bleed at the nose

ㄴ 그는 심하게 넘어져서 코피를 흘렸다

The voice is a second face

ㄴ 말하는 목소리는 제2의 얼굴이다

The way of a fool is right in his own eyes, but he who heeds counsel is wise

ㄴ 미련한 자는 자기 행위를 바른 줄로 여기나 지혜로운 자는 권고를 받느니라

The way she behaved like that will cause tongues to wag

· **havoc** wide destruction, great confusion

· **heed** pay attention, attention

ㄴ 그 여자가 그런 짓을 했으니 입방아에 오르겠군

The way to a man's heart is through his stomach

ㄴ 남자의 사랑을 얻으려면 그가 좋아하는 음식을 만들어 줘라

The wind in one's face make one wise

ㄴ 역경은 사람을 현명하게 해준다

The window was jammed with the girl's head stuck and nobody could get it open

ㄴ 소녀의 목이 창문에 끼어 꼼짝 못한 채 아무도 창문을 열 수가 없었다

The wound will scar over, but his leg will never be the same as it was before the accident

ㄴ 그의 상처는 흉터를 남긴 채 아물겠지만 다리는 이전의 상태로는 회복될 수 없을 겁니다

The wounded man levered himself up(out) on his elbow and shouted for help

ㄴ 상처를 입은 사람은 힘들게 팔꿈치로 몸을 일으켜 도와달라고 소리쳤다

The wounds on his face lend(give) color to his story that he was beaten by his fellow criminals

ㄴ 그의 얼굴에 있는 상처로 인해 동료 재소자들에게 얻어맞았다는 얘기가 그럴듯해 보인다

Their arms and legs were stuck fast, caught between the two pieces of twisted wreckage

ㄴ 그들의 팔과 다리는 파손된 차의 비틀어진 부속 두 조각에 끼어서 꼼짝을 안했다

Their face to face talks squared the matter

ㄴ 그들은 얼굴을 맞대고 얘기해서 문제를 풀었다

Theory and practice do not always go hand in hand

▸ **square** form into a square, multiply a number by itself, conform, settle

▸ **theory** general principles of a subject, plausible or scientifically acceptable explanation

↳ 이론과 실제가 반드시 동행하지는 않아

There are too many eyes around here
↳ 여긴 보는 눈이 너무 많다

There is tremendous pressure to keep up face in our society
↳ 우리사회는 체면치레라는 보이지 않는 압력이 있다

There's more to be the problem than meets the eye
↳ 그 문제는 겉보기와는 달라

There's no point in running our head against a brick wall
↳ 우린 오르지도 못할 나무는 쳐다볼 필요도 없잖아

There's nothing to choose between bad tongues and wicked ears
↳ 남의 험담을 들어주는 사람은 그 험담을 하는 사람과 다를 바 없다

These knapsacks are made with specially padded straps so that they do not rub against the shoulders
↳ 이 배낭들은 어깨에 시달리지 않도록 특수하게 가죽끈을 덧붙여 만들었다

These words from your mouth sound queer
↳ 네가 이런 소리를 하니 이상해

They are always at each other's throats
↳ 그들은 늘 티격태격이야

They folded their arms and waited for hell to break loose
↳ 그들은 팔짱만 끼고 난장판이 되기를 기다리고 있었다

They fought hand to hand
↳ 주먹다짐이 벌어졌어

They found out that no idea would come; their brains seemed to be lying fallow
↳ 그들은 묘안이 떠오르지 않고 머리도 잘 돌아가지 않고 있는 것만 같았다

▸ **pressure**   burden of distress or urgent business, direct application of force

▸ **fallow**   land plowed but not planted

They have spent years rubbing elbows with the movers and shakers
↳ 그들은 권력자들과 수년간 교제해왔다

They have to stomach it less than perfection
↳ 그들은 적당한 선에서 자제해야해

They joined hands(forces) to raise money when the church burned down
↳ 교회가 전소되자 그들은 모금에 협력했다

They proposed to give the shipbuilder his head in the construction of these ships
↳ 그들은 이들 배를 만들 때 조선업자에게 자신의 방식대로 하게 해 주자고 제안했다

They recharged their batteries and put their shoulders to the wheel
↳ 그들은 재충전해서 본격적으로 일했다

They see eye to eye on many things, but this is not one of them
↳ 그들은 많은 문제에 의견이 일치하지만 이번 일은 그렇지 않아

They tried to palm that painting as a real Kim-hong-do
↳ 그들은 그 그림을 진짜 김홍도의 작품이라고 속여 팔려고 했다

Things have gotten out of hand(control)
↳ 사태가 걷잡을 수 없게 됐어

> (=Things have gone too far(to extremes))

Thirty years ago there might not have been a dry eye in the house
↳ 30년 전이었다면(여기 모인)모든 사람이 눈물을 흘렸을 것이다

This medicine lessens pain by blocking the signals from the affected

---

‣ **palm**　conceal in the hand, impose by fraud(+on, upon)

area's nerves to the brain

↳ 이 약은 병에 걸린 부분의 신경에서 뇌로 신호를 보내는 것을 차단함
으로써 통증을 덜어준다

This money is safe in your hands

↳ 이 돈은 네게 맡기는 게 안심이군

Those things which proceed out of the mouth come from the heart, and defile a man

↳ 입에서 나오는 것들은 마음에서 나오나니 이것이야말로 사람을 더럽
게 하느니라

Time was when we ate from hand to mouth

↳ 우리가 호구지책으로 살아가던 때가 있다

To be a judge you have to be skilled at picking shrapnel out of your head

↳ 판사가 되려면 당신의 머리에서 파편을 끄집어내는데 익숙해야 한다

To see what is in front of one's nose requires a constant struggle

↳ 당신의 코앞에 있는 것을 보는데도 끊임없는 노력이 필요하다

To which team will fortune smile in neck and neck game?

↳ 팽팽한 전력의 양 팀 중 승리의 여신은 누구를 택할까?

Tongues are wagging

↳ 입방아들이 가만히 있질 않고 있어

Truth sits on the lips of dying men

↳ 사람이 죽을 때가 되면 진실을 말한다

Try to keep your nose out of the stuff that doesn't concern you

↳ 너하고 관계없는 일에 끼어 들지마

Trying to get a promotion here is like knocking your head against a brick wall

---

› **shrapnel** metal fragments or a bomb

› **struggle** make strenuous efforts to overcome an adversary, proceed with great effort

ㄴ 여기서 승진을 바라보다가는 철저한 좌절감만 맛볼 뿐이다

Trying to get this office on its feet is harder than I thought
ㄴ 이 사무실이 제대로 돌아가게 돌려놓는 일이 생각보다 어려웠어

Two leading politicians are still at each other's throat
ㄴ 그 두 정치인은 아직도 너 죽고 나죽자는 식으로 나오고 있어

Tyson can beat the other guy with one hand tied behind his back
ㄴ 타이슨은 상대방을 손쉽게 이길 수 있다

Under the tongue men are crushed to death
ㄴ 사람은 혀 밑에 깔려 죽는다

Use your brain
ㄴ 생각을 좀 해봐라

Vitamin plays an important part in the function of the body
ㄴ 비타민은 신진대사에 중요한 역할을 한다

Vivid in memory are the grim faces of those motionless young soldiers clad in uniform
ㄴ 군복차림으로 부동자세를 취하고 있는 젊은 군인들의 섬짓한 모습이 생생하다

Watch that guy with sticky fingers who comes in here
ㄴ 여기 들어오고 있는 저 손버릇 나쁜 녀석을 주의해

We are apt to overlook something worthwhile close at hand
ㄴ 우린 흔히 등잔 밑이 어두운 격이 되기 쉬워

바로 곁에 있는 것을 찾지 못할 때에 쓰이는 표현이다. 서양에서는 "그것이 뱀이라면 당신을 물겠다"라고 하고, 이는 뱀이 물 정도로 가까이 있는 데도 알아채지 못한다는 뜻이다(The husband is always the last to know 등 잔 밑이 어둡다).

› **grim** harsh and forbidding in appearance
› **clad** covered, provide with a covering

We built(made) a fire under his feet, but it did no good
↳ 우린 그에게 자극을 줘봤지만 소용이 없었어

We can see it with the naked eye
↳ 그건 육안으로 보여(eyes가 아님)

We don't see eye to eye on anything
↳ 너랑 나랑은 전혀 맞지 않아

We drank till our tongues tripped
↳ 우린 혀가 꼬부라지게 술을 마셔댔어

We have orders coming out of ears
↳ 우린 주문이 폭주해

We have to hand it to Bong-soo
↳ 봉수의 공은 인정해 주어야해

We have to save money with an eye to the future
↳ 우린 장래를 위해 저축해야해

We have them on hand
↳ 재고준비 있습니다

(=We have them in stock)

We must change our way of thinking if we are to put the nation on its feet after all these struggles
↳ 이 모든 어려움 끝에 나라가 바르게 돌아가자면 우리의 사고방식을 바꿔야 한다

We see eye to eye on many things
↳ 우린 많은 문제에서 의견이 일치해

› **stock** supply of gods kept by a merchant

We should give him some head
↳ 그가 스스로 결정하게 해야 한다

We shouldn't get a swelled head about it
↳ 우리가 그 일로 우쭐해선 안 돼

We won a victory over them that really pinned their ears back
↳ 우리는 그들에게 참패를 안기는 승리를 얻었다

What the eye doesn't see, the heart won't grieve over(crave for)
↳ 차라리 보지 않으면 슬퍼할(가지고 싶은) 일도 없으련만

> 좋은 물건을 보면 가지고 싶은 마음이 생기게 마련이다. 거기다 관리까지 허술하다면 다른 사람으로 하여금 도둑질을 하고 싶은 충동을 느끼게 한다. 비슷한 뜻으로 "A postern door makes a thief 뒷문이 도적을 만든다"도 쓰인다.

What the eye sees not, the ear craves not
↳ 견물생심

> 좋은 물건을 보면 가지고 싶은 마음이 생기게 마련이다. 거기다 관리까지 허술하다면 다른 사람으로 하여금 도둑질을 하고 싶은 충동을 느끼게 한다. 비슷한 뜻으로 "A postern door makes a thief 뒷문이 도적을 만든다"도 쓰인다.

What the heart thinks, the mouth speaks
↳ 마음에 품은 것은 입 밖으로 나오게 돼있어

What's bred in the bone will not go out of the flesh
↳ 세 살 버릇 여든까지

· **grieve** feel or cause to feel grief or sorrow

· **flesh** soft parts of an animal's body

한 번 몸에 밴 습관이 얼마나 중요한 것인지를 알려주는 속담이다. 비슷한 뜻으로 쓰이는 "Once a beggar, always a beggar 한번 거지는 언제나 거지이다"와 "What's learned in the cradle is carried to the grave 요람에서 배운 것은 무덤까지 간다"도 있다.

What's told in the ear of a man is often heard a hundred miles away
ㄴ 발 없는 말이 천리 간다

When he got the punishment he deserved, he laughed on the other side of his face
ㄴ 그가 마땅히 받아야할 벌을 받게되자, 웃다가 우는 꼴이 되었어

When he heard his name called, he pricked up his ears
ㄴ 그의 이름이 호명되자 신경을 곤두세우고 들었어

When she was pregnant and doing a full-time job and all she did was to try to find time to put her feet up
ㄴ 그녀가 임신 중 정규직원으로 일할 때 했던 일이라고는 쉴 틈을 찾는 것뿐이었다

When the facts in this case stared the judge in the face, there was nothing he could do but acquit
ㄴ 이 사건에 대한 사실이 명확해지자 판사는 무죄를 선고할 수 없었다

When the vocal codes vibrate it changes sound that the mouth produce
ㄴ 성대를 진동시키면 입에서 나는 목소리가 달라진다

When we see a secret smile on his lips, he must be telling a lie
ㄴ 그가 입가에 살짝 미소를 지을 때는 거짓말을 하고 있는 게 틀림없어

When wrath speaks, wisdom veils her face
ㄴ 분노가 말을 하면 지혜가 얼굴을 가린다

› **prick** something sharp or pointed

› **vibrate** move or cause to move quickly back and forth or side to side, respond sympathetically

(=Anger begins with folly, and ends with repentance)

When you undergo a general anesthetic, you lose your gag reflex, and are predisposed to choking on stomach contents
↳ 환자가 전신마취를 받게되면 목안에 이물질이 들어와도 반사작용을 못하기 때문에 위장 속의 물질로 인하여 숨이 막히기 쉽다

Whenever he drinks he almost goes out of his head
↳ 그 사람 술만 마시면 제정신이 아냐

Who has a fair wife needs more than two eyes
↳ 예쁜 처를 둔 사람이 마음 편할 날 없다

(=Please your eye and plague your heart)

Who planted that silly idea in your head?
↳ 누가 네게 그런 바보 같은 생각을 하게 만들었지?

Who spits against the wind, it falls on in his face
↳ 바람(하늘)에 데고 침을 뱉어 봐야 자신에게 되돌아온다

다른 사람을 해치려다가 결국은 자신에게 해가 돌아간다는 뜻이다. 한국에서는 '누워서 침 뱉기'가 있고, 영어로는 비슷한 'Spit in the wind 바람에 침 뱉기'와 'Piss in the wind 바람에 오줌누기'가 있다. 바람을 마주보고 침을 뱉거나 오줌을 누면 결국 자신한테로 돌아오는 법이다. 조금 더 점잖은 표현으로는 "Cut off your nose to spite your face 코를 깎아서 얼굴을 망친다"가 있다.

Who will not be deceived must have as many eyes as hairs on his head

---

· **anesthetic** agent that produces anesthesia

· **plague** destructive contagious bacterial disease

┗ 속지 않으려면 머리카락 수만큼의 눈이 있어야 한다

Why are you putting word in my mouth?
┗ 왜 하지도 않은 말을 했다고 그래?

> (=Why are you lying about what I said)
> (=Why are you twisting around my words?)

Why the happy look on your face?
┗ 왜 그리 기분 좋은 표정인가?

Will you please pass your eye over this paper?
┗ 이 서류를 좀 봐주시겠습니까?

Wisdom is found on the lips of him who has understanding
┗ 현명한 자의 입에는 지혜가 있다

With the examination at hand, everyone is nervous
┗ 시험이 다가오자 모두가 긴장해 있다

Words of praise seldom fall from his lips
┗ 좀처럼 그에게 칭찬 받기 힘들어

Words stuck in my throat
┗ 말이 잘 안나왔다

Working overnight three times a week is taking its tolls on my body
┗ 일주일에 세 번씩이나 철야 특근을 했더니 몸이 말이 아니다

Would you raise your hand against your own parents?
┗ 부모님에게 거역하고 나설 수 있겠나?

Wrinkling our brows won't solve a single one of our personal problems
┗ 얼굴은 찌푸린다고 우리들의 개인적인 문제점이 하나라도 해결되지는

› **nervous** relating to or made up of nerves, easily excited, fearful

› **toll** fee paid for a privilege or service, cost of achievement in loss or suffering

않을 것이다

You are a major pain in the ass
> ↳ 넌 참 피곤한 존재군

(=You get on my nerves)

You are all mouth and no chops
> ↳ 넌 입만 살고 실천이 없어

You are just beating your head against the wall(a brick wall)
> ↳ 그래봤자 계란으로 바위 치기야

You are my crying shoulder
> ↳ 넌 나의 든든한 의지가 되고 있어

You are really cutting off your nose to spite your face
> ↳ 그건 정말 누워 침 뱉기야

다른 사람을 해치려다가 결국은 자신에게 해가 돌아간다는 뜻이다. 한국에서는 '누워서 침 뱉기'가 있고, 영어로는 비슷한 'Spit in the wind 바람에 침 뱉기'와 'Piss in the wind 바람에 오줌누기'가 있다. 바람을 마주보고 침을 뱉거나 오줌을 누면 결국 자신한테도 돌아오는 법이다. 조금 더 점잖은 표현으로는 "Cut off your nose to spite your face 코를 깎아서 얼굴을 망친다'가 있다.

You can't scratch your own back
> ↳ 중이 제 머리 못 깎는다

You can't see beyond the end of your nose
> ↳ 등잔 밑이 어두워

› **piss** urinate, discharge urine

바로 곁에 있는 것을 찾지 못할 때에 쓰이는 표현이다. 서양에서는 "그것이 뱀이라면 당신을 물겠다"라고 하고, 이는 뱀이 물 정도로 가까이 있는 데도 알아채지 못한다는 뜻이다(The husband is always the last to know 등잔 밑이 어둡다).

You can't take any action till she shows her hand
　ㄴ 넌 그 여자가 의도를 밝힐 때까지 아무런 조치를 취할 수 없어

You don't have a leg up on anyone
　ㄴ 넌 남들보다 잘난 구석이 하나도 없어

You don't have to rub my nose in it
　ㄴ 창피한 얘기 좀 그만 해라

You don't know your ass from your elbow
　ㄴ 일의 진행을 파악하지 못하고 있군

(=You don't know your left hand from your right hand)

You don't need to carry the weight of the world on your shoulders
　ㄴ 너무 걱정하지 마라

You eat out of his hand
　ㄴ 넌 그가 죽으라면 죽는시늉까지 하잖아

You have excessive concern for your face
　ㄴ 넌 체면을 너무 차리는구나

You have grown slack
　ㄴ 군기 빠졌군

· **concern**　relate to, involve, affair, worry, business

· **slack**　careless, not taut, not busy, part hanging loose, casual trousers(pl)

(=You are not on your toes)

You have to have some heads together to get things done
ㄴ 일이 되게 하려면 네가 관리자답게 일을 시켜야 해

You have to keep a poker face when haggling
ㄴ 흥정할 땐 표정관리를 잘 해야해

You have the upper hand
ㄴ 배부른 흥정이군

> 배부른 흥정이란 말은 유리한 입장에서 흥정을 한다는 뜻이다. Upper Hand는
> 팔씨름(Arm Wrestling)에서 위에 얹는 손이 유리하다는 것에서 나온 말이다.
> 거래를 성사시킬 때에 달변이나 처세술로 흥정을 할 때에 사용하는 속담이다.

You hit the nail right on the head
ㄴ 넌 정곡을 찔렀어

You just run to these arms
ㄴ 내 품으로 달려오기만 하면 돼

You must get on with the job in hand first
ㄴ 현안문제부터 처리해야 해

You need a strong stomach to overcome your weakness
ㄴ 너의 약점을 극복하려면 다부진 마음이 필요해

You seem to have our boss's ear
ㄴ 넌 윗 분의 신임을 받고 있는 것 같구나

You want to see me fall flat on my face
ㄴ 내가 실패하는 꼴을 보고싶다 이 말이군

› **haggle** argue in bargaining

You'd better get out of her face
└ 그녀를 성가시게 하지마

You'd better keep your ears to the ground
└ 상황 판단을 잘 해야 해

You'd better not fly in the face(teeth) of your boss
└ 상사에게 대들어서는 안 돼

You'd better not show your face around here
└ 넌 이제 이 근처에 얼씬도 안 하는 게 좋아

You'd better study the problem before you shoot off your face(mouth)
└ 무책임하게 주절대기 전에 문제를 파악해야 해

You'll be fired if you have your hand in the till
└ 넌 돈을 착복했다가는 해고야

You're talking to the wall
└ 쇠귀에 경 읽기야

> 마음에 있지 않으면 들어도 들리지 않고 보아도 보이지 않는다(There's none so blind as those who will not see = There's none so deaf as those who will not hear).

You've got a hole in your head if you think I'm a dupe
└ 나를 어수룩하게 생각한다면 큰 오산이다

You've got your eyes glued to her
└ 넌 그 여자에게서 눈을 못 떼는 군

Your appearance catches everyone's eyes
└ 네 용모라면 모든 사람의 눈을 끌기에 충분해

· **dupe** one easily deceived or cheated

Your bones are knitting together exactly as expected
     ㄴ 너의 뼈는 예상대로 정확히 아물어 붙고 있어

Your head is in the clouds
     ㄴ 마음이 콩밭에 있군

> (=Where are you?)
> (=Are you daydreaming?)

Your nose is turned up
     ㄴ 너 콧대가 높군

> (=You have your nose in the air)

Your red tie really caught my eye(is really eye-catching)
     ㄴ 빨간 타이가 눈에 확 띄네

Your tongue can make or break you
     ㄴ 말 한마디로 천냥 빚 갚는다

Your very face puts me off
     ㄴ 네 꼴만 봐도 밥맛 떨어져

· **knit**   link firmly or closely, form a fabric
        by interlacing yarn or thread

113. 일   Work & Job

A woman's work is never done
            ↳ 여자의 일은 끝이 없어

All I can do has already been done
              ↳ 내가 할 수 있는 일은 다 했어

All my work is falling into place
              ↳ 모든 일이 잘 풀리고 있어

> (=Everything is going like clockwork(working out perfectly))

All your work got was a lick and a promise
              ↳ 넌 일을 아무렇게나 해놨군

All these things cooperated to make this work a success
              ↳ 모든 상황이 겹쳐서 이 일이 성공했다

All they have done is only a lick and a promise
              ↳ 그 사람들 해 놓은 일이란 날림(하는 둥 마는 둥)이야

At least I landed on both feet when it was all over
              ↳ 그 일이 끝났을 때 난 무사히 버텨냈어

At this time everybody winds up their annual work and reflects on what they have done this year
              ↳ 이맘때면 모두가 1년간의 일을 마무리하고 올해 한 일을 되돌아 본다

› **annual**   occurring once a year, living only one year

Bong-soo had a big head and can't go to work this morning
> ↳ 오늘 아침 봉수는 숙취가 심해서 출근을 못한다(**have a big head** 에는 "자만하다"의 뜻도 있으며 잘 이해하지 못하는 경우도 있음)

Bong-soo is weltering in work, eager to take a break
> ↳ 봉수는 일에 파묻혀서 휴가(식)를 절실히 바라고 있어

Byung-soo wanted a job where he would be calling the shots himself
> ↳ 병수는 자신이 책임지고 지휘할 수 있는 일을 원했다

Byung-soo's work is just bouncing along
> ↳ 병수의 일은 잘 돼가고 있다

Can you call this work?
> ↳ 이걸 일이라고 해 왔나?

Cessation of work is not accompanied by cessation of expenses
> ↳ 일을 그만둔다해서 지출이 없어지는 것이 아니다

Chang-ho will manage if we leave him to his own devices(resources)
> ↳ 창호를 제 멋대로 내버려두면 잘해 나갈 거야

Chang-soo didn't take that crappy job for(due to) his health
> ↳ 창수가 좋아서 그 시시한 일을 하고 있는 게 아니다(목구멍이 포도청이라 하고 있는 거지)

Chul-soo was so tied up with his work that it slipped his mind
> ↳ 철수가 일에 너무 몰두하다보니 그걸 깜박 잊어버린 거야

Do your job right
> ↳ 일에 차질 없도록 해

Do your work first. First things first
> ↳ 네가 할 일이나 먼저 해. 일에는 순서가 있어

Don't do things by halves
> ↳ 일을 어중간하게 하지마

› **welter** toss about, wallow

› **cessation** a halting

Don't gallop through this work
  ↳ 이 일은 급하게 해치워서는 안 돼

Don't have too many irons in the fire
  ↳ 한꺼번에 여러 가지 일을 하려고 하지마

Don't have(hold) a big tiger by the tail. You've already bit off more than you can chew
  ↳ 큰 일을 벌려놓지 마라. 넌 벌써 과욕을 부리고 있어

Don't just bulldoze through your work
  ↳ 일을 밀어 부치기 식으로만 하지마

Don't let yourself in for a lot of extra work
  ↳ 많은 남의 일을 자청해서 하지마

Don't shoot the works
  ↳ 다 쓰지 말고 어려울 때를 대비해서 아껴두어라

Don't spread yourself too thin
  ↳ 너무 여러 가지 일을 벌려놓고 한 가지도 제대로 안되면 안 돼

Don't you know that it is just for you
  ↳ 그 일을 할 사람이 바로 너란 걸 알아야지

Don't work too hard
  ↳ 수고해

Dong-soo just floated through his work yesterday
  ↳ 동수는 어제 일을 아무렇게나 했어

Dong-soo's got a way of disappearing if he thinks there might be work for him to do
  ↳ 동수는 일이 있겠다 싶으면 슬쩍 피하는데 이골이 났어

Doo-chul is always dilly-dallying around with his work
  ↳ 두철인 노상 일을 하는 둥 마는 둥 노닥거리기만 해

› **gallop** fast 3-beat gait of a horse
› **dilly-dally** waste time by delay

Education is a necessity because automation has replaced unskilled labor in many fields of work

    ↳ 많은 업무분야에서 자동화가 미숙련 노동자들을 대체함에 따라 교육은 필수적이다

Everybody's work(business) is nobody's work(business)

    ↳ 여럿이 함께 하는 일은 아무도 책임지려 하지 않는다

> 여러 사람이 같이 하는 일은 서로 책임을 미루게 되어 결국엔 망한다는 뜻이다. 아리스토텔레스는 정치론에서 "A matter common to most men receives least attention 많은 사람이 관심을 갖는 일은 항상 소홀히 취급된다"고 하였다.

First things first

    ↳ 중요한 것부터 먼저(일에는 순서가)

From where I stand(my point of view, my perspective), our new boss has a lot of work to do

    ↳ 내가 보는 바로는 사장에게 일거리가 산더미 같이 있어

Gil-soo got his feet on the ground and is hard at work

    ↳ 길수는 땅에 발을 딱 붙이고 열심히 일하고 있다

Gil-soo is just going through the motions

    ↳ 길수는 공부(일) 하는 척 할 뿐이야

Gil-soo's already fully answered the bell

    ↳ 길수는 벌써 충분히 의무를 수행했다

Gil-soo's getting nowhere fast in this job

    ↳ 길수가 하는 이 일은 잘 되고 있지 않아

Hard work is never wasted

‣ **perspective**   view of things in their true relationship or importance

ㄴ 공든 탑이 무너지랴

He doesn't have regular work
ㄴ 그는 일정한 직업이 없다

He doesn't know when to play and when to work
ㄴ 일할 때와 놀 때를 구분 못해

He has a good thing going, working at home without his boss
ㄴ 그는 감독하는 상사 없이 집에서 일하게 됐으니 잘된 일이지

He is just not performing but she's terrific at her job
ㄴ 그는 자기 일은 제대로 못해내고 있지만 그 여자는 자신의 일을 완벽
하게 해내고 있다

He keeps a dog and barks himself
ㄴ 그는 남들에게 일을 시켜 놓고 스스로 해버린다

**He read the riot act to us for doing such poor work on the assembly
line**
ㄴ 그는 우리들의 일관작업이 형편없다고 심히 꾸짖었다

He rose through the ranks due to his hard work
ㄴ 그는 열심히 일해서 평사원으로부터 빨리 출세했다

He sweated to get it done
ㄴ 그는 그걸 끝내는데 피땀 깨나 흘렸어

He was in the job for ten years and certainly left his mark
ㄴ 그는 **10**년 동안 재직하면서 큰 업적을 남겼다

He worked all day and only made a dent in his work
ㄴ 그는 하루 종일 일했지만 아주 조금밖에 못했다

He worked and worked until he felt utterly exhausted
ㄴ 그는 일하고 또 일하여 결국 지쳐버렸다

He works days and goes to school nights

▸ **assembly**   meeting, a fitting together or parts   ▸ **utter**   absolute, express with the voice

    ↳ 낮에 일하고 밤에 학교에 다녀

He'll get you out of doing all that grunt work
    ↳ 그 사람이라면 그런 따분한 일에서 널 구해줄 거야

He'll rise up to the challenge
    ↳ 그 일은 해낼 거야

He's been working for years at this dead-end job
    ↳ 그는 별로 전망도 없는 일에 오래 동안 일하고 있다

He's been working hard on that pork barrel
    ↳ 그는 그 선심예산을 따놓으려고 열심이야

He's supposed to work hard, but he's just going through the motions
    ↳ 그는 열심히 일해야 하지만 건성으로 일하는 척 할 뿐이다

Heavy sleepiness crept over me after a day's hard work
    ↳ 낮에 열심히 일했더니 잠이 막 쏟아졌다

Heavy work in youth is quiet resting in old age
    ↳ 젊어서 고생은 사서도 한다

Her project is on the up-and-up
    ↳ 그 여자의 일은 잘 돼가고 있어

Her sitting up all that night was her last straw
    ↳ 그 날밤 철야한 것이 끝내 그녀를 쓰러지게 했다

His continuous tantrums in-dispose anyone to work hard
    ↳ 그 사람이 끝없이 짜증을 내니 누구도 열심히 일 할 맘이 안나

How soon do you want to have it done?
    ↳ 그 일은 언제까지 해드리면 되겠습니까?

I can't put my hands on anything
    ↳ 일이 손에 안 잡혀

▸ **grunt** deep guttural sound
▸ **tantrum** fit of bad temper

I hate doing things by half
> ↳ 일을 어중간히 하는 건 질색이다

I have 't's to be crossed and 'i's to be dotted
> ↳ 할 일이 많이 남아있어

I have a lot of catching up to do
> ↳ 할 일이 많이 밀려있어

I have other fish to fry
> ↳ 다른 할 일이 있어

I have some work to catch up on
> ↳ 밀린 일을 좀 해야해

I shuffled through my work
> ↳ 내 할 일은 그럭저럭 해 놓았지

I was all hot and bothered that things didn't turn out the way I wanted
> ↳ 일이 뜻대로 되질 않아서 애태웠지

I'll be there when this is done
> ↳ 하던 일 마저 끝내고 갈께

(=I'll come after what I'm doing)

I'll do what I can
> ↳ 제가 할 수 있는 일은 뭐든지 할게요

I'm not in the vein for work
> ↳ 일할 기분이 아냐

I'm taking a busman's holiday

› **shuffle** mix together, walk with a sliding movement

ㄴ 쉬는 날에 일하고 있는 거야

I'm too backed up
ㄴ 밀린 일이 너무 많아

I'm way ahead of you on that
ㄴ 그 일은 잘 처리해 두었어

I've made a career out of cleaning up your mess
ㄴ 네가 어질러 놓은 것 치우는 게 내 일이 돼 버렸어

If I'm lucky at first, I don't press my work
ㄴ 처음에 잘 됐다해서 계속 요행을 바라진 않아

If you were as free with your help as you are with your advice we could have had the job finished by now
ㄴ 네가 말로 우릴 도와주듯 실제로 쾌히 우릴 도와주었다면 지금쯤 그 일을 끝낼 수 있었을 거야

In the end I have to go it alone
ㄴ 결국 나 혼자 고군분투해야 했어

In-ho will soon get through with his work
ㄴ 진수는 일을 곧 끝낼 거야

It won't kill you to do a bit of work
ㄴ 그 일 좀 한다고 죽니?

It'd be better all around if you'd take that thing off your eyes
ㄴ 그 일을 관심 밖으로 내보내는 것이 어느 모로 보나 훨씬 낫다

It'll be all(as much as) I can do to finish that
ㄴ 내가 그 일을 끝내려면 몹시 애를 먹을 것이다

It'll just take some doing, though not impossible
ㄴ 그 일이 불가능한 일은 아니지만 꽤 힘들 것이다

It'll take a lot of elbow grease

› **back up** become congested
› **mess** confused, dirty, or offensive state

↳ 그걸 해내자면 꽤 힘들 거야

It'll work out for the best
↳ 그 일은 잘 풀릴 거다

It's all on the up and up. There's no catch
↳ 그 일은 잘 돼가고 있어. 아무 문제없어

It's downhill from here on
↳ 지금부터는 수월한 일만 남았어

It's easy to relapse into lazy habits when we have been away from work for a while
↳ 한동안 일손을 놓고 지내면 도로 게으른 버릇에 빠져들기 쉽다

It's every man for himself
↳ 각자 자기 일을 챙겨야 해

It's indelibly impressed upon my mind
↳ 그 일은 내 머리에서 사라지지 않아

It's just one of those things
↳ 그건 어쩔 수 없는 일이야

It's my duty to explore every avenue
↳ 내가 할 일은 모든 일을 검토하는 것이다

It's my job to try
↳ 시도라도 해 보는 게 내 일이야

It's no less a pleasure than a duty for me to work hard
↳ 열심히 일하는 것은 의무이자 즐거움이다

It's not that easy. It'll cost him his neck this time
↳ 그렇게 쉽게 끝날 일이 아냐. 이번엔 그의 목이 걸려 있어

It's run-of-the-mill office work
↳ 되풀이되는 따분한 일이야

› **relapse** recurrence of illness after a period of improvement

› **indelible** not capable of being removed orerased

It's still on the drawing board
> ↳ 그건 아직 계획단계에 불과해

It's the least I can do
> ↳ 제가 할 수 있는 일을 다 했을 뿐입니다

It's work, work, work from one year's end to the next
> ↳ 작년에도 올해도 후년에도 늘 직장에 매달리는 거지 뭐

Jin-soo had been lying down on the job and not getting his work done
> ↳ 진수는 일을 농땡이 치고 제대로 안하고 있어

Joining the army might improve your chances of getting out of that humdrum job
> ↳ 군에 입대하면 그 따분한 일에서 너를 벗어나게 해줄지도 몰라

Keeping busy was the only thing that kept him from going to pieces during the divorce
> ↳ 그가 이혼하고 있을 동안 자제력을 잃지 않게 해준 유일한 것은 계속 바쁘게 일하는 것이었다

Let us try to move forward with the project at a fast pace
> ↳ 이 일을 빨리 진척시켜 나가도록 합시다

Let's finish the project no matter what
> ↳ 무슨 일이 있어도 그 일은 끝내자

Let's put our back into this job
> ↳ 벗어 부치고 이 일을 좀 해보자

Let's work it out together
> ↳ 같이 타결해 나가자

Matters go along somehow
> ↳ 일이 그럭저럭 되어간다

Much yet remains to be done
> ↳ 아직도 할 일이 많이 남아있다

My family comes first, my work next(second)
> ↳ 가족이 먼저고 일은 그 다음이야

My mind keeps wandering from my work
> ↳ 일이 손에 안잡혀

> (=I can't concentrate(focus) on my work)
> (=I can't pay my attention to my work)

Myong-soo marks the time and pays no mind to the job
> ↳ 명수는 시간만 죽이면서 일에는 마음을 쓰지 않아

Nam-soo wears more than one hat
> ↳ 남수는 여러 가지 일에 간여하고 있어

Never let your personal emotions into your work
> ↳ 개인감정을 업무에까지 개입시키지 마라

No boss, no work
> ↳ 왕초가 없으니 농땡이나 칠 수밖에

No work can be done without concentration and self-sacrifice and toil and doubt
> ↳ 집중, 자기희생, 수고, 의심이 없이는 아무 일도 되지 않는다

Not only does a guy live through his work, his work is who he is
> ↳ 남성은 그의 일로서 사는 것일 뿐 아니라 그의 일 자체가 그 사람이 어떤 사람인가를 말해준다

Nothing can be done at once hastily and prudently
> ↳ 무슨 일이고 급히 하면서 동시에 신중을 기할 수는 없는 일이다

› **toil** work hard and long
› **prudent** shrewd, cautious, thrifty

Nothing is more unbearable than the sheer drudgery of that job
ㄴ 순전히 그 따분한 일만 하는 것보다 더 견딜 수 없는 일이 없다

Now I can see daylight
ㄴ 이제야 마무리되어 가는 것 같아

Now that our hectic schedule is over, we'll breathe again
ㄴ 눈코 뜰새 없이 바쁜 일이 끝났으니 이젠 숨 좀 쉬겠다

Now that the big project was done, I can breathe more freely(easily)
ㄴ 이제 큰 일은 마쳤으니 한 시름 놓게 됐지 뭐

One should do what he must even if he is unwilling to do
ㄴ 누구든지 싫더라도 할 일은 해야 한다

One thing at a time
ㄴ 한 번에 두 가지 일을 하지 마라

Only riveting my attention on my work can I forget my sorrows and worries
ㄴ 일에 몰두하는 것만이 내 슬픔과 고통을 잊는 길이다

Our boss will give you the works if you're loafing off again
ㄴ 또 농땡이 쳤다간 사장님한테 혼날 거야

Our boss won't sit still for his coming to work late
ㄴ 그가 늦게 출근하면 사장이 가만 안 둘걸

Our job really keeps on our toes
ㄴ 우리의 일은 우리를 항상 긴장케 하는 작업이다

Pay beforehand and your work will be behindhand
ㄴ 돈부터 미리 냈다가는 시키는 일이 늦어지게 되어있다

Please make a practice of being on time for work
ㄴ 출근시간에 늦지 않는 습관을 기르도록 해

· **sheer**   pure, very steep, very thin and transparent   · **hectic**   filled with excitement or confusion

Pull in your ears and mind your own business
  ↳ 못들은 일로 하고 네 일이나 해

Put it on the front(back) burner
  ↳ 그 일은 먼저 처리해야해(나중 처리해도 돼)

Put some life into your work
  ↳ 일에 좀 더 정력을 쏟아라

Recurring illness forced her to retire from work prematurely
  ↳ 그녀는 병이 재발해서 부득이 조기 퇴직했다

Sang-soo has been sweating out his guts all day, and hardly anything to show for it
  ↳ 상수는 온 종일 죽어라하고 일하고도 이렇다 하고 내놓을게 없게 되었어

Sang-soo has the world on his shoulders
  ↳ 상수에게는 책임이 많아

She can do a better job if you're not on her back so often
  ↳ 네가 그 여자를 성가시게 안 하면 일을 더 잘할 수 있어

She has tons of things to do
  ↳ 그 여자는 할 일이 태산같다

She immersed herself in work so as to stop thinking about the problem
  ↳ 그녀는 그 문제를 더 이상 생각하지 않기 위해 일에 몰두했다

She knows where she is going
  ↳ 그 여자는 자기가 하고 있는 일의 목적(동기)을 알고 있어

She's always on the job unlike the rest of them
  ↳ 그 여자는 다른 사람들과는 달리 늘 열심히 일해왔다

She's running behind schedule

› **immerse** vast

↳ 그녀는 계획보다 진척이 늦다

She's tired of her work, but she still keeps on
↳ 그 여자는 일하기 싫으면서도 그냥 버티고 있어

Some new work has cropped up
↳ 갑자기 새로운 일이 생겼다

Some people expect the main computer to able to do all the donkey work
↳ 메인 컴퓨터가 따분한 일을 다 해줄 것으로 기대하는 사람들도 있다

Some people work out of their house these days
↳ 요즘은 재택 근무를 하는 사람들도 있어

Something has come up
↳ 갑자기 일이 생겼어

Something is likely to happen
↳ 무슨 일이 일어날 것만 같다

Sometimes we stay after hours to finish up our work
↳ 우린 가끔씩 근무시간 후에도 일을 마무리하기 위해 남는 때가 있다

Stay the course on this
↳ 이 일은 끝까지 해봐

Stop flapping about, I'll get the job done in time
↳ 시간 내에 일을 끝내 놓을 테니 염려 붙들어매

Stop freeloading and do some work
↳ 공짜로 얻어먹을 생각말고 일을 해

Such a trifle thing can wait
↳ 그런 하찮은 일은 나중에 해도 돼

Such hot weather in-disposes anyone to work hard
↳ 이렇게 더워서는 누구나 일할 마음이 없어진다

› **flap**   slap, something flat that hangs loose
› **freeload**   live off another's generosity

Such things are earned by use

↳ 그런 일은 자꾸 하다보면 배우게 돼

Sung-soo never stands aside when there's something that wants doing

↳ 성수는 하고자 하는 일이 있을 때는 가만히 있지 않아

Sung-soo set(put) his hand to the plow

↳ 성수는 큰 일에 착수했다

Tai-ho has been slaving all day, and he has hardly made a dent in his work

↳ 태호는 종일 죽도록 일했지만 거의 진척이 없었어

Tai-ho is climbing the walls to get back to work

↳ 태호는 다시 일하기 위해 필사적이다

Tai-ho is right on the top of it

↳ 태호는 그 일에만 매달려 있어

Tai-ho knocks himself out everyday to support his family

↳ 태호는 가족을 위해 매일 열심히 일한다

Tai-ho's been tying up the(his) loose ends

↳ 태호는 하던 일을 마무리해 오고 있다

Taking place for his sick father, he had to work for his brothers and sisters

↳ 앓고 계신 아버지를 대신해서 그는 동생들을 위해서 일했다

Tell your children they can't hang around while we are working

↳ 우리가 일하고 있을 때 여기에 얼씬거리지 말라고 아이들에게 말해 주십시오

Thank you for a job well done

↳ 재임 중의 업적에 사의를 표합니다

That all depends on how much of a risk-taker you are

› **dent** small depression

ㄴ 모든 일은 네가 얼마나 위험을 감수하느냐에 달렸다

That didn't enter into their calculations

ㄴ 그 일은 그들도 생각해 보지 못했다

That'll hurt me more than it hurts you

ㄴ 그 일은 너보다 내가 더 손해볼(고생할) 사람이다(그 일은 어쩔수 없다)

That's not my kind of job

ㄴ 그건 나한테 딱 맞는 일이다

That's what he gets paid to do

ㄴ 그것은 그가 돈받고 하는 일

The best cure for unhappiness is to fling yourself onto your work

ㄴ 불행을 치유하는 가장 좋은 방법은 일에 모든 정력을 쏟는 일이다

The hardest work is to go idle

ㄴ 가장 힘드는 일은 아무 것도 안하는 일이다

The job was completed between them

ㄴ 둘이서 공동으로 그 일을 마무리했다

The only way most people perform well is with some external validation

ㄴ 사람이 능률적으로 일할 수 있는 유일한 길은 타인이 인정해 줄 때다

The reward of a thing well done is to have done it

ㄴ 어떤 일을 잘 해 낸데 대한 보상은 그 일이 잘되었다는 그 자체이다

The rich man has lived well and not done a stroke of work all his life

ㄴ 그 부자는 유복하게 살면서 평생 일이라고는 하나도 안했다

The sight of this mountain of work depresses me

ㄴ 산적한 일을 보니 진저리난다

‣ **idle** worthless, inactive, lazy

‣ **validation** establish as valid

The work is in full swing
> ↳ 일은 착착 진행중이다

The work is in hand
> ↳ 그 일은 처리중이야

Their motives in taking on the job were mixed
> ↳ 그들이 그 일을 맡은 데는 여러 가지 이유가 있다

Their work spread over into the following month
> ↳ 그들의 일은 다음달로 연장되었다

There's a lot to do today, so let's hop to it
> ↳ 오늘 할 일이 많으니 일을 시작하자

There's more to life than money(success , this office)
> ↳ 돈(성공)만이 인생의 전부가 아니다

There's no need to throw him to the wolves yet
> ↳ 아직 그에게 힘든 일을 시킬 필요는 없어

They are doing so many things that I can't stay ahead of them
> ↳ 그들이 너무 많은 일을 하고 있어서 일일이 상황파악 할 수가 없어

They have got a lot on the plate
> ↳ 그들은 할 일이 많아

They recharged their batteries and put their shoulders to the wheel
> ↳ 그들은 재충전해서 본격적으로 일했다

They were exhausted as they had been working for three hours at a stretch to finish it
> ↳ 그들은 일을 끝내려고 세 시간씩이나 단숨에 쉬지 않고 일해서 녹초가 되었다

They worked on alternate days, not every day
> ↳ 그들은 매일이 아니라 하루 걸러서 일한다

› **motive** cause of a person's action

› **alternate** arranged or succeeding by turns, every other, occur or cause to occur by turns

They worked their shifts alternately
> ↳ 그들은 작업 조에게 교대로 일을 시킨다

They'll brace themselves up and work harder
> ↳ 그들은 맘을 가다듬고 더욱 힘차게 일할 것이다

Things are all anyhow
> ↳ 모든 일이 대강대강 되어 있었다

Things are apt to go against our will
> ↳ 일은 우리 뜻대로 안 되기 쉬워

Things are going good
> ↳ 일은 잘 돼가고 있어

Things are running behind, and you'll not finish on time
> ↳ 넌 일이 늦어지고 있어서 시간 내에 끝내지 못하겠군

Things aren't going my way(working out)=Everything seems to be working against me lately
> ↳ 요즘 되는 일이 없어

Things began to fall into place
> ↳ 일이 제대로(제자리에) 되어가게(들어맞아) 됐어

Things fell out of the way they had to
> ↳ 일은 그렇게 될 수밖에 없는 방향으로 된 거야

Things have come to a pretty(nice) pass
> ↳ 일이 성가시게 되었네

Things seem fluctuate between the very good and the very bad
> ↳ 일이 매우 좋아지기도 하고 아주 나빠지기도 하는 것 같아

This and that remains to be done
> ↳ 이것저것 할 일이 많아

▸ **shift** change place, position, or direction; get by

▸ **fluctuate** change rapidly especially up and down

This is a matter of a first(last) importance
↳ 이 일은 매우 중요해(이 경우 **first**와 **last**가 같은 뜻임)

This is just my job
↳ 이게 내 분수에 맞는 일이다

This is such short notice
↳ 갑작스러운 일

This job is sure boring. So what else is new?
↳ 이 일은 지겨워. 항상 하는 일인데 뭘 그래?

This work has a bright outlook
↳ 이 일은 전망이 있어

This work has taken all my time
↳ 이 일을 하는데 애 먹었다

> (=I've had a time doing this work)

This work is far beyond your capacity
↳ 네 능력으로 이 일은 어림없어

This work really takes a lot of me
↳ 이 일은 정말 진 빠지는군

Those who work much do not work hard
↳ 일을 많이 하는 사람은 열심히 하지 않는다

Touch all basis in this matter
↳ 이 일은 사방으로 알아봐

Try to make a low profile until you learn this job
↳ 이 일을 배울 때까지는 저 자세로 참아라

› **outlook** viewpoint, prospect for the future   › **capacity** ability to contain, volume, ability, role or job

Understanding human need is half the job of meeting them
　　　└ 사람들에게 필요한 것이 무엇인지를 아는 것은 그 필요에 응하는 일의 절반이다

Wan-soo did a sloppy job, so he may be whisle for his money
　　　└ 완수는 건성으로 일했기 때문에 돈을 받지 못할 것이다

Wan-soo has been working his butt(tail) off for months now
　　　└ 완수는 몇 달 동안 뼈 빠지게 일하고 있어

Wan-soo has come a long way
　　　└ 완수가 큰 일을 해냈다

We have a long way to go
　　　└ 우린 할 일이 많아

We have no rivals(are second to none) in the care with which we do our work
　　　└ 일의 꼼꼼함에 있어서 우리를 따를 자가 없다

We have to do things in stages
　　　└ 일에는 순서가 있다

We have to make this job successful whatever the cost
　　　└ 어떤 대가를 치러도 이 일은 성공시켜야 해

What must be done must be done
　　　└ 꼭 해야할 일은 꼭 해놔야 한다

When a thing is not worth overdoing, leave it alone
　　　└ 어떤 일을 지나치게 해도 좋을만한 가치가 없다면 하지말고 내버려두어라

When we gallop through our work, we are more likely to make mistakes
　　　└ 일을 서두르면 실수하기 쉽다

‣ **rival** competitor, peer

‣ **overdo** do too much

‣ **gallop** fast 3-beat gait of a horse

When work is a duty, life is slavery
> ↳ 일이 의무일 때 삶은 노역이다

When you want to hurry something, that means you no longer care about it and want to get on to other things
> ↳ 어떤 일을 서두른다는 것은 그 일에 관심이 없고 다른 일을 시작하겠다는 뜻이다

Where there is muck there is money
> ↳ 궂은 일 있는 곳에 돈 있다

Whoever is in a hurry shows that the thing he's about is too big for him
> ↳ 누구든지 허둥대고 있는 사람은 그 일이 그에게 감당하기 벅차다는 것을 말해준다

Why don't you zero in on just the basic necessities
> ↳ 기본적으로 필요한 일에만 전념하도록 해

With so many things on the go at the one time, how can I give them my proper attention?
> ↳ 한꺼번에 할 일이 태산 같은데 내가 어찌 제대로 신경을 쓸 수 있겠나?

Work is just coasting along
> ↳ 일은 잘 돼가고 있다

Work is not the curse, but the drudgery is
> ↳ 일은 지겨운 것이 아니고 따분한 일이 지겨운 것이다

Work spares us three great evils: boredom, vice, and need
> ↳ 일은 지겨움, 해악, 필요라는 세 가지 큰 악을 막아준다

Working freelance means that you are your own boss and can work at your own pace
> ↳ 프리랜서로 일한다는 것은 자신이 경영자가 되어 자기 페이스대로 일

▸ **muck** manure, dirt, or mud; clear of muck; dress soil with muck; soil

▸ **freelance** one who pursues a profession without long-term contracts with any one employer

한다는 것을 말한다

Working overnight three times a week is taking its tolls on my body
ㄴ 일주일에 세 번씩이나 철야 특근을 했더니 몸이 말이 아니다

Working too hard, coupled with not getting enough sleep, will make you ill
ㄴ 일을 너무 열심히 하면서 잠을 충분히 안자면 병나게 돼

Working twenty hours a day completely burned him out
ㄴ 그는 하루 **20**시간을 일하자 완전히 녹초가 되었다

Would you clue me in on this matter?
ㄴ 이 일을 내게 좀 알려줘

You are almost there
ㄴ 네가 하는 일은 거의 다 돼가는구나(**Just about** 거의 끝나가지)

You are cut out for this work
ㄴ 네겐 이 일이 안성맞춤이다

You are dawdling over your work
ㄴ 일을 꽤 꾸물대고 있군

You are lucky to have a job at all, as it is
ㄴ 현 상태로는 네게 일이 있는 것만 해도 다행이다

You can follow your heart in this matter
ㄴ 이 일에는 마음 내키는 대로 해

You can't do it with safety
ㄴ 그런 일을 하려면 위험이 따르게 되어있어

You can't make them do a donkey work
ㄴ 그 사람들에게 따분한 일을 시킬 수는 없어

You did all that work for nothing
ㄴ 네가 한 일은 소용이 없었어

▸ **burn out** exhaust

You have to learn how to dress windows when you work there
↳ 넌 거기서 일할 때 상품 진열 법을 배워야 해

You have to push forward to complete the project on time
↳ 그 일을 끝내려면 일을 추진해 나가야 해

You have your work cut out
↳ 네가 할 일은 얼마든지 있어

You must get on with the job in hand first
↳ 현안문제부터 처리해야 해

You should put first things first
↳ 일은 순서대로 해야 해

You should put this matter on the front(back) burner
↳ 이 일은 먼저(나중) 처리해야 해

You will get nowhere if you work by fits and starts
↳ 공부(일)를 하다 말다 해서는 아무 것도 안 돼

You work long hours
↳ 넌 아주 열심히 일 하는구나

You'd better let the matter ride for the time being
↳ 당분간 이 일은 되는 대로 내버려두는 게 나아

You'll be crippled in your future career unless you have a good command of English
↳ 영어를 잘 구사하지 못하면 너의 전도에 큰 장애가 될 것이다

You'll be taken care of if things work out
↳ 일만 잘 풀리면 남부럽지 않게 해주지

You've no clue as to what's going on
↳ 넌 무슨 일이 일어나고 있는지 잘 모르는군

› **cripple** disabled person, disable

› **clue** piece of evidence that helps solve a problem

Your business is my business
> ㄴ 네 일이 내 일이잖아

Your concentration is so focused
> ㄴ 넌 한가지 일에 푹 빠지는군

> (=You have one-track mind)
> (=You really focus on one thing at a time)
> (=You really get lost in your work)

Your enthusiasm for this project is about to run out of gas
> ㄴ 이 일에 대한 너의 열정이 식어가고 있군

Your experience in dealing with your office work will stand you in good stead no matter what line of work you go into
> ㄴ 네가 앞으로 무슨 일을 하든 사무실 일 처리의 경험이 크게 유익할 것이다

Yung-soo is moonlighting these days
> ㄴ 영수는 요즘 부업 해

· **moonlight** hold a second job

114. 일상 대화   Useful Daily Expressions

A little something for you
     ↳ 약소하지만 선물로 드리지요

A short trip
     ↳ 잠깐 나갔다가 올게

A thinking robot? That's a new one to me
     ↳ 생각하는 로봇이라? 야, 그거 놀랠 노자네

Actually, this is one of the better days
     ↳ 이건 약과야

Adults can be so childish
     ↳ 어른이나 애나 똑같아!=어른들도 유치하긴!

> (=Sometimes adults are so childish)
> (=Sometimes adults act so childishly)

All right, I'll call his bluff
     ↳ 좋아, 해볼테면 해보라지

Big deal!
     ↳ 너 잘났다

› **bluff**   rising steeply with a broad flat front, frank, cliff

> (=I know you are Mr. Perfect(Genius))

Bite the bullet!
> ↳ 부딪쳐 봐!

Blame me if I do
> ↳ 그런 짓 할 사람이 어디 있나

Blow it
> ↳ 될대로 되라지!

Brace yourself(up)
> ↳ 정신차려

> (=Pull yourself together)

Break a leg
> ↳ 잘해봐

But then again we never know
> ↳ 하지만 또 모르지

Call it a hunch
> ↳ 육감이라고나 해두자

Can't complain
> ↳ 별일 없어요

Catch me later
> ↳ 나중에 또 얘기하자

Coffee break's over. Back to the salt mines
> ↳ 쉬는 시간 끝났어. 일과 시작하자

· **hunch** assume or cause to assume a
bent or crooked posture

· **mine** excavation from which mineral
substances are taken

Come hell or high water
      ↳ 이판사판이다

Come on, get into the groove
      ↳ 자, 신나게 놀자

Considering circumstances, I did okay
      ↳ 내 처지를 고려할 때 난 그럭저럭 했어

Couldn't be better
      ↳ 지금 기분 최고야

Couldn't care less
      ↳ 하든지 말든지 맘대로 해

Count me out=I'm out of it
      ↳ 난 손 떼겠어

> (=I don't want any part of it)

Cut ahead to page 50
      ↳ 건너뛰어 50쪽을 봐

Damned if you do, damned if you don't
      ↳ 이것도 저것도 잘 안 된단 말이군

Didn't I tell you so
      ↳ 거봐, 내가 뭐라 했어

> (=Told you)

Do as you see fit

› **groove**   long narrow channel, fixed routine
› **damn**   condemn to hell, curse

ㄴ 네가 알아서 해

Do it however you can
ㄴ 할 수 있는데 까지 해 봐

Do it just in case
ㄴ 혹시 모르니까 해 둬

(=Do it just to be safe)

Doesn't that beat all!
ㄴ 별 희한한 소릴 듣겠군

Don't be longer than you can help
ㄴ 가급적 빨리 해

Don't bet on it
ㄴ 그렇게는 안될걸

Don't get your hopes up
ㄴ 마음을 비워라

(=Don't expect to win)

Don't I know it
ㄴ 말 안해도 알고 있어

Done!
ㄴ 좋아, 그렇게 해(내기에 응할 때)

‣ **case** particular instance, convincing argument,
fact, lawsuit in case if

(=Agreed!)

Draw near, please
> ↳ 가까이 오십시오

Drop everything and let off some steam
> ↳ 만사 잊어버리고 스트레스나 좀 풀자

Drop me a line as soon as you have time to turn around
> ↳ 짬나는 대로 소식 줘

Ed left to pay a call. He should be back soon
> ↳ 에드는 화장실 갔어. 곧 올 거야

Either will do
> ↳ 어느 편이나 좋아

Enjoy the ride
> ↳ 맘 편히 살아(지내)

Even a blind sow finds an acorn
> ↳ 참 재수 좋구먼

Every little bit counts
> ↳ 조금이라도 있으면 도움이 돼

Everyone is out to lunch these days
> ↳ 요즘 모두 멍청해졌나봐

Everything is hurry and confusion
> ↳ 허둥지둥 야단이군

Everything is in confusion
> ↳ 모든 게 엉망이군

Everything is up in the air

‣ **acorn** nut of the oak

    ↳ 모든 게 미정이야

Fair is fair
    ↳ 좋은 게 좋아

Figure it out yourself
    ↳ 네가 알아서 해라

Fill in the blanks
    ↳ 더 이상 말 안 해도 알겠지?

Fine, have it your way
    ↳ 좋아, 맘대로 해

Fix it well in your mind
    ↳ 머리 속에 잘 간직해 둬

For better, for worse
    ↳ 어쩔 수 없지 뭐(기쁠 때나 슬플 때나)

For crying out loud!
    ↳ 맙소사. 짜증나네

Garbage in, garbage out
    ↳ 쓰레기를 넣었으니 쓰레기밖에 더 나오겠니

Get a grip on yourself
    ↳ 진정해라

(=Calm down)

Get a life
    ↳ 그렇게 할 일이 없나

Get off the fast track

›**track**   trail left by wheels or footprints, racing course, train rails

↳ 너무 서둘지(무리하지) 마

Get on with it

↳ 계속해봐

Get this straight

↳ 이점을 분명히 해둔다

(=I'll make this clear)

Get with it!

↳ 뭘 좀 알고 말해(살아)!

Give him some line

↳ 잠시 그에게 여유를 주어라

(=Give him a break)

Give it your best shot

↳ 힘껏 해봐

Give or take a few

↳ 적당히 가감해

Go and get miserable

↳ 네 멋대로 해서 혼 좀 나봐라

Go for it. You've got the qualifications

↳ 해 보는 거야(밀어 부쳐 봐). 넌 적임자야

Go get the door

↳ 가서 누가 왔는지 봐

▸ **qualification**   limitation or stipulation, special
skill or experience for a job

Go on! Tell me another one

        ㄴ 설마 또 그런 일이

Go on!

        ㄴ 말도 안돼. 설마

> (=No way!)

Go to the back of the line

        ㄴ 줄 뒤쪽으로 가 주십시오

Go to the shower

        ㄴ 내가 할 테니 가 보아라(볼일 봐)

Going to be a man in motion

        ㄴ 네 뜻대로 하지(**I'm** 생략)

Have done!

        ㄴ 그만둬! 아서!

He asked for it

        ㄴ 자업자득

> 자기가 한 일이나 말에 대해 책임을 져야 한다는 말이다. '자업자득 As you make your bed, so you must lie upon it'이나 '뿌린 데로 거둔다 You must sow, before you reap'과도 뜻이 통한다. 일상 대화에서는 'He got what he bargained(asked) for'이라고도 한다.

He make(makes가 아님) a donation

        ㄴ 그 사람이 기부금을 내다니! 사람 웃기네

Hell if I know

› **motion** proposal for action, act or instance of moving

› **donate** make a gift of

ㄴ 정말 모른다니까

Here comes the bus in the nick of time

ㄴ 때마침 버스가 오는군

Here goes my vacation

ㄴ 휴가는 물 건너갔군

Here goes nothing

ㄴ 잘하지 못하지만 한번 해볼게

Here we go again

ㄴ 또 시작이군

Here you are

ㄴ 다 왔어. 여기 있어(여럿이 물건을 찾다가)

Here you go

ㄴ 여기 있습니다(물건 건네줄 때)

Here's looking at you(mud in your eye)! Bottoms up!

ㄴ 자, 위하여! 원 샷!

Here's something that might interest you

ㄴ 이게 네 맘에 들지 모르겠어

Here's to our friendship!

ㄴ 건배!

Here's where you are wrong

ㄴ 네가 틀린 건 이 점이야

Hold it right there

ㄴ 꼼짝 마라

Hold(hang) on to your hat

ㄴ 놀라지 말아

▸ **nick** small broken area or chip, critical moment

How I envy you!
> ↳ 정말 부럽군!

Hurry with a capital 'H'
> ↳ 빨리 빨리 서둘러

I agree
> ↳ 맞아요

(=Check)

I am a natural
> ↳ 그거야 기본이죠

(=It's just in me)
(=It's God's given)

I am just bluffing
> ↳ 말이 그렇다는 거지

(=I am just exaggerating it a bit)

I am what I am
> ↳ 나는 나야

I am what I am, and I do what I do
> ↳ 나는 나고 내 일은 내가 알아서 해

I can but try

› **envy**   resentful awareness of another's advantage; object of envy

↳ 하여간 해볼게

I can hardly believe my ears

↳ 그 말은 정말 놀라운 일이네

I can identify with that

↳ 남의 일 같지 않네

> (=I can relate to that)
> (=I understand what that's like)

I can live

↳ 그만한 일에 죽을 내가 아니다

I can make this all work out

↳ 이 일을 모두 해결할 수 있다

I can read the whole story in your face

↳ 얼굴에 다 씌었군

I can read you like a book

↳ 속보인다 속보여

> (=I can read your mind)
> (=I can see right through you)
> (=You are so transparent)

I can see the handwriting on the wall

↳ 뻔할 뻔 자지 뭐

I can see why

↳ 알만하군

› **identify**　associate, establish the identity of

› **handwrite**　write by hand

I can't afford civility
> ↳ 예의는 사양하겠어

I can't be what I am not
> ↳ 내가 아닌 다른 사람이 될 수는 없어요(내 방식 또는 모습대로 하겠다)

I can't believe what's going on
> ↳ 귀신이 곡할 노릇

> (=This is unreal(unbelievable))
> (=I don't believe what has happened)
> (=This can't be happening)

I can't feel so strong
> ↳ 난 그리 뻔뻔하지 못해

I can't hear you very well
> ↳ 말씀이 잘 안 들립니다

I can't make it out at all
> ↳ 무슨 소린지 모르겠어

I can't tell which is(are) which
> ↳ 뭐가 뭔지 모르겠다

I couldn't ask for more
> ↳ 최고야(더 이상 바랄 게 없어)

I defy you to do this
> ↳ 할 수 있거든 해봐(네가 감히)

I didn't catch your name
> ↳ 성함을 잊어버렸습니다

I don't believe this

› **civility** courtesy

ㄴ 세상에 이럴 수가

I don't give a shit

ㄴ 상관 안 해

I don't hold grudges

ㄴ 난 뒤가 없어

(=I hold no grievances)
(=I don't stay resentful)
(=I don't hold ill will against people)

I don't mean what I say

ㄴ 농담이야

I don't mind if I do

ㄴ 그것도 괜찮지 뭐(술, 담배, 게임 등에 응할 때)

(=I won't say no to that)

I don't want to make a trip for nothing

ㄴ 헛걸음 하고 싶지 않아

I doubt that

ㄴ 과연 그렇게 될까?

(=That's not likely)
(=That's what you think)
(=I don't think so)

‣ **grudge** be reluctant to give

I get confused
> ㄴ 헷갈리네

(=I get mixed up)

I have been done
> ㄴ 당했어

I have some late-breaking news
> ㄴ 바로 전에 들어온 새로운 뉴스가 있다

I just ran out of excuses
> ㄴ 이젠 변명거리도 떨어졌어

I knew she would do that
> ㄴ 그럴 줄 알았어

(=That's typical of her)

I know where you are coming from
> ㄴ 무슨 말인지 알겠어

I know where you live
> ㄴ 두고보자

I learnt it to my cost
> ㄴ 그 일은 넌더리 나(데었어)

I like your impudence
> ㄴ 그 뻔뻔스러운 게 놀랍군

I never thought I'd live to see the day

> **impudent** insolent

ㄴ 오래 살고 볼일이군

> (=Will wonders ever cease?)

I only have myself to thank
ㄴ 스스로를 탓할 수밖에

I read you loud and clear
ㄴ 네 말 잘 알겠어=무슨 말인지 잘 알겠다

I shall be glad to do what I can
ㄴ 할 수 있는 일은 기꺼이 도와 드리죠

I stand corrected
ㄴ 제가 잘못했습니다

I think I'll pass
ㄴ 싫어(사양하겠어)

I'll be damned if it's true
ㄴ 그럴 리가 있나

I'll be right with you
ㄴ 잠시만 기다려 주십시오

I'll do what I please
ㄴ 내 맘이야

> (=I'm free to do anything)

I'll lay you a bet
ㄴ 내기를 하자

· **cease** stop
· **bet** agreement that one whose guess about a result proves wrong will give something to one whose guess proves right

I'll let everything go
> ↳ 모든 걸 잊어버릴게

I'll take care of you next
> ↳ 다음은 당신차례입니다(이발, 미용, 의사 등)

> (=I'll do you next)

I'm beyond help
> ↳ 도와줘서 될 일이 아냐

I'm in for it
> ↳ 이거 낭패 났는걸

I'm so confused
> ↳ 헛갈려

I'm so embarrassed
> ↳ 아유 창피해

I'm sorry I'm too much
> ↳ 미안해, 내가 너무 심했어

> (=I was way out of line)
> (=I've gone too far)

I'm sorry to disoblige you
> ↳ 뜻을 거슬러 죄송합니다

I'm speechless
> ↳ 기가 막혀 말이 안 나오네, 정말 감동했어

› **confuse**   make mentally uncertain, jumble

I'm tackling one mountain after another
> ↳ 산 너머 산이군

> (=I'm faced with one mountain after another)
> (=I'm in a never ending nightmare)
> (=What a nightmare!)

If you must, you must
> ↳ 그렇다면 할 수 없지

If you twist my arm
> ↳ 꼭 해야 한다면

> (=If you insist)

Imagine how big my eyes got!
> ↳ 내가 얼마나 놀랐겠는가 상상을 해봐

In a manner of speaking
> ↳ 어쩌면 그럴지도 몰라

In case of anything happening, call this number
> ↳ 무슨 일이 있으면 이 번호로 연락해

In fact, everything in the garden is rosy(lovely)
> ↳ 모든 일이 만족스러워

In-ho won't be long(in) coming back
> ↳ 인호는 곧 올거다

It backfired
> ↳ 역효과 났어

› **nightmare** frightening dream

It beats me too
↳ 나도 모르겠어

It can wait
↳ 그건 나중에 해도 돼

It cost me dearly
↳ 그 때문에 큰코다쳤어

It doesn't amount to(be) a hill of beans
↳ 별거 아니군

It doesn't bother me
↳ 난 상관 안 해

It doesn't have to be this way
↳ 꼭 이래야 하는 건 아냐

It doesn't hurt to ask
↳ 그냥 한 번 물어보는 거야

It figures
↳ 그럴 줄 알았지

It had me in stitches
↳ 배꼽 빼더라

It hangs by the wall
↳ 이제 그런 건 소용없어

It has much sound but little(no) sense
↳ 공연한 법석이군

It is getting(going) nowhere
↳ 그런 식은 안 통해

It is I who am to blame
↳ 내 탓이야

› **figure** be important, calcuate

It isn't worth it
> ↳ 그래봤자 소용없어

It makes a good picture
> ↳ 그림 좋다

It makes sense
> ↳ 그거 말 되네

It serves you right for putting on airs(being haughty)
> ↳ 잘난 척 하더니 꼴 좋다

It shouldn't be this(that) way
> ↳ 이래선 안 돼

It shouldn't happen to a dog
> ↳ 그 생각만 해도 지긋지긋해

It was just a stab(shot) in the dark(wild guess)
> ↳ 어림짐작이었어

It was text book
> ↳ 원칙대로 했지

It weighs on my mind
> ↳ 그거 부담되네

It would have been better(convenient, helpful)
> ↳ 좋다 말았어

It would have gone ill with me
> ↳ 혼날 뻔했어

It'll put the whammy on you
> ↳ 그런 건 재수 없어

It'll speak for itself
> ↳ 그건 자연히 알게 돼 있어

· **haughty** disdainfully proud
· **whammy** misfortune

It'll lead nowhere

ㄴ 그래봤자 소용없어

It's a big joke

ㄴ 정말 웃기는 일이지

It's a figure of speech

ㄴ 말하자면 그렇다는 거지

It's a go

ㄴ 그건 잘됐어(**It's a no go**그건 헛수고야)

It's a miracle

ㄴ 별일이네(해가 서쪽에서 뜨겠군)

(=What's the occasion)
(=This is not something you see everyday)

It's as plain as the nose on your face

ㄴ 그건 뻔한 거잖아

It's awesome

ㄴ 죽여주네

It's crumbled

ㄴ 꽝이야

(=It wasn't anything)
(=It was nothing)
(=It didn't work out well)
(=It didn't go well)

› **awe** respectful fear of wonder

It's exactly like you
ㄴ 정말 너답군

> (=It's just what I'd expected from you)
> (=It suits you perfectly)

It's for the best
ㄴ 차라리 잘 됐어, 최선을 위한 거다

> (=It's better this way)
> (=Things are better this way)

It's getting too close and personal
ㄴ 너무 꼬치꼬치 캐물으시는군요

It's going around
ㄴ 그런 것쯤은 보통이야

> (=There's no shortage of that)
> (=It's more common than you think)

It's highly improbable(hardly possible)
ㄴ 설마 그렇겠어

> (=It's not at all(never) likely to happen)

· **improbable** unlikely to be true or to occur

It's in the nature of things
> ↳ 그건 당연한 거야

It's just a theory
> ↳ 그건 단지 추측일 뿐이야

It's no joke(=laughing matter)
> ↳ 장난 아니네(**=serious**)

It's no news to you(us)
> ↳ 뻔할 뻔 자야

It's not fun and games
> ↳ 장난이 아냐

It's not going to happen
> ↳ 어림없어

> (=No way in hell)
> (=Not in your dreams)

It's the same as usual(always)
> ↳ 늘 그렇지 뭐

> (=It's how it's always been)
> (=It's no different from other time)

It's you
> ↳ 너에게 정말 잘 어울린다(맞는다)

I'll catch up
> ↳ 곧 뒤따라 갈께

› **catch up** provide with the latest information,
travel fast enough to overtake

Just be yourself

  ↳ 평소처럼 하면 돼

Just my luck

  ↳ 어유, 재수 없어

> (=Why me?)
> (=What's going on?)

Let me get back to you

  ↳ 차후에 알려 주지

Let me get this straight

  ↳ 내가 제대로 알아들었는지 보자

Let me guess

  ↳ 말 안 해도 알아

Let me have it back soon

  ↳ 곧 돌려줘야 해

Let's get going(rolling)

  ↳ 슬슬 시작할까

> (=Let's get the show on the road)

Let's get it out into the open

  ↳ 터놓고 얘기하자

Let's get it over at once

  ↳ 얼른 끝내자

▸ **roll** move by turning over and over, move
  on wheels

Let's go for it
ㄴ 잘해봅시다

> (=Let's do our best to be successful)

Let's go slow
ㄴ 쉬엄쉬엄 하자

> (=Let's take it slow)

Let's go halves
ㄴ 분담해 내자

> (=Let's split the bill)

Likewise
ㄴ 동감이야

Live and learn
ㄴ 오래 살고 볼일이다**(Learn something everyday)**

Make no mistake
ㄴ 착각하지마

My mind was on other things
ㄴ 깜박했어

· **split** divide lengthwise or along a grain,
separate(+up)

> (=I was preoccupied)

Nice try!

    ↳ 잘했어!

No harm done

    ↳ 그 사람 말짱해

> (=He's not hurt)
> (=He's still in one piece)

No means no

    ↳ 안 되는 것은 안 돼

None of your hot air

    ↳ 큰소리 좀 집어치워

Not in a million years

    ↳ 어림없는 소리 마

> (=Not in your wildest dreams)
> (=Not a chance)

Not that I can't, but that I'll not

    ↳ 못하는 게 아니라 안하는 거다

Not to get off the track, what's holding you up?

    ↳ 원래 얘기로 돌아와서, 넌 왜 우물쭈물 하는 거냐?

Not too much. I am serious

· **preoccupy** occupy the attention of

　　　　↳ 아냐. 내 진심이야

Nothing doing
　　　　↳ 그런 일은 없을걸=안 돼(거부의 응답)

Nothing escapes you
　　　　↳ 넌 무엇이나 기억하고 있군

Nothing(Not) to speak of
　　　　↳ 별 거 아냐

Now that's one for the books!
　　　　↳ 야! 이건 놀랠 노자네!

Now you look like yourself
　　　　↳ 이제야 너답다

Now you see it, now you don't
　　　　↳ 장담할 일이 아냐

Now, that's more like it
　　　　↳ 그렇게 나와야지

Now, there's a way to go
　　　　↳ 이제야 방법을 찾았군

Oh, I've seen better
　　　　↳ 뭐. 대단한 건 아냐

Oh, no. Not again
　　　　↳ 저런. 또 그랬군

Okay. Catch you later
　　　　↳ 알았어. 나중에 다시 얘기할게

Catch me later
　　　　↳ 나중에 얘기해 줘

› **escape**　get away or get away from

On my mother's grave
> ↳ 맹세할게

Pardon my language
> ↳ 험한 말을 해서 미안해

Pass on, please
> ↳ 자, 앞을 지나가십시오

Really? It's about time
> ↳ 정말? 진작 그랬어야지

Refuse the offer point-blank
> ↳ 딱 잘라 거절해 버려

Says who?
> ↳ 그런 법이 어디 있어(웃기지마)

Sharp's the word
> ↳ 서둘러라(Mum's the word 입 다물어).

Shove it up your ass
> ↳ 집어치워

Shut up before I mace your face up
> ↳ 박살내기 전에 입 닥쳐

Slip me five - Lend me five
> ↳ 악수합시다 - 도와주세요

Small world
> ↳ 세상 참 좁구먼

Smile when you say that
> ↳ 농담이겠지

So much the better
> ↳ 그렇다면 더욱 좋다

‣ **pardon**   excuse of an offense
‣ **shove**   push along, aside, or away

Sometimes I could kill myself
> ↳ 난 왜이리 똑똑하지

> (I'm so good I scare myself 내가 생각해도 난 똑똑해)

Sorry is not enough
> ↳ 죄송하다면 다냐?

Sounds good
> ↳ 괜찮은(반가운) 소린데

> (=I like the sound of that)

Stay like this
> ↳ 계속 그렇게 해

Take a wild guess
> ↳ 맞혀봐

Take no chances
> ↳ 쉽게 끝내(모험하지마)

Take your time
> ↳ 서둘지마

That beats me
> ↳ 정말 놀라게 하는군

That can't be helped
> ↳ 그건 부득이해

› **scare** frighten

> (=There's no help for it)

That covers a lot of ground
↳ 의미심장하군

That depends
↳ 경우에 따라 달라

> (=That's iffy)
> (=Let's see how things go)
> (=Let's see what comes up)
> (=That depends on circumstances)

That explanation satisfied me
↳ 이제야 이해가 가는군

> (=That explains everything)

That is par for the course
↳ 그게 어제오늘 일이냐

That makes us even
↳ 피장파장이군

> (=Let's call it even)
> (=I'd say we are even now)
> (=Now we are even)

· **iffy** uncertain

· **par** stated value, common level, accepted
standard or normal condition

That was close
> ↳ 아슬아슬했지

(=That was a close call(shave))

That was so close
> ↳ 너무 안타깝게 됐군

(=You almost made it)

That'll be the days
> ↳ 내 손에 장을 지져라

(=In your dreams)

That'll do me very well
> ↳ 난 그걸로 족해

That'll never do
> ↳ 그걸로는 부족해

That'll never happen
> ↳ 그럴리 없어(그렇게는 안 돼)

(=That'll be the time)

That's a dig at me

› **dig** discover, poke(+into), cutting remark

    ↳ 나한테 트집 잡는 게로군

That's a dirty shame
    ↳ 치사하게 그게 뭐야

That's a long shot
    ↳ 가망 없는 일이야

That's a matter of degree
    ↳ 그건 정도문제

That's a new one on me
    ↳ 야 그거 신기하네

That's a no-no
    ↳ 그건 안 돼

That's a part of it
    ↳ 그것도 이유는 되지

That's a real win-win solution
    ↳ 그렇게 하면 정말 누이 좋고 매부 좋지

That's a step too far
    ↳ 그건 좀 지나쳐

That's a twice-told tale
    ↳ 그건 김빠진 얘기다

That's a waste
    ↳ 아까운 재주를 썩히는군

(=What a waste of talent)

That's about and about

‣ **solution** answer to a problem, homogeneous liquid mixture

‣ **talent** natural mental, creative, or artistic ability

↳ 오십보 백보야(진척이 없어)

That's about the size of it
↳ 사연인즉 그렇게 된 거야

That's all history
↳ 그건 옛날 얘기(과거지사)

That's all I'm going to tell you
↳ 그 이상은 대답 못해

That's all she wrote
↳ 그게 전부다

That's all you are
↳ 네가 그렇지 뭐

That's all you know about it
↳ 넌 그 일을 제대로 모르고 있군

That's an old story
↳ 흔한 일이지

That's as old as hills
↳ 케케묵은 소리군

That's bargain
↳ 그렇게 하기로 합시다

That's enough to drive me to drink
↳ 거참 짜증나는군

That's fine
↳ 됐어요

› **bargain** agreement, something bought for
less than its value

(=That'll do(just fine))
(It's fine by me 난 됐어요)

That's flat
　　　↳ 그렇다마다 지 뭐(단연코 그렇지)

That's for the birds
　　　↳ 그런 수에는 안 넘어가

That's forcing things
　　　↳ 그건 무리야

That's going too far
　　　↳ 장난이 심하군

That's icing on the cake
　　　↳ 그건 금상첨화야

"좋은데 더 좋은 것을 더한다"는 뜻이다. 영어로는 'Icing on the cake 케익 위의 크림'이라고 한다. 케익만으로도 맛있는데, 거기에 크림을 더해 더욱 맛 있어졌다는 얘기이다. Icing 대신에 Frosting 으로 대체 할 수도 있다.

That's it(that)
　　　↳ 이만 끝

That's much better
　　　↳ 이제 살 것 같다

(=I feel much better)
(=That's exactly what I needed)

› **icing**　sweet usually creamy coating for baked goods

That's neither here no there
> ↳ 그건 별거 아냐. 상관없어

(=That's beside the point)

That's news from nowhere
> ↳ 그건 뻔할 뻔 자야(누구나 다 알아)

That's no bad, considering
> ↳ 그런 대로 그리 나쁘지 않군

That's quite news to me
> ↳ 금시초문인데

That's really something
> ↳ 그거 대단한데

That's so cheap
> ↳ 정말 유치해

That's something
> ↳ 정말 대단해

That's the(whole) lot
> ↳ 그게 전부야

That's the card for it
> ↳ 바로 그거야

That's the end of the ball game
> ↳ 이제 다 끝났어

That's the last straw
> ↳ 더 이상 참을 수가 없어

‣ **straw** grass stems after grain is removed

That's the story
ㄴ 일이 그렇게 된 거야

That's your funeral
ㄴ 그건 네가 할 일

The feeling is mutual
ㄴ 피차 일반이야=동감이야

The game is not worth the candle
ㄴ 그럴만한 가치(필요)가 있는 거냐?(산책, 등산, 낚시, 바둑, 운동 등의
제안에 거절하면서)

The inevitable has come
ㄴ 올 것이 왔어

The lot fell(up)on me
ㄴ 제비뽑기에서 뽑혔지 뭐

The trip here was for nothing
ㄴ 헛걸음했군(괜히 왔군)

> (=This was a wasted trip)

There are a dime a dozen
ㄴ 많고 많다(천지다)

There are talkers and there are doers
ㄴ 허풍떨고 있네

> (=You are all blow and no go)

› **mutual** given or felt by one another in
equal amount, common

› **inevitable** incapable of being avoided or
escaped

There you are. That kid always gets his own way
ㄴ 그거 봐(내 말 대로군). 그 애는 언제나 자기 생각대로 해

There's no getting around it
ㄴ 그건 엄연한 사실이다

There's no more to it than that
ㄴ 그 이상도 이하도 아냐

There's no need to make a big deal about it
ㄴ 그 일로 소란 피울 필요가 없잖아

There's nothing I can do
ㄴ 속수무책이다

There's room for misunderstanding
ㄴ 오해의 소지가 있어

(=It's not absolutely clear to me)

There's(That's) dear
ㄴ 착하지. 잘했어. 울지마(*아이를 달래는 말)

These things happen
ㄴ 그런 일도 종종 있다

This is a big no-no
ㄴ 이건 절대 안 돼

This is a fire in my own backyard
ㄴ 이건 발등의 불

This is all we need
ㄴ 이거 낭패로군

› **absolute** pure, free from restriction, definite

This time I know it's real
> ↳ 이번엔 진짜야

Use this as a makeshift
> ↳ 아쉬운대로 이걸 써라

Use your brain
> ↳ 생각을 좀 해봐라

Wait for me to say "Stop"
> ↳ "그만"이라고 할 때까지 기다려

Watch how I do it
> ↳ 내가 하는걸 봐

We are even
> ↳ 피장파장이야(=all squared up)

(=We don't owe each other anything)
(=We are two of a kind)
(=You are just like me)
(=Aren't we a pair?)
(=We are all square)

We are in for it
> ↳ 벌린 춤이다

(=Over shoes, over boots)
(=We have gone too far to go back)

We are off for the weekend. Be good now

› **makeshift**　temporary substitute

ㄴ 이제 주말이다. 그럼 안녕

We have to see about that
ㄴ 그건 두고봐야 알지

We only get one shot
ㄴ 한 번의 기회 뿐이야

We should be grateful in any circumstances
ㄴ 감지덕지 해야지요

> (=We should be thankful for what we have)
> (=We should count our blessing)

What a(total) mess
ㄴ 난리도 아니네

> (=Look at this mess)

What a big racket that is!
ㄴ 그게 얼마나 손쉽게 수지 맞추는 일이냐

What a break!
ㄴ 너 정말 운 좋구나

> (=You've got a break)

What a curious quirk of fate this is!
ㄴ 이 무슨 운명의 장난이란 말인가!

› **grateful** thankful or appreciative
› **quirk** peculiarity of action or behavior

What a drag!

        └ 아 지겨워

What a night-mare

        └ 산 너머 산이군

> (=I'm tackling one mountain after another)
> (=I'm faced with one problem after another)
> (=I'm in a never-ending night-mare)

What a relief

        └ 10년 묵은 체증이 다 내려가네

> (=I feel much so better now)
> (=It's a huge weight off my shoulders)
> (=It's one less worry for me)

What a windfall!

        └ 횡재했군!

What must be, must be

        └ 운명은 바꿀 수 없다(될 대로 되어라)

> 꼭 일어나야 할 일은 무슨 일이 있어도 일어난다. 그렇기 때문에 운명에 거역하지 말고 순종하여야 한다. 그건 뜻을 가진 영어 명언 중에서 일상적으로 많이 쓰는 말은 "What must be, must be"이다.

What'll be, will be

· **drag**   something dragged over a surface or through water, something that hinders progress or is boring

· **windfall**   thing blown down by wind, unexpected benefit

ㄴ 운명에 맡겨라

Whatever you are, get real(get a life = get a grip)
ㄴ 당신이 누구든 정신차려야 해

Whatever you say(want)
ㄴ 좋으실 대로 하세요. 네 맘대로 해

When pigs fly
ㄴ 절대 안 돼(허용 불가)

Wish me luck
ㄴ 행운을 빌어 줘

Wouldn't we all?
ㄴ 누군들 안 그러겠어?

You ain't seen nothing(anything) yet
ㄴ 아직 진짜를 못 봤어(지금부터가 진짜야)

You are a caution!
ㄴ 너 보통내기 아니구나!

You are asking the wrong person
ㄴ 전 그런 것 잘 몰라요

You are better so
ㄴ 넌 그대로가 좋아

You are getting warm. Keep guessing
ㄴ 정답에 가까워지고 있어. 더 생각해 봐

You are giving me goose bumps
ㄴ 닭살 돋게 하네

(=You make my flesh creep)

› **caution** warning, care or prudence
› **bump** strike or knock forcibly

You are grasping at straws
> ↳ 그래봐야 소용없어

You are not wanted here
> ↳ 여긴 네가 올 자리가 아니야

You are out of it
> ↳ 물정을 모르는군. 정신 나갔군

You are out to lunch
> ↳ 바보 같으니

You are speaking to the wrong person
> ↳ 당신은 사람을 착각하고 있습니다

You are telling me
> ↳ 나도 알아. 동감이야

(=Your thoughts echo mine)

You are too much
> ↳ 너 멋쟁이구나. 넌 너무해

You can all go to hell
> ↳ 엿 먹어라

You can say that again
> ↳ 지당한 말씀

(=You hit the nail right on the head)

You can't beat(top) that

· **grasp** take or seize firmly, understand

↳ 엄청나군(굉장하군)

You can't get help that way
↳ 그래선 안 돼

You can't take it with you
↳ 죽을 때 무덤에 가져갈 수 없어

You don't get it
↳ 뭘 모르시나보군

> (=You don't understand)

You don't have to worry about it
↳ 너한텐 해당 안 돼

> (=It doesn't apply to you(your case))
> (=It has nothing to do with you)

You don't say!
↳ 정말이야?

You have really done it again
↳ 또 일을 저질렀군

You have the first try
↳ 너부터 해봐

You know better than that
↳ 그게 아니란 것은 너도 알잖아=알만한 사람이 왜 그래

・**apply**　place in contact, put to practical
use, devote attention or effort to

something

(Am I being punished? 에 대한 응답이며 벌받을 리 없다는 말임)

You must have been dropped on your head as a baby. Hold it together
> ↳ 너 돌았구나. 정신차려

You said a mouthful there
> ↳ 그렇고 말고, 바로 그거야

(=You said it)

You'll pay for it
> ↳ 이러면 재미없어

You're just being silly
> ↳ 바보 같은 소리하는군

You're out of your mind
> ↳ 네가 제정신이냐? 돌았군 돌았어

(=You've got to be out of your mind)

You've got a break
> ↳ 정말 운 좋구나

(=What a break)

Your apology is no longer due

· **silly** foolish or stupid

· **apology** formal justification, expression of regret for a wrong

ㄴ 진작 사과했어야지

(These words are no longer overdue 이런 말은 진작 했어야 했어)

Your head is in the clouds
ㄴ 마음이 콩밭에 있군

(=Where are you?)
(=Are you daydreaming?)

› **overdue** passed the due date

115. 일상 생활　　　Daily Habits

A hundred thousand won doesn't go very far these days, with the prices rising all the time
> ↳ 물가가 오르기만 하니 십만원 이라야 얼마 못 가

A line of small holes is punched out to show us where to tear the card
> ↳ 카드를 어디서 절취할지 알 수 있게 한 줄로 작은 구멍이 나 있다

After the recession, we had to draw(pull) in our horns
> ↳ 불경기 이후 우린 씀씀이를 줄일 수밖에 없었다

All night you ground your teeth, keeping me awake
> ↳ 네가 밤새도록 이를 가는 바람에 잠을 못잤다

All you do is screw around all day
> ↳ 한다는 일이 하루종일 빈둥거리는 일이군

An-do got(gained) access to the Library by showing his identity card
> ↳ 안도는 신분증을 보여주고 도서관에 들어갔다

As he droned on, the listeners(audience) fell asleep one by one
> ↳ 그가 데데한 소리만 늘어놓자 청중들이 하나씩 잠이 들어버렸다

At this rate, you'll be caught short soon
> ↳ 이런 식으로 나가면 곧 필요한 게(돈, 물건 능력) 떨어져 곤란하게 돼

Back away from the heater a little
> ↳ 히터에서 좀 떨어져 서(앉)지 그래

· **recession** departing procession, period of reduced economic activity

· **drone** make a dull monotonous sound

Back in a second. I've got to take a leak
> ↳ 금방 올게. 소변보고 올 테니까

Be gentle when you are handling the equipment
> ↳ 그 장비를 조심스럽게 다뤄라

Beat a traffic signal
> ↳ 빨간 불 오기 전에 건너가라

Better be out of the world than out of the fashion
> ↳ 유행에 뒤지느니 지구를 떠나겠단 말이군

Bong-soo made a fair guess as to how much I weighed
> ↳ 봉수는 내 체중이 얼마인지 가깝게 맞혔어

Chan-soo always photographs well(badly)
> ↳ 찬수는 언제나 사진이 잘 받아(잘 안 받아)

Choon-ho can make it through the night
> ↳ 춘호는 밤새워 놀(춤출, 해낼)수 있어

Clay binds when it is baked
> ↳ 점토를 구우면 굳어진다

Coal is formed from peat, which consists of different kinds of organic matter that have decomposed
> ↳ 석탄은 분해된 모든 다른 종류의 유기물들로 구성된 도탄에서 형성된다

Cross over at the traffic lights
> ↳ 신호등 있는데서 길을 건너라

Do you think the floor will bear up under the weight of the new machinery?
> ↳ 마루바닥이 새로 구입한 기계무게를 감당할 것 같니?

Dong-soo could only flounder through his song
> ↳ 동수는 떠듬떠듬 겨우 노래를 불렀어

> **leak** become or make known
> **decompose** separate into parts, decay

> **flounder** struggle for footing, proceed clumsily

Doo-chul broke away from this and went straight
> ↳ 두철인 그 일에서 손떼고 손을 씻었어

Doo-chul ran like everything
> ↳ 두철인 전속력으로 달렸어

Doo-chul's answer doesn't sit right with me
> ↳ 두만이의 해명엔 수긍이 안가

Doo-soo began to saw wood(logs) twenty seconds after his head hit the pillow
> ↳ 두수는 드러누워 **20**초가 되자마자 코를 골기 시작했다

Don't fall behind in your payments
> ↳ 계산이 밀리면 안돼

During(the) rush hours, there's always a lot of pushing and shoving to get on trains
> ↳ 러시아워 시간에는 열차를 타기 위해 항상 밀고 비집고 들어가야 한다

Ed 's got some legal eagle to find a loophole in the contract
> ↳ 에드는 한 꾀돌이 변호사를 사서 계약상 빠져나갈 구멍을 찾으려 했

Ed took a long pull(drag) on his cigarette, exhaled and coughed loudly
> ↳ 에드는 담배를 길게 한 모금 빨아 내뱉더니 큰기침을 했다

Every prison that man build is built with bricks of shame
> ↳ 사람이 지은 모든 교도소는 치욕의 벽돌로 지은 집이다

Expensive repairs to sewer systems often result when large trees spread their roots
> ↳ 커다란 나무의 뿌리가 뻗는데서 종종 비싼 복구비가 드는 하수처리
> 시설의 고장이 생긴다

Feeling at loose ends, I went for a stroll

› **loophole** means of evading

› **stroll** walk leisurely

↳ 별로 할 일도 없는 것 같아서 산책하러 갔었지

Flip the envelope to see who it comes from
　　　　↳ 누구에게서 온 편지인지 봉투를 뒤집어봐

For some reason only known to himself he gave up the whole thing
　　　　↳ 그는 개인사정으로 모든 것을 포기했다

For some years he's held the fields
　　　　↳ 그는 몇 년 동안 버티어 왔다

Get off your ass(butt, tail) and mow the lawn
　　　　↳ 썩 일어나서 잔디나 좀 깎아라

Get up against one another to stay warm
　　　　↳ 춥지 않게 서로 바짝 붙어 서(앉아)라

Get(make) the room in order. The room needs straightening up
　　　　↳ 방 좀 정리해라. 이 방은 정돈해야 해

Give me the outline, I'll flesh it out
　　　　↳ 개요만 주면 세부 사항은 내가 할게

Go get your stuff(shit, act) together and be right with us
　　　　↳ 너의 뒷일(소지품 등)을 정리하고 곧바로 따라와

Good care improves durability
　　　　↳ 손질을 잘 하면 오래 쓸 수 있다

He doesn't know whether(if) he's on his head or heels
　　　　↳ 그는 정신 없이 바빠(그의 일은 두서가 없어)

He has gone God knows where
　　　　↳ 그가 어딜 갔는지 아무도 몰라

He has no daily necessities, much less luxuries
　　　　↳ 그에게는 사치품은 말할 것도 없고 필수품조차 없다

› **mow**　cut with a machine
› **durable**　lasting a long time

He makes nothing of sitting(staying) up all night
> ↳ 그는 밤샘을 예사로 한다

He must have seen things
> ↳ 그가 헛것을 봤음이 틀림없어

He sleeps in once in a blue moon
> ↳ 그는 좀체로 늦잠 자는 일이 없다

He was(went) on a binge last night
> ↳ 그는 어젯밤 진탕 마시고 놀았어

He works days and goes to school nights
> ↳ 낮에 일하고 밤에 학교에 다녀

He's already in the hay(in bed)
> ↳ 그는 벌써 잠자리에 들었어

He's home
> ↳ 귀가 중(at home=집에 있어)

Her house is somewhere in the sticks
> ↳ 그 여자의 집은 벽촌 어딘가에 있어

His eyes made the round of the room
> ↳ 그는 방을 휘 둘러보았다

His house is the sixth door on the left
> ↳ 그의 집은 왼쪽으로 여섯 번째이다

How much do you need to see you through until June
> ↳ 6월까지 버티는데 얼마가 필요하니?

Hyun-soo lay on his knapsack
> ↳ 현수는 배낭을 멘 채로 잤어('배낭 위에'가 아님)

I can't carry a tune in a bucket=I'm tone-deaf
> ↳ 난 음치야

▸ **binge** spree

I can't find my book. It must have been spirited away(off)
> ㄴ 내 책이 어디 갔을까 귀신이 곡할 노릇이네

I can't keep pitch
> ㄴ 고음이 안 올라가요

I can't put this book down
> ㄴ 이 책 참 재미있어

I can't well do that
> ㄴ 난 그걸 아무리 해도 안 된다

I don't have time to catch my breath
> ㄴ 눈코 뜰 새 없이 바빠

> (=I don't have time to breathe)

I feel lazy
> ㄴ 만사가 귀찮아

> (=I don't want to do anything)
> (=I don't feel like doing anything)

I got a good night's sleep
> ㄴ 어젯밤엔 밀린 잠을 좀 잤지

> (=I caught up on my sleep last night)
> (=I turned in early last night)

· **spirit** raise the spirit or productivity of(+up),
carry off secretly(+away)

I have a frog in my throat
> ㄴ 목이 쉬었어

(=I have lost my voice)

I have seen better days
> ㄴ 좋은 때도 있었지. 오늘은 별로 이었어

I haven't got all day
> ㄴ 나 바쁘단 말이야

I kept(remained) standing for an hour
> ㄴ 한시간이나 계속 서 있었어(**keep on standing** 은 "몇 번이고 일어서 다"임)

I must have an off day today
> ㄴ 오늘은 하는 일 마다 안 돼

I need to go bad
> ㄴ 나 급하단 말이야(화장실)

I received much company yesterday
> ㄴ 어제는 손님이 많았어

I strolled as fancy led me
> ㄴ 발 가는 대로 걸었어

I thought my number was up yesterday
> ㄴ 어제는 죽는 줄만 알았다

I threw some water on my face
> ㄴ 고양이 세수했어(후닥닥 세수를 하는 둥 마는 둥 했을 때)

› **fancy** liking, whim, imagination

> (=I couldn't wash my face properly)
> (=I quickly washed my face)

I want to do number one
ㄴ 오줌 마려워(이해 못할 수도 있음)

I want to pay a call
ㄴ 화장실 좀 가야겠어

I was cooped up all day
ㄴ 두문불출했지

I went to sleep before I knew it
ㄴ 어느새 잠이 들었어

I would do anything before that
ㄴ 뭐든지 하겠지만 그건 싫어

I'll be at liberty tomorrow
ㄴ 내일이면 한가해지겠지

I'll drop your packages off at the post office. Thanks. I owe you one.
ㄴ 제가 소포를 우체국에서 부쳐드리지요. 고마워. 신세를 져서 어쩌나

I'll meet your flight(plane)
ㄴ 공항으로 마중 갈게

I'll only be gone for a moment
ㄴ 잠깐 어디 좀 갔다 올께

I'm adjusted to living alone now in Dai-jun
ㄴ 이젠 대전에 혼자 사는 게 익숙해졌어

I'm expecting your coming any moment
ㄴ 이제나저제나 하고 기다리고 있어

› **coop**   confine in or as if in a coop
› **adjust**   fix, adapt, or set right

I'm having a bad hair day
> ↳ 오늘은 끔찍한 하루군

I'm not at home today
> ↳ 오늘은 면회 사절('집에 없음'의 뜻도 있음)

I'm out of it today
> ↳ 오늘은 도통 정신이 없어

I'm sorry about back then(yesterday)
> ↳ 그때 일(어제일)은 미안하다

I've been busy about nothing
> ↳ 무사 분주했을 뿐이야

I've got a number two real bad
> ↳ 나 화장실(대변)이 급하단 말이야(이해하지 못할 수도 있음)

I've got to take a leak
> ↳ 소변 좀 보아야겠어

I've got two left feet
> ↳ 저는 춤을 잘 못춰요

If it's for me, tell them(say) I'm not in(here)
> ↳ 나를 찾으면 없다고 해줘

If she doesn't come to the picnic she'll miss out on all the fun
> ↳ 그녀가 야유회에 나오지 않는다면 재미있는 시간을 다 놓칠 것이다

If you fail with nylon, why not, try cotton
> ↳ 나일론으로 안 되거든 면으로 해 보아라

In an instant I was again on my feet
> ↳ 난 곧 일어났어

In his mind's eye, he'll picture what's going to happen
> ↳ 그의 육감으로 무슨 일이 일어날지 예상할 것이다

› **instant** moment, immediate, ready to mix

In the summer he often sleeps in his birthday suit(in the raw)
> ↳ 여름이면 그는 발가벗고 자는 때가 많아

In-ho came off probation this month
> ↳ 인호는 이 달로 수습기간이 끝났어

In-ho earns his salt
> ↳ 인호는 밥벌이나 하는 정도지 뭐

In-soo is in - The train is in
> ↳ 인수는 집에 있어 - 열차가 도착해 있어

It feels like yesterday
> ↳ 엊그제 일 같다

It was a long day
> ↳ 정말 힘든 하루였다

It was good riddance when the troublemaker was sent home
> ↳ 말썽꾸러기를 집으로 보내고 나니 속이 후련했어

It would be like going out of the frying pan into the fire
> ↳ 갈수록 태산이군

역경을 넘을수록 더욱 큰 역경이 기다리고 있다는 뜻이다. 영어로는 'Out of
the frying pan into the fire 튀김 팬에서 나와서 불로'라고 하는데, 이는
튀김 팬이 너무 뜨거워 겨우 나왔더니, 밑의 불로 떨어졌다는 뜻이며, 어려운
일에서 헤어 나왔더니 더 어려운 일에 대면했음을 비유한다.
(=It's getting tougher and tougher as we go on(proceed))

It's a must that we brush our teeth after every meal
> ↳ 우린 매 식사 후 반드시 양치질을 해야 한다

It's all in a day's work

› **probation**   period of testing and trial, | good behavior under supervision
free-dom of a convict during

↳ 그건 항상 있는 일이야(그 정도야 보통이지)

It's all right for somebody. I've got to stay home and look after my baby

↳ 누구는 좋겠다. 난 집에서 아이나 보아야하니

It's been a long time

↳ 피곤한 하루였어

It's best to avoid the main roads at busy times, and remain clear of them until the worst of the traffic is over

↳ 혼잡한 시간에는 최악의 혼잡상태가 지나갈 때까지 큰 도로를 피하는 게 제일 낫다

It's dawning on us that the most intimate details of daily lives are meticulously monitored, searched, recorded and stored

↳ 사람들은 일상생활의 가장 은밀한 일까지 세밀히 감시당하고 조사 당하며 기록되고 저장되고 있다는 사실을 깨닫기 시작했다

It's delicious enough to make a cat speak

↳ 정말 맛있어

It's just a routine check

↳ 그냥 일상 하는 검사야

It's just another day

↳ 오늘도 어제 같은 그저 그런 하루로군

It's just one of those things. Nothing much

↳ 그런 건 일상 있는 일이야. 대단치는 않아

It's mean of you to rush for a seat

↳ 빈자리를 향해 돌진하는 것은 꼴사나워

It's murder in the rush hours in Seoul

↳ 서울의 러시아워엔 말도 못해

▸ **meticulous**   extremely careful in attending
to details

It's my home away from home

↳ 마치 집 같은 곳이지

It's obvious things will get tough

↳ 고생문이 훤하군

> (=Things are sure to get tough)
> (=Things will clearly get tough)
> (=It looks like tough times are ahead)

It's only a step(stone' throw)

↳ 바로 코앞이야

It's something I cherish(treasure)

↳ 그건 내 보물단지

> (=It's very dear to me)

It's staring you in the face

↳ 네 눈(코) 앞에 있잖아

It's time to go to bed and there's to be no nonsense

↳ 객쩍은 소리(수작) 그만하고 잠이나 자

Jin-soo made my day

↳ 진수 덕분에 신나는 하루였어

Jung-ah had her mouth full and couldn't get the words out

↳ 정아는 입에 밥이 들어있어서 말하기 힘들었어(get something out 은 "입이 안 떨어지다"의 뜻도 있음)

Just ride it out until the end of the month

· **obvious** plain or unmistakable

· **cherish** hold dear

↳ 월말까지만 참고 견뎌라

Keep your voice down

↳ 목소리 좀 줄여라

Knock before you barge in on people taking showers

↳ 샤워하는데 마구 들어오기 전에 노크를 해

Ladies and gentlemen, I give you the National Statistical Office

↳ 여러분, 통계청의 발전을 위하여 건배합시다

Less noise, please

↳ 좀 조용히 해

Let me dash off a letter to him before we go shopping

↳ 쇼핑 가기 전에 그에게 보낼 편지를 재빨리 쓸게

Let my things alone

↳ 내 물건은 그대로 둬

Let's check out(visit) the plumbing before we go

↳ 떠나기 전에 화장실에 들러서 가자

Let's draw for it

↳ 제비뽑기하자

Let's drink to the guest of honor, Mr. Song

↳ 우리의 주빈 송 선생님을 위하여 건배합시다

Let's eat, drink, and be merry, for tomorrow is another day

↳ 내일은 내일이니 오늘을 즐기자

Let's have a ball

↳ 신나게 놀아보자

Let's have a big round of applause

↳ 박수를 보내자

› **barge** move rudely or clumsily
› **applause** a clapping in approval

Let's have a night out together
↳ 하룻밤 어울려 놀자구나

Let's not see this uninteresting part, I'll see the film on to the exciting scene
↳ 이 재미없는 대목은 보지말고 필름을 돌려서 재미있는 대목을 볼 거야

Let's play first, whatever may happen afterwards
↳ 나중에야 어찌되든 놀고 보자

Let's raise our glasses to Jong-moon
↳ 종문을 위해서 건배합시다

Let's see if we can get them wholesale and save ourselves some money
↳ 그 물건들을 도매로 사서 얼마간의 돈이라도 절약할 수 있을지 한 번 보자

Let's see what the bad news is
↳ 계산(청구서, 고지서)이 얼마나 나왔는지 어디 보자

Let's see who gets there fastest
↳ 저기까지 누가 먼저가나 내기할까?

(=I'll race you to see who gets there fastest)

Let's sleep on it
↳ 하룻밤 자며 생각하자, 신중히 생각하자

Let's trim off(away) the unnecessary parts of our spending
↳ 불필요한 비용을 줄이자

Living on my uncle make me feel small
↳ 아저씨 댁에 기식하자니 눈치가 보여

› **wholesale** sale of goods in quantity for resale by a retail merchant

› **trim** decorate, make neat or reduce by cutting

Living out of a suitcase can make a person get homesick
↳ 떠돌이 생활은 사람을 향수에 젖게 한다

Living out there in the middle of nowhere will be fun sometimes
↳ 가끔씩 아무도 없는 그런 외딴 곳에 사는 것도 재미있을 거야

Look at all this rubbish and broken glass everywhere. Words fail me
↳ 사방에 널려있는 이 쓰레기며 유리조각 좀 봐. 말이 안 나오네

Lots of people have been driven back on cheaper clothes by the rises in prices
↳ 물가가 오르자 많은 사람들이 싼 옷을 다시 입게됐다

Lulu'll be late for her own funeral, let's not wait for her
↳ 루루는 항상 늦게 오는 사람이니 기다리지 말자

Make a few holes in the bottom of this plant pot to allow the water to drain out
↳ 화분 밑바닥에 구멍을 몇 개 뚫어 물을 빼어라

Make each day count
↳ 하루하루를 의미 있게 살아라

Make it up as you go along
↳ 임기응변으로 해라

Make no sorrows of something you lost
↳ 한 번 잃어버린 것을 한탄하지 마라

Make sure that your picnic doesn't clash with the alumni meeting
↳ 너의 야유회 날짜가 동창회와 중복이 안되도록 해

Make sure to sort out the recyclables
↳ 재활용 쓰레기를 확실히 분리해 둬라

Make your presence known before you come in
↳ 인기척이나 하고 들어와

· **homesick** longing for home
· **alumni** graduate

Man-soo always sings out of tune
↳ 만수는 음치야

Many city dwellers yearn for the idyllic life of the country
↳ 많은 도시 거주자들은 시골의 목가적인 생활을 동경한다

Many farmers are pouring away gallons of milk that has gone sour everyday
↳ 많은 농장에서 매일 다량의 쉬어진 우유를 쏟아버린다

Many taxpayers are up in arms when they got their tax bills
↳ 많은 납세자가 고지서를 받아보고는 화를 내었다

Min-ho was spoken to by a stranger
↳ 민호에게 낯선 사람이 말을 걸었다

Moo-ho has moved so often that he finds no difficulty in putting down roots
↳ 무호는 너무 자주 여기저기 이사를 다녔기 때문에 새로 자리를 잡아
나가는데는 어려움 없이 대처해 나갔다

Moon-soo can't call his time his own
↳ 문수는 정신없이 바빠

Moon-soo has a frog in the throat
↳ 문수는 목이 쉬어있어

(=Moon-soo has lost his voice)

Morning comes whether you set the alarm or not
↳ 알람을 맞춰놓든 아니든 아침은 온다

Mountain-climbing over the weekend made me ready to drop
↳ 주말에 등산을 갔더니 몸이 천근이다

· **idyll**   poem describing peaceful country
life, fit subject for an idyll

My body won't listen to me
> ㄴ 몸이 전혀 말을 안 들어

> (=My energy level has dropped)
> (=I'm not feeling well)
> (=My body is feeling week)

My brain isn't working today
> ㄴ 오늘은 머리가 잘 안 돌아

My daughter ties up the bathroom every morning
> ㄴ 우리 딸이 화장실을 오래 쓰는 통에 아무도 쓸수 가 없어

My days are full
> ㄴ 매일 바빠

My days are pretty much the same
> ㄴ 매일 생활이 똑같아요

My dogs are killing me after walking around town all day
> ㄴ 온 종일 시내를 돌아다녔더니 발이 아파

My fingers have gone stiff from lack of practice
> ㄴ 연습을 안 했더니 손가락이 굳었어

My handwriting is nothing but chicken scratches
> ㄴ 내 필적은 괴발개발이야

My name in Korean alphabet goes like this
> ㄴ 홍길동. 내 이름은 한글로 '홍 길동'이라고 써

My shoes have worn down since I started walking so much
> ㄴ 내가 이 신을 신고 많이 돌아다녔더니 해져버렸다

My shoes take a high polish

› **stiff** not bending easily, tense, formal, strong

› **polish** make smooth and glossy, develop or refine

ㄴ 내 구두는 광이 잘 나

My shoes were caked with mud

ㄴ 내 신발에는 진흙이 달라붙었다

My sides hurt=It kept me in stitches

ㄴ 배꼽 빠지는 줄 알았어

My socks keep slipping down

ㄴ 양말이 자꾸 미끄러져 내려오네

My wife got after me to hang up the clothes

ㄴ 집사람이 내게 옷을 걸어놓으라고 성화였어

Nam-soo was in the neighborhood

ㄴ 남수는 근처에 왔다가 들렀대

Never mind, I've got a well-lined pocket today

ㄴ 걱정 마, 오늘은 주머니 사정이 괜찮으니까

No end is in sight

ㄴ 오리무중이다

No goose eggs this week. We are on a roll

ㄴ 이번 주에는 공치는 날이 없군. 행운이 겹치는군

No more than I have to

ㄴ 그냥 슬슬 하면서 지내고 있어

No peace(rest) for the wicked

ㄴ 죄지은 사람은 발뻗고 못자

No, I don't put any stock in such superstition

ㄴ 아니, 난 그런 비과학적인 건 안 믿어

Nobody observed him ever trying the door

ㄴ 아무도 그가 한 번이라도 문단속 확인하는 것을 본 적이 없다

› **wicked** morally bad, harmful or troublesome, very unpleasant, mischievous

› **superstition** beliefs based on ignorance, fear of the unknown, or trust in magic

Not for at least an hour
> ↳ 한 시간 이상 기다려야 해

Nothing can go right toady
> ↳ 오늘은 되는 일이 없어

Nothing costs so much as what's given us
> ↳ 공짜보다 더 비싼 건 없다

Nothing makes a man more reverent than a library
> ↳ 도서관보다 더 사람을 경건하게 만드는 것은 없다

Nothing works out the way I want it to
> ↳ 마음대로 되는 일이 없어

Now is now, and then was then
> ↳ 지금은 지금이고 그 때는 그 때다

Now this is the life
> ↳ 이제야 살맛이 나는군

Now we must reconcile ourselves to a reduced standard of living
> ↳ 이제 우리는 줄어든 생활비를 감수해야 한다

Now you are burning
> ↳ 궁금해 죽겠지(퀴즈 등)

Now you have learned to stay afloat, you'll feel better about water from now on
> ↳ 넌 이제 물위에 뜨는 법을 배웠으니 이제 물에 대한 두려움은 없어질 거야

Now you have to make your living by the sweat of your brow
> ↳ 이제 열심히 일 해서 생활비를 벌어 와야 해

Nowadays smoking is no longer the in thing to do
> ↳ 담배를 피우는 건 더 이상 인기 없어

› **revere** show honor and devotion to

› **reconcile** cause to be friendly again, adjust or settle, bring to acceptance

Number one or number two?
> ↳ 소변이냐 대변이냐?

Oh-yung will now oblige us with a song
> ↳ 이제 오영이가 노래를 한 곡 부르겠습니다

Old people these days tend to keep to themselves
> ↳ 요즈음의 노인들은 고독하게 지내게 마련이다

On his way home, he visited all of his stamping(stomping) ground
> ↳ 집에 오다가 단골이란 단골은 다 들렀어

Once he falls asleep, he's dead to the world
> ↳ 그가 일단 잠들고 나면 세상 모르고 잔다

Once prices go up, they stay up
> ↳ 물가는 한 번 오르면 떨어질 줄 몰라

One day is quite like another
> ↳ 그 날이 그 날이야

One of these days are none of these days
> ↳ 조만간 이란 말은 아무 날에도 안 하겠다는 말이다

One who has the reputation of an early riser may safely lie abed till noon
> ↳ 일찍 일어나는 것으로 알려진 사람이 정오까지 일어나지 않을 수도 있다

Only a few people questioned said they ignored TV newscasts
> ↳ 질문 받은 사람들 중 몇 사람만이 텔레비전 뉴스방송에 관심을 쓰지 않는 것으로 답했다

Our fingers had gone dead and we couldn't write our names
> ↳ 우리는 손가락이 곱아서 이름을 쓸 수가 없었다

Our memories are independent of our wills

> ‣ **stamp** pound with the sole of the foot or a heavy implement, impress with a mark

> ‣ **independent** not governed by another, not requiring or relying on something or somebody else

↳ 우리의 기억은 우리의 의지와는 별개이다

Our(My) house is your house

↳ 우리 집에서 편히 지내세요

Paying my monthly bills always leaves me high and dry

↳ 매월 청구서를 지불하고 나면 항상 무일푼이야

People are getting hard-hearted in these days of high prices

↳ 요즘 물가가 올라 인심이 각박해지고 있다

Plants usually respond to proper treatment

↳ 식물은 보통 돌보기만 잘하면 잘 자란다

Please insert the ticket in the slot to the right of the gate entrance and retrieve the ticket when passing through the gate

↳ 티켓을 입구 오른쪽에 있는 길쭉한 구멍에 집어넣은 뒤 문을 통과하고 난 뒤 되찾아 주십시오

Please pitch in with the dishes

↳ 설거지하는데 좀 도와줄래

Please tell me when you need a nature stop

↳ 화장실 갈 일 있으면 말만 해

Plug this hole up so the cold air doesn't get in

↳ 찬바람이 안 들어오게 구멍을 메워라

Poke your hand through this crack and see if you can reach any coins there

↳ 이 벌어진 틈 사이로 손을 푹 집어넣어 거기 동전이 있는지 찾아봐

Practice gives facility

↳ 연습을 하면 솜씨가 늘게 돼 있어

Prayer is when you talk to God; meditation is when you listen to God

---

› **retrieve** search for and bring in game, recover

› **meditate** contemplate

ㄴ 기도는 하나님에게 말씀을 드리는 것이며, 명상은 하나님으로부터의
소리를 듣는 것이다

Prices for everyday item rise
ㄴ 기본 생필품 가격이 오르고 있다

Prices will keep up
ㄴ 물가가 계속 오를 것 같아

Procrastination is the art of keeping up with yesterday
ㄴ 뒤로 미루는 것은 어제와의 연락을 끌어가는 기술이다

Procrastination is the thief of time
ㄴ 뒤로 미루는 것은 시간을 도둑맞는 일이다

Put your room to right
ㄴ 방 좀 치워라

> (=Put(Set) you room in order)
> (=Straighten(Tidy) your room)

Pyung-soo puts a portion of his salary in the savings account each month
ㄴ 평수는 월급의 일부를 매달 보통예금 계좌에 넣는다

Pyung-soo always comes out well in his picture
ㄴ 평수는 언제나 사진이 잘 나와

Pyung-soo was reduced to a pulp
ㄴ 평수는 몹시 지쳐 있었어

Pyung-soo's picture didn't come out right
ㄴ 평수의 사진은 잘 안나왔어

Quite a few theatergoers began to trickle in an hour before the show

---

· **procrastinate** put something off until later | · **pulp** soft part of a fruit or vegetable, softmoist mass

ㄴ 영화 상영 한시간 전에 모여들기 시작한 관객들이 꽤 많아졌다

Remain under the umbrella so you don't get wet
    ㄴ 비 맞지 않게 우산을 쓰고 다녀라

Return me the novel when you have done it
    ㄴ 그 소설을 다 읽거든 돌려 줘

Run back the tape and listen again
    ㄴ 테이프를 되돌려서 또 한 번 들어봐라

Sang-soo has moved in before I knew what had happened and sponged on us for three months
    ㄴ 영문도 모르는 사이에 상수는 우리 집으로 이사해 왔고 석달씩 이나 얹혀 살았다

Sang-soo paid all that money to see the concert and slept through the whole thing
    ㄴ 상수는 그 큰돈을 주고 음악회에 갔다가 내내 잠만 쿨쿨 자고 왔다

Sang-soo stole away without anyone seeing him
    ㄴ 상수는 아무도 모르게 슬쩍 가버렸다

Sang-soo will make himself ill if he tries to squeeze any more activities in
    ㄴ 상수가 더 이상 무리한 시간을 내어 다른 활동까지 하려고 한다면 병이 나고 말 거야

Seal up the envelope in order to make it confidential
    ㄴ 봉투를 남이 뜯어볼 수 없게 봉해라

See if you can drop out that ugly wall at the side of the house
    ㄴ 사진에 집 한쪽의 벽이 나오지 않게 찍어봐

Set the camera lens to infinity
    ㄴ 카메라의 렌즈를 무한대에 맞추어라

· **sponge**   living at another's expense
· **infinity**   quality or state of being infinite

She always goes into her song and dance about the subway being delayed
> ↳ 그 여자는 항상 지하철이 연착됐다고 그럴싸하게 둘러대

She always waits until the eleventh hour
> ↳ 그 여자는 늘 최후 순간까지 미룬다

She barred herself in
> ↳ 그 여자는 자기 집에 처박혀서 아무도 안 만났어

She can no longer pay her way alone
> ↳ 그 여자는 이제 더 이상 혼자서는 밥값도 못해

She chose to drop out of the picture and live in obscurity
> ↳ 그녀는 스스로 사람들에게서 멀어져 나가는 길을 택하여 사람들의 눈에 띄지 않게 살았다

She could only flounder through her song
> ↳ 그녀는 노래를 더듬더듬 간신히 불렀다

She couldn't see her way to allowing us to rent the house
> ↳ 그 여자는 우리에게 집을 세놓을 사정이 아니었다

She crept toward the door, hugging the pillar so as not to be seen
> ↳ 그녀는 들키지 않으려고 살며시 현관문 쪽으로 기어갔다

She earns very hard bread by sewing
> ↳ 바느질로 겨우 생계를 이어

She flickered away(off) the butterfly from her sleeve
> ↳ 그녀는 소매에 붙은 나비를 탁 쳐서 쫓아 버렸다

She got one of her fingers trapped in the door
> ↳ 그녀는 손가락이 문에 끼었다

She has a brain like a sieve and always forget the secret number
> ↳ 그녀는 너무 기억력이 나빠서 늘 비밀번호를 잊어버린다

- **delay**   postpone, stop or hinder for a time
- **flicker**   waver, burn unsteadily

She has been banging away at her typewriter full steam ahead all day
> ↳ 그녀는 종일 있는 속력을 다 내어 타이프를 치고 있다

She knows enough Chinese to get by in it
> ↳ 그녀는 중국어로 일상생활을 하는 데는 충분하다

She said her period was irregular
> ↳ 그 여자는 생리가 불순하다고 했어

She was out like a light when she went to bed
> ↳ 그 여자는 잠자리에 들자마자 골아 떨어졌다

She went down on her knees and began to pray
> ↳ 그 여자는 무릎을 꿇고 기도하기 시작했다

She'll be in and out all day today
> ↳ 그 여자는 오늘 하루종일 들락날락 할 거야

She's been after her daughter all day to clean up her room
> ↳ 그 여자는 자기 딸에게 방 좀 치우라고 하루종일 성화다

She's been in and out all day today
> ↳ 그 여자는 오늘 외출이 많았어

She's going to add to this house as soon as she moves in
> ↳ 그 여자는 이사 들자마자 이 집을 증축하려고 해

She's long sung the praise of country life and finally moved to Yong-in
> ↳ 그녀는 오랫동안 전원생활에 찬사를 보내더니 끝내 용인으로 이사를 갔다

She's taking a hard breath because she's late and hurried
> ↳ 그녀는 늦어서 서두르느라고 숨을 몰아쉬고 있다

Shut the door after you
> ↳ 들어올 때에 문을 닫아라

‣ **pray** entreat, ask earnestly for something, address a divinity

Slick up this room before company gets home
↳ 손님이 집에 오시기 전에 이 방을 정돈해 놔

Some land goes with the house
↳ 그 집에는 약간의 토지가 딸려 있어

Some people sprawl about on the seat so that there's no room for anyone else
↳ 어떤 사람들은 자리에 퍼져 앉아서 다른 사람이 앉을 자리가 없다

Somebody left the umbrella behind
↳ 누군가가 우산을 두고 갔어

Sometimes I lie awake at night
↳ 난 가끔씩 밤잠을 설쳐

Sometimes this table doubles as a desk
↳ 이 식탁이 책상으로 쓰이는 때도 있어

Sometimes we have to serve a cracked cup
↳ 때로는 달갑지 않은 손님도 대접해야 해

Sorry. I'm behind the eight ball(broke) this month
↳ 미안하지만 이번 달엔 돈이 없어

Spread the umbrella over your head
↳ 머리에 우산을 받쳐라

State the contents of the package
↳ 소포내용을 써 주라

Stop coming home at all hours
↳ 아무 때나(늦게) 집에 와서 식사하는 버릇은 고쳐라

Stop fluttering about and sit still
↳ 왔다 갔다 하지말고 가만히 앉아 있어

› **slick** very smooth, clever
› **sprawl** lie or sit with limbs spread out

Stop playing at doing the dishes and get the job done
> ↳ 설거지하는 체 하지 말고 일을 제대로 해

Stress is building up day in and day out
> ↳ 밤 낮 스트레스가 쌓인다

Stretch your foot to the length of your blanket
> ↳ 당신의 발을 담요의 길이까지만 뻗어라

Sung-hi is dead to the world
> ↳ 성희는 세상 모르게 자고 있어

Sure, I would like to kick in for the gift
> ↳ 좋아, 선물 사는데 같이 돈 낼께

Tai-ho takes a very good(bad) picture
> ↳ 태호는 사진이 잘 나와

Tai-ho tapped out the ashes on his heels
> ↳ 태호는 담배 재를 구두 뒤축에 대고 털었다

Take litter with you
> ↳ 쓰레기를 버리지 맙시다

Tap your cigarette ash out into the ash tray, not onto the floor
> ↳ 담배 재를 마루바닥에 털지 말고 재떨이에 털어라

That guy got to the front by shouldering his way forward, I'll make him move to the back
> ↳ 저 사람이 남들을 밀어 제치고 앞쪽으로 나갔으니 내가 가서 줄 뒤에 서라고 해야겠다

That's not the very good way to start the day
> ↳ 일진이 안 좋군

That's something between a bench and a sofa
> ↳ 그건 벤치도 소파도 아닌 어중간한 것이다

› **ash**   matter left when something is burned

The boxes are untrue to type
ㄴ 이 상자들은 규격이 안 맞아

The clothes have been out in the sun all day and they should be dry as a bone by now
ㄴ 빨래를 하루종일 햇빛에 말렸으니 지금쯤 바싹 말랐을 것이다

The color of this dress will not run when you wash it
ㄴ 이 옷은 세탁해도 번지지 않아

The concierge asked me gruffly for my identity card
ㄴ 관리인은 퉁명한 목소리로 내게 신분증을 요구했다

The coverage made the news seem lifelike
ㄴ 생중계가 뉴스를 실감나게 만들더군

The crowd became thin as we got a little farther from the downtown
ㄴ 번화가에서 멀어질수록 사람들이 한산해 졌다

The day is closing in
ㄴ 하루해가 저물어 가네(유사 표현: **Night is closing in**밤이 되어 어두워 지는군)

The days are drawing(closing) in(out)
ㄴ 해가 점점 짧아(길어)지고 있어

The dirt clinging to the collar can't be washed out
ㄴ 옷깃에 묻은 때가 지워지지 않는다

The Dragon year is often characterized by bustle and activity
ㄴ 용띠 해에는 바쁘고 여러 가지 일이 생겨

The enormous bills every month clean me out
ㄴ 매월 쏟아지는 공과금 때문에 알거지 꼴이야

The faucet had fallen into disuse and joints had rusted solid
ㄴ 수도꼭지를 사용하지 않아 이음매 부분이 녹이 나서 굳어져 버렸어

› **concierge** manager and doorkeeper of an apartment building

› **gruffly** rough in speech or manner

The fish market springs to life at dawn
> ↳ 새벽이 되면 어시장이 활기를 띠지

The fluorescent tube is going out(flickering, blinking)
> ↳ 형광등이 깜박거려

The gas and water bills really set me back on my heels
> ↳ 가스비와 수도세 때문에 깜짝 놀랐어

The good news followed on the neck of the letter
> ↳ 그 편지에 이어 좋은 소식이 전해졌어

The iron gate jarred against the wall
> ↳ 철문이 담벼락에 부딪쳐 쾅 하고 소리가 났다

The letters were all broken up
> ↳ 글자가 다 깨졌어

The line of people waiting to have meals snaked along slowly
> ↳ 식사하려고 늘어선 사람들의 열이 구불구불 움직였다

The longest day must have an end
> ↳ 기나긴 날도 끝이 있는 법

The man least dependent upon tomorrow goes to meet the tomorrow most cheerfully
> ↳ 내일에 가장 적게 의지하는 사람이 내일을 가장 즐겁게 맞이한다

The mirror fogged up(over), I couldn't see to shave
> ↳ 거울이 부옇게 흐려서 들여다보고 면도를 할 수 없게 됐어

The mist has clouded the mirror over(up)
> ↳ 김이 나서 거울이 흐려졌다

The neighborhood of the airport is a drawback
> ↳ 공항에 가까운 것이 결점이다

› **drawback** disadvantage

The odor soon penetrated the whole building
> ㄴ 그 냄새는 곧 건물 전체에 스며들었다

The people poured back into the village as soon as the floods had gone down
> ㄴ 홍수 물이 빠지자마자 사람들이 몰려서 마을로 되돌아 왔다

The plot was weak(solid)
> ㄴ 애기의 구성이 허술해(잘 짜였어)(영화, **TV**,소설 등)

(=There was no plot)

The postage costs more than the goods
> ㄴ 배보다 배꼽이군

The rent falls due today, don't forget to pay it
> ㄴ 오늘 방세 내는 날이니 잊어버리지마

The slightest touch can cut off the electricity
> ㄴ 조금만 건드려도 전기가 나가게 돼있어

The squalor of that room has to be seen
> ㄴ 그 방은 말도 못하게 더러워(눈으로 봐야 알아)

The washing machine was rattling away so we could hardly hear each other speak
> ㄴ 세탁기가 시끄럽게 움직이고 있어서 서로의 얘기가 들리지 않았다

The window crashed open and voices in the room fell silent
> ㄴ 창문이 쾅 열리자 방안에서 들려오던 말소리가 뚝 끊어졌다

The window was jammed with the girl's head stuck and nobody could get it open

---

› **squalor** quality or state of being squalid | › **rattle** make a series of clattering sounds, say briskly, confuse or upset

↳ 소녀의 목이 창문에 끼어 꼼짝 못한 채 아무도 창문을 열 수가 없었다

Then you have to dip into your savings to pay your bills

↳ 그렇다면 넌 공과금을 내기 위해 저축을 꺼내 쓸 수밖에 없겠구나

Then you have to shift for yourself

↳ 그렇다면 넌 이제 자력으로 생계를 꾸려야겠군

Then you have to trim your sails and give up such luxuries

↳ 그렇다면 씀씀이(활동범위)를 줄이고 그런 사치품은 포기해야 해

There are daily cycles in commuter traffic that correspond with when people go to work and when they return home

↳ 사람들이 출근할 때와 귀가할 때가 일치하는 매일 매일의 출근주기가 있다

There are too many eyes around here

↳ 여긴 보는 눈이 너무 많다

There is a nick(chip) in the plate(dish)

↳ 접시에 이가 나갔군

> (=The dish(plate) is chipped)

There'll be no name-calling in this house

↳ 집안에서 욕을 해선 안 돼

There's no doubt concerning the genuineness of this gem

↳ 이 보석이 진짜라는데 대한 의혹은 없다

There's no harm in trying

↳ 밑져야 본전

There's no hot water running

↳ 따뜻한 물이 안나와요

› **commute** reduce, travel back and forth regularly

› **genuine** being the same in fact as in appearance

There's nothing better than being on good terms with your neighbors
↳ 이웃과 잘 지내는 것보다 좋은 게 없어

There's only so much I can take
↳ 참을 만큼 참았어

These old buildings have a touch of class
↳ 이 오래된 건물들은 품위가 있다

These tickets are good for ten days
↳ 이 표는 10일간 유효

These walls are made of light materials and thus will not support heavy roof structures
↳ 이 벽들은 가벼운 소재로 되어 있어서 무거운 구조물로 된 지붕은 버티지 못할 것이다

They are being nickel-and-dimed to death by these small daily expenses
↳ 그들은 매일 생기는 세세한 경비 때문에 죽을 지경이다

They are getting by from day to day
↳ 그들은 그날그날 견디어 나가고 있다

They bought a little house to get away from it all
↳ 그들은 도시생활이 싫어서 시골에 작은 집을 샀다

They can just scrape along(by) the little money she earns from her sewing
↳ 그들은 그 여자가 버는 작은 돈으로 연명이나 할 정도야

They caught him dead to rights with the keys in his pocket
↳ 그들은 그의 주머니에 열쇠가 있어 꼼짝 못하게 된 그를 붙잡았다

They commiserated with each other and returned home empty-handed
↳ 그들은 서로 동정하면서 맨손으로 귀가했다

› **scrape**   get along with difficulty
› **commiserate**   sympathize

They couldn't hear(speak) themselves think in there
> ↳ 그들은 거기에 주변이 시끄러워서 아무 소리도 들을 수 없었다

They decided not pull the historic house down
> ↳ 그들인 역사적인 가옥을 헐지 않기로 결정했다

They had to trim their spending down to fit their income
> ↳ 그들은 수입에 맞게 씀씀이를 줄여야 했다

They hardly have enough money to keep body and soul together
> ↳ 그들은 겨우 밥이나 먹고살기에도 급급할 정도야

They have gone so far as to call broadcasters to impose a complete ban on entertainers who are implicated in any wrong-doings
> ↳ 그들은 비행에 연루된 전 연예인들에게 일체의 방송 출연을 금해야 한다고 방송인들에게 요구하게까지 이르렀다

They have never had it so good until now
> ↳ 그들은 그 어느 때 보다도 지금 경제적인 형편이 낫다

They really missed out on wonderful time
> ↳ 그들은 정말 멋진 시간을 놓친 거야

They were pressed to the wall with all their medical bills
> ↳ 그들의 많은 병원비가 큰 부담이 되었다

They'll pull the place down and rebuild. No half measures
> ↳ 그들은 그 곳을 헐고 새 집을 지을 것이다(추호의 양보도 없다)

They've lived in Seoul 50 years upwards
> ↳ 그들은 50년 이상 서울에 살고 있다

They've tried to keep a considerable amount of money tucked away for their retirement
> ↳ 그들은 퇴직에 대비해서 상당한 금액을 따로 저축해 왔다

They'll let the translation run along the bottom of the screen for

---

› **implicate** involve

› **tuck** pull up into a fold

audiences
> ㄴ 그들은 시청자들을 위해 화면 아래쪽에 번역문을 흘려 보낼 것이다

Things are getting down
> ㄴ 살기가 어려워지고 있어

Things command a higher price when they are scarce
> ㄴ 물자가 부족하면 값이 오르게 되어 있지

This amount will tide me over until next month
> ㄴ 이만한 양이면 다음 달까지 견디겠다

This bag weighs a ton
> ㄴ 이 가방은 엄청나게 무거워

This building is being renovated(under renovation)
> ㄴ 이 건물은 내부수리중입니다

This can't be
> ㄴ 그건 말도 안 돼

(=I can't believe it)

This color really jars with the wall color
> ㄴ 이 색은 벽 색깔과 너무 안 어울려

This didn't start yesterday
> ㄴ 어제오늘 일이 아니야

(=This is nothing new)
(=This has been going on way back)

· **tide** be enough to allow to get by for a time

· **renovate** make like new again

This doesn't amount to much
  ↳ 이건 별거 아냐

This door gives onto the garden, leading into the rest room
  ↳ 이 문으로 나가면 정원을 통해서 화장실로 통하게 된다

This evening I'm going to eat in
  ↳ 오늘 저녁은 집에서 식사해요

This has been a real bad hair day
  ↳ 오늘은 정말 되는 일이 없어

This house is a diamond in the rough
  ↳ 이 집을 사 두면 큰 이익이 될 거야

This house is built to last
  ↳ 이 집은 튼튼하게 지어 졌어

This huge house is a milestone about my neck
  ↳ 이 커다란 집이 내게는 무거운 짐이야

This is a fine time of night to come back home
  ↳ 이렇게 밤늦게 집에 돌아오는 녀석이 어디 있어

This is a small token of my good wishes
  ↳ 하찮은 것이지만 축하의 뜻으로 드립니다

This is how I go about it
  ↳ 이게 내 방식

(This is what I believe 이것이 내 신조다)

This is my day
  ↳ 오늘은 일진이 좋은가 봐

› **milestone** significant point in development

This is sink or swim for me
> ↳ 이건 나의 사활이 걸린 문제다

This is the last day I'll come here
> ↳ 다시는 여기에 오나봐라

This is the utmost I can do
> ↳ 난 기껏 그 정도밖엔 못해

This is what I believe
> ↳ 이것이 나의 신조다

This is where we came in
> ↳ 우린 시작단계로 되돌아 온 거야

This means the world to me
> ↳ 이건 내게 중요해(의미가 있어)

This picture does not do her justice
> ↳ 이 사진은 그 여자 실물보다 못하다

This place is too fancy for my blood
> ↳ 여긴 내 취향에는 너무 고급이다

This place stinks to high heaven
> ↳ 냄새가 코를 찌르는군

This record has been gathering dust on my shelves for the past twenty years
> ↳ 이 레코드는 지난 **20**년간 선반에 얹힌 채 한번도 쓰인 일이 없어

This river can kill you in a thousand ways
> ↳ 이 강엔 곳곳에 위험이 도사리고 있다

This room is not large enough; but we'll make it do
> ↳ 이 방은 약간 좁지만 그런 대로 지낼만해

· utmost   most distant, of the greatest or
highest degree or amount

This shelter is framed to resist any storm
ㄴ 이 피신처는 어떤 폭풍에도 견딜 수 있게 만들어졌다

This sofa does double as a bed
ㄴ 이것은 소파와 침대로 겸용할 수 있다

This soft hair brush can hold a large amount of paint
ㄴ 이 부드러운 솔은 페인트를 많이 머금을 수 있다

This tack on the floor was playing hob with the carpet
ㄴ 마룻바닥에 있는 압정이 카페트를 망가뜨리고 있었군

This tape is warped(=broken)
ㄴ 테이프가 늘어났다

This used to be a home away from home
ㄴ 여기는 자주 들렀던 곳이지

This will save the day for you
ㄴ 이걸로 네 얼굴은 설 것이다

Those houses were knocked together after the war
ㄴ 그 집들은 전후에 급조된 것이다

Those were the salad(dog) days
ㄴ 그 땐 한창이었지(고생을 했었지)

Thousands of people poured along the street during the rush hour
ㄴ 출퇴근 시간에 수 천명의 인파가 길거리를 따라 쏟아져 나왔다

Time has jammed the pipe up with dust
ㄴ 오랜 시간에 먼지가 끼어서 파이프가 막혔어

Toss out all those rusty junks
ㄴ 녹슬어있는 저 잡동사니들을 버려라

Under no circumstances should you walk around at night
ㄴ 어떤 일이 있어도 밤에 돌아다니면 안된다

› **tack** small sharp nail, course of action

› **warp** twist out of shape, lead astray, distort

Unexpected company at dinner time caught me flat-footed
> ↳ 저녁준비 없을 때 뜻밖의 손님이 찾아와 당황했어

Wait, I'm not decent yet
> ↳ 난 아직 옷을 안 입었어(목욕, 알몸상태)

Wait. It's being processed(in the works)
> ↳ 처리 중이니 기다리세요

Wan-soo whipped round(whirl about, whirl round) to the mention of his name
> ↳ 완수는 자신의 이름을 부르는 소리를 듣고 홱 돌아보았다

Wardrobes have been built into walls
> ↳ 옷장은 붙박이로 만들어져 있어

Watch where you are going from now on
> ↳ 앞을 똑바로 보고 다녀

We are almost finished(home, there)
> ↳ (목적지에) 거의 다 됐어

> (=We are in the homestretch now)

We are nearly there
> ↳ 이제 거의 다 왔어

We are on different sides of the line
> ↳ 우린 사는 곳이(분야가) 달라

We are running low on groceries and you'd better get some at the store
> ↳ 식료품이 떨어져가고 있으니 가게에 가서 좀 사와야겠다

› **wardrobe** clothes closet, collection or wearing apparel

› **homestretch** last part of a racetrack, final stage

We can see it with the naked eye
> ↳ 그건 육안으로 보여(eyes가 아님)

We can spit on it from here
> ↳ 엎어지면 코 닿을 거리야

> 아주 가까운 거리를 두고 '엎어지면 코 닿을 거리'라고 한다. 영어로는
> 'Within a stone's throw 돌을 던지면 닿을 거리'라고 한다.

We find it very difficult to make both ends meet these days
> ↳ 요즘은 적자 없이 살아가기 힘들어

We get bombarded with mail towards the end of the year
> ↳ 연말에는 우편물이 폭주해요

We have been walking a tight-rope
> ↳ 우린 파산 직전이야

We have to make it through the night here
> ↳ 우린 여기서 밤을 새워야겠는데

We have to straighten our house before company comes
> ↳ 손님 오시기 전에 집을 정돈해야 해

We haven't got a can opener, but this spoon will do the turn
> ↳ 우리에게 깡통따개는 없지만 이 스푼이 그 역할을 해줄 것이다

We need to earn our keeps
> ↳ 우린 모두 밥값은 해야 해

> (=We need to do our part)
> (=We need to contribute)
> (=We need to pitch in)

> **bombard** attack with or as if with artillery

We'll be back after this message
> ↳ 전하는 말씀을 듣고 다시(방송을) 시작하겠습니다

We've been asked up(down, over) before
> ↳ 우린 집으로 초대받은 일이 있어

What a horrible day! I should have stood in bed
> ↳ 끔찍한 날이었어. 이 꼴 안보고 방안에서나 죽치고 있을 걸 그랬어

What a pity to stick(keep) in on a lovely day like this!
> ↳ 이렇게 좋은날 네가 집구석에 틀어박혀 있다니

When he heard his name called, he pricked up his ears
> ↳ 그의 이름이 호명되자 신경을 곤두세우고 들었어

When I let the rent fall into arrears, I'll be asked to leave
> ↳ 방세를 제때에 못 내면 쫓겨나게 돼

When is it on?
> ↳ 언제 중계됩니까?

When it comes to the handwriting, I'm the weakest link
> ↳ 필적으로 말하면 내게 가장 약한 부분이다

When Sung-moon won the lottery, he shouted the news from the roof(house) tops
> ↳ 성문이가 복권에 당첨되자 동네방네 떠들고 다녔어

Who has left the tab running?
> ↳ 누가 수도꼭지를 틀어놓은 채 내버려두었나?

Why don't you settle for a smaller house considering the cost of a big one
> ↳ 큰집에 대한 비용을 생각해서 작은 집으로 하는 게 어때?

Why should he go poking round his house?
> ↳ 왜 그는 집에서 빈들거리며 놀고 지내야 하나?

· **lottery**　drawing of lots with prizes going to winners
· **poke**　prod, dwindle

Will you let me walk under your umbrella
↳ 우산 좀 같이 쓰실 수 있을까요?

(=May I share your umbrella?)

Will you pass me the air?
↳ 담배연기 이쪽으로 안 오게 해 주시겠습니까?

Will you pose for me for a picture?
↳ 사진 한 장 같이 찍지 않겠습니까?

With everyone falling over Ed after he won the big jackpot, he's been living in the fast line
↳ 에드가 거금을 손에 쥐자 모두가 굽실대게 되었으니 흥청거리며 살고 있지

You are always down to the wire at tax-time
↳ 넌 세금 낼 때만 되면 항상 막판까지 가서 내는군

You are very photogenic
↳ 넌 사진 발 잘 받네

(=You turn out well in pictures)

You have never lost the key!
↳ 설마 열쇠를 잃어버린 건 아니겠지

You have the wrong house
↳ 집을 잘못 찾으셨군요

You have to go to bed with chickens and get up early too

› **jackpot** sum of money won

↳ 넌 일찍 자고 일찍 일어나야 해

You look better in photo than in person

↳ 넌 실물보다 사진이 더 잘나왔어

You look much better in person

↳ 실물이 훨씬 낫네

> (=You are better looking than pictures)
> (=Pictures don't do you justice)

You must be putting on a show

↳ 너 쇼(꾀병 등) 하지마

You must beat me two out of three

↳ 삼세판으로 하자

> (=It's two out of three)

You must have been seeing things

↳ 넌 헛것을 본 모양이구나

You must keep track of current affairs

↳ 매일 매일 일어나는 일에 주의를 기울여야 해

You really can carry a tune

↳ 너 정말 노래 잘 하는구나

You'll get six feet under if you continue to smoke a lot

↳ 네가 계속해서 담배를 많이 피우면 죽게 돼있어

You'll kick yourself for not getting up earlier

· **current** occurring in or belonging to the present

ㄴ 넌 좀 더 일찍 일어나지 못한 걸 후회하게 될 거야

You're holding up the line

ㄴ 너 때문에 줄이 늦어지고 있잖아(줄에서 한눈 팔 때)

You're in the wrong line

ㄴ 줄을 잘못 서셨군요

You've been spaced out these days

ㄴ 넌 요즘 필름이 끊어져 있어

Your cigarette ash is very long; knock it off before it falls on the floor

ㄴ 네 담배재가 길게 늘어나고 있어, 바닥에 떨어지기 전에 털어 버려라

Your name flashed across the television screen

ㄴ 네 이름이 텔레비전 화면에 확 지나가더구나

Your smoking may bring on a fit of coughing

ㄴ 흡연은 발작적인 기침을 일으킬 수 있다

› **knock off** stop doing something, do
hurriedly, deduct, kill

116. 자신 & 자만   Self-Esteem

A man is valued as he makes himself valuable
> ↳ 사람은 자신을 얼마나 가치 있는 사람으로 만드느냐에 따라 평가된다

Chul-hee feels more himself
> ↳ 철희는 자신에 대한 긍지를 느끼고 있다

Diffidence is the better part of knowledge
> ↳ 자신 없다고 생각하는 것이 지식의 태반이다

Education is the ability to listen to almost anything without losing your temper or self-confidence
> ↳ 교육이란 화내지 않고 자신감을 잃지 않으며 거의 모든 것을 경청하는 능력이다

Gil-soo has been getting above himself since he won the prize
> ↳ 길수는 상을 받고 나서 자만에 빠져있다

He that is proud eats himself up
> ↳ 자만하는 자는 자신을 먹어치운다

I did a really good job on this, if I say so myself
> ↳ 내 입으로 말하기는 뭐하지만 이건 썩 잘했어

It's not easy for that ambitious man to realize he's a nobody
> ↳ 그 야심에 찬 사람에게 자신이 시시한 사람이라는 걸 인식시키기는 쉽지 않다

Let others mind their own business

› **diffident** reserved

ㄴ 남은 남이고 나는 나다

No matter what I do, I give it my best shot
ㄴ 난 무슨 일을 하던지 최선을 다해

No one can make you feel inferior without your consent
ㄴ 당신의 동의가 없다면 아무도 당신이 열등감을 느끼게 하지 못한다

None are so empty as those who are full of ourselves
ㄴ 자아로 가득 찬 사람처럼 공허한 사람은 없다

Not all things fit all persons - Every man after his fashion
ㄴ 모든 것이 모든 사람에게 맞는 건 아니다 - 사람마다 각자의 방식이 있다

Now I can hold my head up again
ㄴ 이제 다시 당당하게 나가도 되겠군

Now I'm my own boss(master)
ㄴ 이젠 내 세상이다

One learns to know oneself best behind one's back
ㄴ 자기가 없을 때 남들이 하는 말을 들어봐야 자기를 가장 잘 알 수 있다

Pride goes before a fall
ㄴ 교만은 오래 못 가

Pride is a mask of one's own faults
ㄴ 자랑은 자신의 결함을 가리기 위한 것이다

Pride is over-estimation of oneself by reason of self-love
ㄴ 자랑은 자기사랑에서 나온 자신에 대한 과대평가이다

She has climbed into her coffin and pulled down the lid for herself
ㄴ 그 여자는 자신만만하게 살아왔어

Small things make base men proud
ㄴ 하찮은 사람은 하찮은 일에 자부심을 느낀다

› **consent** give permission or approval
› **coffin** box for burial

Such radiant cultural heritage, timeless fragrance of tradition, and unique culture are the pride of every Korean
> ↳ 찬란한 문화유산, 은은한 전통의 향기, 문화적 독창성은 한국인의 자부심이다

Tai-ho thinks no small beer of himself
> ↳ 태호는 꽤 자만심이 있는 사람이다

That's a dodge to win your confidence
> ↳ 그건 너의 신임을 얻으려는 속임수

The best throw of the dice is to throw away himself
> ↳ 주사위를 가장 잘 던지는 것은 자신을 던져버리는 것이다

There is no such flatterer than a man's self
> ↳ 자기 자신보다 자신에게 더 아부하는 사람은 없다

There's but a step between a proud man's glory and disgrace
> ↳ 자부심 있는 자의 영광과 치욕 사이에는 단 한 발자국의 거리에 불과하다

This pretension itself is a very great prejudice
> ↳ 이런 자만 자체가 매우 큰 편견이다

We should put our own house in order before criticizing others
> ↳ 우린 남을 비판하기에 앞서 자기 자신을 돌아봐야 해

Who spits against the wind, it falls on in his face
> ↳ 바람(하늘)에 데고 침을 뱉어 봐야 자신에게 되돌아온다

다른 사람을 해치려다가 결국은 자신에게 해가 돌아간다는 뜻이다. 한국에서는 '누워서 침 뱉기'가 있고, 영어로는 비슷한 'Spit in the wind 바람에 침 뱉기'와 'Piss in the wind 바람에 오줌누기'가 있다. 바람을 마주보고 침을 뱉거나 오줌을 누면 결국 자신한테도 돌아오는 법이다. 조금 더 점잖은 표현으로는 "Cut off your nose to spite your face 코를 깎아서 얼굴을 망친다"가 있다.

- **radiant** glowing, beaming with happiness, transmitted by radiation
- **prejudice** damage especially to one's rights

You're forgetting yourself
ㄴ 네 자신을 알아라

(=Know your limitation)

Yung-joh burst at the seams with pride
ㄴ 영조는 가슴이 벅차 오르는 자부심을 느꼈다

› **pride** quality or state of being proud

117. 자유　　　　　　Freedom

A hungry man is more interested in four sandwiches than four freedoms
　　　↳ 배고픈 사람에게는 네 가지 자유보다 네 개의 샌드위치가 낫다

Emancipation from the bondage of the soil is no freedom for the tree
　　　↳ 나무가 땅의 속박에서 해방된다는 것은 자유가 아니다

Fettered by old customs, they are unable to act freely
　　　↳ 그들은 낡은 관습에 묶여 자유롭게 행동하지 못한다

Freedom is not free
　　　↳ 자유는 거저 주어지는 것이 아니다

Freedom is the greatest fruit of self-sufficiency
　　　↳ 자유는 자급자족에 대한 최상의 열매이다

Freedom is the will to be responsible to ourselves
　　　↳ 자유는 우리 자신에게 책임지겠다는 의지이다

He only earns his freedom and existence who daily conquers them anew
　　　↳ 매일 매일 자유와 생존을 정복해 나가는 사람만이 그것을 쟁취한다

If we were free to make any remark individually, we wouldn't have to seek safety in numbers or resort to group activities
　　　↳ 우리가 개인적으로 아무 말이나 할 수 있는 자유를 가졌다면 다수를

▸ **emancipate** set free
▸ **fetter** chain or shackle for the feet

빌린 안전을 찾거나 단체행동에 호소하려하지 않을 것이다

If you can't be free, be as free as you can
↳ 자유롭게 되고 싶거든 할 수 있는데까지 자유를 가져라

In the truest sense freedom can't be bestowed, it must be achieved
↳ 가장 진정한 의미에서 자유는 주어지는 게 아니라 쟁취하는 것이다

It's unconscionable for us to ignore the prisoners of war that dedicated their lives to guarding our country's freedom and democracy
↳ 우리는 자유와 민주주의를 위해 헌신한 전쟁포로들을 잊는다는 것은 비양심적인 일이다

Liberty doesn't work as good in practice as it does in speech
↳ 자유를 실행하는 것이 말처럼 쉽게 이루어지는 것이 아니다

Liberty entails responsibility
↳ 자유에는 책임이 따른다

Liberty exists in proportion to wholesome resistance
↳ 자유는 건전한 저항에 비례한다

Liberty is apt to degenerate into lawlessness
↳ 자유는 방종으로 흐르기 쉬워

Liberty is the right to do what the laws permit
↳ 자유는 법률이 허용한 권리이다

People demand freedom only when they have no power
↳ 사람들은 힘이 없을 때에만 자유를 요구한다

Perfect freedom is preserved for the man who lives by his own work and in that work what he wants to do
↳ 완전한 자유는 자신의 일 때문에 살고 그 일이 자신이 하고싶은 일일 때 유지된다

› **bestow** give
› **entail** involve as a necessary result

The best road to progress is freedom's road
ㄴ 진보를 위한 최상의 길은 자유의 길이다

The best use of man can of his freedom is to place limitation on it
ㄴ 사람이 그의 자유를 최대한 누리는 것은 그의 자유에 제한을 두는 일이다

The history of liberty is a history of limitation of government, not the increase of it
ㄴ 자유의 역사는 정부의 확대가 아닌 축소의 역사이다

The history of the world is none other than the progress of the conscience of the freedom
ㄴ 세계역사는 바로 양심의 자유의 진로이다

The shallow consider liberty a release from all law, from every constraint
ㄴ 생각이 얕은 사람들은 자유를 모든 법률과 모든 구속으로부터의 해방으로 여긴다

The true charter of liberty is independence, maintained by force
ㄴ 참된 자유의 선언은 힘으로 지켜내는 독립이다

The tyrant claims freedom to kill freedom
ㄴ 독재자는 자유를 말살할 자유를 요구한다

The upside of their proposal is that it would give him the freedom of act
ㄴ 그들의 제안에서 긍정적인 면은 그에게 행동의 자유가 주어진다는 점이다

There can be no real freedom without the freedom to fail
ㄴ 실패할 자유 없이는 참된 자유가 없다

To renounce liberty is to renounce being a man

› **charter** document granting rights
› **tyrant** harsh ruller having absolute power

› **renounce** give up, refuse, or resign

ㄴ 자유를 포기하는 것은 인간이기를 포기하는 것이다

Too little liberty brings stagnation, and too much brings chaos

ㄴ 자유가 너무 적으면 침체해지고 너무 많으면 혼란해진다

True freedom is to share all the chains our brothers wear

ㄴ 진정한 자유란 우리의 형제들이 차고있는 족쇄의 고통을 함께 하는데 있다

True individual freedom can't exist without economic security and independence

ㄴ 경제적 안정과 독립 없이는 진정한 개인적 자유가 보장될 수 없다

Tyranny is always better organized than freedom

ㄴ 압제정치는 늘 자유보다 조직화 되어있다

What space and time have been to physicists, liberty and quality have been and still are to democratic theories

ㄴ 공간과 시간이 물리학자에게 관련되는 것처럼, 자유와 평등이 민주주의 이론에 관련되어 왔고 여전히 계속 관련이 있다

What the proponents of sexual freedom have grossly overlooked is that without a sense of responsibility there's no genuine freedom

ㄴ 성의 자유를 옹호하는 사람들이 크게 간과하고 있는 것은 책임감 없이는 어떠한 진정한 자유도 없다는 사실이다

While we strive to live most free, we are caught in our own toils

ㄴ 우리가 가장 자유롭게 살기 위해 애쓰는 가운데 우리 자신이 그 수고에서 벗어나지 못한다

You can(are free to) think what you want

ㄴ 착각은 자유다

> (=You can believe whatever you want)
> (=You are entitled to think what you want)

· **stagnant** not moving or active | · **overlook** look down on, fail to see, ignore, pardon

118. 재판   Trials

All the evidence makes in the same direction
↳ 모든 증거가 같은 방향을 가리키고 있다

Bong-doo finally pulled a confession out of Jong-soo
↳ 봉두는 마침내 종수에게서 자백을 받아냈어

For their money, you'd be better off forgetting about the lawsuit
↳ 그들의 의견으로는 너의 소송 따위는 그만두는 게 좋겠다는 거야

He'll sue your pants off if you are not obedient
↳ 네가 고분고분하게 나오지 않으면 그가 고소를 해서 큰돈이 들것이다

Judges must be incorruptible and everything must be done according to the law
↳ 판사는 청렴해야 하고 모든 일은 법대로 처리돼야 한다

Only a minuscule fraction of all litigation reaches the Supreme Court
↳ 모든 소송 중에 극소수만 대법원까지 가게된다

Pyung-ho made a petition to have his case heard in court
↳ 평수는 법정소송을 위해 탄원서를 제출했다

She may have to answer for it before a judge
↳ 그녀는 판사 앞에서 벌을 받아야할지 몰라

She retracted her confession later, saying it was made under duress
↳ 그녀는 자신의 자백이 강박에 의해 이루어졌다면서 나중에 자백을 취소했다

› **minuscule** very small   › **duress** coercion
› **litigate** carry on a lawsuit

She rushed out of the court with a pack of reporters at her heels
      ㄴ 그녀는 기자들이 대거 몰려오자 황급히 법정을 빠져나갔다

She was cited for violating the regulation and sought to have her heavy fines absolved
      ㄴ 그녀는 그 규정을 어겼기 때문에 소환장을 받고는 무거운 벌금을 면할 방법을 찾고 있다

She's already out of the picture
      ㄴ 그 여자는 이미 검토대상에서 제외됐어

Show no partiality in your decisions
      ㄴ 판정에 편파성이 있으면 안 돼

The auditors and the lawmakers began to grill him for answers to why and how the vital waterways were allowed to reach an abominable state
      ㄴ 감사관들과 국회의원들은 그에게 왜 그리고 어떻게 그 중요한 수로가 그렇게 지독하게 방치되었는지 답변을 요구하며 닦달했다

The Constitutional Court ruled that a law banning out-of-school tutoring is unconstitutional and infringes the basic rights of the people more than is necessary
      ㄴ 헌법재판소는 과외 금지가 헌법에 어긋나며 국민의 기본권을 필요 이상으로 침해하는 것이라고 판결했다

The crooked lawyer did them out of twenty million won
      ㄴ 그 악덕변호사는 그들에게서 이천만원을 우려먹었다

The defendant turned pale and went head over heels onto the courtroom floor
      ㄴ 피고인은 창백해지더니 마루바닥으로 고꾸라져 쓰러졌다

The detective is on a fishing expedition now

· **cite** summon before a court, quote | · **absolve** set free of the consequences of guilt

ㄴ 형사가 진상조사 중이다

The investigation blew the lid off
ㄴ 조사를 통해 사실이 드러났어

The judge severely castigated the criminal before remitting him to the custody of the prison
ㄴ 판사는 죄수를 교도소에 구금토록 보내기 전에 크게 꾸짖었다

The judge threw the book at him for a gamut of felony charges running from the armed robbery to trickery
ㄴ 판사는 그가 무장강도에서 사기범에 이르기까지 모든 범죄를 종횡무진하게 저질러왔기 때문에 그를 엄벌에 처했다

The jury is still on that issue
ㄴ 그 문제에 대해서는 아직도 결정을 못 내리고 있다

The last 5 minutes determine the issue
ㄴ 최후의 5분이 중요해

The young man went to pieces when the judge said he would have to go to prison
ㄴ 판사가 젊은이를 징역형에 처한다고 하자 그는 정신(자제력)을 잃었다

There's much to be said on both sides
ㄴ 양쪽 다 할 말은 많아

There's no evidence to the contrary
ㄴ 그렇지 않다는 증거는 없다

They are still grilling the suspect for the kidnapping
ㄴ 그들은 아직도 유괴 혐의자를 심문하고 있어

They are waiting for him to come round so they can question him about the attack
ㄴ 그들은 그가 의식이 돌아와서 그의 공격적 행위에 대해 질문할 수 있

› **castigate** chastise severely
› **gamut** entire range or series

게 되기를 기다리고 있다

They have not been able to get past the finger-pointing stage
ㄴ 그들은 아직도 누구의 잘못인가를 찾아내는 단계에서 벗어나지 못하고 있다

They'll be clear if they all stick to the same story
ㄴ 그들이 모두 입을 맞춘다면 무죄로 판정될 것이다

We filed for court receivership
ㄴ 우린 법정관리 신청했어

When he got the punishment he deserved, he laughed on the other side of his face
ㄴ 그가 마땅히 받아야할 벌을 받게되자, 웃다가 우는 꼴이 되었어

When the facts in this case stared the judge in the face, there was nothing he could do but acquit
ㄴ 이 사건에 대한 사실이 명확해지자 판사는 무죄를 선고할 수 없었다

Witnesses ought to stick to the facts and leave aside all emotion and sentiment
ㄴ 증인은 사실에 벗어나지 않게 증언해야 하며 감정과 정서는 배제해야 한다

You have the right to be silent
ㄴ 넌 묵비권을 행사할 수 있어

› **acquit** pronounce not guilty
› **sentiment** belief, feeling

119. 제안   Proposal

All he has done is put a damper on every suggestion
> 그가 한 일은 모든 제안에 대해 생트집 잡는 것이었어

Am I to understand you have agreed to the proposal?
> 그 제안에 동의한 것으로 이해해도 되겠습니까?

Bong-soo raised a few good points, but An-do shot him down immediately
> 봉수가 몇 가지 좋은 안을 제기했지만 안도가 즉각 묵살해 버렸다

Don't forget that your suggestion can backfire
> 네 제안이 역효과를 낼 수도 있다는 걸 잊지 마라

Her idea of hiring a convicted sex offender went over like a lead balloon
> 성 범죄자를 고용하자던 그 여자의 제안은 차가운 반응에 부딪쳤다

His proposal is dead in the water this year
> 그의 제안이 금년 중에는 거론도 안 돼

If he makes(offers) new proposals, we should seize them with both hands
> 그가 새로운 제안들은 내놓는다면 감지덕지 할 일이지

Let him down easily(gently)
> 창피하지 않게 살며시 알려주어라

Let him stew in his own juice

› **damper** movable plate to regulate a flue draft   › **seize** take by force

ㄴ 그가 자승자박하게 내버려둬

Let it go at that
ㄴ 그 정도로 넘어가자

Let me feel out Jung-soo about this matter
ㄴ 이 일은 정수한테 알아볼게

Let nature take its course
ㄴ 일이 되는 대로 내버려둬

Let the future take care of itself
ㄴ 나중에 어떻게 되겠지 뭐

Let things drift
ㄴ 될 대로 내버려둬

Let your fingers do the walking
ㄴ 손가락으로 짚어가며 찾아봐라

Let's address ourselves to the matters at hand
ㄴ 현안 문제부터 해결하자

Let's adopt his plan in its integrity
ㄴ 그의 계획을 그대로 받아들이자

Let's agree to bury the whole thing
ㄴ 모든 걸 잊어버리기로 하자

Let's beat(get) the show on the road
ㄴ 본격적으로 시작해 볼까

Let's brazen it through
ㄴ 밀어 부쳐 보자

Let's call it quits
ㄴ 없었던 일로 하자

› **drift** float or be driven along

› **braze** solder with an alloy that has a relatively lower melting temperature

> (=Let bygones be bygones)
> (=Let's say the incident never happened)
> (=Let's ignore that incident)

Let's cash up some money to have a party
ㄴ 돈을 좀 추렴해서 회식하자

Let's chip in some money for his farewell gift
ㄴ 그에게 줄 작별선물 사게 돈을 좀 추렴하자

Let's concentrate on one problem at a time
ㄴ 문제를 하나 하나 생각해 보자

Let's do away with all ceremony
ㄴ 형식적인 것은 그만 두자

Let's do away with these lots of red tape
ㄴ 이 번잡스러운 절차를 없애자

Let's do it now and have(get) done with it
ㄴ 곧 착수해서 해치우자

Let's face it
ㄴ 인정할 건 인정하자

Let's follow the path of least resistance
ㄴ 제일 쉬운 방법을 택하자

Let's get on with the job at hand first
ㄴ 우선 현안문제부터 처리하자

Let's go and give it the once-over
ㄴ 가서 어떤 건지 대충 보자

Let's go and see if I lost my touch
ㄴ 가서 내 실력이 살아있는지 한번 보자

› **farewell** wish or welfare at parting, departure

Let's have done with it
ㄴ 그 일은 손떼기로 하자(이해 못할 수도 있음)

Let's have separate checks(pay our own bills). I'm a little short
ㄴ 각자 내기로 하자. 난 돈이 약간 모자라

Let's just forget that we had that talk
ㄴ 없었던 일(이야기)로 하자

Let's just hold it in abeyance until things get better
ㄴ 사정이 나아질 때까지 보류하자

Let's keep it that way
ㄴ 그렇게 놔두자

> (=Let's leave it alone)

Let's kick around some of the details and decide what projects to take
ㄴ 세부사항을 논의해서 어떤 사업을 해야할지 결정합시다

Let's leave aside the current situation and talk about the future
ㄴ 현 상황은 접어놓고 장래 일을 논의하자

Let's leave it at that
ㄴ 이 일은 이 정도에서 그치기로 하자

Let's not drag this out
ㄴ 이 일은 끌지 말자

Let's pull together on it. I read you loud and clear
ㄴ 모두 힘을 합하자. 네 말은 잘 알았다

Let's put our heads together

› **abeyance** state of iinactivity

ㄴ 중지를 모읍시다

Let's put it off till some other time
ㄴ 그건 나중에 하기로 하자

Let's see if we can get them wholesale and save ourselves some money
ㄴ 그 물건들을 도매로 사서 얼마간의 돈이라도 절약할 수 있을지 한 번 보자

Let's see how they respond
ㄴ 그들이 어떻게 나오는지 보자

Let's sit on the fence for the present
ㄴ 당분간 형세를 관망하자

Let's stick to the plan
ㄴ 계획대로 버티어 보자

Let's stop differing with each other on these small things
ㄴ 이런 작은 일로 서로 논란하지 말자

Let's take to the hills before she finds out what she has done
ㄴ 우리가 한 일을 그녀가 알아채기 전에 빨리 도망가자

Let's try to crown our project with perfection
ㄴ 우리의 사업에 유종의 미를 거두도록 합시다

Let's wait and see what line he takes
ㄴ 그가 어떻게 나오는지 두고보자

Lie low until this whole mess is over
ㄴ 저지른 일이 잠잠해질 때까지 죽은 듯이 지내라

My assent to the proposal clinched the bargain
ㄴ 내가 그의 제안에 찬성하여 거래는 이루어졌다

Nobody supported his supposition that the earnings should be

· clinch fasten securely, settle, hold fast or firmly

pooled
> ↳ 수입의 일부를 공동자금으로 하자는 그의 제안을 아무도 지지하지 않
> 았다

Our director didn't listen to our proposal, so we went over(above) him
> ↳ 우리 과장이 우리의 안을 들어주지 않아서 과장 위의 상사에게 가져
> 갔지

Such a proposal may be received with rather ill grace
> ↳ 그런 제의는 불쾌하게 받아들여질 수 있어

Sung-soo's suggestion will be brought(put) forward to committee at a suitable date
> ↳ 성수의 제안은 적절한 날짜에 위원회에 회부될 것이다

The proposal failed to go through
> ↳ 그 제안은 받아들여지지 않았다

The suggestion does you credit
> ↳ 네가 그런 제안을 하다니 훌륭하군

The upside of their proposal is that it would give him the freedom of act
> ↳ 그들의 제안에서 긍정적인 면은 그에게 행동의 자유가 주어진다는 점
> 이다

Their suggestion for improving the nation's exports were very well put(said)
> ↳ 국가의 수출을 늘이겠다는 그들의 제안은 옳은 말이었다

They have to play along with his suggestion, although it's not exactly what they want
> ↳ 그의 제안이 꼭 그들의 원하는 바가 아니라 하더라도 동의하는 체 할
> 수밖에 없었다

› **propose** plan or intend, make an offer of
marriage, present for consideration

They proposed to give the shipbuilder his head in the construction of these ships
> ㄴ 그들은 이들 배를 만들 때 조선업자에게 자신의 방식대로 하게 해 주자고 제안했다

This proposal is bound to flutter the dove-cotes
> ㄴ 이 제안은 평지풍파를 일으킬 게 틀림없어

Wan-soo said their proposal was incredible, or words to that effect
> ㄴ 완수는 그 사람들의 제안이 믿을 수 없다던가

You'd better spy out the land before accepting the offer
> ㄴ 제안을 수락하기 전에 상황판단을 하는 게 좋아

‣ **incredible** too extraordinary to be believed

120. 전쟁 　　　　　　　　　　 War

A blackout is the action of turning off all the lights against an air raid

ㄴ 등화관제란 적의 야간공습에 대비하여 모든 등불을 끄게 하는 조치이다

A search behind enemy lines requires a tremendous test of our endurance and nerves

ㄴ 적진의 후방을 탐색하는 데는 대단한 참을성과 담력을 요한다

All progress means war with society

ㄴ 모든 진보는 사회와의 싸움이다

Although he stayed out of the Korean War, he always spins us a yarn about his daring deeds in the war

ㄴ 그는 **6.25** 전쟁 때 참전하지도 않았으면서 늘 우리들에게 무용담을 늘어놓는다

As the threat of nuclear war receded, other things began to worry us

ㄴ 핵전쟁의 위협이 수그러들자 다른 걱정이 생겨나기 시작했다

During the Korean War, Korean soldiers disputed every inch of ground

ㄴ 한국전쟁 때 한국군은 한 치의 땅이라도 양보하지 않으려고 항쟁했다

He hits the high spots only

ㄴ 그는 눈에 확 띄는 일만 해(전시행정 등)

His courage brought the people through the war

▸ **blackout** darkness due to electrical failure

ㄴ 그의 용기에 사람들이 전쟁에서 버티어 낼 수 있었다

How can we manage to get the wounded out of the battlefield under this heavy fire from all sides

    ㄴ 사방의 심한 포화 속의 전쟁터에서 어떻게 부상자를 구해올 수 있을까?

In the eyes of the people, the general who wins a battle has made no mistakes

    ㄴ 사람들의 눈에는 전투에 이긴 장군은 아무런 실수도 하지 않는 사람처럼 보인다

In war there can be no substitute for victory

    ㄴ 전쟁에서는 승리 외에 아무 대안이 없다

It's unconscionable for us to ignore the prisoners of war that dedicated their lives to guarding our country's freedom and democracy

    ㄴ 우리는 자유와 민주주의를 위해 헌신한 전쟁포로들을 잊는다는 것은 비양심적인 일이다

Let's hide ourselves behind this rock and pick the enemy off before they fire at us

    ㄴ 이 바위 뒤에 몸을 숨기고 적이 우리에게 사격하기 전에 조준사격을 가하자

No man has tasted full flavor of life until he has known poverty, love, and war

    ㄴ 가난, 사랑, 전쟁을 알기 전에는 아무도 인생을 안다고 할 수 없다

Once war is forced upon us, there is no alternative than to apply every available means to bring it to a swift end

    ㄴ 일단 전쟁을 수행해야할 상황이 닥치면 전쟁을 신속히 종식시키기 위해 모든 수단을 동원하는 것 외에 아무 대안이 없다

› **substitute** replacement

The battle for people's mind is more important than military struggle

      ↳ 민심을 얻기 위한 전쟁은 군대를 동원한 전투보다 중요하다

The battle was won by brain rather than brawn

      ↳ 전투는 완력이 아닌 두뇌로 승부가 났다

The enemy peppered our lines with their shot

      ↳ 적은 아군의 진지에 총탄을 퍼부었다

The fighter-bomber drew the enemy soldier's fire away from the ships

      ↳ 전투기는 적의 포화가 선박으로 쏠리지 않고 자신에게 쏠리도록 유도
했다

The growing hostility between the two parties is threatening to plunge the country into civil war

      ↳ 양 정당간에 커져 가는 적대감은 나라를 내전에 빠뜨릴 지경의 위험
으로 몰아가고 있다

The Korean War brought all Koreans together; there was no upper class and lower class in those days

      ↳ 6.25 전쟁은 전 한국인들을 단합시켜 주었고, 그 때에는 귀천이 없었다

The mere absence of war is not peace

      ↳ 전쟁이 없다는 것만으로 평화는 아니다

The most persistent sound which reverberates through man's history is the beating of war drums

      ↳ 인류 역사를 통해 끈질기게 울려 퍼지는 소리는 전쟁의 북소리이다

The race is not to the swift, nor the battle to the strong

      ↳ 경주에서 빠른 자가 반드시 이기는 것도 아니고 전투에서 강한 자가
반드시 이기는 것도 아니다

The whole city was laid flat by the heavy bombing

      ↳ 심한 폭격으로 도시 전체가 초토화되었다

▸ **plunge**   thrust or dive into something, begin an action suddenly

▸ **reverberate**   resound in a series of echoes

There never was a good war or a bad peace
ㄴ 역사상 좋은 전쟁이나 나쁜 평화는 없었다

They banded together to protect the villagers against the raiders
ㄴ 그들은 마을 사람들을 침략군으로부터 보호하기 위해 단합했다

They dropped(died) like flies in that battle
ㄴ 그들은 그 전투에서 파리목숨처럼 죽어갔다

They fired ceaseless rolling barrage so that their troops could creep forward behind it and attack enemy lines
ㄴ 그들은 아군이 유도탄막 속에 포복으로 적진을 돌파해서 공격하려고 끊임없이 사격을 가했다

Those houses were knocked together after the war
ㄴ 그 집들은 전후에 급조된 것이다

War is a continuation of policy by other means
ㄴ 전쟁은 방법을 달리하여 수행하는 정책의 하나이다

We do more to decimate our population in automobile accidents than we do in war
ㄴ 전쟁에서보다 자동차 사고에서 더 많은 사람들이 죽는다

We played our guns on the fortress
ㄴ 아군은 요새에 포화를 퍼부었다

We should protect our own security from conflicts that pose the risk of wider war and threaten our common humanity
ㄴ 우리는 전쟁 확산의 위험성을 가지고 인간성을 위협하는 분쟁으로부터 안전을 지켜야 한다

When the war ended, Korea was carved up by the powers of the world
ㄴ 전쟁이 끝나자 한국은 강대국들에 의해 분단되었다

· **barrage**   heavy artillery fire
· **decimate**   destroy a large part of

When war is declared, truth is first casualty

  ㄴ 전쟁이 선포되면 진실이 첫 희생물이 된다

Where drums beat, laws are silent

  ㄴ 북소리 나는 곳에 법은 침묵한다(전쟁 때는 법이 소용없다)

With confidence in our armed forces, with the un-bounding determination of our people, we will gain the inevitable triumph

  ㄴ 우리 군대에 대한 신뢰와 우리 국민의 결연한 의지로써 우리는 기필코 승리를 거두게 될 것이다

› **casualty**　serious or fatal accident, one injured, lost, or destroyed

121. 전화   **Phone Callings**

Anybody will drop a dime these days
> ↳ 요즘은 아무나 전화신고를(밀고) 해

Are you here? Put him on
> ↳ 너 전화 받을래(옆에서 살며시)? 바꿔 줘

Are you there? - Yes I am(still here)
> ↳ 여보세요. 듣고있니? - 듣고있어

Are you through with your call?
> ↳ 통화 끝났니?

Bong-soo broke off from telling the story to answer the telephone
> ↳ 전화가 와서 봉수는 하던 얘기를 중단했다

Calls are flooding(pouring) in
> ↳ 전화가 빗발치고 있다

> (=Calls are coming in torrents)

Click the phone downstairs
> ↳ 전화를 아래층으로 돌려줘

Could you keep it short(brief)
> ↳ 통화를 간단히 해

Could you tell me what the call is about?

▸ **dime**   US coin worth one tenth of a dollar
▸ **brief**   short or concise

↳ 무슨 용건으로 전화 하셨는지요?

(=May I ask what the call is concerning?)

Dong-ho gave me a disconnect
↳ 동호가 전화를 끊었어(이해하지 못하는 경우도 있음)

555-1112 is no longer in service
↳ 결번

Get hold of Mi-jah and put her through(put her on)
↳ 미자에게 연결해서 내게 좀 연결해 줘

He can't come to the phone
↳ 전화 받을 수 없는 상태입니다(목욕 등)

He's on another line
↳ 다른 전화 받음

How may I direct your call?
↳ 전화를 어디로 대 드릴까요?

I can't get through
↳ 통화가 안 돼

I don't get a dial tone
↳ 전화가 먹통이야

I feel bad about not returning your call
↳ 네가 전화해 달라는데 못해줘서 맘에 걸렸지

I have someone on hold
↳ 난 지금 다른 사람과 통화 중이야

I have to let you go

· **disconnect** undo the connection of

ㄴ 이제 전화 끊어야겠어

(=I'll talk to you later)

I was cut off while talking by telephone
ㄴ 전화 통화중 끊겼어

I was cut off
ㄴ 통화가 끊겼어

I'd like to speak to someone in charge
ㄴ 담당자 바꿔 주십시오(전화)

I'd rather not burn the line
ㄴ 전화를 길게 하지 말아야겠군

I'll connect you to the right department
ㄴ 담당 부서로 전화 돌려 드리죠

I'll get her on the phone
ㄴ 그 여자분 전화 바꿔 드리죠

I'm getting Seoul
ㄴ 서울에 통화가 되기 시작했어(이해 못할 수도 있음)

I'm in the middle of something, can you call me later?
ㄴ 지금 다른 것 하고 있으니 나중에 전화할래?

If you have any questions, I can be reached at 256-7488
ㄴ 문의사항이 있으시면 **256-7488**로 문의하시기 바랍니다

In case of anything happening, call this number
ㄴ 무슨 일이 있으면 이 번호로 연락해

Is this a good time to call?

› **cut off** terminate

ㄴ 바쁜 시간에 전화 한 건 아닌지요?

It looks like we were disconnected
ㄴ 전화가 끊어졌던 것 같아

It's no use ringing around(round) to find the best place to eat
ㄴ 식당을 여기저기 전화 해봐야 소용없어

Just call us and we'll make Mt. Sorak come alive for you
ㄴ 전화만 해 주시면 설악산이 생생하게 눈앞에 다가올 여행 프로그램을 제공하겠습니다

Let me transfer this call to the man in charge
ㄴ 담당자에게 전화를 돌려 드리겠습니다

Make it collect
ㄴ 수신인 부담으로 해 주세요

May I speak to Mi-jah?(Give me Mi-jah)
ㄴ 미자 좀 바꿔 주십시오(친숙할 경우)

My mobile phone makes only outgoing calls. I can't get(receive) any incoming calls
ㄴ 내 이동전화는 발신 전용이야. 수신용으로는 못써

Please feel free to contact me at any time with any questions you may have
ㄴ 의문사항이 있으면 언제든지 연락해 주시기 바랍니다

Please get Mr. Joo on the phone
ㄴ 주 선생님 전화 좀 바꿔 주십시오

Please keep the line clear
ㄴ 다른 곳에 전화하지 말고 내 전화 기다려(통화중이면 내 전화 받을 수 없으니까)

Please leave your message after the beep tone

› **outgo**   going out, surpass

↳ "삐" 소리가 난 다음에 메시지를 남기세요

Please speak after beep and press the star(asterisk) key

↳ "삐" 소리가 나면 녹음하시고 끝나면 별표를 눌러주세요

Please try to keep the line clear today

↳ 오늘은 전화를 사용하지 말아 줬으면 좋겠어

Shall I hang up and call you back?

↳ 전화를 끊고 다시 걸어도 되겠습니까?

Some office girls are always going blah-blah on the phone

↳ 사무실에는 종일 전화통에 대고 수다떠는 여직원들도 있다

Stop running up the telephone bill

↳ 긴 통화는 하지 마세요(통화료 오르니까요)

That suspicious fellow just breezed into our office, used the phone, and then breezed out again

↳ 그 수상한 사람이 우리 사무실에 슬쩍 들어와서 전화를 하더니 다시 슬쩍 나가버렸다

The number you dialed(called) is a vacant number

↳ 지금 전화하신 번호는 결번입니다

The number you have reached(call) is not in service at this time

↳ 지금 거신 전화는 국번이 없거나 결번입니다

The phone started ringing off the hook

↳ 전화가 끊이지 않고 오기 시작했어

The telephone gets(brings) distant people into contact with each other

↳ 전화 덕분에 멀리 있는 사람들의 접촉이 가능하다

To whom am I speaking?

↳ 전화하신 분이 누구죠?

We had a bad connection and he hung up on me

› **asterisk** a character * used as a reference mark or as an indication of | omission of words

› **vacant** not occupied, filled, or in use

ㄴ 전화 상태가 나빠지더니 그가 일방적으로 끊었어

We seem to have bad(poor) connection

ㄴ 전화 상태가 나쁘군요

We've got a lot of cut-offs today

ㄴ 오늘은 전화가 잘 끊겨

What name shall I give?

ㄴ 누구시라 할까요?

(=Who's calling?)
(=May I have your name?)

What name shall I say?

ㄴ 누구시라고 여쭐까요?

Who shall I tell him called?

ㄴ 어느 분이 전화(방문) 하셨다고 말씀드릴까요?

Who's the person at the other end of the line?

ㄴ 전화 받는 사람이 누구니?

(=Who are you talking to?)

Who(m) do you wish to speak to?

ㄴ 누구를 바꿔 드릴까요?

Will someone else do?

ㄴ 다른 사람에게 전화를 바꿔도 되겠습니까?

Will you hold my calls?

› **hold a call**　keep someone waiting on the phone

└ 나한테 오는 전화 좀 받아줄래?

You are in connection
> └ 전화 왔습니다

You are welcome to call us if you need additional names of credit references or require more information before granting credit
> └ 신용추천인이 추가로 필요하거나 신용증인을 위한 정보가 더 필요할 경우 전화를 주시면 감사하겠습니다

You caught me at a bad time
> └ 지금은 전화하기 곤란한 상황이야

Your call can't be completed at this line. Please call again
> └ 지금은 전화를 할 수 없사오니 잠시 후 다시 걸어 주십시오

Your continuing lack of response to our letters and telephone calls, and your unwillingness to cooperate leave us no choice
> └ 귀하가 지속적으로 당사의 서신 및 전화에 거부함에 따라 당사로서는 다른 선택의 여지가 없음을 알려드립니다

Your daughter was burning up the(phone) line
> └ 너희 딸은 전화통에 불이 나더군

Your party is on the line
> └ 전화 연결되었습니다

› **reference** a bearing on a matter, consultation
for information

You are in connection.

You are welcome to call us if you need additional names of credit references or require more information before granting credit.

You caught me at a bad time.

Your call can't be completed at this time. Please call again.

Your continuing lack of response to our letters and telephone calls, and your unwillingness to cooperate leave us no choice.

Your daughter was hanging up the telephone line.

Your party is on the line.

122. 전통 & 역사　　Traditions & History

A dragon's appearance has been regarded not only as an auspicious sign, but also as a mysterious object of folk worship in Korea
> ↳ 한국에서 용의 출현은 상서로운 조짐일 뿐 아니라 사람들이 숭배하는 신비의 대상으로 여겨왔다

A woman's whole life is a history of the affections
> ↳ 여자의 전 생애는 애정의 역사이다

Abstaining from pork is a law that applies to the entire country in Saudi Arabia
> ↳ 사우디아라비아에서는 돼지고기를 삼가는 것을 전국적으로 적용하는 법으로 시행하고 있다

Admiral Yi(Soon-shin) went down in history as a loyalist
> ↳ 이순신 장군은 충신으로 역사에 남아 있어

After the spirits of ancestors taste the food on New Year's day, it'll be served as the first meal of the year to the family
> ↳ 설날 아침 조상들이 음식을 맛본 후 그 음식은 가족들에게 주어지는 새해 첫 음식이 된다

Anyone can rattle off the names of all the kings from Taejo to Soonjong
> ↳ 태조부터 순종까지 역대 왕의 이름쯤이야 누구라도 술술 외운다

Can you date this crown?

‣ **auspicious** favorable
‣ **abstain** refrain from doing something

ㄴ 왕관의 제작 년대를 아니?

Families prepare 'charye' for their deceased ancestors, serving rice, soup, side dishes, fruit, and rice cakes to spirits visiting their homes

ㄴ 가족들은 집으로 찾아오는 돌아가신 조상들의 귀신들에게 밥, 국, 찬, 떡 등을 차례 올릴 차례를 준비한다

Families visit tombs to pay respects to their ancestors on the occasion of Chusok

ㄴ 가족들은 추석에 즈음하여 조상의 묘를 찾아 성묘를 한다

Fettered by old customs, they are unable to act freely

ㄴ 그들은 낡은 관습에 묶여 자유롭게 행동하지 못한다

For a state to survive more than a fleeting historical moment, it must have the loyalty of its residents

ㄴ 국가가 절박한 역사적인 순간에서 살아남기 위하여 국가는 주민의 충성심을 얻어내어야 한다

For this I give him full marks and I hope history will do the same

ㄴ 이 일에 나는 최대의 찬사를 그에게 보내는 바이며 역사도 그에게 최대의 찬사를 보내길 바란다

General Yi(Soon-shin) earned his place in history

ㄴ 이(순신) 장군은 후세에 이름을 남겼다

Bong-soo is flying blind when he talks about history

ㄴ 봉수는 역사 얘길 할 때면 자기가 무슨 소릴 하는지도 모르는 얘기를 하고 있어

He knows a thing or two about Chinese history

ㄴ 그는 중국 역사에 조예가 깊어

He waded through slaughter to the throne

ㄴ 그는 피비린내 나는 싸움을 치르고 왕위를 차지하였다

› **fetter** chain or shackle for the feet

Her life spans the last years of classicism and the eve of revolutionary era
> ㄴ 그녀의 생애는 고전주의 말기에서 시작해서 혁명기의 직전까지 걸쳐있다

History has finally come full circle(History repeats itself)
> ㄴ 역사는 돌고 도나봐(온고지신)

"옛 것을 익혀서 새 것을 안다"라는 뜻의 '온고지신(溫故知新)'은 영어로는 "History repeats itself 역사는 돌고 돈다'나 "History is the best prophesy 역사는 최선의 예언이다'라고 한다. 역사는 돌고, 사람은 같은 일을 반복한다는 것을 뜻하는 명언 중에 'As a dog returns to its vomit 개는 토해낸 것을 다시 먹는 것 같이' 라는 비유의 표현이 있다.
(=History is the best prophecy)

History is a continuous process of interaction between the historian and his facts, and unbending dialogue between the present and the past
> ㄴ 역사는 사학가와 그가 본 사실간의 지속적인 상호작용의 과정이고, 현재와 과거 사이의 끊임없는 대화이다

History is an unending dialogue between the present and the past
> ㄴ 역사는 현재와 과거간의 끝없는 대화이다

History must repeat itself because we pay such little attention to it the first time
> ㄴ 우리는 역사의 첫 경험에서 별로 주의를 하지 않으니 역사는 반복되어야 한다

▸ **classicism**　a period when classics were in fashion

▸ **vomit**　throw up the contents of the stomach

"옛 것을 익혀서 새 것을 안다"라는 뜻의 '온고지신(溫故知新)'은 영어로는 "History repeats itself 역사는 돌고 돈다"나 "History is the best prophesy 역사는 최선의 예언이다"라고 한다. 역사는 돌고, 사람은 같은 일을 반복한다는 것을 뜻하는 명언 중에 'As a dog returns to its vomit 개는 토해낸 것을 다시 먹는 것 같이' 라는 비유의 표현이 있다.

History teaches us that men and nations behave wisely once they have exhausted all other alternatives
　　ㄴ 역사는 국민과 국가에게 모든 대안이 고갈됐을 때 현명하게 행동한다는 것을 가르쳐 준다

In Korea traditionally any mother-in-law provides her son-in-law with a feast fit for a king
　　ㄴ 한국에서는 전통적으로 장모가 사위에게 진수성찬으로 대접한다

It's a Korean custom to stay up all night until the cock crows on New Year's Eve
　　ㄴ 섣달 그믐날 저녁 닭이 울 때까지 자지 않고 있는 것이 한국의 관습이다

It's our custom to give money during holidays as a token of appreciation
　　ㄴ 명절에 감사의 표시로 돈을 주는 것이 우리의 관습이다

Junior generations kowtow before senior generations as the first greeting of the year and then exchange 'dugdam', wishes concerning health, success, and/or prosperity
　　ㄴ 새해 첫 인사로 젊은이들은 어른들에게 세배를 드리면서 건강, 성공, 혹은 번영 등을 비는 덕담을 나눈다

King Se-jong is as great a man as ever lived
　　ㄴ 세종대왕은 다시없는 위대한 인물이다

▸ **kowtow** show excessive deference

King Se-jong's valuable pioneering work will be ever remembered
↳ 세종대왕의 값지고 창의적인 업적은 길이 잊혀지지 않을 것이다

Knowledge and history are the enemies of religion
↳ 지식과 역사는 종교의 적이다

Koreans also consult fortunetelling books and hold rituals so that they may avoid bad luck by taking precautions against possible sources of jeopardy
↳ 한국인은 또한 닥쳐올지도 모를 재앙의 근원에 대비하여 주의함으로써 불운을 막기 위해 토정비결을 보기도 하고 의식행사를 가지기도 한다

Koreans are creating a new future and shaping a bountiful life today on the basis of their history and tradition
↳ 한국은 과거의 역사와 전통을 바탕으로 현재의 풍요로운 삶을 이루어 내고 미래를 새롭게 창조해 나가고 있다

Much money and time are spent to prepare sacrificial food to offer the spirits of ancestors
↳ 조상신들에게 드릴 제사음식을 준비하느라고 많은 돈과 시간이 소비된다

Nam-chul is history(a has-been)
↳ 남철인 한물 갔어

> (=Nam-chul is washed-up)
> (=Nam-chul lost his get-up and go)

On the occasion of the traditional holiday 'Solal', all roads lead home out of the cities
↳ 전통 명절인 설날을 맞아 모든 도로가 귀성 차량으로 가득 찬다

› **bountiful**   generous, rewarding

On this day, many engage in rituals to banish evil spirits or bring abundant productions
> ↳ 이 날 많은 사람들은 악귀를 내쫓고, 풍년을 맞기 위한 행사를 열게 된다

Our navy led by Admiral Yi(Soon-shin) bore(carried) off the palm in the battle
> ↳ 이순신 장군이 이끄는 우리 해군이 승전했다

Perhaps full moon signified plenty and bliss, so that the people would launch celebrations under the full moon
> ↳ 보름달은 풍요와 복을 의미하게 되어 보름 때 축제를 열게 되었던 것 같다

Stone implements had to be produced in order for man to live
> ↳ 인간이 살아가기 위해서 석기를 제조해야 했다

Such radiant cultural heritage, timeless fragrance of tradition, and unique culture are the pride of every Korean
> ↳ 찬란한 문화유산, 은은한 전통의 향기, 문화적 독창성은 한국인의 자부심이다

Suck-ho aced out the history
> ↳ 석호는 요행히 역사 시험에 합격했어

That idea changed the current of history
> ↳ 그 사상이 역사의 흐름을 바꾸어 놓았다

That men do not learn very much from the lessons of history is the most important of all the lessons that history has to teach
> ↳ 역사가 우리에게 가르쳐 줄 일 중에서 가장 중요한 것은 우리가 역사로부터 별로 배우지 못하고 있다는 사실이다

That's all history

· **banish** force by authority to leave a country, expel

ㄴ 그건 옛날 얘기(과거지사)

The conquistadors caused the annihilation of native South American cultures through their abject disregard and uncontrolled plundering

ㄴ 정복자들은 경멸할만한 무관심과 약탈로 아메리카 원주민들의 문화를 전멸시켰다

The elders remain at home and receive the younger ones, who make the New Year bow called 'sebae' in which the forehead touches the floor

ㄴ 어른들은 집에 남아서 젊은이들을 맞이하는데 젊은이들은 어른들에게 이마가 바닥에 닿는 '세배'라고 하는 절을 올린다

The first full moon of the year used to be much more festive than the first day of the year

ㄴ 옛날에는 정월 대보름을 정월 초하루보다 더 크게 지냈다

The history of liberty is a history of limitation of government, not the increase of it

ㄴ 자유의 역사는 정부의 확대가 아닌 축소의 역사이다

The history of the world is none other than the progress of the conscience of the freedom

ㄴ 세계역사는 바로 양심의 자유의 진로이다

The most persistent sound which reverberates through man's history is the beating of war drums

ㄴ 인류 역사를 통해 끈질기게 울려 퍼지는 소리는 전쟁의 북소리이다

The older generation are respectful of tradition

ㄴ 나이든 사람들은 전통을 존중한다

The only lesson history has taught us is that man has not yet learned from history

---

▸ **conquistador** leader in the Spanish conquest of America

▸ **abject** low in spirit or hope

▸ **reverberate** resound in a series of echoes

ㄴ 역사가 우리에게 가르쳐 준 것은 우리가 역사로부터 아직 아무 것도 배우지 못 했다는 사실이다

There's no precedent for it and the rest is history

ㄴ 그 일은 선례가 없던 일이고 그 후의 일은 아시는 바와 같습니다

They decided not pull the historic house down

ㄴ 그들인 역사적인 가옥을 헐지 않기로 결정했다

This castle dates as far back as 16th century

ㄴ 이 성은 16세기로 거슬러 올라가

This is our family tradition to hand this ring down(on) from mother-in-law to daughter-in-law

ㄴ 시어머니가 며느리에게 이 반지를 물러주는 게 우리 집 전통이다

This tradition reaches back into ancient times

ㄴ 이 전통은 태고 적까지 거슬러 올라가

Tradition and culture are often at variance with needs of modern living

ㄴ 전통과 문화는 현대 생활의 필요성과 상충하는 일이 많다

Tradition is a guide and not a jailor

ㄴ 전통은 선도자이고 재소자가 아니다

Traditional Asian extended family consists of at least three generations

ㄴ 전통적으로 동양의 대가족은 3대 이상으로 이루어진다

Try to find out what's the history on it

ㄴ 그 일의 연유를 알아봐

We are like ignorant shepherds living on a site where great civilization once flourished

ㄴ 우리는 위대한 문명이 번영했던 곳에 살고있는 셰퍼드 개만큼 역사에

▸ **precedent** something said or done earlier that serves as an example

▸ **jailor** prisoner

▸ **shepherd** one that tends sheep

대해 무식하다

We Koreans are traditionally forced not to smile or laugh freely in the presence of others
> ↳ 우리 한국인들은 전통적으로 남들 앞에서 미소짓거나 마음껏 웃는 것이 금기시 되어 있다

We release kites on the first full moon of the lunar year carrying pieces of papers noting potential adversities we may face
> ↳ 우리는 정월 대보름이 되면 우리에게 닥쳐올지도 모를 액운을 여러 장의 종이에 그려 넣어 매단 연을 날린다

When Koreans start a business, they have a unique ceremony for good luck on the first day of the business
> ↳ 한국인들은 사업을 시작할 때 행운이 따르기를 기원하면서 사업 첫날 독특한 의식을 치른다

When people get together they bow to the pig and put money into the pig's mouth
> ↳ 사람들이 모두 모일 때에 그 돼지 앞에서 절을 하고 돼지주둥이에 돈을 넣는다

Where does the Emperor Sejoh stand in the Josun Imperial line?
> ↳ 세조는 조선 왕조의 몇 번째 임금이지?

You'll be history if you have a fling at other guys
> ↳ 다른 남자들하고 바람을 피웠다간 끝장인줄 알아

▸ **kite** covered framework flown at the end of a string

▸ **imperial** relating to an empire or an emperor

123. 정치 & 정부   Government

A small group of party members splintered(split) off and formed a new political party
> ↳ 당원 중 소수 일파가 당을 깨고 나가 신당을 만들었다

All signs point to heavy voter turnout, despite disgust with the current crop of candidates
> ↳ 몇몇 후보들에 대한 염증에도 불구하고 모든 것이 투표에 높은 참여율을 보일 것으로 나타나고 있다

Any artificial attempt to realign political power is not desirable at the moment as it would only trigger further partisanship
> ↳ 정치권을 인위적으로 개편하려는 어떠한 시도도 당파성을 더 조장할 뿐이므로 지금으로서는 바람직하지 않다

Any attempts to revive the outdated campaign tactics of using regional rivalries to drum up support will further exacerbate the loss of public confidence in politicians
> ↳ 표를 모으기 위해 지역감정을 부추기는 낡은 전략을 부활시키려는 어떠한 시도도 정치인에 대한 신뢰상실을 악화시킬 것이다

Are you trying to muscle in on their turf?
> ↳ 그들의 세력권 안으로 밀고 들어가려는 거냐?

Aristocracy in a republic is like a chicken whose head is cut off
> ↳ 공화국에서의 금권정치는 머리가 잘려나간 닭과 같다

- **splinter** break into splinters
- **partisan** adherent, guerrilla
- **aristocracy** upper class

As an independent organization we have enough elbow room to try out new methods
ㄴ 이제 독립된 기관으로서 새로운 방법을 시험해 볼 여지가 생겼다

As soon as the decision is irrevocably pronounced, everyone is silent, and the friends as well as the opponents of the measure unite in assenting to its propriety
ㄴ 일단 돌이킬 수 없는 결정이 내려지면 모두 침묵을 치키고 법안에 찬성하던 사람이든 반대하던 사람이든 그 정당성에 동의하고 단결한다

At this rate, the present government will not remain long in power
ㄴ 이대로 가서는 현 정권이 오래 버티지 못할 것이다

Back on the front burner are unfinished tasks of reform in the financial and labor-management sectors
ㄴ 개혁의 우선과제는 금융과 노사부문이다

Ballots are the rightful and peaceful successor to bullets
ㄴ 투표는 총탄의 가장 정당하고 평화로운 계승자이다

Capitalism and democracy have their costs
ㄴ 자본주의와 민주주의는 비용이 든다

Chan-soo has all the moves(rights)
ㄴ 찬수는 실(유)력자 이다(실세)

Civil servants should endeavor to deal with the affairs of the public sympathetically, efficiently, promptly and without bias or maladministration
ㄴ 공무원들은 편견이나 실책 없이 온정 있고, 효율적이고, 신속히 공무를 처리해야 한다

Critics say that the government is turning a blind eye to signs of overheating to press ahead with expansionary policy in an attempt to

---

· **irrevocable** incapable of being revoked

· **ballot** paper used to cast a vote, system of voting

gain votes
> ↳ 비평가들은 정부가 투표의 지지율을 높이려고 확장정책을 밀고 나가기 위해 과열증세를 무시하고 있다고 비난하고 있다

Decision by the(a) majority is one of the most important principles of democracy
> ↳ 다수결은 민주주의의 가장 중요한 원리이다

Democracy means government by the uneducated, while aristocracy means government by the badly educated
> ↳ 민주주의는 무식한 사람들에 의한 정부이며 귀족정치는 잘못 배운 사람들에 의한 정부이다

Dictators ride to and fro upon tigers which they dare not dismount
> ↳ 권력자는 호랑이 등에 앉아 두려워서 내리지 못한 채 이리 저리 타고 다니는 사람이다

Discussions about poverty are laden with value judgments and are often motivated by political rather than humanitarian concerns
> ↳ 빈곤에 대한 논의는 가치판단이 개입되며 인도적인 관심보다는 정치적인 동기에서 이루어지는 일이 더 흔하다

Eliminating prejudice should be among the primary concerns of democracy
> ↳ 편견을 제거하는 것이 민주주의에 제1차 적인 관심사 중에 하나가 되어야 한다

Equal authority would lead to an absence of government
> ↳ 평등한 권위만 존재한다면 정부가 없어지는 상황이 될 수도 있다

Even though prices have risen drastically, the government is not entirely to blame
> ↳ 물가가 엄청나게 올랐지만 정부만의 탓은 아니다

▸ **dismount** get down from something, take apart   ▸ **laden** loaded, load

Every penny(vote) counts
> ↳ 한푼이(표)라도 중요해

Everyone who is born, holds dual citizenship, in the kingdom of the well and in the kingdom of the sick
> ↳ 사람은 누구에게나 두 가지 시민권이 있는데, 한 가지는 건강한 왕국의 시민권이고 다른 하나는 환자 왕국의 시민권이다

Fluctuating government policies becomes(has become) the rule of the day these days
> ↳ 요즈음 불안정한 정부정책은 관례처럼 되고 있다

For all that, democracy is probably the best form of government we can devise
> ↳ 그럼에도 불구하고 민주주의는 아마 생각해 낼 수 있는 최상의 정부 형태일 것이다

Gil-soo started government service in 1980
> ↳ 길수는 1980년에 공직생활을 시작했다

Good citizenship is indispensable in building a better democracy
> ↳ 보다 나은 민주주의를 구축해 나가는 데는 훌륭한 시민정신이 절대 필요하다

Government departments have been urged to cut down on bureaucracy in order to save money
> ↳ 정부 부처들은 예산절감을 위해 관료적인 형식절차를 줄여나가야 했다

Government support should focus on raising a entrepreneur's awareness of the survival instinct
> ↳ 정부의 지원은 기업의 자생본능을 불러일으키는데 주안을 두어야 한다

Having been left out of(off) the list of the candidates, they are now finding faults with the nomination process

---

› **indispensable** absolutely essential | › **entrepreneur** organizer or promoter of an enterprise

ㄴ 공천 후보들이 공천자 명부에서 빠지자 공천과정에 대해 헐뜯고 있다

He carries little weight in the party

ㄴ 그는 당에서 별로 중요한 인물이 못돼

He is a long shot

ㄴ 그 사람은 이길(당선) 가능성이 없어

He is trying to sweep his failure to keep his election promise under the mat(carpet)

ㄴ 그는 선거공약을 지키지 못한 것을 슬며시 덮어두려고 하고 있다

He never knows how the pendulum will swing

ㄴ 그는 민심동향이 어떻게 변할지 몰라

Health authorities unveiled an array of measurements to protect people from various health risks

ㄴ 보건당국은 각종 질환의 위험으로부터 국민들을 보호하기 위한 일련의 조치들을 내 놓았다

His political apostasy to the opposing party did not lessen his popularity

ㄴ 그가 탈당하여 반대당으로 갔지만 그의 인기는 줄지 않았다

How many committee members are up for re-election this time?

ㄴ 이번에 위원 몇 명이 재선 대상에 들어있습니까?

How many voters drank in his lies?

ㄴ 얼마나 많은 유권자가 그 사람의 거짓말에 귀를 기울이겠니?

In line with the historic implementation of a law acknowledging brain death, the government launched a state-run agency to manage all matters related to organ transplants

ㄴ 정부는 뇌사를 인정하는 장기이식에 관한 법률 시행과 연계해 장기이식을 총괄하기 위한 공공기구를 발족시켰다

› **pendulum** weight that swings from a fixed point

› **apostasy** abandonment of a former loyalty

In many countries' political elections, the candidates that win are usually the ones who have green power backing them
> ㄴ 보통 많은 나라의 선거에서 도움을 주는 자금력이 있는 후보가 승자가 된다

In order to prevent party-hopping we must institute a measure such as a recall system
> ㄴ 당적을 바꾸는 것을 막으려면 소환제와 같은 조치를 취해야 한다

Instead of wasting energy in extended partisan confrontation, they should join in efforts to tackle the many crucial issues pending
> ㄴ 그들은 더 이상 당파간 대결대신 많은 중요 현안들을 처리하는 데 합심해 노력해 나가야 한다

Interest groups taking illegal job actions to capitalize on the general election will be punished in accordance with the law
> ㄴ 총선 분위기에 편승하여 불법행위를 하는 이익집단들은 법에 따라 처벌될 것이다

It just goes to show you that the political world is moved by money
> ㄴ 정치의 세계는 돈으로 움직인다는 게 명백해

It's supported to a man
> ㄴ 만장일치로 지지 받고 있어

It's time government pulled in its belt too
> ㄴ 이제 정부도 지출을 줄여 경제적으로 운영할 때다

It's unconscionable for us to ignore the prisoners of war that dedicated their lives to guarding our country's freedom and democracy
> ㄴ 우리는 자유와 민주주의를 위해 헌신한 전쟁포로들을 잊는다는 것은 비양심적인 일이다

› **institute** establish, start

It's perfectly true that the government is(the) best which governs least
  ↳ 최소한의 정부가 최고의 정부라는 것은 정말 진실이다

Jong-shick reached a high place in the government in Seoul
  ↳ 종식이는 서울에서 정부 고관으로 올라가 있었다

Jong-soo is making a pitch for his favorite candidate, Jin-soo
  ↳ 종수는 가장 좋아하는 후보인 진수를 위해 지지(원)연설을 하고 있다

Justice delayed is democracy delayed
  ↳ 정의는 허용되지 않은 민주주의이다

Lots of voters are still on the fence about who to vote for
  ↳ 많은 유권자들이 아직도 누구에게 투표할지 결정하지 못하고 있다

Love of nature is a common language that can transcend political and social boundaries
  ↳ 자연에 대한 사랑은 정치적 사회적 경계선을 초월할 수 있는 공통의 언어이다

Many of our newspapers and television networks still tend to be subservient to the authorities
  ↳ 많은 우리의 신문과 텔레비전 방송은 아직도 정부당국의 시녀노릇을 하는 경향이 있다

Many public servants have clean hands as regards money
  ↳ 많은 공무원들이 금전문제에 깨끗해

Min-ho filed candidacy just under the wire
  ↳ 민호는 마감시간이 다 돼서야 후보등록을 했다

Moo-hyun is a shoo-in
  ↳ 무현인 당선(우승)이 확실한 후보

Most politicians are playing politics merely to advance their political

› **transcend** rise above or surpass
› **shoo** scare, drive, or send away

ambitions
> ↳ 대부분의 정치인들은 다만 자신들의 정치적 야망을 이루기 위해 정치적 문제를 잘 이용하고 있을 뿐이다

Moving to another party after winning the election on the nomination of or affiliation with one party is a form of cheating
> ↳ 한 정당에서 공천을 받은 사람이나 그 당원인 사람이 선거에 당선된 후 다른 당으로 옮긴다면 일종의 속임수이다

Mr. Ahn has started a whispering campaign against the mayor, saying that he's not honest
> ↳ 안씨가 시장이 정직하지 못하다는 흑색선전을 시작했어

Narrowing the gap between the rich and poor should receive the government's highest priority
> ↳ 정부는 빈부격차를 줄이는 것을 최고의 우선 과제로 해야한다

New members must fit in with rest of the committee
> ↳ 신규 회원은 여타 위원들과 잘 어울려 나가야 해

No government can be long secure without formidable opposition
> ↳ 무서운 반대 없는 정부는 장기적으로 안정된 정부가 될 수 없다

None of these unproductive debates between the ruling and opposition camps is helpful to their efforts to recover confidence of voters
> ↳ 여야간의 이러한 비생산적인 논쟁은 그들이 유권자들의 신뢰를 회복하려고 기울이는 노력에 전혀 도움이 되지 않는다

Normally public officials confront all embarrassments with a stale formula
> ↳ 일반적으로 공무원들은 모든 당혹스러운 일에 틀에 박힌 일반적인 방법으로 대처한다

Obtaining(Gaining) the support from the grassroots will be crucial for

---

› **formidable**　causing fear or dread, very difficult　　› **stale**　not fresh

reforms to bear fruit

    ↳ 개혁이 결실을 맺기 위해서는 일반대중으로부터 지지를 얻는 것이 결정적인 관건이다

Oh-yung overreached himself this time, aiming for the contract with the government

    ↳ 오영이는 정부의 계약을 따려는 과도한 의욕 때문에 실패했다

One can't reign and be honest

    ↳ 통치자가 되고서도 무죄가(정직하게) 될 수는 없다

One of the best things come out of the scandal is an increased public awareness of the politicians' morality

    ↳ 그 스캔들에서 얻는 것은 정치인들의 도덕성에 대하여 국민들의 관심이 커져가고 있다는 것이다

One of them concerns the ongoing investigation by the prosecution into draft irregularities involving politicians

    ↳ 그 중 하나가 현재 진행중인 정치인들의 병역비리에 관한 조사와 관련된다

Our democracies must build a culture of mutual trust and respect and re-learn the value of strategic thinking

    ↳ 우리의 민주주의는 상호신뢰와 존중의 문화를 증진시키고 전략적 사고의 가치를 다시 배워나가야 한다

Overseas travel fad comes back to regional and city council members

    ↳ 지방의회 의원들의 외유 병이 재발하고 있다

Policies that are intended to redistribute income or wealth from the haves to the have-nots can be counter-productive

    ↳ 소득과 부를 가진 자에게서 못 가진 자에게 재분배토록 하는 의도의 정책은 생산성 향상에 역행한다

・**prosecute**   follow to the end, seek legal
                  punishment of

Political gloom spread, with no ends of clouds in sight
> ㄴ 우울한 정치의 암운이 사라질 기색을 보이지 않고 있다

Political leaders also need to do everything by the book so that no one catch them out
> ㄴ 아무도 자신들의 잘못을 고집을 수 없도록 정치인들도 원칙을 따를 필요가 있다

Political parties in this country have long been criticized for their undemocratic, behind-closed-door nominating processes
> ㄴ 우리나라의 정당은 비민주적 밀실공천에 대해 오랜 지탄을 받아왔다

Politicians can do worse than display their emotions in public
> ㄴ 정치인이 자기 감정을 대중 앞에 토로한다해서 뭐가 이상해

Politicians love to create grassroots movements
> ㄴ 정치인들은 민중운동을 일으키기를 좋아한다

Politicians often try to sway undecided voters by promising lower taxes
> ㄴ 정치인들은 부동 투표자들에게 세금을 낮추어 준다고 약속함으로써 마음을 사로잡으려 한다

Politicians say anything to get votes, but once the elections are over, they don't act on their words
> ㄴ 정치인들은 득표를 위해 온갖 말을 늘어놓지만 선거가 끝나고 나면 그들이 한 말을 이행치 않는다

Politicians who are in the public eye have a responsibility to behave in a sensible way
> ㄴ 세인의 주목을 받는 정치인은 지각 있는 행동을 할 책임이 있다

Politics is a game at which two can play
> ㄴ 정치에서 상대방을 비방하면 그 사람도 같이 비방하게 돼 있어

› **gloom**   darkness, sadness

Politics is an area where thick-skinned people with unquenchable greed and filthy mouths come to play their foolish games

    ↳ 정치는 억누를 수 없는 탐욕과 낯두껍고 입심 사나운 사람들이 바보 게임을 하는 분야이다

Politics is war without bloodshed while war is politics with bloodshed

    ↳ 정치는 유혈 없는 전쟁이고 전쟁은 유혈정치이다

Pre-election surveys are aimed at providing a prior glimpse at voter support

    ↳ 사전 선거 여론조사는 유권자들의 지지를 미리 엿볼 수 있게 하는 것이 목적이다

Public opinion became vocal about the new financial policy

    ↳ 새로운 정책에 대한 여론이 분분해졌다

Public servants(Government employees) must eat their honest bread

    ↳ 공무원은 정직한 월급으로 살아야 한다

Quite a few lawmakers climbed on the bandwagon

    ↳ 꽤 많은 국회의원들이 시류에 편승했어

Rumors have been getting round(going about) the government's big deal

    ↳ 정부의 빅딜에 대한 소문이 퍼지고 있다

Several high level delegation have done the rounds to inspect the party organization

    ↳ 여러 번에 걸쳐 당의 고위 간부대표가 당 조직 점검을 위해 순회 방문했다

Some politicians are digging their own graves

    ↳ 일부 정치인들은 스스로 무덤을 파고 있어

Some politicians still try to buy their way to the top

‣ **unquenchable**   not capable to be put out, unsatisfied   ‣ **bloodshed**   slaughter

↳ 일부 정치인들은 아직도 돈을 써서 높은 자리를 사려고 하고 있다

Some public servants feather their own nest by getting money from contractors

↳ 일부 공무원들은 건설업자들에게 뇌물을 받아 사복을 채운다

Some successful candidates may have to resign if the authorities find them guilty of electioneering offences

↳ 당국에서 일부 당선자들의 선거운동 위반 사실을 적발할 경우 사임해야 할지도 모른다

Such debates can lead rival camps to base their campaigns on policy issues rather than simply bickering over irresponsible accusation and groundless rumors

↳ 이러한 논쟁은 적대진영으로 하여금 무책임한 비난과 근거 없는 소문에 대한 입씨름보다 정책문제를 근거로 논쟁하게 해준다

Such half-hearted reforms can't do much more than serve as palliative for the time being

↳ 그런 미온적인 개혁은 임시 경감 책밖에 안 돼

Such regulatory measures will help to close loopholes that can be used in order to misappropriate funds

↳ 이러한 조치는 자금의 오용을 하기 위해 빠져나갈 구멍을 만들려는 것을 규제하는데 도움을 줄 것이다

Tai-ho stepped on someone's toes during the last campaign

↳ 태호는 지난 유세 중 누군가의 감정을 건드린 일이 있어

That arrest is part of a new government campaign to stamp out the corruption

↳ 그 체포는 부패를 일소하기 위한 새 정부 운동의 일환이었다

The aim of the article is to cause the greatest embarrassment to the

---

› **bicker** squabble	› **palliate** ease without curing, cover or conceal by excusing

ruling party just before the general election
> ↳ 그 기사는 총선 직전에 여당을 최대한 곤혹스럽게 하려는 데 목적을 둔다

The basis of effective government is public confidence
> ↳ 효율적인 정부의 기본은 국민의 신뢰에 있다

The bolting opposition members may resort to stoking regional rivalries to win public support for their new party
> ↳ 야당에서 탈당한 이들은 신당에 대한 국민의 지지를 얻기 위해 지역 감정을 부추길지 모른다

The breakaway party being formed around former ruling and opposition members is shifting into a high gear
> ↳ 여·야의 탈당자들로 구성된 그 당은 발 빠른 행보로 전향해 가고 있다

The candidates suck up to the voters
> ↳ 입후보자들은 유권자들에게 감언이설을 하고 있는 거야

The cutthroat nature of the competition between candidates has added to our concerns
> ↳ 후보자들 간의 치열한 경쟁이 우리의 우려를 가중시켜주고 있다

The dead hand of bureaucracy exerts its paralyzing influence everywhere
> ↳ 마비시킬 듯한 관료적 병폐는 어디서나 맹위를 떨치고 있다

The decision is in the hands of the power that be
> ↳ 그 결정은 당국의 손에 달려있다

The degree of government involvement in private affairs became an embarrassment to the nation when it was revealed that directors had been contacted regarding their decisions
> ↳ 중역들은 결정을 내리는 과정에서 정부로부터 접촉을 받았다는 사실이 드러남으로써 민간 업무에 관한 정부의 개입정도는 나라를 떠들

· **cutthroat** murderer, ruthless

· **bureaucracy** body of government officials

· **paralyze** affect with paralysis

썩하게 만들었다

The dependence on connections to influential people and cronyism are encouraging illegal lobbying
ㄴ 인맥과 연고에 의존하는 우리의 문화가 음성로비를 활개치게 하는 환경을 조성하고 있다

The dictator finally came to the power
ㄴ 그 독재자는 결국 권좌에 올랐다

The domestic political scene is rife with all kinds of allegations of all political conspiration
ㄴ 국내 정치권에서는 온갖 음모 주장이 난무하고 있다

The equitable distribution of resources and wealth should be a priority of the government
ㄴ 자원과 부의 공정한 배분이 정부의 우선 과제여야 한다

The few that really control things are not honest and that tips(turns) the balance(scales)
ㄴ 소수의 부정직한 사람들이 매사를 좌지우지하고 그들의 세력이 우선권을 가진다

The government always costs more and the results are worse than if we had handled ourselves
ㄴ 정부가 하는 일은 항상 우리자신이 처리하는 것 보다 비용이 많이 들고 그 결과도 더 나쁘다

The government and the ruling party argue that the increasing debt has stemmed from their efforts to clean up the problems created under the rule of past administration
ㄴ 정부와 여당은 늘어나는 빚을 전 정권이 저지른 문제점들을 정리해 나가는 노력에서 생겨난 것이라고 주장한다

· **cronyism** depending on close friends

The government has called an emergency session to beef up computer security after hackers broke into official web site
> ㄴ 정부는 웹사이트 해커들의 침입사건이 발생하자 보안 강화를 위한 회의를 소집했다

The government is hoping to ease import restrictions soon
> ㄴ 정부는 수입제한제도를 완화하기를 희망하고 있다

The government is trying hard to downplay the seriousness of the situation
> ㄴ 정부는 사태의 심각성을 애써 대단치 않게 보고 있다

The government must try to distribute the country's wealth, so that they help those who need it most
> ㄴ 정부는 국가의 부를 가장 필요로 하는 사람들을 도울 수 있도록 국가의 부를 분배해야 한다

The government need not have complete control over the dissemination of information within a country
> ㄴ 정부가 국내의 정보 유통을 완전히 장악할 필요는 없다

The government offers incentives to recycle waste
> ㄴ 정부는 폐기물 재활용에 대한 장려 책을 내놓고 있다

The government should adopt policies that promote sustainable growth through increased access to markets
> ㄴ 정부는 시장 접근을 높임으로써 지속적인 성장을 촉진할 수 있게 하는 정책을 채택하여야 할 것이다

The government will have a job to prevent a recession
> ㄴ 정부가 불경기를 막으려면 애를 먹을 것이다

The government will not stand idly by as they take public health hostage in the pursuit of financial gains

---

› **downplay** neglect
› **disseminate** spread around

› **incentive** inducement to do something

ㄴ 정부는 그들이 경제적인 이익을 추구하여 국민의 건강을 볼모로 하는 그들을 좌시하지 않을 것이다

The government will soon move to halt the won's slide against the dollar

ㄴ 정부는 달러에 대한 원화 가치 하락에 조치를 취할 것이다

The government's action only increases suspicions that the public is not being warned about the dangers of rising pollution levels

ㄴ 정부의 그런 행동은 증가하고있는 대기오염의 위험수위에 대해 경고하지 않았다는 의심을 증폭시킬 뿐이다

The government's commitment to a balanced public finance position will be called into question

ㄴ 정부가 공약한 균형재정이라는 입장에 의문이 제기될 것이다

The government-controlled press painted a very different picture

ㄴ 정부 관리하의 언론들은 매우 다르게 보도(묘사, 기술)했다

The greatest ill of all in a democracy may be silence

ㄴ 아마 민주주의에서 가장 좋지 않는 것은 침묵일 것이다

The growing clamor for political reform has brought about change among lawmakers

ㄴ 커져 가는 정치개혁의 요구는 국회의원들에게 변화를 가져다주었다

The growing hostility between the two parties is threatening to plunge the country into civil war

ㄴ 양 정당간에 커져 가는 적대감은 나라를 내전에 빠뜨릴 지경의 위험으로 몰아가고 있다

The history of liberty is a history of limitation of government, not the increase of it

ㄴ 자유의 역사는 정부의 확대가 아닌 축소의 역사이다

› **clamor** uproar, protest
› **plunge** thrust or dive into something, begin

an action suddenly, dive or throw oneself forward or down

The insufferable pain of the impoverished masses outweighs any fear of the consequences of striking out against those in power
> ↳ 피폐해진 대중들의 참을 수 없는 고통이 권력을 쥔 사람들에 대항해 일어남의 결과에 대한 두려움을 넘어설 정도였다

The irrational racialism has generated(contributed) more heat than light
> ↳ 이성을 잃은 민족주의는 분란만 일으킬 뿐 도움이 되지 않는다

The lawmakers showed a glaring lack of respect for the solemnity of the occasion
> ↳ 국회의원들은 그 행사의 엄숙성에 대해 빤히 들여다보일 만큼 존중심이 없음을 보여줬다

The legislature should revise the election law in order to make up for this problem and other shortcomings
> ↳ 입법부는 이 문제와 다른 결함들을 보완하기 위해 선거법을 개정해야 한다

The local authorities ought to take their orders from the central government
> ↳ 지방정부는 중앙정부의 지시에 따라야 한다

The magnitude of a progress is gauged by the greatness of the sacrifice it requires
> ↳ 진보의 크기는 그 진보가 요하는 희생의 크기에 달렸다

The mayor couldn't face down the entire city council
> ↳ 시장은 전체 시의회를 꺾을 수 없었다

The movement contributed tremendously to raising the awareness that politicians should keep clean records
> ↳ 그 운동은 정치인들이 깨끗한 경력을 유지해야 한다는 것을 일깨워

› **racialism** racism
› **solemn** dignified and ceremonial, highly

serious, of great importance or responsibility

주는데 크게 기여했다

The only way for them to prove changes is to conduct the upcoming elections in a fair and transparent manner
> ㄴ 그들이 변했다는 것을 보여주는 유일한 길은 오는 선거를 공정하고 투명하게 치르는 일이다

The opposition attacked the statements as a phony gesture to woo voters' support for his party in the coming election
> ㄴ 야당에서는 그가 자기 당이 오는 선거에서 유권자들에게 지지를 얻는 것을 돕기 위한 제스츄어라고 공격했다

The party is divided against itself
> ㄴ 당은 내분상태

The party's choice dashed public hopes for the extensive replacement of old political hands with young bloods
> ㄴ 그 정당의 선택은 낡은 정치인들을 젊은 정치인으로 대폭 교체시키기 바라는 사람들의 희망을 무산시켰다

The political parties are expected to seek alliances with other groups to secure a legislative majority
> ㄴ 정당들은 의회의 과반수를 확보하기 위해 타 집단과의 연대를 모색할 것 같다

The program for rebuilding the town withered(died) on the vine
> ㄴ 읍을 재건하겠다던 계획은 초보단계에서 무너졌어

The project is obviously a pork barrel that he inserted into the budget to please the citizens of the home town
> ㄴ 그 계획은 분명히 그가 자신의 선거구 주민에게 환심을 사려고 예산안에 끼워 넣은 선심 사업이다

The rampant negative campaigns against candidates before the elections

---

> ‣ **woo** try to gain the love or favor of
> ‣ **alliance** association

> ‣ **wither** shrivel, lose or cause to lose energy, force, or freshness

made many voters turn away from the polls
> ↳ 선거전에 상대 후보들에 대한 판을 치는 흑색선전이 많은 유권자들로 하여금 투표장을 외면케 했다

The religions are obsolete when the reforms do not proceed from them
> ↳ 개혁이 종교 때문에 진척되지 않는다면 그 종교는 쓸모가 없다

The ruling and opposition camps are urged to cooperate in seeking effective ways to reduce the state debt
> ↳ 여·야는 나라의 빚을 줄이기 위한 효과적인 방법을 찾는데 협조해야 한다

The ruling and opposition parties are making all-out efforts to win a majority in the next general elections
> ↳ 여야는 오는 총선에서 다수의석당의 위치를 확보하려고 전면적인 노력을 기울이고 있다

The ruling party and the government frequently push pork-barrel projects which brought about massive budget burdens
> ↳ 여당과 정부는 예산상 큰 부담을 가져오는 선심예산 사업을 추진한 일이 많았다

The ruling party is playing hard ball
> ↳ 여당이 강경 노선으로 치닫고 있어

The tide had turned in favor of fiscal restraint
> ↳ 대세는 재정억제를 찬성하는 쪽으로 기울었다

The two leaders are expected to pave the way for establishing new politics and provide a basis for reconciliation
> ↳ 두 지도자는 새로운 정치 확립의 길을 트고 화해의 기초를 마련할 것으로 기대된다

› **rampant** widespread
› **fiscal** relating to money

The two parties couldn't hammer out a contract
ㄴ 쌍방이 계약에 대하여 논의했으나 합의에 이르지 못했어

The tyrant claims freedom to kill freedom
ㄴ 독재자는 자유를 말살할 자유를 요구한다

The vote was 5 in favor, 3 against with 2 absentations
ㄴ 투표 결과는 찬성 5, 반대 3, 기권 2 이었다

The voters are getting tired of politicians loading the dice like that
ㄴ 유권자들은 그처럼 부당하게 조작하는 정치인들에게 염증을 느끼고 있어

The voters lists are placed on the public review for correction
ㄴ 선거인 명부가 일반인들에게 열람되고 있다

The who's who of the political scene was at the party
ㄴ 파티에는 정계에서 내노라 하는 사람들이 다 왔어

The wining-and-dining revelations will unravel the plan to use taxpayer money
ㄴ 뇌물성 접대 사실이 드러나면 국민의 세금을 사용하려던 계획이 밝혀질 것이다

Their interpretation of polls is arbitrary and in many cases designed to meet hidden goals
ㄴ 여론조사에 대한 그들의 해석은 자의적이고 많은 경우 숨겨진 목적이 있다

Then he's done for as president
ㄴ 그러다간 대통령으로선 끝장이지 뭐

There are still enough of these little leaks to drain off millions from the public treasury
ㄴ 국가 재원으로부터 수십 억 달러의 돈을 들어먹을 이 작은 구멍들은

› **tyrant** harsh ruler having absolute power

› **unravel** separate the threads of, solve

› **arbitrary** selected at random, autocratic

아직도 있다

There must be a shift in political emphasis from individual profit to social equality

ㄴ 정치적으로 강조돼야 할 것은 개인의 이익에서 사회적 평등으로의 전환이다

There's always the possibility that the poll results were manipulated by researchers to suit the purposes of those who commission them

ㄴ 투표 여론조사의 결과는 조사자들이 자신들을 채용해준 사람들의 목적에 부합시키려고 조작될 가능성이 언제나 있다

There's been a credibility gap between the government and the people

ㄴ 정부와 국민들과의 불신감이 심각하다

There's scarcely a great truth or principle but has to fight its way to public recognition in the face of opposition

ㄴ 공적인 인정을 받기 위해서 반대와 비난에 맞서 싸워 나가지 않아도 되는 대 진리나 대 원칙은 없다

They are naturally making a play for the agricultural vote

ㄴ 그들이 농민들의 표에 환심을 사려는 건 당연해

They are now under fire for attempting to use the tax surplus to woo voters

ㄴ 그들은 지금 여분의 세금으로 유권자들에게 선심을 쓰려하고 있다는 비난을 받고 있다

They are trying to work out measures to spend surplus tax revenue for the less privileged in society

ㄴ 그들은 소외계층을 위해 잉여세입을 사용할 계획을 마련하고 있다

They are undergoing severe after-shocks derived from the danger and

---

· **poll**   cut off, receive or record votes, question in a poll

discontent of incumbent lawmakers who have failed to get nominated

     └ 그들은 공천에서 탈락된 현직의원들의 분노와 불만으로 인한 심한 후유증을 겪고 있다

They blindly supported the new legislation out of a misplaced sense of loyalty to the leadership

     └ 그들은 지도체제에 대한 잘못된 충성심에서 새로운 법률 제정에 맹목적으로 지지했다

They don't tell the necessary but unpleasant truths because they are afraid that the voters will kill the messenger

     └ 필요하면서도 귀에 거슬리는 말을 그들이 하지 않는 이유는 유권자들이 그런 말하는 사람을 오히려 망칠까봐 두려워하기 때문이다

They lined up behind Jong-soo and got him elected

     └ 그들은 정수의 지원(지) 조직을 만들어 그를 당선시켰어

They originally planned to help the people most in need, but backed away due to opposition critics

     └ 그들은 당초 가장 어려운 사람들을 도우려 계획했었으나 야당 비평자들 때문에 철회했다

They succeeded in isolating extreme left by winning massive popular support

     └ 그들은 대중의 큰 지지에 힘입어 극좌분자를 색출하는데 성공했다

They suspect the prosecution's decision to probe draft-dodging allegations as part of the ruling party's ploy to dig up dirt on some opposition members

     └ 그들은 검찰의 병역기피 주장에 대한 조사를 여당이 야당의원들에 대한 비리를 들춰내려는 속셈의 일환이라고 의심했다

They tend to take sides with the weaker party

› **incumbent**   obligatory, holder of an office

└ 그들은 소수당의 편에서는 경향이 있다

They were sitting on the pins and needles as the slain politician's followers threatened to riot in retaliation
> └ 살해당한 정치인의 지지자들이 폭동을 일으키겠다고 협박해 오자 그들은 바늘방석이었다

They'll be out of business if they don't offer sweet heart deals to the politicians
> └ 그들이 정치인들에게 누이 좋고 매부 좋을 일을 제시하지 않다가는 망하고 말 것이다

This initiative by the civic group met with a quick response from the government
> └ 그 시민단체의 그러한 움직임에 대해 정부는 신속한 반응을 보였다

This is his will to place his party under his complete control and defeat challenges from non-mainstream factions
> └ 이는 그가 당을 완전히 장악하여 비주류의 도전을 꺾어놓겠다는 의지이다

This letter shall remain confidential among two parties
> └ 이 편지는 우리 양측의 기밀로 해야 합니다

This state of things cries for reform
> └ 이 사태는 기필코 개혁을 요한다

This unpopular tax must be scrapped altogether instead of modification
> └ 평이 나쁜 이 조세는 내용 수정이 아니라 폐지되어야 한다

Those who make peaceful revolution impossible will make violent revolution inevitable
> └ 평화적인 혁명을 불가능하게 하는 사람은 폭력적 혁명을 불가피하게 할 것이다

› **slay** kill
› **retaliate** get revenge

› **riot** violent public disorder, random or disorderly profusion

Though sympathetic relationship between the media and public figures exists everywhere, it is particularly strong in Korea

    ㄴ 언론과 공인과의 공생관계는 어디서나 볼 수 있는 현상이지만 한국에서는 그것이 유달리 두드러진다

To begin another investigation with the general elections two months away is enough to raise suspicions about their motivations

    ㄴ 총선을 2개월 앞두고 또다시 조사를 하겠다는 것은 그들의 동기에 대해 충분히 의문을 제기할 만한 일이다

To pardon the oppressor is to deal harshly with the oppressed

    ㄴ 독재자를 용서하는 것은 피압박자들을 가혹하게 대하는 행위이다

To the extent that we are a democracy we share a responsibility in what our country does

    ㄴ 민주국가인 이상 우리는 국가가 하는 일에 대하여 책임을 분담하고 있는 셈이다

Two candidates are in dead heat

    ㄴ 두 후보는 백중지세다

Two leading politicians are still at each other's throat

    ㄴ 그 두 정치인은 아직도 너 죽고 나죽자는 식으로 나오고 있어

Tyranny is always better organized than freedom

    ㄴ 압제정치는 늘 자유보다 조직화 되어있다

Tyrants are but the spawn of ignorance

    ㄴ 독재자는 무지의 소산일 뿐이다

Very few people know the score of the politics

    ㄴ 정치의 내막을 아는 사람은 거의 없어

Virtually no candidate of any party will be elected in those provinces controlled by an opposing party

---

• **spawn** produce oggs or offspring, bring forth

↳ 반대당이 장악하고 있는 도에서 선거에 당선될 후보는 사실상 없을 것이다

Vote for the man who promises least
↳ 공약이 제일 적은 사람에게 표를 찍어라

Voters have traditionally been regarded as onlookers alienated from the legislative activities of their representatives once the balloting is over
↳ 유권자들은 전통적으로 일단 투표가 끝나면 의원들의 의정활동과는 분리된 방관자로 여겨져 왔다

Voters should shop around among the different candidates to see who will truly represent their interests best, rather than guided by party loyalty
↳ 유권자들은 후보자 가운데서 정당정책에 이끌려가기보다 유권자들의 이익을 가장 잘 대변 할 사람이 누구인가 잘 가려서 뽑아야 한다

Voting is a right we shouldn't take lightly
↳ 투표는 우리가 가볍게 여길 권리가 아니다

We call on both ruling and opposition camps to stop bickering at once and work out a compromise
↳ 우리는 여·야 모두 즉각 불화를 종식시키고 타협안을 찾아낼 것을 원한다

We have finally reached across party lines to reach our first balanced budget
↳ 우리의 초당적인 노력의 결과 마침내 처음으로 균형예산을 이루었다

We must bring down him at the next vote
↳ 다음 투표에서 그를 낙선시켜야 해

We must bring our actions into line with party beliefs if we are to remain a member

---

▸ **province**   administrative district, all of a country outside the metropolis(pl)

ㄴ 우리가 당원으로 남아 있으려면 당 노선에 따라야 한다

We must drum out the crooked politicians
ㄴ 부정직한 정치인은 추방해야 해

We must not forget the duties in a public official
ㄴ 우린 공무원의 직무를 잊어선 안 돼

We must search for a renewed strategy in seeking to be an advanced nation
ㄴ 우리는 선진화의 길을 찾기 위한 새로운 전략을 찾아야 한다

We public servants earn(turn) an honest penny
ㄴ 우리 공무원은 정직하게 일하고 보수를 받는다

We should take the next big step and make that tax credit refundable for low-income families
ㄴ 이러한 세금감면제도가 저소득층 가정으로 돌아갈 수 있도록 해야 한다

We'll take a vote on this matter
ㄴ 이 건은 표결로 처리하겠습니다

What space and time have been to physicists, liberty and quality have been and still are to democratic theories
ㄴ 공간과 시간이 물리학자에게 관련되는 것처럼, 자유와 평등이 민주주의 이론에 관련되어 왔고 여전히 계속 관련이 있다

When are you supposed to square off the budget?
ㄴ 예산은 언제 결산하게 되나요?

When the government didn't have transparency, the fundamental structure of the economy weakened and economic progress ground to a halt
ㄴ 정부가 투명성이 없을 때 경제의 기본구조가 약화되어 경제발전이 정지되었다

› **refund** give or put back (money)

Whenever election time rolls around, we all pay lip service to the idea of rooting out regional animosity
> ↳ 선거철만 돌아오면 우리는 모두 지역감정을 뿌리뽑아야 한다고 말로만 떠들어댄다

With government debts rising so fast, it's preposterous to use the excess taxes for purposes other than reducing it
> ↳ 정부의 부채가 이토록 빨리 늘어나고 있는데 여분의 조세로 이를 줄이는데 쓰지 않고 다른 목적으로 쓰는 것은 모순이다

Without approval, our budget plan is history
> ↳ 승인을 못 받으면 우리의 예산계획은 무용지물이다

You have to be the meat in the sand-witch if you try to resolve this disputes
> ↳ 당들의 분쟁을 해결하려고 나섰다가는 고래싸움에 새우 등 터지는 꼴을 하게 돼 있어

You have to raise additional funds to meet your current expenses
> ↳ 현재 너의 지출을 충당해 나가려면 추가자금을 조달해야 해

You should put out some feelers
> ↳ 넌 여론을 수렴해봐야 해

Your vote will tip the scale(balance)
> ↳ 네 한 표가 결정을 좌우해

› **animosity** resentment
› **preposterous** absurd

124. 좋은 관계   Good Relationships

A sense of duty is useful in work, but offensive in personal relations
    ㄴ 의무감이 일에는 유용하나 대인관계에는 기분을 언짢게 하는 요인이
    된다

Chan-soo put a bug in my ear
    ㄴ 찬수가 내게 귀띔(경고, 부추김) 하더군

Doo-chul doesn't stand on ceremony whenever we meet him
    ㄴ 언제 두철일 만나도 격식을 안 따져

Doo-chul knows well enough what I am
    ㄴ 두철인 내가 어떤 사람인지 잘 알아

He felt himself called upon to do something to help
    ㄴ 그는 무언가 거들어줘야 한다고 느꼈다

He pressed a gift on me that I couldn't refuse
    ㄴ 내가 사양해도 그가 선물을 주는 바람에 거절을 못했어

He told me he would see me through
    ㄴ 그는 내게 끝까지 돕겠다고 했어

He would give you the shirt off his back if you curry favor with him
    ㄴ 네가 그의 비위만 잘 맞추면 있는 것 없는 것 다 줄 것이다

He's always given me a fair shake
    ㄴ 그는 내게 항상 공정해

He's using smoking and mirrors to make them believe there's a

---

▸ **refuse**   decline to accept, do, or give

budget deficit
> ↳ 그는 그들로 하여금 결손이 있었다고 믿도록 연막작전을 펴고 있다

Hee-jung is eating out of your hand
> ↳ 희정인 네가 죽으라면 죽는시늉이라도 하는 사람이잖아

Help me to help you
> ↳ 내가 널 도와 줄 수 있게 해 줘

Hee-jung shall not be the loser by it
> ↳ 그 때문에 희정이에게 손해가 되진 않아

How can you write him off as a non-entity?
> ↳ 어떻게 그를 시시한 사람으로 빼어버릴 수 있어?

How come you have a callous attitude toward the sufferings of others?
> ↳ 어떻게 남의 고통을 나 몰라라 할 수 있니?

How could you do that to me?
> ↳ 네가 내게 그럴 수 있나?

Hyun-soo is hard to get hold of
> ↳ 현수에게는 연락하기가 힘들어

Hyun-soo stopped by my place time and time again
> ↳ 현수는 우리 집에 여러 번 왔어

I couldn't agree with you more
> ↳ 전적으로 동감

I couldn't hate you if I tried
> ↳ 넌 미워하려 해도 미워할 수 없구나

> (=I could never hate you)
> (=Nothing could make me hate you)

› **callous** thickened and hardened, unfeeling,
make callous

I have a great surprise in store for you
ㄴ 너를 놀래줄 것이 하나있다

I have heard more than enough of your talking-to
ㄴ 네 잔소리는 신물나게 들었어

I have tried to get hold of you
ㄴ 네게 연락하려고 애 먹었지

I know of him
ㄴ 그 사람 이름 정도는 알지(**I know him** 은 "직접 알다"임)

I know them like the back of my hand
ㄴ 그 사람들이야 손바닥 들여다보듯 알지

I know you backwards and forwards
ㄴ 너에 대해선 샅샅이 알고 있어

I need some company
ㄴ 누구라도 옆에 있어줬으면 좋겠어

I think I have claim on your compassion
ㄴ 조금은 내 맘을 알아줘야지

I would never do you wrong
ㄴ 하지만 네게 함부로 대하지는 않을게

I'm doing it the way you told me to
ㄴ 네가 하라는 대로 하고 있는 거야

I'm not playing games
ㄴ 힘 겨루기 하자는 게 아냐

I'm ready when you are
ㄴ 너만 좋다면 나도 좋아(네가 원한다면 언제나)

I've been saving(preserving, keeping) myself for you
ㄴ 난 네가 부를(올) 때까지 기다리는 중이야

› **compassion** pity

If anyone keeps bugging Jim any longer, he may cancel their Christmas
┗ 이제 더 이상 짐을 괴롭히는 사람이 있다면 그런 사람을 죽일지도 몰라

If I'm an idiot, you are another
┗ 내가 바보라면 너도 바보다

If you try to get with me, I'll end up unhappy
┗ 네가 나를 간섭하려고 한다면 난 불행해지고 말 거야

If you won't do it, no more will I
┗ 네가 안 하겠다면 나도 안 해

In-ho talks about you whenever you're not around
┗ 네가 자리를 비우기만 하면 인호는 네 얘길 해

It gets past me how you do it
┗ 네 방식은 너무 어려워

It is always the case with you
┗ 넌 늘 그 모양이야

It never dawned on me where I had seen him before
┗ 내가 그를 어디서 보았는지 도무지 생각이 안나

It seemed an eternity before you appeared
┗ 널 기다리기가 일각이 여삼추였어

> 힘든 일을 하거나 무엇을 기다릴 때에는 시간이 늦게 가는 것처럼 느껴진다. 이
> 럴 때에는 "일각이 여삼추다"라는 말을 쓴다. 한 순간이 삼년 같다는 말이다. 영
> 어로는 "Every minute seems like a thousand 일분이 천 분 같다"라는 표현
> 을 쓴다. 아주 지루할 때에는 "Time drags 시간이 질질 끈다"라는 표현을 쓰기
> 도 하는데, 이는 "Time flies 시간이 날아간다"와 반대되는 표현이다.

It take two to tango

› **bug** pester, conceal a microphone in

↳ 그 일은 손발이 맞아야 해

It won't do good to play up to me
↳ 비행기 태워야 소용없어

It'll be a pleasure to help you in any way
↳ 할 수 있는 한 어떻게든 도와 드리겠습니다(서한문)

It'll be so nice to see you after such a long absence
↳ 오랜만에 너를 보면 무척 반가울 거다

It'll go hard with him if we don't help him
↳ 우리가 그를 도와주지 않으면 큰 타격을 받을 것이다

It's a chance in a thousand we met
↳ 우리가 만난 건 천우신조

It's beneath you to say such a thing
↳ 그런 말하는 건 너 답지 않아

It's hard to catch you these days
↳ 요즘 얼굴보기 힘들군

> (=It's currently difficult to see you)
> (=I haven't seen much of you lately)

It's more blessed to give than to receive
↳ 받는 것보다 주는 것이 복이 있다

It's my turn to pick up the tab
↳ 이번엔 내가 살 차례

It's okay whatever turns you on
↳ 너만 좋다면 그걸로 됐어

▸ **bless** consecrate by religious rite, invoke
divine care for, make happy

It's on you
> 한턱 내

(=It's your treat)

It's safer not to burn your bridges
> 유대관계를 끊지 않는 것이 낫다

It's the very last time I forgive you
> 이번에 마지막으로 용서하는 거다

It's you
> 그건 널 위한 것(네게 맞는 것)

Jang-soo. Just the person I wanted to see
> 장수야. 마침 만나고 싶던 참이다

Jung-soo lost no time in making acquaintances with them
> 정수는 곧 그들과 친해졌어

Just do what you are told, or else!
> 내가 말한 대로 하기나 해, 안 하기만 해봐라

Just try to have(get) the goods on him
> 그 사람 발목(약점)을 잡아두기만 해

Keep away from such company
> 그런 패거리들과 가까이 하지마

Leave out your name from gift
> 선물은 누가 주는 줄 모르게 주라

Let's chip in some money for his farewell gift
> 그에게 줄 작별선물 사게 돈 좀 추렴하자

› **acquaintance**   person with who one is acquainted

› **farewell**   wish of welfare at parting, departure

Let's go Dong-soo. I feel a draft

    ↳ 동수야 가자. 우리를 반가워하지 않는 것 같아

Look like he'll be a no-show

    ↳ 그 사람은 안 올 것 같아

Look me in the face eyeball to eyeball(face to face)

    ↳ 내 얼굴을 똑바로 쳐다봐

Lulu looked after me with scrupulous care

    ↳ 루루는 가려운 데를 긁어주듯이 나를 돌봐주었다

My heart still bleeds for Mi-sook

    ↳ 미숙이 생각에 아직도 가슴 미어져

My job never bothers him

    ↳ 그는 내 일에 상관하지 않는다

My meager effort paled beside your masterpiece

    ↳ 너의 대단한 일(걸작)에 비하면 나의 미미한 노력은 아무 것도 아니지 뭐

My support gives them confidence

    ↳ 그들은 내가 있어서 든든하게 생각해

> (=They feel strong with me side by side)

Myung-ho was disappointed at missing my visit because he was out of town

    ↳ 명호가 출장 중 이어서 내가 찾아갔는데도 만나지 못하여 서운해 했다

Nam-soo will go the whole nine yards for you

    ↳ 남수가 네 일이라면 끝까지 도와 줄 거야

Nam-soo will surely nail your hide to the wall

› **scruple** reluctance due to ethical
          considerations

    ↳ 남수가 정말 너를 가만히 안 둘 거야

No use getting on my good side

    ↳ 나한테 잘 보이려 해도 소용없어

Nobody can come close to Jin-hee in caring for me

    ↳ 날 위하는 덴 아무도 진희를 못 따라가

Nobody gets me the way you do

    ↳ 너만큼 날 이해해 주는 사람이 없어

Nobody is going to nail your ears back

    ↳ 아무도 널 호되게 나무랄 사람은 없어

Nobody knows he has it in him

    ↳ 그가 실력 있다는 것을 아무도 몰라

Nobody knows where I'm coming from

    ↳ 내 생각이 뭔지 아무도 이해 못해

Nobody wants you to put up emotional shields

    ↳ 아무도 네가 마음의 문을 닫기를 원치 않아

Nobody will hold things against you when you goof up

    ↳ 네가 실수할 때 앙심 품을 사람은 없어

None knows the weight of another's burden

    ↳ 남의 무거운 짐을 알아주는 사람은 없다

Nothing in the world I could keep from you

    ↳ 네게는 아무 것도 숨길 게 없어

Nothing in the world I would keep from you

    ↳ 네게 뭐가 아까울 게 있겠니

Nothing passed between Chang-ho and me

    ↳ 창호와 나 사이엔 아무 일도 없었어

· **shield**   broad piece of armor carried on
the arm, something that protects

Nothing personal
> ↳ 개인적인 유감은 없어

Nothing works because of you - I should be saying that
> ↳ 너 때문에 되는 일이 없어 - 그건 내가 할 말이다

Now I must put his behind to the test
> ↳ 이제 그의 배후를 알아봐야겠어

Now nobody can sweep their difficulties aside in that easy manner
> ↳ 아무도 그리 쉽게 그들의 어려움을 무시할 수 없게 되어 있다

Now you are embarrassing me
> ↳ 무안하게 만들지마

Oh, don't let me keep you
> ↳ 저런, 그러시면 붙잡진 않겠습니다

One bad general is better than two good ones
> ↳ 한 사람의 시원찮은 장군은 똑똑한 장군 둘이 있는 것보다 낫다(불화
> 에 대한 경고)

One can bear grief, but it takes two to be glad
> ↳ 슬픔은 혼자서 견딜 수 있지만 기쁨을 나누는데는 둘이 있어야 한다

One has fear on every side of a fool
> ↳ 바보는 어느 쪽에서 봐도 두렵다

One man's superstition is another man's religion
> ↳ 한 사람의 미신이 다른 사람에게는 종교가 된다

One man's trash is another man's treasure
> ↳ 어떤 사람에게는 쓰레기일지라도 어떤 사람에게는 보물이 된다

One should mind ones own business
> ↳ 쓸데없이 남의 일에 간섭해서는 안돼

Opposites attract

› **superstition**   beliefs based on ignorance,   trust in magic
              fear of the unknown, or

↳ 극과 극은 통한다

이 세상에는 좋은 것과 나쁜 것이 따로 있는 것이 아니고 사람의 생각에 의해서 결정된다. 좋은 것이 상황에 따라서는 나쁜 것이 될 수도 있고, 그 반대가 될 수도 있다. 선(善)의 반대는 악(惡)이지만 악(惡)이 없이는 선(善)도 아무런 의미가 없다.

Pay them for what they did to you

↳ 그들에게 본때를 보여줘라(혼내줘라)

Picking on me won't help

↳ 나한테 화풀이 해봐야 소용없어

Pretend you don't know me, or you'll blow my cover

↳ 네가 날 모른 척 하지 않으면 내 정체가 발각돼

Putting your ass on the line for somebody else

↳ 다른 사람을 위해 목숨을 걸겠다는 거로군

Pyung-soo tries to hold out the olive branch to the person he had hurt

↳ 평수는 그가 때려줬던 사람과 화해하려고 하고 있어

Pyung-soo's affected manners are quite provoking

↳ 평수의 젠체하는 꼴은 못 봐주겠다

Remember that time I saved your hide(bacon, neck)

↳ 그때 내가 널 위기에서 구해줬다는 걸 잊지마

Sang-soo doesn't have any idea about what to do

↳ 상수에게 어떻게 해 보겠다는 생각이라곤 쥐뿔도 없어

Sang-soo rubs shoulders with rich people only

↳ 상수는 돈 많은 사람들하고만 사귄다

See it from other person's point of view(perspective)

› **bacon**   salted and smoked meat from a
pig

    ↳ 다른 사람의 입장에서 생각을 좀 해봐

She and I go way back
    ↳ 그 여자와 나는 오래 전부터 알고 지내

She finally reached(came to) an accommodation with him
    ↳ 결국 그녀는 그와 화해하게 되었다

She has bent over backwards to please you
    ↳ 그 여자는 너를 기쁘게 해주려고 안달해 왔었단 말이야

She has something for your private ear
    ↳ 그 여자가 네게 은밀히 할 얘기가 있대

She is hanging on my coattail
    ↳ 그 여자가 내게 달라붙고(아쉬운 소리하고) 있단 말이야

She is so shy to notice you
    ↳ 그 여자는 너무 수줍어서 네게 아는 체를 안 하는 거야

She made a joke and it cleared the air between them
    ↳ 그 여자가 농담을 하자 그들 사이의 오해가 풀렸다

She means much to me
    ↳ 그 여자에게 신세를 많이 지고있지

She nursed along the invalid
    ↳ 그 여자가 환자를 줄곧 돌봐왔어

She saved the situation and now it's up to you not to let her down
    ↳ 그 여자가 어려움은 해결했으니 이제 네가 할 일은 그 여자를 실망시
    키지 않는 일이다

She stood surety for me
    ↳ 그 여자가 내 보증을 서 주었다

She understood me heart to heart
    ↳ 그 여자는 진심으로 나를 이해했어

› **accommodation** quarters(pl), act of accommodating

› **invalid** not true or legal

She wears her feet(is on the go) for us
> ↳ 그 여자는 우리를 위해 동분서주 하고 있어

She won't have it any other way
> ↳ 그렇게 하지 않는다면 그녀가 허용치 않을 거야

She's been up to here now
> ↳ 그 여자는 이제 네게 신물이 난 거야

She's my soul sister
> ↳ 그 여자는 나하고 마음이 통해

Since then she's been negatively friendly
> ↳ 그 후 그녀와의 사이는 좋지도 않고 나쁘지도 않아

Somehow he managed to slip through their fingers
> ↳ 어쨌든 그는 그들에게서 빠져나갔어

Soon-ho's nothing like me
> ↳ 순호는 나하곤 달라

> (=Soon-ho's very different from me)

Sung-mi tried to get a hold of me for a month
> ↳ 성미가 한달 동안이나 내게 연락하려고 애썼대

Tai-ho was just trying to find out how you feel
> ↳ 태호는 그냥 너를 한번 떠 본 것 뿐이야

Tai-jung just sat on his hands
> ↳ 태정인 전혀 도와주려고 하지 않더군

Take(draw, pull) him aside and let him know your views
> ↳ 그를 한 쪽으로 데려가서 네 생각을 알려라

▸ **negative** marked by denial or refusal, showing a lack of something suspected or desirable, less than zero, having more electrons than protons, having light and shadow images reversed

That guy is a strange bed fellow
 ↳ 저 친구는 속마음을 알 수가 없어

That guy now has kind of grown on me
 ↳ 저 사람이 이젠 점점 마음에 들게 됐어

That's between you and me
 ↳ 너와 나와의 문제

The circumstances being what they are(The situation being what it is) we'll overlook it
 ↳ 사정이 사정인 만큼 너그럽게 봐주자

The fault is as much mine as yours
 ↳ 잘못은 내게만 있는 게 아니라 네게도 있다

The fault is in ourselves, not in our stars
 ↳ 잘 안 되는 일은 복이 없어서가 아니라 자신의 탓이다

The fault lies with you, not with me
 ↳ 잘못이 네 탓이지 내 탓이 아냐

The prompter the refusal, the less the disappointment
 ↳ 거절이 빠를수록 실망이 적다

There is a difference between not thinking of someone and forgetting him
 ↳ 누군가를 생각하지 않는 것과 잊는 것에는 차이가 있다

They are all boys(girls) together
 ↳ 그들은 모두 한 마음 한 뜻이었다

They are all of a mind(size)
 ↳ 전부 같은 마음(크기)이다

They are all parts of the same
 ↳ 그들은 한통속이다

› **disappoint** fail to fulfill the expectation or hope of

They are in tune with each other
　ㄴ 그들은 죽이 잘 맞아

They are like peas and carrots
　ㄴ 그들은 붙어 다니는 짝꿍이야

They are trying to help you out if you play your cards right
　ㄴ 네가 처신만 잘하면 그들이 너를 도와주려는 거야

They are trying to reduce their difficult relationship to a simple form of shared love and common interests
　ㄴ 그들은 어려워진 관계를 서로간의 사랑과 상호 이익이라는 단순한 형
　　태로 이끌어 가려고 애쓰고 있다

They can't pull anything over on me when it comes to journalism
　ㄴ 저널리즘에 관한 한 그들이 나를 속일 수는 없어

They crossed each other on the way
　ㄴ 그들은 중도에서 서로 스쳐지나갔다

They did fine by me
　ㄴ 그 분들이 내게 잘 해 줬어

They exchanged gifts to one another
　ㄴ 그들은 서로 선물을 교환했다

They finally came to a parting of the ways
　ㄴ 그들은 마침내 각자의 갈 길로 갔다

They have spent years rubbing elbows with the movers and shakers
　ㄴ 그들은 권력자들과 수년간 교제해 왔다

They often pal around(up) with each other
　ㄴ 그 사람들은 자주 같이 잘 어울려

They rarely have their signals crossed(mixed)
　ㄴ 그들은 죽이 잘 맞아

›**journalism** business of reporting or printing news

They went their respective ways
> ㄴ 그들은 저마다 제 갈 길을 갔다

They'll understand you with time
> ㄴ 그들은 시간이 지나면 널 이해할 것이다

They've got a lot in common
> ㄴ 그들은 공통점이 많아

We are apt to judge our fellowmen in comparison with ourselves
> ㄴ 우리는 우리자신과 비교하여 남을 판단하기 쉽다

We are getting along
> ㄴ 우린 죽이 잘 맞아

(=We are on the same wavelength)

We are not quite together today
> ㄴ 오늘은 손발이 안 맞아

We can't forgive another for not being ourselves
> ㄴ 우리는 남이라는 이유만으로 그들을 용서할 줄 모른다

We mingled our tears
> ㄴ 우리는 함께 울었어

We work together in perfect harmony
> ㄴ 우리는 손발이 척척 맞아

We've got a lot in common
> ㄴ 우린 공통점이 많아

Who will not be deceived must have as many eyes as hairs on his head

---

› **respective** individual and specific

ㄴ 속지 않으려면 머리카락 수만큼의 눈이 있어야 한다

Why are you always dangling about(after) him?

ㄴ 왜 넌 그 사람하고 붙어 다녀?

Would that he were here to help us!

ㄴ 그가 우리를 돕기 위해 여기 있었으면

You and I are on the same wavelength

ㄴ 너와 내 생각이 서로 통하는군

You are going to see a lot of me

ㄴ 앞으로 자주 만나게 될 거야

You are in your own conceit

ㄴ 딴엔 영리하다고 자만하고 있군

You are my crying shoulder

ㄴ 넌 나의 든든한 의지가 되고 있어

You are no worse than the others

ㄴ 너도 다른 사람과 다를 바 없군

You are on deck

ㄴ 이번엔 네 차례

You are too curious about other people's business

ㄴ 넌 공연히 남의 일을 알고 싶어하고 있는 거야

You can't fool(please) the people all the time

ㄴ 모든 사람을 언제나 속일(즐겁게 할) 수는 없다

You don't care a bag of beans for me

ㄴ 내게 눈곱만큼도 관심을 안 주는군

You eat out of his hand

ㄴ 넌 그가 죽으라면 죽는시늉까지 하잖아

· **dangle** hang and swing freely, be left without support or connection, allow or cause to hang

· **wavelength** distance from crest to crest in the line of advance of a wave

You go your way and I'll go my way
> ↳ 넌 네 뜻대로 난 내 뜻대로 하겠어

You guys are two of a kind
> ↳ 너희 둘은 똑같아

You need not stand on ceremony with me
> ↳ 너와 나 사이에 무슨 격식이냐

You need someone to whom you can pour your heart out
> ↳ 네게는 마음을 털어놓을 만한 사람이 있어야 해

You need to give a little to get a little
> ↳ 가는 정이 있어야 오는 정이 있다

> (=It's all about give-and-take(helping each other))
> (=You can't just be on the receiving end)

You're the only kind of person I can open myself up to
> ↳ 마음을 터놓을 수 있는 사람이라곤 너 밖에 없다

You've been hard to get in touch with
> ↳ 너한테 연락하기 힘들었어

› **pour** flow or supply copiously, rain hard

125. 주문   **Orders**

Are you adding it to your order?
> ↳ 별도(추가)로 주문하는 겁니까?

(=Is that a separate order?)
(=Do you want that as well?)

Are you going to will-call it?
> ↳ 물건을 직접 찾아가시겠습니까?

It should come in a few days
> ↳ 2~3일 내에 주문이 도착합니다

It's on order
> ↳ 주문해 뒀습니다

Last year they swamped us with orders
> ↳ 작년에 주문이 쇄도했다

Orders for the new kind of ware flowed in upon him
> ↳ 그 신제품의 주문이 그에게 쇄도했다

Our order reached us 10 units short
> ↳ 주문품이 열 개 모자라게 왔습니다

Please sign the duplicate of the enclosed order form and return it to us as your acknowledgement

---

· **swamp**   wet spongy land, deluge
· **duplicate**   consisting of 2 identical items,   exact copy, make an exact copy of, repeat or equal

ㄴ 주문서의 사본에 수취확인 서명 후 저희에게 반송해 주십시오

This trial order could lead to many substantial orders in the future

ㄴ 이 시험발주는 장래 본격적인 주문으로 연결될 수 있을 것이다

We are backlogged

ㄴ 밀린 주문이 많습니다

We have orders coming out of ears

ㄴ 우린 주문이 폭주해

We just filled a large order that cleaned us out of stock

ㄴ 대량 주문을 받아서 재고가 떨어졌습니다

We'll ship your order right away

ㄴ 주문품을 바로 선적해 드리겠습니다

What's your normal turnaround?

ㄴ 주문(신청)하면 얼마나 걸립니까?

› **substantial** plentiful, considerable

› **backlog** reserve of unfilled orders, accumulation of things to be done

126. 주식   **Stock**

A crash in the stock market like that is too much for a lot of people
    ㄴ 이런 주가 폭락은 많은 사람들에게 큰 타격이다

An-do made a fortune by wheeling and dealing on the stock market
    ㄴ 안도는 증권시장에서 수완(실력)을 발휘하여 큰돈을 벌었어

As some of the thinking now collapses with share prices, concrete consequences are beginning to emerge
    ㄴ 이 같은 생각이 주가폭락과 함께 붕괴되면서 구체적인 결과들이 나타나기 시작했다

Because of increased costs(profits), we have come out in the wrong(right) side this month
    ㄴ 이 달에는 수익(비용)이 늘어서 이익(손해)을 보았다

Byung-soo burned his fingers in the stock market, and didn't want to try again
    ㄴ 병수는 주식에 혼이 나서 다시는 주식할 생각이 없어졌어

Don't burn your fingers on the stock market
    ㄴ 주식에 손대었다가 큰코다치지 않도록 해

Pyung-soo took a bath on that construction stock
    ㄴ 평수는 그 건설업 주식을 샀다가 크게 날렸어

She struck gold by picking the right tech stocks at the right time
    ㄴ 그녀는 확실한 기술 주(식)를 선택해서 큰돈을 벌었다

› **emerge**   rise, come forth, or appear

Stock prices go through the roof these days
> ㄴ 요즘 주가가 천장부지로 오르고 있다

The market is risen(fallen)
> ㄴ 시세가 올랐어(내렸어)

The rapid changes in the market placed the bank stocks at a premium
> ㄴ 주식시장의 변동으로 은행주 값이 확 올랐어

The recession knocked the bottom out of my profits
> ㄴ 불경기로 내 이익금의 최저 수준이 무너졌어

The share carries 6% interest
> ㄴ 그 증권에는 6% 이자가 붙는다

The stock market has swung from one extreme to another over the past two years
> ㄴ 지난 2년간 주식시장은 극단에서 극단으로 움직였다

The stock market is going south
> ㄴ 증권시장은 내림세야

These factors will never show any growth or spark any rally in the stock market
> ㄴ 이들 요인으로는 주식시장의 반등세를 보여주거나 반등을 이끌어 내
> 지는 못할 것이다

› **spark** emit or produce sparks, stir to activity

127. 죽음   Death

A great man will be remembered for his achievements

         ↳ 호랑이는 죽어서 가죽을 남기고 사람은 죽어서 이름을 남긴다

> (=A man dies; his name remains)

A person's death makes us exaggerate the importance of his place

         ↳ 사람의 죽음은 그의 중요성을 과장하게 만들어

A pig that has two owners is sure to die of hunger

         ↳ 주인이 둘인 돼지는 굶어죽게 마련이다

> 여러 사람이 같이 하는 일은 서로 책임을 미루게 되어 결국엔 망한다는 뜻이다. 아리스토텔레스는 정치론에서 "A matter common to most men receives least attention 많은 사람이 관심을 갖는 일은 항상 소홀히 취급된다"고 하였다.

A useless life is early death

         ↳ 쓸데없는 인생은 일찍 죽는 것과 같다

A will gives detailed instructions to your family in case of your sudden death

         ↳ 유언장에는 사람이 갑자기 사망할 경우에 대비하여 가족들에게 상세

› **exaggerate** say more than is true

히 전할 말을 명시해 두는 것이다

All interest in disease and death is only another expression of interest in life
> ↳ 질병과 죽음에 대한 모든 관심은 삶에 대한 관심의 또 다른 표현이다

Be careful not to flog it to death, or your customers will lose interest
> ↳ 같은 소리를 또 하고 또 해서 손님들의 흥미가 덜어지지 않도록 해

Better a living dog than a dead lion
> ↳ 죽은 정승은 살아있는 개보다 못하다

Bong-soo's seen many a man meet his maker in the electric chair
> ↳ 봉수는 많은 사람들이 전기의자로 처형되는 것을 보아왔다

Confucian beliefs have it that cutting open corpses would kill a person once again after death
> ↳ 유교에서는 사체에서 조직을 떼어내는 것은 죽은 자를 또 한 번 죽이는 것이라고 주장한다

Cross my heart and hope to die
> ↳ 정말이지 믿어줘

Death cancels everything but truth
> ↳ 죽음은 진실 외의 모든 것을 취소한다

Death is but an instant, life a long torment
> ↳ 죽음은 순간이지만 삶은 고문이다

Do it or die
> ↳ 죽을 각오로 해야 해

Don't slip up on me and scare me to death like that
> ↳ 그렇게 슬며시 다가와 깜짝 놀라게 하지마

Every violation of truth is not only a sort of suicide in the liar, but

---

› **confucian** relating to the Chinese philosopher Confucius or his teachings

› **torment** extreme pain or anguish or a source of this, harass

is a stab at the health of human society
> ↳ 진실에 어긋나는 모든 일은 거짓말한 사람의 자살일 뿐 아니라 인간 사회의 건전성에도 타격이 된다

Everyone knew he'd come to a bad end
> ↳ 그의 말로가 안 좋으리란 건 모두가 알았어

Expect not praise without envy until you are dead
> ↳ 죽기 전에는 질투 없는 칭찬을 기대하지 마라

Fire-safety inspectors described the basement beer hall as a death trap
> ↳ 화재 안전 검사단은 그 지하실 맥주집을 매우 위험한 장소라고 기록했다

Getting deeply in debt to a loan-shark finally led him to his suicide
> ↳ 그의 고리대금업자에게 지게된 큰 빚이 자살을 불러왔다

Hares may pull the dead lion by the beard
> ↳ 토끼도 죽은 사자는 깔본다

Hate is a prolonged form of suicide
> ↳ 증오는 오랜 시간에 걸친 자살행위다

He all but died for his wounds
> ↳ 그는 중상을 입고 죽을 뻔했어

He attempted to disembowel himself to death
> ↳ 그는 할복자살을 시도했다

He begins to die that quits his desire
> ↳ 소망을 포기하는 사람은 죽어가기 시작한 사람이다

인간은 살아가면서 여러 가지 절망에 부딪히는데, 이럴 때마다 희망을 버리면 살수가 없다. "하늘이 무너져도 솟아날 구멍이 있다(If the sky falls we shall catch larks)"고 하였다(Hope springs eternal = 희망의 샘은 영원히 샘솟는다). (=He's perspective)

› **disembowel** remove the bowels of

He has gone to a better place
↳ 그는 천국에 갔을 거야

He is long dead
↳ 그는 죽은 지 오래 되었어

He's dead but won't lie down
↳ 그는 여기 없지만 그가 남긴 영향은 사라지지 않을 것이다

He's dead from the memory of the world
↳ 그는 세상에서 버림받았어

Her death struck me dumb with astonishment
↳ 그녀의 죽음에 나는 아연실색했다

Her father's been in the pits ever since her mother passed away
↳ 그 여자의 어머니가 돌아가신 후 그 여자의 아버지는 생지옥이었지 뭐

Her remarkable life and tragic death poignantly express the hopes and disappointments of a whole generation
↳ 그녀의 눈부신 생애와 비극적인 죽음은 모든 세대들의 희망과 절망을 찡하게 표현해준다

His anguish at not being able to be at his father's deathbed preyed on his mind for a long time
↳ 그에게는 아버지의 임종을 못본데 대한 고뇌가 오랫동안 마음을 괴롭혔다

His death followed close on his failure
↳ 그는 실패한지 얼마 후 결국 죽었다

His death will fall heavy on his family
↳ 그가 죽으면 가족들 살 길이 난감해

His life was fled = He already passed away
↳ 그는 이미 숨을 거두었다(이해하지 못할 경우도 있음)

‣ **astonish** amaze
‣ **poignant** emotionally painful, deeply moving

If you do that again, you'll sign your own death warrant
> ↳ 또 그랬다간 네 죽을 짓 하는 거야

In fact those amazing acrobats have to dice with death on that high trapeze
> ↳ 사실 저 놀라운 곡예사들은 목숨을 내걸고 공중그네를 타야 해

In line with the historic implementation of a law acknowledging brain death, the government launched a state-run agency to manage all matters related to organ transplants
> ↳ 정부는 뇌사를 인정하는 장기이식에 관한 법률 시행과 연계해 장기이식을 총괄하기 위한 공공기구를 발족시켰다

In old times, property was usually handed down to the oldest son upon his father's death
> ↳ 옛날엔 보통 아버지의 사망 때 장남에게 재산을 대물림했다

In the way of righteous is life, and in its pathway there's no death
> ↳ 의로운 길에 생명이 있나니 그 길에는 사망이 없느니라

It's going to be do or die
> ↳ 죽기 아니면 살기 식이야(이판사판)

> (=It's make or die)
> (=It's throwing caution or discretion to the wind)

Life is ephemeral and it's what happens after death that's important
> ↳ 인생은 덧없는 것이고 중요한 것은 사후에 어떻게 될 것이냐 이다

Lots of insects have met their death playing about a flame
> ↳ 많은 곤충들이 불꽃 주위에 접근하다가 죽었다

Lots of people live in momentary expectation of death

› **acrobat** performer of tumbling feats
› **ephemeral** short-lived

↳ 많은 사람들은 금방이라도 죽음이 닥쳐오리라 각오하면서 살고 있다

Many huge monuments built over some people's graves in an effort to achieve some degree of immortal presence long after their death are disgusting

↳ 죽은 지 오랜 후에도 상당한 정도로 불멸의 존재로 인식됨을 달성해 보려는 시도에서 무덤에 거대한 많은 비석들을 세우는 것은 역겹다

My father lay at death's door for a week, but he began to get better

↳ 아버지가 1주일 동안 사경을 헤매었으나 곧 나아지기 시작하셨어

Nam-soo must be laughing up his sleeve as his nagging wife is dead

↳ 바가지 긁는 부인이 죽었으니 남수가 화장실에서 웃고 있겠지

Nothing is certain but death and taxes

↳ 인생에 있어서 확실한 건 죽음과 세금이다

One may die at any moment

↳ 사람은 언제 죽을지 몰라

People aged 60 and older who have a certain type of high blood pressure and who are particularly thin face have higher risks of stroke and death

↳ 60세 이상인 사람으로서 특정한 종류의 고혈압이 있고 특히 얼굴이 야윈 사람이 더 뇌졸중에 걸리거나 사망할 위험이 더 크다

Sang-mi gained ground after being near death

↳ 상미는 죽도록 아프다가(망했다가) 많이 회복했어

She is too young to buy the farm

↳ 그 여자가 죽기에는 너무 젊다

She left a great name behind her

↳ 그 여자는 위대한 이름을 남기고 세상을 떠났다

She made a good end(death)

› **immortal** not mortal, having lasting fame

↳ 그 여자는 아름다운 죽음을 했다

She promised never to reveal her secrets on pain of death
↳ 그 여자는 목숨을 걸고라도 그 비밀을 지키겠다고 약속했다

She was energetic woman who cut off her prime by scarlet fever
↳ 그녀는 정력적인 여성이었으나 한창때 성홍열로 요절했다

She's too young to end up in cement city
↳ 그 여자가 죽기에는 너무 아까운 나이다

Surrendering herself to her feelings of shame, she killed herself
↳ 그 여자는 부끄러운 마음을 이기지 못하여 자살했다

That would be signing your own death warrant
↳ 그런 짓 하는 건 네 죽을 짓이야

The act is forbidden under penalty of death
↳ 그 행위는 이를 범하면 사형에 처한다는 규정 하에 금지되고 있다

The dead pheasant spiraled down into the valley, where the hunting dog picked it up
↳ 죽은 꿩이 빙글빙글 돌면서 골짜기로 떨어지자 사냥개가 물어왔다

The good die young
↳ 곧은 나무가 먼저 찍힌다

'미인박명(美人薄命)', "곧은 나무가 먼저 찍힌다"라는 말이 한국에선 자주 쓰인다. 세상에 이로운 사람이 요절할 때 아쉬움을 표현하는 말이다. 영어에서는 말 그래도 "The good die young 좋은 사람은 어려서 죽는다"라고 한다. (=The best go first)

The loneliness after his wife's death made my heart bleed
↳ 부인을 잃은 그의 외로움에 내 가슴이 아팠어

▸ **reveal** make known, show plainly

The man was rushed to the hospital but was pronounced dead on arrival
    └ 그 남자를 급히 병원으로 보냈으나 병원에 도착할 때 이미 사망한 것으로 판명됐다

The man who is always the life of the party will be the death of his wife
    └ 항상 파티에서 잘 나가는 남자를 둔 부인은 죽을 맛이다

The memory of my late uncle revives unexpectedly from time to time
    └ 문득문득 돌아가신 아저씨 생각이 난다

The memory of those who died is very green
    └ 죽은 사람들에 대한 기억이 매우 생생하다

The miser and the pig are of no use until dead
    └ 구두쇠와 돼지는 죽기 전엔 쓸모가 없다

The poet came to an untimely end
    └ 그 시인은 요절했어

The story you use has been worked to death many time and is no longer interesting
    └ 너의 그 얘긴 지겹게 써먹었던 터라 더 이상 흥미가 없어

There could be no worse misfortune than her death
    └ 그녀의 죽음보다 더한 불행은 없다

They are being nickel-and-dimed to death by these small daily expenses
    └ 그들은 매일 생기는 세세한 경비 때문에 죽을 지경이다

They lived together in happy union till parted by death
    └ 그들은 백년해로했다

This is dedicated to those who did not live to tell the tale
    └ 자신들이 겪은 일을 말도 못해보고 죽은 사람들을 위해 이것을 바

› **miser** person who hoards money
› **nickel** US 5-cent coin

친다

To achieve great things we must live as though we were never going to die
> ㄴ 큰 일을 이루기 위해서는 영원히 죽지 않을 것처럼 살아야 한다

To know the great man dead is compensation for having to live with the mediocre
> ㄴ 이미 죽은 사람의 위대함을 인정해 주는 것은 그가 평범한 사람들과 같이 살았던데 대한 보상이다

To the ashes of the dead glory comes too late
> ㄴ 영광은 죽음의 유골 앞에 너무나 늦게 온다

Truth sits on the lips of dying men
> ㄴ 사람이 죽을 때가 되면 진실을 말한다

Under the tongue men are crushed to death
> ㄴ 사람은 혀 밑에 깔려 죽는다

We'll always remember her in our prayers
> ㄴ 항상 그 여자의 명복을 빌겠습니다

Well, I mean, death's(ages) something that comes to us all
> ㄴ 죽음(나이 먹음)은 누구에게나 오게 돼 있다 이 말이야

You are a long time dead
> ㄴ 언제 죽을지 모르는 몸, 살았을 때 즐겨라(활동적으로 살아라)

You are history＝Enjoy your life while you can
> ㄴ 넌 이제 죽었어(오늘이 제삿날이야)

You had a lucky escape from death
> ㄴ 구사일생이었군

You have flogged it to death
> ㄴ 넌 그 일을 신물나게 토의(검토) 하고 있잖아

▸ **flog** beat with a rod or whip

128. 즐거움   **Pleasure**

All good things must come to an end
    ㄴ 모든 즐거운 일에는 끝이 있다

> 쾌락을 구하는 마음은 한이 없고 그것이 극에 달하면 권태와 절망이 기다리
> 고 있다. 높은 산이 있으면 깊은 골짜기가 있듯이 아무리 즐거운 일이라도
> 오래가지 못한다(Pleasure cannot go on forever).

Can she maintain the balancing act of pleasing her parents and her parent-in-law?
    ㄴ 그녀가 친부모와 시부모 모두를 기쁘게 할 균형 있는 행동을 유지할
       수 있을까?

Chang-soo never fails to please
    ㄴ 창수는 절대 남의 비위를 건드리지 않아

Danger and delight grow on one stalk
    ㄴ 위험과 즐거움은 같은 줄기에서 자란다

Diseases are the interests of pleasure
    ㄴ 질병은 쾌락의 이자이다

Don't mix business with pleasure
    ㄴ 공과 사를 구분하라

Eat at pleasure, drink by measure

› **parent-in-law**   parent of spouse

↳ 즐겁게 먹고 적당히 마셔라

Eat to please yourself, but dress to please others

 ↳ 자신을 위해서 먹고 남을 위해서 옷을 입어라

Few people want the pleasure they are free to take

 ↳ 마음대로 즐길 수 있는 즐거움을 욕심내는 사람은 없다

For lawless joys a bitter ending awaits

 ↳ 무절제한 즐거움 끝에는 쓰라린 결말이 기다리고 있다

Have I the pleasure of addressing Mr. Bahk?

 ↳ 박 선생님이십니까?

He always colors up his adventures to please his listeners(audience)

 ↳ 그는 늘 듣는 사람들을 즐겁게 해주려고 모험담에 그럴듯한 살을 붙인다

He is a good boy to his parents

 ↳ 그는 그의 부모님에게는 좋은 아들이다

> (=He tries to please his parents)
> (=He tries to make)

He that is of a merry heart has a continual feast

 ↳ 즐거운 마음을 가지는 것은 계속되는 잔치에 가는 것과 같다

I can't tell you how pleased I am

 ↳ 말로 할 수 없을 만큼 기뻐

I don't believe I've had the pleasure

 ↳ 초면인 것 같습니다

I'll do what I please

 ↳ 내 맘이야

› **await** wait for

› **feast** large or fancy meal, religious festival

> (=I'm free to do anything)

It'll be a pleasure to help you in any way
  ↳ 할 수 있는 한 어떻게든 도와 드리겠습니다(서한문)

It's no less a pleasure than a duty for me to work hard
  ↳ 열심히 일하는 것은 의무이자 즐거움이다

Long ailments wear out pain, long hopes, and joy
  ↳ 긴 고통은 아픔도, 오랜 희망도, 기쁨도 사라지게 한다

Marriage has many pains, but celibacy has no pleasure
  ↳ 결혼은 많은 고통을 수반하지만 혼자 살면 아무런 즐거움도 없다

Money may procure pleasure but not happiness
  ↳ 돈으로 향락은 살 수 있을지 몰라도 행복은 사지 못한다

Men seldom give pleasure when they are not pleased themselves
  ↳ 사람은 자신이 기쁘지 않으면서 남에게 기쁨을 주지는 않는다

Mustard is a good sauce, but mirth is better
  ↳ 겨자가 좋은 소스지만 즐거움은 더 좋은 소스이다

Not joy but joylessness is the mother of debauchery
  ↳ 방탕은 즐거움에서가 아닌 즐거움이 없는데서 생겨난다

One joy scatters a hundred griefs
  ↳ 한가지 기쁨은 백가지 슬픔을 몰아낸다

One moment may with bliss repay unnumbered hours of pain
  ↳ 한 순간의 큰 기쁨은 수많은 시간의 아픔을 보상할 수 있다

Perfect understanding will sometimes almost extinguish pleasure
  ↳ 완벽한 이해가 때로는 즐거움의 대부분을 소멸시키는 때가 있다

Please all, and you will please none

· **aliment** nourishment

· **mirth** gladness and laughter

· **celibacy** state of being unmarried, abstention from sexual intercourse

↳ 모든 사람을 즐겁게 하려다가는 아무도 즐겁게 할 수 없다

Pleasure has a sting in its tail
↳ 쾌락의 뒤에는 쏘는 맛이 있다

Pleasure is not pleasure unless it cost dear
↳ 비싸게 먹히지 않는 즐거움은 즐거움이 아니다

Pleasures of love lasts but a moment
↳ 사랑의 즐거움은 잠깐 뿐이다

Present joys are more to flesh and blood than a dull prospect of a distant good
↳ 장래에 다가올 미지근한 희망보다는 현실적인 즐거움이 낫다

Saving is to put aside present pleasure for future happiness
↳ 저축이란 장래의 행복을 위해 현재의 쾌락을 억제하는 것

She has bent over backwards to please you
↳ 그 여자는 너를 기쁘게 해주려고 안달해 왔었단 말이야

Sudden joy kills sooner than excessive grief
↳ 갑작스러운 기쁨은 지나친 슬픔보다 더 사람을 빨리 죽인다

Tai-ho will take you out of yourself
↳ 태호가 너를 즐겁게 해줄 것이다

The fine day added to our pleasure
↳ 날씨가 좋아서 더 즐거웠다

The greatest pleasure is to do a good action by stealth, and to have it found out by chance
↳ 몰래 선행을 한 다음 그것이 우연히 말해지게 되는 것이 가장 큰 기쁨이다

The remembrance of past sorrows is joyful
↳ 지나간 슬픔을 떠올리는 것은 즐거운 일이다

› **stealth** secret or underhand procedure

The way to rise is to obey and please
ㄴ 성공의 방법은 남의 말을 따르고 남을 기쁘게 하는 일이다

There's nothing pleases me more
ㄴ 이 보다 더 기쁜 일이 없다

They are half on business and half on pleasure
ㄴ 그들은 업무 겸 관광차 온 거야

They greeted me with every sign of pleasure
ㄴ 그들은 만면에 기쁨의 빛을 띠우면서 나를 맞이했다

They that sow in tears shall reap in joy
ㄴ 눈물로 씨를 뿌린 자는 기쁨으로 거두리라

To please people is a great step towards persuading them
ㄴ 사람들을 기쁘게 하는 것이 그들을 설득하는 큰 발걸음이다

To some life means pleasure, to others suffering
ㄴ 인생이란 어떤 사람에겐 기쁨을 뜻하고 어떤 사람에겐 괴로움을 뜻한다

We request the pleasure of your company at our party
ㄴ 파티에 참석해 주시면 감사하겠습니다

When the first fine rapture had worn off, he seemed none too pleased
ㄴ 그는 처음의 열광이 지나가자 그다지 즐거워하는 기색이 아니었다

Women have many faults, but the worst of them all is that they are too pleased with themselves and take too little pains to please the men
ㄴ 여자들에게는 많은 결함이 있는데 그 중에서도 가장 나쁜 것은 자신들에게 너무 만족해하고 남자들을 위해서 거의 아무 수고도 하지 않는다는 점이다

You can't fool(please) the people all the time
ㄴ 모든 사람을 언제나 속일(즐겁게 할) 수는 없다

› **greet** address with expressions of kind wishes, react to

› **rapture** spiritual or emotional ecstasy

You picked me up when I was down
ㄴ 우울할 땐 내게 기쁨을 주었지

Your joy is your sorrow unmasked
ㄴ 기쁨은 가면을 벗은 슬픔이다

Your worst humiliation is only someone else's momentary entertainment
ㄴ 당신에게 있어 최대의 굴욕도 타인에게는 잠시의 즐거움일 뿐이다

· **humiliate** injure the self-respect of

129. 지식   Knowledge

A blackout is the action of turning off all the lights against an air raid
      ↳ 등화관제란 적의 야간공습에 대비하여 모든 등불을 끄게 하는 조치이다

A dam is a thick bank or wall built to control water and prevent flooding
      ↳ 댐은 수량을 통제하고 홍수를 예방하려는 목적으로 축조한 두터운 둑이나 제방이다

A diet is what helps a person gain weight more slowly
      ↳ 식이요법이란 살이 천천히 붙도록 도와주는 것이다

A dynamiter is used to measure muscle power
      ↳ 근력계는 근력을 측정하는 데 쓰인다

A fable is a story intended to teach a moral truth
      ↳ 우화는 도덕적 진실을 가르치려는 의도가 담긴 이야기다

A good memory is one trained to forget the trivial
      ↳ 우수한 기억력은 시시한 일을 잊어버리는데 단련되는 일이다

A line of small holes is punched out to show us where to tear the card
      ↳ 카드를 어디서 절취할지 알 수 있게 한 줄로 작은 구멍이 나 있다

A literal translation is not always the closest to the original meaning
      ↳ 직역이 언제나 원 의미에 가장 가까운 것은 아니다

A major application of the science of the logic is to help distinguish between correct and incorrect reasoning

---

› **distinguish**   perceive as different, set apart, discern, make outstanding

    ㄴ 논리학을 사용하는 주된 이유는 정확한 추론과 정확하지 못한 추론을
구별하기 위함이다

A new pragmatism is replacing the old emphasis on the size, prestige and face

    ㄴ 크기, 명성, 체면을 생각했던 옛 생각은 새로운 실용주의로 바뀌고
있다

A number is an abstraction that has no physical existence

    ㄴ 숫자는 물리적 형체가 없는 추상적 개념이다

A person's attention is attracted not so much by the intensity of different signals as by their context, significance, and information contents

    ㄴ 사람의 주의력은 서로 다른 신호들의 강도보다는 신호들의 상황, 중
요성, 그리고, 정보의 내용에 보다 더 끌린다

A sentence that isn't coherent is hard to understand

    ㄴ 조리 없는 문장은 이해하기 힘들어

A sneeze cannot be performed voluntarily, nor can it be easily suppressed

    ㄴ 재채기는 마음대로 나오게 할 수도 없고 쉽게 멈추게 할 수도 없다

A strong memory is commonly coupled with infirm judgement

    ㄴ 강한 기억력은 보통 허약한 판단력과의 결합으로 이루어진다

A traveller without knowledge is a bird without wings

    ㄴ 지식 없는 여행자는 날개 없는 새와 같다

A will gives detailed instructions to your family in case of your sudden death

    ㄴ 유언장에는 사람이 갑자기 사망할 경우에 대비하여 가족들에게 상세
히 전할 말을 명시해 두는 것이다

All great discoveries are made by men whose feelings run ahead of

---

› **abstraction** abstract idea or work of art

their thinking
> ↳ 모든 위대한 발명은 느낌이 생각보다 앞서가는 사람들에 의해 이루어진다

All port cities generally have lots of establishments catering to sailors on shore leave
> ↳ 어느 항구도시나 일반적으로 선원들의 기항을 겨냥한 시설들이 많다

Allegories are still written today although modern authors generally prefer less abstract, more personal symbolism
> ↳ 현대의 작가들이 덜 추상적이고 더 개인적인 상징을 선호하지만 우화는 오늘날에도 여전히 사용되고 있다

Although the emission volumes remain high, natural winds usually blow the pollutants away, keeping the dense of pollution in check
> ↳ 배출량은 높은 수치를 유지하고 있으나 자연에서 오는 바람이 공해물질을 불어 없애 줌으로써 그 밀도를 억제해 준다

An acre is the amount of land a yoke of oxen can plow in one day
> ↳ 에이커는 황소 두 필이 하루에 갈 수 있는 밭의 넓이 이다

An ideal is a standard by which people judge real phenomena
> ↳ 이상이란 사람들이 그것에 의해서 판단하는 표준이다

An organ is a group of tissues capable of performing some special function
> ↳ 신체기관이란 어떤 특수한 기능을 이행할 수 있는 일단의 조직들이다

Antibiotics can be conveniently grouped according to species of microorganisms they inhibit
> ↳ 항생물질은 편의상 이들이 억제하는 미생물의 종류에 따라 분류될 수 있다

Apples are valued nowadays for their aid to digestion and their help in keeping teeth clean and healthy

---

› **cater** provide food for, supply what is wanted(+to)

› **inhibit** hold in check

ㄴ 사과는 소화를 돕고 이를 깨끗하게 하고 건강을 유지시켜줌으로써 오늘날 소중히 여겨진다

As soon as microbes enter the body they would kill all living matter, if it were not for the tiny defenders that rush immediately to fight them

ㄴ 만일 침입자들과 싸우기 위해 즉시 달려가는 작은 방어 균이 없다면 세균이 몸 속에 들어가자마자 살아있는 모든 것을 죽일 것이다

Cigarette ads in magazines and newspapers carry a health warning because they are obliged to

ㄴ 잡지와 신문에 나오는 광고는 이들 회사의 의무 때문에 건강에 대한 광고를 싣는다

Clay binds when it is baked

ㄴ 점토를 구우면 굳어진다

Coal is formed from peat, which consists of different kinds of organic matter that have decomposed

ㄴ 석탄은 분해된 모든 다른 종류의 유기물들로 구성된 도탄에서 형성된다

Confucian beliefs have it that cutting open corpses would kill a person once again after death

ㄴ 유교에서는 사체에서 조직을 떼어내는 것은 죽은 자를 또 한 번 죽이는 것이라고 주장한다

Conversation is unlike a discussion, insofar as one is not trying to arrive at any definite conclusion

ㄴ 대화란 어떤 명확한 결론에 도달하려고 하지 않는 점에 있어서 토론과 다르다

Danggwi not only helps stimulate circulation and manufacture blood, but it also purifies existing blood

ㄴ 당귀는 혈액순환을 촉진하고 조혈작용을 도울 뿐만 아니라 몸에 있던

› **peat** decay organic deposit often dried for fuel

피를 정화하기도 한다

Diffidence is the better part of knowledge
> ↳ 자신 없다고 생각하는 것이 지식의 태반이다

Don't forget to earth up the roots firmly when you plant the tree
> ↳ 나무를 심을 때 뿌리에 흙을 단단히 덮어야 한다

Double-think means the power of holding two contradictory beliefs in one's mind simultaneously
> ↳ 이중사고란 두 가지의 모순된 신념을 동시에 가진다는 말이다

Duty largely consists of pretending that the trivial is critical
> ↳ 의무란 주로 시시한 일을 중요한 일인 것처럼 가장하는 일이다

Every prison that man build is built with bricks of shame
> ↳ 사람이 지은 모든 교도소는 치욕의 벽돌로 지은 집이다

Every step by which men add to their knowledge and skills is a step also by which they can control other men
> ↳ 자신의 지식과 기술에 보탬이 되어 나가는 모든 과정은 다른 사람들을 관리할 수 있는 과정이 되기도 한다

Examination papers are usually marked on the basis of 100
> ↳ 시험은 보통 100점 만점으로 채점해

Expensive repairs to sewer systems often result when large trees spread their roots
> ↳ 커다란 나무의 뿌리가 뻗는데서 종종 비싼 복구비가 드는 하수처리 시설의 고장이 생긴다

Exposed topsoil can lose its ability to support plant growth and to hold moisture
> ↳ 노출된 표토는 식물의 성장을 도와줄 능력과 습기를 머금는 능력을 잃게된다

› **contradict** state the contrary of

› **topsoil** surface soil in which plants have most of their roots

Exposure to the brilliant sunlight is the acid test for showing this fabric won't fade

       ↳ 이 천이 탈색하지 않는지 엄밀히 검사하기 위해서는 화창한 햇빛에 내놔 봐야 한다

4 goes into 8 two times, but two won't go into 7

       ↳ 8에 4를 나누면 2가 되지만 7은 2로 나눌 수 없다

Fluorescent high-lighters are easy to accentuate the main ideas in our reading

       ↳ 형광 펜은 우리가 읽고있는 내용을 두드러지게 표시하기 쉽다

Four from six leaves two

       ↳ 6에서 4를 빼면 2가 남는다

Ginseng helps warm up the body, strengthen immunity and even fight cancer

       ↳ 인삼은 몸을 따뜻하게 하고 면역성을 강화시키며 암에 대한 저항력까지 강화해 준다

He that increases knowledge increases sorrow

       ↳ 지식을 늘이는 사람은 슬픔도 늘이게 된다

Hormone-disturbing chemicals cause cancer, reduce the number of sperm, hamper growth, and disturb the reproductive system

       ↳ 환경호르몬은 암을 발생시킬 뿐 아니라 사람의 정자 수를 줄이고 성적 억제와 생식이상 등을 초래한다

(I'm sorry) I'm only armed with knowledge

       ↳ 지식 외엔 믿는 게 없어

If the population of one species rises too much a new epidemic will come along to redress the balance

       ↳ 한 종족의 총 수가 너무 늘어나면 전염병이 생겨나서 그 생존 수를

▸ **accentuate**   stress or show off by a contrast   ▸ **hamper**   impede

▸ **sperm**   semen or a germ cell in it

균형 시킨다

If you don't know one word but you know the others, your knowledge should help you in figuring out the meaning of the unknown word

↳ 만일 당신이 한가지 단어를 모르지만 다른 단어를 알 때 당신이 가지고 있는 지식은 알지 못하는 단어의 의미를 추리해 내도록 도울 것이다

Ignorance, if recognized, is often more fruitful than the appearance of knowledge

↳ 무지를 깨닫기만 한다면 지식을 내보이는 것보다 값질 때가 많다

In order to produce electricity by power, a dam is built to utilize a stream

↳ 수력발전을 위해서 댐을 건설하여 강물을 막는다

In the new world of e-commerce, there's concern that information is being exchanged more easily, resulting in unwelcome intrusions into consumers' personal lives

↳ 새로운 전자 상거래 세계에서는 정보가 한층 용이하게 교환되며 결과적으로 소비자들의 사생활을 침범하는 결과를 낳게 된다는 문제가 있다

Inbreeding may suggest an array of idiots, imbeciles, monsters, weaklings, deaf mutes, and other defects among the offspring

↳ 동종번식을 하면 자식들에게 천치, 저능아, 기형, 농아, 그리고 여러 가지 장애 등이 나타나는 것을 암시할 수 있다

Infestation by pests and inimical organisms can be obviated by using benign insects and natural odor that ward off harmful elements

↳ 해충이나 다른 유해한 유기체가 번지는 것은, 해로운 요소를 물리치는 이로운 곤충이나 자연 향을 사용함으로써 미연에 방지할 수 있다

It won't be profitable to exploit the sea, no matter what great riches

---

› **commerce** business

› **infest** swarm or grow in or over

› **obviate** make unnecessary

it has
> ㄴ 바다가 아무리 많은 부를 가지고 있을지라도 바다를 개발하는 것은 수익성이 없다

It's a mistake to seek a single usual explanation
> ㄴ 단일한 보편적인 설명을 찾는 것은 잘못이다

It's just as important to keep some wildlife from being too plentiful as it is to keep others from becoming too scarce
> ㄴ 야생 생물들이 수적으로 너무 희박해 지지 않도록 하는 것만큼이나 이들이 너무 많아지지 않도록 하는 것도 중요하다

It's now possible to fabricate many parts of a new house in a factory and then put them together at the site
> ㄴ 이제는 새 집에 필요한 많은 부품들을 공장에서 만든 뒤 현장에서 조립하는 것이 가능해졌다

It's only when a rough diamond is faceted that its brilliance and beauty are revealed to us
> ㄴ 다이아몬드 원광이 깎일 때 비로소 그 광택과 아름다움이 사람의 눈에 띈다

Jesus used parables to explain moral questions in a way that people could understand
> ㄴ 예수는 사람들이 알아들을 수 있도록 도덕성에 관한 문제를 설명하기 위해 비유를 사용했다

Jiwhang can be a great help for people who get easily stressed and fatigued working long hours
> ㄴ 지황은 장시간 일을 해서 쉽게 스트레스가 쌓이고 쉽게 피곤해지는 사람에게 큰 도움이 된다

Jiwhang helps prevent the symptoms of senility and supplements the

---

› **facet** surface of a cut gem, phase

substances essential for marrow production
> ↳ 지황은 노화현상을 막아주고 골수형성에 꼭 필요한 성분을 보충해준다

Kimchi is prepared with Chinese cabbage and many other natural ingredients, then stored underground in clay containers to ferment for at least three weeks
> ↳ 김치는 배추와 여러 가지 자연산 재료들을 섞어 질그릇에 넣어 땅 속에서 최소한 3주 이상 발효시켜 만든다

Knowledge and history are the enemies of religion
> ↳ 지식과 역사는 종교의 적이다

Knowledge can be communicated, but wisdom not
> ↳ 지식은 전해질 수 있지만 지혜는 그렇지 않다

Licorice root counteracts the effects of poisons and helps to increase and harmonize effects of other herbs
> ↳ 감초는 독성을 중화시키고 다른 한약재들의 효능을 강화시키고 조화시켜 준다

Lots of apartment blocks were so badly designed they had to be demolished within a few years of being built
> ↳ 많은 아파트들이 크게 잘못 설계되어서 지은 지 몇 년 안 가서 무너지기에 이르렀다

Maintaining objectivity and a sense of balance are cardinal rules for all self-respecting members the media news
> ↳ 객관성과 균형감각의 유지는 새로운 대중매체의 모든 자존심 있는 종사자들에게 핵심적인 규칙이다

Many detergents are chemical compounds made by combining bleaches and other ingredients into mixture of tablets
> ↳ 많은 세제들은 표백제와 다른 재료들을 섞어 작은 알갱이로 만든 화

› **marrow** soft tissue in the cavity of bone

› **demolish** tear down or smash, put an end to

학 혼합물이다

Many useful substances are now recovered from materials that used to be thrown away
ㄴ 옛날에 폐기되었던 물질에서 지금은 유용한 물질이 많이 재생되고 있다

Milk is a suspension of nourishing materials in water
ㄴ 우유는 물 속에 녹아있는 영양성분 물질의 현탁액이다

Modulating the sound of the words we say adds feeling, intentions or emphasis to them
ㄴ 말하는 단어들의 소리를 조절함으로써 그 말에 감정이나 의도, 혹은 강조의 의미를 덧붙이게 된다

Most books now available simply enumerate words without identifying any proper etymological thread running through them
ㄴ 현재 시중에 나와있는 대부분의 책들은 책의 내용 속에 흐르고 있는 어원적 실마리를 제대로 적시하지 못한 채 단지 단어들을 나열하고 있음에 불과하다

Mt. Halla rises 1950 meters above sea level
ㄴ 한라산은 해발 1950 미터이다

9 divides 45=45 divides by 9
ㄴ 45는 9로 나누어져

Negotiable instruments such as personal checks may ordinarily be transferred to another person by endorsement
ㄴ 개인수표와 같은 양도가능 약속어음은 보통 배서를 통해 남에게 양도 될 수 있다

Our increased knowledge and skill may augment our capacity for evil if our purposes are unwise
ㄴ 우리의 목적이 어리석다면 우리에게 늘어난 지식과 기술이 나쁜 일에

› **modulate** keep in proper measure or proportion, vary a radio wave

› **etymology** history of a word, study of etymologies

대처할 능력을 증가시킬 수 있다

Paleontology, which is closely related to the study of evolution, is a discipline that examines life as it exited in past geological times
> ↳ 진화론과 밀접하게 관련되어 있는 고생물학은 지난 지질시대에 퇴장한 생물에 대해서 연구하는 학문이다

Pedantry is the dotage of knowledge
> ↳ 학자연하는 태도는 맹목적인 지식 사랑이다

Philosophy triumphs easily over past evils and future evils; but present evils triumph over it
> ↳ 철학은 과거와 미래의 재앙을 쉽게 이기지만 현재의 재앙은 철학을 이겨낸다

Photography is a dynamic way to capture and preserve fleeting moments in time
> ↳ 사진술은 시간의 흐름 속에 지나가는 순간을 포착해 보존하는 역동적인 방법이다

Picked-up knowledge is useful, too
> ↳ 귀동냥도 쓸모는 있다

Pocket all your knowledge with your watch, and never pull it out in company unless desired
> ↳ 당신의 모든 지식은 시계와 함께 주머니에 넣어주고 필요할 때 외에는 절대로 남 앞에서 꺼내지 마라

Relaxation therapy teaches not to fret about small things
> ↳ 이완요법은 사소한 일에 너무 걱정하지 말라고 가르친다

Root up the whole tree, otherwise it will grow again from any remaining roots
> ↳ 나무를 뿌리째 뽑아버리지 않으면 뿌리가 조금만 있어도 싹이 난다

• **paleontology** science of life in past geological periods
• **dotage** senility

She found she couldn't keep her secret from becoming public knowledge
ㄴ 그녀는 자신의 비밀이 새는 것을 어찌할 수 없었다

Slash-and-burn farmers work one farm of land until it is exhausted, then move on to virgin soil and start again
ㄴ 화전민들은 땅의 힘이 고갈될 때까지 농사를 짓다가 또 새로운 땅으로 이동하여 다시 시작한다

Statistics can easily mislead the man in the street
ㄴ 통계는 보통사람들을 쉽게 오도할 수 있다

Steamers can float in water in spite of their being heavier than water
ㄴ 기선은 물보다 무겁지만 물에 뜬다

Suffering need not be embittering but be a source of knowledge
ㄴ 고난이 반드시 가혹할 필요는 없지만 지식의 원천이 될 수는 있다

Tampering with the smoke detectors is federal offense and will set off an alarm in the cockpit
ㄴ 화재 감지기에 손을 대면 연방법을 위반하게 되며 조종석에 부착된 알람을 작동시키게 됩니다

That library has a whole range of user-friendly encyclopedias and dictionaries
ㄴ 저 도서관에는 모든 부문에 걸친 이용자 위주의 백과서전과 사전들이 비치되어 있다

The amount of water used in industry is enormous but the amount wasted is even greater
ㄴ 산업에 사용되는 물의 양은 엄청나지만 낭비되는 양은 그보다 훨씬 더 많다

The bamboo is a plant which finishes its growth in one year

› **embitter** make bitter

› **tamper** interfere so as to change for the worse(+with)

       ↳ 대나무는 1년 내에 성장을 끝낸다

The binding power of any adhesive depends on the cohesion of the adhesive itself and how well the adhesive adheres
       ↳ 접착제의 접착력은 접착제 자체의 응집력과 부착물의 표면에 접착제가 얼마나 잘 붙는가에 달려있다

The bushes may die back(down) in this cold autumn but they will grow again next spring
       ↳ 이 관목들은 이 추운 겨울에 지상부분이 말라죽을 수 있지만 다음 봄엔 다시 싹이 난다

The difference between libel and slander is that libel is printed while slander is spoken
       ↳ 중상문과 중상의 차이는 중상문이 글로 되어있는데 반해 중상은 말로 한다는데 있다

The great end of life is not knowledge but action
       ↳ 인생의 큰 목표는 지식이 아닌 행동에 있다

The pursuit of knowledge should be combined with wisdom
       ↳ 지식의 추구에는 지혜가 수반돼야 한다

The thing came to my knowledge later
       ↳ 그 일은 나중에 알았어

This brochure provides a brief description of some of the salient features of the insurance policy
       ↳ 이 소책자에는 보험증서의 두드러진 특징 및 가치에 대한 간략한 설명이 들어있다

This is one hundredth the life size of a turtle-shaped warship
       ↳ 이것은 거북선 실물 크기의 100분의 1이다

This lead to a dichotomous view of people and events as good versus bad

---

› **libel** action, crime, or an instance of injuring a person's reputation especially by

› **dichotomy** division into 2 contrasting groups   something written

ㄴ 이는 인물이나 사건에 대해 이분법적인 관점으로 귀결된다

Three into nine goes three times
ㄴ 9에 3을 나누면 3이 된다

To be conscious that you are ignorant is a great step to knowledge
ㄴ 자신의 무지를 깨닫는다는 것은 지식을 향한 큰 발걸음이다

To be proud of knowledge is to blind with light
ㄴ 지식을 자랑하는 것은 빛이 있을 때 보지 못하는 것과 같다

Two goes into six three times
ㄴ 6을 2로 나누면 3이 된다

Whoever acquires knowledge and does not practise it resembles him who ploughs his land and leaves it unsown
ㄴ 알면서 행하지 않음은 땅만 갈고 파종하지 않음과 같다

Wisdom sets bounds even to knowledge
ㄴ 지혜는 지식까지도 한계를 정해준다

With that much knowledge, you can hardly said to know statistics
ㄴ 그 정도를 가지고 통계를 안다고 해서는 안 돼

Zeal without knowledge is fire without light
ㄴ 지식 없는 열정은 빛 없는 불과 같다

· **resemble** be like or similar to

130. 지혜　　　　　　　　　　**Wisdom**

A chain is only as strong as its weakest link
　　ㄴ 어느 한 모퉁이라도 취약한 면이 있어서는 안 된다

> 허술한 곳이 있으면 결국에는 몰락한다는 뜻이다. 전쟁 중에도 한 곳의 허술한 방어가 함락의 원인이 되고, 사회도 소외 받은 계층이 사회 문제를 일으킨다. 영어에서는 "A chain is no stronger than its weakest link 체인은 가장 약한 부분만큼 강하다"라는 속담이 있다.

A fool's wrath is known at once, but a prudent man covers shame
　　　　ㄴ 미련한 자는 분노를 당장 나타내거니와 슬기로운 자는 치욕을 참느니라

A god could hardly love and be wise
　　　　ㄴ 신이라 하더라도 사랑에 빠지면 현명할 수 없다

> "Love is blind 사랑에 빠지면 눈이 먼다"라는 얘기가 있다. 사랑과 이성은 공존할 수 없다는 뜻이다(Love and reason do not go togther).

A great mind is one that can forget or look beyond itself
　　　　ㄴ 위대한 사람은 잊어버릴 줄 알거나 그보다 더 저쪽을 볼 수 있는 사람이다

A hero is a man who does what he can
　　　　ㄴ 영웅은 그가 할 수 있는 일을 하는 사람이다

› **link** connecting structure, bond

A privilege often gives rise to abuses
  ↳ 특권은 흔히 남용을 야기시킨다

A rod is found the back of him who is devoid of understanding
  ↳ 지혜 없는 자의 등에는 채찍이 있느니라

A wise man cares not for what he cannot have
  ↳ 현명한 사람은 허욕을 부리지 않는다

A wise man gets more use from his enemies than a fool
  ↳ 어리석은 자가 친구에게서 얻는 것 이상으로 현명한 자는 적으로부터 쓸모 있는 것을 얻는다

A wise man never refuses anything to necessity
  ↳ 현명한 사람은 필요 앞에 아무 것도 거부하지 않는다

A wise man profits by his mistakes
  ↳ 현명한 사람은 실수도 좋은 경험으로 삼는다

> 보통 사람들은 자신의 경험으로 지혜를 쌓아 나간다. 좋은 경험과 나쁜 경험을 통해 참된 지혜를 얻는다. 그보다 더 앞선 사람은 자신의 경험이 아닌 남의 경험을 통해서도 지혜를 얻는다(By other's faults wise men correct their own = 현인은 남의 허물을 보고 스스로의 허물을 시정한다).

Admit your errors before someone else exaggerates them
  ↳ 남들이 당신의 실수를 과장하기 전에 그 실수를 인정하라

Adversity makes a man wise
  ↳ 역경은 사람을 현명하게 만든다

> 사람은 역경을 통하여 참된 지혜를 얻는다. 또한 사람은 역경을 통하여 진정한 친구를 가려낼 수도 있다(Adversity makes strange bedfellows).

› **devoid** entirely lacking

All envy is proportionate to desire
> 모든 질투는 열망과 비례한다

All faults may be forgiven of him who has perfect candor
> 완전히 솔직한 사람은 모든 허물을 용서받을 수 있다

All that is human must retrograde itself if it does not advance
> 인간은 진보하지 않으면 퇴보할 수밖에 없다

An error doesn't become a mistake until you refuse to correct it
> 잘못은 고치기를 거부할 때 까지는 될 수 없다

Anger restrained is wisdom gained
> 화를 참으면 지혜를 얻는다

Answer a fool according to his folly
> 어리석은 자에게는 어리석음의 정도에 따라 대답해 줘라

Any man can make mistakes, but only an idiot persists in his error
> 누구나 잘못을 저지를 수 있지만 바보만이 그 실수를 고집한다

As iron is eaten away by rust, so the envious are consumed by their own passion
> 녹이 쇠를 부식하듯이 질투하는 자의 열정이 마음을 부식한다

At least she knows how to look after number one
> 그 여자는 적어도 자기 실속은 챙길 줄 알아

Attributing everything to one cause is too simple and not very realistic
> 모든 일을 한 가지 원인의 탓으로 도리는 것은 너무 단순하고 현실적이지 않다

Bad is never good until worse happens
> 더 나쁜 것이 나타나기 전에는 나쁜 것이 좋은 것으로 되지는 않는다

Being tactful in audacity is knowing how far one can go too far

---

› **candor** frankness

› **audacity** boldness or insolence

› **retrograde** moving backward, becomingworse

ㄴ 요령 있는 대담성이란 자신이 얼마나 너무 멀리 갈 수 있는가를 아는 데 있다

Better be wise by the misfortunes of others than by your own

ㄴ 자신의 불운을 통해서 현명해지기보다는 남의 불운을 통해 현명해지는 것이 낫다

Better mad with the rest of the world than wise alone

ㄴ 혼자 현명하기보다는 세상의 다른 사람들과 더불어 함께 미치는 게 낫다

Better to flatter the devil than fight him

ㄴ 악마와 싸우기보다는 그를 추켜 주어라

Better to wear out than to rust out

ㄴ 녹슬게 하느니 써 없애는 게 나아

Brevity is the soul of wit

ㄴ 말은 짧을수록 좋아

> 말이란 뜻을 전달하기 위한 수단이다. 거창하고 긴 말은 말의 초점을 흐릴 뿐만 아니라, 진실성이 없어진다. 비슷한 뜻으로 "Short answer is often the most eloquent 간단한 말은 웅변과 같다"도 쓰인다.

Caution is a virtue

ㄴ 조심이 미덕

Come back wiser for experience

ㄴ 경험 쌓아 지혜롭게 돌아 오라

Coming events cast their shadows before

ㄴ 무슨 일이 닥치기 전에 조짐이 있게 마련이다

Chance favors a prepared mind

ㄴ 기회는 준비된 사람의 편이다

› **eloquent** forceful and persuasive in speech

Chance governs all
> ↳ 모든 것이 운

Condemn the offence and not its perpetrator
> ↳ 죄는 미워해도 사람은 미워하지 마라

Content lodges oftener(more often) in cottages than palaces
> ↳ 만족은 대궐보다 오두막집에 들어오는 때가 많다

Could everything be done twice everything would be done better
> ↳ 무슨 일이고 두 번씩 한다면 훨씬 잘 될 것이다

Curses come home to roost
> ↳ 해치려하다가는 자기가 먼저 해 입어

> 남을 욕하거나 저주하면 결국에는 자신에게 다시 돌아온다는 말이다. 남에게
> 상처를 주는 말은 하지 말아야 한다는 뜻과 일맥상통한다(Reckless words
> pierce like a sword = 무분별한 말은 칼과 같이 사람을 찌른다).

Cut this off from the start
> ↳ 미연에 방지하다

> (=Put the brakes on this right now)
> (=Nipping in the bud)

Danger is next neighbor to true security
> ↳ 위험을 겪어보지 않고는 참된 안정을 얻을 수 없다

Dangers are indifferent to us
> ↳ 위험 따위는 우리 안중에도 없다

Debauchery is perhaps an act of despair in the face of infinity

---

· **perpetrate** be guilty of doing
· **debauch** seduce or corrupt

· **lodge** provide quarters for, come to rest, file

ㄴ 타락은 무한대에 대한 절망감일 수 있다

Desire to have things done quickly prevents their being done thoroughly

    ㄴ 일을 급하게 처리하겠다는 욕심은 그 일이 제대로 되는 것을 방해한다

Doing nothing is doing ill

    ㄴ 아무 일도 안 하는 것은 나쁜 일을 하는 것이다

Don't despise the bottom rungs in the ascent to greatness

    ㄴ 높은 곳에 오를 때 디디는 사다리의 바닥 가로장을 경시하지 마라

Don't judge a man until you've walked in his boots

    ㄴ 남의 처지가 되어보지도 않고 남을 판단하지 마라

Don't trade your passion for (cheap) glory

    ㄴ 값 싼 영광 때문에 열정을 팔지마

Enough is as good as a feast

    ㄴ 배부르면 진수성찬이 부럽지 않다(충분한 것 이상은 오히려 해가 될 수 있다)

Even the gods are moved by the voice of entreaty

    ㄴ 간청하면 신의 마음도 움직인다

Every advantage has its tax

    ㄴ 모든 유리한 일에는 부담이 따르게 되어있다

Every man has a fool in his sleeve

    ㄴ 약점 없는 사람은 없다

Every slip is not a fall

    ㄴ 미끄러진다고 다 쓰러지는 것은 아니다

Everything eventually comes back to number one

    ㄴ 모든 일이 결국은 본인에게 돌아오게 돼있어

› **entreat** ask earnestly

> 남을 욕하거나 저주하면 결국에는 자신에게 다시 돌아온다는 말이다. 남에게 상처를 주는 말은 하지 말아야 한다는 뜻과 일맥상통한다(Reckless words pierce like a sword = 무분별한 말은 칼과 같이 사람을 찌른다).

Evil communications corrupt good manners
  ↳ 먹물 옆에 가면 먹물이 묻게 마련이다

> 나쁜 친구를 사귀면 나쁜 사람이 된다는 뜻이다. 성경에는 "Bad company corrupts good character 나쁜 친구는 좋은 성격을 방해한다"라는 표현이 있다. 영어 속담으로는 "Evil communication corrupts good manners"라는 성경에서 유래한 표현이 있다.

Expect poison from the standing water
  ↳ 고인 물에는 독이 있을 것으로 생각하라

Faith will move mountains=Sincerity moves heaven
  ↳ 지성이면 감천

> "뜻이 있는 곳에 길이 있다"라는 말이 있다. 신념을 가지고 정진하면 길이 보이게 마련이다. 영어 속담에는 "Faith moves mountains 신념이 산을 움직인다"라고 한다.

Fashionably amusing table manners are a matter of breaking the rule at the right time
  ↳ 식탁의 좌중을 상황에 맞게 웃기는 것은 적절한 때에 법을 어기는 것과 같다

Fear is an instructor of great sagacity
  ↳ 두려움은 큰 지혜의 스승이다

· **reckless** lacking caution
· **sagacity** shrewd

Few things are impossible to diligence and skill
ㄴ 근면과 숙련 앞에 안 되는 일이 거의 없다

Fine manners need the support of fine manners in others
ㄴ 한 사람의 훌륭한 태도는 다른 사람의 훌륭한 태도를 필요로 한다

Force without reason falls of its own weight
ㄴ 도리에 맞지 않는 폭력은 그 자체의 무게로 쓰러진다

Forgiving the unrepentant is like making pictures on water
ㄴ 회개하지 않는 자를 용서함은 물위에 그림을 그리는 것과 같다

Forgotten is forgiven
ㄴ 잊어버린 것은 용서한 것이다

Fortune brings in some boats that are not steered
ㄴ 어떤 보트에게 행운은 조종하지 않은 방향으로 나아가게 한다

Fortune is not the side of the faint-hearted
ㄴ 행운은 겁쟁이의 편을 들지 않는다

Fortune rarely accompanies any one to the door
ㄴ 행운은 좀처럼 사람을 문간까지 동행하지 않는다

Generosity is the flower of justice
ㄴ 후함은 도리(정의)의 꽃이다

Gladly we desire to make other people perfect but we will not amend our own faults
ㄴ 우리는 남들이 완벽해지기를 기꺼이 바라면서도 우리 자신의 허물은 고치려 하지 않는다

Grammar will never prevail against usage
ㄴ 문법이 실용에 앞설 수는 없다

Great things are done more through courage than wisdom
ㄴ 큰 일은 지혜보다 용기를 통하여 이루어지는 일이 많다

· **faint-hearted**　cowardly or spiritless, weak and dizzy, lacking vigor　ǀ　· **amend**　omprove, alter in writing

Greed has no limits
ㄴ 말 타면 경마 잡히고 싶어한다

> 사람은 쉽게 만족하지 않아서 욕심이 끝이 없다. 한국의 "말 타면 경마 잡히고 싶다"는 그런 사람의 심리를 잘 표현하였다. 영어로는 "Greed has no limits 욕심은 한계가 없다" 또는 "The more you get, the more you want 많이 가질수록 더 원한다"라고 한다.

Hasty climbers have sudden falls
ㄴ 급히 올라가는 사람은 갑자기 떨어지게 돼있어

Hate a priest, and you will hate his surplice
ㄴ 중이 미우면 가사도 밉다

He deserves paradise who makes his company laugh
ㄴ 동료를 웃게 하는 자는 천국에 갈 자격이 있다(마호멭)

He is no wise man that can't play the fools sometimes
ㄴ 가끔씩 바보짓을 할 줄 모르는 사람은 현명한 사람이 아니다

He knows peace who has forgotten desire
ㄴ 욕망을 잊는 사람은 평온을 아는 사람이다

He may find the fault that cannot mend
ㄴ 잘못을 발견하기는 쉬워도 고치기는 어렵다

He that flings dirt at another, dirties himself most
ㄴ 남에게 진흙을 던지는 사람은 자신이 제일 많이 더러워진다

He that idles is tempted by a legion
ㄴ 할 일이 없는 사람은 무수한 사람의 유혹을 받는다

He that serves everybody is paid by nobody
ㄴ 모든 사람에게 봉사하는 사람은 아무에게도 보답 받지 못한다

▸ **surplice**　loose white outer ecclesiastical vestment

He that stumbles twice over one stone, deserves to break his shins
ㄴ 같은 돌부리에 두 번씩 걸려 넘어지는 사람은 정강이가 부러져도 싸다

He who digs a pit for others falls in himself
ㄴ 남을 함정에 빠뜨리려면 자기가 먼저 빠진다

He who envies admits his inferiority
ㄴ 질투하는 사람은 자신의 열등함을 인정하는 것이다

He who has never learned to obey can't be a good commander
ㄴ 명령에 따르는 것을 배우지 않는 사람은 훌륭한 지도자가 될 수 없다

He who lives without folly is not so wise as he believes
ㄴ 바보짓을 하지 않고 사는 사람은 자신이 믿고 있는 것만큼은 현명하지 않다

He who restrains his lips is wise
ㄴ 입술을 제어하는 자는 지혜가 있느니라

He who wants a rose must respect the thorn
ㄴ 장미를 원하는 사람은 가시를 존경해야 한다

History teaches us that men and nations behave wisely once they have exhausted all other alternatives
ㄴ 역사는 국민과 국가에게 모든 대안이 고갈됐을 때 현명하게 행동한다는 것을 가르쳐 준다

Honor and profit lie not in one sack
ㄴ 명예와 이익은 같은 자루 속에 들어있지 않다

Horror causes men to clench their fists, and in horror men join together
ㄴ 공포는 사람들의 주먹을 꽉 쥐게 만들고 사람들은 두려움 속에서 단합한다

Human progress is furthered, not by conformity, but by aberration

---

› **restrain** limit or keep under control

› **clench** hold fast, close tightly

› **aberration** deviation or distortion

ㄴ 인간의 진보는 일치성이 아닌 불일치성에서 더욱 진척된다

If the shoe fits, wear it
ㄴ 마음에 찔린다면 네게 맞는 말이기 때문

If we are not foolish young, we are foolish old
ㄴ 젊어서 어리석은 짓을 해보지 않으면 나이를 먹어서 어리석어진다

If you can't stand the heat, keep out of the kitchen
ㄴ 문제의 해법이 보이지 않으면 처음부터 끼어 들지 마라=무거운 절보
다 가벼운 중이 먼저 떠나라

If you desire many things, many things will seem but a few
ㄴ 많은 것을 탐내면 그 많은 것들이 불과 몇 개로밖에 안 보일 것이다
(욕심은 끝이 없어)

사람은 쉽게 만족하지 않아서 욕심이 끝이 없다. 한국의 "말 타면 경마 잡히
고 싶다"는 그런 사람의 심리를 잘 표현하였다. 영어로는 "Greed has no
limits 욕심은 한계가 없다"또는 "The more you get, the more you
want 많이 가질수록 더 원한다"라고 한다.

If you don't make mistakes you don't make anything
ㄴ 실수를 하지 않으면 아무 것도 해낼 수 없다(구더기 무서워 장 못 담그랴)

실패를 두려워하는 사람은 아무것도 성취할 수 없다는 뜻이다. 사람은 실수를
하면서 배워가기 때문이다. 영어로는 "If you don't make mistakes you
don't make anything 실수를 하지 않으면 아무 것도 이루지 못한다"이다.

If you get lost, it's best to double back the way you came
ㄴ 길을 잃을 때는 왔던 길로 되돌아가는 게 제일 낫다

If you hold your tongue, no one will be any wiser

› **greed**   selfish desire beyond reason

↳ 네가 잠자코 있으면 누가 알겠나

Ignorance is the womb of monsters
↳ 무지는 괴물들이 생겨나는 자궁이다

In the multitude of counsellors there's wisdom(safety)
↳ 여럿이 모이면 좋은 꾀가 나온다(실수가 없다)

> 한 사람의 지혜보다 여럿이 힘을 합치면 더욱 좋은 생각을 낼 수 있다는 뜻이다. "Two heads are better than one 두 사람의 머리가 한 사람의 머리보다 낫다"라는 영어 속담도 있다.

Industry is fortune's right hand, and frugality her left
↳ 근면은 행운의 오른손이고 검소함은 왼손이다

It is important to stand by your own principle
↳ 자기 나름대로의 원칙을 지키는 게 중요하다

It is very foolish to be wise exclusively
↳ 혼자만 현명하겠다는 것은 매우 어리석은 일이다

It takes a wise man to recognize a wise man
↳ 현자가 현자를 알아본다

It takes backbone to be a pioneer
↳ 선구자가 되려면 불굴의 정신이 필요해

It'll be wise for you to be tight-lipped about what you have done
↳ 네가 한 일에 대하여는 입을 다무는 게 현명해

It's easier to be wise on behalf of others than to be so for ourselves
↳ 자신을 위할 때보다 남을 위할 때 더 현명해지기 쉽다

It's easier to commend poverty than to endure it
↳ 가난을 찬양하기는 쉬워도 참아내기는 어렵다

› **multitude** great number
› **frugal** thrifty

It's easy to be wise after the event
> ↳ 사후에 현명해지기는 쉬운 일이다

It's easy to bear the misfortunes of others
> ↳ 남의 불행을 참아내기는 쉽다

It's foolish to have to go to a certain place just because others go
> ↳ 남들이 간다고 해서 자기도 그곳에 가야 한다는 것은 어리석은 일이다

It's more easier to get a favor from fortune than to keep it
> ↳ 공성은 쉬워도 수성은 어려워(행운을 잡기는 쉬워도 지키기는 어려워)

It's not knowing much, but what is useful, that makes a wise man
> ↳ 현명한 사람을 만드는 것은 많이 안다는 것이 아니라 유용한 것을 아
> 는 것이다

It's only through restraint that man can manage not to suppress himself
> ↳ 사람은 절제가 있어야만 자신에 대한 속박 없이 견딜 수 있다

Just as our eyes need light in order to see, our minds need ideas in order to conceive
> ↳ 우리의 눈이 보는데는 빛이 필요하듯이 우리의 마음에 아이디어가 있
> 어야 궁리를 하게 된다

Knowing what is right does not make a sagacious man
> ↳ 무엇이 옳은지 아는 것으로 현명한 사람이 되는 것은 아니다

Knowledge can be communicated, but wisdom not
> ↳ 지식은 전해질 수 있지만 지혜는 그렇지 않다

Korea possesses the potential and wisdom to meet any challenge
> ↳ 한국은 어떠한 난관도 이겨낼 수 있는 저력과 지혜를 가지고 있다

Let another's shipwreck be your sea-mark
> ↳ 다른 배가 좌초하거든 당신의 항해에 지표로 삼아라

Let's not burden our remembrance with a heaviness that's gone

---

› **sagacious** shrewd

ㄴ 지난 일의 마음 무거움으로 우리의 마음을 더 무겁게 짓누르지 마라

Luck never made a wise man

ㄴ 행운은 현명한 사람을 만든 일없다

Measure is treasure medicine

ㄴ 절제(중용)가 보배다

> 중용이란 한쪽으로 치우침이 없고 항상 변함 없음을 말한다. 자신을 과소평가나 과대평가 하지말고, 항상 겸손한 마음으로 중도를 걷는 것이 중요하다. 예부터 우리나라에서는 공자의 사상을 받들어 중용을 강조하였다.
> (=Virtue is found in the middle)
> (=Safety lies in the middle course)

Much will have more

ㄴ 욕심은 한이 없어

> 사람은 쉽게 만족하지 않아서 욕심이 끝이 없다. 한국의 "말 타면 경마 잡히고 싶다"는 그런 사람의 심리를 잘 표현하였다. 영어로는 "Greed has no limits 욕심은 한계가 없다"또는 "The more you get, the more you want 많이 가질수록 더 원한다"라고 한다.

Nature and books belong to the eyes that see them

ㄴ 자연과 책은 알아보는 눈을 가진 사람의 것이다

Nature gave us fear to protect us from danger

ㄴ 자연은 우리를 위험으로부터 보호하기 위해 공포심을 주었다

Nature's instructions are always slow, those of men are generally premature

ㄴ 자연의 가르침은 언제나 늦지만 사람의 지시는 대체로 너무 이르다

› **premature**   coming before the usual or proper time

Necessity relieves us from embarrassment of choice
> ↳ 절실한 필요는 선택의 어려움으로부터 구제해 준다

Necessity turns lion into fox
> ↳ 필요는 사자를 여우로 만든다

Nine-tenths of wisdom is being wise in time
> ↳ 대부분의 지혜는 시간이 가면서 생겨난다

No legacy is so rich as honesty
> ↳ 어떤 것도 정직만큼 풍성한 유산은 없다

No man is born wise or learned
> ↳ 태어날 때부터 현명하거나 배우고 나온 사람은 없다

> 아무리 위대한 사람도 태어났을 때부터 위대하지는 않았다. "Alexander himself was once a crying babe 알렉산더 대왕도 한 때는 우는 아기였다"라는 말이 있다. 예전엔 왕족이 있어서 태어날 때부터 고귀한 사람이 있었기 때문에 "Not every man is born with a silver spoon in his mouth 모두 입에 은수저를 물고 태어난 것은 아니다"라는 말이 있었지만, 요즘은 모두 평등하기 때문에 태생으로 운명이 결정 나는 일은 드물다.

No man so wise but he may be deceived
> ↳ 아무리 현명한 사람도 속을 때가 있다

Not by years but by disposition is the wisdom acquired
> ↳ 지혜는 나이가 아닌 성품으로 얻게 된다

Nothing dries sooner than tears
> ↳ 눈물보다 빨리 마르는 건 없다(슬픔은 지나가게 마련)

Obstinacy alone is not a virtue
> ↳ 고집만으로는 덕성이 아니다

▸ **disposition** act or power of disposing or, arrangement, natural attitude

Obstinacy and dogmatism are the surest sign of stupidity

ㄴ 고집과 독선은 가장 확실한 어리석음의 표시이다

Old and new wisdom mix admirably

ㄴ 오랜 지혜와 새로운 지혜는 기막히게 잘 어울린다

One can't love and be wise

ㄴ 사랑에 빠지고도 현명할 수는 없다

> "Love is blind 사랑에 빠지면 눈이 먼다"라는 얘기가 있다. 사랑과 이성은 공존할 수 없다는 뜻이다(Love and reason do not go togther).

One man's fault is another man's lesson

ㄴ 남의 잘못을 보고 자기의 잘못을 고쳐라

> (=Learn from the follies from others)

One of the greatest disadvantages of hurry is that it takes such a long time

ㄴ 서두름에서 오는 가장 큰 손해는 그 서두름으로 인하여 오히려 매우 오랜 시간이 걸린다는 점이다

Our increased knowledge and skill may augment our capacity for evil if our purposes are unwise

ㄴ 우리의 목적이 어리석다면 우리에게 늘어난 지식과 기술이 나쁜 일에 대처할 능력을 증가시킬 수 있다

Pain is forgotten where gain follows

ㄴ 이익이 있으면 고통을 잊어버린다

Pain makes man think, thought makes man wise, wisdom makes life

---

› **dogmatism** unwarranted stubbornness of opinion, viewpoint based on insufficiently examined premises

› **augment** enlarge or increase

endurable
> ↳ 고통은 사람을 생각하게 하고, 사색은 현명하게 하며, 지혜는 삶의 인내심을 키워준다

Plots sometimes recoils on plotters
> ↳ 음모는 음모자 자신에게 되돌아가는 수가 있다

Power tends to corrupt and absolute power corrupts absolutely
> ↳ 권력은 썩기 쉽고 절대권력은 절대로 썩는다

Prejudice is the child of ignorance
> ↳ 편견은 무지의 소치이다

Principles often clash with interests
> ↳ 주의와 이해관계는 흔히 상충한다

Prospect is often better than possession
> ↳ 소유에 대한 기대는 소유 그 자체보다 나은 때가 많다

Punishment deferred commonly falls the heavier
> ↳ 매도 먼저 맞는 게 낫다

Pure logic is the ruin of the spirit
> ↳ 순수한 논리는 정신을 망친다

Put conscience before profits
> ↳ 이익보다 양심을 앞세워라

Reason governs the wise and cudgels the fool
> ↳ 현자는 이치에 따르고 어리석은 자는 몽둥이에게 따른다

Reason is only a harmony among irrational impulses
> ↳ 이성은 비이성적 충동간의 조화에 불과하다

Regrets and recriminations only hurt your soul
> ↳ 후회와 남의 탓 하기는 자신의 마음만 상하게 할 뿐이다

Repentance comes too late

› **recoil** draw or spring back

› **cudgel** club, beat with a cudgel

› **recrimination** accuation

↳ 후회는 언제나 때늦게 온다

Repentance is a pill unwillingly swallowed
↳ 후회는 억지로 삼킨 알약이다

Restrictions do have to be tightened
↳ 제한은 엄격하게 해야한다

Retorting blow for blow is never good
↳ 주먹에 주먹으로 응수하는 것은 결코 좋은 일이 아니다

Science may be learned by rote, but wisdom not
↳ 학문은 기계적으로 배울 수도 있지만 지혜는 그렇지 않다

Service without reward is punishment
↳ 보답 없는 봉사는 형벌이다

Silence can seem so loud
↳ 때로는 침묵이 더 큰 의미를 갖게 돼

Silence can't always be read as agreement
↳ 침묵을 언제나 승낙으로 이해해서는 안 된다

Silence gives consent
↳ 침묵은 승낙의 표시

Simple honesty doesn't pay
↳ 고지식해서 득 볼 게 없어

Sin again reared its ugly head
↳ 죄악이 다시 그 추한 머리를 들었다

Singularity is dangerous in everything
↳ 별난 것은 무슨 일에나 위험하다

Small sacrifice may be inevitable in order to achieve great things
↳ 큰 일을 위해선 작은 희생을 감수해야 한다

› **retort** say in reply

› **rear** back, position at the back of something, being at the back

So many people, so many solitudes
> ↳ 군중 속의 고독이로군

Sorrows remembered sweeten present joy
> ↳ 잊지 않고 있는 슬픔은 현재의 기쁨을 달게 해 준다

Spare to speech and spare to speed
> ↳ 입을 다물고 있으면 아무 일도 진척이 안 된다

Step after step the ladder is ascended
> ↳ 사다리는 한 단계 한 단계씩 올라가야 한다

Such homely virtues as thrifty, hard work, and simplicity seem old-fashioned in these days
> ↳ 절약, 근면, 검소와 같은 소박한 덕목들이 오늘날에 와서는 시대에 뒤진 것으로 비쳐진다

Take the backtrack if anything goes wrong(amiss)
> ↳ 여의치 않으면 왔던 길로 되돌아가라

Take whatever measure you think the best
> ↳ 무엇이든지 적절하다고 생각되는 조치를 취하라

That fault of his can be redeemed by his good points
> ↳ 그의 장점이 결점을 보충할 수 있다

The art of being wise is the art of knowing what to overlook
> ↳ 현명해지는 요령은 무엇을 무시해야할지를 아는 요령이다

The best cure for unhappiness is to fling yourself onto your work
> ↳ 불행을 치유하는 가장 좋은 방법은 일에 모든 정력을 쏟는 일이다

The crown of the wise is the riches, but the foolishness of fools is folly
> ↳ 지혜로운 자의 재물은 그의 면류관이요 미련한 자의 소유는 다만 그 미련한 것이니라

The direction of the mind is more important than its progress

---

› **solitude**   state of being alone
› **backtrack**   retrace one's course

ㄴ 마음의 방향은 마음의 진행보다 중요하다

The first degree of folly is to hold one's self wise
ㄴ 자신이 현명하다고 생각하는 사람이 가장 바보다

The first step in wisdom is to open the windows of ego as wide as possible
ㄴ 지혜의 첫 걸음은 이기심의 창문을 열 수 있는데 까지 활짝 여는 것이다

The fool asks much, but he is more fool that grants it
ㄴ 바보는 많은 것을 요구하고 그 요구를 들어주는 사람은 더 바보다

The fool is always satisfied with himself
ㄴ 바보는 늘 자신에게 만족해한다

The fool is the man who doesn't know enough to cash in on his foolishness
ㄴ 어리석은 사람은 자신의 어리석음을 충분히 활용하지 못 하는 사람이다

The function of wisdom is to discriminate between good and evil
ㄴ 지혜의 기능은 선악을 구분하는 것이다

The growth of wisdom may be gauged accurately by the decline of ill temper
ㄴ 지혜의 상승은 못된 성질의 감소에 의해 측정될 수 있다

The growth of wisdom may be gauged exactly by the diminution of ill-temper
ㄴ 지혜의 성장은 정확히 언짢은 마음을 줄임으로써 평가될 수도 있다

The higher the mountain the greater the descent
ㄴ 산을 높이 오를수록 내려오는 길도 힘들다

The higher you climb the harder you fall
ㄴ 높이 올라갈수록 떨어질 때 비참해진다

› **gauge** measure
› **diminution** decrease

The higher-ups are apt to blind themselves to all their faults
↳ 위 사람들은 자신의 허물을 잘 알기 힘들어

The impossible takes a longer time
↳ 불가능한 일은 좀 더 시간을 요할 뿐 결국은 할 수 있다

The infliction of cruelty with a good conscience is a delight to moralists
↳ 잔인한 짓이 착한 마음에서 저질러졌을 때 도덕군자에게는 기쁨이 된다

The learning of books that you do not make your own wisdom is money in the hands of other in time of need
↳ 자신의 지혜로 만들 수 없는 책을 공부한다는 것은 돈이 필요할 때 남의 주머니에 있는 것과 같다

The loftiest edifices need the deepest foundation
↳ 가장 높은 건물은 가장 깊은 기반을 필요로 한다

The longer you vacillate, the less time you'll have to do anything worthwhile
↳ 오래 망설일수록 가치 있는 일을 할 수 있는 시간이 더 짧아진다

The loss which is unknown is no loss at all
↳ 잃는 줄도 모르고 잃는 것은 잃는 것이 아니다

The man occupies the first place seldom plays the principal part
↳ 윗자리를 차지한 사람이 주된 역할을 하는 사람은 드물다

The man who obeys is nearly always better than the man who commands
↳ 명령에 따르는 사람은 거의 언제나 명령하는 사람보다 낫다

The misfortune of the wise is better than the prosperity of the fool
↳ 현명한 사람에게 닥치는 불운은 어리석은 사람의 번영보다 낫다

The noblest vengeance is to forgive

› **lofty** tall or high, being of a noble or spiritual nature

› **vengeance** punishment in retaliation for an injury or offense

ㄴ 가장 훌륭한 보복은 참는 것이다

The pursuit of knowledge should be combined with wisdom
ㄴ 지식의 추구에는 지혜가 수반돼야 한다

The real fault is to have faults and not to amend them
ㄴ 허물을 알고도 고치지 않음이 진짜 허물이다

The tongue of the wise promotes health
ㄴ 지혜로운 자의 혀는 양약 같으니라

The tree casts its shade upon all, even upon the woodcutter
ㄴ 나무는 모든 사물에게 그림자를 골고루 던진다, 자신을 찍을 나무꾼
에게까지

The way of a fool is right in his own eyes, but he who heeds counsel is wise
ㄴ 미련한 자는 자기 행위를 바른 줄로 여기나 지혜로운 자는 권고를 받
느니라

The wind in one's face make one wise
ㄴ 역경은 사람을 현명하게 해준다

The wise forget insults, as the ungrateful a kindness
ㄴ 배은망덕한 사람이 남의 친절을 잊어버리듯이 현인은 모욕을 잊어버린다

The wise man lives so long as he ought, not so long as he can
ㄴ 현인은 살아야 할 만큼 살고 살 수 있는 것만큼 사는 게 아니다

Their ignorance was their own enemy
ㄴ 그들은 자신들의 무지를 탓해야 했다

There is always danger for those who are afraid of it
ㄴ 위험을 두려워하는 자에게는 항상 위험이 따르게 되어있다

They that stands high have many blasts to shake them
ㄴ 우뚝 솟은 나무는 흔들어 대는 바람을 많이 받는다

▸ **blast** violent gust of wind, explosion

Those who wish to be learned to fools, seem fool to the learned
↳ 어리석은 자들에게 배운 사람으로 보이고 싶어하는 사람은 배운 사람에게 어리석은 사람으로 보여진다

Though a tree grow ever so high, the falling leaves return to the root
↳ 나무가 아무리 높아도 낙엽은 결국 뿌리 쪽으로 떨어진다

Throw out a sprat to catch a mackerel
↳ 큰 것을 위해서 작은 것을 희생 해야해(버려야 한다)

> (=We must sacrifice a small good for the sake of a greater good)
> (=You must lose a fly to catch a trout)

To be wiser than others is to be honester than they
↳ 남들보다 현명해지려면 그들보다 정직해야 한다

To do evil is like sport to a fool, but a man of understanding has wisdom
↳ 미련한 자가 나쁜 것을 낙으로 삼는 것 같이 명철한 자는 지혜로 낙을 삼는다

To err is human
↳ 한번 실수는 병가상사다

To refuse and give tardily is all the same
↳ 주기를 거부하거나 늑장부리며 주는 것은 매 한가지다

To the sublime the ridiculous is only a step
↳ 숭고한 것과 우스꽝스러운 것은 한 발자국 차이에 불과하다

To the victors belong the spoils
↳ 이기면 충신, 지면 역적

To understand all is to forgive all

› **sprat** small or young herring

› **mackerel** North Atlantic food fish

› **sublime** pass or cause to pass directly from the solid to the vapor state

↳ 모든 사실을 제대로 이해하게 되면 용서할 마음이 생긴다

To understand is to forgive, even oneself

↳ 이해한다는 것은 용서하는 것이다, 자기 자신까지도

To win without risk is to triumph without glory

↳ 위험 없이 이기는 것은 영광 없이 이기는 것이다

Too often we seek justice just for us

↳ 우리는 너무나 자주 우리 자신만을 위한 정의를 추구한다

Too swift arrives as tardy as too slow

↳ 너무 서두르는 것은 너무 천천히 하는 것과 똑같이 느리다

Trouble brings experience and experience brings wisdom

↳ 고통은 경험을 주고 경험은 지혜를 준다

직접 경험은 책이나 학교에서 배운 지혜나 간접 경험을 통해 얻은 지혜보다
값진 것이다. "Seeing is believing = 백 번 듣는 것보다 한번 보는 것이
낫다"라는 속담도 경험의 중요성을 말해준다.

Two wrongs don't make a right

↳ 나쁜 짓에 대하여 나쁜 짓으로 앙갚음한다면 그 앙갚음이 옳은 일이
아니다

Understanding and love require a wisdom that comes only with age

↳ 이해와 사랑은 나이를 먹어야만 찾아온다

Use prudence in whatever you do

↳ 무슨 일이고 경솔히 해서는 안 된다

**Villainous weeds grow in uncultivated minds and they are the haunt
of toad**

↳ 마음을 교화시키지 않으면 지독한 잡초가 자라고 그 잡초 속에 두꺼

› **haunt**   visit often, visit or inhabit as a
ghost

비가 우글거린다

We are all wise for others, none for himself
ㄴ 남의 일에는 누구나 현명하지만 자신의 일에는 아무도 현명하지 못하다

We can't at once catch the applauses of the vulgar and expect the approbation of the wise
ㄴ 우리는 속된 사람에게서 박수도 받으면서 동시에 현명한 사람의 칭찬을 받을 수는 없다

We often despise what is most useful to us
ㄴ 우리는 가장 유용한 것을 멸시하는 때가 많다

We only admit to minor faults to persuade ourselves that we have no major ones
ㄴ 우리에게 중대한 허물이 없다는 것을 우리 자신에게 설득하려고 단지 작은 허물만을 자백한다

When people make wise choices, the environment stays healthy
ㄴ 사람들이 현명한 선택을 할 때 환경은 건강하게 유지된다

When wrath speaks, wisdom veils her face
ㄴ 분노가 말을 하면 지혜가 얼굴을 가린다

(=Anger begins with folly, and ends with repentance)

Where ignorance is bliss, it's folly to be wise
ㄴ 식자우환

› **wrath** violent anger

알아서 좋은 일이 있지만, 몰라야 될 일도 있는 법이다. 언제나 좋은 일만 생길 수는 없기 때문이다. 한국에서는 "모르는 게 약이다"라고 하지만, 영어로는 "Ignorance is bliss 무지는 곧 안심이다"라고 한다. 무엇인지 알기 전에는 걱정을 할 필요는 없기 때문이다.

Will and wisdom are both mighty leaders
↳ 의지와 지혜는 힘있는 지도자이다

Wisdom comes alone through suffering
↳ 지혜는 고통을 통해서 혼자 온다

Wisdom consists of knowing what to do
↳ 지혜란 다음의 할 일을 아는 것이다

Wisdom is an always overmatch for strength
↳ 힘으로는 지혜를 절대 감당할 수 없다

Wisdom is found on the lips of him who has understanding
↳ 현명한 자의 입에는 지혜가 있다

Wisdom is often nearer when we stoop than when we soar
↳ 지혜는 우리가 높은 데로 오를 때보다 몸을 수그릴 때 우리에게 더 가까이 다가올 때가 많다

Wisdom rises upon the ruins of folly
↳ 지혜는 어리석음의 잔해 위에서 일어선다

Wisdom sets bounds even to knowledge
↳ 지혜는 지식까지도 한계를 정해준다

Wise distrust is the parent of security
↳ 현명한 의심은 안전으로 보장해준다

Wise living consists less in acquiring good habits than acquiring as few habits as possible

---

› **overmatch** facing something or someone that is powerful than the sel

ᄂ 현명한 삶은 좋은 습관을 붙이는 것보다 오히려 가능한 한 나쁜 습관을 줄여나가는 데 있다

Wise men learn from others' harms, fools scarcely by their own

ᄂ 현명한 사람은 다른 사람들이 해를 입는 것을 보고 배우지만 바보는 자신이 해를 입고도 거의 아무 것도 배우지 못한다

Wishers were ever fools

ᄂ 어리석은 자는 헛된 희망에 의지한다

Years know more than books

ᄂ 노인의 지혜는 책보다 낫다

You can catch more flies with honey than with vinegar

ᄂ 식초보다 꿀이 더 많은 파리를 잡는다(부드러움은 강함을 이긴다)

You may have much to lose by precipitate action and much to gain from patience

ᄂ 넌 경솔한 짓을 했다가는 손해보기 십상이고 참아서 이익 볼일이 많아

Youth is the time to study wisdom; old is time to practice it

ᄂ 젊어서는 지혜를 배우고 나이가 들어서는 실행할 때다

▸ **precipitate** cause to happen quickly or abruptly, cause to separate | out of a liquid

131. 직업　　　　　Occupation

A good doctor can net(clear) over 50 million won a year
　　↳ 괜찮은 의사라면 1년에 5천만원 이상의 순수익을 올린다

A good salesman will not encroach on his customer's time
　　↳ 훌륭한 판매원은 고객에게 시간을 낭비시키지 않는다

A large amount of money goes through banker's hands, but none of it is his
　　↳ 은행원은 하루에도 거금을 만지지만 자기 돈은 하나도 없다

A lot of National Statistical Office colleagues cut me dead somehow
　　↳ 왠지 많은 통계청 직원들이 날 모른 척 해

A lot of police take ice
　　↳ 많은 경찰이 뇌물을 받지(잘 이해하지 못하는 경우도 있음)

A man who runs to be a lawmaker has a lot of camp-flowers
　　↳ 국회의원 후보에게는 많은 정상배들이 있어

A man who works with his hand and his brain, and his heart is an artist
　　↳ 손과 머리와 가슴으로 일하는 사람은 예술가이다

A number of mobs forced their way in, pushing security guards aside
　　↳ 다수의 폭도들이 경비원들을 밀어젖히고 힘으로 밀고 들어왔다

A police comedy action centered on a cop fooling around at headquarters, was one of the biggest box-office draw in Korea last year
　　↳ 경찰서에서 빈둥거리는 형사 이야기를 그린 경찰 코미디 영화가 국내

· **encroach**　enter upon another's property orrights | · **mob**　large disorderly crowd, criminal gang

에서 지난해 가장 큰 흥행을 기록한 영화의 하나다

A writer must know the facts on both sides of the issue he's addressing

ㄴ 훌륭한 작가는 그가 말하고 있는 문제에 대한 양면의 사실을 모두 알 아야한다

Absence of occupation is not rest

ㄴ 하는 일이 없다는 것은 휴식이 아니다

Admiral Yi(Soon-shin) went down in history as a loyalist

ㄴ 이순신 장군은 충신으로 역사에 남아있어

Advertisers always play up the good qualities of the house for sale and fail to mention its disadvantage

ㄴ 광고주들은 팔려는 집의 장점만 내세우고 불리한 점은 어물쩍 넘어간다

All legitimate trades are equally honorable

ㄴ 직업은 귀천이 없어

> (=All occupations are equally honorable)
> (=Every honest occupation deserves esteem)

All morning the garage men had to pound my car out to its proper shape again

ㄴ 차량 정비공들이 오전 내내 내 차를 본래의 모양으로 두드려 폈다

All port cities generally have lots of establishments catering to sailors on shore leave

ㄴ 어느 항구도시나 일반적으로 선원들의 기항을 겨냥한 시설들이 많다

All public servants must shoot straight(square) with the general public(their customers)

› **admiral** senior commissioned officer in the navy

› **legitimate** lawfully begotten, genuine, conforming with law or accepted standards

↳ 전 공무원은 국민(고객)에게 공정하고 정직해야 한다

All the actor(actress) wanna-bes are always hanging around Choong-moo-ro
↳ 모든 배우지망생들은 충무로에서 서성거린다

As a baseball player, he doesn't come up to his brother's shoulder
↳ 그가 야구선수로서는 형보다 못해

Although young, he has the makings of a first-class salesman
↳ 그는 젊지만 일류 판매원의 자질을 갖추고 있다

At last Sook-hee found herself as a teacher
↳ 마침내 숙희는 학교 교사직이 맞는다는 것을 알았어

Authors are often fearsome adversaries of the editors who correct their manuscripts
↳ 교정원이 원고를 교정할 때 그들에게는 저자가 무서운 장애가 되는 수가 흔히 있다

By tracking the eye of a hurricane, forecasters can determine the speed at which a storm is moving
↳ 기상통보관들은 허리케인의 중심점을 추적하여 허리케인의 이동속도를 알 수 있다

Chan-soo bowed out as a train engineer after ten years of railroading
↳ 찬수는 철도 사업에 10년 근무한 후 기관사직을 그만 두었어

Chang-soo carved out a name for himself in business
↳ 창수는 자력으로 사업가로서의 명성을 얻었다

Chang-soo's been cooking the books for years, but the auditors have never caught it
↳ 창수가 회계장부를 몇 년씩이나 조작해 왔지만 감사원이 적발하지 못했어

Civil servants should endeavor to deal with the affairs of the public

---

› **manuscript** something written or typed
› **bow out** withdraw

sympathetically, efficiently, promptly and without bias or maladministration
> ↳ 공무원들은 편견이나 실책 없이 온정 있고, 효율적이고, 신속히 공무
> 를 처리해야 한다

Computer skills are necessary in any profession, whereas some people refuse to learn these skills out of fear
> ↳ 컴퓨터기술은 거의 모든 직업에 필요한데 반하여 어떤 사람들은 두려
> 움 때문에 이 기술을 배우기를 거부한다

Credit is everything for a merchant
> ↳ 장사꾼에게는 신용이 무엇보다 중요해

Creditors have better memories than debtors
> ↳ 채권자는 채무자 보다 기억력이 좋다

Do your own thing(stuff)
> ↳ 적성(전문)에 맞는 일을 해라

Doctors took to the streets yesterday demanding a redress of the nation's medical system
> ↳ 의사들은 어제 의료서비스제도의 개정을 요구하면서 거리로 뛰쳐나갔다

Doctors won't be able to avoid public condemnation if they continue to push their plans to boycott services for patients
> ↳ 의사들이 환자들의 진료를 거부하겠다는 계획을 강행한다면 국민들의
> 비난을 면치 못할 것이다

Don't shoot the pianist
> ↳ 호의로 그랬던 사람을 책하지 마라

Dong-soo's going to fire the manager, and you'll be in the driver's seat soon
> ↳ 동수가 지배인을 내보내게 되면 네가 중책을 맡게될 거야

· **merchant** one who buys and sells
· **boycott** refrain from dealing with

Drought and pestilence dogged the poor farmers' footsteps
↳ 가뭄과 역병이 불쌍한 농민들을 떠나지 않았다

Duck-soo is doing this on doctor's orders only, but he doesn't like it
↳ 덕수는 이 일을 어쩔 수 없어서 하는 것이지 좋아서 하는 게 아니다

Each reporter is trying to get the jump on the others with the story of the scandal
↳ 신문기자들은 저마다 그 스캔들의 기사를 다른 기자들 보다 앞질러 보도하려고 기를 쓰고 있어

Every calling is great when greatly pursued
↳ 훌륭히 수행한다면 모든 직업이 위대하다

Everybody thinks the accountant had his hand in the till
↳ 모두들 경리가 돈을 훔친 것으로 생각한다

Feed by measure and defy the physician
↳ 절제 있게 먹으면 의사가 필요 없다

Fire-safety inspectors described the basement beer hall as a death trap
↳ 화재 안전 검사단은 그 지하실 맥주 집을 매우 위험한 장소라고 기록했다

Gil-soo was a good boxer until he became rich and went to seed
↳ 기수는 돈이 붙고 한물 가기 전까지는 훌륭한 권투선수였어

God heals, and the doctor takes the fees
↳ 치료는 신이 하고 치료비는 의사가 받는다

Hate a priest, and you will hate his surplice
↳ 중이 미우면 가사도 밉다

He builds for a living
↳ 건축업을 하고 있어

He deserves well(ill) of the National Statistical Office
↳ 통계청에 공로자(통계청에서 벌받아야 할 사람)

· **pestilence** plague

He doesn't want anything like supporting the leading actor
> ↳ 그는 조연 따윈 결코 바라지 않아

He is nothing, if not a sales man
> ↳ 그는 매우 훌륭한 판매원이야

He's a statistician of a sort
> ↳ 그는 엉터리 통계인 이다

He's retired as a player, but he keeps his hand in by giving us tennis lessons
> ↳ 그가 테니스 선수로서는 은퇴했지만 우리들에게 레슨을 해 주면서 손
> 을 놓지는 않고 있다

How do you rate the future of your job?
> ↳ 네 직업의 전망은 어때?

I'm sure that he will be an asset to your company and I highly recommend him for the position of software programing supervisor
> ↳ 그는 귀사의 훌륭한 인적자산이 되리라 확신하며 귀사의 소프트웨어
> 프로그래밍 매니저 자리에 강력히 추천합니다

In fact those amazing acrobats have to dice with death on that high trapeze
> ↳ 사실 저 놀라운 곡예사들은 목숨을 내걸고 공중그네를 타야 해

In our life there is a single color; as on an artist's palette, which provides the meaning of life and art
> ↳ 우리의 삶에는 화가의 팔레트처럼 삶과 예술의 의미를 주는 한가지
> 색깔이 있다

In-ho is between jobs(out of work, out of a job)
> ↳ 인호는 실업자

Jobs are one of the evaluations of the success on any society

---

› **evaluate** appraise

↳ 직업은 어느 사회에서나 성공 여부를 평가하는 기준이 될 수 있다

Lawyers and painters can soon change white to black
↳ 변호사와 화가는 흰 것을 금방 검게 만들 수 있다

Many public servants have clean hands as regards money
↳ 많은 공무원들이 금전문제에 깨끗해

Mr. Ahn has started a whispering campaign against the mayor, saying that he's not honest
↳ 안씨가 시장이 정직하지 못하다는 흑색선전을 시작했어

My calling requires a good deal of traveling
↳ 난 직업상 출장이 많아

My wife's been hounding me to see a doctor
↳ 집사람이 병원에 가 보라고 성화야

Myung-soo made a mess when trying to make a wooden box as he was not a carpenter
↳ 명수는 목수가 아니었기에 나무상자를 만들 때 엉망이 되었다

Nam-soo is a novelist, a singer, and a baseball player rolled into one
↳ 남수는 소설가이자, 가수이자, 야구선수 모두를 다 잘 해

Newspaper reporters must be primed with facts before they start to write their article
↳ 신문기자들은 기사를 쓰기 전에 사실을 파악해야 한다

Once a pilot starts the descent of his airplane, it will not be easy to abort its landing
↳ 조종사가 일단 항공기의 하강을 시작하면 중단시키기 어렵게 된다

Our scientists are trying to beat them to the punch
↳ 우리의 과학자들은 선수를 치려고 노력하고 있어

▸ **prime** fill or load, lay a preparatory coating on   ▸ **abort** terminate prematurely

Reporters shouldn't slant their stories against one political party
> ↳ 신문기자는 어느 한 정당에 불리하게 편향된 기사를 써서는 안 된다

Sang-soo tried a number of different jobs before he finally found himself to be an accountant
> ↳ 상수는 여러 직종을 찾아 본 후에 적임인 회계원이 되었다

Scholars tend to lack a sense of proportion
> ↳ 학자는 사물을 균형 있게 보는 눈이 결여되기 쉬워

Scientists already learned to build and maintain artificial wombs to give premature infants a fighting chance
> ↳ 과학자들은 이미 인공자궁을 만들고 유지하여 조산아에게 살아날 수 있는 기회를 제공하는 법을 알게되었다

Scientists can't predict what'll happen to the earth's atmosphere if the ozone layer continues to be depleted
> ↳ 과학자들은 오존층이 파괴될 때 지구의 대기에 어떤 일이 일어날지 예측하지 못한다

Several miners hung by a thread while the rescuers worked toward them
> ↳ 몇 명의 광원들은 구조대가 굴진해 들어갈 동안 생명이 경각에 달려 있었다

She decided not to become a doctor because medicine is not her bag
> ↳ 그 여자는 의학이 취향에 맞지 않아 의사가 되지 않기로 결정했다

She has something of a actress in her nature
> ↳ 그 여자는 배우 기질을 타고났어

She is counted among the top(best) ten actresses in Korea
> ↳ 그 여자는 한국에서 손꼽히는 배우 중 한 사람이다

She is the person we have to do the washing
> ↳ 그 여자는 우리가 세탁을 맡기고 있는 고용인이다

› **deplete** use up resources of

She is well on her way to becoming an famous actress
> ↳ 그 여자는 이름난 배우가 될 단계에 와 있어

She knows how to doctor the figures
> ↳ 그 여자가 숫자를 조작하는데는 선수다

She, who is a reporter, pounded out the story, racing to meet the deadline
> ↳ 그 여기자는 마감시간에 맞추기 위해 서둘러 기사를 입력했다

She put her job on the line to save their lives
> ↳ 그 여자는 그들의 생명을 구하기 위해 자신의 직업까지 걸었다

She rushed out of the court with a pack of reporters at her heels
> ↳ 그녀는 기자들이 대거 몰려오자 황급히 코트를 빠져나갔다

She's had a variety of jobs in her own line of country
> ↳ 그 여자는 자신의 다양한 전문분야에 종사했다

Some people start out to train career in medicine, but drop(fall) by the wayside
> ↳ 어떤 사람들은 직업의사가 되려고 공부하다가 도중에 팽개치곤 해

Sung-soo wears two hats
> ↳ 성수는 두 직업(부업)을 가졌어

That actor still packs'em in
> ↳ 그 배우는 아직도 인기 있어

That ex-army-officer runs his business with a rod of iron
> ↳ 그 육군장교출신의 관리자는 사업을 군대식으로 운영한다

That job is made for you
> ↳ 그건 꼭 널 위한 직업

That man lined his pocket(purse) by permitting contractors to use

---

› **rod** straight slender stick

› **permit** give approval for, make possible

poor building materials

ㄴ 저 사람이 건설업자들에게 부실건축자재 사용을 허용해준 사람이다

That salesman caught them off guard with his sales pitch

ㄴ 저 판매원은 그들의 허술한 틈을 이용하여 그럴듯한 입담으로 설득했다

That would be just what the doctor ordered

ㄴ 그건 꼭 필요한 것

That's not my bag, I want to be a historian

ㄴ 그건 내 취향이 아니니 역사학자가 되고싶어

The anesthesiologist has to administer small doses of drugs to sedate the patient throughout the operation

ㄴ 마취의사는 수술 중 내내 환자를 진정시키기 위해 소량의 약을 투여 해야 한다

The band-master doubles in brass as a pianist

ㄴ 악단 장은 피아니스트 역할도 겸해

The detective is on a fishing expedition now

ㄴ 형사가 진상조사 중이다

The doctor arrived none too soon

ㄴ 의사가 딱 맞게 도착했다

The doctor gave me a clean bill of health

ㄴ 의사는 내가 아주 건강하다고 했어

The drum majorette performed her routine, twirling her batons in the air

ㄴ 여자 고적대장은 지휘봉을 휘저으면서 판에 박은 묘기를 보여줬다

The farmer has strived to slip bonds of earth in vain

ㄴ 그 농부는 땅의 속박에서 벗어나려고 몸부림 쳤으나 허사였다

The farmers are taking(bringing) the rice in early this year because

---

· **anesthesiology** branch of medicine dealing with anesthesia

· **majorette** girl or woman who leads or accompanies a marching band

of clear weather
> ↳ 금년에는 맑은 날씨 덕분에 농민들이 벼를 일찍 수확하고 있다

The farmers have a way of trapping locusts at night, using bright lights
> ↳ 농부들은 밝은 등불을 이용하여 밤에 메뚜기들을 잡는 법을 잘 알고 있다

The kindergarten teacher doubles as a novelist
> ↳ 그 유치원 교사는 소설가로서의 일까지 겸한다

The laborer is worthy of his hire
> ↳ 남에게 봉사해 주는 사람에게는 정당한 보상이 있어야 한다

The man got into the house by masquerading(posing) as a plumber
> ↳ 그 사람은 배관공인체 하면서 집으로 들어갔다

The mayor couldn't face down the entire city council
> ↳ 시장은 전체 시의회를 꺾을 수 없었다

The mechanic will get around to you in no time
> ↳ 수리공이 곧 손님 차를 봐줄 겁니다

The newspaper boy makes his rounds every morning
> ↳ 신문배달 소년은 매일아침 이집 저집 신문을 배달한다

The plan prohibits physicians from selling medicines and does not allow pharmacists to prescribe without the doctor's prescription
> ↳ 이 지침에는 의사들의 매약을 금하고 약사들은 의사의 처방 없이 약을 조제하지 못하도록 되어있다

The plumber did a lousy job on my sink
> ↳ 배관 수리공이 싱크대를 엉망으로 해놨어

The poet came to an untimely end
> ↳ 그 시인은 요절했어

The real estate operator turned a pretty penny in selling that house
> ↳ 그 부동산 업자는 그 집을 팔아서 거금을 벌었다

› **masquerade** costume party, disguise, disguise oneself, take part | in a costume party

The reporters fired away at the news conference
> ↳ 기자들이 기자회견에서 질문공세를 펴왔다

The salesman tried to cozy up to me
> ↳ 판매원이 간지러운 말로 접근해 왔어

The singer thought he had fully made a name for himself and decided to ride off into the sunset at the height of his career
> ↳ 그 가수는 충분히 출세했다는 생각에서 인기 절정에서 무대에서 은퇴하기로 결심했다

The singer you mentioned is still around
> ↳ 네가 말한 가수는 아직도 인기 있어

The writer needs no audience other than the few who understand
> ↳ 작가는 작품을 이해해 주는 몇 사람 외의 관중은 필요 없다

The writer will come out with a sequel
> ↳ 작가는 속편을 내놓을 것이다

The writer's life seethes within but not without
> ↳ 글쓰는 사람의 삶은 마음속에서 끓고 밖으로는 끓지 않는다

They are convinced the salesman did them out of lots of money
> ↳ 그들은 판매원이 큰돈을 떼어먹었다고 확신하고 있다

They must have been done in by that foxy salesman
> ↳ 그들은 그 교활한 외판원에게 속아넘어간 게 틀림없어

They must place an emphasis on the moral integrity of entertainers in addition to their talent
> ↳ 그들은 연예인들의 재능에 부가하여 도덕적 무결함을 중시해야 한다

This is a totally National Statistical Office staff thing to do
> ↳ 이건 순전히 통계청 직원다운 행동

Thousands upon thousands of youngsters set out to be film stars but

---

› **sequel** consequence or result, continuation of a story

only a handful make it
> ↳ 무수한 젊은이들이 일류배우를 지망하지만 성공하는 사람은 불과 소수이다

To be a judge you have to be skilled at picking shrapnel out of your head
> ↳ 판사가 되려면 당신의 머리에서 파편을 끄집어내는데 익숙해야 한다

Top lawyers rake it in these days
> ↳ 잘 나가는 변호사들은 요즈음 돈을 쓸어 담는다

True scientists are often inspired men and women of unbending curiosity for new facts
> ↳ 진정한 과학자들은 새로운 사실에 대해서 끝없는 호기심에 사로잡힌 영감을 받은 사람들인 경우가 많다

Under the new law physicians will be limited to diagnosing patients and writing prescriptions
> ↳ 새로운 법에 따라 의사들은 환자들은 진료하고 처방전을 써 주는 것으로 제한 받게된다

Wan-soo is wearing a very different hat this time
> ↳ 완수가 이번엔 전혀 다른 역할을 하고 있어

With us, once a man over forty loses his own particular job, he's done for
> ↳ 우리들에게 있어서, 마흔 살이 넘어서 해오던 직업을 잃으면 모든 게 끝이다

You are a welder, do your thing
> ↳ 넌 용접공이니 용접 일은 네가 해

You'll get your start if he recommends you to the manager
> ↳ 그가 널 지배인으로 추천해 준다면 때를 만나게 되는 거야

> ‣ **shrapnel** metal fragments of a bomb

> ‣ **weld** unite by heating, hammering, or pressing

132. 직장   **Workplace**

A growing number of people work in part-time and insecure work
> ↳ 시간제로 일하며 불안정한 직장에서 근무하는 사람들의 수가 점차 증가하고 있다

A lot of National Statistical Office colleagues cut me dead somehow
> ↳ 왠지 많은 통계청 직원들이 날 모른 척 해

After a certain period of in-house training you'll be taken on to the full-time staff
> ↳ 일정 기간의 사내 훈련기간을 거치면 정식 직원으로 채용된다

After heated discussion they came down in favor of accepting the new pay offer
> ↳ 그들은 열띤 논의 끝에 새로운 급여방식을 수용하는 쪽으로 결정했다

After his impossible behavior, they froze him out from(of) the organization
> ↳ 그의 그 역겨운 행동 이후 사람들이 그를 조직에서 못 배기게 한 거야

After Sang-mee had worked there for a while, she began to warm up
> ↳ 상미가 거기서 한동안 일한 후 친숙감이 생겨나기 시작했어

All government workers have had their salaries frozen for three years
> ↳ 모든 공무원들의 봉급이 3년간 동결되었다

All public servants must shoot straight(square) with the general public(their customers)

‣ **insecure** uncertain, unsafe, fearful

┗ 전 공무원은 국민(고객)에게 공정하고 정직해야 한다

An-do didn't want to burn himself out on this job
┗ 안도가 직장에서 퇴물이 되긴 싫었지

An-do is new here and doesn't yet know what's what
┗ 안도는 여기 온지 얼마 안돼서 뭐가 뭔지(무엇이 중요한지) 잘 몰라

An-do never seemed to be in the same job for more than three months at a time
┗ 안도는 한 직장에서 세 달 이상 눌러앉아 있질 못하는 것 같았어

Anybody in this office will be a part of this plan
┗ 이 사무실에 있는 사람은 누구나 이 계획의 대상이 된다

Are you at work now?
┗ 직장에 나가니?

Are you going to install yourself as the boss of the department?
┗ 네가 그 부서 책임자의 일을 맡겠다는 거니?

Are you going to put(cast) our plan into the melting pot?
┗ 우리 계획을 전면적으로 고치겠다는 거냐?

Are you trying to pull rank on me?
┗ 지위가 높다고 이래라 저래라 하는 겁니까?

Aren't you a little premature in forming such a plan?
┗ 그런 계획을 세우기엔 조금 빠르지 않나?

As a protest over their work-mate's getting sacked, the other workers downed their tools until he was reinstated
┗ 동료직원의 해임에 항의해서 근로자들은 그 실직자가 복직될 때까지 파업했다

As he did most of the hard spade-work, he was given all credit for it
┗ 그가 가장 힘드는 준비작업을 해 내자 그 일의 모든 공로가 그에게

· **install** induct into office, set up for use
· **sack** dismiss

· **reinstate** restore to a former position

돌아갔다

Be sure to get it down in black and white
> ↳ 그건 꼭 문서화해야 해

Because we refuse to astray from the path, we are doing something that would have seemed unimaginable seven years ago
> ↳ 우리는 이러한 원칙을 고수했기 때문에 7년 전에는 할 수 없었던 일들을 현재 추진하고 있다

Bong-soo puts himself ahead of his colleagues and expects special treatment
> ↳ 봉수는 자신을 동료들보다 중요한 사람으로 생각하고 특별 대우를 기대하고 있어

Byung-soo is too tied-up(backed) in his paperwork
> ↳ 병수는 서류작업이 너무 많이 밀려있다

Byung-soo will get his feet off the ground
> ↳ 병수는 곧 자리를 확고히 잡게 될 것이다

Byung-soo will take the rap for us
> ↳ 병수가 총대를 멜 거야

Byung-soo's idea will stand well with the management
> ↳ 병수의 안은 중역진에게 호감을 살 것이다

Byung-soo's services fell below the standards we normally require
> ↳ 병수의 근무실적은 우리가 필요로 하는 수준에 미달했다

Chan-soo bowed out as a train engineer after ten years of railroading
> ↳ 찬수는 철도 사업에 10년 근무한 후 기관사직을 그만 두었어

Chan-soo has been falling down on the job
> ↳ 찬수는 일을 농땡이 쳐 오고 있어

Chan-soo is working for Samsung Company and he is raking(coining)

· **astray** off the right way

it in
> ↳ 찬수는 삼성회사에 다니는데 엄청나게 돈을 벌고 있다

Chan-soo worked at two jobs in order to eke out a salary
> ↳ 찬수는 봉급액수를 늘리려고 두 직장을 다녔어

Chang-soo has forty men under his command
> ↳ 창수에게는 **40**명의 부하직원이 있다

Chang-soo's been cooking the books for years, but the auditors have never caught it
> ↳ 창수가 회계장부를 몇 년씩이나 조작해 왔지만 감사원이 적발하지 못했어

Come what may, I'll call him to account this time
> ↳ 이번엔 어떤 일이 있어도 그에게 책임을 물을 것이다

Coming up with a Sunday punch isn't going to be a walk in the park
> ↳ 산뜻한 아이디어를 짜내기란 그리 간단치 않아

Credit should be given where credit is due
> ↳ 모든 일은 공과에 따라 정당하게 평가해야 한다

Disciplinary proceedings against employees at issue is under way
> ↳ 문제의 종업원들에 대한 징계절차가 진행 중이다

Do you know any idea about how I can get off the hook?
> ↳ 이 곤경에서 빠져나갈 묘안 없어?

Do you spend a lot of time on the road?
> ↳ 업무상 외근이 많습니까?

Do you want to box in the whole staff?
> ↳ 전 직원을 묶어 놓겠다는 겁니까?

Dong-soo's going to fire the manager, and you'll be in the driver's seat soon
> ↳ 동수가 지배인을 내보내게되면 네가 중책을 맡게될 거야

› **auditor** a person who examines financial accounts

› **discipline** field of study, training that corrects, molds, or perfects, punishment

Don't bust your ass(gut), but try to get just the thing we need
ㄴ 너무 무리할 것까진 없지만 우리가 필요로 하는 건 구해와

Don't go(get) out of line in this office
ㄴ 사무실에서 주제넘은(사리에 안 맞는) 짓은 하지마

Don't ice me in front of my colleagues
ㄴ 동료들 앞에서 무안 주지마

Don't just sit around the office all day
ㄴ 하루종일 사무실에서 빈들거리기만 하지마

Don't leave anything lying about the office, it makes it difficult to clean
ㄴ 사무실에 아무 것도 어질러놓지 마라, 어지르면 깨끗이 청소하기 어렵잖아

Don't try to palm(pass) that idea off as your own
ㄴ 그 안을 네가 내놓은 것처럼 하지 마라

Doo-soo is the only man for the job
ㄴ 두수야말로 적임자다

Duck-soo's down for the count in the office
ㄴ 덕수는 사무실에서 힘을 못 써(제 구실을 못 해)

Each questionnaire goes through a foolproof system of checking which ensures that there are no errors in the final report
ㄴ 각각의 조사표는 최종 보고서에 착오가 없도록 확실한 점검 체계를 거치게 된다

Ed is only a low man on the totem pole here
ㄴ 에드가 여기서는 말단사원이야

Ed's foul language in the office caused our eyebrows to rise
ㄴ 에드가 사무실에서 상스러운 말을 하는 바람에 우리가 놀랐어

Either you must obey my order or you must leave here

› **questionnaire** of doubtful truth or morality › **totem** often carved figure used as a family or tribe emblem

ㄴ 내 명령을 따르지 않으려면 여기서 나가라

Employees generally appreciate feedback about their performance on the job

ㄴ 직원들은 일반적으로 자기가 하는 일의 성과에 대해 보답해(알아) 주는 것을 고마워한다

Employers who want two-way communication with their staff must be ready to listen to what they have to say

ㄴ 직원들과 상호 대화를 원하는 고용주는 그들이 꼭 해야 할 말을 들어줄 준비가 돼 있어야 한다

Everybody in this office is in his pocket

ㄴ 그는 사무실에 있는 모든 사람을 떡 주무르듯 해

Everybody knew that their mission entailed a certain amount of risk

ㄴ 그들의 임무에는 어느 정도 위험이 수반한다는 것을 누구나 알고 있었다

Everything seems to be in order

ㄴ 모든 게 제대로 돼 있는 것 같군

Falling out with people she works with becomes difficult for her

ㄴ 그녀와 같은 직장에 있는 사람들과 불화 하면 직장이 힘들어져

Finally the internal strife came to the fore(surface)

ㄴ 마침내 내부의 불화가 표면화되었다

From time to time, you should step back and let your men run their own way

ㄴ 때로는 한 발작 물러나서 직원들이 자신의 일을 스스로 처리하게 해야 해

Get in good with him, he's on the fast track in this office

ㄴ 그 사람은 사무실에서 잘 나가는 사람이니 가까이 사귀어 둬

Gil-soo is a man with a finger in every pie in our office

ㄴ 우리 사무실에서 길수는 약방에 감초지

› **feedback**   the return of part of the output to the point of input for   monitoring of self-regulating

Hard enough to call it a raise
> 그 정도 가지고 월급 인상이라 할 수 있나

Hard work and honesty should be placed at a premium in our office
> 우리 사무실에서는 열심히 일 하는 것과 정직성을 높이 쳐줘야 한다

Haven't you nothing better to do than making repeated bows day in and day out?
> 그렇게 할 일이 없어서 밤이나 낮이나 졸고만 있니?

Having all the time in the world is hard for an office worker
> 사무원에게 시간이 남아돈다는 것은 흔한 일이 아니다

He approved this with reservation
> 그는 석연치 않아 하면서 이걸 승인했어

He can no longer kick the workers around(about) and make them do whatever he wants
> 이제 그는 더 이상 근로자들에게 이래라 저래라 하면서 원하는 일이면 무엇이든 시킬 수는 없게 되었다

He couldn't work late because his mind kept jumping the track to thinking about the new girl in the office
> 그는 사무실에 새로 온 여직원 생각으로 마음이 흔들려 늦게까지 일 할 수 없었다

He gathered his courage to take the plunge, resign from his job and start his own business
> 그는 용단을 내어서 모험을 걸어 직장을 그만 두고 자신의 사업을 시작했다

He has gone for the day
> 퇴근 하셨습니다

▸ **plunge**　thrust of dive into something, begin an action suddenly, dive　|　or throw oneself forward or down

> (=He got off work)

He is all out to get the edge on his colleagues
　　ㄴ 그는 동료들보다 우위에 서려고 혈안이야

He is always trying to get in(good) with the people in charge
　　ㄴ 그는 늘 관계(책임)자들에게 환심을 사려고 해

He is dragging his feet on this project
　　ㄴ 그는 이 계획을 일부러 질질 끌고있어

He is not at(away from) his desk now
　　ㄴ 지금 자리에 안 계십니다

He is off the rest of the day
　　ㄴ 그는 조퇴했다

He is tied up at the moment
　　ㄴ 그 분은 지금 바빠요

He is with a client
　　ㄴ 그 분은 지금 손님과 상담중입니다

He made me feel second-best
　　ㄴ 그가 와서 내가 뒷전에 밀려난 기분이야

He may not be the best worker in the office, but he's right up there
　　ㄴ 그가 사무실에서 가장 우수한 직원은 못 될지 몰라도 상위 급이야

He mixes well in any company
　　ㄴ 그는 어떤 동료하고나 사이 좋게 지내

He turned in(=took off) his badge
　　ㄴ 그 사람 옷 벗었다(사임)(=leave the post)

He will haul us over the coals for not finishing on time

▸ **badge** symbol of status

ㄴ 우린 제때 일을 못 끝냈다고 호되게 야단 맞을 것이다

He would have been fired if he weren't the fair-haired boy

ㄴ 그 친구 마음에 드는 구석이 없었으면 진작 잘렸을 거다

He would have my head

ㄴ 난 모가지야

> (=My head's gonna roll)

He'll be out for the rest of the day

ㄴ 그는 조퇴했어(오늘 중 오지 않음)

He'll call the shots. Do what you're told

ㄴ 명령은 그가 하는 거야. 넌 하라는 대로하기만 하면 돼

He's a giant among his colleagues

ㄴ 동료 중 아무도 너의 발뒤꿈치도 못 따라가

He's away from his desk

ㄴ 잠시 자리에 없습니다(옆 사람이 자리 비울 때의 대답)

He's engaged for the occasion

ㄴ 그는 임시로 고용돼 있다

He's really plugged into what's going on in this office

ㄴ 그는 사무실에서 정통한 소식통이야

Heads will roll when he gets back to the office

ㄴ 그가 사무실에 돌아오면 벼락이 떨어질 것이다

**Her house was burgled(robbed) last night and she took a day off
work today**

ㄴ 그녀의 집이 어젯밤 도둑을 맞아서 오늘은 허락 받아 직장을 안 나왔다

› **engage** participate or cause to participate,
bring or come into working contact

Her idea of hiring a convicted sex offender went over like a lead balloon

↳ 성 범죄자를 고용하자던 그 여자의 제안은 차가운 반응에 부딪쳤다

Her record eclipses everything she has done up to now

↳ 그녀의 실적은 그녀가 지금까지 이루어 낸 모든 일 보다 낫다

Her sleeplessness and loss of appetite are symptoms of too much pressure at work

↳ 그녀가 잠을 못 자고 입맛이 떨어진 것은 직장에서 스트레스가 너무 심해서 오는 증상이다

His continuous tantrums in-dispose anyone to work hard

↳ 그 사람이 끝없이 짜증을 내니 누구도 열심히 일 할 맘이 안나

His job may be in jeopardy

↳ 그 사람 해고될지 몰라

> (=He's walking on a tight rope)
> (=He's risking his job)

How are you going to shape up the salespeople overnight?

↳ 어떻게 판매부 직원들을 금방 개조해 놓겠다는 거니?

How can you deride a long-serving man as a spent force?

↳ 장기 근속한 직원을 어떻게 쓸모 없는 사람이라고 조롱할 수 있는가

How can you expect these indignant workers to tolerate appalling working conditions and low quality, outdated equipment?

↳ 이 끔직한 근로조건, 질 낮고 낡아빠진 장비를 성난 근로자들이 어떻게 참아낼 수 있을 것으로 기대하나?

How did your first day on the job go?

· **eclipse** total or partial obscuring of one celestial body by another

· **jeopardy** exposure to death, loss, or injury
· **appall** fill with horror or dismay

↳ 첫 출근은 어땠어?

How does it feel being the top-dog in the Sales Department?
↳ 판매부의 부장 된 기분이 어때?

How many members of the office share this copying machine?
↳ 사무실 직원 몇 명이 이 복사기를 사용하고 있나?

How much are you in your job?
↳ 직장에서 얼마 받니?

Hyun-soo is going places in his company
↳ 현수는 회사에서 잘나가(인기 있어)

Hyun-soo threw up his hands in disgust and quit his job
↳ 현수는 속이 뒤틀려서 손을 털어 버리고 직장을 그만 두었어

I don't want to go over your head, but I will if necessary
↳ 당신을 무시하고 당신 상사에게 따지고 싶지 않지만 계속 이러시면 어쩔 수 없어요

I don't work here by choice
↳ 여기가 좋아서 일 하고 있는 게 아냐

I feel out of myself in this new line of business
↳ 새 일을 맡고 보니 어리벙벙해

I have read better reports than this
↳ 이 보고서는 맘에 안 들어

You'll drink yourself out of your job
↳ 그러다간 술로 직장을 잃게 돼

I work for chicken feed(peanuts)
↳ 쥐꼬리 월급 받고 있어

› **disgust** strong aversion

(=I'm making slave wages)

I'm up against a deadline
    ↳ 마감시간에 쫓기고 있어

I've been around the National Statistical Office
    ↳ 난 통계청에서 산전수전 다 겪었어

If he makes(offers) new proposals, we should seize them with both hands
    ↳ 그가 새로운 제안들은 내 놓는다면 감지덕지 할 일이지

If he runs with the ball, he'll know how to get the project done
    ↳ 그가 책임을 떠맡기만 한다면 그 프로젝트를 어떻게 추진할지 알게 될 것이다

If the master copy is ready, he'll run some more copies off
    ↳ 원본이 준비되면 그가 몇 부 복사해 줄 것이다

If there are no corrections, the minutes stand approved as read
    ↳ 의사록에 바꿀 것이 없으면 읽은 대로 승인됩니다

If you go on behaving like that, you'll get yourself talked about in the office
    ↳ 네가 계속 이렇게 행동하면 사무실에서 소문나겠다

If you lay down on the job, you'll get marching orders(walking papers)
    ↳ 업무를 게을리 하면 해고야

In his work, he has been moved about from city to city
    ↳ 그는 직장 일로 이 도시 저 도시로 옮겨다녔다

In my office, lots of people are cozing up to the higher-ups
    ↳ 사무실에선 많은 사람들이 위 사람과 친하려고 애를 쓰고 있어

‣ **deadline**   time by which something must be finished

‣ **cozing**   act friendly to

In our office you'll report to your director on all matters
  ↳ 우리 사무실에서 자네는 모든 일을 전무의 지시대로 근무해야 해

In these respects our production is home and dry
  ↳ 이런 면에서 우리의 생산라인은 고비를 넘겼다

In-ho knows the National Statistical Office inside out
  ↳ 인호는 통계청 일이라면 모르는 게 없어

In-ho quit his job for personal reasons
  ↳ 인호는 개인 사정으로 직장을 그만뒀어

Individual indifferences in mental traits assume importance in fitting workers to jobs
  ↳ 근로자를 업무에 적응시키는데는 개개인이 가지고있는 특성의 차이가 중요하다

Is there any law against double-dippers?
  ↳ 월급을 두 군데서 받으면 안 되는 일이라도 있나?

It'll take a few months for them to get into the swing of things
  ↳ 그들이 익숙해지기까지는 두 세 달 걸릴 것이다

It's now your barbecue
  ↳ 이제 이건 네 소관이야

It's out of my hands
  ↳ 이젠 네 손을 떠났어

It's really preposterous that unemployment is sky-high while so many companies are understaffed
  ↳ 실업률이 엄청나게 높은데도 회사들은 인력난에 허덕이는 것은 모순이다

Jai-ho showed Gwang-woo the ropes when he was doing his office work
  ↳ 광우가 사무실 일을 할 때 재호가 요령을 가르쳐 줬어

Jung-soo couldn't be kept on the payroll

› **trait** distinguishing quality

› **understaffed** lack numbers of staff

› **payroll** list of employees, money to be distributed to those on a payroll

ㄴ 정수는 직장에서 배겨낼 수 없었어

Let him have it by reducing his pay by 10%

ㄴ 그의 봉급을 10% 깎아서 본때를 보여줘라

Let's get our co-workers on the same sheet of music

ㄴ 우리 직장 동료들은 한 목소리를 내도록 합시다

Let's go easy on our office supplies

ㄴ 사무용품을 아껴 씁시다

Let's knock off work today early and go have a few beers

ㄴ 오늘은 일찍 퇴근해서 맥주나 한 잔 하러 가자

Look at it this way. A boring job is better than no job at all

ㄴ 따분한 직장도 그나마 없는 것보다야 낫지

Lost papers will probably turn up in the wrong file or something like that

ㄴ 잃어버린 문서는 아마 엉뚱한 문서철이나 그와 비슷한 문서철에 있을지 몰라

Lots of office workers have been frozen out of this office

ㄴ 이 사무실에서 많은 사무원들이 배겨나지 못하고 떠나버렸다

Lots of workers just don't move up in the world

ㄴ 많은 근로자들은 입신이라곤 못해(이름이라곤 못내)보고 살아

Man-soo's father changed jobs several times a year, and the family was moved from pillar to post

ㄴ 만수의 아버지는 1년에 여러 번 직장을 옮겨서 가족들이 여기 저기 이사를 다녔어

Many employers in Korea are turning to South-East Asia for workers who are still not unwilling to sweat for their pay

ㄴ 한국의 많은 고용주들은 보수를 받기 위해 땀흘리며 일하기를 마다하

› **unwilling** not inclined nor favorably disposed in mind

지 않는 노동자들을 찾기 위해 동남아시아에 의존하고 있다

Many foreign workers are relegated to illegal alien status where low pay and bad working conditions force them to flee their work-places
> ↳ 많은 외국인들은 낮은 급료와 열악한 근무조건으로 인해 직장을 이탈 하게되는 외국인의 신분으로 떨어지고 있다

Many male superintendents consider that it is not acceptable for women to assume leadership roles
> ↳ 남자 관리자들은 여성이 관리자 역할을 맡는 것을 허용할 수 없다고 여긴다

Mi-sook is a draw in the office
> ↳ 미숙이는 사무실의 꽃이다

Min-gyoo hit the skids after he ended up on the street himself(lost his job)
> ↳ 민규는 실직 후 타락의 길로 빠졌어

Moon-soo moves from job to job so often that I don't see how he can amount(come) to much
> ↳ 문수는 이 직장 저 직장을 너무 옮겨다녀서 성공할 것 같지 않다

Most people have to start at the bottom and work up
> ↳ 대부분의 사람들은 말단에서 시작해서 차차 지위가 올라가게 돼 있다

Nam-soo has quickly entrenched himself in the new office, and is liked by everyone
> ↳ 남수는 새로운 사무실에서 재빨리 자리잡았고 모두가 그를 좋아한다

Nam-soo is on top of everything going on in the office
> ↳ 남수는 사무실 일을 모르는 게 없어(모두 그의 통제 하에 움직여)

Nobody is allowed to use any barn yard language in the office
> ↳ 사무실에서는 누구도 십원짜리 문자를 써서는 안 된다

› **relegate** remove to some less prominent position, assign to a particular

class or sphere
› **entrench** establish in a strong position

Not when I last looked at it

      ㄴ 아까(저번에) 내가 봤을 때 안 해놨더군

Of those who work part-time in industry, the vast majority are women

      ㄴ 파트타임으로 일하고있는 산업근로자 중 태반 이상이 여자들이다

On May 2, a 3% price increase will become effective on all over vehicles as a result of increased production and labor costs

      ㄴ 생산비 및 인건비 인상으로 자사의 전 차종에 대해 **5**월 **2**일자로 **3%**
의 가격인상이 있을 것입니다

On our office picnic, we count our noses(heads)

      ㄴ 사무실 야유회 때 우린 인원 점검을 해

Once you pay your dues, I'm sure you'll get a more important assignment

      ㄴ 일단 네가 경력을 쌓게되면 더욱 중요한 일을 맡게 될 게 틀림없어

Our director didn't listen to our proposal, so we went over(above) him

      ㄴ 우리 과장이 우리의 안을 들어주지 않아서 과장 위의 상사에게 가져갔지

Our division has good chemistry

      ㄴ 우리 과 직원은 잘 지내고 있다

좋은 관계, 마음이 통하는 관계를 사자성어로 '이심전심(以心傳心)'이라고 한
다. 이 것을 영어로 하면, 'To have the right chemistry 잘 맞는 화학 반
응' 정도가 된다. 이는 잘 어울리는 두 가지의 화학 성분을 혼합할 때, 폭발
하거나 분리되지 않고 잘 섞이는 것을 비유하는 표현이다.

Our division is 12 strong

      ㄴ 우리 과 인력은 **12**명이다

· **chemistry** composition and chemical
properties of a substance

Our office has come a long way since 1960s
> ↳ 우리 사무실은 1960년대 이후 크게 발전했어

Our office has statistical data on call for twenty-four hours
> ↳ 우리 사무실은 전화만 오면 언제나 알아볼 수 있는 통계자료를 준비
> 해 두고 있다

Our office runs like a well-oiled machine
> ↳ 우리 사무실은 기름 친 기계처럼 잘 돌아가

Our office seems to run on all cylinders
> ↳ 우리 사무실은 잘 돌아가는 것 같다

Our on-the-job training system should be tailored to the needs of the trainees, and not the other way around
> ↳ 우리의 사내 직무훈련은 훈련생들의 필요에 부합해야 하고, 이와 다
> 른 방식으로 나아가서는 안 된다

Our unending losses are ascribable to over-manning in our production department
> ↳ 우리의 끝없는 손실은 생산부의 인력 과잉에 기인한다

Overcoming this red tape really encumbers our operation and put us at a disadvantage
> ↳ 번잡한 절차들을 이겨 나간다는 것은 우리의 경영을 방해하고 불리하
> 게 만들어주고 있다

Part-time employees often deal with resentment from full-time workers who envy their less demanding schedules
> ↳ 파트타임 종사자들은 종종 그들의 시간여유 있음을 시기하는 정식 근
> 로자들의 눈총을 대해야 했다

Petty officials are given no scope for original thought
> ↳ 말단공무원에게는 창의적인 생각을 할 여지가 없다

› **data** factual information

› **ascribe** attribute

› **encumber** burden

Please don't go into your song and dance about being the best in this office
> ↳ 이 사무실에서 네가 최고라는 그 단골메뉴 좀 그만할 수 없니

Please inform me of the course of the affair(business)
> ↳ 일의 진행을 알려 주시오

Please lick this report into shape by Monday
> ↳ 월요일까지 이 보고서(기사)를 정리해 줘

Please look at the question from various angles
> ↳ 문제를 다각도로 검토해 주십시오

Please make a practice of being on time for work
> ↳ 출근시간에 늦지 않는 습관을 기르도록 해

Proper praise can improve work relationships
> ↳ 제대로 한 칭찬은 직장의 대인관계를 개선시킨다

Put(Lay) your final offer and we'll consider it open-mindedly
> ↳ 솔직히 제의하면 우리가 허심탄회하게 검토하겠습니다

Putting in overtime without pay is above and beyond the call of duty
> ↳ 무급으로 초과근무를 하는 것은 업무상 요구하는 정도를 벗어난 것이다

Pyung-soo pulled some strings to get his daughter hired
> ↳ 평수는 자기 딸이 고용되도록 몰래 영향력을 행사했다

Pyung-soo's got a real soft job in this office
> ↳ 이 사무실에서 평수가 하는 일은 거저먹기야

Quite a lot of people lost their jobs through no fault of their own
> ↳ 많은 사람들은 자신들의 잘못이 아닌데도 직장을 잃게된다

Quite a lot of wage earners live for the day when they will be able to stop work
> ↳ 많은 근로자들은 일 하지 않아도 될 날을 간절히 고대한다

‣ **open-mindly** act receptively to arguments
       or appeals

Raise a glass for everyone
> ↳ 모두를 위해 건배(Here's to you 당신을 위해 건배)

Recurring illness forced her to retire from work prematurely
> ↳ 그녀는 병이 재발해서 부득이 조기 퇴직했다

Sexually explicit magazines have no place in a business setting
> ↳ 노골적으로 성적인 내용을 담은 잡지를 직장 내에 비치해선 안 돼

She drops in at our office at long intervals
> ↳ 그 여자는 이따금씩 우리 사무실에 들러

She filled in for the manager until the replacement was found
> ↳ 그녀는 교체할 사람이 올 때까지 전무 자리를 맡았었다

She had to make a mark early on her career to achieve her ambition
> ↳ 그녀는 야망을 달성하기 위해 직장에서 일찍부터 두각을 내어야 했다

She took the rest of the day off
> ↳ 그 여직원은 조퇴했습니다

She was forced out to our Daejun branch office
> ↳ 그 여자는 우리 회사의 대전 지사로 좌천되었다

She was in the same position as when she started like a chipmunk spinning the wheel
> ↳ 그녀는 입사할 때와 똑 같은 직급으로 개미 쳇바퀴 돌 듯 일했다

She worked her way up to the top of the corporate ladder
> ↳ 그녀는 열심히 매진하여 그 회사의 최고 지위에 올랐다

She'll stop short of firing you
> ↳ 그 여자가 너를 해고까지는 안 할 것이다

She's been still working to make the ends meet
> ↳ 그녀는 살림에 보태려고 아직도 직장에 나가

› **explicit** absolutely clear or precise

› **chipmunk** small striped ground-dwelling squirrel

She's gone from job to job for years
> ↳ 그녀는 수년간 이 직장 저 직장을 옮겨다녔다

Some office girls are always going blah-blah on the phone
> ↳ 사무실에는 종일 전화통에 대고 수다떠는 여직원들도 있다

Some people don't belong here
> ↳ 어떤 직원은 여기(맡은 일)가 체질에 안 맞아

Some people don't know what to do with themselves when they retire
> ↳ 퇴직 때 무엇하며 시간 보내야 할지 모르는 사람들이 있다(do oneself
> 에는 "행동 또는 처신하다"의 뜻도 있음)

Sometimes he has his fingers in the till
> ↳ 그는 가끔씩 회사(가게)에서 돈을 슬쩍 훔쳐

Sometimes the office staff buffeted documents from one desk to another
> ↳ 사무실 직원들이 때로는 문서를 이곳 저곳으로 핑퐁치곤 했어

Soon-ho is a low man on the totem pole
> ↳ 순호는 말단직원

Stop going after girls and get a proper job
> ↳ 여자들 꽁무니만 쫓아다니는 것 그만하고 제대로 된 직장을 찾아라

Sung-soo put in an appearance at work, but he goofed off all day
> ↳ 성수는 직장에 얼굴을 내밀었지만 하루종일 빈둥거리기만 했어

Tai-gyung is going to root out all the deadwood from the office staff
> ↳ 태경이는 모든 직원들 중 쓸모 없는 사람들을 추려내려고 하고 있어

Tai-ho made a clean sweep of the office to find the lost money
> ↳ 태호는 잃어버린 돈을 찾으려고 샅샅이 사무실을 뒤졌다

Temporary and part-time workers make up a higher proportion of the work force than they did in the past

---

› **deadwood** something useless
› **temporary** lasting for a short time only

ㄴ 현재 임시직이나 파트타임 근로자 수는 과거에 비해 더 높은 비율을
차지하고 있다

Tens of firms have plans to trim their operations in the hopes of turning around

ㄴ 수십 개의 업체가 사태 호전을 위해 운영을 축소할 계획을 추진중이다

That he didn't need her services is only a roundabout way of giving a pink slip

ㄴ 그가 그녀에게 더 이상 일하지 않아도 된다고 말 한 건 해고란 말을
둘러서 표현한 것뿐이다

That poor-mouth won't even chip in to buy flowers to our hospitalized employee

ㄴ 돈타령만 하는 그 사람은 입원한 종업원에게 줄 꽃을 사는데도 한푼
내지 않을 사람이야

That suspicious fellow just breezed into our office, used the phone, and then breezed out again

ㄴ 그 수상한 사람이 우리 사무실에 슬쩍 들어와서는 전화를 하더니 다
시 슬쩍 나가버렸다

That's not my idea of an office girl

ㄴ 여직원이 그러면 안되지

The beginning of understanding men is understanding how men act at work

ㄴ 남자를 이해하는 것은 남자가 직장에서 어떻게 행동하는가를 이해할
때 시작된다

The body count will be about 30, when the pink slips come out

ㄴ 인력 감축시 **30**명 정도 해고 될 것이다

The bottom dropped out of the day for Bong-soo when he lost his job

---

▸ **roundabout** indirect

↳ 봉수가 실직하게 되자 기가 팍 죽었어

The deadline is ticking closer and closer
↳ 마감시간이 임박해 오고 있다

The facts add together to give a hopeless picture of the firm
↳ 상황을 종합해 보면 회사는 전망이 전혀 없어

The figures send up a red alert to this month's target
↳ 통계수치는 이 달 목표에 적신호를 보내고 있다

The figures you have don't square with those I have
↳ 네가 가진 수치는 내 것과 맞지 않아

The frosting(icing) on the cake is that I can earn more overtime
↳ 게다가 시간외 근무수당도 더 벌 수 있게 됐으니 금상첨화지 뭐

The greatest threat to privacy comes from employers and from all-seeing Web sites and advertizing networks that track every move we make in cyberspace
↳ 사생활 침해의 가장 큰 주범은 고용주들이며 모든 정보를 꿰뚫어 보고 있는 웹사이트들과 사이버 공간에서 우리의 일거수 일투족을 감시하는 광고 네트웍이다

The issue has exposed a gaping fault line in the workplace
↳ 그 문제로 인해 직원들간에 큰 갈등이 노출될 것이다

The new manager will certainly make things go
↳ 이번 경영자는 일을 잘 처리할 것이다

The plan received a lukewarm response
↳ 그 계획에 대해 별다른 반응이 없었다

The previous regulations are in effect through this project
↳ 종전 규정들은 이 사업까지 적용된다

The question of pay mushroomed into a major problem

› **lukewarm** moderately warm, not enthusiastic

ㄴ 급여문제가 갑자기 주요 문제로 대두되었어

The rest is up to the powers that be
ㄴ 남은 일은 실권 있는 사람들이 할 일이야

The sales department will initiate you into our office routines
ㄴ 판매부에서 너에게 사무실의 기초적인 일상 업무를 가르쳐 줄 것이다

The secret percolated through the office until everyone knew
ㄴ 그 비밀은 차츰 사무실에 새어나오더니 모두가 알게 됐다

The theft must have been an inside job considering only the staff knew the money was there
ㄴ 돈이 거기 있었다는 것을 직원들만이 알았던 점으로 보아 도난사건은 내부 소행이 틀림 없을 것이다

The trend toward computerization of an ever-increasing number of airline function is accelerating rapidly and is beginning to embrace even the world's smallest carriers
ㄴ 항공사들은 점점 증가하고 있는 기능을 전산화하는 경향이 가속화되고 있으며 이러한 추세가 소규모 항공사에까지 미치기 시작했다

The worker's impaired hearing is attributable to the unremitting, incessant ear-piercing noises
ㄴ 그 근로자의 청각손상은 끊임없이 귀청을 찢는 소음 때문이다

Their disarmament talks fell through because neither side was prepared for risking the initiative
ㄴ 그들의 군축회의는 어느 쪽도 먼저 나서려는 자세가 아니었기 때문에 실패하고 말았다

There're a lot of idle workmen these days
ㄴ 요즘 실업자가 많아(게으른 노동자 아님)

There's no one at work I can be open with

› **percolate** trickle or cause to trickle down through a substance

› **disarm** take weapons from, reduce armed forces, make harmless or friendly

ㄴ 직장에서는 마음을 털어 놓을만한 사람이 없어

There's nobody in this office I can depend on if I ever get into a tight spot

ㄴ 내가 곤경에 빠지면 사무실에서 의지할 수 있는 사람은 아무도 없다

These final reports are going to be a handful

ㄴ 이 마지막 보고서 작성은 만만찮은 일이야

These price increases are always hardest on the pocket of the lowest-paid workers

ㄴ 이들 물가 인상은 가장 낮은 급료를 받는 근로자에게 제일 타격이 크다

They are casting their nets farther and farther(wider)

ㄴ 그들은 범위(규모)를 자꾸만 키우고 있어

They are cheap but never free

ㄴ 그들은 쥐꼬리 월급쟁이인 데다가 시간이라곤 전혀 내질 못해

They are going to hang tough on the salary raise

ㄴ 그들은 봉급인상을 강경하게 주장 할 태세다

They are oscillating between approval and opposition

ㄴ 그들은 승인할까 반대할까 망설이고 있다

They are refusing to be ordered about(around)

ㄴ 그들은 고용주가 이래라 저래라 하는 걸 거부(싫어)하고 있다

They are trying to muscle you out of your job

ㄴ 그들이 너를 직장에서 내보내려고 하고 있어

They are trying to weed the poor workers out of the work force

ㄴ 그들은 근로자 중에서 성적이 나쁜 사람을 추려내려고 하고 있어

They had kittens when they found out what was going on

ㄴ 그들이 일의 진행을 보고는 당황해 했다

› **oscillate** swing back and forth

They have regular meetings where workers are given an opportunity to air their grievances
> ㄴ 그들은 정기적으로 고충을 토로할 모임을 갖는다

They have streamlined the whole business by introducing a new computer system which provides easy access to the information
> ㄴ 그들은 정보에 대한 접근을 쉽게 해 주는 새로운 컴퓨터 시스템을 도입함으로써 전반적인 업무를 효율화했다

They have to put right everything that their predecessors did wrong
> ㄴ 그들은 전임자들이 저지른 모든 잘못을 바로잡아 놓아야 해

They mark their time and pay no mind to the job
> ㄴ 그들은 퇴근시간만 기다리고 일에는 관심 없어

They offer a salary and benefits package consistent with their leadership position in the field of nursing and health related facilities
> ㄴ 그들은 요양이나 시설관련 분야에서 근무하는 지휘자의 직위에 어울리는 봉급과 복리후생을 제공한다

They proposed to give the shipbuilder his head in the construction of these ships
> ㄴ 그들은 이들 배를 만들 때 조선업자에게 자신의 방식대로 하게 해 주자고 제안했다

They require all employees to wear identification badges at all times as part of the new security system
> ㄴ 그들은 새로운 보안체계의 일환으로 전 종업원들에게 항상 식별배지를 달도록 하고있다

They succeeded in their cost-cutting program by getting rid of a fourth of their manpower
> ㄴ 그들은 인력의 1/4을 감원시킴으로써 비용절감에 성공했다

› **streamline** made with contours to reduce air or water resistance,　　　simplified, modernized

They tend to give a wide berth to their boss when he's in a bad mood
ㄴ 그들은 사장의 심기가 불편할 때 접근을 꺼려하는 경향이 있다

They want to have at least every other weekend off
ㄴ 그들은 적어도 주말의 격주근무를 원한다

They will get the feel of the job after they've been there a few months
ㄴ 그들이 두 세 달 지나면 업무에 대한 감을 잡게 될 것이다

They would like to put the clock back to the good old days when employees were under their control
ㄴ 그들은 근로자들이 고분고분하던 그리운 옛날로 되돌아 가고 싶어했다

They'll bring the workers out and make them to stay out until their demands are met
ㄴ 그들은 근로자들을 파업으로 몰고 가서 주장이 관철 될 때까지 직장에 복귀하지 않게 할 것이다

They'll furnish you with credit information about our financial responsibility and promptness of our payments
ㄴ 그들은 저희회사의 재정지불 능력 및 신속한 어음상환에 대한 신용정보를 제공해 줄 것입니다

They'll get a big raise when the economy turns around
ㄴ 경기가 좋아지면 그들은 월급을 크게 올려 받을 것이다

They'll put some of the older executives out to pasture
ㄴ 그들은 일부 나이가 든 중역들을 내보내기로 하고 있어

They've been having trouble keeping pace with their colleagues
ㄴ 그들은 동료들에게 뒤지지 않으려고 애를 먹고 있어

They've been short-handed, overworked and under considerable strain
ㄴ 그들은 일손 부족에, 업무량 과중에, 상당한 스트레스를 받고 있다

They've let the office go since the boss retired

› **berth** place where a ship lies at anchor, place to sit or sleep especially on a ship

› **pasture** land used for grazing, graze

    ㄴ 전임 사장이 퇴직한 후 그들은 사무실을 엉망으로 만들었다

This door leads into the conference room
    ㄴ 이 문은 회의실로 통해

This in-house training course is aimed at eliminating some of the mystique usually associated with your job
    ㄴ 이번 사내 훈련 과정은 보통 여러분들의 직무와 관련하여 업무 수행 상 일어나는 신비적인 거리감을 다소나마 해소하려는데 목적을 둡니다

This maxim indicates everybody to be the boss of something small, rather than a follower of something big
    ㄴ 이 속담은 누구나 큰 회사 같은 곳의 말단이 되기보다 하찮은 곳이라도 우두머리가 되라는 것을 말해준다

This was an inside job
    ㄴ 이건 내부 소행이야

This won't look good on your performance record
    ㄴ 계속 그러면 인사과에 나쁘게 반영시킬 거야

Thousands of demonstrators demanded a bigger slice of cake
    ㄴ 수천 명의 근로자들은 보다 나은 급료(배당)을 요구했다

Today three meetings clash
    ㄴ 오늘은 세 건의 모임이 중복된다

Try not to push your employees too far
    ㄴ 종업원들을 혹사하지 않도록 해

Try not your employees be down on you
    ㄴ 종업원들에게 원망을 듣지 않도록 해

Try to keep pace with the other colleagues
    ㄴ 다른 동료들과 보조를 맞춰 주시오

Trying to get this office on its feet is harder than I thought

---

· **mystique**   air or attitude of mystery or reverence about something

↳ 이 사무실이 제대로 돌아가게 돌려놓는 일이 생각보다 어려웠어

Two employees were killed in the line of duty when they tried to stop a robbery

↳ 종업원 두 명이 근무 중 강도를 잡으려다가 피살됐다

Upon his returning from work, he was running on empty

↳ 그가 직장에서 귀가할 때쯤이면 기진맥진이었다

Wan-soo did a sloppy job, so he may be whisle for his money

↳ 완수는 건성으로 일했기 때문에 돈을 받지 못할 것이다

We are right on schedule

↳ 계획대로 진행 중

We are waiting anxiously to see if the group will remain faithful to its promise of reform

↳ 우리는 그 기업그룹이 구조조정 약속을 충실히 지킬지 눈 여겨 지켜 보고 있다

We did our bit and it's up to you to keep your side of the bargain and increase overtime pay

↳ 우리가 해야 할 일을 다 했으니 이제 사장님이 약속을 지켜 초과근무 수당을 올려줘야 합니다

We have a few loose ends to clear up

↳ 우린 몇 가지 정리할 사항이 있어

We have a lot of fifth wheels in our office

↳ 우리 사무실에는 일도 안하고 노는 사람이 많다

We have no choice but to let you go=We should let you go

↳ 당신을 해고해야 겠어요

We have to comply with the new regulatory policies until we receive official notice that we are exempted from doing so

---

› **reform** make or become better by correcting bad habits

› **exempt** being free from some liability

↳ 우리는 우리 회사가 면제되었다는 공식적인 통보를 받을 때까지는 새 규정을 따라야 한다

We have to fly the coop today
↳ 우린 오늘 재빨리 퇴근해야해

We should place the right man in the right place
↳ 우린 인력을 적재 적소에 둬야 해

We've got to learn to take our lumps in this job
↳ 우린 직무상의 잔소리(징계)쯤 감수하는 걸 익혀야 해

What's the average starting wage in your line of work?
↳ 당신 직종의 평균 초임은 얼마입니까?

When I transferred to this office, I found myself a small(little) frog in a big pond
↳ 내가 이 사무실로 전입해왔을 때 나 같은 사람은 극히 미미한 존재란 걸 실감했어

When she was pregnant and doing a full-time job and all she did was to try to find time to put her feet up
↳ 그녀가 임신 중 정규직원으로 일할 때 했던 일이라고는 쉴 틈을 찾는 것 뿐 이었다

When they retire they'll due for a rude awakening
↳ 그들이 퇴직하면 언짢은 일을 당하게 돼 있어

When we watch our best office worker going into his act, we can learn a lot from him
↳ 사무실 내에 우수사원의 일상 행동을 보면 배울게 많다

When you don't play your card well this time, you''ll have to end up with a pink slip
↳ 네가 이번 일을 잘 처리하지 못하면 해고를 당하게 돼있어

‣ **pregnant** containing unborn young, meaningful

Who made the hamburger(mincemeat)out of my paper?
　　　ㄴ 누가 내 서류를 엉망으로 만들어 놨어?

Who's made it hot for you in the office?
　　　ㄴ 사무실에서 누가 널 힘들게 만들고 있니?

Will you advance me a month's salary?
　　　ㄴ 한 달치 월급을 가불해 주시겠습니까?

Will you be around next week?
　　　ㄴ 다음주에 휴가나 출장 안가시죠?

Will you please pass your eye over this paper?
　　　ㄴ 이 서류를 좀 봐주시겠습니까?

With our labor union fully in operation we'll soon be able to protect our interests
　　　　　　ㄴ 우리의 노조가 기능을 다하면 우리의 권익을 보호받게 될 것이다

With skill workers it makes very little odds which method is used
　　　　　ㄴ 숙련된 일꾼들에겐 어떤 방법을 쓰건 별 문제가 안 돼

With the feud clearly settled, many hope that the group will now be able to refocus on its business operation
　　　　　　ㄴ 많은 사람들은 불화가 말끔히 해소되는 가운데 이 기업그룹이 사업경
　　　　　　영에 다시 총력을 기울일수 있게 되기를 희망한다

Won-suck was dissatisfied at getting a raw deal
　　　　　ㄴ 원석인 정당치 못한 대우를 받아 불만이었어

Would you stay here in the office and hold the fort until I get back?
　　　　　ㄴ 내가 돌아올 때까지 사무실에 남아서 내가 할 일을 대신 해줄래?

Would you work the graveyard shift?
　　　ㄴ 심야근무를 하시겠습니까?

Wrap things up before you quit for the day

· **feud**　lasting conflict between families or clans

· **graveyard**　place of burial

↳ 퇴근하기 전에 끝내고 가

Write your paper on every other line

↳ 문서를 작성할 때 한 줄씩 띄어 써라

You are best suited for active duty=You belong on street

↳ 넌 현장근무가 제격이야

You are supposed to do what you are told to

↳ 시키는 대로만 하면 돼

You can get an advance of one million won on your salary=You can draw one million won against your salary

↳ 넌 월급에서 백만원 가불 할 수 있어

You can reach me at work

↳ 직장으로 연락하면 돼

You come up short again this month

↳ 이번 달 또 할당량을 못 채웠군

You have to have some heads together to get things done

↳ 일이 되게 하려면 네가 관리자답게 일을 시켜야 해

You have to pick your way through report after report to find the information

↳ 넌 보고서(기사)를 하나하나 훑어보고 자료(정보)를 찾아내야 해

You have to provide your employees with a healthy outlet for tension and stress

↳ 넌 종업원들의 긴장과 스트레스에 대한 건전한 해소대책을 마련해 줘야 해

You must make the loss up next month

↳ 다음달에 손실을 만회해야 해

You should ask that of the data base

↳ 그건 데이터베이스에 보면 나와 있어

› **suit** be appropriate or becoming to, meet the needs of

› **tension** tension condition, state of mental unrest or of potential hostility or opposition

You'd better light(make, build) a fire under your staff

└ 직원들이 빠릿빠릿하게 움직이도록 만드는 게 좋아

You'll be back in the thick of the action before you know

└ 곧 활동이 활발한 부서에 복직하게 될 거야

You'll be brought to book if you're regularly late for work

└ 항상 출근이 늦으면 문책 받게 돼 있어

You'll be fired if you have your hand in the till

└ 넌 돈을 착복했다가는 해고야

You'll surely get promoted; you have everything going for you

└ 모든 일이 네게 유리하게 돌아가고 있으니 틀림없이 성공할거야

Your vacation is over. Back to salt mines

└ 휴가는 끝났으니 지겹지만 직장에 나가 일 해야지

‣ **mine** excavation from which mineral
substances are taken

133. 진실   Truth

A lie has speed, but truth has endurance
> ↳ 거짓은 속도를 자랑하지만 진실은 인내력을 가지고 있다

A platitude is a truth repeated until people get tired of hearing of it
> ↳ 진부한 문구는 사람들이 듣기 싫을 만큼 반복해서 말해온 진실일 뿐이다

Add a few drops of venom to a half truth and you have an absolute truth
> ↳ 얼치기 진실에 독약을 몇 방울 떨어뜨리면 확실한 진실을 얻는다

All truths that are silent become poisonous
> ↳ 모든 침묵하는 진실은 독성을 띠게 된다

Although we now enjoy complete freedom of speech, we still seem to instinctively flinch from telling the truth to others
> ↳ 우리가 완전한 언론의 자유를 누리고 있지만 아직도 본능적으로 남들에게 진실을 말하기를 꺼리는 것 같다

An accumulation of facts is no more a science than a heap of stones is a house
> ↳ 돌무더기를 쌓아올린 것이 집이 아니듯이 사실들을 쌓아 올린 것도 과학이 아니다

An-do was brought down to earth by the revelation of the truth
> ↳ 사실을 밝힘으로써 안도가 현실을 깨닫게 되었지

At that time, I couldn't dare to tell you the truth

› **platitude** trite remark
› **venom** poison secreted by certain, ill will

ㄴ 그때 진실을 얘기할 용기가 없었죠

Be the matter what it may, always speak the truth
ㄴ 무슨 일이든지 언제나 진실을 말하라

Better a lie that heals than a truth that wounds
ㄴ 남에게 상처를 입히는 진실보다 상처를 낫게 해주는 거짓이 낫다

Call a spade a spade
ㄴ 솔직히 털어놔라

Craft must have clothes, but truth loves to go naked
ㄴ 책략에는 옷을 입혀야 하지만 진실은 옷을 벗고 있기를 좋아한다

Death cancels everything but truth
ㄴ 죽음은 진실 외의 모든 것을 취소한다

Every violation of truth is not only a sort of suicide in the liar, but is a stab at the health of human society
ㄴ 진실에 어긋나는 모든 일은 거짓말 한 사람의 자살일 뿐 아니라 인간 사회의 건전성에도 타격이 된다

Fact(Truth) is stranger than fiction
ㄴ 사실이 소설보다 더 기이하다

Facts are stubborn things
ㄴ 진실은 밝혀진다

Facts do not cease to exist because they are ignored
ㄴ 사실은 무시된다고 해서 없어지는 것은 아니다

Great is truth and strongest of all
ㄴ 진실은 위대하고 무엇보다 강하다

Hair perhaps divides the truthfulness and falsehood
ㄴ 머리카락 하나로 진실과 거짓을 가려낸다

He that does not speak truth to me does not believe me when I

· **spade** dig with a spade

· **fiction** a made-up story or literature consisting of these

speak truth
> ↳ 진실을 말하지 않는 사람은 남이 진실을 말할 때 믿지 않는다

His accounts of what happened approached the truth, but there were a few errors
> ↳ 발생한 사건에 대한 그의 설명은 사실에 가까웠으나 다소 잘못이 있었다

His words have a ring of truth
> ↳ 그의 말에는 진실이 담겨있다

Hope is a great falsifier of truth
> ↳ 희망은 진실을 크게 왜곡시킨다

In too much dispute truth is lost
> ↳ 너무 시비를 일삼으면 진실을 놓친다

In wine there's truth
> ↳ 취중진담

> (=What soberness conceals drunkeness reveals)
> (=There is truth in wine)

Irrationally held truths may be more harmful than reasoned errors
> ↳ 이치에 안 맞게 마음에 담고있는 진실은 조리가 선 착오보다 더 해롭다

It is only too true
> ↳ 틀림없는 사실이다

It proves the truth of the proverb
> ↳ 그 속담이 맞다 는 걸 알 수 있어

It will be long(not long)before we know the truth
> ↳ 진상은 여간해서 알기 어려울(얼마 안 가서 알게 될) 것이다

> ‣ **sober** not drunk, serious or solemn
> ‣ **proverb** short meaningful popular saying

It's one thing to show a man that he's in an error, and another to put him in possession of truth
> ↳ 잘못을 지적해 주는 것과 진리를 갖도록 하는 것은 별개 문제이다

It's stretching the truth to say he's a born sharper
> ↳ 그가 타고난 사기꾼이라고 말하는 건 과장된 말이다

Let others say what they will, I always speak the truth
> ↳ 남이야 무엇이라고 말하든 나는 언제나 진실을 말하겠다

Let the facts speak for themselves
> ↳ 진실이 저절로 밝혀지게 내버려 둬

Let's go over the facts
> ↳ 사실을 한 번 검토해 보자

Life is a system of half-truths and lies
> ↳ 인생은 반의 사실과 반의 거짓으로 된 체계이다

Logic is the art of making truth prevail
> ↳ 논리는 진실이 통하게 하는 기술이다

Love truth, but pardon error
> ↳ 진실을 사랑하되 실수를 용서하라

Many a true word is spoken in jest
> ↳ 수많은 진담이 농담으로 말해진다

> 사자성어 중에 '언중유골'이라는 성어가 있다. 사람의 감정을 상하게 할 수도 있는 진실을 농담으로 말하는 것이 인간 관계를 유연하게 이끌어 나가는 지혜이다.

Newspapers should not give currency to frightening news without making sure of their facts

---

› **logic** science of reasoning, sound reasoning
› **currency** general use or acceptance, money

 ↳ 신문이 사실 확인도 안하고 겁주는 뉴스를 보도해서는 안 된다

No one believes a liar when you tell the truth
 ↳ 콩으로 메주를 쑨데도 네 말은 못 믿겠구나(이솝이야기에서)

> 자주 쓰이는 영어 속담중에 'You are crying wolf too often'이 있다. 이것은 이솝이야기의 '양치기 소년'이라는 이야기에서 유래하였다. 양치기 소년이 늑대가 나타났다고 거짓말을 여러 번 했기 때문에 진짜로 늑대가 나타났을 때에는 아무도 믿지 않았다는 내용이다. 여기서 직역을 하면 "너는 늑대를 너무 여러 번 외쳤어"이고, 그렇기 때문에 믿을 수 없다는 뜻이다.

Nothing could be farther from the truth
 ↳ 어처구니없는(얼토당토 않는) 소리

One falsehood spoils a thousand truths
 ↳ 한 가지의 거짓은 천 가지의 진실을 망친다

Our enemies approach nearer to truth in their judgements of us than we do ourselves
 ↳ 적은 우리를 판단함에 있어서 우리 자신보다 더 진실에 가까이 접근한다

Repetition doesn't transform a lie into a truth
 ↳ 거짓은 반복해서 말해도 거짓말이 참말로 바뀌지 않는다

Right or not, it's a fact
 ↳ 옳건 그르건 간에 그건 사실이다

She must tell the truth and shame the devil
 ↳ 그 여자는 입을 열기 어려운 상황이지만 사실대로 말해야 해

Tell it like it is
 ↳ 이실직고해

▸ **shame**   distress over guilt or disgrace, cause of shame or regret

> (=Tell your story without diverging from the truth)

That swindler is clever enough to twist the truth until it fits his needs
ㄴ 그 사기꾼이라면 능히 자신의 필요에 맞아 들어갈 때까지 사실을 왜곡할 수 있어

That's when you'll know the truth
ㄴ 그 때가 되면 너도 알게 돼

The facts are patient of two interpretations
ㄴ 그 사실에 대해선 두 가지 해석이 가능하다

The sting of a reproach is in the truth of it
ㄴ 꾸지람의 통렬함은 꾸짖는 내용의 진실성에 달려있다

The stories were neither of them true
ㄴ 어느 쪽의 이야기도 진실이 아니었다

The theory failed to converge on the truth
ㄴ 그 이론은 사실에 부합하지 못했어

The truthful lip shall be established forever, but a lying tongue is but for a moment
ㄴ 진실한 입술은 영원히 보존되거니와 거짓 혀는 눈깜짝일 동안 있을 뿐이니라

There's many a true word said in jest
ㄴ 농담 속이 진실 있다

> 사자성어 중에 '언중유골'이라는 성어가 있다. 사람의 감정을 상하게 할 수도 있는 진실을 농담으로 말하는 것이 인간 관계를 유연하게 이끌어 나가는 지혜이다.

› **diverge**   move in different directions, differ
› **converge**   approach a single point

There's no worse lie than a truth misunderstood who hear it
> ↳ 사실을 듣고서 그 사실을 오해하는 것 보다 더 나쁜 거짓말이 없다

There's not an atom of truth in the rumor
> ↳ 그 소문은 전혀 사실무근이었다

There's nothing you can do after the fact
> ↳ 사전에 잘해야지 사후엔 소용없어

There's scarcely a great truth or principle but has to fight its way to public recognition in the face of opposition
> ↳ 공적인 인정을 받기 위해서 반대와 비난에 맞서 싸워 나가지 않아도 되는 대 진리나 대 원칙은 없다

This fact lends probability to the story
> ↳ 이 사실로 보면 그 얘기가 그럴듯하다

Time can shout the truth where words lie
> ↳ 말이 거짓을 지껄이고 있을 경우에도 시간은 진실을 외칠 수 있다

> 인간의 악행에 대한 처벌이나, 선행에 대한 보답은 즉시 일어나지 않을 수도 있지만 시간이 흐르면 틀림없이 일어난다. 하나님의 맷돌은 천천히 돌아가지만 아주 곱게 갈아진다는 뜻의 "The mills of God grind slowly, yet they grind exceeding small"과도 같은 뜻이다.

True scientists are often inspired men and women of unbending curiosity for new facts
> ↳ 진정한 과학자들은 새로운 사실에 대해서 끝없는 호기심에 사로잡힌 영감을 받은 사람들인 경우가 많다

Truth disappears with the telling of it
> ↳ 진실을 말하자마자 그 진실은 사라진다

› **inspire**   inhale, influence by example, bring about, stir to action

Truth fears no trial
ㄴ 진실은 시험을 두려워하지 않는다

Truth has already ceased to be itself if polemically said
ㄴ 따지듯이 말하는 진실은 이미 진실이 아니다

Truth is more of a stranger than fiction
ㄴ 진실은 가공보다 더 생소하다

Truth lives on in the midst of deception
ㄴ 진실은 속임수가 난무하는 가운데에 있다

Truth looks tawdry when she is overdressed
ㄴ 진실이 옷을 너무 입으면 천박해 보인다

Truth sits on the lips of dying men
ㄴ 사람이 죽을 때가 되면 진실을 말한다

Veracity is the heart of morality
ㄴ 진실은 도덕의 핵심이다

When money speaks the world(truth) is in silence
ㄴ 돈이 말을 하면 세상(진실)이 침묵한다

When the wine is in, wit(truth) is out
ㄴ 술먹은 개

When war is declared, truth is first casualty
ㄴ 전쟁이 선포되면 진실이 첫 희생물이 된다

With the trowel of patience we dig out roots of truth
ㄴ 인내의 삽으로 진실을 캐낸다

Witnesses ought to stick to the facts and leave aside all emotion and sentiment
ㄴ 증인은 사실에 벗어나지 않게 증언해야 하며 감정과 정서는 배제해야 한다

› **polemic** practice of disputation
› **tawdry** cheap and gaudy

› **veracity** truthfulness or accuracy

Your remarks deviate from the truth
ㄴ 네 말은 사실과 동떨어져

‣ **deviate** change especially from a course
  or standard

134. 질문   Useful Questions

Am I asking a lot?

    ↳ 욕심이 과한 건가요?

> (=Am I asking for the impossible?)
> (=Is my request too much to ask for?)

Am I getting through to you?

    ↳ 내 말 알아듣겠어?

Am I seen through?

    ↳ 내 속이 들여다보이니?

Am I to understand you have agreed to the proposal?

    ↳ 그 제안에 동의 한 것으로 이해해도 되겠습니까?

Am I up next?

    ↳ 다음이 내 차례인가?

Any good ideas?

    ↳ 뭐 뾰족한 수가 있나?

Anything good on tonight?

    ↳ 오늘저녁 뭐 좋은 프로 있나?

Are the fish biting?

    ↳ 낚시는 잘 하니?

▸ **request** ask for

> (=Any luck fishing?)
> (=Have you caught any fish?)
> (=Is it a good day to fish?)

Are there any landmarks along the way?
> ↳ 길을 가면 길 찾는 표적이 될만한 게 있습니까?

Are there enough oil supplies to see the world to(through to) the end of the century?
> ↳ 세기말까지 기름 공급이 유지될 수 있을까?

Are they going to name names?
> ↳ 그들이 대상(비행 등)자들을 거명 하겠다는 거니?

Are we there?
> ↳ (목적지에) 다 왔어?

Are you adding it to your order?
> ↳ 별도(추가)로 주문하는 겁니까?

> (=Is that a separate order?)
> (=Do you want that as well?)

Are you always this lukewarm about everything?
> ↳ 넌 언제나 모든 일에 이렇게 뜨뜻미지근하냐?

Are you at work now?
> ↳ 직장에 나가니?

Are you available today?
> ↳ 오늘 시간 좀 있어?

Are you being attended to?

· **landmark** object that marks a boundary
　　　　　　or serves as a guide

· **lukewarm** moderately warm, not enthusiastic

↳ (손님에게)주문 하셨습니까?

Are you being helped(served)?

↳ 주문하셨어요?

Are you directing your remark at(to) me?

↳ 내게 한 말이냐?

Are you getting somewhere with Moon-Soo?

↳ 문수하고는 얘기가 잘 돼가니?

Are you giving me ultimatums?

↳ 한 번 해 보자는 거냐?

Are you going to blow off the meeting?

↳ 회의를 빼 먹으(망치)려는 거냐?

Are you going to install yourself as the boss of the department?

↳ 네가 그 부서 책임자의 일을 맡겠다는 거니?

Are you going to let your hair grow long?

↳ 머리를 기를 생각이냐?

Are you going to make him pay?

↳ 그에게 앙갚음하겠다는 거니?

Are you going to prepare charges against the driver who ruined your lawns

↳ 넌 너희 잔디를 망친 운전자를 고발할 생각이니?

Are you going to put him through the paces?

↳ 그의 능력을 시험해보려는 거냐?

Are you going to put(cast) our plan into the melting pot?

↳ 우리 계획을 전면적으로 고치겠다는 거냐?

Are you going to put the chill(freeze) on me?

↳ 나를 상대하지 않겠다(무시하겠다)는 거니?

· chill   make or become cold or chilly

Are you going to will-call it?
ㄴ 물건을 직접 찾아가시겠습니까?

Are you holding out on me?
ㄴ 내 발목을 잡겠다는 거니?

Are you holding something back from me?
ㄴ 너 나한테 뭔가 숨기고 있는 거지?

Are you in a position to say that?
ㄴ 그렇게 말 할 자격 있니?

(=Are you entitled to say that?)

Are you muffled up against the cold?
ㄴ 감기 안 들게 옷을 두껍게 입었니?

Are you playing with a full deck?
ㄴ 넌 지금 제정신으로 하는 짓이냐?

Are you quite rested?
ㄴ 충분히 휴식했니?

Are you ready to put down roots here?
ㄴ 여기서 정착할 준비가 된 거냐?

Are you seeing anyone?
ㄴ 너 사귀는 사람 있니?

Are you short of breath at all?
ㄴ 조금이라도 숨이 차는 일이 있습니까?

Are you through with your call?
ㄴ 통화 끝났니?

▸ **entitle** name, give a right to

Are you trying to move on his date?
> ㄴ 넌 그의 애인을 꼬시겠다는 거니?

Are you trying to muscle in on their turf?
> ㄴ 그들의 세력권 안으로 밀고 들어가려는 거냐?

Are you trying to pull rank on me?
> ㄴ 지위가 높다고 이래라 저래라 하는 겁니까?

Are you up or down today?
> ㄴ 오늘 기분(몸 상태)이 좋으냐 나쁘냐?

Are you with me?
> ㄴ 내 말 알아듣겠어?

Are your talks with your boss getting anywhere?
> ㄴ 사장과의 얘긴 잘 돼가니?

Aren't you a little premature in forming such a plan?
> ㄴ 그런 계획을 세우기엔 조금 빠르지 않나?

At the risk of sounding stupid, can I ask a simple question?
> ㄴ 바보같이 들릴지 모르지만 간단한 질문 하나 해도 될까요?

Can he measure up to the new boss's expectations?
> ㄴ 그가 사장의 기대에 부응할 수 있을까?

Can I bum a cigarette off you?
> ㄴ 담배 한 대 있어?

Can I buy them singularly?
> ㄴ 낱개로 살 수 있습니까?

(=Can you break up the set?)

› turf   upper layer of soil bound by grass and roots

Can I check my valuables with you?
  ↳ 귀중품을 맡아 주시겠습니까?

(I'd like my valuables back 맡긴 귀중품을 돌려주십시오)

Can I digress for a moment?
  ↳ 잠시 본론에서 벗어나도 되겠습니까?

Can I entice you with a piece of cake?
  ↳ 과자 하나 먹어볼래?

(=Can I oblige you with a piece of cake?)

Can I get some directions?
  ↳ 길 좀 물어보겠습니다

Can I help you to some more soup?
  ↳ 수프를 좀 더 드시겠습니까?

Can I leave my resume with you just in case anything opens up?
  ↳ 혹시 새로 자리가 날지 모르니까 이력서를 놓고 가겠습니다

Can I make good connections for Seoul?
  ↳ 서울로 가는 연결 교통편이 있습니까?

Can I move it up a day?
  ↳ 하루 앞당길 수 있을까요?

Can I put in my two cents?
  ↳ 제 의견을 덧붙여도 될까요?

Can I see a statement showing all accrued interest?

› **digress** wander from the main subject
› **entice** tempt

ㄴ 전체 발생한 이자에 대해서 알려 주시겠습니까?

Can I shame him out of such un-acceptable behavior?
ㄴ 그에게 창피를 주어서 그런 용납할 수 없는 행동을 못하게 할 수 있을까?

Can I share your umbrella?
ㄴ 우산 좀 같이 쓰십시다

(=Can I walk under your umbrella?)

Can I stop over on route?
ㄴ 도중에 내릴 수 있습니까?

Can I tempt you with another glass of beer?
ㄴ 맥주 한 잔 더 하시겠습니까?

Can I top off your glass?
ㄴ 술을 더(첨가해서) 따를까요?

Can she maintain the balancing act of pleasing her parents and her parent-in-law?
ㄴ 그녀가 친부모와 시부모 모두를 기쁘게 할 균형 있는 행동을 유지할 수 있을까?

Can such things be?
ㄴ 이런 일이 있을 수 있나?

Can the leopard change his spots?
ㄴ 제 버릇 개 주랴

Can this money carry you through this month?
ㄴ 이 돈이면 이 달을 넘길 수 있나?

Can we make it off the record?
ㄴ 비밀로 하기로 합시다

· **tempt** coax or persuade to do wrong, attract or provoke

Can we patch up our differences?
　　　↳ 우리가 견해차를 조정(수습할 수 있을까?)

Can you call this work?
　　　↳ 이걸 일이라고 해 왔나?

Can you balance a coin on its edge?
　　　↳ 이 동전을 가장자리로 세워놓을 수 있겠니?

Can you bring him around to your way of thinking?
　　　↳ 그를 설득해서 동의를 얻어낼 수 있겠나?

Can you come down a little more?
　　　↳ 조금 더 깎아줄 수 없겠습니까?

Can you date this crown?
　　　↳ 왕관의 제작 년대를 아니?

Can you debug the program to make it run right?
　　　↳ 이 컴퓨터 프로그램이 제대로 가동되도록 점검해 줄 수 있겠니?

Can you drive a car with a manual transmission?
　　　↳ 수동 변속 차를 운전할 수 있니?

Can you find a way to persuade the fence-hangers to come over to our side?
　　　↳ 마음을 정하지 못한 사람들을 우리편으로 설득해 올 방법이 없을까?

Can you fit(squeeze, crowd) in a game of bowling with me on the weekend?
　　　↳ 주말에 보울링 한판 칠래?(crowd in 스케줄에 넣어주다)

Can you fit them all in your trunk?
　　　↳ 그것들을 전부 네 트렁크에 넣을 수 있겠나?

Can you fold this paper into a little bird?
　　　↳ 이 종이를 접어서 작은 새를 만들 수 있니?

> **debug** eliminate malfunctions in

> **manual** involving the hands or physical force

Can you forgive the fool that I've been?
↳ 저의 바보 같은 짓을 용서해 주시겠어요?

Can you gain on(get ahead of) the car in front?
↳ 앞차를 추월할 수 있겠니?

Can you get everything on him?
↳ 그 사람에 대한 모든 걸 알아줄 수 있나?

Can you get it through your head?
↳ 그게 무슨 말인지 납득이 가니?

Can you get them round the table to agree on this point?
↳ 그들이 이 문제에 합의할 수 있도록 협상 테이블로 끌어 올 수 있겠나?

Can you help me understand one reason why I should keep you around?
↳ 당신을 이 회사에 계속 고용할 이유가 있는 건지 한 가지라도 대 보시오

Can you keep this business on its feet for another year?
↳ 이 사업을 1년 더 버티어 낼 수 있겠나?

Can you make just one exception?
↳ 한 번만 봐 주십시오

Can you move(push) the date back a little?
↳ 날짜를 조금 늦출 수 있겠나?

Can you oblige(us) with a song?
↳ 노래 한 곡 해 주시겠습니까?

Can you open up the engine a little?
↳ 차를 좀 빨리 몰 수 없겠니?

Can you pick me out in this old school photograph?
↳ 이 옛날 학생 때 사진에서 나를 알아볼 수 있겠나?

▸ **photograph** picture taken by photography

Can you place me with a company that makes electronic goods?
ㄴ 전자제품 만드는 회사에 취직시켜줄 수 있겠습니까?

Can you pull the thread through the eye of the needle?
ㄴ 이 실을 바늘귀에 꿸 수 있겠니?

> (=Can you thread the needle?)

Can you put your finger on it?
ㄴ 그걸 딱 꼬집어 낼 수 있겠니?

Can you run that by me again?
ㄴ 다시 한번 말해 줄 수 있겠니?

Can you run this wire in through this hole in the top?
ㄴ 꼭대기에 있는 이 구멍에 철사를 꿸 수 있겠니?

Can you smooth over this matter?
ㄴ 네가 이 일을 수습할 수 있겠니?

Can you squeeze a few kilometers out of this tank of gas before you fill up again?
ㄴ 주유소에 닿기 전에 차에 있는 기름으로 몇 킬로 더 갈 수 있겠니?

Can you stall(play) for time till the end of the year?
ㄴ 연말까지 시간을 늦춰줄 수 있겠니?

Can you stand on your hands?
ㄴ 너 물구나무서기 할 수 있겠니?

Can you sweat any information out of him?
ㄴ 그에게서 정보 좀 얻어낼 수 있겠나?

Can you take my car in exchange(as a trade)?

› **needle** incite to action by repeated gibes ┆ › **stall** delay, evade, or keep a situation going to gain advantage or time

    ↳ 받을 돈 대신 차를 가져가시면 안되겠습니까?

Can you take(let) these pants in(out)?

    ↳ 이 바지 좀 넓혀(줄여) 주시겠어요?

Can you tell the twins from one another?

    ↳ 그 쌍둥이들을 구별할 수 있겠니?

Can you whip the players into shape before the game?

    ↳ 게임 전에 선수들의 몸 만들기를 해낼 수 있겠습니까?

Could everyone come up front?

    ↳ 앞쪽으로 와 주시겠습니까?(회의장에서)

Could I be excused?

    ↳ 일어나도 되겠습니까?(먼저 자리 뜰 때)

Could I get by?

    ↳ 앞을 좀 지나가도 되겠습니까?

Could stupidity(imbecility) go further?

    ↳ 이보다 더 바보짓이 있을까?

Could you be more specific?

    ↳ 좀더 구체적으로 말씀해 주시겠습니까?

Could you clean the fish?

    ↳ 비늘과 내장을 제거해 주시겠어요?

Could you fix another one?

    ↳ 한 잔 더 주시겠어요?

Could you go for a cup of tea?

    ↳ 차 한 잔 드릴까요?

Could you have a person paged for me?

    ↳ 사람 좀 찾아주세요(사람 찾는 방송 부탁합니다)

› **imbecile** feebleminded or foolish person

Could you let me go with a warning?
> ↳ 경고정도로 처리해 줄 수 없겠습니까?

Could you let us know when the shipment comes in?
> ↳ 언제 선적물이 들어오는지 알려주시겠어요?

Could you move over(down) a little so we can have some room
> ↳ 자리가 생기게 좀 죄어 앉아(서) 주시겠습니까?

Could you please put your car at my disposal today?
> ↳ 오늘 네 차를 좀 사용할 수 있겠나?

Could you put it on my credit card?
> ↳ 카드로 지급해도 되나요?

Could you put that more simply?
> ↳ 조금 설명을 해 주시겠어요?

Could you save my seat for me?
> ↳ 제 자리 좀 봐 주시겠습니까?(잠시 자리 뜰 때)

Could you squeeze a little?
> ↳ 좀 지나가겠습니다

Could you start the ball rolling?
> ↳ 먼저 발언해 주시겠습니까?

Could you tell me what the call is about?
> ↳ 무슨 용건으로 전화 하셨는지요?

(=May I ask what the call is concerning?)

Did that piss you off?
> ↳ 그래서 열 받았나?

· **disposal** give a tendency to, settle

Did the boss ream you out?
> ↳ 윗분이 야단 치셨어요?

Did the punishment really fit the crime?
> ↳ 그 처벌이 정말 그 죄과에 합당했을까?

Did you enjoy your stay with us?
> ↳ 계속 즐겁게 시청 하셨습니까?

Did you remember to take care of the waiter?
> ↳ 웨이터에게 팁 주는 것 잊지 않았겠지?

Did you see the shameless way she was chucking(hurling, throwing, flinging) herself at him?
> ↳ 그 여자가 창피한 줄도 모르고 그에게 매달리는 것 보았니?

Did you tie one on again?
> ↳ 또 술을 진탕 마셨나?

Didn't you have sense enough to offer your seat to the old lady?
> ↳ 그 노부인에게 자리를 양보 할 생각 없습니까?

Do I always have to be the heavy?
> ↳ 왜 내가 항상 악역을 맡아야 하니?

Do I have to spell it out?
> ↳ 일일이 설명할 필요가 있나요?

> (=Do I have to paint a picture?)

Do I have to take the slack up?
> ↳ 내가 마무리해야 하나?

Do I get a discount if I buy in bulk?

› **chuck** tap, toss
› **hurl** throw with violence

ㄴ 대량으로 사면 할인해 줍니까?

(=Do you give discounts on volume purchases?)

Do I know you?
　　　ㄴ 누구시던가요? 저를 아십니까?

Do I make myself clear?
　　　ㄴ 내 말 알아듣겠어?

(=Do you get(follow) me?)

Do I turn right here or at the next corner?
　　　ㄴ 여기서 좌회전해야 합니까 아니면 다음 모퉁이에서 해야 합니까?

Do I understand that I am no longer welcome here?
　　　ㄴ 내가 더 이상 여기서 환영받지 못하단 말인가?

Do those chatterboxes ever stop talking big?
　　　ㄴ 저 수다쟁이들의 허풍은 못 말린다니까

Do we have enough heating oil to last out this winter?
　　　ㄴ 이 겨울을 넘길만한 난방용 기름이 우리한테 있나?

Do we not all spend the greater part of our lives under the shadow of an event that has not yet come to pass?
　　　ㄴ 우리 모두는 아직 다가오지 않은 사건의 그늘 아래서 인생의 태반 이상을 소비하고 있지 않을까?

Do you have a time for a quick one?
　　　ㄴ 한잔 할 시간 있니?

› **chatterbox** incessant talker

Do you have any preference about which airline you fly?
  ㄴ 특별히 선호하는 항공사가 있습니까?

Do you have any theory about the case?
  ㄴ 그 일에 뭐 집히는 일이라도 있나?

Do you have anything on this evening?
  ㄴ 오늘 저 무슨 계획(약속)이라도 있니?

Do you have enough paper to see you through?
  ㄴ 하던 일 끝낼 만큼 종이가 충분해?

Do you have that many on hand?
  ㄴ 그만한 수량의 재고가 있습니까?

Do you have to bark your orders out at everyone?
  ㄴ 아무한테나 이래라 저래라 명령조로 말해야 하니?

Do you have something against me?
  ㄴ 내게 유감 있니?

Do you keep the household accounts?
  ㄴ 가계부를 적습니까?

Do you know any idea about how I can get off the hook?
  ㄴ 이 곤경에서 빠져나갈 묘안 없어?

Do you spend a lot of time on the road?
  ㄴ 업무상 외근이 많습니까?

Do you take cream and sugar in your coffee?
  ㄴ 커피에 크림이나 설탕 넣습니까?

Do you think your hat will stay on in this high wind?
  ㄴ 이렇게 센바람에 모자가 안 날아갈 것 같으냐?

Do you want me to give you a rundown?
  ㄴ 개요를 말해줄까?

› **bark** speak in a loud curt tone, make the sound of a dog

› **rundown** summary

Do you want to get out of a promise(back out of from a promise)?
    ↳ 약속을 취소하고 싶어?

Do you want to order dinner in?
    ↳ 저녁을 배달시켜 먹을 거냐?

Do you want to box in the whole staff?
    ↳ 전 직원을 묶어 놓겠다는 겁니까?

Do you make any discount for cash?
    ↳ 현금으로 사면 할인해 줍니까?

Do you mind?
    ↳ 그러면 안돼요(줄을 설 때 밀치거나 툭툭 부딪칠 때)

Do you think he doesn't know his way around?
    ↳ 그를 아무 것도 모르는 사람으로 아나?

Do you think I have the golden goose that lays the golden eggs?
    ↳ 난 뭐 도깨비 방망이라도 가진 줄(돈이 무한정 있는 줄) 아나?

Do you think I'm a clay pigeon?
    ↳ 나를 동네북으로 아나?(clay pigeon 에는 '누워 떡 먹기'의 뜻이 있음)

Do you think I'm getting a gut?
    ↳ 내가 점점 배가 나오는 것 같니?

Do you think I'm loaded or something?
    ↳ 내가 재력가라도 되는 줄 아는 모양이군

Do you think the floor will bear up under the weight of the new machinery?
    ↳ 마루바닥이 새로 구입한 기계무게를 감당할 것 같니?

Do you think your hat will stay on in this high wind?
    ↳ 이렇게 센바람에 모자가 안 날아갈 것 같으냐?

‣ **discount**   reduction from a regular price, reduce the amount of, disregard

Do you want a piece of that?
  ↳ 그 여자 어떻게 해보고 싶어?

Do you want to go one on one with me?
  ↳ 나하고 맞붙어 보겠다는 거냐?

Do you want to share(use) this umbrella with me?
  ↳ 저와 우산을 같이 쓸까요?

Does a bear shit in the woods?
  ↳ 나하고 관계없는 일을 왜 자꾸 들먹거려

Does anyone claim this ring?
  ↳ 반지 잃으신 분계십니까?

Does that answer your question(explain it)?
  ↳ 질문에 답이 되었습니까?

Does that ring a bell?
  ↳ 이제 생각나나?

Does the advertising bring in any business?
  ↳ 광고를 하면 일거리가 들어오나?

Does the house have gas, electricity and water laid on?
  ↳ 이 집에는 가스, 전기, 수도가 부설되어 있습니까?

Don't I know you from somewhere?
  ↳ 어디선가 만난 적이 있던가요?

Don't you feel embarrassed?
  ↳ 부끄럽지 않니?

Don't you know how much you mean to me?
  ↳ 네가 내게 얼마나 소중한지 알잖아

Don't you think it's time we sent in the second string?
  ↳ 이제 제2진을 내보내는 게 어때?

▸ **advertise** call public attention to

Don't you think she's had a basinful(bellyfull) of your company this week?

     ↳ 그 여자가 이번 주 내내 지겹도록 너와 같이 있어주었다고 생각 안 해?

Excuse me, but don't I know you from somewhere?

     ↳ 실례합니다만, 어디서 만난 적이 있던가요?

Has the fax gone through yet? Yes, the receiver confirmed it

     ↳ 팩스가 들어갔나? 그래, 수신기에 확인이 됐어

Has the world another man to show like him?

     ↳ 세상에 그런 사람 또 있을까?

Has your ship come home?

     ↳ 큰돈이라도 들어왔나?

Have I the pleasure of addressing Mr. Bahk?

     ↳ 박 선생님이 십니까?

Have you been keeping out of trouble?

     ↳ 요즘 별일 없나?

Have you been on any medication for this pain?

     ↳ 이 통증 때문에 약을 드신 적이 있습니까?

Have you done it? - Like hell

     ↳ 그거 해놨니? - 내가 그런 거 할 것 같아?

Have you ever had someone steal your heart away?

     ↳ 누군가에게 마음을 뺏겨 본 일이 있나?

Have you fed the data into the computer?

     ↳ 컴퓨터에 자료 입력했니?

Have you got everything?

     ↳ 잊으신 것 없습니까?

· **confirm** ratify, verify, admit as a full member of a church or synagogue

Have you got your eyes then?
ㄴ 그러면 봐둔 사람이 있다는 거니?

Have you gotten over your jet lag?
ㄴ 시차병은 나았나요?

Have you lost all your marbles?
ㄴ 너 정신 나갔니?

Have you lost your tongue?
ㄴ 꿀 먹은 벙어리냐?

> (=Are you dumb-struck?)
> (=What's with the silence?)

Have you met before?
ㄴ 두 분이 아시는 사이십니까?

Have you run out of gas?
ㄴ 너 벌써 피곤하다는 거니?

Have you run out of resources?
ㄴ 밑천 다 떨어졌니?

Have you taken leave of your senses?
ㄴ 너 머리가 돈 거냐?

Have you taken out an insurance policy?
ㄴ 보험 들었니?

Haven't you got a home to go to?
ㄴ 할 일이 그렇게 없니?(그런 건 너희 집 안방에서나 해)

Haven't you nothing better to do than making repeated bows day in
ㄴ 기도문을 염해도? ... 이게 뭐 할 짓 없어

› **marble** crystallized limestone
› **insure** guarantee against loss, make certain

and day out?

    ↳ 그렇게 할 일이 없어서 밤이나 낮이나 졸고만 있니?

How about shifting gears?

    ↳ 방식을 바꿔보는 게 어때?

How am I doing?

    ↳ 나 잘 하고 있는 것 같니?

How are you going to call the tune when you are tone-deaf(flat)?

    ↳ 음치인 주제에 어떻게 선창을 하겠다는 거니?

How are you going to fill in this afternoon?

    ↳ 오늘 오후에 뭐하면서 시간 보낼 거니?

How are you going to shape up the salespeople overnight?

    ↳ 어떻게 판매부 직원들을 금방 개조해 놓겠다는 거니?

How are you keeping?

    ↳ 넌 어떻게 지내니?

How are you making out in your job?

    ↳ 하는 일은 잘 돼 가니?

How are you with your hands?

    ↳ 네 솜씨 좀 보고싶은데

How can he get a job after being behind bars for many years?

    ↳ 교도소에서 몇 년씩이나 복역한 사람이 어떻게 취직을 할까?

How can I persuade you of my plight?

    ↳ 어떻게 하면 나의 곤란한 입장을 이해할 수 있겠니?

How can I reach you?

    ↳ 어떻게 연락되죠?

How can that be?

    ↳ 어찌 그런 일이 있을 수 있나?

▸ **persuade**   cause to do or believe by argument or entreaty

▸ **plight**   pledge, bad state

How can we abuse a man of collaboration for doing what he had to?
ㄴ 어쩔 수 없어서 협력했던 사람을 어떻게 비난할 수 있겠나?

How can we wear out this dull afternoon?
ㄴ 이 지겨운 오후시간을 어떻게 때워 넘기지?

How can you be out from under that loan?
ㄴ 넌 어떻게 그 빚을 갚아 낼 거냐?

How can you deride a long-serving man as a spent force?
ㄴ 장기 근속한 직원을 어떻게 쓸모 없는 사람이라고 조롱할 수 있는가

How can you do(live) without your wife?
ㄴ 부인 없이 어떻게 지내려고 그러세요?

How can you expect respect when you are so condescending?
ㄴ 그리 잘난 척 하면서 어떻게 존경을 기대할 수 있겠니?

How can you expect these indignant workers to tolerate appalling working conditions and low quality, outdated equipment?
ㄴ 이 끔찍한 근로조건, 질 낮고 낡아빠진 장비를 성난 근로자들이 어떻게 참아낼 수 있을 것으로 기대하나?

How can you go through your allowance so fast?
ㄴ 어쩜 용돈을 그리도 빨리 써버리니?

How can you leave me on the mat?
ㄴ 날 문전박대 하다니

How can you think other than logically?
ㄴ 어찌 논리적이 아닌 방식으로 생각할 수 있겠는가?

How can you write him off as a non-entity?
ㄴ 어떻게 그를 시시한 사람으로 빼어버릴 수 있어?

How come you have a callous attitude toward the sufferings of others?

> collaborate   work jointly with others, help the enemy

> **deride**   make fun of
> **condescend**   lower oneself, act haughtily

ㄴ 어떻게 남의 고통을 나 몰라라 할 수 있니?

How could anyone be like that?
ㄴ 뭐 그런 사람이 다 있어

How could I have known?
ㄴ 내가 어떻게 알 수 있었겠어?

How could you?
ㄴ 어떻게 그럴 수 있나?

How could you behave so shamefully in public?
ㄴ 여러 사람 앞에서 그런 추태를 보이다니

How could you do that to me?
ㄴ 네가 내게 그럴 수 있나?

How could you have the gut to say so?
ㄴ 어디서 감히 그런 말이 나와?

How dare you say such a thing?
ㄴ 감히 네가 어찌 그런 말을

How did I get here?
ㄴ 어쩌다 내가 이 꼴이 됐지?

How did she clear up that matter?
ㄴ 그 여자가 그 일을 어떻게 처리했나?

How did such a foolish statement find its way into print?
ㄴ 이런 엉터리 기사가 어떻게 인쇄되어 나왔을까?

How did you get your first break?
ㄴ 넌 그 첫 취직자리를 어떻게 구했니?

How did you leave your parents?
ㄴ 떠날 때 양친은 어떠셨습니까?

▸ **public**   relating to the people as a whole,
civic, not private

How did you make it through?
    ㄴ 어떻게 견뎌냈어?

How did you take the wrong exit off the freeway?
    ㄴ 어쩌다가 고속도로에서 엉뚱한 출구로 빠져 나오게 되었나?

How did your first day on the job go?
    ㄴ 첫 출근은 어땠어?

How did your new idea rate with your boss?
    ㄴ 너의 새 아이디어가 사장에게 어느 정도 호평을 얻었니?

How do things stand now?
    ㄴ 현재 상태는 어때?

How do you earn your living?
    ㄴ 무슨 일 하세요?

How do you feel?
    ㄴ 몸은 어때?

How do you find my new car?
    ㄴ 내 새차 어때?

How do you find yourself today?
    ㄴ 오늘 기분이 어때?

> (=How goes it with you today?)

How do you rate the future of your job?
    ㄴ 네 직업의 전망은 어때?

How do you stay so fresh?
    ㄴ 넌 어찌 그리 팔팔하냐?

› **freeway**   limited-access expressway

How do you stand among the runners in your class?
　　　　　ㄴ 넌 달리기 할 때 반에서 몇 번째 가니?

How do you stand in your class?
　　　　　ㄴ 네 성적은 반에서 몇 등이냐?

How do you think you got here?
　　　　　ㄴ 네가 어떻게 세상에 태어났는지 아니?

How does it feel being the top-dog in the Sales Department?
　　　　　ㄴ 판매부의 부장 된 기분이 어때?

How does this song go?
　　　　　ㄴ 이 노래 시작이 어떻게 되더라?

（=How do you begin this song?）

How easy is that?
　　　　　ㄴ 그게 얼마나 쉬운 거냐?

How else can I say it?
　　　　　ㄴ 그렇게 밖에 말 할 수 없잖아

How far are you going?
　　　　　ㄴ 어디까지 가십니까?

How far did you go?
　　　　　ㄴ (데이트) 어느 단계까지 갔니?

How far does this road reach?
　　　　　ㄴ 이 도로는 어디까지 뻗어있지?

How have you put up with him treating you like dirt for all the years?
　　　　　ㄴ 그가 그토록 긴 세월에 걸쳐 너를 개떡같이 취급해 오는 것을 어떻게
　　　　　　참아왔나?

· **treat**　have as a topic, pay for the food or entertainment of, act toward or　　regorard in a certain way, give medical care for

How is he placed in his company?
↳ 회사에서 그 사람 지위가 뭐니?

How is sugar(the dollar)?
↳ 설탕(달러) 시세 어때?(이해하지 못할 수도 있음)

How long can I check it out?
↳ 대여기간이 며칠입니까?

> (=When is it due?)
> (=How long can I keep it?)

How long do I have to keep this act up?
↳ 언제까지 이런 연극을 해야 해?

How long is it since? I knew it many years since
↳ 얼마전 일인가? 그 일은 몇 년이나 전에 알았어

How long is it since?
↳ 얼마전 일이냐?

How long is the wait?
↳ 얼마나 오래 기다려야 해?

How long should I stay(remain) on these pills?
↳ 이 알약을 얼마동안 복용해야 합니까?

How long will it keep(last)?
↳ 얼마동안 먹어도 됩니까?(식품)

How long will the next train be?
↳ 다음 열차는 얼마나 기다려야 오죠?

How long will you remain in?
↳ 얼마동안 회원으로 남겠습니까?

‣ **pill** small rounded mass of medicine

How many committee members are up for re-election this time?
ㄴ 이번에 위원 몇 명이 재선 대상에 들어있습니까?

How many copies shall I do(make)?
ㄴ 몇 장 복사할까요?

How many members of the office share this copying machine?
ㄴ 사무실 직원 몇 명이 이 복사기를 사용하고 있나?

How many shots did you have?
ㄴ 몇 잔 마셨어?

How many stops is Sung-soo from here
ㄴ 여기서 성수까지 몇 번째 정거장입니까?

How many suits will this piece of cloth cut up into?
ㄴ 이 옷감으로 옷 몇 벌을 지을 수 있나?

How many times should I tell you?
ㄴ 한 번 얘기하면 알아들어야지

How many voters drank in his lies?
ㄴ 얼마나 많은 유권자가 그 사람의 거짓말에 귀를 기울이겠니?

How many will there be in your party?
ㄴ 일행이 몇 분이십니까?

How may I direct your call?
ㄴ 전화를 어디로 대 드릴까요?

How much are you in your job?
ㄴ 직장에서 얼마 받니?

How much did it cost to juice your car up?
ㄴ 네 차를 힘 좋은 엔진으로 개조하는데 얼마 들었니?

How much did your car go for in the end?
ㄴ 결국 너의 차가 얼마에 팔렸니?

· **committee**　panel that examines or acts
　　　　　　　　on something

How much finer things are in composition than alone?
> ㄴ 얼마나 많은 일이 혼자 하는 것보다 협조를 통하여 보다 잘 이루어져 왔던가

How much front money do we need?
> ㄴ 착수(선불)금은 얼마나 필요해?

How much interest will your loan bear?
> ㄴ 당신 돈의 이자는 얼마입니까?

How much money are we talking about?
> ㄴ 어느 정도 금액을 말씀하시는 겁니까?

How often have I not watched him?
> ㄴ 그를 눈 여겨 본 일이 몇 번인지 모른다

How soon do you want to have it done?
> ㄴ 그 일은 언제까지 해 드리면 되겠습니까?

How the rich get richer and the poor get poorer?
> ㄴ 어떻게 부자는 더 부자가 되고 가난한 사람은 더 가난하게 되지?

How's the world treating(using) you?
> ㄴ 어떻게 지내니?

I make bold to ask you
> ㄴ 실례지만 여쭤보겠습니다

I'll bite, what is it?
> ㄴ 모르겠어, 뭐야?(질문, 수수께끼)

I'm in the middle of something, can you call me later?
> ㄴ 지금 다른 것하고 있으니 나중에 전화할래?

If you'll get tanked up, who'll drive me home?
> ㄴ 네가 술에 취하면 누가 나를 집까지 태워주나

Is a million won anything to sneeze at?

· **compose** create or put together, calm, set type

· **sneeze** force the breath out with sudden and involuntary violence

↳ 백만원이 누구 이름인줄 아나

Is everything all right?

↳ 뭐 도와드릴까요

Is he on your case again?

↳ 그가 네게 또 싫은 소리 하나?

Is he visible?

↳ 그를 만날 수 있을까요?

Is it an isolated incident or does it happen routinely?

↳ 그 때 한 번 그런 거냐 아니면 툭하면 그런 거냐?

Is it going to suit everybody?

↳ 이제 모두 이의 없지?

Is it too much for you to handle(manage)?

↳ 무리한 부탁(주문)인가?

(=Am I asking too much?)

Is it worth going for?

↳ 해볼만한 일인가?

Is our schedule carved in stone?

↳ 우리 계획은 변동 없는 거지?

Is Samchunpo on the map?

↳ 삼천포가 널리 알려진(찾기 쉬운) 곳이냐?

Is something eating you up?

↳ 속상한 일이라도 있니?

Is that seat taken?

› **routine**   procedure or course of action
regularly followed

↳ 자리에 사람 있어요?

Is that what you insinuating to me?
↳ 그게 나를 두고 한 말이니?

Is the money good?
↳ 돈벌이 잘 되니?

Is the Saturday still on you?
↳ 토요일 약속 아직 변동 없는 거지?(약속 확인. 그러나 이해 못할 수 있음)

Is there any good in arguing with the inevitable?
↳ 피할 수 없는 일을 이러쿵저러쿵 해 본들 무슨 소용이냐

Is there any green in my eye?
↳ 내가 만만해 보이니?

Is there any hurry?
↳ 서두를 필요 있겠어?

Is there any law against double-dippers?
↳ 월급을 두 군데서 받으면 안 되는 일이라도 있나?

Is there any law against my eating out?
↳ 나라고 외식 못 하라는 법 있나?

Is there any need to rub my nose in it(rub it in)?
↳ 그 일을 두고두고 들먹거려야 하겠니?

Is there any time to pull it out of the fire?
↳ 늦기 전에 이 일에 조치할 시간이 있을까?(잘못된 일의 사후조치)

Is there anything to eat?
↳ 안주 있습니까?

Is this a good time to call?
↳ 바쁜 시간에 전화 한 건 아닌지요?

› **insinuate** imply, bring in artfully

› **inevitable** incapable of being avoided or escaped

Is this still yours to give?

    ↳ 이게 아직도 네 것이라고 믿니?

Is this the road leading me to the seashore?

    ↳ 이 길로 가면 해변이 나옵니까?

Is this what life is at(after) all?

    ↳ 이렇게라도 살아야 하나?

> (=Is this how I'm to live my life?)

Is your baby potty-trained?

    ↳ 너희 아이는 대소변 가리니?

Is your journey necessary?

    ↳ 꼭 그래야만 하는 거니?

Isn't that making mountains out of mole hills?

    ↳ 그거 지나친 생각(과장) 아냐?

Isn't there any way out(way of getting around it)?

    ↳ 어떤 묘안이 없을까?

It's sheeting(pelting, pouring) down outside, hadn't you better wait a few minutes before going out?

    ↳ 밖에 비가 억수로 쏟아지고 있으니 몇 분 기다렸다가 가는 게 어때?

May I be excused?

    ↳ 잠시 자리를 떠도 될까요?

May I direct your attention to this young lady?

    ↳ 이 젊은 여자 분에게 주목해 주시기 바랍니다

May I serve you in any way?

› **pelt** strike with blows or missiles

       ↳ 뭔가 도와드릴 일이 있습니까?

May I speak to Mi-jah?(Give me Mi-jah)
       ↳ 미자 좀 바꿔 주십시오(친숙할 경우)

May I take your order?
       ↳ 주문하시겠어요?

Mind backing up a little?
       ↳ 차(car) 좀 빼 주시겠어요?

Must he pontificate on his virtues so much?
       ↳ 그 사람은 자신의 장점(공로)을 건방진 태도로 얘기해야만 하나?

Must you nitpick all the time?
       ↳ 넌 항상 그렇게 꼬투리를 잡아야 하니?

No problem. I can live with that, can you?
       ↳ 상관없어. 난 그래도 괜찮지만, 넌 어때?

Not to get off the track, what's holding you up?
       ↳ 원래 얘기로 돌아와서, 넌 왜 우물쭈물 하는 거냐?

Now what do I do?
       ↳ 이제 와서 어떻게 하라고?

Now, what's the damage?
       ↳ 자, 손해가 얼마죠?

Number one or number two?
       ↳ 소변이냐 대변이냐?

On which of the week does Christmas fall this year?
       ↳ 금년의 성탄절은 무슨 요일이지?

Says who?
       ↳ 그런 법이 어디 있어(웃기지마)

▸ **pontificate**　talk pompously

Shall I dust him off?
> ↳ 경고를 한 번 줄까?(투수가 위협구를 던지면 타자가 쓰러졌다 일어나 먼지를 터는데서)

Shall I go down the list for you?
> ↳ 일일이 말해줘야 하나?

Shall I hang up and call you back?
> ↳ 전화를 끊고 다시 걸어도 되겠습니까?

Shall we change the channel here?
> ↳ 이쯤에서 화제를 바꾸는 게 어때?

Shall we do a trial run of the presentation?
> ↳ 예행연습을 좀 할까?

Shall we make believe we are pirates looking for buried treasure?
> ↳ 우리 숨겨둔 보물찾기를 하는 해적놀이를 해 볼까?

Shall we pick up where we left off before our lunch?
> ↳ 점심 전에 했던 데에서 다시 시작할까요?

Shall we raise the bar?
> ↳ 목표를 올려 잡는 게 어때?

Shall we recur to what was said yesterday?
> ↳ 이제 우리가 어제 했던 얘기로 되돌아갑시다

Shall we split the difference?
> ↳ 우리 타협할까?

Shall we take a puff outside?
> ↳ 우리 담배 한 대 피우러 밖으로 나갈래?

Shall we throw stones at the can on that tree until we knock it over?
> ↳ 저 나무 위에 있는 깡통에 돌을 던져 떨어뜨리기 할래?

Since when have you developed a taste for money?

· **pirate**   one who commits piracy
· **puff**   blow in short gusts, pant, enlarge

↳ 너 언제부터 돈맛 들였니?

Suppose everyone knows it
↳ 모든 사람에게 알려지면 어쩌지?

That's a loaded question
↳ 유도심문이로군(넘겨짚기)

That's news to me. Anybody I know?
↳ 금시초문인데. 내가 아는 사람인가?

This is your fair play, isn't it?
↳ 이게 네가 말하는 공정한 게임이라는 거였군(어처구니없군)

This job is sure boring. So what else is new?
↳ 이 일은 지겨워. 항상 하는 일인데 뭘 그래?

To whom am I speaking?
↳ 전화하신 분이 누구죠?

Wasn't that hilarious?
↳ 너무 법석댄 것 아냐?

Were you out hunting for the meat?
↳ 돼지를 사냥해서 잡아오는 겁니까?(주문한 돼지고기가 오래 걸릴때)

What about the warranty?
↳ 품질보증 기간은요?

What are the do's and dont's here?
↳ 여기서 해야 할 것과 안 해야 할 것이 무엇입니까?

What are the store('s) hours?
↳ 영업시간이 몇 시에서 몇 시까지입니까?

What are you driving about?
↳ 무슨 객쩍은 소리냐?

‣ **hilarious** extremely funny
‣ **drivel** drool, talk stupidly

What are you getting at?
> ↳ 무슨 뜻이냐?

What are you leading up to?
> ↳ 무슨 수작이야?

> (=What are you playing at?)
> (=What are you up to?)
> (=What 's the catch?)

What are your measurements?
> ↳ 몸 치수가 어떻게 되시죠?

What can be done to preserve the world's dwindling natural resources?
> ↳ 세계에서 줄어들고 있는 자연자원을 보존하기 위해 어떻게 해야 할까?

What can be(is) the cause of a rainbow?
> ↳ 무지개가 서는 것은 무슨 까닭일까?(**reason**이 아님)

What can I do to get you there?
> ↳ 어떻게 해야 날 사랑하게 할 수 있나요?

What can I say?
> ↳ 입이 열 개라도 할 말이 없다

What did he look like?
> ↳ 인상착의는?

What did I do wrong?
> ↳ 내가 뭘 잘못 했다는 거냐?

What difference would it make?
> ↳ 그런다고 뭐 달라지나?

What do you do to unwind after working hours?

• **dwindle** become steadily less

↳ 일과 후 긴장을 풀기 위해 무엇을 하십니까?

What do you do when you are a weekend warrior(playing soldier)?
↳ 당직 때 무엇하고 시간을 보내니?

What do you expect?
↳ 그건 당연한 결과야

What do you say we bypass the hostilities?
↳ 이제 적개심 따윈 접어두는 게 어때

What do you say we cruise(stop) by the bar?
↳ 술자리 옮기는 게 어때?

What do you see in him?
↳ 그의 어디가 맘에 드니?

What do you shoot?
↳ 얼마(몇 점) 치니?(당구 등)

What do you take me for?
↳ 사람을 무엇으로 보는 거냐

What do you want me to say?
↳ 내가 뭐라고 말해야 시원하겠니?

What do you want to make out of him?
↳ 그에게 뭘 바라는 거야?

What does it matter if he forgets it?
↳ 그가 잊어버린들 무슨 상관이 있어?

What does the man on the street think about this?
↳ 일반인이 이 일을 어떻게 생각할까?

What else can I do to stop him from throwing caution to the wind?
↳ 그가 이판사판으로 나오는데 더 이상 무슨 수로 말리나?

› **bypass** go around

› **cruise** sail to several ports, travel at the most efficient speed

What else is it good for?

    ㄴ 그게 그밖에 무슨 도움이 되니?

What features does it have?

    ㄴ 어떤 특징들이 있습니까?

What good is it?

    ㄴ 그게 무슨 소용이냐?

What have you been up to?

    ㄴ 요즘 재미가 어때?

What have you got to lose by trying?

    ㄴ 밑져야 본전

> (=What's there to lose)
> (=There's nothing to lose)
> (=There's not much to lose)

What hour do you open?

    ㄴ 가게문을 몇 시에 엽니까?

What I have got to lose?

    ㄴ 이판사판이다

What is dignity without honesty?

    ㄴ 정직 없는 위엄이 무슨 가치가 있는가?

What is its composition?

    ㄴ 그게 무엇으로(구성) 되어있나?

What is she leading up to?

    ㄴ 그녀의 속셈이 무엇일까?

What is the good of a sundial in the shade?

· **dignity** quality of state of being worthy or honored, formal reserve

· **sundial** device for showing time by the sun's shadow

ㄴ 지나친 겸양은 악덕

What is the lowest price you'll go down to?

ㄴ 최하로 싸게 해서 얼마입니까?

What it'll be?

ㄴ 뭘 드시겠어요?

What kept you away yesterday?

ㄴ 무슨 일로 어제 못 왔어?

What kind of gas mileage do you get?

ㄴ 차의 연비는 어떻습니까?

What kind of money can I make?

ㄴ 돈은 얼마나 벌 수 있을까?

What landmarks are on the way?

ㄴ 도중의 경계표시(뚜렷한 표지물 또는 지형지물)를 알려주십시오

What line(of business) are you in?

ㄴ 무슨 사업하십니까?

What more could you ask for?

ㄴ 더 바랄게 뭐 있니?

What name shall I give?

ㄴ 누구시라 할까요?

(=Who's calling?)
(=May I have your name?)

What name shall I say?

ㄴ 누구시라고 여쭐까요?

› **mileage** allowance per mile for traveling expenses, amount or rate of   use expressed in miles

What name should I make the reservation under?
    ㄴ 누구 이름으로 예약할까요?

What reduction do you make for a prolonged day?
    ㄴ 호텔에 오래 머물면 할인해 줍니까?

What possessed you to say such a thing?
    ㄴ 도대체 무슨 생각으로 그런 말을 하는 거냐?

What price range do you have in mind?
    ㄴ 생각하시는 가격수준은 얼마입니까?

What shape is it in?
    ㄴ 현재 상태가 어때?

What that thug will do when he's back on the street?
    ㄴ 저 악당이 풀려나면 무엇을 할까?

What time does the last train go?
    ㄴ 막차가 몇 시에 떠납니까?

What time shall we make it?
    ㄴ 몇 시에 만날까요?

> (=When is the best time for you?)
> (=When do you have time?)
> (=What time is good for you?)

What track does the next train leave from?
    ㄴ 다음 열차는 몇 번 선에서 떠납니까?

What was the result of your blind date(marriage meeting)?
    ㄴ 너 선 본 결과가 어떻게 되었니?

What would life be if we had no courage to attempt anything?

· **thug** ruffian or gangster

    ↳ 무언가를 시도할만한 용기가 없다면 삶이 무슨 의미가 있겠는가

What's all this commotions?
    ↳ 웬 호들갑이냐?

What's come over(influence) you?
    ↳ 왜 이래?

What's cooking?
    ↳ 어떻게 지내?

What's eating you?
    ↳ 언짢은 일이라도 있나?

What's got into you?
    ↳ 도대체 무슨 일이냐?(이상한 행동에 대해)

> (=What's come over you?)

What's he on about this time?
    ↳ 그 사람이 이번엔 무슨 얘기를 그리 길게 하고 있나?

What's her story(background)?
    ↳ 그녀의 내력은? 어떤 여자?

What's in it for me?
    ↳ 그게 내게 어떤 이익(도움)이 되지?

What's on tap for today?
    ↳ 오늘 스케줄이 뭐지?

What's showing on channel 6 tonight?
    ↳ 오늘밤 6번 채널에서 뭐하지?

What's taking our order so long?

▸ **commotion** disturbance

       ↳ 주문한 게 왜 이리 늦어

What's the answer?
       ↳ 날더러 어쩌란 말이냐?

What's the airline distance between Seoul and Daejun?
       ↳ 서울과 대전간 직선거리가 얼마냐?

What's the average starting wage in your line of work?
       ↳ 당신 직종의 평균 초임은 얼마입니까?

What's the big deal?
       ↳ 그게 뭐 대수(별거)냐

> (=That's no big deal)

What's the buzz?
       ↳ 무슨 소문이니?

What's the catch?
       ↳ 뭘 노리고 그런 거지?

What's the deal?
       ↳ 도대체 무슨 소동이야?

What's the good word?
       ↳ 재미가 어때?

What's the lie of the land?
       ↳ 상황이 어때?(lie=형세, 방향 *골프코스의 지형에서)

What's the occasion?
       ↳ 해가 서쪽에서 뜨겠군

›**buzz** make a low humming sound

> (=This is not something you see everyday)
> (=It's a miracle)

What's the right thing to do?
> ↳ 어떻게 하는 게 좋을까요?

What's the scene?
> ↳ 왜들 다 법석이야

What's the seating capacity?
> ↳ 좌석수가 얼마입니까?

What's the story on it?
> ↳ 그게 어떻게 된 일이냐?

What's the use of children?
> ↳ 무자식 상팔자지

What's the use of saving life?
> ↳ 살아남은들 무슨 의미가 있겠나?

What's the world coming to?
> ↳ 세상이 어떻게 돌아가는 거냐?

What's this all about?
> ↳ 도대체 무슨 일이야?

What's to be made out of this?
> ↳ 이에 대해 어떤 의견이 나올까?

What's your day like?
> ↳ 오늘 일정은 어때?

What's your normal turnaround?
> ↳ 주문(신청)하면 얼마나 걸립니까?

› **turnaround**   reversal in thinking or acting,
　　　　　　　time required for a round trip

What's your secret to get his account?
    ↳ 그와 거래선을 개척하게 된 비결이 뭐냐?

What's your sign of zodiac(Chinese astrological sign)?
    ↳ 넌 무슨 띠냐?

What's $5 equivalent to Korean won?
    ↳ 5달러는 한국의 원으로 얼마냐?

When are you going to take me out of this black hole?
    ↳ 언제쯤 날 이 슬픔에서 구해줄 건가요?

When are you going to tie(untie) the knot?
    ↳ 언제 결(이)혼 해요?

When are you supposed to square off the budget?
    ↳ 예산은 언제 결산하게 되나요?

Where did the time go?
    ↳ 벌써 시간이 그렇게 됐나?

When did the old tree blow down?
    ↳ 저 큰 나무가 언제 바람에 쓰러졌지?

When did you come on the scene?
    ↳ 현장엔 언제 왔나요?

When did your dog come in season(heat)?
    ↳ 너희 개는 언제 발정했니?

When is it on?
    ↳ 언제 중계됩니까?

When is the big day?
    ↳ 혼사 날이 언제니?

When is the due date?
    ↳ 반납일(납기, 출산 등)이 언제입니까?

› **zodiac**   imaginary belt in the heavens encompassing the paths of the   planets and divided into 12 signs used in astrology

When is the last bus for this line?

    ↳ 이 노선의 막차는 몇 시까지입니까?

When is traffic at its worst around here?

    ↳ 여기에 차가 가장 많이 막히는 시간이 언제지?

When will you have it working?

    ↳ 언제 작동 되도록 할 겁니까?

When will you take your car out for a spin?

    ↳ 너의 차는 언제 시승할 거냐?

Where am I going?

    ↳ 어디로 데려가는 거야?

Where are my manners?

    ↳ 제가 큰 실례를 했군요

Where are you going?

    ↳ 앞으로 뭐 할 거냐?

Where are your eyes(=wits, brains, swallows)?

    ↳ 똑똑히 보고 다녀, 정신을 어디다 빼고 다녀(핀잔 줄 때)

Where did he place(finish)?

    ↳ 그 사람 몇 등 했니?

Where did I go wrong?

    ↳ 내가 어디서 잘못 했지?

Where did we left off last time?

    ↳ 요 전에 어디까지 나가다 그만뒀죠?

Where do I go from here?

    ↳ 더 이상 어쩌자는 거냐?

Where do I stand in regards to the promotion?

    ↳ 나의 승진 가능성은 어떻습니까?

› **regard**   consideration, feeling of approval
               or liking, friendly greeting(pl)

Where do the books go?

    ㄴ 책은 어디다 둬야 합니까?

Where do you get off telling me how to run my life?

    ㄴ 네가 뭔데 내 인생을 이래라 저래라 하는 거니?

Where do you plan to live out your days(life)?

    ㄴ 여생을 어디서 보내실 계획입니까?

Where do you want your hair parted?

    ㄴ 가르마는 어느 쪽으로 하십니까?

Where does the Emperor Sejoh stand in the Josun Imperial line?

    ㄴ 세조는 조선 왕조의 몇 번째 임금이지?

Where does this street go?

    ㄴ 이 길로 가면 어디로 가지?

(=Where this road lead to?)

Where has my mind gone?

    ㄴ 내 정신 좀 봐

Where is the pair to this sock?

    ㄴ 이 양말의 짝은 어디 있니?

Where is this supposed to go?

    ㄴ 이걸 어디다 놓을까?

Where were we?

    ㄴ 우리가 어디까지 얘기했지?

Where will I find you?

    ㄴ 우리 어디서 만날까?

· **emperor**　ruler of an empire

Where(do you think) you get off?
> ↳ 네가 뭔가 되는 것으로 아는 모양이군(주제넘군, 건방지군)

Where's harm in that?
> ↳ 그래서 나쁠 게 뭐야

Where's my violin?
> ↳ 웃기고 자빠졌네

Where's your judgement?
> ↳ 분별력이 그렇게 없니?

Where's your service?
> ↳ 서비스가 이게 뭡니까?

Who are the movers and shakers here?
> ↳ 여기서 좌지우지하는 사람들이 누구니?

Who are you banking with?
> ↳ 어느 은행에 거래하니?

Who are you playing against?
> ↳ 상대팀이 누구니?

Who are you putting on the dog(ritz) for?
> ↳ 누굴 위해 쪽 빼 입은 거지?

Who came first in the race?
> ↳ 경주에서 누가 우승했지?

Who can he be?
> ↳ 도대체 그가 누구냐?

Who did a number on that poor old woman?
> ↳ 누가 저 불쌍한 나이든 여자에게 못된 짓을 했나?

Who do I make this check out to?
> ↳ 이 수표를 누구 앞으로 끊어 드릴까요?

› number   count, assign a number to, comprise
in number

Who do you think you are?

↳ 네가 뭔데 네 맘대로야

Who has left the tab running?

↳ 누가 수도꼭지를 틀어놓은 채 내버려두었나?

Who is running the show?

↳ 이 일은 누가 주관합니까?

Who is to blame?

↳ 누가 나쁜 거냐?

Who knows if it may be so?

↳ 그렇지 않다고 장담 못해. 그럴지도 몰라

Who made the hamburger(mincemeat) out of my paper?

↳ 누가 내 서류를 엉망으로 만들어놨어?

Who planted that silly idea in your head?

↳ 누가 네게 그런 바보 같은 생각을 하게 만들었지?

Who shall I say, sir?

↳ 누구시라고 할까요?

Who shall I tell him called?

↳ 어느 분이 전화(방문) 하셨다고 말씀드릴까요?

Who should come into my room at night but a thief?

↳ 도둑이 아닌 다음에야 밤중에 내 방에 누가 들어오겠나

Who spoke to a certain party about the matter he mentioned?

↳ 그가 그 일에 대해 한 말을 누가 아무개한테 일러바쳤나?

Who that can work dare stay idle?

↳ 일할 수 있는데 빈둥거릴 사람이 어디 있니?

Who was making advances to whom?

↳ 누가 누굴 유혹했단 말인가?

› **mention** refer to

› **idle** worthless, inactive, lazy

Who was that cute number we saw you with yesterday?

　　　↳ 어제 너하고 같이 있던 잘 빠진 여자 누구니?

Who will pick the tab up for dinner?

　　　↳ 저녁은 누가 사는 거지?

Who would(could) have thought?

　　　↳ 전혀 믿을 수 없어

Who's been messing(playing) about my books?

　　　↳ 누가 내 책을 마구 어질러 놓았어?

Who's going to break the ice?

　　　↳ 어색한 분위기를 누가 깨지?(처음 시작할 때의 서먹서먹한 분위기)

Who's going to call the tune?

　　　↳ 누가 선창하지?

Who's got the nod for that job?

　　　↳ 누가 그 일에 낙점 받았지?

Who's high man on the totem pole here?

　　　↳ 여기서 책임자가 누구야?

Who's made it hot for you in the office?

　　　↳ 사무실에서 누가 널 힘들게 만들고 있나?

Who's the light bulb over there?

　　　↳ 저기 있는 임신한 여자는 누구니?

Who's the person at the other end of the line?

　　　↳ 전화 받는 사람이 누구니?

(=Who are you talking to?)

› **nod**　bend the head downward or forward,
　　　move up and down

Who(m) do you wish to speak to?
> ↳ 누구를 바꿔드릴까요?

Whom did you fly with?
> ↳ 어느 항공사 비행기로 왔니?

Would this date suit you?
> ↳ 이 날이면 되겠어?

Would you please inform us when we may expect the payment of this balance?
> ↳ 언제쯤 이 잔금을 지급해 주실지 알려 주시겠습니까?

Would you share your thoughts with the others?
> ↳ 네 생각을 다른 사람에게 얘기해 보지 그래

Would you teach a fish how to swim?
> ↳ 공자 앞에 문자 쓰려고 그래?

> 박식한 사람 앞에서 아는 체 하는 사람을 비웃을 때 쓰는 말이다. 직역하면
> "물고기에게 수영을 가르친다"이다.

Wouldn't we all?
> ↳ 누군들 안 그르겠어?

Why all this ceremony today?
> ↳ 오늘은 왜 이리 서먹서먹해?

Why am I not surprised?
> ↳ 놀랠 일도 아니잖아. 뻔할 뻔 자지 뭐

Why are all these clothes lying about?
> ↳ 이 옷들이 왜 마구 널려있어?

› **share** divide into shares(+out), use with others

Why are you always at me about everything?

       ㄴ 넌 어쩨서 내게 따지러 드니?

Why are you always dangling about(after) him?

       ㄴ 왜 넌 그 사람하고 붙어 다녀?

Why are you always furtive(in your manner)?

       ㄴ 어쩨서 넌 늘 남의 눈치를 살피니?

Why are you always selling yourself short?

       ㄴ 넌 왜 항상 낮춰 말하니?

Why are you bothered by it?

       ㄴ 왜 그 일에 신경을 쓰니?

Why are you driving me to drink?

       ㄴ 왜 날 달달 볶고 있지?

Why are you getting your jaws so tight?

       ㄴ 왜 그리 화가 나 있나?(**What made your jaw drop a mile?** 뭣 때문에 그리 놀란 거냐?)

Why are you running around like chickens with their heads cut off?

       ㄴ 호떡집에 불났나?

> "Running around like a hen with its head cut off"는 한국식으로 표현하면 "호떡집에 불났다"이다. 양계장에서 닭 잡는 날의 혼란스러움에 빗대어 만든 속담이다.

Why are you putting word in my mouth?

       ㄴ 왜 하지도 않은 말을 했다고 그래

› **furtive**   slyly or secretly done

› **bother**   annoy or worry, take the trouble

> (=Why are you lying about what I said?)
> (=Why are you twisting around my words?)

Why are you so buddy-buddy with me?
　ㄴ 왜 나하고 친한 척 하는 거니?

Why are you so keyed up about nothing?
　ㄴ 아무 것도 아닌 일을 왜 흥분하고 야단이야

Why can't you play ball with me?
　ㄴ 왜 넌 내게 협조를 못하는 거니?

Why can't you see anything straight?
　ㄴ 넌 어째서 만사를 삐딱하게만 보니?

Why did she marry such a mouse?
　ㄴ 그 여자가 어째서 그런 꽁생원과 결혼을 했지?

Why did you make it hard on her?
　ㄴ 왜 그 여자에게 모질게 굴었니?

Why did you settle for second best then?
　ㄴ 그런데 넌 왜 차선을 택했지?

Why did you take a dig(jab) at him?
　ㄴ 넌 왜 그에게 쥐어박는 소릴 했어?

Why do I always get the short end of the stick?
　ㄴ 왜 난 항상 억울한 꼴을 당해야 하나?

Why do I always have to pick up after you?
　ㄴ 내가 왜 늘 네 뒤치다꺼리해야 하니?

Why do I have to stay out until all the hours of day and night?
　ㄴ 난 어째서 밤낮 일찍 오고 늦게까지 있어야 하나?

· **jab**　thrust quickly or abruptly

Why do people treat me like a doormat?
> ↳ 왜 사람들이 나를 함부로 대할까?

Why do these eyes of mine cry?
> ↳ 두 눈에서 왜 눈물이 나는 걸까?

Why do you always enmesh(entangle) yourself in someone else's business?
> ↳ 넌 어째서 늘 남의 일에 끼어(말려)드는 거니?

Why do you always have to do a dump on me?
> ↳ 넌 어째서 늘 내게 마구 해대는 거냐?

Why do you bend yourself out of shape?
> ↳ 왜 네가 화내는 거니?

Why do you dump all over(criticize) me?
> ↳ 왜 날 못 잡아먹어서 야단이야

Why do you hang around with that nowhere bum
> ↳ 어째서 그 쓰레기 같은 건달하고 어울려 다니는 거냐?

Why do you have to cross me up all the time?
> ↳ 넌 어째서 내 일이라면 쌍심지를 켜고 나서니?

Why do you have to ingratiate yourself with everyone?
> ↳ 어째서 모든 사람의 비위만 맞추려고 드니?

Why do you keep bugging(pestering) me?
> ↳ 왜 자꾸 시비야

> (=Why are you such a pest?)
> (=Why are you being such a rat?)

› **enmesh** catch in or as if in a net

› **ingratiate** gain favor for oneself

› **pester** harass persistently with petty matters

Why do you keep harping on the same subject?
> ↳ 어째서 넌 늘 같은 말만 되풀이하고 있어?

Why do you keep him on then?
> ↳ 그렇다면 넌 왜 그를 내쫓지 않고 있나?

Why does the rain have pour on me all the time?
> ↳ 왜 항상 내게만 액운이 닥치지?

Why does your heart sink like that?
> ↳ 넌 왜 그렇게 축 처져있니?

Why doesn't that surprise me?
> ↳ 그거 놀랠 일도 아니네

Why don't we make it another time?
> ↳ 다음에 하기로 합시다

Why don't we team up and do it together?
> ↳ 우리가 힘을 합해 함께 하는 게 어때?

Why don't you ask around?
> ↳ 이 사람 저 사람에게 물어봐

Why don't you boil it down to a page?
> ↳ 한 페이지로 요약하지 그래

Why don't you give it a shot?
> ↳ 한 번 해보지 그래

Why don't you pop over for a moment?
> ↳ 잠시 나한테 와 줄 수 있겠나?

Why don't you stop ordering me around(about)?
> ↳ 날 마구 부려먹으려 하지마

Why don't you too get together?
> ↳ 어째서 너희 둘은 마음이 안 맞니?

› **harp** dwell on a subject tiresomely

Why isn't the traffic moving?
> ↳ 왜 차가 꼼짝도 안 하는 거야

Why should he go poking round his house?
> ↳ 왜 그는 집에서 빈들거리며 놀고 지내야 하나?

Why should I stick my neck for you?
> ↳ 내가 왜 너 때문에 목숨을 걸어야 하니?

Why the change of heart?
> ↳ 어째서 심경의 변화를 일으켰지?

> (=what made your change of heart?)

Why the happy look on your face?
> ↳ 왜 그리 기분 좋은 표정인가?

Why today of all days?
> ↳ 왜 하필 오늘이야

Will it work now? It should
> ↳ 이제 작동되나요? 그럴 거예요

Will school keep all day?
> ↳ 오늘 수업이 종일 있나?

Will someone else do?
> ↳ 다른 사람에게 전화를 바꿔도 되겠습니까?

Will the cops drag it out of him?
> ↳ 경찰이 그에게서 정보를 끌어낼 수 있을까?

Will you advance me a month's salary?
> ↳ 한 달치 월급을 가불해 주시겠습니까?

› **poke** prod, dawdle

Will you be around next week?
└ 다음주에 휴가나 출장 안가시죠?

Will you be getting more in?
└ 물건이 더 들어옵니까?

Will you chalk(notch, log, clock, score) it up to me?
└ 내 이름으로(외상으로) 달아주시오

(=Will you charge it to me?)
(=Will you charge it against my account?)

Will you do the honors this evening?
└ 오늘 밤 주빈 역할을 좀 해 주시겠습니까?

Will you favor me with your company at our meeting?
└ 모임에 참석해 주시겠습니까?

Will you get real?
└ 정신 좀 차려

Will you hold my calls?
└ 나한테 오는 전화 좀 받아줄래?

Will you let me walk under your umbrella
└ 우산 좀 같이 쓰실 수 있을까요?

(=May I share your umbrella?)

Will you pass me the air?
└ 담배연기 이쪽으로 안 오게 해 주시겠습니까?

‣ **notch**   V-shaped hollow

Will you permit me a few words?
> ↳ 몇 마디 말씀드려도 되겠습니까?

Will you pose for me for a picture?
> ↳ 사진 한 장 같이 찍지 않겠습니까?

Will you please pass your eye over this paper?
> ↳ 이 서류를 좀 봐주시겠습니까?

With so many things on the go at the one time, how can I give them my proper attention?
> ↳ 한꺼번에 할 일이 태산 같은데 내가 어찌 제대로 신경을 쓸 수 있겠나?

Would you chip in(with) some money on a gift for Sung-woo's housewarming?
> ↳ 성우네 집들이 선물 사는데 추렴 좀 안 할래?

Would you clue me in on this matter?
> ↳ 이 일을 내게 좀 알려줘

Would you like some company?
> ↳ 같이 앉아도 되겠습니까?

> (=May I sit here?)

Would you like this printed back-to-back?
> ↳ 이걸 양면으로 복사해 드릴까요?

Would you mind the store while I go out?
> ↳ 외출 때 집 좀 봐줄래?

Would you please double for me while I'm on holiday?
> ↳ 내가 연가 내는 날 네가 할 일을 좀 해줄래?

› **double**   make or become twice as great, fold or bend, clench

Would you please inform us when we may expect the payment of this balance?

↳ 언제쯤 이 잔금을 지급해 주실 지 알려 주시겠습니까?

Would you put a plug in for me?

↳ 나를 위해 남들에게 얘기 좀 해줘

Would you stay here in the office and hold the fort until I get back?

↳ 내가 돌아올 때까지 사무실에 남아서 내가 할 일을 대신 해줄래?

Would you teach a fish how to swim?

↳ 공자 앞에 문자 쓰려고 그래?

Would you work the graveyard shift?

↳ 심야근무를 하시겠습니까?

You can bear your own faults, and why not a fault in your wife?

↳ 당신은 자신의 허물에 그리도 관대하면서 아내의 허물을 참지 못하는가?

You can really dish it out, but can you take it?

↳ 남에게 마구 해대기는 잘도 하는군, 남들이 너한테 그렇게 해대면 참 아닐 수 있겠니?

You smelled something? Yeah, I smelled a rat

↳ 뭔가 수상하지 않니? 그래 뭔가 수상했어

You want to make something out of it?

↳ 시비를 한번 걸어보겠다는 거냐?

"Can I fill a glass again?" "Can a duck swim?"

↳ "한 잔 더 따라 드릴까요?" "물어보면 잔소리지"

› **shift**   change place, position, or direction; get by

135. 질문 & 대답 　Questions & Answers

A soft answer turned away wrath
　　ㄴ 웃는 낮에 침 뱉으랴

> 웃음으로 어떠한 나쁜 상황도 대처할 수 있다는 얘기이다. "A soft answer turneth away wrath 부드러운 대답은 화를 없앤다"는 성서에서 유래한 말로서 구어를 사용한 것이 특징이다.

An answer will oblige
　　ㄴ 회답을 받았으면 합니다

Ask a stupid(silly) question and you'll get a stupid(silly) answer
　　ㄴ 현문현답, 우문우답

> (=Like question, like answer)

Ask no questions and I'll tell you no lies
　　ㄴ 거짓말 하고 싶지 않으니 묻지마

By and large the more question you ask in a survey, the less polite people tend to be
　　ㄴ 대체로 사람들은 조사시 질문을 많이 할수록 불친절해지기 쉽다

Catch him off balance with a lot of unexpected questions

› **silly** foolish or stupid

ㄴ 그에게 예상하지 못한 질문공세를 펴서 허를 찔러라

Chan-soo had a bit of whiskey to get corkscrewed to pop the question
ㄴ 찬수는 술김에 결혼 얘기를 꺼내보려고 위스키를 약간 마셨다

Cut out that knee-jerk reaction and think them through
ㄴ 덮어놓고 대답하지 말고 잘 생각해서 대답해

Don't ask me. I take the fifth
ㄴ 내게 묻지마. 난 말 안 하기로 했으니까

Don't be inquisitive
ㄴ 꼬치꼬치 캐묻지마

(=You'll find out soon)
(=Don't be so nosey)
(=Don't be so prying)
(=Don't stick your nose in other people's affairs)

Doo-chul's answer doesn't sit right with me
ㄴ 두만이의 해명엔 수긍이 안가

He answered in monosyllables
ㄴ 그의 대답은 무뚝뚝했어

He managed to pass off the shower of questions
ㄴ 그는 질문공세를 그럭저럭 받아넘겼다

He raised his hand to answer the question, but I gave him the go-by
ㄴ 그가 대답하려고 손을 들었지만 무시해버렸어

He that nothing questions nothing learns(He that questions nothing learns nothing)
ㄴ 아무 것도 묻지 않는 사람은 아무 것도 배우지 못해

· **monosyllable** word of one syllable

They are waiting for him to come round so they can question him about the attack
> ↳ 그들은 그가 의식이 돌아와서 그의 공격적 행위에 대해 질문할 수 있게 되기를 기다리고 있다

This question involves embarrassing explanation
> ↳ 이 문제에는 구차한 설명이 필요하다

Wan-soo has a way of whipping out a reply when we least expect it
> ↳ 완수는 우리가 대답을 거의 기대할 수 없을 때 잽싸게 대답해내는 요령이 있어

We urge you to promote our environmental policy when you respond to customer questions and issues
> ↳ 우리는 여러분이 고객들의 질문과 문제들에 대하여 대답할 때 우리회사의 환경친화 방침을 홍보할 것을 당부합니다

We'll get back to you tomorrow with our answer
> ↳ 내일 회답해 드리겠습니다

You can't answer me because of a guilty conscience
> ↳ 대답을 못 하는 걸 보니 켕기는 데가 있는 모양이지

You caught me off guard
> ↳ 갑자기 물으면 어떻게 대답하나

You stole my question
> ↳ 나도 그 점을 네게 물어보려던 참이었어

Your question is too up close and personal
> ↳ 너무 꼬치꼬치 캐묻는군

> • **reply**　say or do in answer

> • **issue**　go, out, or flow out descend from a specified ancestor

136. 집   **Houses**

A big house like that is going to cost you a nice piece of change
>↳ 저런 큰집을 사려면 큰돈이 들어야 해

A quarter of my income goes in(on) for housing
>↳ 월급에서 평균 4분의 1은 주거비에 들어간다

A stately mansion? You can't get there from here
>↳ 근사한 저택이라? 꿈도 야무지군

A trail runs across the field to my house
>↳ 한 가닥의 작은 길이 들판을 가로질러 우리 집까지 나 있다

Advertisers always play up the good qualities of the house for sale and fail to mention its disadvantage
>↳ 광고주들은 팔려는 집의 장점만 내세우고 불리한 점은 어물쩍 넘어간다

After a certain period of in-house training you'll be taken on to the full-time staff
>↳ 일정 기간의 사내 훈련기간을 거치면 정식 직원으로 채용된다

After he bought that house, the bottom dropped out of the market and he lost a lot of money
>↳ 그가 집을 사고 난 뒤 집 값이 바닥으로 떨어져 큰 손해를 보았다

After he sold his house, he was ten million won to the good(ahead of the game)
>↳ 그는 집을 팔아 천만원 이익을 봤어

› **stately** having impressive dignity

› **trail** hang down and drag along the ground, draw along behind, follow the track of

Allowing the pricing of houses entirely to market forces will undoubtedly raise housing prices greatly
> ↳ 주택가격책정을 전적으로 시장 실정에 맡기는 어떠한 결정도 주택가격을 크게 올릴 것이 틀림없다

An accumulation of facts is no more a science than a heap of stones is a house
> ↳ 돌무더기를 쌓아올린 것이 집이 아니듯이 사실들을 쌓아 올린 것도 과학이 아니다

An-do has a big house, but I wouldn't change places
> ↳ 안도가 큰집을 가졌다해서 그 사람 처지가 되고싶진 않아

As he managed to sell his house for a tidy sum he was elated at the unexpected windfall
> ↳ 그가 상당히 좋은 값으로 집을 팔게되자 굴러 들어온 호박에 한껏 고무되었다

Before getting married, you have to set your house in order
> ↳ 결혼하기 전에 주변정리부터 해

Before you criticize others, you should set your house in order
> ↳ 다른 사람을 욕하기 전에 행실부터 고쳐라

Bong-soo's business fell apart like a house of cards
> ↳ 봉수의 사업은 사상누각처럼 망했어

> '사상누각', 즉 '모래 위의 집'이다. 비슷한 뜻으로 '공중누각'이라는 표현도 있고, 이는 영어에는 'Castle in the air'라는 비슷한 표현이 있다. 또한 'House of cards 카드로 지은 집'라는 표현도 쓰인다.

Burn not your house to frighten the mouse away

› **elate** fill with joy

    ↳ 쥐가 놀라 도망가게 하려고 집을 태우지 마라(빈대 한 마리 잡으려고 초가삼간 태우지 마라)

Buying our house privately will cut out the middleman and save money on agent's fees
    ↳ 우리 집을 당사자 개인간에 사고 팔면 중개인 없는 거래여서 중개 수수료가 절약된다

By the look of your huge house and new car, you are getting up in the world
    ↳ 너의 큰집이며 새차를 보니 출세했구나

Dong-soo dashed back to the burning house without a second thought
    ↳ 동수는 즉각 불타고있는 집으로 다시 뛰어들었다

Doo-chul was under house arrest
    ↳ 두철인 가택연금을 당했었다

Gil-soo bought the house for a song and sold it a few months later at a good price
    ↳ 길수는 집을 헐값에 사서 두 세 달 후 큰 이익보고 팔았어

Has your ship come home?
    ↳ 큰돈이라도 들어왔나?

He who heard and did nothing is like a man who built a house on earth without a foundation
    ↳ 듣고 행치 아니하는 자는 주춧돌 없이 집을 지은 사람과 같다

Her house is somewhere in the sticks
    ↳ 그 여자의 집은 벽촌 어딘가에 있어

Her house was burgled(robbed) last night and she took a day off work today
    ↳ 그녀의 집이 어젯밤 도둑을 맞아서 오늘은 허락 받아 직장을 안 나왔다

› **middleman**   dealer or agent between the producer and consumer

› **burgle** commit burglary on or in

His acting carried the house
> ↳ 그의 연기가 만장의 박수를 받았어

His house is the sixth door on the left
> ↳ 그의 집은 왼쪽으로 여섯 번째이다

His mother got after him for tracking mud into the house
> ↳ 그의 어머니가 그에게 흙을 묻혀 집에 들어오지 말라고 야단치셨어

Home is where the heart is
> ↳ 네 마음이 있는 곳이 바로 집이다=가정은 마음의 지주다

I did my daughter over for coming home late
> ↳ 딸아이가 늦게 집에 오기에 야단쳐줬지

I wouldn't give it a house room
> ↳ 거저 줘도 싫어

If you buy the house, they will fling in a car
> ↳ 그 집을 사신다면 자동차를 얹어준답니다

It's on the house
> ↳ 이건 서비스입니다(접객업소 등)

It's now possible to fabricate many parts of a new house in a factory and then put them together at the site
> ↳ 이제는 새 집에 필요한 많은 부품들을 공장에서 만든 뒤 현장에서 조립하는 것이 가능해졌다

It's sad to see him mooning(moping) about the house like this
> ↳ 그가 집안에서 울적한 세월을 보내고 있는 게 안 됐어

My children eat me out of house and home
> ↳ 애들이 기둥뿌리 뽑아먹고 있다네

Nam-soo and Bong-hee keep house these days
> ↳ 남수하고 봉희는 결혼 안하고 동거하고 있어(**she keeps house**그 여자

▸ **fabricate** construct, invent
▸ **moon** spend time in idle reverie

는 가사를 돌보고 있어)

Our(My) house is your house
↳ 우리 집에서 편히 지내세요

See if you can drop out that ugly wall at the side of the house
↳ 사진에 집 한쪽의 벽이 나오지 않게 찍어봐

She couldn't see her way to allowing us to rent the house
↳ 그 여자는 우리에게 집을 세놓을 사정이 아니었다

She had just made it to the house when the heavens opened
↳ 그 여자는 막 비가 억수로 쏟아질 때 집에 돌아갔다

She was a woman living in a nondescript brick-house in the boonies
↳ 그녀는 오지에서 평범한 벽돌집에서 살던 여자였다

**She was flabbergasted to learn that she didn't legally own the house
she bought**
↳ 그녀는 자기가 산 집이 법적으로 자기 소유가 아니라는 것을 알고 어
이가 없었다

She's going to add to this house as soon as she moves in
↳ 그 여자는 이사 들자마자 이 집을 증축하려고 해

Some land goes with the house
↳ 그 집에는 약간의 토지가 딸려 있어

Some people work out of their house these days
↳ 요즘은 재택 근무를 하는 사람들도 있어

The house praises the carpenter
↳ 사람은 이루어놓은 업적에 따라 평가된다

**The officials assume that patients contracted the epidemic from
contaminated underground water at the prayer house**
↳ 관계 공무원들은 전염병에 걸린 환자들이 기도원의 오염된 지하수를

› **flabbergast** astound

› **epidemic** affecting many persons at one time

마신 데서 일어난 것으로 추정한다

The little house nestled among the trees
> ㄴ 그 작은 집은 나무 사이에서 보일락 말락 했다

The man got into the house by masquerading(posing) as a plumber
> ㄴ 그 사람은 배관공인체 하면서 집으로 들어갔다

The real estate operator turned a pretty penny in selling that house
> ㄴ 그 부동산 업자는 그 집을 팔아서 거금을 벌었다

The woman was looking forlornly at her gutted roofless house and the farmer pointed at his seared seed potatoes
> ㄴ 여인은 지붕이 다 타버린 집을 쓸쓸히 쳐다보고 있었고 농부는 그을린 씨감자를 가리켰다

There'll be no name-calling in this house
> ㄴ 집안에서 욕을 해선 안 돼

They(집, 물건) are going fast
> ㄴ 살 사람(세입자)이 빨리 나서거든요

They bought a little house to get away from it all
> ㄴ 그들은 도시생활이 싫어서 시골에 작은 집을 샀다

They decided not pull the historic house down
> ㄴ 그들인 역사적인 가옥을 헐지 않기로 결정했다

They had broken into the house while we were away, and turned the place inside out looking for money
> ㄴ 그들은 우리가 집을 비운 사이에 무단침입해서 돈이 있는지 샅샅이 뒤졌다

Thirty years ago there might not have been a dry eye in the house
> ㄴ 30년 전이었다면(여기 모인)모든 사람이 눈물을 흘렸을 것이다

This house is a diamond in the rough

· **forlorn** deserted, wretched

↳ 이 집을 사 두면 큰 이익이 될 거야

This house is built to last

↳ 이 집은 튼튼하게 지어졌어

This huge house is a milestone about my neck

↳ 이 커다란 집이 내게는 무거운 짐이야

This in-house training course is aimed at eliminating some of the mystique usually associated with your job

↳ 이번 사내 훈련 과정은 보통 여러분들의 직무와 관련하여 업무 수행 상 일어나는 신비적인 거리감을 다소나마 해소하려는데 목적을 둡니다

Those houses were knocked together after the war

↳ 그 집들은 전후에 급조된 것이다

Those who live in glass-houses should not throw stones

↳ 자식 있는 사람은 남의 자식 욕 못해

To dispute a drunkard is to debate with an empty house

↳ 술주정뱅이와 논쟁하는 것은 빈집과 말씨름하는 것과 같다

We have to straighten our house before company comes

↳ 손님 오시기 전에 집을 정돈해야 해

We should put our own house in order before criticizing others

↳ 우린 남을 비판하기에 앞서 자기 자신을 돌아봐야 해

Why don't you settle for a smaller house considering the cost of a big one

↳ 큰집에 대한 비용을 생각해서 작은 집으로 하는 게 어때?

Why should he go poking round his house?

↳ 왜 그는 집에서 빈들거리며 놀고 지내야 하나?

Would you chip in(with) some money on a gift for Sung-woo's housewarming?

‣ **eliminate** get rid of
‣ **drunkard** a person who is drunk

ㄴ 성우네 집들이 선물 사는데 추렴 좀 안 할래

You have the wrong house

ㄴ 집을 잘못 찾으셨군요

· **have** hold in possession, service, or affection;   receive; undergo; cause to; bear

be compelled or forced to; obtain or

137. 차   **Cars**

A reckless driver who crashes into another car may be guilty of a crime in endangering public safety
> ↳ 무모하게 다른 차와 충돌하는 운전자는 공동의 안전을 위협하는 죄를 짓는 짓이다

A white cab came out of nowhere and rolled over him
> ↳ 별안간 하얀 택시가 나타나서 그를 치었어

About the only thing lost by politeness is a seat on a crowded bus
> ↳ 친절해서 손해본다 해봤자 만원버스에서 좌석 하나 잃는 정도뿐이다

All morning the garage men had to pound my car out to its proper shape again
> ↳ 차량 정비공들이 오전 내내 내 차를 본래의 모양으로 두드려 폈다

An oil tanker came careering along the road, banging into all other vehicles in its path
> ↳ 유조차가 거리를 질주해 오면서 마주치는 모든 차량을 마구 부딪쳤다

Are you going to prepare charges against the driver who ruined your lawns?
> ↳ 넌 너희 잔디를 망친 운전자를 고발할 생각이니?

As the old bus route has become unpopular, they decided to discontinue it
> ↳ 종전의 버스노선에 이용자가 적어지자 그들은 버스운행을 중단시키기

› **endanger** bring into danger

로 했다

Buses stop here only by request
ㄴ 버스가 요청이 있을 때에만 정차한다

Buying a good car won't come cheap, but it's worth it for you
ㄴ 좋은 차를 사는 건 비싸게 먹히지만 네게 그만한 가치는 있다

Buying a new car is sure to draw fire
ㄴ 새차를 사면 사람들이 말이 많을 것이다

Can you fit them all in your trunk?
ㄴ 그것들을 전부 네 트렁크에 넣을 수 있겠나?

Can you take my car in exchange(as a trade)?
ㄴ 받을 돈 대신 차를 가져가시면 안되겠습니까?

Chang-soo's car has it all over that piece of junk
ㄴ 창수의 차가 저 고물차 보다 훨씬 낫지

Could you please put your car at my disposal today?
ㄴ 오늘 네 차를 좀 사용할 수 있겠나?

Dong-soo scared(scraped) up the money for his speeding ticket
ㄴ 동수는 겨우 속도위반 벌금을 마련했어

Dong-soo's car flew apart on his way to Seoul
ㄴ 동수의 차는 서울로 오다가 박살이 났어

Doo-chul gave me a long song and dance about his new car
ㄴ 두철인 새차를 샀다고 한참 얘길 늘어놓았어

Doo-man went to flag down a taxi
ㄴ 두만이는 택시 잡으러 갔어

Every fourth man has a car in Korea
ㄴ 한국에는 4명당 한 명 꼴로 차가 있다

· **scrap** get rid of as useless, fight

Gil-soo sold Sung-min the car at a cheap price and included the tape recorder for good measure
> ↳ 길수는 성민이에게 차를 싸게 팔면서 녹음기를 덤으로 주었어

He barely missed being knocked down by the car
> ↳ 그는 하마터면 차에 치일 뻔했다

He can kiss his car goodbye
> ↳ 그는 차를 망치게 될 것이다

He finally bought a new car. He's glad to get it out of his system
> ↳ 그는 결국 새차를 샀다. 이제 소망하던 일이 달성되어 기뻐하고 있다

Here comes the bus in the nick of time
> ↳ 때마침 버스가 오는군

His car has many nice options which are sort of the icing(frosting) on the cake
> ↳ 그의 차에는 덤(금상첨화)이라 할 수 있는 멋진 옵션이 많이 붙어 있어

> "좋은 데 더 좋은 것을 더한다"는 뜻이다. 영어로는 'Icing on the cake 케익위의 크림'이라고 한다. 케익만으로도 맛있는데, 거기에 크림을 더해 더욱 맛있어 졌다는 얘기이다. Icing 대신에 Frosting으로 대체할 수도 있다.

His car has stood the test of time and he can't bear to part with it
> ↳ 그는 그 차를 오래 써서 떨어질 수 없게 된 거야

How do you find my new car?
> ↳ 내 새차 어때?

How much did it cost to juice your car up?
> ↳ 네 차를 힘 좋은 엔진으로 개조하는데 얼마 들었니?

How much did your car go for in the end?

› **juice** add juice to, extract the juice from

ㄴ 결국 너의 차가 얼마에 팔렸니?

I have been averaging 20 minutes to get a taxi
ㄴ 택시 잡는데 **20**분이나 걸렸어

If a new car is having teething troubles, nine times out of ten free servicing is available
ㄴ 새차의 길들이기(초창기 어려움)에 문제가 있으면 대개의 경우 해당 지역에서 서비스를 제공받는다

If you buy the house, they will fling in a car
ㄴ 그 집을 사신다면 자동차를 얹어준답니다

In-ho barely missed being knocked out by the car
ㄴ 인호는 하마터면 그 차에 치일 뻔했어

In-soo shelled out a lot of money for his new car
ㄴ 인수는 새차 구입에 큰 돈 들었어

Most drivers do not even dare to touch the intricate pattern of adjunct devices compacted under their cars' hoods
ㄴ 대부분의 자동차 운전자들은 자동차 후드 밑에 꽉 차게 뒤엉켜 있는 부속품들을 감히 건드려 보지도 않는다

My car is still under warranty
ㄴ 내 차는 아직 수리보증기간 중이야

My car won't kick over because weather's too cold this morning
ㄴ 오늘아침 날씨가 너무 추워서 시동이 잘 안 걸려

My father gave me a blank check to use his car for month
ㄴ 차를 맘대로 쓰라고 아버지가 허락하셨어

Nearly thirty cars piled up on the highway yesterday
ㄴ 어제 고속도로에서 거의 **30**중 충돌이 있었다

No rest room in the bus

› **intricate** very complex and delicate | › **adjunct** something joined or added but not essential

└ 버스 타기 전에 용변을 미리 보십시오

On the occasion of the traditional holiday 'Solal', all roads lead home out of the cities

└ 전통 명절인 설날을 맞아 모든 도로가 귀성 차량으로 가득 찬다

Please take the next bus, I can't cram any more passengers in

└ 이 차는 만원이니 다음 버스를 타십시오

Pyung-soo's fancy car is too-too, if you ask

└ 내 생각으로는 평수의 으리으리한 차는 너무 티를 내는 것 같아

She caught the wrong bus and wound up going in the opposite direction

└ 그녀는 차를 잘못 타서 반대방향으로 가게되고 말았다

She certainly sold you a bill of goods when she induced you to buy that car

└ 그 여자가 네게 그 차를 사라고 권한 것은 널 속였음이 틀림없어

She didn't give a fair shake on my trade-in for a new car

└ 내가 헌차를 새차로 바꿀 때 그 여자는 헌 차 값을 정당하게 쳐주지 않았다

She has more money than sense when she bought that luxury car

└ 그 여자가 거금을 들여 고급 차를 산 것은 지각없는 짓이다

She's cut it fine. The bus's just leaving

└ 그 여자는 아슬아슬하게 버스에 탔어. 버스가 막 떠나던 참이거든

Somebody pushed me aside and got on the bus ahead of me

└ 어떤 사람이 나를 옆으로 밀어버리고 나보다 먼저 버스를 탔다

Someone has jumped in the taxi just ahead of us

└ 어떤 사람이 우리보다 먼저 택시를 잡아타고 갔어

Strangely, the perfectly good car was abandoned like that in the middle of nowhere

---

› **cram** eat greedily, pack in tight, study intensely for a test

› **abandon** give up without intent to reclaim

ㄴ 이상하게도 완전할 만큼 좋은 차가 이렇게 한적한 곳에 버려져 있었다

Tai-ho tore his new trousers on something sharp on the side of the car
　　　ㄴ 태호는 차 옆의 뾰족한 무엇에 걸려서 새 바지를 찢었다

Take care not to miss out on the car sale
　　　ㄴ 자동차 세일을 놓치지 않도록 주의해

That car cost the equivalent of my year's salary
　　　ㄴ 저 차는 내 1년 월급에 맞먹는 비용이 들었어

That car is a must-see in your price range
　　　ㄴ 너의 차 구입비로 봐서 그 차는 꼭 봐야 해

**That nerd caught wrong bus and wound up going in the opposite
direction**
　　　　　ㄴ 그 멍청이 녀석이 버스를 잘못 타서 반대방향으로 가게되고 말았어

**The best safety device in a car is a rear-view mirror with a
policeman in it**
　　　　　ㄴ 차량의 최고 안전장치는 경찰의 얼굴이 보이는 백미러이다

The bus goes in a different direction
　　　　　ㄴ 그 버스는 돌아서 거기로 가

(=The bus goes there a different way(around another way))
(=The bus takes a different route)

**The bus line launched with a lot of fanfare and fizzled out just in
one month**
　　　　　ㄴ 요란하게 떠들어대며 착수한 버스노선이 한 달만에 흐지부지 끝나버렸다

The bus was nowhere(not) near full
　　　　　ㄴ 버스는 거의 비어 있었어

› **fanfare**　a sounding of trumpets, showy
　　　　　display

› **fizzle**　fizz, fail

The bus was so packed that people were actually clinging to sides
  ↳ 버스가 너무 꽉 차서 사람들이 사실상 차의 옆에 매달릴 정도였다

The car was totalled
  ↳ 그 차는 박살이 났어

The cars arrived one after the other
  ↳ 차들이 차례차례 도착했다

The company has focused on autos, shunning the finger-in-very-pie approach of other conglomerates
  ↳ 그 회사는 다른 재벌들의 문어발 식 경영관행에서 탈피하여 자동차 사업에만 주력했다

The crash left the remains of the vehicles, distorted out of all recognition
  ↳ 충돌사고로 차량들의 잔해가 형체를 알아보기 힘들 정도로 찌그러져 있었다

The driver forced to double up
  ↳ 운전사가 합승을 강요했다

The heavy truck hit the curb and then veered across the road
  ↳ 무거운 트럭이 연석에 부딪치더니 도로 건너편으로 홱 방향을 틀었다

The heavy-laden oil tank went out of control and ploughed into a cluster of people on the sidewalk
  ↳ 육중하게 짐을 실은 유조차가 것 잡을 수 없게되어 인도에 모여있던 사람들에게 덮쳐왔다

The mechanic will get around to you in no time
  ↳ 수리공이 곧 손님 차를 봐줄 겁니다

The new car could negotiate the desert
  ↳ 새차는 사막을 무사히 넘을 수 있었어

› **total** add up, amount to
› **veer** change course gradually

The new car that Dong-soo is driving is a real hot number

    ㄴ 동수가 몰고 다니는 새차 정말 캡이다

The packed buses and overflowing trains speak joyfully of the home they are heading for

    ㄴ 꽉 찬 버스와 미어져 터지는 열차에 탄 승객들은 자기들이 가고있는 가정에 대한 즐거운 얘기로 꽃을 피운다

The police appealed for information concerning the whereabouts of the stolen car used in the robbery

    ㄴ 경찰은 강도행위에 사용되었던 차의 소재에 대한 제보를 호소했다

The police are putting the heat on the motorists who show any signs of driving while under the influence(of alcohol)

    ㄴ 경찰이 조금이라도 기미가 있는 음주운전자에게는 단속을 강화하고 있다

The road is a three-ring circus of cars, people, noise and lights

    ㄴ 도로는 자동차, 사람들, 소음, 가로등으로 시끌벅적해

The robber came out of the jewelry shop and jumped into his car

    ㄴ 강도는 보석상에서 달려나와 자신의 차에 뛰어 올라 탔다

The robber lit out on a stolen car which was waiting for him outside the shop

    ㄴ 강도는 가게 밖에 있던 차를 훔쳐 타고 급히 달아났다

The taxi did no such thing

    ㄴ 택시는 내가 하자는(계획) 대로 해주지 않았다

The taxi driver had no fares all morning

    ㄴ 그 택시 운전사는 오전 내내 승객이 없었다

The well-trained nurses and paramedics climbed the toppled van and administered aid to those trapped

    ㄴ 잘 훈련된 간호원들과 응급 치료원들은 전복된 승합차로 올라가 차에

› **paramedic** person trained to give first aid and some medical treatment as an aid to a doctor

› **topple** fall or cause to fall

서 나오지 못한 사람들을 치료했다

Then you are bound to run a foul of the traffic officer
> ↳ 그랬다가는 영락없이 교통경찰한테 걸리게 돼 있어

There were a couple of fender-benders on the expressway this morning
> ↳ 오늘아침 고속도로상에서 가벼운 접촉사고가 두 건 있었다

They gave you a good deal on this car
> ↳ 그들이 이 차를 네게 싸게 팔았군

They put a new bridge across the river to take the increased traffic
> ↳ 그들은 늘어난 교통량을 감당하기 위해 강에 다리를 놓았다

They've been trying to soft-pedal the fact that their cars are polluting the air seriously
> ↳ 그들의 차가 아직도 대기를 심각하게 오염시키고 있다는 사실을 그들은 은폐시키려 기를 써 오고 있다

This bus is on a regular run between Dae-jun and Jin-ju
> ↳ 이 버스는 대전과 진주간을 정가 운행해

This car carries only four
> ↳ 이 차는 4인승 이다

This car has my name on it
> ↳ 이 차 맘에 쏙 든다

This car is beginning to date
> ↳ 이 차는 고물이 되어가고 있어

This car is too rich for my blood
> ↳ 내겐 이 차가 너무 고급이다

This car outperforms my initial expectations
> ↳ 이 차는 나의 당초 기대보다 좋은 성능을 보여주고 있어

This car will stand up to all kinds of strain

· **outperform** do better than

ㄴ 이 차는 아무리 험하게 사용해도 끄떡없다

Those wrecked vehicles were riddled with bullet holes
ㄴ 그 부서진 차량들은 총알 맞은 구멍 투성이였다

Traffic is often congested around the city, creating problems for motorists many blocks away
ㄴ 시내 한 가운데에는 자주 교통이 혼잡하여 몇 블록씩이나 떨어진 곳에 있는 자동차 운전자들도 힘들게 되었다

Traffic jams during rush hour ought to be averted by keeping the openings and closings of the street commensurate
ㄴ 거리의 개통과 폐쇄를 균형 있게 유지함으로써 출퇴근 시간의 교통체증이 해소돼야 한다

Traffic tailed back for ten kilometers when the highway was blocked by the accident
ㄴ 고속도로가 사고로 막혔을 때 차량이 10킬로도 넘게 늘어섰다

Traffic there is badly backed up
ㄴ 그 곳은 교통체증이 심해

Using your un-repaired car in its present state is at your own risk
ㄴ 수리하지도 않은 차를 그 상태로 타는 것은 자신이 위험을 감수해야 해

Violating the traffic law cost me hundred thousand won
ㄴ 교통위반으로 십만원 물었다

We do more to decimate our population in automobile accidents than we do in war
ㄴ 전쟁에서보다 자동차 사고에서 더 많은 사람들이 죽는다

We have to pen in the kids to keep them away from the traffic
ㄴ 아이들이 차 다니는 길에 나가지 않도록 못나가게 해야해

We offset the greater distance by the better roads

› **avert** turn away

› **commensurate** equal in measure or extent

› **decimate** destroy a large part of

ㄴ 도로가 좋으면 거리가 먼 것이 별로 문제가 되지 않는다

We'll make our connection if this bus hurries up
ㄴ 이 버스가 서둘러서 가면 연결차를 탈 수 있을 것이다

We've been stuck in traffic for hours
ㄴ 우리는 몇 시간동안 교통에 막혀 꼼짝 못했어(**Traffic is at a standstill** 교통이 꽉 막혔어)

What kind of gas milage do you get?
ㄴ 차의 연비는 어떻습니까?

When is the last bus for this line?
ㄴ 이 노선의 막차는 몇 시까지입니까?

When is traffic at its worst around here?
ㄴ 여기에 차가 가장 많이 막히는 시간이 언제지?

When will you take your car out for a spin?
ㄴ 너의 차는 언제 시승할 거냐?

Where does this street go?
ㄴ 이 길로 가면 어디로 가지?

> (=Where this road lead to?)

Why isn't the traffic moving?
ㄴ 왜 차가 꼼짝도 안 하는 거야

You are going the wrong way
ㄴ 차를 잘못 타셨군요

You can keep yourself amused on the bus by listening to this music
ㄴ 버스를 탈 때 이 음악을 들으면 심심하지 않게 갈 수 있어

› **amuse** engage the attention of in an interesting and pleasant way,   make laugh

You might as well ask for the moon as for a car
┗ 차는 사줄 수 없어

You should pay double
┗ 왕복요금을 내셔야 합니다

You will beat the traffic
┗ 교통혼잡은 피할 수 있을 거야

You'd better come over to a diesel-powered car
┗ 디젤차로 바꾸지 그래

› **diesel** engine in which high compression
cause ignition of the fuel

138. 추측   **Supposition**

Anybody's guess is nobody's guess
↳ 사람마다 예상이 다를 경우 누구의 예상도 옳다고 할 수 없다

By no stretch of the imagination
↳ 아무리 생각해 보아도 힘들 거야

Byung-soo will land on his feet
↳ 병수는 어려운 상황에서 잘 벗어날 것이다

Castigating and punishing her would only exacerbate the shame she's suffering
↳ 그녀를 나무라고 벌주는 것은 수치심을 더 악화시킬 뿐이다

He is going to play hardball with you, and you'll get a little more difficulty to deal with
↳ 그가 네게 심(엄)하게 나올 테니 견디기가 좀 어려워질 거야

He'll continue to cook the books to his own greater glory
↳ 그는 자신을 더욱 돋보이게 하려고 사실을 계속 조작할 것이다

He'll never go to any greater length than a protest
↳ 그는 기껏 항의하는 정도에 그칠 것이다

It is reduced to conjecture
↳ 추측해 보는 수밖에 없어

It's just a theory
↳ 그건 단지 추측일 뿐이야

‣ **castigate**   chastise severely
‣ **conjecture**   guess

My guess was just a shot in the dark
> ↳ 모르고 그냥 추측한 것 뿐이야

She could have averted a conflagration if any member of her family had reacted to the first flames
> ↳ 그녀의 가족 중 누구든 한 사람이라도 첫 번째 불길에 조치를 취했더라면 큰불은 피할 수 있었을 것이다

The ice will not bear
> ↳ 얼음에 올라서면 깨질 것이다

The last shall be first
> ↳ 제일 꼴찌라고 여긴 사람(일)이 실은 최고일거야

Their estimate was in the ball park
> ↳ 그들의 추측은 대충 맞았어

Their predictions were way off the beam
> ↳ 그들의 예상은 아주 어긋났다

There's no way to tell
> ↳ 예측할 수 없어

Your guess is wide of the mark
> ↳ 네 추측은 얼토당토않아

› **conflagration** great fire

139. 충고   Advices

A fault confessed is half redressed
> 실토한 잘못은 반은 고쳐진 것이다

A once over lightly is not enough
> 대충해서는 안 돼

A warlike atmosphere will prevail if you rock the boat again
> 네가 다시 분란을 일으켰다가는 분위기가 살벌해 질 것이다

Aim high and you'll strike high
> 큰걸 노려야 큰걸 얻지

All clouds not bring rain
> 겉만 보고 속단하지 마라

(=All are not thieves that dogs bark at)
(=Not all clouds bring rain)

All good things must come to an end
> 모든 즐거운 일에는 끝이 있다

All things are easy, that are done willingly
> 하겠다는 마음으로 하면 안 되는 일이 없다

▸ **confess** acknowledge or disclose one's misdeed, fault, or sin; declare   faith in

속담 중에도 "뜻이 있는 곳에 길이 있다(Where there is a will, there is a way)"라는 말이 있다. 아무리 힘들고 어려운 일이라도 목적을 가지고 끈기 있게 도전하면 안 되는 일이 없다는 뜻이다(=Nothing is impossible to a willing heart).

All you have to do is to be the right man for(at) the right time
↳ 네가 할 일은 시대가 꼭 필요로 하는 사람이 되는 것뿐이다

All you have to do is to do as you think right
↳ 네가 할 일은 네가 옳다고 생각하는 대로 하기만 하면 돼

Allow me to give you the benefit of my advice(experience)
↳ 달갑지 않겠지만 내 충고(경험담)를 들어줘

Be careful about which make-up you wear under these strong lights
↳ 이 강렬한 조명아래 무슨 화장을 해야할지 주의해라

Be careful about your appearance
↳ 옷차림에 유의해야해

Be careful not to be dashed with mud
↳ 흙탕물에 튀기지 않도록 조심해

Be careful not to blow a deal
↳ 고객 놓치지 않게 주의해야해

Be careful not to come down on the wrong horse
↳ 줄을 잘못 서지 않도록 주의해라

Be careful not to flog it to death, or your customers will lose interest
↳ 같은 소리를 또 하고 또 해서 손님들의 흥미가 덜어지지 않도록 해

Be careful not to get any on your fingers when you are putting on the glue
↳ 아교를 바를 때 손가락에 묻지 않도록 해

› **benefit** something that does good, help, fund-raising event

Be careful not to get off on the wrong foot
> ↳ 처음부터 잘되게 주의해

Be careful not to give a handle to him
> ↳ 약점 잡히지 않도록 해(많이 쓰이는 용법은 아님)

Be careful not to glide into bad habits
> ↳ 나쁜 버릇 붙이지 않도록 주의해야 해

Be careful not to let your tongue run away with you again
> ↳ 또다시 말을 못 참는 일이 없도록 조심해

Be careful not to play(talk) down to your hearers, they are very sensitive about being treated as stupid
> ↳ 청중들이 바보취급 당하는 일에 매우 민감하니 수준을 낮추어 얘기하
> 지 않도록 해라

Be careful not to price yourself out of business(market)
> ↳ 너무 비싼 값을 매겨 물건이 안 팔려 사업이 망하지 않도록 주의해

Be careful not to run the needle into your finger by mistake
> ↳ 잘못해서 바늘에 손가락이 찔리지 않도록 주의해

Be careful not to shoot from the hip
> ↳ 준비 없이 행동(말) 하지 않도록 주의해

Be careful not to slip on the wet spot on the floor
> ↳ 바닥의 젖은 곳에 밟아 미끄러지지 않게 주의해

Be careful what you say
> ↳ 함부로 말하지마

```
(=Watch what you say)
(=Watch your mouth)
(=Don't say things you'll regret)
```

> **spot** blemish, distinctive small part, location,
> see or recognize

Be careful what you wish for
> ↳ 종아리 맞고 싶어 간지러운 거냐?

Be cautious in all your movements
> ↳ 일거일동에 조심해

Be just before you are generous
> ↳ 관대하기에 앞서 공정히 하라

Be on sure ground before you suspect anyone
> ↳ 공연히 남을 의심해선 안 돼(자주 쓰이지는 않음)

Be prepared
> ↳ 유비무환

Better bad now than worse later
> ↳ 지금은 나쁘더라도 나중 일을 생각해야 해

Better learn all the do's and don'ts immediately
> ↳ 즉시 모든 규칙을 알아두는 게 좋아

Better make yourself scarce
> ↳ 자리를 피하는 게 좋아

Better never to begin than never to make an end
> ↳ 끝맺지 않을 바에 시작을 안 하는 게 낫다

Better not a hero than work oneself up into heroism by shouting
> ↳ 거짓말로 떠들어서 영웅이 되느니 보다 안되는 게 낫다

Better to be ignorant of a matter than half known
> ↳ 얼치기로 아는 것보다 모르는 게 낫다

Beware lest you lose the substance by grasping at the shadow
> ↳ 그림자를 잡으려다 실체를 놓치지 않는지 주의하라

Beware of bedroom eyes
> ↳ 유혹의 눈길에 주의하라

· **ignorant** lacking knowledge, stupid, unaware
· **beware** be cautious

Beware of one who flatters unduly
↳ 당치도 않게 아첨하는 사람을 경계하라

Beware of the man who does not return your blow
↳ 매 맞고도 가만히 있는 사람을 주의하라

Beware the people weeping when they bare the iron and
↳ 압제에서 벗어나면서 우는 사람들을 주의하라

Character before career
↳ 먼저 사람이 되어라

Come down to earth
↳ 냉수 먹고 속차려

Count your blessings
↳ 불행할 때 좋은 일을 생각하라

Do it or die
↳ 죽을 각오로 해야 해

Don't act the cock of the walk
↳ 으스대지마

Don't badmouth everybody like that
↳ 그렇게 아무나 막 헐뜯지마

Don't be a camel sticking his nose under the tent
↳ 그렇게 참견하지마

Don't be a party to the conspiracy
↳ 그 음모에 가담해선 안 돼

Don't be a sore(poor) loser
↳ 진 것 가지고 트집 잡지 마라

Don't be an armchair quarterback
↳ 뒷전에 앉아서 이러쿵저러쿵 하지마

▸ **unduly** excessively

Don't be coy with me
> 내숭떨지마

Don't be impossible
> 짜증나게 하지마

Don't be inquisitive
> 꼬치꼬치 캐묻지마

> (=You'll find out soon)
> (=Don't be so nosey)
> (=Don't be so prying)
> (=Don't stick your nose in other people's affairs)

Don't be so cheap
> 그리 쩨쩨하게 굴지마

Don't be so dense
> 그런 눈치 없는 소리하지마

Don't be so difficult
> 너무 그리 까다롭게 굴지마

Don't be so upright
> 그렇게 짜증 부리지마

Don't be such a basket case about it
> 그런 일에 안달복달하지마

Don't be such a mother hen
> 이것해라 저것해라 하지마

Don't be such a space cadet like that
> 그렇게 우왕좌왕하지마(멍청한 짓 하지마)

· **coy** shy or pretending shyness | · **upright** vertical, erect in posture, morally correct

Don't be such a stick in the mud
  ↳ 그런 고리타분한 식으로 나오지마

Don't big talk me(boss me around)
  ↳ 나한테 이래라 저래라 하지마

Don't bite the hand that feeds you
  ↳ 배은망덕한 짓은 하지 마라

Don't boss everyone around
  ↳ 남들에게 이래라 저래라 하지마

Don't breed bad blood between them
  ↳ 그들에게 불화를 조장하지 말라

Don't bring it up again
  ↳ 그 얘기 또 꺼내지마

Don't burn the candle at both ends
  ↳ 과도한 정력 소비하지마

Don't burst in like that
  ↳ 그렇게 불쑥 들어오지마

Don't chase after another
  ↳ 우물을 파도 한 우물을 파라

Don't clutter your head up with unimportant details
  ↳ 하찮은 일로 머리 속을 어지럽게 하지마

Don't confound the means with the end
  ↳ 수단과 목적을 혼동하지마

Don't cross the line
  ↳ 규칙을 어기지 마라

Don't drop(fall) by the wayside
  ↳ 도중에 포기하지마

· **confound** confuse

Don't find fault. Find a remedy
> ↳ 흠을 잡지말고 해결책을 찾아라

Don't flatter yourself
> ↳ 잘난 척 하지마

> (=Don't get a big head)
> (=Don't get a swell(big, swollen) head=)
> (Don't put on airs)

Don't follow in my tracks
> ↳ 나의 전철을 밟지마

Don't forget that your suggestion can backfire
> ↳ 네 제안이 역효과를 낼 수도 있다는 걸 잊지 마라

Don't give up in the middle
> ↳ 한 번 시작한 일은 끝까지 해라

> (=Finish what you planned(started))
> (=See it through to the end)

Don't give yourself away
> ↳ 속맘을 털어놓지마

Don't go off half-cocked
> ↳ 성급하게 굴지마

Don't hide(bury) your head in the sand
> ↳ 현실도피(눈감고 아웅) 식으로 나와선 안 돼

· **suggest** put into someone's mind, remind
one by association of ideas

> 'The cat that ate the canary 카나리아를 잡아먹은 고양이'란 한국 속담
> 으로 표현하면 "눈감고 아웅한다"이다. 이는 자신이 잘못한 일을 다른 사람이
> 모를 것이라 생각하고 시치미 떼는 상황을 말한다. 영어 속담은 주인이 아끼
> 는 카나리아를 잡아먹고 시치미 떼는 고양이에 비유하였다.

Don't just mouth off
ㄴ 나설 차례가 아닐 때 나서지 마라

Don't let anyone say you have a long bottom
ㄴ 아무에게도 엉덩이가 무겁다는 말을 듣지 않도록 해

Don't let anyone say you're talking to hear your own voice
ㄴ 남들에게서 네가 말이 많다는 소릴 듣게 해선 안 돼

Don't let anyone think you're a loose cannon
ㄴ 남들에게서 못 말리는 위험인물(떠버리)이란 소릴 들어선 안 돼

Don't let it become an obsession
ㄴ 너무 빠지지마

Don't let it happen again
ㄴ 다시는 그런 일이 없어야 해

Don't let the grass grow under your feet
ㄴ 시간낭비 하지 마라

Don't let this opportunity slip though your fingers
ㄴ 이번 기회를 놓치지 마라

Don't let your guard down
ㄴ 방심하지마

Don't like being a small(little) fish in a big pond
ㄴ 시시한 사람으로 안주할 생각은 하지마

Don't live in a happy-go-lucky way

▸ **cannon** artillery piece

ㄴ 되는 대로 살아선 안 돼

Don't make a pig of yourself
ㄴ 돼지같이 욕심부리지마

Don't press your luck
ㄴ 운만 믿고 너무 무리하지마

Don't procrastinate until an opportunity is lost
ㄴ 차일피일 하다가 시기를 놓치지 마라

Don't push to all your limits
ㄴ 극한 상황으로 가지마

Don't push your luck any more
ㄴ 더 이상 운을 믿고 욕심부리지마

Don't put a false construction on his action
ㄴ 남을 일부러 곡해하지마

Don't rush to the judgment on that
ㄴ 그 일은 성급히 판단하지마

Don't shoot the pianist
ㄴ 호의로 그랬던 사람을 책하지 마라

Don't stick your neck out
ㄴ 위험을 자초하지마

Don't take chances
ㄴ 너무 무리하지마

Even then you don't have to burn the bridge with him
ㄴ 그렇더라도 그와 적대감을 가질 필요는 없어

Everybody gave me advice about what to do with my problem but kept his own counsel
ㄴ 모두가 내 문제에 대해 한 마디씩 했는데도 그는 자신의 생각을 말하

› **rush** move forward or act with too great haste, perform in a short time

지 않았어

Everyone must pay his dues
↳ 누구나 대가는 치러야 해

For lawless joys a bitter ending awaits
↳ 무절제한 즐거움 끝에는 쓰라린 결말이 기다리고 있다

He gave ear to my advice
↳ 그는 내 충고를 들어줬어

Gambling will undo him someday
↳ 도박이 언젠가는 그를 망칠게다

Get organized and stop running around like a hen with its head cut off(in circles)
↳ 정신 좀 차리고 호떡집에 불난 것처럼 허둥대지마

"Running around like a hen with its head cut of"는 한국식으로 표현하면 "호떡집에 불났다"이다. 양계장에서 닭 잡는 날의 혼란스러움에 빗대어 만든 속담이다.

Get yourself straitened out and don't cry in your beer
↳ 생활태도를 고치고 후회 할 일 없도록 해

Gil-soo should keep his wits about him all the time
↳ 길수는 늘 정신 바짝 차리고 있어야 해

Give it your concentration
↳ 그 일에 집중해라

Give neither counsel nor salt till you are asked for it
↳ 요청 받기 전에는 충고와 소금을 남에게 주지 마라

Her joke(advice) was not lost(up)on him

· **gamble**   play a game for stakes, bet, take a chance

    ↳ 그 여자의 농담(충고)을 그가 금방 알아듣더군

Hold your course through good and evil report
    ↳ 남들이 뭐라고 하든 개의치 말고 네 방침대로 해 나가라

Hope for the best and prepare for the worst
    ↳ 유비무환이다

How can you expect respect when you are so condescending?
    ↳ 그리 잘난 척 하면서 어떻게 존경을 기대할 수 있겠니?

Hyun-soo needs your stupid advice like a hole in the head
    ↳ 현수가 뭐가 아쉬워서 너의 서푼어치 조언이 필요하겠니

You'll drink yourself out of your job
    ↳ 그러다간 술로 직장을 잃게 돼

If he wants to move ahead in his job, he should take advice from more experienced workers
    ↳ 그가 업무에 앞서 나가려면 경험 많은 동료들에게 조언을 받아야 한다

If the counsel be good, no matter who gave it
    ↳ 좋은 충고라면 누가 충고 했느냐가 중요한 게 아니다

If you are not sure what you're doing, ask for advice
    ↳ 아는 길도 물어서 가라

If you know what's good for you, don't let him know what you really think
    ↳ 네가 그렇게 생각하는 것을 드러내지 않는 것이 너 자신을 위하는 일이야

If you make the most of the situation, you can still come out ahead
    ↳ 현재 처한 상황을 최대한으로 활용하면 자신에게 유리하게 될 것이다

If you want it done right, do it yourself
    ↳ 잘되기 바라면 직접 해라

› **situation**   location, condition, job

If you want people to notice your faults, start giving advice
> ↳ 사람들에게 당신의 약점을 알리고 싶거든 그들에게 충고를 시작하라

If you want work well done, select a busy man
> ↳ 일이 잘 되기 원한다면 부지런히 일하는 사람을 골라라

If you were as free with your help as you are with your advice we could have had the job finished by now
> ↳ 네가 말로 우릴 도와주듯 실제로 쾌히 우릴 도와주었다면 지금쯤 그 일을 끝낼 수 있었을 거야

Ignore this warning at your own peril
> ↳ 이 경고를 무시하면 목숨이 위태로운 줄 알아라

In vain he craves advice that he will not follow
> ↳ 행하지 않으면서 조언만 구하는 것은 헛일이다

It can save you a lot of trouble if you'll listen to reason
> ↳ 남의 충고를 따르면 많은 어려움을 피할 수 있어

It was like talking to a stone wall
> ↳ 쇠귀에 경 읽기였어(그는 내 말을 전혀 안 들었어)

마음에 있지 않으면 들어도 들리지 않고 보아도 보이지 않는다(There's none so blind as those who will not see = There's none so deaf as those who will not hear).
(=He was deaf to my advice)

It'll be wise for you to be tight-lipped about what you have done
> ↳ 네가 한 일에 대하여는 입을 다무는 게 현명해

It'll cost you dear
> ↳ 그 일 때문에 혼날 거다

› **peril** danger, put in danger

It'll do more harm than good
> 얻는 것 보다 잃는 게 많아

It's all for your own sake
> 다 너 좋게 하려고 하는 소리(일)이야

It's best to err on the safe side
> 잘못 하더라도 조심하는 게 나아

It's better to be safe than sorry
> 후회하는 것 보다 안전한 게 나아

It's the last straw that breaks the camel's back
> 작은 일일지라도 한도를 넘으면 돌이킬 수 없게 된다

It's better to be safe than sorry
> 후회하는 것 보다 안전한 게 나아

Just paper over the cracks
> 적당히 마무리 해

Lacking anything better, use what you have
> 좋은 것이 없다면 지금 있는 것을 사용하라

Learn to concentrate as early in life as possible
> 될 수 있는 한 젊을 때부터 주의를 집중하는 법을 배워라

Learn to obey before you command
> 남에게 명령하기 전에 남의 명령을 듣는 것을 배워라

Leave somebody there to hold the fort
> 뒷일을 위해 한 사람 남겨놓아라

Let the dog see the rabbit
> 도움이 안될 일에는 나서지 말고 구경이나 해

Live my words everyday
> 매일매일 내 말을 실천하며 살아라

› **err** be or do wrong

Look after yourself
> ↳ 네 일은 네가 알아서 해라

Look out for number one first
> ↳ 너 자신의 일이나 먼저 돌봐라

Make assurance doubly(double) sure
> ↳ 물샐틈없이 주의하라

My advice(joke) was not lost upon her
> ↳ 그 여자는 내 충고(농담)를 잘 알아들었다

Nice guys finish last
> ↳ 이기려면 야비하게 굴어라(또는 좋은 사람일수록 출세가 늦어)

No one should make fun of or ridicule others who are trying to improve themselves
> ↳ 자기발전을 위해 노력하려는 사람들을 놀리거나 비웃어서는 안 된다

Now just do what you are told, or else!
> ↳ 내가 말 한대로 해야해, 안 하기만 해봐라!

Of the evils choose the less
> ↳ 부득이한 선택이라면 그 중에서 나은 것을 골라라

One hour's cold will spoil seven year's warming
> ↳ 일순간의 잘못으로 공든 탑도 무너진다

> (=One slip of the knife will spoil the work of months)

Open confession is good for the soul
> ↳ 잘못을 인정하고 고치기를 주저하지 마라

› **ridicule** laugh at or make fun of

죄를 짓느냐 짓지 않느냐가 문제가 아니라 죄를 고백하고 반성하고 고치려고 노력을 하는 것이 중요한 것이다. 죄를 짓지 않는 인간은 없기 때문이다 (Confession can be described as a medicine that heals the mind = 고백은 마음의 상처를 치료하는 치료제와 같다).

Outspoken advice is(sounds) harsh to the ear
ㄴ 바른 말은 귀에 거슬린다

자신의 결점을 꼬집어서 말하는 충고를 들을 때에는 기분이 좋을 수가 없다. 그렇기 때문에 함부로 남에게 충고를 해서는 안되고, 충고를 들어서 기분이 나쁘더라도 받아들일 수 있는 아량이 있어야 한다.
(=Unpleasant advice is a good medicine)
(=A good medicine taste bitter)

Please do what you can to get yourself up-to-date
ㄴ 가능한 한 신식 물결(최신 정보)에서 빠지지 않도록 해

Please treat us equally
ㄴ 편파적으로 나가선 안 돼

(=Please stop being biased(playing favorites))

Possess yourself in patience
ㄴ 꾹 눌러 참아라

Rights come together with duties
ㄴ 권리에는 의무가 따른다

Rigid justice is the greatest injustice

‣ **outspoken** direct and open in speech
‣ **rigid** lacking flexibility

↳ 경직된 정의는 가장 큰 불의이다

Shape up or ship out

↳ 제대로 하던지 그만두던지 해

Shoot for the highest attainable goal

↳ 성취 가능한 최고의 목표를 잡아라

Simmer down and get a grip on yourself

↳ 맘을 가라앉히고 이성을 찾아라

Stay(be) on the ball all the time

↳ 항상 방심해서는 안 돼

Stick to your first plan

↳ 초지일관해야 해

Stop chopping around(about) and make up your mind

↳ 이랬다저랬다 하지말고 마음을 정해라

Take my warning for the future

↳ 차후에 조심해

The only thing against you is your greed

↳ 너의 유일한 결함은 탐욕이다

There's no looking aside from your responsibility

↳ 책임감을 잊고 한눈을 팔아서는 안 돼

There's no sense in riding off in all directions

↳ 한꺼번에 이것저것 하려는 건 어리석은 일이야

They were advised to keep their own counsel

↳ 그들은 속마음을 말하지 말라고 충고 받았다

This thing will get you sometime soon

↳ 이러다간 네 몸 상한다(신세 망친다)

› **attainable** able to achieve or accomplish, able to reach

› **simmer down** become calm or peachful

Throw away that cancer stick(Stop smoking)
ㄴ 담배 좀 끊어

Too much adherence to form will defeat its own end
ㄴ 형식에 너무 치우치면 목적을 그르칠 수 있어

Too much is as bad as little
ㄴ 지나침은 부족한 것과 같다

Too much of a good thing can be bad
ㄴ 좋은 것도 지나치면 안 좋아

> (=Too much of anything can be bad)
> (=You can ruin anything with excess)

Too much of something is bad enough
ㄴ 뭐든지 너무 많은 건 좋지 않아

Too much water drowned the miller
ㄴ 지나침은 모자람만 못해

Trees that don't bend before the wind will break
ㄴ 바람에 휘지 않는 나무는 부러진다

Try every trick in the book to get their support
ㄴ 그들의 지원을 받도록 온갖 수단을 동원해 봐

Try not to alienate any supporters you may have at this moment
ㄴ 현재 너를 지지하고 있을 사람들을 소외시키지 않도록 해라

Try not to back the wrong horse
ㄴ 승산 없는 사람을 지지(원) 하지마

Try not to see anything through tinted spectacles
ㄴ 무슨 일이나 색안경을 쓰고 보지마

· **alienate** cause to be no longer friendly
· **spectacle** impressive public display

Undo this hurt you caused
↳ 네가 남긴 상처는 네가 치료해라

Wan-soo's good advice doesn't seem to work on Sang-soo
↳ 완수의 좋은 충고가 상수에게 아무 효과가 없는 것 같아

Watch that guy with sticky fingers who comes in here
↳ 여기 들어오고 있는 저 손버릇 나쁜 녀석을 주의해

We have better counsel to give than to take
↳ 좋은 충고를 하기는 쉬워도 받아들이기는 어렵다

We must be up and doing
↳ 우린 무사안일로 지내선 안 돼

We must bow to necessity
↳ 불가항력(운명)은 받아들여야 해

We'd better smarten up if we want to survive around here
↳ 우리가 여기서 살아남으려면 똑똑하게 굴어야 해

When a thing is done, advice comes too late
↳ 일이 끝난 뒤에는 조언이 필요 없다

When you jump for joy, be aware that no one moves the ground from beneath your feet
↳ 기뻐서 펄쩍펄쩍 뛸 때에 뛰어내리는 발 밑에 누군가가 흙을 치워버리지나 않는지 주의하라

You can't get away with that
↳ 그러다간 벌(꾸지람, 보복 등)을 면치 못할걸

You must make up your mind to that
↳ 넌 체념하고 받아들여(각오해)야 해

Your admonition has struck home to me
↳ 훈계가 가슴에 사무칩니다

· **admonish** rebuke

Your advice hits home with me
ㄴ 네 충고가 가슴에 와 닿는다

‣ **hit**   reach with a blow, come or cause to come in contact, affect detrimentally | discover or achieve something(+on, upon)

140. 취미 & 흥미   Hobbies & Interests

A dull subject like this is enough to switch me off
> ↳ 이런 시시한 얘기는 나한테는 너무나 흥미가 떨어져

An interesting thought just past through my mind
> ↳ 재미있는 생각이 막 떠올랐어

Are the fish biting?
> ↳ 낚시는 잘 하니?

> (=Any luck fishing?)
> (=Have you caught any fish?)
> (=Is it a good day to fish?)

Baduk requires strong concentration
> ↳ 바둑은 강한 집중력을 요해

Be careful not to flog it to death, or your customers will lose interest
> ↳ 같은 소리를 또 하고 또 해서 손님들의 흥미가 덜어지지 않도록 해

Bong-soo cleaned up at the Wha-tu card game last night
> ↳ 봉수는 어젯밤 화투판을 쓸었어

Calligraphy looks difficult, and it is
> ↳ 서예는 어려워 보이고 실제로도 어렵다

Can you fit(squeeze, crowd) in a game of bowling with me on the

---

‣ **calligraphy** beautiful penmanship

weekend?
　　ㄴ 주말에 볼링 한판 칠래?(crowd in 스케줄에 넣어주다)

Can you fold this paper into a little bird?
　　ㄴ 이 종이를 접어서 작은 새를 만들 수 있니?

Card game tomorrow? You are on
　　ㄴ 내일 카드게임 한판 하자고? 좋아(너도 끼워주지)

Cards are game, in disguise of a sport
　　ㄴ 카드게임은 게임을 가장한 전쟁이다

Chan-soo tried to duck out of going mountain-climbing
　　ㄴ 찬수는 등산 가는데 빠지려고 했어

Chang-soo bought a tape recorder and used it day and night
　　ㄴ 창수는 녹음기를 사서 밤낮 귀 따갑게 듣고 있어

Chang-soo has forgotten more about camping out than most people ever knew
　　ㄴ 창수는 대부분의 사람들이 알고 있던 것 이상으로 캠핑에 대해서 잘 안다

Chang-soo is like a kid in a candy store
　　ㄴ 참새(창수)가 방아간을 그냥 지나가겠나

Chul-soo is licking his chops because he beat me at a card game yesterday
　　ㄴ 철수는 어제 카드게임에서 나한테 이겨서 승리를 만끽하고 있어

Deal the cards. I'm hot today
　　ㄴ 카드(패) 돌려. 오늘은 계속 끝발 나네

Different strokes for different folks
　　ㄴ 사람이 다르면 취향도 달라

Doo-man is a good Baduk player, and he can beat me coming and

---

› **disguise** hide the true identity or nature of

going
> ↳ 두만이는 바둑이 세어서 나를 마음대로 이길 수 있어

Doo-soo loves skin-flicks
> ↳ 두수는 야한 영화를 좋아해

Ed likes living on the edge
> ↳ 에드는 위태로운 짓 하는 걸 즐겨해

Every man has his own taste
> ↳ 사람은 각각 좋고 싫은 것이 있다

사람마다 추구하는 취향이 다른 법이다. 우리는 사자성어로 '십인십색(十人十色)'이라고 한다. 영어에는 "To each his own 각각 그들 자신만의 것이 있다", "So many man, so many minds 사람도 많고 마음도 많다", "Tastes differ 취향은 다르다", "One man's meat is another man's poison 한 사람의 약이 다른 사람의 독이 된다" 등등의 표현이 있다.

Everyone has different standards(their own opinion)
> ↳ 제 눈에 안경이다

사람은 자신만의 관점으로 세상을 바라본다. 한국 속담에는 "제 눈에 안경이다"가 있고, 영어에는 "There is no disputing about taste 맛을 가지고 다투는 것 아니다", "Everyone to his taste 각각의 취향은 다르다", "There is no accounting for tastes 취향을 애써 설명할 필요 없다"가 있다.

Everyone has his humor
> ↳ 각인 각색

Everyone is more or less mad on one point
> ↳ 한가지 면에서는 모든 사람이 얼마간 미쳐있다

› **taste**　individual preference, critical appreciation of quality

Everyone wants to see him

    ㄴ 그는 선망의 대상이다

> (=He's everyone's idol)
> (=Everyone wants to be him)
> (=Everyone loves(admires) him)

Familiarize yourself with the rules of this game

    ㄴ 이 게임의 규칙을 잘 익혀둬

Games and recreation provide a release from tension and make people both more willing and fitting to resume their daily routines

    ㄴ 게임과 레크레이션은 긴장이완을 제공하고 사람들의 일상생활을 기꺼이 다시 시작하고 잘 적응하게 한다

Golf is so expensive that only the carriage trade play it

    ㄴ 골프는 돈이 많이 들어서 상류층만 골프를 친다

He goes on a mountain-climbing every time he turns around

    ㄴ 그는 등산을 매우 자주 가

He likes nothing better than pottering(puttering) around(about) in the garden, doing a few odd jobs

    ㄴ 그는 정원에서 자잘한 일로 소일하는 것을 무엇보다 좋아한다

He ran the table again

    ㄴ 그가 또 판을 쓸었어

He really like flying into the face of danger

    ㄴ 그는 위험에 뛰어드는 걸 너무 즐겨

Ho-yung keeps trying to beat me in Baduk, each time he tries it, he draws a blank

---

› **potter**   occupy oneself with casual or unimportant work, waste(+away)

↳ 호영이가 내게 바둑을 이기려고 애를 쓰고 있지만 매 번 실패야

I hear you(what you are saying). But I sure would like to go fishing
↳ 알(이해하)고 있어. 하지만 꼭 낚시는 가고싶어

I play Baduk in between
↳ 난 틈틈이 바둑을 둬

If fishing doesn't float your boat, there's wildlife to be seen and rapids to be rafted
↳ 낚시가 구미에 당기지 않으면 야생식물들을 볼 수 있고 급류 타기 할 급류도 있다

If life were eternal all interest and anticipation would vanish
↳ 인생이 영원하다면 모든 관심과 기대가 사라질 것이다

If they like that kind of thing, they would find it funny
↳ 그런 걸 좋아하는 사람들에게는 그게 재미있겠지(난 흥미 없어)

If you're not interested, you can jump ship
↳ 흥미 없으면 탈퇴해도 돼(무거운 절보다 가벼운 중이 떠나라)

> 꼭 필요한 불편에 대해 불평을 해서는 안 된다는 뜻이다. 맘에 안 맞는 직장이나 희망도 없는 사업에 매달려 불평만 하고 있을 것이 아니라 빨리 다른 일을 찾아보라는 충고이다. 그래서 영어로 "If you don't like the heat, get out of the kitchen 열이 싫으면 부엌에서 나가라"라고 한다.

It'll be hard for you to quit gambling once you get your feet wet
↳ 노름에 한번 손대면 끊기 힘든다

Keep your hearers interested, don't let them go off the boil
↳ 듣는 사람에게 흥미를 잃지 않게 하라, 시들하게 내버려두지 마라

Little fishes slip through nets, but great fishes are taken

‣ **raft** travel or transport by raft

ㄴ 작은 물고기들은 그물을 빠져나가지만 큰 물고기들은 잡힌다

Little minds are attracted by little minds
ㄴ 소인은 하찮은 일에 흥미를 가져

Most people like his singing, but it doesn't do anything to me
ㄴ 대부분의 사람들이 그의 노래를 좋아하지만 내겐 전혀 흥미 없어

Mountain-climbing over the weekend made me ready to drop
ㄴ 주말에 등산을 갔더니 몸이 천근이다

Music is not in my way
ㄴ 음악은 내게 취미에 맞지 않아

Newspaper reports and magazines are usually flavored with sex and violence
ㄴ 신문과 잡지는 대개 섹스와 폭력으로 독자들의 흥미를 끌려한다

Once and for all, I don't like mountain-climbing
ㄴ 딱 잘라 말해서 등산은 싫어

Patience is the name of the game in fishing
ㄴ 낚시에서 가장 중요한 것은 인내심이다

Reading such silly stories, you'll pervert your taste for good books
ㄴ 그런 저속한 얘기를 읽는다면 양서에 대한 취미를 상실하게 될 것이다

She can really make her guitar talk
ㄴ 그 여자는 기타를 기막히게 잘 쳐

She's just playing hard to get
ㄴ 그 여자는(관심 끌려고 좋아하지 않는 척) 빼고 있을 뿐이야

Sung-soo puts in five hours a day reading
ㄴ 성수는 독서하는데 하루 다섯 시간 사용한다

Tai-gyung is a square peg in a round hole when it comes to books
ㄴ 태경인 책하곤 거리가 멀어

› **flavor** give flavor to
› **peg** small pinlike piece

The card game sometimes takes us by storm

↳ 때론 우리가 카드게임에 빠지기도 해

The story you use has been worked to death many time and is no longer interesting

↳ 너의 그 얘긴 지겹게 써먹었던 터라 더 이상 흥미가 없어

There's no disputing about tastes

↳ 취미란 좋고 나쁨을 따질게 못돼

> 사람마다 추구하는 취향이 다른 법이다. 우리는 사자성어로 '십인십색(十人十色)'이라고 한다. 영어에는 "To each his own 각각 그들 자신만의 것이 있다", "So many man, so many minds 사람도 많고 마음도 많다", "Tastes differ 취향은 다르다", "One man's meat is another man's poison 한 사람의 약이 다른 사람의 독이 된다" 등등의 표현이 있다.

They played computer games non-stop for a day or so, but the novelty soon wore off

↳ 그들은 처음 하루 이틀 동안은 컴퓨터게임에 쉬지 않고 빠졌지만 신통해하던 기분이 곧 사그라졌다

They would like to see a real no-holds-barred nude show

↳ 그들은 있는 그대로 홀랑 벗는 누드 쇼를 원해

Time passes quickly when I'm absorbed in reading an interesting book

↳ 재미있는 책읽기에 빠지면 시간 가는 줄 몰라

To each his own

↳ 십인십색이다

› **novelty** something new or unusual, newness

› **absorb** suck up or take in as a sponge does, engage

사람마다 추구하는 취향이 다른 법이다. 우리는 사자성어로 '십인십색(十人十色)'이라고 한다. 영어에는 "To each his own 각각 그들 자신만의 것이 있다", "So many man, so many minds 사람도 많고 마음도 많다", "Tastes differ 취향은 다르다", "One man's meat is another man's poison 한 사람의 약이 다른 사람의 독이 된다" 등등의 표현이 있다.

To read means to borrow; to create out of one's reading is paying off one's debts
> ㄴ 독서는 남의 것을 빌리는 일이고 독서를 통한 창조는 그 빚을 갚는 일이다

We can live several lives while reading several books
> ㄴ 여러 책을 읽음으로써 여러 삶을 맛보게 된다

We have different temperaments
> ㄴ 우린 취향이 달라

Whang-dae really shines among his colleagues in Baduck
> ㄴ 바둑에서 황대는 동료들간에 빛나는 존재다

When he warmed up to his subject, his speech became very interesting
> ㄴ 그의 주제가 열기를 띄자 연설이 매우 재미있게 진행되었다

When it comes to Whatu card game, he lets himself go
> ㄴ 그 사람은 화투라면 완전히 빠져버리는 사람이야

When you play this game, don't forget to come up for air every so often
> ㄴ 이 게임을 할 때 자주 숨 돌릴 시간을 가져라

Whoever plays deep must necessarily lose his money or his character
> ㄴ 큰 도박을 하면 누구나 반드시 돈 아니면 품위를 잃게 된다

Worms will do us for bait

· **temperament** characteristic frame of mind

ㄴ 지렁이로 미끼를 하지

Would you persuade, speak of interest, not of reason

ㄴ 남을 설득하려거든 이치로 설득하지 말고 흥미 있는 말로 설득하라

"Do you want to go fishing or go on a picnic?" "I'm easy"

ㄴ "낚시하러 갈래 아니면 야유회 갈래?" "난 아무래도 좋아"

・**persuade** cause to do or believe by
argument or entreaty

141. 취직   Getting a Job

Allow me to recommend myself to your kindness, such as it is
    ↳ 부족한 점이 많지만 잘 봐주십시오

At last you have made the last cut
    ↳ 드디어 네가 최종 합격자로 뽑혔군

Bong-soo accepted the offer of a job after a week of backing and filling
    ↳ 봉수는 한 주일의 망설임 끝에 그 일자리에 취업하기로 했다

Bong-soo has to straighten out(up) if he wants to get a job
    ↳ 봉수가 취직을 하려면 행동을 바로잡아야 해

Bong-soo passed the test in one go
    ↳ 봉수는 한 번에 시험에 합격했어

Can I leave my resume with you just in case anything opens up?
    ↳ 혹시 새로 자리가 날지 모르니까 이력서를 놓고 가겠습니다

Can you place me with a company that makes electronic goods?
    ↳ 전자제품 만드는 회사에 취직시켜줄 수 있겠습니까?

Cash in on it and get a job this time
    ↳ 기회를 살려서 이번엔 취직을 해라

Comparison of my background and professional qualifications with your candidate descriptions, as specified in this advertizement, suggest that I would be an excellent candidate for this interesting position
    ↳ 이 광고에 기재된 구인조건과 제 전문성 및 배경을 비교해 보니 제가

▸ **recommend**   present as deserving of acceptance or trial, advice   ▸ **resume**   return to or take up again after interruption

이 직책에 적격이라는 걸 알았습니다

Don't sell yourself short at the interview or you'll never get the job
↳ 면접에서 주눅들지 마라, 주눅들면 일자리를 얻지 못해

Dong-soo is divided between joining the army and taking a job
↳ 동수는 군에 입대할지 취직을 할지 마음을 정하지 못하고 있다

Ed did fine on the orals but fell down on the written exam
↳ 에드가 구술시험은 잘 했지만 필기시험에 잡쳤어

Everything seems to be going(coming) his way with offers of work from all over the place
↳ 그에게 사방에서 일자리가 쇄도하니 신났어

Face up to the facts of life and get a job
↳ 현실에 뛰어들어 직장을 가져라(**facts of life** 에는 '성교육'의 뜻도 있음)

Fill it out and leave nothing blank
↳ 한 칸도 남김없이 다 기입하시오

He has been pounding the pavement
↳ 그는 직장을 구하고 다녀

He was short-listed for the job
↳ 그는 입사시험 1차에 합격했어

He'll fully justify your confidence if you offer him a position with your firm
↳ 그가 귀사에 취직된다면 기대를 저버리지 않을 겁니다

How can he get a job after being behind bars for many years?
↳ 교도소에서 몇 년씩이나 복역한 사람이 어떻게 취직을 할까?

How did you get your first break?
↳ 넌 그 첫 취직자리를 어떻게 구했니?

· **oral** spoken, relating to the mouth

I appreciate your time in reviewing my enclosed resume and would welcome the opportunity to meet and discuss my qualifications and experience with you

    ↳ 제 이력서를 읽어주셔서 감사 드리며 귀하를 뵙고 저의 자격과 경력에 대해서 더 많은 말씀을 드리고 싶습니다

I believe that my background, qualifications and work experience are well-suited to your company's specific requirements

    ↳ 저의 학력, 자격, 경력이 귀사의 요구조건에 잘 맞는다고 생각합니다

I'm sure that he will be an asset to your company and I highly recommend him for the position of software programing supervisor

    ↳ 그는 귀사의 훌륭한 인적자산이 되리라 확신하며 귀사의 소프트웨어 프로그래밍 매니저 자리에 강력히 추천합니다

It's a good idea to let him in on the ground floor, so that he is keen to learn on the job

    ↳ 그가 업무에 대해서 열성을 가지고 배우도록 말단에서 시작하게 하는 게 좋아

Jin-soo just barely squeaked through the exam, but he got the job

    ↳ 진수는 간신히 시험에 합격했지만 취직은 됐어

Jin-soo wants to know what prospects such work hold out

    ↳ 진수는 그 일자리의 전망에 대하여 알고싶어해

Jung-soo has taken a new job with an automobile company but is quite out of his depth with that kind of work

    ↳ 정수는 자동차회사에 새로 취업했지만 그런 일은 그에게 매우 어려웠다

Large firms recruit by preference with pretence of open competition

    ↳ 대기업들이 겉으로는 공채를 하는 척 하면서 속으로는 특채를 하고 있다

Looking for someone with the right stuff is not easy

‣ **supervisor** one who has charge of

‣ **squeak** make a thin high-pitched sound

‣ **recruit** newly enlisted member, enlist the membership or service of

ㄴ 그런 요건을 갖춘 사람을 구하기란 쉽지 않아

Many are called, but few are chosen

ㄴ 대상은 많지만 뽑히기는 어려워

My services are at your disposal

ㄴ 무슨 일이든 시켜만 주십시오

Nobody is going to hand a job to you on a silver platter

ㄴ 취직이란 게 누가 자리 비워놓고 "어서 오십시오" 하는 게 아냐

Poor handwriting is a liability in getting a job

ㄴ 악필은 취업에 불리하다

Sang-soo has been knocking on doors

ㄴ 상수는 일자리를 찾고있는 중

Sang-soo is in between jobs now

ㄴ 상수는 실(구)직 중이야

Screen out undesirable job applicants through several rounds of acid test

ㄴ 여러 차례 엄격한 시험을 거쳐서 부적합한 지원자들을 걸러내어라

She can smooth the way for me to get a job with that company

ㄴ 그녀는 내가 그 회사에 취직하는데 쉽도록 도와 줄 수 있어

She had nothing to write home about her career and her bag of tricks was soon empty at the job interview

ㄴ 그녀는 자신의 경력에 대해 이렇다하게 내세울 것이 없고 보니 입사 면접시험에서 이내 답변할 밑천이 떨어지고 말았다

She is in need of someone with a proven track record in accounting

ㄴ 그녀는 회계부문에서 경력이 검증된 사람을 필요로 한다

Since I got a job, a lot of water passed under the bridge

ㄴ 내가 취직하고 난 후에 많은 것이 변했다

The application was tried and found(to be) wanting

· **platter** large serving plate

ㄴ 지원자는 응시했으나 부적격 판정을 받았다

Their office is stocked with applications
ㄴ 그들 사무(영업)소에 응시원서를 비치하고 있다

There's a growing number of openings for women in business
ㄴ 여자들에게 취업기회가 점점 늘어나고 있다

They need someone who is hard-working and who knows what the score is
ㄴ 그들에게는 열심히 일하면서도 기민한 사람이 필요해

Ugly looks and poor writing are a liability in getting a job
ㄴ 흉한 외모와 악필은 취직에 불리해

We need someone neat, enthusiastic, and quick on the uptake
ㄴ 우리는 깔끔하고, 열정적이고, 머리가 잘 돌아가는 사람이 필요해

What I need is a cushy job with business trips to Hawaii every month
ㄴ 매월 하와이로 출장이나 다니면서 쉽게 돈버는 일자리가 있었으면 좋으련만

When the rising prices are combined with a lack of jobs, many people suffer and the nation becomes poorer
ㄴ 물가가 오르는데 취업마저 어려워지면 나라가 점점 가난해진다

Who's got the nod for that job?
ㄴ 누가 그 일에 낙점 받았지?

You can recommend him without reservation
ㄴ 그 사람을 전적으로 추천해도 돼

You have to realize that I'm acting against my better judgement in allowing you to be engaged
ㄴ 너보다 더 나은 사람이 있는데도 네게 일자리를 준다는 걸 알아야 해

You will come to your own when you get a job

▸ **enthusiasm** strong excitement of feeling ▸ **cushy** easy
▸ **uptake** understanding

ㄴ 넌 취직하면 제 자리를 찾게 될 거야

Your brother is the manager, you've got your job in the bag

ㄴ 네 형이 책임자이니 일자리야 따 논 당상이잖아

▸ **manage**   control, direct or carry on business
           or affairs, cope

142. 친구   Friends

A broken friendship may be soldered, but will never be sound
   ↳ 깨어진 우정에 땜질을 할 수는 있으나 온전해 지지는 않는다

A doubtful friend is worse than a certain enemy
   ↳ 의심스러운 친구는 확실한 적보다 더 나쁘다

A false friend and a shadow attend only while the sun shines
   ↳ 신의 없는 친구와 그림자는 햇빛이 비칠 때에만 따라다닌다

A few people go a long way with me
   ↳ 사람이 두·세 명만 있어도 내겐 큰 도움이 된다

A friend in court is better than a penny in purse
   ↳ 높은 자리에 있는 친구는 지갑 속의 돈보다 낫다

A friend in power is a friend lost
   ↳ 권력을 쥐고있는 친구는 잃어버린 친구이다

A friend is easier lost than found
   ↳ 친구를 잃기는 쉬워도 구하기는 어렵다

A friend is one who knows all about you and still likes you
   ↳ 진정한 친구는 너에 대해 모든 것을 알면서도 당신을 좋아한다

A friend that you buy with presents will be bought from you
   ↳ 선물을 주고 사는 친구는 또다시 너에게서 팔려나갈 것이다

A friend to everybody and to nobody is the same thing
   ↳ 모든 사람에게 친구가 되는 사람과 아무에게도 친구가 못 되는 사람

› **solder**   metallic alloy melted to join metallic
          surfaces, cement with solder

은 마찬가지로 문제 있는 사람이다

A good friend is better than a hundred relatives

    ㄴ 좋은 친구 한 명이 친척 100명보다 낫다

A near neighbour is better than a far dwelling kinsman

    ㄴ 이웃사촌

> 가까운 이웃, 친구가 먼 친척보다 낫다는 말이다. 한국에 '이웃사촌'이란 말이 있듯이 영어로는 'Near neighbor is better than a distant cousin'이라고 풀어서 표현한다.

A true friend would have acted differently

    ㄴ 진정한 친구라면 그렇게 행동하진 않았을 것이다

A wise king wouldn't want his friends and officials to lick his boots

    ㄴ 현명한 왕이라면 그의 친구와 신하들에게 아부하기를 원치 않을 것이다

A wise man gets more use from his enemies than a fool

    ㄴ 어리석은 자가 친구에게서 얻는 것 이상으로 현명한 자는 적으로부터 쓸모 있는 것을 얻는다

As a man is, so is his company

    ㄴ 친구를 보면 사람됨을 알 수 있다

Better a neighbor near than a brother far

    ㄴ 가까운 이웃이 먼 친척보다 낫다

› **relative**   person connected with another by blood or marriage

› **kinsman**   male relative

Better to be alone than in bad company
↳ 나쁜 친구와 사귀는 것보다 혼자 있는 게 낫다

> 나쁜 친구를 경계하라는 뜻이다. 앞에 'You had'가 생략된 충고형 문장이다.
> 비슷한 뜻으로 "A man is known by the company he keeps 사람은 그
> 의 친구로서 평가된다"가 있다.

Between friends there's no need of justice
↳ 친구간에는 정의가 필요 없다

Books and friends should be few and good
↳ 책과 친구의 수는 적어야 좋고 내용이 알차야 한다

Chang-soo has other fish to fry and is out of circulation with his friends
↳ 창수는 다른 중요한 일이 있어서 친구들하고 어울리지 않아

Count not him among your friends who'll retail your privacies to the world
↳ 당신의 개인적인 일을 여기 저기 떠들고 다니는 사람을 친구로 삼지 말라

Defend me from my friends!
↳ 알랑쇠는 딱 질색이야!

Doo-chul cheated me under the name of friendship
↳ 두철이는 우정이란 이름으로 나를 속였어

Duck-soo's been deceiving his girl friend with other girls
↳ 덕수는 여자친구를 배신한 채 다른 여자들을 사귀어 왔어

Ed's friend threw him a lifeline in the form of a million won loan when he was in a pinch
↳ 에드가 어려움을 당했을 때 그의 친구가 백만원을 빌려줘서 구원해 주었다

‣ **company** guests, infantry unit

‣ **lifeline** line to which persons may cling to save or protect their lives

Friends show their love in time of trouble, not in happiness
ㄴ 친구는 행복할 때가 아닌 어려울 때 애정을 나타낸다

> 어려움에 부딪혀 봐야 진정으로 친구를 알아 볼 수 있다는 말이다. 더 자주 쓰이는 표현으로 "A friend in need is the friend indeed 필요할 때 옆에 있어주는 친구가 진정한 친구이다"가 있다.

Friendship admits the difference of character, as love does that of sex
ㄴ 우정은 성격 차를 용납한다, 사랑에서 이성을 허용하듯이

Friendship is a plant which must be often watered
ㄴ 우정은 물을 자주 주어야 하는 식물이다

Friendship is a single-soul dwelling in two bodies
ㄴ 우정은 두 몸에 따로 있는 한 개의 정신이다

Friendship is a two-way street
ㄴ 우정이란 서로에게 도움이 되어야 이루어진다

Friendship makes prosperity more brilliant, and lightens adversity by dividing and sharing it
ㄴ 우정은 친구의 번영을 더욱 빛나게 하고 친구의 역경을 나누어 가짐으로써 가볍게 해준다

Friendship ought to be immortal, hostilities mortal
ㄴ 우정은 영원하고 적대감은 일시적이어야 한다

Friendship, stability, and trust are frequently mentioned as criteria for a worthwhile relationship between two people
ㄴ 우정, 안정성, 신뢰가 두 사람간의 가치 있는 관계의 기준으로 종종 언급된다

Friendships provoked become the bitterest enemy

· **admit** allow to enter, permit
· **criteria** standard

· **provoke** incite to anger, stir up on purpose

ㄴ 친구의 성질을 건드리면 가장 잔인한 적이 된다

Gratitude preserves old friendships, and procures new ones

ㄴ 감사의 표시는 옛 우정을 유지시켜 줄 뿐 아니라 새로운 우정을 쌓게
해 준다

He gave his friend away to the police, hoping to escape punishment

ㄴ 그는 처벌을 면할 생각에서 친구의 행적을 경찰에 불어버렸다

**He had enough presence of mind to rescue his friend from the
wreckage**

ㄴ 그는 매우 침착하게 잔해에서 친구를 구조했다

He has been carrying on with his wife's best friend

ㄴ 아내의 가장 친한 친구와 바람을 피워

He is my friend who speaks well of me behind my back

ㄴ 내가 없는 데서 내게 좋은 말을 해 주는 사람이야말로 참다운 친구다

He makes no friends who never made a foe

ㄴ 적을 만들지 않은 사람은 친구를 만들지 못한다

**He regretted the number of acquaintanceships in his life that had
never developed into friendships**

ㄴ 그의 생애에서 친구로까지 진전되지 못했던 많은 지인 관계를 아쉽게
여겼다

He who is afraid of making enemies will never have true friends

ㄴ 적을 만들까봐 두려워하는 사람은 친구를 만들지 못한다

**He who touches pitches shall be defiled therewith=Who keeps
company with the wolf will learn to howl**

ㄴ 近墨者黑(근묵자흑)

- **gratitude** state of being grateful
- **procure** get possession of

- **acquaintance** personal knowledge, person
with who one is acquainted

> 나쁜 친구를 사귀면 나쁜 사람이 된다는 뜻이다. 성경에는 "Bad company corrupts good character 나쁜 친구는 좋은 성격을 방해한다"라는 표현이 있다. 영어 속담으로는 "Evil communication corrupts good manners"라는 성경에서 유래한 표현이 있다.

He who treats his friends and enemies alike, has neither love nor justice
> ㄴ 친구와 적을 똑같이 취급하는 사람은 사랑도 정의도 없는 사람이다

He's a buddy from my old stomping ground
> ㄴ 그는 죽마고우야

> 영어에는 한국의 '죽마고우(竹馬故友)'처럼 향수를 불러일으키는 표현은 없지만, 보통 'my buddy'라고 소개하면 아주 가까운 친구, 어릴 적부터 친구를 뜻한다. 또한, 'My buddy from my old stomping ground 옛날부터 같이 다니는 친구'라는 표현도 간혹 쓴다. 'Stomping ground'는 '늘 다니던 길'이란 뜻을 가졌다.

He's my bosom friend(soul brother)
> ㄴ 그는 뜻이 통하는 친구다

Her boyfriend has been stepping out on her
> ㄴ 그녀의 남자친구가 바람을 피우고 있어

Here's to our friendship!
> ㄴ 건배!

However rare true love may be, it is less so than true friendship
> ㄴ 진정한 사랑을 아무리 찾기 어렵다해도 진정한 우정만큼 찾기 어렵지는 않다

I have a boy(girl) friend
> ㄴ 난 사귀는 사람이 있어요

· **corrupt** change from good to bad, bribe | · **bosom** breast, intimate
· **stomp** stamp

(=I'm not single)
(=I have a relationship)
(=I'm with somebody)
(=I'm not available)

I would like to associate on friendly terms with you
> 허물없이 지내고 싶어

If he's willing to go half way with me(meet me halfway), we'll be friends again
> 그가 타협으로 나오면 다시 친해질 수 있어

If you'll pardon the liberty, you cheated him under pretence of friendship
> 주제넘은 말 같지만 넌 친한 척 하면서 그를 속였어

In adversity friends stay away of their own accord
> 역경에 처하면 누가 시키지 않아도 친구가 멀어진다

It's easier to forgive an enemy than to forgive a friend
> 친구보다 적을 용서하는 것이 더 쉽다

It's like they are joined at the hips
> 바늘 가는데 실 간다(단짝)

(=where the needle goes, the thread will follow)
(=They are like two peas in a pod)
(=They are like peanut butter and jelly)

It's curious how often one prefers his enemies to his friends
> 친구보다 적을 더 좋아했던 일이 얼마나 많았던가는 희한한 일이다

> **associate** join in companionship or partnership, connect in though

> **accord** grant, agree, agreement

Jin-soo should stay at arm's length from any liquor(such a friend)
> 진수는 술이란 술(그런 친구)을 멀리 해야 해

Let's stay friends
> 계속 우정을 나누며 지내자

Money gone, friends gone
> 돈 떨어지면 죽는 날이다

My friend cast out his daughter when she married against his wishes
> 우리 친구는 딸이 뜻을 거역해 결혼하자 다시는 안 본다며 의절을 선언했어

My friend stabbed me in the back
> 믿는 도끼에 발등 찍혔어

"믿는 도끼에 발등 찍혔다"에 해당하는 영어 표현은 "Stabbed in the back 등을 찔렸다"이다. 또한 강아지가 주인의 손을 무는 상황에 비유하여 "Bite the hand that feeds you 먹이를 주는 손을 문다"라고도 한다.

My friend was getting old then long before his time
> 친구는 그 때 나이보다 훨씬 겉늙어 있었다

Nothing broadens your horizons as having friends
> 친구를 사귀는 이상으로 견문을 넓혀 주는 것은 없다

One friend in a lifetime is much; two are many; three are hardly possible
> 일생에 한 사람의 친구를 사귀는 일은 대단한 일이고, 두 사람은 너무 많으며, 세 사람은 거의 불가능하다

One of my friends rolled around(round) when I was getting coffee ready this morning

---

· **stab** wound given by a pointed weapon, quick thrust, attempt

· **broaden** widen, clear or open

ㄴ 오늘 오전 커피를 마시려 할 때 친구 하나가 불쑥 찾아왔다

One sheep follows another
ㄴ 친구 따라 강남 간다

Over a bottle many a friend is found
ㄴ 술자리에 가면 많은 친구가 생긴다

Prosperity is full of friends
ㄴ 잘 나갈 때는 친구가 넘쳐난다

Prosperity makes friends, adversity tries them
ㄴ 번영은 친구를 만들고 역경은 친구를 시험한다

Real friendship does not freeze in winter
ㄴ 진정한 우정은 겨울이 되어도 얼지 않는다

She had her head in the clouds until her friend was promoted
ㄴ 그 여자는 자기 친구가 승진할 때까지 건성으로 일하고 있었다

Short debts make long friends
ㄴ 빚을 빨리 갚아야 우정이 길어져

> 가까운 사이일수록 금전 관계를 조심해야 한다는 뜻이다. 친구끼리의 빚 독촉도 곤란하고, 돈을 갚지 못하는 입장도 곤란하다. 비슷한 뜻으로 "Lend your money and lose your friend 돈을 빌려주면 친구를 잃는다"도 쓰인다.

Slight misunderstanding may sever lifelong friendship
ㄴ 사소한 오해가 평생의 우정을 갈라놓을 수 있다

Small gifts make friends, great ones make enemies
ㄴ 작은 선물은 친구를 만들고 큰 선물은 적을 만든다

Sook-hee moved in on Jung-hee's boy friend and now they are not talking to each other

---

- **prosperity** economic well-being
- **adversity** hard times

↳ 숙회가 정희의 남자친구를 가로채는 바람에 이제 서로 말도 안하고 지내

The enemy's enemy is your friend
　　　　↳ 적의 적은 친구이다

The firmest friendships have been formed in mutual adversity
　　　　↳ 가장 단단한 우정은 역경을 같이할 때 생겨난다

The friends we rub up against in our early years in school make a great difference to our future
　　　　↳ 초년 학생시절에 사귄 친구가 우리의 장래에 큰 영향을 미친다

The only good friend is a dead friend
　　　　↳ 그까짓 친구라면 없는 게 낫지

The quarrels of friends are the opportunities of foes
　　　　↳ 친구의 싸움이 적에게는 기회가 된다

The rich knows not who is his friend
　　　　↳ 부자는 누가 자신의 친구인지 모른다

The stillest tongue can be the truest friend
　　　　↳ 가만히 있는 혀가 참된 친구가 될 수 있다

There should be courtesy even between close friends
　　　　↳ 친한 사이에도 예절은 지켜야해

> 처음 만나는 사람에게는 모두가 예의를 갖추지만, 친해지면 상대를 함부로 대하기 쉽다. 그렇지만 친한 사이일수록 거래도 조심해야 하며 예의도 지켜야 한다. 너무 친하면 공경하는 태도가 없어지지만, 거리를 두고 지내면 존경심을 갖게 된다(Familiarity breeds contempt, while rarity wins admiration).

They are like peas and carrots

· **mutual**　given or felt by one another in equal amount, common

· **courtesy**　courteous behavior

↳ 그들은 붙어 다니는 짝꿍이야

Time, which strengthens friendship, weakens love
↳ 시간은 우정을 두텁게 하지만 사랑은 약하게 한다

> 사랑은 시간이 지나면 퇴색한다는 뜻이다. 비슷한 뜻으로 'Love me little, love me long 사랑은 가늘고 길게'도 많이 쓰인다. 직역하면 "나는 조금씩 오래 사랑하라"이다. '백년해로'란 말을 결혼하는 커플들에게 많이 얘기하지만 말처럼 쉽지만은 않다.

Treat a friend as if he might become a foe
↳ 친구가 원수로 변할 수도 있다는 조심스러운 마음으로 친구를 대하라

We are bosom bodies
↳ 우린 죽마고우야

> 영어에는 한국의 '죽마고우(竹馬故友)'처럼 향수를 불러일으키는 표현은 없지만, 보통 'my buddy'라고 소개하면 아주 가까운 친구, 어릴 적부터 친구를 뜻한다. 또한, 'My buddy from my old stomping ground 옛날부터 같이 다니던 친구'라는 표현도 간혹 쓴다. 'Stomping ground'는 '늘 다니던 길'이란 뜻을 가졌다(=We go way back).

We make our friends; we make our enemies; but God makes our next door neighbor
↳ 우리는 친구를 만들고 적을 만든다; 그러나 신은 우리의 이웃을 만드셨다

Why are you so buddy-buddy with me?
↳ 왜 나하고 친한 척 하는 거니?

Wishing to be friendship is quick work, but friendship is a slow-ripening fruit

---

› **buddy** friend

↳ 우정을 만들고 싶은 마음은 재빨리 생겨나지만 우정은 더디게 익는 과일이다

You can't be friends upon any other terms than upon the terms of equality

↳ 동등한 관계가 아니고서는 친구가 될 수 없다

You shall judge of a man by his foes as well as by his friends

↳ 그의 친구 뿐 아니라 그의 적이 누군가에 따라 사람을 판단하라

You'll always find a friend in me

↳ 언제라도 힘이 되어 줄께

Your friend's name flitted through my mind, only to be forgotten again

↳ 네 친구 이름은 언뜻 생각이 났다가도 그저 잊어버려져

‣ **equality** of the same quantity, value, quality, number, or status as another

‣ **foe** enemy

‣ **flit** dart

143. 칭찬   Compliments

A voice like that is few and far between(very rare, one in a million)
　└ 그런 목소리는 100년에 한 번 있을까 말까 해

A woman will doubt everything you say except if it compliments herself
　└ 여자는 자신에 대한 찬사 외에는 무슨 말을 해도 의심한다

All the credit goes to you
　└ 모두 너의 공이다

An-do has the Midas touch
　└ 안도의 손에만 가면 신품 같이 돼(안 되는 일이 없어)

Anything(Everything) looks good on you
　└ 옷걸이가 좋군요

Appreciation begets ambition
　└ 칭찬은 야망을 낳아

Aren't you dressed to kill!
　└ 야, 멋지다(멋지게 입었네)

Awesome!
　└ 끝내주는군(너무 좋아)

(＝This is incredible!)
(＝Cool!)

▸ **rare**   having a portion relatively uncooked

▸ **compliment**   flattering remark, pay a compliment to

Backhanded compliments are insults in disguise
ㄴ 빈정거리는 투로 칭찬하는 말은 위장된 모욕이다

Byung-ho is as innocent as a new-born baby
ㄴ 병호는 정말 깨끗해

Chang-ho has the patience of a saint(Job)
ㄴ 창호는 돌부처 같은 인내심을 가졌어

Chang-ho really plays it safe(enough)
ㄴ 창호는 정말 신중해

Chang-soo is very good(much) in command of himself
ㄴ 창수는 자제력이 대단해

Chul-soo has something of the boss in him(his nature)
ㄴ 철수는 윗 사람다운 데가 있어

Don't damn me with faint praise
ㄴ 나를 칭찬하는 듯 하면서 헐뜯지마

Don't let all this praise go to your head
ㄴ 칭찬 좀 들었다고 우쭐해 하지마

Dong-soo damns others with faint praise
ㄴ 동수는 남들을 칭찬하는 척 하면서 곧잘 헐뜯는다

Dong-soo is a monument of industry
ㄴ 동수는 보기 드문 근면가이다

Dong-soo is sincerity personified
ㄴ 동수는 성실의 귀감이야

Ed looks a little tacky, but he's a diamond in the rough
ㄴ 에드가 볼품 없어 보이지만 싹수가 있는 사람이다

Every single thing you do is right
ㄴ 당신이 하는 일은 뭐든지 옳아요

› **disguise** hide the true identity or nature of, something that conceals	› **sincere** genuine or honest
	› **personify** represent as a human being

Expect not praise without envy until you are dead
> ↳ 죽기 전에는 질투 없는 칭찬을 기대하지 마라

For my money, he's one of the best I've had
> ↳ 내 생각에 그는 어느 누구보다 좋은 사람중의 하나지

For this I give him full marks and I hope history will do the same
> ↳ 이 일에 나는 최대의 찬사를 그에게 보내는 바이며 역사도 그에게 최대의 찬사를 보내기 바란다

Generally we praise to be praised
> ↳ 대개 우리는 칭찬을 받기 위해서 칭찬한다

Gil-soo's good qualities and his faults cancel out
> ↳ 길수의 훌륭한 점이 그의 허물을 덮어준다

He goes heart and soul into anything
> ↳ 그는 무슨 일이고 열심히 해

He has a finger in every pie
> ↳ 그는 약방의 감초다

He has more goodness in his little finger than you have altogether
> ↳ 그는 너보다 훨씬 훌륭한 사람이야

He has no respect of persons
> ↳ 그는 편파심이 없다

> (He respects persons 그는 편파심이 있다)
> (have respect for people 존경하다)

He is nothing, if not a sales man
> ↳ 그는 매우 훌륭한 판매원이야

He is nothing, if not kind

▸ **praise** express approval of, glorify
▸ **generally** relating to the whole, applicable to all of a group, common or widespread

ↆ 그는 무척 친절하다(친절 빼면 시체)

He is the last word in architecture
ↆ 그는 건축의 최고 권위자이다

He made the right move
ↆ 그가 한 일은 잘한 일이다

He's a quick child
ↆ 그는 머리회전이 빨라

He's good news in many ways
ↆ 그는 여러 가지 면에서 나무랄 데 없는 사람이다

His idea is out of this world
ↆ 그의 생각은 훌륭해

How big of you to obtain the scholarship
ↆ 네가 장학금을 타다니 장하기도 하구나

I don't want any more back-handed compliments
ↆ 더 이상의 겉치레 찬사는 원치 않아

I feel much flattered by your compliments
ↆ 그렇게 말씀해 주시니 송구합니다

I know you have your feet on the ground
ↆ 넌 사리분별이 있는 사람이잖아

I'm begging(looking) for a compliment(congratulations, gratitude)
ↆ 엎드려 절 받기로군

I'm so glad I finally caught you
ↆ 겨우 연락이 되어 기쁘군요

I'm sure you more than deserve the recognition
ↆ 넌 인정을 받고도 남을 사람

· **obtain** gain by effort, be generally recognized | · **back-hand** stroke made with the back of the hand turned forward

If you want your children to improve, let them overhear the nice things you say about them to others
> ↳ 당신의 자녀가 나아지기를 원한다면 다른 사람들에게 그들의 칭찬을 하면서 그들이 엿듣게 하라

In-ho is laying it on thick because he wants you to do him a favor
> ↳ 인호는 네게 아쉬운 소리가 있어서 혀가 닳게 찬사를 늘어놓고 있는 거야

It's a good lookout for you
> ↳ 넌 전도가 밝아

Jong-soo will surely make things go
> ↳ 종수는 일을 끝내주게 처리할거야

Joo-young is always forward to help(in helping) others
> ↳ 주영이는 언제나 자진해서 남을 도우려 하고 있어

Let's all give Guang-woo a pat on the back
> ↳ 우리 모두 광우에게 축하(찬사)해 줍시다

Modesty is the only sure angle bait when you angle for praise
> ↳ 칭찬을 받으려면 겸손함이 유일한 미끼가 된다

Moon-soo has an memory like an elephant
> ↳ 문수는 기억력이 굉장히 좋아

Newspapers acclaimed Whang Young-Jo an exemplary national hero, extolled the virtues of his diligent, assiduous training
> ↳ 신문에서는 황영조 선수를 크게 칭찬하고, 그의 근면함, 정성을 다하는 미덕을 높이 칭찬했다

Nobody feels offended by compliments
> ↳ 칭찬 받고 화내는 사람은 없어

Not only does sucking up help your relationship with peers, it does wonders for the boss

---

‣ **lookout** one who watches, careful watch	‣ **extol** praise highly
‣ **acclaim** give praise to, declare	‣ **assiduous** diligent

↳ 칭찬(아부)은 동료들과의 관계개선에 도움을 줄 뿐 아니라 상사에게 신통한 효과가 있다

People ask you for criticism, but they only want praise
↳ 사람들은 자신을 비판해 달라고 말하지만 실은 단지 칭찬만을 원한다

Praise by evil men is dispraise
↳ 악한 사람의 칭찬은 비방이다

Praise is more obstructive than a reproach
↳ 칭찬은 꾸지람보다 더 큰 방해가 된다

Praise is the reflection of virtue
↳ 칭송은 덕행을 반영한다

Praise makes good men better and wicked men worse
↳ 칭찬은 착한 사람을 더욱 착하게 만들고 나쁜 사람을 더욱 나쁘게 만든다

Praise owes it's value only to it's scarcity
↳ 칭찬의 가치는 그 희소성에 있다

Praise without profits puts little in the pot
↳ 실속 없는 칭찬은 밥 먹여 주지 않는다

Praises from wicked men are reproaches
↳ 악한 사람으로부터의 칭찬은 꾸지람이다

Proper praise can improve work relationships
↳ 제대로 한 칭찬은 직장의 대인관계를 개선시킨다

Refuse of praise is a desire to be praised twice
↳ 칭찬에 대한 사양은 곱으로 칭찬하기를 바라는 것이다

She praised her dog and rewarded him a tidbit when her dog obeyed her instructions
↳ 그녀는 개가 시키는 대로하자 칭찬을 하면서 먹을 것을 한 입 감 주었다

She's drawn a great deal of praise for the way she handled that case

---

▸ **reproach** disgrace, rebuke, express disapproval to	▸ **scarcity** not plentiful, rare
	▸ **tidbit** choice morsel

↳ 그녀가 그 일을 처리한 방법에 대하여 큰 찬사를 얻었다

She's long sung the praise of country life and finally moved to Yong-in
↳ 그녀는 오랫동안 전원생활에 찬사를 보내더니 끝내 용인으로 이사를 갔다

Such a person commands our spontaneous respect
↳ 저런 사람에 대해서는 존경심이 저절로 우러난다

Sung-soo sound his wife's praises far and wide
↳ 성수는 어디로 가나 부인 칭찬만 해

Tai-gyung is not out for compliments
↳ 태경이는 칭찬을 들으려는 게 아냐

Take his praise as a kind of lip service
↳ 그의 칭찬을 입 발린 소리쯤으로 알아라

That's a compliment
↳ 과찬이시군요

(=I'm flattered)

That's admirable
↳ 장하다

(=I really admire you)
(=You should be commended for)

That's where you are so great
↳ 그게 너의 훌륭한 점이지

The house praises the carpenter

▸ **spontaneous** done, produced, or occurring naturally or without planning

▸ **admire** have high regard for

ㄴ 사람은 이루어놓은 업적에 따라 평가된다

The suggestion does you credit

ㄴ 네가 그런 제안을 하다니 훌륭하군

There is not much to be said for it

ㄴ 별로 칭찬할게 못돼

Virtue is praised by all, but practised by few

ㄴ 덕은 모든 사람이 칭송하지만 행하는 사람은 거의 없다

We can't at once catch the applauses of the vulgar and expect the approbation of the wise

ㄴ 우리는 속된 사람에게서 박수도 받으면서 동시에 현명한 사람의 칭찬을 받을 수는 없다

We have to hand it to Bong-soo

ㄴ 봉수의 공은 인정해 주어야 해

What you say is shot through with the praise for the boss

ㄴ 네 말은 상사에 대한 칭찬 일색이군

Words of praise seldom fall from his lips

ㄴ 좀처럼 그에게 칭찬 받기 힘들어

You always do the nicest things

ㄴ 넌 하는 일 마다 예쁘구나

(=You are such a nice person)
(=you are so thoughtful)

You are above praise

ㄴ 너를 뭐라고 칭찬해야 할지 모르겠구나

You are complimenting me against your will

‣ **vulgar** relating to the common people, lacking refinement

‣ **approbation** approval

ㄴ 엎드려 절 받기로군

(=I'm pressing(forcing, burdening) you to compliment me)

You are really going to town this month
ㄴ 너 이 달에 잘 나가는구나(실적 좋구나)

You are really onto something this time
ㄴ 이번엔 정말 한 건 한 것 같구나

You are really something else
ㄴ 야, 넌 정말 훌륭하구나

You are something else
ㄴ 너 대단하구나

You are still the same person
ㄴ 너 여전하구나

(=Just the same as ever)

You deserve a pat on the back
ㄴ 넌 칭찬 받을만해

You did the right thing
ㄴ 잘 했어

You have come a long way
ㄴ 너 많이 발전했구나

You look fit to kill
ㄴ 너 끝내 주게 멋있네

· **pat** light tap, small mass, tap gently, apt
or glib

You look like a million dollars

     ㄴ 너 신수가 훤해 보이는구나

You must be gifted with second sight

     ㄴ 넌 틀림없이 천리안을 가졌어

Yours is a real rags to riches story

     ㄴ 너 정말 개천에서 용 났구나

> 한국에서 용은 귀함을 대표하지만, 서양에서는 괴물, 악마를 뜻한다. 따라서
> 비슷한 뜻으로 'A white egg laid by a black hen(검은 닭이 난 하얀 알)'
> 이나, 'A rag to riches story(누더기에서 부자가 된 이야기)'가 쓰인다.

› **rag** waste piece of cloth

144. 태도   Attitude

Being a star soccer player goes to Jong-soo's head
ㄴ 종수가 이름 있는 축구선수가 되더니 교만해졌어

Byung-soo's innocent air is all put on
ㄴ 병수의 천진난만한 태도는 연기에 불과해

Chan-soo's in-your-face confrontational style turns a lot of people off
ㄴ 찬수의 안하무인격인 태도에 많은 사람들이 밥맛 떨어지고 있어

He began to sing a different tune
ㄴ 그의 태도가 달라지기 시작했어

He has an equable way of dealing with people
ㄴ 그는 누구에게나 한결같은 태도로 대한다

He was very off-putting with a very abrupt manner that made everyone feel uncomfortable
ㄴ 그는 모든 사람들을 불편하게 하는 불쑥불쑥한 태도로 매우 불쾌감을 준다

His manner, if patronizing, was not unkind
ㄴ 선심 쓰는 척 했지만 그의 태도가 불친절하지는 않았다

Manners are the happy ways of doing things
ㄴ 훌륭한 태도는 행복하게 일하는 방법이다

Morality is simply the attitude we adopt towards people whom we personally dislike
ㄴ 도덕은 단지 우리가 개인적으로 싫어하는 사람에 대해 취하는 태도이다

› **abrupt** sudden, so quick as to seem rude | › **patronize** be a customer of, treat with condescension

Nobody likes his devil-may-care attitude about flying
ㄴ 그의 조심성 없는 비행기 조종 태도를 아무도 좋아하지 않아

Our boss will take a drastic measure and won't let the contumacious, discordant behavior of any employees ruin the harmonious atmosphere
ㄴ 사장은 단호한 태도로 직장의 조화로운 분위기를 깨는 어떤 직원의 불손하고 거슬리는 행동도 가만두지 않을 것이다

Sang-soo stormed off and came back with hat in hand when he ran out of money
ㄴ 상수는 휭 하니 떠났다가 돈이 떨어지자 공손한 태도로 돌아왔다

She whistled a different tune later
ㄴ 그 여자는 나중에 태도를 바꾸었다

Soon-ho is wedded to smoke-and-mirrors posturing
ㄴ 순호는 애매한 태도야

Tai-ho's obstinate refusal to tell you about his bankruptcy is typical of him
ㄴ 태호가 파산에 대해서 네게 말하기를 완강히 거부하는 것은 태호다운 모습이다

Tai-ho's truculent attitude alienated all supporters he had won to his cause
ㄴ 태호의 거친 태도 때문에 그를 지지하던 모든 사람들을 등돌리게 만들었다

Their behavior should suffice to illustrate how social attitudes are changing
ㄴ 그들의 행동은 사회풍조가 어떻게 변하고 있는가를 잘 보여주기에 충분할 것이다

Their outmoded attitudes are dragging the country back into the

---

· **contumacious** stubborn or insubordinate
· **truculent** aggressively self-assertive

· **outmode** cause to be old-fashioned or out-of-date

twentieth century
       ㄴ 그들의 낡은 태도가 나라를 **20**세기로 퇴보시키고 있다

They are being quite cynical that the reason why we have such a large turnout is that we are serving refreshments
       ㄴ 그들은 우리가 음료수를 제공하기 때문에 참석자들이 그렇게 많은 것
        이라는 냉소적인 태도이다

Your attitude really grates on me
       ㄴ 네 태도가 몹시 거슬려

› **grate** pulverize by rubbing against something rough, irritate

145. 파티 & 행사   Parties & Ceremonies

A wedding anniversary is the celebration of love, trust, partnership, tolerance and tenacity. The order varies for any given year
> ↳ 결혼 기념일은 사랑, 믿음, 협조, 관용, 인내에 대한 축하이다. 그 중 무엇이 중요한가의 순서는 해마다 다르다

A wedding is an event, but marriage is an achievement
> ↳ 결혼식은 하나의 행사지만 결혼생활은 성취이다

After you wrote out invitations, it was all systems go
> ↳ 네가 초청장을 다 쓰고 나니 모든 준비가 완료됐어

All the prize-winners were called forward to receive their prizes
> ↳ 모든 수상자들은 상을 받기 위해 앞으로 불리어 나갔다

Another big party? I'll be there with bells on
> ↳ 또 근사한 파티라? 만사 전폐하고 가지

At parties he usually outstays all the other guests
> ↳ 회합 때 그는 대체로 다른 손님보다 오래있다

Bong-soo went to the fair, and only hit the high spots
> ↳ 종수는 품평회에 가서 중요한 것만 보았다

Both celebrations were held on the same day by a(n) happy(unhappy) coincidence
> ↳ 두 행사가 요행히(하필) 같은 날 열렸다

Byung-soo will do the honors at the banquet

› **tenacious**   holding fast, retentive
› **banquet**   ceremonial dinner

ㄴ 연회에서는 병수가 주빈 역할을 할 것이다

Chan-soo fell to pieces and didn't attend the meeting

ㄴ 찬수는 속이 뒤틀려서 모임에도 안 나왔어

Chan-soo is a real party animal

ㄴ 찬수는 정말 노는 것 좋아해

> (Don't be a party pooper 잔치 분위기 깨지마)
> (Don't be a wallflower 빼지 말고 같이 어울려 놀자)

Chan-soo was grooving at the party

ㄴ 찬수는 파티에서 신나게 놀더군

Chang-soo began to call off the names on the list

ㄴ 창수가 명단을 보고 호명했다

Don't feel small at parties any more

ㄴ 더 이상 파티장에서 기죽지마

Don't think the test will be a tea party

ㄴ 그 시험을 식은 죽 먹기로 여기지마

During the ceremony, the host sets the table with food, rice cakes, and the head of a pig

ㄴ 사업주는 음식과 떡을 차려놓은 상위에 돼지머리를 올려놓는다

Ed zoomed in on a real cutie as soon as he walked into the party

ㄴ 에드는 파티장에 들어서자마자 정말 예쁜 아가씨에게 마음이 확 끌렸다

Everybody who is anybody at all was there

ㄴ 이렇다할 만한 사람은 모두 있었다

Everyone really cut loose and had a very good time

ㄴ 우리들은 진짜 흥청거리면서 아주 재미있게 보냈다

▸ **poop** enclosed superstructure at the stern of a ship

▸ **zoom** move or increase with great speed

Everyone was dancing wildly when the radio was at full volume
  ↳ 라디오를 크게 켜자 모두 신나게 춤을 추었다

Fly right when you get to the party
  ↳ 파티에 가서 올바르게 행동해

Gil-soo let himself go yesterday and was the life of the party
  ↳ 어제 길수가 분위기잡고 나서서 파티를 확 살렸지

He was banking on my attending the party
  ↳ 그는 내가 파티에 오는 줄 알고 있었어

His family celebrates birthdays in a big way
  ↳ 그의 가족들은 생일을 성대하게 치른다

It's no longer the fashion to get drunk after the party
  ↳ 잔치 끝에 술에 취하는 풍습은 사라졌다

Let's cash up some money to have a party
  ↳ 돈을 좀 추렴해서 회식하자

Let's flock(get, gather) around the birthday cake
  ↳ 생일 케익 옆에 둥그렇게 모이자

Lots of people go to the party just to network
  ↳ 많은 사람들은 각계 인사들과 교제를 넓히려고 파티에 간다

My father remembered me on my birthday
  ↳ 아버지는 내 생일을 잊지 않고 선물을 주셨다

No party is complete without you
  ↳ 네가 있어야 파티지(네가 있어야 파티가 어울리지)

Put you out of your misery and announce who's won the first prize
  ↳ 애간장 태우지 말고 1등이 누구인지 발표해 주시오

She always seems to fall all over her guests at her parties
  ↳ 그 여자는 항상 자신의 파티에 오는 손님들에게 친절히 대해주는 것 같아

› **flock** gather or move as a group
› **announce** make known publicly

She drank so much before we got there that she fell asleep and missed all the fun of the fair

↳ 그 여자는 우리가 거기 가기 전에 너무 취한 채 잠이 들어 즐거운 행사를 다 놓쳐버렸어

That ugly guy latched on to me at the party and I couldn't get rid of him

↳ 저 못생긴 녀석이 파티에서 달라붙어서 안 떨어져

The annual Miss Korea pageant features over 100 would-be beauty queens, each aspiring to be throned as the most beautiful woman in Korea

↳ 매년 열리는 미스코리아 대회에는 한국에서 가장 아름다운 여성으로서의 권좌에 오르길 열망하는 100명 이상의 지망생들이 참가한다

The hall was crammed with many people standing

↳ 홀은 입추의 여지가 없었어

The man who is always the life of the party will be the death of his wife

↳ 항상 파티에서 잘 나가는 남자를 둔 부인은 죽을 맛이다

The party fizzled out when everyone went home early

↳ 파티에 왔던 사람들이 일찍 귀가하자 파티가 깨져버렸어

The party was dull until Sang-ho jazzed it up with his song

↳ 파티가 맹숭맹숭하다가 상호가 노래를 불러서 분위기를 띄웠다

The party was turning into a shouting match between the host and guests

↳ 파티장은 주인과 손님간에 고성이 오가는 소란한 분위기로 변했다

The shout of applause reverberated through the hall

↳ 환성이 회장 안에 울려 퍼졌다

- › **latch**　catch or get hold
- › **aspire**　have an ambition

- › **fizzle**　fizz, fail
- › **reverberate**　resound in a serious of echoes

The who's who of the political scene was at the party
> ↳ 파티에는 정계에서 내노라 하는 사람들이 다 왔어

The wild music made us switched on and we started to dance
> ↳ 신나는 음악에 우리는 신이 나서 춤을 추었다

They came on like gang-busters when they had their housewarming party
> ↳ 그들이 집들이 잔치를 할 때 시끌벅적했다

They trickled out as the evening wore on
> ↳ 밤이 깊어가자 그들은 하나씩 가버렸다

We are expecting company
> ↳ 더 올 사람이 있습니다

We are expecting a lot of people
> ↳ 많은 손님들이 올 거야

We request the pleasure of your company at our party
> ↳ 파티에 참석해 주시면 감사하겠습니다

Why all this ceremony today?
> ↳ 오늘은 왜 이리 서먹서먹해?

Will you do the honors this evening?
> ↳ 오늘 밤 주빈 역할을 좀 해 주시겠습니까?

Will you make it to the party? - I should be there
> ↳ 파티에 시간 맞춰 올 수 있겠니? - 갈 수 있을 거야

You've already organized more events than you have had hot dinners
> ↳ 넌 벌써 행사를 한 두 번 치러 본 게 아니잖아

Your presence is a great compliment
> ↳ 참석해 주셔서 무한 영광입니다

› **housewarming** party to celebrate moving into a house

› **trickle** run in drops or a thin stream

146. 평가   **Evaluation**

A false step could prove fatal(disastrous)
> ↳ 한 발작만 잘못 디디면 큰일이다

A man is valued as he makes himself valuable
> ↳ 사람은 자신을 얼마나 가치 있는 사람으로 만드느냐에 따라 평가된다

Everyone did what they pleased and the whole thing turned into a mess
> ↳ 각자가 제멋대로 하는 바람에 사태를 악화시킨 거야

Half a loaf is better than no bread(none)
> ↳ 소량이라도 없는 것 보다 낫지

He got what he bargained for
> ↳ 그 사람 자업자득이지 뭐

> 자기가 한 일이나 말에 대해 책임을 져야 한다는 말이다. '자업자득 As you make your bed, so you must lie upon it' 이나 "뿌린 데로 거둔다 You must sow, before you reap"과도 뜻이 통한다. 일상 대화에서는 "He got what he bargained(asked) for"이라고도 한다.

He was a mere instrument, not an agent
> ↳ 그는 하수인에 불과했고 주모자는 아니다

He was deservedly punished
> ↳ 당연한 벌을 받은 거지

› **fatal** causing death or ruin

› **instrument** means, implement, something that produces music, legal document

He was deceived by his own trick
> ㄴ 제 꾀에 제가 넘었어

He was finally knocked down to size
> ㄴ 마침내 그는 코(기)가 꺾였어

He was pinned down for a definite answer
> ㄴ 그는 확답을 안 할 수 없게 되었다

He was pushed to the verge of exhaustion
> ㄴ 그는 더 이상 견딜 수 없을 만큼 지쳐버렸다

He was then at the height of popularity
> ㄴ 그는 그 당시 인기절정이었어

He will never condescend to little things
> ㄴ 그는 시시한 일은 거들떠보지도 않아

He'd take it in a minute
> ㄴ 그 사람이야 감지덕지지

He's all bark and no bite
> ㄴ 그는 입으로만 큰소리치지 대단치 않아

He's always on the ball
> ㄴ 그는 늘 신경 쓰고 있어

He's been accused of being spineless in the face of the aggression
> ㄴ 그는 공격에 대해 줏대가 없다는 비난을 받고 있다

He's fond of contending with everything
> ㄴ 그는 무슨 일이고 시비를 걸려고 해

He's getting much too personal
> ㄴ 그는 시시콜콜한 개인 비밀을 너무 건드려

He's got some other reason, I'll be bound
> ㄴ 틀림없이 그에게 다른 이유가 있어

› **verge** be almost on the point, of happening or doing something

› **condescend** lower oneself, act haughtily

› **spineless** without backbone

He's over the hill
> ㄴ 그 사람 한 물 갔어

He's quite worked out
> ㄴ 그는 기진해 있다

He's rich enough that he wants for nothing
> ㄴ 그는 부자여서 부족한 게 없다

Her inertia continues to exacerbate the situation
> ㄴ 그녀의 무사 안일함이 상황을 계속 악화시키고 있다

Her sense of humor is sick
> ㄴ 그 여자의 유머감각은 넌더리난다

Ho-yung glossed over his errors
> ㄴ 호영인 자신의 과실을 용케 둘러댔어

Holiday-makers left the place in a shambles
> ㄴ 소풍객들이 그 장소를 마구 어질러 놓았다

Hyun-soo showed his displeasure and shot it full of holes
> ㄴ 현수는 불쾌감을 표하면서 그것을 심하게 비판했다

Hyun-soo's alibi doesn't hold water
> ㄴ 현수의 알리바이는 앞뒤가 안 맞아

I am off to a great start
> ㄴ 시작은 좋았지

I don't want this to become a precedent
> ㄴ 이게 전례가 돼선 안 돼

I feel it in my bones
> ㄴ 내 짐작이 틀림없어

I guess I've been blessed
> ㄴ 난 축복 받은 사람 같아

› **inertia** tendency of matter to remain at rest or in motion

› **shamble** shuffle along

I guess you jumped the gun
    ↳ 너무 성급했던 것 같군

I had(have) an idea
    ↳ 짐작이 갔지(좋은 생각이 있어)

I have only myself to thank for it
    ↳ 다 내 책임이야

I have taken all I have
    ↳ 참을 만큼 참았어

I know right from wrong
    ↳ 난 옳고 그름은 알아

I put a lot into it and it paid off
    ↳ 정성을 들였더니 효과가 있었지

I think it's quite the opposite
    ↳ 그 반대라고 생각해

I won't lose any sleep over it
    ↳ 그런 일에 구애받지 않아

I won't pull my(any) punches
    ↳ 사정 봐 주지 않을 거야

I wouldn't give it a house room
    ↳ 거저 줘도 싫어

I wouldn't have missed it for the world
    ↳ 절대 놓칠 수 없었지

I'll see you farther(further) first
    ↳ 그런 일은 딱 질색이야

I'm new at this kind of thing
    ↳ 이런 일은 첨이야

▸ **opposite** one that is opposed, set facing
something that is at the other

side or end, opposed or contrary

If he had done his homework, he would have known that guy was likely to skip town without paying
> ↳ 그가 미리 낌새를 알아냈더라면 그 녀석이 돈을 떼어먹고 도망하리라는 것을 알았으련만

If worst comes to worst
> ↳ 최악의 경우

If you can't get there in time, that's your tough luck
> ↳ 시간 내에 거기 안 오면 끝장이야

If you're spewing(spilling) your guts, they'll cancel your Christmas
> ↳ 네가 모든 걸 털어놓는다면 그들이 널 죽일 것이다

Improvement is within the bounds(range) of the possibility
> ↳ 개선의 가능성도 있다

In a sense, it's a must
> ↳ 어떤 면에서 그건 당연하지

It comes with the territory
> ↳ 그건 당연히 수반하는 거야

It cuts two ways
> ↳ 그 일에는 양면성이 있어

It didn't have a firm ending
> ↳ 호지부지 끝났어

(=The end was weak)
(=The end left us hanging(lingering))

It doesn't matter, one way or the other
> ↳ 이렇든 저렇든 내겐 문제가 안 돼

› **spew** gush out in a stream
› **territory** particular geographical region

It doesn't seem to get anywhere
 ↳ 그건 별로 쓸모(효과)가 없는 것 같다

It doesn't add up
 ↳ 그건 말이 안 돼

> (=None of it adds up)
> (=It doesn't make sense)

It escapes me right now
 ↳ 딱 집어 말하기 어려워

> (=I can't quite figure(make)it out)

It happened for the best
 ↳ 그런 일이 일어난 건(차라리) 잘된 일

It is and it isn't
 ↳ 그럴 수도 있고 아닐 수도 있어

It is beneath all your notice
 ↳ 그런 건 문제시 할 것이 못된다

It seems like a no-win situation because it cuts both ways
 ↳ 그것은 양쪽 다 이치에 맞기 때문에 어느 쪽도 편들 수 없을 것 같다

It serves you right
 ↳ 네가 자초한 것이지 않나(당해서 싸지)

› **beneath** below
› **situation** location, condition, job

자기가 한 일이나 말에 대해 책임을 져야 한다는 말이다. '자업자득 As you make your bed, so you must lie upon it' 이나 "뿌린 데로 거둔다 You must sow, before you reap"과도 뜻이 통한다. 일상 대화에서는 "He got what he bargained(asked) for"이라고도 한다.
(=You asked for it)

It stands up to comparison
ㄴ 이건 어디 내놓아도 손색이 없다

(=This is the best)
(=This is second to none)

It started out big, but now it's kind of petering out
ㄴ 시작은 요란했으나 흐지부지해지고 있어

'용두사미(龍頭蛇尾)'란 '작심삼일'과 비슷한 말이다. 거창하게 시작해 놓고 흐지부지 끝나는 것을 설명한 말이다. 영어로는 "Starts off with a bang and ends with a whimper 큰소리로 시작해서 낑낑대며 끝난다"이다.

It struck me as singular
ㄴ 그것이 이상하게 생각되었어

It takes a miracle to find
ㄴ 그걸 찾긴 쉽지 않아

It takes time to do it right
ㄴ 제대로 하려면 시간이 걸려

It takes two to tango

· **comparison** act of comparing
· **peter out** diminish gradually

↳ 네게도 절반의 책임은 있어

It was all for the best
↳ 전화위복이었어

It was less than I expected
↳ 생각보다는 별 게 아니었어

It will avail you little or nothing
↳ 그건 네게 이로울 데가 별로 없다

It will do in a pinch
↳ 그건 유사시 필요해

It won't count against you
↳ 그게 너한테 해롭진 않을 거야

It'll just fill the bill
↳ 그게 기준은 통과할 것 같아

It's a big challenge, but she'll rise to the occasion
↳ 그건 큰 도전이지만 그 여자는 위기에도 잘 대처할 거야

It's a bitter pill to swallow
↳ 그건 받아들이기 힘든 사실이다

It's a case of the blind leading the blind
↳ 그건 자신도 잘 모르면서 남들을 가르치는(이끌어 가는)일이지

It's a choice of evils for him
↳ 그가 부득이 일을 당했지만 그래도 나은 편이다

It's a disgrace the way we waste food and energy
↳ 우리가 음식과 에너지를 낭비하는걸 보면 한심해

It's a good bet that the spy will soon be caught
↳ 그 스파이는 곧 붙잡힐 가능성이 높아

› **pinch** squeeze between the finger and thumb or between the jaws of a tool, compress painfully

› **swallow** take into the stomach through the throat, envelop or take in, accept too easily

It's a matter of taking calculated risks in the right way at the right time
  ㄴ 그건 적시에 적당한 방법으로 승산 있는 모험을 거느냐의 문제지

It's a no-win situation
  ㄴ 그건 싹수가 없는 일이야

It's a one-time offer
  ㄴ 다시없는 기회

It's a sorry state of affairs
  ㄴ 참 한심한 일(상황)이군

It's a tough call
  ㄴ 처리(결정)하기 어려운 일

> (=I'm not sure what to do)
> (=It's not an easy call)

It's all in your mind
  ㄴ 그건 네 마음먹기에 달렸다

It's an old story
  ㄴ 뻔할 뻔 자지

It's as broad as it's long
  ㄴ 결국은 마찬가지

It's as difficult as the argument over whether which come first chickens or the eggs
  ㄴ 그건 닭이 먼저냐 달걀이 먼저냐 하는 논쟁만큼이나 어렵다

It's back to square one
  ㄴ 다시 원점이야

‣ **calculate**   determine by mathematical
      processes, judge, rely(+on, upon)

‣ **call**   summon, demand

It's none the worse for wear
> ↳ 그건 낡았지만(피곤해 보이지만) 말짱해(얼마든지 더 활동할 수 있어)

It's not a gift from the gods
> ↳ 그건 뜻밖의 선물은 아니다

It's not all it's hyped up to be
> ↳ 소문만 요란했지 영 아니더라

It's not always the case
> ↳ 늘 그런 건 아냐

It's not bad for the first time
> ↳ 개시치고는 좋은 편이다

It's not up to par yet
> ↳ 아직 미흡하다

> (=rough round the edges)

It's not worth it
> ↳ 그럴 필요가 없어(그럴만한 가치가 없다)

It's nothing more, nothing less
> ↳ 그 이상도 그 이하도 아냐

> (=That's all it is)
> (=It's that simple)
> (=That's all there's to it)

It's poison
> ↳ 백해무익

› **hype up** exaggerate

(=It'll only harm you)
(=It'll only do(cause) you harm)

It's premature for that
ㄴ 시기상조

(=Now is not the time)

It's running out of steam
ㄴ 그건 한물 간 얘기야

(=The story is evaporating)

It's shaping up very well
ㄴ 잘 돼가고 있어

It's so unlike you
ㄴ 너답지 않다

It's stamped on your forehead
ㄴ 네 얼굴에 다 씌었어

It's still open to dispute
ㄴ 반박 여지가 있군

It's still too close to call
ㄴ 아직도 막상막하야

It's the best conceivable
ㄴ 그 이상의 것은 생각할 수 없어

▸ **evaporate**　pass off in or convert into vapor, disappear quickly

It's the double standard
> ↳ 그건 이중 잣대

It's the tail wagging the dog
> ↳ 본말이 전도된 꼴이군. 하극상이로군

It's time you laid your(place) cards on the table and spoke honestly
> ↳ 이제 네 입장을 밝히고 솔직히 말해야 될 때가 됐어

It's too rich for your blood
> ↳ 그건 네겐 과중한 비용이야

It's you all over
> ↳ 네가 늘 그 모양이잖아

Its last state is worse than the first
> ↳ 그건 개선이 아니고 개악이야

Jin-ho messes everything up
> ↳ 진호는 제대로 하는 게 없어

> (=Jin-ho is beyond help)
> (=Jin-ho is hopeless)
> (=Jin-ho is incompetent)

Joo-il is famous now, but in no time he'll sink into oblivion
> ↳ 주일이가 지금은 유명하지만 얼마 안 가서 세인들에게서 잊혀질 것이다

Jung-man is just a square peg in a round hole
> ↳ 정만이는 그 일에 부적합해

Jung-soo has a screw loose to do such a thing
> ↳ 정수가 그런 짓 하다니 머리가 어떻게 된 모양이지

Jung-soo rose to the occasion

‣ **oblivion**   state of having lost conscious awareness

‣ **peg**   small pinlike piece, put a peg into, fix or mark with or as if with pegs

ㄴ 정수는 난국에 잘 대처했어

Jung-tae is a rotten apple to spoil it for the rest of us

    ㄴ 정태는 미꾸라지 한 마리가 웅덩이 전체를 흐려놓을 사람이다

> 하나가 전체에게 나쁜 영향을 미친다는 말이다. 영어 속담에는 여러 가지가
> 있는데, 가장 자주 쓰이는 표현은 "One rotten apple spoils the barrel
> 썩은 사과 하나가 한 통을 썩게 한다"이다. 악한 한 사람이 한 가문, 한 나라
> 를 욕되게 하는 것은 "It is an ill bird that fouls its own nest 자기의
> 둥지를 더럽히는 새는 나쁜 새이다"로 표현한다.
> (=One scabbed sheep will mar a whole flock)
> (=A hog that's bemired endeavors to bemire others)

Just play it cool and he'll probably appoint you because of your past success

    ㄴ 그저 차분하게 해나가면 아마 전에 네가 거둔 성과 덕분에 네가 임명
       될 것이다

Justice has to be served

    ㄴ 정의가 바로 서야 한다

Making himself out to be some kind of expert in modern art is all he did

    ㄴ 그가 한 일이라고는 자기가 제법 현대예술에 대한 전문가인체 한 것
       뿐이다

Man-soo doesn't miss a trick(any tricks) in anything

    ㄴ 만수는 무슨 일에나 소홀함이 없어

Man-soo seems to have fallen off the map

    ㄴ 만수는 한물 간 것 같아

Man-soo shot himself in the foot

▸ **expert** thoroughly skilled

↳ 만수는 화를 자초했어

Man-soo stood on his dignity to the very end
↳ 창호는 끝까지 품위를 잃지 않았다

Many huge monuments built over some people's graves in an effort to achieve some degree of immortal presence long after their death are disgusting
↳ 죽은지 오랜 후에도 상당한 정도로 불멸의 존재로 인식됨을 달성해 보려는 시도에서 무덤에 거대한 많은 비석들을 세우는 것은 역겹다

Marketable progress was made within a relatively short span of time then
↳ 그 때에 비교적 짧은 기간에 경이적인 발전을 이루었다

Mere cleverness without sound principles does not count for anything
↳ 건전한 신념 없이 머리만 좋아서는 아무 쓸모 없어

Mere report is not enough to go upon
↳ 단순한 풍문 따위는 믿을만한 것이 못된다

Mi-sook stands out in the crowd
↳ 미숙인 군계일학이다

> '군계일학(群鷄一鶴)'은 '여러 닭 중에 섞인 한 마리의 학'이란 뜻이며, 이는 군중 속에서 뛰어난 한 사람을 뜻한다. 영어로는 'Stands out in the crowd'라고 한다. 'Stand out'은 "구별되다"라는 뜻의 숙어이다.

Moo-ho will rise up to the challenge
↳ 무호는 해낼 거다

Moon-soo took his medicine like a man
↳ 문수는 남자답게 처벌을 감수했다

> **dignity** quality or state of being worthy or honored, formal reserve

> **disgust** strong aversion, provoke disgust in

Moon-sook is more than a pretty face
> ↳ 문숙이는 보기보다 능력 있어

My efforts were rewarded(bore fruit)
> ↳ 애쓴 보람이 있었어

> (=My hard work paid out)

My father has a mind like a steel trap
> ↳ 아버지는 기억력이 매우 좋으셔

Nam-chul is history(a has-been)
> ↳ 남철인 한물 갔어

> (=Nam-chul is washed-up)
> (=Nam-chul lost his get-up and go)

Nam-soo used to hang around with the wrong people, but now he's a real together guy(has it together)
> ↳ 남수가 왕년엔 나쁜 사람들과 어울려 다녔지만 지금은 건실해

New fashions seem to come in and go out again more quickly these days
> ↳ 요즈음 신 유행이 생겨났다가 사라지는 것이 훨씬 빨라진 것 같다

No one else deserves the position better
> ↳ 그 자리에 너 만한 적임자가 어디 있니

No two ways about it
> ↳ 확실히 그렇다

Nobody seemed to be sold on the idea by your presentation

▸ **reward**   give a reward to or for

ㄴ 너의 설명(발표)에도 그 생각을 믿으려는 사람은 없는 것 같더라

Not everyone is cut out for that
　　ㄴ 아무나 쉽게 할 수 있는 일이 아냐

> (=It doesn't come naturally to everyone)
> (=Not everyone is good at it(can do that well))

Not only do they rob us they smash everything too
　　ㄴ 그들은 우리에게서 강탈할 뿐 아니라 모든 것을 박살낸다

Not that great right now
　　ㄴ 현재론 신통치 않아

> (=It's not going that well right now)
> (=It's not going as well as I hoped)

Nothing in life will induce him to give up the plan
　　ㄴ 어떤 것도 그에게 그 계획을 포기하게 할 수는 없을 것이다

Nothing matters any more
　　ㄴ 그 이상 중요한게 없어

Nothing more nothing less
　　ㄴ 그 이상도 이하도 아냐

Nothing stays the same
　　ㄴ 변하지 않는 건 없어

Now the tail is wagging the dog
　　ㄴ 이제 보니 하극상이로군

Please judge us on our own merits

› **smash**　break or be broken into pieces

› **induce**　persuade, bring about

› **merit**　praiseworthy quality, rights and wrongs
　　　　　　of a legal case(pl)

ㄴ 우리들의 진가(공적)에 따라 평가해 주십시오

Pyung-ho is first and foremost a pighead
ㄴ 평호는 무엇보다도 벽창호야

Pyung-ho is not poor, only he seems such
ㄴ 평호가 가난한 게 아니라 단지 가난하게 보일 뿐이다

Pyung-soo arranges all his affairs to make himself good
ㄴ 평수는 자신의 일에 대해 겉으로만 근사해 보이려고 한다

Pyung-soo has a commanding presence but lacks brains
ㄴ 평수가 풍채는 있지만 머리가 모자라

Sang-soo never falls for any snow job
ㄴ 상수는 감언이설에 안 넘어가

'감언이설'은 줄여서 '감언'이라고도 하는데, 말 그대로 '달콤한 말', 즉 듣기 좋은 말을 뜻한다. 이는 영어로도 그대로 'sweet talk'라고 한다.

She can do it all in good time
ㄴ 그 여자는 그 일을 시간 내에 해낼 수 있어

She gets her point across and is entertaining at the same time
ㄴ 그 여자는 요점을 제대로 집어내면서도 아주 웃겨

She had it coming
ㄴ 그 여자는 벌을 받아 마땅했다

She is as snobbish as she comes
ㄴ 그 여자의 속물근성은 이루 말할 수 없어

She is headed for an early grave
ㄴ 그 여자는 자기 명을 재촉하고 있어

▸ **pigheaded** stubborn
▸ **snob** one who acts superior to others

She is making a lot of wind
↳ 공연한 야단법석만 떨고있군

She is on a roll
↳ 그 여잔 잘 나가

She is on the skids
↳ 그 여잔 죽 쑤고 있어

She is really magnetic
↳ 그 여잔 끼가 있어

She is really too much
↳ 저 여자 멋져

She is stuck up(conceited, uppish, snotty)
↳ 그 애 공주병에 걸려있어

(=She's a snob)

She must be talked to
↳ 그 여자는 혼내줘야 해

She must have a screw loose somewhere
↳ 그 여자 정신 나갔군

She never gets upset, she just takes everything in her stride
↳ 그녀는 언짢아하지 않고 모든 어려움을 극복해 나간다

She never goes halfway with anything
↳ 그 여자는 일을 하다가 마는 사람이 아니다

She pouts over nothing
↳ 저 애는 잘도 삐쳐

› **magnetic** attractive

› **stride** walk or run with long steps

› **pout** look sullen

(=She often gets pouty)

She sleeps around
> ↳ 그 여자는 정조관념이 없어

She tends to pigeonhole any people according to her first impression of them
> ↳ 그녀는 사람을 누구나 첫 인상으로 평가 분류해 버리는 경향이 있다

She's a very fastidious woman but her exhaustive reporting is well worth the trouble
> ↳ 그녀는 몹시 까다로운 여자지만 그녀의 철저한 보도는 충분히 그 수고의 가치가 있다

She's been up and up ever since I have known her
> ↳ 그 여자는 내가 알게된 후 늘 성실했어

She's got a curvy(shapely) figure
> ↳ 그 여자 멋지다

She's got two left feet
> ↳ 그 여자는 도무지 춤 솜씨가 늘지 않아

She's got you pegged as very strict and impatient person
> ↳ 그 여자는 너를 아주 엄격하고 조급한 사람으로 평가하고 있어

She's in the blissful ignorance of the world
> ↳ 그 여자는 세상 물정을 모르고 잘난 척 한다

She's just trying to smell like a rose
> ↳ 그 여자는 순진하게 보이려고 하고 있을 뿐이야

She's nobody's fool
> ↳ 그 여자는 바보가 아냐

› **fastidious** hard to please

She's past(beyond) her prime
↳ 그 여자 한물갔어

> (=She's no longer in her prime)
> (=Her best days are over)

She's pretty much set in her ways
↳ 그 여자는 상당히 옹고집이야

She's really a hot number
↳ 저 여자 정말 멋있다

She's stingy, arrogant and stupid, at that
↳ 그 여자는 쩨쩨하고, 거만하고, 게다가 멍청해

She's whistling in the dark all the time
↳ 그 여자는 항상 허세를 부려

Singing comes naturally to her
↳ 그녀는 노래에 타고난 소질이 있어

Some are good, some are bad, some are indifferent
↳ 좋은 것도 있고, 나쁜 것도 있고, 그 중간 것도 있다

Sometimes social workers are often regarded as only interfering do-gooders
↳ 사회사업가들은 단지 쓸데없이 남의 일에 간섭이나 하는 사람으로 취급받는 일이 흔히 있다

Such a wicked fellow deserves to be wiped off the face of the earth
↳ 저런 나쁜 놈은 지구를 떠나야 해

Such practice should be done away with
↳ 이런 관행은 없어져야 한다

› **arrogant** showing an offensive sense of superiority

Such things are more than flesh and blood can bear(stand)

    ↳ 그런 일은 인간으로서 도저히 견딜 수 없는 일이다

Suffice it to say we did our best

    ↳ 우리가 최선을 다 했다고나 해 두자

Sung-gyoo has a very good hand

    ↳ 성규는 매우 글씨를 잘 써

> (=Sung-gyoo's handwriting is very good)

Sung-ho couldn't well do that

    ↳ 성호가 아무리 해봐도 못하고 말았어

Sung-mi doesn't play it straight

    ↳ 성미는 정당하지 못해

Sung-moon is a very obliging man

    ↳ 성문이는 말만하면 무엇이든 들어줘

Sung-soo's wit is sometimes a thing

    ↳ 성수가 때로는 재치가 번득여

Tai-gyung is a meat-eater(grass-eater)

    ↳ 태경인 뇌물을 밝혀(돈주면 받아)

Tai-ji is now at a discount

    ↳ 태지의 인기는 한물갔어

Tai-ji was then at the height of popularity

    ↳ 태지는 그 당시 인기 절정이었지

That actor still packs'em in

    ↳ 그 배우는 아직도 인기 있어

› **suffice** be sufficient

› **popularity** wide acceptance

That building was just slapped together
　　ㄴ 저 건물은 정말 날림으로 지었어

That building will go any moment
　　ㄴ 저 건물이 언제 쓰러질지 몰라

That guy has sticky fingers
　　ㄴ 저 친구 손버릇이 나빠

That matter may be left out of consideration
　　ㄴ 그 일은 문제삼지 않아도 된다

That may pass in a crowd
　　ㄴ 보통 정도는 될 거야(눈에 띄진 않을 거다)

That remains to be seen
　　ㄴ 그건 두고봐야 알아

That still remains a question
　　ㄴ 그건 아직도 알 수 없어

That style went out of fashion a long time ago
　　ㄴ 그런 스타일은 예전에 한물 갔어

That was a passing fad in the '80s
　　ㄴ 그건 80년대의 한때 유행이었지

That way of doing things died out a long time ago
　　ㄴ 그런 식으로 하는 건 오래 전에 사라졌어

That will be a reflection upon our honor
　　ㄴ 그것은 우리의 명예를 손상시키게 될 것이다

That would be just what the doctor ordered
　　ㄴ 그건 꼭 필요한 것

That'll do except that it's too long
　　ㄴ 너무 긴 것만 빼면 괜찮아

· **consideration**　thinking about, thoughtful
　　　　　　　　　　attention

· **honor**　good name, outward respect or
　　　　　　symbol of this, privilege

That's a blessing in disguise
> ↳ 그건 전화위복이야

That's a kind of a tax for being famous
> ↳ 그게 일종의 유명세지

That's an interesting scent you are wearing
> ↳ 네가 뿌린 향수는 독특해

That's between the cup and the lip
> ↳ 그건 아직 더 두고봐야 알아

That's just because he likes playing hard to get
> ↳ 그건 그가 필요이상으로 힘들게 해 나가고 있기 때문일 뿐이야

That's more like it. You should think before you speak
> ↳ 그렇게 하는 게 훨씬 좋아. 말하기 전에 충분히 생각해야 해

That's not the way to do it
> ↳ 그런 식으론 안 돼

That's one for the books
> ↳ 그거 이상한 일이군

That's one of his crucial blind spots as a leader
> ↳ 그게 바로 그가 가진 지도자로서의 치명적 맹점중의 하나다

That's only par for the course for me
> ↳ 그건 내게 일상적인 일일 뿐이야 내 그럴 줄 알았지

That's the last thing I expected
> ↳ 설마 그러리라고는 생각 못했지

That's the last thing I meant to do
> ↳ 일부러 그런 게 아니다

That's the last thing to do
> ↳ 그건 해볼만한 일이 아냐

› **disguise** hide the true identity or nature of
› **crucial** vitally important

That's the luck of the draw
> ↳ 그건 복이 굴러 들어온 거야

That's the only thing that really counts
> ↳ 정말 중요한 것은 그 한가지뿐이다

That's the thing nowadays
> ↳ 그게 요즘 유행이야

That's too far, to say the least
> ↳ 아무리 그래도 그건 너무해

That's what comes of the clobber not sticking to his last
> ↳ 그건 그가 주제파악을 못한 탓이야

That's no bad, considering
> ↳ 그런 대로 그리 나쁘진 않군

The advantage of the scheme outweighs its disadvantages
> ↳ 그 계획은 장점이 단점보다 낫다

The building is on its last legs
> ↳ 그 건물은 낡았어

The first isn't good, and the neither is the second
> ↳ 처음 것도 좋지 않고, 둘째 것도 좋지 않았어

The left hand doesn't know what the right hand is doing
> ↳ 하고있는 일이 제 각각이구면

The matter can't wait any longer
> ↳ 그 문제를 방치할 수 없다

The matter hangs in doubt
> ↳ 그 일은 확실치 않아

The matter will keep till tomorrow
> ↳ 그 일은 내일까지 해도 된다

› **clobber** hit hard
› **scheme** crafty plot, systematic design

The outcome caught me off guard(was unexpected)
> ↳ 예상 밖의 결과였어

The outcome is doubtful
> ↳ 결과는 불투명해

The plan ended up a fade-out
> ↳ 계획은 우물쭈물 끝났어

The project bumped along to an uncertain conclusion
> ↳ 그 일은 삐걱거리며 진행되다가 이렇다 할 결과 없이 끝나버렸어

The question is not so much what it is as what it looks
> ↳ 문제는 본질에 있다기보다 외관에 있다

The result tells its own tale
> ↳ 결과를 보니 알만하군

The results exceed my hope
> ↳ 기대이상이다

The road ahead of him is rough
> ↳ 그의 앞에 갈 길은 험난해

The ultimate measure of a man is where he stands at times of challenge and controversy
> ↳ 사람은 결국 도전과 논쟁에 어떻게 대처하는가에 따라 평가된다

The value of a man can only be measured with regard to other men
> ↳ 사람의 가치는 다른 사람과의 관련으로 평가된다

Their survey covered only too few cases to make findings statistically significant
> ↳ 그들의 조사는 너무나 적은 불과 몇 건에 불과해서 통계적인 유의성
> 이 있는 자료를 만들지는 못한다

There's more behind

› **controversy**　clash of opposing views
› **significant**　meaning, importance

ㄴ 이면에 속셈이 있어

There's more to it than meets the eye

ㄴ 겉보기와는 달라

There's no shadow of a doubt

ㄴ 전혀 의심의 여지가 없어

There's nothing that he wouldn't do

ㄴ 그는 못 할 일이 없다

There's nothing to it

ㄴ 그건 쉬운 일이야("그 말은 근거가 없어"의 뜻도 있음)

There's something about you

ㄴ 너 하는 짓이 뭔가 수상해

There's something at the back of it

ㄴ 배후에 뭔가 있어

There's something in it

ㄴ 일리 있군(뭔가 꿍꿍이가 있겠군)

There's something missing in your plan of operation

ㄴ 네 작전에는 허점이 있어

They are breaking a looking-glass

ㄴ 그들은 불행을 자초하고 있는 거야

They are drawing benefit too, you bet your life

ㄴ 그 사람들도 득을 보고 있음이 확실해

They are holding the ring

ㄴ 그들은 수수방관하고 있어

They are in good spirits

ㄴ 그들은 신바람 났어

› **shadow**   shade cast upon a surface by
something blocking light, trace

They are of a kind
↳ 모두 같은 종류

They are on a losing streak
↳ 그들은 연패의 늪에 빠져있어

They didn't take a beating
↳ 그들은 손해본 거 없어

They don't have the luxury
↳ 그들에게는 그럴만한 여유가 없어(그들에게는 사치다)

They have certainly come a long way
↳ 그 사람들 큰 일 해냈구나

They have to stomach it less than perfection
↳ 그들은 적당한 선에서 자제해야 해

They were not on the right track from the beginning
↳ 그들은 첫 단추부터 잘못 끼웠다

They're just jogging along(on)
↳ 그들은 그럭저럭 해 나가고 있어

They've been spinning their wheels
↳ 그 사람들은 헛일만 하고 있는 거야

Things are coming along
↳ 차차 나아지고 있어

Things can't get any worse
↳ 이제 갈데까지 가버린 거야

Things do not bode well for him
↳ 그에게 좋은 조짐이 아냐

Things go badly(wrong) with Song-joo
↳ 송주가 하는 일은 어그러지기만 해

▸ **streak** mark of a different color, narrow band of light, trace, run or series

▸ **bide** indicate by signs, wait, dwell

This is a worse way in the long run
ㄴ 긴 안목으로 보면 이게 더 나쁜 방법이다

This is so typical of you
ㄴ 이건 너다운 일이군

This method is a better bet
ㄴ 이 방식이 더 나아

This move is uncalled-for
ㄴ 이번 조치는 너무 심해

This reason preponderates over all others
ㄴ 이 이유는 다른 모든 이유보다도 중요하다

Though he never uses your name, the allusion to you is obvious
ㄴ 그가 너를 직접 거명 하진 않았지만 은근히 너를 가리키는 건 분명해

Wan-soo is beginning to throw his weight around
ㄴ 완수가 폼을 잡기 시작하는군

We must have our signals crossed
ㄴ 우리가 잘못 알렸음이 틀림없어

We've gone as far as we can go
ㄴ 그건 너무 지나쳐

> (=We'll be over the limit)
> (=That's pushing it)

When they find out about this, you're going to be in the firing line
ㄴ 그들이 이 사실에 대하여 알게 될 경우 넌 문책을 받게 돼있다

You are a minute late
ㄴ 넌 한 발 늦었어

› **preponderate** exceed in weight, power, importance, or numbers

You are a real hot one
    └ 너 정말 인기 있구나

You are crying(asking) for the moon
    └ 그건 터무니없는 요구야

You are just beating your head against the wall(a brick wall)
    └ 그래봤자 계란으로 바위 치기야

You are making too much fuss about it
    └ 넌 그 일로 공연히 소동을 벌이고 있는 거야

You are not within your rights
    └ 그건 네 권한 밖이야

You are putting on a poker face
    └ 시치미 떼고있군

You are rather hasty in your generalization
    └ 넌 지레짐작이야

You are really cutting off your nose to spite your face
    └ 그건 정말 누워 침 뱉기야

You don't have to be a rocket scientist
    └ 그건 어렵지 않아

You don't review the performance; you just pick them apart(to pieces)
    └ 넌 연기를 비평하는 게 아니라 그저 혹평만 하고 있어

› **generalize**   reach a general conclusion   particular instances
                  especially on the basis of

You are a real hot one

You are crying (asking) for the moon

You are just beating your head against the walls (brick wall)

You are making too much fuss about it

You are not within your rights

You are putting on a poker face

You are rather hasty in your generalization

You are really cutting off your nose to spite your face

You don't have to be a rocket scientist

You don't review the performance; you just pick them apart (to pieces)

147. 평등   Equality

Equal authority would lead to an absence of government
     ↳ 평등한 권위만 존재한다면 정부가 없어지는 상황이 될 수도 있다

All men are equal but some men are more equal than others
     ↳ 모든 사람이 평등해 보이지만 어떤 사람들은 특권을 누린다

Every man should have a fair opportunity to make the best of himself
     ↳ 누구에게나 자신의 힘을 최대한 발휘할 기회가 공평히 주어져야 한다

Ignorance and narrow-mindedness have long stood in the way of equality for women
     ↳ 무지와 편협이 여성의 평등에 오랫동안 큰 장애가 되어왔다

Natural barriers to equality begin with the unequal distribution of natural abilities
     ↳ 평등에 장애가 되는 원초적인 장벽은 재능이 불균등하게 분배되는데서 시작된다

Nobody can get over being abused by a court system that preaches justice and equality
     ↳ 정의와 평등을 공언하는 법원이 학대한다는 사실에 대해 그냥 넘어갈 사람은 없다

The enormous en-equality is the real cause of speculative investment in property, which remains a leading social issue in Korea
     ↳ 그 막심한 불평등이 한국의 주요 사회문제로 되어 온 부동산 투기의

| ▸ **authority**   expert; right, responsibility or power to influence | ▸ **speculate**   think about things yet unknown, risk money in a business deal in hope of high profit |

진정한 원인이다

There must be a shift in political emphasis from individual profit to social equality

ㄴ 정치적으로 강조돼야 할 것은 개인의 이익에서 사회적 평등으로의 전환이다

What space and time have been to physicists, liberty and equality have been and still are to democratic theories

ㄴ 공간과 시간이 물리학자에게 관련되는 것처럼, 자유와 평등이 민주주의 이론에 관련되어왔고 여전히 계속 관련이 있다

Women become on a par with men

ㄴ 여성들은 남성들과 거의 동등해지고 있다

You can't be friends upon any other terms than upon the terms of equality

ㄴ 동등한 관계가 아니고서는 친구가 될 수 없다

▸ **emphasis** stress

148. 표정　　　Facial Expressions

A faint smile played on his lips
> ↳ 엷은 미소가 그의 입가를 스쳤다

A puzzled look(expression) crossed(passed) over his face
> ↳ 곤혹스러운 표정이 그의 얼굴을 스쳤다

All he got was blank looks when he made some simple remark in this matter
> ↳ 그가 이 일에 몇 마디 했을 때 모두 멍한 표정이었어

Don't just stand there with your bare face hanging out
> ↳ 그냥 그렇게 바보 같은 얼굴로 서 있지마

Don't sit there like a wall-flower
> ↳ 꿔다놓은 보릿자루처럼 앉았지마

He flashed a smile(glance) at her
> ↳ 그는 그녀에게 살짝 미소(시선)를 던졌다

He had a very worried look on his face
> ↳ 그는 몹시 근심스러운 표정이었어

He is just putting on a brave face
> ↳ 그는 그저 태연한 체 할 뿐이야

He made a face at me when I was talking to the boss
> ↳ 사장에게 얘기를 막 하려는데 그가 내게 얼굴(표정)로 신호를 보냈다

▸ **faint**　cowardly or spiritless, weak and dizzy, lacking vigor

▸ **bare**　naked, not concealed, empty, leaving nothing to spare, plain

Her smile is her best feature
↳ 그녀의 웃는 얼굴이 가장 예쁘다

His face fell
↳ 그 사람 실망의 빛이 보였어

I can read the whole story in your face
↳ 얼굴에 다 씌었군

In-ho's smile was rather forced
↳ 인호는 억지 웃음을 지어 보였다

It's coming out(written on) of your face
↳ 네 얼굴에 씌었어

It's stamped on your forehead
↳ 네 얼굴에 다 씌었어

One could tell his face was distorted by rage
↳ 그가 화가 나서 얼굴이 일그러졌다는 것은 누구나 알 수 있었다

She colored up when he spoke to her
↳ 그가 그녀에게 말을 하자 그녀는 얼굴을 붉혔다

She's laughing all over her face
↳ 그 여자는 희색이 만면해

Sung-mo was guiltless of smiles
↳ 성모는 방긋도 안 했어

The color mounted to her face as she saw him staring at her
↳ 그 여자는 그가 자신을 뚫어지게 쳐다보고 있는 걸 보고 얼굴을 확 붉혔다

The girl flamed up when I spoke to her
↳ 내가 말을 건네자 소녀는 얼굴을 붉혔다

The lines in his face reflect a hard life
↳ 그의 얼굴에 새겨진 주름들은 그가 많은 고생을 했음을 보여준다

▸ **distort** twist out of shape, condition, or
true meaning

When we see a secret smile on his lips, he must be telling a lie
> ↳ 그가 입가에 살짝 미소를 지을 때는 거짓말을 하고 있는 게 틀림없어

Why the happy look on your face?
> ↳ 왜 그리 기분 좋은 표정인가?

Wrinkling our brows won't solve a single one of our personal problems
> ↳ 얼굴은 찌푸린다고 우리들의 개인적인 문제점이 하나라도 해결되지는 않을 것이다

You have to keep a poker face when haggling
> ↳ 흥정할 땐 표정관리를 잘 해야 해

› **haggle**   argue in bargaining

149. 풍경   Scenery

A beautiful rainbow hangs(spans) in the sky
> ↳ 예쁜 무지개가 서있다

A brook cuts that field
> ↳ 시냇물이 벌판을 가로질러 흐른다

A path wound through the woods, leading us to the main road
> ↳ 숲 속에는 구불구불한 오솔길이 있어서 우리는 큰 도로로 나가게 되었다

A road had been cut up the hillside
> ↳ 산허리에 길이 나있었지

A trail runs across the field to my house
> ↳ 한 가닥의 작은 길이 들판을 가로질러 우리 집까지 나있다

After the long hot dry summer, the soil is cracking up
> ↳ 장기간 비가 안 오는 여름 날씨에 땅이 갈라지고 있다

As the sea receded from the shore, a lot of shells were left behind
> ↳ 바닷물이 빠지자 많은 조가비들이 바닷가에 있었다

As the vine grows, it twined around the lamp-post
> ↳ 덩굴이 자라서 가로등 기둥을 감고 올라갔다

Barbed wire and concrete walls delineate the DMZ that physically separate the two Korea
> ↳ 철조망과 콘크리트 벽이 두 개의 한국을 물리적으로 분리해 놓고 있
> 는 비무장지대를 표시하고 있다

▸ **brook**   tolerate, small stream
▸ **twin**   couple, duplicate

Bushes and trees prepare for the day when they will burst into full bloom
> ㄴ 수풀과 나무들은 활짝 만개할 날을 위해 채비를 한다

Clouds were floating across the blue sky
> ㄴ 푸른 하늘에 구름이 떠 있었다

Darkness began to invest the earth
> ㄴ 땅거미가 대지를 덮기 시작했다

Don't trample out a path in the barley field
> ㄴ 보리밭을 밟고 다녀서 길을 내지마

Every path has a puddle
> ㄴ 어느 길에나 패인 곳이 있다(결함 없는 것이 없다)

Everything comes to a standstill here when the darkness falls
> ㄴ 여긴 어두움이 내리면 세상이 조용해져

Flags fly high up in the sky
> ㄴ 깃발이 하늘높이 휘날리고 있다

Four avenues radiate from the square
> ㄴ 네 갈래의 가로수 길이 그 광장에서 사방으로 뻗쳐있다

Here the river divides into two branches
> ㄴ 이 강은 여기서 둘로 갈라진다

It seems that the yellow dust in the sky has become as regular as birds showing up in spring
> ㄴ 봄철에 누른 색 먼지는 철새처럼 정기적으로 공중에 떠오르는 것 같다

It's medicine, not scenery, for which a sick man must go searching
> ㄴ 병든 사람은 경치 좋은 곳이 아닌 약을 찾아 헤매게 된다

Korea becomes greener every year
> ㄴ 한국의 산은 해마다 짙어가고 있어

‣ trample walk or step on so as to bruise or crush	**‣ radiate** issue rays or in rays, spread from a center

Lamps were strung up across the street
  ↳ 전등이 길을 가로질러 죽 매달려 있었다

Look at those trees reaching for the sky
  ↳ 저 하늘을 찌를 듯 서있는 나무들을 좀 봐

Lots of balloons fly up deep into the sky
  ↳ 많은 풍선이 하늘높이 날아간다

Mountain Sorak is ever changing in color with the season and displays exquisite beauty on every slope
  ↳ 설악산은 계절마다 새 옷을 갈아입고 기묘한 봉우리마다 절묘한 조화를 이룬다

Mt. Jiri is noted for its beautiful shape
  ↳ 지리산은 그 수려한 모습으로 유명하다

Mt. Sorak is all red and yellow
  ↳ 설악산은 단풍이 절정이다

Nestling among the magnificent hills were the crumbling ruins of old monastery
  ↳ 언덕의 여기저기에는 산산조각 난 옛 수도원의 잔해들만 흩어져 있었다

Our paths diverged at the fork in the road
  ↳ 우리가 가는 길은 분기점에서 두 갈래로 나 있었어

Rice has been turned golden yellow
  ↳ 벼가 황금빛으로 물들었다

Rock is perched on the edge of the cliff
  ↳ 벼랑의 가장자리에 바위가 있다

She branched away from the path and cut across the grass
  ↳ 그녀는 길에서 갈라져 나와 풀밭을 건너갔다

Some sprouts have pushed up toward the sun

› **exquisite** flawlessly beautiful and delicate, keenly discriminating

› **diverge** move in different directions, differ
› **perch** roost

↳ 새싹이 햇빛 쪽으로 돌아났다

Soon the moon lost itself in the clouds
↳ 이내 달은 구름 속으로 사라졌다

The boat eased away slowly
↳ 그 보트는 천천히 사라져 갔다

The breakwater projects far into the sea
↳ 방파제가 바다 멀리까지 뻗쳐있다

The church, when the sun catches it, is of a dazzling whiteness
↳ 교회에 햇빛이 비치자 눈부시게 하얀 색으로 보였다

The creek from mountain is running full
↳ 산에서 내려오는 개울물이 넘치도록 흐르고 있다

The curtains were flapping against the window
↳ 커튼이 펄럭거려 창문에 부딪치고 있었다

The darkest hour is that before the dawn
↳ 동트기 전이 가장 어두운 시간이다(절망하지 마라)

아무리 힘들고 어렵더라고 참고 견디면 좋은 일이 생긴다(An unfavourable situation will eventually change for the better = 계속되는 불행도 참 아내다 보면 기회가 온다).

The fence divides my lands from his
↳ 나의 땅과 그의 땅은 울타리를 경계로 한다

The fence goes round the whole of my property
↳ 내 소유지는 이 울타리 안에 다 있다

The ferry steamed off(out), all the flags flying
↳ 연락선은 온통 깃발을 펄럭이며 떠나갔다

› **breakwater**　offshore structure to protect harbors from waves

› **dazzle**　overpower with light, impress greatly

The fields where we played as children have been built up(over)
↳ 우리가 뛰놀던 들이 건물로 꽉 찼다

The flowers exploded with blossoms(came into full bloom)
↳ 꽃이 만개했었지

The grapevines grew over the roof and almost hid it from view
↳ 포도덩굴이 자라서 지붕을 덮어 지붕이 거의 안 보이게 됐어

The ice began to thaw and broke into pieces that floated on the surface of the lake
↳ 얼음이 녹기 시작하더니 산산조각으로 깨어져서 호수의 표면에 떠다녔다

The leaves are turning fast these days
↳ 요즘 나뭇잎 색깔이 빨리 변하고 있어

The little house nestled among the trees
↳ 그 작은 집은 나무 사이에서 보일락말락했다

The little lane ends in a field
↳ 그 작은 길은 밭으로 이어져 있다

The mountain road began to twist up, steeper and steeper
↳ 산길은 점점 더 가파르게 빙빙 돌아 올라가기 시작했다

The numerous craggy peaks in fanciful shapes and the meandering gorges are incredibly beautiful
↳ 수많은 울퉁불퉁한 기묘한 모양의 봉우리들과 굽이쳐 흐르는 계곡들은 참으로 아름답다

The path to the city is lined up with cherry trees
↳ 그 도시로 가는 길에는 벚꽃나무가 줄지어 서있었다

The path twisted in and out among rocks
↳ 길은 꼬불꼬불 바위산 속을 누비듯이 나아갔다

The river has overflowed its banks, the water is running across the fields

---

▸ **explode** discredit, burst or cause to burst violently

▸ **meander** follow a winding course, wander aimlessly

ㄴ 강물이 둑을 넘쳐서 들판을 덮쳐 흐르고 있다

The river is fed by two tributaries
ㄴ 그 강에는 두 갈래의 지류가 흘러들고 있다

The road curves gently to the left
ㄴ 길은 완만하게 왼쪽으로 굽어진다

The road twisted down the side of the mountain
ㄴ 길이 산 가장자리를 따라 구불구불 나있었다

The sea had gone down during the night
ㄴ 바다는 밤사이에 좀 잔잔해졌다

The selling wave bursted through a fire wall
ㄴ 매도세력이 성난 파도처럼 밀어닥쳤다

The ship was laboring through the heavy seas
ㄴ 배는 거친 바다에서 난항을 계속하고 있었다

The smog persisted in the heart of the city throughout the city
ㄴ 스모그가 도심부에 하루종일 자욱히 끼어있었다

The soft ground was marked with lots of indentations where people walked all over
ㄴ 사람들이 마구 밟아놓은 그 곳의 무른 땅 위에는 움푹움푹한 많은 자국이 나있었다

The sun sank down and the darkness spread across the land
ㄴ 해가 지고 대지에 어둠이 깔렸다

The trees are in full leaf
ㄴ 나무들이 잎이 무성해(**leaves**가 아님)

The trees leafed out late this year
ㄴ 올해는 나뭇잎이 늦게 피었다

The turbulent river, swollen by the heavy rain, rushed down to the sea

---

‣ **tributary** stream that flows into a river or lake

‣ **indentation** notch, recess, or dent; action of indenting

↳ 큰비로 물이 불어 강물이 요동치며 바다로 흘러 들어갔다

The water of the fountain was playing in the air
↳ 분수가 공중으로 내뿜고 있었다

The waves knocked against rocks
↳ 파도가 바위에 부딪쳤다

The waves pounded the boat to pieces
↳ 파도는 보트를 산산조각으로 내어버렸다

The waves pounded to pieces against the rocks
↳ 파도는 바위에 부딪쳐서 산산조각이 났다

The waves washed up a bottle
↳ 병이 파도에 바닷가로 떠밀려왔다

The wind laid the garden with leaves
↳ 바람이 정원에 나뭇잎을 흩뿌렸다

The Yalu river rises in Mt. Baekdu and empties(flows) into the Yellow Sea
↳ 압록강은 백두산에서 시작하여 황해로 흐른다

There are trees dotted about the field
↳ 들판에 나무들이 여기저기 서 있다

There was a breeze playing on the water
↳ 미풍이 수면에 잔물결을 일으키며 지나갔다

There's less and less water available as the wells become exhausted
↳ 샘이 말라가서 쓸 수 있는 물이 점점 줄어들고 있다

They are blasting away the sides of valleys and destroying footpaths and woodland
↳ 그들은 골짜기의 변두리를 폭파해 없애고 사람들이 다니던 소로와 숲 지대를 파괴했다

› **fountain** spring of water, source, artificial jet of water

› **footpath** small path made by walking through

Thick smoke billowed up into the sky from the fire

    ↳ 화재로 발생한 짙은 연기가 소용돌이치듯 올라갔다

This ash tree is six meters long from root to tip

    ↳ 이 물푸레나무는 높이가 6미터 정도다

This river has its source among the hills

    ↳ 이 강은 그 작은 산들 사이에서 발원한다

This stream rises from that mountain valley and weaves across the plain towards the sea

    ↳ 이 개울은 저 산골짜기에서 발원해서 들을 굽이쳐 흘러 바다로 간다

Utility poles are installed every ten meters along the street

    ↳ 도로에 전주가 10미터 간격으로 서 있다

We drank in the beautiful view

    ↳ 우린 아름다운 광경에 넋을 잃었어

When the moon is not full, the stars shine more brightly

    ↳ 보름달이 아닐 때에 별들이 더 빛난다

When the pipes burst, water poured across the street

    ↳ 파이프가 터졌을 때에 물이 길을 가로질러 넘쳐흘렀다

› **billow** swell out

› **utility** usefulness, regulated business providing a public service

150. 핑계 & 변명   **Excuses**

But me no buts
> ↳ 구차한 변명하지마

(=Not so many buts)

Don't give me a song and dance
> ↳ 변명하지마

Don't give me the runaround
> ↳ 요 핑계 저 핑계 대지마(말돌리지마)(**A pretext is never wanting** 핑계 없는 무덤 없다)

Ed's poor explanation of his being late didn't fly with the boss
> ↳ 늦게 출근한 에드의 구차한 변명이 사장에게 먹히지 않았다

Equal authority would lead to an absence of government
> ↳ 평등한 권위만 존재한다면 정부가 없어지는 상황이 될 수도 있다

Every vice has its excuse ready
> ↳ 모든 악은 변명을 준비해 두고 있다

I just ran out of excuses
> ↳ 이젠 변명거리도 떨어졌어

Lie if you must
> ↳ 변명할 생각 마

▸ **pretext** falsely stated purpose | ▸ **authority** expert, right responsibility, or power to influence

Nothing can excuse this
    ㄴ 변명의 여지가 없습니다

> (=There's no excuse for this)

Stop trying to get away with such a poor excuse
    ㄴ 그런 서툰 변명으로 면하겠다는 짓은 하지 마라

Such a poor excuse will not answer
    ㄴ 그런 어설픈 변명으로는 안 된다

Such action admits of no excuse(is unjustifiable)
    ㄴ 입이 열 개라도 할 말이 없을 거다

That's a fine excuse
    ㄴ 서툰 변명하지마

That's a sorry excuse
    ㄴ 정말 구차한 변명을 하는군

That's another slim(slender) excuse
    ㄴ 또 속보이는 변명을 하는군

The absent are never without fault, nor the present without excuse
    ㄴ 그 자리에 없는 사람 치고 죄를 안 뒤집어쓰는 사람 없고 그 자리에
    있는 사람 치고 변명 없는 사람 없다

· **unjustifiable** can not be proven to be just,
        right, or reasonable

151. 하지마   **Don't**

Beat it! Get out of my face
       ↳ 꺼져. 더 이상 얘기하지마

Don't act contrary to rules
       ↳ 규칙에 어긋나는 행동은 말아라

Don't act the cock of the walk
       ↳ 으스대지마

Don't ask me. I take the fifth
       ↳ 내게 묻지마. 난 말 안 하기로 했으니까

Don't badmouth everybody like that
       ↳ 그렇게 아무나 막 헐뜯지마

Don't be a camel sticking his nose under the tent
       ↳ 그렇게 참견하지마

Don't be a party to the conspiracy
       ↳ 그 음모에 가담해선 안 돼

Don't be a sore(poor) loser
       ↳ 진 것 가지고 트집 잡지 마라

Don't be an armchair quarterback
       ↳ 뒷전에 앉아서 이러쿵저러쿵 하지마

Don't be coy with me
       ↳ 내숭떨지마

› **conspire** secretly plan an unlawful act   › **quarterback** offensive back in football
                                                      whodirects the offensive action

Don't be cut up about the defeat
    ↳ 패배를 애석해 하지마

Don't be familiar with that girl
    ↳ 저 아가씨에게 치근대지마

Don't be impossible
    ↳ 짜증나게 하지마

Don't be inquisitive
    ↳ 꼬치꼬치 캐묻지마

> (=You'll find out soon)
> (=Don't be so nosey)
> (=Don't be so prying)
> (=Don't stick your nose in other people's affairs)

Don't be longer than you can help
    ↳ 가급적 빨리 해

Don't be so cheap
    ↳ 그리 쩨쩨하게 굴지마

Don't be so dense
    ↳ 그런 눈치 없는 소리하지마

Don't be so difficult
    ↳ 너무 그리 까다롭게 굴지마

Don't be so upright
    ↳ 그렇게 짜증 부리지마

Don't be such a basket case about it
    ↳ 그런 일에 안달복달하지마

· **inquisitive** curious
· **pry** look closely or inquisitively

Don't be such a mother hen
> ↳ 이것해라 저것해라 하지마

Don't be such a space cadet like that
> ↳ 그렇게 우왕좌왕하지마(멍청한 짓 하지마)

Don't be such a stick in the mud
> ↳ 그런 고리타분한 식으로 나오지마

Don't be such a wuss with your wife
> ↳ 아내한테 그렇게 쥐어 살지마

Don't be too hard on me
> ↳ 너무 그러지마

Don't beat around the bush, come straight to the point
> ↳ 번죽만 울리지 말고 요점을 말해

Don't beat(bang) your head against a brick wall
> ↳ 바보짓 그만둬

Don't believe a person on his bare word
> ↳ 남의 말만 듣고 믿어선 안 돼

Don't bet on it
> ↳ 그렇게는 안될걸

Don't big talk me(boss me around)
> ↳ 나한테 이래라 저래라 하지마

Don't bite the hand that feeds you
> ↳ 배은망덕한 짓은 하지 마라

Don't blow up over minor things
> ↳ 사소한 일로 화 내지마

Don't boss everyone around
> ↳ 남들에게 이래라 저래라 하지마

› **cadet** student in a military academy

Don't bottle up all your feelings
↳ 감정을 모두 억제하려고만 하지마

Don't breathe a word of this
↳ 입도 뻥끗 말아라

Don't breed bad blood between them
↳ 그들에게 불화를 조장하지 말라

Don't bring it up again
↳ 그 얘기 또 꺼내지마

Don't bug me
↳ 귀찮게 하지마

Don't burn the candle at both ends
↳ 과도한 정력 소비하지마

Don't burn your bridge behind you
↳ 배수진을 치지 마라

> '배수지진(背水之陣)'이란 "강을 등지고 진을 친다"라는 뜻으로 사마천의 사기에 나오는 내용이다. 도망갈 곳이 없으면 죽기 살기로 싸우기 때문에 오히려 더 어려운 곳에다 진을 치라는 내용이다. 그러나 잘못하면 자신을 궁지에 몰아넣는 수가 있다. 때에 따라서 위기 상황에는 배수진이 필요하기도 하다 (Desperate diseases must have desperate remedies 중병에는 극약 처방이 필요하다). 이는 암 치료를 위한 항암치료를 빗댄 말이다. 항암치료는 암세포뿐만 아니라 정상적인 세포까지도 파괴하는 부작용이 있기 때문이다.

Don't burn your bridges, you might need their help someday
↳ 돌이킬 수 없는 사이를 만들지 마라. 언젠가 그들의 도움을 필요로 할지 모르니까

Don't burn your fingers on the stock market

› **breed** give birth to, propagate, raise
› **remedy** medicine that cures

↳ 주식에 손대었다가 큰코다치지 않도록 해

Don't burst in like that

    ↳ 그렇게 불쑥 들어오지마

Don't buy that fish, it's crawling with flies

    ↳ 그 생선은 파리가 득시글거리는데 사지마

Don't call me Mr. it's very distant

    ↳ 우리 서먹서먹하게 **Mr.**라 부르지 말자

Don't call me names if you like the way your teeth are arranged

    ↳ 이빨이 성하고 싶거든 날 욕하지마

Don't change the subject

    ↳ 말 돌리지마

Don't chase after another

    ↳ 우물을 파도 한 우물을 파라

Don't chew the scenery

    ↳ 과잉연기 하지마

Don't chop(cut) me off

    ↳ 내 말 막지마(안 끝났어)

Don't come between Jung-soo and Mi-yun

    ↳ 정수와 미연이 사이에 끼어 들어 파경으로 이끌지마

Don't con me into believing what you said

    ↳ 네 말을 믿어달라고 우기지마

Don't confound the means with the end

    ↳ 수단과 목적을 혼동하지마

Don't consider this problem from your own angle

    ↳ 그 문제를 너의 독자적인 각도에서 고찰해선 안 돼

› **chase** follow trying to catch, drive away

› **confound** confuse

Don't clatter those dishes about
> ↳ 그 접시들을 달가닥 달가닥 하지마

Don't clutter your head up with unimportant details
> ↳ 하찮은 일로 머리 속을 어지럽게 하지마

Don't crank it out of water
> ↳ 거짓말 만들어내지마

Don't crash about the living room while I have visitors
> ↳ 손님들이 와 계실 동안 거실에서 쿵쿵거리면서 시끄럽게 굴지마

Don't cross the line
> ↳ 규칙을 어기지 마라

Don't cut across the street
> ↳ 거리를 가로질러 건너지마

Don't cut the grass from under my feet
> ↳ 말꼬리 물고 늘어지지마(방해하지마)

> (=Don't pick at my words or find fault with my remark)
> (=Don't pick at(nitpick, criticize) everything I say)
> (=Don't pick at my every word)

Don't damn me with faint praise
> ↳ 나를 칭찬하는 듯 하면서 헐뜯지마

Don't dare to touch me
> ↳ 내 몸에 손대기만 해봐라

Don't dawdle over your meal, we don't want to be late for the bus
> ↳ 버스시간 늦으면 안되니까 밥 먹는데 꾸물대지마

Don't dive in head first

› **clatter** make a rattling sound
› **clutter** fill with things that get in the way

↳ 무모한 짓 하지마

> (=Don't make a leap in the dark)

Don't do something you'll regret
↳ 똑바로 행동해

> (=Don't shoot yourself in the foot)

Don't drag me in
↳ 날 끌어들이지마

Don't draw me out about this scandal
↳ 이 스캔들에 대해 나한테 말시키지마

Don't drive drunk(under the influence)
↳ 음주 운전은 안 돼

> (=Drinking and driving do not mix)
> (=Don't drive under the influence)

Don't drop(fall) by the wayside
↳ 도중에 포기하지마

Don't dwell on the past
↳ 과거에 연연하지 마라

> (=Don't think too much of what's already happened)

· **leap** jump
· **wayside** side of a road

Don't eat your heart out
ㄴ 너무 슬퍼하지마

Don't expect that jack-off to get ahead in life
ㄴ 저 식충이 녀석에게 잘 되리라는 기대는 하지마

Don't feel small at parties any more
ㄴ 더 이상 파티장에서 기죽지마

Don't fight a losing battle
ㄴ 승산 없는 싸움(일, 게임) 하지마

(=Don't play losing games)

Don't find fault. Find a remedy
ㄴ 흠을 잡지말고 해결책을 찾아라

Don't flatter yourself
ㄴ 잘난 척 하지마

(=Don't get a big head)
(=Don't get a swell(big, swollen) head=)
(Don't put on airs)

Don't fling about all your books and clothes
ㄴ 책이며 옷을 마구 팽개쳐 놓지마

Don't fling your arms and legs like that, make the proper swimming strokes
ㄴ 아무렇게나 손발을 허우적거리지 말고 제대로 수영동작을 취해라

Don't flip the police officer off again

› **fling** move brusquely, throw

↳ 다시는 경찰관한테 삿대질하지마

Don't follow in my tracks
↳ 나의 전철을 밟지마

Don't forget people who made you what you are today
↳ 오늘의 네가 있기까지 도와준 사람들을 잊지 마라

Don't forget that old habits die hard and she likes to fool around
↳ 사람의 버릇은 고쳐지지 않는 법인데 그 여자는 바람기가 있다는 점을 잊지 마라

Don't forget that your customers are worth their weight in gold
↳ 너의 고객이야말로 매우 소중하다는 것을 잊지 마라

Don't forget that your suggestion can backfire
↳ 네 제안이 역효과를 낼 수도 있다는 걸 잊지 마라

Don't forget they are playing chicken with you
↳ 그들이 네가 나가떨어질 때까지 버티고 있다는 걸 잊지마

Don't forget to keep a tally of everything that you spend
↳ 네가 지출하는 모든 계산을 잊지 말고 적어둬라

Don't forget to return the favor
↳ 신세진 일은 잊지 말고 갚아라

Don't forget your legs can go to sleep if you swim a long distance
↳ 장거리 수영을 하면 다리에 쥐가 날 수 있다는 걸 잊지 마라

Don't fritter away all your money and time
↳ 보람 없는 일에 돈과 시간을 허비해선 안 돼

Don't fuss about so much. Things will take care of themselves
↳ 너무 수선 피우지마. 일은 저절로 잘 풀릴 테니까

Don't get a rise out of him by teasing
↳ 그를 놀려서 약오르게 하지마

▸ **fritter** waste little by little

Don't get after me all the time
  ↳ 나를 노상 들볶(괴롭히)지마(**get after** 에는 "추격하다"의 뜻도 있음)

Don't get emotional on me
  ↳ 내게 감정으로 대하지마

Don't get me set up as an outsider
  ↳ 날 이방인 취급 마

Don't get me started on the food
  ↳ 음식얘기는 꺼내지도 마라

Don't get me upset
  ↳ 신경 긁지마

Don't get me wrong
  ↳ 오해하지마

Don't get(become) personal with him any more
  ↳ 그에게 더 이상 인신공격 하지마

Don't get physical with anyone
  ↳ 남들에게 완력으로 대해선 안 돼(**get physical** 에는 **touch someone in love-making**)이란 뜻도 있음)

Don't get sentimental on me
  ↳ 아양떨지마

Don't get smart with me
  ↳ 건방지게 굴지마(**love-making**)이란 뜻도 있음)

Don't get your bowels in an uproar
  ↳ 너무 속상해 하지마

Don't get your hopes up
  ↳ 마음을 비워라

› **outsider** one who does not belong to a
group

(=Don't expect to win)

Don't get your nose out of joint
  ↳ 속상해(부러워) 하지마

Don't give it another thought(a second thought)
  ↳ 그 일은 이제 잊어버려

(=Don't sweat it)

Don't give me a line
  ↳ 마음에도 없는 소리하지마

Don't give me any of that nonsense
  ↳ 그 따위 소리 마

Don't give me none of your noise
  ↳ 그런 헛소리하지마

Don't give me such a bum steer any more
  ↳ 더 이상 그처럼 나를 오도하지마

Don't give me that
  ↳ 그런 소리 마

(=Don't talk like that)

Don't give me that cock-and-bull story
  ↳ 말도 안 되는 소리하지마

Don't give me that line about how hard things are for you

› **steer** direct the course of, guide

ㄴ 네가 얼마나 어려운 처지에 있는지 장황하게 늘어놓지마

Don't give her a glad eye
  ㄴ 그 여자에게 추파 던지지마

> (=Don't make googoo eyes to her)

Don't give him a black look
  ㄴ 그에게 언짢은 내색하지마

Don't give the game(show) away
  ㄴ 미리 산통 깨지마

Don't give them the back of your hand
  ㄴ 그들을 함부로 대하지마

Don't give up in the middle
  ㄴ 한 번 시작한 일은 끝까지 해라

> (=Finish what you planned(started))
> (=See it through to the end)

Don't give your customers a runaround any more
  ㄴ 더 이상 네 고객들에게 이리 가라 저리 가라 하지 마라

Don't give yourself away
  ㄴ 속맘을 털어놓지마

Don't go by what he says, he's very untrustworthy
  ㄴ 그 사람 믿지 못할 사람이니 그 사람 말만 믿고 판단해선 안 돼

Don't go off half-cocked

› **customer** buyer

↳ 성급하게 굴지마

Don't go(get) out of line in this office
↳ 사무실에서 주제넘은(사리에 안 맞는) 짓은 하지마

Don't go out of your way to do it
↳ 일부러 그렇게까지 하지마

Don't go overboard(for me)
↳ (나 때문에) 무리하지마

Don't go snitching to her
↳ 그 여자에게 고자질하지마

Don't hang(ride) on to somebody else's coattails
↳ 남에게 신세를 지지 마라

Don't have(hold) a big tiger by the tail. You've already bit off more than you can chew
↳ 큰 일을 벌려놓지 마라. 넌 벌써 과욕을 부리고 있어

Don't have a cow
↳ 징징거리지마

Don't have a double standard
↳ 사람차별 하지마

Don't hide(bury) your head in the sand
↳ 현실도피(눈감고 아웅) 식으로 나와선 안 돼

'The cat that ate the canary 카나리아를 잡아먹은 고양이'란 한국 속담으로 표현하면 "눈감고 아웅한다"이다. 이는 자신이 잘못한 일을 다른 사람이 모를 것이라 생각하고 시치미 떼는 상황을 말한다. 영어 속담은 주인이 아끼는 카나리아를 잡아먹고 시치미 떼는 고양이에 비유하였다.

▸ **overboard** over the side into the water

Don't ice me in front of my colleagues
> ↳ 동료들 앞에서 무안 주지마

Don't interfere with other people's comfort
> ↳ 다른 사람을 불편하게 하지마

Don't jostle everyone around
> ↳ 아무에게나 함부로 대하지마

Don't just breeze along through life
> ↳ 인생을 얼렁뚱땅 살아선 안 돼

Don't just gobble your food down
> ↳ 음식을 게걸스레 먹기만 해서는 안 돼

Don't just mouth off
> ↳ 나설 차례가 아닐 때 나서지 마라

Don't just sit around the office all day
> ↳ 하루종일 사무실에서 빈들거리기만 하지마

Don't just stand there with your bare face hanging out
> ↳ 그냥 그렇게 바보 같은 얼굴로 서 있지마

Don't keep me in suspense any longer
> ↳ 더 이상 나를 마음 조리게 하지 마라

Don't kid yourself
> ↳ 착각하지마

Don't kill yourself to get here in time
> ↳ 무리하게 시간 내에 여기 오려고 하지마

Don't lay down the law to me
> ↳ 내게 이래라 저래라 하지(야단치지)마

Don't lay that guilt trip on me
> ↳ 날 모함하려 하지마

› **ice** freeze, chill, cover with icing
› **jostle** push or shove

Don't leave anything lying about the office, it makes it difficult to clean
> ↳ 사무실에 아무 것도 어질러놓지 마라, 어지르면 깨끗이 청소하기 어렵잖아

Don't leave me up in the air
> ↳ 나를 맘 조리게(궁금해하게) 하지마(**The matter is left up in the air** 미결상태)

Don't leave things about
> ↳ 물건을 어질러 놓지마

Don't leave your clothes(lying) around
> ↳ 옷을 아무렇게나 널어놓지마

Don't leave your things(belongings) unattended
> ↳ 소지품을 아무렇게나 방치하지 마라

Don't let all this praise go to your head
> ↳ 칭찬 좀 들었다고 우쭐해 하지마

Don't let anyone feel isolated
> ↳ 누구든 외톨이가 된(소외감이 드는) 기분으로 만들어선 안 돼

Don't let anyone say you have a long bottom
> ↳ 아무에게도 엉덩이가 무겁다는 말을 듣지 않도록 해

Don't let anyone say you're talking to hear your own voice
> ↳ 남들에게서 네가 말이 많다는 소릴 듣게 해선 안 돼

Don't let anyone think you're a loose cannon
> ↳ 남들에게서 못 말리는 위험인물(떠버리)이란 소릴 들어선 안 돼

Don't let all this praise go to your head
> ↳ 칭찬 좀 들었다고 우쭐해 하지마

Don't let her rest till she consents
> ↳ 그녀가 승낙할 때까지 떼를 써라

Don't let him kick you around

‣ **isolate**   place or keep by itself

↳ 그 사람이 널 함부로 대하게 내버려둬선 안 돼

Don't let him pump you
↳ 그의 유도신문에 넘어가선 안 돼

Don't let him slip through your fingers this time
↳ 이번엔 그를 놓치지 마라

Don't let it become an obsession
↳ 너무 빠지지마

Don't let it bother you
↳ 신경 쓰지마

Don't let it get you down
↳ 그 일로 기죽지마

Don't let it happen again
↳ 다시는 그런 일이 없어야 해

Don't let me catch you at that again
↳ 또 그 짓 하다가 내게 발각되면 그냥 안 돼

Don't let the grass grow under your feet
↳ 시간낭비 하지 마라

Don't let this matter pull you apart
↳ 이 일로 상심하지마

Don't let this opportunity slip though your fingers
↳ 이번 기회를 놓치지 마라

Don't let your eyes wander when you are driving
↳ 운전시 항상 도로를 주의해야해

Don't let your file rasp
↳ 줄로 싹싹 소리 내지마

› **obsess** preoccupy intensely or abnormally
› **rasp** rub with or as if with a rough file

Don't let your guard down
ㄴ 방심하지마

Don't let yourself get cowed down by his heavy scolding
ㄴ 그에게 큰 꾸지람 받았다고 의기소침하지마

Don't let yourself loose
ㄴ 함부로 지껄이지마

Don't like being a small(little) fish in a big pond
ㄴ 시시한 사람으로 안주할 생각은 하지마

Don't linger over your meal, we don't have all day
ㄴ 우린 급하니까 밥 먹는데 시간 끌지 말자

Don't live in a happy-go-lucky way
ㄴ 되는 대로 살아선 안 돼

Don't look that way at me
ㄴ 그런 눈길로 쳐다보지마

Don't lose any sleep over the matter
ㄴ 그 일에 마음 쓰지마

Don't make a big deal out of it
ㄴ 그 일로 소란 피우지마

Don't make a big fuss
ㄴ 엄살떨지마

> (=Stop whining)
> (=Stop complaining)

Don't make a big production out of it
ㄴ 요란 떨지마

· **whine** utter a high-pitched plaintive or distress cry, complain

Don't make a(federal) case out of nothing
　　ㄴ 아무 것도 아닌 걸 가지고 큰 문제를 만들지마

Don't make a pig of yourself
　　ㄴ 돼지같이 욕심부리지마

Don't make it bad
　　ㄴ 나쁘게 생각지마(비관하지마)

Don't make him feel like a fish out of water
　　ㄴ 그가 서먹서먹하지 않게 해줘

Don't make me the scapegoat
　　ㄴ 나만 잘못했다고 탓하지마

Don't make yourself conspicuous
　　ㄴ 유별나게(튀려고)굴지마

Don't mess around with me
　　ㄴ 날 좀 괴롭히지마

Don't mess with me
　　ㄴ 나한테 함부로 굴지마

Don't miss out on life
　　ㄴ 인생을 즐기며 살아라

Don't mix business with pleasure
　　ㄴ 공과 사를 구분하라

Don't nose into another's affairs
　　ㄴ 남의 일에 끼어 들지마

Don't palm(pawn, pass) that pest on me
　　ㄴ 그 귀찮은걸 내게 떠넘기지마

Don't pick up after children who are old enough to keep their own

---

› **federal**　of or constituting a government
withpower distributed between a
central authority and constituent units

› **conspicuous**　very noticeable

things in order
> ↳ 자기 물건을 정돈해 놓을만한 나이의 아이들을 위해 뒤치다꺼리 해 주지마

Don't pin that on me
> ↳ 내 탓이라고 하지마

Don't play deaf
> ↳ 못 들은 척 하지마

Don't play doctor with anybody any more
> ↳ 더 이상 남의 옷을 벗기고 만지는 짓은 하지마

Don't play games
> ↳ 튕기지마

> (=Come on, I don't like a chasing game)
> (He likes the chase 그는 튕기는 것 좋아해)

Don't play hard-to-get with me any more
> ↳ 더 이상 내게 내숭떨지마

Don't play possum
> ↳ 오리발 내밀지마

Don't play(toy) with your food
> ↳ 음식을 먹지는 않고 건드리기만 해선 안 돼

Don't press your luck
> ↳ 운만 믿고 너무 무리하지마

Don't price yourself out of the market
> ↳ 터무니없이 비싼 값을 불러서 물건이 팔리지 않게 하지마

Don't procrastinate until an opportunity is lost

› **possum**   opossum, common tree-dwelling
          mammal

ㄴ 차일피일 하다가 시기를 놓치지 마라

Don't pull in anyone else
ㄴ 다른 사람을 끌어들이지마

Don't push her to get it done
ㄴ 그 여자에게 그 일을 독촉하지 마라

Don't push so hard against the door; the lock will give
ㄴ 문을 너무 세게 밀어서는 안 돼, 자물쇠가 망가져 버리니까

Don't push to all your limits
ㄴ 극한 상황으로 가지마

Don't push your luck any more
ㄴ 더 이상 운을 믿고 욕심부리지마

Don't put a false construction on his action
ㄴ 남을 일부러 곡해하지마

Don't put it on the street
ㄴ 그 일을 모든 사람에게 알려선 안 돼

Don't put the cart before the horse
ㄴ 주객을 전도하지 마라

Don't put this on the street
ㄴ 이 일을 동네방네 불고 다니지마

Don't put your nose out of joint
ㄴ 언짢아하지마

Don't rain on my parade
ㄴ 내 일에 초치지마

Don't rake up the past
ㄴ 지난 일을 꼬치고치 캐지 마라

› **construct** build or make

› **rake** gather, loosen, or smooth with or as if with a rake, sweep with gunfire

Don't rank me among such people
> ↳ 나를 그런 사람들과 똑같이 취급하지 마라

Don't ride for a fall any more
> ↳ 더 이상 무모한 짓 하지마

Don't rock the boat
> ↳ 긁어 부스럼 만들지 말라

> 그냥 놔두면 될 것을 건드려서 화를 자초할 때 쓰이는 속담이다. 영어에서는
> "자는 개(호랑이)는 깨우지 마라", "구더기 깡통은 열지 마라" 등으로 쓴다.

Don't run to meet trouble
> ↳ 걱정을 사서하지 마라

Don't rush to the judgment on that
> ↳ 그 일은 성급히 판단하지마

Don't saddle yourself with such a big debt before you are sure of your professional success
> ↳ 사업상 성공이 보장되기 전에는 그 큰 빚을 떠맡지 마라

Don't say anything you don't mean
> ↳ 마음에 없는 말하지마

Don't sell me short
> ↳ 날 만만하게 보지마

Don't sell the skin before you have killed the bear
> ↳ 너구리 굴 보고 빚돈 내 써서는 안 돼

Don't shake your leg, it's bad luck
> ↳ 다리 떨지마, 복 나간다

› **rock** sway or cause to sway back and
forth

> (=It causes(or brings) bad luck)
> (=It's unlucky)

Don't shoot the pianist
> ↳ 호의로 그랬던 사람을 책하지 마라

Don't shoot yourself in the foot
> ↳ 경솔하게 말하지마

> (=Don't put your foot into your mouth)
> (=Don't say the wrong thing)

Don't shove your idea down my throat
> ↳ 네 생각을 내게 강요하지마

Don't show him your hand too soon
> ↳ 그에게 너무 빨리 속마음을 보여주지 마라

Don't shuffle; give a clear answer
> ↳ 얼렁뚱땅 하지 말고 똑똑히 말해

Don't sit there like a wall-flower
> ↳ 꿔다놓은 보릿자루처럼 앉았지마

Don't skip(miss) meals
> ↳ 끼니를 거르지 마라

> (=Eat at every mealtime)

Don't slip up on me and scare me to death like that

› **shuffle**   mix together, walk with a sliding
         movement

↳ 그렇게 슬며시 다가와 깜짝 놀라게 하지마

Don't sneak up on me like that, you gave me a shock!

↳ 그렇게 소리 기척 없이 다가오지마, 깜짝 놀랐잖아

Don't speak out of order

↳ 차례가 아닐 때 말하지 마라

Don't speak out of place

↳ 자다가 봉창 두드리지마

Don't speak too soon

↳ 그렇게 말하기는 아직 일러

Don't speak with a forked tongue

↳ 일구이언하지마

Don't speak with your mouth full

↳ 입에 음식을 넣은 채 말하지마

Don't split hairs about who's to blame for such trifles

↳ 그런 하찮은 일에 누구 잘못인지 따위의 시시콜콜한 얘기는 집어 치워

Don't spoil him

↳ 애를 오냐오냐하지 마라

> (＝He is growing up spoiled)
> (＝Don't let him have his way)

Don't spur a willing horse

↳ 필요 이상으로 재촉하지 마라

Don't squirt the hose at me

↳ 호스를 내게 대고 물 뿌리지마

› **sneak** move or take in a furtive manner

› **squirt** eject liquid in a spurt

Don't start with me
    ㄴ 내 성질 건드리지마

Don't steam
    ㄴ 흥분하지마

> (=Calm down)
> (=Take it easy)

Don't step into something that doesn't concern you
    ㄴ 무관한 일에 끼어 들지 마라

Don't step out on your wife
    ㄴ 집사람 놔두고 바람피우지마

Don't stick like glue to me
    ㄴ 나한테 붙어 다니지마

Don't stick your neck out
    ㄴ 위험을 자초하지마

Don't stick your nose into other people's private affairs
    ㄴ 남의 사생활에 간섭하지마

Don't stir up a hornet's nest again
    ㄴ 긁어 부스럼 만들지마

> 그냥 놔두면 될 것을 건드려서 화를 자초할 때 쓰이는 속담이다. 영어에서는
> "자는 개(호랑이)는 깨우지 마라", "구더기 깡통은 열지 마라"등으로 쓴다.
> (=Let sleeping dogs lie)
> (=That would be opening a can of worms)
> (=Wake not sleeping lion)

› **hornet** large social wasp

Don't tailgate that car, he must be drunk
↳ 저 차 운전자가 술 취한 게 틀림없으니 너무 바싹 따라가지마

Don't take a candy from a baby
↳ 비열한 짓 하지마

Don't take chances
↳ 너무 무리하지마

Don't take it hard
↳ 심각하게 받아들이지마

Don't take it out on me
↳ 그걸 내게 분풀이하지마

Don't take me the wrong way
↳ 오해하지마

Don't tear yourself down(apart) for making a small error
↳ 조그만 잘못에 자책하지마

Don't tell me that. What I don't know won't(can't) hurt me
↳ 그런 건 내게 말하지마. 모르면 기분 상할 일도 없으니까

Don't tell the whole world
↳ 사사로운 일을 남들에게 얘기하지마

Don't think I haven't been onto your little game
↳ 너의 시시한 게임에 넘어가리라고 생각지 마라

Don't think I'm going to let it pass
↳ 슬쩍 넘어갈 생각하지마

> (=Dont thing I'm going to let it slide)
> (=Don't think I'm going to let you off so easily)
> (=Don't think I'm going to go at that)

▸ **tear down** knock down and break into pieces

Don't think the test will be a tea party
    ↳ 그 시험을 식은 죽 먹기로 여기지마

Don't touch a sore point with her
    ↳ 그 여자 속 뒤집어놓을 소린 하지 마라

Don't trifle with your meal
    ↳ 음식을 깨지락거리지마

Don't trouble trouble till trouble troubles you
    ↳ 고통이 당신을 괴롭히기 전에는 고통에 손대지 마라

Don't try and run my life
    ↳ 나에게 이런 저런 간섭하지마

Don't try to be all think to all men
    ↳ 모든 사람의 마음에 들려고 하지 마라

Don't try to earn time
    ↳ 시간만 벌려고 하지마

Don't try to gloss over your criminal past by drawing our attention to your recent good behavior
    ↳ 요즘 행실이 좀 좋아졌다는 걸 가지고 과거 비행을 호도하려 하지 마라

Don't try to have the last word
    ↳ 억지쓰지마

Don't try to keep(hold) it in
    ↳ 그걸 마음속으로만 삭이려 하지마

Don't try to make him the heavy because he's watching out for his own interests
    ↳ 그가 자신의 이익만 챙긴다고 매도하지마

Don't try to palm(pass) that idea off as your own
    ↳ 그 안을 네가 내놓은 것처럼 하지 마라

‣ **recent**   lately made or used, of the present time or time just past

Don't try to paper over it
  ↳ 그 일을 쉬쉬해서 넘기려 하지마

Don't try to paper over the mess you have made
  ↳ 네가 엉망으로 만들어 놓은걸 덮어 감추려 하지마

Don't try to poison their minds against me
  ↳ 그들이 내게 편견을 가지도록 사주하지마

Don't try to put a fast one on me
  ↳ 나를 감쪽같이 속이려 하지 마라

(＝Don't try to put your best face to him)

Don't try to reason him out of his obstinacy
  ↳ 그의 고집을 꺾으려 하지마

Don't try to stick it to me with all the little extras
  ↳ 잡다한 비목을 붙여서 내게 바가지 씌우러 하지 마시오

Don't try to weasel out of it
  ↳ 꽁무니 빼려 하지마

Don't try to weasel out of your responsibility
  ↳ 책임을 벗어나려고 하지마

Don't turn it off with a joke
  ↳ 농담으로 얼버무리지마

Don't turn on waterworks. Cheer up
  ↳ 울지만 말고 용기를 내어라

Don't use bad language
  ↳ 상소리 하지마

‣ **obstinacy** stubbornness

Don't waffle about. Make up your mind
> ↳ 엉거주춤 하지 말고 마음을 정해라

Don't wake a sleeping dog
> ↳ 일을 시끄럽게 만들지 마라

Don't want to communicate
> ↳ 아무 말도 하고싶지 않아(**I**가 생략되어 있음)

Don't wear your heart on your sleeve
> ↳ 맘속에 있는 대로 표시(말) 해선 안 돼

Don't worry, I'll keep my end up
> ↳ 걱정 마, 내 일(몫)은 내가 할 테니까

Don't you bigmouth this, but she's going to have a baby
> ↳ 소문내지마, 그 여자 아이 가졌어

Dry up
> ↳ 입 다물어. 그만 좀 해 둬

> (=Give it a break(rest))

Enough is enough
> ↳ 그만 해둬

Flowers in the garden mustn't be gathered
> ↳ 공원에서 꽃을 꺾어서는 안 돼

Get organized and stop running around like a hen with its head cut off(in circles)
> ↳ 정신 좀 차리고 호떡집에 불난 것처럼 허둥대지마

› **waffle** equivocate

> "Running around like a hen with its head cut off"는 한국식으로 표현하면 "호떡집에 불났다"이다. 양계장에서 닭 잡는 날의 혼란스러움에 빗대어 만든 속담이다.

Give it up
> ↳ 그만 좀 해둬

> (=Get over it)

I don't need your instructions
> ↳ 이래라 저래라 하지마

Keep your hands to yourself
> ↳ 남의 것(깨지는 것) 손대지마(아이들에게는 "남을 때리지마"이고, 어른들에게는 "내 몸에 손대지마"가 될 수 있음)

Keep off the grass
> ↳ 참견하지 마시오. 잔디에 들어가지 마시오

Kindle not a fire that you can't extinguish
> ↳ 끌 수 없는 불을 일으키지 마라

Leave me out of it
> ↳ 나를 끌어들이지마

> (=Leave me out)

Let me breathe
> ↳ 이제 그만 좀 해둬

‣ **extinguish** put out (as a fire)

Look at your future just from the pink pleasant side of it but not the dark angle of it
> ㄴ 너의 장래를 장미 빛 측면으로 보고 어두운 측면으로 보지 마라

Never is a long time(word, day)
> ㄴ '결코'라고 말하지 마라

> (=Never say never)

Never lose your temper till it would be detrimental to keep it
> ㄴ 참아서 해로울 때까지는 화를 내지 마라

Never oppose violence to violence
> ㄴ 폭력을 폭력으로 대항하지 마라

Never present a gun at anyone, even in fun
> ㄴ 장난으로라도 총을 누구에게든 겨누지 마라

Never tell him anything. He's telling out of school
> ㄴ 그 사람한테 아무 것도 말하지마. 비밀을 지킬 줄 모르니까

Never try to prove that nobody doubts
> ㄴ 아무도 의심하지 않는 것을 밝히려 하지 마라

No ifs, ands or buts about it
> ㄴ 핑계 대지마

No matter how broke you are, never go to a juicer
> ㄴ 아무리 돈이 없어도 고리대금업자(일수업자)에게 가지 마라

No more strong arm tactics
> ㄴ 더 이상 고압적인 수단을 사용하지 마라

Please don't argue back all the time

▸ **detriment** damage	▸ **oppose** place opposite or against something, resist

ᄂ 노상 말대꾸만 하지마

Please don't bring back those blotted-out memories
ᄂ 나의 지워(잊어)졌던 기억을 되살아나게 하지마

Please don't gloat over others' misfortunes
ᄂ 다른 사람의 불행을 고소해 하지마

Please don't go behind my back
ᄂ 나 몰래 무슨 짓 하지마(내 뒤를 캐지마)

Please don't hold that over me anymore
ᄂ 더 이상 내 발목 쥐고 흔들지마

Please don't intrude(yourself)into this matter
ᄂ 이 일에 훼방 놓지(끼어 들지) 말아 줘

Please don't jump down on his throat(all over him)
ᄂ 그 사람 호되게 나무라지 마

Please don't pull a trick(stunt) that on me again
ᄂ 내게 또 그런 장난하지마

Please don't warm that matter over again
ᄂ 그 일은 재론하지 맙시다

Please stop fanning the breeze any more
ᄂ 제발 더 이상 조잘대지마

Please stop getting on my case all the time
ᄂ 이제 날 좀 괴롭히(트집 잡)지마

Stop bandying about someone else's business
ᄂ 남의 일을 이러쿵저러쿵 하지마

Stop barging in here
ᄂ 불쑥 들어오지마

› **intrude** thrust in, encroach
› **bandy** exchange in rapid succession

Stop being stingy(a miser, cheap)
ㄴ 짜게 굴지마

Stop breathing down my neck, I make mistakes when I'm being watched
ㄴ 옆에서 지켜보지마, 누가 지켜보면 실수한단 말이야

Stop buttering me up
ㄴ 사탕발림 그만해

(=Stop sucking up to me)

Stop chain-smoking, or else you'll wind up a basket case
ㄴ 담배 피우지마, 담배를 안 끊고선 네 병을 못 고쳐

Stop crying before you are hurt
ㄴ 미리 설치지마. 지레 짐작으로 떠들지마

Stop dishing on me behind my back
ㄴ 내가 없을 때 나를 술안주(화제 거리) 삼지마

Stop dishing the dirt
ㄴ 남의 말 함부로 하지마

Stop doing the impossible
ㄴ 되지도 않는 일을 하지 마라

Stop drooling over it
ㄴ 눈독들이지마

(=Stop coveting it with your eyes)

Stop dwelling on the little things

› **butter up** flatter
› **drool** let liquid run from the mouth

ㄴ 작은 일에 연연하지마

> (=Don't be so worried about the little things)
> (=Concentrate on more important things)

Stop following the crowd blindly
ㄴ 남들이 하는 대로 맹목적으로 따라하지 마라

Stop going wool gathering
ㄴ 헛된 생각 마

Stop harping on the same string(thing)
ㄴ 같은 얘기 계속 하지마

Stop keeping after me and after me
ㄴ 좀 보채지마

Stop Monday morning quarter-backing
ㄴ 끝난 일에 뒷공론은 집어치워

Stop noising that rumor around
ㄴ 그 소문을 여기저기 퍼뜨리고 다니지마

Stop picking holes in everything I say
ㄴ 말끝마다 토를 달고 나서지마

Stop playing innocent
ㄴ 오리발 내밀지마

Stop putting your words into my mouth
ㄴ 내가 하지도 않은 말을 했다고 하지마

Stop rushing me
ㄴ 보채지마

▸ **gather** bring or come together, harvest, pick up little by little, deduce

> (=I'm moving as fast I can)

Stop slapping him down every time he says something
↳ 그 사람이 말할 때마다 윽박지르지마

Stop talking to a stone wall now
↳ 이제 쇠귀에 경 읽기는 그만해

> 마음에 있지 않으면 들어도 들리지 않고 보아도 보이지 않는다(There's none so blind as those who will not see = There's none so deaf as those who will not hear).

Stop that for decency's sake
↳ 체면 깎일 짓 하지마

Stop trying to do any snow job on me any more
↳ 더 이상 내게 속임수나 쓰려고 하지마

Stop trying to get away with such a poor excuse
↳ 그런 서툰 변명으로 면하겠다는 짓은 하지 마라

Stop trying to stretch out time
↳ 퇴근시간까지 질질 시간 채우려 들지마

Stop walking in and out of here
↳ 들락날락 하지마

Stop whacking all the flower heads off with your stick
↳ 작대기로 꽃을 마구 때려 떨어뜨리는 짓은 그만해

Whatever you can lose, reckon of no account
↳ 잃을 수 있는 것이면 무엇이나 중히 여기지 마라

› **decency** goodness, righteousness, or justification

› **whack** strike sharply

152. 행동   Actions & Behaviors

A man is not good or bad for one action
> ↳ 사람이 한 번의 행동으로 좋고 나쁨이 가려지는 것이 아니다

A true friend would have acted differently
> ↳ 진정한 친구라면 그렇게 행동하진 않았을 것이다

Act quickly, think slowly
> ↳ 행동(실천)은 빨리, 생각은 천천히

After his impossible behavior, they froze him out from(of) the organization
> ↳ 그의 그 역겨운 행동 이후 사람들이 그를 조직에서 못 배기게 한 거야

After the way you behaved, nobody will ask you back
> ↳ 그 따위로 행동하니 아무도 널 다시 초청하지 않을 거다

All he is doing is going through the motions
> ↳ 그가 하는 모든 일은 일 하는 체 하는 것 뿐이야

All they have done is only a lick and a promise
> ↳ 그 사람들 해 놓은 일이란 날림(하는 둥 마는 둥)이야

All you have done so far is talk in circles
> ↳ 지금까지 네가 한 것이라곤 했던 말을 또 하고 또 한 것 뿐이야

All you have to do is to screw(squeeze) the soapy water out of the cloth before you dip it in the clean water
> ↳ 이제 네가 할 일이라곤 이 빨래를 맑은 물에 담그기 전에 짜기만 하면 돼

› **organization**   a group of people gathered for same purpose

Almost all absurdity of conduct arises from the imitation of those whom we can't resemble
>↳ 어리석은 행동의 태반은 자신이 닮을 수 없는 사람의 흉내를 내는데서 비롯된다

An ounce of practice is worth a pound of precept
>↳ 교훈보다 실행이 중요하다

An-do is just beating his head against the wall
>↳ 안도는 부질없는 짓만 하고 있는 거야

An-do is just dragging his feet on this matter
>↳ 안도는 이 일에 늑장만 부리고 있어

An-do only added fuel to the fire
>↳ 안도는 불난 집에 부채질만 했지 뭐

(=An-do only rubbed salt into the an open wound)

And I've got to do it now
>↳ 지금 당장 해야한다

Any firm can be tainted to a great extent by dishonesty and sharp practice
>↳ 어느 회사나 부정직과 교활한 행위로 명성을 크게 손상할 수 있다

Anyone with his head screwed on straight wouldn't have done something so dumb
>↳ 제정신이 있는 사람이라면 그런 멍청한 짓을 하려고 안 했을 것이다

Are you playing with a full deck?
>↳ 넌 지금 제정신으로 하는 짓이냐?

› **absurd** ridiculous or unreasonable

› **taint** affect or become affected with something bad and decay

As you broke the window, you have to take your medicine
> ↳ 네가 유리창을 깼으니 뒷일은 감수해야지

At it again
> ↳ 또 그 짓이군

Be careful not to shoot from the hip
> ↳ 준비 없이 행동(말) 하지 않도록 주의해

Be careful what you wish for
> ↳ 종아리 맞고 싶어 간지러운 거냐?

Be cautious in all your movements
> ↳ 일거일동에 조심해

Be slow to promise, quick to perform
> ↳ 약속은 천천히, 실천은 빨리

Be yourself in public
> ↳ 많은 사람들 앞에서 자연스럽게 행동해

Before you criticize others, you should set your house in order
> ↳ 다른 사람을 욕하기 전에 행실부터 고쳐라

Being with this company cramps my style
> ↳ 이 회사에 다니다보니 행동제약이 따를 수밖에 없어

Blame me if I do
> ↳ 그런 짓 할 사람이 어디 있나

Bong-soo has to straighten out(up) if he wants to get a job
> ↳ 봉수가 취직을 하려면 행동을 바로잡아야 해

Bong-soo sits like a bump on a log and criticizes what everyone does
> ↳ 봉수는 할 일 없이 앉아서 다른 사람이 하는 일을 트집이나 잡고 있어

Bong-soo smiled and put up a good front
> ↳ 봉수는 웃으며 자신을 위장했어

› **criticize** judge as a critic, find fault

› **cramp** restrain

Brave men's deeds live after them
ㄴ 용기 있는 사람의 위업은 사후에도 남는다

By doing nothing we learn to do ill
ㄴ 아무 것도 안 하고 있으면 못된 짓을 배우게 된다

By this act you blotted out all your previous disgraces
ㄴ 이번 일로 지난번의 불명예는 씻었어

Byung-soo stepped out of line once too often and got bawled at
ㄴ 병수는 못된 짓을 너무 자주 해서 호되게 야단 맞았어

Can I shame him out of such un-acceptable behavior?
ㄴ 그에게 창피를 주어서 그런 용납할 수 없는 행동을 못하게 할 수 있을까?

Can you forgive the fool that I've been?
ㄴ 저의 바보 같은 짓을 용서해 주시겠어요?

Chan-ho nosed out of the room quickly and stealthily
ㄴ 찬호는 민첩하게 살며시 방을 빠져 나왔어

Chan-ho went down the line, passing out handouts
ㄴ 찬호는 광고지를 이 사람 저 사람에게 돌렸다

Chan-soo also wants to fall in line
ㄴ 찬수도 행동을 같이 하기를 원해

Chang-soo barely squeezed himself into the crowded elevator
ㄴ 창수는 겨우 비좁은 엘리베이터에 비집고 들어갔다

Chang-soo has been up to no good again
ㄴ 창수가 또 못된 짓 했어

Chul-hee comes on too strong
ㄴ 철희는 너무 적극적으로 나오고 있어

Circumstances warrant(justify) such conduct
ㄴ 사정이 사정이니 만큼 그런 행위가 허용돼

› **bawl** cry loudly

› **warrant** declare or maintain positively, guarantee, approve

Could stupidity(imbecility) go further?
> ↳ 이보다 더 바보짓이 있을까?

Deeds are better than words
> ↳ 말보다 실천

Divorce can provoke aberrant behavior on the part of both parents and children when emotional resources to deal with aberrant are completely drained
> ↳ 이혼은 이상행위를 다룰 정서수단이 완전히 없어지게 될 때 부모와 아이들 모두에게 일탈행위를 유발시킬 수 있다

Dong-soo doesn't strike me as the type of person to do something like that
> ↳ 동수가 그런 짓 할 사람 같지 않아

Dong-soo was decorated for his good conduct
> ↳ 동수는 선행에 대한 포상을 받았다

Don't act contrary to rules
> ↳ 규칙에 어긋나는 행동은 말아라

Don't beat(bang) your head against a brick wall
> ↳ 바보짓 그만둬

Don't dive in head first
> ↳ 무모한 짓 하지마

> (=Don't make a leap in the dark)

Don't do something you'll regret
> ↳ 똑바로 행동해

· **imbecile** feebleminded or foolish person

· **decorate** add something attractive to, honor with a medal

> (=Don't shoot yourself in the foot)

Don't let me catch you at that again
> ↳ 또 그 짓 하다가 내게 발각되면 그냥 안 돼

Don't ride for a fall any more
> ↳ 더 이상 무모한 짓 하지마

Don't take a candy from a baby
> ↳ 비열한 짓 하지마

Don't try to gloss over your criminal past by drawing our attention to your recent good behavior
> ↳ 요즘 행실이 좀 좋아졌다는 걸 가지고 과거 비행을 호도 하려 하지 마라

Doo-man made an exhibition of himself
> ↳ 두만인 바보짓을 했어(창피 당해)

Even then your action didn't constitute lawful behavior
> ↳ 그렇더라도 네 행동은 합법적인 것이 아니었어

Every deed is judged by the doer's intention
> ↳ 모든 행위는 행위자의 의도에 따라 평가된다

Everybody makes a boo-boo every now and then
> ↳ 누구나 가끔씩은 멍청한 짓을 한다

Fettered by old customs, they are unable to act freely
> ↳ 그들은 낡은 관습에 묶여 자유롭게 행동하지 못한다

Finish with this foolishness
> ↳ 이 어리석은 짓은 그만 둬

Follow your heart
> ↳ 마음내키는 대로(진정 원하는걸) 해

› **exhibit** display especially publicly

› **constitute** establish, be all or a basic part of

Follow(stick to) your own judgement
> ↳ 소신껏 밀고 나가

> (=Believe in what you think)
> (=Have faith in yourself)

Good acts are better than good intentions
> ↳ 선행은 선의보다 났다

Good deeds generate other good deeds
> ↳ 선행이 선행을 낳는다

Good words without deeds are rushes and reeds
> ↳ 행동이 따르지 않는 말은 골풀과 갈대와 같다

Great talkers are not great doers
> ↳ 말 잘하는 사람 치고 실행이 따르는 사람 없다

> "빈 수레가 요란하다 Empty vessels make the greatest noise"와도 뜻이 통한다. 말이 많고 허풍이 많은 사람일수록 실천이 뒤따르는 사람은 드물다.

He acts as if he were somebody
> ↳ 그는 제가 뭐나 되는 것처럼 으스댄다

He always runs off in all directions and doesn't focus his energy
> ↳ 그는 늘 이것저것 다하려 하고 한 가지도 집중을 안 해

He didn't actually say anything offensive, but his expression was sulky, insolent and hostile
> ↳ 그가 실제 남의 비위를 건드릴 말은 안 했지만 표정은 뽀루퉁하고, 무례하고 적대적이었다

› **vessel** container for a liquid

› **sulky** be moodily silent

› **insolent** contemptuously rude

He goes out of his way to insult me
    ㄴ 그는 일부러 내게 버릇없이 군다

He has a great need of a fool, that plays the fool himself
    ㄴ 자신이 바보짓 하는 사람은 절실히 바보를 필요로 한다

He is all mouth and no chops
    ㄴ 그 사람은 입만 살고 행동이 없어

He is always nosing about something
    ㄴ 그는 여기저기 돌아다니면서 뭔가를 탐지한다

He let his zeal over-run his discretion
    ㄴ 그는 열중한 나머지 무분별한 짓을 했다

He made vain resolutions never to repeat the act
    ㄴ 그가 다시는 그 행동을 되풀이하지 않겠다고 결심했으나 허사였다

He never lets the grass grow from under his feet
    ㄴ 그는 행동이 민첩해(기회를 안 놓쳐)

He often wanders from proper conduct
    ㄴ 그는 때때로 정도를 벗어나

He put his finger and thumb in his mouth and gave a piercing whistle
    ㄴ 그는 손가락을 입에 넣고 귀청이 떨어지게 휘파람을 불었다

He who defines his conduct by ethics imprisons his song-bird in a cage
    ㄴ 자신의 행동을 도덕으로 정의하는 사람은 노래하는 새를 새장에 가두는 사람이다

He who heard and did nothing is like a man who built a house on earth without a foundation
    ㄴ 듣고 행치 아니하는 자는 주춧돌 없이 집을 지은 사람과 같다

He who is quick-tempered acts foolishly
    ㄴ 노하기를 속히 하는 자는 어리석은 일을 행한다

› **zeal**   enthusiasm
› **discretion**   discreet quality

He who lives without folly is not so wise as he believes
> ↳ 바보짓을 하지 않고 사는 사람은 자신이 믿고 있는 것만큼은 현명하지 않다

He who walks with integrity walks securely, but he who perverts his ways will become known
> ↳ 바른 길로 행하는 자는 걸음이 평안하려니와 굽은 길로 행하는 자는 그 일이 곧 알려지리라

He's always telling, never doing
> ↳ 그는 언제나 말만하고 실행은 하지 않는다

He's always on when he's out in public
> ↳ 그가 대중 앞에 나설 때는 늘 가식적이야

His behavior was not in the best of taste
> ↳ 그의 행동은 경우에 없는 짓이었어

His career was paved with good intentions
> ↳ 그의 생애는 선의로 일관되어 있었다

His conduct is next door to madness
> ↳ 그의 행위는 거의 미친 짓이다

His deliberate provocation made me think furiously
> ↳ 그의 고의적인 도발이 골 때리게 만들었어

His words and actions do not correspond
> ↳ 그는 언행이 일치하지 않아

History teaches us that men and nations behave wisely once they have exhausted all other alternatives
> ↳ 역사는 국민과 국가에게 모든 대안이 고갈됐을 때 현명하게 행동한다는 것을 가르쳐 준다

I can't let his wrongdoing go unchallenged

› **pervert** corrupt or distort
› **furious** fierce or angry

↳ 그 사람 비행을 그대로 놔둘 수 없어

I couldn't have acted otherwise
↳ 그럴 수밖에 없었어

I would have never believed it of him
↳ 그걸 그 사람 소행으로 생각지 않아

I'm not given that way
↳ 난 그런 짓 할 사람이 아니야

If you do that again, you'll sign your own death warrant
↳ 또 그랬다간 네 죽을 짓 하는 거야

If you go on behaving like that, you'll get yourself talked about in the office
↳ 네가 계속 이렇게 행동하면 사무실에서 소문나겠다

If you keep acting that way, you'll get your lumps
↳ 계속 그런 식으로 나가면 응분의 벌을 받아야 해

Impatience will not mend matters
↳ 조급히 굴어봤자 소용없어

In vain he craves advice that he will not follow
↳ 행하지 않으면서 조언만 구하는 것은 헛일이다

It takes guts to do something like that
↳ 배짱 없으면 그런 일 못해

It's a case of sleeping on a volcano
↳ 그건 무모한 짓이다

It's better to suffer wrong than do it
↳ 남에게 못된 짓을 하는 것보다 남의 못된 짓을 참는 것이 낫다

It's superfluous to strain at a gnat
↳ 큰 일을 놔두고 작은 일에 애를 쓰는 것은 쓸데없는 짓이다

› **superfluous** more than necessary
› **gnat** small biting fly

Jung-soo has a screw loose to do such a thing
> 정수가 그런 짓 하다니 머리가 어떻게 된 모양이지

Just keep your own place
> 분별 있게 행동해야 해

Lack of love in early children can induce criminal behavior in the young
> 어릴 적 사랑의 결핍은 청년기에 범죄행위로 빠지게 할 수 있다

Let's not overplay our hand
> 무리한 짓은 말자

Manners require time, as nothing is as vulgar than haste
> 매너는 시간을 요한다, 서두르는 것보다 더 보기 싫은 것이 없기 때문이다

Min-ho's acts belies his words
> 민호는 언행이 다른 사람이야

Moon-soo had better mend his way or he's going to end up in prison
> 문수가 행동을 고치지 않으면 교도소 가게 되어있어

More faults are often committed while we are trying to oblige than while we are giving offense
> 사람은 남들에게 무례한 짓을 할 때보다는 좋은 일을 해 주려고 하다가 잘못을 저지르는 일이 더 흔하다

More people are flattered into virtue than bullied out of vice
> 을러서 악행을 안 하게 된 사람보다 칭찬으로 덕을 행하게 된 사람이 많다

Most firms slip into questionable business practices as a way to keep paces with competitors
> 대부분의 회사들은 다른 경쟁자들에게 뒤지지 않기 위한 방편으로 의심스러운 행위를 은밀히 할 수 있다

No man in their senses would do it(his 또는 once가 아님)

‣ **pace** walking step, rate of progress

ㄴ 제정신으로 그런 짓 할 사람은 아무도 없다

Noble deeds are most estimable when hidden

ㄴ 남몰래 행한 고귀한 행동이 가장 값진 행동이다

Nobody could utter a syllable when he exhorted them to reform their conduct

ㄴ 그가 그들에게 행동을 고치라고 훈계할 때 아무도 끽소리 못했다

None so good that it's good to all

ㄴ 모든 사람에게 다 좋은 덕행이란 없다

Not if I know it

ㄴ 누가 그런 짓을 하겠나

Nothing prevents our being natural so much as the desire to appear so

ㄴ 자연스럽게 보이려는 생각보다 더 자연스러움을 방해하는 것은 없다

Now there's a way to go

ㄴ 이젠 죽을 짓을 하는구먼

Now you are done it

ㄴ 큰 일을 저질렀군

> (=See what you've done)

Now, I've seen everything

ㄴ 별꼴 다 보겠네

Often a noble face hides filthy ways

ㄴ 고상한 얼굴로 더러운 수단을 덮어 가리는 일은 흔히 있다

Once the way to proceed on is fixed upon, everything will be done accordingly

---

› **estimable** worthy of esteem

› **syllable** unit of a spoken word

› **exhort** urge earnestly

↳ 일단 나아갈 길이 결정되면 모든 걸 그에 따라 행해야 한다

One of the most important things for you is to take orders

↳ 네게 가장 중요한 일의 하나는 고분고분 해야할 일이다

People always overdo the matter when they attempt deception

↳ 사람들이 남을 속이려 할 때는 늘 과잉행위를 한다

Please come to yourself and stop acting strangely

↳ 평소에 하던 대로하고 이상한 짓은 집어치워

Please don't lecture me about my behavior

↳ 내 행동에 대해 뭐라고(꾸중) 하지마

Please straighten up and fly right before you get into trouble

↳ 어려운 일 당하기 전에 자세를 고쳐서 바르게 행동해라

Please undo this mess you made

↳ 네가 어지른 건 원래대로 해둬

Politicians who are in the public eye have a responsibility to behave in a sensible way

↳ 세인의 주목을 받는 정치인은 지각 있는 행동을 할 책임이 있다

Rudeness is the weak man's imitation of strength

↳ 무례는 약자의 힘 자랑 흉내이다

Sang-soo raised up and set down one of his feet after the other

↳ 상수는 발을 차례로 들었다 놓았다 했다

Sang-soo spun out at the sound of his name, ready to defend himself

↳ 상수는 자신의 이름을 부르는 소리에 방어자세를 취하면서 홱 돌아섰다

Sang-soo will nail you to the wall if he finds out what you've done

↳ 네가 한 짓을 상수가 알기라도 한다면 혼 줄이 날거다

Saying and doing are two things

↳ 말로는 쉬워도 실천은 어렵다

› **attempt** make an effort toward
› **lecture** instructive talk

> "빈 수레가 요란하다 Empty vessels make the greatest noise"와도 뜻이
> 통한다. 말이 많고 허풍이 많은 사람일수록 실천이 뒤따르는 사람은 드물다.
> (=From word to deed is a great space)

Set the action to the word
> ↳ 말한 대로 행하라

She always acts big and talks big
> ↳ 그 여자는 늘 허장성세이다(**She is big** 그 여자는 육체파이다)

She gave me hard time
> ↳ 그 여자는 까다롭게 굴었다

She is no better than she should be
> ↳ 그 여자는 행실이 좋지 못해

She never referred to his conduct, though she sometimes alluded to it by hinting
> ↳ 그녀는 가끔 그의 행동에 대해서 암시는 했으나 결코 공공연히 말하
> 지는 않았다

She put that kind of behavior above you
> ↳ 그 여자는 그런 행동을 너답지 않다고 생각해

She was a woman who gave free play to her emotions
> ↳ 그 여자는 자신의 감정대로 행동하는 사람이었어

She'll never ever do that again
> ↳ 그 여자는 두 번 다시 그런 짓을 안 할 사람이다

She's been long on threats to do something about me and short on action
> ↳ 그 여자가 내게 어떤 조치를 취할 것이라고 위협만 해왔지 실제 행동
> 으로 옮긴 일은 거의 없었다

› **allude** refer indirectly

She's slow in putting her ideas into practice
ㄴ 그녀는 생각을 실천으로 옮기는 데 느리다

Simple believes every word, but the prudent man considers well his steps
ㄴ 어리석은 자는 온갖 말을 믿으나 슬기로운 자는 행동을 삼가느니라

Speech is the mirror of the action
ㄴ 말은 행동의 거울이다

Such behavior is like you
ㄴ 과연 너다운 행동이다

Such conduct is not becoming in a gentleman
ㄴ 그런 행동은 신사에게 어울리지 않아

Such conduct is not becoming in you(very well with you)
ㄴ 그런 행동은 너답지 않아

Tai-ho always sets tongues wagging by his actions
ㄴ 태호는 늘 자기 행동으로 입방아에 오르고 있어

Tai-ho's truculent attitude alienated all supporters he had won to his cause
ㄴ 태호의 거친 태도 때문에 그를 지지하던 모든 사람들을 등돌리게 만들었다

Talk will not avail without work
ㄴ 실행 없이 말만 앞세우는 건 소용없어

Talkers are no great doers
ㄴ 말이 많은 사람이 실행가는 아니다

That guy fell(went)to pieces at the funeral
ㄴ 저 녀석이 장례식에서 망나니짓을 하더구먼

That would be signing your own death warrant
ㄴ 그런 짓 하는 건 네 죽을 짓이야

· **prudent** shrewd, cautious, thrifty
· **truculent** aggressively self-assertive

That's a fine how-do-you-do after all I've done for him
ㄴ 내가 저한테 어떻게 해 줬는데 그런 실망스러운 행동이라니

That's not all he does
ㄴ 그 사람 그보다 더한 짓도 해

The act is forbidden under penalty of death
ㄴ 그 행위는 이를 범하면 사형에 처한다는 규정 하에 금지되고 있다

The act of evil breeds others to follow
ㄴ 악행은 타인이 따라 할 악행을 낳는다

The acts of good men live after them in our memories
ㄴ 훌륭한 사람들의 행동은 그들이 죽은 후에도 우리의 기억에 남는다

The beginning of understanding men is understanding how men act at work
ㄴ 남자를 이해하는 것은 남자가 직장에서 어떻게 행동하는가를 이해할 때 시작된다

The behavior that once was condemned as deviant is now considered quite normal
ㄴ 한때 비정상적인 행위로 비난받던 일이 지금은 상당히 정상적인 것으로 받아들여지고 있다

The government's action only increases suspicions that the public is not being warned about the dangers of rising pollution levels
ㄴ 정부의 그런 행동은 증가하고 있는 대기오염의 위험수위에 대해 경고하지 않았다는 의심을 증폭시킬 뿐이다

The great end of life is not knowledge but action
ㄴ 인생의 큰 목표는 지식이 아닌 행동에 있다

The greatest pleasure is to do a good action by stealth, and to have it found out by chance

---

▸ **condemn**   declare to be wrong, guilty, or unfit for use, sentence

▸ **deviant**   change especially from a course or standard

↳ 몰래 선행을 한 다음 그것이 우연히 말해지게 되는 것이 가장 큰 기
쁨이다

The happiness and unhappiness of a rational, social animal depend on his or her deeds

↳ 이성적이고 사회적인 동물의 행복과 불행은 그들의 행위에 달렸다

The misfortune is he who would act the angel acts the beast

↳ 천사처럼 행동하려고 하는 사람이 실은 야수같이 행동하는 것은 불행
한 일이다

The project muddled through until the new manager got hold of it

↳ 그 사업은 새로운 책임자가 떠맡을 때까지 그럭저럭 넘어갔어

The test of any man lies in action

↳ 사람은 행동으로 평가된다

The time has come for us to call a halt to such a bad behavior

↳ 이제 우린 이런 무질서한 행동을 중지시킬 때가 됐다

The upside of their proposal is that it would give him the freedom of act

↳ 그들의 제안에서 긍정적인 면은 그에게 행동의 자유가 주어진다는 점이다

The way she behaved like that will cause tongues to wag

↳ 그 여자가 그런 짓을 했으니 입방아에 오르겠군

Their behavior should suffice to illustrate how social attitudes are changing

↳ 그들의 행동은 사회풍조가 어떻게 변하고 있는가를 잘 보여주기에 충
분할 것이다

There are no tall people who know how to behave

↳ 키 크고 싱겁지 않은 사람 없다

There are talkers and there are doers

· **muddle** make, be, or act confused; make a mess of; waste(+away)   · **upside** advantage, positive side

    ↳ 허풍떨고있네

> (=You are all blow and no go)

There's no fool like an old fool
    ↳ 저런 멍청이 짓은 죽어도 못 버려

They are being quite cynical that the reason why we have such a large turnout is that we are serving refreshments
    ↳ 그들은 우리가 음료수를 제공하기 때문에 참석자들이 그렇게 많은 것이라는 냉소적인 태도이다

They do least who talk most
    ↳ 다변가일수록 실천이 적다

They'll really give it to you if you don't keep straight
    ↳ 제대로 행동하지 않으면 그들에게 혼날 것이다

This conduct shows what stuff you are made of
    ↳ 이 행위로 너의 인물됨을 볼 수 있군

This is a totally National Statistical Office staff thing to do
    ↳ 이건 순전히 통계청 직원다운 행동

Those who can, do; those who cannot, teach
    ↳ 제대로 할 줄 아는 사람은 직접 행하고, 제대로 못하는 사람은 남에게 가르친다

To explain any aspect of society the sociologist must determine the law influencing human behavior
    ↳ 사회의 어떤 양상을 설명하기 위해서 사회학자는 사회적인 맥락에서 인간 행동에 영향을 주는 법칙을 알아내야 한다

To resume our story, your behavior isn't in keeping

‣ **cynic**   one who attributes all actions to selfish motives

ㄴ 각설하고 너의 행동은 상식 선을 벗어나고 있어

Try to keep a low profile

ㄴ 남의 눈에 띄지 않도록 행동해

Virtue can bring more than its own reward

ㄴ 선행은 그 선행 자체가 가져오는 이상의 보상을 가져올 수 있다

Virtue is its own reward

ㄴ 선행의 보람은 선행 그 자체에 있다

Virtue is more clearly shown in the performance of fine actions than in the nonperformance of base ones

ㄴ 덕행은 비열한 행위를 행하지 않았을 때보다 훌륭한 행동을 행하였을 때 더 두드러진다

Virtue is praised by all, but practised by few

ㄴ 덕은 모든 사람이 칭송하지만 행하는 사람은 거의 없다

Virtue must shape itself in deed

ㄴ 덕은 행동함으로써 생겨나야 한다

Virtue wouldn't go to such lengths if vanity did not keep her company

ㄴ 허영심을 동반하지 않은 덕행은 그리 멀리 가지 않을 것이다

Virtues and happiness are mother and daughter

ㄴ 덕행과 행복은 어머니와 딸과의 관계다

Wan-soo tries to take the high road whenever he can

ㄴ 완수는 가능하다면 늘 양심적으로 행동하려고 하는 사람이야

We are judged by how we act

ㄴ 사람은 행동 여하에 따라 판단된다

We are more apt to catch the more vices of others than their virtues

ㄴ 사람은 덕행보다 악행을 더 잘 지적하기 쉽다

We as often repent the good as ills

‣ **repent** turn from sin, regret

↳ 사람은 악행을 후회했던 만큼이나 자주 선행을 했던 일도 후회한다

We must give awards to them strictly in line with their deeds done

↳ 그들에게 상을 줄 때에는 그들이 행한 행동과 일치하도록 주어야 한다

We must live out our dreams to transform them into action

↳ 우리의 꿈을 실현하고 이를 행동으로 옮겨야 해

What he does is out of keeping with his words

↳ 그의 행동은 말과 일치하지 않아

What you do is out of keeping with your words

↳ 넌 언행이 일치하지 않아

When we watch our best office worker going into his act, we can learn a lot from him

↳ 사무실 내에 우수사원의 일상 행동을 보면 배울게 많다

Whenever you want to do, do it now. There are only so many tomorrow

↳ 하고자 하는 일이 무엇이든 당장 실천에 옮겨라. 내일은 얼마 남지 않았다

Whoever acquires knowledge and does not practise it resembles him who ploughs his land and leaves it unsown

↳ 알면서 행하지 않음은 땅만 갈고 파종하지 않음과 같다

Words without actions are of little use

↳ 실천이 안 따르는 말은 소용없어

You are acting against your own interest

↳ 그러다간 네게 이롭지 못해

You are young man, act like one

↳ 젊은이가 젊은이답게 행동해야지

You brought you pigs to a fine(pretty) market

· **strict** severe and unyielding, precise

· **transform** to change in structure, appearance, or character

↳ 넌 엉뚱한 짓을 한 거야

You can't take any action till she shows her hand

↳ 넌 그 여자가 의도를 밝힐 때까지 아무런 조치를 취할 수 없어

You give a false color to your statement(conduct)

↳ 정말인 것 같이 말(행동)하고 있군

You have grown slack = You are not on your toes

↳ 군기 빠졌군

You have my leave to act as you like

↳ 허락할 테니 네 맘대로 해

You look like you couldn't care less

↳ 강 건너 불구경이로군

> (=You act like it doesn't concern you)

You should carry yourself well

↳ 훌륭하게 행동해야 해

You were so very awkward in doing that

↳ 형편없이 서툰 짓 했군

You'd better clean your act up now

↳ 이제 넌 개심 해야 해

You're no better than you should be

↳ 넌 행실이 좋지 못해

You've been going around in circles(the bend) all day

↳ 넌 종일 정신 나간 짓만 하고 있잖아

Your chilly manner holds people off

‣ **awkward** clumsy, embarrassing

ㄴ 너의 쌀쌀한 태도 때문에 사람들이 가까이 안 오는 거야

Your conduct in society was impeccable
ㄴ 사람들 앞에서 너의 행동은 나무랄 데 없었다

Your continual goofing off has got past a joke
ㄴ 너의 계속되는 농땡이는 그냥 넘어갈 일이 아냐

Your style is to say one thing to one person and to opposite to another and then play both ends against the middle
ㄴ 네 행동은 여기 가서 이 말 하고 저기 가서 저 말해서 사람을 이간시켜 어부지리를 얻으려는 거로군

Youth is the time to study wisdom; old is time to practice it
ㄴ 젊어서는 지혜를 배우고 나이가 들어서는 실행할 때다

· **impeccable** faultless

153. 행복   **Happiness**

A great obstacle to happiness is to anticipate too great a happiness
    ↳ 행복에 대한 큰 장애는 너무 큰 행복을 기대하는 것이다

A happy family is but an earlier heaven
    ↳ 행복한 가정은 한 발 앞서 찾아 온 천국이다

A happy marriage is the world's best bargain
    ↳ 행복한 결혼생활은 이 세상 최고의 계약이다

A sense of happiness stole over(upon) him
    ↳ 그는 어느새 행복감에 젖었다

Ain't nothing better
    ↳ 이보다 더 큰 행복은 없어(Ain't=There isn't anything)

An-do is now quite at his ease
    ↳ 안도가 지금은 팔자가 늘어졌어

Being with you makes me happy
    ↳ 당신과 함께 있는 건 즐거워

Caution in love is the most fatal to true happiness
    ↳ 사랑의 신중함은 진정한 행복에 치명적 장애이다

Deviation from nature is deviation from happiness
    ↳ 자연에서 벗어나는 일은 행복에서 벗어나는 일이다

Different men seek after happiness in different ways
    ↳ 사람이 다르면 행복을 추구하는 방법도 다르다

‣ **anticipate**   be prepared for, look forward to | ‣ **deviate**   change especially from a course or standard

Everyone hopes to spin out happy times and shorten bad days
　　　↳ 모든 사람은 행복한 시간이 길어지기를 바라고 안 좋은 시간은 짧아
　　　지기를 바란다

Friends show their love in time of trouble, not in happiness
　　　↳ 친구는 행복할 때가 아닌 어려울 때 애정을 나타낸다

> 어려움에 부딪혀 봐야 진정을 친구를 알아 볼 수 있다는 말이다. 더 자주 쓰
> 이는 표현으로 "A friend in need is the friend indeed 필요할 때 옆에
> 있어주는 친구가 진정한 친구이다"가 있다.

Growth itself contains the germ of happiness
　　　↳ 성장(숙) 그 자체에 행복의 씨앗이 들어있다

Happiness always looks small while you hold it in your hand
　　　↳ 손에 들어온 행복은 늘 작아 보인다

Happiness consists in working toward one's goals
　　　↳ 행복은 목표를 향해 노력하는데 있다

Happiness doesn't lie in happiness, but in the achievement of it
　　　↳ 행복은 행복 그 자체에 있는 것이 아니라 그 행복을 이루어 내는데 있다

Happiness is beneficial for the body, but it is grief that develops the powers of mind
　　　↳ 행복은 신체에 이롭지만 슬픔은 마음에 힘을 길러준다

Happiness is composed of misfortunes avoided
　　　↳ 행복은 불행을 피함으로서 이루어진다

Happiness is not best achieved by those who seek it directly
　　　↳ 직접 행복을 구하는 사람들에게는 그리 만족스럽게 구해지는 것이 아니다

Happiness lies in trying to do our duty

› **avoid**　keep away from, prevent the
　　　occurrence of, refrain from

ㄴ 행복은 우리의 의무를 다 하려는 데 있다

Happiness makes up in height what it lacks in length
ㄴ 행복은 길이에서 부족한 것을 높이로 보충해준다

Happy are they that hear their detractions and put them to mending
ㄴ 남에게 욕을 얻어먹고 이를 고칠 수 있는 사람은 행복한 사람이다

Happy is a man while he is smiling and that smile makes others happy too
ㄴ 미소로서 남들을 행복하게 해주는 사람들이야말로 행복한 사람이다

Happy is he who chastens himself
ㄴ 자신을 벌할 줄 아는 사람은 행복한 사람이다

He comes on as a happy camper, but he's just putting it on
ㄴ 그가 행복한 척 티를 내지만 행복한 척 하고 있을 뿐이야

I can't keep my happiness to myself
ㄴ 이 행복을 혼자 지니기엔 너무 벅차

I wouldn't change places with him. I'm happier the way I am
ㄴ 그 사람하고 처지를 바꾸고 싶지 않아. 난 이대로가 더 행복해

I'd like nothing better
ㄴ 더 이상 바랄게 없어

I'm as happy as happy can be
ㄴ 지금이 최대로 행복해

In every kind of adversity, the bitterest part of a man's affliction is to remember that he once was happy
ㄴ 어떤 역경에서나 사람에게 가장 쓰라린 고통은 그가 과거에 행복했다는 것을 기억하고 있다는 일이다

It is comparison that makes men happy or miserable
ㄴ 사람은 남들과의 비교를 통해서 행복해지거나 비참해진다

‣ **detract** take away(+from)
‣ **chasten** discipline

‣ **afflict** cause pain and distress to

It is misery enough to have once been happy
> ↳ 한때 행복을 누린 일이 있다는 것은 불행한 일이다

It's not enough to be happy, it is also necessary that others not be
> ↳ 자신이 행복한 것만으로는 부족하며 다른 사람들이 절대로 불행해져서는 안 된다

Knowledge of what's possible is the beginning of happiness
> ↳ 가능한 일이 무엇인지 아는 것이 행복의 시작이다

Let us all be happy, and live within means
> ↳ 분수를 지키면서 행복하게 살자

Man's real life is happy, chiefly because he's ever expecting that it soon will be so
> ↳ 인간의 실제 생활은 행복하다, 주된 원인은 그가 행복해지리라고 기대하기 때문이다

Manners are the happy ways of doing things
> ↳ 훌륭한 태도는 행복하게 일하는 방법이다

Misfortunes tell us what fortune is
> ↳ 불행을 당해봐야 행복을 안다

Money may procure pleasure but not happiness
> ↳ 돈으로 향락은 살 수 있을지 몰라도 행복은 사지 못한다

My happiness is bitter-sweet=I have mixed feelings
> ↳ 시원섭섭한(착잡) 심정이야

Nor silver nor gold can buy our happiness
> ↳ 은이나 금으로도 행복은 살 수 없다

Riches alone make no man happy
> ↳ 돈만 있다고 행복해지는 건 아니다

Rob the average man of his life-illusion and you rob him of his

---

‣ **procure** get possession of

happiness at one stroke
> ↳ 보통사람에게서 그의 평소의 환상을 빼앗으면 단번에 그의 행복을 앗아가게 된다

Saving is to put aside present pleasure for future happiness
> ↳ 저축이란 장래의 행복을 위해 현재의 쾌락을 억제하는 것

The first thing to learn in intercourse with others is non-interference with their own ways of being happy
> ↳ 남들과의 교제에서 먼저 알아야 할 것은 그들 고유의 특수한 방식으로 행복해지는데 대한 불간섭이다

The greatest happiness you can have is knowing that you do not necessarily require happiness
> ↳ 최대의 행복은 당신 자신에게 꼭 그 행복이 필요한 것이 아니라는 것을 깨닫는 데 있다

The happiness and unhappiness of a rational, social animal depend on his or her deeds
> ↳ 이성적이고 사회적인 동물의 행복과 불행은 그들의 행위에 달렸다

The happy man is not he who seems happy to others, but who seems thus to himself
> ↳ 행복한 사람은 남들에게 행복해 보이는 사람이 아니라 자신에게 행복해 보이는 사람이다

The search of the happiness is one of the chief sources of happiness
> ↳ 행복추구야말로 주된 행복의 근원 중 하나이다

The secret of happiness is to admire without desiring
> ↳ 행복의 비결은 탐하지 않으면서 경탄하는 것이다

The secret of happiness is to fill one's life with activity
> ↳ 행복의 비결은 인생을 활동적으로 사는 일이다

› **intercourse**   relations between persons or nations, copulation

The supreme happiness of life is the conviction that we are loved
ㄴ 인생 최고의 행복은 자신이 사랑을 받고 있다는 확신이다

The way to be happy is to make others so
ㄴ 행복해지려거든 타인을 행복하게 해 주어라

There's no way home
ㄴ 옛날의 행복으로 되돌아갈 수는 없어

Unhappiness does make people look stupid
ㄴ 불행은 사람을 정말 바보처럼 보이게 한다

Virtues and happiness are mother and daughter
ㄴ 덕행과 행복은 어머니와 딸과의 관계다

We are never so happy or unhappy as we suppose
ㄴ 우린 생각하는 것만큼 행복하거나 불행하지가 않아

We felt so happy that we did not know what to do with ourselves
ㄴ 우리는 너무 기뻐서 어쩔 줄 몰랐다

A fine gentleman will justy forgive others but it is not appropriate for him to be the position of being forgiven by others
ㄴ 대장부는 마땅히 남을 용서할지언정 남에게서 용서를 받아서는 안된다

Where fear is, happiness is not
ㄴ 두려움 있는 곳에 행복은 없다

› **suppose**　assume to be true, expect, think probable

154. 협력   **Co-operation**

An-do chickened out on us at the last minute
> ↳ 안도는 최종 순간에 우리와 동행(협조)하지 않기로 했어

Discord gives a relish to concord
> ↳ 불화는 화합의 향미를 제공한다

Facing a common enemy keeps the nation together
> ↳ 국가 공동의 적을 앞에 두면 국민이 단합하게 된다

Harmony would lose its attractiveness if it did not have a background of discord
> ↳ 의견차이를 바탕으로 끌어내지 않은 화합은 그 빛을 잃게 된다

Horror causes men to clench their fists, and in horror men join together
> ↳ 공포는 사람들의 주먹을 꽉 쥐게 만들고 사람들은 두려움 속에서 단합한다

How can we abuse a man of collaboration for doing what he had to?
> ↳ 어쩔 수 없어서 협력했던 사람을 어떻게 비난할 수 있겠나?

How much finer things are in composition than alone?
> ↳ 얼마나 많은 일이 혼자 하는 것보다 협조를 통하여 보다 잘 이루어져 왔던가

I hope this opportunity will inaugurate a long and fruitful cooperation between our firms

---

· **concord**   agreement

· **inaugurate**   install in office, start

· **collaborate**   work jointly with others, help the enemy

ㄴ 이번 일을 계기로 양사 간에 유익한 협력관계를 여는 출발점이 되기 바랍니다

If they don't stand together, they'll be defeated one by one

ㄴ 그들이 단합하지 않으면 한사람씩 각개 격파되고 말 것이다

If we pull together, you can get this job done on time

ㄴ 너희들이 협력하면 시간 내에 이 일을 해낼 수 있을 것이다

Let's cooperate with each other

ㄴ 우리 서로 협력하자(**with**가 있어야 함)

Man and wife must help each other, for better or for worse

ㄴ 부부는 장래에 잘살건 못살건 서로 협조해 나가야 한다

Nobody goes by the rules here

ㄴ 여기서는 아무도 규정대로 하지 않아

Our membership has been rolling up for the past few years

ㄴ 우리의 회원 수가 지난 몇 년 동안 점점 늘어나고 있다

There is strength in unity

ㄴ 뭉치면 살고 헤치면 죽는다

(=To gain strength, we need to stick together)
(=United we stand, divided we fall)

They'll be better off if they'll play ball with me

ㄴ 그들은 내게 협력하는 것이 그들에게 유리할 것이다

Together we can win

ㄴ 우리가 힘을 합하면 이길 수 있어

Uniforms symbolize the oneness of the spirit and coordination essential to the winning

---

· **unite** put or join together

· **essential** basic or necessary

ㄴ 유니폼은 승리하는데 필수적인 단일정신과 일치를 상징한다

We beat the odds together

ㄴ 우린 함께 난국을 헤쳐 나왔어

We must all hang together, or assuredly we shall all hang separately

ㄴ 모두가 단결하지 않으면 모두가 교수형에 처해질 것이다

We must band against the common enemy

ㄴ 우리는 공동의 적에 대항해서 단합해야 한다

We must hang together when one of us in trouble

ㄴ 우리들 중 한 사람이 어려움에 처할 때 우린 단합해야 해

We must learn to live together as brothers or perish together as fools

ㄴ 우리는 형제같이 같이 살지 않으면 바보같이 같이 망하게 된다는 것
을 깨달아야 한다

Why can't you play ball with me?

ㄴ 왜 넌 내게 협조를 못하는 거니?

Why don't we team up and do it together?

ㄴ 우리가 힘을 합해 함께 하는 게 어때?

› **odd**   additional to what is usual or to the   › **perish**   die or spoil
number mentioned, queer

155. 회사   Company

A careful and impartial review of the bank reference and the two references you gave to us indicate that your company is experiencing considerable financial difficulties in making prompt payments

    ↳ 귀사가 거래하는 은행과 신용거래처 두 곳의 신중하고 공정한 의견은 귀사가 현재 대금 지급을 하기엔 심각한 자금 압박을 받고 있다고 말하고 있습니다

A foreign corporation with a fixed business location can voluntarily calculate and file for corporate tax on its income

    ↳ 고정된 영업장이 있는 외국기업은 그들의 소득에 대해 자진하여 법인세를 계산해서 신고할 수 있다

An inability to identify potential high-volume customers are a major failing of the marketing department, but the lack of credit in general has contributed to the company's poor performance

    ↳ 잠재적인 많은 고객을 찾아내지 못하는 것이 마케팅부의 중요 실패이지만 전반적인 신용결여가 이 회사의 나쁜 실적의 원인이 되고 있다

Any firm can be tainted to a great extent by dishonesty and sharp practice

    ↳ 어느 회사나 부 정직과 교활한 행위로 명성을 크게 손상할 수 있다

As your company rewards enterprising employees with accelerated promotions and responsibilities, you'll go far into the job

    ↳ 너희 회사가 진취적인 사원에게 빠른 승진과 책임 있는 일의 보임을

· **impartial** not partial   · **enterprise** an undertaking, business organization, initiative

보장하고 있으니 넌 그 직무에서 성공할 것이다

At six the workers began to leave the company in dribs and drabs
ㄴ 여섯 시가 되자 직원들이 하나씩 둘씩 회사에서 나갔다

At that time, quite a lot of firms suffered from a shrinkage of(in) the work force
ㄴ 그 당시 많은 회사들이 인력난으로 고통을 겪었다

Being with this company cramps my style
ㄴ 이 회사에 다니다보니 행동제약이 따를 수밖에 없어

Bong-soo had to bail out of the company because he decided it was failing
ㄴ 병수는 회사가 파산하리라는 판단에서 회사를 그만 뒀어

Bulk buying has enabled the company to cut costs
ㄴ 회사에서 대량으로 구입함에 따라 비용을 절감할 수 있게 되었다

Can you help me understand one reason why I should keep you around?
ㄴ 당신을 이 회사에 계속 고용할 이유가 있는 건지 한 가지라도 대보시오

Can you place me with a company that makes electronic goods?
ㄴ 전자제품 만드는 회사에 취직시켜줄 수 있겠습니까?

Chan-ho can't wait to get inside the company and see what makes it tick
ㄴ 찬호는 얼른 회사 업무를 파악하여 회사가 어떻게 돌아가는지 알고싶어해

Chan-soo is working for Samsung Company and he is raking(coining) it in
ㄴ 찬수는 삼성회사에 다니는데 엄청나게 돈을 벌고 있다

Companies that are slow to respond to customers' ever-changing needs will find themselves squeezed out by those possessing the

---

· **bail out** abruptly get out of a predicament

necessary celerity
> ↳ 끊임없이 변하는 고객의 요구에 응하는 속도가 느린 회사들은 필요한 민첩성을 갖춘 회사들에게 밀려나게 됨을 알게 될 것이다

Control of a whole industry by a single company tends to eliminate competition
> ↳ 한 회사가 전체 산업을 장악하면 경쟁력이 없어지기 쉽다

Desert and reward seldom keep company
> ↳ 공이 있다고 보답이 따르는 건 아니다

Despite the much ballyhooed exodus of workers from large companies to venture firms, many who left for startups are returning to their former employers
> ↳ 벤처기업으로 떠들썩하게 대이동 했던 대기업 직원 중 많은 수가 옛 직장으로 되돌아가고 있다

Don't blunder(blurt) out your company secrets again
> ↳ 또 회사 비밀을 불쑥 말하지마

Factories will have to go all out for business if they are not to fail in these hard times
> ↳ 이 어려운 시기에 공장들이 견디어 내려면 전력을 다 해야 한다

Generally the basic policy of most advertizing agencies is to assume the general public are all morons
> ↳ 일반적으로 대부분 광고회사들의 기본 방침은 모든 일반 대중들을 멍청이라는 가정 하에 세워진다

Hai-tai Department Store finally folded(up) because of the recession
> ↳ 불경기로 해태백화점이 문 닫았어

He is trying to pump you for your company secrets
> ↳ 그는 네게서 회사 기밀을 얻어내려는 거야

> • **celerity** speed
> • **exodus** mass departure

He left the company after 30 years' service without a single black mark against him
> ↳ 그는 **30**년간 단 하나의 과오도 없이 회사를 물러났다

He took it in the shorts when his company went bankrupt
> ↳ 그의 회사가 망하자 그는 참담하게 몰락했다

He vowed to clean the company up and get rid of any lazy workers
> ↳ 그는 회사의 기강을 바로잡아 게으른 직원들을 해고시키겠다고 언명했다

He was caught diverting the company's money into his own bank account
> ↳ 그는 회사 자금을 자신의 은행 계좌에 유용하다가 들통났어

How is he placed in his company?
> ↳ 회사에서 그 사람 지위가 뭐니?

I hope this opportunity will inaugurate a long and fruitful cooperation between our firms
> ↳ 이번 일을 계기로 양사 간에 유익한 협력관계를 여는 출발점이 되기 바랍니다

I'm sure that he will be an asset to your company and I highly recommend him for the position of software programing supervisor
> ↳ 그는 귀사의 훌륭한 인적자산이 되리라 확신하며 귀사의 소프트웨어 프로그래밍 매니저 자리에 강력히 추천합니다

If we get unlimited sick leave, severance pay, two week paid vacation and coffee break, it'll fold any day
> ↳ 회사에서 무제한의 병가, 해직수당, **2**주간 유급휴가, 커피타임을 주었 다간 회사가 금방 망할 거야

If you back out of(from) your contract(promise), you'll have to pay the penalty to the firm

---

· **divert** turn from a course or purpose, distract, amuse

ㄴ 계약(약속)을 이행치 않으면 회사에 벌금을 물어야 해

In recent years lots of companies have spared no expense on new technology

ㄴ 요즘 많은 회사들은 신기술에 많은 비용을 아끼지 않는다

It turned up trumps after all, and the firm made a lot of money

ㄴ 그 일이 결국 예상외로 잘되어 그 회사는 큰돈을 벌었다

Jung-soo has taken a new job with an automobile company but is quite out of his depth with that kind of work

ㄴ 정수는 자동차회사에 새로 취업했지만 그런 일은 그에게 매우 어려웠다

Lots of companies cleaned up in the real estate

ㄴ 많은 이름 있는 회사들이 부동산으로 떼돈을 벌었어

Most firms slip into questionable business practices as a way to keep paces with competitors

ㄴ 대부분의 회사들은 다른 경쟁자들에게 뒤지지 않기 위한 방편으로 의심스러운 행위를 은밀히 할 수 있다

Most refineries had allowed their stocks to run low and subsequently had to scramble to recover requirements at higher prices

ㄴ 대부분의 정유회사들이 재고량을 적게 유지해서 그 결과 필요한 양을 더 비싼 가격으로 채워 넣어야 했다

Most workers will sit there and watch their business go down the tubes

ㄴ 대부분의 근로자들은 뒷짐지고 서서 회사가 망해 가는 꼴을 지켜보기만 할 것이다

Nam-soo invested a couple of nickel-and-dime in the company that went belly-up

ㄴ 남수는 영세업자 두 군데를 투자했는데 부도가 나버렸어

No companies want to make workers redundant because of the

▸ **refinery** place for refining(as oil or sugar)　　▸ **redundant** using more words than necessary
▸ **subsequent** following after

recession, but they have no alternative
　↳ 어느 회사든 불경기로 인해 여분의 인력을 두기를 원치 않지만 대안이 없다

Our company is currently in full blast
　↳ 우리 회사는 요즈음 풀 가동이야

Our company is restructuring the marketing division to reach the sophisticated consumer interested in growth opportunities
　↳ 우리 회사는 성장 가능성에 관심이 있는 세련된 수요자의 요구에 부응하기 위하여 마케팅부를 구조조정 하는 중이다

Our company's been struggling to stay afloat
　↳ 우리 회사는 살아남으려고 발버둥 쳐 오고 있다

Please don't leave the company, we shall be lost without you
　↳ 회사를 그만 두어서는 안 돼, 네가 없으면 우리가 어렵게 돼

Please furnish us with information about that company, particularly the regularity with which management meets their financial obligations
　↳ 그 회사에 관한 정보, 특히 재정채무관계에 관한 일반적인 규정을 알려 주십시오

She allows me almost no say at all in running the company
　↳ 그녀는 회사 운영에 대해 거의 전혀 내게 운영권을 허용치 않아

She can smooth the way for me to get a job with that company
　↳ 그녀는 내가 그 회사에 취직하는데 쉽도록 도와 줄 수 있어

She has the built-up-from-the-bottom career with the company
　↳ 그 여자는 회사에서 말단부터 한 단계씩 쌓아 올라갔다

She has to shoot straight in business or her company will fail
　↳ 그 여자가 정직하게 사업을 하지 않으면 회사가 실패하고 말 것이다

She performed her responsibilities as an assistant sales manager with our

---

▸ **recession** departing procession, period of reduced economic activity　　▸ **sophisticate** make worldly-wise

company with competence, diligence, discretion and complete loyalty
> ㄴ 그녀는 우리 회사의 판매부 차장으로 책임감 있게 맡은바 일을 끝까지 수행하고 신중하며 애사심이 충만한 직원이다

Sometimes unscrupulous employers even call the police to have foreign workers deported to avoid paying the salary money they owe
> ㄴ 때로는 사업주가 고용인들에게 대한 급료 지급을 회피하기 위하여 외국인 근로자들을 추방시키도록 경찰에 신고하기까지 한다

Sun-gyoo's company went out of business
> ㄴ 선규의 회사는 문 닫았어

The biggest slice of the cake goes to the multinational oil companies
> ㄴ 제일 큰 알짜는 다국적 석유회사들이 다 쓸어간다

The company arranges 10 blind dates for each of its members
> ㄴ 그 회사는 10건의 맞선을 주선하고 있다

The company has focused on autos, shunning the finger-in-very-pie approach of other conglomerates
> ㄴ 그 회사는 다른 재벌들의 문어발 식 경영관행에서 탈피하여 자동차 사업에만 주력했다

The company has yet to turn a profit
> ㄴ 그 회사는 아직 이익을 못 올리고 있다

The company held the line on employment
> ㄴ 회사는 더 이상 직원을 해고하지 않았다

The company is floundering around and getting nowhere
> ㄴ 회사가 기를 쓰고 버티고 있지만 되는 게 없어

The company will be a blue chip again
> ㄴ 그 회사는 다시 우량기업이 될 거야

The company will go public soon

▸ **loyalty** faithful to a country, cause or friend	▸ **flounder** struggle for footing, proceed clumsily

↳ 그 회사는 곧 주식공개를 할 것이다

The conglomerate pledged to speed up its downsizing efforts during recent financial jitters caused by the liquid problem of its financial arm

↳ 그 기업그룹은 금융계열사의 유동성 문제로 야기된 최근의 자금 불안감이 팽배해진 가운데 조직의 축소개편 노력을 가속시킬 것을 다짐했다

The lack of credit in general has contributed to our company's poor performance

↳ 전반적인 신용결여가 우리 회사의 빈약한 실적의 원인이 되고 있다

The oiling companies are raking in lots of money selling all that heating oil

↳ 석유 회사들은 난방용 연료를 팔아 큰돈을 벌어들이고 있다

The two companies preyed on each other to their mutual destruction

↳ 두 회사는 서로 잡아먹기를 하다가 같이 망했어

The wearing of appropriate personal protective equipment for hazardous jobs is required by company safety regulations

↳ 회사의 안전규칙에 따라 위험한 업무에는 적절한 개인장비의 착용을 요한다

Their company has pulled out all the stops because there is a lot of competition for the contract

↳ 그 계약에 대한 경쟁이 치열하니 그 회사는 최선을 다 해야 해

They denied their liability in the accidents, but that was only the standard insurance company response

↳ 그들은 그 사고에 대한 책임을 부인했지만 그것은 단지 배상청구에 대하여 표준적으로 취하는 보험회사의 반응일 뿐이다

They have already reneged on their commitment to full employment

↳ 그들은 이미 완전고용에 대한 공약을 어겼어

· **regulation** rule dealing with details of procedure

· **renege** go back on a promise

They held out for several years against the policy of the company
> ㄴ 그들은 회사의 방침에 맞서서 몇 년씩이나 싸웠다

They plan to dispose of less viable companies and focus on core businesses
> ㄴ 그들은 자생력이 약한 회사들을 처분하고 핵심사업에 주력하기로 하고 있다

They set up the company in prospect of large profits
> ㄴ 그들은 커다란 수익을 내다보고 회사를 만들었다

They'll furnish you with credit information about our financial responsibility and promptness of our payments
> ㄴ 그들은 저희회사의 재정지불 능력 및 신속한 어음상환에 대한 신용정보를 제공해 줄 것입니다

Those who have any legitimate grievance against the company can take it to the arbitration committee
> ㄴ 회사에 정당한 불평이 있는 사람은 이를 조정위원회에 제기할 수 있다

Try to keep what the company has decided, even if it goes against your personal opinions
> ㄴ 회사가 결정한 일은 네 생각과 어긋나더라도 따르도록 해라

Venture companies need to be put under greater scrutiny, with requirements that they produce financial statements periodically
> ㄴ 벤처회사들에게는 정기적으로 재무제표를 제출하도록 요구하여 보다 엄밀히 조사할 필요가 있다

We absolutely deny your allegation that our company is at fault in this matter
> ㄴ 우리는 이 문제에 대한 책임이 저희 회사에 있다는 귀 측의 주장을 절대로 인정할 수 없습니다

› **viable**   capable of surviving or growing, practical or workable

› **furnish**   provide with what is needed, make available for use

We are waiting anxiously to see if the group will remain faithful to its promise of reform
> ↳ 우리는 그 기업그룹이 구조조정 약속을 충실히 지킬지 눈여겨 지켜보고 있다

We have to keep our company from going under
> ↳ 우린 회사가 망하는걸 막아야 해

> (go under 에는 "마쳐되다, 침몰하다"의 뜻이 있음)

We parted company on where our new office should be built
> ↳ 우리는 새 사무실을 어디다 지어야 할지 의견이 분분했다

We will hold you liable for all losses caused by this inexcusable delay
> ↳ 이유 없이 지연된 귀사의 물품 송달로 야기된 모든 피해의 책임을 귀사에 요구할 것입니다

We urge you to promote our environmental policy when you respond to customer questions and issues
> ↳ 우리는 여러분이 고객들의 질문과 문제들에 대하여 대답할 때 우리회사의 환경친화 방침을 홍보할 것을 당부합니다

When major companies in an industry raise prices, the smaller ones usually follow suit
> ↳ 대기업들이 가격을 올리면 중소기업들은 대체로 그 뒤를 따른다

When the company representative gave him the fifth degree, he began to suffer the pangs of conscience
> ↳ 회사의 대표가 꼬치꼬치 캐어 물어오자 그는 양심에 찔려오기 시작했다

You can't let up on your efforts to compete with other firms
> ↳ 다른 회사와의 경쟁을 위한 노력을 소홀히 해서는 안 돼

› **anxious** uneasy, earnestly wishing

156. 휴가&휴식   **Vacation**

A nice cool glass of beer(a paid vacation) is just what the doctor ordered
> ↳ 시원한 맥주 한 잔(유급휴가)이야 말로 내게 가장 필요한 것이다

As our boss's on vacation, I've got the run of the place now
> ↳ 사장님이 휴가중이니 이제 여긴 내 맘대로야

Bong-soo is weltering in work, eager to take a break
> ↳ 봉수는 일에 파묻혀서 휴가(식)를 절실히 바라고 있어

Doo-chul sounded out his boss about a few days off
> ↳ 두철인 2~3일 휴가를 얻으려고 사장님에게 떠보았어

Ed is climbing the walls to take a vacation
> ↳ 에드는 휴가를 얻고싶어 좀이 쑤신다

Everybody needs to get away from it all now and then
> ↳ 누구나 가끔은 만사를 잊은 채 푹 쉬어야 할 때가 있어

Here goes my vacation
> ↳ 휴가는 물 건너갔군

I shall be away for the summer
> ↳ 피서 계획 중

I want to get the most out of this vacation
> ↳ 이번 휴가를 의미 있게 보내고 싶어

If this diet doesn't work, go to a fat farm on you next vacation

---

› **welter**　toss about, wallow

ㄴ 이번 다이어트에 효과가 없거든 다음 휴가 때 살빼기 훈련원에 가봐

If we get unlimited sick leave, severance pay, two week paid vacation and coffee break, it'll fold any day

ㄴ 회사에서 무제한의 병가, 해직수당, **2**주간 유급휴가, 커피타임을 주었 다간 회사가 금방 망할 거야

It was a regular holiday

ㄴ 즐거운(휴일다운) 휴일이었어

Let it all hang out and take a week off

ㄴ 만사를 잊어버리고 일주일을 푹 쉬어라

Let's take advantage of the off-peak reduction for package holidays

ㄴ 휴일 여행 때 비수기 할인 기회를 활용하자

Make yourself at home. there's no need to stand on ceremony

ㄴ 편하게 쉬세요. 격식을 따질 필요가 없거든요

Man-soo wants to get the most out of this vacation

ㄴ 만수는 이번 휴가를 의미 있게 보내기를 원해

Nam-soo's vacation plans went into(down) the toilet when one of his colleagues got sick

ㄴ 남수의 직장동료 한 사람이 병이 나는 바람에 휴가계획이 물 건너 가 버렸다

Our vacation went off like clockwork and everyone had a good time

ㄴ 우리의 휴가는 원활하게 진행되었고 모두가 즐거운 시간을 가졌다

Prices are higher at certain seasons and holidays than at other times of the year

ㄴ 물가는 일년 중 다른 때 보다 특정 계절이나 휴가 때 더 높다

Recreation facilities need atmosphere

ㄴ 휴양지는 분위기가 있어야 해

› **sever** cut off or apart

Rest is sauce of labor
    ↳ 휴식은 노동의 소스이다

Take a few days off and get away from it all
    ↳ 며칠 휴가를 내어 이 복잡한 일에서 벗어나지 그래

The heavy rain spoiled the long-awaited holiday
    ↳ 비가 와서 모처럼의 휴일을 망쳤어

There's a long weekend next week
    ↳ 다음 주엔 연휴

Time dragged toward my vacation
    ↳ 그럭저럭 휴가 때가 다가왔군

To be able to fill leisure intelligently is the last product of civilization
    ↳ 여가시간을 슬기롭게 채우는 것은 문명의 최종 산물이다

We are going to take a brief break to let you hear from our sponsors before I continue to blast you with smashes from the past
    ↳ 잠시 협찬회사들의 광고를 들으면서 휴식시간을 가진 다음 불멸의 히트곡을 들려 드리겠습니다

Why don't you wind down on this sofa a bit
    ↳ 이 소파에 잠시 앉아 쉬지 그래

With lots of unexpected snags hanging over us, we can't enjoy our holidays
    ↳ 예상치 못한 많은 걸림돌들이 우리에게 다가오고 있으니 우리는 휴일을 즐길 형편이 아니다

Would you please double for me while I'm on holiday?
    ↳ 내가 연가 내는 날 내가 할 일을 좀 해줄래?

You can do it at your leisure
    ↳ 여가 날 때 하면 돼

› **snag**   unexpected difficulty

You need to take a day off and get your head together
ㄴ 하루쯤 시간을 내어 머리 좀 식히지 그래

You'd better wait his leisure
ㄴ 그 사람 여가 날 때까지 기다려야 할거야

Your exciting vacation took years off(of) you
ㄴ 너의 신나는 휴가 덕분에 몇 년은 젊어 보이는군

Your vacation is over. Back to salt mines
ㄴ 휴가는 끝났으니 지겹지만 직장에 나가 일해야지

The person who knows how to be content or pleased, though not wealthy and of low social status, is happy free from anxiety and worry
ㄴ 만족할줄 아는 사람은 가난하고 신분이 낮아도 즐겁다

› **take a day off**   rest for a day

157. TV, 미디어　　Television & Media

Allowing unethical figures to appear on the TV programs will only serve to numb the sense of viewers
>↳ 비도덕적인 인물들을 TV 프로그램에 출연시킨다는 것은 시청자들의 도덕관념을 마비시킬 뿐이다

An embarrassment of riches is perennial on TV
>↳ TV를 보면 항상 무엇을 골라야 할지 모르겠어

Anything good on tonight?
>↳ 오늘저녁 뭐 좋은 프로 있나?

Did you enjoy your stay with us?
>↳ 계속 즐겁게 시청 하셨습니까?

He used the opportunity of appearing on TV to give his product a plug
>↳ 그는 TV에 출연해서 자기회사 제품을 선전할 기회로 활용했다

How can we ensure that our message reaches the maximum number of listeners
>↳ 우리가 전할 말을 어떻게 하면 가장 많은 청취자에게 확실히 전달할 수 있을까?

Maintaining objectivity and a sense of balance are cardinal rules for all self-respecting members the media news
>↳ 객관성과 균형감각의 유지는 새로운 대중매체의 모든 자존심 있는 종사자들에게 핵심적인 규칙이다

▸ **perennial**　present at all season of the year, continuing to live from year to year

▸ **cardinal**　of basic importance

Many of our newspapers and television networks still tend to be subservient to the authorities

↳ 많은 우리의 신문과 텔레비전 방송은 아직도 정부당국의 시녀노릇을 하는 경향이 있다

Only a few people questioned said they ignored TV newscasts

↳ 질문 받은 사람들 중 몇 사람만이 텔레비전 뉴스방송에 관심을 쓰지 않는 것으로 답했다

She tried to deflect the attention of the media by disowning her own son

↳ 그녀는 자신의 아들을 모르는 사람이라고 잡아뗌으로써 매스컴의 주목을 피하려 했다

Some people are glued to their tubes

↳ 텔레비전 앞에서 떠나지 못하는 사람들도 있다

Television has robbed the cinema of its former popularity

↳ 텔레비전이 영화의 옛 인기를 빼앗아 갔다

The government-controlled press painted a very different picture

↳ 정부 관리하의 언론들은 매우 다르게 보도(묘사, 기술)했다

The media turned him into an idol

↳ 언론이 그를 우상으로 만들었어

That drama gives an amusing but wildly inaccurate account of historical evidence

↳ 그 드라마는 재미는 있지만 역사적인 사실에 부정확한 이야기 투성이다

That man looks much fatter in real life than he does on TV

↳ 저 사람은 TV에서 보다 실제로 더 뚱뚱해 보인다

That TV program about cruelty to women brought thousands of letters from worried viewers

---

· **subservient** obsequious submission
· **idol** image of god, object of devotion

↳ 여성에게 잔인했던 그 텔레비전 프로를 우려하는 수 천 통의 시청자 편지가 쇄도했다

The late-night talk show tonight promises to be good

↳ 오늘 밤 토크쇼가 좋은 것 같아

The picture is not sharp enough

↳ (TV)화면이 선명치 않아요

The plot was weak(solid)

↳ 얘기의 구성이 허술해(잘 짜였어)(영화, TV,소설 등)

> (=There was no plot)

The TV program was so exciting that I could hardly tear myself away from it

↳ 텔레비전 프로가 너무 신이 나서 안 볼 수가 없었어

The use of television in the auditorium is a departure from generally held views of education

↳ 강당에서 텔레비전을 사용하는 것은 평상시 생각하는 교육방식과는 상이한 것이다

There's nothing but junk on the tube tonight

↳ 오늘저녁 TV에는 시시한 프로밖에 없군

These comedy programs are pitched at the lowest level of mentality

↳ 이런 코미디는 지능이 가장 낮은 사람들을 대상으로 만든 거야

They'll let the translation run along the bottom of the screen for audiences

↳ 그들은 시청자들을 위해 화면 아래쪽에 번역문을 흘려 보낼 것이다

We'll be back after this message

› **auditorium**   room or building used for public gatherings   › **mentality**   mind or its disorders

ↆ 전하는 말씀을 듣고 다시(방송을) 시작하겠습니다

What's showing on channel 6 tonight?

ↆ 오늘밤 6번 채널에서 뭐하지?

When is it on?

ↆ 언제 중계됩니까?

Your name flashed across the television screen

ↆ 네 이름이 텔레비전 화면에 확 지나가더구나

▸ **channel** broadcast frequency

◈ 편 저 ◈
대한영어교육연구원

◈ 대한영어교육연구원 저서 ◈
Word Origins and Vocabulary 77,000
뿌리부터 알아가는 VOCABULARY & IDIOMS
영어가 우리말처럼(Voca Idiom)

영어로 표현하기 힘든 각 분야별 문장과 회화의 해법

영어문장·회화 대사전　　정가 160,000원

2016年 04月 10日 인쇄
2016年 04月 15日 발행

편 저 : 대한영어교육연구원
발행인 : 김 현 호
발행처 : 법문 북스
공급처 : 법률미디어

152-050
서울 구로구 경인로 54길 4
TEL : (대표) 2636-2911, FAX : 2636~3012
등록 : 1979년 8월 27일 제5-22호
Home : www.lawb.co.kr

❙ ISBN 978-89-7535-345-1 13740
❙ 이 도서의 국립중앙도서관 출판예정도서목록(CIP)은 서지정보유통지원시스템 홈페이지
　(http://seoji.nl.go.kr)와 국가자료공동목록시스템(http://www.nl.go.kr/kolisnet)에서
　이용하실 수 있습니다.(CIP제어번호: CIP2016007914)
❙ 파본은 교환해 드립니다.
❙ 본서의 무단 전재·복제행위는 저작권법에 의거, 3년 이하의
　징역 또는 3,000만원 이하의 벌금에 처해집니다.

❀ 참 고 ❀

❀ 《英語‧日本語辭典》에 付함 ❀
Word Origin and Vocabulary (7,000)
영어의 語源과 VOCABULARY & IDIOMS
영어 숙어(영영숙어사전 포함)

영어‧일한‧일영 대사전

2008년 9월 10일 인쇄
2008년 9월 15일 발행

저 자 : 배명수외공저
발행인 : 배 명 수
발행처 : 명 문 당

─ (주) 명 문 당 ─
TEL : (代)733‑3039‧734‧ FAX : 734‑9209
등록 : 1977년 11월 19일 제1‑148호
home : www.myungmundang.net